BUTTERWORTHS
PROPERTY LAW
HANDBOOK

KU-450-629

DISPOSED OF
BY LIBRARY
HOUSE OF LORDS

BUTTERWORTHS
PROPERTY LAW
HANDBOOK

THIRD EDITION

Consultant Editor

ERNEST H SCAMELL, LLB, LLM, AKC

*Barrister, Emeritus Professor of English Law
in the University of London*

BUTTERWORTHS
LONDON, DUBLIN, EDINBURGH
1994

United Kingdom	Butterworth & Co (Publishers) Ltd, 88 Kingsway, LONDON WC2B 6AB and 4 Hill Street, EDINBURGH EH2 3JZ
Australia	Butterworths, SYDNEY, MELBOURNE, BRISBANE, ADELAIDE, PERTH, CANBERRA and HOBART
Belgium	Butterworth & Co (Publishers) Ltd, BRUSSELS
Canada	Butterworths Canada Ltd, TORONTO and VANCOUVER
Ireland	Butterworth (Ireland) Ltd, DUBLIN
Malaysia	Malayan Law Journal Sdn Bhd, KUALA LUMPUR
New Zealand	Butterworths of New Zealand Ltd, WELLINGTON and AUCKLAND
Puerto Rico	Butterworth of Puerto Rico, Inc, SAN JUAN
Singapore	Butterworths Asia, SINGAPORE
USA	Butterworth Legal Publishers, CARLSBAD, California; and SALEM, New Hampshire

All rights reserved. No part of this publication may be reproduced in any material form (including photocopying or storing it in any medium by electronic means and whether or not transiently or incidentally to some other use of this publication) without the written permission of the copyright owner except in accordance with the provisions of the Copyright, Designs and Patents Act 1988 or under the terms of a licence issued by the Copyright Licensing Agency Ltd, 90 Tottenham Court Road, London, England W1P 9HE. Application for the copyright owner's written permission to reproduce any part of this publication should be addressed to the publisher.

Warning: The doing of an unauthorised act in relation to a copyright work may result in both a civil claim for damages and criminal prosecution.

© Butterworth & Co (Publishers) Ltd 1994

A CIP Catalogue record for this book is available from the British Library.

ISBN 0 406 03254 8

Typeset, printed and bound in Great Britain by
William Clowes Limited, Beccles and London

PREFACE

As with previous editions of this Handbook, the aim underlying this edition has been to provide the serious student of land law, trusts, succession and conveyancing with as comprehensive a collection of statutes and statutory provisions as is practicable in the space of a single volume of moderate size. Since the last edition was published, some of the Acts and Statutory Instruments which featured in it now appear as re-enactments and replacements (with amendments) and many of the others have been amended by later Acts and Statutory Instruments. In the former case, the relevant provisions of the replacement Act or Statutory Instrument are, of course, reproduced in the form of their latest livery (as, for example, in the case of the Town and Country Planning Act 1990, the Land Registration (Open Register) Rules 1991 and the Charities Act 1993) whilst in the latter case the earlier provisions are printed as amended by the later Act or Statutory Instrument. The amendments falling into this category have been numerous but fortunately for the manageability of the present volume, have not in themselves added significantly to its length.

In addition to the process of renovation referred to above, Parliament has been by no means idle in producing entirely new property legislation and where germane to the general parameters of property law (as particularised above) it is hoped that an appropriate choice has been made in including new legislation in this volume. In this connection, there has been much heart-searching as to whether to include selected provisions from the Leasehold Reform, Housing and Urban Development Act 1993 and the Property Misdescriptions Act 1991 but in the end it was decided not to do so. As to the 1993 Act (containing 188 sections and 22 Schedules), whilst the provisions relating to the "right to collective enfranchisement" conferred upon certain lessees of flats in blocks of flats and the "right to acquire a new lease" conferred upon certain individual lessees of flats, are unquestionably of far-reaching importance in the realm of Landlord and Tenant, they nevertheless constitute a highly specialised aspect of that realm and are therefore considered to be more appropriate to a Handbook on Landlord and Tenant rather than to such a volume as the present. (The same consideration has hitherto led to the exclusion of provisions in the Leasehold Reform Act 1967 and the Rent Acts.) At the same time, it is still considered appropriate to include a selection of the "right to buy" provisions in the Housing Act 1985 (as now amended) since unlike the right to buy provisions of the 1993 Act, the provisions of the Housing Act 1985 (in addition to being far less complex) provide some revealing sidelights on certain interesting aspects of general property law, (including rights of pre-emption and "claw-back" provisions in relation to the discounted purchase price on re-sale within a prescribed period). As to the Property Misdescriptions Act 1991, this will be found, on close examination, to be confined to enlarging the scope of criminal sanctions for property misdescription, and not to affect civil rights or remedies. Again, therefore, this Act appears more suitable (despite its beguiling title!) for inclusion in a different kind of Handbook.

As indicated above, the exercise of choice as to what should or should not form part of a collection of this nature is sometimes tantalising, and it can but

be hoped that those who turn to the present volume for enlightenment on the
up-to-date text of some Act or Statutory Instrument dealing with general
property law will much more frequently find themselves pleasantly surprised
than forlornly disappointed.

The contents are reproduced as amended to 1 January 1994, although later
developments have been noted wherever possible.

Ernest H Scamell
Lincoln's Inn
January 1994

CONTENTS

PART 2 STATUTORY INSTRUMENTS

PART 1
STATUTES

FIRES PREVENTION (METROPOLIS) ACT 1774
(c 78)

An Act ... for the more effectually preventing Mischiefs by Fire within the Cities of London and Westminster and the Liberties thereof, and other the Parishes, Precincts, and Places within the Weekly Bills of Mortality, the Parishes of Saint Mary-le-bon, Paddington, Saint Pancras and Saint Luke at Chelsea, in the County of Middlesex ... [1774]

NOTES
Words omitted repealed by the Statute Law Revision Act 1887.

83. Money insured on houses burnt, how to be applied

And in order to deter and hinder ill-minded persons from wilfully setting their house or houses or other buildings on fire with a view of gaining to themselves the insurance money, whereby the lives and fortunes of many families may be lost or endangered: Be it further enacted by the authority aforesaid, that it shall and may be lawful to and for the respective governors or directors of the several insurance offices for insuring houses or other buildings against loss by fire, and they are hereby authorised and required, upon the request of any person or persons interested in or intitled unto any house or houses or other buildings which may hereafter be burnt down, demolished or damaged by fire, or upon any grounds of suspicion that the owner or owners, occupier or occupiers, or other person or persons who shall have insured such house or houses or other buildings have been guilty of fraud, or of wilfully setting their house or houses or other buildings on fire, to cause the insurance money to be laid out and expended, as far as the same will go, towards rebuilding, reinstating or repairing such house or houses or other buildings so burnt down, demolished or damaged by fire, unless the party or parties claiming such insurance money shall, within sixty days next after his, her or their claim is adjusted, give a sufficient security to the governors or directors of the insurance office where such house or houses or other buildings are insured, that the same insurance money shall be laid out and expended as aforesaid, or unless the said insurance money shall be in that time settled and disposed of to and amongst all the contending parties, to the satisfaction and approbation of such governors or directors of such insurance office respectively.   **[1]**

86. No action to lie against a person where the fire accidentally begins

And ... no action, suit or process whatever shall be had, maintained or prosecuted against any person in whose house, chamber, stable, barn or other building, or on whose estate any fire shall ... accidentally begin, nor shall any recompence be made by such person for any damage suffered thereby, any law, usage or custom to the contrary notwithstanding: ... provided that no contract or agreement made between landlord and tenant shall be hereby defeated or made void.   **[2]**

NOTES
First words omitted repealed by the Statute Law Revision Act 1888; second words omitted repealed by the Statute Law Revision Act 1948; final words omitted repealed by the Statute Law Revision Act 1958.

PRESCRIPTION ACT 1832
(c 71)

ARRANGEMENT OF SECTIONS

An Act for shortening the Time of Prescription in certain cases   [1 August 1832]

1. Claims to right of common and other profits à prendre (except tithes, etc), not to be defeated after thirty years enjoyment by merely showing the commencement of the right—After sixty years enjoyment the right to be absolute, unless shown to be had by consent or agreement

... No claim which may be lawfully made at the common law, by custom, prescription, or grant, to any right of common or other profit or benefit to be taken and enjoyed from or upon any land of our sovereign lord the King ... or any land being parcel of the duchy of Lancaster or the duchy of Cornwall, or of any ecclesiastical or lay person, or body corporate, except such matters and things as are herein specially provided for, and except tithes, rent, and services, shall, where such right, profit, or benefit shall have been actually taken and enjoyed by any person claiming right thereto without interruption for the full period of thirty years, be defeated or destroyed by showing only that such right, profit, or benefit was first taken or enjoyed at any time prior to such period of thirty years, but nevertheless such claim may be defeated in any other way by which the same is now liable to be defeated; and when such right, profit, or benefit shall have been so taken and enjoyed as aforesaid for the full period of sixty years, the right thereto shall be deemed absolute and indefeasible, unless it shall appear that the same was taken and enjoyed by some consent or agreement expressly made or given for that purpose by deed or writing.   **[3]**

NOTES
   Words omitted repealed by the Statute Law Revision Act 1890.

2. In claims of rights of way or other easements the periods to be twenty years and forty years

... No claim which may be lawfully made at the common law, by custom, prescription, or grant, to any way or other easement, or to any watercourse, or the use of any water, to be enjoyed or derived upon, over, or from any land or water of our said lord the King ... or being parcel of the duchy of Lancaster or of the duchy of Cornwall, or being the property of any ecclesiastical or lay person, or body corporate, when such way or other matter as herein last before mentioned shall have been actually enjoyed by any person claiming right thereto without interruption for the full period of twenty years, shall be defeated or destroyed by showing only that such way or other matter was first enjoyed at any time prior to such period of twenty years, but nevertheless such claim may be defeated in any other way by which the same is now liable to be defeated; and where such way or other matter as herein last before mentioned shall have been so enjoyed as aforesaid for the full period of forty years, the right thereto shall be deemed absolute and indefeasible, unless it shall appear that the same was enjoyed by some consent or agreement expressly given or made for that purpose by deed or writing.　　　　　　　　　　　　　　　　　　　　　　　**[4]**

NOTES
　　Words omitted repealed by the Statute Law Revision (No 2) Act 1888 and the Statute Law Revision Act 1890.

3. Right to the use of light enjoyed for twenty years, indefeasible, unless shown to have been by consent

. . . When the access and use of light to and for any dwelling house, workshop, or other building shall have been actually enjoyed therewith for the full period of twenty years without interruption, the right thereto shall be deemed absolute and indefeasible, any local usage or custom to the contrary notwithstanding, unless it shall appear that the same was enjoyed by some consent or agreement expressly made or given for that purpose by deed or writing.　　　　　　　**[5]**

NOTES
　　Words omitted repealed by the Statute Law Revision (No 2) Act 1888.

4. The periods to be those next before the suit or action—What shall constitute an interruption

. . . Each of the respective periods of years herein-before mentioned shall be deemed and taken to be the period next before some suit or action wherein the claim or matter to which such period may relate shall have been or shall be brought into question; and . . . no act or other matter shall be deemed to be an interruption, within the meaning of this statute, unless the same shall have been or shall be submitted to or acquiesced in for one year after the party interrupted shall have had or shall have notice thereof, and of the person making or authorizing the same to be made.　　　　　　　　　　　　　　　　**[6]**

NOTES
　　Words omitted repealed by the Statute Law Revision (No 2) Act 1888.

5. What claimant may allege

. . . In all actions upon the case and other pleadings, wherein the party claiming may now by law allege his right generally, without averring the existence of such right from time immemorial, such general allegation shall still be deemed sufficient, and if the same shall be denied, all and every the matters in this Act mentioned and provided, which shall be applicable to the case, shall be admissible in evidence to sustain or rebut such allegation; and . . . in all pleadings to actions of trespass, and in all other pleadings wherein before the passing of this Act it would have been necessary to allege the right to have existed from time immemorial, it shall be sufficient to allege the enjoyment thereof as of right by the occupiers of the tenement in respect whereof the same is claimed for and during such of the periods mentioned in this Act as may be applicable to the case, and without claiming in the name or right of the owner of the fee, as is now usually done; and if the other party shall intend to rely on any proviso, exception, incapacity, disability, contract, agreement, or other matter herein-before mentioned, or on any cause or matter of fact or of law not inconsistent with the simple fact of enjoyment, the same shall be specially alleged and set forth in answer to the allegation of the party claiming, and shall not be received in evidence on any general traverse or denial of such allegation.

[7]

NOTES
Words omitted repealed by the Statute Law Revision (No 2) Act 1888.

6. No presumption to be allowed

... In the several cases mentioned in and provided for by this Act, no presumption shall be allowed or made in favour or support of any claim, upon proof of the exercise or enjoyment of the right or matter claimed for any less period of time or number of years than for such period or number mentioned in this Act as may be applicable to the case and to the nature of the claim.   [8]

NOTES
Words omitted repealed by the Statute Law Revision (No 2) Act 1888.

7. Proviso where any person capable of resisting a claim is an infant, etc

Provided also, that the time during which any person otherwise capable of resisting any claim to any of the matters before mentioned shall have been or shall be an infant, idiot, non compos mentis, feme covert, or tenant for life, or during which any action or suit shall have been pending, and which shall have been diligently prosecuted, until abated by the death of any party or parties thereto, shall be excluded in the computation of the periods herein-before mentioned, except only in cases where the right or claim is hereby declared to be absolute and indefeasible.   [9]

8. Time to be excluded in certain cases in computing the term of forty years appointed by this Act

Provided always, ... that when any land or water upon, over or from which any such way or other convenient watercourse or use of water shall have been or shall be enjoyed or derived hath been or shall be held under or by virtue of any term of life, or any term of years exceeding three years from the granting thereof, the time of the enjoyment of any such way or other matter as herein last before mentioned, during the continuance of such term, shall be excluded in the computation of the said period of forty years, in case the claim shall within three years next after the end or sooner determination of such term be resisted by any person entitled to any reversion expectant on the determination thereof.

[10]

NOTES
Words omitted repealed by the Statute Law Revision (No 2) Act 1888.

9. Extent of Act

This Act shall not extend to Scotland ...   [11]

NOTES
Words omitted repealed by the Statute Law Revision Act 1874.

FINES AND RECOVERIES ACT 1833
(c 74)

ARRANGEMENT OF SECTIONS

An Act for the Abolition of Fines and Recoveries and for the Substitution of more simple Modes of Assurance   [28 August 1833]

15. Power of actual tenants in tail, after 31 December 1833, to dispose of entailed lands in fee simple or for less estate, saving the rights of certain persons

. . . After the thirty-first day of December one thousand eight hundred and thirty-three every actual tenant in tail, whether in possession, remainder, contingency or otherwise, shall have full power to dispose of for an estate in fee simple absolute or for any less estate the lands entailed, as against all persons claiming the lands entailed by force of any estate tail which shall be vested in or might be claimed by, or which but for some previous act would have been vested in or might have been claimed by, the person making the disposition at the time of his making the same, and also as against all persons, including the King's most excellent Majesty, whose estates are to take effect after the determination or in defeasance of any such estate tail; saving always the rights of all persons in respect of estates prior to the estate tail in respect of which such disposition shall be made, and the rights of all other persons, except those against whom such disposition is by this Act authorized to be made.   **[12]**

NOTES
     Words omitted repealed by the Statute Law Revision (No 2) Act 1888.

18. The power of disposition not to extend to certain tenants in tail restrained by 34 & 35 Hen 8 c 20 etc

Provided always, . . . that the power of disposition hereinbefore contained shall not extend to tenants of estates tail who, by an Act passed in the thirty-fourth and thirty-fifth years of the reign of his Majesty King Henry the Eighth, intituled "An Act to embar feigned recovery of lands wherein the King is in reversion", or by any other Act, are restrained from barring their estates tail, or to tenants in tail after possibility of issue extinct.   **[13]**

NOTES
     Words omitted repealed by the Statute Law Revision (No 2) Act 1888.

19. Power after 31 December 1833, to enlarge base fees; saving the rights of certain persons

... After the thirty-first day of December one thousand eight hundred and thirty-three, in every case in which an estate tail in any lands shall have been barred and converted into a base fee, either before or on or after that day, the person who, if such estate tail had not been barred, would have been actual tenant in tail of the same lands, shall have full power to dispose of such lands as against all persons, including the King's most excellent Majesty, whose estates are to take effect after the determination or in defeasance of the base fee into which the estate tail shall have been converted, so as to enlarge the base fee into a fee simple absolute; saving always the rights of all persons in respect of estates prior to the estate tail which shall have been converted into a base fee, and the rights of all other persons, except those against whom such disposition is by this Act authorized to be made. **[14]**

NOTES
Words omitted repealed by the Statute Law Revision (No 2) Act 1888.

22. The owner of the first existing estate under a settlement, prior to an estate tail under the same settlement, to be the protector of the settlement

... If, at the time when there shall be a tenant in tail of lands under a settlement, there shall be subsisting in the same lands or any of them, under the same settlement, any estate for years determinable on the dropping of a life or lives, or any greater estate (not being an estate for years), prior to the estate tail, then the person who shall be the owner of the prior estate, or the first of such prior estates if more than one then subsisting under the same settlement, or who would have been so if noe absolute disposition thereof had been made, (the first of such prior estates, if more than one, being for all the purposes of this Act deemed the prior estate), shall be the protector of the settlement so far as regards the lands in which such prior estate shall be subsisting, and shall for all the purposes of the Act be deemed the owner of such prior estate, although the same may have been charged or incumbered either by the owner thereof or by the settlor, or otherwise howsoever, and although the whole of the rents and profits be exhausted or required for the payment of the charges and incumbrances on such prior estate, and although such prior estate may have been absolutely disposed of by the owner thereof, or by or in consequence of the bankruptcy or insolvency of such owner, or by any other act or default of such owner; and an estate by the curtesy, in respect of the estate tail, or of any prior estate created by the same settlement, shall be deemed a prior estate under the same settlement within the meaning of this clause; and an estate by way of resulting use or trust to or for the settlor shall be deemed an estate under the same settlement within the meaning of this clause. **[15]**

NOTES
Words omitted repealed by the Statute Law Revision (No 2) Act 1888.

34. Where there is a protector, his consent shall be requisite to enable an actual tenant in tail to create a larger estate than a base fee

Provided always, ... that if at the time when any person, actual tenant in tail of lands under a settlement, but not entitled to the remainder or reversion in fee immediately expectant on the determination of his estate tail, shall be desirous of making under this Act a disposition of the lands entailed, there shall be a protector of such settlement, then and in every such case the consent of such protector shall be requisite to enable such actual tenant in tail to dispose of the lands entailed to the full extent to which he is herein-before authorized to dispose of the same; but such actual tenant in tail may, without such consent, make a disposition under this Act of the lands entailed, which shall be good against all persons who, by force of any estate tail which shall be vested in or might be claimed by, or which but for some previous act or default would have been vested in or might have been claimed by, the person making the disposition at the time of his making the same, shall claim the lands entailed.   **[16]**

NOTES
Words omitted repealed by the Statute Law Revision (No 2) Act 1888.

35. Where there is a base fee, and a protector, his consent shall be requisite to the exercise of the power of disposition

Provided always, . . . that where an estate tail shall have been converted into a base fee, in such case, so long as there shall be a protector of the settlement by which the estate tail was created, the consent of such protector shall be requisite to enable the person who would have been tenant of the estate tail if the same had not been barred to exercise, as to the lands in respect of which there shall be such protector, the power of disposition herein-before contained.   **[17]**

NOTES
Words omitted repealed by the Statute Law Revision (No 2) Act 1888.

39. Base Fees, when united with the immediate reversions, enlarged, instead of being merged

. . . If a base fee in any lands, and the remainder or reversion in fee in the same lands, shall at the time of the passing of this Act, or at any time afterwards, be united in the same person, and at any time after the passing of this Act there shall be no intermediate estate between the base fee and the remainder or reversion, then and in such case the base fee shall not merge, but shall be ipso facto enlarged into as large an estate as the tenant in tail, with the consent of the protector, if any, might have created by any disposition under this Act, if such remainder or reversion had been vested in any other person.   **[18]**

NOTES
Words omitted repealed by the Statute Law Revision (No 2) Act 1888.

WILLS ACT 1837
(c 26)

ARRANGEMENT OF SECTIONS

An Act for the amendment of the Laws with respect to Wills   [3 July 1837]

1. Meaning of certain words in this Act

. . . the words and expressions herein-after mentioned, which in their ordinary signification have a more confined or a different meaning, shall in this Act, except where the nature of the provisions or the context of the Act shall exclude such construction, be interpreted as follows; (that is to say,) the word "will" shall extend to a testament, and to a codicil, and to an appointment by will or by writing in the nature of a will in exercise of a power, [and also to an appointment by will of a guardian of a child], . . . and to any other testamentary disposition; and the words "real estate" shall extend to manors, advowsons, messuages, lands, tithes, rents, and hereditaments, . . . whether corporeal, incorporeal, or personal, and to any undivided share thereof, and to any estate, right, or interest (other than a chattel interest) therein; and the words "personal estate" shall extend to leasehold estates and other chattels real and also to monies, shares of government and other funds, securities for money (not being real estates), debts, choses in action, rights, credits, goods, and all other property whatsoever which by law devolves upon the executor or administrator, and to any share or interest therein; and every word importing the singular number only shall extend and be applied to several persons or things as well as one person or thing; and every word importing the masculine gender only shall extend and be applied to a female as well as a male.   **[19]**

NOTES
    First words omitted repealed by the Statute Law Revision Act 1893; words in square brackets substituted by the Children Act 1989, s 108(5), Sch 13, para 1; other words omitted repealed by the Statute Law (Repeals) Act 1969, s 1, Schedule, Part III.

3. All property may be disposed of by will

. . . it shall be lawful for every person to devise, bequeath, or dispose of, by his will executed in manner herein-after required, all real estate and all personal estate which he shall be entitled to, either at law or in equity, at the time of his death, and which, if not so devised, bequeathed, and disposed of, would devolve . . . upon his executor or administrator; and . . . the power hereby given shall extend . . . to all contingent, executory or other future interests in any real or personal estate, whether the testator may or may not be ascertained as the person or one of the persons in whom the same respectively may become vested, and whether he may be entitled thereto under the instrument by which the same respectively were created, or under any disposition thereof by deed or will; and also to all rights of entry for conditions broken, and other rights of entry; and also to such of the same estates, interests, and rights respectively, and other real and personal estate, as the testator may be entitled to at the time of his death, notwithstanding that he may become entitlted to the same subsequently to the execution of his will. **[20]**

NOTES
First and third words omitted repealed by the Statute Law Revision (No 2) Act 1888; other words omitted repealed by the Statute Law (Repeals) Act 1969.

7. No will of a person under age valid

. . . no will made by any person under the age of [eighteen years] shall be valid.
[21]

NOTES
Words omitted repealed by the Statute Law Revision (No 2) Act 1888; words in square brackets substituted by the Family Law Reform Act 1969, s 3(1)(a).

[9. Signing and attestation of wills

No will shall be valid unless—

    (*a*) it is in writing, and signed by the testator, or by some other person in his presence and by his direction; and

    (*b*) it apears that the testator intended by his signature to give effect to the will; and

    (*c*) the signature is made or acknowledged by the testator in the presence of two or more witnesses present at the same time; and

    (*d*) each witness either—

        (i) attests and signs the will; or

        (ii) acknowledges his signature, in the presence of the testator (but not necessarily in the presence of any other witness),

but no form of attestation shall be necessary.] **[22]**

NOTES
Substituted with a saving by the Administration of Justice Act 1982, ss 17, 73(6).

10. Appointments by will to be executed like other wills, and to be valid, although other required solemnities are not observed

. . . no appointment made by will, in exercise of any power, shall be valid, unless the same be executed in manner herein-before required; and every will executed in manner herein-before required shall, so far as respects the execution and attestation thereof, be a valid execution of a power of appointment by will, notwithstanding it shall have been expressly required that a will made in exercise of such power should be executed with some additional or other form of execution or solemnity. **[23]**

NOTES
Words omitted repealed by the Statute Law Revision (No 2) Act 1888.

11. Saving as to wills of soldiers and mariners.

Provided always, . . . that any soldier being in actual military service, or any mariner or seaman being at sea, may dispose of his personal estate as he might have done before the making of this Act. **[24]**

NOTES
Words omitted repealed by the Statute Law Revision (No 2) Act 1888.

13. Publication of will not requisite

. . . every will executed in manner herein-before required shall be valid without any other publication thereof. **[25]**

NOTES
Words omitted repealed by the Statute Law Revision (No 2) Act 1888.

14. Will not be void on account of incompetency of arresting witness

. . . if any person who shall attest the execution of a will shall at the time of the execution thereof or at any time afterwards be incompetent to be admitted a witness to prove the execution thereof, such will shall not on that account be invalid. **[26]**

NOTES
Words omitted repealed by the Statute Law Revision (No 2) Act 1888.

15. Gifts to an attesting witness, or his or her wife or husband, to be void

. . . if any person shall attest the execution of any will to whom or to whose wife or husband any beneficial devise, legacy, estate, interest, gift, or appointment, of or affecting any real or personal estate (other than and except charges and directions for the payment of any debt or debts), shall be thereby given or made, such devise, legacy, estate, interest, gift, or appointment shall, so far only as concerns such person attesting the execution of such will, or the wife or husband of such person, or any person claiming under such person or wife or husband, be utterly null and void, and such person so attesting shall be admitted as a witness to prove the execution of such will, or to prove the validity or invalidity thereof, notwithstanding such devise, legacy, estate, interest, gift, or appointment mentioned in such will. **[27]**

NOTES
Words omitted repealed by the Statute Law Revision (No 2) Act 1888.

16. Creditor attesting a will charging estate with debts shall be admitted a witness.

. . . in case by any will any real or personal estate shall be charged with any debt or debts, and any creditor, or the wife or husband of any creditor, whose debt is so charged, shall attest the execution of such will, such creditor notwithstanding such charge shall be admitted a witness to prove the execution of such will, or to prove the validity or invalidity thereof. **[28]**

NOTES
Words omitted repealed by the Statute Law Revision (No 2) Act 1888.

17. Executor shall be admitted a witness

. . . no person shall, on account of his being an executor of a will, be incompetent to be admitted a witness to prove the execution of such will, or a witness to prove the validity or invalidity thereof.   **[29]**

NOTES
Words omitted repealed by the Statute Law Revision (No 2) Act 1888.

[18. Wills to be revoked by marriage, except in certain cases

(1) Subject to subsections (2) to (4) below, a will shall be revoked by the testator's marriage.

(2) A disposition in a will in exercise of a power of appointment shall take effect notwithstanding the testator's subsequent marriage unless the property so appointed would in default of appointment pass to his personal representatives.

(3) Where it appears from a will that at the time it was made the testator was expecting to be married to a particular person and that he intended that the will should not be revoked by the marriage, the will shall not be revoked by his marriage to that person.

(4) Where it appears from a will that at the time it was made the testator was expecting to be married to a particular person and that he intended that a disposition in the will should not be revoked by his marriage to that person,—

    (*a*) that disposition shall take effect notwithstanding the marriage; and

    (*b*) any other disposition in the will shall take effect also, unless it appears from the will that the testator intended the disposition to be revoked by the marriage.]   **[30]**

NOTES
Substituted with a saving by the Administration of Justice Act 1982, ss 18(1), 73(6).

[18A. Effect of dissolution or annulment of marriage on wills

(1) Where, after a testator has made a will, a decree of a court [of civil jurisdiction in England and Wales] dissolves or annuls his marriage [or his marriage is dissolved or annulled and the divorce or annulment is entitled to recognition in England and Wales by virtue of Part II of the Family Law Act 1986],—

    (*a*) the will shall take effect as if any appointment of the former spouse as an executor or as the executor and trustee of the will were omitted; and

    (*b*) any devise or bequest to the former spouse shall lapse,

except in so far as a contrary intention appears by the will.

(2) Subsection (1)(*b*) above is without prejudice to any right of the former spouse to apply for financial provision under the Inheritance (Provision for Family and Dependants) Act 1975.

(3) Where—

    (*a*) by the terms of a will an interest in remainder is subject to a life interest; and (*b*) the life interest lapses by virtue of subsection (1)(*b*) above,

the interest in remainder shall be treated as if it had not been subject to the life interest and, if it was contingent upon the termination of the life interest, as if it had not been so contingent.] **[31]**

NOTES

Inserted with a saving by the Administration of Justice Act 1982, ss 18(2), 73(6).
Sub-s (1): first words in square brackets substituted and second words in square brackets inserted by the Family Law Act 1986, s 53.

19. No will to be revoked by presumption from altered circumstances

. . . no will shall be revoked by any presumption of an intention on the ground of an alteration in circumstances. **[32]**

NOTES

Words omitted repealed by the Statute Law Revision (No 2) Act 1888.

20. No will to be revoked otherwise than as aforesaid or by another will or codicil, or by destruction thereof

. . . no will or codicil, or any part thereof, shall be revoked otherwise than as aforesaid, or by another will or codicil executed in manner herein-before required, or by some writing declaring an intention to revoke the same and executed in the manner in which a will is herein-before required to be executed, or by the burning, tearing, or otherwise destroying the same by the testator, or by some person in his presence and by his direction, with the intention of revoking the same. **[33]**

NOTES

Words omitted repealed by the Statute Law Revision (No 2) Act 1888.

21. No alteration in a will after execution except in certain cases, shall have any effect, unless executed as a will

. . . no obliteration, interlineation, or other alteration made in any will after the execution thereof shall be valid or have any effect, except so far as the words or effect of the will before such alteration shall not be apparent, unless such alteration shall be executed in like manner as herein-before is required for the execution of the will; but the will, with such alteration as part thereof, shall be deemed to be duly executed if the signature of the testator and the subscription of the witnesses be made in the margin or on some other part of the will opposite or near to such alteration, or at the foot or end of or opposite to a memorandum referring to such alteration, and written at the end of some other part of the will. **[34]**

NOTES

Words omitted repealed by the Statute Law Revision (No 2) Act 1888.

22. No revoked will shall be revived otherwise than by re-execution or a codicil, etc

. . . no will or codicil, or any part thereof, which shall be in any manner revoked, shall be revived otherwise than by the re-execution thereof or by a codicil executed in manner herein-before required and showing an intention to revive the same; and when any will or codicil which shall be partly revoked, and afterwards wholly revoked, shall be revived, such revival shall not extend to so much thereof as shall have been revoked before the revocation of the whole thereof, unless an intention to the contrary shall be shown.   [35]

NOTES
Words omitted repealed by the Statute Law Revision (No 2) Act 1888.

23. Subsequent conveyance or other act not to prevent operation of will

... no conveyance or other act made or done subsequently to the execution of a will of or relating to any real or personal estate therein comprised, except an act by which such will shall be revoked as aforesaid, shall prevent the operation of the will with respect to such estate or interest in such real or personal estate as the testator shall have power to dispose of by will at the time of his death.   [36]

NOTES
Words omitted repealed by the Statute Law Revision (No 2) Act 1888.

24. Wills shall be construed as to the estate comprised, to speak from the death of the testator

... every will shall be construed, with reference to the real estate and personal estate comprised in it, to speak and take effect as if it had been executed immediately before the death of the testator, unless a contrary intention shall appear by the will.   [37]

NOTES
Words omitted repealed by the Statute Law Revision (No 2) Act 1888.

25. Residuary devises shall include estates comprised in lapsed and void devises

... unless a contrary intention shall appear by the will, such real estate or interest therein as shall be comprised or intended to be comprised in any devise in such will contained, which shall fail or be void by reason of the death of the devisee in the lifetime of the testator, or by reason of such devise being contrary to law or otherwise incapable of taking effect shall be included in the residuary devise (if any) contained in such will.   [38]

NOTES
Words omitted repealed by the Statute Law Revision (No 2) Act 1888.

26. A general devise of the testator's lands shall include copyhold and leasehold as well as freehold lands, in the absence of a contrary intention

... a devise of the land of the testator, or of the land of the testator in any place or in the occupation of any person mentioned in his will, or otherwise described in a general manner, and any other general devise which would describe a ... leasehold estate if the testator had no freehold estate which could be described by it, shall be construed to include the ... leasehold estates of the testator, or his ... leasehold estates, or any of them, to which such description shall extend, as the case may be, as well as freehold estates, unless a contrary intention shall appear by the will.   [39]

NOTES
First words omitted repealed by the Statute Law Revision (No 2) Act 1888; other words omitted repealed by the Statute Law (Repeals) Act 1969.

27. A general gift of realty or personalty shall include property over which the testator has a general power of appointment

. . . a general devise of the real estate of the testator, or of the real estate of the testator in any place or in the occupation of any person mentioned in his will, or otherwise described in a general manner, shall be construed to include any real estate, or any real estate to which such description shall extend (as the case may be), which he may have power to appoint in any manner he may think proper, and shall operate as an execution of such power, unless a contrary intention shall appear by the will; and in like manner a bequest of the personal estate of the testator, or any bequest of personal property described in a general manner, shall be construed to include any personal estate, or any personal estate to which such description shall extend (as the case may be), which he may have power to appoint in any manner he may think proper, and shall operate as an execution of such power, unless a contrary intention shall appear by the will.   **[40]**

NOTES
 Words omitted repealed by the Statute Law Revision (No 2) Act 1888.

28. A devise of real estate without any words of limitation shall pass the fee, etc

. . . where any real estate shall be devised to any person without any words of limitation, such devise shall be construed to pass the fee simple, or other the whole estate or interest which the testator had power to dispose of by will in such real estate, unless a contrary intention shall appear by the will.   **[41]**

NOTES
 Words omitted repealed by the Statute Law Revision (No 2) Act 1888.

29. The words "die without issue," or "die without leaving issue," etc, shall mean a want or failure of issue in the lifetime or at the death of the person, except in certain cases

. . . in any devise or bequest of real or personal estate the words "die without issue" or "die without leaving issue," or "have no issue," or any other words which may import either a want or failure of issue of any person in his lifetime or at the time of his death, or an indefinite failure of his issue, shall be construed to mean a want or failure of issue in the lifetime or at the time of the death of such person, and not an indefinite failure of his issue, unless a contrary intention shall appear by the will, by reason of such person having a prior estate tail, or of a preceding gift, being, without any implication arising from such words, a limitation of an estate tail to such person or issue, or otherwise: Provided, that this Act shall not extend to cases where such words as aforesaid import if no issue described in a preceding gift shall be born, or if there shall be no issue who shall live to attain the age or otherwise answer the description required for obtaining a vested estate by a preceding gift to such issue.   **[42]**

NOTES
 Words omitted repealed by the Statute Law Revision (No 2) Act 1888.

30. Devise of realty to trustees or executors shall pass the fee, etc, except in certain cases

. . . where any real estate (other than or not being a presentation to a church) shall be devised to any trustee or executor, such devise shall be construed to pass the fee simple or other the whole estate or interest which the testator had power to dispose of by will in such real estate, unless a definite term of years, absolute or determinable, or an estate of freehold, shall thereby be given to him expressly or by implication. **[43]**

NOTES

Words omitted repealed by the Statute Law Revision (No 2) Act 1888.

31. Trustees under an unlimited devise, where the trust may endure beyond the life of a person beneficially entitled for life, shall take the fee, etc

... where any real estate shall be devised to a trustee, without any express limitation of the estate to be taken by such trustee, and the beneficial interest in such real estate, or in the surplus rents and profits thereof, shall not be given to any person for life, or such beneficial interest shall be given to any person for life, but the purposes of the trust may continue beyond the life of such person, such devise shall be construed to vest in such trustee the fee simple, or other the whole legal estate which the testator had power to dispose of by will in such real estate, and not an estate determinable when the purposes of the trust shall be satisfied. **[44]**

NOTES

Words omitted repealed by the Statute Law Revision (No 2) Act 1888.

32. Devises of estates tail shall not lapse where inheritable issue survives, etc

... where any person to whom any real estate shall be devised for an estate tail or an estate in quasi entail shall die in the lifetime of the testator leaving issue who would be heritable under such entail, and any such issue shall be living at the time of the death of the testator, such devise shall not lapse, but shall take effect as if the death of such person had happened immediately after the death of the testator, unless a contrary intention shall appear by the will. **[45]**

NOTES

Words omitted repealed by the Statute Law Revision (No 2) Act 1888.

[33. Gifts to children or other issue who leave issue living at the testator's death shall not lapse

(1) Where—

    (*a*) a will contains a devise or bequest to a child or remoter descendant of the testator; and

    (*b*) the intended beneficiary dies before the testator, leaving issue; and

    (*c*) issue of the intended beneficiary are living at the testator's death,

then, unless a contrary intention appears by the will, the devise or bequest shall take effect as a devise or bequest to the issue living at the testator's death.

    (2) Where—

    (*a*) a will contains a devise or bequest to a class of person consisting of children or remoter descendants of the testator; and

    (*b*) a member of the class dies before the testator, leaving issue, and

    (*c*) issue of that member are living at the testator's death,

then, unless a contrary intention appears by the will, the devise or bequest shall take effect as if the class included the issue of its deceased member living at the testator's death.

    (3) Issue shall take under this section through all degrees, according to their stock, in equal shares if more than one, any gift or share which their parent

would have taken and so that no issue shall take whose parent is living at the testator's death and that no issue shall take whose parent is living at the testator's death and so capable of taking.

(4) For the purposes of this section—

(*a*) the illegitimacy of any person is to be disregarded; and

(*b*) a person conceived before the testator's death and born living thereafter is to be taken to have been living at the testator's death.]

[46]

NOTES

Substituted with a saving by the Administration of Justice Act 1982, ss 19, 73(6).

34. Act not to extend to wills made before 1838, or to estates pur autre vie of persons who die before 1838

... this Act shall not extend to any will made before the first day of January one thousand eight hundred and thirty-eight; and every will re-executed or republished, or revived by any codicil, shall for the purposes of this Act be deemed to have been made at the time at which the same shall be so re-executed, republished or revived; and this Act shall not extend to any estate pur autre vie of any person who shall die before the first day of January one thousand eight hundred and thirty-eight. **[47]**

NOTES

Words omitted repealed by the Statute Law Revision (No 2) Act 1888.

SCHOOL SITES ACT 1841
(c 38)

An Act to afford further facilites for the Conveyance and Endowment of Sites for Schools [21 June 1841]

2. Limited owners may convey land to be used as sites for schools etc—Land to revert on ceasing to be used for a school

Any person, being seised in fee simple, fee tail, or for life, of and in any manor or lands of freehold, copyhold, or customary tenure, and having the beneficial interest therein, ... may grant, convey, or enfranchise by way of gift, sale, or exchange, in fee simple or for a term of years, any quantity not exceeding one acre of such land, as a site for a school for the education of poor persons, or for the residence of the schoolmaster or schoolmistress, or otherwise for the purposes of the education of such poor persons in religious and useful knowledge; provided that no such grant made by any person seised only for life of and in any such manor or lands shall be valid, unless the person next entitled to the same in remainder, in fee simple or fee tail, (if legally competent,) shall be a party to and join in such grant: Provided also, that where any portion of waste or commonable land shall be gratuitously conveyed by any lord or lady of a manor for any such purposes as aforesaid, the rights and interest of all persons in the said land shall be barred and divested by such conveyance; Provided also, that upon the said land so granted as aforesaid, or any part thereof, ceasing to be used for the purposes in this Act mentioned, the same shall thereupon immediately revert to and become a portion of the said estate held in fee simple or otherwise, or of any manor or land as aforesaid, as fully to all intents and purposes as if this Act had not been passed, any thing herein contained to the contrary notwithstanding. **[48]**

NOTES

Words omitted repealed by the Education (Scotland) Act 1945, Sch 5.

LANDS CLAUSES CONSOLIDATION ACT 1845
(c 18)

ARRANGEMENT OF SECTIONS

Purchase of lands otherwise than by agreement

An Act for consolidating in one Act certain Provisions usually inserted in Acts authorizing the taking of Lands for Undertakings of a Public Nature
[8 May 1845]

Purchase of lands otherwise than by agreement

68. Compensation to be settled by arbitration or jury, at the option of the party claiming compensation

If any party shall be entitled to any compensation in respect of any lands, or of any interest therein which shall have been taken for or injuriously affected by the execution of the works, and for which the promoters of the undertaking shall not have made satisfaction under the provisions of this or the special Act, or any Act incorporated therewith, ... such party may have the same settled ... **[49]**

NOTES

Words omitted repealed by the Compulsory Purchase Act 1965, s 39(4), Sch 8, Part III.

Conveyances

81. Forms of Conveyances

And with respect to the conveyances of lands, be it enacted as follows:

Conveyances of lands to be purchased under the provisions of this or the special Act, or any Act incorporated therewith, may be according to the forms in the schedules (A) and (B) respectively to this Act annexed, or as near thereto as the circumstances of the case will admit, or by deed in any other form which the promoters of the undertaking may think fit; and all conveyances made according to the forms in the said schedules, or as near thereto as the circumstances of the case will admit, shall be effectual to vest the lands thereby conveyed in the promoters of the undertaking, and shall operate . . . to bar and to destroy all such estates tail, and all other estates, rights, titles, remainders, reversions, limitations, trusts, and interests whatsoever, of and in the lands comprised in such conveyances, which shall have been purchased or compensated for by the consideration therein mentioned . . .   **[49A]**

NOTES

Words omitted repealed by the Compulsory Purchase Act 1965, ss 39(4), 40(3), Sch 8, Part II.

Sale of Superfluous Land

127. Lands not wanted to be sold within 10 years after expiration of time limited for completion of works, or in default to vest in owners of adjoining lands

And with respect to lands acquired by the promoters of the undertaking under the provisions of this or the special Act, or any Act incorporated therewith, but which shall not be required for the purposes thereof, be it enacted as follows:

Within the prescribed period, or if no period be prescribed within ten years after the expiration of the time limited by the special Act for the completion of the works, the promoters of the undertaking shall absolutely sell and dispose of all such superfluous lands, and apply the purchase money arising from such sales to the purposes of the special Act; and in default thereof all such superfluous lands remaining unsold at the expiration of such period shall thereupon vest in and become the property of the owners of the lands adjoining thereto, in proportion to the extent of their lands respectively adjoining the same.   **[50]**

128. Lands not in a town or built upon, etc, to be offered to owner of lands from which they were originally taken, or to adjoining owners

Before the promoters of the undertaking dispose of any such superfluous lands they shall, unless such lands be situate within a town, or be lands built upon or used for building purposes, first offer to sell the same to the person then entitled to the lands (if any) from which the same were originally severed; or if such person refuse to purchase the same, or cannot after diligent inquiry be found, then the like offer shall be made to the person or to the several persons whose lands shall immediately adjoin the lands so proposed to be sold, such persons being capable of entering into a contract for the purchase of such lands; and where more than one such person shall be entitled to such right of pre-emption such offer shall be made to such persons in succession, one after another, in such order as the promoters of the undertaking shall think fit.   **[51]**

129. Right of pre-emption to be claimed within six weeks from offer— Evidence of refusal, etc, to exercise right

If any such persons be desirous of purchasing such lands, then within six weeks after such offer of sale they shall signify their desire in that behalf to the promoters of the undertaking; or if they decline such offer, or if for six weeks they neglect to signify their desire to purchase such lands, the right of pre-emption of every such person so declining or neglecting in respect of the lands included in such offer shall cease; and a declaration in writing made before a justice by some person not interested in the matter in question, stating that such offer was made, and was refused, or not accepted within six weeks from the time of making the same, or that the person or all the persons entitled to the right of pre-emption were out of the country, or could not after diligent inquiry be found, or were not capable of entering into a contract for the purchase of such lands, shall in all courts be sufficient evidence of the facts therein stated.

[52]

130. Differences as to price to be settled by arbitration

If any person entitled to such pre-emption be desirous of purchasing any such lands, and such person and the promoters of the undertaking do not agree as to the price thereof, then such price shall be ascertained by arbitration, and the costs of such arbitration shall be in the discretion of the arbitrators.   **[53]**

COMMON LAW PROCEDURE ACT 1852
(c 76)

An Act to amend the Process, Practice, and Mode of Pleading in the Superior Courts of Common Law at Westminster, and in the Superior Courts of the Counties Palatine of Lancaster and Durham   [30 June 1852]

Ejectment

210. Proceedings in ejectment by landlord for non-payment of rent

In all cases between landlord and tenant, as often as it shall happen that one half year's rent shall be in arrear, and the landlord or lessor, to whom the same is due, hath right by law to re-enter for the non-payment thereof, such landlord or lessor shall and may, without any formal demand or re-entry, serve a writ in ejectment for the recovery of the demised premises, . . . which service . . . shall stand in the place and stead of a demand and re-entry; and in case of judgment against the defendant for nonappearance, if it shall be made appear to the court where the said action is depending, by affidavit, or be proved upon the trial in case the defendant appears, that half a year's rent was due before the said writ was served, and that no sufficient distress was to be found on the demised premises, countervailing the arrears then due, and that the lessor had power to re-enter, then and in every such case the lessor shall recover judgment and execution, in the same manner as if the rent in arrear had been legally demanded, and a re-entry made; and in case the lessee or his assignee, or other person claiming or deriving under the said lease, shall permit and suffer judgment to be had and recovered on such trial in ejectment, and execution to be executed thereon, without paying the rent and arrears, together with full costs, and without proceeding for relief in equity within six months after such execution executed, then and in such case the said lessee, his assignee, and all other persons claiming and deriving under the said lease, shall be barred and foreclosed from all relief or remedy in law or equity, other than by bringing error for reversal of such judgment, in case the same shall be erroneous, and the said landlord or lessor shall from thenceforth hold the said demised premises discharged from such lease; . . . provided that nothing herein contained shall extend to bar the right of any mortgagee of such lease, or any part thereof, who shall not be in possession, so as such mortgagee shall and do, within six months after such judgment obtained and execution executed pay all rent in arrear, and all costs and damages sustained by such lessor or person entitled to the remainder or reversion as aforesaid, and perform all the covenants and agreements which, on the part and behalf of the first lessee, are and ought to be performed.   [54]

NOTES
Words omitted repealed with savings by the Statute Law Revision Act 1892.

211. Lessee proceeding in equity not to have injunction or relief without payment of rent and costs

In case the said lessee, his assignee, or other person claiming any right, title, or interest, in law or equity, of, in, or to the said lease, shall, within the time aforesaid, proceed for relief in any court of equity, such person shall not have or continue any injunction against the proceedings at law on such ejectment, unless he does or shall, within forty days next after a full and perfect answer shall be made by the claimant in such ejectment, bring into court, and lodge with the proper officer such sum and sums of money as the lessor or landlord shall in his answer swear to be due and in arrear over and above all just allowances, and also the costs taxed in the said suit, there to remain till the hearing of the cause, or to be paid out to the lessor or landlord on good security, subject to the decree of the court; and in case such proceedings for relief in equity shall be taken within the time aforesaid, and after execution is executed, the lessor or landlord shall be accountable only for so much and no more as he shall really and bona fide, without fraud, deceit, or wilful neglect, make of the demised premises from the time of his entering into the actual possession thereof; and if what shall be so made by the lessor or landlord happen to be less than the rent reserved on the said lease, then the said lessee or his assignee, before he shall be restored to his possession, shall pay such lessor or landlord what the money so by him made fell short of the reserved rent for the time such lessor or landlord held the said lands.   [55]

212. Tenant paying all rent, with costs, proceedings to cease

If the tenant or his assignee do or shall, at any time before the trial in such ejectment, pay or tender to the lessor or landlord, his executors or administrators, or his or their attorney in that cause, or pay into the court where the same cause is depending, all the rent and arrears, together with the costs, then and in such case all further proceedings on the said ejectment shall cease and be discontinued; and if such lessee, his executors, administrators, or assigns, shall, upon such proceedings as aforesaid, be relieved in equity, he and they shall have, hold, and enjoy the demised lands, according to the lease thereof made, without any new lease.   [56]

APPORTIONMENT ACT 1870
(c 75)

An Act for the better Apportionment of Rents and other periodical Payments
[1 August 1870]

1. Short title

This Act may be cited for all purposes as "The Apportionment Act 1870".
[56A]

2. Rents, etc to be apportionable in respect of time

. . . All rents, annuities, dividends, and other periodical payments in the nature of income (whether reserved or made payable under an instrument in writing or otherwise) shall, like interest on money lent, be considered as accruing from day to day, and shall be apportionable in respect of time accordingly. **[56B]**

NOTES
Words omitted repealed by the Statute Law Revision (No 2) Act 1893.

3. Apportioned part of rent, etc to be payable when the next entire portion shall have become due

The apportioned part of any such rent, annuity, dividend, or other payment shall be payable or recoverable in the case of a continuing rent, annuity, or other such payment when the entire portion of which such apportioned part shall form part shall become due and payable, and not before, and in the case of a rent, annuity, or other such payment determined by re-entry, death, or otherwise when the next entire portion of the same would have been payable if the same had not so determined, and not before. **[56C]**

4. Persons shall have the same remedies for recovering apportioned parts as for entire portions—Proviso as to rents reserved in certain cases

All persons and their respective heirs, executors, administrators, and assigns, and also the executors, administrators, and assigns respectively of persons whose interests determine with their own deaths, shall have such or the same remedies at law and in equity for recovering such apportioned parts as aforesaid when payable (allowing proportionate parts of all just allowances) as they respectively would have had for recovering such entire portions as aforesaid if entitled thereto respectively; provided that persons liable to pay rents reserved out of or charged on lands or other hereditaments of any tenure, and the same lands or other hereditaments, shall not be resorted to for any such apportioned part forming part of an entire or continuing rent as aforesaid specifically, but the entire or continuing rent, including such apportioned part, shall be recovered and received by the heir or other person who, if the rent had not been apportionable under this Act, or otherwise, would have been entitled to such entire or continuing rent, and such apportioned part shall be recoverable from such heir or other person by the executors or other parties entitled under this Act to the same by action at law or suit in equity. **[56D]**

5. Interpretation

In the construction of this Act—

The word "rents" includes rent service, rentcharge, and rent seck, and also tithes and all periodical payments or renderings in lieu of or in the nature of rent of tithe.

The word "annuities" includes salaries and pensions.

The word "dividends" includes (besides dividends strictly so called) all payments made by the name of dividend, bonus or otherwise out of the revenue of trading or other public companies, divisible between all or any of the members of such respective companies, whether such payments shall be usually made or declared, at any fixed times or otherwise; and all such divisible revenue shall, for the purposes of this Act, be deemed to have accrued by equal daily increment during and within the period for or in respect of which the payment of the same revenue shall be declared or expressed to be made, but the said word "dividend" does not include payments in the nature of a return or reimbursement of capital. **[56E]**

6. Act not to apply to policies of assurance

Nothing in this Act contained shall render apportionable any annual sums made payable in policies of assurance of any description. **[56F]**

7. Nor where stipulation made to the contrary

The provisions of this Act shall not extend to any case in which it is or shall be expressly stipulated that no apportionment shall take place. **[56G]**

MARRIED WOMEN'S PROPERTY ACT 1882
(c 75)

An Act to consolidate and amend the Acts relating to the Property of Married Women [18 August 1882]

11. Moneys payable under policy of assurance not to form part of estate of the insured

A married woman may . . . effect a policy upon her own life or the life of her husband for her [own benefit]; and the same and all benefit thereof shall enure accordingly.

A policy of assurance effected by any man on his own life, and expressed to be for the benefit of his wife, or of his children, or of his wife and children, or any of them, or by any woman on her own life, and expressed to be for the benefit of her husband, or of her children, or of her husband and children, or any of them, shall create a trust in favour of the objects therein named, and the moneys payable under any such policy shall not, so long as any object of the trust remains unperformed, form part of the estate of the insured, or be subject to his or her debts: Provided, that if it shall be proved that the policy was effected and the premiums paid with intent to defraud the creditors of the insured, they shall be entitled to receive, out of the moneys payable under the policy, a sum equal to the premiums so paid. The insured may by the policy, or by any memorandum under his or her hand, appoint a trustee or trustees of the moneys payable under the policy, and from time to time appoint a new trustee or new trustees thereof, and may make provision for the appointment of a new trustee or new trustees thereof, and for the investment of the moneys payable under such policy. In default of any such appointment of a trustee, such policy, immediately on its being effected, shall vest in the insured and his or her legal personal representatives, in trust for the purposes aforesaid . . . The receipt of a trustee or trustees duly appointed, or in default of any such appointment, or in default of notice to the insurance office, the receipt of the legal personal representatives of the insured shall be a discharge to the office for the sum secured by the policy, or for the value thereof, in whole or in part.   **[57]**

NOTES
First words omitted repealed and words in square brackets substituted by the Law Reform (Married Women and Tortfeasors) Act 1935, ss 5(1), (2), 8(2), Schs 1, 2; second words omitted repealed by the Statute Law (Repeals) Act 1969.

17. Questions between husband and wife as to property to be decided in a summary way

In any question between husband and wife as to the title to or possession of property, either party, ... may apply by summons or otherwise in a summary way [to the High Court or such county court as may be prescribed and the court may, on such an application (which may be heard in private), make such order with respect to the property as it thinks fit.

In this section "prescribed" means prescribed by rules of court and rules made for the purposes of this section may confer jurisdiction on county courts whatever the situation or value of the property in dispute.]   **[58]**

NOTES
Words omitted repealed by the Statute Law (Repeals) Act 1969; words in square brackets substituted by the Matrimonial and Family Proceedings Act 1984, s 43.

WILLS (SOLDIERS AND SAILORS) ACT 1918
(c 58)

ARRANGEMENT OF SECTIONS

An Act to amend the Law with respect to Testamentary Dispositions by Soldiers and Sailors   [6 February 1918]

1. Explanation of s 11 of Wills Act 1837

In order to remove doubts as to the construction of the Wills Act 1837, it is hereby declared and enacted that section eleven of that Act authorises and always has authorised any soldier being in actual military service, or any mariner or seaman being at sea, to dispose of his personal estate as he might have done before the passing of that Act, though under the age of [eighteen years].   **[59]**

NOTES
Words in square brackets substituted by the Family Law Reform Act 1969, s 3(1)(b).

2. Extension of s 11 of Wills Act 1837

Section eleven of the Wills Act 1837 shall extend to any member of His Majesty's naval or marine forces not only when he is at sea but also when he is so circumstanced that if he were a soldier he would be in actual military service within the meaning of that section. **[60]**

3. Validity of testamentary dispositions of real property made by soldiers and sailors

(1) A testamentary disposition of any real estate in England or Ireland made by a person to whom section eleven of the Wills Act 1837 applies, and who dies after the passing of this Act, shall, notwithstanding that the person making the disposition was at the time of making it under [eighteen years] of age or that the disposition has not been made in such manner or form as was at the passing of this Act required by law, be valid in any case where the person making the disposition was of such age and the disposition has been made in such manner and form that if the disposition had been a disposition of personal estate made by such a person domiciled in England or Ireland it would have been valid.

(2) A testamentary disposition of any heritable property in Scotland made after the passing of this Act by a person to whom section eleven of the Wills Act 1837 applies or to whom it would apply if he were domiciled in England, shall not be invalid by reason only of the fact that such person is under twenty-one years of age, provided always that he is of such age that he could, if domiciled in Scotland, have made a valid testamentary disposition of moveable property. **[61]**

NOTES

Sub-s (1): words in square brackets substituted by the Family Law Reform Act 1969, s 3(1)(*b*).

4. Power to appoint testamentary guardians

Where any person dies after the passing of this Act having made a will which is, or which, if it had been a disposition of property, would have been rendered valid by section eleven of the Wills Act 1837, any appointment contained in that will of any person as guardian of the infant children of the testator shall be of full force and effect. **[62]**

5. Short title and interpretation

(1) This Act may be cited as the Wills (Soldiers and Sailors) Act 1918.

(2) For the purposes of section eleven of the Wills Act 1837 and this Act the expression "soldier" includes a member of the Air Force, and references in this Act to the said section eleven include a reference to that section as explained and extended by this Act. **[63]**

LAW OF PROPERTY ACT 1922
(c 16)

An Act to assimilate and amend the law of Real and Personal Estate, to abolish copyhold and other special tenures, to amend the law relating to commonable lands and of intestacy, and to amend the Wills Act 1837, the Settled Land Acts 1882 to 1890, the Conveyancing Acts 1881 to 1911, the Trustee Act 1893, and the Land Transfer Acts 1875 and 1897 [29 June 1922]

PART VII

PROVISIONS RESPECTING LEASEHOLDS

Conversion of Perpetually Renewable Leaseholds into Long Terms

145. Conversion of perpetually renewable leaseholds

For the purpose of converting perpetually renewable leases and underleases (not being an interest in perpetually renewable copyhold land enfranchised by Part V of this Act, but including a perpetually renewable underlease derived out of an interest in perpetually renewable copyhold land) into long terms, for preventing the creation of perpetually renewable leasehold interests and for providing for the interests of the persons affected, the provisions contained in the Fifteenth Schedule to this Act shall have effect.   **[64]**

SCHEDULES

SCHEDULE 15

Section 145
PROVISIONS RELATING TO PERPETUALLY RENEWABLE LEASES AND UNDERLEASES

1. Conversion of perpetually renewable leases into long terms

(1) Land comprised in a perpetually renewable lease which was subsisting at the commencement of this Act shall, by virtue of this Act, vest in the person who at such commencement was entitled to such lease, for a term of two thousand years, to be calculated from the date at which the existing term or interest commenced, at the rent and subject to the lessees' covenants and conditions (if any) which under the lease would have been payable or enforceable during the subsistence of such term or interest.

(2) The rent, covenants and conditions (if any) shall (subject to the express provisions of this Act to the contrary) be payable and enforceable during the subsistence of the term created by this Act; and that term shall take effect in substitution for the term or interest created by the lease, and be subject to the like power of re-entry (if any) and other provisions which affected the term or interest created by the lease, but without any right of renewal.   **[65]**

2. Conversion of perpetually renewable underleases into long terms

(1) Land comprised in any underlease, which at the commencement of this Act was perpetually renewable and was derived out of a head term affected by this Act, shall, be virtue of this Act, vest in the person who at such commencement was entitled to the subterm or interest for a term of two thousand years less one day, to be calculated from the date at which the head term created by this Act commenced, at the rent and subject to the underlessee's covenants and conditions (if any) which under the underlease would have been payable or enforceable during the subsistence of such subterm or interest.

(2) The rent, covenants and conditions (if any) shall (subject to the express provisions of this Act to the contrary) be payable and enforceable during the subsistence of the subterm created by this Act; and that subterm shall take effect in substitution for the subterm or interest created by the underlease, and be subject to the like power of re-entry (if any) and other provisions which affected the subterm or interest created by the underlease, but without any right of renewal.

(3) The foregoing provisions of this section shall also apply to any perpetually renewable subterm or interest which, at the commencement of this Act, was derived out of any other subterm or interest, but so that in every case the subterm created by this Act shall be one day less in duration that the derivative term created by this Act, out of which it takes effect.   **[66]**

5. Dispositions purporting to create perpetually renewable leaseholds

A grant, after the commencement of this Act, of a term, subterm, or other leasehold interest with a covenant or obligation for perpetual renewal, which would have been valid if this Part of this Act had not been passed, shall (subject to the express provisions of this Act) take effect as a demise for a term of two thousand years or in the case of a subdemise for a term less in duration by one day than the term out of which it is derived, to commence from the date fixed for the commencement of the term, subterm, or other interest, and in every case free from any obligation for renewal or for payment of any fines, fees, costs, or other money in respect of renewal. **[67]**

SETTLED LAND ACT 1925

(c 18)

ARRANGEMENT OF SECTIONS

PART I

GENERAL PRELIMINARY PROVISIONS

Settlements and Settled Land

An Act to consolidate the enactments relating to Settled Land in England and Wales.   **[9 April 1925]**

PART I

GENERAL PRELIMINARY PROVISIONS

Settlements and Settled Land

1. What constitutes a settlement

(1) Any deed, will, agreement for a settlement or other agreement, Act of Parliament, or other instrument, or any number of instruments, whether made or passed before or after, or partly before and partly after, the commencement of this Act, under or by virtue of which instrument or instruments and land, after the commencement of this Act, stands for the time being—

(i) limited in trust for any persons by way of succession; or

(ii) limited in trust for any person in possession—

(a) for an entailed interest whether or not capable of being barred or defeated;

(b) for an estate in fee simple or for a term of years absolute subject to an executory limitation, gift, or disposition over on failure of his issue or in any other event;

(c) for a base or determinable fee or any corresponding interest in leasehold land;

(d) being an infant, for an estate in fee simple or for a term of years absolute; or

(iii) limited in trust for any person for an estate in fee simple or for a term of years absolute contingently on the happening of any event; or

(iv) ...

(v) charged, whether voluntarily or in consideration of marriage or by way of family arrangement, and whether immediately or after an interval, with the payment of any rentcharge for the life of any person, or any less period, or of any capital, annual, or periodical sums for the portions, advancement, maintenance, or otherwise for the benefit of any persons, with or without any term of years for securing or raising the same;

creates or is for the purposes of this Act a settlement and is in this Act referred to as a settlement, or as the settlement, as the case requires;

Provided that, where land is the subject of a compound settlement, references in this Act to the settlement shall be construed as meaning such compound settlement, unless the context otherwise requires.

(2) Where an infant is beneficially entitled to land for an estate in fee simple or for a term of years absolute and by reason of an intestacy or otherwise there is no instrument under which the interest of the infant arises or is acquired, a settlement shall be deemed to have been made by the intestate, or by the person whose interest the infant has acquired.

(3) An infant shall be deemed to be entitled in possession notwithstanding any subsisting right of dower (not assigned by metes and bounds) affecting the land, and such a right of dower shall be deemed to be an interest comprised in the subject of the settlement and coming to the dowress under or by virtue of the settlement.

Where dower has been assigned by metes and bounds, the letters of administration or probate granted in respect of the estate of the husband of the dowress shall be deemed a settlement made by the husband.

(4) An estate or interest not disposed of by a settlement and remaining in or reverting to the settlor, or any person deriving title under him, is for the purposes of this Act an estate or interest comprised in the subject of the settlement and coming to the settlor or such person under or by virtue of the settlement.

(5) Where—

(a) a settlement creates an entailed interest which is incapable of being barred or defeated, or a base or determinable fee, whether or not the reversion or right of reverter is in the Crown, or any corresponding interest in leasehold land; or

(b) the subject of a settlement is an entailed interest, or a base or determinable fee, whether or not the reversion or right of reverter is in the Crown, or any corresponding interest in leasehold land;

the reversion or right of reverter upon the cesser of the interest so created or settled shall be deemed to be an interest comprised in the subject of the settlement, and limited by the settlement.

(6) Subsection (4) and (5) of this section bind the Crown.

[(7) This section does not apply to land held upon trust for sale.]   **[68]**

NOTES
    Sub-s (1): para (iv) repealed by the Married Women (Restraint upon Anticipation) Act 1949, s 1(4), Sch 2.
    Sub-s (7): added by the Law of Property (Amendment) Act 1926, s 7, Schedule.

2. What is settled land

Land which is or is deemed to be the subject of a settlement is for the purposes of this Act settled land, and is in relation to the settlement referred to in this Act as the settled land.   **[69]**

3. Duration of settlements

Land [not held upon trust for sale] which has been subject to a settlement shall be deemed for the purposes of this Act to remain and be settled land, and the settlement shall be deemed to be subsisting settlement for the purposes of this Act so long as—

(a) any limitation, charge, or power of charging under the settlement subsists, or is capable of being exercised; or

(b) the person who, if of full age, would be entitled as beneficial owner to have that land vested in him for a legal estate is an infant.   **[70]**

NOTES
    Words in square brackets added by the Law of Property (Amendment) Act 1926, s 7, Schedule.

4. Authorised method of settling land inter vivos

(1) Every settlement of a legal estate in land inter vivos shall, save as in this Act otherwise provided, be effected by two deeds, namely, a vesting deed and a trust instrument and if effected in any other way shall not operate to transfer or create a legal estate.

(2) By the vesting deed the land shall be conveyed to the tenant for life or statutory owner (and if more than one as joint tenants) for the legal estate the subject of the intended settlement:

Provided that, where such legal estate is already vested in the tenant for life or statutory owner, if shall be sufficient, without any other conveyance, if the vesting deed declares that the land is vested in him for that estate.

(3) The trust instrument shall—

(*a*) declare the trusts affecting the settled land;

(*b*) appoint or constitute trustees of the settlement:

(*c*) contain the power, if any, to appoint new trustees of the settlement;

(*d*) set out, either expressly or by reference, any powers intended to be conferred by the settlement in extension of those conferred by this Act;

(*e*) bear any ad valorem stamp duty which may be payable (whether by virtue of the vesting deed or otherwise) in respect of the settlement.

[71]

5. Contents of vesting deeds

(1) Every vesting deed for giving effect to a settlement or for conveying settled land to a tenant for life or statutory owner during the subsistence of the settlement (in this Act referred to as a "principal vesting deed") shall contain the following statements and particulars, namely:—

(*a*) A description, either specific or general, of the settled land;

(*b*) A statement that the settled land is vested in the person or persons to whom it is conveyed or in whom it is declared to be vested upon the trusts from time to time affecting the settled Land;

(*c*) The names of the persons who are the trustees of the settlement;

(*d*) Any additional or larger powers conferred by the trust instrument relating to the settled land which by virtue of this Act operate and are exercisable as if conferred by this Act on a tenant for life;

(*e*) The name of any person for the time being entitled under the trust instrument to appoint new trustees of the settlement.

(2) The statements or particulars required by this section may be incorporated by reference to an existing vesting instrument, and, where there is a settlement subsisting at the commencement of this Act, by reference to that settlement and to any instrument whereby land has been conveyed to the uses or upon the trusts of that settlement, but not (save as last aforesaid) by reference to a trust instrument nor by reference to a disentailing deed.

(3) A principal vesting deed shall not be invalidated by reason only of any error in any of the statements or particulars by this Act required to be contained therein.

[72]

6. Procedure in the case of settlements by will

Where a settlement is created by the will of an estate owner who dies after the commencement of this Act—

(*a*) the will is for the purposes of this Act a trust instrument; and

(*b*) the personal representatives of the testator shall hold the settled land on trust, if and when required so to do, to convey it to the person who, under the will, or by virtue of this Act, is the tenant for life or statutory owner, and, if more than one, as joint tenants.

[73]

7. Procedure on change of ownership

(1) If, on the death of a tenant for life or statutory owner, or of the survivor of two or more tenants for life or statutory owners, in whom the settled land was vested, the land remains settled land, his personal representatives shall hold the

settled land on trust, if and when required so to do, to convey it to the person who under the trust settlement or by virtue of this Act becomes the tenant for life or statutory owner and, if more than one, as joint tenants.

(2) If a person by reason of attaining full age becomes a tenant for life for the purposes of this Act of settled land, he shall be entitled to require the trustees of the settlement, personal representatives, or other persons in whom the settled land is vested, to convey the land to him.

(3) If a person who, when of full age, will together with another person or other persons constitute the tenant for life for the purposes of this Act of settled land attains that age, he shall be entitled to require the tenant for life, trustees of the settlement, personal representatives or other persons in whom the settled land is vested to convey the land to him and the other person or persons who together with him constitute the tenant for life as joint tenants.

(4) If by reason of forfeiture, surrender, or otherwise the estate owner of any settled land ceases to have the statutory powers of a tenant for life and the land remains settled land, he shall be bound forthwith to convey the settled land to the person who under the trust instrument, or by virtue of this Act, becomes the tenant for life or statutory owner and, if more than one, as joint tenants.

(5) If any person of full age becomes absolutely entitled to the settled land (whether beneficially, or as personal representative, or as trustee for sale, or otherwise) free from all limitations, powers, and charges taking effect under the settlement, he shall be entitled to require the trustees of the settlement, personal representatives, or other persons in whom the settled land is vested, to convey the land to him, and if more persons than one being of full age become so entitled to the settled land they shall be entitled to require such persons as aforesaid to convey the land to them as joint tenants.   **[74]**

8. Mode and costs of conveyance, and saving of rights of personal representative and equitable charges

(1) A conveyance by personal representatives under either of the last two preceding sections may be made by an assent in writing signed by them which shall operate as a conveyance.

(2) Every conveyance under either of the last two preceding sections shall be made at the cost of the trust estate.

(3) The obligations to convey settled land imposed by the last two preceding sections are subject and without prejudice—

(a) where the settlement is created by a will, to the rights and powers of the personal representatives for purposes of administration; and

(b) in any case, to the person on whom the obligation is imposed being satisfied that provision has been or will be made for the payment of any unpaid death duties in respect of the land or any interest therein for which he is accountable, and any interest and costs in respect of such duties, or that he is otherwise effectually indemnified against such duties, interest and costs.

(4) Where the land is or remains settled land a conveyance under either of the last two preceding sections shall—

(a) if by deed, be a principal vesting deed; and

(b) if by an assent, be a vesting assent, which shall contain the like statements and particulars as are required by this Act in the case of a principal vesting deed.

(5) Nothing contained in either of the last two preceding sections affects the right of personal representatives to transfer or create such legal estates to take effect in priority to a conveyance under either of those sections as may be required for giving effect to the obligations imposed on them by statute.

(6) A conveyance under either of the last two preceding sections, if made by deed, may contain a reservation to the person conveying of a term of years absolute in the land conveyed, upon trusts for indemnifying him against any unpaid death duties in respect of the land conveyed or any interest therein, and any interest and costs in respect of such duties.

(7) Nothing contained in either of the last two preceding sections affects any right which a person entitled to an equitable charge for securing money actually raised, and affecting the whole estate the subject of the settlement, may have to require effect to be given thereto by a legal mortgage, before the execution of a conveyance under either of those sections.   [75]

9. Procedure in the case of settlement and of instruments deemed to be trust instruments

(1) Each of the following settlements or instruments shall for the purposes of this Act be deemed to be a trust instrument, and any reference to a trust instrument contained in this Act shall apply thereto, namely:—

(i) An instrument executed, or, in case of a will, coming into operation, after the commencement of this Act which by virtue of this Act is deemed to be a settlement;

(ii) A settlement which by virtue of this Act is deemed to have been made by any person after the commencement of this Act;

(iii) An instrument inter vivos intended to create a settlement of a legal estate in land which is executed after the commencement of this Act, and does not comply with the requirements of this Act with respect to the method of effecting such a settlement; and

(iv) A settlement made after the commencement of this Act (including a settlement by the will of a person who dies after such commencement) of any of the following interests—

(a) an equitable interest in land which is capable, when in possession, of subsisting at law; or

(b) an entailed interest; or

(c) a base or determinable fee or any corresponding interest in leasehold land,

but only if and when the interest settled takes effect free from all equitable interests and powers under every prior settlement (if any).

(2) As soon as practicable after a settlement, or an instrument which for the purposes of this Act is deemed to be a trust instrument, takes effect as such, the trustees of the settlement may, and on the request of the tenant for life or statutory owner shall, execute a principal vesting deed, containing the proper statements and particulars, declaring that the legal estate in the settled land shall vest or is vested in the person or persons therein named, being the tenant for life or statutory owner, and including themselves if they are the statutory owners, and such deed shall, unless the legal estate is already so vested, operate

to convey or vest the legal estate in the settled land to or in the person or persons aforesaid and, if more than one, as joint tenants.

(3) If there are no trustees of the settlement, then (in default of a person able and willing to appoint such trustees) an application under this Act shall be made to the court for the appointment of such trustees.

(4) The provisions of the last preceding section with reference to a conveyance shall apply, so far as they are applicable, to a principal vesting deed under this section.   **[76]**

10. Procedure on acquisition of land to be made subject to a settlement

(1) Where after the commencement of this Act land is acquired with capital money arising under this Act or in exchange for settled land, or a rentcharge is reserved on a grant of settled land, the land shall be conveyed to, and the rentcharge shall by virtue of this Act become vested in, the tenant for life or statutory owner, and such conveyance or grant is in this Act referred to as a subsidiary vesting deed:

Provided that, where an instrument is subsisting at the commencement of this Act, or is made or comes into operation after such commencement, by virtue of which any money or securities are liable under this Act, or the Acts which it replaces, or under a trust or direction contained in the instrument, to be invested in the purchase of land to be conveyed so as to become settled land, but at the commencement of this Act, or when such instrument is made or comes into operation after such commencement, as the case may be, there is no land in respect of which a principal vesting deed is capable of being executed, the first deed after the commencement of this Act by which any land is acquired as aforesaid shall be a principal vesting deed and shall be framed accordingly.

(2) A subsidiary vesting deed executed on the acquisition of land to be made subject to a settlement shall contain the following statements and particulars, namely—

    (*a*) particulars of the last or only principal vesting instrument affecting land subject to the settlement;

    (*b*) a statement that the land conveyed is to be held upon and subject to the same trusts and powers as the land comprised in such last or only principal vesting instrument;

    (*c*) the names of the persons who are the trustees of the settlement;

    (*d*) the name of any person for the time being entitled to appoint new trustees of the settlement.

(3) A subsidiary vesting deed reserving a rentcharge on a grant of settled land shall contain the following statements and particulars—

    (*a*) a statement that the rentcharge is vested in the grantor and is subject to the settlement which, immediately before the grant, was subsisting with respect to the land out of which it was reserved;

    (*b*) particulars of the last or only principal vesting instrument affecting such land.

(4) A subsidiary vesting deed shall not be invalidated by reason only of any error in any of the statements or particulars by this Act required to be contained therein.

(5) The acquisition of the land shall not operate to increase or multiply charges or powers of charging.   **[77]**

11. As to contracts for the settlement of land

(1) A contract made or other liability created or arising after the commencement of this Act for the settlement of land—

> (i) by or on the part of an estate owner; or
> (ii) by a person entitled to—
>
> > (*a*) an equitable interest which is capable when in possession of subsisting at law; or
> > (*b*) an entailed interest; or
> > (*c*) a base or determinable fee or any corresponding interest in leasehold land;

shall, but in cases under paragraph (ii) only if and when the interest of the person entitled takes effect free from all equitable interests and powers under every prior settlement, if any, be deemed an estate contract within the meaning of the Land Charges Act 1925, and may be registered as a land charge accordingly, and effect shall be given thereto by a vesting deed and a trust instrument in accordance with this Act.

(2) A contract made or other liability created on arising before the commencement of this Act to make a settlement of land shall be deemed to be sufficiently complied with if effect is given thereto by a vesting deed and a trust instrument in accordance with this Act. **[78]**

12. Power to make vesting orders as to settled land

(1) If—

> (*a*) any person who is bound under this Part of this Act to execute a conveyance, vesting deed or vesting assent or in whom settled land is wrongly vested refuses or neglects to execute the requisite conveyance, vesting deed or vesting assent within one month after demand in writing; or
> (*b*) any such person is outside the United Kingdom, or cannot be found, or it is not known whether he is alive or dead; or
> (*c*) for any reason the court is satisfied that the conveyance, vesting deed or vesting assent cannot be executed, or cannot be executed without undue delay or expense;

the court may, on the application of any person interested, make an order vesting the settled land in the tenant for life or statutory owner or person, if any, of full age absolutely entitled (whether beneficially or as personal representative or trustee for sale or otherwise), and, if the land remains settled land, the provisions of this Act relating to a principal vesting deed or a subsidiary vesting deed, as the case may be, shall apply to any order so made and every such order shall contain the like statements and particulars.

(2) No stamp duty shall be payable in respect of a vesting order made in place of a vesting or other assent. **[79]**

13. Dispositions not to take effect until vesting instrument is made

Where a tenant for life or statutory owner has become entitled to have a principal vesting deed or a vesting assent executed in his favour, then until a vesting instrument is executed or made pursuant to this Act in respect of the settled land, any purported disposition thereof inter vivos by any person, other than a personal representative (not being a disposition which he has power to make in right of his equitable interests or powers under a trust instrument), shall not take effect except in favour of a purchaser of a legal estate [without notice of such tenant for life or statutory owner having become so entitled as aforesaid] but, save as aforesaid, shall operate only as a contract for valuable consideration to carry out the transaction after the requisite vesting instrument has been executed or made, and a purchaser of a legal estate shall not be concerned with such disposition unless the contract is registered as a land charge.

[Nothing in this section affects the creation or transfer of a legal estate by virtue of an order of the court or the Minister or other competent authority.]
[80]

NOTES
    First words in square brackets substituted and second words in square brackets added by the Law of Property (Amendment) Act 1926, ss 6, 7, Schedule.

14. Forfeiture and stamps

(1) Any vesting effected under the powers conferred by this Act in relation to settled land shall not operate as a breach of a covenant or condition against alienation or give rise to a forfeiture.

(2) Nothing in this Act shall operate to impose any stamp duty on a vesting or other assent.   **[81]**

15. Examples of instruments

Examples of instruments framed in accordance with the provisions of this Act are contained in the First Schedule to this Act.   **[82]**

Enforcement of Equitable Interests and powers against Estate Owner and discharge on termination of Settlements

16. Enforcement of equitable interests and powers against estate owner

(1) All equitable interests and powers in or over settled land (whether created before or after the date of any vesting instrument affecting the legal estate) shall be enforceable against the estate owner in whom the settled land is vested (but in the case of personal representatives without prejudice to their rights and powers for purposes of administration) in manner following (that is to say):—

    (i) The estate owner shall stand possessed of the settled land and the income thereof upon such trusts and subject to such powers and provisions as may be requisite for giving effect to the equitable interests and powers affecting the settled land or income thereof of which he has notice according to their respective priorities;

    (ii) Where any person of full age becomes entitled to require a legal estate in the settled land to be vested in him in priority to the settlement, by reason of a right of reverter, statutory or otherwise, or an equitable right of entry taking effect, or on the ground that his interest ought no longer to be capable of being overreached under the powers of this Act, the estate owner shall be bound, if so requested in writing, to transfer or create such legal estate as may be required for giving legal effect to the rights of the person so entitled;

    (iii) Where—

        (a) any principal sum is required to be raised on the security of the settled land, by virtue of any trust, or by reason of the exercise of an equitable power affecting the settled land, or by any person or persons who under the settlement is or are entitled or together entitled to or has or have a general power of appointment over the settled land, whether subject to any equitable charges or powers of charging subsisting under the settlement or not; or

(b) the settled land is subject to any equitable charge for securing money actually raised and affecting the whole estate the subject of the settlement;

the estate owner shall be bound, if so requested in writing, to create such legal estate or charge by way of legal mortgage as may be required for raising the money or giving legal effect to the equitable charge:

Provided that, so long as the settlement remains subsisting, any legal estate or charge by way of legal mortgage so created shall take effect and shall be expressed to take effect subject to any equitable charges or powers of charging subsisting under the settlement which have priority to the interests or powers of the person or persons by or on behalf of whom the money is required to be raised or legal effect is required to be given to the equitable charge, unless the persons entitled to the prior charges or entitled to exercise the powers consent in writing to the same being postponed, but it shall not be necessary for such consent to be expressed in the instrument creating such legal estate or charge by way of legal mortgage.

(2) Where a mortgage or charge is expressed to be made by an estate owner pursuant to this section, then, in favour of the mortgagee or chargee and persons deriving title under him, the same shall take effect in priority to all the trusts of the settlement and all equitable interests and powers subsisting or to arise under the settlement except those to which it is expressly made subject, and shall so take effect, whether the mortgagee or chargee has notice of any such trusts, interests, or powers, or not, and the mortgagee or chargee shall not be concerned to see that a case had arisen to authorise the mortgage or charge, or that no more money than was wanted was raised.

(3) Nothing contained in paragraph (iii) of subsection (1) of this section affects the power conferred by this Act on a tenant for life of raising money by mortgage or of directing money to be applied in discharge of incumbrances.

(4) Effect may be given by means of a legal mortgage to an agreement for a mortgage, or a charge or lien, whether or not arising by operation of law, if the agreement charge or lien ought to have priority over the settlement.

(5) Save as hereinbefore expressly provided, no legal estate shall, so long as the settlement is subsisting, be transferred or created by the estate owner for giving effect to any equitable interest or power under the settlement.

(6) If a question arises or a doubt is entertained whether any and what legal estate ought to be transferred or created pursuant to this section, an application may be made to the court for directions as hereinafter provided.

(7) If an estate owner refuses or neglects for one month after demand in writing to transfer or create any such legal estate, or if by reason of his being outside the United Kingdom, or being unable to be found, or by reason of the dissolution of a corporation, or for any other reason, the court is satisfed that the transaction cannot otherwise be effected, or cannot be effected without undue delay or expense, the court may, on the application of any person

interested, make a vesting order transferring or creating the requisite legal estate.

(8) This section does not affect a purchaser of a legal estate taking free from any equitable interest or power. **[83]**

17. Deed of discharge on termination of settlement

(1) Where the estate owner of any settled land holds the land free from all equitable interests and powers under a trust instrument, the persons who in the last or only principal vesting instrument or the last or only endorsement on or annex thereto are declared to be the trustees of the settlement or the survivors of them shall, save as hereinafter mentioned, be bound to execute, at the cost of the trust estate, a deed declaring that they are discharged from the trust so far as regards that land;

Provided that, if the trustees have notice of any derivative settlement, trust for sale or equitable charge affecting such land, they shall not execute a deed of discharge until—

(a) in the case of a derivative settlement, or trust for sale, a vesting instrument or a conveyance has been executed or made for giving effect thereto; and

(b) in the case of an equitable charge, they are satisfied that the charge is or will be secured by a legal mortgage, or is protected by registration as a land charge, or by deposit of the documents of title, or that the owner thereof consents to the execution of the deed of discharge.

Where the land is affected by a derivative settlement or trust for sale, the deed of discharge shall contain a statement that the land is settled land by virtue of such vesting instrument as aforesaid and the trust instrument therein referred to, or is held on trust for sale by virtue of such conveyance as aforesaid, as the case may require.

(2) If, in the circumstances mentioned in subsection (1) of this section and when the conditions therein mentioned have been complied with, the trustees of a settlement on being requested to execute a deed of discharge—

(a) by the estate owner; or

(b) by a person interested under, or by the trustees of, a derivative settlement; or

(c) by the trustees of a conveyance on trust for sale;

refuse to do so, or if for any reason the discharge cannot be effected without undue delay or expense, the estate owner, person interested, or trustees may apply to the court for an order discharging the first mentioned trustees as respects the whole or any part of the settled land, and the court may make such order as it may think fit.

(3) Where a deed or order of discharge contains no statement to the contrary, a purchaser of a legal estate in the land to which the deed or order relates shall be entitled to assume that the land has ceased to be settled land, and is not subject to any trust for sale. **[84]**

Restrictions on dispositions of Settled Land where Trustees have not been Discharged

18. Restrictions on dispositions of settled land where trustees have not been discharged

(1) Where land is the subject of a vesting instrument and the trustees of the settlement have not been discharged under this Act, then—

(a) any disposition by the tenant for life or statutory owner of the land, other than a disposition authorised by this Act or any other statute, or made in pursuance of any additional or larger powers mentioned in the vesting instrument, shall be void, except for the purpose of conveying or creating such equitable interests as he has power, in right of his equitable interests and powers under the trust instrument, to convey or create; and

(b) if any capital money is payable in respect of a transaction, a conveyance to a purchaser of the land shall only take effect under this Act if the capital money is paid to or by the direction of the trustees of the settlement or into court; and

(c) notwithstanding anything to the contrary in the vesting instrument, or the trust instrument, capital money shall not, except where the trustee is a trust corporation, be paid to or by the direction of fewer persons than two as trustees of the settlement.

(2) The restrictions imposed by this section do not affect—

(a) the right of a personal representative in whom the settled land may be vested to convey or deal with the land for the purposes of administration;

(b) the right of a person of full age who has become absolutely entitled (whether beneficially or as trustee for sale or personal representative or otherwise) to the settled land, free from all limitations, powers, and charges taking effect under the trust instrument, to require the land to be conveyed to him;

(c) the power of the tenant for life, statutory owner, or personal representative in whom the settled land is vested to transfer or create such legal estates, to take effect in priority to the settlement, as may be required for giving effect to any obligations imposed on him by statute, but where any capital money is raised or received in respect of the transaction the money shall be paid to or by the direction of the trustees of the settlement or in accordance with an order of the court.

[85]

Tenants for Life and Persons with Powers of Tenant for Life

19. Who is tenant for life

(1) The person of full age who is for the time being beneficially entitled under a settlement to possession of settled land for his life is for the purposes of this Act the tenant for life of that land and the tenant for life under that settlement.

(2) If in any case there are two or more persons of full age so entitled as joint tenants, they together constitute the tenant for life for the purposes of this Act.

(3) If in any case there are two or more persons so entitled as joint tenants and they are not all of full age, such one or more of them as is or are for the time being of full age is or (if more than one) together constitute the tenant for life for the purposes of this Act, but this subsection does not affect the beneficial interests of such of them as are not for the time being of full age.

(4) A person being tenant for life within the foregoing definitions shall be deemed to be such notwithstanding that, under the settlement or otherwise, the settled land, or his estate or interest therein, is incumbered or charged in any manner or to any extent, and notwithstanding any assignment by operation of

law or otherwise of his estate or interest under the settlement, whether before or after it came into possession, other than an assurance which extinguishes that estate or interest. [86]

20. Other limited owners having powers of tenant for life

(1) Each of the following persons being of full age shall, when his estate or interest is in possession, have the powers of a tenant for life under this Act, (namely):—

    (i) A tenant in tail, including a tenant in tail after possibility of issue extinct, and a tenant in tail who is by Act of Parliament restrained from barring or defeating his estate tail, and although the reversion is in the Crown, but not including such a tenant in tail where the land in respect whereof he is so restrained was purchased with money provided by Parliament in consideration of public services;

    (ii) A person entitled to land for an estate in fee simple or for a term of years absolute with or subject to, in any of such cases, an executory limitation, gift, or disposition over on failure of his issue or in any other event;

    (iii) A person entitled to a base or determinable fee, although the reversion or right of reverter is in the Crown, or to any corresponding interest in leasehold land;

    (iv) A tenant for years determinable on life, not holding merely under a lease at a rent;

    (v) A tenant for the life of another, not holding merely under a lease at a rent;

    (vi) A tenant for his own or any other life, or for years determinable on life, whose estate is liable to cease in any event during that life, whether by expiration of the estate, or by conditional limitation, or otherwise, or to be defeated by an executory limitation, gift, or disposition over, or is subject to a trust for accumulation of income for any purpose;

    (vii) A tenant by the curtesy;

    (viii) A person entitled to the income of land under a trust or direction for payment thereof to him during his own or any other life, whether or not subject to expenses of management or to a trust for accumulation of income for any purpose, or until sale of the land, or until forfeiture, cesser or determination by any means of his interest therein, unless the land is subject to an immediate binding trust for sale;

    (ix) A person beneficially entitled to land for an estate in fee simple or for a term of years absolute subject to any estates, interests, charges, or powers of charging, subsisting or capable of being exercised under a settlement;

    (x) ...

(2) In every such case as is mentioned in subsection (1) of this section, the provisions of this Act referring to a tenant for life, either as conferring powers on him or otherwise, shall extend to each of the persons aforesaid, and any reference in this Act to death as regards a tenant for life shall, where necessary, be deemed to refer to the determination by death or otherwise of the estate or interest of the person on whom the powers of a tenant for life are conferred by this section.

(3) For the purposes of this Act the estate or interest of a tenant by the

curtesy shall be deemed to be an estate or interest arising under a settlement made by his wife.

(4) Where the reversion of right or reverter or other reversionary right is in the Crown, the exercise by a person on whom the powers of a tenant for life are conferred by this section of his powers under this Act, binds the Crown. **[87]**

NOTES
Sub-s (1): para (x) repealed by the Married Women (Restraint upon Anticipation) Act 1949, s 1(4), Sch 2.

21. Absolute owners subject to certain interests to have the powers of tenant for life

(1) Where a person of full age is beneficially entitled in possession to a legal estate subject to any equitable interests or powers, then, for the purpose of overreaching such interests or powers, he may, notwithstanding any stipulation to the contrary, by deed (which shall have effect as a principal vesting deed within the meaning of this Act) declare that the legal estate is vested in him on trust to give effect to all equitable interests and powers affecting the legal estate, and that deed shall be executed by two or more individuals approved or appointed by the court or a trust corporation, who shall be stated to be the trustees of the settlement for the purposes of this Act.

Thereupon so long as any of the equitable interests and powers are subsisting the following provisions shall have effect:—

(a) The person so entitled as aforesaid and each of his successors in title being an estate owner shall have the powers of a tenant for life and the land shall be deemed to be settled land;

(b) The instrument (if any) under which his estate arises or is acquired, and the instrument (if any) under which the equitable interests or powers are subsisting or capable of taking effect shall be deemed to be the trust instrument:

Provided that where there is no such instrument as last aforesaid then a deed (which shall take effect as a trust instrument) shall be executed contemporaneously with the vesting deed, and shall declare the trusts affecting the land;

(c) The persons stated in the principal vesting deed to be the trustees of the settlement for the purposes of this Act shall also be the trustees of the trust instrument for those purposes; and

(d) Capital money arising on any disposition of the land shall be paid to or by the direction of the trustees of the settlement or into court, and shall be applicable towards discharging or providing for payment in due order of any principal money payable in respect of such interests or charges as are overreached by such disposition, and until so applied shall be invested or applied as capital money under the trust instrument, and the income thereof shall be applied as the income of such capital money, and be liable for keeping down in due order any annual or periodical sum which may be overreached by the disposition.

(2) The following equitable interests and powers are excepted from the operation of subsection (1) of this section namely—

(i) an equitable interest protected by a deposit of documents relating to the legal estate affected;

(ii) the benefit of a covenant or agreement restrictive of the user of land;

   (iii) an easement, liberty or privilege over or affecting land and being merely an equitable interest;
   (iv) the benefit of a contract to convey or create a legal estate, including a contract conferring either expressly or by statutory implication a valid option of purchase, a right of pre-emption, or any other like right;
   (v) any equitable interest protected by registration under the Land Charges Act 1925, other than—

   (*a*) an annuity within the meaning of Part II of that Act;
   (*b*) a limited owner's charge or a general equitable charge within the meaning of that Act.

(3) Subject to the powers conferred by this Act on a tenant for life, nothing contained in this section shall deprive an equitable chargee of any of his rights or of his remedies for enforcing those rights.   **[88]**

22. Provisions applicable where interest in settled land is restored.

(1) Where by a disentailing assurance settled land is expressed to be limited (whether subject or not to any estates, interests, charges or powers expressly created or conferred thereby) upon the trusts subsisting with respect thereto immediately before the execution of such disentailing assurance, or any of such trusts then, for the purposes of this Act and otherwise, a person entitled to any estate or interest in the settled land under any such previously subsisting trust is entitled thereto after the execution of such disentailing assurance as of his former estate or interest.

(2) Where by a resettlement of settled land any estate or interest therein is expressed to be limited to any person (whether subject or not to any estate, interest, charge or power expressly created or conferred by the resettlement) in restoration or confirmation of his estate or interest under a prior settlement, then, for the purposes of this Act and otherwise, that person is entitled to the estate or interest so restored or confirmed as of his former estate or interest and in addition to the powers exercisable by him in respect of his former estate or interest, he is capable of exercising all such further powers as he could have exercised by virtue of the resettlement, if his estate or interest under the prior settlement had not been so restored or confirmed, but he had been entitled under the resettlement only.   **[89]**

23. Powers of trustees, etc, when there is no tenant for life

(1) Where under a settlement there is no tenant for life nor, independently of this section, a person having by virtue of this Act the powers of a tenant for life then—

   (*a*) any person of full age on whom such powers are by the settlement expressed to be conferred; and
   (*b*) in any other case the trustees of the settlement;

shall have the powers of a tenant for life under this Act.

(2) This section applies to trustees of settlements of land purchased with money provided by Parliament in consideration of public services where the tenant in tail is restrained from barring or defeating his estate tail, except that, if the tenant in tail is of full age and capacity, the powers shall not be exercised without his consent, but a purchaser shall not be concerned to see or inquire whether such consent has been given.   **[90]**

24. As to a tenant for life who has parted with his interest

(1) If it is shown to the satisfaction of the court that a tenant for life, who has by reason of bankruptcy, assignment, imcumbrance, or otherwise ceased in the opinion of the court to have a substantial interest in his estate or interest in the settled land or any part thereof, has unreasonably refused to exercise any of the powers conferred on him by this Act, or consents to an order under this section, the court may, on the application of any person interested in the settled land or the part thereof affected, make an order authorising the trustees of the settlement, to exercise in the name and on behalf of the tenant for life, any of the powers of a tenant for life under this Act, in relation to the settled land or the part thereof affected, either generally and in such manner and for such period as the court may think fit, or in a particular instance, and the court may by the order direct that any documents of title in the possession of the tenant for life relating to the settled land be delivered to the trustees of the settlement.

(2) While any such order is in force, the tenant for life shall not, in relation to the settled land or the part thereof affected, exercise any of the powers thereby authorised to be exercised in his name and on his behalf, but no person dealing with the tenant for life shall be affected by any such order, unless the order is for the time being registered as an order affecting land.

(3) An order may be made under this section at any time after the estate or interest of the tenant for life under the settlement has taken effect in possession, and notwithstanding that he disposed thereof when it was an estate or interest in remainder or reversion. [91]

25. Married woman, how to be affected

(1) The foregoing provisions of this Act apply, to a married woman of full age, whether or not she is entitled to her estate or interest for her separate use or as her separate property, and she, without her husband, may exercise the powers of a tenant for life under this Act.

(2) ... [92]

NOTES
Sub-s (2): repealed by the Married Women (Restraint upon Anticipation) Act 1949, s 1(4), Sch 2.

26. Infants, how to be affected

(1) Where an infant is beneficially entitled in possession to land for an estate in fee simple or for a term of years absolute or would if of full age be a tenant for life of or have the powers of a tenant for life over settled land, then, during the minority of the infant—

(a) if the settled land is vested in a personal representative, the personal representative, until a principal vesting instrument has been executed pursuant to the provisions of this Act; and

(b) in every other case, the trustees of the settlement;

shall have, in reference to the settled land and capital money, all the powers conferred by this Act and the settlement on a tenant for life, and on the trustees of the settlement.

(2) If the settled land is vested in a personal representative, then, if and when during the minority the infant, if of full age, would have been entitled to have the legal estate in the settled land conveyed to or otherwise vested in him pursuant to the provisions of this Act, a principal vesting instrument shall, if

the trustees of the settlement so require, be executed, at the cost of the trust estate, for vesting the legal estate in themselves, and in the meantime the personal representative shall, during the minority, give effect to the directions of the trustees of the settlement, and shall not be concerned with the propriety of any conveyance directed to be made by those trustees if the conveyance appears to be a proper conveyance under the powers conferred by this Act or by the settlement, and the capital money, if any, arising under the conveyance is paid to or by the direction of the trustees of the settlement or into court, but a purchaser dealing with the personal representative and paying the capital money, if any, to him shall not be concerned to see that the money is paid to trustees of the settlement or into court, or to inquire whether the personal representative is liable to give effect to any such directions, or whether any such directions have been given.

(3) Subsection (2) of this section applies whether the infant becomes entitled before or after the commencement of this Act, and has effect during successive minorities until a person of full age becomes entitled to require the settled land to be vested in him.

(4) This section does not apply where an infant is beneficially entitled in possession to land for an estate in fee simple or for a term of years absolute jointly with a person of full age (for which case provision is made in the Law of Property Act 1925), but it applies to two or more infants entitled as aforesaid jointly, until one of them attains full age.

(5) This section does not apply where an infant would, if of full age, constitute the tenant for life or have the powers of a tenant for life together with another person of full age, but it applies to two or more infants who would, if all of them were of full age, together constitute the tenant for life or have the powers of a tenant for life, until one of them attains full age.

(6) Nothing in this section affects prejudicially any beneficial interest of an infant.   **[93]**

27. Effect of conveying legal estate to infant

(1) A conveyance of a legal estate in land to an infant alone, or to two or more persons jointly, both or all of whom are infants, for his or their own benefit shall operate only as an agreement for valuable consideration to execute a settlement by means of a principal vesting deed and a trust instrument in favour of the infant or infants, and in the meantime to hold the land in trust for the infant or infants.

(2) Nothing in this Act prevents an equitable interest in settled land being vested in or transferred to an infant.

(3) . . .   **[94]**

NOTES

Sub-s (3): repealed with a saving by the Family Law Reform Act 1969, s 11(*a*).

29. Charitable and public trusts

(1) For the purposes of this section, all land vested or to be vested in trustees on or for charitable, ecclesiastical, or public trusts or purposes shall be deemed to be settled land, and the trustees shall, without constituting them statutory owners, have in reference to the land, all the powers which are by this Act conferred on a tenant for life and on the trustees of a settlement.

In connection only with the exercise of those powers, and not so as to impose any obligation in respect of or to affect—

  (a) the mode of creation or the administration of such trusts; or
  (b) the appointment or number of trustees of such trusts;

the statute or other instrument creating the trust or under which it is administered shall be deemed the settlement, and the trustees shall be deemed the trustees of the settlement, and, save where the trust is created by a will coming into operation after the commencement of this Act, a separate instrument shall not be necessary for giving effect to the settlement.

Any conveyance of land held on charitable, ecclesiastical or public trusts shall state that the land is held on such trusts, and, where a purchaser has notice that the land is held on charitable, ecclesiastical, or public trusts, he shall be bound to see that any consents or orders requisite for authorising the transaction have been obtained.

(2) The said powers shall be exercisable subject to such consents or orders, if any, being obtained as would, if this Act had not been passed, have been requisite if the transaction were being effected under an express power conferred by the instrument creating the trust, and where the land is vested in . . . persons having no powers of management, the said powers shall be exercisable by the managing trustees or committee of management, and the . . . persons aforesaid shall not be liable for giving effect to directions given by the managing trustees or committee of management:

Provided that where—

  (a) a disposition or dealing is to be effected for a nominal price or rent, or for less than the best price or rent that can be reasonably obtained or gratuitously; or
  (b) any interest in land is to be acquired;

the like consent or order (if any) shall be required in reference to the disposition, dealing or acquisition, as would have been requisite if the intended transaction were a sale.

(3) Nothing in this section affects the jurisdiction of the court, Charity Commissioners, Board of Education, or other competent authority, in regard to the administration of charitable, ecclesiastical, or public trusts.

(4) . . .

(5) Where any trustees or the majority of any set of trustees have power to transfer or create any legal estate, that estate shall be transferred or created by them in the names and on behalf of the persons . . . in whom the legal estate is vested.

(6) This section applies (save as otherwise provided) whether the trust was created before or after the commencement of this Act, but does not apply to land to which the Universities and College Estates Act 1925, applies.   [95]

NOTES
  Sub-s (4): repealed by the Charities Act 1960, s 48(2), Sch 7, Part I.
  Sub-s (5): words omitted repealed by the Charities Act 1960, s 48(2), Sch 7, Part I.

Trustees of Settlement

30. Who are trustees for purposes of Act

(1) Subject to the provisions of this Act, the following persons are trustees of a settlement for the purposes of this Act, and are in this Act referred to as the "trustees of the settlement" or "trustees of a settlement", namely—

> (i) the persons, if any, who are for the time being under the settlement trustees with power of sale of the settled land (subject or not to the consent of any person), or with power of consent to or approval of the exercise of such a power of sale, or if there are no such persons; then
>
> (ii) the persons, if any, for the time being, who are by the settlement declared to be trustees thereof for the purposes of the Settled Land Acts 1882 to 1890, or any of them, or this Act, or if there are no such persons; then
>
> (iii) the persons, if any, who are for the time being under the settlement trustees with power of or upon trust for sale of any other land comprised in the settlement and subject to the same limitations as the land to be sold or otherwise dealt with, or with power of consent to or approval of the exercise of such a power of sale, or, if there are no such persons; then
>
> (iv) the persons, if any, who are for the time being under the settlement trustees with future power of sale, or under a future trust for sale of the settled land, or with power of consent to or approval of the exercise of such a future power of sale, and whether the power or trust takes effect in all events or not, or, if there are no such persons; then
>
> (v) the persons, if any, appointed by deed to be trustees of the settlement by all the persons who at the date of the deed were together able, by virtue of their beneficial interests or by the exercise of an equitable power, to dispose of the settled land in equity for the whole estate the subject of the settlement.

(2) Paragraphs (i) (iii) and (iv) of the last preceding subsection take effect in like manner as if the powers therein referred to had not by this Act been made exercisable by the tenant for life or statutory owner.

(3) Where a settlement is created by will, or a settlement has arisen by the effect of an intestacy, and apart from this subsection there would be no trustees for the purposes of this Act of such settlement, then the personal representatives of the deceased shall, until other trustees are appointed, be by virtue of this Act the trustees of the settlement, but where there is a sole personal representative, not being a trust corporation, it shall be obligatory on him to appoint an additional trustee to act with him for the purposes of this Act, and the provisions of the Trustee Act 1925, relating to the appointment of new trustees and the vesting of trust property shall apply accordingly.   [96]

31. As to trustees of compound settlements

(1) Persons who are for the time being trustees for the purposes of this Act of an instrument which is a settlement, or is deemed to be a subsisting settlement for the purposes of this Act, shall be the trustees for the purposes of this Act of any settlement constituted by that instrument and any instruments subsequent in date or operation.

[Where there are trustees for the purposes of this Act of the instrument under which there is a tenant for life or statutory owner but there are no trustees for those purposes of a prior instrument, being one of the instruments by which a compound settlement is constituted, those trustees shall, unless and until trustees are appointed of the prior instrument or of the compound settlement, be the trustees for the purposes of this Act of the compound settlement.]

(2) This section applies to instruments coming into operation before as well as after the commencement of this Act, but shall have effect without prejudice to any appointment made by the court before such commencement of trustees of a settlement constituted by more than one instrument, and to the power of the court in any case after such commencement to make any such appointment, and where any such appointment has been made before such commencement or is made thereafter this section shall not apply or shall cease to apply to the settlement consisting of the instruments to which the appointment relates. [97]

NOTES
    Sub-s (1): words in square brackets added by the Law of Property (Amendment) Act 1926, s 7, Schedule.

32. As to trustees of referential settlements

(1) Where a settlement takes or has taken effect by reference to another settlement, the trustees for the time being of the settlement to which reference is made shall be the trustees of the settlement by reference, but this section does not apply if the settlement by reference contains an appointment of trustees thereof for the purposes of the Settled Land Acts 1882 to 1890, or any of them, or this Act.

(2) This section applies to instruments coming into operation before as well as after the commencement of this Act, but shall have effect without prejudice to any appointment made by the court before such commencement of trustees of a settlement by reference, or of the compound settlement consisting of a settlement and any other settlement or settlements made by reference thereto, and to the power of the court in any case after such commencement to make any such appointment, and where any such appointment has been made before such commencement or is made thereafter this section shall not apply or shall cease to apply.

(3) In this section "a settlement by reference to another settlement" means a settlement of property upon the limitations and subject to the powers and provisions of an existing settlement, with or without variation.   [98]

33. Continuance of trustees in office, and as to certain compound settlements

(1) Where any persons have been appointed or constituted trustees of a settlement, whether by an order of the court or otherwise, or have by reason of any power of sale, or trust for sale, or by reason of a power of consent to, or approval of, the exercise of a power of sale, or by virtue of this Act, or otherwise at any time become trustees of a settlement for the purposes of the Settled Land Acts 1882 to 1890, or this Act, then those persons or their successors in office shall remain and be trustees of the settlement as long as that settlement is subsisting or deemed to be subsisting for the purposes of this Act.

In this subsection "successors in office" means the persons who, by appointment or notherwise, have become trustees for the purposes aforesaid.

(2) Where settled land is or has been expressed to be disposed of under a compound settlement of which trustees were appointed by the court, and the

capital money (if any) arising on the disposition is or was paid to the persons who by virtue of the order or any subsequent appointment appear to be or to have been the trustees of that settlement, and where the person by or on whose behalf the disposition is or was made is or was the tenant for life or statutory owner of the land disposed of under an instrument mentioned in the order as constituting part of such compound settlement (in this subsection called "the principal instrument") then the title of the person to whom the disposition is made shall not be impeachable on the ground—

(a) that the instruments mentioned in the order did not constitute a compound settlement; or

(b) that those instruments were not all the instruments at the date of the order or of the disposition constituting the compound settlement of the land disposed of; or

(c) that any of the instruments mentioned in the order did not form part of the settlement of the land disposed of, or had ceased to form part of the settlement at the date of the disposition;

but nothing in this subsection shall prejudice the rights of any person in respect of any estate, interest or charge under any instrument existing at the date of the order and not mentioned therein which would not have been overreached if the disposition had been made by or on behalf of the tenant for life or statutory owner under the principal instrument as such, and there had been trustees of that instrument for the purposes of the Settled Land Acts 1882 to 1890, or this Act, and the capital money, if any, arising on the disposition had been paid to the trustees.

(3) The foregoing provisions of this section operate to confirm all dispositions made before the commencement of this Act, but not so as to render invalid or prejudice any order of the court, or any title or right acquired before the commencement of this Act, and operates without prejudice to any appointment already made by the court of trustees of a settlement, and to the power of the court in any case hereafter to make any such appointment. **[99]**

34. Appointment of trustees by court

(1) If at any time there are no trustees of a settlement, or where in any other case it is expedient, for the purposes of this Act, that new trustees of a settlement be appointed, the court may, if it thinks fit, on the application of the tenant for life, statutory owner, or of any other person having, under the settlement, an estate or interest in the settled land, in possession, remainder or otherwise, or, in the case of an infant, of his testamentary or other guardian or next friend, appoint fit persons to be trustees of the settlement.

(2) The persons so appointed, and the survivors and survivor of them, while continuing to be trustees or trustee, and, until the appointment of new trustees, the personal representatives or representative for the time being of the last surviving or continuing trustee, shall become and be the trustees or trustee of the settlement. **[100]**

35. Procedure on appointment of new trustees

(1) Whenever a new trustee for the purposes of this Act is appointed of a trust instrument or a trustee thereof for the purposes aforesaid,[is discharged from the trust without a new trustee being appointed, a deed shall be executed supplemental to the last or only principal vesting instrument containing a declaration that the persons therein named, being the persons who after such appointment or discharge, as the case may be, are the trustees of the trust

instrument for the purposes aforesaid, are the trustees of the settlement for those purposes; and a memorandum shall be endorsed on or annexed to the last or only principal vesting instrument in accordance with the Trustee Act 1925.

(2) Every such deed as aforesaid shall, if the trustee was appointed or discharged by the court be executed by such person as the court may direct, and, in any other case, shall be executed by—

(i) the person, if any, named in the principal vesting instrument as the person for the time being is entitled to appoint new trustees of the settlement, or if no person is so named, or the person is dead or unable or unwilling to act, the persons who if the principal vesting instrument had been the only instrument constituting the settlement would have had power to appoint new trustees thereof;

(ii) the persons named in the deed of declaration as the trustees of the settlement; and

(iii) any trustee who is discharged as aforesaid or retires.

(3) A statement contained in any such deed of declaration as is mentioned in this section to the effect that the person named in the principal vesting instrument as the person for the time being entitled to appoint new trustees of the settlement is unable or unwilling to act, or that a trustee has remained outside the United Kingdom for more than twelve months, or refuses or is unfit to act, or is incapable of acting, shall in favour of a purchaser of a legal estate be conclusive evidence of the matter stated. **[101]**

Provisions as to Undivided Shares

36. Undivided shares to take effect behind a trust for sale of the land

(1) If and when, after the commencement of this Act, settled land is held in trust for persons entitled in possession under a trust instrument in undivided shares, the trustees of the settlement (if the settled land is not already vested in them) may require the estate owner in whom the settled land is vested (but in the case of a personal representative subject to his rights and powers for purposes of administration), at the cost of the trust estate, to convey the land to them, or assent to the land vesting in them as joint tenants, and in the meantime the land shall be held on the same trusts as would have been applicable thereto if it had been so conveyed to or vested in the trustees.

(2) If and when the settled land so held in trust in undivided shares is or becomes vested in the trustees of the settlement, the land shall be held by them (subject to any incumbrances affecting the settled land which are secured by a legal mortgage, but freed from any incumbrances affecting the undivided shares or not secured as aforesaid, and from any interests, powers and charges subsisting under the trust instrument which have priority to the trust for the persons entitled to the undivided shares) upon the statutory trusts.

(3) If the estate owner refuses or neglects for one month after demand in writing to convey the settled land so held in trust in undivided shares in manner aforesaid, or if by reason of his being outside the United Kingdom or being unable to be found, or by reason of the dissolution of a corporation, or for any other reason, the court is satisfied that the conveyance cannot otherwise be made, or cannot be made without undue delay or expense, the court may, on the application of the trustees of the settlement, make an order vesting the settled land in them on the statutory trusts.

(4) An undivided share in land shall not be capable of being created except

under a trust instrument or under the Law of Property Act 1925, and shall then only take effect behind a trust for sale.

(5) Nothing in this section affects the priority inter se of any incumbrances whether affecting the entirety of the land or an undivided share.

(6) For the purposes of this section land held upon the statutory trusts shall be held upon the trusts and subject to the provisions following, namely, upon trust to sell the same, with power to postpone the sale of the whole or any part thereof, and to stand possessed of the net proceeds of sale, after payment of costs, and of the net rents and profits until sale, after payment of rates, taxes, costs of insurance, repairs, and other outgoings, upon such trusts and subject to such powers and provisions as may be requisite for giving effect to the rights of the persons interested in the settled land [and the right of a person who, if the land had not been made subject to a trust for sale by virtue of this Act, would have been entitled to an entailed interest in an undivided share in the land, shall be deemed to be a right to a corresponding entailed interest in the net proceeds of sale attributable to that share].

(7) The provisions of this section bind the Crown.   **[102]**

NOTES
    Sub-s (1): words in square brackets added by the Law of Property (Entailed Interests) Act 1932, s 1(1).

Transitional Provisions

37. Transitional provisions with respect to existing settlements, etc

The transitional provisions set out in the Second Schedule to this Act shall have effect as regards settlements existing at the commencement of this Act.   **[103]**

PART II

POWERS OF A TENANT FOR LIFE

Sale and Exchange

38. Powers of sale and exchange.

A tenant for life—

(i) May sell the settled land, or any part thereof, or any easement, right or privilege of any kind over or in relation to the land; and

(ii) . . .

(iii) May make an exchange of the settled land, or any part thereof, or of any easement, right, or privilege of any kind, whether or not newly created, over or in relation to the settled land: or any part thereof, for other land, or for any easement, right or privilege of any kind, whether or not newly created, over or in relation to other land, including an exchange in consideration of money paid for equality of exchange.   **[104]**

NOTES
    Para (ii): repealed by the Statute Law (Repeals) Act 1969.

39. Regulations respecting sales

(1) Save as hereinafter provided every sale shall be made for best consideration in money that can reasonably be obtained.

(2) A sale may be made in consideration wholly or partially of a perpetual rent, or a terminable rent consisting of principal and interest combined, payable yearly or half yearly to be secured upon the land sold, or the land to which the easement, right or privilege sold is to be annexed in enjoyment or an adequate part thereof.

In the case of a terminable rent, the conveyance shall distinguish the part attributable to principal and that attributable to interest, and the part attributable to principal shall be capital money arising under this Act:

Provided that, unless the part of the terminable rent attributable to interest varies according to the amount of the principal repaid, the trustees of the settlement shall, during the subsistence of the rent, accumulate the income of the said capital money in the way of compound interest by investing it and the resulting income thereof in securities authorised for the investment of capital money and shall add the accumulations to capital.

(3) The rent to be reserved on any such sale shall be the best rent that can reasonably be obtained, regard being had to any money paid as part of the consideration, or laid out, or to be laid out, for the benefit of the settled land, and generally to the circumstances of the case, but a peppercorn rent, or a nominal or other rent less than the rent ultimately payable, may be made payable during any period not exceeding five years from the date of the conveyance.

(4) Where a sale is made in consideration of a rent, the following provisions shall have effect:—

  (i) The conveyance shall contain a convenant by the purchaser for payment of the rent, and [the statutory powers and remedies for the recovery of the rent shall apply];

  (ii) A duplicate of the conveyance shall be executed by the purchaser and delivered to the tenant for life or statutory owner, of which execution and delivery the execution of the conveyance by the tenant for life of statutory owner shall be sufficient evidence;

  (iii) A statement, contained in the conveyance or in an indorsement thereon, signed by the tenant for life of statutory owner, respecting any matter of fact or of calculation under this Act in relation to the sale, shall, in favour of the purchaser and of those claiming under him, be sufficient evidence of the matter stated.

(5) The consideration on a sale to any company incorporated by special Act of Parliament or by provisional order confirmed by Parliament or by any other order, scheme or certificate having the force of an Act of Parliament, may, with the consent of the tenant for life, consist, wholly or in part, of fully-paid securities of any description of the company, and such securities shall be vested in the trustees of the settlement and shall be subject to the provisions of this Act relating to securities representing capital money arising under this Act, and may be retained and held by the trustees in like manner as if they had been authorised by this Act for the investment of capital money.

(6) A sale may be made in one lot or in several lots, and either by auction or by private contract, and may be made subject to any stipulations respecting title, or evidence of title, or other things.

(7) On a sale the tenant for life may fix reserve biddings and may buy in at an auction.   **[105]**

NOTES
   Sub-s (4): words in square brackets substituted by the Law of Property (Amendment) Act 1926,
Schedule.

40. Regulations respecting exchanges

(1) Save as in this Part of this Act provided, every exchange shall be made for the best consideration in land or in land and money that can reasonably be obtained.

(2) An exchange may be made subject to any stipulations respecting title, or evidence of title, or other things.

(3) Settled land in England or Wales shall not be given in exchange for land out of England or Wales.   **[106]**

Leasing Powers

41. Power to lease for ordinary or building or mining or forestry purposes

A tenant for life may lease the settled land, or any part thereof, or any easement, right, or privilege of any kind over or in relation to the land, for any purpose whatever, whether involving waste or not, for any term not exceeding—

    (i) In case of a building lease, nine hundred and ninety-nine years;
    (ii) In case of a mining lease, one hundred years;
    (iii) In case of a forestry lease, nine hundred and ninety-nine years;
    (iv) In case of any other lease, fifty years.   **[107]**

42. Regulations respecting leases generally

(1) Save as hereinafter provided, every lease—

    (i) shall be by deed, and be made to take effect in possession not later than twelve months after its date, or in reversion after an existing lease having not more than seven years to run at the date of the new lease;

    (ii) shall reserve the best rent that can reasonably be obtained, regard being had to any fine taken, and to any money laid out or to be laid out for the benefit of the settled land, and generally to the circumstances of the case;

    (iii) shall contain a covenant by the lessee for payment of the rent, and a condition of re-entry on the rent not being paid within a time therein specified not exceeding thirty days.

(2) A counterpart of every lease shall be executed by the lessee and delivered to the tenant for life or statutory owner, of which execution and delivery the execution of the lease by the tenant for life or statutory owner shall be sufficient evidence.

(3) A statement, contained in a lease or in an indorsement thereon, signed by the tenant for life or statutory owner, respecting any matter of fact or of calculation under this Act in relation to the lease, shall, in favour of the lessee and of those claiming under him, be sufficient evidence of the matter stated.

(4) A fine received on the grant of a lease under any power conferred by this Act shall be deemed to be capital money arising under this Act.

(5) A lease at the best rent that can be reasonably obtained without fine,

and whereby the lessee is not exempted from punishment for waste, may be made—

    (i) Where the term does not exceed twenty-one years—

        (*a*) without any notice of an intention to make the lease having been given under this Act; and

        (*b*) notwithstanding that there are no trustees of the settlement; and

    (ii) Where the term does not extend beyond three years from the date of the writing, by any writing under hand only containing an agreement instead of a covenant by the lessee for payment of rent.   **[108]**

43. Leasing powers for special objects

The leasing power of a tenant for life extends to the making of—

    (i) a lease for giving effect (in such manner and so far as the law permits) to a covenant of renewal, performance whereof could be enforced against the owner for the time being of the settled land; and

    (ii) a lease for confirming, as far as may be, a previous lease being void or voidable, but so that every lease, as and when confirmed, shall be such a lease as might at the date of the original lease have been lawfully granted under this Act or otherwise, as the case may require.   **[109]**

Provisions as to building, mining and forestry leases

44. Regulations respecting building leases

(1) Every building lease shall be made partly in consideration of the lessee, or some person by whose direction the lease is granted, or some other person, having erected or agreeing to erect buildings, new or additional, or having improved or repaired or agreeing to improve or repair buildings, or having executed or agreeing to execute on the land leased, an improvement authorised by this Act for or in connexion with building purposes.

(2) A peppercorn rent or a nominal or other rent less than the rent ultimately payable, may be made payable for the first five years or any less part of the term.

(3) Where the land is contracted to be leased in lots, the entire amount of rent to be ultimately payable may be apportioned among the lots in any manner:

Provided that—

    (i) the annual rent reserved by any lease shall not be less than [50p]; and

    (ii) the total amount of the rents reserved on all leases for the time being granted shall not be less than the total amount of the rents which, in order that the leases may be in conformity with this Act, ought to be reserved in respect of the whole land for the time being leased; and

    (iii) the rent reserved by any lease shall not exceed one-fifth part of the full annual value of the land comprised in that lease with the buildings thereon when completed.   **[110]**

NOTES
Sub-s (3): sum in square brackets substituted by virtue of the Decimal Currency Act 1969, s 10(1).

---

45. Regulations respecting mining leases

(1) In a mining lease—

    (i) the rent may be made to be ascertainable by or to vary according to the acreage worked, or by or according to the quantities of any mineral or substance gotten, made merchantable, converted, carried away, or disposed of, in or from the settled land, or any other land, or by or according to any facilities given in that behalf; and

    (ii) the rent may also be made to vary according to the price of the minerals or substances gotten, or any of them, and such price may be the saleable value, or the price or value appearing in any trade or market or other price list or return from time to time, or may be the marketable value as ascertained in any manner prescribed by the lease (including a reference to arbitration), or may be an average of any such prices of values taken during a specified period; and

    (iii) a fixed minimum rent may be made payable: with or without power for the lessee, in case the rent, according to acreage or quantity or otherwise, in any specified period does not produce an amount equal to the fixed or minimum rent, to make up the deficiency in any subsequent specified period, free of rent other than the fixed or minimum rent.

(2) A lease may be made partly in consideration of the lessee having executed, or agreeing to execute, on the land leased an improvement authorised by this Act, for or in connexion with mining purposes. **[111]**

46. Variation of building or mining lease according to circumstances of district

(1) Where it is shown to the court with respect to the district in which any settled land is situate, either—

    (i) that it is the custom for land therein to be leased for building or mining purposes for a longer term or on other conditions than the term or conditions specified in that behalf in this Act; or

    (ii) that it is difficult to make leases for building or mining purposes of land therein, except for a longer term or on other conditions than the term and conditions specified in that behalf in this Act;

the court may, if it thinks fit, authorise generally the tenant for life or statutory owner to make from time to time leases of or affecting the settled land in that district, or parts thereof for any term or on any conditions as in the order of the court expressed, or may, if it thinks fit, authorise the tenant for life or statutory owner to make any such lease in any particular case.

(2) Thereupon the tenant for life or statutory owner, and, subject to any direction in the order of the court to the contrary, each of his successors in title being a tenant for life or statutory owner, may make in any case, or in the particular case, a lease of the settled land, or part thereof, in conformity with the order. **[112]**

47. Capitalisation of part of mining rent

Under a mining lease, whether the mines or minerals leased are already opened or in work or not, unless a contrary intention is expressed in the settlement there shall be from time to time set aside, as capital money arising under this Act, part of the rent as follows, namely—where the tenant for life or statutory owner is impeachable for waste in respect of minerals, three fourth parts of the rent, and otherwise one fourth part thereof, and in every such case the residue of the rent shall go as rents and profits. **[113]**

48. Regulations respecting forestry leases

(1) In the case of a forestry lease—

    (i) a peppercorn rent or a nominal or other rent less than the rent ultimately payable, may be made payable for the first ten years or any less part of the term;

    (ii) the rent may be made to be ascertainable by, or to vary according to the value of the timber on the land comprised in the lease, or the produce thereof, which may during any year be cut, converted carried away, or otherwise disposed of;

    (iii) a fixed or minimum rent may be made payable, with or without power for the lessee, in case the rent according to value in any specified period does not produce an amount equal to the fixed or minimum rent, to make up the deficiency in any subsequent specified period, free of rent other than the fixed or minimum rent; and

    (iv) any other provisions may be made for the sharing of the proceeds or profits of the user of the land between the reversioner and the Forestry Commissioners.

(2) In this expression "timber" includes all forest products. **[114]**

Miscellaneous Powers

49. Power on dispositions to impose restrictions and make reservations and stipulations

(1) On a sale or other disposition or dealing under the powers of this Act—

    (a) any easement, right, or privilege of any kind may be reserved or granted over or in relation to the settled land or any part thereof or other land, including the land disposed of, and, in the case of an exchange, the land taken in exchange; and

    (b) any restriction with respect to building on or other user of land, or with respect to mines and minerals, or with respect to or for the purpose of the more beneficial working thereof, or with respect to any other thing, may be imposed and made binding, as far as the law permits, by covenant, condition or otherwise, on the tenant for life or statutory owner and the settled land or any part thereof, or on the other party and any land disposed of to him; and

    (c) the whole or any part of any capital or annual sum (and in the case of an annual sum whether temporary or perpetual) charged on or payable out of the land disposed of, or any part thereof, and other land subject to the settlement, may as between the tenant for life or statutory owner and his successors in title, and the other party and persons deriving title under or in succession to him (but without prejudice to the rights of the person entitled to such capital or annual sum) be charged exclusively on the land disposed of, or any part thereof, or such other land as aforesaid, or any part thereof, in exoneration of the rest of the land on or out of which such capital or annual sum is charged or payable.

(2) A sale of land may be made subject to a stipulation that all or any of the timber and other trees, pollards, tellers, underwood, saplings and plantations on the land sold (in this section referred to as "timber") or any articles attached to the land (in this section referred to as "fixtures") shall be taken by the purchaser at a valuation and the amount of the valuation shall form part of the price of the land, and shall be capital money accordingly.

(3) Where on a sale the consideration attributable to any timber or fixtures is by mistake paid to a tenant for life or other person not entitled to receive it, then, if such person or the purchaser or the persons deriving title under either of them subsequently pay the aforesaid consideration, with such interest, if any, thereon as the court may direct to the trustees of the settlement or other persons entitled thereto or into court, the court may, on the application of the purchaser or the persons deriving title under him, declare that the disposition is to take effect as if the whole of the consideration had at the date thereof been duly paid to the trustees of the settlement or other persons entitled to receive the same.

The person, not entitled to receive the same, to whom the consideration is paid, and his estate and effects shall remain liable to make good any loss attributable to the mistake.   **[115]**

50. Separate dealing with surface and minerals with or without wayleaves, etc.

A sale, exchange, lease or other authorised disposition, may be made either of land, with or without an exception or reservation of all or any of the mines and minerals therein, or of any mines and minerals, and in any such case with or without a grant or reservation of powers of working, wayleaves or rights of way, rights of water and drainage, and other powers, easements, rights, and privileges for or incident to or connect with mining purposes, in relation to the settled land, or any part thereof, or any other land.   **[116]**

51. Power to grant options

(1) A tenant for life may at any time, either with or without consideration, grant by writing an option to purchase or take a lease of the settled land, or any part thereof, or any easement, right, or privilege over or in relation to the same at a price or rent fixed at the time of the granting of the option.

(2) Every such option shall be made exercisable within an agreed number of years not exceeding ten.

(3) The price or rent shall be the best which, having regard to all the circumstances, can reasonably be obtained and either—

    (a) may be a specified sum of money or rent, or at a specified rate according to the superficial area of the land with respect to which the option is exercised: or the frontage thereof or otherwise; or

    (b) in the case of an option to purchase contained in a lease or agreement for a lease, may be a stated number of years' purchase of the highest rent reserved by the lease or agreement; or

    (c) if the option is exercisable as regards part of the land comprised in the lease or agreement, may be a proportionate part of such highest rent;

and any aggregate price or rent may be made to be apportionable in any manner, or according to any system, or by reference to arbitration.

(4) An option to take a mining lease may be coupled with the grant of a licence to search for and prove any mines or minerals under the settled land, or any part thereof, pending the exercise of the option.

(5) The consideration for the grant of the option shall be capital money arising under this Act.   **[117]**

52. Surrenders and regrants

(1) A tenant for life may accept, with or without consideration, a surrender of any lease of settled land, whether made under this Act or not, or a regrant of any land granted in fee simple, whether under this Act or not, in respect of the whole land leased or granted, or any part thereof, with or without an exception of all or any of the mines and minerals therein, or in respect of mines and minerals, or any of them, and with or without an exception of any easement, right or privilege of any kind over or in relation to the land surrendered or regranted.

(2) On a surrender of a lease, or a regrant of land granted in fee simple, in respect of part only of the land or mines and minerals leased or granted, the rent or rentcharge may be apportioned.

(3) On a surrender or regrant, the tenant for life may in relation to the land or mines and minerals surrendered or regranted, or of any part thereof, make a new or other lease, or grant in fee simple, or new or other leases, or grants in fee simple, in lots.

(4) A new or other lease, or grant in fee simple, may comprise additional land or mines and minerals, and may reserve any apportioned or other rent or rentcharge.

(5) On a surrender or regrant, and the making of a new or other lease, whether for the same or for any extended or other term, or of a new of other grant in fee simple, and whether or not subject to the same or to any other covenants, provisions, or conditions, the value of the lessee's or grantee's interests in the lease surrendered, or the land regranted, may be taken into account in the determination of the amount of the rent or rentcharge to be reserved, and of any fine or consideration in money to be taken, and of the nature of the covenants, provisions, and conditions to be inserted in the new or other lease, or grant in fee simple.

(6) Every new or other lease, or grant in fee simple, shall be in conformity with this Act.

(7) All money, not being rent or rentcharge, received on the exercise by the tenant for life of the powers conferred by this section, shall, unless the court, on an application made within six months after the receipt thereof or within such further time as the court may in special circumstances allow, otherwise directs, be capital money arising under this Act.

(8) A regrant shall be made to the tenant for life or statutory owner, and shall be deemed a subsidiary vesting deed, and the statements and particulars required in the case of subsidiary vesting deeds shall be inserted therein.

(9) In this Section, "land granted in fee simple" means land so granted with

or subject to a reservation thereout of a perpetual or terminable rentcharge which is or forms part of the settled land, and "grant in fee simple" has a corresponding meaning. **[118]**

53. Acceptance of leases

(1) A tenant for life may accept a lease of any land, or of any mines and minerals or of any easement, right, or privilege, convenient to be held or worked with or annexed in enjoyment to the settled land, or any part thereof, for such period, and upon such terms and conditions, as the tenant for life thinks fit:

Provided that no fine shall be paid out of capital money in respect of such lease.

(2) The lease shall be granted to the tenant for life or statutory owner, and shall be deemed a subsidiary vesting deed, and the statements and particulars required in the case of subsidiary vesting deeds shall either be inserted therein or endorsed thereon.

(3) The lease may contain an option to purchase the reversion expectant on the term thereby granted. **[119]**

54. Power to grant water rights to statutory bodies

(1) For the development, improvement, or general benefit of the settled land, or any part thereof, a tenant for life may make a grant in fee simple or absolutely, or a lease for any term of years absolute, for a nominal price or rent, or for less than the best price or rent that can reasonably be obtained, or gratuitously, to any statutory authority, of any water or streams or springs of water in, upon, or under the settled land, and of any rights of taking, using, enjoying and conveying water, and of laying, constructing, maintaining, and repairing mains, pipes, reservoirs, dams, weirs and other works of any kind proper for the supply and distribution of water, and of any part of the settled land required as a site for any of the aforesaid works, and of any easement, right or privilege over or in relation to the settled land or any part thereof in connexion with any of the aforesaid works.

(2) This section does not authorise the creation of any greater rights than could have been created by a person absolutely entitled for his own benefit to the settled land affected.

(3) In this section "statutory authority" means an authority or company for the time being empowered by any Act of Parliament, public general, or local or private, or by any order or certificate having the force of an Act of Parliament, to provide with a supply of water any town, parish or place in which the settled land or any part thereof is situated.

(4) All money, not being rent, received on the exercise of any power conferred by this section shall be capital money arising under this Act. **[120]**

55. Power to grant land for public and charitable purposes

(1) For the development, improvement, or general benefit of the settled land, or any part thereof, a tenant for life may make a grant in fee simple, or absolutely, or a lease for any term of years absolute, for a nominal price or rent, or for less than the best price or rent that can reasonably be obtained, or gratuitously, of any part of the settled land, with or without any easement, right or privilege over or in relation to the settled land or any part thereof, for all or any one or more of the following purposes, namely:—

(i) For the site, or the extension of any existing site, of a place of religious worship, residence for a minister of religion, school house, town hall, market house, public library, public baths, museum, hospital, infirmary, or other public building, literary or scientific institution, drill hall, working-men's club, parish room, reading room or village institute, with or without in any case any yard, garden, or other ground to be held with any such building; or

(ii) For the construction, enlargement, or improvement of any railway, canal, road (public or private), dock, sea-wall, embankment, drain, watercourse, or reservoir; or

(iii) For any other public or charitable purpose in connexion with the settled land, or any part thereof, or tending to the benefit of the persons residing, or for whom dwelling may be erected, on the settled land, or any part thereof.

Not more than one acre shall in any particular case be conveyed for any purpose mentioned in paragraphs (i) and (iii) of this subsection, nor more than five acres for any purpose mentioned in paragraph (ii) of this subsection, unless the full consideration be paid or reserved in respect of the excess.

(2) All money, not being rent, received on the exercise of any power conferred by this section shall be capital money arising under this Act.   **[121]**

56. Dedication for streets, open spaces, etc

(1) On or after or in connexion with a sale or grant for building purposes, or a building lease, or the development as a building estate of the settled land, or any part thereof, or at any other reasonable time, the tenant for life, for the general benefit of the residents on the settled land, or on any part thereof—

(i) may cause or require any parts of the settled land to be appropriated and laid out for streets, roads, paths, squares, gardens, or other open spaces, for the use, gratuitously or on payment, of the public or of individuals, with sewers, drains, water courses, fences, paving, or other works necessary or proper in connexion therewith; and

(ii) may provide that the parts so appropriated shall be conveyed to or vested in the trustees of the settlement, or other trustees, or any company or public body, on trusts or subject to provisions for securing the continued appropriation thereof to the purposes aforesaid, and the continued repair or maintenance of streets and other places and works aforesaid, with or without provision for appointment of new trustees when required; and

(iii) may execute any general or other deed necessary or proper for giving effect to the provisions of this section (which deed may be inrolled in the Central Office of the Supreme Court), and thereby declare the mode, terms, and conditions of the appropriation, and the manner in which and the persons by whom the benefit thereof is to be enjoyed, and the nature and extent of the privileges and conveniences granted.

(2) In regard to the dedication of land for the public purposes aforesaid, a tenant for life shall be in the same position as if he were an absolute owner.

(3) A tenant for life shall have power—

(a) to enter into any agreement for the recompense to be made for any part of the settled land which is required for the widening of a highway under [the Highways Act 1980], or otherwise;

(b) to consent to the diversion of any highway over the settled land under [the Highways Act 1980], or otherwise; and

(c) . . .

and any agreement or consent so made or given shall be valid and effectual, for all purposes, as if made or given by an absolute owner of the settled land.

(4) All money, not being rent, received on the exercise of any power conferred by this section shall be capital money arising under this Act.   **[122]**

NOTES
Sub-s (3): words in square brackets substituted and para (c) repealed by the Highways Act 1980, s 343(2), Sch 24.

57. Provision of land for small dwellings, small holdings and dwellings for working classes

(1) Where land is sold, or given in exchange or leased—

(a) for the purpose of the erection on such land of small dwellings; or

(b) to the council of a county or county borough for the purposes of small holdings;

the sale, exchange, or lease may, notwithstanding anything contained in this Act, be made for such consideration in money, or land, or in land and money, or may reserve such rent, as having regard to the said purposes and to all the circumstances of the case, is the best that can reasonably be obtained, notwithstanding that a better consideration or rent might have been obtained if the land were sold, exchanged, or leased, for another purpose.

(2) Notwithstanding anything contained in, and in addition to the other powers conferred by this Act, a tenant for life may at any time—

(a) for the purpose of the erection of dwellings for the working classes, or the provision of gardens to be held therewith; or

(b) for the purpose of the Small Holdings and Allotments Acts 1908 to 1919;

make a grant in fee simple or absolutely, or a lease for any term of years absolute of any part of the settled land, with or without any easement, right or privilege of any kind over or in relation to the settled land or any part thereof, for a nominal price or rent, or for less than the best price or rent that can reasonably be obtained or gratuitously:

Provided that, except under an order of the court, not more than two acres in the case of land situate in an urban district, or ten acres in the case of land situate in a rural district, in any one parish shall be granted or leased under the powers conferred by this subsection, unless the full consideration be paid or reserved in respect of the excess.

(3) All money, not being rent, received on the exercise of any power conferred by this section shall be capital money arising under this Act.   **[123]**

58. Power to compromise claims and release restrictions, etc

(1) A tenant for life may, with the consent in writing of the trustees of the settlement, either with or without giving or taking any consideration in money or otherwise, compromise, compound, abandon, submit to arbitration, or

otherwise settle any claim, dispute, or question whatsoever relating to the settled land, or any part thereof, including in particular claims, disputes or questions as to boundaries, the ownership of mines and minerals, rights and powers of working mines and minerals, local laws and customs relative to the working of mines and minerals and other matters . . . easements, and restrictive covenants, and for any of those purposes may enter into, give, execute, and do such agreements, assurances, releases, and other things as the tenant for life may, with such consent as aforesaid, think proper.

(2) A tenant for life may, with the consent in writing of the trustees of the settlement, at any time, by deed or writing, either with or without consideration in money or otherwise, release, waive, or modify, or agree to release, waive, or modify any covenant, agreement, or restriction imposed on any other land for the benefit of the settled land, or any part thereof, or release, or agree to release, any other land from any easement, right or privilege, including a right of pre-emption, affecting the same for the benefit of the settled land, or any part thereof.

(3) A tenant for life may contract that a transaction effected before or after the commencement of this Act, which (whether subject or not to any variation authorised by this subsection) is affected by section seventy-eight of the Railway Clauses Consolidation Act 1845, or by section twenty-two of the Waterworks Clauses Act 1847 (relating to support by minerals) shall take effect as if some other distance than forty yards or the prescribed distance had been mentioned in such sections or had been otherwise prescribed.

In any case where section seventy-eight aforesaid has effect as amended and re-enacted by Part II of the Mines (Working Facilities and Support) Act 1923, a tenant for life may make any agreement authorised by section eighty-five A of the Railway Clauses Consolidation Act 1845, as enacted in the said Part II.   **[124]**

NOTES
Sub-s (1): words omitted repealed by the Statute Law (Repeals) Act 1969.

59. Power to vary leases and grants and to give licences and consents

(1) A tenant for life may, at any time, by deed, either with or without consideration in money or otherwise, vary, release, waive or modify, either absolutely or otherwise, the terms of any lease whenever made of the settled land or any part thereof, or any covenants or conditions contained in any grant in fee simple whenever made of land with or subject to a reservation thereout of a rent which is or forms part of the settled land, and in either case in respect of the whole or any part of the land comprised in any such lease or grant, but so that every such lease or grant shall, after such variation, release, waiver or modification as aforesaid, be such a lease or grant as might then have been lawfully made under this Act if the lease had been surrendered, or the land comprised in the grant had never been so comprised, or had been regranted.

(2) Where land is or has been disposed of subject to any covenant requiring the licence, consent, or approval of the covenantee or his successors in title as to—

(a) the user of the land in any manner; or
(b) the erection construction or alteration of or addition to buildings or works of any description on the land; or
(c) the plans or elevations of any proposed buildings or other works on the land; or

(*d*) any other act, matter, or thing relating to the land, or any buildings or works thereon; or

(*e*) any assignment, under-letting or parting with the possession of all or any part of the property comprised in any lease affecting the settled land;

and the covenant enures for the benefit of settled land (including, where the disposition is a lease, the reversion expectant on the determination thereof), the licence, consent or approval may be given by the tenant for life of the settled land affected. **[125]**

60. Power to apportion rents

(1) A tenant for life may, at any time, by deed, either with or without consideration in money or otherwise, agree for the apportionment of any rent reserved or created by any such lease or grant as mentioned in the last preceding section, or any rent being or forming part of the settled land, so that the apportioned parts of such rent shall thenceforth be payable exclusively out of or in respect of such respective portions of the land subject thereto as may be thought proper, and also agree that any covenants, agreements, powers, or remedies for securing such rent and any other covenants or agreements by the lessee or grantee and any conditions shall also be apportioned and made applicable exclusively to the respective portions of the land out of or in respect of which the apportioned parts of such rent shall thenceforth be payable.

(2) Where the settled land, or any part thereof, is held or derived under a lease, or under a grant reserving rent, or subject to covenants, agreements or conditions, whether such lease or grant comprised other land or not, the tenant for life may at any time by deed, with or without giving or taking any consideration in money or otherwise, procure the variation, release, waiver, or modification, either absolutely or otherwise, of the terms, covenants, agreements, or conditions contained in such lease or grant, in respect of the whole or any part of the settled land comprises therein, including the apportionment of any rent, covenants, agreements, conditions, and provisions reserved, or created by, or contained in, such lease or grant.

(3) This section applies to leases or grants made either before or after the commencement of this Act. **[126]**

61. Provisions as to consideration

(1) All money, not being rent, payable by the tenant for life in respect of any transaction to which any of the three last preceding sections relates shall be paid out of capital money arising under this Act, and all money, not being rent, received on the exercise by the tenant for life of the powers conferred by any of those sections, shall, unless the court, on an application made within six months after the receipt thereof or within such further time as the court may in special circumstances allow, otherwise directs, be capital money arising under this Act.

(2) For the purpose of the three last preceding sections "consideration in money or otherwise" means—

(*a*) a capital sum of money or a rent;

(*b*) land being freehold or leasehold for any term of years whereof not less than sixty years shall be unexpired;

(*c*) any easement, right or privilege over or in relation to the settled land, or any part thereof, or any other land;

(*d*) the benefit of any restrictive covenant or condition; and (*e*) the release of the settled land, or any part thereof, or any other land, from any easement, right or privilege, including a right of pre-emption, or from the burden of any restrictive covenant or condition affecting the same.　　　　　　　　　　　　　　**[127]**

62. Special provisions as to manorial incidents, etc

(1)–(3) ...

(4) In reference to the conversion of a perpetually renewable lease or underlease into a long term, a tenant for life may enter into such agreements and do such acts and things as the lessor or lessee or under lessee, as the case may require, is, by any enactment authorised to enter into or do.　　**[128]**

NOTES

Sub-ss (1)–(3): repealed by the Statute Law (Repeals) Act 1969.

63. Power to complete predecessor's contracts

A tenant for life may make any disposition which is necessary or proper for giving effect to a contract entered into by a predecessor in title, and which if made by that predecessor would have been valid as against his successors in title.　.　　　　　　　　　　　　　　　　　　　　　　**[129]**

64. General power for the tenant for life to effect any transaction under an order of the court

(1) Any transaction affecting or concerning the settled land, or any part thereof, or any other land (not being a transaction otherwise authorised by this Act, or by the settlement) which in the opinion of the court would be for the benefit of the settled land, or any part thereof, or the persons interested under the settlement, may, under an order of the court, be effected by a tenant for life, if it is one which could have been validly effected by an absolute owner.

(2) In this section "transaction" includes any sale, ... exchange, assurance, grant, lease, surrender, reconveyance, release, reservation, or other disposition, and any purchase or other acquisiton, and any covenant, contract, or option, and any application of capital money ... and any compromise or other dealing, or arrangement ... ; and "effected" has the meaning appropriate to the particular transaction; and the references to land include references to restrictions and burdens affecting land.　　　　　　　　　　**[130]**

NOTES

Sub-s (2): first words omitted repealed by the Statute Law (Repeals) Act 1969; other words omitted repealed by the Settled Land and Trustee Acts (Court's General Powers) Act 1943, s 2.

Provisions as to special classes of property

65. Power to dispose of mansion

(1) The powers of disposing of settled land conferred by this Act on a tenant for life may be exercised as respects the principal mansion house, if any, on any settled land, and the pleasure grounds and park and lands, if any, usually occupied therewith:

Provided that those powers shall not be exercised without the consent of the trustees of the settlement or an order of the court—

    (*a*) if the settlement is a settlement made or coming into operation before the commencement of this Act and the settlement does not expressly provide to the contrary; or

    (*b*) if the settlement is a settlement made or coming into operation after the commencement of this Act and the settlement expressly provides that these powers or any of them shall not be exercised without such consent or order.

(2) Where a house is usually occupied as a farmhouse, or where the site of any house and the pleasure grounds and park and lands, if any, usually occupied therewith do not together exceed twenty-five acres in extent, the house is not to be deemed a principal mansion house within the meaning of this section, and may accordingly be disposed of in like manner as any other part of the settled land.   **[131]**

66. Cutting and sale of timber, and capitalisation of part of proceeds

(1) Where a tenant for life is impeachable for waste in respect of timber, and there is on the settled land timber ripe and fit for cutting, the tenant for life, on obtaining the consent of the trustees of the settlement or an order of the court, may cut and sell that timber, or any part thereof.

(2) Three fourths part of the net proceeds of the sale shall be set aside as and be capital money arising under this Act, and the other fourth part shall go as rents and profits.   **[132]**

67. Sale and purchase of heirlooms under order of court

(1) Where personal chattels are settled so as to devolve with settled land, or to devolve therewith as nearly as may be in accordance with the law or practice in force at the date of the settlement, or are settled together with land, or upon trusts declared by reference to the trusts affecting land, a tenant for life of the land may sell the chattels or any of them.

(2) The money arising by the sale shall be capital money arising under this Act, and shall be paid, invested, or applied and otherwise dealt with in like manner in all respects as by this Act directed with respect to other capital money arising under this Act, or may be invested in the purchase of other chattels of the same or any other nature, which, when purchased, shall be settled and held on the same trusts, and shall devolve in the same manner as the chattels sold.

(3) A sale or purchase of chattels under this section shall not be made without an order of the court.

(4) Any reference in any enactment to personal chattels settled as heirlooms shall extend to any chattels to which this section applies.   **[133]**

Dealings as between tenants for life and the estate

68. Provision enabling dealings with tenant for life

(1) In the manner mentioned and subject to the provisions contained in this section—

    (*a*) a sale, grant, lease, mortgage, charge or other disposition of settled land, or of any easement, right, or privilege over the same may be made to the tenant for life; or

    (*b*) capital money may be advanced on mortgage to him; or

(*c*) a purchase may be made from him of land to be made subject to the limitations of the settlement; or

(*d*) an exchange may be made with him of settled land for other land; and

(*e*) any such disposition, advance, purchase, or exchange as aforesaid may be made to, from, or with any persons of whom the tenant for life is one.

(2) In every such case the trustees of the settlement shall, in addition to their powers as trustees, have all the powers of a tenant for life in reference to negotiating and completing the transaction, and shall have power to enforce any covenants by the tenant for life, or, where the tenant for life is himself one of the trustees, then the other or others of them shall have such power, and the said powers of a tenant for life may be exercised by the trustees of the settlement in the name and on behalf of the tenant for life.

(3) This section applies, notwithstanding that the tenant for life is one of the trustees of the settlement, or that an order has been made authorising the trustees to act on his behalf, or that he is [suffering from mental disorder] but does not apply to dealings with any body of persons which inlcudes a trustee of the settlement, not being the tenant for life, unless the transaction is either previously or subsequently approved by the court.   **[134]**

NOTES
Sub-s (3): words in square brackets substituted by the Mental Health Act 1959, s 149, Sch 7, Part I.

Incumbrances

69. Shifting of incumbrances

Where there is an incumbrance affecting any part of the settled land (whether capable of being overreached on the exercise by the tenant for life of his powers under this Act or not), the tenant for life, with the consent of the incumbrancer, may charge that incumbrance on any other part of the settled land, or on all or any part of the capital money or securities representing capital money subject or to become subject to the settlement, whether already charged therewith or not, in exoneration of the first mentioned part, and, by a legal mortgage, or otherwise, make provision accordingly.   **[135]**

70. Power to vary provisions of an incumbrance and to charge by way of additional security

(1) Where an incumbrance affects any part of the settled land, the tenant for life may, with the consent of the incumbrancer, vary the rate of interest charged and any of the other provisions of the instrument, if any, creating the incumbrance, and with the like consent charge that incumbrance on any part of the settled land, whether already charged therewith or not, or on all or any part of the capital money or securities representing capital money subject or to become subject to the settlement, by way of additional security, or of consolidation of securities, and by a legal mortgage or otherwise, make provision accordingly.

(2) "Incumbrance" in this section includes any annual sum payable during a life or lives or during a term of years absolute or determinable, but in any such case an additional security shall be effected so as only to create a charge or security similar to the original charge or security.   **[136]**

Raising of Money

71. Power to raise money by mortgage

(1) Where money is required for any of the following purposes namely:—

    (i) Discharging an incumbrance on the settled land or part thereof;

    (ii) Paying for any improvement authorised by this Act or by the settlement;

    (iii) Equality of exchange;

    (iv), (v) . . . ;

    (vi) Redeeming a compensation rentcharge in respect of the extinguishment of manorial incidents and affecting the settled land;

    (vii) Commuting any additional rent made payable on the conversion of a perpetually renewable leasehold interest into a long term;

    (viii) Satisfying any claims for compensation on the conversion of a perpetually renewable leasehold interest into a long term by any officer, solicitor, or other agent of the lessor in respect of fees or remuneration which would have been payable by the lessee or under-lessee on any renewal;

    (ix) Payment of the costs of any transaction authorised by this section or either of the two last preceding sections;

the tenant for life may raise the money so required, on the security of the settled land, or of any part thereof, by a legal mortgage, and the money so raised shall be capital money for that purpose, and may be paid or applied accordingly.

(2) "Incumbrance" in this section does not include any annual sum payable only during a life or lives or during a term of years absolute or determinable.

(3) The restrictions imposed by this Part of this Act on the leasing powers of a tenant for life do not apply in relation to a mortgage term created under this Act.   **[137]**

NOTES

Sub-s (1): paras (iv), (v) repealed by the Statute Law (Repeals) Act 1969.

Conveyance

72. Completion of transactions by conveyance

(1) On a sale, exchange, lease, mortgage, charge, or other disposition, the tenant for life may, as regards land sold, given in exchange, leased, mortgaged, charged, or otherwise disposed of, or intended so to be, or as regards easements or other rights or privileges sold, given in exchange, leased, mortgaged, or otherwise disposed of, or intended so to be, effect the transaction by deed to the extent of the estate or interest vested or declared to be vested in him by the last or only vesting instrument affecting the settled land or any less estate or interest, in the manner requisite for giving effect to the sale, exchange, lease, mortgage, charge, or other disposition, but so that a mortgage shall be effected by the creation of a term of years absolute in the settled land or by charge by way of legal mortgage, and not otherwise.

(2) Such a deed, to the extent and in the manner to and in which it is expressed or intended to operate and can operate under this Act, is effectual to pass the land conveyed, or the easements, rights, privileges or other interests created, discharged from all the limitations, powers, and provisions of the settlement, and from all estates, interests, and charges subsisting or to arise thereunder, but subject to and with the exception of—

(i) all legal estates and charges by way of legal mortage having priority to the settlement; and

(ii) all legal estates and charges by way of legal mortgage which have been conveyed or created for securing money actually raised at the date of the deed; and

(iii) all leases and grants at fee-farm rents or otherwise, and all grants of easements, rights of common, or other rights or privileges which—

(a) were before the date of the deed granted or made for value in money or money's worth, or agreed so to be, by the tenant for life or statutory owner, or by any of his predecessors in title, or any trustees for them, under the settlement, or under any statutory power, or are at that date otherwise binding on the successors in title of the tenant for life or statutory owner; and

(b) are at the date of the deed protected by registration under the Land Charges Act 1925, if capable of registration thereunder.

(3) Notwithstanding registration under the Land Charges Act 1925, of—

(a) an annuity within the meaning of Part II of that Act;

(b) a limited owner's charge or a general equitable charge within the meaning of that Act;

a disposition under this Act operates to overreach such annuity or charge which shall, according to its priority, take effect as if limited by the settlement.

(4) Where a lease is by this Act authorised to be made by writing under hand only, such writing shall have the same operation under this section as if it had been a deed. **[138]**

PART III

INVESTMENT OR OTHER APPLICATION OF CAPITAL MONEY

73. Modes of investment or application

(1) Capital money arising under this Act, subject to payment of claims properly payable thereout and to the application thereof for any special authorised object for which the capital money was raised, shall, when received, be invested or otherwise applied wholly in one, or partly in one and partly in another or others, of the following modes (namely):—

(i) In investment in Government securities, or in other securities in which the trustees of the settlement are by the settlement or by law authorised to invest trust money of the settlement, with power to vary the investment into or for any other such securities;

(ii) In discharge, purchase, or redemption of incumbrances affecting the whole estate the subject of the settlement, or of ... , rentcharge in lieu of tithe, Crown rent, chief rent, or quit rent, charged on or payable out of the settled land, or of any charge in respect of an improvement created on a holding under the [Agricultural Holdings Act 1986], or any similar previous enactment;

(iii) In payment for any improvement authorised by this Act;

(iv) In payment as for an improvement authorised by this Act of any money expended and costs incurred by a landlord under or in pursuance of the *Agricultural Holdings Act 1923* [Agricultural

Holdings Act 1986], or any similar previous enactment, or under custom or agreement or otherwise, in or about the execution of any improvement comprised in *Part I or Part II of the First Schedule* [Schedule 7] to the said Agricultural Holdings Act;

(v) In payment for equality of exchange of settled land;

(vi), (vii) . . . ;

(viii) In redemption of any compensation rentcharge created in respect of the extinguishment of manorial incidents, and affecting the settled land;

(ix) In commuting any additional rent made payable on the conversion of a perpetually renewable leasehold interest into a long term, and in satisfying any claim for compensation on such conversion by any officer, solicitor, or other agent of the lessor in respect of fees or remuneration which would have been payable by the lessee or under-lessee on any renewal;

(x) In purchase of the freehold reversion in fee of any part of the settled land, being leasehold land held for years;

(xi) In purchase of land in fee simple, or of leasehold land held for sixty years or more unexpired at the time of purchase, subject or not to any exception or reservation of or in respect of mines or minerals therein, or of or in respect of rights or powers relative to the working of mines or minerals therein, or in other land;

(xii) In purchase either in fee simple, or for a term of sixty years or more, of mines and minerals convenient to be held or worked with the settled land, or of any easement, right, or privilege convenient to be held with the settled land for mining or other purposes;

(xiii) In redemption of an improvement rentcharge, that is to say, a rentcharge (temporary or permanent) created, whether before or after the commencement of this Act, in pursuance of any Act of Parliament, with the object of paying off any money advanced for defraying the expenses of an improvement of any kind authorised by Part I of the Third Schedule to this Act;

(xiv) In the purchase, with the leave of the court, of any leasehold interest where the immediate reversion is settled land, so as to merge the leasehold interest (unless the court otherwise directs) in the reversion, and notwithstanding that the leasehold interest may have less than sixty years to run;

(xv) In payment of the costs and expenses of all plans, surveys, and schemes, including schemes under the Town Planning Act 1925, or any similar previous enactment, made with a view to, or in connexion with the improvement or development of the settled land, or any part thereof, or the exercise of any statutory powers, and of all negotiations entered into by the tenant for life with a view to the exercise of any of the said powers, notwithstanding that such negotiations may prove abortive, and in payment of the costs and expenses of opposing any such proposed scheme as aforesaid affecting the settled land, whether or not the scheme is made;

(xvi) In the purchase of an annuity charged under section four of the Tithe Act 1918, on the settled land or any part thereof, or in the discharge of such part of any such annuity as does not represent interest;

(xvii) In payment to a local or other authority of such sum as may be agreed in consideration of such authority taking over and becoming liable to repair a private road on the settled land or a road for the maintenance whereof a tenant for life is liable ratione tenurae;

(xviii) In financing any person who may have agreed to take a lease or grant for building purposes of the settled land, or any part thereof, by making advances to him in the usual manner on the security of an equitable mortgage of his building agreement;

(xix) In payment to any person becoming absolutely entitled or empowered to give an absolute discharge;

(xx) In payment of costs, charges, and expenses of or incidental to the exercise of any of the powers, or the execution of any of the provisions of this Act including the costs and expenses incidental to any of the matters referred to in this section;

(xxi) In any other mode authorised by the settlement with respect to money produced by the sale of the settled land.

(2) Notwithstanding anything in this section capital money arising under this Act from settled land in England or Wales shall not be applied in the purchase of land out of England and Wales, unless the settlement expressly authorises the same.   **[139]**

NOTES

Sub-s (1): first words omitted repealed by the Finance Act 1963, s 73 (8)(*b*), Sch 11, Part VI; paras (vi), (vii) repealed by the Statute Law (Repeals) Act 1969; words in square brackets substituted with savings by the Agricultural Holdings Act 1986, ss 99, 100, Sch 13, para 3, Sch 14, para 11.

74. Power to acquire land subject to certain incumbrances

(1) Land may be acquired on a purchase or exchange to be made subject to a settlement, notwithstanding that the land is subject to any Crown rent, quit rent, chief rent, or other incident of tenure, or to any easement, right or privilege, or to any restrictive covenant, or to any liability to maintain or repair walls, fences, sea-walls, river banks, dykes, roads, streets, sewers, or drains, or to any improvement rentcharge which is capable under this Act of being redeemed out of capital money.

(2) The acquisition on a purchase or exchange before the commencement of this Act of any land subject to any such burden as aforesaid is hereby confirmed.   **[140]**

75. Regulations respecting investment, devolution, and income of securities, etc

(1) Capital money arising under this Act shall, in order to its being invested or applied as aforesaid, be paid either to the trustees of the settlement or into court at the option of the tenant for life, and shall be invested or applied by the trustees, or under the direction of the court, as the case may be, accordingly.

(2) The investment or other application by the trustees shall be made according to the direction of the tenant for life, and in default thereof according to the discretion of the trustees, but in the last-mentioned case subject to any consent required or direction given by the settlement with respect to the investment or other application by the trustees of trust money of the settlement, and any investment shall be in the names or under the control of the trustees.

(3) The investment or other application under the direction of the court shall be made on the application of the tenant for life, or of the trustees.

(4) Any investment or other application shall not during the subsistence of the beneficial interest of the tenant for life be altered without his consent.

(5) Capital money arising under this Act while remaining uninvested or unapplied, and securities on which an investment of any such capital money is made shall for all purposes of disposition, tranmission and devolution be treated as land, and shall be held for and go to the same persons successively, in the same manner and for and on the same estates, interests, and trusts, as the land wherefrom the money arises would, if not disposed of, have been held and have gone under the settlement.

(6) The income of those securities shall be paid or applied as the income of that land, if not disposed of, would have been payable or applicable under the settlement.

(7) Those securities may be converted into money, which shall be capital money arising under this Act.

(8) All or any part of any capital money paid into court may, if the court thinks fit, be at any time paid out to the trustees of the settlement.   **[141]**

76. Application of money in court under Lands Clauses and other Acts

Where, under an Act, or an order or scheme confirmed by or having the force of an Act of Parliament, incorporating or applying, wholly or in part, the Lands Clauses Acts, or under any Act, public general or local or private, money is at the commencement of this Act in court, or is afterwards paid into court, and is liable to be laid out the in purchase of land to be made subject to a settlement, then, in addition to any mode of dealing therewith authorised by the Act under which the money is in court, that money may be invested or applied as capital money arising under this Act, on the like terms, if any, respecting costs and other things, as nearly as circumstances admit, and notwithstanding anything in this Act according to the same procedure, as if the modes of investment or application authorised by this Act were authorised by the Act under which the money is in court.   **[142]**

77. Application of money in hands of trustees under powers of settlement

Where—

    (a) under any instrument coming into operation either before or after the commencement of this Act money is in the hands of trustees, and is liable to be laid out in the purchase of land to be made subject to the trusts declared by that instrument; or

    (b) under any instrument coming into operation after the commencement of this Act money or securities or the proceeds of sale of any property is or are held by trustees on trusts creating entailed interests therein;

then, in addition to such powers of dealing therewith as the trustees have independently of this Act, they may, at the option of the tenant for life, invest or apply the money securities or proceeds as if they were capital money arising under this Act.   **[143]**

78. Provision as to personal estate settled by reference to capital money, or on trusts corresponding with the limitations of land

(1) Where money or securities or the proceeds of sale of any property is or are by any instrument coming into operation either before or after the commencement of this Act directed to be held on trusts declared by reference to capital

money arising under this Act from land settled by that instrument or any other instrument, the money securities or proceeds shall be held on the like trusts as if the same had been or represented money which had actually arisen under this Act from the settled land.

[This sub-section operates without prejudice to the rights of any person claiming under a disposition for valuable consideration of any such money securities or proceeds, made before the commencement of this Act].

(2) Where money or securities or the proceeds of sale of any property is or are by any instrument coming into operation after the commencement of this Act directed to be held on the same trusts as, or on trusts corresponding as nearly as may be with the limitations of land settled by that instrument or any other instrument, the money, securities or proceeds shall be held on the like trusts as if the same had been or represented capital money arising under this Act from the settled land.

(3) Such money, securities, or proceeds of sale shall be paid or transferred to or retained by the trustees of the settlement of the settled land, or paid or transferred into court, and invested or applied accordingly.

(4) Where the settled land includes freehold land, the money, securities, or proceeds of sale aforesaid shall be held on the like trusts as if the same had been or represented capital money arising from the freehold land.

(5) This section has effect notwithstanding any direction in the instrument creating the trust that the trust property is not to vest absolutely in any tenant in tail or in tail male or in tail female under the limitations of the settled land who dies under a specified age, or before the happening of a specified event, but, save as aforesaid, has effect with any variations and subject to any contrary intention expressed in the instrument creating the trust.   **[144]**

NOTES
  Sub-s (1): words in square brackets added by the Law of Property (Amendment) Act 1926, Schedule.

79. Application of money paid for lease or reversion

Where capital money arising under this Act is purchase-money paid in respect of—

  (*a*) a lease for years; or
  (*b*) any other estate or interest in land less than the fee simple; or
  (*c*) a reversion dependent on any such lease, estate, or interest;

the trustees of the settlement or the court, as the case may be, and in the case of the court on the application of any party interested in that money, may, notwithstanding anything in this Act, require and cause the same to be laid out, invested, accumulated, and paid in such manner as, in the judgment of the trustees or of the court, as the case may be, will give to the parties interested in that money the like benefit therefrom as they might lawfully have had from the lease, estate, interest, or reversion in respect whereof the money was paid, or as near thereto as may be.   **[145]**

80. As to money received by way of damages for breach of covenant

(1) Money, not being rent, received by way of damages or compensation for breach of any covenant by a lessee or grantee contained in any lease or grant of settled land shall, unless in any case the court on the application of the tenant for life or the trustees of the settlement otherwise directs, be deemed to be

capital money arising under this Act, and shall be paid to or retained by the trustees of the settlement, or paid into court, and invested or applied, accordingly.

(2) In addition to the other modes in which capital money may be applied under this Act or the settlement, money so received as aforesaid or any part thereof may, if the circumstances permit, be applied at any time within twelve months after such receipt, or such extended period as the court may allow, in or towards payment of the costs of making good in whole or in part the breach of covenant in respect of which it was so received, or the consequences thereof, and the trustees of the settlement, if they think fit, may require any money so received or any part thereof to be so applied.

(3) In the application of any such money in or towards payment of the cost of making good any such breach or the consequences of any such breach as aforesaid, the work required to be done for the purpose shall be deemed to be an improvement authorised by Part I of the Third Schedule to this Act.

(4) This section does not apply to money received by way of damages or compensation for the breach of a covenant to repay to the lessor or grantor money laid out or expended by him, or to any case in which if the money received were applied in making good the breach of covenant or the consequences thereof such application would not enure for the benefit of the settled land, or any buildings thereon.

(5) This section does not apply to money received by way of damages or compensation before the commencement of this Act, but it applies whether the lease or grant was made before or after the commencement of this Act, and whether under the powers conferred by the Settled Land Acts 1882 to 1890, or this Act or not.

(6) The provisions of this section apply only if and as far as a contrary intention is not expressed in the settlement, and have effect subject to the terms of the settlement, and to any provisions therein contained, but a contrary intention shall not be deemed to be expressed merely by words negativing impeachment for waste. **[146]**

81. As to capital arising otherwise than under the Act

Any money which after the commencement of this Act arises from settled land otherwise than under this Act, as well as any money or securities in the names or under the control of the tenant for life or the trustees of the settlement, being or representing money which had arisen before the commencement of this Act from the settled land otherwise than under the Settled Land Acts 1882 to 1890, and which ought, as between the persons interested in the settled land, to be or to have been treated as capital, shall (without prejudice to any other statutory provisions affecting the same) be deemed to be or to represent capital money arising under this Act, and shall be paid or transferred to or retained by the trustees of the settlement, or paid or transferred into court, and invested or applied, accordingly. **[147]**

82. Land acquired may be made a substituted security for released charges

(1) Land acquired by purchase or in exchange or otherwise under the powers of this Act, may be made a substituted security for any charge from which the settled land or any part thereof has theretofore been released on the occasion and in order to the completion of a sale, exchange or other disposition:

Provided that, where a charge does not affect the whole of the settled land, the land acquired shall not be subjected thereto, unless the land is acquired either by purchase with money arising from sale of land which was before the sale subject to the charge, or by an exchange of land which was before the exchange subject to the charge.

(2) On land being so acquired, any person who, by the direction of the tenant for life, so conveys the land as to subject it to any legal estate or charge by way of legal mortgage, is not concerned to inquire whether or not it is proper that the land should be subjected to such legal estate or charge. **[148]**

PART IV

IMPROVEMENTS

Improvements with Capital Money

83. Description of improvements authorised by Act

Improvements authorised by this Act are the making or execution on, or in connexion with, and for the benefit of settled land, of any of the works mentioned in the Third Schedule to this Act, or of any works for any of the purposes mentioned in that Schedule, and any operation incident to or necessary or proper in the execution of any of those works, or necessary or proper for carrying into effect any of those purposes, or for securing the full benefit of any of those works or purposes. **[149]**

84. Mode of application of capital money

(1) Capital money arising under this Act may be applied in or towards payment for any improvement authorised by this Act or by the settlement, without any scheme for the execution of the improvement being first submitted for approval to, or approved by, the trustees of the settlement or the court.

(2) Where the capital money to be expended is in the hands of the trustees of the settlement, they may apply that money in or towards payment for the whole or any part of any work or operation comprised in the improvement, on—

    (i) a certificate to be furnished by a competent engineer or able practical surveyor employed independently of the tenant for life, certifying that the work or operation comprised in the improvement or some specific part thereof, has been properly executed, and what amount is properly payable in respect thereof, which certificate shall be conclusive in favour of the trustees as an authority and discharge for any payment made by them in pursuance thereof; or

    (ii) an order of the court directing or authorising the trustees so to apply a specified portion of the capital money:

Provided that—

    (a) In the case of improvements not authorised by Part I of the Third Schedule to this Act or by the settlement, the trustees may, if they think fit, and shall if so directed by the court, before they make any such application of capital money require that that money, or any part thereof, shall be repaid to them out of the income of the settled land by not more than fifty half-yearly instalments, the first of such instalments to be paid or to be deemed to have become payable at the expiration of six months from the date when the work or operation, in payment for which the money is to be applied, was completed;

(b) No capital money shall be applied by the trustees in payment for improvements not authorised by Parts I and II of the Third Schedule to this Act, or by the settlement, except subject to provision for the repayment thereof being made in manner mentioned in the preceding paragraph of this proviso.

(3) Where the capital money to be expended is in court, the court may, if it thinks fit, on a report or certificate of the Minister, or of a competent engineer or able practical surveyor approved by the court, or on such other evidence as the court may think sufficient, make such order and give such directions as it thinks fit for the application of the money, or any part thereof, in or towards payment for the whole or any part of any work or operation comprised in the improvement.

(4) Where the court authorises capital money to be applied in payment for any improvement or intended improvement not authorised by Part I of the Third Schedule to this Act or by the settlement, the court, as a condition of making the order, may in any case require that the capital money or any part thereof, and shall as respects an improvement mentioned in Part III of that Schedule (unless the improvement is authorised by the settlement), require that the whole of the capital money shall be repaid to the trustees of the settlement out of the income of the settled land by a fixed number of periodical instalments to be paid at the times appointed by the court, and may require that any incumbrancer of the estate or interest of the tenant for life shall be served with notice of the proceedings.

(5) All money received by the trustees of the settlement in respect of any instalments under this section shall be held by them as capital money arising from freehold land under the settlement, unless the court otherwise directs.

[150]

85. Creation of rentcharges to discharge instalments

(1) When the tenant for life is required by the trustees to repay by instalments the capital money expended, or any part thereof, the tenant for life is by this section authorised to create out of the settled land, or any part thereof, a yearly rentcharge in favour of the trustees of the settlement sufficient in amount to discharge the said half-yearly instalments.

(2) Where an order is made requiring repayment by instalments, the settled land shall stand charged with the payment to the trustees of the settlement of a yearly rentcharge sufficient in amount to discharge the periodical instalments, and the rentcharge shall accrue from day to day, and be payable at the times appointed for payment of the periodical instalments, and shall have effect as if limited by the settlement prior to the estate of the tenant for life, and the trustees of the settlement shall have all statutory and other powers for recovery thereof.

(3) A rentcharge created by or under this section shall not be redeemed out of capital money, but may be overreached in like manner as if the same were limited by the settlement, and shall cease if and when the land affected by the improvement ceases to be settled or is sold or exchanged, but if part of the land so affected remains subject to the settlement the rentcharge shall remain in force in regard to the settled land.   **[151]**

Sundry Provisions as to Improvements

86. Concurrence in improvements

The tenant for life may join or concur with any other person interested in executing any improvement authorised by this Act, or in contributing to the cost thereof. **[152]**

87. Court may order payment for improvements executed

The court may, in any case where it appears proper, make an order directing or authorising capital money to be applied in or towards payment for any improvement authorised by the Settled Land Acts 1882 to 1890, or this Act, notwithstanding that a scheme was not, before the execution of the improvement, submitted for approval, as required by the Settled Land Act 1882, to the trustees of the settlement or to the court, and notwithstanding that no capital money is immediately available for the purpose. **[153]**

88. Obligation on tenant for life and successors to maintain, insure, etc

(1) The tenant for life, and each of his successors in title having under the trust instrument a limited estate or interest only in the settled land, shall, during such period, if any, as the Minister by certificate in any case prescribes, maintain and repair, at his own expense, every improvement executed under the foregoing provisions of this Act or the enactments replaced thereby, and where a building or work in its nature insurable against damage by fire is comprised in the improvement, shall at his own expense insure and keep insured the improvement in such amount, if any, as the Minister by certificate in any case prescribes.

(2) The tenant for life, or any of his successors as aforesaid, shall not cut down or knowingly permit to be cut down, except in proper thinning, any trees planted as an improvement under the foregoing provisions of this Act, or under the enactments replaced by those provisions.

(3) The tenant for life, and each of his successors as aforesaid, shall from time to time, if required by the Minister on or without the application of any person having under the trust instrument any estate or interest in the settled land in possession, remainder, or otherwise, report to the Minister the state of every improvement executed under this Act, and the fact and particulars of fire insurance, if any.

(4) The Minister may vary any certificate made by him under this section in such manner or to such extent as circumstances appear to him to require, but not so as to increase the liabilities of the tenant for life, or any of his successors as aforesaid.

(5) If the tenant for life, or any of his successors as aforesaid, fails in any respect to comply with the requisitions of this section, or does any act in contravention thereof, any person having, under the trust instrument, any estate or interest in the settled land in possession, remainder, or reversion, shall have a right of action, in respect of that default or act, against the tenant for life; and the estate of the tenant for life, after his death, shall be liable to make good to the persons entitled under the trust instrument any damages occasioned by that default or act.

(6) Where in connection with any improvement an improvement rentcharge,

as hereinbefore defined, has been created, and that rentcharge has been redeemed out of capital money, this section shall apply to the improvement as if it had been an improvement executed under this Act.   **[154]**

89. Protection as regards waste in execution and repair of improvements

The tenant for life, and each of his successors in title having, under the trust instrument, a limited estate or interest only in the settled land and all persons employed by or under contract with the tenant for life or any such successor, may from time to time enter on the settled land, and, without impeachment of waste by any remainderman or reversioner, thereon execute any improvement authorised by this Act, or inspect, maintain, and repair the same, and for the purposes thereof do, make, and use on the settled land, all acts, works, and conveniences proper fo the execution, maintenance, repair, and use thereof, and get and work freestone, limestone, clay, sand, and other substances, and make tramways and otherways, burn and make bricks, tiles, and other things, and cut down and use timber and other trees not planted or left standing for shelter or ornament.   **[155]**

PART V

MISCELLANEOUS PROVISIONS

90. Power for tenant for life to enter into contracts

(1) A tenant for life—

    (i) may contract to make any sale, exchange, mortgage, charge or other disposition authorised by this Act; and (ii) may vary or rescind, with or without comsideration, the contract in the like cases and manner in which, if he were absolute owner of the settled land, he might lawfully vary or rescind the same, but so that the contract as varied be in conformity with this Act; and

    (iii) may contract to make any lease, and in making the lease may vary the terms, with or without consideration, but so that the lease be in conformity with this Act; and

    (iv) may accept a surrender of a contract for a lease or a grant in fee simple at a rent, in like manner and on the like terms in and on which he might accept a surrender of a lease or a regrant, and thereupon may make a new or other contract for or relative to a lease or leases, or a grant or grants in fee simple at a rent, in like manner and on the like terms in and on which he might make a new or other lease or grant, or new or other leases or grants, where a lease or a grant in fee simple at a rent had been executed; and

    (v) may enter into a contract for or relating to the execution of any improvement authorised by this Act, and may vary or rescind any such contract; and

    (vi) may, in any other case, enter into a contract to do any act for carrying into effect any of the purposes of this Act, and may vary or rescind any such contract.

(2) Every contract, including a contract arising by reason of the exercise of an option, shall be binding on and shall enure for the benefit of the settled land, and shall be enforceable against and by every successor in title for the time being of the tenant for life, or statutory owner, and may be carried into effect by

any such successor, but so that it may be varied or rescinded by any such successor, in the like case and manner, if any, as if it had been made by himself.

(3) The court may, on the application of the tenant for life, or statutory owner, or of any such successor as aforesaid, or of any person interested in any contract, give directions respecting the enforcing, carrying into effect, varying, or rescinding thereof.

(4) A preliminary contract under this Act for or relating to a lease, and a contract conferring an option, shall not form part of the title or evidence of the title of any person to the lease, or to the benefit thereof, or to the land the subject of the option.

(5) All money, not being rent, received on the exercise by the tenant for life or statutory owner of the powers conferred by subsection (1) of this section, shall, unless the court on an application made within six months after the receipt of the money, or within such further time as the court may in special circumstances allow, otherwise directs, be capital money arising under this Act. **[156]**

91. Provisions as to different estates settled upon the same limitations

(1) Where estates are settled by different settlements upon the same limitations, whether by reference or otherwise, the following provisions shall have effect:—

> (i) The estates or any two or more of them, as the case may require, may be treated as one aggregate estate, in which case the aggregate estate shall be the settled land for all the purposes of this Act;
>
> (ii) Where the trustees for the purposes of this Act of the two or several settlements are the same persons they shall be the trustees of the settlement of the aggregate estate for all the purposes of this Act, and all or any part of the capital money arising from one of the estates may be applied by the direction of the tenant for life or statutory owner as if the same had arisen from any other of the estates;
>
> (iii) Where the trustees for the purposes of this Act of the settlements or of any two or more of them are not the same persons—
>
>> (*a*) any notice required to be given by this Act to the trustees of the settlement and to the solicitor of such trustees shall be given to the trustees of every settlement which comprises any part of the land to which such notice relates and to the solicitor of such trustees;
>>
>> (*b*) any capital money arising on any sale, exchange, lease, mortgage, charge, or other disposition of land comprised in more than one settlement, shall be apportioned between the trustees of the different settlements in such manner as the tenant for life or statutory owner may think fit;
>>
>> (*c*) all or any part of the capital money arising from the land comprised in one of the settlements may be paid by the trustees of that settlement, by such direction as aforesaid, to the trustees of any of the other settlements, to be applied by such last-mentioned trustees as if the same had arisen from land comprised in that other settlement:
>
> (iv) For the purposes of this subsection, money liable to be laid out in the purchase of land to be settled upon the same limitations as other land may be applied and dealt with in like manner in all

respects as if land had been purchased and settled, and the money were capital money arising therefrom.

(2) Estates shall be deemed to be settled upon the same limitations, notwithstanding that any of them may be subject to incumbrances, charges, or powers of charging to which the other or others of them may not be subject:

Provided that, in any such case as last aforesaid, the powers of this section relating to the payment or application of capital money shall not, unless the settlement under which the capital money is held otherwise provides, be exercisable without an order of the court.

(3) This section has effect without prejudice to any appointment made by the court before the commencement of this Act of trustees of the settlement of an aggregate estate, and to the power of the court in any case after such commencement to make any such appointment, and where any such appointment has been made before such commencement, or is made thereafter, this section has effect as if the trustees so appointed and their successors in office were the trustees for the purposes of this Act of each of the settlements constituting the settlement of the aggregate estate, and there were no other trustees thereof for the purposes of this Act.

(4) In this section "estate" means the land, capital money, and securities representing capital money for the time being subject to a particular settlement.   **[157]**

92. Proceedings for protection or recovery of land settled or claimed as settled

The court may, if it thinks fit, approve of any action, defence, petition to Parliament, parliamentary opposition, or other proceeding taken or proposed to be taken for the protection of settled land, or of any action or proceeding taken or proposed to be taken for the recovery of land being or alleged to be subject to a settlement, and may direct that any costs, charges, or expenses incurred or to be incurred in relation thereto, or any part thereof, be paid out of property subject to the settlement.   **[158]**

93. Reference of questions to court

If a question arises or a doubt is entertained—

- (a) respecting the exercise or intended exercise of any of the powers conferred by this Act, or any enactment replaced by this Act, or the settlement, or any matter relating thereto; or
- (b) as to the person in whose favour a vesting deed or assent ought to be executed, or as to the contents thereof; or
- (c) otherwise in relation to property subject to a settlement;

the tenant for life or statutory owner, or the trustees of the settlement, or any other person interested under the settlement, may apply to the court for its decision or directions thereon, or for the sanction of the court to any conditional contract, and the court may make such order or give such directions respecting the matter as the court thinks fit.   **[159]**

PART VI
GENERAL PROVISIONS AS TO TRUSTEES

94. Number of trustees to act

(1) Notwithstanding anything in this Act, capital money arising under this Act shall not be paid to fewer than two persons as trustees of a settlement, unless the trustee is a trust corporation.

(2) Subject as aforesaid the provisions of this Act referring to the trustees of a settlement apply to the surviving or continuing trustees or trustee of the settlement for the time being.   **[160]**

95. Trustees' receipts

The receipt or direction in writing of or by the trustees of the settlement, or where a sole trustee is a trust corporation, of or by that trustee, or of or by the personal representatives of the last surviving or continuing trustee, for or relating to any money or securities, paid or transferred to or by the direction of the trustees, trustee, or representatives, as the case may be, effectually discharges the payer or transferor therefrom, and from being bound to see to the application or being answerable for any loss or misapplication thereof, and, in case of a mortgagee or other person advancing money, from being concerned to see that any money advanced by him is wanted for any purpose of this Act, or that no more than is wanted is raised.   **[161]**

96. Protection of each trustee individually

Each person who is for the time being a trustee of a settlement is answerable for what he actually receives only, notwithstanding his signing any receipt for conformity, and in respect of his own acts, receipts, and defaults only, and is not answerable in respect of those of any other trustee, or of any banker, broker, or other person, or for the insufficiency or deficiency of any securities, or for any loss not happening through his own wilful default.   **[162]**

97. Protection of trustees generally

The trustees of a settlement, or any of them—

    (a) are not liable for giving any consent, or for not making, bringing, taking, or doing any such application, action, proceeding, or thing, as they might make, bring, take, or do; and

    (b) in case of a purchase of land with capital money arising under this Act, or of an exchange, lease, or other disposition, are not liable for adopting any contract made by the tenant for life or statutory owner, or bound to inquire as to the propriety of the purchase, exchange, lease, or other disposition, or answerable as regards any price, consideration, or fine; and

    (c) are not liable to see to or answerable for the investigation of the title, or answerable for a conveyance of land, if the conveyance purports to convey the land in the proper mode; and

    (d) are not liable in respect of purchase-money paid by them by the direction of the tenant for life or statutory owner to any person joining in the conveyance as a conveying party, or as giving a receipt for the purchase-money, or in any other character, or in respect of any other money paid by them by the direction of the tenant for life or statutory owner on the purchase, exchange, lease, or other disposition.   **[163]**

98. Protection of trustees in particular cases

(1) Where the tenant for life or statutory owner directs capital money to be invested on any authorised security or investment, the trustees of the settlement shall not be liable for the acts of any agent employed by the tenant for life or statutory owner in connexion with the transaction, or for not employing a separate agent in or about the valuation of the subject of the security or the investigation of the title thereto, or for the form of the security or of any deed conveying the subject thereof to the trustees.

(2) The trustees of the settlement shall not be liable for paying or applying any capital money by the direction of the tenant for life or statutory owner for any authorised purpose.

(3) The trustees of the settlements shall not be liable in any way on account of any vesting instrument or other documents of title relating to the settled land, other than securities for capital money, being placed in the possession of the tenant for life or statutory owner:

Provided that where, if the settlement were not disclosed, it would appear that the tenant for life had a general power of appointment over, or was absolutely and beneficially entitled to the settled land, the trustees of the settlement shall, before they deliver the documents to him, require that notice of the last or only principal vesting instrument be written on one of the documents under which the tenant for life acquired his title, and may, if the documents are not in their possession, require such notice to be written as aforesaid, but, in the latter case, they shall not be liable in any way for not requiring the notice to be written.

(4) This section applies to dealings and matters effected before as well as after the commencement of this Act. **[164]**

99. Indemnities to personal representatives and others

Personal representatives, trustees, or other persons who have in good faith, pursuant to this Act, executed a vesting deed, assent, or other conveyance of the settled land, or a deed of discharge of trustees, shall be absolutely discharged from all liability in respect of the equitable interests and powers taking effect under the settlement, and shall be entitled to be kept indemnified at the cost of the trust estate from all liabilities affecting the settled land, but the person to whom the settled land is conveyed (not being a purchaser taking free therefrom) shall hold the settled land upon the trusts, if any, affecting the same. **[165]**

100. Trustees' reimbursements

The trustees of a settlement may reimburse themselves or pay and discharge out of the trust property all expenses properly incurred by them. **[166]**

101. Notice to trustees

(1) Save as otherwise expressly provided by this Act, a tenant for life or statutory owner, when intending to make a sale, exchange, lease, mortgage, or charge or to grant an option—

    (*a*) shall give notice of his intention in that behalf to each of the trustees of the settlement, by posting registered letters, containing the notice, addressed to the trustees severally, each at his usual or last known place of abode in the United Kingdom; and

(b) shall give a like notice to the solicitor for the trustees, if any such solicitor is known to the tenant for life or statutory owner, by posting a registered letter, containing the notice, addressed to the solicitor at his place of business in the United Kingdom;

every letter under this section being posted not less than one month before the making or granting by the tenant for life or statutory owner of the sale, exchange, lease, mortgage, charge, or option, or of a contract for the same:

Provided that a notice under this section shall not be valid unless at the date thereof the trustee is a trust corporation, or the number of trustees is not less than two.

(2) The notice required by this section of intention to make a sale, exchange, or lease, or to grant an option, may be notice of a general intention in that behalf.

(3) The tenant for life or statutory owner is, upon request by a trustee of the settlement, to furnish to him such particulars and information as may reasonably be required by him from time to time with reference to sales, exchanges, or leases effected, or in progress, or immediately intended.

(4) Any trustee, by writing under his hand, may waive notice either in any particular case, or generally, and may accept less than one month's notice.

(5) A person dealing in good faith with the tenant for life is not concerned to inquire respecting the giving of any such notice as is required by this section. **[167]**

102. Management of land during minority or pending contingency

(1) If and as long as any person who is entitled to a beneficial interest in possession affecting land is an infant, the trustees appointed for this purpose by the settlement, or if there are none so appointed, then the trustees of the settlement, unless the settlement or the order of the court whereby they or their predecessors in office were appointed to be such trustees expressly provides to the contrary, or if there are none, then any persons appointed as trustees for this purpose by the court on the application of a guardian or next friend of the infant, may enter into and continue in possession of the land on behalf of the infant, and in every such case the subsequent provisions of this section shall apply.

(2) The trustees shall manage or superintend the management of the land, with full power—

(a) to fell timber or cut underwood from time to time in the usual course for sale, or for repairs or otherwise; and

(b) to erect, pull down, rebuild, and repair houses, and other buildings and erections; and

(c) to continue the working of mines, minerals, and quarries which have usually been worked; and

(d) to drain or otherwise improve the land or any part thereof; and

(e) to insure against loss by fire; and

(f) to make allowances to and arrangements with tenants and others; and

(g) to determine tenancies, and to accept surrenders of leases and tenancies; and

(h) generally to deal with the land in a proper and due course of management;

but so that, where the infant is impeachable for waste, the trustees shall not commit waste, and shall cut timber on the same terms only, and subject to the same restrictions, on and subject to which the infant could, if of full age, cut the same.

(3) The trustees may from time to time, out of the income of the land, including the produce of the sale of timber and underwood, pay the expenses incurred in the management, or in the exercise of any power conferred by this section, or otherwise in relation to the land, and all outgoings not payable by any tenant or other person, and shall keep down any annual sum, and the interest of any principal sum, charged on the land.

(4) This section has effect subject to an express appointment by the settlement, or the court, of trustees for the purposes of this section or of any enactment replaced by this section.

(5) Where any person is contingently entitled to land, this section shall, subject to any prior interests or charges affecting that land, apply until his interest vests, or, if his interest vests during his minority, until he attains [the age of eighteen years].

This sub-section applies only where a person becomes contingently entitled under an instrument coming into operation after the commencement of this Act.

(6) This section applies only if and as far as a contrary intention is not expressed in the instrument, if any, under which the interest of the infant or person contingently entitled as aforesaid arises, and has effect subject to the terms of that instrument and to the provisions therein contained.   **[168]**

NOTES
    Sub-s (5): words in square brackets substituted by the Family Law Reform Act 1969, s 1(3), Sch 1.

PART VII

RESTRICTIONS, SAVINGS AND PROTECTION OF PURCHASERS

103. Legal estate in settled land not to vest in trustee in bankruptcy of estate owner

[For the purposes of determining, where the estate owner of any settled land is bankrupt, whether the legal estate in the settled land is comprised in, or is capable of being claimed for, the bankrupt's estate, the legal estate in the settled land shall be deemed not to vest in the] estate owner unless and until the estate owner becomes absolutely and beneficially entitled to the settled land free from all limitations, powers, and charges taking effect under the settlement.   **[169]**

NOTES
    Words in square brackets substituted by the Insolvency Act 1985, s 235, Sch 8, para 3.

104. Powers not assignable, and contract not to exercise powers void

(1) The powers under this Act of a tenant for life are not capable of assignment or release, and do not pass to a person as being, by operation of law or otherwise, an assignee of a tenant for life, and remain exercisable by the tenant for life after and notwithstanding any assignment, by operation of law or otherwise, of his estate or interest under the settlement.

This subsection applies notwithstanding that the estate or interest of the tenant for life under the settlement was not in possession when the assignment was made or took effect by operation of law.

(2) A contract by a tenant for life not to exercise his powers under this Act or any of them shall be void.

(3) Where an assignment for value of the estate or interest of the tenant for life was made before the commencement of this Act, this section shall operate without prejudice to the rights of the assignee, and in that case the asignee's rights shall not be affected without his consent, except that—

(a) unless the assignee is actually in possession of the settled land or the part thereof affected, his consent shall not be requisite for the making of leases thereof by the tenant for life or statutory owner, provided the leases are made at the best rent that can reasonably be obtained, without fine, and in other respects are in conformity with this Act; and

(b) the consent of the assignee shall not be required to an investment of capital money for the time being affected by the assignment in securities authorised by statute for the investment of trust money.

(4) Where such an assignment for value is made or comes into operation after the commencement of this Act, the consent of the assignee shall not be requisite for the exercise by the tenant for life of any of the powers conferred by this Act:

Provided that—

(a) the assignee shall be entitled to the same or the like estate or interest in or charge on the land, money, or securities for the time being representing the land, money, or securities comprised in the assignment, as he had by virtue of the assignment in the last-mentioned land, money, or securities; and

(b) if the assignment so provides, or if it takes effect by operation of the law of bankruptcy, and after notice thereof to the trustees of the settlement, no investment or application of capital money for the time being affected by the assignment shall be made without the consent of the assignee, except an investment in securities authorised by statute for the investment of trust money; and

(c) notice of the intended transaction shall, unless the assignment otherwise provides, be given to the assignee, but a purchaser shall not be concerned to see or inquire whether such notice has been given.

(5) Where such an assignment for value was made before the commencement of this Act, then on the exercise by the tenant for life after such commencement of any of the powers conferred by this Act—

(a) a purchaser shall not be concerned to see or inquire whether the consent of the assignee has been obtained; and

(b) the provisions of paragraph (a) of the last subsection shall apply for the benefit of the assignee.

(6) A trustee or personal representative who is an assignee for value shall have power to consent to the exercise by the tenant for life of his powers under this Act, or to any such investment or application of capital money as aforesaid, and to bind by such consent all persons interested in the trust estate, or the estate of the testator or intestate.

(7) If by the original assignment, or by any subsequent disposition, the estate or interest assigned or created by the original assignment, or any part

thereof, or any derivative interest is settled on persons in succession, whether subject to any prior charge or not, and there is no trustee or personal representative in whom the entirety of the estate or interest so settled is vested, then the person for the time being entitled in possession under the limitations of that settlement, whether as trustee or beneficiary, or who would, if of full age, be so entitled, and notwithstanding any charge or incumbrance subsisting or to arise under such settlement, shall have power to consent to the exercise by the tenant for life of his powers under this Act, or to any such investment or application of capital money as aforesaid, and to bind by such consent all persons interested or to become interested under such settlement.

(8) Where an assignee for value, or any person who has power to consent as aforesaid under this section, is an infant, the consent may be given on his behalf by his parents or parent or testamentary or other guardian in the order named.

(9) The court shall have power to authorise any person interested under any assignment to consent to the exercise by the tenant for life of his powers under this Act, or to any such investment or application of capital money as aforesaid on behalf of himself and all other persons interested, or who may become interested under such assignment.

(10) An assignment by operation of the law of bankruptcy, where the assignment comes into operation after the commencement of this Act, shall be deemed to be an assignment for value for the purposes of this section.

(11) An instrument whereby a tenant for life, in consideration of marriage or as part or by way of any family arrangement, not being a security for payment of money advanced, makes an assignment of or creates a charge upon his estate or interest under the settlement is to be deemed one of the instruments creating the settlement, and not an assignment for value for the purposes of this section:

Provided that this subsection shall not have effect with respect to any disposition made before the eighteenth day of August, eighteen hundred and ninety, if inconsistent with the nature or terms of the disposition.

(12) This section extends to assignments made or coming into operation before or after the commencement of this Act, and in this section "assignment" includes assignment by way of mortgage, and any partial or qualified assignment, and any charge or incumbrance, "assignee" has a corresponding meaning, and "assignee for value" includes persons deriving title under the original assignee.

[170]

105. Effect of surrender of life estate to the next remainderman

(1) Where the estate or interest of a tenant for life under the settlement has been or is absolutely assured with intent to extinguish the same, either before or after the commencement of this Act, to the person next entitled in remainder or reversion under the settlement, then, . . . the statutory powers of the tenant for life under this Act shall, in reference to the property affected by the assurance, and notwithstanding the provisions of the last preceding section, cease to be exercisable by him, and the statutory powers shall thenceforth become exercisable as if he were dead, but without prejudice to any incumbrance affecting the estate or interest assured, and to the rights to which any incumbrancer would have been entitled if those powers had remained exercisable by the tenant for life.

This subsection applies whether or not any term of years or charge intervenes, or the estate of the remainderman or reversioner is liable to be defeated, and whether or not the estate or interest of the tenant for life under the settlement was in possession at the date of the assurance.

This subsection does not prejudice anything done by the tenant for life before the commencement of this Act, in exercise of any power operating under the Settled Land Acts 1882 to 1890, or, unless the assurance provides to the contrary, operate to accelerate any such intervening terms of years or charge as aforesaid.

(2) In this section "assurance" means any surrender, conveyance, assignment or appointment under a power (whether vested in any person solely, or jointly in two or more persons) which operates in equity to extinguish the estate or interest of the tenant for life, and "assured" has a corresponding meaning.

[171]

NOTES
Sub-s (1): words omitted repealed by the Law of Property (Amendment) Act 1926, s 7, Schedule.

106. Prohibition or limitation against exercise of powers void, and provision against forfeiture

(1) If in a settlement, will, assurance, or other instrument executed or made before or after, or partly before and partly after, the commencement of this Act a provision is inserted—

    (a) purporting or attempting, by way of direction, declaration, or otherwise, to forbid a tenant for life or statutory owner to exercise any power under this Act, or his right to require the settled land to be vested in him; or

    (b) attempting, or tending, or intended, by a limitation, gift, or disposition over of settled land, or by a limitation, gift, or disposition of other real or any personal property, or by the imposition of any condition, or by forfeiture, or in any other manner whatever, to prohibit or prevent him from exercising, or to induce him to abstain from exercising, or to put him into a position inconsistent with his exercising any power under this Act, or his right to require the settled land to be vested in him;

that provision, as far as it purports, or attempts, or tends, or is intended to have, or would or might have, the operation aforesaid, shall be deemed to be void.

(2) For the purposes of this section an estate or interest limited to continue so long only as a person abstains from exercising any such power or right as aforesaid shall be and take effect as an estate or interest to continue for the period for which it would continue if that person were to abstain from exercising the power or right, discharged from liability to determination or cesser by or on his exercising the same.

(3) Notwithstanding anything in a settlement, the exercise by the tenant for life or statutory owner of any power under this Act shall not occasion a forfeiture. **[172]**

107. Tenant for life trustee for all parties interested

(1) A tenant for life or statutory owner shall, in exercising any power under this Act, have regard to the interests of all parties entitled under the settlement, and shall, in relation to the exercise thereof by him, be deemed to be in the position and to have the duties and liabilities of a trustee for those parties.

(2) The provision by a tenant for life or statutory owner, at his own expense, of dwellings available for the working classes on any settled land shall not be deemed to be an injury to any interest in reversion or remainder in that land, but such provision shall not be made by a tenant for life or statutory owner without the previous approval in writing of the trustees of the settlement. **[173]**

108. Saving for and exercise of other powers

(1) Nothing in this Act shall take away, abridge, or prejudicially affect any power for the time being subsisting under a settlement, or by statute or otherwise, exercisable by a tenant for life, or (save as hereinafter provided) by trustees with his consent, or on his request, or by his direction, or otherwise, and the powers given by this Act are cumulative.

(2) In case of conflict between the provisions of a settlement and the provisions of this Act, relative to any matter in respect whereof the tenant for life or statutory owner exercises or contracts or intends to exercise any power under this Act, the provisions of this Act shall prevail; and, notwithstanding anything in the settlement, any power (not being merely a power of revocation or appointment) relating to the settled land thereby conferred on the trustees of the settlement or other persons exercisable for any purpose, whether or not provided for in this Act, shall, after the commencement of this Act, be exercisable by the tenant for life or statutory owner as if it were an additional power conferred on the tenant for life within the next following section of this Act and not otherwise.

(3) If a question arises or a doubt is entertained respecting any matter within this section, the tenant for life or statutory owner, or the trustees of the settlement, or any other person interested, under the settlement may apply to the court for its decision thereon, and the court may make such order respecting the matter as the court thinks fit. **[174]**

109. Saving for additional or larger powers under settlement

(1) Nothing in this Act precludes a settlor from conferring on the tenant for life, or (save as provided by the last preceding section) on the trustees of the settlement, any powers additional to or larger than those conferred by this Act.

(2) Any additional or larger powers so conferred shall, as far as may be, notwithstanding anything in this Act, operate and be exercisable in the like manner, and with all the like incidents, effects, and consequences, as if they were conferred by this Act, and, if relating to the settled land, as if they were conferred by this Act on a tenant for life. **[175]**

110. Protection of purchasers, etc

(1) On a sale, exchange, lease, mortgage, charge, or other disposition, a purchaser dealing in good faith with a tenant for life or statutory owner shall, as against all parties entitled under the settlement, be conclusively taken to have given the best price, consideration, or rent, as the case may require, that could reasonably be obtained by the tenant for life or statutory owner, and to have complied with all the requisitions of this Act.

(2) A purchaser of a legal estate in settled land shall not, except as hereby expressly provided, be bound or entitled to call for the production of the trust instrument or any information concerning that instrument or any ad valorem stamp duty thereon, and whether or not he has notice of its contents he shall, save as hereinafter provided, be bound and entitled if the last or only principal

vesting instrument contains the statements and particulars required by this Act to assume that—

(a) the person in whom the land is by the said instrument vested or declared to be vested is the tenant for life or statutory owner and has all the powers of a tenant for life under this Act, including such additional or larger powers, if any, as are therein mentioned;

(b) the persons by the said instrument stated to be the trustees of the settlement, or their successors appearing to be duly appointed, are the properly constituted trustees of the settlement;

(c) the statements and particulars required by this Act and contained (expressly or by reference) in the said instrument were correct at the date thereof;

(d) the statements contained in any deed executed in accordance with this Act declaring who are the trustees of the settlement for the purposes of this Act are correct;

(e) the statements contained in any deed of discharge, executed in accordance with this Act, are correct:

Provided that, as regards the first vesting instrument executed for the purpose of giving effect to—

(a) a settlement subsisting at the commencement of this Act; or

(b) an instrument which by virtue of this Act is deemed to be a settlement; or

(c) a settlement which by virtue of this Act is deemed to have been made by any person after the commencement of this Act; or

(d) an instrument inter vivos intended to create a settlement of a legal estate in land which is executed after the commencement of this Act and does not comply with the requirements of this Act with respect to the method of effecting such a settlement; a purchaser shall be concerned to see—

(i) that the land disposed of to him is comprised in such settlement or instrument;

(ii) that the person in whom the settled land is by such vesting instrument vested, or declared to be vested, is the person in whom it ought to be vested as tenant for life or statutory owner;

(iii) that the persons thereby stated to be the trustees of the settlement are the properly constituted trustees of the settlement.

(3) A purchaser of a legal estate in settled land from a personal representative shall be entitled to act on the following assumptions:—

(i) If the capital money, if any, payable in respect of the transaction is paid to the personal representative, that such representative is acting under his statutory or other powers and requires the money for purposes of administration;

(ii) If such capital money is, by the direction of the personal representative, paid to persons who are stated to be the trustees of a settlement, that such persons are the duly constituted trustees of the settlement for the purposes of this Act, and that the personal representative is acting under his statutory powers during a minority;

(iii) In any other case, that the personal representative is acting under his statutory or other powers.

(4) Where no capital money arises under a transaction, a disposition by a tenant for life or statutory owner shall, in favour of a purchaser of a legal estate,

have effect under this Act notwithstanding that at the date of the transaction there are no trustees of the settlement.

(5) If a conveyance of or an assent relating to land formerly subject to a vesting instrument does not state who are the trustees of the settlement for the purposes of this Act, a purchaser of a legal estate shall be bound and entitled to act on the assumption that the person in whom the land was thereby vested was entitled to the land free from all limitations, powers, and charges taking effect under that settlement, absolutely and beneficially, or, if so expressed in the conveyance or assent, as personal representative, or trustee for sale or otherwise, and that every statement of fact in such conveyance or assent is correct.   **[176]**

111. Purchaser of beneficial interest of tenant for life to have remedies of a legal owner

Where—

    (*a*) at the commencement of this Act the legal beneficial interest of a tenant for life under a settlement is vested in a purchaser; or

    (*b*) after the commencement of this Act a tenant for life conveys or deals with his beneficial interest in possession in favour of a purchaser, and the interest so conveyed or created would, but for the restrictions imposed by statute on the creation of legal estates, have been a legal interest;

the purchaser shall (without prejudice to the powers conferred by this Act on the tenant for life) have and may exercise all the same rights and remedies as he would have had or have been entitled to exercise if the interest had remained or been a legal interest and the reversion, if any, on any leases or tenancies derived out of the settled land had been vested in him:

Provided that, where the conveyance or dealing is effected after the commencement of this Act, the purchaser shall not be entitled to the possession of the documents of title relating to the settled land, but shall have the same rights with respect thereto as if the tenant for life had given to him a statutory acknowledgment of his right to production and delivery of copies thereof, and a statutory undertaking for the safe custody thereof.

The tenant for life shall not deliver any such documents to a purchaser of his beneficial interest, who is not also a purchaser of the whole of the settled land to which such documents relate.   **[177]**

112. Exercise of powers; limitation of provisions, etc

(1) Where a power of sale, exchange, leasing, mortgaging, charging, or other power is exercised by a tenant for life, or statutory owner or by the trustees of a settlement, he and they may respectively execute, make, and do all deeds, instruments, and things necessary or proper in that behalf.

(2) Where any provision in this Act refers to sale, purchase, exchange, mortgaging, charging, leasing, or other disposition or dealing, or to any power, consent, payment, receipt, deed, assurance, contract, expenses, act, or transaction, it shall (unless the contrary appears) be construed as extending only to sales, purchases, exchanges, mortgages, charges, leases, dispositions, dealings, powers, consents, payments, receipts, deeds, assurances, contracts, expenses, acts, and transactions under this Act.   **[178]**

PART VIII

COURT, MINISTRY OF AGRICULTURE AND FISHERIES, PROCEDURE

113. Jurisdiction and procedure

(1) All matters within the jurisdiction of the court under this Act shall, subject to the enactments for the time being in force with respect to the procedure of the Supreme Court of Judicature, be assigned to the Chancery Division of the High Court.

(2) ...

[(3) The powers of the court may, as regards land not exceeding in capital value the county court limit, or in net annual value for rating the county court limit, and, as regards capital money arising under this Act, and securities in which the same is invested, not exceeding in amount or value the county court limit, and as regards personal chattels settled or to be settled, as in this Act mentioned, not exceeding the county court limit, be exercised by any county court. Section 147(2) and (3) of the County Courts Act 1984 (construction of references to net annual value for rating) shall apply for the purposes of this subsection as it applies for the purposes of that Act.]

[(3A) In the preceding subsection "the county court limit" means the county court limit for the time being specified by an Order in Council under [section 145 of the County Courts Act 1984] as the county court limit for the purposes of that subsection.]

(4) Payment of money into court effectually exonerates therefrom the person making the payment.

(5) Every application to the court under this Act shall, subject to any rules of court to the contrary, be by summons at Chambers.

(6) On an application by the trustees of a settlement notice shall be served in the first instance on the tenant for life.

(7) On any application notice shall be served on such persons, if any, as the court thinks fit.

(8) The court shall have full power and discretion to make such order as it thinks fit respecting the costs, charges, or expenses of all or any of the parties to any application, and may, if it thinks fit, order that all or any of those costs, charges, or expenses be paid out of property subject to the settlement.

(9) The provisions of the Trustee Act 1925 relating to vesting orders and orders appointing a person to convey shall apply to all vesting orders authorised to be made by this Act.   **[179]**

NOTES
Sub-s (2): repealed by the Courts Act 1971, s 56(4), Sch 11, Part II.
Sub-s (3): substituted by the County Courts Act 1984, s 148(1), Sch 2, para 20.
Sub-s (3A): inserted by the Administration of Justice Act 1982, s 37, Sch 3, Part II, para 4; words in square brackets substituted by the County Courts Act 1984, s 148(1), Sch 2, para 20.

114. Payment of costs out of settled property

Where the court directs that any costs, charges, or expenses be paid out of property subject to a settlement, the same shall, subject and according to the directions of the court, be raised and paid—

    (*a*) out of capital money arising under this Act, or other money liable to be laid out in the purchase of land to be made subject to the settlement; or

    (*b*) out of securities representing such money, or out of income of any such money or securities; or

    (*c*) out of any accumulations of income of land, money, or securities; or

    (*d*) by means of a sale of part of the settled land in respect whereof the costs, charges or expenses are incurred, or of other settled land comprised in the same settlement and subject to the same limitations; or

    (*e*) by means of a legal mortgage of the settled land or any part thereof to be made by such person as the court directs;

or partly in one of those modes and partly in another or others, or in any such other mode as the court thinks fit.   **[180]**

115. Powers of the Minister of Agriculture

(1) The Minister shall, by virtue of this Act, have for the purposes of any Act, public general or local or private, making provision for the execution of improvements on settled land, all such powers and authorities as he has for the purposes of the Improvement of Land Act 1864.

(2) The provisions of the last-mentioned Act relating to proceedings and inquiries, and to authentication of instruments, and to declarations, statements, notices, applications, forms, security for expenses, inspections and examinations, shall extend and apply, as far as the nature and circumstances of the case admit, to acts and proceedings done or taken by or in relation to the Minister under any Act making provision as last aforesaid.

(3) The provisions of any Act relating ... to security for costs to be taken in respect of the business transacted under the Acts administered by the Minister as successor of the Land Commissioners for England shall extend and apply to the business transacted by or under the direction of the Minister under any Act, public general or local or private, by which any power or duty is conferred or imposed on him as such successor.   **[181]**

NOTES

    Sub-s (3): words omitted repealed by the Agriculture (Miscellaneous Provisions) Act 1963, s 28, Schedule, Part II.

116. Filing of certificates, etc at the Ministry of Agriculture

(1) Every certificate and report approved and made by the Minister under this Act shall be filed in the office of [the Minister of Agriculture, Fisheries and Food].

(2) An office copy of any certificate or report so filed shall be delivered out of such office to any person requiring the same, on payment of the proper fee, and shall be sufficient evidence of the certificate or report whereof it purports to be a copy.   **[182]**

NOTES

Sub-s (1): words in square brackets substituted by virtue of the Transfer of Functions (Ministry of Food) Order 1955, SI 1955 No 554.

PART IX
SUPPLEMENTARY PROVISIONS

117. Definitions

(1) In this Act, unless the context otherwise requires, the following expressions have the meanings hereby assigned to them respectively, that is to say:—

    (i) "Building purposes" include the erecting and the improving of, and the adding to, and the repairing of buildings; and a "building lease" is a lease for any building purposes or purposes connected therewith;

    (ii) "Capital money arising under this Act" means capital money arising under the powers and provisions of this Act or the Acts replaced by this Act, and receivable for the trusts and purposes of the settlement and includes securities representing capital money;

    (iii) "Death duty" means estate duty . . . and every other duty leviable or payable on death;

    (iv) "Determinable fee" means a fee determinable whether by limitation or condition;

    (v) "Disposition" and "conveyance" include a mortgage, charge by way of legal mortgage, lease, assent, vesting declaration, vesting instrument, disclaimer, release and every other assurance of property or of an interest therein by any instrument, except a will, and "dispose of" and "convey" have corresponding meanings;

    (vi) "Dower" includes "freebench";

    (vii) "Hereditaments" mean real property which on an intestacy might before the commencement of this Act have devolved on an heir;

    (viii) "Instrument" does not include a statute unless the statute creates a settlement;

    (ix) "Land" includes land of any tenure, and mines and minerals whether or not held apart from the surface, buildings or parts of buildings (whether the division is horizontal, vertical or made in any other way) and other corporeal hereditaments; also a manor, an advowson, and a rent and other incorporeal hereditaments, and an easement, right, privilege, or benefit in, over, or derived from land, and any estate or interest in land not being an undivided share in land;

    (x) "Lease" includes an agreement for a lease, and "forestry lease" means a lease to the Forestry Commissioners for any purpose for which they are authorised to acquire land by the Forestry Act 1919;

    (xi) "Legal mortgage" means a mortgage by demise or sub-demise or a charge by way of legal mortgage, and "legal mortgagee" has a corresponding meaning; "legal estate" means an estate interest or charge in or over land (subsisting or created at law) which is by statute authorised to subsist or to be created at law; and "equitable interests" mean all other interests and charges in or over land or in the proceeds of sale thereof; an equitable interest "capable of subsisting at law" means such an equitable interest as could validly subsist at law, if clothed with the legal estate; and "estate owner" means the owner of a legal estate;

(xii) "Limitation" includes a trust, and "trust" includes an implied or constructive trust;

(xiii) ...

(xiv) "Manor" includes lordship, and reputed manor or lordship; and "manorial incident" has the same meaning as in the Law of Property Act 1922;

(xv) "Mines and minerals" mean mines and minerals whether already opened or in work or not, and include all minerals and substances in, on, or under the land, obtainable by underground or by surface working; and "mining purposes" include the sinking and searching for, winning, working, getting, making merchantable, smelting or otherwise converting or working for the purposes of any manufacture, carrying away, and disposing of mines and minerals, in or under the settled land, or any other land, and the erection of buildings, and the execution of engineering and other works suitable for those purposes; and a "mining lease" is a lease for any mining purposes or purposes connected therewith, and includes a grant or licence for any mining purposes;

(xvi) "Minister" means [the Minister of Agriculture, Fisheries and Food];

(xvii) "Notice" includes constructive notice;

(xviii) "Personal representative" means the executor, original or by representation, or administrator, for the time being of a deceased person, and where there are special personal representatives for the purposes of settled land means those personal representatives;

(xix) "Possession" includes receipt of rents and profits, or the right to receive the same, if any; and "income" includes rents and profits;

(xx) "Property" includes any thing in action, and any interest in real or personal property;

(xxi) "Purchaser" means a purchaser in good faith for value, and includes a lessee, mortgagee or other person who in good faith acquires an interest in settled land for value; and in reference to a legal estate includes a chargee by way of legal mortgage;

(xxii) "Rent" includes yearly or other rent, and toll, duty, royalty, or other reservation, by the acre, or the ton, or otherwise; and in relation to rent, "payment" includes delivery; and "fine" includes premium or fore-gift, and any payment, consideration, or benefit in the nature of a fine, premium, or fore-gift;

(xxiii) "Securities" include stocks, funds, and shares;

(xxiv) "Settled land" includes land which is deemed to be settled land; "settlement" includes an instrument or instruments which under this Act or the Acts which it replaces is or are deemed to be or which together constitute a settlement, and a settlement which is deemed to have been made by any person or to be subsisting for the purposes of this Act; "a settlement subsisting at the commencement of this Act" includes a settlement created by virtue of this Act immediately on the commencement thereof; and "trustees of the settlement" mean the trustees thereof for the purposes of this Act howsoever appointed or constituted;

(xxv) "Small dwellings" mean dwelling-houses of a rateable value not exceeding one hundred pounds per annum;

(xxvi) "Statutory owner" means the trustees of the settlement or other persons who, during a minority, or at any other time when there is no tenant for life, have the powers of a tenant for life under this Act, but does not include the trustees of the settlement, where by virtue of an order of the court or otherwise the trustees have power to convey the settled land in the name of the tenant for life;

(xxvii) "Steward" includes deputy steward, or other proper officer, of a manor;

(xxviii) "Tenant for life" includes a person (not being a statutory owner) who has the powers of a tenant for life under this Act, and also (where the context requires) one of two or more persons who together constitute the tenant for life, or have the powers of a tenant for life; and "tenant in tail" includes a person entitled to an entailed interest in any property; and "entailed interest" has the same meaning as in the Law of Property Act 1925;

(xxix) A "term of years absolute" means a term of years, taking effect either in possession or in reversion, with or without impeachment for waste, whether at a rent or not and whether subject or not to another legal estate, and whether certain or liable to determination by notice, re-entry, operation of law, or by a provision for cesser on redemption, or in any other event (other than the dropping of a life, or the determination of a determinable life interest), but does not include any term of years determinable with life or lives or with the cesser of a determinable life interest, nor, if created after the commencement of this Act, a term of years which is not expressed to take effect in possession within twenty-one years after the creation thereof where required by statute to take effect within that period; and in this definition the expression "term of years" includes a term for less than a year, or for a year or years and a fraction of a year or from year to year;

(xxx) "Trust corporation" means the Public Trustee or a corporation either appointed by the court in any particular case to be a trustee or entitled by rules made under subsection (3) of section four of the Public Trustee Act 1906, to act as custodian trustee, and "trust for sale" "trustees for sale" and "power to postpone a sale" have the same meanings as in the Law of Property Act 1925;

(xxxi) In relation to settled land "vesting deed" or "vesting order" means the instrument whereby settled land is conveyed to or vested or declared to be vested in a tenant for life or statutory owner; "vesting assent" means the instrument whereby a personal representative, after the death of a tenant for life or statutory owner, or the survivor of two or more tenants for life or statutory owners, vests settled land in a person entitled as tenant for life or statutory owner; "vesting instrument" means a vesting deed, a vesting assent or, where the land affected remains settled land, a vesting order; "principal vesting instrument" includes any vesting instrument other than a subsidiary vesting deed; and "trust instrument" means the instrument whereby the trusts of the settled land are declared, and includes any two or more such instruments and a settlement or instrument which is deemed to be a trust instrument;

(xxxii) "United Kingdom" means Great Britain and Northern Ireland;

(xxxiii) "Will" includes codicil.

[(1A) Any reference in this Act to money, securities or proceeds of sale being paid or transferred into court shall be construed as referring to the money, securities or proceeds being paid or transferred into the Supreme Court or any other court that has jurisdiction, and any reference in this Act to the court, in a context referring to the investment or application of money, securities or proceeds of sale paid or transferred into court, shall be construed, in the case of money, securities or proceeds paid or transferred into the Supreme Court, as referring to the High Court, and, in the case of money, securities or proceeds paid or transferred into another court, as referring to that other court.]

(2) Where an equitable interest in or power over property arises by statute or operation of law, references to the "creation" of an interest or power include any interest or power so arising.

(3) References to registration under the Land Charges Act 1925, apply to any registration made under any statute which is by the Land Charges Act 1925, to have effect as if the registration had been made under that Act. **[183]**

NOTES
Sub-s (1): first words omitted repealed by the Finance Act 1949, s 52, Sch 11, Part IV; para (xiii) repealed by the Mental Health Act 1959, s 149(2), Sch 8, Part I; words in square brackets substituted by virtue of the Transfer of Functions (Ministry of Food) Order 1955, SI 1955 No 554.
Sub-s (1A): inserted by the Administration of Justice Act 1965, s 17(1), Sch 1.

118. Retrospective amendment of certain provisions of Settled Land Acts

For the purpose of removing certain doubts as to the construction and operation of the Settled Land Acts 1882 to 1890, and validating past transactions, the provisions contained in the Fourth Schedule to this Act shall have effect.

Subject as aforesaid, this Act does not affect the validity of anything done or any order made or directions given by the court before the commencement of this Act. **[184]**

119. Repeals, savings, and construction

(1) ... without prejudice to the provisions of section thirty-eight of the Interpretation Act 1889:—

(a) Nothing in this repeal shall affect the validity or legality of any dealing in land or other transaction completed before the commencement of this Act, or any title or right acquired or appointment made before the commencement of this Act, but, subject as aforesaid, this Act shall, except where otherwise expressly provided, apply to and in respect of settlements and other instruments whether made or coming into operation before or after the commencement of this Act;

(b) Nothing in this repeal shall affect any rules, orders, or other instruments made under any enactment so repealed, but all such rules, orders and instruments shall continue in force as if made under the corresponding enactment in this Act;

(c) References in any document to any enactment repealed by this Act shall be construed as references to this Act or the corresponding enactment in this Act.

(2) References in any statute to the Settled Estates Act 1877, and to any enactment which it replaced shall be construed as references to this Act.

(3) This Act, as respects registered land, takes effect subject to the provisions of the Land Registration Act 1925. **[185]**

NOTES

Sub-s (1): words omitted repealed by the Statute Law Revision Act 1950.

120. Short title, commencement and extent

(1) This Act may be cited as the Settled Land Act 1925.

(2) ...

(3) This Act extends to England and Wales only.   **[186]**

NOTES

Sub-s (2): repealed by the Statute Law Revision Act 1950.

SCHEDULES
SCHEDULE 1

Section 15

FORMS OF INSTRUMENTS

FORM NO. 1

VESTING DEED FOR GIVING EFFECT TO A SETTLEMENT SUBSISTING AT THE COMMENCEMENT
OF THIS ACT

This Vesting Deed is made [etc.] between *X.* of [etc.] and *Y.* of [etc.] (hereinafter called the trustees) of the one part and *T.L.* of [etc.] of the other part.

[*Recite the Settlement under which T.L. is a tenant for life of full age in possession of the freeholds and leaseholds respectively described in the First and Second Schedules and has power to appoint new trustees, and the trustees are trustees for the purposes of the Settled Land Act 1925, also the request by T.L. that the trustees should execute the requisite vesting deed.*]

Now for giving effect to the requirements of the Settled Land Act 1925, this deed witnesseth as follows:—

1. The trustees as Trustees hereby declare that—

All and singular the hereditaments and premises respectively mentioned in the First and Second Schedules hereto and all other (if any) the premises capable of being vested by this declaration which are now by any means subject to the limitations of the recited settlement are vested in the said as to the freehold hereditaments mentioned in the First Schedule hereto in fee simple, and as to the leasehold hereditaments mentioned in the Second Schedule hereto, for all the residue of the terms of years for which the same are respectively held.

2. The said *T.L.* shall stand possessed of the premises upon the trusts and subject to the powers and provisions upon and subject to which under the recited settlement or otherwise the same ought to be held from time to time.

3. The trustees are the trustees of the settlement for the purposes of the Settled Land Act 1925.

4. The following additional or larger powers are conferred by the said settlement in relation to the settled land, and by virtue of the Settled Land Act 1925, operate and are exercisable as if conferred by that Act on a tenant for life [*Here insert the additional powers*].

5. [*Add the usual covenant by T.L. with the trustees to pay the rent in respect of leasehold hereditaments, observe the lessee's covenants and keep the trustees indemnified.*]

6. The power to appoint a new trustee or new trustees of the settlement is vested in the said *T.L.* during his life.

In witness [etc.].

[NOTE.—Add the schedules. In the first part of the First Schedule give particulars of the manors, advowsons and other incorporeal hereditaments. In the second part give particulars of the freehold land referring, if practicable, to annexed plans, so that the vesting deed may ultimately become a convenient root of title. Unless this is done the deeds referred to will for purposes of the parcels remain part of the title. In the Second Schedule give particulars of the dates of and parties to the leases of the leasehold hereditaments, and short particulars of the properties demised, the terms and the rents. If there are any mortgages having priority to the settlement these should be mentioned in another schedule and referred to in the recitals.]

FORM NO. 2

VESTING DEED ON THE SETTLEMENT OF LAND

This Vesting Deed made [etc.] between *John H.* of [etc.] of the first part, *Jane W.* of [etc.] of the second part, and *X.* of [etc.], *Y.* of [etc.], and *Z.* of [etc.] (hereinafter called the trustees) of the third part.

Witnesseth and it is hereby declared as follows:—

1. In consideration of the intended marriage between *John H.* and *Jane W.* the said *John H.* as Settlor hereby declares that

All that (*setting out the parcels by reference to a schedule or otherwise*) are vested in *John H.* in fee simple (*or in the case of leaseholds refer to the terms*).

Upon the trusts declared concerning the same by a Trust Instrument bearing even date with but intended to be executed contemporaneously with these presents and made between the same parties and in the same order as these presents or upon such other trusts as the same ought to be held from time to time.

2. The trustees are the trustees of the settlement for the purposes of the Settled Land Act 1925.

3. The following additional or larger powers are conferred by the said trust instrument in relation to the settled land and by virtue of the Settled Land Act 1925, operate and are exercisable as if conferred by that Act on a tenant for life. [*Here insert the additional powers.*]

4. The power of appointing a new trustee or new trustees of the settlement is vested in the said [*John H.*] during his life.

In witness [etc.].

FORM NO. 3

TRUST INSTRUMENT ON THE SETTLEMENT OF LAND

This Trust Instrument is made [etc.] between *John H.* of [etc.] (hereinafter called the Settlor) of the first part, *Jane W.* of [etc.] of the second part, and *X.* of [etc.], *Y.* of [etc.], and *Z.* of [etc.] (hereinafter called the trustees) of the third part.

Whereas by a deed (hereinafter called the Vesting Deed) bearing even date with but executed contemporaneously with these presents, and made between the same parties and in the same order as these presents, certain hereditaments situated at in the county of were vested in the Settlor Upon the trusts declared concerning the same by a trust instrument of even date therein referred to (meaning these presents).

Now in consideration of the intended marriage between the Settlor and *Jane W.*, this Deed Witnesseth as follows:—

1. The Settlor hereby agrees that he will hold the hereditaments and property comprised in the Vesting Deed In trust for himself until the solemnisation of the said marriage and thereafter Upon the trusts following, that is to say:—

2. Upon trust for the Settlor during his life without impeachment of waste with remainder Upon trust if *Jane W.* survives him that she shall receive out of the premises

during the residue of her life a yearly jointure rentcharge of [etc.] and subject thereto Upon trust for the trustees for a term of 800 years from the date of the death of the Settlor without impeachment of waste Upon the trusts hereinafter declared concerning the same. And subject to the said term and the trusts thereof Upon trust for the first and other sons of the said intended marriage successively according to seniority in tail male with remainder [etc.] *with an ultimate remainder in trust for the Settlor in fee simple.*

[Here add the requisite trusts of the portions term, and any other proper provisions including the appointment of the trustees to be trustees of the settlement for the purposes of the Settled Land Act 1925, extension of Settled Land Act powers, and a power for the tenant for life for the time being of full age to appoint new trustees of the settlement.]

In witness [etc.]

[NOTE.—The Vesting Deed and the Trust Instrument can be executed as escrows till the marriage.]

FORM NO. 4

SUBSIDIARY VESTING DEED ON SALE WHEN THE LAND IS PURCHASED WITH CAPITAL MONEY

This Subsidiary Vesting Deed is made [etc.] between *Henry V.* of [etc.] (hereinafter called the Vendor) of the first part, *X.* of [etc.], *Y.* of [etc.], and *Z.* of [etc.] (hereinafter called the trustees) of the second part, and *John H.* [etc.] (hereinafter called the Purchaser) of the third part.

Whereas the Vendor is entitled for an estate in fee simple in possession free from incumbrances to the hereditaments hereinafter conveyed and has agreed to sell the same to the Purchaser at the price of pounds.

And whereas by a principal vesting deed (hereinafter called the principal deed) dated [etc.], and made [etc.] *[Form No. 2]*, certain hereditaments were vested in the Purchaser Upon the trusts of a trust instrument of even date therewith, and by [endorsements on] the principal deed the trustees were stated to be the trustees of the settlement for the purposes of the Settled Land Act 1925.

Now this Deed witnesseth as follows:—

1. In consideration of the sum of pounds now paid to the Vendor by the trustees by the direction of the Purchaser (the receipt of which sum the Vendor hereby acknowledges) the Vendor as Beneficial Owner hereby conveys unto the Purchaser All those [etc.].

To hold unto the Purchaser [in fee simple] upon and subject to the same trusts and powers as are declared by the principal deed by reference as aforesaid with respect to the hereditaments therein comprised.

2 and 3. *[Same as 2 and 4 in Form No. 2.]*

In witness [etc.].

NOTE.—On a purchase of a term of years absolute out of capital money, the term must be conveyed to the tenant for life, if any, of full age, instead of to the trustees of the settlement. If there is a minority the land will be conveyed to the personal representatives or to the Settled Land Act trustees.

FORM NO. 5

VESTING ASSENT BY PERSONAL REPRESENTATIVE

1. *E.F.* of [etc.] and *G.H.* of [etc.] as the personal representatives of *X.Y.*, late of [etc.] deceased, do this day of 19 hereby, As Personal Representatives, assent to the vesting in *C.D.* of [etc.] of [All that farm, etc.] *or* [All the property described in the Schedule hereto] for all the estate or interest of the said *X.Y.* at the time of his death [*or*, for an estate in fee simple].

2. The premises are vested in the said *C.D.* upon the trusts declared concerning the same by [etc.].

3. The said *E.F.* and *G.H.* are the trustees of the settlement for the purposes of the Settled Land Act 1925.

4 and 5. [*Same as 3 and 4 in Form No. 2*].

As witness, etc.

NOTE.—The expression "conveyance" includes an assent, but an assent will relate back to the death unless a contrary intention appears.

An assent will not be properly postponed merely because death duty remains to be paid. The representatives have only to be satisfied (*e.g.*, where the tenant for life has directed payment out of capital money or has executed a mortgage for raising the money as and when an instalment becomes due) that the duty will be paid.   **[187]**

SCHEDULE 2

Section 37

TRANSITIONAL PROVISIONS AFFECTING EXISTING SETTLEMENTS

Paragraph 1

PROVISIONS FOR VESTING LEGAL ESTATE IN TENANT FOR LIFE OR STATUTORY OWNER

1.—(1) A settlement subsisting at the commencement of this Act is, for the purposes of this Act, a trust instrument.

(2) As soon as practicable after the commencement of this Act, the trustees for the purposes of this Act of every settlement of land subsisting at the commencement of this Act (whether or not the settled land is already vested in them), may and on the request of the tenant for life or statutory owner, shall at the cost of the trust estate, execute a principal vesting deed (containing the proper statements and particulars) declaring that the legal estate in the settled land shall vest or is vested in the person or persons therein named (being the tenant for life or statutory owner, and including themselves if they are the statutory owners), and such deed shall (unless the legal estate is already so vested) operate to convey or vest the legal estate in the settled land to or in the person or persons aforesaid and, if more than one, as joint tenants.

(3) If there are no trustees of the settlement then (in default of a person able and willing to appoint such trustees), an application shall be made to the court by the tenant for life or statutory owner, or by any other person interested, for the appointment of such trustees.

(4) If default is made in the execution of any such principal vesting deed, the provisions of this Act relating to vesting orders of settled land shall apply in like manner as if the trustees of the settlement were persons in whom the settled land is wrongly vested.

(5) This paragraph does not apply where, at the commencement of this Act, settled land is held at law or in equity in undivided shares vested in possession.

(6) In the case of settlements subsisting at the commencement of this Act, all the estates, interests and powers thereby limited which are not by statute otherwise converted into equitable interests or powers, shall, as from the date of the principal vesting deed or the vesting order, take effect only in equity.

[This sub-paragraph shall not apply to any legal estate or interest vested in a mortgagee or other purchaser for money or money's worth.]

(7) This paragraph does not apply where settled land is vested in personal representatives at the commencement of this Act, or where settled land becomes vested in personal representatives before a principal vesting deed has been executed pursuant to this paragraph.

(8) No ad valorem stamp duty shall be payable in respect of a vesting deed or order made for giving effect to an existing settlement.   **[188]**

NOTES
Sub-para (6): words in square brackets added by the Law of Property (Amendment) Act 1926, s 7, Schedule.

Paragraph 2

PROVISIONS WHERE SETTLED LAND IS AT COMMENCEMENT OF ACT VESTED IN PERSONAL REPRESENTATIVES

2.—(1) Where settled land remains at the commencement of this Act vested in the personal representatives of a person who dies before such commencement, or becomes vested in personal representatives before a principal vesting deed has been executed pursuant to the last preceding paragraph, the personal representatives shall hold the settled land on trust, if and when required so to do, to convey the same to the person who, under the trust instrument, or by virtue of this Act, is the tenant for life or statutory owner and, if more than one, as joint tenants.

(2) A conveyance under this paragraph shall be made at the cost of the trust estate and may be made by an assent in writing signed by the personal representatives which shall operate as a conveyance. No stamp duty is payable in respect of a vesting assent.

(3) The obligation to convey settled land imposed on the personal representatives by this paragraph is subject and without prejudice—

(a) to their rights and powers for purposes of administration, and
(b) to their being satisfied that provision has been or will be made for the payment of any unpaid death duties in respect of the land or any interest therein for which they are accountable, and any interest and costs in respect of such duties, or that they are otherwise effectually indemnified against such duties, interest and costs.

(4) A conveyance under this paragraph shall—

(a) if by deed, be a principal vesting deed, and
(b) if by an assent, be a vesting assent, which shall contain the like statements and particulars as are required by this Act in the case of a principal vesting deed.

(5) Nothing contained in this paragraph affects the rights of personal representatives to transfer or create such legal estates to take effect in priority to a conveyance under this paragraph as may be required for giving effect to the obligations imposed on them by statute.

(6) A conveyance by personal representatives under this paragraph, if made by deed, may contain a reservation to themselves of a term of years absolute in the land conveyed upon trusts for indemnifying them against any unpaid death duties in respect of the land conveyed or any interest therein, and any interest and costs in respect of such duties.

(7) Nothing contained in this paragraph affects any right which a person entitled to an equitable charge for securing money actually raised, and affecting the whole estate the subject of the settlement, may have to require effect to be given thereto by a legal mortgage, before the execution of a conveyance under this section.   **[189]**

Paragraph 3

PROVISIONS AS TO INFANTS

3.—(1) Where, at the commencement of this Act, an infant is beneficially entitled to land in possession for an estate in fee simple or for a term of years absolute, or would, if of full age, be a tenant for life or have the powers of a tenant for life, the settled land shall, by virtue of this Act, vest in the trustees (if any) of the settlement upon such trusts as may be requisite for giving effect to the rights of the infant and other persons (if any) interested:

Provided that, if there are no such trustees, then—

(i) Pending their appointment, the settled land shall, by virtue of this Act, vest in the Public Trustee upon the trusts aforesaid:

    (ii) The Public Trustee shall not be entitled to act in the trust, or charge any fee, or be liable in any manner unless and until requested in writing to act on behalf of the infant by his parents or parent or testamentary or other guardian in the order named:

    (iii) After the Public Trustee has been so requested to act, and has accepted the trust, he shall become the trustee of the settlement, and no trustee shall (except by an order of the court) be appointed in his place without his consent:

    (iv) If there is no other person able and willing to appoint trustees the parents or parent or testamentary or other guardian of the infant, if respectively able and willing to act, shall (in the order named) have power by deed to appoint trustees of the settlement in place of the Public Trustee in like manner as if the Public Trustee had refused to act in the trust, and to vest the settled land in them on the trusts aforesaid, and the provisions of the Trustee Act 1925, relating to the appointment of new trustees, and the vesting of trust property shall apply as if the persons aforesaid (in the order named) had been nominated by the settlement for the purpose of appointing new trustees thereof; and in default of any such appointment the infant by his next friend, may, at any time during the minority, apply to the court for the appointment of trustees of the settlement, and the court may make such order as it thinks fit, and if thereby trustees of the settlement are appointed, the settled land shall, by virtue of this Act, vest in the trustees as joint tenants upon the trusts aforesaid:

        Provided that in favour of a purchaser a statement in the deed of appointment that the father or mother or both are dead or are unable or unwilling to make the appointment shall be conclusive evidence of the fact stated.

    (v) If land to which an infant is beneficially entitled in possession for an estate in fee simple or for a term of years absolute vests in the Public Trustee, but the Public Trustee does not become the trustee of the settlement, and trustees of the settlement are not appointed in his place, then, if and when the infant attains the age of twenty-one years, the land shall vest in him.

(2) The provisions of this paragraph shall extend to the legal estate in the settled land, except where such legal estate is, at or immediately after the commencement of this Act, vested in personal representatives, in which case this paragraph shall have effect without prejudice to the provisions of paragraph two of this Schedule.

(3) Where, at the commencement of this Act, any persons appointed under section sixty of the Settled Land Act 1882, have power to act generally or for any specific purpose on behalf of an infant, then those persons shall, by virtue of this Act, become and be the trustees of the settlement.

(4) Notwithstanding that the settled land is by virtue of this paragraph vested in the trustees of the settlement, they shall, at the cost of the trust estate, in accordance with this Act, execute a principal vesting deed declaring that the settled land is vested in them.

(5) This paragraph does not apply where an infant is beneficially entitled in possession to land for a estate in fee simple or for a term of years absolute jointly with a person of full age (for which case provision is made in the Law of Property Act 1925), but it applies to two or more infants entitled as aforesaid jointly.

(6) This paragraph does not apply where an infant would, if of full age, constitute the tenant for life or have the powers of a tenant for life together with another person of full age, but it applies to two or more infants who would, if all of them were of full age, together constitute the tenant for life or have the powers of a tenant for life.   **[190]**

SCHEDULE 3
Section 83

PART I

IMPROVEMENTS, THE COSTS OF WHICH ARE NOT LIABLE TO BE REPLACED BY INSTALMENTS

(i) Drainage, including the straightening, widening, or deepening of drains, streams, and watercourses:

(ii) Bridges:

(iii) Irrigation; warping:

(iv) Drains, pipes, and machinery for supply and distribution of sewage as manure:

(v) Embanking or weiring from a river or lake, or from the sea, or a tidal water:

(vi) Groynes; sea walls; defences against water:

(vii) Inclosing; straightening of fences; re-division of fields:

(viii) Reclamation; dry warping:

(ix) Farm roads; private roads; roads or streets in villages or towns:

(x) Clearing; trenching; planting:

(xi) Cottages for labourers, farm-servants, and artisans, employed on the settled land or not:

(xii) Farmhouses, offices, and outbuildings, and other buildings for farm purposes:

(xiii) Saw-mills, scutch-mills, and other mills, water-wheels, engine-houses, and kilns, which will increase the value of the settled land for agricultural purposes or as woodland or otherwise:

(xiv) Reservoirs, tanks, conduits, watercourses, pipes, wells, ponds, shafts, dams, weirs, sluices, and other works and machinery for supply and distribution of water for agricultural, manufacturing, or other purposes, or for domestic or other consumption:

(xv) Tramways; railways; canals; docks:

(xvi) Jetties, piers, and landing places on rivers, lakes, the sea, or tidal waters, for facilitating transport of persons and of agricultural stock and produce, and of manure and other things required for agricultural purposes, and of minerals, and of things required for mining purposes:

(xvii) Markets and market-places:

(xviii) Streets, roads, paths, squares, gardens, or other open spaces for the use, gratuitously or on payment, of the public or of individuals, or for dedication to the public, the same being necessary or proper in connexion with the conversion of land into building land:

(xix) Sewers, drains, watercourses, pipe-making, fencing, paving, brick-making, tile-making, and other works necessary or proper in connexion with any of the objects aforesaid:

(xx) Trial pits for mines, and other preliminary works necessary or proper in connexion with development of mines:

(xxi) Reconstruction, enlargement, or improvement of any of those works:

(xxii) The provision of small dwellings, either by means of building new buildings or by means of the reconstruction, enlargement, or improvement of existing buildings, if that provision of small dwellings is, in the opinion of the court, not injurious to the settled land or is agreed to by the tenant for life and the trustees of the settlement:

(xxiii) Additions to or alterations in buildings reasonably necessary or proper to enable the same to be let:

(xxiv) Erection of buildings in substitution for buildings within an urban sanitary district taken by a local or other public authority, or for buildings taken under compulsory powers, but so that no more money be expended than the amount received for the buildings taken and the site thereof:

(xxv) The rebuilding of the principal mansion house on the settled land:

Provided that the sum to be applied under this head shall not exceed one-half of the annual rental of the settled land.   **[191]**

PART II

IMPROVEMENTS, THE COSTS OF WHICH THE TRUSTEES OF THE SETTLEMENT OR THE COURT MAY REQUIRE TO BE REPLACED BY INSTALMENTS

(i) Residential houses for land or mineral agents, managers, clerks, bailiffs, woodmen, gamekeepers and other persons employed on the settled land, or in connexion with the management or development thereof:

(ii) Any offices, workshops and other buildings of a permanent nature required in connexion with the management or development of the settled land or any part thereof:

(iii) The erection and building of dwelling houses, shops, buildings for religious, educational, literary, scientific, or public purposes, market places, market houses, places of amusement and entertainment, gasworks, electric light or power works, or any other works necessary or proper in connexion with the development of the settled land, or any part thereof as a building estate:

(iv) Restoration or reconstruction of buildings damaged or destroyed by dry rot:

(v) Structural additions to or alterations in buildings reasonably required, whether the buildings are intended to be let or not, or are already let:

(vi) Boring for water and other preliminary works in connexion therewith.   **[192]**

PART III

IMPROVEMENTS, THE COSTS OF WHICH THE TRUSTEES OF THE SETTLEMENT AND THE COURT MUST REQUIRE TO BE REPLACED BY INSTALMENTS

(i) Heating, hydraulic or electric power apparatus for buildings, and engines, pumps, lifts, rams, boilers, flues, and other works required or used in connexion therewith:

(ii) Engine houses, engines, gasometers, dynamos, accumulators, cables, pipes, wiring, switchboards, plant and other works required for the installation of electric, gas, or other artificial light, in connexion with any principal mansion house, or other house or buildings; but not electric lamps, gas fittings, or decorative fittings required in any such house or building:

(iii) Steam rollers, traction engines, motor lorries and moveable machinery for farming or other purposes.   **[193]**

TRUSTEE ACT 1925
(c 19)

ARRANGEMENT OF SECTIONS

PART I

INVESTMENTS

An Act to consolidate certain enactments relating to trustees in England and Wales
                                                              [9 April 1925]

                                    PART I

                                 INVESTMENTS

2. Purchase at a premium of redeemable stocks; change of character of investment

(1) A trustee may under the powers of this Act invest in any of the securities mentioned or referred to in section one of this Act, notwithstanding that the same may be redeemable, and that the price exceeds the redemption value.

. . .

(2) A trustee may retain until redemption any redeemable stock, fund, or security which may have been purchased in accordance with the powers of this Act, or any statute replaced by this Act.   **[194]**

NOTES
Sub-s (1): words omitted repealed by Trustee Investments Act 1961, s 16(2), Sch 5.

3. Discretion of trustees

Every power conferred by the preceding sections shall be exercised according to the discretion of the trustee, but subject to any consent or direction required by the instrument, if any, creating the trust or by statute with respect to the investment of the trust funds.   **[195]**

4. Power to retain investment which has ceased to be authorised

A trustee shall not be liable for breach of trust by reason only of his continuing to hold an investment which has ceased to be an investment authorised by the trust instrument or by the general law.   **[196]**

5. Enlargement of powers of investment

(1) A trustee having power to invest in real securities may invest and shall be deemed always to have had power to invest—

    (*a*) . . .

    (*b*) on any charge,or upon mortgage of any charge, made under the Improvement of Land Act, 1864.

(2) A trustee having power to invest in real securities may accept the security in the form of a charge by way of legal mortgage, and may, in exercise of the statutory power, convert an existing mortgage into a charge by way of legal mortgage.

(3) A trustee having power to invest in the mortgages or bonds of any railway company or of any other description of company may invest in the debenture stock of a railway company or such other company as aforesaid.

    (4)–(6) . . .   **[197]**

NOTES
Sub-s (1): para (*a*) repealed by the Trustee Investments Act 1961, s 16(2), Sch 5.
Sub-ss (4)-(6): repealed by the Trustee Investments Act 1961, s 16(2), Sch 5.

6. Power to invest in land subject to drainage charges

A trustee having power to invest in the purchase of land or on mortgage of land may invest in the purchase or on mortgage of any land notwithstanding the same is charged with a rent under the powers of . . . the Landed Property Improvement (Ireland) Act 1847, or by an absolute order made under the Improvement of Land Act 1864, unless the terms of the trust expressly provide that the land to be purchased or taken in mortgage shall not be subject to any such prior charge.   **[198]**

NOTES
Words omitted repealed by the Statute Law Revision Act 1963.

7. Investment in bearer securities

(1) A trustee may, unless expressly prohibited by the instrument creating the trust, retain or invest in securities payable to bearer which, if not so payable, would have been authorised investments:

Provided that securities to bearer retained or taken as an investment by a trustee (not being a trust corporation) shall, until sold, be deposited by him for safe custody and collection of income with a banker or banking company.

A direction that investments shall be retained or made in the name of a trustee shall not, for the purposes of this subsection, he deemed to be such an express prohibition as aforesaid.

(2) A trustee shall not be responsible for any loss incurred by reason of such deposit, and any sum payable in respect of such deposit and collection shall be paid out of the income of the trust property. [199]

8. Loans and investments by trustees not chargeable as breaches of trust

(1) A trustee lending money on the security of any property on which he can properly lend shall not be chargeable with breach of trust by reason only of the proportion borne by the amount of the loan to the value of the property at the time when the loan was made, if it appears to the court—

   (a) that in making the loan the trustee was acting upon a report as to the value of the property made by a person whom he reasonably believed to be an able practical surveyor or valuer instructed and employed independently of any owner of the property, whether such surveyor or valuer carried on business in the locality where the property is situate or elseWhere; and

   (b) that the amount of the loan does not exceed two third parts of the value of the property as stated in the report; and

   (c) that the loan was made under the advice of the surveyor or valuer expressed in the report.

(2) A trustee lending money on the security of any leasehold property shall not be chargeable with breach of trust only upon the ground that in making such loan he dispensed either wholly or partly with the production or investigation of the lessor's title.

(3) A trustee shall not be chargeable with breach of trust only upon the ground that in effecting the purchase, or in lending money upon the security, of any property he has accepted a shorter title than the title which a purchaser is, in the absence of a special contract, entitled to require, if in the opinion of the court the title accepted be such as a person acting with prudence and caution would have accepted.

(4) This section applies to transfers of existing securities as well as to new securities and to investments made before as well as after the commencement of this Act. [200]

9. Liability for loss by reason of improper investment

(1) Where a trustee improperly advances trust money on a mortgage security which would at the time of the investment be a proper investment in all respects for a smaller sum than is actually advanced thereon, the security shall be deemed an authorised investment for the smaller sum, and the trustee shall only be liable to make good the sum advanced in excess thereof with interest.

(2) This section applies to investments made before as well as after the commencement of this Act. [201]

10. Powers supplementary to powers of investment

(1) Trustees lending money on the security of any property on which they can lawfully lend may contract that such money shall not be called in during any period not exceeding seven years from the time when the loan was made, provided interest be paid within a specified time not exceeding thirty days after every half-yearly or other day on which it becomes due, and provided there be no breach of any covenant by the mortgagor contained in the instrument of mortgage or charge for the maintenance and protection of the property.

(2) On a sale of land for an estate in fee simple or for a term having at least five hundred years to run by trustees or by a tenant for life or statutory owner, the trustees, or the tenant for life or statutory owner on behalf of the trustees of the settlement, may, where the proceeds are liable to be invested, contract that the payment of any part, not exceeding two-thirds, of the purchase money shall be secured by a charge by way of legal mortgage or a mortgage by demise or sub-demise for a term of at least five hundred years (less a nominal reversion when by sub-demise), of the land sold, with or without the security of any other property, such charge or mortgage, if any buildings are comprised in the mortgage, to contain a covenant by the mortgagor to keep them insured against loss or damage by fire to the full value thereof.

The trustees shall not be bound to obtain any report as to the value of the land or other property to be comprised in such charge or mortgage, or any advice as to the making of the loan, and shall not be liable for any loss which may be incurred by reason only of the security being insufficient at the date of the charge or mortgage; and the trustees of the settlement shall be bound to give effect to such contract made by the tenant for life or statutory owner.

(3) Where any securities of a company are subject to a trust, the trustees may concur in any scheme or arrangement—

    (*a*) for the reconstruction of the company;
    (*b*) for the sale of all or any part of the property and undertaking of the company to another company;
    [(*bb*)for the acquisition of the securities of the company, or of control thereof by another company];
    (*c*) for the amalgamation of the company with another company;
    (*d*) for the release, modification, or variation of any rights, privileges or liabilities attached to the securities or any of them;

in like manner as if they were entitled to such securities beneficially, with power to accept any securities of any denomination or description of the reconstructed or purchasing or new company in lieu of or in exchange for all or any of the first-mentioned securities; and the trustees shall not be responsible for any loss occasioned by any act or thing so done in good faith, and may retain any securities so accepted as aforesaid for any period for which they could have properly retained the original securities.

(4) If any conditional or preferential right to subscribe for any securities in any company is offered to trustees in respect of any holding in such company, they may as to all or any of such securities, either exercise such right and apply capital money subject to the trust in payment of the consideration, or renounce such right, or assign for the best consideration that can be reasonably obtained the benefit of such right or the title thereto to any person, including any beneficiary under the trust, without being responsible for any loss occasioned by any act or thing so done by them in good faith:

Provided that the consideration for any such assignment shall be held as capital money of the trust.

(5) The powers conferred by this section shall be exercisable subject to the consent of any person whose consent to a change of investment is required by law or by the instrument, if any, creating the trust.

(6) Where the loan referred to in subsection (1), or the sale referred to in subsection (2), of this section is made under the order of the court, the powers conferred by those subsections respectively shall apply only if and as far as the court may by order direct.   **[202]**

NOTES

Sub-s (3): para (*bb*) added by the Trustee Investments Act 1961, s 9(1).

11. Power to deposit money at bank and to pay calls

(1) Trustees may, pending the negotiation and preparation of any mortgage or charge, or during any other time while an investment is being sought for, pay any trust money into a bank to a deposit or other account, and all interest, if any, payable in respect thereof shall be applied as income.

(2) Trustees may apply capital money subject to a trust in payment of the calls on any shares to the same trust.   **[203]**

PART II

GENERAL POWERS OF TRUSTEES AND PERSONAL REPRESENTATIVES

General Powers

12. Power of trustees for sale to sell by auction, etc

(1) Where a trust for sale or a power of sale of property is vested in a trustee, he may sell or concur with any other person in selling all or any part of the property, either subject to prior charges or not, and either together or in lots, by public auction or by private contract, subject to any such conditions respecting title or evidence of title or other matter as the trustee thinks fit, with power to vary any contract for sale, and to buy in at any auction, or to rescind any contract for sale and to re-sell, without being answerable for any loss.

(2) A trust or power to sell or dispose of land includes a trust or power to sell or dispose of part thereof, whether the division is horizontal, vertical, or made in any other way.

(3) This section does not enable an express power to sell settled land to be exercised where the power is not vested in the tenant for life or statutory owner.   **[204]**

13. Power to sell subject to depreciatory conditions

(1) No sale made by a trustee shall be impeached by any beneficiary upon the ground that any of the conditions subject to which the sale was made may have been unnecessarily depreciatory, unless it also appears that the consideration for the sale was thereby rendered inadequate.

(2) No sale made by a trusteee shall, after the execution of the conveyance, be impeached as against the purchaser upon the ground that any of the conditions subject to which the sale was made may have been unnecessarily

depreciatory, unless it appears that the purchaser was acting in collusion with the trustee at the time when the contract for sale was made.

(3) No purchaser, upon any sale made by a trustee, shall be at liberty to make any objection against the title upon any of the grounds aforesaid.

(4) This section applies to sales made before or after the commencement of this Act. **[205]**

14. Power of trustees to give receipts

(1) The receipt in writing of a trustee for any money, securities, or other personal property or effects payable, transferable, or deliverable to him under any trust or power shall be a sufficient discharge to the person paying, transferring, or delivering the same and shall effectually exonerate him from seeing to the application or being answerable for any loss or misapplication thereof.

(2) This section does not, except where the trustee is a trust corporation, enable a sole trustee to give a valid receipt for—

    (*a*) the proceeds of sale or other capital money arising under a . . . trust for sale of land;

    (*b*) capital money arising under the Settled Land Act 1925.

(3) This section applies notwithstanding anything to the contrary in the instrument, if any, creating the trust. **[206]**

NOTES

    Sub-s (2): words omitted repealed by the Law of Property (Amendment) Act 1926, ss 7, 8(2), Schedule.

---

15. Power to compound liabilities

A personal representative, or two or more trustees acting together, or, subject to the restrictions imposed in regard to receipts by a sole trustee not being a trust corporation, a sole acting trustee where by the instrument, if any, creating the trust, or by statute, a sole trustee is authorised to execute the trusts and powers reposed in him, may, if and as he or they think fit—

    (*a*) accept any property, real or personal, before the time at which it is made transferable or payable; or

    (*b*) sever and apportion any blended trust funds or property; or

    (*c*) pay or allow any debt or claim on any evidence that he or they think sufficient; or

    (*d*) accept any composition or any security, real or personal, for any debt or for any property, real or personal, claimed; or

    (*e*) allow any time of payment of any debt; or

    (*f*) compromise, compound, abandon, submit to arbitration, or otherwise settle any debt, account, claim, or thing Whatever relating to the testator's or intestate's estate or to the trust;

and for any of those purposes may enter into, give, execute, and do such agreements, instruments of composition or arrangement, releases, and other things as to him or them seem expedient, without being responsible for any loss occasioned by any act or thing so done by him or them in good faith. **[207]**

16. Power to raise money by sale, mortgage, etc.

(1) Where trustees are authorised by the instrument, if any, creating the trust or by law to pay or apply capital money subject to the trust for any purpose or in any manner, they shall have and shall be deemed always to have had power to raise the money required by sale, conversion, calling in, or mortgage of all or any part of the trust property for the time being in possession.

(2) This section applies notwithstanding anything to the contrary contained in the instrument, if any, creating the trust, but does not apply to trustees of property held for charitable purposes, or to trustees of a settlement for the purposes of the Settled Land Act 1925, not being also the statutory owners.

[208]

17. Protection to purchasers and mortgagees dealing with trustees

No purchaser or mortgagee paying or advancing money on a sale or mortgage purporting to be made under any trust or power vested in trustees, shall be concerned to see that such money is wanted; or that no more than is wanted is raised, or otherwise as to the application thereof.   **[209]**

18. Devolution of powers or trusts

(1) Where a power or trust is given to or imposed on two or more trustees jointly, the same may be exercised or performed by the survivors or survivor of them for the time being.

(2) Until the appointment of new trustees, the personal representatives or representative for the time being of a sole trustee, or, where there were two or more trustees of the last surviving or continuing trustee, shall be capable of exercising or performing any power or trust which was given to, or capable of being exercised by, the sole or last surviving or continuing trustee, or other the trustees or trustee for the time being of the trust.

(3) This section takes effect subject to the restrictions imposed in regard to receipts by a sole trustee, not being a trust corporation.

(4) In this section "personal representative" does not include an executor who has renounced or has not proved.   **[210]**

19. Power to insure

(1) A trustee may insure against loss or damage by fire any building or other insurable property to any amount, including the amount of any insurance already on foot, not exceeding three fourth parts of the full value of the building or property, and pay the premiums for such insurance out of the income thereof or out of the income of any other property subject to the same trusts without obtaining the consent of any person who may be entitled wholly or partly to such income.

(2) This section does not apply to any building or property which a trustee is bound forthwith to convey absolutely to any beneficiary upon being requested to do so.   **[211]**

20. Application of insurance money where policy kept up under any trust, power or obligation

(1) Money receivable by trustees or any beneficiary under a policy of insurance against the loss or damage of any property subject to a trust or to a settlement

within the meaning of the Settled Land Act, 1925, whether by fire or otherwise, shall, where the policy has been kept up under any trust in that behalf or under any power statutory or otherwise, or in performance of any covenant or of any obligation statutory or otherwise, or by a tenant for life impeachable for waste, be capital money for the purposes of the trust or settlement, as the case may be.

(2) If any such money is receivable by any person, other than the trustees of the trust or settlement, that person shall use his best endeavours to recover and receive the money, and shall pay the net residue thereof, after discharging any costs of recovering and receiving it, to the trustees of the trust or settlement, or, if there are no trustees capable of giving a discharge therefor, into court.

(3) Any such money—

(a) it was receivable in respect of settled land within the meaning of the Settled Land Act, 1925, or any building or works thereon, shall be deemed to be capital money arising under that Act from the settled land, and shall be invested or applied by the trustees, or, if in court, under the direction of the court, accordingly;

(b) if it was receivable in respect of personal chattels settled as heirlooms within the meaning of the Settled Land Act, 1925, shall be deemed to be capital money arising under that Act; and shall be applicable by the trustees, or, if in court, under the direction of the court, in like manner as provided by that Act with respect to money arising by sale of chattels as heirlooms as aforesaid;

(c) if it was receivable in respect of property held upon trust for sale, shall be held upon the trusts and subject to the powers and provisions applicable to money arising by a sale under such trust;

(d) in any other case, shall be held upon trusts corresponding as nearly as may be with the trusts affecting the property in respect of which it was payable.

(4) Such money, or any part thereof, may also be applied by the trustees, or, if in court, under the direction of the court, in rebuilding, reinstating, replacing, or replacing the property loss or damaged, but any such application by the trustees shall be subject to the consent of any person whose consent is required by the instrument, if any, creating the trust to the investment of money subject to the trust, and, in the case of money which is deemed to be capital money arising under the Settled Land Act, 1925, be subject to the provisions of that Act with respect to the application of capital money by the trustees of the settlement.

(5) Nothing contained in this section prejudices or affects the right of any person to require any such money or any part thereof to be applied in rebuilding reinstating, or repairing the property lost or damaged, or the rights of any mortgagee, lessor, or lessee, whether under any statute or otherwise.

(6) This section applies to policies effected either before or after the commencement of this Act, but only to money received after such commencement. **[212]**

21. Deposit of documents for safe custody

Trustees may deposit any documents held by them relating to the trust, or to the trust property, with any banker or banking company or any other company whose business includes the undertaking of the safe custody of documents, any sum payable in respect of such deposit shall be paid out of the income of the trust property. **[213]**

22. Reversionary interests, valuations, and audit

(1) Where trust property includes any share or interest in property not vested in the trustees, or the proceeds of the sale of any such property, or any other thing in action, the trustees on the same falling into possession, or becoming payable or transferable may—

    (*a*) agree or ascertain the amount or value thereof or any part thereof in such manner as they may think fit;

    (*b*) accept in or towards satisfaction thereof, at the market or current value, or upon any valuation or estimate of value which they may think fit, any authorised investments;

    (*c*) allow any deductions for duties, costs, charges and expenses which they may think proper or reasonable;

    (*d*) execute any release in respect of the premises so as effectually to discharge all accountable parties from all liability in respect of any matters coming within the scope of such release;

without being responsible in any such case for any loss occasioned by any act or thing so done by them in good faith.

(2) The trustees shall not be under any obligation and shall not be chargeable with any breach of trust by reason of any omission—

    (*a*) to place any distringas notice or apply for any stop or other like order upon any securities or other property out of or on which such share or interest or other thing in action as aforesaid is derived, payable or charged; or

    (*b*) to take any proceedings on account of any act, default, or neglect on the part of the persons in whom such securities or other property or any of them or any part thereof are for the time being, or had at any time been, vested; unless and until required in writing so to do by some person, or the guardian of some person, beneficially interested under the trust, and unless also due provision is made to their satisfaction for payment of the costs of any proceedings required to be taken:

Provided that nothing in this subsection shall relieve the trustees of the obligation to get in and obtain payment or transfer of such share or interest or other thing in action on the same falling into possession.

(3) Trustees may, for the purpose of giving effect to the trust, or any of the provisions of the instrument, if any, creating the trust or of any statute, from time to time (by duly qualified agents) ascertain and fix the value of any trust property in such manner as they think proper, and any valuation so made in good faith shall be binding upon all persons interested under the trust.

(4) Trustees may, in their absolute discretion, from time to time, but not more than once in every three years unless the nature of the trust or any special dealings with the trust property make a more frequent exercise of the right reasonable, cause the accounts of the trust property to be examined or audited by an independent accountant, and shall, for that purpose, produce such vouchers and give such information to him as he may require; and the costs of such examination or audit, including the fee of the auditor, shall be paid out of the capital or income of the trust property, or partly in one way and partly in the other as the trustees, in their absolute discretion, think fit, but, in default of any direction by the trustees to the contrary in any special case, costs attributable to capital shall be borne by capital and those attributable to income by income.

23. Power to employ agents

(1) Trustees or personal representatives may, instead of acting personally, employ and pay an agent, whether a solicitor, banker, stockbroker, or other person, to transact any business or any act required to be transacted or done in the execution of the trust, or the administration of the testator's or intestate's estate, including the receipt and payment of money and shall be entitled to be allowed and paid all charges and expenses so incurred, and shall not be responsible for the default of any such agent if employed in good faith.

(2) Trustees or personal representatives may appoint any person to act as their agent or attorney for the purpose of selling, converting, collecting, getting in, and executing and perfecting insurances of, or managing or cultivating, or otherwise administering any property, real or personal, moveable or immoveable, subject to the trust or forming part of the testator's or intestate's estate, in any place outside the United Kingdom or executing or exercising any discretion or trust or power vested in them in relation to any such property, with such ancillary powers, and with and subject to such provisions and restrictions as they may think fit, including a power to appoint substitutes, and shall not, by reason only of their having made such appointment, be responsible for any loss arising thereby.

(3) Without prejudice to such general power of appointing agents as aforesaid—

    (a) A trustee may appoint a solicitor to be his agent to receive and give a discharge for any money or valuable consideration or property receivable by the trustee under the trust, by permitting the solicitor to have the custody of, and to produce, a deed having in the body thereof or endorsed thereon a receipt for such money or valuable consideration or property, the deed being executed, or the endorsed receipt being signed, by the person entitled to give a receipt for that consideration;

    (b) A trustee shall not be chargeable with breach of trust by reason only of his having made or concurred in making any such appointment; and the production of any such deed by the solicitor shall have the same statutory validity and effect as if the person appointing the solicitor had not been a trustee;

    (c) A trustee may appoint a banker or solicitor to be his agent to receive and give a discharge for any money payable to the trustee under or by virtue of a policy of insurance, by permitting the banker or solicitor to have the custody of and to produce the policy of insurance with a receipt signed by the trustee, and a trustee shall not be chargeable with a breach of trust by reason only of his having made or concurred in making any such appointment;

Provided that nothing in this subsection shall exempt a trustee from any liability which he would have incurred if this Act and any enactment replaced by this Act had not been passed, in case he permits any such money, valuable consideration, or property to remain in the hands or under the control of the banker or solicitor for a period longer than is reasonably necessary to enable the banker or solicitor, as the case may be, to pay or transfer the same to the trustee.

This subsection applies whether the money or valuable consideration or property was or is received before or after the commencement of this Act. **[215]**

24. Power to concur with others

Where an undivided share in the proceeds of sale of land directed to be sold, or in any other property, is subject to a trust, or forms part of the estate of a testator or intestate, the trustees or personal representatives may (without prejudice to the trust for sale affecting the entirety of the land and the powers of the trustees for sale in reference thereto), execute or exercise any trust or power vested in them in relation to such share in conjunction with the persons entitled to or having power in that behalf over the other share or shares, and notwithstanding that any one or more of the trustees or personal representatives may be entitled to or interested in any such other share, either in his or their own right or in a fiduciary capacity.   **[216]**

25. Power to delegate trusts during absence abroad

[(1) Notwithstanding any rule of law or equity to the contrary, a trustee may, by power of attorney, delegate for a period not exceeding twelve months the execution or exercise of all or any of the trusts, powers and discretions vested in him as trustee either alone or jointly with any other person or persons.

(2) The persons who may be donees of a power of attorney under this section include a trust corporation but not (unless a trust corporation) the only other co-trustee of the donor of the power.

(3) An instrument creating a power of attorney under this section shall be attested by at least one witness.

(4) Before or within seven days after giving a power of attorney under this section the donor shall give written notice thereof (specifying the date on which the power comes into operation and its duration), the donee of the power, the reason why the power is given and, where some only are delegated, the trusts, powers and discretions delegated) to—

(a) each person (other than himself), if any, who under any instrument creating the trust has power (whether alone or jointly) to appoint a new trustee; and

(b) each of the other trustees, if any;

but failure to comply with this subsection shall not, in favour of a person dealing with the donee of the power, invalidate any act done or instrument executed by the donee.

(5) The donor of a power of attorney given under this section shall be liable for the acts or defaults of the donee in the same manner as if they were the acts or defaults of the donor].

[(6)] For the purpose of executing or exercising the trusts or powers delegated to him, the donee may exercise any of the powers conferred on the donor as trustee by statute or by the instrument creating the trust, including power, for the purpose of the transfer of any inscribed stock, himself to delegate to an attorney power to transfer but not including the power of delegation conferred by this section.

[(7)] The fact that it appears from any power of attorney given under this section, or from any evidence required for the purposes of any such power of attorney or otherwise, that in dealing with any stock the donee of the power is acting in the execution of a trust shall not be deemed for any purpose to affect any person in whose books the stock is inscribed or registered with any notice of the trust.

[(8) This section applies to a personal representative, tenant for life and statutory owner as it applies to a trustee except that subsection (4) shall apply as if it required the notice there mentioned to be given—

    (*a*) in the case of a personal representative, to each of the other personal
        representatives, if any, except any executor who has renounced
        probate;

    (*b*) in the case of a tenant for life, to the trustees of the settlement and to
        each person, if any, who together with the person giving the notice
        constitutes the tenant for life;

    (*c*) in the case of a statutory owner, to each of the persons, if any, who
        together with the person giving the notice constitute the statutory
        owner and, in the case of a statutory owner by virtue of section 23(1)
        (*a*) of the Settled Land Act 1925; to the trustees of the settlement.]

[217]

NOTES

    Sub-ss (1)–(5): substituted for sub-ss (1)–(8), as originally enacted, by the Powers of Attorney
Act 1971, s 9(2).

    Sub-ss (6), (7): renumbered as such by the Powers of Attorney Act 1971, s 9(3).

    Sub-s (8): substituted for sub-s (11), as originally enacted, by the Powers of Attorney Act 1971,
s 9(3).

    This section in its amended form is not restricted to delegation by trustees during absence
abroad.

Indemnities

26. Protection against liability in respect of rents and covenants

(1) Where a personal representative or trustee liable as such for—

    (*a*) any rent, covenant, or agreement reserved by or contained in any
        lease; or

    (*b*) any rent, covenant or agreement payable under or contained in any
        grant made in consideration of a rentcharge; or

    (*c*) any indemnity given in respect of any rent, covenant or agreement
        referred to in either of the foregoing paragaphs;

satisfies all liabilities under the lease or grant [which may have accrued and
been claimed] up to the date of the conveyance hereinafter mentioned, and,
where necessary, sets apart a sufficient fund to answer any future claim that
may be made in respect of any fixed and ascertained sum which the lessee or
grantee agreed to lay out on the property demised or granted, although the
period for laying out the same may not have arrived, then and in any such case
the personal representative or trustee may convey the property demised or
granted to a purchaser, legatee, devisee, or other person entitled to call for a
conveyance thereof and thereafter—

    (i) he may distribute the residuary real and personal estate of the
       deceased testator or intestate, or, as the case may be, the trust
       estate (other than the fund, if any, set apart as aforesaid) to or
       amongst the persons entitled thereto, without appropriating any
       part, or any further part, as the case may be, of the estate of the
       deceased or of the trust estate to meet any future liability under
       the said lease or grant;

    (ii) notwithstanding such distribution, he shall not be personally
       liable in respect of any subsequent claim under the said lease or
       grant.

(2) This section operates without prejudice to the right of the lessor or
grantor, or the persons deriving title under the lessor or grantor, to follow the
assets of the deceased or the trust property into the hands of the persons amongst
whom the same may have been respectively distributed, and applies notwith-

standing anything to the contrary in the will or other instrument, if any, creating the trust.

(3) In this section "lease" includes an underlease and an agreement for a lease or underlease and any instrument giving any such indemnity as aforesaid or varying the liabilities under the lease; "grant" applies to a grant whether the rent is created by limitation, grant, reservation, or otherwise, and includes an agreement for a grant and any instrument giving any such indemnity as aforesaid or varying the liabilities under the grant; "lessee" and "grantee" include persons respectively deriving title under them. **[218]**

NOTES
Sub-s (1): words in square brackets substituted by the Law of Property (Amendment) Act 1926, ss 7, 8(2), Schedule.

27. Protection by means of advertisements

(1) With a view to the conveyance to or distribution among the persons entitled to any real or personal property, the trustees of a settlement or of a disposition on trust for sale or personal representatives, may give notice by advertisement in the Gazette, and [in a newspaper circulating in the district in which the land is situated] and such other like notices, including notices elsewhere than in England and Wales, as would, in any special case, have been directed by a court of competent jurisdiction in an action for administration, of their intention to make such conveyance or distribution as aforesaid, and requiring any person interested to send to the trustees or personal representatives within the time, not being less than two months, fixed in the notice or, where more than one notice is given, in the last of the notices, particulars of his claim in respect of the property or any part thereof to which the notice relates.

(2) At the expiration of the time fixed by the notice the trustees or personal representatives may convey or distribute the property or any part thereof to which the notice relates, to or among the persons entitled thereto, having regard only to the claims, whether formal or not, of which the trustees or personal representatives then had notice and shall not, as respects the property so conveyed or distributed, be liable to any person of whose claim the trustees or personal representatives have not had notice at the time of conveyance or distribution; but nothing in this section—

(a) prejudices the right of any person to follow the property, or any property representing the same, into the hands of any person, other than a purchaser, who may have received it; or

(b) frees the trustees or personal representatives from any obligation to make searches or obtain official certificates of search similar to those which an intending purchaser would be advised to make or obtain.

(3) This section applies notwithstanding anything to the contrary in the will or other instrument, if any, creating the trust. **[219]**

NOTES
Sub-s (1): words in square brackets substituted by the Law of Property (Amendment) Act 1926, ss 7, 8(2), Schedule.

28. Protection in regard to notice

A trustee or personal representative acting for the purposes of more than one trust or estate shall not, in the absence of fraud, be affected by notice of any instrument, matter, fact or thing in relation to any particular trust or estate if he has obtained notice therefore merely by reason of his acting or having acted for the purposes of another trust or estate. **[220]**

30. Implied indemnity of trustees

(1) A trustee shall be chargeable only for money and securities actually received by him notwithstanding his signing any receipt for the sake of conformity, and shall be answerable and accountable only for his own acts, receipts, neglects, or defaults, and not for those of any other trustee, nor for any banker, broker, or other person with whom any trust money or securities may be deposited, nor for the insufficiency or deficiency of any securities, nor for any other loss, unless the same happens through his own wilful default.

(2) A trustee may reimburse himself or pay or discharge out of the trust premises all expenses incurred in or about the execution of the trusts or powers.

[221]

Maintenance Advancement and Protective Trusts

31. Power to apply income for maintenance and to accumulate surplus income during a minority

(1) Where any property is held by trustees in trust for any person for any interest whatsoever, whether vested or contingent, then, subject to any prior interests or charges affecting that property—

    (i) during the infancy of any such person, if his interest so long continues, the trustees may, at their sole discretion, pay to his parent or guardian, if any, or otherwise apply for or towards his maintenance, education, or benefit, the whole or such part, if any, of the income of that property as may, in all the circumstances, be reasonable, whether or not there is—

        (*a*) any other fund applicable to the same purpose; or
        (*b*) any person bound by law to provide for his maintenance or education; and

    (ii) if such person on attaining the age of [eighteen years] has not a vested interest in such income, the trustees shall thenceforth pay the income of that property and of any accretion thereto under subsection (2) of this section to him, until he either attains a vested interest therein or dies, or until failure of his interest:

Provided that, in deciding whether the whole or any part of the income of the property is during a minority to be paid or applied for the purposes aforesaid, the trustees shall have regard to the age of the infant and his requirements and generally to the circumstances of the case, and in particular to what other income, if any, is applicable for the same purposes; and where trustees have notice that the income of more than one fund is applicable for those purposes, then, so far as practicable, unless the entire income of the funds is paid or applied as aforesaid or the court otherwise directs, a proportionate part only of the income of each fund shall be so paid or applied.

(2) During the infancy of any such person, if his interest so long continues, the trustees shall accumulate all the residue of that income in the way of compound interest by investing the same and the resulting income thereof from time to time in authorized investments, and shall hold those accumulations as follows:—

(i) If any such person—

> (a) attains the age of [eighteen years], or marries under that age, and his interest in such income during his infancy or until his marriage is a vested interest; or
>
> (b) on attaining the age of [eighteen years] or on marriage under that age becomes entitled to the property from which such income arose in fee simple, absolute or determinable, or absolutely, or for an entailed interest;
>
> the trustees shall hold the accumulations in trust for such person absolutely, but without prejudice to any provision with respect thereto contained in any settlement by him made under any statutory powers during his infancy, and so that the receipt of such person after marriage, and though still an infant, shall be a good discharge; and

(ii) In any other case the trustees shall, notwithstanding that such person had a vested interest in such income, hold the accumulations as an accretion to the capital of the property from which such acccumulations arose, and as one fund with such capital for all purposes, and so that, if such property is settled land, such accumulations shall be held upon the same trusts as if the same were capital money arising therefrom;

but the trustees may, at any time during the infancy of such person if his interest so long continues, apply those accumulations, or any part thereof, as if they were income arising in the then current year.

(3) This section applies in the case of a contingent interest only if the limitation or trust carries the intermediate income of the property, but it applies to a future or contingent legacy by the parent of, or a person standing in loco parentis to, the legatee, if and for such period as, under the general law, the legacy carries interest for the maintenance of the legatee, and in any such case as last aforesaid the rate of interest shall (if the income available is sufficient, and subject to any rules of court to the contrary) be five pounds per centum per annum.

(4) This section applies to a vested annuity in like manner as if the annuity were the income of property held by trustees in trust to pay the income thereof to the annuitant for the same period for which the annuity is payable, save that in any case accumulations made during the infancy of the annuitant shall be held in trust for the annuitant or his personal representatives absolutely.

(5) This section does not apply where the instrument, if any, under which the interest arises came into operation before the commencement of this Act.

[222]

NOTES

Sub-s (1): words in square brackets substituted by the Family Law Reform Act 1969, s 1(3), Sch 1, Part I.

Sub-s (2): words in square brackets substituted by the Family Law Reform Act 1969, s 1(3), Sch 1, Part I.

32. Power of advancement

(1) Trustees may at any time or times pay or apply any capital money subject to a trust, for the advancement or benefit, in such manner as they may, in their absolute discretion, think fit, of any person entitled to the capital of the trust property or of any share thereof, whether absolutely or contingently on his

attaining any specified age or on the occurrence of any other event, or subject to a gift over on his death under any specified age or on the occurrence of any other event, and whether in possession or in remainder or reversion, and such payment or application may be made notwithstanding that the interest of such person is liable to be defeated by the exercise of a power of appointment or revocation, or to be diminished by the increase of the class to which he belongs:

Provided that—

(a) the money so paid or applied for the advancement or benefit of any person shall not exceed altogether in amount one-half of the presumptive or vested share or interest of that person in the trust property; and

(b) if that person is or becomes absolutely and indefeasibly entitled to a share in the trust property the money so paid or applied shall be brought into account as part of such share; and

(c) no such payment or application shall be made so as to prejudice any person entitled to any prior life or other interest, whether vested or contingent, in the money paid or applied unless such person is in existence and of full age and consents in writing to such payment or application.

(2) This section applies only where the trust property consists of money or securities or of property held upon trust for sale calling in and conversion, and such money or securities, or the proceeds of such sale calling in and conversion are not by statute or in equity considered as land, or applicable as capital money for the purposes of the Settled Land Act, 1925.

(3) This section does not apply to trusts constituted or created before the commencement of this Act. **[223]**

33. Protective trusts

(1) Where any income, including an annuity or other periodical income payment, is directed to be held on protective trusts for the benefit of any person (in this section called "the principal beneficiary") for the period of his life or for any less period, then, during that period (in this section called the "trust period") the said income shall, without prejudice to any prior interest, be held on the following trusts, namely:—

(i) Upon trust for the principal beneficiary during the trust period or until he, whether before or after the termination of any prior interest, does or attempts to do or suffers any act or thing, or until any event happens, other than an advance under any statutory or express power, whereby, if the said income were payable during the trust period to the principal beneficiary absolutely during that period, he would be deprived of the right to receive the same or any part thereof, in any of which cases, as well as on the termination of the trust period, whichever first happens, this trust of the said income shall fail or determine;

(ii) If the trust aforesaid fails or determines during the subsistence of the trust period, then, during the residue of that period, the said income shall be held upon trust for the application thereof for the maintenance or support, or otherwise for the benefit, of all or any one or more exclusively of the other or others of the following persons (that is to say)—

(a) the principal beneficiary and his or her wife or husband, if any, and his or her children or more remote issue, if any; or

(b) if there is no wife or husband or issue of the principal
beneficiary in existence, the principal beneficiary and the
persons who would, if he were actually dead, be entitled to
the trust property or the income thereof or to the annuity
fund, if any, or arrears of the annuity, as the case may be;

as the trustees in their absolute discretion, without being liable
to account for the exercise of such discretion, think fit.

(2) This section does not apply to trusts coming into operation before the
commencement of this Act, and has effect subject to any variation of the implied
trusts aforesaid contained in the instrument creating the trust.

(3) Nothing in this section operates to validate any trust which would, if
contained in the instrument creating the trust, be liable to be set aside.

[(4) In relation to the dispositions mentioned in section 19(1) of the Family
Law Reform Act 1987, this section shall have effect as if any reference (however
expressed) to any relationship between two persons were construed in accordance
with section 1 of that Act.]   **[224]**

NOTES

Sub-s (4): added by the Family Law Reform Act 1987, s 33(1), Sch 2, para 2.

PART III

APPOINTMENT AND DISCHARGE OF TRUSTEES

34. Limitation of the number of trustees

(1) Where, at the commencement of this Act, there are more than four trustees
of a settlement of land, or more than four trustees holding land on trust for sale,
no new trustees shall (except where as a result of the appointment the number
is reduced to four or less) be capable of being appointed until the number is
reduced to less than four, and thereafter the number shall not be increased
beyond four.

(2) In the case of settlements and dispositions on trust for sale of land made
or coming into operation after the commencement of this Act—

(a) the number of trustees thereof shall not in any case exceed four, and
where more than four persons are named as such trustees, the four
first named (who are able and willing to act) shall alone be the trustees,
and the other persons named shall not be trustees unless appointed on
the occurrence of a vacancy;
(b) the number of the trustees shall not be increased beyond four.

(3) This section only applies to settlements and dispositions of land, and the
restrictions imposed on the number of trustees do not apply—

(a) in the case of land vested in trustees for charitable, ecclesiastical, or
public purposes; or
(b) where the net proceeds of the sale of the land are held for like
purposes; or
(c) to the trustees of a term of years absolute limited by a settlement on
trusts for raising money, or of a like term created under the statutory
remedies relating to annual sums charged on land.   **[225]**

35. Appointments of trustees of settlements and dispositions on trust for sale of land

(1) Appointments of new trustees of conveyances on trust for sale on the one hand and of the settlement of the proceeds of sale on the other hand, shall, subject to any order of the court, be effected by separate instruments, but in such manner as to secure that the same persons shall become the trustees of the conveyance on trust for sale as become the trustees of the settlement of the proceeds of sale.

(2) Where new trustees of a settlement are appointed, a memorandum of the names and addresses of the persons who are for the time being the trustees thereof for the purposes of the Settled Land Act 1925, shall be endorsed on or annexed to the last or only principal vesting instrument by or on behalf of the trustees of the settlement, and such vesting instrument shall, for that purpose, be produced by the person having the possession thereof of the trustees of the settlement when so required.

(3) Where new trustees of a conveyance on trust for sale relating to a legal estate are appointed, a memorandum of the persons who are for the time being the trustees for sale shall be endorsed on or annexed thereto by or on behalf of the trustees of the settlement of the proceeds of sale, and the conveyance shall, for that purpose, be produced by the person having the possession thereof to the last-mentioned trustees when so required.

(4) This section applies only to settlements and dispositions of land. **[226]**

36. Power of appointing new or additional trustees

(1) Where a trustee, either original or substituted, and whether appointed by a court or otherwise, is dead, or remains out of the United Kingdom for more than twelve months, or desires to be discharged from all or any of the trusts or powers reposed in or conferred on him, or refuses or is unfit to act therein, or is incapable of acting therein, or is an infant, then, subject to the restrictions imposed by this Act on the number of trustees,—

    (a) the person or persons nominated for the purpose of appointing new trustees by the instrument, if any, creating the trust; or

    (b) if there is no such person, or no such person able and willing to act, then the surviving or continuing trustees or trustee for the time being, or the personal representatives of the last surviving or continuing trustee;

may, by writing, appoint one or more other persons (whether or not being the persons exercising the power) to be a trustee or trustees in the place of the trustee so deceased remaining out of the United Kingdom, desiring to be discharged, refusing, or being unfit or being incapable, or being an infant, as aforesaid.

(2) Where a trustee has been removed under a power contained in the instrument creating the trust, a new trustee or new trustees may be appointed in the place of the trustee who is removed, as if he were dead, or, in the case of a corporation, as if the corporation desired to be discharged from the trust, and the provisions of this section shall apply accordingly, but subject to the restrictions imposed by this Act on the number of trustees.

(3) Where a corporation being a trustee is or has been dissolved, either before or after the commencement of this Act, then, for the purposes of this section and of any enactment replaced thereby, the corporation shall be deemed

to be and to have been from the date of the dissolution incapable of acting in the trusts or powers reposed in or conferred on the corporation.

(4) The power of appointment given by subsection (1) of this section or any similar previous enactment to the personal representatives of a last surviving or continuing trustee shall be and shall be deemed always to have been exercisable by the executors for the time being (whether original or by representation) of such surviving or continuing trustee who have proved the will of their testator or by the administrators for the time being of such trustee without the concurrence of any executor who has renounced or has not proved.

(5) But a sole or last surviving executor intending to renounce, or all the executors where they all intend to renounce, shall have and shall be deemed always to have had power, at any time before renouncing probate, to exercise the power of appointment given by this section, or by any similar previous enactment, if willing to act for that purpose and without thereby accepting the office of executor.

(6) Where a sole trustee, other than a trust corporation, is or has been originally appointed to act in a trust, or where, in the case of any trust, there are not more than three trustees (none of them being a trust corporation) either original or substituted and whether appointed by the court or otherwise, then and in any such case—

    (*a*) the person or persons nominated for the purpose of appointing new trustees by the instrument, if any, creating the trust; or

    (*b*) if there is no such person, or no such person able and willing to act, then the trustee or trustees for the time being;

may, by writing appoint another person or other persons to be an additional trustee or additional trustees, but it shall not be obligatory to appoint any additional trustee, unless the instrument, if any, creating the trust, or any statutory enactment provides to the contrary, nor shall the number of trustees be increased beyond four by virtue of any such appointment.

(7) Every new trustee appointed under this section as well before as after all the trust property becomes by law, or by assurance, or otherwise, vested in him, shall have the same powers, authorities, and discretions, and may in all respects act as if he had been originally appointed a trustee by the instrument, if any, creating the trust.

(8) The provisions of this section relating to a trustee who is dead include the case of a person nominated trustee in a will but dying before the testator, and those relative to a continuing trustee include a refusing or retiring trustee, if willing to act in the execution of the provisions of this section.

[(9) Where a trustee is incapable, by reason of mental disorder within the meaning of [the Mental Health Act 1983], of exercising his functions as trustee and is also entitled in possession to some beneficial interest in the trust property, no appointment of a new trustee in his place shall be made by virtue of paragraph (*b*) of subsection (1) of this section unless leave to make the appointment has been given by the authority having jurisdiction under [Part VII of the Mental Health Act 1983].]   **[227]**

NOTES

    Sub-s (9): substituted by the Mental Health Act 1959, s 149(1), Sch 7, Part I; words in square brackets substituted by the Mental Health Act 1983, s 148, Sch 4, para 4.

37. Supplemental provisions as to appointment of trustees

(1) On the appointment of a trustee for the whole or any part of trust property—

    (a) the number of trustees may, subject to the restrictions imposed by this Act on the number of trustees, be increased; and

    (b) a separate set of trustees, not exceeding four, may be appointed for any part of the trust property held on trusts distinct from those relating to any other part or parts of the trust property, notwithstanding that no new trustees or trustee are or is to be appointed for other parts of the trust property, and any existing trustee may be appointed or remain one of such separate set of trustees, or, if only one trustee was originally appointed, then, save as hereinafter provided, one separate trustee may be so appointed; and

    (c) it shall not be obligatory, save as hereinafter provided, to appoint more than one new trustee where only one trustee was originally appointed, or to fill up the original number of trustees where more than two trustees were originally appointed, but, except where only one trustee was originally appointed, and a sole trustee when appointed will be able to give valid receipts for all capital money, a trustee shall not be discharged from his trust unless there will be either a trust corporation or at least two individuals to act as trustees to perform the trust; and

    (d) any assurance or thing requisite for vesting the trust property, or any part thereof, in a sole trustee, or jointly in the persons who are the trustees, shall be executed or done.

(2) Nothing in this Act shall authorise the appointment of a sole trustee, not being a trust corporation, where the trustee, when appointed, would not be able to give valid receipts for all capital money arising under the trust. **[228]**

38. Evidence as to a vacancy in a trust

(1) A statement, contained in any instrument coming into operation after the commencement of this Act by which a new trustee is appointed for any purpose connected with land, to the effect that a trustee has remained out of the United Kingdom for more than twelve months or refuses or is unfit to act, or is incapable of acting, or that he is not entitled to a beneficial interest in the trust property in possession, shall, in favour of a purchaser of a legal estate, be conclusive evidence of the matter stated.

(2) In favour of such purchaser any appointment of a new trustee depending on that statement, and any vesting declaration, express or implied, consequent on the appointment, shall be valid. **[229]**

39. Retirement of trustee without a new appointment

(1) Where a trustee is desirous of being discharged from the trust, and after his discharge there will be either a trust corporation or at least two individuals to act as trustees to perform the trust, then, if such trustee as aforesaid by deed declares that he is desirous of being discharged from the trust, and if his co-trustees and such other person, if any, as is empowered to appoint trustees, by deed consent to the discharge of the trustee, and to the vesting in the co-trustees alone of the trust property, the trustee desirous of being discharged shall be deemed to have retired from the trust, and shall, by the deed, be discharged therefrom under this Act, without any new trustee being appointed in his place.

(2) Any assurance or thing requisite for vesting the trust property in the continuing trustees alone shall be executed or done. **[230]**

40. Vesting of trust property in new or continuing trustees

(1) Where by a deed a new trustee is appointed to perform any trust, then—

(*a*) if the deed contains a declaration by the appointor to the effect that any estate or interest in any land subject to the trust, or in any chattel so subject, or right to recover or receive any debt or other thing in action so subject, shall vest in the persons who by virtue of the deed become or are the trustees for performing the trust, the deed shall operate, without any conveyance or assignment, to vest in those persons as joint tenants and for the purposes of the trust the estate interest or right to which the declaration relates; and

(*b*) if the deed is made after the commencement of this Act and does not contain such a declaration, the deed shall, subject to any express provision to the contrary therein contained, operate as if it had contained such a declaration by the appointor extending to all the estates interests and rights with respect to which a declaration could have been made.

(2) Where by a deed a retiring trustee is discharged under the statutory power without a new trustee being appointed, then—

(*a*) if the deed contains such a declaration as aforesaid by the retiring and continuing trustees, and by the other person, if any, empowered to appoint trustees, the deed shall, without any conveyance or assignment, operate to vest in the continuing trustees alone, as joint tenants, and for the purposes of the trust, the estate, interest, or right to which the declaration relates; and

(*b*) if the deed is made after the commencement of this Act and does not contain such a declaration, the deed shall, subject to any express provision to the contrary therein contained, operate as if it had contained such a declaration by such persons as aforesaid extending to all the estates, interests and rights with respect to which a declaration could have been made.

(3) An express vesting declaration, whether made before or after the commencement of this Act, shall, notwithstanding that the estate, interest or right to be vested is not expressly referred to, and provided that the other statutory requirements were or are complied with, operate and be deemed always to have operated (but without prejudice to any express provision to the contrary contained in the deed of appointment or discharge) to vest in the persons respectively referred to in subsections (1) and (2) of this section, as the case may require, such estates, interests and rights as are capable of being and ought to be vested in those persons.

(4) This section does not extend—

(*a*) to land conveyed by way of mortgage for securing money subject to the trust, except land conveyed on trust for securing debentures or debenture stock;

(*b*) to land held under a lease which contains any covenant, condition or agreement against assignment or disposing of the land without licence or consent, unless, prior to the execution of the deed containing expressly or impliedly the vesting declaration, the requisite licence or consent has been obtained, or unless, by virtue of any statute or rule of law, the vesting declaration, express or implied, would not operate as a breach of covenant or give rise to a forfeiture;

(c) to any share, stock, annuity or property which is only transferable in books kept by a company or other body, or in manner directed by or under an Act of Parliament.

In this subsection "lease" includes an underlease and an agreement for a lease or underlease.

(5) For purposes of registration of the deed in any registry, the person or persons making the declaration expressly or impliedly, shall be deemed the conveying party or parties, and the conveyance shall be deemed to be made by him or them under a power conferred by this Act.

(6) This section applies to deeds of appointment or discharge executed on or after the first day of January, eighteen hundred and eighty-two.   **[231]**

PART IV

POWERS OF THE COURT

Appointment of new Trustees

41. Power of court to appoint new trustees

(1) The court may, whenever it is expedient to appoint a new trustee or new trustees, and it is found inexpedient difficult or impracticable so to do without the assistance of the court, make an order appointing a new trustee or new trustees either in substitution for or in addition to any existing trustee or trustees, or although there is no existing trustee.

In particular and without prejudice to the generality of the foregoing provision, the court may make an order appointing a new trustee in substitution for a trustee who . . . is [incapable, by reason of mental disorder within the meaning of [the Mental Health Act 1983], of exercising his functions as trustee], or is a bankrupt, or is a corporation which is in liquidation or has been dissolved.

(2) The power conferred by this section may, in the case of a deed of arrangement within the meaning of the Deeds of Arrangement Act 1914, be exercised either by the High Court or by the court having jurisdiction in bankruptcy in the district in which the debtor resided or carried on business at the date of the execution of the deed.

(3) An order under this section, and any consequential vesting order or conveyance, shall not operate further or otherwise as a discharge to any former or continuing trustee than an appointment of new trustees under any power for that purpose contained in any instrument would have operated.

(4) Nothing in this section gives power to appoint an executor or administrator.   **[232]**

NOTES
Sub-s (1): words omitted repealed by the Criminal Law Act 1967, s 10, Sch 3, Part III; first words in square brackets substituted by the Mental Health Act 1959, s 149(1), Sch 7, Part I, words in square brackets therein substituted by the Mental Health Act 1983, s 148, Sch 4, para 4.

42. Power to authorise remuneration

Where the court appoints a corporation, other than the Public Trustee, to be a trustee either solely or jointly with another person, the court may authorise the corporation to charge such remuneration for its services as trustee as the court may think fit.   **[233]**

43. Powers of new trustee appointed by the Court

Every trustee appointed by a court of competent jurisdiction shall, as well before as after the trust property becomes by law, or by assurance, or otherwise, vested in him, have the same powers, authorities, and discretions, and may in all respects act as if he had been originally appointed a trustee by the instrument, if any, creating the trust.   **[234]**

Vesting Orders

44. Vesting orders of land

In any of the following cases, namely:

    (i) Where the court appoints or has appointed a trustee, or where a trustee has been appointed out of court under any statutory or express power;

    (ii) Where a trustee entitled to or possessed of any land or interest therein, whether by way of mortgage or otherwise, or entitled to a contingent right therein, either solely or jointly with any other person—

        (*a*) is under disability; or

        (*b*) is out of the jurisdiction of the High Court; or

        (*c*) cannot be found, or, being a corporation, has been dissolved;

    (iii) Where it is uncertain who was the survivor of two or more trustees jointly entitled to or possessed of any interest in land;

    (iv) Where it is uncertain whether the last trustee known to have been entitled to or possessed of any interest in land is living or dead;

    (v) Where there is no personal representative of a deceased trustee who was entitled to or possessed of any interest in land, or where it is uncertain who is the personal representative of a deceased trustee who was entitled to or possessed of any interest in land;

    (vi) Where a trustee jointly or solely entitled to or possessed of any interest in land, or entitled to a contingent right therein, has been required, by or on behalf of a person entitled to require a conveyance of the land or interest or a release of the right, to convey the land or interest or to release the right, and has wilfully refused or neglected to convey the land or interest or release the right for twenty-eight days after the date of the requirement;

    (vii) Where land or any interest therein is vested in a trustee whether by way of mortgage or otherwise, and it appears to the court to be expedient;

the court may make an order (in this Act called a vesting order) vesting the land or interest therein in any such person in any such manner and for any such estate or interest as the court may direct, or releasing or disposing of the contingent right to such person as the court may direct:

Provided that—

    (*a*) Where the order is consequential on the appointment of a trustee the land or interest therein shall be vested for such estate as the court may direct in the persons who on the appointment are the trustees; and

    (*b*) Where the order relates to a trustee entitled or formerly entitled jointly with another person, and such trustee is under disability or out of the jurisdiction of the High Court or cannot be found, or being a

corporation has been dissolved, the land interest or right shall be
vested in such other person who remains entitled, either alone or with
any other person the court may appoint.   [235]

45. Orders as to contingent rights of unborn persons

Where any interest in land is subject to a contingent right in an unborn person
or class of unborn persons who, on coming into existence would, in respect,
thereof, become entitled to or possessed of that interest on any trust, the court
may make an order releasing the land or interest therein from the contingent
right, or may make an order vesting in any person the estate or interest to or of
which the unborn person or class of unborn persons would, on coming into
existence, be entitled or possessed in the land.   [236]

46. Vesting order in place of conveyance by infant mortgagee

Where any person entitled to or possessed of any interest in land, or entitled to
a contingent right in land, by way of security for money, is an infant, the court
may make an order vesting or releasing or disposing of the interest in the land
or the right in like manner as in the case of a trustee under disability.   [237]

47. Vesting order consequential on order for sale or mortgage of land

Where any court gives a judgment or makes an order directing the sale or
mortgage of any land, every person who is entitled to or possessed of any interest
in the land, or entitled to a contingent right therein, and is a party to the action
or proceeding in which the judgment or order is given or made or is otherwise
bound by the judgment or order, shall be deemed to be so entitled or possessed,
as the case may be, as a trustee for the purpose of this Act, and the court may, if
it thinks expedient, make an order vesting the land or any part thereof for such
estate or interest as that court thinks fit in the purchaser or mortgagee or in any
other person:

   Provided that, in the case of a legal mortgage, the estate to be vested in the
mortgagee shall be a term of years absolute.   [238]

48. Vesting order consequential on judgement for specific performance, etc

Where a judgment is given for the specific performance of a contract concerning
any interest in land, or for sale or exchange of any interest in land, or generally
where any judgment is given for the conveyance of any interest in land either in
cases arising out of the doctrine of election or otherwise, the court may declare—

   (a) that any of the parties to the action are trustees of any interest in the
       land or any part thereof within the meaning of this Act; or
   (b) that the interests of unborn persons who might claim under any party
       to the action, or under the will or voluntary settlement of any deceased
       person who was during his lifetime a party to the contract or
       transaction concerning which the judgment is given, are the interests
       of persons who, on coming into existence, would be trustees within
       the meaning of this Act;

and thereupon the court may make a vesting order relating to the rights of those
persons, born and unborn, as if they had been trustees.   [239]

49. Effect of vesting order

A vesting order under any of the foregoing provisions shall in the case of a vesting order consequential on the appointment of a trustee, have the same effect—

(*a*) as if the persons who before the appointment were the trustees, if any, had duly executed all proper conveyances of the land for such estate or interest as the court directs; or

(*b*) if there is no such person, or no such person of full capacity, as if such person had existed and been of full capacity and had duly executed all proper conveyances of the land for such estate or interest as the court directs;

and shall in every other case have the same effect as if the trustee or other person or description or class of persons to whose rights or supposed rights the said provisions respectively relate had been an ascertained and existing person of full capacity, and had executed a conveyance or release to the effect intended by the order.   **[240]**

50. Power to appoint person to convey

In all cases where a vesting order can be made under any of the foregoing provisions, the court may, if it is more convenient, appoint a person to convey the land or any interest therein or release the contingent right, and a conveyance or release by that person in conformity with the order shall have the same effect as an order under the appropriate provision.   **[241]**

51. Vesting orders as to stock and things in action

(1) In any of the following cases, namely:—

(i) Where the court appoints or has appointed a trustee, or where a trustee has been appointed out of court under any statutory or express power;

(ii) Where a trustee entitled, whether by way of mortgage or otherwise, alone or jointly with another person to stock or to a thing in action—

    (*a*) is under disability; or

    (*b*) is out of the jurisdiction of the High Court; or

    (*c*) cannot be found, or, being a corporation, has been dissolved;

or

    (*d*) neglects or refuses to transfer stock or receive the dividends or income thereof, or to sue for or recover a thing in action, according to the direction of the person absolutely entitled thereto for twenty-eight days next after a request in writing has been made to him by the person so entitled; or

    (*e*) neglects or refuses to transfer stock or receive the dividends or income thereof, or to sue for or recover a thing in action for twenty-eight days next after an order of the court for that purpose has been served on him;

(iii) Where it is uncertain whether a trustee entitled alone or jointly with another person to stock or to a thing in action is alive or dead;

(iv) Where stock is standing in the name of a deceased person whose personal representative is under disability;

(v) Where stock or a thing in action is vested in a trustee whether by way of mortgage or otherwise and it appears to the court to be expedient;

the court may make an order vesting the right to transfer or call for a transfer of stock, or to receive the dividends or income thereof, or to sue for or recover the thing in action, in any such person as the court may appoint:

Provided that—

(a) Where the order is consequential on the appointment of a trustee, the right shall be vested in the persons who, on the appointment, are the trustees; and

(b) Where the person whose right is dealt with by the order was entitled jointly with another person, the right shall be vested in that last-mentioned person either alone or jointly with any other person whom the court may appoint.

(2) In all cases where a vesting order can be made under this section, the court may, if it is more convenient, appoint some proper person to make or join in making the transfer:

Provided that the person appointed to make or join in making a transfer of stock shall be some proper officer of the bank, or the company or society whose stock is to be transferred.

(3) The person in whom the right to transfer or call for the transfer of any stock is vested by an order of the court under this Act, may transfer the stock to himself or any other person, according to the order, and the Bank of England and all other companies shall obey every order under this section according to its tenor.

(4) After notice in writing of an order under this section it shall not be lawful for the Bank of England or any other company to transfer any stock to which the order relates or to pay any dividends thereon except in accordance with the order.

(5) The court may make declarations and give directions concerning the manner in which the right to transfer any stock or thing in action vested under the provisions of this Act is to be exercised.

(6) The provisions of this Act as to vesting orders shall apply to shares in ships registered under the Acts relating to merchant shipping as if they were stock.   **[242]**

52. Vesting orders of charity property

The powers conferred by this Act as to vesting orders may be exercised for vesting any interest in land, stock, or thing in action in any trustee of a charity or society over which the court would have jurisdiction upon action duly instituted, whether the appointment of the trustee was made by instrument under a power or by the court under its general or statutory jurisdiction.   **[243]**

53. Vesting orders in relation to infants' beneficial interests

Where an infant is beneficially entitled to any property the court may, with a view to the application of the capital or income thereof for the maintenance, education, or benefit of the infant, make an order—

(a) appointing a person to convey such property; or

(*b*) in the case of stock, or a thing in action, vesting in any person the right to transfer or call for a transfer of such stock, or to receive the dividends or income thereof, or to sue for and recover such thing in action, upon such terms as the court may think fit. **[244]**

[54. Jurisdiction in regard to mental patients

(1) Subject to the provisions of this section, the authority having jurisdiction under [Part VII of the Mental Health Act 1983], shall not have power to make any order, or give any direction or authority, in relation to a patient who is a trustee if the High Court has power under this Act to make an order to the like effect.

(2) Where a patient is a trustee and a receiver appointed by the said authority is acting for him or an application for the appointment of a receiver has been made but not determined, then, except as respects a trust which is subject to an order for administration made by the High Court, the said authority shall have concurrent jurisdiction with the High Court in relation to—

(*a*) mortgaged property of which the patient has become a trustee merely by reason of the mortgage having been paid off;
(*b*) matters consequent on the making of provision by the said authority for the exercise of a power of appointing trustees or retiring from a trust;
(*c*) matters consequent on the making of provision by the said authority for the carrying out of any contract entered into by the patient;
(*d*) property to some interest in which the patient is beneficially entitled but which, or some interest in which, is held by the patient under an express, implied or constructive trust.

The Lord Chancellor may make rules with respect to the exercise of the jurisdiction referred to in this subsection.

(3) In this section "patient" means a patient as defined by [section 94 of the Mental Health Act 1983], or a person as to whom powers are [exercisable under section 98 of that Act and have been exercised under that section or section 104 of the Mental Health Act 1959].] **[245]**

NOTES
Substituted by the Mental Health Act 1959, s 149(1), Sch 7, Part I.
Sub-s (1): words in square brackets substituted by the Mental Health Act 1983, s 148, Sch 4, para 4.
Sub-s (3): words in square brackets substituted by the Mental Health Act 1983, s 148, Sch 4, para 4.

55. Orders made upon certain allegations to be conclusive evidence

Where a vesting order is made as to any land under this Act or under [Part VII of the Mental Health Act 1983], as amended by any subsequent enactment, or under any Act relating to lunacy in Northern Ireland, founded on an allegation of any of the following matters namely—

(*a*) the personal incapacity of a trustee or mortgagee; or
(*b*) that a trustee or mortgagee or the personal representative of or other person deriving title under a trustee or mortgagee is out of the jurisdiction of the High Court or cannot be found, or being a corporation has been dissolved; or
(*c*) that it is uncertain which of two or more trustees, or which of two or more persons interested in a mortgage, was the survivor; or

(*d*) that it is uncertain whether the last trustee or the personal
representative of or other person deriving title under a trustee or
mortgagee, or the last surviving person interested in a mortgage is
living or dead: or

(*e*) that any trustee or mortgagee has died intestate without leaving a
person beneficially interested under the intestacy or has died and it is
not known who is his personal representative or the person interested;

the fact that the order has been so made shall be conclusive evidence of the
matter so alleged in any court upon any question as to the validity of the order;
but this section does not prevent the court from directing a reconveyance or
surrender or the payment of costs occasioned by any such order it improperly
obtained.   **[246]**

NOTES
Words in square brackets substituted by the Mental Health Act 1983, s 148, Sch 4, para 4.

56. Application of vesting order to property out of England

The powers of the court to make vesting orders under this Act shall extend to
all property in any part of His Majesty's dominions except Scotland.   **[247]**

Jurisdiction to make other Orders

57. Power of court to authorise dealings with trust property

(1) Where in the management or administration of any property vested in
trustees, any sale, lease, mortgage, surrender, release, or other disposition, or
any purchase, investment, acquisition, expenditure, or other transaction, is in
the opinion of the court expedient, but the same cannot be effected by reason of
the absence of any power for that purpose vested in the trustees by the trust
instrument, if any, or by law, the court may by order confer upon the trustees,
either generally or in any particular instance, the necessary power for the
purpose, on such terms, and subject to such provisions and conditions, if any,
as the court may think fit and may direct in what manner any money authorised
to be expended, and the costs of any transaction, are to be paid or borne as
between capital and income.

(2) The court may, from time to time, rescind or vary any order made under
this section, or may make any new or further order.

(3) An application to the court under this section may be made by the
trustees, or by any of them, or by any person beneficially interested under the
trust.

(4) This section does not apply to trustees of a settlement for the purposes
of the Settled Land Act 1925.   **[248]**

58. Persons entitled to apply for orders

(1) An order under this Act for the appointment of a new trustee or concerning
any interest in land, stock, or thing in action subject to a trust, may be made
on the application of any person beneficially interested in the land, stock, or thing
in action, whether under disability or not, or on the application of any person
duly appointed trustee thereof.

(2) An order under this Act concerning any interest in land, stock, or thing

in action subject to a mortgage may be made on the application of any person beneficially interested in the equity of redemption, whether under disability or not, or of any person interested in the money secured by the mortgage.   **[249]**

59. Power to give judgment in absence of a trustee

Where in any action the court is satisfied that diligent search has been made for any person who, in the character of trustee, is made a defendant in any action, to serve him with a process of the court, and that he cannot be found, the court may hear and determine the action and give judgment therein against that person in his character of a trustee as if he had been duly served, or had entered an appearance in the action, and had also appeared by his counsel and solicitor at the hearing, but without prejudice to any interest he may have in the matters in question in the action in any other character.   **[250]**

60. Power to charge costs on trust estate

The court may order the costs and expenses of and incident to any application for an order appointing a new trustee, or for a vesting order, or of and incident to any such order, or any conveyance or transfer in pursuance thereof, to be raised and paid out of the property in respect whereof the same is made, or out of the income thereof, or to be borne and paid in such manner and by such persons as to the court may seem just.   **[251]**

61. Power to relieve trustee from personal liability

If it appears to the court that a trustee, whether appointed by the court or otherwise, is or may be personally liable for any breach of trust, whether the transaction alleged to be a breach of trust occurred before or after the commencement of this Act, but has acted honestly and reasonably, and ought fairly to be excused for the breach of trust and for omitting to obtain the directions of the court in the matter in which he committed such breach, then the court may relieve him either wholly or partly from personal liability for the same.   **[252]**

62. Power to make beneficiary indemnify for breach of trust

(1) Where a trustee commits a breach of trust at the instigation or request or with the consent in writing of a beneficiary, the court may, if it thinks fit, . . . make such order as to the court seems just, for impounding all or any part of the interest of the beneficiary in the trust estate by way of indemnity to the trustee or persons claiming through him.

(2) This section applies to breaches of trust committed as well before as after the commencement of this Act.   **[253]**

NOTES

   Sub-s (1): words omitted repealed by the Married Women (Restraint upon Anticipation) Act 1949, s 1(4), Sch 2.

Payment into Court

63. Payment into court by trustees

(1) Trustees, or the majority of trustees, having in their hands or under their control money or securities belonging to a trust, may pay the same into court;
   . . .

(2) The receipt or certificate of the proper officer shall be a sufficient discharge to trustees for the money or securities so paid into court.

(3) Where money or securities are vested in any persons as trustees, and the majority are desirous of paying the same into court, but the concurrence of the other or others cannot be obtained, the court may order the payment into court to be made by the majority without the concurrence of the other or others.

(4) Where any such money or securities are deposited with any banker, broker, or other depositary, the court may order payment or delivery of the money or securities to the majority of the trustees for the purpose of payment into court.

(5) Every transfer payment and delivery made in pursuance of any such order shall be valid and take effect as if the same had been made on the authority or by the act of all the persons entitled to the money and securities so transferred, paid, or delivered. **[254]**

NOTES
Sub-s (1): words omitted repealed by the Administration of Justice Act 1965, s 36(4), Sch 3.

[63A. Jurisdiction of County Court

(1) The county court has jurisdiction under the following provisions where the amount or value of the trust estate or fund to be dealt with in the court does not exceed the county court limit—

section 41;

section 42;

section 51;

section 57;

section 60;

section 61;

section 62.

(2) The county court has jurisdiction under the following provisions where the land or the interest or contingent right in land which is to be dealt with in the court forms part of a trust estate which does not exceed in amount or value the county court limit—

section 44;

section 45;

section 46.

(3) The county court has jurisdiction—

(a) under sections 47 and 48 of this Act, where the judgment is given or order is made by the court;

(b) under sections 50 and 56, where a vesting order can be made by the court;

(c) under section 53, where the amount or value of the property to be dealt with in the court does not exceed the county court limit; and (*d*) under section 63 (including power to receive payment of money or securities into court) where the money or securities to be paid into court do not exceed in amount or value the county court limit.

(4) Any reference to the court in section 59 of this Act includes a reference to the county court.

(5) In this section, in its application to any enactment, "the county court limit" means the amount for the time being specified by an Order in Council under section 145 of the County Courts Act 1984 as the county court limit for the purposes of that enactment (or, where no such Order in Council has been made, the corresponding limit specified by Order in Council under section 192 of the County Courts Act 1959).]   [255]

NOTES
Inserted by the County Courts Act 1984, s 148(1), Sch 2, para 1.

PART V

GENERAL PROVISIONS

64. Application of Act to Settled Land Act Trustees

(1) All the powers and provisions contained in this Act with reference to the appointment of new trustees, and the discharge and retirement of trustees, apply to and include trustees for the purposes of the Settled Land Act 1925, and trustees for the purpose of the management of land during a minority, whether such trustees are appointed by the court or by the settlement, or under provisions contained in any instrument.

(2) Where, either before or after the commencement of this Act, trustees of a settlement have been appointed by the court for the purposes of the Settled Land Acts 1882 to 1890, or of the Settled Land Act 1925, then, after the commencement of this Act—

(*a*) the person or persons nominated for the purpose of appointing new trustees by the instrument, if any, creating the settlement, though no trustees for the purposes of the said Acts were thereby appointed; or

(*b*) if there is no such person, or no such person able and willing to act, the surviving or continuing trustees or trustee for the time being for the purposes of the said Acts or the personal representatives of the last surviving or continuing trustee for those purposes,

shall have the powers conferred by this Act to appoint new or additional trustees of the settlement for the purposes of the said Acts.

(3) Appointments of new trustees for the purposes of the said Acts made or expressed to be made before the commencement of this Act by the trustees or trustee or personal representatives referred to in paragraph (*b*) of the last preceding subsection or by the persons referred to in paragraph (*a*) of that subsection are, without prejudice to any order of the court made before such commencement, hereby confirmed.   [256]

66. Indemnity to banks, etc

This Act, and every order purporting to be made under this Act, shall be a complete indemnity to the Bank of England, and to all persons for any acts done pursuant thereto, and it shall not be necessary for the Bank of for any person to inquire concerning the propriety of the order, or whether the court by which the order was made had jurisdiction to make it. [257]

67. Jurisdiction of the "court"

(1) In this Act "the court" means the High Court . . . or the county court, where those courts respectively have jurisdiction.

(2) The procedure under this Act in . . . county courts shall be in accordance with the Acts and rules regulating the procedure of those courts. [258]

NOTES
    Sub-s (1): words omitted repealed by the Courts Act 1971, s 56, Sch 11, Part II.
    Sub-s (2): words omitted repealed by the Courts Act 1971, s 56, Sch 11, Part II.

68. Definitions

[(1)] In this Act, unless the context otherwise requires, the following expressions have the meanings hereby assigned to them respectively, that is to say:—

(1) "Authorised investments" mean investments authorised by the instrument, if any, creating the trust for the investment of money subject to the trust, or by law;

(2) "Contingent right" as applied to land includes a contingent or executory interest, a possibility coupled with an interest, whether the object of the gift or limitation of the interest, or possibility is or is not ascertained, also a right of entry, whether immediate or future, and whether vested or contingent;

(3) "Convey" and "conveyance" as applied to any person include the execution by that person of every necessary or suitable assurance (including an assent) for conveying, assigning, appointing, surrendering, or otherwise transferring or disposing of land whereof he is seised or possessed, or wherein he is entitled to a contingent right, either for his whole estate or for any less estate, together with the performance of all formalities required by law for the validity of the conveyance; "sale" includes an exchange;

(4) "Gazette" means the London Gazette;

(5) "Instrument" includes Act of Parliament;

(6) "Land" includes land of any tenure, and mines and minerals, whether or not severed from the surface, buildings or parts of buildings, whether the division is horizontal, vertical or made in any other way, and other corporeal hereditaments; also a manor, an advowson, and a rent and other incorporeal hereditaments, and an easement, right, privilege, or benefit in, over, or derived from land, but not an undivided share in land; and in this definition "mines and minerals" include any strata or seam of minerals or substances in or under any land, and powers of working and getting the same, but not an undivided share thereof; and "hereditaments" mean real property which under an intestacy occurring before the commencement of this Act might have devolved on an heir;

(7) "Mortgage" and "mortgagee" include a charge or chargee by way of legal mortgage, and relate to every estate and interest regarded in equity as merely a security for money, and every person deriving title under the original mortgagee;

(8) . . .

(9) "Personal representative" means the executor, original or by representation, or administrator for the time being of a deceased person;

(10) "Possession" includes receipt of rents and profits or the right to receive the same, if any; "income" includes rents and profits; and "possessed" applies to receipt of income of and to any vested estate less than a life interest in possession or in expectancy in any land;

(11) "Property" includes real and personal property, and any estate share and interest in any property, real or personal, and any debt, and any thing in action, and any other right or interest, whether in possession or not;

(12) "Rights" include estates and interests;

(13) "Securities" include stocks, funds, and shares; . . . and "securities payable to bearer" include securities transferable by delivery or by delivery and endorsement;

(14) "Stock" includes fully paid up shares, and so far as relates to vesting orders made by the court under this Act, includes any fund, annuity, or security transferable in books kept by any company or society, or by instrument of transfer either alone or accompanied by other formalities, and any share or interest therein;

(15) "Tenant for life," "statutory owner," "settled land," "settlement," "trust instrument," "trustees of the settlement" . . . "term of years absolute" and "vesting instrument" have the same meanings as in the Settled Land Act 1925, and "entailed interest" has the same meaning as in the Law of Property Act 1925;

(16) "Transfer" in relation to stock or securities, includes the performance and execution of every deed, power of attorney, act, and thing on the part of the transferor to effect and complete the title in the transferee;

(17) "Trust" does not include the duties incident to an estate conveyed by way of mortgage, but with this exception the expressions "trust" and "trustee" extend to implied and constructive trusts, and to cases where the trustee has a beneficial interest in the trust property, and to the duties incident to the office of a personal representative, and "trustee" where the context admits, includes a personal representative, and "new trustee" includes an additional trustee;

(18) "Trust corporation" means the Public Trustee or a corporation either appointed by the court in any particular case to be a trustee, or entitled by rules made under subsection (3) of section four of the Public Trustee Act 1906, to act as custodian trustee;

(19) "Trust for sale" in relation to land means an immediate binding trust for sale, whether or not exercisable at the request or with the consent of any person, and with or without power at discretion to postpone the sale; "trustees for sale" mean the persons (including a personal representative) holding land on trust for sale;

(20) "United Kingdom" means Great Britain and Northern Ireland.

[(2) Any reference in this Act to paying money or securities into court shall be construed as referring to paying the money or transferring or depositing the securities into or in the Supreme Court or into or in any other court that has jurisdiction, and any reference in this Act to payment of money or securities into court shall be construed—

(*a*) with reference to an order of the High Court, as referring to payment of the money or transfer or deposit of the securities into or in the Supreme Court; and

(*b*) with reference to an order of any other court, as referring to payment of the money or transfer or deposit of the securities into or in that court.]   **[259]**

NOTES

Sub-s (1): para (8), and words omitted from para (13) repealed by the Administration of Justice Act 1965, s 17(1), Sch 1: words omitted from para (15) repealed by the Mental Health Act 1959 s 149(2), Sch, Part I.

Sub-s (2): added by the Administration of Justice Act 1965, s 17(1), Sch 1.

69. Application of Act

(1) This Act, except where otherwise expressly provided, applies to trusts including, so far as this Act applies thereto, executorships and administratorships constituted or created either before or after the commencement of this Act.

(2) The powers conferred by this Act on trustees are in addition to the powers conferred by the instrument, if any, creating the trust, but those powers, unless otherwise stated, apply if and so far only as a contrary intention is not expressed in the instrument, if any, creating the trust, and have effect subject to the terms of that instrument.

(3) ...   **[260]**

NOTES

Sub-s (3): repealed by the Statute Law (Repeals) Act 1978.

70. Enactments repealed

... without prejudice to the provisions of section thirty-eight of the Interpretation Act 1889:

(*a*) Nothing in this repeal shall affect any vesting order or appointment made or other thing done under any enactment so repealed, and any order or appointment so made may be revoked or varied in like manner as if it has been made under this Act;

(*b*) References in any document to any enactment repealed by this Act shall be construed as references to this Act or to the corresponding enactment in this Act.   **[261]**

NOTES

Words omitted repealed by the Statute Law Revision Act 1950.

71. Short title, commencement, extent

(1) This Act may be cited as the Trustee Act, 1925.

(2) ...

(3) This Act, except where otherwise expressly provided, extends to England and Wales only.

(4) The provisions of this Act bind the Crown.   **[262]**

NOTES

Sub-s (2): repealed by the Statute Law Revision Act 1950.

LAW OF PROPERTY ACT 1925
(c 20)

ARRANGEMENT OF SECTIONS

PART I
GENERAL PRINCIPLES AS TO LEGAL ESTATES, EQUITABLE INTERESTS AND POWERS

Section   Para

PART II

CONTRACTS, CONVEYANCES AND OTHER INSTRUMENTS

Contracts

Conveyances and other Instruments

Covenants

PART III

MORTGAGES, RENTCHARGES AND POWERS OF ATTORNEY

Mortgages

PART IV

EQUITABLE INTERESTS AND THINGS IN ACTION

PART V

LEASES AND TENANCIES

An Act to consolidate the enactments relating to Conveyancing and the Law of Property in England and Wales   **[9 April 1925]**

PART I

GENERAL PRINCIPLES AS TO LEGAL ESTATES, EQUITABLE INTERESTS AND POWERS

1. Legal estates and equitable interests

(1) The only estates in land which are capable of subsisting or of being conveyed or created at law are—

(*a*) An estate in fee simple absolute in possession;

(*b*) A term of years absolute.

(2) The only interests or charges in or over land which are capable of subsisting or of being conveyed or created at law are—

(*a*) An easement, right, or privilege in or over land for an interest equivalent to an estate in fee simple absolute in possession or a term of years absolute;

(*b*) A rentcharge in possession issuing out of or charged on land being either perpetual or for a term of years absolute;

(*c*) A charge by way of legal mortgage;

(*d*) . . . and any other similar charge on land which is not created by an instrument;

(*e*) Rights of entry exercisable over or in respect of a legal term of years absolute, or annexed, for any purpose, to a legal rentcharge.

(3) All other estates, interests, and charges in or over land take effect as equitable interests.

(4) The estates, interests, and charges which under this section are authorised to subsist or to be conveyed or created at law are (when subsisting or conveyed or created at law) in this Act referred to as "legal estates," and have the same incidents as legal estates subsisting at the commencement of this Act; and the owner of a legal estate is referred to as "an estate owner" and his legal estate is referred to as his estate.

(5) A legal estate may subsist concurrently with or subject to any other legal estate in the same land in like manner as it could have done before the commencement of this Act.

(6) A legal estate is not capable of subsisting or of being created in an undivided share in land or of being held by an infant.

(7) Every power of appointment over, or power to convey or charge land or any interest therein, whether created by a statute or other instrument or implied by law, and whether created before or after the commencement of this Act (not being a power vested in a legal mortgagee or an estate owner in right of his estate and exercisable by him or by another person in his name and on his behalf), operates only in equity.

(8) Estates, interests, and charges in or over land which are not legal estates are in this Act referred to as "equitable interests," and powers which by this Act are to operate in equity only are in this Act referred to as "equitable powers."

(9) The provisions in any statute or other instrument requiring land to be conveyed to uses shall take effect as directions that the land shall (subject to creating or reserving thereout any legal estate authorised by this Act which may be required) be conveyed to a person of full age upon the requisite trusts.

(10) The repeal of the Statute of Uses (as amended) does not affect the operation thereof in regard to dealings taking effect before the commencement of this Act. **[263]**

NOTES

Sub-s (2): words omitted repealed by the Finance Act 1963, s 73(8)(*b*), Sch 14 and the Tithe Act 1936, s 48(3), Sch 9.

2. Conveyances overreaching certain equitable interests and powers

(1) A conveyance to a purchaser of a legal estate in land shall overreach any equitable interest or power affecting that estate, whether or not he has notice thereof, if—

    (i) the conveyance is made under the powers conferred by the Settled Land Act 1925 or any additional powers conferred by a settlement, and the equitable interest or power is capable of being overreached thereby, and the statutory requirements respecting the payment of capital money arising under the settlement are complied with;

    (ii) the conveyance is made by trustees for sale and the equitable interest or power is at the date of the conveyance capable of being overreached by such trustees under the provisions of sub-section (2) of this section or independently of that sub-section, and the statutory requirements respecting the payment of capital money arising under a disposition upon trust for sale are complied with;

    (iii) the conveyance is made by a mortgagee or personal representative in the exercise of his paramount powers, and the equitable interest or power is capable of being overreached by such conveyance, and any capital money arising from the transaction is paid to the mortgagee or personal representative;

    (iv) the conveyance is made under an order of the court and the equitable interest or power is bound by such order, and any capital money arising from the transaction is paid into, or in accordance with the order of, the court.

(2) [Where the legal estate affected is subject to a trust for sale, then if at the date of a conveyance made after the commencement of this Act under the trust for sale or the powers conferred on the trustees for sale, the trustees (whether original or substituted) are either—]

    (*a*) two or more individuals approved or appointed by the court or the successors in office of the individuals so approved or appointed; or

    (*b*) a trust corporation,

any equitable interest or power having priority to the trust for sale] shall, notwithstanding any stipulation to the contrary, be overreached by the conveyance, and shall, according to its priority, take effect as if created or arising by means of a primary trust affecting the proceeds of sale and the income of the land until sale.

(3) The following equitable interests and powers are excepted from the operation of subsection (2) of this section, namely—

    (i) Any equitable interest protected by a deposit of documents relating to the legal estate affected;

    (ii) The benefit of any covenant or agreement restrictive of the user of land;

      (iii) Any easement, liberty, or privilege over or affecting land and being merely an equitable interest (in this Act referred to as an "equitable easement");

      (iv) The benefit of any contract (in this Act referred to as an "estate contract") to convey or create a legal estate, including a contract conferring either expressly or by statutory implication a valid option to purchase, a right of pre-emption, or any other like right;

      (v) Any equitable interest protected by registration under the Land Charges Act 1925 other than—

          (*a*) an annuity within the meaning of Part II of that Act;

          (*b*) a limited owner's charge or a general equitable charge within the meaning of that Act.

(4) Subject to the protection afforded by this section to the purchaser of a legal estate, nothing contained in this section shall deprive a person entitled to an equitable charge of any of his rights or remedies for enforcing the same.

(5) So far as regards the following interests, created before the commencement of this Act (which accordingly are not within the provisions of the Land Charges Act 1925), namely—

    (*a*) the benefit of any covenant or agreement restrictive of the user of the land;

    (*b*) any equitable easement;

    (*c*) the interest under a puisne mortgage within the meaning of the Land Charges Act 1925 unless and until acquired under a transfer made after the commencement of this Act;

    (*d*) the benefit of an estate contract, unless and until the same is acquired under a conveyance made after the commencement of this Act;

a purchaser of a legal estate shall only take subject thereto if he has notice thereof, and the same are not overreached under the provisions contained or in the manner referred to this section. **[264]**

NOTES

    Sub-s (2): words in square brackets substituted by the Law of Property (Amendment) Act 1926, s 7, Schedule.

3. Manner of giving effect to equitable interests and powers

(1) All equitable interests and powers in or over land shall be enforceable against the estate owner of the legal estate affected in manner following (that is to say):—

    (*a*) Where the legal estate affected is settled land, the tenant for life or statutory owner shall be bound to give effect to the equitable interests and powers in manner provided by the Settled Land Act 1925;

    (*b*) Where the legal estate affected is vested in trustees for sale—

      (i) The trustees shall stand possessed of the net proceeds of sale after payment of costs and of the net rents and profits of the land until sale after payment of rates, taxes, costs of insurance, repairs, and other outgoings, upon such trusts and subject to such powers and provisions as may be requisite for giving effect to the equitable interests and powers affecting the same respectively, of which they have notice, and whether created before or after the disposition upon trust for sale, according to their respective priorities:

(ii) Where, by reason of the exercise of any equitable power or under any trust affecting the proceeds of sale, any principal sum is required to be raised, or any person of full age becomes entitled to require a legal estate in the land to be vested in him in priority to the trust for sale, then, unless the claim is satisfied out of the net proceeds of sale, the trustees for sale shall (if so requested in writing) be bound to transfer or create such legal estates, to take effect in priority to the trust for sale, as may be required for raising the money by way of legal mortgage or for giving legal effect to the rights of the person so entitled:
Provided that, if the proceeds of sale are held in trust for persons of full age in undivided shares absolutely free from incumbrances affecting undivided shares, those persons cannot require the land to be conveyed to them in undivided shares, but may (subject to effect being given by way of legal mortgage to incumbrances affecting the entirety) require the same to be vested in any of them (not exceeding four) as joint tenants on trust for sale; and if the conveyance purports to transfer the land to any of them in undivided shares or to more than four such persons, it shall operate only as a transfer to them or (if more than four) to the four first named therein as joint tenants on trust for sale:

(c) Where the legal estate affected is neither settled land nor vested in trustees for sale, the estate owner shall be bound to give effect to the equitable interests and powers affecting his estate of which he has notice according to their respective priorities. This provision does not affect the priority or powers of a legal mortgagee, or the powers of personal representatives for purposes of administration.

(2) Effect may be given by means of a legal mortgage to an agreement for a mortgage, charge or lien (whether or not arising by operation of law) if the agreement, charge or lien ought to have priority over the trust for sale.

(3) Where, by reason . . . of an equitable right of entry taking effect, or for any other reason, a person becomes entitled to require a legal estate to be vested in him, then and in any such case the estate owner whose estate is affected shall be bound to convey or create such legal estate as the case may require.

(4) If any question arises whether any and what legal estate ought to be transferred or created as aforesaid, any person interested may apply to the court for directions in the manner provided by this Act.

(5) If the trustees for sale or other estate owners refuse or neglect for one month after demand to transfer or create any such legal estate, or if by reason of their being out of the United Kingdom or being unable to be found, or by reason of the dissolution of a corporation, or for any other reason, the court is satisfied that the transaction cannot otherwise be effected, or cannot be effected without undue delay or expense, the court may, on the application of any person interested, make a vesting order transferring or creating a legal estate in the manner provided by this Act.

(6) This section does not affect a purchaser of a legal estate taking free from an equitable interest or power.

[(7) The county court has jurisdiction under this section where the land which is to be dealt with in the court does not exceed [£30,000] in capital value . . .]   [265]

NOTES
   Sub-s (3): words omitted repealed by the Reverter of Sites Act 1987, s 8(2), (3), Schedule.
   Sub-s (7): added by the County Courts Act 1984, s 148(1), Sch 2, para 2; sum in square brackets
substituted and words omitted repealed by the High Court and County Courts Jurisdiction Order
1991, SI 1991 No 724, art 2(8), Schedule.

4. Creation and disposition of equitable interests

(1) Interests in land validly created or arising after the commencement of this
Act, which are not capable of subsisting as legal estates, shall take effect as
equitable interests, and, save as otherwise expressly provided by statute,
interests in land which under the Statute of Uses or otherwise could before the
commencement of this Act have been created as legal interests, shall be capable
of being created as equitable interests:

Provided that, after the commencement of this Act (and save as hereinafter
expressly enacted), an equitable interest in land shall only be capable of being
validly created in any case in which an equivalent equitable interest in property
real or personal could have been validly created before such commencement.

(2) All rights and interests in land may be disposed of, including—

 (a) a contingent, executory or future equitable interest in any land, or a
      possibility coupled with an interest in any land, whether or not the
      object of the gift or limitation of such interest or possibility be
      ascertained;
 (b) a right of entry, into or upon land whether immediate or future, and
      whether vested or contingent.

(3) All rights of entry affecting a legal estate which are exercisable on
condition broken or for any other reason may after the commencement of this
Act, be made exercisable by any person and the persons deriving title under
him, but, in regard to an estate in fee simple (not being a rentcharge held for a
legal estate) only within the period authorised by the rule relating to
perpetuities.   **[266]**

5. Satisfied terms, whether created out of freehold or leasehold land to cease

(1) Where the purposes of a term of years created or limited at any time out of
freehold land, become satisfied either before or after the commencement of this
Act (whether or not that term either by express declaration or by construction
of law becomes attendant upon the freehold reversion) it shall merge in the
reversion expectant thereon and shall cease accordingly.

(2) Where the purposes of a term of years created or limited, at any time,
out of leasehold land, become satisfied after the commencement of this Act,
that term shall merge in the reversion expectant thereon and shall cease
accordingly.

(3) Where the purposes are satisfied only as respects part of the land
comprised in a term, this section shall have effect as if a separate term had been
created in regard to that part of the land.   **[267]**

6. Saving of lessors' and lessees' covenants

(1) Nothing in this Part of this Act affects prejudicially the right to enforce any
lessor's or lessee's covenants, agreements or conditions (including a valid option
to purchase or right of pre-emption over the reversion), contained in any such

instrument as is in this section mentioned, the benefit or burden of which runs with the reversion or the term.

(2) This section applies where the covenant, agreement or condition is contained in any instrument—

   (*a*) creating a term of years absolute, or
   (*b*) varying the rights of the lessor or lessee under the instrument creating the term.   **[268]**

7. Saving of certain legal estates and statutory powers

(1) A fee simple which, by virtue of the Lands Clauses Acts, . . . or any similar statute, is liable to be divested, is for the purposes of this Act a fee simple absolute, and remains liable to be divested as if this Act had not been passed, [and a fee simple subject to a legal or equitable right of entry or re-entry is for the purposes of this Act a fee simple absolute].

(2) A fee simple vested in a corporation which is liable to determine by reason of the dissolution of the corporation is, for the purposes of this Act, a fee simple absolute.

(3) The provisions of—

   (*a*) . . . ;
   (*b*) the Friendly Societies Act 1896, in regard to land to which that Act applies;
   (*c*) any other statutes conferring special facilities or prescribing special modes (whether by way of registered memorial or otherwise) for disposing of or acquiring land, or providing for the vesting (by conveyance or otherwise) of the land in trustees or any person, or the holder for the time being of an office or any corporation sole or aggregate (including the Crown);

shall remain in full force.

This subsection does not authorise an entailed interest to take effect otherwise than as an equitable interest.

(4) Where any such power for disposing of or creating a legal estate is exercisable by a person who is not the estate owner, the power shall, when practicable, be exercised in the name and on behalf of the estate owner.   **[269]**

NOTES
   Sub-s (1): words omitted repealed by the Reverter of Sites Act 1987, s 8(3), Schedule; words in square brackets added by the Law of Property (Amendment) Act 1926, s 7, Schedule.
   Sub-s (3): words omitted repealed by the Criminal Justice Act 1948, s 83, Sch 10.

8. Saving of certain legal powers to lease

(1) All leases or tenancies at a rent for a term of years absolute authorised to be granted by a mortgagor or mortgagee or by the Settled Land Act 1925, or any other statute (whether or not extended by any instrument) may be granted in the name and on behalf of the estate owner by the person empowered to grant the same, whether being an estate owner or not, with the same effect and priority as if this Part of this Act had not been passed; but this section does not (except as respects the usual qualified covenant for quiet enjoyment) authorise any person granting a lease in the name of an estate owner to impose any personal liability on him.

(2) Where a rentcharge is held for a legal estate, the owner thereof may

under the statutory power or under any corresponding power, create a legal term of years absolute for securing or compelling payment of the same; but in other cases terms created under any such power shall, unless and until the estate owner of the land charged gives legal effect to the transaction, takes effect only as equitable interests. **[270]**

9. Vesting orders and dispositions of legal estates operating as conveyances by an estate owner

(1) Every such order, declaration, or conveyance as is hereinafter mentioned, namely—

- (a) every vesting order made by any court or other competent authority;
- (b) every vesting declaration (express or implied) under any statutory power;
- (c) every vesting instrument made by the trustees of a settlement or other persons under the provisions of the Settled Land Act 1925;
- (d) every conveyance by a person appointed for the purpose under an order of the court or authorised under any statutory power to convey in the name or on behalf of an estate owner;
- (e) every conveyance made under any power reserved or conferred by this Act,

which is made or executed for the purpose of vesting, conveying, or creating a legal estate, shall operate to convey or create the legal estate disposed of in like manner as if the same has been a conveyance executed by the estate owner of the legal estate to which the order, declaration, vesting instrument, or conveyance relates.

(2) Where the order, declaration, or conveyance is made in favour of a purchaser, the provisions of this Act relating to a conveyance of a legal estate to a purchaser shall apply thereto.

(3) The provisions of the Trustee Act 1925, relating to vesting orders and orders appointing a person to convey shall apply to all vesting orders authorised to be made by this Part of this Act. **[271]**

10. Title to be shown to legal estates

(1) Where title is shown to a legal estate in land, it shall be deemed not necessary or proper to include in the abstract of title an instrument relating only to interests or powers which will be over-reached by the conveyance of the estate to which title is being shown; but nothing in this Part of this Act affects the liability of any person to disclose an equitable interest or power which will not be so over-reached, or to furnish an abstract of any instrument creating or affecting the same.

(2) A solicitor delivering an abstract framed in accordance with this Part of this Act shall not incur any liability on account of an omission to include therein an instrument which, under this section, is to be deemed not necessary or proper to be included, nor shall any liability be implied by reason of the inclusion of any such instrument. **[272]**

12. Limitation and Prescription Acts

Nothing in this Part of this Act affects the operation of any statute, or of the general law for the limitation of actions or proceedings relating to land or with reference to the acquisition of easements or rights over or in respect of land.
[273]

13. Effect of possession of documents

This Act shall not prejudicially affect the right or interest of any person arising out of or consequent on the possession by him of any documents relating to a legal estate in land, nor affect any question arising out of or consequent upon any omission to obtain or any other absence of possession by any person of any documents relating to a legal estate in land. **[274]**

14. Interests of persons in possession

This Part of this Act shall not prejudicially affect the interest of any person in possession or in actual occupation of land to which he may be entitled in right of such possession or occupation. **[275]**

15. Presumption that parties are of full age

The persons expressed to be parties to any conveyance shall, until the contrary is proved, be presumed to be of full age at the date thereof. **[276]**

Death Duties

16. Liability for death duties

(1) A personal representative shall be accountable for all death duties which may become leviable or payable on the death of the deceased in respect of land (including settled land) which devolves upon him by virtue of any statute or otherwise.

(2) In every other case the estate owner (other than a purchaser who acquires a legal estate after the charge for death duties has attached and free from such charge), shall be accountable for all the duties aforesaid which become leviable or payable in respect of his estate in the land or any interest therein capable of being overreached by his conveyance, being a conveyance to a purchaser made under the Settled Land Act 1925, or pursuant to a trust for sale.

(3) For the purpose of raising the duty, and the costs of raising the same, the personal representative or other person accountable as aforesaid shall have all the powers which are by any statute conferred for raising the duty.

(4) Nothing in this Act shall alter any duty payable in respect of land, or impose any new duty thereon, or affect the remedies of the Commissioners of Inland Revenue against any person other than a purchaser or a person deriving title under him.

(5) Notwithstanding that any duties are by this section made payable by the personal representative or other person aforesaid, nothing in this Part of this Act shall affect the liability of the persons beneficially interested or their respective interests in respect of any duty and they shall accordingly account for or repay the same and any interest and costs attributable thereto to the said Commissioners or to the personal representative or other person accountable as aforesaid, as the case may require.

(6) Nothing in this Part of this Act shall impose on a personal representative, tenant for life, statutory owner, trustee for sale, or other person in a fiduciary position, as such, any liability for payment of duty, in excess of the assets (including land) vested in him or in the trustees of the settlement which may for the time being be available in his hands or in the hands of such trustees for the payment of the duty or which would have been so available but for his or their own neglect or default or impose a charge for duties on leasehold land, or render a mortgagee liable in respect of any charge for duties which is not paramount to his mortgage.

(7) The said Commissioners, on being satisfied that a personal representative or other person accountable has paid or commuted or will pay or commute all death duties for which he is accountable in respect of the land or any part thereof, shall if required by him, give a certificate to that effect, which shall discharge from any further claim for such duty the land to which the certificate extends, and the production of such certificate to the land registrar or other proper officer shall be a sufficient authority to enable him to cancel any land charge registered in respect of the duty so far as it affects the land to which the certificate extends. **[277]**

NOTES
Repealed with savings by the Finance Act 1975, ss 59(5), Sch 13, Part I.

17. Protection of purchasers from liability for death duties

(1) Where a charge in respect of death duties is not registered as a land charge, a purchaser of a legal estate shall take free therefrom, unless the charge for duties attached before the commencement of this Act and the purchaser had notice of the facts giving rise to the charge.

(2) Where a charge in respect of death duties is not registered as a land charge, the person who conveys a legal estate to a purchaser, and the proceeds of sale, funds, and other property (if any) derived from the conveyance and the income thereof shall (subject as in this Act provided) be or remain liable in respect of and stand charged with the payment of the death duties the charge for which is over-reached by the conveyance, together with any interest payable in respect of the same.

(3) Notwithstanding that any death duties may be payable by instalments, on a conveyance of a legal estate by way of sale exchange or legal mortgage all death duties payable in respect of the land dealt with and remaining unpaid shall, if the charge for the duties is over-reached by such conveyance, immediately become payable and carry interest at the rate of [8] [11] pounds per centum per annum [rate applicable under section 178 of the Finance Act 1989] from the date of the conveyance:

Provided that, where by reason of this subsection an amount is paid or becomes payable for duties and interest in excess of the amount which would have been payable if the duties had continued to be paid by instalments, such excess shall be repaid or allowed as a deduction by the Commissioners of Inland Revenue.

(4) Except in the case of a conveyance to a purchaser, a conveyance shall take effect subject to any subsisting charge or liability for payment of the duties and interest, if any, notwithstanding that the charge for duties may not have been registered.

(5) This section does not apply to registered land. **[278]**

NOTES
Repealed with savings by the Finance Act 1975, ss 52(2), 59(5), Sch 13, Part I.
Sub-s (3): first figure in square brackets substituted with respect to interest accruing on or after 6 August 1988, by the Estate Duty (Interest on Unpaid Duty) Order 1988, SI 1988 No 1276, art 2; second figure in square brackets substituted with respect to interest accruing on or after 6 July 1989, by the Estate Duty (Interest on Unpaid Duty) Order 1989, SI 1989 No 998, art 2; words from "rate" where it first appears to "annum" substituted by words in square brackets immediately following in relation to periods beginning on or after 18 August 1989, by the Finance Act 1989, s 179.

18. Application of capital money in discharge of death duties

(1) Capital money liable to be laid out in the purchase of land to be settled in the same manner as the land in respect of which any death duties may have become payable, and personal estate held on the same trusts as the proceeds of sale of land,

being land held on trust for sale in respect of which any such duties may have become payable, may, by the direction of the tenant for life, statutory owner, or trustee for sale who is accountable, and although the duty is only payable in respect of an interest which is or is capable of being over-reached by a conveyance to a purchaser, be applied in discharging all or any of the duties aforesaid and the costs of discharging the same.

(2) Where the duties would not, except by virtue of the last subsection, be payable out of the capital money or personal estate aforesaid—

(a) the amount so paid shall be repaid by the person liable for the duty to the trustees of the settlement or the trustees for sale by the like instalments and at the like rate of interest by and at which the unpaid duty and the interest thereon might have been paid, or, where the land has been conveyed to a purchaser, would have been paid if the land had not been so conveyed;

(b) the interest of the person so liable, remaining subject to the settlement of the land or of the proceeds of sale, shall stand charged with the repayment of the instalments and the interest aforesaid;

(c) the trustees of the settlement or the trustees for sale shall be entitled to recover and receive any excess of duty which may become repayable by the said Commissioners. **[279]**

NOTES

Repealed with savings by the Finance Act 1975, ss 52(2), 59(5), Sch 13, Part I.

Infants and Lunatics

19. Effect of conveyances of legal estates to infants

(1) A conveyance of a legal estate in land to an infant alone or to two or more persons jointly both or all of whom are infants, shall have such operation as is provided for in the Settled Land Act 1925.

(2) A conveyance of a legal estate in land to an infant, jointly with one or more other persons of full age, shall operate to vest the legal estate in the other person or persons on the statutory trusts, but not so as to sever any joint tenancy in the net proceeds of sale or in the rents and profits until sale, or affect the right of a tenant for life or statutory owner to have settled land vested in him.

(3) The foregoing provisions of this section do not apply to conveyances on trust or by way of mortgage.

(4) A conveyance of a legal estate to an infant alone or to two or more persons jointly, both or all of whom are infants, on any trusts, shall operate as a declaration of trust and shall not be effectual to pass any legal estate.

(5) A conveyance of a legal estate in land to an infant jointly with one or more other persons of full age on any trusts shall operate as if the infant had not been named therein, but without prejudice to any beneficial interest in the land intended to be thereby provided for the infant.

(6) A grant or transfer of a legal mortgage of land to an infant shall operate only as an agreement for valuable consideration to execute a proper conveyance when the infant attains full age, and in the meantime to hold any beneficial interest in the mortgage debt in trust for the persons for whose benefit the conveyance was intended to be made:

Provided that, if the conveyance is made to the infant and another person or other persons of full age, it shall operate as if the infant had not been named therein, but without prejudice to any beneficial interest in the mortgage debt intended to be thereby provided for the infant.   **[280]**

20. Infants not to be appointed trustees

The appointment of an infant to be a trustee in relation to any settlement or trust shall be void, but without prejudice to the power to appoint a new trustee to fill the vacancy.   **[281]**

21. Receipts by married infants

A married infant shall have power to give valid receipts for all income (including statutory accumulations of income made during the minority) to which the infant may be entitled in like manner as if the infant were of full age.   **[282]**

[22. Conveyances on behalf of persons suffering from mental disorder and as to land held by them on trust for sale

(1) Where a legal estate in land (whether settled or not) is vested in a person suffering from mental disorder, either solely or jointly with any other person or persons, his receiver or (if no receiver is acting for him) any person authorised in that behalf shall, under an order of the authority having jurisdiction under [Part VII of the Mental Health Act 1983], or of the court, or under any statutory power, make or concur in making all requisite dispositions for conveying or creating a legal estate in his name and on his behalf.

(2) If land held on trust for sale is vested, either solely or jointly with any other person or persons, in a person who is incapable, by reason of mental disorder, of exercising his functions as trustee, a new trustee shall be appointed in the place of that person, or he shall be otherwise discharged from the trust, before the legal estate is dealt with under the trust for sale or under the powers vested in the trustees for sale.]   **[283]**

NOTES
   Substituted by the Mental Health Act 1959, s 149(1), Sch 7, Part I.
   Sub-s (1): words in square brackets substituted by the Mental Health Act 1983, s 148, Sch 4, para 5.

Dispositions on Trust for Sale

23. Duration of trusts for sale

Where land has, either before or after the commencement of this Act, become subject to an express or implied trust for sale, such trust shall, so far as regards the safety and protection of any purchaser thereunder, be deemed to be subsisting until the land has been conveyed to or under the direction of the persons interested in the proceeds of sale.

This section applies to sales whether made before or after the commencement of this Act, but operates without prejudice to an order of any court restraining a sale.   **[284]**

24. Appointment of trustees of dispositions on trust for sale

(1) The persons having power to appoint new trustees of a conveyance of land on trust for sale shall be bound to appoint the same persons (if any) who are for the time being trustees of the settlement of the proceeds of sale, but a purchaser

shall not be concerned to see whether the proper persons are appointed to be trustees of the conveyance of the land.

(2) This section applies whether the settlement of the proceeds of sale or the conveyance on trust for sale comes into operation before or after the commencement of this Act.   [285]

25. Power to postpone sale

(1) A power to postpone sale shall, in the case of every trust for sale of land, be implied unless a contrary intention appears.

(2) Where there is a power to postpone the sale, then (subject to any express direction to the contrary in the instrument, if any, creating the trust for sale) the trustees for sale shall not be liable in any way for postponing the sale, in the exercise of their discretion, for any indefinite period; nor shall a purchaser of a legal estate be concerned in any case with any directions respecting the postponement of a sale.

(3) The foregoing provisions of this section apply whether the trust for sale is created before or after the commencement or by virtue of this Act.

(4) Where a disposition or settlement coming into operation after the commencement of this Act contains a trust either to retain or sell land the same shall be construed as a trust to sell the land with power to postpone the sale.

[286]

26. Consents to the execution of a trust for sale

(1) If the consent of more than two persons is by the disposition made requisite to the execution of a trust for sale of land, then, in favour of a purchaser, the consent of any two of such persons to the execution of the trust or to the exercise of any statutory or other powers vested in the trustees for sale shall be deemed sufficient.

(2) Where the person whose consent to the execution of any such trust or power is expressed to be required in a disposition is not sui juris or becomes subject to disability, his consent shall not, in favour of a purchaser, be deemed to be requisite to the execution of the trust or the exercise of the power; but the trustees shall, in any such case, obtain the separate consent of the parent or testamentary or other guardian of an infant or of the ... receiver (if any) of a [person suffering from mental disorder].

[(3) Trustees for sale shall so far as practicable consult the persons of full age for the time being beneficially interested in possession in the rents and profits of the land until sale, and shall, so far as consistent with the general interest of the trust, give effect to the wishes of such persons, or, in the case of dispute, of the majority (according to the value of their combined interests) of such persons, but a purchaser shall not be concerned to see that the provisions of this subsection have been complied with.

In the case of a trust for sale, not being a trust for sale created by or in pursuance of the powers conferred by this or any other Act, this subsection shall not apply unless the contrary intention appears in the disposition creating the trust.]

(4) This section applies whether the trust for sale is created before or after the commencement or by virtue of this Act.   [287]

Sub-s (2): words omitted repealed and words in square brackets substituted by the Mental Health Act 1959, s 149(1), Sch 7, Part I.
Sub-s (3): substituted by the Law of Property (Amendment) Act 1926, s 7, Schedule.

27. Purchaser not to be concerned with the trusts of the proceeds of sale which are to be paid to two or more trustees or to a trust corporation

(1) A purchaser of a legal estate from trustees for sale shall not be concerned with the trusts affecting the proceeds of sale of land subject to a trust for sale (whether made to attach to such proceeds by virtue of this Act or otherwise), or affecting the rents and profits of the land until sale, whether or not those trusts are declared by the same instrument by which the trust for sale is created.

[(2) Notwithstanding anything to the contrary in the instrument (if any) creating a trust for sale of land or in the settlement of the net proceeds, the proceeds of sale or other capital money shall not be paid to or applied by the direction of fewer than two persons as trustees for sale, except where the trustee is a trust corporation, but this subsection does not affect the right of a sole personal representative as such to give valid receipts for, or direct the application of, proceeds of sale or other capital money, nor, except where capital money arises on the transaction, render it necessary to have more than one trustee.]

[288]

NOTES
Sub-s (2): substituted by the Law of Property (Amendment) Act 1926, s 7, Schedule.

28. Powers of management, etc, conferred on trustees for sale

(1) Trustees for sale shall, in relation to land or to manorial incidents and to the proceeds of sale, have all the powers of a tenant for life and the trustees of a settlement under the Settled Land Act 1925 including in relation to the land the powers of management conferred by that Act during a minority: [and where by statute settled land is or becomes vested in the trustees of the settlement upon the statutory trusts, such trustees and their successors in office shall also have all the additional or larger powers (if any) conferred by the settlement on the tenant for life, statutory owner, or trustees of the settlement], and (subject to any express trust to the contrary) all capital money arising under the said powers shall, unless paid or applied for any purpose authorised by the Settled Land Act 1925 be applicable in the same manner as if the money represented proceeds of sale arising under the trust for sale.

All land acquired under this subsection shall be conveyed to the trustees on trust for sale.

The powers conferred by this subsection shall be exercised with such consents (if any) as would have been required on a sale under the trust for sale, and when exercised shall operate to overreach any equitable interests or powers which are by virtue of this Act or otherwise made to attach to the net proceeds of sale as if created by a trust affecting those proceeds.

(2) Subject to any direction to the contrary in the disposition on trust for sale or in the settlement of the proceeds of sale, the net rents and profits of the land until sale, after keeping down costs of repairs and insurance and other outgoings shall be paid or applied, except so far as any part thereof may be liable to be set aside as capital money under the Settled Land Act 1925 in like manner as the income of investments representing the purchase money would

be payable or applicable if a sale had been made and the proceeds had been duly invested.

(3) Where the net proceeds of sale have under the trusts affecting the same become absolutely vested in persons of full age in undivided shares (whether or not such shares may be subject to a derivative trust) the trustees for sale may, with the consent of the persons, if any, of full age, not being annuitants, interested in possession in the net rents and profits of the land until sale:—

    (a) partition the land remaining unsold or any part thereof; and

    (b) provide (by way of mortgage or otherwise) for the payment of any equality money; and, upon such partition being arranged, the trustees for sale shall give effect thereto by conveying the land so partitioned in severalty (subject or not to any legal mortgage created for raising equality money) to persons of full age and either absolutely or on trust for sale or, where any part of the land becomes settled land, by a vesting deed, or partly in one way and partly in another in accordance with the rights of the persons interested under the partition, but a purchaser shall not be concerned to see or inquire whether any such consent as aforesaid has been given:

Provided that—

    (i) If a share in the net proceeds belongs to a [person suffering from mental disorder] the consent of his . . . receiver shall be sufficient to protect the trustees for sale:

    (ii) If a share in the net proceeds is affected by an incumbrance the trustees for sale may either give effect thereto or provide for the discharge thereof by means of the property alloted in respect of such share, as they may consider expedient.

(4) If a share in the net proceeds is absolutely vested in an infant, the trustees for sale may act on his behalf and retain land (to be held on trust for sale) or other property to represent his share, but in other respects the foregoing power shall apply as if the infant had been of full age.

(5) This section applies to dispositions on trust for sale coming into operation either before or after the commencement or by virtue of this Act.   **[289]**

NOTES

    Sub-s (1): words in square brackets inserted by the Law of Property (Amendment) Act 1926, s 7, Schedule.

    Sub-s (3): words in square brackets substituted and words omitted repealed by the Mental Health Act 1959 s 149(1), Sch 7, Part I.

29. Delegation of powers of management by trustees for sale

(1) The powers of and incidental to leasing, accepting surrenders of leases and management, conferred on trustees for sale whether by this Act or otherwise, may, until sale of the land, be revocably delegated from time to time, by writing, signed by them, to any person of full age (not being merely an annuitant) for the time being beneficially entitled in possession to the net rents and profits of the land during his life or for any less period: and in favour of a lessee such writing shall, unless the contrary appears, be sufficient evidence that the person named therein is a person to whom the powers may be delegated, and the production of such writing shall, unless the contrary appears, be sufficient evidence that the delegation has not been revoked.

(2) Any power so delegated shall be exercised only in the names and on behalf of the trustees delegating the power.

(3) The persons delegating any power under this section shall not, in relation to the exercise or purported exercise of the power, be liable for the acts or defaults of the person to whom the power is delegated, but that person shall, in relation to the exercise of the power by him, be deemed to be in the position and to have the duties and liabilities of a trustee.

(4) Where, at the commencement of this Act, an order made under section seven of the Settled Land Act 1884 is in force, the person on whom any power is thereby conferred shall, while the order remains in force, exercise such power in the names and on behalf of the trustees for sale in like manner as if the power had been delegated to him under this section.　　　　　　　　　　　　**[290]**

30. Powers of court where trustees for sale refuse to exercise powers

[(1)] If the trustees for sale refuse to sell or to exercise any of the powers conferred by either of the last two sections, or any requisite consent cannot be obtained, any person interested may apply to the court for a vesting or other order for giving effect to the proposed transaction or for an order directing the trustees for sale to give effect thereto, and the court may make such order as it thinks fit.

[(2) The county court has jurisdiction under this section . . .]　　　　　　**[291]**

NOTES
　　Sub-s (1): renumbered as such by the County Courts Act 1984, s 148(1), Sch 2, para 2.
　　Sub-s (2): added by the County Courts Act 1984, s 148(1), Sch 2, para 2; words omitted repealed by the High Court and County Courts Jurisdiction Order 1991, SI 1991 No 724, art 2(8), Schedule.

31. Trust for sale of mortgaged property where right of redemption is barred

(1) Where any property, vested in trustees by way of security, becomes, by virtue of the statutes of limitation, or of an order for foreclosure or otherwise, discharged from the right of redemption, it shall be held by them on trust for sale.

(2) The net proceeds of sale, after payment of costs and expenses, shall be applied in like manner as the mortgage debt, if received, would have been applicable, and the income of the property until sale shall be applied in like manner as the interest, if received, would have been applicable; but this subsection operates without prejudice to any rule of law relating to the apportionment of capital and income between tenant for life and remainderman.

(3) This section does not affect the right of any person to require that, instead of a sale, the property shall be conveyed to him or in accordance with his directions.

(4) Where the mortgage money is capital money for the purposes of the Settled Land Act 1925 the trustees shall, if the tenant for life or statutory owner so requires, instead of selling any land forming the whole or part of such property, execute such subsidiary vesting deed with respect thereto as would have been required if the land had been acquired on a purchase with capital money.

(5) This section applies whether the right of redemption was discharged before or after the first day of January, nineteen hundred and twelve, but has effect without prejudice to any dealings or arrangements made before that date.　　　　　　　　　　　　　　　　　　　　　　　　　　　**[292]**

32. Implied trust for sale in personalty settlements

(1) Where a settlement of personal property or of land held upon trust for sale contains a power to invest money in the purchase of land, such land shall, unless the settlement otherwise provides, be held by the trustees on trust for sale; and the net rents and profits until sale, after keeping down costs of repairs and insurance and other outgoings, shall be paid or applied in like manner as the income of investments representing the purchase-money would be payable or applicable if a sale had been made and the proceeds had been duly invested in personal estate.

(2) This section applies to settlements (including wills) coming into operation after the thirty-first day of December, nineteen hundred and eleven, and does not apply to capital money arising under the Settled Land Act 1925 or money liable to be treated as such. **[293]**

33. Application of Part I to personal representatives

The provisions of this Part of this Act relating to trustees for sale apply to personal representatives holding on trust for sale, but without prejudice to their rights and powers for purposes of administration. **[294]**

Undivided Shares and Joint Ownership

34. Effect of future dispositions to tenants in common

(1) An undivided share in land shall not be capable of being created except as provided by the Settled Land Act 1925 or as hereinafter mentioned.

(2) Where, after the commencement of this Act, land is expressed to be conveyed to any persons in undivided shares and those persons are of full age, the conveyance shall (notwithstanding anything to the contrary in this Act) operate as if the land had been expressed to be conveyed to the grantees, or, if there are more than four grantees, to the four first named in the conveyance, as joint tenants upon the statutory trusts hereinafter mentioned and so as to give effect to the rights of the persons who would have been entitled to the shares had the conveyance operated to create those shares:

Provided that, where the conveyance is made by way of mortgage the land shall vest in the grantees or such four of them as aforesaid for a term of years absolute (as provided by this Act) as joint tenants subject to cesser on redemption in like manner as if the mortgage money had belonged to them on a joint account, but without prejudice to the beneficial interests in the mortgage money and interest.

(3) A devise bequest or testamentary appointment, coming into operation after the commencement of this Act, of land to two or more persons in undivided shares shall operate as a devise bequest or appointment of the land to the trustees (if any) of the will for the purposes of the Settled Land Act 1925 or, if there are no such trustees, then to the personal representatives of the testator, and in each case (but without prejudice to the rights and powers of the personal representatives for purposes of administration) upon the statutory trusts hereinafter mentioned.

(4) Any disposition purporting to make a settlement of an undivided share in land shall only operate as a settlement of a corresponding share of the net proceeds of sale and of the rents and profits until sale of the entirety of the land. **[295]**

35. Meaning of the statutory trusts

For the purposes of this Act land held upon the "statutory trusts" shall be held upon the trusts and subject to the provisions following, namely, upon trust to sell the same and to stand possessed of the net proceeds of sale, after payment of costs, and of the net rents and profits until sale after payment of rates, taxes, costs of insurance, repairs, and other outgoings, upon such trusts, and subject to such powers and provisions, as may be requisite for giving effect to the rights of the persons (including an incumbrancer of a former undivided share or whose incumbrance is not secured by a legal mortgage) interested in the land [and the right of a person who, if the land had not been made subject to a trust for sale by virtue of this Act, would have been entitled to an entailed interest in an undivided share in the land, shall be deemed to be a right to a corresponding entailed interest in the net proceeds of sale attributable to that share].

[Where—
    (a) an undivided share was subject to a settlement, and
    (b) the settlement remains subsisting in respect of other property, and
    (c) the trustees thereof are not the same persons as the trustees for sale,

then the statutory trusts include a trust for the trustees for sale to pay the proper proportion of the net proceeds of sale or other capital money attributable to the share to the trustees of the settlement to be held by them as capital money arising under the Settled Land Act 1925.] **[296]**

NOTES
    First words in square brackets added by the Law of Property (Entailed Interests) Act 1932, s 1; second words in square brackets added by the Law of Property (Amendment) Act 1926, s 7.

36. Joint tenancies

(1) Where a legal estate (not being settled land) is beneficially limited to or held in trust for any persons as joint tenants, the same shall be held on trust for sale, in like manner as if the persons beneficially entitled were tenants in common, but not so as to sever their joint tenancy in equity.

(2) No severance of a joint tenancy of a legal estate, so as to create a tenancy in common in land, shall be permissible, whether by operation of law or otherwise, but this subsection does not affect the right of a joint tenant to release his interest to the other joint tenants, or the right to sever a joint tenancy in an equitable interest whether or not the legal estate is vested in the joint tenants:

Provided that, where a legal estate (not being settled land) is vested in joint tenants beneficially, and any tenant desires to sever the joint tenancy in equity, he shall give to the other joint tenants a notice in writing of such desire or do such other acts or things as would, in the case of personal estate, have been effectual to sever the tenancy in equity, and thereupon under the trust for sale affecting the land the net proceeds of sale, and the net rents and profits until sale, shall be held upon the trusts which would have been requisite for giving effect to the beneficial interests if there had been an actual severance.

[Nothing in this Act affects the right of a survivor of joint tenants, who is solely and beneficially interested, to deal with his legal estate as if it were not held on trust for sale.]

(3) Without prejudice to the right of a joint tenant to release his interest to the other joint tenants no severance of a mortgage term or trust estate, so as to create a tenancy in common, shall be permissible. **[297]**

NOTES
Sub-s (2): words in square brackets added by the Law of Property (Amendment) Act 1926, s 7, Schedule.

37. Rights of husband and wife

A husband and wife shall, for all purposes of acquisition of any interest in property, under a disposition made or coming into operation after the commencement of this Act, be treated as two persons. **[298]**

38. Party Structures

(1) Where under a disposition or other arrangement which, if a holding in undivided shares had been permissible, would have created a tenancy in common, a wall or other structure is or is expressed to be made a party wall or structure, that structure shall be and remain severed vertically as between the respective owners, and the owner of each part shall have such rights to support and user over the rest of the structure as may be requisite for conferring rights corresponding to those which would have subsisted if a valid tenancy in common had been created.

(2) Any person interested may, in case of dispute, apply to the court for an order declaring the rights and interests under this section of the persons interested in any such party structure, and the court may make such order as it thinks fit. **[299]**

Transitional Provisions

39. Transitional Provisions

For the purpose of effecting the transition from the law existing prior to the commencement of the Law of Property Act 1922 to the law enacted by that Act (as amended), the provisions set out in the First Schedule to this Act shall have effect—

(1) for converting existing legal estates, interests and charges not capable under the said Act of taking effect as legal interests into equitable interests;

(2) for discharging, getting in or vesting outstanding legal estates;

(3) for making provision with respect to legal estates vested in infants;

(4) for subjecting land held in undivided shares to trusts for sale;

(5) for dealing with party structures and open spaces held in common;

(6) for converting tenancies by entireties into joint tenancies;

(7) for converting existing freehold mortgages into mortgages by demise;

(8) for converting existing leasehold mortgages into mortgages by sub-demise. **[300]–[301]**

PART II

CONTRACTS, CONVEYANCES AND OTHER INSTRUMENTS

Contracts

40. (*Repealed by the Law of Property (Miscellaneous Provisions) Act 1989 ss 2(8), 4, Sch 2 and superseded by s 2(1)–(7) of that Act; see para* **[1240]**).

41. Stipulations not of the essence of a contract

Stipulations in a contract, as to time or otherwise, which according to rules of equity are not deemed to be or to have become of the essence of the contract, are also construed and have effect at law in accordance with the same rules.

[302]

42. Provisions as to contracts

(1) A stipulation that a purchaser of a legal estate in land shall accept a title made with the concurrence of any person entitled to an equitable interest shall be void, if a title can be made discharged from the equitable interest without such concurrence—

    (*a*) under a trust for sale; or

    (*b*) under this Act, or the Settled Land Act 1925, or any other statute.

(2) A stipulation that a purchaser of a legal estate in land shall pay or contribute towards the costs of or incidental to—

    (*a*) obtaining a vesting order, or the appointment of trustees of a settlement, or the appointment of trustees of a conveyance on trust for sale; or

    (*b*) the preparation stamping or execution of a conveyance on trust for sale, or of a vesting instrument for bringing into force the provisions of the Settled Land Act 1925;

shall be void.

(3) A stipulation contained in any contract for the sale or exchange of land made after the commencement of this Act, to the effect that an outstanding legal estate is to be traced or got in by or at the expense of a purchaser or that no objection is to be taken on account of an outstanding legal estate, shall be void.

(4) If the subject matter of any contract for the sale or exchange of land—

    (i) is a mortgage term and the vendor has power to convey the fee simple in the land, or, in the case of a mortgage of a term of years absolute, the leasehold reversion affected by the mortgage, the contract shall be deemed to extend to the fee simple in the land or such leasehold reversion;

    (ii) is an equitable interest capable of subsisting as a legal estate, and the vendor has power to vest such legal estate in himself or in the purchaser or to require the same to be so vested, the contract shall be deemed to extend to such legal estate;

    (iii) is an entailed interest in possession and the vendor has power to vest in himself or in the purchaser the fee simple in the land, (or, if the entailed interest is an interest in a term of years absolute, such term,) or to require the same to be so vested, the contract shall be deemed to extend to the fee simple in the land or the term of years absolute.

(5) This section does not affect the right of a mortgagee of leasehold land to sell his mortgage term only if he is unable to convey or vest the leasehold reversion expectant thereon.

(6) Any contract to convey an undivided share in land made before or after the commencement of this Act, shall be deemed to be sufficiently complied with by the conveyance of a corresponding share in the proceeds of sale of the land in like manner as if the contract had been to convey that corresponding share.

(7) Where a purchaser has power to acquire land compulsorily, and a contract, whether by virtue of a notice to treat or otherwise, is subsisting under which title can be made without payment of the compensation money into court, title shall be made in that way unless the purchaser, to avoid expense or delay or for any special reason, considers it expedient that the money should be paid into court.

(8) A vendor shall not have any power to rescind a contract by reason only of the enforcement of any right under this section.

(9) This section only applies in favour of a purchaser for money or money's worth.   **[303]**

43. Rights protected by registration

(1) Where a purchaser of a legal estate is entitled to acquire the same discharged from an equitable interest which is protected by registration as a pending action, annuity, writ, order, deed of arrangement or land charge, and which will not be overreached by the conveyance to him, he may notwithstanding any stipulation to the contrary, require—

>   (*a*) that the registration shall be cancelled; or
>   (*b*) that the person entitled to the equitable interest shall concur in the conveyance;

and in either case free of expense to the purchaser.

(2) Where the registration cannot be cancelled or the person entitled to the equitable interest refuses to concur in the conveyance, this section does not affect the right of any person to rescind the contract.   **[304]**

44. Statutory commencements of title

(1) After the commencement of this Act [fifteen years] shall be substituted for forty years as the period of commencement of title which a purchaser of land may require; nevertheless earlier title than [fifteen years] may be required in cases similar to those in which earlier title than forty years might immediately before the commencement of this Act be required.

(2) Under a contract to grant or assign a term of years, whether derived or to be derived out of freehold or leasehold land, the intended lessee or assign shall not be entitled to call for the title to the freehold.

(3) Under a contract to sell and assign a term of years derived out of a leasehold interest in land, the intended assign shall not have the right to call for the title to the leasehold reversion.

(4) On a contract to grant a lease for a term of years to be derived out of a

leasehold interest, with a leasehold reversion, the intended lessee shall not have the right to call for the title to that reversion.

(5) Where by reason of any of the three last preceding subsections, an intending lessee or assign is not entitled to call for the title to the freehold or to a leasehold reversion, as the case may be, he shall not, where the contract is made after the commencement of this Act, be deemed to be affected with notice of any matter or thing of which, if he had contracted that such title should be furnished, he might have had notice.

(6) Where land of copyhold or customary tenure has been converted into freehold by enfranchisement, then, under a contract to sell and convey the freehold, the purchaser shall not have the right to call for the title to make the enfranchisement.

(7) Where the manorial incidents formerly affecting any land have been extinguished, then, under a contract to sell and convey the freehold, the purchaser shall not have the right to call for the title of the person entering into any compensation agreement or giving a receipt for the compensation money to enter into such agreement or to give such receipt, and shall not be deemed to be affected with notice of any matter or thing of which, if he had contracted that such title should be furnished, he might have had notice.

(8) A purchaser shall not be deemed to be or ever to have been affected with notice of any matter or thing of which, if he had investigated the title or made enquiries in regard to matters prior to the period of commencement of title fixed by this Act, or by any other statute, or by any rule of law, he might have had notice, unless he actually makes such investigation or enquiries.

(9) Where a lease whether made before or after the commencement of this Act, is made under a power contained in a settlement, will, Act of Parliament, or other instrument, any preliminary contract for or relating to the lease shall not, for the purpose of the deduction of title to an intended assign, form part of the title, or evidence of the title, to the lease.

(10) This section, save where otherwise expressly provided, applies to contracts for sale whether made before or after the commencement of this Act, and applies to contracts for exchange in like manner as to contracts for sale, save that it applies only to contracts for exchange made after such commencement.

(11) This section applies only if and so far as a contrary intention is not expressed in the contract.   **[305]**

NOTES

Sub-s (1): words in square brackets substituted in relation to contracts made after 1 January 1970, by the Law of Property Act 1969, s 23.

45. Other statutory conditions of sale

(1) A purchaser of any property shall not—

    (*a*) require the production, or any abstract or copy, of any deed, will, or other document, dated or made before the time prescribed by law, or stipulated, for the commencement of the title, even though the same creates a power subsequently exercised by an instrument abstracted in the abstract furnished to the purchaser; or

    (*b*) require any information, or make any requisition, objection, or inquiry, with respect to any such deed, will, or document, or the title prior to that time, notwithstanding that any such deed, will, or other document, or that prior title, is recited, agreed to be produced, or noticed;

and he shall assume, unless the contrary appears, that the recitals, contained in the abstracted instruments, of any deed, will, or other document, forming part of that prior title, are correct, and give all the material contents of the deed, will, or other document so recited, and that every document so recited was duly executed by all necessary parties, and perfected, if and as required, by fine, recovery, acknowledgment, inrolment, or otherwise:

Provided that this subsection shall not deprive a purchaser of the right to require the production, or an abstract or copy of—

    (i) any power of attorney under which any abstracted document is executed; or

    (ii) any document creating or disposing of an interest, power or obligation which is not shown to have ceased or expired, and subject to which any part of the property is disposed of by an abstracted document; or

    (iii) any document creating any limitation or trust by reference to which any part of the property is disposed of by an abstracted document.

(2) Where land sold is held by lease (other than an under-lease), the purchaser shall assume, unless the contrary appears, that the lease was duly granted; and, on production of the receipt for the last payment due for rent under the lease before the date of actual completion of the purchase, he shall assume, unless the contrary appears, that all the covenants and provisions of the lease have been duly performed and observed up to the date of actual completion of the purchase.

(3) Where land sold is held by under-lease, the purchaser shall assume, unless the contrary appears, that the under-lease and every superior lease were duly granted; and, on production of the receipt for the last payment due for rent under the under-lease before the date of actual completion of the purchase, he shall assume, unless the contrary appears, that all the covenants and provisions of the under-lease have been duly performed and observed up to the date of actual completion of the purchase, and further that all rent due under every superior lease, and all the covenants and provisions of every superior lease, have been paid and duly performed and observed up to that date.

(4) On a sale of any property, the following expenses shall be borne by the purchaser where he requires them to be incurred for the purpose of verifying the abstract or any other purpose, that is to say—

    (a) the expenses of the production and inspection of all Acts of Parliament, inclosure awards, records, proceedings of courts, court rolls, deeds, wills, probates, letters of administration, and other documents, not in the possession of the vendor or his mortgagee or trustee, and the expenses of all journeys incidental to such production or inspection; and

    (b) the expenses of searching for, procuring, making, verifying, and producing all certificates, declarations, evidences, and information not in the possession of the vendor or his mortgagee or trustee, and all attested, stamped, office or other copies or abstracts of, or extracts from, any Acts of Parliament or other documents aforesaid, not in the possession of the vendor or his mortgagee or trustee;

and where the vendor or his mortgagee or trustee retains possession of any document, the expenses of making any copy thereof, attested or unattested, which a purchaser requires to be delivered to him, shall be borne by that purchaser.

(5) On a sale of any property in lots, a purchaser of two or more lots, held wholly, or partly under the same title, shall not have a right to more than one abstract of the common title, except at his own expense.

(6) Recitals, statements, and descriptions of facts, matters, and parties contained in deeds, instruments, Acts of Parliament, or statutory declarations, twenty years old at the date of the contract, shall, unless and except so far as they may be proved to be inaccurate, be taken to be sufficient evidence of the truth of such facts, matters, and descriptions.

(7) The inability of a vendor to furnish a purchaser with an acknowledgment of his right to production and delivery of copies of documents of title or with a legal covenant to produce and furnish copies of documents of title shall not be an objection to title in case the purchaser will, on the completion of the contract, have an equitable right to the production of such documents.

(8) Such acknowledgments of the right of production or covenants for production and such undertakings or covenants for safe custody of documents as the purchaser can and does require shall be furnished or made at his expense, and the vendor shall bear the expense of perusal and execution on behalf of and by himself, and on behalf of and by necessary parties other than the purchaser.

(9) A vendor shall be entitled to retain documents of title where—

(*a*) he retains any part of the land to which the documents relate; or

(*b*) the document consists of a trust instrument or other instrument creating a trust which is still subsisting, or an instrument relating to the appointment or discharge of a trustee of a subsisting trust.

(10) This section applies to contracts for sale made before or after the commencement of this Act, and applies to contracts for exchange in like manner as to contracts for sale, except that it applies only to contracts for exchange made after such commencement:

Provided that this section shall apply subject to any stipulation or contrary intention expressed in the contract.

(11) Nothing in this section shall be construed as binding a purchaser to complete his purchase in any case where, on a contract made independently of this section, and containing stipulations similar to the provisions of this section, or any of them, specific performance of the contract would not be enforced against him by the court.   [306]

46. Forms of contracts and conditions of sale

The Lord Chancellor may from time to time prescribe and publish forms of contracts and conditions of sale of land, and the forms so prescribed shall, subject to any modification, or any stipulation or intention to the contrary, expressed in the correspondence, apply to contracts by correspondence, and may, but only by express reference thereto, be made to apply to any other cases for which the forms are made available.   [307]

47. Application of insurance money on completion of a sale or exchange

(1) Where after the date of any contract for sale or exchange of property, money becomes payable under any policy of insurance maintained by the vendor in respect of any damage to or destruction of property included in the contract, the money shall, on completion of the contract, be held or receivable by the vendor on behalf of the purchaser and paid by the vendor to the purchaser on completion of the sale or exchange, or so soon thereafter as the same shall be received by the vendor.

(2) This section applies only to contracts made after the commencement of this Act, and has effect subject to—

    (*a*) any stipulation to the contrary contained in the contract,

    (*b*) any requisite consents of the insurers,

    (*c*) the payment by the purchaser of the proportionate part of the premium from the date of the contract.

(3) This section applies to a sale or exchange by an order of the court, as if—

    (*a*) for references to the "vendor" there were substituted references to the "person bound by the order";

    (*b*) for the reference to the completion of the contract there were substituted a reference to the payment of the purchase or equality money (if any) into court;

    (*c*) for the reference to the date of the contract there were substituted a reference to the time when the contract becomes binding. **[308]**

48. Stipulations preventing a purchaser, lessee, or underlessee from employing his own solicitor to be void

(1) Any stipulation made on the sale of any interest in land after the commencement of this Act to the effect that the conveyance to, or the registration of the title of, the purchaser shall be prepared or carried out at the expense of the purchaser by a solicitor appointed by or acting for the vendor, and any stipulation which might restrict a purchaser in the selection of a solicitor to act on his behalf in relation to any interest in land agreed to be purchased, shall be void; and, if a sale is effected by demise or subdemise, then, for the purposes of this subsection, the instrument required for giving effect to the transaction shall be deemed to be a conveyance:

Provided that nothing in this subsection shall affect any right reserved to a vendor to furnish a form of conveyance to a purchaser from which the draft can be prepared, or to charge a reasonable fee therefor, or, where a perpetual rentcharge is to be reserved as the only consideration in money or money's worth, the right of a vendor to stipulate that the draft conveyance is to be prepared by his solicitor at the expense of the purchaser.

(2) Any covenant or stipulation contained in, or entered into with reference to any lease or underlease made before or after the commencement of this Act—

    (*a*) whereby the right of preparing, at the expense of a purchaser, any conveyance of the estate or interest of the lessee or underlessee in the demised premises or in any part thereof, or of otherwise carrying out, at the expense of the purchaser, any dealing with such estate or interest, is expressed to be reserved to or vested in the lessor or underlessor or his solicitor; or (*b*) which in any way restricts the right of the purchaser to have such conveyance carried out on his behalf by a solicitor appointed by him; shall be void:

Provided that, where any covenant or stipulation is rendered void by this subsection, there shall be implied in lieu thereof a covenant or stipulation that the lessee or underlessee shall register with the lessor or his solicitor within six months from the date thereof, or as soon after the expiration of that period as may be practicable, all conveyances and devolutions (including probates or letters of administration) affecting the lease or underlease and pay a fee of one guinea in respect of each registration, and the power of entry (if any) on breach of any covenant contained in the lease or underlease shall apply and extend to the breach of any covenant so to be implied.

(3) Save where a sale is effected by demise or subdemise, this section does not affect the law relating to the preparation of a lease or underlease or the draft thereof.

(4) In this section "lease" and "underlease" include any agreement therefor or other tenancy, and "lessee" and "underlessee" and "lessor" and "underlessor" have corresponding meanings.   **[309]**

49. Applications to the court by vendor and purchaser

(1) A vendor or purchaser of any interest in land, or their representatives respectively, may apply in a summary way to the court, in respect of any requisitions or objections, or any claim for compensation, or any other question arising out of or connected with the contract (not being a question affecting the existence or validity of the contract), and the court may make such order upon the application as to the court may appear just, and may order how and by whom all or any of the costs of and incident to the application are to be borne and paid.

(2) Where the court refuses to grant specific performance of a contract, or in any action for the return of a deposit, the court may, if it thinks fit, order the repayment of any deposit.

(3) This section applies to a contract for the sale or exchange of any interest in land.

[(4) The county court has jurisdiction under this section where the land which is to be dealt with in the court does not exceed [£30,000] in capital value . . .]   **[310]**

NOTES
    Sub-s (4): added by the County Courts Act 1984, s 148(1), Sch 2, para 2; sum in square brackets substituted and words omitted repealed by the High Court and County Courts Jurisdiction Order 1991, SI 1991 No 724, art 2(8), Schedule.

50. Discharge of incumbrances by the court on sales or exchanges

(1) Where land subject to any incumbrance, whether immediately realisable or payable or not, is sold or exchanged by the court, or out of court, the court may, if it thinks fit, on the application of any party to the sale or exchange, direct or allow payment into court of such sum as is hereinafter mentioned, that is to say—

    (*a*) in the case of an annual sum charged on the land, or of a capital sum charged on a determinable interest in the land, the sum to be paid into court shall be of such amount as, when invested in Government securities, the court considers will be sufficient, by means of the dividends thereof, to keep down or otherwise provide for that charge; and

(b) in any other case of capital money charged on the land, the sum to be paid into court shall be of an amount sufficient to meet the incumbrance and any interest due thereon;

but in either case there shall also be paid into court such additional amount as the court considers will be sufficient to meet the contingency of further costs, expenses and interests, and any other contingency, except depreciation of investments, not exceeding one-tenth part of the original amount to be paid in, unless the court for special reason thinks fit to require a larger additional amount.

(2) Thereupon, the court may, if it thinks fit, and either after or without any notice to the incumbrancer, as the court thinks fit, declare the land to be freed from the incumbrance, and make any order for conveyance, or vesting order, proper for giving effect to the sale or exchange, and give directions for the retention and investment of the money in court and for the payment or application of the income thereof.

(3) The court may declare all other land, if any, affected by the incumbrance (besides the land sold or exchanged) to be freed from the incumbrance, and this power may be exercised either after or without notice to the incumbrancer, and notwithstanding that on a previous occasion an order, relating to the same incumbrance, has been made by the court which was confined to the land then sold or exchanged.

(4) On any application under this section the court may, if it thinks fit, as respects any vendor or purchaser, dispense with the service of any notice which would otherwise be required to be served on the vendor or purchaser.

(5) After notice served on the persons interested in or entitled to the money or fund in court, the court may direct payment or transfer thereof to the persons entitled to receive or give a discharge for the same, and generally may give directions respecting the application or distribution of the capital or income thereof.

(6) This section applies to sales or exchanges whether made before or after the commencement of this Act, and to incumbrances whether created by statute or otherwise.   **[311]**

Conveyances and other Instruments

51. Lands lie in grant only

(1) All lands and all interests therein lie in grant and are incapable of being conveyed by livery or livery and seisin, or by feoffment, or by bargain and sale; and a conveyance of an interest in land may operate to pass the possession or right to possession thereof, without actual entry, but subject to all prior rights thereto.

(2) The use of the word grant is not necessary to convey land or to create any interest therein.   **[312]**

52. Conveyances to be by deed

(1) All conveyances of land or of any interest therein are void for the purpose of conveying or creating a legal estate unless made by deed.

(2) This section does not apply to—

    (*a*) assents by a personal representative;

    (*b*) disclaimers made in accordance with ... [sections 178 to 180 or sections 315 to 319 of the Insolvency Act 1986] or not required to be evidenced in writing;

    (*c*) surrenders by operation of law, including surrenders which may, by law, be effected without writing;

    (*d*) leases or tenancies or other assurances not required by law to be made in writing;

    (*e*) receipts [other than those falling within section 115 below];

    (*f*) vesting orders of the court or other competent authority;

    (*g*) conveyances taking effect by operation of law.   **[313]**

NOTES

Sub-s (2): words omitted repealed by the Insolvency Act 1985, s 235, Sch 8, para 4; first words in square brackets substituted by the Insolvency Act 1986, s 439(2), Sch 14; second words in square brackets substituted by the Law of Property (Miscellaneous Provisions) Act 1989, s 1(8), Sch 1, para 2.

53. Instruments required to be in writing

(1) Subject to the provisions hereinafter contained with respect to the creation of interests in land by parol—

    (*a*) no interest in land can be created or disposed of except by writing signed by the person creating or conveying the same, or by his agent thereunto lawfully authorised in writing, or by will, or by operation of law;

    (*b*) a declaration of trust respecting any land or any interest therein must be manifested and proved by some writing signed by some person who is able to declare such trust or by his will;

    (*c*) a disposition of an equitable interest or trust subsisting at the time of the disposition, must be in writing signed by the person disposing of the same, or by his agent thereunto lawfully authorised in writing or by will.

(2) This section does not affect the creation or operation of resulting, implied or constructive trusts.   **[314]**

54. Creation of interests in land by parol

(1) All interests in land created by parol and not put in writing and signed by the persons so creating the same, or by their agents thereunto lawfully authorised in writing, have, notwithstanding any consideration having been given for the same, the force and effect of interests at will only.

(2) Nothing in the foregoing provisions of this Part of this Act shall affect the creation by parol of leases taking effect in possession for a term not exceeding three years (whether or not the lessee is given power to extend the term) at the best rent which can be reasonably obtained without taking a fine.   **[315]**

55. Savings in regard to last two sections

Nothing in the last two foregoing sections shall—

(*a*) invalidate dispositions by will; or
(*b*) affect any interest validly created before the commencement of this Act; or
(*c*) affect the right to acquire an interest in land by virtue of taking possession; or
(*d*) affect the operation of the law relating to part performance.   **[316]**

56. Persons taking who are not parties and as to indentures

(1) A person may take an immediate or other interest in land or other property, or the benefit of any condition, right of entry, covenant or agreement over or respecting land or other property, although he may not be named as a party to the conveyance or other instrument.

(2) A deed between parties, to effect its objects, has the effect of an indenture though not indented or expressed to be an indenture.   **[317]**

57. Description of deeds

Any deed, whether or not being an indenture, may be described (at the commencement thereof or otherwise) as a deed simply, or as a conveyance, deed of exchange, vesting deed, trust instrument, settlement, mortgage, charge, transfer of mortgage, appointment, lease or otherwise according to the nature of the transaction intended to be effected.   **[318]**

58. Provisions as to supplemental instruments

Any instrument (whether executed before or after the commencement of this Act) expressed to be supplemental to a previous instrument, shall, as far as may be, be read and have effect as if the supplemental instrument contained a full recital of the previous instrument, but this section does not operate to give any right to an abstract or production of any such previous instrument, and a purchaser may accept the same evidence that the previous instrument does not affect the title as if it had merely been mentioned in the supplemental instrument.   **[319]**

59. Conditions and certain covenants not implied

(1) An exchange or other conveyance of land made by deed after the first day of October, eighteen hundred and forty-five, does not imply any condition in law.

(2) The word "give" or "grant" does not, in a deed made after the date last aforesaid, imply any covenant in law, save where otherwise provided by statute.   **[320]**

60. Abolition of technicalities in regard to conveyances and deeds

(1) A conveyance of freehold land to any person without words of limitation, or any equivalent expression, shall pass to the grantee the fee simple or other the whole interest which the grantor had power to convey in such land, unless a contrary intention appears in the conveyance.

(2) A conveyance of freehold land to a corporation sole by his corporate designation without the word "successors" shall pass to the corporation the fee simple or other the whole interest which the grantor had power to convey in such land, unless a contrary intention appears in the conveyance.

(3) In a voluntary conveyance a resulting trust for the grantor shall not be

implied merely by reason that the property is not expressed to be conveyed for the use or benefit of the grantee.

(4) The foregoing provisions of this section apply only to conveyances and deeds executed after the commencement of this Act:

Provided that in a deed executed after the thirty-first day of December, eighteen hundred and eighty-one, it is sufficient—

   (a) In the limitation of an estate in fee simple, to use the words "in fee simple", without the word "heirs";
   (b) In the limitation of an estate tail, to use the words "in tail" without the words "heirs of the body"; and
   (c) In the limitation of an estate in tail male or in tail female, to use the words "in tail male" or "in tail female", as the case requires, without the words "heirs male of the body", or "heirs female of the body".

[321]

61. Construction of expressions used in deeds and other instruments

In all deeds, contracts, wills, orders and other instruments executed, made or coming into operation after the commencement of this Act, unless the context otherwise requires—

   (a) "Month" means calendar month;
   (b) "Person" includes a corporation;
   (c) The singular includes the plural and vice versa;
   (d) The masculine includes the feminine and vice versa. **[322]**

62. General words implied in conveyances

(1) A conveyance of land shall be deemed to include and shall by virtue of this Act operate to convey, with the land, all buildings, erections, fixtures, commons, hedges, ditches, fences, ways, waters, watercourses, liberties, privileges, easements, rights, and advantages whatsoever, appertaining or reputed to appertain to the land, or any part thereof, or, at the time of conveyance, demised, occupied, or enjoyed with or reputed or known as part or parcel of or appurtenant to the land or any part thereof.

(2) A conveyance of land, having houses or other buildings thereon, shall be deemed to include and shall by virtue of this Act operate to convey, with the land, houses, or other buildings, all outhouses, erections, fixtures, cellars, areas, courts, courtyards, cisterns, sewers, gutters, drains, ways, passages, lights, watercourses, liberties, privileges, easements, rights, and advantages whatsoever, appertaining or reputed to appertain to the land, houses, or other buildings conveyed, or any of them, or any part thereof, or, at the time of conveyance, demised, occupied, or enjoyed with, or reputed or known as part or parcel of or appurtenant to, the land, houses, other buildings conveyed, or any of them, or any part thereof.

(3) A conveyance of a manor shall be deemed to include and shall by virtue of this Act operate to convey, with the manor, all pastures, feedings, wastes, warrens, commons, mines, minerals, quarries, furzes, trees, woods, underwoods, coppices, and the ground and soil thereof, fishings, fisheries, fowlings, courts leet, courts baron, and other courts, view of frankpledge and all that to view of frankpledge doth belong, mills, mulctures, customs, tolls, duties, reliefs, heriots, fines, sums of money, amerciaments, waifs, estrays, chief-rents, quitrents, rentscharge, rents seck, rents of assize, fee farm rents, services, royalties, jurisdictions, franchises, liberties, privileges, easements, profits, advantages,

rights, emoluments, and hereditaments whatsoever, to the manor appertaining or reputed to appertain, or, at the time of conveyance, demised, occupied, or enjoyed with the same, or reputed or known as part, parcel, or member thereof.

For the purposes of this subsection the right to compensation for manorial incidents on the extinguishment thereof shall be deemed to be a right appertaining to the manor.

(4) This section applies only if and as far as a contrary intention is not expressed in the conveyance, and has effect subject to the terms of the conveyance and to the provisions therein contained.

(5) This section shall not be construed as giving to any person a better title to any property, right, or thing in this section mentioned than the title which the conveyance gives to him to the land or manor expressed to be conveyed, or as conveying to him any property, right, or thing in this section mentioned, further or otherwise than as the same could have been conveyed to him by the conveying parties.

(6) This section applies to conveyances made after the thirty-first day of December, eighteen hundred and eighty-one. **[323]**

63. All estate clause implied

(1) Every conveyance is effectual to pass all the estate, right, title, interest, claim, and demand which the conveying parties respectively have, in, to, or on the property conveyed, or expressed or intended so to be, or which they respectively have power to convey in, to, or on the same.

(2) This section applies only if and as far as a contrary intention is not expressed in the conveyance, and has effect subject to the terms of the conveyance and to the provisions therein contained.

(3) This section applies to conveyances made after the thirty-first day of December, eighteen hundred and eighty-one. **[324]**

64. Production and safe custody of documents

(1) Where a person retains possession of documents, and gives to another an acknowledgment in writing of the right of that other to production of those documents, and to delivery of copies thereof (in this section called an acknowledgment), that acknowledgment shall have effect as in this section provided.

(2) An acknowledgment shall bind the documents to which it relates in the possession or under the control of the person who retains them, and in the possession or under the control of every other person having possession or control thereof from time to time, but shall bind each individual possessor or person as long only as he has possession or control thereof; and every person so having possession or control from time to time shall be bound specifically to perform the obligations imposed under this section by an acknowledgment, unless prevented from so doing by fire or other inevitable accident.

(3) The obligations imposed under this section by an acknowledgment are to be performed from time to time at the request in writing of the person to whom an acknowledgment is given, or of any person, not being a lessee at a rent, having or claiming any estate, interest, or right through or under that person, or otherwise becoming through or under that person interested in or affected by the terms of any document to which the acknowledgment relates.

(4) The obligations imposed under this section by an acknowledgment are—

    (i) An obligation to produce the documents or any of them at all reasonable times for the purpose of inspection, and of comparison with abstracts or copies thereof, by the person entitled to request production or by any person by him authorised in writing; and

    (ii) An obligation to produce the documents or any of them at any trial, hearing, or examination in any court, or in the execution of any commission, or elsewhere in the United Kingdom, on any occasion on which production may properly be required, for proving or supporting the title or claim of the person entitled to request production, or for any other purpose relative to that title or claim; and

    (iii) An obligation to deliver to the person entitled to request the same true copies or extracts, attested or unattested, of or from the documents or any of them.

(5) All costs and expenses of or incidental to the specific performance of any obligation imposed under this section by an acknowledgment shall be paid by the person requesting performance.

(6) An acknowledgment shall not confer any right to damages for loss or destruction of, or injury to, the documents to which it relates, from whatever cause arising.

(7) Any person claiming to be entitled to the benefit of an acknowledgment may apply to the court for an order directing the production of the documents to which it relates, or any of them, or the delivery of copies of or extracts from those documents or any of them to him, or some person on his behalf; and the court may, if it thinks fit, order production, or production and delivery, accordingly, and may give directions respecting the time, place, terms, and mode of production or delivery, and may make such order as it thinks fit respecting the costs of the application, or any other matter connected with the application.

(8) An acknowledgment shall by virtue of this Act satisfy any liability to give a covenant for production and delivery of copies of or extracts from documents.

(9) Where a person retains possession of documents and gives to another an undertaking in writing for safe custody thereof, that undertaking shall impose on the person giving it, and on every person having possession or control of the documents from time to time, but on each individual possessor or person as long only as he has possession or control thereof, an obligation to keep the document safe, whole, uncancelled, and undefaced, unless prevented from so doing by fire or other inevitable accident.

(10) Any person claiming to be entitled to the benefit of such an undertaking may apply to the court to assess damages for any loss or destruction of, or injury to, the documents or any of them, and the court may, if it thinks fit, direct an inquiry respecting the amount of damages, and order payment thereof by the person liable, and may make such order as it thinks fit respecting the costs of the application, or any other matter connected with the application.

(11) An undertaking for safe custody of documents shall by virtue of this Act satisfy any liability to give a covenant for safe custody of documents.

(12) The rights conferred by an acknowledgment or an undertaking under this section shall be in addition to all such other rights relative to the production,

or inspection, or the obtaining of copies of documents, as are not, by virtue of this Act, satisfied by the giving of the acknowledgment or undertaking, and shall have effect subject to the terms of the acknowledgment or undertaking, and to any provisions therein contained.

(13) This section applies only if and as far as a contrary intention is not expressed in the acknowledgment or undertaking.

(14) This section applies to an acknowledgment or undertaking given, or a liability respecting documents incurred, after the thirty-first day of December, eighteen hundred and eighty-one.   **[325]**

65. Reservation of legal estates

(1) A reservation of a legal estate shall operate at law without any execution of the conveyance by the grantee of the legal estate out of which the reservation is made, or any regrant by him, so as to create the legal estate reserved, and so as to vest the same in possession in the person (whether being the grantor or not) for whose benefit the reservation is made.

(2) A conveyance of a legal estate expressed to be made subject to another legal estate not in existence immediately before the date of the conveyance, shall operate as a reservation unless a contrary intention appears.

(3) This section applies only to reservations made after the commencement of this Act.   **[326]**

66. Confirmation of past transactions

(1) A deed containing a declaration by the estate owner that his estate shall go and devolve in such a manner as may be requisite for confirming any interests intended to affect his estate and capable under this Act of subsisting as legal estates which, at some prior date, were expressed to have been transferred or created, and any dealings therewith which would have been legal if those interests had been legally and validly transferred or created, shall, to the extent of the estate of the estate owner, but without prejudice to the restrictions imposed by this Act in the case of mortgages, operate to give legal effect to the interests so expressed to have been transferred or created and to the subsequent dealings aforesaid.

(2) The powers conferred by this section may be exercised by a tenant for life or statutory owner, trustee for sale or a personal representative (being in each case an estate owner) as well as by an absolute owner, but if exercised by any person, other than an absolute owner, only with the leave of the court.

(3) This section applies only to deeds containing such a declaration as aforesaid if executed after the commencement of this Act.

[(4) The county court has jurisdiction under this section where the land which is to be dealt with in the court does not exceed [£30,000] in capital value . . .]   **[327]**

NOTES
   Sub-s (4): added by the County Courts Act 1984, s 148(1), Sch 2, para 2; sum in square brackets substituted and words omitted repealed by the High Court and County Courts Jurisdiction Order 1991, SI 1991 No 724, art 2(8), Schedule.

67. Receipt in deed sufficient

(1) A receipt for consideration money or securities in the body of a deed shall be a sufficient discharge for the same to the person paying or delivering the same, without any further receipt for the same being indorsed on the deed.

(2) This section applies to deeds executed after the thirty-first day of December, eighteen hundred and eighty-one. [328]

68. Receipt in deed or indorsed evidence

(1) A receipt for consideration money or other consideration in the body of a deed or indorsed thereon shall, in favour of a subsequent purchaser, not having notice that the money or other consideration thereby acknowledged to be received was not in fact paid or given, wholly or in part, be sufficient evidence of the payment or giving of the whole amount thereof.

(2) This section applies to deeds executed after the thirty-first day of December, eighteen hundred and eighty-one. [329]

69. Receipt in deed or indorsed authority for payment to solicitor

(1) Where a solicitor produces a deed, having in the body thereof or indorsed thereon a receipt for consideration money or other consideration, the deed being executed, or the indorsed receipt being signed, by the person entitled to give a receipt for that consideration, the deed shall be a sufficient authority to the person liable to pay or give the same for his paying or giving the same to the solicitor, without the solicitor producing any separate or other direction or authority in that behalf from the person who executed or signed the deed or receipt.

(2) This section applies whether the consideration was paid or given before or after the commencement of this Act. [330]

70. Partial release of security from rentcharge

(1) A release from a rentcharge of part of the land charged therewith does not extinguish the whole rentcharge, but operates only to bar the right to recover any part of the rentcharge out of the land released, without prejudice to the rights of any persons interested in the land remaining unreleased, and not concurring in or confirming the release.

(2) This section applies to releases made after the twelfth day of August, eighteen hundred and fifty-nine. [331]

71. Release of part of land affected from a judgment

(1) A release from a judgment (including any writ or order imposing a charge) of part of any land charged therewith does not affect the validity of the judgment as respects any land not specifically released.

(2) This section operates without prejudice to the rights of any persons interested in the property remaining unreleased and not concurring in or confirming the release.

(3) This section applies to releases made after the twelfth day of August, eighteen hundred and fifty-nine. [332]

72. Conveyances by a person to himself, etc

(1) In conveyances made after the twelfth day of August, eighteen hundred and fifty-nine, personal property, including chattels real, may be conveyed by a person to himself jointly with another person by the like means by which it might be conveyed by him to another person.

(2) In conveyances made after the thirty-first day of December, eighteen hundred and eighty-one, freehold land, or a thing in action, may be conveyed by a person to himself jointly with another person, by the like means by which it might be conveyed by him to another person; and may, in like manner, be conveyed by a husband to his wife, and by a wife to her husband, alone or jointly with another person.

(3) After the commencement of this Act a person may convey land to or vest land in himself.

(4) Two or more persons (whether or not being trustees or personal representatives) may convey, and shall be deemed always to have been capable of conveying, any property vested in them to any one or more of themselves in like manner as they could have conveyed such property to a third party; provided that if the persons in whose favour the conveyance is made are, by reason of any fiduciary relationship or otherwise, precluded from validly carrying out the transaction, the conveyance shall be liable to be set aside.

[333]–[334]

74. Execution of instruments by or on behalf of corporations

(1) In favour of a purchaser a deed shall be deemed to have been duly executed by a corporation aggregate if its seal be affixed thereto in the presence of and attested by its clerk, secretary or other permanent officer or his deputy, and a member of the board of directors, council or other governing body of the corporation, and where a seal purporting to be the seal of a corporation has been affixed to a deed, attested by persons purporting to be persons holding such offices as aforesaid, the deed shall be deemed to have been executed in accordance with the requirements of this section, and to have taken effect accordingly.

(2) The board of directors, council or other governing body of a corporation aggregate may, by resolution or otherwise, appoint an agent either generally or in any particular case, to execute on behalf of the corporation any agreement or other instrument [which is not a deed] in relation to any matter within the powers of the corporation.

(3) Where a person is authorised under a power of attorney or under any statutory or other power to convey any interest in property in the name or on behalf of a corporation sole or aggregate, he may as attorney execute the conveyance by signing the name of the corporation in the presence of at least one witness, . . . and such execution shall take effect and be valid in like manner as if the corporation had executed the conveyance.

(4) Where a corporation aggregate is authorised under a power of attorney or under any statutory or other power to convey any interest in property in the name or on behalf of any other person (including another corporation), an officer appointed for that purpose by the board of directors, council or other governing body of the corporation by resolution or otherwise, may execute the deed or other instrument in the name of such other person; and where an instrument appears to be executed by an officer so appointed, then in favour of

a purchaser the instrument shall be deemed to have been executed by an officer duly authorised.

(5) The foregoing provisions of this section apply to transactions wherever effected, but only to deeds and instruments executed after the commencement of this Act, except that, in the case of powers or appointments of an agent or officer, they apply whether the power was conferred or the appointment was made before or after the commencement of this Act or by this Act.

(6) Notwithstanding anything contained in this section, any mode of execution or attestation authorised by law or by practice or by the statute, charter, memorandum or articles, deed of settlement or other instrument constituting the corporation or regulating the affairs thereof, shall (in addition to the modes authorised by this section) be as effectual as if this section had not been passed.   **[335]**

NOTES

Sub-s (2): words in square brackets substituted by the Law of Property (Miscellaneous Provisions) Act 1989, s 1(8), Sch 1, para 3.

Sub-s (3): words omitted repealed by the Law of Property (Miscellaneous Provisions) Act 1989, s 4, Sch 2.

75. Rights of purchaser as to execution

(1) On a sale, the purchaser shall not be entitled to require that the conveyance to him be executed in his presence, or in that of his solicitor, as such; but shall be entitled to have, at his own cost, the execution of the conveyance attested by some person appointed by him, who may, if he thinks fit, be his solicitor.

(2) This section applies to sales made after the thirty-first day of December, eighteen hundred and eighty-one.   **[336]**

Covenants

76. Covenants for title

(1) In a conveyance there shall, in the several cases in this section mentioned, be deemed to be included, and there shall in those several cases, by virtue of this Act, be implied, a covenant to the effect in this section stated, by the person or by each person who conveys, as far as regards the subject-matter or share of subject-matter expressed to be conveyed by him, with the person, if one, to whom the conveyance is made, or with the persons jointly, if more than one, to whom the conveyance is made as joint tenants, or with each of the persons, if more than one, to whom the conveyance is (when the law permits) made as tenants in common, that is to say:

    (A) In a conveyance for valuable consideration, other than a mortgage, a covenant by a person who conveys and is expressed to convey as beneficial owner in the terms set out in Part I of the Second Schedule to this Act;

    (B) In a conveyance of leasehold property for valuable consideration, other than a mortgage, a further covenant by a person who conveys and is expressed to convey as beneficial owner in the terms set out in Part II of the Second Schedule to this Act;

    (C) In a conveyance by way of mortgage (including a charge) a covenant by a person who conveys or charges and is expressed to convey or charge as beneficial owner in the terms set out in Part III of the Second Schedule to this Act;

(D) In a conveyance by way of mortgage (including a charge) of freehold property subject to a rent or of leasehold property, a further covenant by a person who conveys or charges and is expressed to convey or charge as beneficial owner in the terms set out in Part IV of the Second Schedule to this Act;

(E) In a conveyance by way of settlement, a covenant by a person who conveys and is expressed to convey as settlor in the terms set out in Part V of the Second Schedule to this Act;

(F) In any conveyance, a covenant by every person who conveys and is expressed to convey as trustee or mortgagee, or as personal representative of a deceased person, . . . or under an order of the court, in the terms set out in Part VI of the Second Schedule to this Act, which covenant shall be deemed to extend to every such person's own acts only, and may be implied in an assent by a personal representative in like manner as in a conveyance by deed.

(2) Where in a conveyance it is expressed that by direction of a person expressed to direct as beneficial owner another person conveys, then, for the purposes of this section, the person giving the direction, whether he conveys and is expressed to convey as beneficial owner or not, shall be deemed to convey and to be expressed to convey as beneficial owner the subject-matter so conveyed by his direction; and a covenant on his part shall be implied accordingly.

(3) Where a wife conveys and is expressed to convey as beneficial owner, and the husband also conveys and is expressed to convey as beneficial owner, then, for the purposes of this section, the wife shall be deemed to convey and to be expressed to convey by direction of the husband, as beneficial owner; and, in addition to the covenant implied on the part of the wife, there shall also be implied, first, a covenant on the part of the husband as the person giving that direction, and secondly, a covenant on the part of the husband in the same terms as the covenant implied on the part of the wife.

(4) Where in a conveyance a person conveying is not expressed to convey as beneficial owner, or as settlor, or as trustee, or as mortgagee, or as personal representative of a deceased person, . . . or under an order of the court, or by direction of a person as beneficial owner, no covenant on the part of the person conveying shall be, by virtue of this section, implied in the conveyance.

(5) In this section a conveyance does not include a demise by way of lease at a rent, but does include a charge and "convey" has a corresponding meaning.

(6) The benefit of a covenant implied as aforesaid shall be annexed and incident to, and shall go with, the estate or interest of the implied covenantee, and shall be capable of being enforced by every person in whom that estate or interest is, for the whole or any part thereof, from time to time vested.

(7) A covenant implied as aforesaid may be varied or extended by a deed or an assent, and, as so varied or extended, shall, as far as may be, operate in the like manner, and with all the like incidents, effects, and consequences, as if such variations or extensions were directed in this section to be implied.

(8) This section applies to conveyances made after the thirty-first day of December, eighteen hundred and eighty-one, but only to assents by a personal representative made after the commencement of this Act.   [337]

NOTES

Sub-s (1): words omitted repealed by the Mental Health Act 1959, s 149(2), Sch 8, Part I.

Sub-s (4): words omitted repealed by the Mental Health Act 1959, s 149(2), Sch 8, Part I.

77. Implied covenants in conveyance subject to rents

(1) In addition to the covenants implied under the last preceding section, there shall in the several cases in this section mentioned, be deemed to be included and implied, a covenant to the effect in this section stated, by and with such persons as are hereinafter mentioned, that is to say:—

(A) In a conveyance for valuable consideration, other than a mortgage, of the entirety of the land affected by a rentcharge, a covenant by the grantee or joint and several covenants by the grantees, if more than one, with the conveying parties and with each of them, if more than one, in the terms set out in Part VII of the Second Schedule to this Act. Where a rentcharge has been apportioned in respect of any land, with the consent of the owner of the rentcharge, the covenants in this paragraph shall be implied in the conveyance of that land in like manner as if the apportioned rentcharge were the rentcharge referred to, and the document creating the rentcharge related solely to that land:

(B) In a conveyance for valuable consideration, other than a mortgage, of part of land affected by a rentcharge, subject to a part of that rentcharge which has been or is by that conveyance apportioned (but in either case without the consent of the owner of the rentcharge) in respect of the land conveyed:—

(i) A covenant by the grantee of the land or joint and several covenants by the grantees, if more than one, with the conveying parties and with each of them, if more than one, in the terms set out in paragraph (i) of Part VIII of the Second Schedule to this Act;

(ii) A covenant by a person who conveys or is expressed to convey as beneficial owner, or joint and several covenants by the persons who so convey or are expressed to so convey, if at the date of the conveyance any part of the land affected by such rentcharge is retained, with the grantees of the land and with each of them (if more than one) in the terms set out in paragraph (ii) of Part VIII of the Second Schedule to this Act:

(C) In a conveyance for valuable consideration, other than a mortgage, of the entirety of the land comprised in a lease, for the residue of the term or interest created by the lease, a covenant by the assignee or joint and several covenants by the assignees (if more than one) with the conveying parties and with each of them (if more than one) in the terms set out in Part IX of the Second Schedule to this Act. Where a rent has been apportioned in respect of any land, with the consent of the lessor, the covenants in this paragraph shall be implied in the conveyance of that land in like manner as if the apportioned rent were the original rent reserved, and the lease related solely to that land:

(D) In a conveyance for valuable consideration, other than a mortgage, of part of the land comprised in a lease, for the residue of the term or interest created by the lease, subject to a part of the rent which has been or is by the conveyance apportioned (but in either case without the consent of the lessor) in respect of the land conveyed:—

(i) A covenant by the assignee of the land, or joint and several covenants by the assignees, if more than one, with the conveying parties and with each of them, if more than one, in the terms set out in paragraph (i) of Part X of the Second Schedule to this Act;

(ii) A covenant by a person who conveys or is expressed to convey as beneficial owner, or joint and several covenants by the persons who so convey or are expressed to so convey, if at the date of the conveyance any part of the land comprised in the lease is retained, with the assignees of the land and with each of them (if more than one) in the terms set out in paragraph (ii) of Part X of the Second Schedule to this Act.

(2) Where in a conveyance for valuable consideration, other than a mortgage, part of land affected by a rentcharge, or part of land comprised in a lease is, without the consent of the owner of the rentcharge or of the lessor, as the case may be, expressed to be conveyed—

(i) subject to or charged with the entire rent—

then paragraph (B)(ii) or (D)(i) of the last subsection, as the case may require shall have effect as if the entire rent were the apportioned rent; or

(ii) discharged or exonerated from the entire rent—

then paragraph (B)(ii) or (D)(ii) of the last subsection, as the case may require, shall have effect as if the entire rent were the balance of the rent, and the words "other than the covenant to pay the entire rent" had been omitted.

(3) In this section "conveyance" does not include a demise by way of lease at a rent.

(4) Any covenant which would be implied under this section by reason of a person conveying or being expressed to convey as beneficial owner may, by express reference to this section, be implied, with or without variation, in a conveyance, whether or not for valuable consideration, by a person who conveys or is expressed to convey as settlor, or as trustee, or as mortgagee, or as personal representative of a deceased person, . . . or under an order of the court.

(5) The benefit of a covenant implied as aforesaid shall be annexed and incident to, and shall go with, the estate or interest of the implied covenantee, and shall be capable of being enforced by every person in whom that estate or interest is, for the whole or any part thereof, from time to time vested.

(6) A covenant implied as aforesaid may be varied or extended by deed, and, as so varied or extended, shall, as far as may be, operate in the like manner, and with all the like incidents, effects and consequences, as if such variations or extensions were directed in this section to be implied.

(7) In particular any covenant implied under this section may be extended by providing that—

(*a*) the land conveyed; or

(*b*) the part of the land affected by the rentcharge which remains vested in the covenantor; or

(c) the part of the land demised which remains vested in the covenantor; shall, as the case may require, stand charged with the payment of all money which may become payable under the implied covenant.

(8) This section applies only to conveyances made after the commencement of this Act.   **[338]**

NOTES

Sub-s (4): words omitted repealed by the Mental Health Act 1959, s 149(2), Sch 8, Part I.

78. Benefit of covenants relating to land

(1) A covenant relating to any land of the covenantee shall be deemed to be made with the covenantee and his successors in title and the persons deriving title under him or them, and shall have effect as if such successors and other persons were expressed.

For the purposes of this subsection in connexion with covenants restrictive of the user of land "successors in title" shall be deemed to include the owners and occupiers for the time being of the land of the covenantee intended to be benefited.

(2) This section applies to covenants made after the commencement of this Act, but the repeal of section fifty-eight of the Conveyancing Act 1881 does not affect the operation of covenants to which that section applied.   **[339]**

79. Burden of covenants relating to land

(1) A covenant relating to any land of a covenantor or capable of being bound by him, shall, unless a contrary intention is expressed, be deemed to be made by the covenantor on behalf of himself his successors in title and the persons deriving title under him or them, and, subject as aforesaid, shall have effect as if such successors and other persons were expressed.

This subsection extends to a covenant to do some act relating to the land, notwithstanding that the subject-matter may not be in existence when the covenant is made.

(2) For the purposes of this section in connexion with covenants restrictive of the user of land "successors in title" shall be deemed to include the owners and occupiers for the time being of such land.

(3) This section applies only to covenants made after the commencement of this Act.   **[340]**

80. Covenants binding land

(1) A covenant and a bond and an obligation or contract [made under seal after 31st December 1881 but before the coming into force of section 1 of the Law of Property (Miscellaneous Provisions) Act 1989 or executed as a deed in accordance with that section after its coming into force], binds the real estate as well as the personal estate of the person making the same if and so far as a contrary intention is not expressed in the covenant, bond, obligation, or contract.

This subsection extends to a covenant implied by virtue of this Act.

(2) Every covenant running with the land, whether entered into before or after the commencement of this Act, shall take effect in accordance with any

statutory enactment affecting the devolution of the land, and accordingly the benefit or burden of every such covenant shall vest in or bind the persons who by virtue of any such enactment or otherwise succeed to the title of the covenantee or the covenantor, as the case may be.

(3) The benefit of a covenant relating to land entered into after the commencement of this Act may be made to run with the land without the use of any technical expression if the covenant is of such a nature that the benefit could have been made to run with the land before the commencement of this Act.

(4) For the purposes of this section, a covenant runs with the land when the benefit or burden of it, whether at law or in equity, passes to the successors in title of the covenantee or the covenantor, as the case may be.   **[341]**

NOTES

Sub-s (1): words in square brackets substituted by the Law of Property (Miscellaneous Provisions) Act 1989, s 1(8), Sch 1, para 4.

81. Effect of covenant with two or more jointly

(1) A covenant, and a contract under seal, and a bond or obligation under seal, made with two or more jointly, to pay money or to make a conveyance, or to do any other act, to them or for their benefit, shall be deemed to include, and shall, by virtue of this Act, imply, an obligation to do the act to, or for the benefit of, the survivor or survivors of them, and to, or for the benefit of, any other person to whom the right to sue on the covenant, contract, bond, or obligation devolves, and where made after the commencement of this Act shall be construed as being also made with each of them.

(2) This section extends to a covenant implied by virtue of this Act.

(3) This section applies only if and as far as a contrary intention is not expressed in the covenant, contract, bond, or obligation, and has effect subject to the covenant, contract, bond, or obligation, and to the provisions therein contained.

(4) Except as otherwise expressly provided, this section applies to a covenant, contract, bond, or obligation made or implied after the thirty-first day of December, eighteen hundred and eighty-one.

[(5) In its application to instruments made after the coming into force of section 1 of the Law of Property (Miscellaneous Provisions) Act 1989 subsection (1) above shall have effect as if for the words "under seal, and a bond or obligation under seal," there were substituted the words "bond or obligation executed as a deed in accordance with section 1 of the Law of Property (Miscellaneous Provisions) Act 1989.]   **[342]**

NOTES

Commencement: 31 July 1990 (sub-s (5)); before 1 January 1970 (remainder).

Sub-s (5): added by the Law of Property (Miscellaneous Provisions) Act 1989, s 1(8), Sch 1, para 5.

82. Covenants and agreements entered into by a person with himself and another or others

(1) Any covenant, whether express or implied, or agreement entered into by a person with himself and one or more other persons shall be construed and be

capable of being enforced in like manner as if the covenant or agreement had been entered into with the other person or persons alone.

(2) This section applies to covenants or agreements entered into before or after the commencement of this Act, and to covenants implied by statute in the case of a person who conveys or is expressed to convey to himself and one or more other persons, but without prejudice to any order of the court made before such commencement.   **[343]**

83. Construction of implied covenants

In the construction of a covenant or proviso, or other provision, implied in a deed or assent by virtue of this Act, words importing the singular or plural number, or the masculine gender, shall be read as also importing the plural or singular number, or as extending to females, as the case may require.   **[344]**

84. Power to discharge or modify restrictive covenants affecting land

(1) The Lands Tribunal shall (without prejudice to any concurrent jurisdiction of the court) have power from time to time, on the application of any person interested in any freehold land affected by any restriction arising under covenant or otherwise as to the user thereof or the building thereon, by order wholly or partially to discharge or modify any such restriction on being satisfied—

    (*a*) that by reason of changes in the character of the property or the neighbourhood or other circumstances of the case which the Lands Tribunal may deem material, the restriction ought to be deemed obsolete; or

    (*aa*)that (in a case falling within subsection (1A) below) the continued existence thereof would impede some reasonable user of the land for public or private purposes or, as the case may be, would unless modified so impede such user; or

    (*b*) that the persons of full age and capacity for the time being or from time to time entitled to the benefit of the restriction, whether in respect of estates in fee simple or any lesser estates or interests in the property to which the benefit of the restriction is annexed, have agreed, either expressly or by implication, by their acts or omissions, to the same being discharged or modified; or

    (*c*) that the proposed discharge or modification will not injure the persons entitled to the benefit of the restriction;

and an order discharging or modifying a restriction under this subsection may direct the applicant to pay to any person entitled to the benefit of the restriction such sum by way of consideration as the Tribunal may think it just to award under one, but not both, of the following heads, that is to say, either—

    (i) a sum to make up for any loss or disadvantage suffered by that person in consequence of the discharge or modification; or

    (ii) a sum to make up for any effect which the restriction had, at the time when it was imposed, in reducing the consideration then received for the land affected by it.

(1A) Subsection (1)(*aa*) above authorises the discharge or modification of a restriction by reference to its impeding some reasonable user of land in any case in which the Lands Tribunal is satisfied that the restriction, in impeding that user, either—

    (*a*) does not secure to persons entitled to the benefit of it any practical benefits of substantial value or advantage to them; or (*b*) is contrary to the public interest;

and that money will be an adequate compensation for the loss or disadvantage (if any) which any such person will suffer from the discharge or modification.

(1B) In determining whether a case is one falling within subsection (1A) above, and in determining whether (in any such case or otherwise) a restriction ought to be discharged or modified, the Lands Tribunal shall take into account the development plan and any declared or ascertainable pattern for the grant or refusal of planning permissions in the relevant areas, as well as the period at which and context in which the restriction was created or imposed and any other material circumstances.

(1C) It is hereby declared that the power conferred by this section to modify a restriction includes power to add such further provisions restricting the user of or the building on the land affected as appear to the Lands Tribunal to be reasonable in view of the relaxation of the existing provisions, and as may be accepted by the applicant; and the Lands Tribunal may accordingly refuse to modify a restriction without some such addition.

(2) The court shall have power on the application of any person interested—

(*a*) to declare whether or not in any particular case any freehold land is, or would in any given event be, affected by a restriction imposed by any instrument; or

(*b*) to declare what, upon the true construction of any instrument purporting to impose a restriction, is the nature and extent of the restriction thereby imposed and whether the same is, or would in any given event be, enforceable and if so by whom.

Neither subsections (7) and (11) of this section nor, unless the contrary is expressed, any later enactment providing for this section not to apply to any restrictions shall affect the operation of this subsection or the operation for purposes of this subsection of any other provisions of this section.

(3) The Lands Tribunal shall, before making any order under this section, direct such enquiries, if any, to be made of any government department or local authority, and such notices, if any, whether by way of advertisement or otherwise, to be given to such of the persons who appear to be entitled to the benefit of the restriction intended to be discharged, modified, or dealt with as, having regard to any enquiries, notices or other proceedings previously made, given or taken, the Lands Tribunal may think fit.

(3A) On an application to the Lands Tribunal under this section the Lands Tribunal shall give any necessary directions as to the persons who are or are not to be admitted (as appearing to be entitled to the benefit of the restriction) to oppose the application, and no appeal shall lie against any such direction; but rules under the Lands Tribunal Act 1949 shall make provision whereby, in cases in which there arises on such an application (whether or not in connection with the admission of persons to oppose) any such question as is referred to in subsection (2)(*a*) or (*b*) of this section, the proceedings on the application can and, if the rules so provide, shall be suspended to enable the decision of the court to be obtained on that question by an application under that subsection, or by means of a case stated by the Lands Tribunal, or otherwise, as may be provided by those rules or by rules of court.

(5) Any order made under this section shall be binding on all persons, whether ascertained or of full age or capacity or not, then entitled or thereafter capable of becoming entitled to the benefit of any restriction, which is thereby

discharged, modified or dealt with, and whether such persons are parties to the proceedings or have been served with notice or not.

(6) An order may be made under this section notwithstanding that any instrument which is alleged to impose the restriction intended to be discharged, modified, or dealt with, may not have been produced to the court or the Lands Tribunal, and the court or the Lands Tribunal may act on such evidence of that instrument as it may think sufficient.

(7) This section applies to restrictions whether subsisting at the commencement of this Act or imposed thereafter, but this section does not apply where the restriction was imposed on the occasion of a disposition made gratuitously or for a nominal consideration for public purposes.

(8) This section applies whether the land affected by the restrictions is registered or not, but, in the case of registered land, the Land Registrar shall give effect on the register to any order under this section in accordance with the Land Registration Act 1925.

(9) Where any proceedings by action or otherwise are taken to enforce a restrictive covenant, any person against whom the proceedings are taken, may in such proceedings apply to the court for an order giving leave to apply to the Lands Tribunal under this section, and staying the proceedings in the meantime.

(11) This section does not apply to restrictions imposed by the Commissioners of Works under any statutory power for the protection of any Royal Park or Garden or to restrictions of a like character imposed upon the occasion of any enfranchisement effected before the commencement of this Act in any manor vested in His Majesty in right of the Crown or the Duchy of Lancaster, nor (subject to subsection (11A) below) to restrictions created or imposed—

(a) for naval, military or air force purposes,
[(b) for civil aviation purposes under the powers of the Air Navigation Act 1920, of section 19 or 23 of the Civil Aviation Act 1949 or of section 30 or 41 of the Civil Aviation Act 1982.]

(11A) Subsection (11) of this section—

(a) shall exclude the application of this section to a restriction falling within subsection (11)(a), and not created or imposed in connection with the use of any land as an aerodrome, only so long as the restriction is enforceable by or on behalf of the Crown; and
(b) shall exclude the application of this section to a restriction falling within subsection (11)(b), or created or imposed in connection with the use of any land as an aerodrome, only so long as the restriction is enforceable by or on behalf of the Crown or any public or international authority.

(12) Where a term of more than forty years is created in land (whether before or after the commencement of this Act) this section shall, after the expiration of twenty-five years of the term, apply to restrictions, affecting such leasehold land in like manner as it would have applied had the land been freehold:

Provided that this subsection shall not apply to mining leases.   **[345]**

NOTES
Set out as reprinted with amendments in the Law of Property Act 1969, s 28(1), Sch 3.
Sub-s (11): para (b) substituted by the Civil Aviation Act 1982, s 109, Sch 15, para 1.

PART III

MORTGAGES, RENTCHARGES AND POWERS OF ATTORNEY

Mortgages

85. Mode of mortgaging freeholds

(1) A mortgage of an estate in fee simple shall only be capable of being effected at law either by a demise for a term of years absolute, subject to a provision for cesser on redemption, or by a charge by deed expressed to be by way of legal mortgage:

Provided that a first mortgagee shall have the same right to the possession of documents as if his security included the fee simple.

(2) Any purported conveyance of an estate in fee simple by way of mortgage made after the commencement of this Act shall (to the extent of the estate of the mortgagor) operate as a demise of the land to the mortgagee for a term of years absolute, without impeachment for waste, but subject to cesser on redemption, in manner following, namely:—

  (a) A first or only mortgagee shall take a term of three thousand years from the date of the mortgage:

  (b) A second or subsequent mortgagee shall take a term (commencing from the date of the mortgage) one day longer than the term vested in the first or other mortgagee whose security ranks immediately before that of such second or subsequent mortgagee:

and, in this subsection, any such purported conveyance as aforesaid includes an absolute conveyance with a deed of defeasance and any other assurance which, but for this subsection, would operate in effect to vest the fee simple in a mortgagee subject to redemption.

(3) This section applies whether or not the land is registered under the Land Registration Act 1925, or the mortgage is expressed to be made by way of trust or otherwise.

(4) Without prejudice to the provisions of this Act respecting legal and equitable powers, every power to mortgage or to lend money on mortgage of an estate in fee simple shall be construed as a power to mortgage the estate for a term of years absolute, without impeachment for waste, or by a charge by way of legal mortgage or to lend on such security. **[346]**

86. Mode of mortgaging leaseholds

(1) A mortgage of a term of years absolute shall only be capable of being effected at law either by a subdemise for a term of years absolute, less by one day at least than the term vested in the mortgagor, and subject to a provision for cesser on redemption, or by a charge by deed expressed to be by way of legal mortgage; and where a licence to subdemise by way of mortgage is required, such licence shall not be unreasonably refused:

Provided that a first mortgagee shall have the same right to the possession of documents as if his security had been effected by assignment.

(2) Any purported assignment of a term of years absolute by way of mortgage made after the commencement of this Act shall (to the extent of the estate of the mortgagor) operate as a subdemise of the leasehold land to the mortgagee for a term of years absolute, but subject to cesser on redemption, in manner following, namely:—

(a) The term to be taken by a first or only mortgagee shall be ten days less than the term expressed to be assigned:

(b) The term to be taken by a second or subsequent mortgagee shall be one day longer than the term vested in the first or other mortgagee whose security ranks immediately before that of the second or subsequent mortgagee, if the length of the last mentioned term permits, and in any case for a term less by one day at least than the term expressed to be assigned:

and, in this subsection, any such purported assignment as aforesaid includes an absolute assignment with a deed of defeasance and any other assurance which, but for this subsection, would operate in effect to vest the term of the mortgagor in a mortgagee subject to redemption.

(3) This section applies whether or not the land is registered under the Land Registration Act 1925, or the mortgage is made by way of sub-mortgage of a term of years absolute, or is expressed to be by way of trust for sale or otherwise.

(4) Without prejudice to the provisions of this Act respecting legal and equitable powers, every power to mortgage for or to lend money on mortgage of a term of years absolute by way of assignment shall be construed as a power to mortgage the term by subdemise for a term of years absolute or by a charge by way of legal mortgage, or to lend on such security.   **[347]**

87. Charges by way of legal mortgage

(1) Where a legal mortgage of land is created by a charge by deed expressed to be by way of legal mortgage, the mortgagee shall have the same protection, powers and remedies (including the right to take proceedings to obtain possession from the occupiers and the persons in receipt of rents and profits, or any of them) as if—

(a) where the mortgage is a mortgage of an estate in fee simple, a mortgage term for three thousand years without impeachment of waste had been thereby created in favour of the mortgagee; and

(b) where the mortgage is a mortgage of a term of years absolute, a sub-term less by one day than the term vested in the mortgagor had been thereby created in favour of the mortgagee.

(2) Where an estate vested in a mortgagee immediately before the commencement of this Act has by virtue of this Act been converted into a term of years absolute or sub-term, the mortgagee may, by a declaration in writing to that effect signed by him, convert the mortgage into a charge by way of legal mortgage, and in that case the mortgage term shall be extinguished in the inheritance or in the head term as the case may be, and the mortgagee shall have the same protection, powers and remedies (including the right to take proceedings to obtain possession from the occupiers and the persons in receipt of rents and profits or any of them) as if the mortgage term or sub-term had remained subsisting.

The power conferred by this subsection may be exercised by a mortgagee notwithstanding that he is a trustee or personal representative.

(3) Such declaration shall not affect the priority of the mortgagee or his right to retain possession of documents, nor affect his title to or right over any fixtures or chattels personal comprised in the mortgage.   **[348]**

88. Realisation of freehold mortgages

(1) Where an estate in fee simple has been mortgaged by the creation of a term of years absolute limited thereout or by a charge by way of legal mortgage and the mortgagee sells under his statutory or express power of sale—

  (a) the conveyance by him shall operate to vest in the purchaser the fee simple in the land conveyed subject to any legal mortgage having priority to the mortgage in right of which the sale is made and to any money thereby secured, and thereupon;

  (b) the mortgage term or the charge by way of legal mortgage and any subsequent mortgage term or charges shall merge or be extinguished as respects the land conveyed;

and such conveyance may, as respects the fee simple, be made in the name of the estate owner in whom it is vested.

(2) Where any such mortgagee obtains an order for foreclosure absolute, the order shall operate to vest the fee simple in him (subject to any legal mortgage having priority to the mortgage in right of which the foreclosure is obtained and to any money thereby secured), and thereupon the mortgage term, if any, shall thereby be merged in the fee simple, and any subsequent mortgage term or charge by way of legal mortgage bound by the order shall thereupon be extinguished.

(3) Where any such mortgagee acquires a title under the Limitation Acts, he, or the persons deriving title under him, may enlarge the mortgage term into a fee simple under the statutory power for that purpose discharged from any legal mortgage affected by the title so acquired, or in the case of a chargee by way of legal mortgage may by deed declare that the fee simple is vested in him discharged as aforesaid, and the same shall vest accordingly.

(4) Where the mortgage includes fixtures or chattels personal any statutory power of sale and any right to foreclose or take possession shall extend to the absolute or other interest therein affected by the charge.

(5) In the case of a sub-mortgage by subdemise of a long term (less a nominal period) itself limited out of an estate in fee simple, the foregoing provisions of this section shall operate as if the derivative term, if any, created by the sub-mortgage had been limited out of the fee simple, and so as to enlarge the principal term and extinguish the derivative term created by the sub-mortgage as aforesaid, and to enable the sub-mortgagee to convey the fee simple or acquire it by foreclosure, enlargement, or otherwise as aforesaid.

(6) This section applies to a mortgage whether created before or after the commencement of this Act, and to a mortgage term created by this Act, but does not operate to confer a better title to the fee simple than would have been acquired if the same had been conveyed by the mortgage (being a valid mortgage) and the restrictions imposed by this Act in regard to the effect and creation of mortgages were not in force, and all prior mortgages (if any) not being merely equitable charges had been created by demise or by charge by way of legal mortgage. [349]

89. Realisation of leasehold mortgages

(1) Where a term of years absolute has been mortgaged by the creation of another term of years absolute limited thereout or by a charge by way of legal mortgage and the mortgagee sells under his statutory or express power of sale,—

(a) the conveyance by him shall operate to convey to the purchaser not only the mortgage term, if any, but also (unless expressly excepted with the leave of the court) the leasehold reversion affected by the mortgage, subject to any legal mortgage having priority to the mortgage in right of which the sale is made and to any money thereby secured, and thereupon

(b) the mortgage term, or the charge by way of legal mortgage and any subsequent mortgage term or charge, shall merge in such leasehold reversion or be extinguished unless excepted as aforesaid;

and such conveyance may, as respects the leasehold reversion, be made in the name of the estate owner in whom it is vested.

Where a licence to assign is required on a sale by a mortgagee, such licence shall not be unreasonably refused.

(2) Where any such mortgagee obtains an order for foreclosure absolute, the order shall, unless it otherwise provides, operate (without giving rise to a forfeiture for want of a licence to assign) to vest the leasehold reversion affected by the mortgage and any subsequent mortgage term in him, subject to any legal mortgage having priority to the mortgage in right of which the foreclosure is obtained and to any money thereby secured, and thereupon the mortgage term and any subsequent mortgage term or charge by way of legal mortgage bound by the order shall, subject to any express provision to the contrary contained in the order, merge in such leasehold reversion or be extinguished.

(3) Where any such mortgagee acquires a title under the Limitation Acts, he, or the persons deriving title under him, may by deed declare that the leasehold reversion affected by the mortgage and any mortgage term affected by the title so acquired shall vest in him, free from any right of redemption which is barred, and the same shall (without giving rise to a forfeiture for want of a licence to assign) vest accordingly, and thereupon the mortgage term, if any, and any other mortgage term or charge by way of legal mortgage affected by the title so acquired shall, subject to any express provision to the contrary contained in the deed, merge in such leasehold reversion or be extinguished.

(4) Where the mortgage includes fixtures or chattels personal, any statutory power of sale and any right to foreclose or take possession shall extend to the absolute or other interest therein affected by the charge.

(5) In the case of a sub-mortgage by subdemise of a term (less a nominal period) itself limited out of a leasehold reversion, the foregoing provisions of this section shall operate as if the derivative term created by the sub-mortgage had been limited out of the leasehold reversion, and so as (subject as aforesaid) to merge the principal mortgage term therein as well as the derivative term created by the sub-mortgage and to enable the sub-mortgagee to convey the leasehold reversion or acquire it by foreclosure, vesting, or otherwise as aforesaid.

(6) This section takes effect without prejudice to any incumbrance or trust affecting the leasehold reversion which has priority over the mortgage in right of which the sale, foreclosure, or title is made or acquired, and applies to a mortgage whether executed before or after the commencement of this Act, and to a mortgage term created by this Act, but does not apply where the mortgage term does not comprise the whole of the land included in the leasehold reversion unless the rent (if any) payable in respect of that reversion has been apportioned as respects the land affected, or the rent is of no money value or no rent is

reserved, and unless the lessee's covenants and conditions (if any) have been apportioned, either expressly or by implication, as respects the land affected.

[(7) The county court has jurisdiction under this section where the amount owing in respect of the mortgage or charge at the commencement of the proceedings does not exceed [£30,000].] **[350]**

NOTES
Sub-s (7): added by the County Courts Act 1984, s 148(1), Sch 2, para 3; sum in square brackets substituted by the High Court and County Courts Jurisdiction Order 1991, SI 1991 No 724, art 2(8), Schedule.

90. Realisation of equitable charges by the court

(1) Where an order for sale is made by the court in reference to an equitable mortgage on land (not secured by a legal term of years absolute or by a charge by way of legal mortgage) the court may, in favour of a purchaser, make a vesting order conveying the land or may appoint a person to convey the land or create and vest in the mortgagee a legal term of years absolute to enable him to carry out the sale, as the case may require, in like manner as if the mortgage had been created by deed by way of legal mortgage pursuant to this Act, but without prejudice to any incumbrance having priority to the equitable mortgage unless the incumbrancer consents to the sale.

(2) This section applies to equitable mortgages made or arising before or after the commencement of this Act, but not to a mortgage which has been over-reached under the powers conferred by this Act or otherwise.

[(3) The county court has jurisdiction under this section where the amount owing in respect of the mortgage or charge at the commencement of the proceedings does not exceed [£30,000].] **[351]**

NOTES
Sub-s (3): added by the County Courts Act 1984, s 148(1), Sch 2, para 3; sum in square brackets substituted by the High Court and County Courts Jurisdiction Order 1991, SI 1991 No 724, art 2(8), Schedule.

91. Sale of mortgaged property in action for redemption or foreclosure

(1) Any person entitled to redeem mortgaged property may have a judgment or order for sale instead of for redemption in an action brought by him either for redemption alone, or for sale alone, or for sale or redemption in the alternative.

(2) In any action, whether for foreclosure, or for redemption, or for sale, or for the raising and payment in any manner of mortgage money, the court, on the request of the mortgagee, or of any person interested either in the mortgage money or in the right of redemption, and, notwithstanding that—

(a) any other person dissents; or
(b) the mortgagee or any person so interested does not appear in the action;

and without allowing any time for redemption or for payment of any mortgage money, may direct a sale of the mortgaged property, on such terms as it thinks fit, including the deposit in court of a reasonable sum fixed by the court to meet the expenses of sale and to secure performance of the terms.

(3) But, in an action brought by a person interested in the right of redemption and seeking a sale, the court may, on the application of any defendant, direct the plaintiff to give such security for costs as the court thinks fit, and may give the conduct of the sale to any defendant, and may give such directions as it thinks fit respecting the costs of the defendants or any of them.

(4) In any case within this section the court may, if it thinks fit, direct a sale without previously determining the priorities of incumbrancers.

(5) This section applies to actions brought either before or after the commencement of this Act.

(6) In this section "mortgaged property" includes the estate or interest which a mortgagee would have had power to convey if the statutory power of sale were applicable.

(7) For the purposes of this section the court may, in favour of a purchaser, make a vesting order conveying the mortgaged property, or appoint a person to do so, subject or not to any incumbrance, as the court may think fit; or, in the case of an equitable mortgage, may create and vest a mortgage term in the mortgagee to enable him to carry out the sale as if the mortgage had been made by deed by way of legal mortgage.

[(8) The county court has jurisdiction under this section where the amount owing in respect of the mortgage or charge at the commencement of the proceedings does not exceed [£30,000].]   **[352]**

NOTES
Sub-s (8): added by the County Courts Act 1984, s 148(1), Sch 2, para 3; sum in square brackets substituted by the High Court and County Courts Jurisdiction Order 1991, SI 1991 No 724, art 2(8), Schedule.

92. Power to authorise land and minerals to be dealt with separately

[(1)] Where a mortgagee's power of sale in regard to land has become exercisable but does not extend to the purposes mentioned in this section, the court may, on his application, authorise him and the persons deriving title under him to dispose—

> (a) of the land, with an exception or reservation of all or any mines and minerals, and with or without rights and powers of or incidental to the working, getting or carrying away of minerals; or
> (b) of all or any mines and minerals, with or without the said rights or powers separately from the land;

and thenceforth the powers so conferred shall have effect as if the same were contained in the mortgage.

[(2) The county court has jurisdiction under this section where the amount owing in respect of the mortgage or charge at the commencement of the proceedings does not exceed [£30,000].]   **[353]**

NOTES
Sub-s (1): renumbered as such by the County Courts Act 1984, s 148(1), Sch 2, para 3.
Sub-s (2): added by the County Courts Act 1984, s 148(1), Sch 2, para 3; sum in square brackets substituted by the High Court and County Courts Jurisdiction Order 1991 No 724, art 2(8), Schedule

93. Restriction on consolidation of mortgages

(1) A mortgagor seeking to redeem any one mortgage is entitled to do so without paying any money due under any separate mortgage made by him, or by any person through whom he claims, solely on property other than that comprised in the mortgage which he seeks to redeem.

This subsection applies only if and as far as a contrary intention is not expressed in the mortgage deeds or one of them.

(2) This section does not apply where all the mortgages were made before the first day of January, eighteen hundred and eighty-two.

(3) Save as aforesaid, nothing in this Act, in reference to mortgages, affects any right of consolidation or renders inoperative a stipulation in relation to any mortgage made before or after the commencement of this Act reserving a right to consolidate. [354]

94. Tacking and further advances

(1) After the commencement of this Act, a prior mortgagee shall have a right to make further advances to rank in priority to subsequent mortgages (whether legal or equitable)—

(a) if an arrangement has been made to that effect with the subsequent mortgagees; or

(b) if he had no notice of such subsequent mortgages at the time when the further advance was made by him; or

(c) whether or not he had such notice as aforesaid, where the mortgage imposes an obligation on him to make such further advances.

This subsection applies whether or not the prior mortgage was made expressly for securing further advances.

(2) In relation to the making of further advances after the commencement of this Act a mortgagee shall not be deemed to have notice of a mortgage merely by reason that it was registered as a land charge ... if it was not so registered at the [time when the original mortgage was created] or when the last search (if any) by or on behalf of the mortgagee was made, whichever last happened.

This subsection only applies where the prior mortgage was made expressly for securing a current account or other further advances.

(3) Save in regard to the making of further advances as aforesaid, the right to tack is hereby abolished:

Provided that nothing in this Act shall affect any priority acquired before the commencement of this Act by tacking, or in respect of further advances made without notice of a subsequent incumbrance or by arrangement with the subsequent incumbrancer.

(4) This section applies to mortgages of land made before or after the commencement of this Act, but not to charges registered under the Land Registration Act 1925 or any enactment replaced by that Act. [355]

NOTES
Sub-s (2): words omitted repealed by the Law of Property Act 1969, s 16, Sch 2, Pt I; words in square brackets substituted by the Law of Property (Amendment) Act 1926, s 7, Schedule.

95. Obligation to transfer instead of reconveying, and as to right to take possession

(1) Where a mortgagor is entitled to redeem, then subject to compliance with the terms on compliance with which he would be entitled to require a reconveyance or surrender, he shall be entitled to require the mortgagee, instead of reconveying or surrendering, to assign the mortgage debt and convey the mortgaged property to any third person, as the mortgagor directs; and the mortgagee shall be bound to assign and convey accordingly.

(2) The rights conferred by this section belong to and are capable of being

enforced by each incumbrancer, or by the mortgagor, notwithstanding any intermediate incumbrance; but a requisition of an incumbrancer prevails over a requisition of the mortgagor, and, as between incumbrancers, a requisition of a prior incumbrancer prevails over a requisition of a subsequent incumbrancer.

(3) The foregoing provisions of this section do not apply in the case of a mortgagee being or having been in possession.

(4) Nothing in this Act affects prejudicially the right of a mortgagee of land whether or not his charge is secured by a legal term of years absolute to take possession of the land, but the taking of possession by the mortgagee does not convert any legal estate of the mortgagor into an equitable interest.

(5) This section applies to mortgages made either before or after the commencement of this Act, and takes effect notwithstanding any stipulation to the contrary.   [356]

96. Regulations respecting inspection, production and delivery of documents, and priorities

(1) A mortgagor, as long as his right to redeem subsists, shall be entitled from time to time, at reasonable times, on his request, and at his own cost, and on payment of the mortgagee's costs and expenses in this behalf, to inspect and make copies or abstracts of or extracts from the documents of title relating to the mortgaged property in the custody or power of the mortgagee.

This subsection applies to mortgages made after the thirty-first day of December, eighteen hundred and eighty-one, and takes effect notwithstanding any stipulation to the contrary.

(2) A mortgagee, whose mortgage is surrendered or otherwise extinguished, shall not be liable on account of delivering documents of title in his possession to the person not having the best right thereto, unless he has notice of the right or claim of a person having a better right, whether by virtue of a right to require a surrender or reconveyance or otherwise.

[In this subsection notice does not include notice implied by reason of registration under the Land Charges Act 1925 . . .]   [357]

NOTES
Sub-s (2): words in square brackets added by the Law of Property (Amendment) Act 1926, s 7, Schedule; words omitted spent for certain purposes and repealed for certain purposes by the Law of Property Act 1969, s 16, Sch 2, Part I.

97. Priorities as between puisne mortgages

Every mortgage affecting a legal estate in land made after the commencement of this Act, whether legal or equitable (not being a mortgage protected by the deposit of documents relating to the legal estate affected) shall rank according to its date of registration as a land charge pursuant to the Land Charges Act 1925.

This section does not apply [to mortgages or charges to which the Land Charges Act 1972 does not apply by virtue of section 14(3) of that Act (which excludes certain land charges created by instruments necessitating registration under the Land Registration Act 1925), or] to mortgages or charges of registered land . . .   [358]

NOTES
Words in square brackets substituted by the Land Charges Act 1972, s 18(1), Sch 3; words omitted spent for certain purposes and repealed for certain purposes by the Law of Property Act 1969, s 17, Sch 2, Part II.

98. Actions for possession by mortgagors

(1) A mortgagor for the time being entitled to the possession or receipt of the rents and profits of any land, as to which the mortgagee has not given notice of his intention to take possession or to enter into the receipt of the rents and profits thereof, may sue for such possession, or for the recovery of such rents or profits, or to prevent or recover damages in respect of any trespass or other wrong relative thereto, in his own name only, unless the cause of action arises upon a lease or other contract made by him jointly with any other person.

(2) This section does not prejudice the power of a mortgagor independently of this section to take proceedings in his own name only, either in right of any legal estate vested in him or otherwise.

(3) This section applies whether the mortgage was made before or after the commencement of this Act.   [359]

99. Leasing powers of mortgagor and mortgagee in possession

(1) A mortgagor of land while in possession shall, as against every incumbrancer, have power to make from time to time any such lease of the mortgaged land, or any part thereof, as is by this section authorised.

(2) A mortgagee of land while in possession shall, as against all prior incumbrancers, if any, and as against the mortgagor, have power to make from time to time any such lease as aforesaid.

(3) The leases which this section authorises are—
     (i) agricultural or occupation leases for any term not exceeding twenty-one years, or, in the case of a mortgage made after the commencement of this Act, fifty years; and
     (ii) building leases for any term not exceeding ninety-nine years, or, in the case of a mortgage made after the commencement of this Act, nine hundred and ninety-nine years.

(4) Every person making a lease under this section may execute and do all assurances and things necessary or proper in that behalf.

(5) Every lease shall be made to take effect in possession not later than twelve months after its date.

(6) Every such lease shall reserve the best rent that can reasonably be obtained, regard being had to the circumstances of the case, but without any fine being taken.

(7) Every such lease shall contain a covenant by the lessee for payment of the rent, and a condition of re-entry on the rent not being paid within a time therein specified not exceeding thirty days.

(8) A counterpart of every such lease shall be executed by the lessee and delivered to the lessor, of which execution and delivery the execution of the lease by the lessor shall, in favour of the lessee and all persons deriving title under him, be sufficient evidence.

(9) Every such building lease shall be made in consideration of the lessee,

or some person by whose direction the lease is granted, having erected, or agreeing to erect within not more than five years from the date of the lease, buildings, new or additional, or having improved or repaired buildings, or agreeing to improve or repair buildings within that time, or having executed, or agreeing to execute within that time, on the land leased, an improvement for or in connexion with building purposes.

(10) In any such building lease a peppercorn rent, or a nominal or other rent less than the rent ultimately payable, may be made payable for the first five years, or any less part of the term.

(11) In case of a lease by the mortgagor, he shall, within one month after making the lease, deliver to the mortgagee, or, where there are more than one, to the mortgagee first in priority, a counterpart of the lease duly executed by the lessee, but the lessee shall not be concerned to see that this provision is complied with.

(12) A contract to make or accept a lease under this section may be enforced by or against every person on whom the lease if granted would be binding.

(13) This section applies only if and as far as a contrary intention is not expressed by the mortgagor and mortgagee in the mortgage deed, or otherwise in writing, and has effect subject to the terms of the mortgage deed or of any such writing and to the provisions therein contained.

(14) The mortgagor and mortgagee may, by agreement in writing, whether or not contained in the mortgage deed, reserve to or confer on the mortgagor or the mortgagee, or both, any further or other powers of leasing or having reference to leasing; and any further or other powers so reserved or conferred shall be exercisable, as far as may be, as if they were conferred by this Act, and with all the like incidents, effects, and consequences:

Provided that the powers so reserved or conferred shall not prejudicially affect the rights of any mortgagee interested under any other mortgage subsisting at the date of the agreement, unless that mortgagee joins in or adopts the agreement.

(15) Nothing in this Act shall be construed to enable a mortgagor or mortgagee to make a lease for any longer term or on any other conditions than such as could have been granted or imposed by the mortgagor, with the concurrence of all the incumbrancers, if this Act and the enactments replaced by this section had not been passed:

Provided that, in the case of a mortgage of leasehold land, a lease granted under this section shall reserve a reversion of not less than one day.

(16) Subject as aforesaid, this section applies to any mortgage made after the thirty-first day of December, eighteen hundred and eighty-one, but the provisions thereof, or any of them, may, by agreement in writing made after that date between mortgagor and mortgagee, be applied to a mortgage made before that date, so nevertheless that any such agreement shall not prejudicially affect any right or interest of any mortgagee not joining in or adopting the agreement.

(17) The provisions of this section referring to a lease shall be construed to extend and apply, as far as circumstances admit, to any letting, and to an agreement, whether in writing or not, for leasing or letting.

(18) For the purposes of this section "mortgagor" does not include an incumbrancer deriving title under the original mortgagor.

(19) The powers of leasing conferred by this section shall, after a receiver of the income of the mortgaged property or any part thereof has been appointed by a mortgagee under his statutory power, and so long as the receiver acts, be exercisable by such mortgagee instead of by the mortgagor, as respects any land affected by the receivership, in like manner as if such mortgagee were in possession of the land, and the mortgagee may, by writing, delegate any of such powers to the receiver. **[360]**

100. Powers of mortgagor and mortgagee in possession to accept surrenders of leases

(1) For the purpose only of enabling a lease authorised under the last preceding section, or under any agreement made pursuant to that section, or by the mortgage deed (in this section referred to as an authorised lease) to be granted, a mortgagor of land while in possession shall, as against every incumbrancer, have, by virtue of this Act, power to accept from time to time a surrender of any lease of the mortgaged land or any part thereof comprised in the lease, with or without an exception of or in respect of all or any of the mines and minerals therein, and, on a surrender of the lease so far as it comprises part only of the land or mines and minerals leased, the rent may be apportioned.

(2) For the same purpose, a mortgagee of land while in possession shall, as against all prior or other incumbrancers, if any, and as against the mortgagor, have, by virtue of this Act, power to accept from time to time any such surrender as aforesaid.

(3) On a surrender of part only of the land or mines and minerals leased, the original lease may be varied, provided that the lease when varied would have been valid as an authorised lease if granted by the person accepting the surrender; and, on a surrender and the making of a new or other lease, whether for the same or for any extended or other term, and whether subject or not to the same or to any other covenants, provisions, or conditions, the value of the lessee's interest in the lease surrendered may, subject to the provisions of this section, be taken into account in the determination of the amount of the rent to be reserved, and of the nature of the covenants, provisions, and conditions to be inserted in the new or other lease.

(4) Where any consideration for the surrender, other than an agreement to accept an authorised lease, is given by or on behalf of the lessee to or on behalf of the person accepting the surrender, nothing in this section authorises a surrender to a mortgagor without the consent of the incumbrancers, or authorises a surrender to a second or subsequent incumbrancer without the consent of every prior incumbrancer.

(5) No surrender shall, by virtue of this section, be rendered valid unless:—

    (*a*) An authorised lease is granted of the whole of the land or mines and minerals comprised in the surrender to take effect in possession immediately or within one month after the date of the surrender; and

    (*b*) The term certain or other interest granted by the new lease is not less in duration than the unexpired term or interest which would have been subsisting under the original lease if that lease had not been surrendered; and

    (*c*) Where the whole of the land mines and minerals originally leased has been surrendered, the rent reserved by the new lease is not less than the rent which would have been payable under the original lease if it had not been surrendered; or where part only of the land or mines and minerals has been surrendered, the aggregate rents respectively remaining payable or reserved under the original lease and new lease are not less than the rent which would have been payable under the original lease if no partial surrender had been accepted.

(6) A contract to make or accept a surrender under this section may be enforced by or against every person on whom the surrender, if completed, would be binding.

(7) This section applies only if and as far as a contrary intention is not expressed by the mortgagor and mortgagee in the mortgage deed, or otherwise in writing, and shall have effect subject to the terms of the mortgage deed or of any such writing and to the provisions therein contained.

(8) This section applies to a mortgage made after the thirty-first day of December, nineteen hundred and eleven, but the provisions of this section, or any of them, may, by agreement in writing made after that date, between mortgagor and mortgagee, be applied to a mortgage made before that date, so nevertheless that any such agreement shall not prejudicially affect any right or interest of any mortgagee not joining in or adopting the agreement.

(9) The provisions of this section referring to a lease shall be construed to extend and apply, as far as circumstances admit, to any letting, and to an agreement, whether in writing or not, for leasing or letting.

(10) The mortgagor and mortgagee may, by agreement in writing, whether or not contained in the mortgage deed, reserve or confer on the mortgagor or mortgagee, or both, any further or other powers relating to the surrender of leases; and any further or other powers so conferred or reserved shall be exercisable, as far as may be, as if they were conferred by this Act, and with all the like incidents, effects and consequences:

Provided that the powers so reserved or conferred shall not prejudicially affect the rights of any mortgagee interested under any other mortgage subsisting at the date of the agreement, unless that mortgagee joins in or adopts the agreement.

(11) Nothing in this section operates to enable a mortgagor or mortgagee to accept a surrender which could not have been accepted by the mortgagor with the concurrence of all the incumbrancers if this Act and the enactments replaced by this section had not been passed.

(12) For the purposes of this section "mortgagor" does not include an incumbrancer deriving title under the original mortgagor.

(13) The powers of accepting surrenders conferred by this section shall, after a receiver of the income of the mortgaged property or any part thereof has been appointed by the mortgagee, under the statutory power, and so long as the receiver acts, be exercisable by such mortgagee instead of by the mortgagor, as respects any land affected by the receivership, in like manner as if such mortgagee were in possession of the land; and the mortgagee may, by writing, delegate any of such powers to the receiver.   **[361]**

101. Powers incident to estate or interest of mortgagee

(1) A mortgagee, where the mortgage is made by deed, shall, by virtue of this Act, have the following powers, to the like extent as if they had been in terms conferred by the mortgage deed, but not further (namely):—

(i) A power, when the mortgage money has become due, to sell, or to concur with any other person in selling, the mortgaged property, or any part thereof, either subject to prior charges or not, and either together or in lots, by public auction or by private contract, subject to such conditions respecting title, or evidence of title, or other matter, as the mortgagee thinks fit, with power to vary any contract for sale, and to buy in at an auction, or to rescind any contract for sale, and to re-sell, without being answerable for any loss occasioned thereby; and

(ii) A power, at any time after the date of the mortgage deed, to insure and keep insured against loss or damage by fire any building, or any effects or property of an insurable nature, whether affixed to the freehold or not, being or forming part of the property which or an estate or interest wherein is mortgaged, and the premiums paid for any such insurance shall be a charge on the mortgaged property or estate or interest, in addition to the mortgage money, and with the same priority, and with interest at the same rate, as the mortgage money; and

(iii) A power, when the mortgage money has become due, to appoint a receiver of the income of the mortgaged property, or any part thereof; or, if the mortgaged property consists of an interest in income, or of a rentcharge or an annual or other periodical sum, a receiver of that property or any part thereof; and

(iv) A power, while the mortgagee is in possession, to cut and sell timber and other trees ripe for cutting, and not planted or left standing for shelter or ornament, or to contract for any such cutting and sale, to be completed within any time not exceeding twelve months from the making of the contract.

(2) Where the mortgage deed is executed after the thirty-first day of December, nineteen hundred and eleven, the power of sale aforesaid includes the following powers as incident thereto (namely):—

(i) A power to impose or reserve or make binding, as far as the law permits, by covenant, condition, or otherwise, on the unsold part of the mortgaged property or any part thereof, or on the purchaser and any property sold, any restriction or reservation with respect to building on or other user of land, or with respect to mines and minerals, or for the purpose of the more beneficial working thereof, or with respect to any other thing:

(ii) A power to sell the mortgaged property, or any part thereof, or all or any mines and minerals apart from the surface:—

(a) With or without a grant or reservation of rights of way, rights of water, easements, rights, and prvileges for or connected with building or other purposes in relation to the property remaining in mortgage or any part thereof, or to any property sold: and

(b) With or without an exception or reservation of all or any of the mines and minerals in or under the mortgaged property, and with or without a grant or reservation of powers of working, wayleaves, or rights of way, rights of water and drainage and other powers, easements, rights, and privileges for or connected with mining purposes in relation to the property remaining unsold or any part thereof, or to any property sold: and

(c) With or without covenants by the purchaser to expend money on the land sold.

(3) The provisions of this Act relating to the foregoing powers, comprised either in this section, or in any other section regulating the exercise of those powers, may be varied or extended by the mortgage deed, and, as so varied or extended, shall, as far as may be, operate in the like manner and with all the like incidents, effects, and consequences, as if such variations or extensions were contained in this Act.

(4) This section applies only if and as far as a contrary intention is not expressed in the mortgage deed, and has effect subject to the terms of the mortgage deed and to the provisions therein contained.

(5) Save as otherwise provided, this section applies where the mortgage deed is executed after the thirty-first day of December, eighteen hundred and eighty-one.

(6) The power of sale conferred by this section includes such power of selling the estate in fee simple or any leasehold reversion as is conferred by the provisions of this Act relating to the realisation of mortgages.   [362]

102. Provision as to mortgages of undivided shares in land

(1) A person who was before the commencement of this Act a mortgagee of an undivided share in land shall have the same power to sell his share in the proceeds of sale of the land and in the rents and profits thereof until sale, as, independently of this Act, he would have had in regard to the share in the land; and shall also have a right to require the trustees for sale in whom the land is vested to account to him for the income attributable to that share or to appoint a receiver to receive the same from such trustees corresponding to the right which, independently of this Act, he would have had to take possession or to appoint a receiver of the rents and profits attributable to the same share.

(2) The powers conferred by this section are exercisable by the persons deriving title under such mortgagee.   [363]

103. Regulation of exercise of power of sale

A mortgagee shall not exercise the power of sale conferred by this Act unless and until—

(i) Notice requiring payment of the mortgage money has been served on the mortgagor or one of two or more mortgagors, and default has been made in payment of the mortgage money, or of part thereof, for three months after such service; or

(ii) Some interest under the mortgage is in arrear and unpaid for two months after becoming due; or

(iii) There has been a breach of some provision contained in the mortgage deed or in this Act, or in an enactment replaced by this Act, and on the part of the mortgagor, or of some person concurring in making the mortgage, to be observed or performed, other than and besides a covenant for payment of the mortgage money or interest thereon.   [364]

104. Conveyance on sale

(1) A mortgagee exercising the power of sale conferred by this Act shall have power, by deed, to convey the property sold, for such estate and interest therein as he is by this Act authorised to sell or convey or may be the subject of the mortgage, freed from all estates, interest, and rights to which the mortgage has priority, but subject to all estates, interests, and rights which have priority to the mortgage.

(2) Where a conveyance is made in exercise of the power of sale conferred by this Act, or any enactment replaced by this Act, the title of the purchaser shall not be impeachable on the ground—

(a) that no case had arisen to authorise the sale; or

(b) that due notice was not given; or

(c) where the mortgage is made after the commencement of this Act, that leave of the court, when so required, was not obtained; or

(d) whether the mortgage was made before or after such commencement, that the power was otherwise improperly or irregularly exercised;

and a purchaser is not, either before or on conveyance, concerned to see or inquire whether a case has arisen to authorise the sale, or due notice has been given, or the power is otherwise properly and regularly exercised; but any person damnified by an unauthorised, or improper, or irregular exercise of the power shall have his remedy in damages against the person exercising the power.

(3) A conveyance on sale by a mortgagee, made after the commencement of this Act, shall be deemed to have been made in exercise of the power of sale conferred by this Act unless a contrary intention appears. **[365]**

105. Application of proceeds of sale

The money which is received by the mortgagee, arising from the sale, after discharge of prior incumbrances to which the sale is not made subject, if any, or after payment into court under this Act of a sum to meet any prior incumbrance, shall be held by him in trust to be applied by him, first, in payment of all costs, charges, and expenses properly incurred by him as incident to the sale or any attempted sale, or otherwise; and secondly, in discharge of the mortgage money, interest, and costs, and other money, if any, due under the mortgage; and the residue of the money so received shall be paid to the person entitled to the mortgaged property, or authorised to give receipts for the proceeds of the sale thereof. **[366]**

106. Provisions as to exercise of power of sale

(1) The power of sale conferred by this Act may be exercised by any person for the time being entitled to receive and give a discharge for the mortgage money.

(2) The power of sale conferred by this Act does not affect the right of foreclosure.

(3) The mortgagee shall not be answerable for any involuntary loss happening in or about the exercise or execution of the power of sale conferred by this Act, or of any trust connected therewith, or, where the mortgage is executed after the thirty-first day of December, nineteen hundred and eleven, of any power or provision contained in the mortgage deed.

(4) At any time after the power of sale conferred by this Act has become exercisable, the person entitled to exercise the power may demand and recover

from any person, other than a person having in the mortgaged property an estate, interest, or right in priority to the mortgage, all the deeds and documents relating to the property, or to the title thereto, which a purchaser under the power of sale would be entitled to demand and recover from him. [367]

107. Mortgagee's receipts, discharges, etc

(1) The receipt in writing of a mortgagee shall be a sufficient discharge for any money arising under the power of sale conferred by this Act, or for any money or securities comprised in his mortgage, or arising thereunder; and a person paying or transferring the same to the mortgagee shall not be concerned to inquire whether any money remains due under the mortgage.

(2) Money received by a mortgagee under his mortgage or from the proceeds of securities comprised in his mortgage shall be applied in like manner as in this Act directed respecting money received by him arising from a sale under the power of sale conferred by this Act, but with this variation, that the costs, charges, and expenses payable shall include the costs, charges, and expenses properly incurred of recovering and receiving the money or securities, and of conversion of securities into money, instead of those incident to sale. [368]

108. Amount and application of insurance money

(1) The amount of an insurance effected by a mortgagee against loss or damage by fire under the power in that behalf conferred by this Act shall not exceed the amount specified in the mortgage deed, or, if no amount is therein specified two third parts of the amount that would be required, in case of total destruction, to restore the property insured.

(2) An insurance shall not, under the power conferred by this Act, be effected by a mortgagee in any of the following cases (namely):—

    (i) Where there is a declaration in the mortgage deed that no insurance is required:

    (ii) Where an insurance is kept up by or on behalf of the mortgagor in accordance with the mortgage deed:

    (iii) Where the mortgage deed contains no stipulation respecting insurance, and an insurance is kept up by or on behalf of the mortgagor with the consent of the mortgagee to the amount to which the mortgagee is by this Act authorised to insure.

(3) All money received on an insurance of mortgaged property against loss or damage by fire or otherwise effected under this Act, or any enactment replaced by this Act, or on an insurance for the maintenance of which the mortgagor is liable under the mortgage deed, shall, if the mortgagee so requires, be applied by the mortgagor in making good the loss or damage in respect of which the money is received.

(4) Without prejudice to any obligation to the contrary imposed by law, or by special contract, a mortgagee may require that all money received on an insurance of mortgaged property against loss or damage by fire or otherwise effected under this Act, or any enactment replaced by this Act, or on an insurance for the maintenance of which the mortgagor is liable under the mortgage deed, be applied in or towards the discharge of the mortgage money.

[369]

109. Appointment, powers, remuneration and duties of receiver

(1) A mortgagee entitled to appoint a receiver under the power in that behalf conferred by this Act shall not appoint a receiver until he has become entitled to exercise the power of sale conferred by this Act, but may then, by writing under his hand, appoint such person as he thinks fit to be receiver.

(2) A receiver appointed under the powers conferred by this Act, or any enactment replaced by this Act, shall be deemed to be the agent of the mortgagor; and the mortgagor shall be solely responsible for the receiver's acts or defaults unless the mortgage deed otherwise provides.

(3) The receiver shall have power to demand and recover all the income of which he is appointed receiver, by action, distress, or otherwise, in the name either of the mortgagor or of the mortgagee, to the full extent of the estate or interest which the mortgagor could dispose of, and to give effectual receipts accordingly for the same, and to exercise any powers which may have been delegated to him by the mortgagee pursuant to this Act.

(4) A person paying money to the receiver shall not be concerned to inquire whether any case has happened to authorise the receiver to act.

(5) The receiver may be removed, and a new receiver may be appointed, from time to time by the mortgagee by writing under his hand.

(6) The receiver shall be entitled to retain out of any money received by him, for his remuneration, and in satisfaction of all costs, charges, and expenses incurred by him as receiver, a commission at such rate, not exceeding five per centum on the gross amount of all money received, as is specified in his appointment, and if no rate is so specified, then at the rate of five per centum on that gross amount, or at such other rate as the court thinks fit to allow, on application made by him for that purpose.

(7) The receiver shall, if so directed in writing by the mortgagee, insure to the extent, if any, to which the mortgagee might have insured and keep insured against loss or damage by fire, out of the money received by him, any building, effects, or property comprised in the mortgage, whether affixed to the freehold or not, being of an insurable nature.

(8) Subject to the provisions of this Act as to the application of insurance money, the receiver shall apply all money received by him as follows, namely:—

    (i) In discharge of all rents, taxes, rates, and outgoings whatever affecting the mortgaged property; and

    (ii) In keeping down all annual sums or other payments, and the interest on all principal sums, having priority to the mortgage in right whereof he is receiver; and

    (iii) In payment of his commission, and of the premiums on fire, life, or other insurances, if any, properly payable under the mortgage deed or under this Act, and the cost of executing necessary or proper repairs directed in writing by the mortgagee; and

    (iv) In payment of the interest accruing due in respect of any principal money due under the mortgage; and

    (v) In or towards discharge of the principal money if so directed in writing by the mortgagee;

and shall pay the residue, if any, of the money received by him to the person who, but for the possession of the receiver, would have been entitled to receive the income of which he is appointed receiver, or who is otherwise entitled to the mortgaged property. **[370]**

110. Effect of bankruptcy of the mortgagor on the power to sell or appoint a receiver

(1) Where the statutory or express power for a mortgagee either to sell or to appoint a receiver is made exercisable by reason of the mortgagor . . . being adjudged a bankrupt, such power shall not be exercised only on account of the . . . adjudication, without the leave of the court.

(2) This section applies only where the mortgage deed is executed after the commencement of this Act. . . **[371]**

NOTES
Words omitted repealed by the Insolvency Act 1985, s 235(3), Sch 10, Part III.

111. Effect of advance on joint account

(1) Where—

(*a*) in a mortgage, or an obligation for payment of money, or a transfer of a mortgage or of such an obligation, the sum, or any part of the sum, advanced or owing is expressed to be advanced by or owing to more persons than one out of money, or as money, belonging to them on a joint account; or

(*b*) a mortgage, or such an obligation, or such a transfer is made to more persons than one, jointly;

the mortgage money, or other money or money's worth, for the time being due to those persons on the mortgage or obligation, shall, as between them and the mortgagor or obligor, be deemed to be and remain money or money's worth belonging to those persons on a joint account; and the receipt in writing of the survivors or last survivor of them, or of the personal representative of the last survivor, shall be a complete discharge for all money or money's worth for the time being due, notwithstanding any notice to the payer of a severance of the joint account.

(2) This section applies if and so far as a contrary intention is not expressed in the mortgage, obligation, or transfer, and has effect subject to the terms of the mortgage, obligation, or transfer, and to the provisions therein contained.

(3) This section applies to any mortgage, obligation, or transfer made after the thirty-first day of December, eighteen hundred and eighty-one. **[372]**

113. Notice of trusts affecting mortgage debts

(1) A person dealing in good faith with a mortgagee, or with the mortgagor if the mortgage has been discharged released or postponed as to the whole or any part of the mortgaged property, shall not be concerned with any trust at any time affecting the mortgage money or the income thereof, whether or not he has notice of the trust, and may assume unless the contrary is expressly stated in the instruments relating to the mortgage—

(*a*) that the mortgagees (if more than one) are or were entitled to the mortgage money on a joint account; and

(*b*) that the mortgagee has or had power to give valid receipts for the purchase money or mortgage money and the income thereof (including any arrears of interest) and to release or postpone the priority of the mortgage debt or any part thereof or to deal with the same or the mortgaged property or any part thereof;

without investigating the equitable title to the mortgage debt or the appointment or discharge of trustees in reference thereto.

(2) This section applies to mortgages made before or after the commencement of this Act, but only as respects dealings effected after such commencement.

(3) This section does not affect the liability of any person in whom the mortgage debt is vested for the purposes of any trust to give effect to that trust.

[374]

114. Transfers of mortgages

(1) A deed executed by a mortgagee purporting to transfer his mortgage or the benefit thereof shall, unless a contrary intention is therein expressed, and subject to any provisions therein contained, operate to transfer to the transferee—

    (a) the right to demand, sue for, recover, and give receipts for, the mortgage money or the unpaid part thereof, and the interest then due, if any, and thenceforth to become due thereon; and

    (b) the benefit of all securities for the same, and the benefit of and the right to sue on all covenants with the mortgagee, and the right to exercise all powers of the mortgagee; and

    (c) all the estate and interest in the mortgaged property then vested in the mortgagee subject to redemption or cesser, but as to such estate and interest subject to the right of redemption then subsisting.

(2) In this section "transferee" includes his personal representatives and assigns.

(3) A transfer of mortgage may be made in the form contained in the Third Schedule to this Act with such variations and additions, if any, as the circumstances may require.

(4) This section applies, whether the mortgage transferred was made before or after the commencement of this Act, but applies only to transfers made after the commencement of this Act.

(5) This section does not extend to a transfer of a bill of sale of chattels by way of security. **[375]**

115. Reconveyances of mortgages by endorsed receipts

(1) A receipt endorsed on, written at the foot of, or annexed to, a mortgage for all money thereby secured, which states the name of the person who pays the money and is executed by the chargee by way of legal mortgage or the person in whom the mortgaged property is vested and who is legally entitled to give a receipt for the mortgage money shall operate, without any reconveyance, surrender, or release—

    (a) Where a mortgage takes effect by demise or subdemise, as a surrender of the term, so as to determine the term or merge the same in the reversion immediately expectant thereon;

    (b) Where the mortgage does not take effect by demise or subdemise, as a reconveyance thereof to the extent of the interest which is the subject matter of the mortgage, to the person who immediately before the execution of the receipt was entitled to the equity of redemption;

and in either case, as a discharge of the mortgaged property from all principal money and interest secured by, and from all claims under the mortgage, but without prejudice to any term or other interest which is paramount to the estate or interest of the mortgagee or other person in whom the mortgaged property was vested.

(2) Provided that, where by the receipt the money appears to have been paid by a person who is not entitled to the immediate equity of redemption, the receipt shall operate as if the benefit of the mortgage had by deed been transferred to him; unless—

(*a*) it is otherwise expressly provided; or

(*b*) the mortgage is paid off out of capital money, or other money in the hands of a personal representative or trustee properly applicable for the discharge of the mortgage, and it is not expressly provided that the receipt is to operate as a transfer.

(3) Nothing in this section confers on a mortgagor a right to keep alive a mortgage paid off by him, so as to affect prejudicially any subsequent incumbrancer; and where there is no right to keep the mortgage alive, the receipt does not operate as a transfer.

(4) This section does not affect the right of any person to require a reassignment, surrender, release, or transfer to be executed in lieu of a receipt.

(5) A receipt may be given in the form contained in the Third Schedule to this Act, with such variation and additions, if any, as may be deemed expedient . . .

(6) In a receipt given under this section the same covenants shall be implied as if the person who executes the receipt had by deed been expressed to convey the property as mortgagee, subject to any interest which is paramount to the mortgage.

(7) Where the mortgage consists of a mortgage and a further charge or of more than one deed, it shall be sufficient for the purposes of this section, if the receipt refers either to all the deeds whereby the mortgage money is secured or to the aggregate amount of the mortgage money thereby secured and for the time being owing, and is endorsed on, written at the foot of, or annexed to, one of the mortgage deeds.

(8) This section applies to the discharge of a charge by way of legal mortgage, and to the discharge of a mortgage, whether made by way of statutory mortgage or not, executed before or after the commencement of this Act, but only as respects discharges effected after such commencement.

(9) The provisions of this section relating to the operation of a receipt shall (in substitution for the like statutory provisions relating to receipts given by or on behalf of a building . . . society) apply to the discharge of a mortgage made to any such society, provided that the receipt is executed in the manner required by the statute relating to the society . . .

(10) This section does not apply to the discharge of a charge or incumbrance registered under the Land Registration Act 1925.

(11) In this section "mortgaged property" means the property remaining subject to the mortgage at the date of the receipt. **[376]**

NOTES
Sub-s (5): words omitted repealed by the Finance Act 1971, s 69, Sch 14, Part VI.
Sub-s (9): first words omitted repealed by the Friendly Societies Act 1971, s 14(2), Sch 3 and the
Industrial and Provident Societies Act 1965, s 77(1), Sch 5; second words omitted repealed by the
Finance Act 1971, s 61, Sch 14, Part VI.

116. Cesser of mortgage terms

Without prejudice to the right of a tenant for life or other person having only a
limited interest in the equity of redemption to require a mortgage to be kept
alive by transfer or otherwise, a mortgage term shall, when the money secured
by the mortgage has been discharged, become a satisfied term and shall cease.
[377]

117. Forms of statutory legal charges

(1) As a special form of charge by way of legal mortgage, a mortgage of freehold
or leasehold land may be made by a deed expressed to be made by way of
statutory mortgage, being in one of the forms (No. 1 or 4) set out in the Fourth
Schedule to this Act, with such variations and additions, if any, as circumstances
may require, and if so made the provisions of this section shall apply thereto.

(2) There shall be deemed to be included, and there shall by virtue of this
Act be implied, in such a mortgage deed—

First, a covenant with the mortgagee by the person therein expressed
to charge as mortgagor to the effect following, namely:—

That the mortgagor will, on the stated day, pay to the mortgagee
the stated mortgage money, with interest thereon in the meantime
at the stated rate, and will thereafter, if and as long as the
mortgage money or any part thereof remains unpaid, pay to the
mortgagee (as well after as before any judgment is obtained under
the mortgage) interest thereon, or on the unpaid part thereof, at
the stated rate, by equal half-yearly payments the first thereof to
be made at the end of six months from the day stated for payment
of the mortgage money:

Secondly, a provision to the following effect (namely):—

That if the mortgagor on the stated day pays to the mortgagee
the stated mortgage money, with interest thereon in the meantime
at the stated rate, the mortgagee at any time thereafter, at the
request and cost of the mortgagor, shall discharge the mortgaged
property or transfer the benefit of the mortgage as the mortgagor
may direct.

This subsection applies to a mortgage deed made under section twenty-six
of the Conveyancing Act 1881 with a substitution of a reference to "the person
therein expressed to convey as mortgagor" for the reference in this subsection
to "the person therein expressed to charge as mortgagor." [378]

118. Forms of statutory transfers of legal charges

(1) A transfer of a statutory mortgage may be made by a deed expressed to be
made by way of statutory transfer of mortgage, being in such one of the three
forms (No. 2, 3, or 4) set out in the Fourth Schedule to this Act as may be
appropriate to the case with such variations and additions, if any, as
circumstances may require, and if so made the provisions of this section shall
apply thereto.

(2) In whichever of those three forms the deed of transfer is made, it shall have effect as follows (namely):—

(i) There shall become vested in the person to whom the benefit of the mortgage is expressed to be transferred (who, with his personal representatives and assigns, is in this section designated the transferee), the right to demand, sue for, recover, and give receipts for the mortgage money, or the unpaid part thereof, and the interest then due, if any, and thenceforth to become due thereon, and the benefit of all securities for the same, and the benefit of and the right to sue on all covenants with the mortgagee, and the right to exercise all powers of the mortgagee:

(ii) All the term and interest, if any, subject to redemption, of the mortgagee in the mortgaged land shall vest in the transferee, subject to redemption.

(3) If a covenantor joins in the deed of transfer, there shall also be deemed to be included, and there shall by virtue of this Act be implied therein, a covenant with the transferee by the person expressed to join therein as covenantor to the effect following (namely):—

That the covenantor will, on the next of the days by the mortgage deed fixed for payment of interest pay to the transferee the stated mortgage money, or so much thereof as then remains unpaid, with interest thereon, or on the unpaid part thereof, in the meantime, at the rate stated in the mortgage deed; and will thereafter, as long as the mortgage money or any part thereof remains unpaid, pay to the transferee interest on that sum, or the unpaid part thereof, at the same rate, on the successive days by the mortgage deed fixed for payment of interest

(4) If the deed of transfer is made in the Form No. 4, it shall, by virtue of this Act, operate not only as a statutory transfer of mortgage, but also as a statutory mortgage, and the provisions of this section shall have effect in relation thereto accordingly; but it shall not be liable to any increased stamp duty by reason only of it being designated a mortgage.

(5) This section applies to the transfer of a statutory mortgage created under any enactment replaced by this Act.   [379]

119. Implied covenants, joint and several

In a deed of statutory mortgage, or of statutory transfer of mortgage, where more persons than one are expressed to convey or charge as mortgagors, or to join as covenantors, the implied covenant on their part shall be deemed to be a joint and several covenant by them; and where there are more mortgagees or more transferees than one, the implied covenant with them shall be deemed to be a covenant with them jointly, unless the amount secured is expressed to be secured to them in shares or distinct sums, in which latter case the implied covenant with them shall be deemed to be a covenant with each severally in respect of the share or distinct sum secured to him.   [380]

120. Form of discharge of statutory mortgage or charge

A statutory mortgage may be surrendered or discharged by a receipt in the form (No. 5) set out in the Fourth Schedule to this Act with such variations and additions, if any, as circumstances may require.   [381]

Rentcharges

121. Remedies for the recovery of annual sums charged on land

(1) Where a person is entitled to receive out of any land, or out of the income of any land, any annual sum, payable half-yearly or otherwise, whether charged on the land or on the income of the land, and whether by way of rentcharge or otherwise, not being rent incident to a reversion, then, subject and without prejudice to all estates, interests, and rights having priority to the annual sum, the person entitled to receive the annual sum shall have such remedies for recovering and compelling payment thereof as are described in this section, as far as those remedies might have been conferred by the instrument under which the annual sum arises, but not further.

(2) If at any time the annual sum or any part thereof is unpaid for twenty-one days next after the time appointed for any payment in respect thereof, the person entitled to receive the annual sum may enter into and distrain on the land charged or any part thereof, and dispose according to law of any distress found, to the intent that thereby or otherwise the annual sum and all arrears thereof, and all costs and expenses occasioned by non-payment thereof, may be fully paid.

(3) If at any time the annual sum or any part thereof is unpaid for forty days next after the time appointed for any payment in respect thereof, then, although no legal demand has been made for payment thereof, the person entitled to receive the annual sum may enter into possession of and hold the land charged or any part thereof, and take the income thereof, until thereby or otherwise the annual sum and all arrears thereof due at the time of his entry or afterwards becoming due during his continuance in possession, and all costs and expenses occasioned by nonpayment of the annual sum, are fully paid; and such possession when taken shall be without impeachment of waste.

(4) In the like case the person entitled to the annual sum, whether taking possession or not, may also by deed demise the land charged, or any part thereof, to a trustee for a term of years, with or without impeachment of waste, on trust, by all or any of the means hereinafter mentioned, or by any other reasonable means, to raise and pay the annual sum and all arrears thereof due or to become due, and all costs and expenses occasioned by nonpayment of the annual sum, or incurred in compelling or obtaining payment thereof, or otherwise relating thereto, including the costs of the preparation and execution of the deed of demise, and the costs of the execution of the trusts of that deed:

Provided that this subsection shall not authorise the creation of a legal term of years absolute after the commencement of this Act, save where the annual sum is a rentcharge held for a legal estate.

The surplus, if any, of the money raised, or of the income received, under the trusts of the deed shall be paid to the person for the time being entitled to the land therein comprised in reversion immediately expectant on the term thereby created.

The means by which such annual sum, arrears, costs, and expenses may be raised includes—

   (a) the creation of a legal mortgage or a sale (effected by assignment or subdemise) of the term created in the land charged or any part thereof,
   (b) the receipt of the income of the land comprised in the term.

(5) This section applies only if and as far as a contrary intention is not

expressed in the instrument under which the annual sum arises, and has effect subject to the terms of that instrument and to the provisions therein contained.

(6) The rule of law relating to perpetuities does not apply to any powers or remedies conferred by this section, ...

(7) The powers and remedies conferred by this section apply where the instrument creating the annual sum comes into operation after the thirty-first day of December, eighteen hundred and eighty-one, and whether the instrument conferring the power under which the annual sum was authorised to be created came into operation before or after that date, unless the instrument creating the power or under which the annual sum is created otherwise directs.   **[382]**

NOTES
Sub-s (6): words omitted repealed by the Perpetuities and Accumulations Act 1964, s 11(2).

122. Creation of rentcharges charged on another rentcharge and remedies for recovery thereof

(1) A rentcharge or other annual sum (not being rent incident to a reversion) payable half yearly or otherwise may be granted, reserved, charged or created out of or on another rentcharge or annual sum (not being rent incident to a reversion) charged on or payable out of land or on or out of the income of land, in like manner as the same could have been made to issue out of land.

(2) If at any time the annual sum so created or any part thereof is unpaid for twenty-one days next after the time appointed for any payment in respect thereof, the person entitled to receive the annual sum shall (without prejudice to any prior interest or charge) have power to appoint a receiver of the annual sum charged or any part thereof, and the provisions of this Act relating to the appointment, powers, remuneration and duties of a receiver, shall apply in like manner as if such person were a mortgagee entitled to exercise the power of sale conferred by this Act, and the annual sum charged were the mortgaged property and the person entitled thereto were the mortgagor.

(3) The power to appoint a receiver conferred by this section shall (where the annual sum is charged on a rentcharge) take effect in substitution for the remedies conferred, in the case of annual sums charged on land, by the last preceding section, but subsection (6) of that section shall apply and have effect as if herein re-enacted and in terms made applicable to the powers conferred by this section.

(4) This section applies to annual sums expressed to be created before as well as after the commencement of this Act, and, but without prejudice to any order of the court made before the commencement of this Act, operates to confirm any annual sum which would have been validly created if this section had been in force.   **[383]**

Powers of Attorney

125. Powers of attorney relating to land to be filed

(1) ...

(2) Notwithstanding any stipulation to the contrary, a purchaser of any interest in or charge upon land (not being land or a charge registered [under the Land Registration Act 1925] shall be entitled to have any instrument creating a

power of attorney which affects his title, or [a copy] thereof or of the material portions thereof delivered to him free of expense.

(3) This section only applies to instruments executed after the commencement of this Act, and no right to rescind a contract shall arise by reason of the enforcement of the provisions of this section. **[384]**

NOTES
Sub-s (1): repealed by the Powers of Attorney Act 1971, s 11(2), Sch 2.
Sub-s (2): first words in square brackets substituted by the Powers of Attorney Act 1971, s 11(3); second words in square brackets substituted by the Law of Property (Amendment) Act 1926, s 7, Schedule.

PART IV

EQUITABLE INTERESTS AND THINGS IN ACTION

130. Creation of entailed interests in real and personal property

(1) An interest in tail or in tail male or in tail female or in tail special (in this Act referred to as "an entailed interest") may be created by way of trust in any property, real or personal, but only by the like expressions as those by which before the commencement of this Act a similar estate tail could have been created by deed (not being an executory instrument) in freehold land, and with the like results, including the right to bar the entail either absolutely or so as to create an interest equivalent to a base fee, and accordingly all statutory provisions relating to estates tail in real property shall apply to entailed interests in personal property.

Personal estate so entailed (not being chattels settled as heirlooms) may be invested, applied, and otherwise dealt with as if the same were capital money or securities representing capital money arising under the Settled Land Act 1925, from land settled on the like trusts.

(2) Expressions contained in an instrument coming into operation after the commencement of this Act, which, in a will, or executory instrument coming into operation before such commencement, would have created an entailed interest in freehold land, but would not have been effectual for that purpose in a deed not being an executory instrument, shall (save as provided by the next succeeding section) operate in equity, in regard to property real or personal, to create absolute, fee simple or other interests corresponding to those which, if the property affected had been personal estate, would have been created therein by similar expressions before the commencement of this Act.

(3) Where personal estate (including the proceeds of sale of land directed to be sold and chattels directed to be held as heirlooms) is, after the commencement of this Act, directed to be enjoyed or held with, or upon trusts corresponding to trusts affecting, land in which, either before or after the commencement of this Act an entailed interest has been created, and is subsisting, such direction shall be deemed sufficient to create a corresponding entailed interest in such personal estate.

(4) In default of and subject to the execution of a disentailing assurance or the exercise of the testamentary power conferred by this Act, an entailed interest (to the extent of the property affected) shall devolve as an equitable interest, from time to time, upon the persons who would have been successively entitled thereto as the heirs of the body (either generally or of a particular class) of the tenant in tail or other person, or as tenant by the curtesy, if the entailed interest

had, before the commencement of this Act, been limited in respect of freehold land governed by the general law in force immediately before such commencement, and such law had remained unaffected.

(5) Where personal chattels are settled without reference to settled land on trusts creating entailed interest therein, the trustees, with the consent of the usufructuary for the time being if of full age, may sell the chattels or any of them, and the net proceeds of any such sale shall be held in trust for and shall go to the same persons successively, in the same manner and for the same interests, as the chattels sold would have been held and gone if they had not been sold, and the income of investments representing such proceeds of sale shall be applied accordingly.

(6) An entailed interest shall only be capable of being created by a settlement of real or personal property or the proceeds of sale thereof (including the will of a person dying after the commencement of this Act), or by an agreement for a settlement in which the trusts to affect property are sufficiently declared.

(7) In this Act where the context so admits "entailed interest" includes an estate tail (now made to take effect as an equitable interest) created before the commencement of this Act. **[385]**

131. Abolition of the rule in Shelley's case

Where by any instrument coming into operation after the commencement of this Act an interest in any property is expressed to be given to the heir or heirs or issue or any particular heir or any class of the heirs or issue of any person in words which, but for this section would, under the rule of law known as the Rule in Shelley's case, have operated to give to that person an interest in fee simple or an entailed interest, such words shall operate in equity as words of purchase and not of limitation, and shall be construed and have effect accordingly, and in the case of an interest in any property expressed to be given to an heir or heirs or any particular heir or class of heirs, the same person or persons shall take as would in the case of freehold land have answered that description under the general law in force before the commencement of this Act. **[386]**

132. As to heirs taking by purchase

(1) A limitation of real or personal property in favour of the heir, either general or special, of a deceased person which, if limited in respect of freehold land before the commencement of this Act, would have conferred on the heir an estate in the land by purchase, shall operate to confer a corresponding equitable interest in the property on the person who would, if the general law in force immediately before such commencement had remained unaffected, have answered the description of the heir, either general or special, of the deceased in respect of his freehold land, either at the death of the deceased or at the time named in the limitation, as the case may require.

(2) This section applies whether the deceased person dies before or after the commencement of this Act, but only applies to limitations or trusts created by an instrument coming into operation after such commencement. **[387]**

134. Restriction on executory limitations

(1) Where there is a person entitled to—

    (*a*) an equitable interest in land for an estate in fee simple or for any less interest not being an entailed interest, or (*b*) any interest in other property, not being an entailed interest,

with an executory limitation over on default or failure of all or any of his issue, whether within or at any specified period or time or not, that executory limitation shall be or become void and incapable of taking effect, if and as soon as there is living any issue who has attained the age of [eighteen years] of the class on default or failure whereof the limitation over was to take effect.

(2) This section applies where the executory limitation is contained in an instrument coming into operation after the thirty-first day of December, eighteen hundred and eighty-two, save that, as regards instruments coming into operation before the commencement of this Act, it only applies to limitations of land for an estate in fee, or for a term of years absolute or determinable on life, or for a term of life. **[388]**

NOTES

Sub-s (1): words in square brackets substituted by the Family Law Reform Act 1969, ss 1(3), 28(3), Sch 1.

135. Equitable waste

An equitable interest for life without impeachment of waste does not confer upon the tenant for life any right to commit waste of the description known as equitable waste, unless an intention to confer such right expressly appears by the instrument creating such equitable interest. **[389]**

136. Legal assignments of things in action

(1) Any absolute assignment by writing under the hand of the assignor (not purporting to be by way of charge only) of any debt or other legal thing in action, of which express notice in writing has been given to the debtor, trustee or other person from whom the assignor would have been entitled to claim such debt or thing in action, is effectual in law (subject to equities having priority over the right of the assignee) to pass and transfer from the date of such notice—

(*a*) the legal right to such debt or thing in action;
(*b*) all legal and other remedies for the same; and
(*c*) the power to give a good discharge for the same without the concurrence of the assignor:

Provided that, if the debtor, trustee or other person liable in respect of such debt or thing in action has notice—

(*a*) that the assignment is disputed by the assignor or any person claiming under him; or
(*b*) of any other opposing or conflicting claims to such debt or thing in action;

he may, if he thinks fit, either call upon the persons making claim thereto to interplead concerning the same, or pay the debt or other thing in action into court under the provisions of the Trustee Act 1925.

(2) This section does not affect the provisions of the Policies of Assurance Act 1867.

[(3) The county court has jurisdiction (including power to receive payment of money or securities into court) under the proviso to subsection (1) of this section where the amount or value of the debt or thing in action does not exceed [£30,000].] **[390]**

NOTES
Sub-s (3): added by the County Courts Act 1984, s 148(1), Sch 2, para 4; sum in square brackets substituted by the High Court and County Courts Jurisdiction Order 1991, SI 1991 No 724, art 2(8), Schedule.

137. Dealings with life interests, reversions and other equitable interests

(1) The law applicable to dealings with equitable things in action which regulates the priority of competing interests therein, shall, as respects dealings with equitable interests in land, capital money, and securities representing capital money effected after the commencement of this Act, apply to and regulate the priority of competing interests therein.

(2) This subsection applies whether or not the money or securities are in court.

    (i) In the case of a dealing with an equitable interest in settled land, capital money or securities representing capital money, the persons to be served with notice of the dealing shall be the trustees of the settlement; and where the equitable interest is created by a derivative or subsidiary settlement, the persons to be served with notice shall be the trustees of that settlement.

    (ii) In the case of a dealing with an equitable interest in the proceeds of sale of land or in the rents and profits until sale the persons to be served with notice shall, as heretofore, be the trustees for sale.

    (iii) In any other case the person to be served with notice of a dealing with an equitable interest in land shall be the estate owner of the land affected.

The persons on whom notice is served pursuant to this subsection shall be affected thereby in the same manner as if they had been trustees of personal property out of which the equitable interest was created or arose.

This subsection does not apply where the money or securities are in court.

(3) A notice, otherwise than in writing, given to, or received by, a trustee after the commencement of this Act as respects any dealing with an equitable interest in real or personal property, shall not affect the priority of competing claims of purchasers in that equitable interest.

(4) Where, as respects any dealing with an equitable interest in real or personal property—

    (a) the trustees are not persons to whom a valid notice of the dealing can be given; or

    (b) there are no trustees to whom a notice can be given; or

    (c) for any other reason a valid notice cannot be served, or cannot be served without unreasonable cost or delay;

a purchaser may at his own cost require that—

    (i) a memorandum of the dealing be endorsed, written on or permanently annexed to the instrument creating the trust;

    (ii) the instrument be produced to him by the person having the possession or custody thereof to prove that a sufficient memorandum has been placed thereon or annexed thereto.

Such memorandum shall, as respects priorities, operate in like manner as if notice in writing of the dealing had been given to trustees duly qualified to receive the notice at the time when the memorandum is placed on or annexed to the instrument creating the trust.

(5) Where the property affected is settled land, the memorandum shall be placed on or annexed to the trust instrument and not the vesting instrument.

Where the property affected is land on trust for sale, the memorandum shall be placed on or annexed to the instrument whereby the equitable interest is created.

(6) Where the trust is created by statute or by operation of law, or in any other case where there is no instrument whereby the trusts are declared, the instrument under which the equitable interest is acquired or which is evidence of the devolution thereof shall, for the purposes of this section, be deemed the instrument creating the trust.

In particular, where the trust arises by reason of an intestacy, the letters of administration or probate in force when the dealing was effected shall be deemed such instrument.

(7) Nothing in this section affects any priority acquired before the commencement of this Act.

(8) Where a notice in writing of a dealing with an equitable interest in real or personal property has been served on a trustee under this section, the trustees from time to time of the property affected shall be entitled to the custody of the notice, and the notice shall be delivered to them by any person who for the time being may have the custody thereof; and subject to the payment of costs, any person interested in the equitable interest may require production of the notice.

(9) The liability of the estate owner of the legal estate affected to produce documents and furnish information to persons entitled to equitable interests therein shall correspond to the liability of a trustee for sale to produce documents and furnish information to persons entitled to equitable interests in the proceeds of sale of the land.

(10) This section does not apply until a trust has been created, and in this section "dealing" includes a disposition by operation of law.   **[391]**

138. Power to nominate a trust corporation to receive notices

(1) By any settlement or other instrument creating a trust, a trust corporation may be nominated to whom notices of dealings affecting real or personal property may be given, whether or not under the foregoing section, and in default of such nomination the trustees (if any) of the instrument, or the court on the application of any person interested, may make the nomination.

(2) The person having the possession or custody of any instrument on which notices under that section may be endorsed shall cause the name of the trust corporation to whom notices may be given to be endorsed upon that instrument.

(3) Notice given to any trust corporation whose name is so endorsed shall operate in the same way as a notice or endorsement under the foregoing section.

(4) Where a trust corporation is acting for the purposes of this section a notice given to a trustee of the trust instrument of a dealing relating to the trust property shall forthwith be delivered or sent by post by the trustee to the trust corporation, and until received by the corporation shall not affect any priority.

(5) A trust corporation shall not be nominated for the purposes of this section—

    (a) unless that corporation consents to act; or

(*b*) where that corporation has any beneficial interest in or charge upon the trust property; or

(*c*) where a trust corporation is acting as the trustee or one of the trustees of the instrument creating the trust.

(6) Where a trust corporation acting for the purposes of this section becomes entitled to any beneficial interest in or charge upon the trust property, another trust corporation shall be nominated in its place and all documents relating to notices affecting the trust shall be delivered to the corporation so nominated.

(7) A trust corporation acting for the purposes of this section shall be bound to keep a separate register of notices of dealings in respect of each equitable interest and shall enter therein—

(*a*) the date of the notice;

(*b*) the name of the person giving the notice;

(*c*) short particulars of the equitable interest intended to be affected; and

(*d*) short particulars of the effect of the dealing if mentioned in the notice.

(8) The trust corporation may, before making any entry in the register, require the applicant to pay a fee not exceeding the prescribed fee.

(9) Subject to the payment of a fee not exceeding the prescribed fee, the trust corporation shall permit any person who would, if the corporation had been the trustee of the trust investment, have been entitled to inspect notices served on the trustee, to inspect and take copies of the register and any notices held by the corporation.

(10) Subject to the payment by the applicant of a fee not exceeding the prescribed fee, the trust corporation shall reply to all inquiries respecting notices received by the corporation in like manner and in the same circumstances as if the corporation had been the trustee of the trust instrument.

(11) In this section "prescribed fee" means the fee prescribed by the Treasury, with the sanction of the Lord Chancellor, in cases where the Public Trustee acts as a trust corporation for the purposes of this section.   [392]

PART V

LEASES AND TENANCIES

139. Effect of extinguishment of reversion

(1) Where a reversion expectant on a lease of land is surrendered or merged, the estate or interest which as against the lessee for the time being confers the next vested right to the land, shall be deemed the reversion for the purpose of preserving the same incidents and obligations as would have affected the original reversion had there been no surrender or merger thereof.

(2) This section applies to surrenders or mergers effected after the first day of October, eighteen hundred and forty-five.   [393]

140. Apportionment of conditions on severance

(1) Notwithstanding the severance by conveyance, surrender, or otherwise of the reversionary estate in any land comprised in a lease, and notwithstanding the avoidance or cesser in any other manner of the term granted by a lease as to part only of the land comprised therein, every condition or right of re-entry, and every other condition contained in the lease, shall be apportioned, and shall

remain annexed to the severed parts of the reversionary estate as severed, and shall be in force with respect to the term whereon each severed part is reversionary, or the term in the part of the land as to which the term has not been surrendered, or has not been avoided or has not otherwise ceased, in like manner as if the land comprised in each severed part, or the land as to which the term remains subsisting, as the case may be, had alone originally been comprised in the lease.

(2) In this section "right of re-entry" includes a right to determine the lease by notice to quit or otherwise; but where the notice is served by a person entitled to a severed part of the reversion so that it extends to part only of the land demised, the lessee may within one month determine the lease in regard to the rest of the land by giving to the owner of the reversionary estate therein a counter notice expiring at the same time as the original notice . . .

(3) This section applies to leases made before or after the commencement of this Act and whether the severance of the reversionary estate or the partial avoidance or cesser of the term was effected before or after such commencement:

Provided that, where the lease was made before the first day of January eighteen hundred and eighty-two nothing in this section shall affect the operation of a severance of the reversionary estate or partial avoidance or cesser of the term which was effected before the commencement of this Act.   [394]

NOTES
   Sub-s (2): words omitted repealed with savings by the Agricultural Holdings Act 1948, ss 98, 100(1), Sch 8.

141. Rent and benefit of lessee's covenants to run with the reversion

(1) Rent reserved by a lease, and the benefit of every covenant or provision therein contained, having reference to the subject-matter thereof, and on the lessee's part to be observed or performed, and every condition of re-entry and other condition therein contained, shall be annexed and incident to and shall go with the reversionary estate in the land, or in any part thereof, immediately expectant on the term granted by the lease, notwithstanding severance of that reversionary estate, and without prejudice to any liability affecting a covenantor or his estate.

(2) Any such rent, covenant or provision shall be capable of being recovered, received, enforced, and taken advantage of, by the person from time to time entitled, subject to the term, to the income of the whole or any part, as the case may require, of the land leased.

(3) Where that person becomes entitled by conveyance or otherwise, such rent, covenant or provision may be recovered, received, enforced or taken advantage of by him notwithstanding that he becomes so entitled after the condition of re-entry or forfeiture has become enforceable, but this subsection does not render enforceable any condition of re-entry or other condition waived or released before such person becomes entitled as aforesaid.

(4) This section applies to leases made before or after the commencement of this Act, but does not affect the operation of—

    (a) any severance of the reversionary estate; or
    (b) any acquisition by conveyance or otherwise of the right to receive or enforce any rent covenant or provision;

effected before the commencement of this Act.   [395]

142. Obligation of lessor's covenants to run with reversion

(1) The obligation under a condition or of a covenant entered into by a lessor with reference to the subject-matter of the lease shall, if and as far as the lessor has power to bind the reversionary estate immediately expectant on the term granted by the lease, be annexed and incident to and shall go with that reversionary estate, or the several parts thereof, notwithstanding severance of that reversionary estate, and may be taken advantage of and enforced by the person in whom the term is from time to time vested by conveyance, devolution in law, or otherwise; and, if and as far as the lessor has power to bind the person from time to time entitled to that reversionary estate, the obligation aforesaid may be taken advantage of and entered against any person so entitled.

(2) This section applies to leases made before or after the commencement of this Act, whether the severance of the reversionary estate was effected before or after such commencement:

Provided that, where the lease was made before the first day of January eighteen hundred and eighty-two, nothing in this section shall affect the operation of any severance of the reversionary estate effected before such commencement.

This section takes effect without prejudice to any liability affecting a covenantor or his estate.   [396]

143. Effect of licences granted to lessees

(1) Where a licence is granted to a lessee to do any act, the licence, unless otherwise expressed, extends only—

    (*a*) to the permission actually given; or
    (*b*) to the specific breach of any provision or covenant referred to; or
    (*c*) to any other matter thereby specifically authorised to be done;

and the licence does not prevent any proceeding for any subsequent breach unless otherwise specified in the licence.

(2) Notwithstanding any such licence—

    (*a*) All rights under covenants and powers of re-entry contained in the lease remain in full force and are available as against any subsequent breach of covenant, condition or other matter not specifically authorised or waived, in the same manner as if no licence had been granted; and
    (*b*) The condition or right of entry remains in force in all respects as if the licence had not been granted, save in respect of the particular matter authorised to be done.

(3) Where in any lease there is a power or condition of re-entry on the lessee assigning, subletting or doing any other specified act without a licence, and a licence is granted—

    (*a*) to any one of two or more lessees to do any act, or to deal with his equitable share or interest; or
    (*b*) to any lessee, or to any one of two or more lessees to assign or underlet part only of the property, or to do any act in respect of part only of the property;

the licence does not operate to extinguish the right of entry in case of any breach of covenant or condition by the co-lessees of the other shares or interests in the property, or by the lessee or lessees of the rest of the property (as the case may be) in respect of such shares or interests or remaining property, but the right of entry remains in force in respect of the shares, interests or property not the subject of the licence.

This subsection does not authorise the grant after the commencement of this Act of a licence to create an undivided share in a legal estate.

(4) This section applies to licences granted after the thirteenth day of August, eighteen hundred and fifty-nine.   [397]

144. No fine to be exacted for licence to assign

In all leases containing a covenant, condition, or agreement against assigning, underletting, or parting with the possession, or disposing of the land or property leased without licence or consent, such covenant, condition, or agreement shall, unless the lease contains an express provision to the contrary, be deemed to be subject to a proviso to the effect that no fine or sum of money in the nature of a fine shall be payable for or in respect of such licence or consent; but this proviso does not preclude the right to require the payment of a reasonable sum in respect of any legal or other expense incurred in relation to such licence or consent.

[398]

145. Lessee to give notice of ejectment to lessor

Every lessee to whom there is delivered any writ for the recovery of premises demised to or held by him, or to whose knowledge any such writ comes, shall forthwith give notice thereof to his lessor or his bailiff or receiver, and, if he fails so to do, he shall be liable to forfeit to the person of whom he holds the premises an amount equal to the value of three years' improved or rack rent of the premises, to be recovered by action in any court having jurisdiction in respect of claims for such an amount.   [399]

146. Restrictions on and relief against forfeiture of leases and underleases

(1) A right of re-entry or forfeiture under any proviso or stipulation in a lease for a breach of any covenant or condition in the lease shall not be enforceable, by action or otherwise, unless and until the lessor serves on the lessee a notice—

    (*a*) specifying the particular breach complained of; and
    (*b*) if the breach is capable of remedy, requiring the lessee to remedy the breach; and
    (*c*) in any case, requiring the lessee to make compensation in money for the breach;

and the lessee fails, within a reasonable time thereafter, to remedy the breach, if it is capable of remedy, and to make reasonable compensation in money, to the satisfaction of the lessor, for the breach.

(2) Where a lessor is proceeding, by action or otherwise, to enforce such a right of re-entry or forfeiture, the lessee may, in the lessor's action, if any, or in any action brought by himself, apply to the court for relief; and the court may grant or refuse relief, as the court, having regard to the proceedings and conduct of the parties under the foregoing provisions of this section, and to all the other circumstances, thinks fit; and in case of relief may grant it on such terms, if any, as to costs, expenses, damages, compensation, penalty, or otherwise, including the granting of an injunction to restrain any like breach in the future, as the court, in the circumstances of each case, thinks fit.

(3) A lessor shall be entitled to recover as a debt due to him from a lessee,

and in addition to damages (if any), all reasonable costs and expenses properly incurred by the lessor in the employment of a solicitor and surveyor or valuer, or otherwise, in reference to any breach giving rise to a right of re-entry or forfeiture which, at the request of the lessee, is waived by the lessor, or from which the lessee is relieved, under the provisions of this Act.

(4) Where a lessor is proceeding by action or otherwise to enforce a right of re-entry or forfeiture under any covenant, proviso, or stipulation in a lease, or for non-payment of rent, the court may, on application by any person claiming as under-lessee any estate or interest in the property comprised in the lease or any part thereof, either in the lessor's action (if any) or in any action brought by such person for that purpose, make an order vesting, for the whole term of the lease or any less term, the property comprised in the lease or any part thereof in any person entitled as under-lessee to any estate or interest in such property upon such conditions as to execution of any deed or other document, payment of rent, costs, expenses, damages, compensation, giving security, or otherwise, as the court in the circumstances of each case may think fit, but in no case shall any such under-lessee be entitled to require a lease to be granted to him for any longer term than he had under his original sub-lease.

(5) For the purposes of this section—

    (a) "Lease" includes an original or derivative under-lease; also an agreement for a lease where the lessee has become entitled to have his lease granted; also a grant at a fee farm rent, or securing a rent by condition;

    (b) "Lessee" includes an original or derivative under-lessee, and the persons deriving title under a lessee; also a grantee under any such grant as aforesaid and the persons deriving title under him;

    (c) "Lessor" includes an original or derivative under-lessor, and the persons deriving title under a lessor; also a person making such grant as aforesaid and the persons deriving title under him;

    (d) "Under-lease" includes an agreement for an underlease where the underlessee has become entitled to have his underlease granted;

    (e) "Underlessee" includes any person deriving title under an underlessee.

(6) This section applies although the proviso or stipulation under which the right of re-entry or forfeiture accrues is inserted in the lease in pursuance of the directions of any Act of Parliament.

(7) For the purposes of this section a lease limited to continue as long only as the lessee abstains from committing a breach of covenant shall be and take effect as a lease to continue for any longer term for which it could subsist, but determinable by a proviso for re-entry on such a breach.

(8) This section does not extend—

    (i) To a covenant or condition against assigning, underletting, parting with the possession, or disposing of the land leased where the breach occurred before the commencement of this Act; or

    (ii) In the case of a mining lease, to a covenant or condition for allowing the lessor to have access to or inspect books, accounts, records, weighing machines or other things, or to enter or inspect the mine or the workings thereof.

(9) This section does not apply to a condition for forfeiture on the bankruptcy of the lessee or on taking in execution of the lessee's interest if contained in a lease of—

(a) Agricultural or pastoral land;
(b) Mines or minerals;
(c) A house used or intended to be used as a public-house or beershop;
(d) A house let as a dwelling-house, with the use of any furniture, books, works of art, or other chattels not being in the nature of fixtures;
(e) Any property with respect to which the personal qualifications of the tenant are of importance for the preservation of the value or character of the property, or on the ground of neighbourhood to the lessor, or to any person holding under him.

(10) Where a condition of forfeiture on the bankruptcy of the lessee or on taking in execution of the lessee's interest is contained in any lease, other than a lease of any of the classes mentioned in the last subsection, then—

(a) if the lessee's interest is sold within one year from the bankruptcy or taking in execution, this section applies to the forfeiture condition aforesaid;
(b) if the lessee's interest is not sold before the expiration of that year, this section only applies to the forfeiture condition aforesaid during the first year from the date of the bankruptcy or taking in execution.

(11) This section does not, save as otherwise mentioned, affect the law relating to re-entry or forfeiture or relief in case of non-payment of rent.

(12) This section has effect notwithstanding any stipulation to the contrary.

[(13) The county court has jurisdiction under this section—

(a), (b) . . .]   [400]

NOTES

Sub-s (13): added by the County Courts Act 1984, s 148(1), Sch 2, para 5; paras (a), (b) repealed by the High Court and County Courts Jurisdiction Order 1991, SI 1991 No 724, art 2(8), Schedule.

147. Relief against notice to effect decorative repairs

(1) After a notice is served on a lessee relating to the internal decorative repairs to a house or other building, he may apply to the court for relief, and if, having regard to all the circumstances of the case (including in particular the length of the lessee's term or interest remaining unexpired), the court is satisfied that the notice is unreasonable, it may, by order, wholly or partially relieve the lessee from liability for such repairs.

(2) This section does not apply:—

(i) where the liability arises under an express covenant or agreement to put the property in a decorative state of repair and the covenant or agreement has never been performed;
(ii) to any matter necessary or proper—

(a) for putting or keeping the property in a sanitary condition, or
(b) for the maintenance or preservation of the structure;

(iii) to any statutory liability to keep a house in all respects reasonably fit for human habitation;
(iv) to any covenant or stipulation to yield up the house or other building in a specified state of repair at the end of the term.

(3) In this section "lease" includes an underlease and an agreement for a

lease, and "lessee" has a corresponding meaning and includes any person liable to effect the repairs.

(4) This section applies whether the notice is served before or after the commencement of this Act, and has effect notwithstanding any stipulation to the contrary.

[(5) The county court has jurisdiction under this section . . .]   **[401]**

NOTES
    Sub-s (5): added by the County Courts Act 1984, s 148(1), Sch 2, para 6; words omitted repealed by the High Court and County Courts Jurisdiction Order 1991, SI 1991 No 724, art 2(8), Schedule.

148. Waiver of a covenant in a lease

(1) Where any actual waiver by a lessor or the persons deriving title under him of the benefit of any covenant or condition in any lease is proved to have taken place in any particular instance, such waiver shall not be deemed to extend to any instance, or to any breach of covenant or condition save that to which such waiver specially relates, nor operate as a general waiver of the benefit of any such covenant or condition.

(2) This section applies unless a contrary intention appears and extends to waivers effected after the twenty-third day of July, eighteen hundred and sixty.
[402]

149. Abolition of interesse termini, and as to reversionary leases and leases for lives

(1) The doctrine of interesse termini is hereby abolished.

(2) As from the commencement of this Act all terms of years absolute shall, whether the interest is created before or after such commencement, be capable of taking effect at law or in equity, according to the estate interest or powers of the grantor, from the date fixed for commencement of the term, without actual entry.

(3) A term, at a rent or granted in consideration of a fine, limited after the commencement of this Act to take effect more than twenty-one years from the date of the instrument purporting to create it, shall be void, and any contract made after such commencement to create such a term shall likewise be void; but this subsection does not apply to any term taking effect in equity under a settlement, or created out of an equitable interest under a settlement, or under an equitable power for mortgage, indemnity or other like purposes.

(4) Nothing in subsections (1) and (2) of this section prejudicially affects the right of any person to recover any rent or to enforce or take advantage of any covenants or conditions or, as respects terms or interests created before the commencement of this Act, operates to vary any statutory or other obligations imposed in respect of such terms or interests.

(5) Nothing in this Act affects the rule of law that a legal term, whether or not being a mortgage term, may be created to take effect in reversion expectant on a longer term, which rule is hereby confirmed.

(6) Any lease or underlease, at a rent, or in consideration of a fine, for life or lives or for any term of years determinable with life or lives, or on the marriage of the lessee, or any contract therefor, made before or after the commencement of this Act, or created by virtue of Part V of the Law of Property

Act 1922, shall take effect as a lease, underlease or contract therefor, for a term of ninety years determinable after the death or marriage (as the case may be) of the original lessee, or of the survivor of the original lessees, by at least one month's notice in writing given to determine the same on one of the quarter days applicable to the tenancy, either by the lessor or the persons deriving title under him, to the person entitled to the leasehold interest, or if no such person is in existence by affixing the same to the premises, or by the lessee or other persons in whom the leasehold interest is vested to the lessor or the persons deriving title under him:

Provided that—

(a) this subsection shall not apply to any term taking effect in equity under a settlement or created out of an equitable interest under a settlement for mortgage, indemnity, or other like purposes;

(b) the person in whom the leasehold interest is vested by virtue of Part V of the Law of Property Act 1922, shall, for the purposes of this subsection, be deemed an original lessee;

(c) if the lease, underlease, or contract therefor is made determinable on the dropping of the lives of persons other than or besides the lessees, then the notice shall be capable of being served after the death of any person or of the survivor of any persons (whether or not including the lessees) on the cesser of whose life or lives the lease, underlease, or contract is made determinable, instead of after the death of the original lessee or of the survivor of the original lessees;

(d) if there are no quarter days specially applicable to the tenancy, notice may be given to determine the tenancy on one of the usual quarter days. [403]

150. Surrender of a lease, without prejudice to underleases with a view to the grant of a new lease

(1) A lease may be surrendered with a view to the acceptance of a new lease in place thereof, without a surrender of any under-lease derived thereout.

(2) A new lease may be granted and accepted, in place of any lease so surrendered, without any such surrender of an under-lease as aforesaid, and the new lease operates as if all under-leases derived out of the surrendered lease had been surrendered before the surrender of that lease was effected.

(3) The lessee under the new lease and any person deriving title under him is entitled to the same rights and remedies in respect of the rent reserved by and the covenants, agreements and conditions contained in any under-lease as if the original lease had not been surrendered but was or remained vested in him.

(4) Each under-lessee and any person deriving title under him is entitled to hold and enjoy the land comprised in his under-lease (subject to the payment of any rent reserved by and to the observance of the covenants agreements and conditions contained in the under-lease) as if the lease out of which the under-lease was derived had not been surrendered.

(5) The lessor granting the new lease and any person deriving title under him is entitled to the same remedies, by distress or entry in and upon the land comprised in any such under-lease for rent reserved by or for breach of any covenant, agreement or condition contained in the new lease (so far only as the rents reserved by or the covenants, agreements or conditions contained in the new lease do not exceed or impose greater burdens than those reserved by or

contained in the original lease out of which the under-lease is derived) as he would have had—

    (*a*) If the original lease had remained on foot; or

    (*b*) If a new under-lease derived out of the new lease had been granted to the under-lessee or a person deriving title under him;

as the case may require.

(6) This section does not affect the powers of the court to give relief against forfeiture. [404]

151. Provision as to attornments by tenants

(1) Where land is subject to a lease—

    (*a*) the conveyance of a reversion in the land expectant on the determination of the lease; or

    (*b*) the creation or conveyance of a rentcharge to issue or issuing out of the land;

shall be valid without any attornment of the lessee:

Nothing in this subsection—

    (i) affects the validity of any payment of rent by the lessee to the person making the conveyance or grant before notice of the conveyance or grant is given to him by the person entitled thereunder; or

    (ii) renders the lessee liable for any breach of covenant to pay rent, on account of his failure to pay rent to the person entitled under the conveyance or grant before such notice is given to the lessee.

(2) An attornment by the lessee in respect of any land to a person claiming to be entitled to the interest in the land of the lessor, if made without the consent of the lessor, shall be void.

This subsection does not apply to an attornment—

    (*a*) made pursuant to a judgment of a court of competent jurisdiction; or

    (*b*) to a mortgagee, by a lessee holding under a lease from the mortgagor where the right of redemption is barred; or

    (*c*) to any other person rightfully deriving title under the lessor. [405]

152. Leases invalidated by reason of non-compliance with terms of powers under which they are granted

(1) Where in the intended exercise of any power of leasing, whether conferred by an Act of Parliament or any other instrument, a lease (in this section referred to as an invalid lease) is granted, which by reason of any failure to comply with the terms of the power is invalid, then—

    (*a*) as against the person entitled after the determination of the interest of the grantor to the reversion; or

    (*b*) as against any other person who, subject to any lease properly granted under the power, would have been entitled to the land comprised in the lease;

the lease, if it was made in good faith, and the lessee has entered thereunder, shall take effect in equity as a contract for the grant, at the request of the lessee, of a valid lease under the power, of like effect as the invalid lease, subject to such variations as may be necessary in order to comply with the terms of the power:

Provided that a lessee under an invalid lease shall not, by virtue of any such implied contract, be entitled to obtain a variation of the lease if the other persons who would have been bound by the contract are willing and able to confirm the lease without variation.

(2) Where a lease granted in the intended exercise of such a power is invalid by reason of the grantor not having power to grant the lease at the date thereof, but the grantor's interest in the land comprised therein continues after the time when he might, in the exercise of the power, have properly granted a lease in the like terms, the lease shall take effect as a valid lease in like manner as if it had been granted at that time.

(3) Where during the continuance of the possession taken under an invalid lease the person for the time being entitled, subject to such possession, to the land comprised therein or to the rents and profits thereof, is able to confirm the lease without variation, the lessee, or other person who would have been bound by the lease had it been valid, shall, at the request of the person so able to confirm the lease, be bound to accept a confirmation thereof, and thereupon the lease shall have effect and be deemed to have had effect as a valid lease from the grant thereof.

Confirmation under this subsection may be by a memorandum in writing signed by or on behalf of the persons respectively confirming and accepting the confirmation of the lease.

(4) Where a receipt or a memorandum in writing confirming an invalid lease is, upon or before the acceptance of rent thereunder, signed by or on behalf of the person accepting the rent, that acceptance shall, as against that person, be deemed to be a confirmation of the lease.

(5) The foregoing provisions of this section do not affect prejudicially—

(*a*) any right of action or other right or remedy to which, but for those provisions or any enactment replaced by those provisions, the lessee named in an invalid lease would or might have been entitled under any covenant on the part of the grantor for title or quiet enjoyment contained therein or implied thereby; or

(*b*) any right of re-entry or other right or remedy to which, but for those provisions or any enactment replaced thereby, the grantor or other person for the time being entitled to the reversion expectant on the termination of the lease, would or might have been entitled by reason of any breach of the covenants, conditions or provisions contained in the lease and binding on the lessee.

(6) Where a valid power of leasing is vested in or may be exercised by a person who grants a lease which, by reason of the determination of the interest of the grantor or otherwise, cannot have effect and continuance according to the terms thereof independently of the power, the lease shall for the purposes of this section be deemed to have been granted in the intended exercise of the power although the power is not referred to in the lease.

(7) This section does not apply to a lease of land held on charitable, ecclesiastical or public trusts.

(8) This section takes effect without prejudice to the provision in this Act for the grant of leases in the name and on behalf of the estate owner of the land affected. **[406]**

153. Enlargement of residue of long terms into fee simple estates

(1) Where a residue unexpired of not less than two hundred years of a term, which, as originally created, was for not less than three hundred years, is subsisting in land, whether being the whole land originally comprised in the term, or part only thereof,—

- (*a*) without any trust or right of redemption affecting the term in favour of the freeholder, or other person entitled in reversion expectant on the term; and
- (*b*) without any rent, or with merely a peppercorn rent or other rent having no money value, incident to the reversion, or having had a rent, not being merely a peppercorn rent or other rent having no money value, originally so incident, which subsequently has been released or has become barred by lapse of time, or has in any other way ceased to be payable;

the term may be enlarged into a fee simple in the manner, and subject to the restrictions in this section provided.

(2) This section applies to and includes every such term as aforesaid whenever created, whether or not having the freehold as the immediate reversion thereon; but does not apply to—

- (i) Any term liable to be determined by re-entry for condition broken; or
- (ii) Any term created by subdemise out of a superior term, itself incapable of being enlarged into fee simple.

(3) This section extends to mortgage terms, where the right of redemption is barred.

(4) A rent not exceeding the yearly sum of one pound which has not been collected or paid for a continuous period of twenty years or upwards shall, for the purposes of this section, be deemed to have ceased to be payable:

Provided that, of the said period, at least five years must have elapsed after the commencement of this Act.

(5) Where a rent incident to a reversion expectant on a term to which this section applies is deemed to have ceased to be payable for the purposes aforesaid, no claim for such rent or for any arrears thereof shall be capable of being enforced.

(6) Each of the following persons, namely—

- (i) Any person beneficially entitled in right of the term, whether subject to any incumbrance or not, to possession of any land comprised in the term, and, in the case of a married woman without the concurrence of her husband, whether or not she is entitled for her separate use or as her separate property, . . . ;
- (ii) Any person being in receipt of income as trustee, in right of the term, or having the term vested in him in trust for sale, whether subject to any incumbrance or not;
- (iii) Any person in whom, as personal representative of any deceased person, the term is vested, whether subject to any incumbrance or not;

shall, so far as regards the land to which he is entitled, or in which he is interested in right of the term, in any such character as aforesaid, have power by deed to declare to the effect that, from and after the execution of the deed, the term shall be enlarged into a fee simple.

(7) Thereupon, by virtue of the deed and of this Act, the term shall become and be enlarged accordingly, and the person in whom the term was previously vested shall acquire and have in the land a fee simple instead of the term.

(8) The estate in fee simple so acquired by enlargement shall be subject to all the same trusts, powers, executory limitations over, rights and equities, and to all the same covenants and provisions relating to user and enjoyment, and to all the same obligations of every kind, as the term would have been subject to if it had not been so enlarged.

(9) But where—

(a) any land so held for the residue of a term has been settled in trust by reference to other land, being freehold land, so as to go along with that other land, or, in the case of settlements coming into operation before the commencement of this Act, so as to go along with that other land as far as the law permits; and

(b) at the time of enlargement, the ultimate beneficial interest in the term, whether subject to any subsisting particular estate or not, has not become absolutely and indefeasibly vested in any person, free from charges or powers of charging created by a settlement;

the estate in fee simple acquired as aforesaid shall, without prejudice to any conveyance for value previously made by a person having a contingent or defeasible interest in the term, be liable to be, and shall be, conveyed by means of a subsidiary vesting instrument and settled in like manner as the other land, being freehold land, aforesaid, and until so conveyed and settled shall devolve beneficially as if it had been so conveyed and settled.

(10) The estate in fee simple so acquired shall, whether the term was originally created without impeachment of waste or not, include the fee simple in all mines and minerals which at the time of enlargement have not been severed in right or in fact, or have not been severed or reserved by an inclosure Act or award.   [407]

NOTES
    Sub-s (6): words omitted repealed by the Married Women (Restraint upon Anticipation) Act 1949, s 1, Sch 2.

154. Application Part V to existing leases

This part of this Act, except where otherwise expressly provided, applies to leases created before or after the commencement of this Act, and "lease" includes an under-lease or other tenancy.   [408]

PART VI

POWERS

155. Release of powers simply collateral

A person to whom any power, whether coupled with an interest or not, is given may by deed release, or contract not to exercise, the power.   [409]

156. Disclaimer of power

(1) A person to whom any power, whether coupled with an interest or not, is given may by deed disclaim the power, and, after disclaimer, shall not be capable of exercising or joining in the exercise of the power.

(2) On such disclaimer, the power may be exercised by the other person or persons or the survivor or survivors of the other persons, to whom the power is given, unless the contrary is expressed in the instrument creating the power.

[410]

157. Protection of purchasers claiming under certain void appointments

(1) An instrument purporting to exercise a power of appointment over property, which, in default of and subject to any appointment, is held in trust for a class or number of persons of whom the appointee is one, shall not (save as hereinafter provided) be void on the ground of fraud on the power as against a purchaser in good faith:

Provided that, if the interest appointed exceeds, in amount or value, the interest in such property to which immediately before the execution of the instrument the appointee was presumptively entitled under the trust in default of appointment, having regard to any advances made in his favour and to any hotchpot provision, the protection afforded by this section to a purchaser shall not extend to such excess.

(2) In this section "a purchaser in good faith" means a person dealing with an appointee of the age of not less than twenty-five years for valuable consideration in money or money's worth, and without notice of the fraud, or of any circumstances from which, if reasonable inquiries had been made, the fraud might have been discovered.

(3) Persons deriving title under any purchaser entitled to the benefit of this section shall be entitled to like benefit.

(4) This section applies only to dealings effected after the commencement of this Act. [411]

158. Validation of appointments where objects are excluded or take illusory shares

(1) No appointment made in exercise of any power to appoint any property among two or more objects shall be invalid on the ground that—

    (a) an unsubstantial, illusory, or nominal share only is appointed to or left unappointed to devolve upon any one or more of the objects of the power; or

    (b) any object of the power is thereby altogether excluded;

but every such appointment shall be valid notwithstanding that any one or more of the objects is not thereby, or in default of appointment, to take any share in the property.

(2) This section does not affect any provision in the instrument creating the power which declares the amount of any share from which any object of the power is not to be excluded.

(3) This section applies to appointments made before or after the commencement of this Act. [412]

159. Execution of powers not testamentary

(1) A deed executed in the presence of and attested by two or more witnesses (in the manner in which deeds are ordinarily executed and attested) is so far as respects the execution and attestation thereof, a valid execution of a power of appointment by deed or by any instrument in writing, not testamentary, notwithstanding that it is expressly required that a deed or instrument in writing, made in exercise of the power, is to be executed or attested with some additional or other form of execution or attestation or solemnity.

(2) This section does not operate to defeat any direction in the instrument creating the power that—

> (a) the consent of any particular person is to be necessary to a valid execution;
> (b) in order to give validity to any appointment, any act is to be performed having no relation to the mode of executing and attesting the instrument.

(3) This section does not prevent the donee of a power from executing it in accordance with the power by writing, or otherwise than by an instrument executed and attested as a deed; and where a power is so executed this section does not apply.

(4) This section applies to appointments by deed made after the thirteenth day of August, eighteen hundred and fifty-nine.   **[413]**

160. Application of Part VI to existing powers

This Part of this Act applies to powers created or arising either before or after the commencement of this Act.   **[414]**

PART VII

PERPETUITIES AND ACCUMULATIONS

Perpetuities

161. Abolition of the double possibility rule

(1) The rule of law prohibiting the limitation, after a life interest to an unborn person, of an interest in land to the unborn child or other issue of an unborn person is hereby abolished, but without prejudice to any other rule relating to perpetuities.

(2) This section only applies to limitations or trusts created by an instrument coming into operation after the commencement of this Act.   **[415]**

162. Restrictions on the perpetuity rule

(1) For removing doubts, it is hereby declared that the rule of law relating to perpetuities does not apply and shall be deemed never to have applied—

> (a) To any power to distrain on or to take possession of land or the income thereof given by way of indemnity against a rent, whether charged upon or payable in respect of any part of that land or not; or

(b) To any rentcharge created only as an indemnity against another rentcharge, although the indemnity rentcharge may only arise or become payable on breach of a condition or stipulation; or

(c) To any power, whether exercisable on breach of a condition or stipulation or not, to retain or withhold payment of any instalment of a rentcharge as an indemnity against another rentcharge; or

(d) To any grant, exception, or reservation of any right of entry on, or user of, the surface of land or of any easements, rights, or privileges over or under land for the purpose of—

(i) winning, working, inspecting, measuring, converting, manufacturing, carrying away, and disposing of mines and minerals;

(ii) inspecting, grubbing up, felling and carrying away timber and other trees, and the tops and lops thereof.

(iii) executing repairs, alterations, or additions to any adjoining land, or the buildings and erections thereon;

(iv) constructing, laying down, altering, repairing, renewing, cleansing, and maintaining sewers, watercourses, cesspools, gutters, drains, water-pipes, gas-pipes, electric wires or cables or other like works.

(2) This section applies to instruments coming into operation before or after the commencement of this Act.   **[416]**

Accumulations

164. General restrictions on accumulation of income

(1) No person may by any instrument or otherwise settle or dispose of any property in such manner that the income thereof shall, save as hereinafter mentioned, be wholly or partially accumulated for any longer period than one of the following, namely:—

(a) the life of the grantor or settlor; or

(b) a term of twenty-one years from the death of the grantor, settlor or testator; or

(c) the duration of the minority or respective minorities of any person or persons living or en ventre sa mere at the death of the grantor, settlor or testator; or

(d) the duration of the minority or respective minorities only of any person or persons who under the limitations of the instrument directing the accumulations would, for the time being, if of full age, be entitled to the income directed to be accumulated.

In every case where any accumulation is directed otherwise than as aforesaid, the direction shall (save as hereinafter mentioned) be void; and the income of the property directed to be accumulated shall, so long as the same is directed to be accumulated contrary to this section, go to and be received by the person or persons who would have been entitled thereto if such accumulation had not been directed.

(2) This section does not extend to any provision—

(i) for payment of the debts of any grantor, settlor, testator or other person;

(ii) for raising portions for—

(a) any child, children or remoter issue of any grantor, settlor or testator; or (*b*) any child, children or remoter issue of a person taking any interest under any settlement or other disposition directing the accumulations or to whom any interest is thereby limited;

(iii) respecting the accumulation of the produce of timber or wood;

and accordingly such provisions may be made as if no statutory restrictions on accumulation of income had been imposed.

(3) The restrictions imposed by this section apply to instruments made on or after the twenty-eighth day of July, eighteen hundred, but in the case of wills only where the testator was living and of testamentary capacity after the end of one year from that date.   **[417]**

165. Qualification of restrictions on accumulation

Where accumulations of surplus income are made during a minority under any statutory power or under the general law, the period for which such accumulations are made is not (whether the trust was created or the accumulations were made before or after the commencement of this Act) to be taken into account in determining the periods for which accumulations are permitted to be made by the last preceding section, and accordingly an express trust for accumulation for any other permitted period shall not be deemed to have been invalidated or become invalid, by reason of accumulations also having been made as aforesaid during such minority.   **[418]**

166. Restriction on accumulation for the purchase of land

(1) No person may settle or dispose of any property in such manner that the income thereof shall be wholly or partially accumulated for the purchase of land only, for any longer period than the duration of the minority or respective minorities of any person or persons who, under the limitations of the instrument directing the accumulation, would for the time being, if of full age, be entitled to the income so directed to be accumulated.

(2) This section does not, nor do the enactments which it replaces, apply to accumulations to be held as capital money for the purposes of the Settled Land Act 1925 or the enactments replaced by that Act, whether or not the accumulations are primarily liable to be laid out in the purchase of land.

(3) This section applies to settlements and dispositions made after the twenty-seventh day of June eighteen hundred and ninety-two.   **[419]**

PART IX

VOIDABLE DISPOSITIONS

173. Voluntary disposition of land how far voidable as against purchasers

(1) Every voluntary disposition of land made with intent to defraud a subsequent purchaser is voidable at the instance of that purchaser.

(2) For the purposes of this section, no voluntary disposition, whenever made, shall be deemed to have been made with intent to defraud by reason only that a subsequent conveyance for valuable consideration was made, if such subsequent conveyance was made after the twenty-eighth day of June, eighteen hundred and ninety-three.   **[420]**

174. Acquisitions of reversions at an under value

(1) No acquisition made in good faith, without fraud or unfair dealing, of any reversionary interest in real or personal property, for money or money's worth, shall be liable to be opened or set aside merely on the ground of under value.

In this subsection "reversionary interest" includes an expectancy or possibility.

(2) This section does not affect the jurisdiction of the court to set aside or modify unconscionable bargains.   [421]

PART X

WILLS

175. Contingent and future testamentary gifts to carry the intermediate income

(1) A contingent or future specific devise or bequest of property, whether real or personal, and a contingent residuary devise of freehold land, and a specific or residuary devise of freehold land to trustees upon trust for persons whose interests are contingent or executory shall, subject to the statutory provisions relating to accumulations, carry the intermediate income of that property from the death of the testator, except so far as such income, or any part thereof, may be otherwise expressly disposed of.

(2) This section applies only to wills coming into operation after the commencement of this Act.   [422]

176. Power for tenant in tail in possession to dispose of property by specific devise or bequest

(1) A tenant in tail of full age shall have power to dispose by will, by means of a devise or bequest referring specifically either to the property or to the instrument under which it was acquired or to entailed property generally—

    (a) of all property of which he is tenant in tail in possession at his death; and

    (b) of money (including the proceeds of property directed to be sold) subject to be invested in the purchase of property, of which if it had been so invested he would have been tenant in tail in possession at his death;

in like manner as if, after barring the entail, he had been tenant in fee simple or absolute owner thereof for an equitable interest at his death, but, subject to and in default of any such disposition by will, such property shall devolve in the same manner as if this section had not been passed.

(2) This section applies to entailed interests authorised to be created by this Act as well as to estates tail created before the commencement of this Act, but does not extend to a tenant in tail who is by statute restrained from barring or defeating his estate tail, whether the land or property in respect whereof he is so restrained was purchased with money provided by Parliament in consideration of public services or not, or to a tenant in tail after possibility of issue extinct, and does not render any interest which is not disposed of by the will of the tenant in tail liable for his debts or other liabilities.

(3) In this section "tenant in tail" includes an owner of a base fee in possession who has power to enlarge the base fee into a fee-simple without the concurrence of any other person.

(4) This section only applies to wills executed after the commencement of this Act, or confirmed or republished by codicil executed after such commencement.   **[423]**

177. Wills in contemplation of marriage

(1) A will expressed to be made in contemplation of a marriage shall, notwithstanding anything in section eighteen of the Wills Act 1837 or any other statutory provision or rule of law to the contrary, not be revoked by the solemnisation of the marriage contemplated.

(2) This section only applies to wills made after the commencement of this Act.
                                                                          [424]

NOTES
Repealed with a saving by the Administration of Justice Act 1982, ss 73(7), 75, Sch 9, Part I.

179. Prescribed forms for reference in wills

The Lord Chancellor may from time to time prescribe and publish forms to which a testator may refer in his will, and give directions as to the manner in which they may be referred to, but, unless so referred to, such forms shall not be deemed to be incorporated in a will.   **[425]**

PART XI

MISCELLANEOUS

Miscellaneous

180. Provisions as to corporations

(1) Where either after or before the commencement of this Act any property or any interest therein is or has been vested in a corporation sole (including the Crown), the same shall, unless and until otherwise disposed of by the corporation, pass and devolve to and vest in and be deemed always to have passed and devolved to or vested in the successors from time to time of such corporation.

(2) Where either after or before the commencement of this Act there is or has been a vacancy in the office of a corporation sole or in the office of the head of a corporation aggregate (in any case in which the vacancy affects the status or powers of the corporation) at the time when, if there had been no vacancy, any interest in or charge on property would have been acquired by the corporation, such interest shall notwithstanding such vacancy vest and be deemed to have vested in the successor to such office on his appointment as a corporation sole, or in the corporation aggregate (as the case may be), but without prejudice to the right of such successor, or of the corporation aggregate after the appointment of its head officer, to disclaim that interest or charge.

(3) Any contract or other transaction expressed or purported to be made with a corporation sole, or any appointment of a corporation sole as a custodian or other trustee or as a personal representative, at a time (either after or before the commencement of this Act) when there was a vacancy in the office, shall on the vacancy being filled take effect and be deemed to have taken effect as if the vacancy had been filled before the contract, transaction or appointment was expressed to be made or was capable of taking effect, and on the appointment of a successor shall be capable of being enforced, accepted, disclaimed, or renounced by him.   **[426]**

181. Dissolution of a corporation

[(1)] Where, by reason of the dissolution of a corporation either before or after the commencement of this Act, a legal estate in any property has determined, the court may by order create a corresponding estate and vest the same in the person who would have been entitled to the estate which determined had it remained a subsisting estate.

[(2) The county court has jurisdiction under this section where the amount or value of the property or of the interest in the property which is to be dealt with in the court does not exceed [£30,000].]   **[427]**

NOTES
    Sub-s (1): numbered as such by the County Courts Act 1984, s 148(1), Sch 2, para 7.
    Sub-s (2): added by the County Courts Act 1984, s 148(1), Sch 2, para 7; sum in square brackets substituted by the High Court and County Courts Jurisdiction Order 1991, SI 1991 No 724, art 2(8), Schedule.

182. Protection of solicitor and trustees adopting Act

(1) The powers given by this Act to any person, and the covenants, provisions, stipulations, and words which under this Act are to be deemed to be included or implied in any instrument, or are by this Act made applicable to any contract for sale or other transaction, are and shall be deemed in law proper powers, covenants, provisions, stipulations, and words, to be given by or to be contained in any such instrument, or to be adopted in connexion with, or applied to, any such contract or transaction, and a solicitor shall not be deemed guilty of neglect or breach of duty, or become in any way liable, by reason of his omitting, in good faith, in any such instrument, or in connexion with any such contract or transaction, to negative the giving, inclusion, implication, or application of any of those powers, covenants, provisions, stipulations, or words, or to insert or apply any others in place thereof, in any case where the provisions of this Act would allow of his doing so.

(2) But, save as expressly provided by this Act, nothing in this Act shall be taken to imply that the insertion in any such instrument, or the adoption in connexion with, or the application to, any contract or transaction, of any further or other powers, covenants, provisions, stipulations, or words is improper.

(3) Where the solicitor is acting for trustees, executors, or other persons in a fiduciary position, those persons shall also be protected in like manner.

(4) Where such persons are acting without a solicitor, they shall also be protected in like manner.   **[428]**

183. Fraudulent concealment of documents and falsification of pedigrees

(1) Any person disposing of property or any interest therein for money or money's worth to a purchaser, or the solicitor or other agent of such person, who—

    (a) conceals from the purchaser any instrument or incumbrance material to the title; or

    (b) falsifies any pedigree upon which the title may depend in order to induce the purchaser to accept the title offered or produced;

with intent in any of such cases to defraud, is guilty of a misdemeanour punishable by fine, or by imprisonment for a term not exceeding two years, or by both.

(2) Any such person or his solicitor or agent is also liable to an action for

damages by the purchaser or the persons deriving title under him for any loss sustained by reason of—

(a) the concealment of the instrument or incumbrance; or
(b) any claim made by a person under such pedigree whose right was concealed by such falsification as aforesaid.

(3) In estimating damages, where the property or any interest therein is recovered from the purchaser or the persons deriving title under him, regard shall be had to any expenditure by him or them in improvements of any land.

(4) No prosecution for any offence under this section shall be commenced without the leave of the Attorney-General.

(5) Before leave to prosecute is granted there shall be given to the person intended to be prosecuted such notice of the application for leave to prosecute as the Attorney-General may direct.   **[429]**

184. Presumption of survivorship in regard to claims to property

In all cases where, after the commencement of this Act, two or more persons have died in circumstances rendering it uncertain which of them survived the other or others, such deaths shall (subject to any order of the court), for all purposes affecting the title of property, be presumed to have occurred in order of seniority, and accordingly the younger shall be deemed to have survived the elder.   **[430]**

185. Merger

There is no merger by operation of law only of any estate the beneficial interest in which would not be deemed to be merged or extinguished in equity.   **[431]**

186. Rights of pre-emption capable of release

All statutory and other rights of pre-emption affecting a legal estate shall be and be deemed always to have been capable of release, and unless released shall remain in force as equitable interests only.   **[432]**

187. Legal easements

(1) Where an easement, right or privilege for a legal estate is created, it shall enure for the benefit of the land to which it is intended to be annexed.

(2) Nothing in this Act affects the right of a person to acquire, hold or exercise an easement, right or privilege over or in relation to land for a legal estate in common with any other person, or the power of creating or conveying such an easement right or privilege.   **[433]**

188. Power to direct division of chattels

[(1)] Where any chattels belong to persons in undivided shares, the persons interested in a moiety or upwards may apply to the court for an order for division of the chattels or any of them, according to a valuation or otherwise, and the court may make such order and give any consequential directions as it thinks fit.

[(2) The county court has jurisdiction under this section where the amount or value of the property or of the interest in the property which is to be dealt with in the court does not exceed [£30,000].]   **[434]**

NOTES

Sub-s (1): numbered as such by the County Courts Act 1984, s 148(1), Sch 2, para 8.

Sub-s (2): added by the County Courts Act 1984, s 148(1), Sch 2, para 8; sum in square brackets substituted by the High Court and County Courts Jurisdiction Order 1991, SI 1991 No 724, art 2(8), Schedule.

189. Indemnities against rents

(1) A power of distress given by way of indemnity against a rent or any part thereof payable in respect of any land, or against the breach of any covenant or condition in relation to land, is not and shall not be deemed ever to have been a bill of sale, within the meaning of the Bills of Sale Acts 1878 and 1882, as amended by any subsequent enactment.

(2) The benefit of all covenants and powers given by way of indemnity against a rent or any part thereof payable in respect of land, or against the breach of any covenant or condition in relation to land, is and shall be deemed always to have been annexed to the land to which the indemnity is intended to relate, and may be enforced by the estate owner for the time being of the whole or any part of that land, notwithstanding that the benefit may not have been expressly apportioned or assigned to him or to any of his predecessors in title.

[435]

Redemption and Apportionment of Rents, etc

190. Equitable apportionment of rents and remedies for non-payment or breach of covenant

(1) Where in a conveyance for valuable consideration, other than a mortgage, of part of land which is affected by a rentcharge, such rentcharge or a part thereof is, without the consent of the owner thereof, expressed to be—

    (*a*) charged exclusively on the land conveyed or any part thereof in exoneration of the land retained or other land; or

    (*b*) charged exclusively on the land retained or any part thereof in exoneration of the land conveyed or other land; or

    (*c*) apportioned between the land conveyed or any part thereof, and the land retained by the grantor or any part thereof;

then, without prejudice to the rights of the owner of the rentcharge, such charge or apportionment shall be binding as between the grantor and the grantee under the conveyance and their respective successors in title.

    (2) Where—

    (*a*) any default is made in payment of the whole or part of a rentcharge by the person who, by reason of such charge or apportionment as aforesaid, is liable to pay the same; or

    (*b*) any breach occurs of any of the covenants (other than in the case of an apportionment the covenant to pay the entire rentcharge) or conditions contained in the deed or other document creating the rentcharge, so far as the same relate to the land retained or conveyed, as the case may be;

the owner for the time being of any other land affected by the entire rentcharge who—

        (i) pays or is required to pay the whole or part of the rentcharge which ought to have been paid by the defaulter aforesaid; or

(ii) incurs any costs, damages or expenses by reason of the breach of covenant or condition aforesaid;

may enter into and distrain on the land in respect of which the default or breach is made or occurs, or any part of that land, and dispose according to law of any distress found, and may also take possession of the income of the same land until, by means of such distress and receipt of income or otherwise the whole or part of the rentcharge (charged or apportioned as aforesaid) so unpaid and all costs, damages and expenses incurred by reason of the non-payment thereof or of the breach of the said covenants and conditions, are fully paid or satisfied.

(3) Where in a conveyance for valuable consideration, other than a mortgage, of part of land comprised in a lease, for the residue of the term or interest created by the lease, the rent reserved by such lease or a part thereof is, without the consent of the lessor, expressed to be—

(a) charged exclusively on the land conveyed or any part thereof in exoneration of the land retained by the assignor or other land; or

(b) charged exclusively on the land retained by the assignor or any part thereof in exoneration of the land conveyed or other land; or

(c) apportioned between the land conveyed or any part thereof and the land retained by the assignor or any part thereof;

then, without prejudice to the rights of the lessor, such charge or apportionment shall be binding as between the assignor and the assignee under the conveyance and their respective successors in title.

(4) Where—

(a) any default is made in payment of the whole or part of a rent by the person who, by reason of such charge or apportionment as aforesaid, is liable to pay the same; or

(b) any breach occurs of any of the lessee's covenants (other than in the case of an apportionment the covenant to pay the entire rent) or conditions contained in the lease, so far as the same relate to the land retained or conveyed, as the case may be;

the lessee for the time being of any other land comprised in the lease, in whom, as respects that land, the residue of the term or interest created by the lease is vested, who—

(i) pays or is required to pay the whole or part of the rent which ought to have been paid by the defaulter aforesaid; or

(ii) incurs any costs, damages or expenses by reason of the breach of covenant or condition aforesaid;

may enter into and distrain on the land comprised in the lease in respect of which the default or breach is made or occurs, or any part of that land, and dispose according to law of any distress found, and may also take possession of the income of the same land until (so long as the term or interest created by the lease is subsisting) by means of such distress and receipt of income or otherwise, the whole or part of the rent (charged or apportioned as aforesaid) so unpaid and all costs, damages and expenses incurred by reason of the non-payment thereof or of the breach of the said covenants and conditions, are fully paid or satisfied.

(5) The remedies conferred by this section take effect so far only as they might have been conferred by the conveyance whereby the rent or any part thereof is expressed to be charged or apportioned as aforesaid, but a trustee, personal representative, mortgagee or other person in a fiduciary position has,

and shall be deemed always to have had, power to confer the same or like remedies.

(6) This section applies only if and so far as a contrary intention is not expressed in the conveyance whereby the rent or any part thereof is expressed to be charged or apportioned as aforesaid, and takes effect subject to the terms of that conveyance and to the provisions therein contained.

(7) The remedies conferred by this section apply only where the conveyance whereby the rent or any part thereof is expressed to be charged or apportioned is made after the commencement of this Act, and do not apply where the rent is charged exclusively as aforesaid or legally apportioned with the consent of the owner or lessor.

(8) The rule of law relating to perpetuities does not affect the powers or remedies conferred by this section or any like powers or remedies expressly conferred, before or after the commencement of this Act, by an instrument.

[436]

Redemption and Apportionment of Rents, etc

192. Apportionment of charges payable for redemption of tithe rentcharge

An order of apportionment of a charge on land by way of annuity for redemption of tithe rentcharge may be made by the Minister under sections ten to fourteen (inclusive) of the Inclosure Act 1854 on the application of any person interested, according to the provisions of the Inclosure Acts 1845 to 1882, in the land charged or any part thereof without the concurrence of any other person:

Provided that the Minister may, in any such case, on the application of any person interested in the annuity, require as a condition of making the order that any apportioned part of the annuity which does not exceed the yearly sum of two pounds shall be redeemed forthwith.   [437]

Commons and Waste Lands

193. Rights of the public over commons and waste lands

(1) Members of the public shall, subject as hereinafter provided, have rights of access for air and exercise to any land which is a metropolitan common within the meaning of the Metropolitan Commons Acts 1866 to 1898, or manorial waste, or a common which is wholly or partly situated within [an area which immediately before 1st April 1974 was] a borough or urban district, and to any land which at the commencement of this Act is subject to rights of common and to which this section may from time to time be applied in manner hereinafter provided:

Provided that—

    (a) such rights of access shall be subject to any Act, scheme, or provisional order for the regulation of the land, and to any byelaw, regulation or order made thereunder or under any other statutory authority; and

    (b) the Minister shall, on the application of any person entitled as lord of the manor or otherwise to the soil of the land, or entitled to any commonable rights affecting the land, impose such limitations on and conditions as to the exercise of the rights of access or as to the extent of the land to be affected as, in the opinion of the Minister, are necessary or desirable for preventing any estate, right or interest of a profitable or beneficial nature in, over, or affecting the land from being injuriously affected, or for protecting any object of historical interest and, where any such limitations or conditions are so imposed, the rights of access shall be subject thereto; and

(c) such rights of access shall not include any right to draw or drive upon the land a carriage, cart, caravan, truck, or other vehicle, or to camp or light any fire thereon; and

(d) the rights of access shall cease to apply—

(i) to any land over which the commonable rights are extinguished under any statutory provision;

(ii) to any land over which the commonable rights are otherwise extinguished if the council of the county [or metropolitan district] ... in which the land is situated by resolution assent to its exclusion from the operation of this section, and the resolution is approved by the Minister.

(2) The lord of the manor or other person entitled to the soil of any land subject to rights of common may by deed, revocable or irrevocable, declare that this section shall apply to the land, and upon such deed being deposited with the Minister the land shall, so long as the deed remains operative, be land to which this section applies.

(3) Where limitations or conditions are imposed by the Minister under this section, they shall be published by such person and in such manner as the Minister may direct.

(4) Any person who, without lawful authority, draws or drives upon any land to which this section applies any carriage, cart, caravan, truck, or other vehicle, or camps or lights any fire thereon, or who fails to observe any limitation or condition imposed by the Minister under this section in respect of any such land, shall be liable on summary conviction to a fine not exceeding [level 1 on the standard scale] for each offence.

(5) Nothing in this section shall prejudice or affect the right of any person to get and remove mines or minerals or to let down the surface of the manorial waste or common.

(6) This section does not apply to any common or manorial waste which is for the time being held for Naval, Military or Air Force purposes and in respect of which rights of common have been extinguished or cannot be exercised.

[438]

NOTES

Sub-s (1): first words in square brackets inserted and words omitted repealed by the Local Government Act 1972, ss 189(4), 272(1), Sch 30; second words in square brackets inserted by the Local Government Act 1985, s 16, Sch 8, para 10(5).

Sub-s (4): maximum fine increased and converted to a level on the standard scale by the Criminal Justice Act 1982, ss 37, 38, 46.

194. Restrictions on inclosure of commons

(1) The erection of any building or fence, or the construction of any other work, whereby access to land to which this section applies is prevented or impeded, shall not be lawful unless the consent of the Minister thereto is obtained, and in giving or withholding his consent the Minister shall have regard to the same considerations and shall, if necessary, hold the same inquiries as are directed by the Commons Act 1876 to be taken into consideration and held by the Minister

before forming an opinion whether an application under the Inclosure Acts 1845 to 1882 shall be acceded to or not.

(2) Where any building or fence is erected, or any other work constructed without such consent as is required by this section, the county court within whose jurisdiction the land is situated, shall, on an application being made by the council of any county . . . or district concerned, or by the lord of the manor or any other person interested in the common, have power to make an order for the removal of the work, and the restoration of the land to the condition in which it was before the work was erected or constructed, but any such order shall be subject to the like appeal as an order made under section thirty of the Commons Act 1876.

(3) This section applies to any land which at the commencement of this Act is subject to rights of common:

Provided that this section shall cease to apply—

(a) to any land over which the rights of common are extinguished under any statutory provision;
(b) to any land over which the rights of common are otherwise extinguished, if the council of the county [or metropolitan district] . . . in which the land is situated by resolution assent to its exclusion from the operation of this section and the resolution is approved by the Minister.

(4) This section does not apply to any building or fence erected or work constructed if specially authorised by Act of Parliament, or in pursuance of an Act of Parliament or Order having the force of an Act, or if lawfully erected or constructed in connexion with the taking or working of minerals in or under any land to which the section is otherwise applicable, or to any [telecommunication apparatus installed for the purposes of a telecommunications code system]. **[439]**

NOTES
Sub-s (2): words omitted repealed by the Local Government Act 1972, s 272(1), Sch 30.
Sub-s (3): words in square brackets inserted by the Local Government Act 1985, s 16, Sch 8, para 10(5); words omitted repealed by the Local Government Act 1972, s 272(1), Sch 30.
Sub-s (4): words in square brackets substituted by the Telecommunications Act 1984, s 109, Sch 4, para 16.

Judgments, etc affecting Land

195. Equitable charges in right of judgment debt, etc

(1)–(3) . . .

(4) A recognisance, on behalf of the Crown or otherwise, whether entered into before or after the commencement of this Act, and an inquisition finding a debt due to the Crown, and any obligation or specialty made to or in favour of the Crown, whatever may have been its date, shall not operate as a charge on any interest in land, or on the unpaid purchase money for any land, unless or until a writ or order, for the purpose of enforcing it, is registered in the register of writs and orders at the Land Registry. **[440]**

NOTES
Sub-ss (1)–(3): repealed by the Administration of Justice Act 1956, ss 34(2), 57(2), Sch 2.

Notices

196. Regulations respecting notices

(1) Any notice required or authorised to be served or given by this Act shall be in writing.

(2) Any notice required or authorised by this Act to be served on a lessee or mortgagor shall be sufficient, although only addressed to the lessee or mortgagor by that designation, without his name, or generally to the persons interested, without any name, and notwithstanding that any person to be affected by the notice is absent, under disability, unborn, or unascertained.

(3) Any notice required or authorised by this Act to be served shall be sufficiently served if it is left at the last-known place of abode or business in the United Kingdom of the lessee, lessor, mortgagee, mortgagor, or other person to be served, or, in case of a notice required or authorised to be served on a lessee or mortgagor, is affixed or left for him on the land or any house or building comprised in the lease or mortgage, or, in case of a mining lease, is left for the lessee at the office or counting-house of the mine.

(4) Any notice required or authorised by this Act to be served shall also be sufficiently served, if it is sent by post in a registered letter addressed to the lessee, lessor, mortgagee, mortgagor, or other person to be served, by name, at the aforesaid place of abode or business, office, or counting-house, and if that letter is not returned through the post-office undelivered; and that service shall be deemed to be made at the time at which the registered letter would in the ordinary course be delivered.

(5) The provisions of this section shall extend to notices required to be served by any instrument affecting property executed or coming into operation after the commencement of this Act unless a contrary intention appears.

(6) This section does not apply to notices served in proceedings in the court. **[441]**

198. Registration under the Land Charges Act 1925, to be notice

(1) The registration of any instrument or matter [in any register kept under the Land Charges Act 1972 or any local land charges register] shall be deemed to constitute actual notice of such instrument or matter, and of the fact of such registration, to all persons and for all purposes connected with the land affected, as from the date of registration or other prescribed date and so long as the registration continues in force.

(2) This section operates without prejudice to the provisions of this Act respecting the making of further advances by a mortgagee, and applies only to instruments and matters required or authorised to be registered [in any such register]. **[442]**

NOTES
  Sub-s (1): words in square brackets substituted by the Local Land Charges Act 1975, s 17(2), Sch 1.
  Sub-s (2): words in square brackets substituted by the Local Land Charges Act 1975, s 17(2), Sch 1.

199. Restrictions on constructive notice

(1) A purchaser shall not be prejudicially affected by notice of—

(i) any instrument or matter capable of registration under the provisions of the Land Charges Act 1925, or any enactment which it replaces, which is void or not enforceable as against him under that Act or enactment, by reason of the non-registration thereof;

(ii) any other instrument or matter or any fact or thing unless—

(a) it is within his own knowledge, or would have come to his knowledge if such inquiries and inspections had been made as ought reasonably to have been made by him; or

(b) in the same transaction with respect to which a question of notice to the purchaser arises, it has come to the knowledge of his counsel, as such, or of his solicitor or other agent, as such, or would have come to the knowledge of his solicitor or other agent, as such, if such inquiries and inspections had been made as ought reasonably to have been made by the solicitor or other agent.

(2) Paragraph (ii) of the last subsection shall not exempt a purchaser from any liability under, or any obligation to perform or observe, any covenant, condition, provision, or restriction contained in any instrument under which his title is derived, mediately or immediately; and such liability or obligation may be enforced in the same manner and to the same extent as if that paragraph had not been enacted.

(3) A purchaser shall not by reason of anything in this section be affected by notice in any case where he would not have been so affected if this section had not been enacted.

(4) This section applies to purchases made either before or after the commencement of this Act.   **[443]**

200. Notice of restrictive covenants and easements

(1) Where land having a common title with other land is disposed of to a purchaser (other than a lessee or a mortgagee) who does not hold or obtain possession of the documents forming the common title, such purchaser, notwithstanding any stipulation to the contrary, may require that a memorandum giving notice of any provision contained in the disposition to him restrictive of user of, or giving rights over, any other land comprised in the common title, shall, where practicable, be written or indorsed on, or, where impracticable, be permanently annexed to some one document selected by the purchaser but retained in the possession or power of the person who makes the disposition, and being or forming part of the common title.

(2) The title of any person omitting to require an indorsement to be made or a memorandum to be annexed shall not, by reason only of this enactment, be prejudiced or affected by the omission.

(3) This section does not apply to dispositions of registered land.

(4) Nothing in this section affects the obligation to register a land charge in respect of—

(a) any restrictive covenant or agreement affecting freehold land; or
(b) any estate contract; or
(c) any equitable easement, liberty or privilege.   **[444]**

PART XII

CONSTRUCTION, JURISDICTION, AND GENERAL PROVISIONS

201. Provisions of Act to apply to incorporeal hereditaments

(1) The provisions of this Act relating to freehold land apply to manors, reputed manors, lordships, advowsons, . . . perpetual rentcharges, and other incorporeal hereditaments, subject only to the qualifications necessarily arising by reason of the inherent nature of the hereditament affected.

(2) This Act does not affect the special restrictions imposed on dealings with advowsons by the Benefices Act 1898 or any other statute or measure, nor affect the limitation of, or authorise any disposition to be made of, a title or dignity of honour which in its nature is inalienable.

(3) This section takes effect subject to the express provisions of this Act relating to undivided shares. **[445]**

NOTES
Sub-s (1): words omitted repealed by the Tithe Act 1936, s 48(3), Sch 9.

202. Provisions as to enfranchisement of copyholds, etc

For giving effect to this Act, the enfranchisement of copyhold land, and the conversion into long terms of perpetually renewable leaseholds, and of leases for lives and of leases for years terminable with life or lives or on marriage, effected by the Law of Property Act 1922 as amended by any subsequent enactment, shall be deemed to have been effected immediately before the commencement of this Act. **[446]**

203. Payment into court, jurisdiction and procedure

(1) Payment of money into court effectually exonerates therefrom the person making the payment.

(2) Subject to any rules of court to the contrary—

    (*a*) Every application to the court under this Act shall, save as otherwise expressly provided, be by summons at chambers;

    (*b*) On an application by a purchaser notice shall be served in the first instance on the vendor;

    (*c*) On an application by a vendor notice shall be served in the first instance on the purchaser;

    (*d*) On any application notice shall be served on such person, if any, as the court thinks fit.

(3) In this Act, unless the contrary intention appears, "the court" means the High Court . . . or the county court, where those courts respectively have jurisdiction.

(4) All matters within the jurisdiction of the High Court under this Act shall, save as otherwise expressly provided, and subject to the enactments for the time being in force with respect to the Supreme Court of Judicature, be assigned to the Chancery Division of the court.

(5) The court shall have full power and discretion to make such order as it thinks fit respecting the costs, charges and expenses of all or any of the parties to any application. **[447]**

NOTES
Sub-s (3): words omitted repealed by the Courts Act 1971, s 56(4), Sch 11, Part II.

204. Orders of court conclusive

(1) An order of the court under any statutory or other jurisdiction shall not, as against a purchaser, be invalidated on the ground of want of jurisdiction, or of want of any concurrence, consent, notice, or service, whether the purchaser has notice of any such want or not.

(2) This section has effect with respect to any lease, sale, or other act under the authority of the court, and purporting to be in pursuance of any statutory power notwithstanding any exception in such statute.

(3) This section applies to all orders made before or after the commencement of this Act. **[448]**

205. General definitions

(1) In this Act unless the context otherwise requires, the following expressions have the meanings hereby assigned to them respectively, that is to say:—

    (i) "Bankruptcy" includes liquidation by arrangement; also in relation to a corporation means the winding up thereof;

    (ii) "Conveyance" includes a mortgage, charge, lease, assent, vesting declaration, vesting instrument, disclaimer, release and every other assurance of property or of an interest therein by any instrument, except a will; "convey" has a corresponding meaning; and "disposition" includes a conveyance and also a devise, bequest, or an appointment of property contained in a will; and "dispose of" has a corresponding meaning;

    (iii) "Building purposes" include the erecting and improving of, and the adding to, and the repairing of buildings; and a "building lease" is a lease for building purposes or purposes connected therewith;

    [(iiiA) . . .]

    (iv) "Death duty" means estate duty, . . . and every other duty leviable or payable on a death;

    (v) "Estate owner" means the owner of a legal estate, but an infant is not capable of being an estate owner;

    (vi) "Gazette" means the London Gazette;

    (vii) "Incumbrance" includes a legal or equitable mortgage and a trust for securing money, and a lien, and a charge of a portion, annuity, or other capital or annual sum; and "incumbrancer" has a meaning corresponding with that of incumbrance, and includes every person entitled to the benefit of an incumbrance, or to require payment or discharge thereof;

    (viii) "Instrument" does not include a statute, unless the statute creates a settlement;

    (ix) "Land" includes land of any tenure, and mines and minerals, whether or not held apart from the surface, buildings or parts of buildings (whether the division is horizontal, vertical or made in any other way) and other corporeal hereditaments; also a manor, an advowson, and a rent and other incorporeal hereditaments, and an easement, right, privilege, or benefit in, over, or derived from land; but not an undivided share in land; and "mines and minerals" include any strata or seam of minerals or substances in or under any land, and powers of working and getting the same but not an undivided share thereof; and "manor" includes a lordship, and reputed manor or lordship; and "hereditament" means any real property which on an intestacy occurring before the commencement of this Act might have devolved upon an heir;

(x) "Legal estates" mean the estates, interests and charges, in or over land (subsisting or created at law) which are by this Act authorised to subsist or to be created as legal estates; "equitable interests" mean all the other interests and charges in or over land or in the proceeds of sale thereof; an equitable interest "capable of subsisting as a legal estate" means such as could validly subsist or be created as a legal estate under this Act;

(xi) "Legal powers" include the powers vested in a chargee by way of legal mortgage or in an estate owner under which a legal estate can be transferred or created; and "equitable powers" mean all the powers in or over land under which equitable interests or powers only can be transferred or created;

(xii) "Limitation Acts" means the Real Property Limitation Acts 1833, 1837 and 1874, and "limitation" includes a trust;

[(xiii) "Mental disorder" has the meaning assigned to it by [section 1 of the Mental Health Act 1983] and "receiver" in relation to a person suffering from mental disorder, means a receiver appointed for that person under [Part VIII of the Mental Health Act 1959 or Part VII of the said Act of 1983];]

(xiv) a "mining lease" means a lease for mining purposes, that is, the searching for, winning, working, getting, making merchantable, carrying away, or disposing of mines and minerals, or purposes connected therewith, and includes a grant or licence for mining purposes;

(xv) "Minister" means [the Minister of Agriculture, Fisheries and Food];

(xvi) "Mortgage" includes any charge or lien on any property for securing money or money's worth; "legal mortgage" means a mortgage by demise or subdemise or a charge by way of legal mortgage and "legal mortgagee" has a corresponding meaning; "mortgage money" means money or money's worth secured by a mortgage; "mortgagor" includes any person from time to time deriving title under the original mortgagor or entitled to redeem a mortgage according to his estate interest or right in the mortgaged property; "mortgagee" includes a chargee by way of legal mortgage and any person from time to time deriving title under the original mortgagee; and "mortgagee in possession" is, for the purposes of this Act, a mortgagee who, in right of the mortgage, has entered into and is in possession of the mortgaged property; and "right of redemption" includes an option to repurchase only if the option in effect creates a right of redemption;

(xvii) "Notice" includes constructive notice;

(xviii) "Personal representative" means the executor, original or by representation, or administrator for the time being of a deceased person, and as regards any liability for the payment of death duties includes any person who takes possession of or intermeddles with the property of a deceased person without the authority of the personal representatives or the court;

(xix) "Possession" includes receipt of rents and profits or the right to receive the same, if any; and "income" includes rents and profits;

(xx) "Property" includes any thing in action, and any interest in real or personal property;

(xxi) "Purchaser" means a purchaser in good faith for valuable consideration and includes a lessee, mortgagee or other person who for valuable consideration acquires an interest in property except that in Part I of this Act and elsewhere where so expressly provided "purchaser" only means a person who acquires an interest in or charge on property for money or money's worth; and in reference to a legal estate includes a chargee by way of legal mortgage; and where the context so requires "purchaser" includes an intending purchaser; "purchase" has a meaning corresponding with that of "purchaser"; and "valuable consideration" includes marriage but does not include a nominal consideration in money;

(xxii) "Registered land" has the same meaning as in the Land Registration Act 1925, and "Land Registrar" means the Chief Land Registrar under that Act;

(xxiii) "Rent" includes a rent service or a rentcharge, or other rent, toll, duty, royalty, or annual or periodical payment in money or money's worth, reserved or issuing out of or charged upon land, but does not include mortgage interest; "rentcharge" includes a fee farm rent; "fine" includes a premium or foregift and any payment, consideration, or benefit in the nature of a fine, premium or foregift; "lessor" includes an underlessor and a person deriving title under a lessor or underlessor; and "lessee" includes an underlessee and a person deriving title under a lessee or underlessee, and "lease" includes an underlease or other tenancy;

(xxiv) "Sale" includes an extinguishment of manorial incidents, but in other respects means a sale properly so called;

(xxv) "Securities" include stocks, funds and shares;

(xxvi) "Tenant for life", "statutory owner", "settled land", "settlement", "vesting deed", "subsidiary vesting deed", "vesting order", "vesting instrument", "trust instrument", "capital money" and "trustees of the settlement" have the same meanings as in the Settled Land Act 1925;

(xxvii) "Term of years absolute" means a term of years (taking effect either in possession or in reversion whether or not at a rent) with or without impeachment for waste, subject or not to another legal estate, and either certain or liable to determination by notice, re-entry, operation of law, or by a provision for cesser on redemption, or in any other event (other than the dropping of a life, or the determination of a determinable life interest); but does not include any term of years determinable with life or lives or with the cesser of a determinable life interest, nor, if created after the commencement of this Act, a term of years which is not expressed to take effect in possession within twenty-one years after the creation thereof where required by this Act to take effect within that period; and in this definition the expression "term of years" includes a term for less than a year, or for a year or years and a fraction of a year or from year to year;

(xxviii) "Trust Corporation" means the Public Trustee or a corporation either appointed by the court in any particular case to be a trustee or entitled by rules made under subsection (3) of section four of the Public Trustee Act 1906 to act as custodian trustee;

(xxix) "Trust for sale", in relation to land, means an immediate binding trust for sale, whether or not exercisable at the request or with the consent of any person, and with or without a power at discretion to postpone the sale; "trustees for sale" mean the persons (including a personal representative) holding land on trust for sale; and "power to postpone a sale" means power to postpone in the exercise of a discretion;

(xxx) "United Kingdom" means Great Britain and Northern Ireland;

(xxxi) "Will" includes codicil.

[(1A) Any reference in this Act to money being paid into court shall be construed as referring to the money being paid into the Supreme Court or any other court that has jurisdiction, and any reference in this Act to the court, in a context referring to the investment or application of money paid into court, shall be construed, in the case of money paid into the Supreme Court, as referring to the High Court, and in the case of money paid into another court, as referring to that other court.]

(2) Where an equitable interest in or power over property arises by statute or operation of law, references to the creation of an interest or power include references to any interest or power so arising.

(3) References to registration under the Land Charges Act 1925, apply to any registration made under any other statute which is by the Land Charges Act 1925, to have effect as if the registration had been made under that Act.

[449]

NOTES
  Sub-s (1): para (iiiA) inserted by the County Courts Act 1984, s 148(1), Sch 2, para 10, repealed by the High Court and County Courts Jurisdiction Order 1991, SI 1991 No 724, art 2(8), Schedule; in para (iv) words omitted repealed by the Finance Act 1949, s 52(9), (10), Sch 11, Part IV; para (xiii) substituted by the Mental Health Act 1959, s 149(1), Sch 7, Part I, words in square brackets substituted by the Mental Health Act 1983, s 148, Sch 4, para 5; in para (xv) words in square brackets substituted by virtue of the Transfer of Functions (Ministry of Food) Order 1955, SI 1955 No 554.
  Sub-s (1A): inserted by the Administration of Justice Act 1965, ss 17, 18, Sch 1.

206. Forms of instruments and examples of abstracts

(1) Instruments in the form of, and using the expressions in the forms given in the Fifth Schedule to this Act, or in the like form or using expressions to the like effect, shall, in regard to form and expression be sufficient.

(2) Examples of abstracts of title framed in accordance with the enactments which will take effect at the commencement of this Act are contained in the Sixth Schedule to this Act.   [450]

207. Repeals as respects England and Wales

... without prejudice to the provisions of section thirty-eight of the Interpretation Act 1889:—

(a) Nothing in this repeal shall affect the validity or legality of any dealing in property or other transaction completed before the commencement of this Act, or any title or right acquired or appointment made before such commencement, but, subject as aforesaid, this Act shall, except where otherwise expressly provided, apply to and in respect of instruments whether made or coming into operation before or after such commencement:

(b) Nothing in this repeal shall affect any rules, orders, or other instruments made under any enactment so repealed, but all such rules, orders and instruments shall continue in force as if made under the corresponding enactment in this Act:

(c) References in any document to any enactment repealed by this Act shall be construed as references to this Act or to the corresponding enactment in this Act. [451]

NOTES
Words omitted repealed by the Statute Law Revision Act 1950.

208. Application to the Crown

(1) Nothing in this Act shall be construed as rendering any property of the Crown subject to distress, or liable to be taken or disposed of by means of any distress.

(2) This Act shall not in any manner (save as otherwise expressly provided and except so far as it relates to undivided shares, joint ownership, leases for lives or leases for years terminable with life or marriage) affect or alter the descent, devolution or tenure or the nature of the estates and interests of or in any land for the time being vested in His Majesty either in right of the Crown or of the Duchy of Lancaster or of or in any land for the time being belonging to the Duchy of Cornwall and held in right or in respect of the said Duchy, but so nevertheless that after the commencement of this Act, no estates, interests or charges in or over any such lands as aforesaid shall be conveyed or created, except such estates, interests or charges as are capable under this Act of subsisting or of being conveyed or created.

(3) Subject as aforesaid the provisions of this Act bind the Crown. [452]

209. Short title, commencement, extent

(1) This Act may be cited as the Law of Property Act 1925.

(2) ...

(3) This Act extends to England and Wales only. [453]

NOTES
Sub-s (2): repealed by the Statute Law Revision Act 1950.

SCHEDULES

SCHEDULE 1

Section 39

TRANSITIONAL PROVISIONS

PART I

CONVERSION OF CERTAIN EXISTING LEGAL ESTATES INTO EQUITABLE INTERESTS

All estates, interests and charges in or over land, including fees determinable whether by limitation or condition, which immediately before the commencement of this Act were estates, interests or charges, subsisting at law, or capable of taking effect as such, but which by virtue of Part I of this Act are not capable of taking effect as legal estates, shall as from the commencement of this Act be converted into equitable interests, and shall not fail by reason of being so converted into equitable interests either in the land or in the proceeds of sale thereof, nor shall the priority of any such estate, charge or interest over other equitable interests be affected.   **[454]**

PART II

VESTING OF LEGAL ESTATES

1. Where the purposes of a term of years, created or limited out of leasehold land, are satisfied at the commencement of this Act, that term shall merge in the reversion expectant thereon and shall cease accordingly; but where the term was vested in the owner of the reversion, the merger and cesser shall take effect without prejudice to any protection which would have been afforded to the owner for the time being of that reversion had the term remained subsisting.

Where the purposes are satisfied only as respects part of the land comprised in a term, this provision has effect as if a separate term had been created in regard to that part of the land.

2. Where immediately after the commencement of this Act any owner of a legal estate is entitled, subject or not to the payment of the costs of tracing the title and of conveyance, to require any other legal estate in the same land to be surrendered, released or conveyed to him so as to merge or be extinguished, the last-mentioned estate shall by virtue of this Part of this Schedule be extinguished but without prejudice to any protection which would have been afforded to him had that estate remained subsisting.

3. Where immediately after the commencement of this Act any person is entitled, subject or not to the payment of the costs of tracing the title and of conveyance, to require any legal estate (not vested in trustees for sale) to be conveyed to or otherwise vested in him, such legal estate shall, by virtue of this Part of this Schedule, vest in manner hereinafter provided.

[The divesting of a legal estate by virtue of this paragraph shall not, where the person from whom the estate is so divested was a trustee, operate to prevent the legal estate being conveyed, or a legal estate being created, by him in favour of a purchaser for money or money's worth, if the purchaser has no notice of the trust and if the documents of title relating to the estate divested are produced by the trustee or by persons deriving title under him.]

This paragraph shall (without prejudice to any claim, in respect of fines, fees, and other customary payments) apply to a person who, under a surrender or any disposition having the effect of a surrender, or under a covenant to surrender or otherwise, was, immediately before the commencement of this Act, entitled to require a legal customary estate of inheritance to be vested in him, or who, immediately after such commencement becomes entitled to enfranchised land.

4. Any person who, immediately after the commencement of this Act, is entitled to an equitable interest capable of subsisting as a legal estate which has priority over any legal estate in the same land, shall be deemed to be entitled for the foregoing purposes to require a legal estate to be vested in him for an interest of a like nature not exceeding in extent or duration the equitable interest:

Provided that this paragraph shall not—

(a) apply where the equitable interest is capable of being over reached by virtue of a subsisting trust for sale or a settlement;

(b) operate to prevent such person from acquiring any other legal estate under this Part of this Schedule to which he may be entitled.

5. For the purposes of this Part of this Schedule, a tenant for life, statutory owner or personal representative, shall be deemed to be entitled to require to be vested in him any legal estate in settled land (whether or not vested in the Crown) which he is, by the Settled Land Act 1925, given power to convey.

6. Under the provisions of this Part of this Schedule, the legal estate affected (namely, any estate which a person is entitled to require to be vested in him as aforesaid) shall vest as follows:—

(a) Where at the commencement of this Act land is subject to a mortgage (not being an equitable charge unsecured by any estate), the legal estate affected shall vest in accordance with the provisions relating to mortgages contained in this Schedule;

(b) Where the land is at the commencement or by virtue of this Act or any Act coming into operation at the same time subject or is by virtue of any statute made subject to a trust for sale, the legal estate affected shall vest in the trustees for sale (including personal representatives holding land on trust for sale) but subject to any mortgage term subsisting of created by this Act;

(c) Where at the commencement of this Act or by virtue of any statute coming into operation at the same time the land is settled land, the legal estate affected shall vest in the tenant for life or statutory owner entitled under the Settled Land Act 1925 to require a vesting deed to be executed in his favour, or in the personal representative, if any, in whom the land may be vested or the Public Trustee, as the case may require but subject to any mortgage term subsisting or created by this Act;

(d) In any case to which the foregoing sub-paragraphs do not apply the legal estate affected shall vest in the person of full age who, immediately after the commencement of this Act, is entitled (subject or not to the payment of costs and any customary payments) to require the legal estate to be vested in him, but subject to any mortgage term subsisting or created by this Act.

7. Nothing in this Part of this Schedule shall operate—

(a) To vest in a mortgagee of a term of years absolute any nominal leasehold reversion which is held in trust for him subject to redemption; or

(b) To vest in a mortgagee any legal estate except a term of years absolute; or

(c) To vest in a person entitled to a leasehold interest, as respects such interest, any legal estate except a term of years absolute; or

(d) To vest in a person entitled to a rentcharge (either perpetual or held for a term of years absolute) as respects such rentcharge, any legal estate except a legal estate in the rentcharge; or

(e) To vest in a person entitled to an easement, right or privilege with reference thereto, any legal estate except a legal estate in the easement, right or privilege; or

(f) To vest any legal estate in a person for an undivided share; or

(g) To vest any legal estate in an infant; or

(h) To affect prejudicially the priority of any mortgage or other incumbrance or interest subsisting at the commencement of this Act; or

(i) To render invalid any limitation or trust which would have been capable of taking effect as an equitable limitation or trust; or

(j) To vest in a purchaser or his personal representatives any legal estate which he has contracted to acquire and in regard to which a contract, including an agreement to create a legal mortgage, is pending at the commencement of this Act, although the consideration may have been paid or satisfied and the title accepted, or to render unnecessary the conveyance of such estate; or

(k) To vest in the managing trustees or committee of management of a charity any legal estate vested in the Official Trustee of Charity Lands; or

(l) To vest in any person any legal estate which failed to pass to him by reason of his omission to be registered as proprietor under the Land Transfer Acts 1875 and 1897 until brought into operation by virtue of the Land Registration Act 1925.

[(m) To vest in any person any legal estate affected by any rent covenants or conditions if, before any proceedings are commenced in respect of the rent covenants or conditions, and before any conveyance of the legal estate or dealing therewith *intet vivos* is effected, he or his personal representatives disclaim it in writing signed by him or them.]

8. Any legal estate acquired by virtue of this Part of this Schedule shall be held upon the trusts and subject to the powers, provisions, rents, covenants, conditions, rights of

redemption (as respects terms of years absolute) and other rights, burdens and obligations, if any, upon or subject to which the estate acquired ought to be held.

9. No stamp duty shall become payable by reason only of any vesting surrender or release effected by this Schedule. **[455]**

NOTES

Para 3: words in square brackets added by the Law of Property (Amendment) Act 1926, s 7, Schedule.

Para 7: words in square brackets added by the Law of Property (Amendment) Act 1926, s 7, Schedule.

PART III

PROVISIONS AS TO LEGAL ESTATE VESTED IN INFANT

1. Where immediately before the commencement of this Act a legal estate in land is vested in one or more infants beneficially, or where immediately after the commencement of this Act a legal estate in land would by virtue of this Act have become vested in one or more infants beneficially if he or they had been of full age, the legal estate shall vest in the manner provided by the Settled Land Act 1925.

2. Where immediately before the commencement of this Act a legal estate in land is vested in an infant jointly with one or more other persons of full age beneficially, the legal estate shall by virtue of this Act vest in that other person or those other persons on the statutory trusts, but not so as to sever any joint tenancy in the net proceeds of sale or in the rents and profits until sale:

Provided that, if by virtue of this paragraph the legal estate becomes vested in one person as trustee, then, if no other person is able and willing to do so, the parents or parent testamentary or other guardian of the infant, if respectively able and willing to act, (in the order named) may, and at the request of any person interested shall (subject to the costs being provided for) by writing appoint an additional trustee and thereupon by virtue of this Act the legal estate shall vest in the additional trustee and existing trustee as joint tenants.

3. Where, immediately before the commencement of this Act, a legal estate in land is vested solely in an infant as a personal representative, or a trustee of a settlement, or on trust for sale or on any other trust, or by way of mortgage, or where immediately after the commencement of this Act a legal estate in land would by virtue of any provision of this Act or otherwise have been so vested if the infant were of full age, the legal estate and the mortgage debt (if any) and interest thereon shall, by virtue of this Act, vest in the Public Trustee, pending the appointment of trustees as hereinafter provided—

    (*a*) as to the land, upon the trusts, and subject to the equities affecting the same (but in the case of a mortgage estate for a term of years absolute in accordance with this Act); and

    (*b*) as to the mortgage debt and interest, upon such trusts as may be requisite for giving effect to the rights (if any) of the infant or other persons beneficially interested therein:

Provided that:—

    (i) The Public Trustee shall not be entitled to act in the trust, or charge any fee, or be liable in any manner, unless and until requested in writing to act by or on behalf of the persons interested in the land or the income thereof, or in the mortgage debt or interest thereon (as the case may be), which request may be made on behalf of the infant by his parents or parent, or testamentary or other guardian (in the order named), and those persons may, in the order aforesaid (if no other person is able and willing to do so) appoint new trustees in the place of the Public Trustee, and thereupon by virtue of this Act the land or term and mortgage money shall vest in the trustees so appointed upon the trusts and subject to the equities aforesaid: Provided that the Public Trustee may, before he accepts the trust, but

subject to the payment of his costs, convey to a person of full age who
becomes entitled;

(ii) After the Public Trustee has been so requested to act, and has accepted
the trust, no trustee shall (except by an order of the court) be appointed in
his place without his consent;

(iii) Any person interested in the land or the income thereof, or in the mortgage
debt or in the interest thereon (as the case may be), may, at the time during
the minority, apply to the court for the appointment of trustees of the
trust, and the court may make such order as it thinks fit, and if thereby
new trustees are appointed the legal estate (but in the case of a mortgage
estate only for a term of years absolute as aforesaid) and the mortgage
debt (if any) and interest shall, by virtue of this Act, vest in the trustees as
joint tenants upon the trusts and subject to the equities aforesaid;

(iv) Neither a purchaser of the land nor a transferee for money or money's
worth of the mortgage shall be concerned in any way with the trusts
affecting the legal estate or the mortgage debt and interest thereon;

(v) The vesting in the Public Trustee of a legal estate or a mortgage debt by
virtue of this Part of this Schedule shall not affect any directions previously
given as to the payment of income or of interest on any mortgage money,
but such instructions may, until he accepts the trust, continue to be acted
on as if no such vesting had been effected.

[3A. The county court has jurisdiction under proviso (iii) to paragraph 3 of this Part
where the land which is to be dealt with in the court does not exceed [£30,000] in capital
value . . .]

4. Where, immediately before the commencement of this Act, a legal estate in land
is vested in two or more persons jointly as personal representatives, trustees, or
mortgagees, and anyone of them is an infant, or where immediately after the
commencement of this Act a legal estate in land would, by virtue of this Act, or otherwise
have been so vested if the infant were of full age, the legal estate in the land with the
mortgage debt (if any) and the interest thereon shall by virtue of this Act, vest in the
other person or persons of full age—

(a) as to the legal estate, upon the trusts and subject to the equities affecting the
same (but in the case of a mortgage estate only for a term of years absolute as
aforesaid); and

(b) as to the mortgage debt and interest, upon such trusts as may be requisite for
giving effect to the rights (if any) of the infant or other persons beneficially
interested therein;

but neither a purchaser of the land nor a transferee for money or money's worth of the
mortgage shall be concerned in any way with the trusts affecting the legal estate or the
mortgage debt and interest thereon:

Provided that, if, by virtue of this paragraph, the legal estate and mortgage debt, if
any, become vested in a sole trustee, then, if no other person is able and willing to do so,
the parents or parent, testamentary or other guardian of the infant (in the order named)
may, and at the request of any person interested shall (subject to the costs being provided
for) by writing appoint a new trustee in place of the infant, and thereupon by virtue of
this Act the legal estate and mortgage money shall vest in the new and continuing trustees
upon the trusts and subject to the equities aforesaid.

5. This Part of this Schedule does not affect the estate or powers of an administrator
durante minore aetate, nor, where there is a tenant for life or statutory owner of settled
land, operate to vest the legal estate therein in the Public Trustee. **[456]**

NOTES
Para 3A: inserted by the County Courts Act 1984, s 148(1), Sch 2, para 10; sum in square
brackets substituted by the High Court and County Courts Jurisdiction Order 1991, SI 1991 No 724,
art 2(8), Schedule.

PART IV

PROVISIONS SUBJECTING LAND HELD IN UNDIVIDED SHARES TO A TRUST FOR SALE

1. Where, immediately before the commencement of this Act, land is held at law or in equity in undivided shares vested in possession, the following provisions shall have effect:—

(1) If the entirety of the land is vested in trustees or personal representatives (whether subject or not to incumbrances affecting the entirety or an undivided share) in trust for persons entitled in undivided shares, then—

(a) if the land is subject to incumbrances affecting undivided shares or to incumbrances affecting the entirety which under this Act or otherwise are not secured by legal terms of years absolute, the entirety of the land shall vest free from such incumbrances in such trustees or personal representatives and be held by them upon the statutory trusts; and

(b) in any other case, the land shall be held by such trustees or personal representatives upon the statutory trusts;

subject in the case of personal representatives, to their rights and powers for the purposes of administration.

(2) If the entirety of the land (not being settled land) is vested absolutely and beneficially in not more than four persons of full age entitled thereto in undivided shares free from incumbrances affecting undivided shares, but subject or not to incumbrances affecting the entirety, it shall, by virtue of this Act, vest in them as joint tenants upon the statutory trusts.

(3) If the entirety of the land is settled land (whether subject or not to incumbrances affecting the entirety or an undivided share) held under one and the same settlement, it shall, by virtue of this Act, vest, free from incumbrances affecting undivided shares, and from incumbrances affecting the entirety, which under this Act or otherwise are not secured by a legal [mortgage, and free from any interests, powers and charges subsisting under the settlement, which have priority to the interests of the persons entitled to the undivided shares], in the trustees (if any) of the settlement as joint tenants upon the statutory trusts.

Provided that if there are no such trustees, then—

(i) pending their appointment, the land shall, by virtue of this Act, vest (free as aforesaid) in the Public Trustee upon the statutory trusts;

(ii) the Public Trustee shall not be entitled to act in the trust, or charge any fee, or be liable in any manner, unless and until requested in writing to act by or on behalf of persons interested in more than an undivided half of the land or the income thereof;

(iii) after the Public Trustee has been so requested to act, and has accepted the trust, no trustee shall (except by an order of the court) be appointed in the place of the Public Trustee without his consent;

(iv) if, before the Public Trustee has accepted the trust, trustees of the settlement are appointed, the land shall, by virtue of this Act, vest (free as aforesaid) in them as joint tenants upon the statutory trusts;

(v) if, before the Public Trustee has accepted the trust, the persons having power to appoint new trustees are unable or unwilling to make an appointment, or if the tenant for life having power to apply to the court for the appointment of trustees of the settlement neglects to make the application for at least three months after being requested by any person interested in writing so to do, or if the tenants for life of the undivided shares are unable to agree, any person interested under the settlement may apply to the court for the appointment of such trustees.

[(3A) The county court has jurisdiction under proviso (v) to sub-paragraph (3) of this paragraph where the land to be dealt with in the court does not exceed [£30,000] in capital value . . .]

(4) In any case to which the foregoing provisions of this Part of this Schedule do not

apply, the entirety of the land shall vest (free as aforesaid) in the Public Trustee upon the statutory trusts:

Provided that—

(i) The Public Trustee shall not be entitled to act in the trust, or charge any fee, or be liable in any manner, unless and until requested in writing to act by or on behalf of the persons interested in more than an undivided half of the land or the income thereof;

(ii) After the Public Trustee has been so requested to act, and has accepted the trust, no trustee shall (except by an order of the court) be appointed in the place of the Public Trustee without his consent;

(iii) Subject as aforesaid, any persons interested in more than an undivided half of the land or the income thereof may appoint new trustees in the place of the Public Trustee with the consent of any incumbrancers of undivided shares (but so that a purchaser shall not be concerned to see whether any such consent has been given) and [thereupon the land shall by virtue of this Act vest] in the persons so appointed (free as aforesaid) upon the statutory trusts; or such persons may (without such consent as aforesaid), at any time, whether or not the Public Trustee has accepted the trust, apply to the court for the appointment of trustees of the land, and the court may make such order as it thinks fit, and if thereby trustees of the land are appointed, the same shall by virtue of this Act, vest (free as aforesaid) in the trustees as joint tenants upon the statutory trusts;

(iv) If the persons interested in more than an undivided half of the land or the income thereof do not either request the Public Trustee to act, or (whether he refuses to act or has not been requested to act) apply to the court for the appointment of trustees in his place, within three months from the time when they have been requested in writing by any person interested so to do, then and in any such case, any person interested may apply to the court for the appointment of trustees in the place of the Public Trustee, and the court may make such order as it thinks fit, and if thereby trustees of the land are appointed the same shall by virtue of this Act vest (free as aforesaid) in the trustees upon the statutory trusts.

[(4A) The county court has jurisdiction under provisos (iii) and (iv) to sub-paragraph (4) of this paragraph where the land which is to be dealt with in the court does not exceed [£30,000] in capital value . . .]

(5) The vesting in the Public Trustee of land by virtue of this Part of this Schedule shall not affect any directions previously given as to the payment of income or of interest on any mortgage money, but such instructions may, until he accepts the trust, continue to be acted on as if no such vesting had been effected.

(6) The court or the Public Trustee may act on evidence given by affidavit or by statutory declaration as respects the undivided shares without investigating the title to the land.

(7) Where all the undivided shares in the land are vested in the same mortgagees for securing the same mortgage money and the rights of redemption affecting the land are the same as might have been subsisting if the entirety had been mortgaged by an owner before the undivided shares were created, the land shall, by virtue of this Act, vest in the mortgagees as joint tenants for a legal term of years absolute (in accordance with this Act) subject to cesser on redemption by the trustees for sale in whom the right of redemption is vested by this act, and for the purposes of this Part of this Schedule the mortgage shall be deemed an incumbrance affecting the entirety.

(8) This Part of this Schedule does not (except where otherwise expressly provided) prejudice incumbrancers whose incumbrances affect the entirety of the land at the commencement of this Act, but (if the nature of the incumbrance admits) the land shall vest in them for legal terms of years absolute in accordance with this Act but not so as to affect subsisting priorities.

(9) The trust for sale and powers of management vested in persons who hold the entirety of the land on trust for sale shall, save as hereinafter mentioned, not be

exercisable without the consent of any incumbrancer, being of full age, affected whose incumbrance is divested by this Part of this Schedule, but a purchaser shall not be concerned to see or inquire whether any such consent has been given, nor, where the incumbrancer is not in possession, shall any such consent be required if, independently of this Part of this Schedule or any enactment replaced thereby the transaction would have been binding on him, had the same been effected by the mortgagor.

(10) This Part of this Schedule does not apply to land in respect of which a subsisting contract for sale (whether made under an order in a partition action or by or on behalf of all the tenants in common or coparceners) is in force at the commencement of this Act if the contract is completed in due course (in which case title may be made in like manner as if this Act, and any enactment thereby replaced, had not been passed), nor to the land in respect of which a partition action is pending at such commencement if an order for a partition or sale is subsequently made in such action [within eighteen months from the commencement of this Act].

(11) The repeal of the enactments relating to partition shall operate without prejudice to any proceedings thereunder commenced before the commencement of this Act, and to the jurisdiction of the court to make any orders in reference thereto, and subject to the following provisions, namely:—

   (i) In any such proceedings, and at any stage thereof, any person or persons interested individually or collectively in [one half or upwards] of the land to which the proceedings relate, may apply to the court for an order staying such proceedings;

   (ii) The court may upon such application make an order staying the proceedings as regards the whole or any part, not being an undivided share, of the land;

   (iii) As from the date of such order the said enactments shall cease to apply to the land affected by the order and the provisions of this Part of this Schedule shall apply thereto;

   (iv) The court may by such order appoint trustees of the land and the same shall by virtue of this Act vest (free as aforesaid) in the trustees as joint tenants upon the statutory trusts;

   (v) The court may order that the costs of the proceedings and of the application shall be raised by the trustees, by legal mortgage of the land or any part thereof, and paid either wholly or partially into court or to the trustees;

   (vi) The court may act on such evidence as appears to be sufficient, without investigating the title to the land.

(12) In this Part of this Schedule "incumbrance" does not include [a legal rentcharge affecting the entirety,] land tax, tithe rentcharge, or any similar charge on the land not created by an instrument.

2. Where undivided shares in land, created before the commencement of this Act, fall into possession after such commencement, and the land is not settled land when the shares fall into possession, the personal representatives (subject to their rights and powers for purposes of administration) or other estate owners in whom the entirety of the land is vested shall, by an assent or a conveyance, give effect to the foregoing provisions of this Part of this Schedule in like manner as if the shares had fallen into possession immediately before the commencement of this Act, and in the meantime the land shall be held on the statutory trusts.

3. This Part of this Schedule shall not save as hereinafter mentioned apply to party structures and open spaces within the meaning of the next succeeding Part of this Schedule.

[4. Where, immediately before the commencement of this Act, there are two or more tenants for life of full age entitled under the same settlement in undivided shares, and, after the cesser of all their interests in the income of the settled land, the entirety of the land is limited so as to devolve together (not in undivided shares), their interests shall, but without prejudice to any beneficial interest, be converted into a joint tenancy, and the joint tenants and the survivor of them shall, until the said cesser occurs, constitute the tenant for life for the purposes of the Settled Land Act 1925 and this Act.]   **[457]**

NOTES
Para 1: words in square brackets in sub-paras (3), (4), (11) substituted and words in square brackets in sub-paras (10), (12) added or inserted by the Law of Property (Amendment) Act 1926, s 7, Schedule; sub-paras (3A), (4A) inserted by the County Courts Act 1984, s 148(1), Sch 2, para 10, sums in square brackets substituted and words omitted repealed by the High Court and County Courts Jurisdiction Order 1991, SI 1991 No 724, art 2(8), Schedule.
Para 4: added by the Law of Property (Amendment) Act 1926, s 7, Schedule.

PART V
PROVISIONS AS TO PARTY STRUCTURES AND OPEN SPACES

1. Where, immediately before the commencement of this Act, a party wall or other party structure is held in undivided shares, the ownership thereof shall be deemed to be severed vertically as between the respective owners, and the owner of each part shall have such rights to support and of user over the rest of the structure as may be requisite for conferring rights corresponding to those subsisting at the commencement of this Act.

2. Where, immediately before the commencement of this Act, an open space of land (with or without any building used in common for the purposes of any adjoining land) is held in undivided shares, in right whereof each owner has rights of access and user over the open space, the ownership thereof shall vest in the Public Trustee on the statutory trusts which shall be executed only with the leave of the court, and, subject to any order of the court to the contrary, each person who would have been a tenant in common shall, until the open space is conveyed to a purchaser, have rights of access and user over the open space corresponding to those which would have subsisted if the tenancy in common had remained subsisting.

3. Any person interested may apply to the court for an order declaring the rights and interests under this Part of this Schedule, of the persons interested in any such party structure or open space, or generally may apply in relation to the provisions of this Part of this Schedule, and the court may make such order as it thinks fit.   **[458]**

PART VI
CONVERSION OF TENANCIES BY ENTIRETIES INTO JOINT TENANCIES

Every tenancy by entireties existing immediately before the commencement of this Act shall, but without prejudice to any beneficial interest, as from such commencement be converted into a joint tenancy.   **[459]**

PART VII
CONVERSION OF EXISTING FREEHOLD MORTGAGES INTO MORTGAGES BY DEMISE

1. All land, which immediately before the commencement of this Act, was vested in a first or only mortgagee for an estate in fee simple in possession, whether legal or equitable, shall, from and after the commencement of this Act, vest in the first or only mortgagee for a term of three thousand years from such commencement, without impeachment of waste, but subject to a provision for cesser corresponding to the right of redemption which, at such commencement, was subsisting with respect to the fee simple.

2. All land, which immediately before the commencement of this Act, was vested in a second or subsequent mortgagee for an estate in fee simple in possession, whether legal or equitable, shall, from and after the commencement of this Act, vest in the second or subsequent mortgagee for a term one day longer than the term vested in the first or other mortgagee whose security ranks immediately before that of such second or subsequent mortgagee, without impeachment of waste, but subject to the term or terms vested in such first or other prior mortgagee and subject to a provision for cesser corresponding to the right of redemption which, at such commencement was subsisting with respect to the fee simple.

3. The estate in fee simple which, immediately before the commencement of this

Act, was vested in any such mortgagee shall, from and after such commencement vest in the mortgagor or tenant for life, statutory owner, trustee for sale, personal representative, or other person of full age who, if all money owing on the security of the mortgage and all other mortgages or charges (if any) had been discharged at the commencement of this Act, would have been entitled to have the fee simple conveyed to him, but subject to any mortgage term created by this Part of this Schedule or otherwise and to the money secured by any such mortgage or charge.

4. If a sub-mortgage by conveyance of the fee simple is subsisting immediately before the commencement of this Act, the principal mortgagee shall take the principal term created by paragraphs 1 or 2 of this Part of this Schedule (as the case may require) and the sub-mortgagee shall take a derivative term less by one day than the term so created, without impeachment of waste, subject to a provision for cesser corresponding to the right of redemption subsisting under the sub-mortgage.

5. This Part of this Schedule applies to land enfranchised by statute as well as to land which was freehold before the commencement of this Act, and (save where expressly excepted) whether or not the land is registered under the Land Registration Act 1925, or the mortgage is made by way of trust for sale or otherwise.

6. A mortgage affecting a legal estate made before the commencement of this Act which is not protected, either by a deposit of documents of title relating to the legal estate or by registration as a land charge, shall not, as against a purchaser in good faith without notice thereof, obtain any benefit by reason of being converted into a legal mortgage by this Schedule, but shall, in favour of such purchaser, be deemed to remain an equitable interest.

This Paragraph does not apply to mortgages or charges registered or protected under the Land Registration Act 1925, or to mortgages or charges registered in a local deeds register.

7. Nothing in this Part of this Schedule shall affect priorities or the right of any mortgagee to retain possession of documents, nor affect his title to or rights over any fixtures or chattels personal comprised in the mortgage.

8. This Part of this Schedule does not apply unless a right of redemption is subsisting immediately before the commencement of this Act. **[460]**

Section 39

TRANSITIONAL PROVISIONS

PART VIII

CONVERSION OF EXISTING LEASEHOLD MORTGAGES INTO MORTGAGES BY SUBDEMISE

1. All leasehold land, which immediately before the commencement of this Act, was vested in a first or only mortgagee by way of assignment of a term of years absolute shall, from and after the commencement of this Act, vest in the first or only mortgagee for a term equal to the term assigned by the mortgage, less the last ten days thereof, but subject to a provision for cesser corresponding to the right of redemption which at such commencement was subsisting with respect to the term assigned.

2. All leasehold land, which immediately before the commencement of this Act, was vested in a second or subsequent mortgagee by way of assignment of a term of years absolute (whether legal or equitable) shall, from and after the commencement of this Act, vest in the second or subsequent mortgagee for a term one day longer than the term vested in the first or other mortgagee whose security ranks immediately before that of such second or subsequent mortgagee if the length of the last-mentioned term permits, and in any case for a term less by one day at least than the term assigned by the mortgage, but subject to the term or terms vested in such first or other prior mortgagee, and subject to a provision for cesser corresponding to the right of redemption which, at the commencement of this Act, was subsisting with respect to the term assigned by the mortgage.

3. The term of years absolute which was assigned by any such mortgage shall, from

and after the commencement of this Act, vest in the mortgagor or tenant for life, statutory owner, trustee for sale, personal representative, or other person of full age who, if all the money owing on the security of the mortgage and all other mortgages or charges, if any, had been discharged at the commencement of this Act, would have been entitled to have the term assigned or surrendered to him, but subject to any derivative mortgage term created by this Part of this Schedule or otherwise and to the money secured by any such mortgage or charge.

4. If a sub-mortgage by assignment of a term is subsisting immediately before the commencement of this Act, the principal mortgagee shall take the principal derivative term created by paragraphs 1 or 2 of this Part of this Schedule or the derivative term created by his mortgage (as the case may require), and the sub-mortgagee shall take a derivative term less by one day than the term so vested in the principal mortgagee, subject to a provision for cesser corresponding to the right of redemption subsisting under the sub-mortgage.

5. A mortgage affecting a legal estate made before the commencement of this Act which is not protected, either by a deposit of documents of title relating to the legal estate or by registration as a land charge shall not, as against a purchaser in good faith without notice thereof, obtain any benefit by reason of being converted into a legal mortgage by this Schedule, but shall, in favour of such purchaser, be deemed to remain an equitable interest.

This paragraph does not apply to mortgages or charges registered or protected under the Land Registration Act 1925, or to mortgages or charges registered in a local deeds register.

6. This Part of this Schedule applies to perpetually renewable leaseholds, and to leaseholds for lives, which are by statute converted into long terms, with the following variations, namely:—

(a) The term to be taken by a first or only mortgagee shall be ten days less than the term created by such statute;

(b) The term to be taken by a second or subsequent mortgagee shall be one day longer than the term vested in the first or other mortgagee whose security ranks immediately before that of the second or subsequent mortgagee, if the length of the last-mentioned term permits, and in any case for a term less by one day at least than the term created by such statute:

(c) The term created by such statute shall, from and after the commencement of this Act, vest in the mortgagor or tenant for life, statutory owner, trustee for sale, personal representative, or other person of full age, who if all the money owing on the security of the mortgage and all other mortgages or charges, if any, had been discharged at the commencement of this Act, would have been entitled to have the term assigned or surrendered to him, but subject to any derivative mortgage term created by this Part of this Schedule or otherwise and to the money secured by any such mortgage or charge.

7. This Part of this Schedule applies (save where expressly excepted) whether or not the leasehold land is registered under the Land Registration Act 1925, or the mortgage is made by way of trust for sale or otherwise.

8. Nothing in this Part of this Schedule shall affect priorities or the right of any mortgagee to retain possession of documents, nor affect his title to or rights over any fixtures or chattels personal comprised in the mortgage, but this Part of this Schedule does not apply unless a right of redemption is subsisting at the commencement of this Act.　　　　　**[461]**

SCHEDULE 2

IMPLIED COVENANTS

PART I

COVENANT IMPLIED IN A CONVEYANCE FOR VALUABLE CONSIDERATION, OTHER THAN A MORTGAGE, BY A PERSON WHO CONVEYS AND IS EXPRESSED TO CONVEY AS BENEFICIAL OWNER

That, notwithstanding anything by the person who so conveys or any one through whom he derives title otherwise than by purchase for value, made, done, executed, or omitted, or knowingly suffered, the person who so conveys has, with the concurrence of every other person, if any, conveying by his direction, full power to convey the subject-matter expressed to be conveyed, subject as, if so expressed, and in the manner in which, it is expressed to be conveyed, and that, notwithstanding anything as aforesaid, that subject-matter shall remain to and be quietly entered upon, received, and held, occupied, enjoyed, and taken by the person to whom the conveyance is expressed to be made, and any person deriving title under him, and the benefit thereof shall be received and taken accordingly, without any lawful interruption or disturbance by the person who so conveys or any person conveying by his direction, or rightfully claiming or to claim by, through, under, or in trust for the person who so conveys or any person conveying by his direction, or by, through, or under any one (not being a person claiming in respect of an estate or interest subject whereto the conveyance is expressly made), through whom the person who so conveys, derives title, otherwise than by purchase for value:

And that, freed and discharged from, or otherwise by the person who so conveys sufficiently indemnified against, all such estates, incumbrances, claims, and demands, other than those subject to which the conveyance is expressly made, as, either before or after the date of the conveyance, have been or shall be made, occasioned, or suffered by that person or by any person conveying by his direction, or by any person rightfully claiming by, through, under, or in trust for the person who so conveys, or by, through, or under any person conveying by his direction, by, through, or under any one through whom the person who so conveys derives title, otherwise than by purchase for value:

And further, that the person who so conveys, and any person conveying by his direction, and every other person having or rightfully claiming any estate or interest in the subject-matter of conveyance, other than an estate or interest subject whereto the conveyance is expressly made, by, through, under, or in trust for the person who so conveys, or by, through, or under any person conveying by his direction, or by, through, or under any one through whom the person who so conveys derives title, otherwise than by purchase for value, will, from time to time and at all times after the date of the conveyance, on the request and at the cost of any person to whom the conveyance is expressed to be made, or of any person deriving title under him, execute and do all such lawful assurances and things for further or more perfectly assuring the subject-matter of the conveyance to the person to whom the conveyance is made, and to those deriving title under him, subject as, if so expressed, and in the manner in which the conveyance is expressed to be made, as by him or them or any of them shall be reasonably required.

In the above covenant a purchase for value shall not be deemed to include a conveyance in consideration of marriage. **[462]**

PART II

FURTHER COVENANT IMPLIED IN A CONVEYANCE OF LEASEHOLD PROPERTY FOR VALUABLE CONSIDERATION, OTHER THAN A MORTGAGE, BY A PERSON WHO CONVEYS AND IS EXPRESSED TO CONVEY AS BENEFICIAL OWNER

That, notwithstanding anything by the person who so conveys, or any one through whom he derives title, otherwise than by purchase for value, made, done, executed, or omitted, or knowingly suffered, the lease or grant creating the term or estate for which the land is conveyed is, at the time of conveyance, a good, valid, and effectual lease or grant of the property conveyed, and is in full force, unforfeited, unsurrendered, and has in nowise become void or voidable, and that, notwithstanding anything as aforesaid, all the rents reserved by, and all the covenants, conditions, and agreements contained in, the lease or grant, and on the part of the lessee or grantee and the persons deriving title under him to be paid, observed, and performed, have been paid, observed, and performed up to the time of conveyance.

In the above covenant a purchase for value shall not be deemed to include a conveyance in consideration of marriage.   **[463]**

PART III

COVENANT IMPLIED IN A CONVEYANCE BY WAY OF MORTGAGE BY A PERSON WHO CONVEYS AND IS EXPRESSED TO CONVEY AS BENEFICIAL OWNER

That the person who so conveys, has, with the concurrence of every other person, if any, conveying by his direction, full power to convey the subject-matter expressed to be conveyed by him, subject as, if so expressed, and in the manner in which it is expressed to be conveyed.

And also that, if default is made in payment of the money intended to be secured by the conveyance, or any interest thereon, or any part of that money or interest, contrary to any provision in the conveyance, it shall be lawful for the person to whom the conveyance is expressed to be made, and the persons deriving title under him, to enter into and upon, or receive, and thenceforth quietly hold, occupy, and enjoy or take and have, the subject-matter expressed to be conveyed, or any part thereof, without any lawful interruption or disturbance by the person who so conveys, or any person conveying by his direction, or any other person (not being a person claiming in respect of an estate or interest subject whereto the conveyance is expressly made):

And that, freed and discharged from, or otherwise by the person who so conveys sufficiently indemnified against, all estates, incumbrances, claims, and demands whatever, other than those subject whereto the conveyance is expressly made:

And further, that the person who so conveys and every person conveying by his direction, and every person deriving title under any of them, and every other person having or rightfully claiming any estate or interest in the subject-matter of conveyance, or any part thereof, other than an estate or interest subject whereto the conveyance is expressly made, will from time to time and at all times, on the request of any person to whom the conveyance is expressed to be made, or of any person deriving title under him, but as long as any right of redemption exists under the conveyance, at the cost of the person so conveying, or of those deriving title under him, and afterwards at the cost of the person making the request, execute and do all such lawful assurances and things for further or more perfectly assuring the subject-matter of conveyance and every part thereof to the person to whom the conveyance is made, and to those deriving title under him, subject as, if so expressed, and in the manner in which the conveyance is expressed to be made, as by him or them or any of them shall be reasonably required.

The above covenant in the case of a charge shall have effect as if for references to "conveys", "conveyed" and "conveyance" there were substituted respectively references to "charges", "charged" and "charge".   **[464]**

PART IV

COVENANT IMPLIED IN A CONVEYANCE BY WAY OF MORTGAGE OF FREEHOLD PROPERTY SUBJECT TO A RENT OR OF LEASEHOLD PROPERTY BY A PERSON WHO CONVEYS AND IS EXPRESSED TO CONVEY AS BENEFICIAL OWNER

That the lease or grant creating the term or estate for which the land is held is, at the time of conveyance a good, valid, and effectual lease or grant of the land conveyed and is in full force, unforfeited, and unsurrendered and has in nowise become void or voidable, and that all the rents reserved by, and all the covenants, conditions, and agreements contained in, the lease or grant, and on the part of the lessee or grantee and the persons deriving title under him to be paid, observed, and performed, have been paid, observed, and performed up to the time of conveyance:

And also that the person so conveying, or the persons deriving title under him, will at all times, as long as any money remains owing on the security of the conveyance, pay, observe, and perform, or cause to be paid, observed, and performed all the rents reserved by, and all the covenants conditions and agreements contained in, the lease or grant, and on the part of the lessee or grantee and the persons deriving title under him to be paid, observed, and performed, and will keep the person to whom the conveyance is made, and those deriving title under him, indemnified against all actions, proceedings, costs, charges, damages, claims and demands, if any, to be incurred or sustained by him or them by reason of the non-payment of such rent or the non-observance of non-performance of such covenants, conditions, and agreements, or any of them.

The above convenant in the case of a charge shall have effect as if for references to "conveys", "conveyed" and "conveyance" there were substituted respectively references to "charges", "charged" and "charge". **[465]**

PART V

COVENANT IMPLIED IN A CONVEYANCE BY WAY OF SETTLEMENT, BY A PERSON WHO CONVEYS AND IS EXPRESSED TO CONVEY AS SETTLOR

That the person so conveying, and every person deriving title under him by deed or act or operation of law in his lifetime subsequent to that conveyance, or by testamentary disposition or devolution in law, on his death, will, from time to time, and at all times, after the date of that conveyance, at the request and cost of any person deriving title thereunder, execute and do all such lawful assurances and things for further or more perfectly assuring the subject-matter of the conveyance to the persons to whom the conveyance is made and those deriving title under them, as by them or any of them shall be reasonably required, subject as, if so expressed, and in the manner in which the conveyance is expressed to be made. **[466]**

PART VI

COVENANT IMPLIED IN ANY CONVEYANCE, BY EVERY PERSON WHO CONVEYS AND IS EXPRESSED TO CONVEY AS TRUSTEE OR MORTGAGEE, OR AS PERSONAL REPRESENTATIVE OF A DECEASED PERSON, ... OR UNDER AN ORDER OF THE COURT

That the person so conveying has not executed or done, or knowingly suffered, or been party or privy to, any deed or thing, whereby or by means whereof the subject-matter of the conveyance, or any part thereof, is or may be impeached, charged, affected, or incumbered in title, estate, or otherwise, or whereby or by means whereof the person who so conveys is in anywise hindered from conveying the subject-matter of the conveyance, or any part thereof, in the manner in which it is expressed to be conveyed.

The foregoing covenant may be implied in an assent in like manner as in a conveyance by deed. **[467]**

NOTES
Words omitted from heading repealed by the Mental Health Act 1959, s 149(2), Sch 8, Part I.

PART VII

COVENANT IMPLIED IN A CONVEYANCE FOR VALUABLE CONSIDERATION, OTHER THAN A MORTGAGE, OF THE ENTIRETY OF LAND AFFECTED BY A RENTCHARGE

That the grantees or the persons deriving title under them will at all times, from the date of the conveyance or other date therein stated, duly pay the said rentcharge and observe and perform all the covenants, agreements and conditions contained in the deed or other document creating the rentcharge, and thenceforth on the part of the owner of the land to be observed and performed:

And also will at all times, from the date aforesaid, save harmless and keep indemnified the conveying parties and their respective estates and effects, from and against all proceedings, costs, claims and expenses on account of any omission to pay the said rentcharge or any part thereof, or any breach of any of the said covenants, agreements and conditions. **[468]**

PART VIII

COVENANTS IMPLIED IN A CONVEYANCE FOR VALUABLE CONSIDERATION, OTHER THAN A MORTGAGE, OR PART OF LAND AFFECTED BY A RENTCHARGE, SUBJECT TO A PART (NOT LEGALLY APPORTIONED) OF THAT RENTCHARGE

(i) That the grantees, or the persons deriving title under them, will at all times, from the date of the conveyance or other date stated, pay the apportioned rent and observe and perform all the covenants (other than the covenant to pay the entire rent) and conditions contained in the deed or other document creating the rentcharge, so far as the same relate to the land conveyed:

And also will at all times, from the date aforesaid, save harmless and keep indemnified the conveying parties and their respective estates and effects, from and against all proceedings, costs, claims and expenses on account of any omission to pay the said apportioned rent, or any breach of any of the said covenants and conditions, so far as the same relate as aforesaid.

(ii) That the conveying parties, or the persons deriving title under them, will at all times, from the date of the conveyance or other date therein stated, pay the balance of the rentcharge (after deducting the apportioned rent aforesaid, and any other rents similarly apportioned in respect of land not retained), and observe and perform all the covenants, other than the covenant to pay the entire rent, and conditions contained in the deed or other document creating the rentcharge, so far as the same relate to the land not included in the conveyance and remaining vested in the covenantors:

And also will at times, from the date aforesaid, save harmless and keep indemnified the grantees and their estates and effects, from and against all proceedings, costs, claims and expenses on account of any omission to pay the aforesaid balance of the rentcharge, or any breach of any of the said covenants and conditions so far as they relate aforesaid.

[469]

PART IX

COVENANT IN A CONVEYANCE FOR VALUABLE CONSIDERATION, OTHER THAN A MORTGAGE, OF THE ENTIRETY OF THE LAND COMPRISED IN A LEASE FOR THE RESIDUE OF THE TERM OR INTEREST CREATED BY THE LEASE

That the assignees, or the persons deriving title under them, will at all times, from the date of the conveyance or other date therein stated, duly pay all rent becoming due under the lease creating the term or interest for which the land is conveyed, and observe and perform all the covenants, agreements and conditions therein contained and thenceforth on the part of the lessees to be observed and performed:

And also will at all times, from the date aforesaid, save harmless and keep indemnified the conveying parties and their estates and effects, from and against all proceedings, costs, claims and expenses on account of any omission to pay the said rent or any breach of any of the said covenants, agreements and conditions. **[470]**

PART X

COVENANTS IMPLIED IN A CONVEYANCE FOR VALUABLE CONSIDERATION, OTHER THAN A MORTGAGE, OF PART OF THE LAND COMPRISED IN A LEASE, FOR THE RESIDUE OF THE TERM OR INTEREST CREATED BY THE LEASE, SUBJECT TO A PART (NOT LEGALLY APPORTIONED) OF THAT RENT

(i) That the assignees, or the persons deriving title under them, will at all times, from the date of the conveyance or other date therein stated, pay the apportioned rent and observe and perform all the covenants, other than the covenant to pay the entire rent, agreements and conditions contained in the lease creating the term or interest for which the land is conveyed, and thenceforth on the part of the lessees to be observed and performed, so far as the same relate to the land conveyed:

And also will at all times from the date aforesaid save harmless and keep indemnified, the conveying parties and their respective estates and effects, from and against all proceedings, costs, claims and expenses on account of any omission to pay the said apportioned rent or any breach of any of the said covenants, agreements and conditions, so far as the same relate as aforesaid.

(ii) That the conveying parties, or the persons deriving title under them, will at all times, from the date of the conveyance, or other date therein stated, pay the balance of the rent (after deducting the apportioned rent aforesaid and any other rents similarly apportioned in respect of land not retained) and observe and perform all the covenants, other than the covenant to pay the entire rent, agreements and conditions contained in the lease and on the part of the lessees to be observed and performed so far as the same relate to the land demised (other than the land comprised in the conveyance) and remaining vested in the covenantors:

And also will at all times, from the date aforesaid, save harmless and keep indemnified, the assignees and their estates and effects, from and against all proceedings, costs, claims and expenses on account of any omission to pay the aforesaid balance of the rent or any breach of any of the said covenants, agreements and conditions so far as they relate as aforesaid. **[471]**

SCHEDULE 3

Sections 114, 115

FORMS OF TRANSFER AND DISCHARGE OF MORTGAGES

FORM NO 1

FORM OF TRANSFER OF MORTGAGE

This Transfer of Mortgage made the .. .. day of .. .. 19 .. , between *M.* of [etc.] of the one part and *T.* of [etc.] of the other part, supplemental to a Mortgage dated [etc.], and made between [etc.], and to a Further Charge dated [etc.], and made between [etc.] affecting etc. (*here state short particulars of the mortgaged property*).

WITNESSETH that in consideration of the sums of £ .. .. .. and £ .. .. .. (for interest) now paid by *T.* to *M.*, being the respective amounts of the mortgage money and interest owing in respect of the said mortgage and further charge (the receipt of which sums *M.* hereby acknowledges) *M.*, as mortgagee, hereby conveys and transfers to *T.* the benefit of the said mortgage and further charge.

In witness, etc. **[472]**

FORM NO 2

FORM OF RECEIPT ON DISCHARGE OF A MORTGAGE

I, *A.B., of* [etc.] hereby acknowledge that I have this .. .. day of .. .. 19 .. , received the sum of £ .. .. representing the [aggregate] [balance remaining owing in respect of the] principal money secured by the within [above] written [annexed] mortgage [and by a further charge dated, etc., *or otherwise as required*] together with all interest and costs, the payment having been made by *C.D.* of [etc.] and *E.F.* of [etc.]

As witness, etc.

NOTE.—If the persons paying are not entitled to the equity of redemption state that they are paying the money out of a fund applicable to the discharge of the mortgage. **[473]**

SCHEDULE 4

Sections 117–120

FORMS RELATING TO STATUTORY CHARGES OR MORTGAGES OF FREEHOLD OR LEASEHOLD LAND

FORM NO 1

STATUTORY CHARGE BY WAY OF LEGAL MORTGAGE

This Legal Charge made by way of Statutory Mortgage the .. .. day of .. .. 19 .. , between *A.* of [etc.] of the one part and *M.* of [etc.] of the other part Witnesseth that in consideration of the sum of £ .. .. .. now paid to *A.* by *M.* of which sum *A.* hereby acknowledges the receipt *A.* As Mortgagor and As Beneficial Owner hereby charges by

way of legal mortgage All That [etc.] with the payment to *M*. on the .. .. day of .. .. ..
.. .. 19 .. , of the principal sum of £ .. .. as the mortgage money with interest
thereon at the rate of .. .. .. per centum per annum.

In witness etc.

NOTE.—Variations in this and the subsequent forms in this Schedule to be made, if
required, for leasehold land or for giving effect to special arrangements. *M*. will be in the
same position as if the Charge had been effected by a demise of freeholds or a subdemise
of leaseholds.   [474]

FORM NO 2

STATUTORY TRANSFER, MORTGAGOR NOT JOINING

This Transfer of Mortgage made by way of statutory transfer the .. .. .. day of .. ..
.. .. .. 19 .. , between *M*. of [etc.] of the one part and *T*. of [etc.] of the other part
supplemental to a legal charge made by way of statutory mortgage dated [etc.] and made
[etc.] Witnesseth that in consideration of the sum of £ .. .. .. now paid to *M*. by *T*. (being
the aggregate amount of £ .. .. mortgage money and £ .. .. interest due in respect
of the said legal charge of which sum *M*. hereby acknowledges the receipt) *M*. as
Mortgagee hereby conveys and transfers to *T*. the benefit of the said legal charge.

In witness, etc.

NOTE.—This and the next two forms also apply to a transfer of a statutory mortgage
made before the commencement of this Act, which will then be referred to as a mortgage
instead of a legal charge.   [475]

FORM NO 3

STATUTORY TRANSFER, A COVENANTOR JOINING

This Transfer of Mortgage made by way of statutory transfer the .. .. .. day of .. ..
.. .. .. 19 .. , between *A*. of [etc.] of the first part *B*. of [etc.] of the second part and *C*. of
[etc.] of the third part Supplemental to a Legal Charge made by way of statutory mortgage
dated [etc.] and made [etc.] Witnesseth that in consideration of the sum of £ .. .. .. now
paid by *A*. to *C*. (being the mortgage money due in respect of the said Legal Charge no
interest being now due or payable thereon of which sum *A*. hereby acknowledges the
receipt) *A*. as Mortgagee with the concurrence of *B*. who joints herein as covenantor
hereby conveys and transfers to *C*. the benefit of the said Legal Charge.

In witness, etc.   [476]

FORM NO 4

STATUTORY TRANSFER AND MORTGAGE COMBINED

This Transfer and Legal Charge is made by way of statutory transfer and mortgage
the .. .. day of .. .. 19 .. , between *A*. of [etc.] of the first part *B*. of [etc.] of
the second part and *C*. of [etc.] of the third part Supplemental to a Legal Charge made
by way of statutory mortgage dated [etc.] and made [etc.] Whereas a principal sum of £ ..
.. .. only remains due in respect of the said Legal Charge as the mortgage money and no
interest is now due thereon And Whereas *B*. is seised in fee simple of the land comprised
in the said Legal Charge subject to that Charge.

Now this Deed Witnesseth as follows:—

1. In consideration of the sum of £ .. .. .. now paid to *A*. by *C*. (the receipt and
payment of which sum *A*. & *B*. hereby respectively acknowledge) * *A*. as mortgagee
hereby conveys and transfers to *C*. the benefit of the said Legal Charge.

2. For the consideration aforesaid *B*. *as beneficial owner hereby charges by way of
legal mortgage. All the premises comprised in the said Legal Charge with the payment
to *C*. on the .. .. .. day of .. .. 19 ..*of the sum of £ .. .. .. as the mortgage money
with interest thereon at the rate of .. .. .. per centum per annum In Witness etc. [or in the
case of a further advance after "acknowledge" at**insert* "and of the further sum of
£ .. .. .. now paid by *C*. to *B*. of which sum *B*. hereby acknowledges the receipt" *also at*

before "as beneficial owner" insert "as mortgagor and" *as well as where B. is not the original mortgagor. And after* "of" *at* *insert "the sums of £ .. .. .. and £ .. .. .. making together"

NOTE.—Variations to be made, as required, in case of the deed being by indorsement, or in respect of any other thing. [477]

FORM No 5
RECEIPT ON DISCHARGE OF STATUTORY LEGAL CHARGE OR MORTGAGE

I *A.B.* of [etc.] hereby acknowledge that I have this .. .. .. day of .. .. 19 .. received the sum of £ .. .. .. representing the [aggregate] [balance remaining owing in respect of the] mortgage money secured by the [annexed] within [above] written statutory legal charge [*or* statutory mortgage] [and by the further statutory charge dated etc. *or otherwise as required*] together with all interest and costs the payment having been made by *C.D.* of [etc.] and *E.F.* of [etc.]

As witness etc.

NOTE.—If the persons paying are not entitled to the equity of redemption state that they are paying the money out of a fund applicable to the discharge of the statutory legal charge or mortgage. [478]

SCHEDULE 5
Section 206
FORMS OF INSTRUMENTS

FORM No 1
CHARGE BY WAY OF LEGAL MORTGAGE

This Legal Charge is made [etc.] between *A.* of [etc.] of the one part and *B.* of [etc.] of the other part.

[*Recite the title of A. to the freeholds or leaseholds in the Schedule and agreement for the loan by B.*]

Now in consideration of the sum of .. .. .. pounds now paid by *B.* to *A.* (the receipt etc.) this Deed witnesseth as follows:—

1. *A.* hereby covenants with *B.* to pay [*Add the requisite covenant to pay principal and interest*].

2. *A.* as Beneficial Owner hereby charges by way of legal mortgage All and Singular the property mentioned in the Schedule hereto with the payment to *B.* of the principal money, interest, and other money hereby covenanted to be paid by *A.*

3. [*Add covenant to insure buildings and any other provisions desired.*]

In witness [etc.] [*Add Schedule*].

NOTE.—*B.* will be in the same position as if a mortgage had been effected by a demise of freeholds or a subdemise of leaseholds. [479]

FORM No 2
FURTHER CHARGE BY WAY OF LEGAL MORTGAGE

This Further Charge made [etc.] between [etc.] [*same parties as foregoing legal charge*] Supplemental to a Legal Charge (hereinafter called the Principal Deed) dated [etc.] and made between the same parties as are parties hereto and in the same order for securing the sum of £ .. .. .. and interest at .. .. .. per centum per annum on [freehold] [leasehold] land at [etc.]

Witnesseth as follows:—

1. In consideration of the further sum of £ .. .. .. now paid to *A.* by *B.* [*add receipt and covenant to pay the further advance and interest*].

2. For the consideration aforesaid *A.* as Beneficial Owner hereby charges by way of

legal mortgage the premises comprised in the Principal Deed with the payment to *B*. of the principal money and interest hereinbefore covenanted to be paid as well as the principal money, interest, and other money secured by the Principal Deed.

In witness [etc.] [480]

FORM NO 3
COVEYANCE ON SALE, LEGAL CHARGEES OR MORTGAGEES CONCURRING

This Conveyance is made [etc.] between *A*. of [etc.] (hereinafter called the Vendor) of the first part *B*. of [etc.] and *C*. of [etc.] (hereinafter called the Mortgagees) of the second part and *D*. of [etc.] (hereinafter called the Purchaser) of the third part (*Recite the Charge by way of legal mortgage, the state of the debt, the agreement for sale and for the mortgagees to concur*].

Now in the consideration of the sum of £ .. .. .. paid by the Purchaser by the direction of the Vendor to the Mortgagees (*the receipt etc*.) and of the sum of £ .. .. .. paid by the Purchaser to the Vendor (*the receipt etc*.) this Deed witnesseth as follows:—

1. The Vendor As Beneficial Owner hereby conveys and the Mortgagees As Mortgagees hereby [surrender and] release unto the Purchaser All That etc.

To Hold unto the Purchaser [in fee simple] discharged from all claims under the recited Legal Charge [Mortgage and to the intent that the term subsisting thereunder shall as respects the premises conveyed merge and be extinguished].

2. [*Add any necessary acknowledgments and undertakings with respect to documents not handed over which relate to the title and any other special provisions.*]

In witness etc. [481]

FORM NO 4
CONVEYANCE ON SALE BY LEGAL CHARGEES OR MORTGAGEES

This Conveyance is made [etc.] between *A*. of [etc.] and *B*. of [etc.] (hereinafter called the Vendors) of the one part and *C*. of [etc.] (hereinafter called the Purchaser) of the other part [*Recite the Legal Charge or the Mortgage, with or without a deed converting the Mortgage into a legal charge and the agreement for sale*].

Now in consideration of the sum of £ .. .. .. paid by the Purchaser to the Vendors (the receipt etc.) this Deed witnesseth as follows:—

1. The Vendors As Mortgagees in exercise of the power for this purpose conferred on them by the Law of Property Act 1925 and of all other powers hereby convey unto the Purchaser All Those etc.

To Hold unto the Purchaser [in fee simple] discharged from all right of redemption and claims under the recited Legal Charge [Mortgage].

2. [*Add any necessary acknowledgements as to documents retained and any other special provisions.*]

In witness etc. [482]

FORM NO 5
CONVEYANCE BY PERSONAL REPRESENTATIVES OF A FEE SIMPLE RESERVING THEREOUT A TERM OF YEARS ABSOLUTE FOR GIVING LEGAL EFFECT TO A MORTGAGE

This Conveyance is made [etc.] between *James Cook* of [etc.] and *Harry Cook* of [etc.] of the first part, *L*. of [etc.] and *M*. of [etc.] of the second part, and *Thomas Wilson* of [etc.] of the third part.

Whereas on the first day of October 1927 Letters of Administration to the real and personal estate of *Henry Wilson*, late of [etc.], who died [etc.], were granted by the principal probate registry to *James Cook* and *Harry Cook*.

And whereas *Henry Wilson* was at his death solely entitled to the hereditaments hereinafter conveyed for an estate in fee simple.

Now this Deed witnesseth that *James Cook* and *Harry Cook, as Personal Representatives of the said Henry Wilson* deceased, hereby convey unto the said *Thomas Wilson.*

All that [etc.]

Reserving out of the premises nevertheless unto *L.* and *M.* a term of eight hundred years, without impeachment of waste, to commence from the date hereof but subject to cesser on redemption by *Thomas Wilson* under a Mortgage dated [etc.] and made between [etc.] on payment of the sum of five thousand pounds, and interest thereon at the rate of five pounds per centum per annum.

To hold the premises subject to the said term unto *Thomas Wilson* [in fee simple].

In witness [etc.]

NOTE.—The reservation will be valid at law, though the deed may not be executed by *Thomas Wilson.* **[483]**

FORM No 6

CONVEYANCE ON SALE RESERVING MINERALS AND RIGHT TO WORK AND A PERPETUAL RENTCHARGE

This Conveyance made [etc.] between *A.* of [etc.] of the one part and *B.* of [etc.] of the other part.

Witnesseth that in consideration of the sum of .. .. .. pounds now paid by *B.* to *A.* (the receipt, etc.) and of the rentcharge hereinafter reserved *A.* as Beneficial Owner hereby conveys unto *B.*

All those [etc.] except and reserving unto *A.* in fee simple all mines and minerals Together with full power to work [etc.]

To hold (except and reserved as aforesaid) unto *B.* in fee simple reserving out of the premises to *A.* in fee simple a perpetual yearly rentcharge of .. .. .. pounds, to be for ever charged upon and issuing out of the premises hereby conveyed clear of all deductions (except landlord's property tax), and payable by equal half-yearly payments on [etc.], the first payment to be made on [etc.]

And *B.* hereby covenants with *A.*, and the persons deriving title under him to pay [etc.]

In witness [etc.]

NOTE.—The reservations will be valid at law even if the deed is not executed by *B.* **[484]**

FORM No 7

DEED FOR CONFIRMING LEGAL ESTATES WHICH HAVE NOT BEEN VALIDLY CREATED

To All to whom this Further Assurance shall come *A.B.* of etc. sends greeting this .. .. day of .. .. 19 .. .

[*Recite the invalid dealings, giving short particulars in schedules of the Conveyances, Grants and Leases which purport to transfer or create legal estates, that A.B. is entitled in fee simple or for a term of years absolute in the land affected and desires to confirm the dealings.*]

Now these presents witness and the said *A.B.* hereby declares that his legal estate in the premises affected to which he is entitled as aforesaid shall go and devolve in such manner as may be requisite for legally confirming the interests capable of subsisting as legal estates expressed to have been transferred or created by the documents mentioned in the schedules hereto or any of those documents and any dealings with the interests so confirmed which would have been legal if those interests had in the first instance been validly transferred or created:

Provided always that subject to such confirmation of interests and dealings nothing herein contained shall affect the legal estate of the said *A.B.* in the premises.

In witness, etc. [*Add Schedules.*]

NOTE.—This form takes the place of a conveyance to uses for confirming past transactions and is applicable to a term of years absolute as well as a fee simple. **[485]**

FORM No 8

ASSENT BY PERSONAL REPRESENTATIVE IN FAVOUR OF A PERSON ABSOLUTELY ENTITLED FREE FROM INCUMBRANCES

I, *A.B.*, of [etc.] as the personal representative of *X.Y.*, late of [etc.] deceased, do this .... day of .... 19 .. hereby, As Personal Representative, assent to the vesting in *C.D.* of [etc.] of [All that farm, etc.] *or* [All the property described in the Schedule hereto] for all the estate or interest of the said *X.Y.* at the time of his death [*or*, for an estate in fee simple].

As witness, etc.

NOTE.—The expression "conveyance" includes an assent, but an assent will relate back to the death unless a contrary intention appears. An assent may be properly given though duties remain to be paid if the personal representative is satisfied in regard to the arrangements made for payment. **[486]**

FORM No 9

ASSENT BY PERSONAL REPRESENTATIVES IN FAVOUR OF TRUSTEES FOR SALE

We, *A.B.*, of [etc.] and *C.D.*, of [etc.] as the Personal Representatives of *X.Y.*, late of [etc.] deceased do this .. ... day of .... 19 .. hereby:—

1. As Personal Representatives assent to the vesting in [ourselves *or*] *T.A.* of [etc.] and *T.B.* of [etc.] of All Those etc. To Hold unto [ourselves *or*] the said *T.A.* and *T.B.* in fee simple Upon trust to sell the same or any part thereof with full power to postpone the sale and to stand possessed of the net proceeds of sale and other money applicable as capital and the net rents and profits until sale upon the trusts respectively declared concerning the same [*or* the proceeds of sale and the rents and profits of certain property at ....] by the Will dated [etc.] of [etc.] [*or* by the Settlement dated etc. *or otherwise as the case may require*].

2. And declare that *F.* of [etc.] and *M.* of [etc.] during their joint lives and the survivor of them during his or her life have or has power to appoint new trustees of this Assent [*or* "that the statutory power to appoint new trustees applies to this Assent" *or otherwise as the case requires to correspond with the power applicable to the Will or Settlement*].

As witness etc. **[487]**

SCHEDULE 6
Section 206

EPITOMES OF ABSTRACTS OF TITLE

SPECIMEN No 1
OF THE TITLE OF JOHN WILLIAMS TO BLACKACRE WHERE THE TITLE COMMENCES BEFORE THE COMMENCEMENT OF THIS ACT

The italics show how the abstract is to be framed and what documents are to be
   abstracted. After the commencement of this Act, the parts not in italics may be
   ignored.

10TH JUNE, 1897.—*Will of H. Jones, appointing Maria Jones and W. Jones executors and
   Settled Land Act trustees.*
Devises, Blackacre.
*To the use that Maria Jones may receive a yearly rentcharge of five hundred pounds for her
   life, and, subject thereto,*
To the use of W. Jones for life with remainder,
To the use of *X.* and *Y.*, for a term of one thousand years, and subject thereto,

To the use of the first and other sons of W. Jones in tail with remainders over.

Trusts of term of one thousand years declared for raising ten thousand pounds for portions for younger children of W. Jones, as he shall appoint, and in default equally.

Hotchpot Clause. Power to appoint new trustees.

4TH JUNE, 1898.—*Death of H. Jones.*

1ST AUGUST, 1898.—*Will of H. Jones proved.*

> [NOTE.—After the execution of the Vesting Deed the will only takes effect in equity and can be withdrawn from the abstract when not required as a root of title.]

20TH AUGUST, 1899.—*Conveyance by the executors to the uses of the Will.*

2ND SEPTEMBER, 1915.—*Appointment of R. and S. to be Settled Land Act trustees of the will in place of Maria Jones and W. Jones who retire.*

1ST JANUARY, 1926.—The Settled Land and Law of Property Acts, 1925, come into operation.

> [NOTE.—The legal estate in fee simple will vest in W. Jones in fee simple, but he cannot deal with it till the vesting deed is executed.]

20TH JANUARY, 1926.—*Deed by the Settled Land Act trustees declaring the fee simple is vested in W. Jones on the trusts of the Will and stating that they are the trustees of the settlement.*

2ND FEBRUARY, 1926.—Appointment by W. Jones of five thousand pounds, part of the ten thousand pounds, to his daughter, Ann Jones.

3RD FEBRUARY, 1926.—Assignment by Ann Jones of her five thousand pounds, part of the ten thousand pounds raisable for portions, to trustees *F.* and *G.* on her marriage to J. Robinson.

4TH FEBRUARY, 1926.—Will of W. Jones, appointing T. Brooks his executor.

6TH MARCH, 1926.—Death of W. Jones leaving three children, Frederick Jones, his eldest son, and E. Jones and Ann Robinson.

2ND APRIL, 1926.—Disentail by Frederick Jones in trust for himself in fee simple.

3RD MAY, 1926.—*Will of W. Jones proved by R. and S. in regard to the settled land.*

6TH JUNE, 1926.—Mortgage by E. Jones of his one-half of the ten thousand pounds to *K.*

1ST DECEMBER, 1926.—Death of Maria Jones, jointress.

2ND JANUARY, 1927.—Release by *F.* and *G.* on payment to them of the five thousand pounds of Ann Robinson.

SAME DATE.—Release by E. Jones and *K.*, his mortgagee, of the five thousand pounds raisable for E. Jones.

3RD JANUARY, 1927.—*Assent by R. and S., as personal representatives to Frederick Jones in fee, without nominating Settled Land Act trustees.*

> [NOTE.—If the Assent had been made before the family charges had been cleared, the personal representatives would have nominated themselves as being the trustees of the settlement, and a discharge from them would have been required when the charges were cleared.]

6TH FEBRUARY, 1927.—*Mortgage either by charge by way of legal mortgage or for a term of one thousand years by Frederick Jones to the Estate Trustees of the C. Assurance Society to secure five thousand pounds and interest.*

20TH MARCH, 1927.—Second mortgage either by charge by way of legal mortgage or for a term of two thousand years by Frederick Jones to *D.*, to secure three thousand pounds and interest.

1ST JUNE, 1927.—Third mortgage either by charge by way of legal mortgage or for a term of three thousand years by Frederick Jones to *E.*, to secure two thousand pounds and interest.

8TH AUGUST, 1927.—Conveyance by Frederick Jones on his marriage (subject to above mortgages) to *M.* and *N.* upon trust for sale, the proceeds of sale being settled by a deed of even date.

12TH NOVEMBER, 1927.—Death of *M.*

20TH DECEMBER, 1927.—Appointment of *F.* as trustee of the conveyance on trust for sale in the place of *M.*, and jointly with *N.*

10TH JUNE, 1928.—*Conveyance by the then Estate Trustees of the C. Assurance Society, under their power of sale as first mortgagees, to John Williams in fee.*

> [NOTE.—The title being made under the power of sale of the Estate Trustees, the fee simple passes and not merely the mortgage term. They can if desired convey the fee in the names of *N.* and *F.* It is unnecessary to disclose the second and third

mortgages or the conveyance on trust for sale. It would have been necessary to disclose them if title had been made by the trustees for sale, as the mortgages and the conveyance all dealt with legal estates. The right to vest the debt and mortgaged property in Estate Trustees by memorial enrolled under a Private Act is preserved.

No evidence of deaths, births, etc., is required. Probate of the will of H. Jones is conveyancing evidence of his death.]

12TH JANUARY, 1929.—John Williams leaves Great Britain and Northern Ireland is believed to be alive but cannot be found.

10TH AUGUST, 1929.—*Private Act passed authorising the X. Company to acquire Blackacre under compulsory powers.*

15TH JUNE, 1930.—*Statutory declaration as to facts known with reference to John Williams.*

16TH JUNE, 1930.—*Deed Poll by X. Company (who by their agent also execute in the name of John Williams) under section seventy-seven of the Lands Clauses Consolidation Act, 1845, vesting the land in themselves.*

[NOTE.—This is an example of an exercise of a power over a legal estate the operation of which is expressly preserved.] **[488]**

SPECIMEN NO 2
OF THE TITLE OF THE TRUSTEES OF FRANK SMITHERS TO GREENACRE RELATING TO UNDIVIDED SHARES

2ND JANUARY, 1910.—*Mortgage by James Smith of Greenacre to M. Coy., Ltd. in fee to secure £1,000 and interest.*

4TH FEBRUARY, 1910.—*Will of James Smith devising Greenacre to his ten children named therein in equal shares and appointing E. to be his executor.*

1ST MARCH, 1910.—Death of James Smith, leaving the ten children surviving.

3RD APRIL, 1910.—*Probate by E.*

4TH DECEMBER, 1910.—*Assent by E. to the devise to the ten children.*

5TH JANUARY, 1911.—Mortgage by one of the sons of his tenth share.

15TH APRIL, 1911.—Conveyance by one of the daughters on her marriage of a tenth share to trustees on trust for sale the net proceeds to be held on the trusts of her settlement of even date.

20TH MAY, 1911.—Settlement by another of the sons of his tenth share and appointing Settled Land Act trustees.

8TH JUNE, 1913.—Will of another daughter devising her tenth to her husband and appointing him executor.

20TH JUNE, 1913.—Death of the testatrix.

4TH AUGUST, 1913.—Probate by her husband.

2ND MAY, 1918.—Death of another son intestate.

30TH JULY, 1918.—Letters of administration granted to two of his brothers.

1ST JANUARY, 1926.—The Law of Property Act, 1925, comes into operation and vests Greenacre, subject only to the mortgage of 1910 affecting the entirety (which is converted into a mortgage for a term of three thousand years), in the Public Trustee, pending the appointment of new trustees, on trust for sale.

4TH JUNE, 1926.—*Order of the court (Chancery Division) made on the application of persons entitled to six tenths, appointing M. and N. to be trustees of the trust affecting Greenacre in place of the Public Trustee.*

7TH MAY, 1927.—*Conveyance on sale to Walter Robinson by M. and N., the M. Company, Limited, being paid off out of part of the purchase money, and joining to surrender the three thousand years term.*

[NOTE.—The balance of the purchase money is available in the hands of the trustees to answer the claims of the mortgagee and other persons interested in undivided shares.]

4TH JUNE, 1927.—Will of Walter Robinson devising and bequeathing Greenacre and his residuary real and personal estate to X. and Y. upon trust for his son John Robinson for life with remainder upon trust for his first and other sons successively according to seniority in tail male with remainder upon trust for the same sons in tail general with remainder upon trust for all the daughters of John Robinson as tenants in common in tail with cross remainders in tail between them in equal shares. Appointment of X. and Y. to be executors and Settled Land Act trustees.

1ST DECEMBER, 1927.—Death of testator.

20TH APRIL, 1928.—*Probate by X. and Y.*

3RD MAY, 1928.—*Assent by X. and Y. vesting the settled land in John Robinson upon the trusts of the will of Walter Robinson, and stating that they are the trustees of the settlement.*

14TH JULY, 1928.—Will of John Robinson appointing his daughters Mary Robinson and Jane Robinson his executors.

16TH MARCH, 1930.—Death of John Robinson without having had a son and leaving five daughters.

12TH JUNE, 1930.—*Probate by X. and Y. in regard to the settled land.*

25TH JULY, 1930.—*Assent by X. and Y. to the vesting of the settled land in themselves on trust for sale, the net proceeds to be held on the trusts of the will of Walter Robinson.*

7TH JANUARY, 1931.—*Conveyance on sale by X. and Y. of Greenacre to Frank Smithers in fee.*

8TH JANUARY, 1931.—Equitable charge by Frank Smithers to James Montagu by way of indemnity and agreement to vest Greenacre in a trust corporation on trust for sale to raise the money when the amount is ascertained and for other purposes.

> [NOTE.—A mere equitable charge not secured by deposit of documents can be overridden when the land is made subject to a trust for sale without joining the chargee.]

9TH JANUARY, 1932.—*Lease by Frank Smithers of part of Greenacre to his wife for life at a rent.*

> [NOTE.—A lease for life is made to take effect as a demise for a term of ninety years determinable by notice after the death of the lessee by his representatives or by the lessor.]

23RD JUNE, 1933.—*Conveyance by Frank Smithers, of Greenacre, to a trust corporation on trust for sale subject to the lease.* The net proceeds to be held on the trusts of a deed of even date, under which effect is given to the Agreement of 1931. **[489]**

SPECIMEN NO 3
OF THE TITLE OF R. HORNE TO WHITEACRE WHERE THE TITLE COMMENCES AFTER THE
COMMENCEMENT OF THIS ACT

4TH JULY, 1926.—*Settlement by John Wilson, being a deed declaring that Whiteacre is vested in himself in fee upon the trusts of a deed of even date.*
Appointment of R. and S. to be trustees for the purposes of the Settled Land Act, 1925.
Provisions extending the powers conferred by the Settled Land Act, so far as they relate to dealings with land, and giving power for John Wilson during his life to appoint new trustees.

SAME DATE.—Trust Instrument.
Trusts declared for John Wilson for life, with remainder.

> Upon trust that Elizabeth Wilson, if she survives him shall have a rent-charge of £200 during the residue of her life, and subject thereto.
> Upon trust for R. and S. for a term of five hundred years to raise five thousand pounds portions for younger children of John Wilson, with remainder.
> Upon trust for Henry Wilson for life, with remainder.
> Upon trust for H. and K. for a term of one thousand years to raise five thousand pounds portions for younger children of Henry Wilson, with remainder.
> Upon trust for the first and other sons of Henry Wilson successively in tail, with further remainders over. Appointment of R. and S. to be Settled Land Act trustees. Extension of Settled Land Act powers by reference to the Vesting Deed of even date or otherwise. Power for tenant for life of full age to appoint new trustees.

4TH SEPTEMBER, 1926.—Appointment of a new trustee of the Trust Instrument and of the five hundred years' term.
Recites that S. is incapable of acting. Appointment by John Wilson of P. to be trustee of the term of five hundred years and for the purposes of the Trust Deed in the place of S. and jointly with R. Declaration (express or implied) vesting the equitable term of five hundred years in R. and P.

SAME DATE.—*Deed stating that R. and P. are the trustees of the settlement. Memorandum of the deed endorsed on the Vesting Deed.*

7TH JANUARY, 1927.—Will of John Wilson appointing Isaac James and Joseph James executors.

3RD SEPTEMBER, 1927.—Death of John Wilson, leaving younger children and his widow.

4TH APRIL, 1928.—*Will of John Wilson proved by R. and P. in regard to the settled land.*

1ST OCTOBER, 1928.—Assignment by *R.* and *P.* to *B.* of term of five hundred years by way of mortgage for securing five thousand pounds and interest.

[NOTE.—As money has been raised on the term the mortgagee could call on the executors to create a legal term for securing it in priority to the settlement.]

2ND DECEMBER, 1928.—*Assent by R. and P., as personal representatives, to the vesting of the settled land in Henry Wilson in fee upon the trusts of the Trust Deed.*

Statement that R. and P. are the trustees of the settlement. Power for Henry Wilson during his life to appoint new trustees.

The same provisions for extending powers conferred by the Settled Land Act as are contained in the Vesting Deed.

[NOTE.—These may be inserted either expressly, if short, or by reference to the former Vesting Deed, if long.]

2ND JUNE, 1929.—Appointment of James Cook and Harry Cook to be trustees of the Trust Deed.

2ND JUNE, 1929.—*Deed stating that they are the trustees of the settlement. Endorsement of notice on the Vesting Deed.*

4TH NOVEMBER, 1929.—Transfer of the mortgage for five thousand pounds by *B.* to *C.*

10TH JULY, 1930.—Death of Henry Wilson, leaving Thomas Wilson, his eldest son, and two younger children.

1ST OCTOBER, 1930.—*Letters of Administration to the settled land of Henry Wilson granted to James Cook and Harry Cook.*

3RD NOVEMBER, 1930.—Disentail by Thomas Wilson.

4TH NOVEMBER, 1930.—Release by *C.* on payment off of his mortgage debt of five thousand pounds and surrender of the equitable term of five hundred years.

10TH NOVEMBER, 1930.—Death of Elizabeth Wilson.

[NOTE.—Though her jointure took effect in equity only she has power to create a term of years absolute for raising arrears of the jointure, and the estate owner would be bound to give legal effect to a mortgage of the term.]

20TH NOVEMBER, 1930.—Release by two younger children of Henry Wilson of their portions.

SAME DATE.—Demise by Thomas Wilson to *L.* and *M.* for an equitable term of eight hundred years, subject to cesser on payment of five thousand pounds and interest.

SAME DATE.—*Demise by James Cook and Harry Cook to L. and M. for the term of eight hundred years, subject to cesser on redemption or charge by way of legal mortgage.*

SAME DATE.—*Assent by them to the vesting of the settled land, subject to the term or legal charge, in Thomas Wilson in fee, without nominating Settled Land Act trustees.*

10TH MARCH, 1931.—*Conveyance by Thomas Wilson and L. and M. to R. Horne in fee.*

[490]

SPECIMEN NO 4

OF THE TITLE OF THE ADMINISTRATORS OF M. CURTIS TO RICH AND MIDDLE FARMS RELATING TO INFANTS

2ND JANUARY, 1922.—Will of James Wilcox devising Rich Farm and Middle Farm to the use of his elder son John Wilcox (an infant) for his life with remainders over for the issue of John Wilcox which failed with remainder to the use of his younger son Gilbert Wilcox (an infant) for his life with remainders over Appointment of *X.* and *Y.* to be executors and Settled Land Act trustees.

4TH FEBRUARY, 1922.—Death of testator, leaving his two sons, giving dates of their births.

12TH MAY, 1922.—*Probate by X. and Y.*

15TH DECEMBER, 1922.—Assent to the devise, John Wilcox being still an infant.

1ST JANUARY, 1926.—The Settled Land Act, 1925, and The Law of Property Act, 1925, come into force and vest the settled land in *X.* and *Y.* as Settled Land Act trustees by reason of John Wilcox being an infant.

4TH JANUARY, 1926.—*Instrument declaring that the settled land is vested in X. and Y.*

3RD JUNE, 1926.—Death of John Wilcox a bachelor and an infant.

29TH SEPTEMBER, 1926.—*Conveyance on sale of Rich Farm by X. and Y. to M. Curtis.*

12TH OCTOBER, 1927.—*Conveyance by X. and Y. vesting Middle Farm in Gilbert Wilcox (who had attained full age) on the trusts of the will of James Wilcox with a statement that they are the trustees of the settlement.*

10TH NOVEMBER, 1927.—*Conveyance on sale of Middle Farm by Gilbert Wilcox to M. Curtis, X. and Y. joining to receive the purchase money.*

1ST FEBRUARY, 1928.—Will of M. Curtis purporting to appoint his infant son John Curtis executor.

3RD APRIL, 1928.—Death of M. Curtis.

5TH SEPTEMBER, 1928.—*Letters of administration with the will annexed granted to M. and N.*

> [NOTE.—Administration will either be granted to a trust Corporation or to not less than two individuals, if there are Settled Land Act trustees, it will, as respects the settled land, be granted to them.] **[491]**

SPECIMEN NO 5
OF THE TITLE OF GEORGE SMITH TO HOUSES IN JOHN STREET RELATED TO LEASEHOLD PROPERTY

25TH MARCH, 1921.—*Lease by Charles Robinson to Henry Chubb, of 10 to 16 (even numbers) John Street, in the city of X., for 99 years from date at a yearly rent of £5 for each house.*

26TH MARCH, 1921.—*First Mortgage (by subdemise) by Henry Chubb to A. for the residue of the term less 3 days for securing £3,000 and interest. Declaration by Henry Chubb that he holds the head term in trust for A. subject to redemption.*

SAME DATE.— Second Mortgage (by subdemise) to B. for the residue of the term less 2 days for securing £1,000 and interest. Declaration by Henry Chubb that (subject to the First Mortgage) he holds the head term in trust for B. subject to redemption.

SAME DATE.—Third Mortgage (by subdemise) to C. for residue of term less 1 day for securing £500 and interest.

24TH DECEMBER, 1924.—*Transfer of First Mortgage by A. to T. in trust for Henry Chubb, who pays off the First Mortgage debt.*

1ST JANUARY, 1926.—The Law of Property Act, 1925, comes into operation.

> [NOTE.—It extinguishes the first mortgage term, because Henry Chubb was not entitled to keep it alive to the prejudice of his mesne incumbrancers.]

1ST JULY, 1926.—Order of Court directing Henry Chubb to hand over the Lease, First Mortgage, and Transfer of that Mortgage to *B.*

20TH JULY, 1926.—*Assignment on sale by B., under his power, to George Smith.*

> [NOTE.—This conveys the head term created by the Lease and extinguishes all the mortgage terms. The head term may, if desired, be conveyed in the name of Henry Chubb.] **[492]**

LAND REGISTRATION ACT 1925
(c 21)

ARRANGEMENT OF SECTIONS

PART I
PRELIMINARY

PART VII

RECTIFICATION OF REGISTER AND INDEMNITY

PART VIII

APPLICATION TO PARTICULAR CLASSES OF LAND

PART IX

UNREGISTERED DEALINGS WITH REGISTERED LAND

Powers of dealing with Registered Land off the Register

PART X

MISCELLANEOUS PROVISIONS

An Act to consolidate the Land Transfer Acts and the statute law relating to
registered land [9 April 1925]

PART I

PRELIMINARY

1. Registers to be continued

There shall continue to be kept at His Majesty's Land Registry, a register of
title to freehold land and leasehold land. **[493]**

2. What estates may be registered

(1) After the commencement of this Act, estates capable of subsisting as legal estates shall be the only interests in land in respect of which a proprietor can be registered and all other interests in registered land (except overriding interests and interests entered on the register at or before such commencement) shall take effect in equity, as minor interests, but all interests (except undivided shares in land) entered on the register at such commencement which are not legal estates shall be capable of being dealt with under this Act:

Provided that, on the occasion of the first dealing with any such interest, the register shall be rectified in such manner as may be provided by rules made to secure that the entries therein shall be similar to those which would have been made if the title to the land had been registered after the commencement of this Act.

(2) Subject as aforesaid, and save as otherwise expressly provided by this Act, this Act applies to land registered under any enactment replaced by this Act in like manner as it applies to land registered under this Act.   **[494]**

3. Interpretation

In this Act unless the context otherwise requires, the following expressions have the meanings hereby assigned to them respectively, that is to say:—

     (i) "Charge by way of legal mortgage" means a mortgage created by charge under which, by virtue of the Law of Property Act 1925, the mortgagee is to be treated as an estate owner in like manner as if a mortgage term by demise or subdemise were vested in him, and "legal mortgage" has the same meaning as in that Act;

   [(ii) "the court" means the High Court or, where county courts have jurisdiction by virtue of rules made under section 138(1) of this Act, the county court;]

    (iii) . . .

    (iv) "Estate owner" means the owner of a legal estate, but an infant is not capable of being an estate owner:

     (v) "Gazette" means the London Gazette;

    (vi) "Income" includes rents and profits;

   (vii) "Instrument" does not include a statute, unless the statute creates a settlement;

  (viii) "Land" includes land of any tenure (including land, subject or not to manorial incidents, enfranchised under Part V of the Law of Property Act 1922), and mines and minerals, whether or not held with the surface, buildings or parts of buildings (whether the division is horizontal, vertical or made in any other way) and other corporeal hereditaments; also a manor, . . ., and a rent and other incorporeal hereditaments, and an easement, right, privilege, or benefit in, over, or derived from land; but not an undivided share in land; and "hereditaments" mean real property which on an intestacy might, before the commencement of this Act, have devolved on an heir;

    (ix) ["Land charge" means a land charge of any class described in section 2 of the Land Charges Act 1972 or a local land charge;]

     (x) "Lease" includes an under-lease and any tenancy or agreement for a lease, under-lease or tenancy;

    (xi) "Legal estates" mean the estates interests and charges in or over land subsisting or created at law which are by the Law of

Property Act 1925, authorised to subsist or to be created at law; and "Equitable interests" mean all the other interests and charges in or over land or in the proceeds of sale thereof; an equitable interest "capable of subsisting at law" means such as could validly subsist at law if clothed with the legal estate;

(xii) "Limitation Acts" mean the Real Property Limitation Acts 1833, 1837 and 1874, and any Acts amending those Acts;

(xiii) "Manorial incidents" have the same meaning as in Part V of the Law of Property Act 1922;

(xiv) "Mines and minerals" include any strata or seam of minerals or substances in or under any land, and powers of working and getting the same, but not an undivided share thereof;

(xv) "Minor interests" mean the interests not capable of being disposed of or created by registered dispositions and capable of being overridden (whether or not a purchaser has notice thereof) by the proprietors unless protected as provided by this Act, and all rights and interests which are not registered or protected on the register and are not overriding interests, and include—

(a) in the case of land held on trust for sale, all interests and powers which are under the Law of Property Act 1925, capable of being overridden by the trustees for sale, whether or not such interests and powers are so protected; and

(b) in the case of settled land, all interests and powers which are under the Settled Land Act 1925, and the Law of Property Act 1925, or either of them, capable of being overridden by the tenant for life or statutory owner, whether or not such interests and powers are so protected as aforesaid;

(xvi) "Overriding interests" mean all the incumbrances, interests, rights, and powers not entered on the register but subject to which registered dispositions are by this Act to take effect, and in regard to land registered at the commencement of this Act include the matters which are by any enactment repealed by this Act declared not to be incumbrances;

(xvii) "Personal representative" means the executor, original or by representation, or administrator for the time being of a deceased person, and as regards any liability for the payment of death duties includes any person who takes possession of or intermeddles with the property of a deceased person without the authority of the personal representatives or the court; and where there are special personal representatives for the purposes of any settled land, it means, in relation to that land, those representatives;

(xviii) "Possession" includes receipt of rents and profits or the right to receive the same, if any;

(xix) "Prescribed" means prescribed by general rules made in pursuance of this Act;

(xx) "Proprietor" means the registered proprietor for the time being of an estate in land or of a charge;

(xxi) "Purchaser" means a purchaser in good faith for valuable consideration and includes a lessee, mortgagee, or other person who for valuable consideration acquires any interest in land or in any charge on land;

(xxii) "Registered dispositions" mean dispositions which take effect under the powers conferred on the proprietor by way of transfer, charge, lease or otherwise and to which (when required to be registered) special effect or priority is given by this Act on registration;

(xxiii) "Registered estate", in reference to land, means the legal estate, or other registered interest, if any, as respects which a person is for the time being registered as proprietor, but does not include a registered charge and a "registered charge" includes a mortgage or incumbrance registered as a charge under this Act;

(xxiv) "Registered land" means land or any estate or interest in land the title to which is registered under this Act or any enactment replaced by this Act, and includes any easement, right, privilege, or benefit which is appurtenant or appendant thereto, and any mines and minerals within or under the same and held therewith;

(xxv) "Rent" includes a rent service or a rentcharge, or other rent, toll, duty, royalty, or annual or periodical payment, in money or money's worth, issuing out of or charged upon land, but does not include mortgage interest;

(xxvi) "Settled land" "settlement" "tenant for life" "statutory owner" "trustees of the settlement" "capital money" . . . "trust corporation" "trust instrument" "vesting deed" "vesting order" "vesting assent" and "vesting instrument" have the same meanings as in the Settled Land Act 1925;

(xxvii) A "term of years absolute" means a term of years, whether at a rent or not, taking effect either in possession or in reversion, with or without impeachment for waste, subject or not to another legal estate and either certain or liable to determination by notice, re-entry, operation of law, or by a provision for cesser on redemption, or in any other event (other than the dropping of a life, or the determination of a determinable life interest), but does not include any term of years determinable with life or lives or with the cesser of a determinable life interest, nor, if created after the commencement of this Act, a term of years which is not expressed to take effect in possession within twenty-one years after the creation thereof where required by the Law of Property Act 1925, to take effect within that period; and in this definition the expression "term of years" includes a term for less than a year, or for a year or years and a fraction of a year or from year to year;

(xxviii) "Trust for sale", in relation to land, means an immediate binding trust for sale, whether or not exercisable at the request or with the consent of any person, and with or without a power at discretion to postpone the sale;

(xxix) "Trustees for sale" mean the persons (including a personal representative) holding land on trust for sale;

(xxx) "United Kingdom" means Great Britain and Northern Ireland;

(xxxi) "Valuable consideration" includes marriage, but does not include a nominal consideration in money;

(xxxii) "Will" includes codicil.   **[495]**

NOTES

Para (ii): substituted by the Administration of Justice Act 1982, s 67, Sch 5.

Para (iii): repealed by the Finance Act 1975, ss 52(2), 59(5), Sch 13, Part I.

Para (viii): words omitted repealed (with effect from the end of the registration period) by the Patronage (Benefices) Measure 1986 (No 3), s 6.

Para (ix): substituted by the Local Land Charges Act 1975, s 17(2), Sch 1.

Para (xxvi): words omitted repealed by the Mental Health Act 1959, s 149(2), Sch 8, Part I.

PART II
REGISTRATION OF LAND
Freehold Land

4. Application for registration of freehold land

Where the title to be registered is a title to a freehold estate in land—

    (*a*) any estate owner holding an estate in fee simple (including a tenant for life, statutory owner, personal representative, or trustee for sale) whether subject or not to incumbrances; or

    (*b*) any other person (not being a mortgagee where there is a subsisting right of redemption or a person who has merely contracted to buy land) who is entitled to require a legal estate in fee simple whether subject or not to incumbrances, to be vested in him;

may apply to the registrar to be registered in respect of such estate, or, in the case of a person not in a fiduciary position, to have registered in his stead any nominee, as proprietor with an absolute title or with a possessory title:

    Provided that—

        (i) Where an absolute title is required the applicant or his nominee shall not be registered as proprietor until and unless the title is approved by the registrar;

       (ii) Where a possessory title is required the applicant or his nominee may be registered as proprietor on giving such evidence of title and serving such notices, if any, as may for the time being be prescribed;

      (iii) If, on an application for registration with possessory title, the registrar is satisfied as to the title to the freehold estate, he may register it as absolute, whether the applicant consents to such registration or not, but in that case no higher fee shall be charged than would have been charged for registration with possessory title.   **[496]**

5. Effect of first registration with absolute title

Where the registered land is a freehold estate, the registration of any person as first proprietor thereof with an absolute title shall vest in the person so registered an estate in fee simple in possession in the land, together with all rights, privileges, and appurtenances belonging or appurtenant thereto, subject to the following rights and interests, that is to say,—

    (*a*) Subject to the incumbrances, and other entries, if any, appearing on the register; and

    (*b*) Unless the contrary is expressed on the register, subject to such overriding interests, if any, as affect the registered land; and

    (*c*) Where the first proprietor is not entitled for his own benefit to the registered land subject, as between himself and the persons entitled to minor interests, to any minor interests of such persons of which he has notice,

but free from all other estates and interests whatsoever, including estates and interests of His Majesty.   **[497]**

6. Effect of first registration with possessory title

Where the registered land is a freehold estate, the registration of any person as first proprietor thereof with a possessory title only shall not affect or prejudice the enforcement of any estate, right or interest adverse to or in derogation of the title of the first proprietor, and subsisting or capable of arising at the time of registration of that proprietor; but save as aforesaid, shall have the same effect as registration of a person with an absolute title.   **[498]**

7. Qualified title

(1) Where an absolute title is required, and on the examination of the title it appears to the registrar that the title can be established only for a limited period, or only subject to certain reservations, the registrar may, on the application of the party applying to be registered, by an entry made in the register, except from the effect of registration any estate, right, or interest—

   (*a*) arising before a specified date; or
   (*b*) arising under a specified instrument or otherwise particularly described in the register,

and a title registered subject to such excepted estate, right, or interest shall be called a qualified title.

(2) Where the registered land is a freehold estate, the registration of a person as first proprietor thereof with a qualified title shall have the same effect as the registration of such person with an absolute title, save that registration with a qualified title shall not affect or prejudice the enforcement of any estate, right or interest appearing by the register to be excepted.   **[499]**

Leasehold Land

8. Application for registration of leasehold land

(1) Where the title to be registered is a title to a leasehold interest in land—

   (*a*) any estate owner (including a tenant for life, statutory owner, personal representative, or trustee for sale, but not including a mortgagee where there is a subsisting right of redemption), holding under a lease for a term of years absolute of which more than twenty-one are unexpired, whether subject or not to incumbrances; or
   (*b*) any other person (not being a mortgagee as aforesaid and not being a person who has merely contracted to buy the leasehold interest) who is entitled to require a legal leasehold estate held under such a lease as aforesaid (whether subject or not to incumbrances) to be vested in him,

may apply to the registrar to be registered in respect of such estate, or in the case of a person not being in a fiduciary position to have registered in his stead any nominee, as proprietor with an absolute title, with a good leasehold title or with a possessory title:

Provided that—

   (i)   Where an absolute title is required, the applicant or his nominee shall not be registered as proprietor until and unless the title both to the leasehold and to the freehold, and to any intermediate leasehold that may exist, is approved by the registrar;
   (ii) Where a good leasehold title is required, the applicant or his nominee shall not be registered as proprietor until and unless the title to the leasehold interest is approved by the registrar;
   (iii) Where a possessory title is required, the applicant or his nominee may be registered as proprietor on giving such evidence of title and serving such notices, if any, as may for the time being be prescribed;

(iv) If on an application for registration with a possessory title the registrar is satisfied as to the title to the leasehold interest, he may register it as good leasehold, whether the applicant consents to such registration or not, but in that case no higher fee shall be charged than would have been charged for registration with possessory title.

[(1A) An application for registration in respect of leasehold land held under a lease in relation to the grant or assignment of which section 123(1) of this Act applies (whether by virtue of this Act or any later enactment) may be made within the period allowed by section 123(1), or any authorised extension of that period, notwithstanding that the lease was granted for a term of not more than twenty-one years or that the unexpired term of the lease is not more than twenty-one years.]

[(2) Leasehold land held under a lease containing a prohibition or restriction on dealings therewith inter vivos shall not be registered under this Act unless and until provision is made in the prescribed manner for preventing any dealing therewith in contravention of the prohibition or restriction by an entry on the register to that effect, or otherwise.]

(3) Where on an application to register a mortgage term, wherein no right of redemption is subsisting, it appears that the applicant is entitled in equity to the superior term, if any, out of which it was created, the registrar shall register him as proprietor of the superior term without any entry to the effect that the legal interest in that term is outstanding, and on such registration the superior term shall vest in the proprietor and the mortgage term shall merge therein:

Provided that this subsection shall not apply where the mortgage term does not comprise the whole of the land included in the superior term, unless in that case the rent, if any, payable in respect of the superior term has been apportioned, or the rent is of no money value or no rent is reserved, and unless the covenants, if any, entered into for the benefit of the reversion have been apportioned (either expressly or by implication) as respects the land comprised in the mortgage term. **[500]**

NOTES
Sub-s (1A): inserted by the Land Registration Act 1986, s 2(2).
Sub-s (2): substituted by the Land Registration Act 1986, s 3(1).

9. Effect of first registration with absolute title

Where the registered land is a leasehold interest, the registration under this Act of any person as first proprietor thereof with an absolute title shall be deemed to vest in such person the possession of the leasehold interest described, with all implied or expressed rights, privileges, and appurtenances attached to such interest, subject to the following obligations, rights, and interests, that is to say,—

(a) Subject to all implied and express covenants, obligations, and liabilities incident to the registered land; and
(b) Subject to the incumbrances and other entries (if any) appearing on the register; and
(c) Unless the contrary is expressed on the register, subject to such overriding interests, if any, as affect the registered land; and
(d) Where such first proprietor is not entitled for his own benefit to the registered land subject, as between himself and the persons entitled to

minor interests, to any minor interests of such persons of which he has notice;

but free from all other estates and interests whatsoever, including estates and interests of His Majesty.   **[501]**

10. Effect of first registration with good leasehold title

Where the registered land is a leasehold interest, the registration of a person as first proprietor thereof with a good leasehold title shall not affect or prejudice the enforcement of any estate, right or interest affecting or in derogation of the title of the lessor to grant the lease, but, save as aforesaid, shall have the same effect as registration with an absolute title.   **[502]**

11. Effect of first registration with possessory title

Where the registered land is a leasehold interest, the registration of a person as first proprietor thereof with a possessory title shall not affect or prejudice the enforcement of any estate, right, or interest (whether in respect of the lessor's title or otherwise) adverse to or in derogation of the title of such first registered proprietor, and subsisting or capable of arising at the time of the registration of such proprietor; but, save as aforesaid, shall have the same effect as registration with an absolute title.   **[503]**

12. Qualified title

(1) Where on examination it appears to the registrar that the title, either of the lessor to the reversion or of the lessee to the leasehold interest, can be established only for a limited period, or subject to certain reservations, the registrar may, upon the request in writing of the person applying to be registered, by an entry made in the register, except from the effect of registration any estate, right or interest—

    (*a*) arising before a specified date, or

    (*b*) arising under a specified instrument, or otherwise particularly described in the register.

and a title registered subject to any such exception shall be called a qualified title.

(2) Where the registered land is a leasehold interest, the registration of a person as first proprietor thereof with a qualified title shall not affect or prejudice the enforcement of any estate, right, or interest appearing by the register to be excepted, but, save as aforesaid, shall have the same effect as registration with a good leasehold title or an absolute title, as the case may be.   **[504]**

Preliminaries to Registration

13. Regulations as to examination of title by registrar

The examination by the registrar of any title under this Act shall be conducted in the prescribed manner:

    Provided that—

    (*a*) Due notice shall be given, where the giving of such notice is prescribed, and sufficient opportunity shall be afforded to any persons desirous of objecting to come in and state their objections to the registrar; and (*b*) The registrar shall have jurisdiction to hear and determine any such objections, subject to an appeal to the court in the prescribed manner and on the prescribed conditions; and

(*c*) If the registrar, upon the examination of any title, is of opinion that the title is open to objection, but is nevertheless a title the holding under which will not be disturbed, he may approve of such title, or may require the applicant to apply to the court, upon a statement signed by the registrar, for its sanction to the registration. [505]

14. Evidence required before registration

(1) Before the completion of the registration of any estate in land in respect of which an examination of title is required, the applicant for registration and his solicitor, shall each, if required by the registrar, make an affidavit or declaration that to the best of his knowledge and belief all deeds, wills, and instruments of title, and all charges and incumbrances affecting the title which is the subject of the application, and all facts material to such title, have been disclosed in the course of the investigation of title made by the registrar.

(2) The registrar may require any person making an affidavit or declaration in pursuance of this section to state in his affidavit or declaration what means he has had of becoming acquainted with the several matters referred to in this section; and if the registrar is of opinion that any further or other evidence is necessary or desirable, he may refuse to complete the registration until such further or other evidence is produced.

(3) Before the registration of any person who has not previously acquired the estate intended to be registered, the registrar shall be satisfied that all ad valorem stamp duty, if any, which, if the estate had been acquired by him, would have been payable in respect of the instrument vesting that estate in him, has been discharged. [506]

15. Production of deeds

(1) When an application has been made to the registrar for the registration of any title to land, then if any person has in his possession or custody any deeds, instruments, or evidence of title relating to or affecting such title, to the production of which the applicant or any trustee for him is entitled, the registrar may require such person to show cause, within a time limited, why he should not produce such deeds, instruments, or evidences of title to the registrar, or otherwise, as the registrar may deem fit; and, unless cause is shown to the satisfaction of the registrar within the time limited, such deeds, instruments, and evidences of title may be ordered by the registrar to be produced at the expense of the applicant, at such time and place, and in such manner, and on such terms, as the registrar thinks fit.

(2) Any person aggrieved by an order of the registrar under this section may appeal in the prescribed manner to the court, which may annul or confirm the order of the registrar with or without modification.

(3) If any person disobeys any order of the registrar made in pursuance of this section, the registrar may certify such disobedience to the court, and thereupon such person, subject to such right of appeal as aforesaid, may be punished by the court in the same manner in all respects as if the order made by the registrar were the order of the court. [507]

16. Deeds to be marked with notice of registration

A person shall not be registered as proprietor until, if required by the registrar, he has produced to him such documents of title, if any, as will, in the opinion of the registrar, when stamped or otherwise marked, give notice to any purchaser or other person dealing with the land of the fact of the registration, and the registrar shall stamp or otherwise mark the same accordingly, unless the registrar is satisfied that without such stamping or marking the fact of such registration cannot be concealed from a purchaser or other person dealing with the land:

Provided that, in the case of registration with a possessory title, the registrar may act on such reasonable evidence as may be prescribed as to the sufficiency of the documents produced, and as to dispensing with their production in special circumstances.   **[508]**

17. Costs of application for registration

(1) All costs, charges, and expenses that are incurred by any parties in or about any proceedings for registration shall, unless the parties otherwise agree, be taxed by the taxing officer of the court as between solicitor and client, but the persons by whom and the proportions in which such costs, charges, and expenses are to be paid shall be in the discretion of the registrar, and shall be determined according to orders of the registrar, regard being had to the following provision, namely, that any applicant under this Act is liable prima facie to pay all costs, charges, and expenses incurred by or in consequence of his application, except—

    (*a*) in a case where parties object whose rights are sufficiently secured without their appearance; and

    (*b*) where any costs, charges, or expenses are incurred unnecessarily or improperly:

Provided that any party aggrieved by any order of the registrar under this section may appeal in the prescribed manner to the court, which may annul or confirm the order of the registrar, with or without modification.

(2) If any person disobeys any order of the registrar made in pursuance of this section, the registrar may certify such disobedience to the court, and thereupon such person, subject to such right of appeal as aforesaid, may be punished by the court in the same manner in all respects as if the order made by the registrar were the order of the court.   **[509]**

PART III

REGISTERED DEALINGS WITH REGISTERED LAND

Dispositions of Freehold Land

18. Powers of disposition of registered freeholds

(1) Where the registered land is a freehold estate the proprietor may, in the prescribed manner, transfer the registered estate in the land or any part thereof, and, subject to any entry in the register to the contrary, may in the prescribed manner—

    (*a*) transfer the fee simple in possession of all or any mines or minerals apart from the surface; or of the surface without all or any of the mines and minerals;

(b) grant an annuity or a rentcharge in possession (either perpetual or for a term of years absolute) in any form which sufficiently refers in the prescribed manner to the registered land charged;

(c) grant in fee simple in possession any easement, right, or privilege in, over, or derived from the registered land or any part thereof, in any form which sufficiently refers, in the prescribed manner, to the registered servient tenement and to the dominant tenement, whether being registered land or not;

(d) transfer the fee simple in possession of the registered land or any part thereof, subject to the creation thereout, by way of reservation, in favour of any person of an annuity or a rentcharge in possession (either perpetual or for a term of years absolute), or of any easement, right, or privilege in possession (either in fee simple or for a term of years absolute);

(e) grant (subject or not to the reservation of an easement, right, or privilege) a lease of the registered land or any part thereof, or of all or any mines and minerals apart from the surface, or of the surface without all or any of the mines and minerals, or of an easement, right or privilege in or over the land, or any part thereof, for any term of years absolute for any purpose (but where by way of mortgage subject to the provisions of this Act and the Law of Property Act 1925, relating thereto), and in any form which sufficiently refers, in the prescribed manner, to the registered land.

(2) A perpetual annuity or rentcharge in possession may be granted or reserved to any person with or without a power of re-entry, exercisable at any time, on default of payment thereof, or on breach of covenant, and shall have incidental thereto all the powers and remedies (as varied if at all by the disposition creating the rentcharge) for recovery thereof conferred by the Law of Property Act 1925; and where an easement, right, or privilege is reserved in a registered disposition for a legal estate, the reservation shall operate to create the same for the benefit of the land for the benefit of which the right is reserved.

(3) A lease for a term, not exceeding twenty-one years, to take effect in possession or within one year from the date thereof ... may be granted and shall take effect under this section notwithstanding that a caution, notice of deposit of a certificate, restriction, or inhibition (other than a bankruptcy inhibition) may be subsisting, but subject to the interests intended to be protected by any such caution, notice, restriction, or inhibition.

(4) The foregoing powers of disposition shall (subject to the express provisions of this Act and of the Law of Property Act 1925, relating to mortgages) apply to dispositions by the registered proprietor by way of charge or mortgage; but no estate, other than a legal estate, shall be capable of being disposed of, or created under, this section.

(5) In this Act "transfer" or "disposition" when referring to registered freehold land includes any disposition authorised as aforesaid; and "transferee" has a corresponding meaning. **[510]**

NOTES

Sub-s (3): words omitted repealed by the Land Registration Act 1986, s 4(2).

19. Registration of disposition of freeholds

(1) The transfer of the registered estate in the land or part thereof shall be completed by the registrar entering on the register the transferee as the

proprietor of the estate transferred, but until such entry is made the transferor shall be deemed to remain proprietor of the registered estate; and, where part only of the land is transferred, notice thereof shall also be noted on the register.

(2) All interests transferred or created by dispositions by the proprietor, other than a transfer of the registered estate in the land, or part thereof, shall, subject to the provisions relating to mortgages, be completed by registration in the same manner and with the same effect as provided by this Act with respect to transfers of registered estates and notice thereof shall also be noted on the register:

Provided that nothing in this subsection—

(a) shall authorise the registration of a lease granted for a term not exceeding twenty-one years, or require the entry of a notice of such a lease . . .; or

(b) shall authorise the registration of a mortgage term where there is a subsisting right of redemption; or

(c) shall render necessary the registration of any easement, right, or privilege except as appurtenant to registered land, or the entry of notice thereof except as against the registered title of the servient land.

Every such disposition shall, when registered, take effect as a registered disposition, and a lease made by the registered proprietor under the last foregoing section which is not required to be registered or noted on the register shall nevertheless take effect as if it were a registered disposition immediately on being granted.

(3) The general words implied in conveyances under the Law of Property Act 1925, shall apply, so far as applicable thereto, to dispositions of a registered estate. **[511]**

NOTES
Sub-s (2): words omitted repealed by the Land Registration Act 1986, s 4(3).

20. Effect of registration and dispositions of freeholds

(1) In the case of a freehold estate registered with an absolute title, a disposition of the registered land or of a legal estate therein, including a lease thereof, for valuable consideration shall, when registered, confer on the transferee or grantee an estate in fee simple or the term of years absolute or other legal estate expressed to be created in the land dealt with, together with all rights, privileges, and appurtenances belonging or appurtenant thereto, including (subject to any entry to the contrary in the register) the appropriate rights and interests which would, under the Law of Property Act 1925, have been transferred if the land had not been registered, subject—

(a) to the incumbrances and other entries, if any, appearing on the register [and any charge for capital transfer tax subject to which the disposition takes effect under section 73 of this Act]; and

(b) unless the contrary is expressed on the register, to the overriding interests, if any, affecting the estate transferred or created,

but free from all other estates and interests whatsoever, including estates and interests of His Majesty, and the disposition shall operate in like manner as if the registered transferor or grantor were (subject to any entry to the contrary in the register) entitled to the registered land in fee simple in possession for his own benefit.

(2) In the case of a freehold estate registered with a qualified title a disposition of the registered land or of a legal estate therein, including a lease thereof, for valuable consideration shall, when registered, have the same effect as it would have had if the land had been registered with an absolute title, save that such disposition shall not affect or prejudice the enforcement of any right or interest appearing by the register to be excepted.

(3) In the case of a freehold estate registered with a possessory title, a disposition of the registered land or of a legal estate therein, including a lease thereof, for valuable consideration shall not affect or prejudice the enforcement of any right or interest adverse to or in derogation of the title of the first registered proprietor, and subsisting or capable of arising at the time of the registration of such proprietor; but, save as aforesaid, shall when registered have the same effect as it would have had if the land had been registered with an absolute title.

(4) Where any such disposition is made without valuable consideration, it shall, so far as the transferee or grantee is concerned, be subject to any minor interests subject to which the transferor or grantor held the same, but, save as aforesaid, shall, when registered, in all respects, and in particular as respects any registered dealings on the part of the transferee or grantee, have the same effect as if the disposition had been made for valuable consideration. **[512]**

NOTES
Sub-s (1): words in square brackets inserted by the Finance Act 1975, s 52(1), Sch 12, paras 2, 5(1), (2).

Dispositions of Leasehold Land

21. Powers of disposition of registered leaseholds

(1) Where the registered land is a leasehold interest the proprietor may, in the prescribed manner, transfer the registered estate in the land or any part thereof, and, subject to any entry in the register to the contrary may in the prescribed manner—

(a) transfer all or any of the leasehold mines and minerals apart from the surface; or the surface without all or any of the leasehold mines and minerals;

(b) grant (to the extent of the registered estate) any annuity or rentcharge in possession, easement, right or privilege in, over, or derived from the registered land or any part thereof, in any form which sufficiently refers, in the prescribed manner, to the registered lease, and to the dominant tenement, whether being registered land or not;

(c) transfer the registered land or any part thereof subject to a reservation to any person of any such annuity, rentcharge, easement, right, or privilege;

(d) grant (subject or not to the reservation of an easement, right or privilege) an underlease of the registered land, or any part thereof, or of all or any mines and minerals apart from the surface, or of the surface without all or any of the mines and minerals, or of an easement, right or privilege, in or over the registered land or any part thereof, for any term of years absolute of less duration than the registered estate and for any purpose (but where by way of mortgage, subject to the provisions of this Act and of the Law of Property Act 1925, relating thereto), and in any form which sufficiently refers in the prescribed manner to the registered land, and in the case of an easement, right, or privilege, to the dominant tenement, whether being registered land or not.

(2) A disposition of registered leasehold land may be made subject to a rent legally apportioned in the prescribed manner, or to a rent not so apportioned.

(3) An underlease for a term, not exceeding twenty-one years, to take effect in possession or within one year from the date thereof, . . ., may be granted and shall take effect under this section, notwithstanding that a caution, notice of deposit of a certificate, restriction, or inhibition (other than a bankruptcy inhibition) may be subsisting, but subject to the interests intended to be protected by any such caution, notice, restriction or inhibition.

(4) The foregoing powers of disposition shall (subject to the express provisions of this Act and of the Law of Property Act 1925, relating to mortgages) apply to dispositions by the registered properietor by way of charge or mortgage, but no estate, other than a legal estate, shall be capable of being disposed of or created under this section.

(5) In this Act "transfer" or "disposition" when referring to registered leasehold land includes any disposition authorised as aforesaid and "transferee" has a corresponding meaning. **[513]**

NOTES

Sub-s (3): words omitted repealed by the Land Registration Act 1986, s 4(2).

22. Registration of dispositions of leaseholds

(1) A transfer of the registered estate in the land or part thereof shall be completed by the registrar entering on the register the transferee as proprietor of the estate transferred, but until such entry is made the transferor shall be deemed to remain the proprietor of the registered estate; and where part only of the land is transferred, notice thereof shall also be noted on the register.

(2) All interests transferred or created by dispositions by the registered proprietor other than the transfer of his registered estate in the land or in part thereof shall (subject to the provisions relating to mortgages) be completed by registration in the same manner and with the same effect as provided by this Act with respect to transfers of the registered estate, and notice thereof shall also be noted on the register in accordance with this Act:

Provided that nothing in this subsection—

(a) shall authorise the registration of an underlease originally granted for a term not exceeding twenty-one years, or require the entry of a notice of such an underlease . . .; or

(b) shall authorise the registration of a mortgage term where there is a subsisting right of redemption; or

(c) shall render necessary the registration of any easement, right, or privilege except as appurtenant to registered land, or the entry of notice thereof except as against the registered title of the servient land.

Every such disposition shall, when registered, take effect as a registered disposition, and an underlease made by the registered proprietor which is not required to be registered or noted on the register shall nevertheless take effect as if it were a registered disposition immediately on being granted.

(3) The general words implied in conveyances under the Law of Property Act 1925 shall apply, so far as applicable thereto, to transfers of a registered leasehold estate. **[514]**

NOTES
Sub-s (2): words omitted repealed by the Land Registration Act 1986, s 4(3).

23. Effect of registration of dispositions of leaseholds

(1) In the case of a leasehold estate registered with an absolute title, a disposition (including a subdemise thereof) for valuable consideration shall, when registered, be deemed to vest in the transferee or underlessee the estate transferred or created to the extent of the registered estate, or for the term created by the subdemise, as the case may require, with all implied or expressed rights, privileges, and appurtenances attached to the estate transferred or created, including (subject to any entry to the contrary on the register) the appropriate rights and interests which would under the Law of Property Act 1925, have been transferred if the land had not been registered, but subject as follows:—

(a) To all implied and express covenants, obligations, and liabilities incident to the estate transferred or created; and

(b) To the incumbrances and other entries (if any) appearing on the register [and any charge for capital transfer for subject to which the disposition takes effect under section 73 of this Act]; and

(c) Unless the contrary is expressed on the register, to the overriding interests, if any, affecting the estate transferred or created,

but free from all other estates and interests whatsoever, including estates and interests of His Majesty; and the transfer or subdemise shall operate in like manner as if the registered transferor or sublessor were (subject to any entry to the contrary on the register) absolutely entitled to the registered lease for his own benefit.

(2) In the case of a leasehold estate registered with a good leasehold title, a disposition (including a subdemise thereof) for valuable consideration shall, when registered, have the same effect as it would have had if the land had been registered with an absolute title, save that it shall not affect or prejudice the enforcement of any right or interest affecting or in derogation of the lessor to grant the lease.

(3) In the case of a leasehold estate registered with a qualified title, a disposition (including a subdemise thereof) for valuable consideration shall, when registered, have the same effect as it would have had if the land had been registered with an absolute title, save that such disposition shall not affect or prejudice the enforcement of any right or interest (whether in respect of the lessor's title or otherwise) appearing by the register to be excepted.

(4) In the case of a leasehold estate registered with a possessory title, a disposition (including a subdemise thereof) for valuable consideration shall not affect or prejudice the enforcement of any right or interest (whether in respect of the lessor's title or otherwise) adverse to or in derogation of the title of the first registered proprietor, and subsisting or capable of arising at the time of the registration of such proprietor, but save as aforesaid shall, when registered, have the same effect as it would have had if the land had been registered with an absolute title.

(5) Where any such disposition is made without valuable consideration it shall, so far as the transferee or underlessee is concerned, be subject to any minor interests subject to which the transferor or sublessor held the same; but,

save as aforesaid, shall, when registered, in all respects, and in particular as respects any registered dealings on the part of the transferee or underlessee, have the same effect as if the disposition had been made for valuable consideration.   **[515]**

NOTES

Sub-s (1): words in square brackets inserted by the Finance Act 1975, s 52(1), Sch 12, paras 2, 5(1), (3).

---

24. Implied covenants on transfers of leaseholds

(1) On the transfer, otherwise than by way of underlease, of any leasehold interest in land under this Act, unless there be an entry on the register negativing such implication, there shall be implied—

(*a*) on the part of the transferor, a covenant with the transferee that, notwithstanding anything by such transferor done, omitted, or knowingly suffered, the rent, covenants, and conditions reserved and contained by and in the registered lease, and on the part of the lessee to be paid, performed, and observed, have been so paid, performed, and observed up to the date of the transfer; and

(*b*) on the part of the transferee, a covenant with the transferor, that during the residue of the term the transferee and the persons deriving title under him will pay, perform, and observe the rent, covenants, and conditions by and in the registered lease reserved and contained, and on the part of the lessee to be paid, performed, and observed, and will keep the transferor and the persons deriving title under him indemnified against all actions, expenses, and claims on account of the non-payment of the said rent or any part thereof, or the breach of the said covenants or conditions, or any of them.

(2) On a transfer of part of the land held under a lease, the covenant implied on the part of the transferee by this section shall be limited to the payment of the apportioned rent, if any, and the performance and observance of the covenants by the lessee and conditions in the registered lease so far only as they affect the part transferred. Where the transferor remains owner of part of the land comprised in the lease, there shall also be implied on his part, as respects the part retained, a covenant with the transferee similar to that implied on the part of the transferee under this subsection.   **[516]**

Charges on Freehold and Leasehold Land

25. Proprietor's power to create charges

(1) The proprietor of any registered land may by deed—

(*a*) charge the registered land with the payment at an appointed time of any principal sum of money either with or without interest;

(*b*) charge the registered land in favour of a building society [(within the meaning of the Building Societies Act 1986), in accordance with] the rules of that society.

(2) A charge may be in any form provided that—

(*a*) the registered land comprised in the charge is described by reference to the register or in any other manner sufficient to enable the registrar to identify the same without reference to any other document;

(*b*) the charge does not refer to any other interest or charge affecting the land which—

    (i) would have priority over the same and is not registered or protected on the register;

    (ii) is not an overriding interest.

(3) Any provision contained in a charge which purports to—

    (i) take away from the proprietor thereof the power of transferring it by registered disposition or of requiring the cessation thereof to be noted on the register; or

    (ii) affect any registered land or charge other than that in respect of which the charge is to be expressly registered,

shall be void. **[517]**

NOTES

    Sub-s (1): words in square brackets substituted by the Building Societies Act 1986, s 120, Sch 18, Part I, para 2.

26. Registration of charges

(1) The charge shall be completed by the registrar entering on the register the person in whose favour the charge is made as the proprietor of such charge, and the particulars of the charge.

(2) A charge may be registered notwithstanding that it contains any trust, power to appoint new trustees, or other provisions for giving effect to the security.

(3) Where the land, in respect of which a charge is registered, is registered with a good leasehold, qualified or possessory title, the charge shall take effect subject to the provisions of this Act with respect to land registered with such a title. **[518]**

27. Terms of years implied in or granted by charges

(1) A registered charge shall, unless made or taking effect by demise or subdemise, and subject to any provision to the contrary contained in the charge, take effect as a charge by way of legal mortgage.

(2) Subject to the provisions of the Law of Property Act 1925, a registered charge may contain in the case of freehold land, an express demise, and in the case of leasehold land an express subdemise of the land to the creditor for a term of years absolute, subject to a proviso for cesser on redemption.

(3) Any such demise or subdemise or charge by way of legal mortgage shall take effect from the date of the delivery of the deed containing the same, but subject to the estate or interest of any person (other than the proprietor of the land) whose estate or interest (whenever created) is registered or noted on the register before the date of registration of the charge.

(4) Any charge registered before the commencement of this Act shall take effect as a demise or subdemise of the land in accordance with the provisions of the Law of Property Act 1925, and the registered estate shall (without prejudice to any registered charge or any term or subterm created by a charge or by this Act) vest in the person appearing by the register to be entitled to the ultimate equity of redemption. **[519]**

28. Implied covenants in charges

(1) Where a registered charge is created on any land there shall be implied on the part of the person being proprietor of such land at the time of the creation

of the charge, unless there be an entry on the register negativing such implication—

(a) a covenant with the proprietor for the time being of the charge to pay the principal sum charged, and interest, if any, thereon, at the appointed time and rate; and

(b) a covenant, if the principal sum or any part thereof is unpaid at the appointed time, to pay interest half-yearly at the appointed rate as well after as before any judgment is obtained in respect of the charge on so much of the principal sum as for the time being remains unpaid.

(2) Where a registered charge is created on any leasehold land there shall (in addition to the covenants aforesaid) be implied on the part of the person being proprietor of such land at the time of the creation of the charge, unless there be an entry on the register negativing such implication, a covenant with the proprietor for the time being of the charge, that the person being proprietor of such land at the time of the creation of the charge, or the persons deriving title under him, will pay, perform, and observe the rent, covenants, and conditions, by and in the registered lease reserved and contained, and on the part of the lessee to be paid, performed, and observed, and will keep the proprietor of the charge, and the persons deriving title under him, indemnified against all proceedings, expenses, and claims, on account of the non-payment of the said rent, or any part thereof, or the breach of the said covenants or conditions, or any of them. [520]

29. Priorities of registered charges

Subject to any entry to the contrary on the register, registered charges on the same land shall as between themselves rank according to the order in which they are entered on the register, and not according to the order in which they are created. [521]

30. Protection of charges for securing further advances

(1) When a registered charge is made for securing further advances, the registrar shall, before making any entry on the register which would prejudicially affect the priority of any further advance thereunder, give to the proprietor of the charge at his registered address, notice by registered post of the intended entry, and the proprietor of the charge shall not, in respect of any further advance, be affected by such entry, unless the advance is made after the date when the notice ought to have been received in due course of post.

(2) If, by reason of any failure on the part of the registrar or the post office in reference to the notice, the proprietor of the charge suffers loss in relation to a further advance, he shall be entitled to be indemnified under this Act in like manner as if a mistake had occurred in the register; but if the loss arises by reason of an omission to register or amend the address for service, no indemnity shall be payable under this Act.

[(3) Where the proprietor of a charge is under an obligation, noted on the register, to make a further advance, a subsequent registered charge shall take effect subject to any further advance made pursuant to the obligation.] [522]

NOTES

Sub-s (3): added by the Law of Property (Amendment) Act 1926, s 5.

31. Alteration of charges

(1) The proprietor of a charge may by deed, in the prescribed manner, alter the terms of the charge, with the consent of the proprietor of the registered land and of the proprietors of all registered charges (if any) of equal or inferior priority, affected by the alteration.

(2) A deed of alteration of a charge may contain an express demise or subdemise in like manner as an original deed of charge, and the provisions of this Act relating to a demise or subdemise contained in a deed of charge shall apply accordingly.

(3) The alteration shall be completed by the registrar entering it on the register.   [523]

32. Provisions when charge registered in names of several proprietors

Where a charge is registered in the names of two or more proprietors (whether jointly or in undivided shares) the mortgage term implied or comprised in the charge shall (but without prejudice to the beneficial interests in the mortgage money) vest in them as joint tenants, and the proprietors or the survivors or survivor of them or the personal representatives of the last survivor, shall have power to give valid receipts, notwithstanding that the mortgage money may be held in undivided shares, in like manner as if the money had been held on a joint account.   [524]

33. Transfer of charges

(1) The proprietor of any registered charge may, in the prescribed manner, transfer the charge to another person as proprietor.

(2) The transfer shall be completed by the registrar entering on the register the transferee as proprietor of the charge transferred, but the transferor shall be deemed to remain proprietor of the charge until the name of the transferee is entered on the register in respect thereof.

(3) A registered transferee for valuable consideration of a charge and his successors in title shall not be affected by any irregularity or invalidity in the original charge itself of which the transferee did not have notice when it was transferred to him.

(4) On registration of any transfer of a charge, the term or subterm (if any) granted expressly or by implication by the charge or any deed of alteration shall, without any conveyance or assignment and notwithstanding anything to the contrary in the transfer or any other instrument, vest in the proprietor for the time being of the charge.

(5) Subject to any entry to the contrary on the register, the vesting of any term or subterm in accordance with this section in the proprietor of a charge shall, subject to the right of redemption, have the same effect as if such proprietor had been registered as the transferee for valuable consideration of the term or subterm.   [525]

34. Powers of proprietor of charge

(1) Subject to any entry on the register to the contrary, the proprietor of a charge shall have and may exercise all the powers conferred by law on the owner of a legal mortgage.

(2) Subject to any entry to the contrary on the register and subject to the

right of any persons appearing on the register to be prior incumbrancers, the proprietor of a charge may, after entry into possession and after having acquired a title under the Limitation Acts, execute a declaration, in the prescribed form, that the right of redemption is barred, and thereupon he shall be entitled, subject to furnishing any evidence which may be prescribed in support thereof, to be registered as proprietor of the land, with the same consequences as if he had been a purchaser for valuable consideration of the land under the power of sale.

(3) An order for foreclosure shall be completed by the registration of the proprietor of the charge (or such other person as may be named in the foreclosure order absolute for that purpose) as the proprietor of the land, and by the cancellation of the charge and of all incumbrances and entries inferior thereto; and such registration shall operate in like manner and with the same consequences as if the proprietor of the charge or other person aforesaid had been a purchaser for valuable consideration of the land under a subsisting power of sale.

(4) A sale by the court or under the power of sale shall operate and be completed by registration in the same manner, as nearly as may be (but subject to any alterations on the register affecting the priority of the charge), as a transfer for valuable consideration by the proprietor of the land at the time of the registration of the charge would have operated or been completed, and, as respects the land transferred, the charge and all incumbrances and entries inferior thereto shall be cancelled.

(5) Notwithstanding the creation of a term or subterm, expressly or by implication, under this Act, such transfer shall (subject to any prior incumbrances or other entries on the register) operate to transfer the registered estate, and the mortgage term or subterm shall become merged, and any purported disposition of or dealing with the mortgage term or subterm apart from the charge, and any process or act purporting to keep alive that term or subterm after the cessation of the charge shall be void.

(6) For the purposes of this section an incumbrance or entry on the register shall not be deemed to be inferior to the charge in right of which title is made if the incumbrance or other interest is given the requisite priority by statute or otherwise.   **[526]**

35. Discharge of charges

(1) The registrar shall, on the requisition of the proprietor of any charge, or on due proof of the satisfaction (whole or partial) thereof, notify on the register in the prescribed manner, by cancelling or varying the original entry or otherwise, the cessation (whole or partial) of the charge, and thereupon the charge shall be deemed to have ceased (in whole or in part) accordingly.

(2) On the notification on the register of the entire cessation of a registered charge, whether as to the whole or part only of the land affected thereby, the term or sub-term implied in or granted by the charge or by any deed or alteration, so far as it affects the land to which the discharge extends, shall merge and be extinguished in the registered estate in reversion without any surrender.   **[527]**

36. Rules as to subcharges

Rules shall be made for applying the provisions of the Law of Property Act 1925 and of this Act to the case of charges by way of submortgage, whether registered before or after the commencement of this Act.   **[528]**

As to Dealings generally

37. Powers of persons entitled to be registered

(1) Where a person on whom the right to be registered as proprietor of registered land or of a registered charge has devolved by reason of the death of the proprietor, or has been conferred by a disposition or charge, in accordance with this Act desires to dispose of or charge the land or to deal with the charge before he is himself registered as proprietor, he may do so in the prescribed manner, and subject to the prescribed conditions.

(2) Subject to the provisions of this Act with regard to registered dealings for valuable consideration, a disposition or charge so made shall have the same effect as if the person making it were registered as proprietor.

(3) Rules may be made for extending the provisions of this section to the case of any person entitled to be registered as first proprietor, and to any other case for which it may be deemed expedient to prescribe. **[529]**

38. Certain provisions of the Law of Property Act to apply

(1) The provisions as to the execution of a conveyance on sale contained in the Law of Property Act 1925 shall apply, so far as applicable thereto, to transfers on sale of registered land.

(2) Rules may be made for prescribing the effect of covenants implied by virtue of the Law of Property Act 1925 in dispositions of registered land. **[530]**

39. Deeds off register, how far to be void

(1) Where any transaction relating exclusively to registered land or to a registered charge is capable of being effected and is effected by a registered disposition, then, subject to any prescribed exceptions, any deed or instrument, other than the registered disposition, which is executed by the proprietor for the purpose of giving effect to the transaction shall be void, but only so far as the transaction is carried out by the registered disposition.

(2) Rules may be made for providing for cases in which any additional deed or instrument may be properly executed and for enabling the registrar to certify that in any special cases an additional deed or instrument will be proper and valid. **[531]**

40. Creation and discharge of restrictive covenants

(1) Subject to any entry to the contrary on the register, and without prejudice to the rights of persons entitled to overriding interests (if any) and to any incumbrances entered on the register, who may not concur therein, the proprietor may in any registered disposition or other instrument by covenant, condition, or otherwise, impose or make binding, so far as the law permits, any obligation or reservation with respect to the building on or other user of the registered land or any part thereof, or with respect to mines and minerals (whether registered separately or as part of the registered land), or with respect to any other thing in like manner as if the proprietor were entitled to the registered land for his own benefit.

(2) The proprietor may (subject as aforesaid) release or waive any rights arising or which may arise by reason of any covenant or condition, or release any obligation or reservation the benefit of which is annexed or belongs to the registered land, to the same extent and in the same manner as if the rights in

respect of the breach or the benefit of the covenant, condition obligation, or reservation had been vested in him absolutely for his own benefit.

This subsection shall authorise the proprietor in reference to the registered land to give any licence, consent or approval which a tenant for life is by the Settled Land Act 1925, authorised to give in reference to settled land.

(3) Entries shall be made on the register in the prescribed manner of all obligations and reservations imposed by the proprietor, of the release or waiver of any obligation or reservation, and of all obligations and reservations acquired by him for the benefit of the registered estate.   **[532]**

Transmissions of Land and Charges on Death and Bankruptcy

41. Transmissions of land and charges on death of proprietor

(1) On the death of the sole proprietor, or of the survivor of two or more joint proprietors, of any registered land or charge, the personal representative of such sole deceased proprietor, or of the survivor of such joint proprietors, shall be entitled to be registered as proprietor in his place:

Provided that, where a special or additional personal representative is appointed by the court in reference to a registered estate, then on production of the order he shall be registered as proprietor either solely or jointly with any of the other personal representatives, as the case may require, and a copy of the order shall be filed at the registry.

(2) Pending an application for the appointment of a special or additional personal representative, a caution against dealings may be lodged under this Act by any person intending to apply to the court for the appointment.

(3) Subject as aforesaid, provision shall be made by rules for the manner in which effect is to be given on the register to transmissions on death.

(4) An assent by a personal representative shall, in the case of registered land, be in the prescribed form and the production of the assent in that form shall authorise the registrar to register the person named in the assent as the proprietor of the registered land.   **[533]**

42. Transmissions on bankruptcy of proprietor

(1) Upon the bankruptcy of the proprietor of any registered land or charge his trustee shall (on production of the prescribed evidence to be furnished by the official receiver or trustee in bankruptcy that the land or charge is [comprised in the bankrupt's estate]) be entitled to be registered as proprietor in his place.

The official receiver shall be entitled to be registered pending the appointment of a trustee.

(2) Where a trustee in bankruptcy disclaims a registered lease under [sections 315 to 319 of the Insolvency Act 1986], and an order is made by the court vesting the lease in any person, the order shall direct the alteration of the register in favour of the person in whom the lease is so vested, and in such case the registrar shall, on being served with such order, forthwith (without notice to the bankrupt or any other person and without requiring production of the land certificate) alter the register accordingly, and no right to indemnity under this Act shall arise by reason of such alteration.   **[534]**

NOTES

Sub-s (1): words in square brackets substituted by the Insolvency Act 1985, s 235, Sch 8, para 5.

Sub-s (2): words in square brackets substituted by the Insolvency Act 1986, s 439(2), Sch 14.

43. Effect of transmissions

Any person registered in the place of a deceased or bankrupt proprietor shall hold the land or charge in respect of which he is registered upon the trusts and for the purposes upon and subject to which the same is applicable by law, and subject to any minor interests subject to which the deceased or bankrupt proprietor held the same; but, save as aforesaid, he shall in all respects, and in particular as respects any registered dealings with such land or charge, be in the same position as if he had taken such land or charge under a transfer for valuable consideration. **[535]**

44. Vesting of term or subterm on transmission of charge

(1) On the registration of any transmission of a charge the term or subterm granted (expressly or by implication) by the charge or any deed of alteration shall without any conveyance or assignment vest in the proprietor for the time being of the charge.

(2) Subject to any entry to the contrary on the register, the vesting of a term or subterm in accordance with this section in the proprietor of a charge, shall, subject to the right of redemption, have the same effect as if such proprietor had been registered as the transferee for valuable consideration of the term or subterm. **[536]**

45. Proof of transmission of registered proprietorship

The fact of any person having become entitled to any registered land or charge in consequence of the death or bankruptcy of any proprietor shall be proved in the prescribed manner. **[537]**

Subsidiary Provisions

46. Determination or variation of leases, incumbrances, etc

The registrar shall, on proof to his satisfaction of—

    (a) the determination of any lease, rentcharge, or other estate or interest the title of which is registered under this Act; or

    (b) the discharge or determination (whole or partial) or variation of any lease, incumbrance, rentcharge, easement, right or other interest in land which is noted on the register as an incumbrance,

notify in the prescribed manner on the register the determination (whole or partial) or variation of such lease or other interest. **[538]**

47. Vesting instruments and dispositions in name of proprietor

(1) The registrar shall give effect on the register to any vesting order or vesting declaration (express or implied) made on the appointment or discharge of a trustee or otherwise, and to dispositions made in the name and on behalf of a proprietor by a person authorised to make the disposition; and the provisions of the Trustee Act 1925, relating to the appointment and discharge of trustees and the vesting of trust property, shall apply to registered land subject to the proper entry being made on the register.

(2) The registrar shall also give effect on the register in the prescribed manner to any vesting instrument which may be made pursuant to any statutory power.   **[539]**

PART IV

NOTICES, CAUTIONS, INHIBITIONS, AND RESTRICTIONS

Notices

48. Registration of notice of lease

(1) Any lessee or other person entitled to or interested in a lease of registered land, where the term granted is not an overriding interest, may apply to the registrar to register notice of such lease in the prescribed manner, and when so registered, every proprietor and the persons deriving title under him shall be deemed to be affected with notice of such lease, as being an incumbrance on the registered land in respect of which the notice is entered:

Provided that a proprietor of a charge or incumbrance registered or protected on the register prior to the registration of such notice shall not be deemed to be so affected by the notice unless such proprietor is, by reason of the lease having been made under a statutory or other power or by reason of his concurrence or otherwise, bound by the terms of the lease.

(2) In order to register notice of a lease, if the proprietor of the registered land affected does not concur in the registration thereof, the applicant shall obtain an order of the court authorising the registration of notice of the lease, and shall deliver the order to the registrar, accompanied with the original lease or a copy thereof, and thereupon the registrar shall make a notice in the register identifying the lease or copy so deposited, and the lease or copy so deposited shall be deemed to be the instrument of which notice is given; but if the proprietor concurs in the notice being registered, notice may be entered in such manner as may be agreed upon:

Provided that, where the lease is binding on the proprietor of the land, neither the concurrence of such proprietor nor an order of the court shall be required.   **[540]**

49. Rules to provide for notices of other rights, interests and claims

(1) The provisions of the last foregoing section shall be extended by the rules so as to apply to the registration of notices of or of claims in respect of—

(a) The grant or reservation of any annuity or rentcharge in possession, either perpetual or for a term of years absolute:

(b) The severance of any mines or minerals from the surface, except where the mines and minerals severed are expressly included in the registration:

(c) Land charges until the land charge is registered as a registered charge:

(d) The right of any person interested in the proceeds of sale of land held on trust for sale or in land subject to a settlement to require that (unless a trust corporation is acting as trustee) there shall be at least two trustees of the disposition on trust for sale or of the settlement:

(e) The rights of any widow in respect of dower or under the Intestates' Estates Act 1890, and any right to free bench or other like right saved by any statute coming into force concurrently with this Act (which rights shall take effect in equity as minor interests):

(*f*) Creditors' notices and any other right, interest, or claim which it may be deemed expedient to protect by notice instead of by caution, inhibition, or restriction:

[(*g*) Charging orders (within the meaning of the Charging Orders Act 1979 [, the Drug Trafficking Offences Act 1986 or the Criminal Justice Act 1988] [, or regulations under paragraph 11 of Schedule 4 to the Local Government Finance Act 1988] [, or regulations under paragraph 11 of Schedule 4 to the Local Government Finance Act 1988] [, or regulations under paragraph 11 of Schedule 4 to the Local Government Finance Act 1992]) which in the case of unregistered land may be protected by registration under the Land Charges Act 1972 and which, notwithstanding section 59 of this Act, it may be deemed expedient to protect by notice instead of by caution:]

[(*h*) Acquisition orders (within the meaning of Part III of the Landlord and Tenant Act 1987) which in the case of unregistered land may be protected by registration under the Land Charges Act 1972 and which, notwithstanding section 59 of this Act, it may be deemed expedient to protect by notice instead of by caution:]

[(*j*) Access orders under the Access to Neighbouring Land Act 1992 which, notwithstanding section 59 of this Act, it may be deemed expedient to protect by notice instead of by caution:]

[(*k*) orders made under section 26(1) or 50(1) of the Leasehold Reform, Housing and Urban Development Act 1993 which in the case of unregistered land may be protected by registration under the Land Charges Act 1972 and which, notwithstanding section 59 of this Act, it may be deemed expedient to protect by notice instead of by caution.]

(2) A notice shall not be registered in respect of any estate, right, or interest which (independently of this Act) is capable of being overriden by the proprietor under a trust for sale or the powers of the Settled Land Act 1925, or any other statute, or of a settlement, and of being protected by a restriction in the prescribed manner:

Provided that notice of such an estate right or interest may be lodged pending the appointment of trustees of a disposition on trust for sale or a settlement, and if so lodged, shall be cancelled if and when the appointment is made and the proper restriction (if any) is entered.

(3) A notice when registered in respect of a right, interest, or claim shall not affect prejudicially—

(*a*) The powers of disposition of the personal representative of the deceased under whose will or by the operation of whose intestacy the right, interest, or claim arose; or

(*b*) The powers of disposition (independently of this Act) of a proprietor holding the registered land on trust for sale. **[541]**

NOTES
Sub-s (1): para (*g*) added by the Charging Orders Act 1979, s 3(3), first words in square brackets substituted by the Criminal Justice Act 1988, s 170(1), Sch 15, para 6, second words in square brackets inserted by the Community Charges (Administration and Enforcement) Regulations 1989, SI 1989 No 438, reg 45(5), third words in square brackets inserted by the Council Tax (Administration and Enforcement) Regulations 1992, SI 1992 No 613, reg 51(5); para (*h*) added by the Landlord and Tenant Act 1986, s 61(1), Sch 4; para (*j*) added by the Access to Neighbouring Land Act 1992, s 5(2); para (*k*) added by the Leasehold Reform, Housing and Urban Development Act 1993, s 187(1), Sch 21, para 1.

50. Notices of restrictive covenants

(1) Any person entitled to the benefit of a restrictive covenant or agreement (not being a covenant or agreement made between a lessor and lessee) with

respect to the building on or other user of registered land may apply to the registrar to enter notice thereof on the register, and where practicable the notice shall be by reference to the instrument, if any, which contains the covenant or agreement, and a copy or abstract of such instrument shall be filed at the registry; and where any such covenant or agreement appears to exist at the time of first registration, notice thereof shall be entered on the register. In the case of registered land the notice aforesaid shall take the place of registration as a land charge.

(2) When such a notice is entered the proprietor of the land and the persons deriving title under him (except incumbrancers or other persons who at the time when the notice is entered may not be bound by the covenant or agreement) shall be deemed to be affected with notice of the covenant or agreement as being an incumbrance on the land.

(3) Where the covenant or agreement is discharged [modified or dealt with] by an order under the Law of Property Act 1925, or otherwise, or the court refuses to grant an injunction for enforcing the same, the entry shall either be cancelled or reference made to the order or other instrument and a copy of the order, judgment, or instrument shall be filed at the registry.

(4) The notice shall, when practicable, refer to the land, whether registered or not, for the benefit of which the restriction was made.   **[542]**

NOTES

Sub-s (3): words in square brackets substituted by the Law of Property Act 1969, s 28(7).

51. Notice of manorial incidents

Where land is affected by manorial incidents, the registrar may enter a note of that fact on the register, and may cancel such note when extinguishment of the manorial incidents has been proved to his satisfaction.   **[543]**

52. Effect of notices

(1) A disposition by the proprietor shall take effect subject to all estates, rights, and claims which are protected by way of notice on the register at the date of the registration or entry of notice of the disposition, but only if and so far as such estates, rights, and claims may be valid and are not (independently of this Act) overriden by the disposition.

(2) Where notice of a claim is entered on the register, such entry shall operate by way of notice only, and shall not operate to render the claim valid whether made adversely to or for the benefit of the registered land or charge.

[544]

Cautions

53. Cautions against first registration

(1) Any person having or claiming such an interest in land not already registered as entitles him to object to any disposition thereof being made without his consent, may lodge a caution with the registrar to the effect that the cautioner is entitled to notice in the prescribed form, and to be served in the prescribed manner, of any application that may be made for the registration of an interest in the land affecting the right of the cautioner.

(2) The caution shall be supported by an affidavit or declaration in the prescribed form, stating the nature of the interest of the cautioner, the land and

estate therein to be affected by such caution, and such other matters as may be prescribed.

(3) After a caution has been lodged in respect of any estate, which has not already been registered, registration shall not be made of such estate until notice has been served on the cautioner to appear and oppose, if he thinks fit, such registration, and the prescribed time has elapsed since the date of the service of such notice, or the cautioner has entered an appearance, whichever may first happen. **[545]**

54. Cautions against dealings

(1) Any person interested under any unregistered instrument, or interested as a judgment creditor, or otherwise howsoever, in any land or charge registered in the name of any other person, may lodge a caution with the registrar to the effect that no dealing with such land or charge on the part of the proprietor is to be registered until notice has been served upon the cautioner:

Provided that a person whose estate, right, interest, or claim has been registered or protected by a notice or restriction shall not be entitled (except with the consent of the registrar) to lodge a caution in respect of such estate, right, interest, or claim, . . .

(2) A caution lodged under this section shall be supported by such evidence as may be prescribed. **[546]**

NOTES
Sub-s (1): words omitted repealed by the Land Registration Act 1986, s 5(5)(*a*).

55. Effect of cautions against dealings

(1) After any such caution against dealings has been lodged in respect of any registered land or charge, the registrar shall not, without the consent of the cautioner, register any dealing or make any entry on the register for protecting the rights acquired under a deposit of a land or charge certificate or other dealing by the proprietor with such land or charge until he has served notice on the cautioner, warning him that his caution will cease to have any effect after the expiration of the prescribed number of days next following the date at which such notice is served; and after the expiration of such time as aforesaid the caution shall cease unless an order to the contrary is made by the registrar, and upon the caution so ceasing the registered land or charge may be dealt with in the same manner as if no caution had been lodged.

(2) If before the expiration of the said period the cautioner, or some person on his behalf, appears before the registrar, and where so required by the registrar gives sufficient security to indemnify every party against any damage that may be sustained by reason of any dealing with the registered land or charge, or the making of any such entry as aforesaid, being delayed, the registrar may thereupon, if he thinks fit to do so, delay registering any dealing with the land or charge or making any such entry for such period as he thinks just. **[547]**

56. General provisions as to cautions

(1) Any person aggrieved by any act done by the registrar in relation to a caution under this Act may appeal to the court in the prescribed manner.

(2) A caution lodged in pursuance of this Act shall not prejudice the claim or title of any person and shall have no effect whatever except as in this Act mentioned.

(3) If any person lodges a caution with the registrar without reasonable cause, he shall be liable to make to any person who may have sustained damage by the lodging of the caution such compensation as may be just, and such compensation shall be recoverable as a debt by the person who has sustained damage from the person who lodged the caution.

(4) The personal representative of a deceased cautioner may consent or object to registration or a dealing in the same manner as the cautioner.   **[548]**

Inhibitions

57. Power for court or registrar to inhibit registered dealings

(1) The court, or, subject to an appeal to the court, the registrar, upon the application of any person interested, made in the prescribed manner, in relation to any registered land or charge, may, after directing such inquiries (if any) to be made and notices to be given and hearing such persons as the court or registrar thinks expedient, issue an order or make an entry inhibiting for a time, or until the occurrence of an event to be named in such order or entry, or generally until further order or entry, the registration or entry of any dealing with any registered land or registered charge.

(2) The court or registrar may make or refuse to make any such order or entry, and annex thereto any terms or conditions the court or registrar may think fit, and discharge such order or cancel such entry when granted, with or without costs, and generally act in the premises in such manner as the justice of the case requires.

(3) Any person aggrieved by any act done by the registrar in pursuance of this section may appeal to the court in the prescribed manner.

(4) The court or the registrar may, in lieu of an inhibition, order a notice or restriction to be placed on the register.   **[549]**

Restrictions

58. Power to place restrictions on register

(1) Where the proprietor of any registered land or charge desires to place restrictions on transferring or charging the land or on disposing of or dealing with the land or charge in any manner in which he is by this Act authorised to dispose of or deal with it, or on the deposit by way of security of any certificate, the proprietor may apply to the registrar to make an entry in the register that no transaction to which the application relates shall be effected, unless the following things, or such of them as the proprietor may determine, are done—

    (*a*) unless notice of any application for the transaction is transmitted by post to such address as he may specify to the registrar;

    (*b*) unless the consent of some person or persons, to be named by the proprietor, is given to the transaction;

    (*c*) unless some such other matter or thing is done as may be required by the applicant and approved by the registrar:

Provided that no restriction under this section shall extend or apply to dispositions of or dealings with minor interests.

(2) The registrar shall thereupon, if satisfied of the right of the applicant to give the directions, enter the requisite restrictions on the register, and no transaction to which the restriction relates shall be effected except in conformity

therewith; but it shall not be the duty of the registrar to enter any such restriction, except upon such terms as to payment of fees and otherwise as may be prescribed, or to enter any restriction that the registrar may deem unreasonable or calculated to cause inconvenience.

(3) In the case of joint proprietors the restriction may be to the effect that when the number of proprietors is reduced below a certain specified number no disposition shall be registered except under an order of the court, or of the registrar after inquiry into title, subject to appeal to the court, and, subject to general rules, such an entry under this subsection as may be prescribed, shall be obligatory unless it is shown to the registrar's satisfaction that the joint proprietors are entitled for their own benefit, or can give valid receipts for capital money, or that one of them is a trust corporation.

(4) Any such restrictions, except such as are in this section declared to be obligatory, may at any time be withdrawn or modified at the instance of all the persons for the time being appearing by the register to be interested in such directions, and shall also be liable to be set aside by an order of the court.

(5) Rules may be made to enable applications to be made for the entry of restrictions by persons other than the proprietor. **[550]**

Protection of various Interests

59. Writs, orders, deeds of arrangement, pending actions, etc

(1) A writ, order, deed of arrangement, pending action, or other interest which in the case of unregistered land may be protected by registration under the Land Charges Act 1925, shall, where the land affected or the charge securing the debt affected is registered, be protected only by lodging a creditor's notice, a bankruptcy inhibition or a caution against dealings with the land or the charge.

(2) Registration of a land charge (other than a local land charge) shall, where the land affected is registered, be effected only by registering under this Act a notice caution or other prescribed entry:

Provided that before a land charge including a local land charge affecting registered land (being a charge to secure money) is realised, it shall be registered and take effect as a registered charge under this Act in the prescribed manner, without prejudice to the priority conferred by the land charge.

(3) . . .

(4) When a land charge protected by notice has been discharged as to all or any part of the land comprised therein, the notices relating thereto and to all devolutions of and dealings therewith shall be vacated as to the registered land affected by the discharge.

(5) The foregoing provisions of this section shall apply only to writs and orders, deeds of arrangement, pending actions and land charges which if the land were unregistered would for purposes of protection be required to be registered or re-registered after the commencement of this Act under the Land Charges Act 1925; and for the purposes of this section a land charge does not include a puisne mortgage . . .

(6) Subject to the provisions of this Act relating to fraud and to the title of a trustee in bankruptcy, a purchaser acquiring title under a registered disposition, shall not be concerned with any pending action, writ, order, deed of arrangement, or other document, matter, or claim (not being an overriding interest [or a

charge for capital transfer tax subject to which the disposition takes effect under section 73 of this Act]) which is not protected by a caution or other entry on the register, whether he has or has not notice thereof, express, implied, or constructive.

(7) In this section references to registration under the Land Charges Act 1925 apply to any registration made under any other statute which, in the case of unregistered land, is by the Land Charges Act 1925 to have effect as if the registration had been made under that Act. **[551]**

NOTES
Sub-s (3): repealed by the Land Registration Act 1988, ss 1(2), 2, Schedule.
Sub-s (5): words omitted repealed by the Finance Act 1975, ss 52(2), 59(5), Sch 13.
Sub-s (6): words in square brackets inserted by the Finance Act 1975, s 52(1), Sch 12, paras 2, 5(1).
Capital transfer tax: except in relation to a liability to tax arising before 25 July 1986 capital transfer tax shall be known as inheritance tax and the Capital Transfer Tax Act 1984 may be cited as the Inheritance Tax Act 1984, by virtue of the Finance Act 1986, s 100.

60. Notice of incumbrances registered under the Companies Act

(1) Where a company, registered under the Companies (Consolidation) Act 1908, is registered as proprietor of any estate or charge already registered, the registrar shall not be concerned with any mortgage, charge, debenture, debenture stock, trust deed for securing the same, or other incumbrance created or issued by the company, whether or not registered under that Act, unless the same is registered or protected by caution or otherwise under this Act.

(2) No indemnity shall be payable under this Act by reason of a purchaser acquiring any interest under a registered disposition from the company free from any such incumbrance. **[552]**

61. Protection of creditors prior to registration of trustee in bankruptcy

(1) The registrar shall as soon as practicable after registration of a petition in bankruptcy as a pending action under the Land Charges Act 1925, register a notice (in this Act called a creditors' notice) against the title of any proprietor of any registered land or charge which appears to be affected, and such notice shall protect the rights of all creditors, and unless cancelled by the registrar in the prescribed manner such notice shall remain in force until a bankruptcy inhibition is registered or the trustee in bankruptcy is registered as proprietor.

No fee shall be charged for the registration of the notice.

(2) . . .

(3) The registrar shall, as soon as practicable after registration of a [bankruptcy order] under the Land Charges Act 1925, enter an inhibition (in this Act called a bankruptcy inhibition) against the title of any proprietor of any registered land or charge which appears to be affected.

No fee shall be charged for the registration of the inhibition.

(4) From and after the entry of a bankruptcy inhibition (but without prejudice to dealings with or in right of interests or charges having priority over the estate or charge of the bankrupt proprietor), no dealing affecting the registered land or charge of the proprietor, other than the registration of the trustee in bankruptcy, shall be entered on the register until the inhibition is vacated as to the whole or part of the land or charge dealt with.

(5) If and when a proprietor of any registered land or charge is adjudged bankrupt, his registered estate or interest, if belonging to him beneficially, and whether acquired before or after the date of adjudication, shall vest in the trustee in bankruptcy in accordance with the statutory provisions relating to bankruptcy for the time being in force.

(6) Where under a disposition to a purchaser in good faith for money or money's worth such purchaser is registered as proprietor of an estate or a charge, then, [notwithstanding that the person making the disposition is adjudged bankrupt,] the title of his trustee in bankruptcy acquired after the commencement of this Act shall, as from the date of such disposition, be void as against such purchaser unless at the date of such disposition, either a creditors' notice or a bankruptcy inhibition has been registered, but a purchaser who, at the date of the execution of the registered disposition, has notice of [the bankruptcy petition or the] adjudication, shall not be deemed to take in good faith.

Nothing in this section shall impose on a purchaser a liability to make any search under the Land Charges Act 1925.

(7) Where the estate or assets of a bankrupt proprietor suffer loss by reason of the omission of the registrar to register a creditors' notice or bankruptcy inhibition, as required by this section, or on account of the execution or registration of a disposition after a petition is registered as a pending action or after [a bankruptcy order] is registered and before the registration of a creditors' notice or bankruptcy inhibition, the trustee in bankruptcy shall be entitled to indemnity as a person suffering loss by reason of an error or omission in the register.

(8) If neither a creditors' notice nor a bankruptcy inhibition is registered against a bankrupt proprietor, nothing in this section shall prejudicially affect a registered disposition of any registered land or charge acquired by the bankrupt after adjudication . . .

(9) If and when a bankruptcy inhibition is wholly or partially vacated, for any cause other than by reason of the registration of the trustee in bankruptcy, any registered estate or interest vested in the trustee in bankruptcy shall, as respects the registered land or charge to which the vacation extends, be divested and the same shall vest in the proprietor in whom it would have been vested if there had been no adjudication in bankruptcy.

(10) . . .   [553]

NOTES

Sub-s (2): words omitted repealed by the Insolvency Act 1985, s 235, Sch 10, Part III.
Sub-s (3): words in square brackets substituted by the Insolvency Act 1985, s 235, Sch 8, para 5.
Sub-s (6): words in square brackets substituted by the Insolvency Act 1985, s 235, Sch 8, para 5.
Sub-s (7): words in square brackets substituted by the Insolvency Act 1985, s 235, Sch 8, para 5.
Sub-s (8): words omitted repealed by the Insolvency Act 1985, s 235, Sch 10, Part III.
Sub-s (10): repealed by the Land Registration Act 1988, ss 1(2), 2, Schedule.

62. Rules to be made as to certain details

Rules shall be made under this Act—

> (a) For postponing the registration of a creditors' notice or bankruptcy inhibition, where the name, address and description of the debtor [or bankrupt] appearing in the application for the registration of the pending action or [bankruptcy order] are not identical with those

stated in the register, until the registrar is satisfied as to the identity of the debtor [or bankrupt];

(b) For requiring the official receiver to notify to the registrar any mistake occurring in the [bankruptcy order] or any other fact relevant to any proposed amendment in the register; and for enabling the registrar to make any consequential amendment;

(c) For providing for the whole or partial vacation (subject to notice to the official receiver or trustee in bankruptcy and to his right to appeal to the court) of a bankruptcy inhibition, where . . . the bankruptcy is annulled, or the registrar is satisfied that the bankruptcy proceedings do not affect or have ceased to affect the statutory powers of the bankrupt to deal with the registered land or charge.   **[554]**

NOTES

Para (a): first and fourth words in square brackets inserted or added and second and third words in square brackets substituted by the Insolvency Act 1985, s 235, Sch 8, para 5.

Para (b): words in square brackets substituted by the Insolvency Act 1985, s 235, Sch 8, para 5.

Para (c): words omitted repealed by the Insolvency Act 1985, s 235, Sch 10, Part III.

PART V

LAND AND CHARGE CERTIFICATES

63. Issue of land and charge certificates

(1) On the first registration of a freehold or leasehold interest in land, and on the registration of a charge, a land certificate, or charge certificate, as the case may be, shall be prepared in the prescribed form; it shall state whether the title is absolute, good leasehold, qualified or possessory, and it shall be either delivered to the proprietor or deposited in the registry as the proprietor may prefer.

(2) If so deposited in the registry it shall be officially endorsed from time to time, as in this Act provided, with notes of all subsequent entries in the register affecting the registered land or charge to which it relates.

(3) The proprietor may at any time apply for the delivery of the certificate to himself or to such person as he may direct, and may at any time again deposit it in the land registry.

(4) The preparation, issue, endorsement, and deposit in the registry of the certificate shall be effected without cost to the proprietor.   **[555]**

64. Certificates to be produced and noted on dealings

(1) So long as a land certificate or charge certificate is outstanding, it shall be produced to the registrar—

(a) on every entry in the register of a disposition by the proprietor of the registered land or charge to which it relates; and

(b) on every registered transmission; and

(c) in every case (except as hereinafter mentioned) where under this Act or otherwise notice of any estate right or claim or a restriction is entered or placed on the register, adversely affecting the title of the proprietor of the registered land or charge, but not in the case of the lodgment of a caution or of an inhibition or of a creditors' notice, or of the entry of a notice of a lease at a rent without taking a fine [or a notice of a charge for capital transfer tax].

(2) A note of every such entry or transmission shall be officially entered on the certificate and the registrar shall have the same powers of compelling the production of certificates as are conferred on him by this Act as to the production of maps, surveys, books, and other documents.

(3) On the completion of the registration of a transferee or grantee of any registered land or charge the registrar shall deliver to him a land certificate or charge certificate, and where part only of the land is dealt with shall also deliver to the transferor or grantor a land certificate containing a description of the land retained by him.

(4) Where a transfer of land is made by the proprietor of a registered charge in exercise of any power vested in him, it may be registered, and a new land certificate may be issued to the purchaser, without production of the former land certificate (when not deposited at the registry), but the charge certificate, if any, must be produced or accounted for in accordance with this section.

The provisions of this subsection shall be extended in the prescribed manner to the cases of—

(*a*) an order for foreclosure absolute;
(*b*) a proprietor of a charge or a mortgagee obtaining a title to the land under the Limitation Acts;
(*c*) title being acquired under a title paramount to the registered estate, including a title acquired pursuant to a vesting or other order of the court or other competent authority.

[(5) Subsection (1) above shall not require the production of the land certificate when a person applies for the registration of a notice by virtue of [section 2(8) of the Matrimonial Homes Act 1983] (spouse's charge in respect of rights of occupation).]

[(6) Subsection (1) above shall also not require the production of the land certificate when a person applies for—

(*a*) the registration of a notice of any variation of a lease affected by or in pursuance of an order under section 38 of the Landlord and Tenant Act 1987 (orders by the court varying leases), including any variation as modified by an order under section 39(4) of that Act (effect of orders varying leases: applications by third parties), or
(*b*) the cancellation of any such notice where a variation is cancelled or modified by an order under section 39(4) of that Act.]

[(7) Subsection (1) above shall also not require the production of the land certificate or of any charge certificate when a person applies for the registration of a notice in respect of an access order under the Access to Neighbouring Land Act 1992.] **[556]**

NOTES
   Sub-s (1): words in square brackets added by the Finance Act 1975, s 52(1), Sch 12, paras 2, 5(1), (5).
   Sub-s (5): added by the Matrimonial Homes and Property Act 1981, s 4(1); words in square brackets substituted by the Matrimonial Homes Act 1983, s 12, Sch 2.
   Sub-s (6): added by the Landlord and Tenant Act 1987, s 61(1), Sch 4.
   Sub-s (7): added by the Access to Neighbouring Land Act 1992, s 5(3).
   Capital transfer tax: except in relation to a liability to tax arising before 25 July 1986 capital transfer tax shall be known as inheritance tax and the Capital Transfer Tax Act 1984 may be cited as the Inheritance Tax Act 1984, by virtue of the Finance Act 1986, s 100.

65. Deposit at registry of certificate of mortgaged land

Where a charge or mortgage (otherwise than by deposit) is registered, or is protected by a caution in a specially prescribed form, the land certificate shall be deposited at the registry until the charge or mortgage is cancelled. **[557]**

66. Creation of liens by deposit of certificates

The proprietor of any registered land or charge may, subject to the overriding interests, if any, to any entry to the contrary on the register, and to any estates, interests, charges, or rights registered or protected on the register at the date of the deposit, create a lien on the registered land or charge by deposit of the land certificate or charge certificate; and such lien shall, subject as aforesaid, be equivalent to a lien created in the case of unregistered land by the deposit of documents of title or of the mortgage deed by an owner entitled for his own benefit to the registered estate, or a mortgagee beneficially entitled to the mortgage, as the case may be. **[558]**

67. Issue of new certificates

(1) The registrar may when a land certificate or charge certificate is produced to him grant a new land certificate or charge certificate in the place of the one produced.

(2) A new land certificate or charge certificate may be issued in place of one lost or destroyed, or in the possession of a person out of the jurisdiction of the High Court, on such terms as to advertisement notice or delay as may be prescribed. **[559]**

68. Certificates to be evidence

Any land certificate or charge certificate shall be admissible as evidence of the several matters therein contained. **[560]**

PART VI
GENERAL PROVISIONS AS TO REGISTRATION AND THE EFFECT THEREOF

69. Effect of registration on the legal estate

(1) The proprietor of land (whether he was registered before or after the commencement of this Act) shall be deemed to have vested in him without any conveyance, where the registered land is freehold, the legal estate in fee simple in possession, and where the registered land is leasehold the legal term created by the registered lease, but subject to the overriding interests, if any, including any mortgage term or charge by way of legal mortgage created by or under the Law of Property Act 1925, or this Act or otherwise which has priority to the registered estate.

(2) Where any legal estate or term left outstanding at the date of first registration (whether before or after the commencement of this Act), or disposed of or created under section forty-nine of the Land Transfer Act 1875, before the commencement of this Act, becomes satisfied, or the proprietor of the land becomes entitled to require the same to be vested in or surrendered to him, and the entry, if any, for protecting the same on the register has been cancelled, the same shall thereupon, without any conveyance, vest in the proprietor of the land, as if the same had been conveyed or surrendered to him as the case may be.

(3) If and when any person is registered as first proprietor of land in a compulsory area after the commencement of this Act, the provisions of the Law of Property Act 1925, for getting in legal estates shall apply to any legal estate in the land which was expressed to be conveyed or created in favour of a purchaser or lessee before the commencement of this Act but which failed to pass or to be created by reason of the omission of such purchaser or lessee to be registered as proprietor of the land under the Land Transfer Acts 1875 and 1897, and shall operate to vest that legal estate in the person so registered as proprietor on his registration, but subject to any mortgage term or charge by way of legal mortgage having priority thereto.

(4) The estate for the time being vested in the proprietor shall only be capable of being disposed of or dealt with by him in manner authorised by this Act.

(5) Nothing in this section operates to render valid a lease registered with possessory or good leasehold title. **[561]**

70. Liability of registered land to overriding interests

(1) All registered land shall, unless under the provisions of this Act the contrary is expressed on the register, be deemed to be subject to such of the following overriding interests as may be for the time being subsisting in reference thereto, and such interests shall not be treated as incumbrances within the meaning of this Act, (that is to say):—

(*a*) Rights of common, drainage rights, customary rights (until extinguished), public rights, profits à prendre, rights of sheepwalk, rights of way, watercourses, rights of water, and other easements not being equitable easements required to be protected by notice on the register;

(*b*) Liability to repair highways by reason of tenure, quit-rents, crown rents, heriots, and other rents and charges (until extinguished) having their origin in tenure;

(*c*) Liability to repair the chancel of any church;

(*d*) Liability in respect of embankments, and sea and river walls;

(*e*) . . . , payments in lieu of tithe, and charges or annuities payable for the redemption of tithe rentcharges;

(*f*) Subject to the provisions of this Act, rights acquired or in course of being acquired under the Limitation Acts;

(*g*) The rights of every person in actual occupation of the land or in receipt of the rents and profits thereof, save where enquiry is made of such person and the rights are not disclosed;

(*h*) In the case of a possessory, qualified, or good leasehold title, all estates, rights, interests, and powers excepted from the effect of registration;

(*i*) Rights under local land charges unless and until registered or protected on the register in the prescribed manner;

(*j*) Rights of fishing and sporting, seignorial and manorial rights of all descriptions (until extinguished), and franchises;

[(*k*) Leases granted for a term not exceeding twenty-one years;]

(*l*) In respect of land registered before the commencement of this Act, rights to mines and minerals, and rights of entry, search, and user, and other rights and reservations incidental to or required for the purpose of giving full effect to the enjoyment of rights to mines and minerals or of property in mines or minerals, being rights which, where the title was first registered before the first day of January, eighteen hundred and ninety-eight, were created before that date, and where the title was first registered after the thirty-first day of December, eighteen hundred and ninety-seven, were created before the date of first registration:

Provided that, where it is proved to the satisfaction of the registrar that any land registered or about to be registered is exempt from land tax, or tithe rentcharge or payments in lieu of tithe, or from charges or annuities payable for the redemption of tithe rentcharge, the registrar may notify the fact on the register in the prescribed manner.

(2) Where at the time of first registration any easement, right, privilege, or benefit created by an instrument and appearing on the title adversely affects the land, the registrar shall enter a note thereof on the register.

(3) Where the existence of any overriding interest mentioned in this section is proved to the satisfaction of the registrar or admitted, he may (subject to any prescribed exceptions) enter notice of the same or of a claim thereto on the register, but no claim to an easement, right, or privilege not created by an instrument shall be noted against the title to the servient land if the proprietor of such land (after the prescribed notice is given to him) shows sufficient cause to the contrary. **[562]**

NOTES
Sub-s (1): words omitted from para (*e*) repealed by the Finance Act 1963, s 73(8)(*b*), Sch 14, Part IV, and by the Tithe Act 1936, s 48(3), Sch 9; para (*k*) substituted by the Land Registration Act 1986, s 4(1).

71. Dispositions by virtue of overriding interests

Where by virtue of any interest or power which is an overriding interest a mortgagee or other person disposes of any estate, charge, or right in or upon a registered estate, and the disposition is capable of being registered, the registrar shall, if so required, give effect to the disposition on the register. **[563]**

72. Appurtenances

If before the registration of any freehold or leasehold interest in land with an absolute or good leasehold title any easement, right, or privilege has been acquired for the benefit thereof, then, on such registration, the easement, right, or privilege shall, subject to any entry to the contrary on the register, become appurtenant to the registered land in like manner as if it had been granted to the proprietor who is registered as aforesaid. **[564]**

[73. Inland Revenue charge for inheritance tax

A disposition shall take effect subject to any subsisting Inland Revenue charge under [the Inheritance Tax Act 1984] unless—

(*a*) the disposition is in favour of a purchaser within the meaning of [that Act]; and

(*b*) the charge is not, at the time of registration of the disposition, protected by notice on the register.] **[565]**

NOTES
Substituted by the Finance Act 1975, s 52(1), Sch 12, paras 2, 5(1), (6); words in square brackets substituted by the Inheritance Tax Act 1984, ss 274, 276, Sch 8, para 1.

Capital transfer tax: except in relation to a liability to tax arising before 25 July 1986 capital transfer tax shall be known as inheritance tax and the Capital Transfer Tax Act 1984 may be cited as the Inheritance Tax Act 1984, by virtue of the Finance Act 1986, s 100.

74. Notice of trust not to affect registered dealing

Subject to the provisions of this Act as to settled land, neither the registrar nor any person dealing with a registered estate or charge shall be affected with notice of a trust express implied or constructive, and references to trusts shall, so far as possible, be excluded from the register. **[566]**

75. Acquisition of title by possession

(1) The Limitation Acts shall apply to registered land in the same manner and to the same extent as those Acts apply to land not registered, except that where, if the land were not registered, the estate of the person registered as proprietor would be extinguished, such estate shall not be extinguished but shall be deemed to be held by the proprietor for the time being in trust for the person who, by virtue of the said Acts, has acquired title against any proprietor, but without prejudice to the estates and interests of any other person interested in the land whose estate or interest is not extinguished by those Acts.

(2) Any person claiming to have acquired a title under the Limitation Acts to a registered estate in the land may apply to be registered as proprietor thereof.

(3) The registrar shall, on being satisfied as to the applicant's title, enter the applicant as proprietor either with absolute, good leasehold, qualified, or possessory title, as the case may require, but without prejudice to any estate or interest protected by any entry on the register which may not have been extinguished under the Limitation Acts, and such registration shall, subject as aforesaid, have the same effect as the registration of a first proprietor; but the proprietor or the applicant or any other person interested may apply to the court for the determination of any question arising under this section.

(4) ...

(5) Rules may be made for applying (subject to any necessary modifications) the provisions of this section to cases where an easement, right or privilege has been acquired by prescription. **[567]**

NOTES
Sub-s (4): repealed by the Land Registration and Land Charges Act 1971, s 14(1)(*b*), Sch 2, Part I.

76. Description of registered land

Registered land may be described—

   (*a*) by means of a verbal description and a filed plan or general map, based on the ordnance map; or
   (*b*) by reference to a deed or other document, a copy or extract whereof is filed at the registry, containing a sufficient description, and a plan or map thereof; or
   (*c*) otherwise as the applicant for registration may desire, and the registrar, or, if the applicant prefers, the court, may approve,

regard being had to ready identification of parcels, correct descriptions of boundaries, and, so far as may be, uniformity of practice; but the boundaries of all freehold land and all requisite details in relation to the same, shall whenever practicable, be entered on the register or filed plan, or general map, and the filed plan, if any, or general map shall be used for assisting the identification of the land. **[568]**

[77. Conversion of title

(1) Where land is registered with a good leasehold title, or satisfies the conditions for such registration under this section, the registrar may, and on application by the proprietor shall, if he is satisfied as to the title to the freehold and the title to any intermediate leasehold, enter the title as absolute.

(2) Where land is registered with a possessory title, the registrar may, and on application by the proprietor shall—

(*a*) if he is satisfied as to the title, or

(*b*) if the land has been so registered for at least twelve years and he is satisfied that the proprietor is in possession,

enter the title in the case of freehold land as absolute and in the case of leasehold land as good leasehold.

(3) Where land is registered with a qualified title, the registrar may, and on application by the proprietor shall, if he is satisfied as to the title, enter it in the case of freehold land as absolute and in the case of leasehold land as good leasehold.

(4) If any claim adverse to the title of the proprietor has been made, an entry shall not be made in the register under this section unless and until the claim has been disposed of.

(5) No fee shall be charged for the making of an entry in the register under this section at the instance of the registrar or on an application by the proprietor made in connection with a transfer for valuable consideration of the land to which the application relates.

(6) Any person, other than the proprietor, who suffers loss by reason of any entry on the register made by virtue of this section shall be entitled to be indemnified under this Act as if a mistake had been made in the register.] **[569]**

NOTES

Substituted by the Land Registration Act 1986, s 1.

78. Provisions as to undivided shares in land

(1) Where in the case of land belonging to persons in undivided shares the entirety of the land is registered at the commencement of this Act, and the persons entitled to the several undivided shares are registered as proprietors, the registrar shall, on the occasion of the first dealing affecting the title after the commencement of this Act, rectify the register by entering as the proprietors of the entirety of the land the persons in whom the legal estate therein has become vested by virtue of the Law of Property Act 1925, and it shall be the duty of the persons registered as the proprietors of the undivided shares in the land to furnish to the registrar such evidence as he may require to enable him to ascertain the persons in whom such legal estate has become so vested as aforesaid.

(2) Where at the commencement of this Act the title to an undivided share in land is registered but the entirety of the land is not registered, the registrar may, at any time, after giving notice to the proprietor and to the other persons, if any, who appear by the register to be interested therein, remove from the register the title to the undivided share, and such removal shall have the like effect as if it had been effected by the proprietor with the assent of such other persons as aforesaid in pursuance of the power in that behalf contained in this Act:

Provided that, if within one year from the commencement of this Act or such extended time as the registrar may allow, and before the removal of the undivided share from the register in manner aforesaid, the persons in whom the legal estate of the entirety of the land is vested by virtue of the Law of Property Act 1925, or any persons interested in more than an undivided half of the land or the income thereof, make an application in the prescribed manner for the purpose and furnish the prescribed evidence, the registrar shall, without charging any fee, register the persons in whom such legal estate is so vested as proprietors of that estate, subject to any incumbrance capable of registration affecting the entirety of the land, but free from any charge or incumbrance (whether formerly registered or not) affecting an undivided share, and when the title to the entirety of the land is so registered, the title to the undivided share shall be closed.

(3) If the person in whom the legal estate in the entirety of the land is so vested is the Public Trustee, he shall not be registered as proprietor pursuant to this section unless and until he has been duly requested to act in accordance with the Law of Property Act 1925, and has accepted the trust.

(4) After the commencement of this Act, no entry other than a caution against dealings with the entirety shall be made in the register as respects the title to an undivided share in land. **[570]**

79. Addresses for service and notices

(1) Every person whose name is entered on the register as proprietor of any registered land or charge, or as cautioner, or as entitled to receive any notice, or in any other character shall furnish to the registrar a place of address in the United Kingdom.

(2) Every notice by this Act required to be given to any person shall be served personally, or sent through the post in a registered letter marked outside "His Majesty's Land Registry," and directed to such person at the address furnished to the registrar, and, unless returned, shall be deemed to have been received by the person addressed within such period, not less than seven days, exclusive of the day of posting, as may be prescribed.

(3) The Postmaster-General shall give directions for the immediate return to the registrar of all letters marked as aforesaid, and addressed to any person who cannot be found, and on the return of any letter containing any notice, the registrar shall act in the matter requiring such notice to be given in such manner as may be prescribed.

(4) A purchaser shall not be affected by the omission to send any notice by this Act directed to be given or by the non-receipt thereof. **[571]**

80. Bona vacantia and forfeiture

Subject to the express provisions of this Act relating to the effect of first registration of title and the effect of registration of a disposition for valuable consideration, nothing in this Act affects any right of His Majesty to any bona vacantia or forfeiture. **[572]**

81. Power to remove land from the register

(1) The proprietor of registered land not situated in an area where the registration of title is compulsory, and, in every case where the entirety of the land is not registered, the proprietor of an undivided share in land, may, with

the consent of the other persons (if any) for the time being appearing by the register to be interested therein, and on delivering up the land certificate and, if the land is subject to any registered charges, the charge certificates, remove the land (including an undivided share) from the register.

(2) After land is removed from the register no further entries shall be made respecting it, and inspection of the register may be made and office copies of the entries therein may be issued, subject to such regulations as may be prescribed.

(3) If the land so removed from the register is situated within the jurisdiction of the Middlesex or Yorkshire registries, it shall again be subject to such jurisdiction as from the date of the removal.   **[573]**

PART VII

RECTIFICATION OF REGISTER AND INDEMNITY

82. Rectification of the register

(1) The register may be rectified pursuant to an order of the court or by the registrar, subject to an appeal to the court, in any of the following cases, but subject to the provisions of this section:—

(a) Subject to any express provisions of this Act to the contrary, where a court of competent jurisdiction has decided that any person is entitled to any estate right or interest in or to any registered land or charge, and as a consequence of such decision such court is of opinion that a rectification of the register is required, and makes an order to that effect;

(b) Subject to any express provision of this Act to the contrary, where the court, on the application in the prescribed manner of any person who is aggrieved by any entry made in, or by the omission of any entry from, the register, or by any default being made, or unnecessary delay taking place, in the making of any entry in the register, makes an order for the rectification of the register;

(c) In any case and at any time with the consent of all persons interested;

(d) Where the court or the registrar is satisfied that any entry in the register has been obtained by fraud;

(e) Where two or more persons are, by mistake, registered as proprietors of the same registered estate or of the same charge;

(f) Where a mortgagee has been registered as proprietor of the land instead of as proprietor of a charge and a right of redemption is subsisting;

(g) Where a legal estate has been registered in the name of a person who if the land had not been registered would not have been the estate owner; and

(h) In any other case where, by reason of any error or omission in the register, or by reason of any entry made under a mistake, it may be deemed just to rectify the register.

(2) The register may be rectified under this section, notwithstanding that the rectification may affect any estates, rights, charges, or interests acquired or protected by registration, or by any entry on the register, or otherwise.

(3) The register shall not be rectified, except for the purpose of giving effect to an overriding interest [or an order of the court], so as to affect the title of the proprietor who is in possession—

[(*a*) unless the proprietor has caused or substantially contributed to the error or omission by fraud or lack of proper care; or]

(*b*)   ...

(*c*) unless for any other reason, in any particular case, it is considered that it would be unjust not to rectify the register against him.

(4) Where a person is in possession of registered land in right of a minor interest, he shall, for the purposes of this section, be deemed to be in possession as agent for the proprietor.

(5) The registrar shall obey the order of any competent court in relation to any registered land on being served with the order or an official copy thereof.

(6) On every rectification of the register the land certificate and any charge certificate which may be affected shall be produced to the registrar unless an order to the contrary is made by him.   **[574]**

NOTES
Sub-s (3): first words in square brackets inserted, para (*a*) substituted and para (*b*) repealed by the Administration of Justice Act 1977, ss 24, 32, Sch 5, Part IV.

83. Right to indemnity in certain cases

(1) Subject to the provisions of this Act to the contrary, any person suffering loss by reason of any rectification of the register under this Act shall be entitled to be indemnified.

(2) Where an error or omission has occurred in the register, but the register is not rectified, any person suffering loss by reason of such error or omission, shall, subject to the provisions of this Act, be entitled to be indemnified.

(3) Where any person suffers loss by reason of the loss or destruction of any document lodged at the registry for inspection or safe custody or by reason of an error in any official search, he shall be entitled to be indemnified under this Act.

(4) Subject as hereinafter provided, a proprietor of any registered land or charge claiming in good faith under a forged disposition shall, where the register is rectified, be deemed to have suffered loss by reason of such rectification and shall be entitled to be indemnified under this Act.

(5) No indemnity shall be payable under this Act in any of the following cases:—

[(*a*) Where the applicant or a person from whom he derives title (otherwise than under a disposition for valuable consideration which is registered or protected on the register) has caused or substantially contributed to the loss by fraud or lack of proper care;]

(*b*) On account of any mines or minerals or of the existence of any rights to work or get mines or minerals, unless a note is entered on the register that the mines or minerals are included in the registered title;

(*c*) On account of costs incurred in taking or defending any legal proceedings without the consent of the registrar.

(6) Where an indemnity is paid in respect of the loss of an estate or interest in or charge on land the amount so paid shall not exceed—

(*a*) Where the register is not rectified, the value of the estate, interest or charge at the time when the error or omission which caused the loss was made;

(*b*) Where the register is rectified, the value (if there had been no rectification) of the estate, interest or charge, immediately before the time of rectification.

(7) . . .

[(8) Subject to subsection (5) (*c*) of this section, as amended by section 2 (2) of the Land Registration and Land Charges Act 1971—

    (*a*) an indemnity under any provision of this Act shall include such amount, if any, as may be reasonable in respect of any costs or expenses properly incurred by the applicant in relation to the matter; and

    (*b*) an applicant for an indemnity under any such provision shall be entitled to an indemnity thereunder of such amount, if any, as may be reasonable in respect of any such costs or expenses, notwithstanding that no other indemnity money is payable thereunder.]

(9) Where indemnity is paid for a loss, the registrar, on behalf of the Crown, shall be entitled to recover the amount paid from any person who has caused or substantially contributed to the loss by his fraud.

(10) The registrar shall be entitled to enforce, on behalf of the Crown, any express or implied covenant or other right which the person who is indemnified would have been entitled to enforce in relation to the matter in respect of which indemnity has been paid.

(11) A liability to pay indemnity under this Act shall be deemed a simple contract debt; and for the purposes of[the Limitation Act 1980] the cause of action shall be deemed to arise at the time when the claimant knows, or but for his own default might have known, of the existence of his claim:

Provided that, when a claim to indemnity arises in consequence of the registration of an estate in land with an absolute or good leasehold title, the claim shall be enforceable only if made within six years from the date of such registration, except in the following cases:—

    (*a*) Where at the date of registration the person interested is an infant, the claim by him may be made within six years from the time he attains full age;

    (*b*) In the case of settled land, or land held on trust for sale, a claim by a person interested in remainder or reversion, may be made within six years from the time when his interest falls into possession;

    (*c*) Where a claim arises in respect of a restrictive covenant or agreement affecting freehold land which by reason of notice or the registration of a land charge or otherwise was binding on the first proprietor at the time of first registration, the claim shall only be enforceable within six years from the breach of the covenant or agreement;

    (*d*) Where any person interested is entitled as a proprietor of a charge or as a mortgagee protected by a caution in the specially prescribed form, the claim by him may be made within six years from the last payment in respect of principal or interest.

(12) This section applies to the Crown in like manner as it applies to a private person.   **[575]**

NOTES

Sub-s (5): words in square brackets substituted by the Land Registration and Land Charges Act 1971, s 3.

Sub-s (7): repealed by the Land Registration and Land Charges Act 1971, ss 2(4), 14(2)(*b*), Sch 2, Part II.

Sub-s (8): substituted by the Land Registration and Land Charges Act 1971, s 2(4).

Sub-s (11): words in square brackets substituted by the Limitation Act 1980, s 40(2), Sch 3, para 1.

84. Application of indemnity in case of settled land

Where any indemnity is paid in respect of settled land, and not in respect of any particular estate, remainder, or reversion therein, the money shall be paid to the trustees of the settlement and held by them as capital money for the purposes of the Settled Land Act 1925, arising from the settled land. **[576]**

PART VIII
APPLICATION TO PARTICULAR CLASSES OF LAND

86. Registration of settled land

(1) Settled land shall be registered in the name of the tenant for life or statutory owner.

(2) The successive or other interests created by or arising under a settlement shall (save as regards any legal estate which cannot be overridden under the powers of the Settled Land Act 1925, or any other statute) take effect as minor interests and not otherwise; and effect shall be given thereto by the proprietor of the settled land as provided by statute with respect to the estate owner, with such adaptations, if any, as may be prescribed in the case of registered land by rules made under this Act.

(3) There shall also be entered on the register such restrictions as may be prescribed, or may be expedient, for the protection of the rights of the persons beneficially interested in the land, and such restrictions shall (subject to the provisions of this Act relating to releases by the trustees of a settlement and to transfers by a tenant for life whose estate has ceased in his lifetime) be binding on the proprietor during his life, but shall not restrain or otherwise affect a disposition by his personal representative.

(4) Where land already registered is acquired with capital money, the same shall be transferred by a transfer in a specially prescribed form to the tenant for life or statutory owner, and such transfer shall state the names of the persons who are trustees of the settlement for the purposes of the Settled Land Act 1925, and contain an application to register the prescribed restrictions applicable to the case; a transfer made in the specially prescribed form shall be deemed to comply with the requirements of that Act, respecting vesting deeds; and where no capital money is paid but land already registered is to be made subject to a settlement, it shall not be necessary for the trustees of the settlement to concur in the transfer.

(5) References in this Act to the "tenant for life" shall, where the context admits, be read as referring to the tenant for life, statutory owner, or personal representative who is entitled to be registered. **[577]**

87. Changes of ownership of settled land

(1) On the death of a proprietor, or of the survivor of two or more joint proprietors of settled land (whether the land is settled by his will or by an instrument taking effect on or previously to his death), his personal representative

shall hold the settled land subject to payment or to making provision for payment of all death duties and other liabilities affecting the land, and having priority to the settlement, upon trust to transfer the same by an assent in the prescribed manner to the tenant for life or statutory owner, and in the meantime upon trust to give effect to the minor interests under the settlement; but a transfer shall not be made to an infant.

(2) Rules may be made—

    (a) for enabling a personal representative or proprietor in proper cases to create legal estates by registered dispositions for giving effect to or creating interests in priority to the settlements;

    (b) to provide for the cases in which application shall be made by the personal representative or proprietor for the registration of restrictions or notices; and

    (c) for discharging a personal representative or former proprietor who has complied with the requirements of this Act and rules from all liability in respect of minor interests under a settlement.

(3) Where a tenant for life or statutory owner who, if the land were not registered, would be entitled to have the settled land vested in him, is not the proprietor, the proprietor shall (notwithstanding any stipulation or provision to the contrary) be bound at the cost of the trust estate to execute such transfers as may be required for giving effect on the register to the rights of such tenant for life or statutory owner.

(4) Where the trustees of a settlement have in the prescribed manner released the land from the minor interests under such settlement, the registrar shall be entitled to assume that the settlement has determined, and the restrictions for protecting the minor interests thereunder shall be cancelled.

(5) Where an order is made under the Settled Land Act 1925, authorising the trustees of the settlement to exercise the powers on behalf of a tenant for life who is registered as proprietor, they may in his name and on his behalf do all such acts and things under this Act as may be requisite for giving effect on the register to the powers authorised to be exercised in like manner as if they were registered as proprietors of the land, but a copy of the order shall be filed at the registry before any such powers are exercised.

(6) Where a proprietor ceases in his lifetime to be a tenant for life, he shall transfer the land to his successor in title, or, if such successor is an infant, to the statutory owner, and on the registration of such successor in title or statutory owner it shall be the duty of the trustees of the settlement, if the same be still subsisting, to apply for such alteration, if any, in the restrictions as may be required for the protection of the minor interests under the settlement.   [578]

88. Settlement may be filed in registry

(1) The settlement, or an abstract or copy thereof, may be filed in the registry for reference in the prescribed manner, but such filing shall not affect a purchaser from the proprietor with notice of its provisions, or entitle him to call for production of the settlement, or for any information or evidence as to its contents.

(2) In this section "settlement" includes any deed stating who are the trustees of the settlement, and the vesting instrument, and any transfer or assent

in the prescribed form taking the place, in the case of registered land, of a vesting instrument, as well as the trust instrument and any other instruments creating the settlement. [579]

89. Registrar's certificate authorising proposed dealing with settled land

The registrar may, notwithstanding any restriction entered on the register, grant a certificate that an intended registered disposition is authorised by a settlement or otherwise, and will be registered, and a purchaser who obtains such a certificate shall not be concerned to see that the disposition is authorised, but where capital money is paid to the persons to whom the same is required to be paid by a restriction or into court no such certificate shall be required. [580]

90. Charges for money actually raised

The proprietor of settled land which is registered and all other necessary parties, if any, shall, on the request, and at the expense of any person entitled to an estate, interest, or charge conveyed or created for securing money actually raised at the date of such request, charge the land in the prescribed manner with the payment of the money so raised, but so long as the estate, interest or charge is capable of being overridden under the Settled Land Act 1925, or the Law of Property Act 1925, no charge shall be created or registered under this section.

[581]

91. Minorities

The following provisions shall have effect as respects settled land (being registered land) during a minority:—

(1) The personal representatives under the will or intestacy under which the settlement is created or arises shall, during the minority, be registered as proprietors, and in reference to the settled land shall have all the powers conferred by the Settled Land Act 1925, on a tenant for life and on the trustees of the settlement; but if and when the personal representatives would, if the infant had been of full age, have been bound to transfer the registered land to him, the personal representatives shall (unless themselves the statutory owners) thenceforth during the minority give effect on the register to the directions of the statutory owner, and shall apply for the registration of any restriction which may be prescribed, but shall not be concerned with the propriety of any registered disposition so directed to be made if the same appears to be a proper disposition under the powers of the statutory owner and the capital money, if any, arising under the disposition is paid to the trustees of the settlement or into court; but a purchaser dealing with the personal representatives, who complies with the restrictions, if any, which may be entered on the register, shall not be concerned to see or inquire whether any such directions have been given:

(2) If an infant becomes entitled in possession (or will become entitled in possession on attaining full age) to registered land otherwise than on a death, the statutory owners during the minority shall be entitled to require the settled land to be transferred to them and shall be registered as proprietors accordingly:

(3) If and when the registered land would (if not registered) have become vested in the trustees of the settlement pursuant to the Law of Property Act 1925, such trustees shall (unless they are already registered) be entitled to be registered as proprietors thereof, and shall in the prescribed manner apply for registration accordingly, and no fee shall be charged in respect of such registration or consequential alteration in the register. [582]

92. Rights of tenants for life and statutory owners to be registered as proprietors

The foregoing provisions of this Part of this Act relating to settled land apply in every case where pursuant to the Settled Land Act 1925, settled land is to be vested in a tenant for life or statutory owner whether the estate was registered before or after the commencement of this Act, and the proprietor of settled land (not being the tenant for life or statutory owner entitled to the same) shall be bound to make such dispositions as may be required for giving effect to the rights of the tenant for life or statutory owner:

Provided that, where the registered land is not, at the commencement of this Act, registered in the name of a tenant for life or statutory owner, or personal representative who, if the land were not registered, would by virtue of the Settled Land Act 1925, or of the Law of Property Act 1925, be entitled to have the settled land vested in him, any such person shall (without any transfer) be entitled to be registered as proprietor thereof, and shall in the prescribed manner apply for registration accordingly, and no fee shall be charged in respect of such registration or consequential alteration in the register.   **[583]**

93. As to persons in a fiduciary position

A person in a fiduciary position may apply for, or concur in, or assent to, any registration authorised by the provisions of this Act, and, if he is a proprietor, may execute a charge or other disposition in favour of any person whose registration is so authorised.   **[584]**

94. Land held on trust for sale

(1) Where registered land is subject to a trust for sale, express or implied, whether or not there is power to postpone the sale, the land shall be registered in the names of the trustees for sale.

(2) Where an order, obtained under section seven of the Settled Land Act 1884, is in force at the commencement of this Act, the person authorised by the order to exercise any of the powers conferred by the Settled Land Act 1925, may, in the names and on behalf of the proprietors, do all such acts and things under this Act as may be requisite for giving effect on the register to the powers authorised to be exercised in like manner as if such person were registered as proprietor of the land, and a copy of the order shall be filed at the registry.

(3) Where, by virtue of any statute, registered land is made subject to a trust for sale, the trustees for sale (unless already registered) shall be registered as proprietors thereof, and shall in the prescribed manner apply for registration accordingly, and no fee shall be charged in respect of such registration or consequential alteration of the register, but this subsection has effect subject to the provisions of this Act relating to the registration of the Public Trustee and the removal of an undivided share from the register the title to the entirety of the land is registered.   **[585]**

95. Restriction on number of trustees

The statutory restrictions affecting the number of persons entitled to hold land on trust for sale and the number of trustees of a settlement apply to registered land.   **[586]**

96. Crown and Duchy land

(1) With respect to land or any estate, right, or interest in land vested in His Majesty, either in right of the Crown or of the Duchy of Lancaster, or otherwise, or vested in any public officer or body in trust for the public service, the public officer or body having the management thereof, if any, or, if none, then such person as His Majesty may by writing under his sign manual appoint, may represent the owner of such land, estate, right, or interest for all the purposes of this Act, and shall be entitled to such notices, and may make and enter any such application or cautions, and do all such other acts as any owner of land, or of any estate, right, or interest therein, as the case may be, is entitled to receive, make, enter, or do under this Act.

(2) With respect to land or any estate, right, or interest in land belonging to the Duchy of Cornwall, such person as the Duke of Cornwall for the time being, or as the person for the time being entitled to the revenues and possessions of the Duchy of Cornwall, may in writing appoint, may act as and represent the owner of such land, estate, right, or interest for all the purposes of this Act, and shall be entitled to receive such notices, and may make and enter any such application or cautions, and do all such other acts as any owner of land or of any estate, right, or interest in land (as the case may be) is entitled to make, enter, or do under this Act. **[587]**

97. Foreshore

(1) If it appears to the registrar that any land, application for registration whereof is made to him, comprises foreshore, he shall not register an estate in the land unless and until he is satisfied that at least one month's notice in writing of the application has been given ... —

    (*a*) in case of land in the county palatine of Lancaster, ... to the proper officer of the Duchy of Lancaster; and

    (*b*) in case of land in the counties of Cornwall or Devon, ... to the proper officer of the Duke of Cornwall; and

    (*c*) in the case of land within the jurisdiction of the Port of London Authority, ... to that authority; and

    (*d*) in all ... cases, ... the Commissioners of Woods.

(2) This section does not apply to the registration of an estate with a possessory title or with a good leasehold title. **[588]**

NOTES

    Sub-s (1): words omitted repealed by the Crown Estate Act 1961, s 9(4), Sch 3, Part I.

98. Land subject to charitable trusts

Where an application is made to register a legal estate in land subject to charitable trusts and that estate is vested in the [official custodian for charities], he shall, notwithstanding that the powers of disposition are vested in the managing trustees or committee, be registered as proprietor thereof. **[589]**

NOTES

    Words in square brackets substituted by the Charities Act 1960, s 48(1), Sch 6.

99. Land belonging to benefices

(1) Where the incumbent of a benefice and his successors are the registered proprietors of land—

(i) No disposition thereof shall be registered unless a certificate in the prescribed form has been obtained [from the Church Commissioners].

(ii) No lien shall be created by deposit of the land certificate, and an inhibition shall be placed on the register and on the land certificate accordingly.

The production of a certificate from [the Church Commissioners] shall be a sufficient authority to the registrar to register the disposition in question, and it shall be the duty of [the Church Commissioners] to grant such certificate in all cases in which the facts admit thereof.

(2) On the registration of the incumbent of a benefice and his successors as the proprietors of a legal estate in land, if it is certified by [the Church Commissioners] or otherwise appears, that the land was originally purchased by Queen Anne's Bounty [or the said Commissioners] or was otherwise appropriated or annexed by or with the consent or the concurrence of Queen Anne's Bounty [or the said Commissioners] to the benefice for the augmentation thereof, the registrar shall enter a note to that effect on the register.

(3) Where the incumbent of a benefice is entitled to indemnity under the provisions of this Act, the money shall be paid to [the Church Commissioners] and appropriated by them to the benefice.

(4) "Benefice" in this section includes all rectories with cure of souls, vicarages, perpetual curacies, donatives, endowed public chapels and parochial chapelries, and chapelries or districts belonging, or reputed to belong, or annexed, or reputed to be annexed, to any church or chapel. **[590]**

NOTES
Sub-s (1): words in square brackets substituted by the Endowments and Glebe Measure 1971, s 47(1), Sch 5, para 1(*a*).
Sub-s (2): first words in square brackets substituted and second and third words in square brackets inserted by the Endowments and Glebe Measure 1971, s 47(1), Sch 5, para 1(*b*).
Sub-s (3): words in square brackets substituted by the Endowments and Glebe Measure 1971, s 47(1), Sch 5, para 1(*c*).

100. Small holdings

(1) Where a county council apply in pursuance of the Small Holdings and Allotments Act 1908, for registration as proprietors, they may be registered as proprietors with any such title as is authorised by this Act.

(2) Where a county council, after having been so registered, dispose of any interest in the land for the purposes of a small holding to a purchaser or lessee, he shall be registered as proprietor of the interest transferred or created (being an interest capable of registration) with an absolute title, subject only to such incumbrances as may be created under the Small Holdings and Allotments Act 1908, but freed from all other liabilities not being overriding interests, and in any such case the remedy of any person claiming by title paramount to the county council in respect either of title or incumbrances shall be in damages only, and such damages shall be recoverable against the county council.

(3) Where under the powers conferred by subsection (4) of section twelve of the said Act, a county council by notice require registered land to be sold to themselves, the council shall, after such date as may be specified by the notice mentioned in that subsection and on production to the registrar of evidence—

(*a*) of service of such notice; and

(*b*) of the payment of the sum agreed or determined in manner provided by that subsection or of the tender of such payment

be registered as the proprietors of the land in place of the proprietor, and such registration shall operate as a registration on a transfer for valuable consideration under this Act.

(4) Rules under this Act may—

    (*a*) adapt this Act to the registration of small holdings with such modifications as appear to be required; and

    (*b*) on the application and at the expense of a county council provide by the appointment of local agents or otherwise for the carrying into effect of the objects of this section; and

    (*c*) enable the registrar to obtain production of the land certificate.

(5) . . .   **[591]**

NOTES
Sub-s (5): repealed by the Local Government Act 1985, s 102, Sch 17.

PART IX

UNREGISTERED DEALINGS WITH REGISTERED LAND

Powers of dealing with Registered Land off the Register

101. Dispositions off register creating "minor interests"

(1) Any person, whether being the proprietor or not, having a sufficient interest or power in or over registered land, may dispose of or deal with the same, and create any interests or rights therein which are permissible in like manner and by the like modes of assurance in all respects as if the land were not registered, but subject as provided by this section.

(2) All interests and rights disposed of or created under subsection (1) of this section (whether by the proprietor or any other person) shall, subject to the provisions of this section, take effect as minor interests, and be capable of being overridden by registered dispositions for valuable consideration.

(3) Minor interests shall, subject to the express exceptions contained in this section, take effect only in equity, but may be protected by entry on the register of such notices, cautions, inhibitions and restrictions as are provided for by this Act or rules.

(4) A minor interest in registered land subsisting or capable of taking effect at the commencement of this Act, shall not fail or become invalid by reason of the same being converted into an equitable interest; but after such commencement a minor interest in registered land shall only be capable of being validly created in any case in which an equivalent equitable interest could have been validly created if the land had not been registered.

(5) Where after the commencement of this Act, the proprietor of the registered estate which is settled, disposes of or deals with his beneficial interest in possession in favour of a purchaser, and accordingly the minor interest disposed of or created would, but for the restrictions imposed by the Law of Property Act 1925, and this section, on the creation of legal estates, have been a legal estate, the purchaser (subject as provided by the next following section in regard to priorities) may exercise all such rights and remedies as he might have exercised had the minor interest been a legal estate, and the reversion (if

any) on any leases or tenancies derived out of the registered estate had been vested in him.

(6) A minor interest created under this section does not operate to prevent a registered estate passing to the personal representative of a deceased proprietor, or to the survivor or survivors of two or more joint proprietors, nor does this section affect the right of any person entitled to an overriding interest, or having any power to dispose of or create an overriding interest, to dispose of or create the same.   **[592]**

102. Priorities as between minor interests

(1) If a minor interest subsisting or capable of taking effect at the commencement of this Act, would, if the Law of Property Acts 1922 and 1925, and this Act had not been passed have taken effect as a legal estate, then (subject and without prejudice to the estate and powers of the proprietor whose estate is affected) the conversion thereof into an equitable interest shall not affect its priority over other minor interests.

(2), (3) . . .   **[593]**

NOTES
Sub-s (2), (3): repealed by the Land Registration Act 1986, s 5(1), (5)(*b*).

103. Obligation to give effect on the register to certain minor interests

(1) Where by the operation of any statute or statutory or other power, or by virtue of any vesting order of any court or other competent authority, or an order appointing a person to convey, or of a vesting declaration (express or implied) or of an appointment or other assurance, a minor interest in the registered land is disposed of or created which would, if registered, be capable of taking effect as a legal estate or charge by way of legal mortgage, then—

(i) if the estate owner would, had the land not been registered, have been bound to give effect thereto by conveying or creating a legal estate or charge by way of legal mortgage, the proprietor shall, subject to proper provision being made for payment of costs, be bound to give legal effect to the transaction by a registered disposition:

(ii) if the proprietor is unable or refuses to make the requisite disposition or cannot be found, or if for any other reason a disposition by him cannot be obtained within a reasonable time, or if, had the land not been registered, no conveyance by the estate owner would have been required to give legal effect to the transaction, the registrar shall give effect thereto in the prescribed manner in like manner and with the like consequences as if the transaction had been carried out by a registered disposition:

Provided that—

(*a*) So long as the proprietor has power under the Settled Land Act 1925, or any other statute conferring special powers on a tenant for life or statutory owner, or under the settlement, to override the minor interest so disposed of or created, no estate or charge shall be registered which would prejudicially affect any such powers:

(*b*) So long as the proprietor holds the land on trust for sale, no estate or charge shall be registered in respect of an interest which, under the Law of Property Act 1925, or otherwise, ought to remain liable to be overridden on the execution of the trust for sale:

(c) Nothing in this subsection shall impose on a proprietor an obligation to make a disposition unless the person requiring the disposition to be made has a right in equity to call for the same:

(d) Nothing in this subsection shall prejudicially affect the rights of a personal representative in relation to the administration of the estate of the deceased.

(2) On every alteration in the register made pursuant to this section the land certificate and any charge certificate which may be affected shall be produced to the registrar unless an order to the contrary is made by him.   **[594]**

104. Protection of leases granted under statutory powers by persons other than registered proprietor and restriction on power

All leases at a rent for a term of years absolute authorised by the powers conferred by the Law of Property Act 1925, or the Settled Land Act 1925, or any other statute (whether or not as extended by any instrument) may be granted in the name and on behalf of the proprietor by any other person empowered to grant the same, and shall be valid at law or in equity (as the case may require) and shall be protected by notice on the register and registered in the same cases, in like manner and with the same effect as if the lease had been granted by the proprietor of the land, and without prejudice to any priority acquired by the exercise of the power; but nothing in this section shall authorise any person granting any lease in the name of the proprietor to impose (save in regard to such usual qualified covenant for quiet enjoyment) any personal liability on such proprietor.   **[595]**

105. As to minor interests in mortgage debts

Rules may be made for applying the provisions of this Part of this Act as to minor interests to the case of minor interests in a debt secured by a registered charge.   **[596]**

[106. Creation and protection of mortgages of registered land

(1) The proprietor of any registered land may, subject to any entry to the contrary on the register, mortgage, by deed or otherwise, the land or any part of it in any manner which would have been permissible if the land had not been registered and, subject to this section, with the like effect.

(2) Unless and until the mortgage becomes a registered charge,—

(a) it shall take effect only in equity, and

(b) it shall be capable of being overriden as a minor interest unless it is protected as provided by subsection (3) below.

(3) A mortgage which is not a registered charge may be protected on the register by—

(a) a notice under section 49 of this Act,

(b) any such other notice as may be prescribed, or

(c) a caution under section 54 of this Act.

(4) A mortgage which is not a registered charge shall devolve and may be transferred, discharged, surrendered or otherwise dealt with by the same instruments and in the same manner as if the land had not been registered.]   **[597]**

NOTES
Substituted by the Administration of Justice Act 1977, s 26(1).

107. Power for proprietors to bind successors and to enforce contracts

(1) Subject to any entry to the contrary on the register, the proprietor of any registered land or charge may enter into any contract in reference thereto in like manner as if the land or charge had not been registered, and, subject to any disposition for valuable consideration which may be registered or protected on the register before the contract is completed or protected on the register, the contract may be enforced as a minor interest against any succeeding proprietor in like manner and to the same extent as if the land or charge had not been registered.

(2) A contract entered into for the benefit of any registered land or charge may (if the same would have been enforceable by the owner for the time being of the land or charge, if not registered, or by a person deriving title under the party contracting for the benefit) be enforced by the proprietor for the time being of the land or charge. **[598]**

108. Acquisition of easements and other benefits

The proprietor of registered land may accept for the benefit thereof the grant of any easement, right, or privilege or the benefit of any restrictive covenant or provision (affecting other land, whether registered or not) in like manner and to the same extent as if he were legally and beneficially entitled to the fee simple in possession, or to the term created by the registered lease, for his own benefit free from incumbrances. **[599]**

109. Restriction on exercise of powers off the register

Subject to the express provisions relating to leases and mortgages, nothing in this Part of this Act shall be construed as authorising any disposition of any estate, interest, or right or other dealing with land to be effected under this Part of this Act if the disposition or dealing is one which could be effected under another Part of this Act, and any such disposition or dealing shall be effected under and in the manner required by such other Part of this Act, and when so required shall be registered or protected as provided by this Act or the rules. **[600]**

PART X

MISCELLANEOUS PROVISIONS

110. Provisions as between vendor and purchaser

On a sale or other disposition of registered land to a purchaser other than a lessee or chargee—

(1) The vendor shall, notwithstanding any stipulation to the contrary, at his own expense furnish the purchaser . . ., if required, with a copy of the subsisting entries in the register and of any filed plans and copies or abstracts of any documents or any part thereof noted on the register so far as they respectively affect the land to be dealt with (except charges or incumbrances registered or protected on the register which are to be discharged or overridden at or prior to completion):

Provided that—

　(*a*) unless the purchase money exceeds one thousand pounds the costs of the copies and abstracts of the said entries plans and documents shall, in the absence of any stipulation to the contrary, be borne by the purchaser requiring the same;

(b) nothing in this section shall give a purchaser a right to a copy or abstract of a settlement filed at the registry:

(2) The vendor shall, subject to any stipulation to the contrary, at his own expense furnish the purchaser with such copies, abstracts and evidence (if any) in respect of any subsisting rights and interests appurtenant to the registered land as to which the register is not conclusive, and of any matters excepted from the effect of registration as the purchaser would have been entitled to if the land had not been registered:

(3) Except as aforesaid, and notwithstanding any stipulation to the contrary, it shall not be necessary for the vendor to furnish the purchaser with any abstract or other written evidence of title, or any copy or abstract of the land certificate, or of any charge certificate:

(4) Where the register refers to a filed abstract or copy of or extract from a deed or other document such abstract or extract shall as between vendor and purchaser be assumed to be correct, and to contain all material portions of the original, and no person dealing with any registered land or charge shall have a right to require production of the original, or be affected in any way by any provisions of the said document other than those appearing in such abstract, copy or extract, and any person suffering loss by reason of any error or omission in such abstract, copy or extract shall be entitled to be indemnified under this Act:

(5) Where the vendor is not himself registered as proprietor of the land or the charge giving a power of sale over the land, he shall, at the request of the purchaser and at his own expense, and notwithstanding any stipulation to the contrary, either procure the registration of himself as proprietor of the land or of the charge, as the case may be, or procure a disposition from the proprietor to the purchaser:

(6) Unless the certificate is deposited at the registry the vendor shall deliver the land certificate, or the charge certificate, as the case may be, to the purchaser on completion of the purchase, or, if only a part of the land comprised in the certificate is dealt with, or only a derivative estate is created, he shall, at his own expense, produce, or procure the production of, the certificate in accordance with this Act for the completion of the purchaser's registration. Where the certificate has been lost or destroyed, the vendor shall, notwithstanding any stipulation to the contrary, pay the costs of the proceedings required to enable the registrar to proceed without it:

(7) The purchaser shall not, by reason of the registration, be affected with notice of any pending action, writ, order, deed of arrangement or land charge (other than a local land charge) to which this subsection applies, which can be protected under this Act by lodging or registering a creditors' notice, restriction, inhibition, caution or other notice, or be concerned to make any search therefor if and so far as they affect registered land.

This subsection applies only to pending actions, writs, orders, deeds of arrangement and land charges (not including local land charges) required to be registered or re-registered after the commencement of this Act, either under the Land Charges Act 1925, or any other statute registration whereunder has effect as if made under that Act. **[601]**

NOTES
Sub-s (1): words omitted repealed by the Land Registration Act 1988, ss 1(2), 2, Schedule.

111. Infants, defectives and lunatics

(1) A purported disposition of any registered land or charge to an infant made after the commencement of this Act, or by the will of a proprietor dying after such commencement, shall not entitle the infant to be registered as proprietor of the registered land or charge until he attains full age, but in the meantime shall operate only as a declaration binding on the proprietor or personal representative that the registered land or charge is to be held on trust to give effect to minor interests in favour of the infant corresponding, as nearly as may be, with the interests which the disposition purports to transfer or create; and the disposition or a copy thereof or extract therefrom shall be deposited at the registry, and shall, unless and until the tenants for life, statutory owners, personal representatives or trustees for sale are registered as proprietors, be protected by means of a restriction or otherwise on the register:

Provided that—

(a) If the disposition is made to the infant jointly with another person of full age, that person shall, during the minority, be entitled to be registered as proprietor, and the infant shall not be registered until he attains full age;

(b) Where the registered land or charge is subject to any trusts or rights of redemption in favour of any person other than the infant, nothing in this section shall affect such trusts or rights of redemption;

(c) Where by reason of the minority or otherwise the land is settled land, the provisions of this Act relating to settled land shall apply thereto.

(2) Where an infant becomes entitled under a will or on an intestacy to any registered land or charge, the same shall not be transferred by the personal representative to the infant until he attains full age.

(3) Where an infant becomes entitled to the benefit of a registered charge, the charge shall during the minority be registered in the names of the personal representatives, trustees, or other persons who if the charge had affected unregistered land would have been able to dispose of the same, and they shall for the purposes of this Act have the same powers in reference thereto as the infant would have had if of full age.

(4) A caution may be lodged in the name or on behalf of an infant by his parent, trustee or guardian.

(5) Where a proprietor of any registered land or charge is [incapable, by reason of mental disorder within the meaning of [the Mental Health Act 1983], of managing and administering his property and affairs, his receiver or (if no receiver is acting for him) any person authorised in that behalf shall, under an order of the authority having jurisdiction under [Part VII of the Mental Health Act 1983], or] of the court, or under any statutory power, have and may exercise in the name and behalf of [the proprietor] all the powers which under this Act [the proprietor] could have exercised if free from disability, and a copy of every such order shall be filed with the registrar and may be referred to on the register.

(6) All the provisions of the Trustee Act 1925, and of [Part VII of the Mental Health Act 1983] and of any Act amending the same, shall apply to estates and charges registered under this Act, subject to the express provisions of this Act and to the rules made thereunder. **[602]**

NOTES
Sub-s (5): first (outer), fourth and fifth words in square brackets substituted by the Mental Health Act 1959, s 149(1), Sch 7, Part I; second and third words in square brackets substituted by the Mental Health Act 1983, s 148, Sch 4, para 6.
Sub-s (6): words in square brackets substituted by the Mental Health Act 1983, s 148, Sch 4, para 6.

[112. Inspection of register and other documents at land registry

(1) Any person may, subject to such conditions as may be prescribed and on payment of any fee payable, inspect and make copies of and extracts from—

(*a*) entries on the register, and
(*b*) documents referred to in the register which are in the custody of the registrar (other than leases or charges or copies of leases or charges).

(2) Documents in the custody of the registrar relating to any land or charge but not falling within subsection (1)(*b*) of this section may be inspected, and copies of and extracts from them may be made—

(*a*) as of right, in such cases as may be prescribed, and
(*b*) at the discretion of the registrar, in any other case,

but subject in all cases to such conditions as may be prescribed and on payment of any fee payable.

(3) References in this section to documents include references to things kept otherwise than in documentary form.] **[603]–[607]**

NOTES
Substituted for ss 112–112C by the Land Registration Act 1988, s 1(1).

113. Office copies to be evidence

Office copies of and extracts from the register and of and from documents . . . filed in the registry shall be admissible in evidence in all actions and matters, and between all persons or parties, to the same extent as the originals would be admissible, but any person suffering loss by reason of the inaccuracy of any such copy or extract shall be entitled to be indemnified under this Act, and no solicitor, trustee, personal representative, or other person in a fiduciary position shall be answerable in respect of any loss occasioned by relying on any such copy or extract. **[608]**

NOTES
Words omitted repealed by the Land Registration Act 1988, s 2, Schedule.

[113A. Inspections etc - supplementary

(1) Any duty under this Act to make a thing available for inspection is a duty to make it available for inspection in visible and legible form.

(2) Any reference in this Act to copies of and extracts from the register and of and from documents . . . filed in the registry includes a reference to reproductions of things which are kept by the registrar under this Act otherwise than in documentary form.] **[609]**

NOTES
Inserted by the Administration of Justice Act 1982, s 66(2).
Sub-s (2): words omitted repealed by the Land Registration Act 1988, s 2, Schedule.

114. Fraudulent dispositions how far to be void

Subject to the provisions in this Act contained with respect to indemnity and to registered dispositions for valuable consideration, any disposition of land or of a charge, which if unregistered would be fraudulent and void, shall, notwithstanding registration, be fraudulent and void in like manner. **[610]**

115. Penalty for suppression of deeds and evidence

If in the course of any proceedings before the registrar or the court in pursuance of this Act any person concerned in such proceedings as principal or agent, with intent to conceal the title or claim of any person, or to substantiate a false claim, suppresses, attempts to suppress, or is privy to the suppression of, any document or fact, the person so suppressing, attempting to suppress, or privy to suppression, shall be guilty of a misdemeanor. **[611]**

116. Penalty for certain fraudulent acts

(1) If any person fraudulently procures, attempts fraudulently to procure, or is privy to the fraudulent procurement of, any entry on, erasure from or alteration of the register, or any land or charge certificate, he shall be guilty of a misdemeanor.

(2) Any entry, erasure, or alteration so made by fraud, shall be void as between all persons who are parties or privy to the fraud. **[612]**

117. Punishment of misdemeanors

A person guilty of a misdemeanor under this Act shall—

    (*a*) on conviction on indictment, be liable to imprisonment for a term not exceeding two years, or to a fine . . .;

    (*b*) on summary conviction, be liable to imprisonment for a term not exceeding three months or to a fine not exceeding [the prescribed sum]. **[613]**

NOTES

    Para (*a*): words omitted repealed by virtue of the Criminal Law Act 1977, s 32.
    Para (*b*): words in square brackets substituted by virtue of the Magistrates' Courts Act 1980, s 32.

119. Civil remedies and discovery

(1) No proceeding or conviction for any act declared by this Act to be a misdemeanor affects any remedy to which any person aggrieved by such act may be entitled, either at law or in equity.

(2) Nothing in this Act entitles any person to refuse to make a complete discovery by answer in any legal proceeding, or to answer any question or interrogatory in any civil proceeding, in any court of law; but no answer to any such question or interrogatory shall be admissible in evidence against such person [or the husband or wife of such person] in any criminal proceeding under this Act. **[614]**

NOTES

    Sub-s (2): words in square brackets inserted by the Civil Evidence Act 1968, s 17(3), Schedule.

PART XI

COMPULSORY REGISTRATION

120. Power to make orders rendering registration compulsory in certain areas

(1) His Majesty may, by Order in Council, declare, as respects any county or part of a county mentioned or defined in the Order, that, on and after a day specified in the Order, registration of title to land is to be compulsory on sale:

Provided that nothing in this Act or in any such Order shall render compulsory the registration of the title to an incorporeal hereditament or to mines and minerals apart from the surface, or to corporeal hereditaments parcel of a manor and included in the sale of a manor as such.

(2)–(5) . . .

(6) Any Order made under this Part of this Act or under any corresponding provision in any enactment replaced by this Act may be revoked or varied by a subsequent Order.

(7) For the purposes of this Part of this Act, "county" means the administrative county . . .   **[615]**

NOTES
 Sub-ss (2), (3): repealed by the Land Registration Act 1966, ss 1(1), 2, Schedule.
 Sub-ss (4), (5): repealed by the Local Government Act 1972, ss 251, 272(1), Sch 29, para 26(2), Sch 30.
 Sub-s (7): words omitted repealed by the Local Government Act 1972, s 272(1), Sch 30.

123. Effect of Act in areas where registration is compulsory

(1) In any area in which an Order in Council declaring that registration of title to land within that area is to be compulsory on sale is for the time being in force, every conveyance on sale of freehold land and every grant of [a term of years absolute of more than twenty-one years from the date of delivery of the grant], and every assignment on sale of leasehold land held for a term of years absolute [having more than twenty-one years to run from the date of delivery of the assignment], shall (save as hereinafter provided), on the expiration of two months from the date thereof or of any authorised extension of that period, become void so far as regards the grant or conveyance of the legal estate in the freehold or leasehold land comprised in the conveyance, grant, or assignment, or so much of such land as is situated within the area affected, unless the grantee (that is to say, the person who is entitled to be registered as proprietor of the freehold or leasehold land) or his successor in title or assign has in the meantime applied to be registered as proprietor of such land:

Provided that the registrar, or the court on appeal from the registrar, may, on the application of any persons interested in any particular case in which the registrar or the court is satisfied that the application for first registration cannot be made within the said period, or can only be made within that period by incurring unreasonable expense, or that the application has not been made within the said period by reason of some accident or other sufficient cause, make an order extending the said period; and if such order be made, then, upon the registration of the grantee or his successor or assign, a note of the order shall be endorsed on the conveyance, grant or assignment:

In the case of land in an area where, at the date of the commencement of this Act, registration of title is already compulsory on sale, this subsection shall apply to every such conveyance, grant, or assignment, executed on or after that date.

(2) Rules under this Act may provide for applying the provisions thereof to dealings with the land which may take place between the date of such conveyance, grant, or assignment and the date of application to register as if such dealings had taken place after the date of first registration, and for registration to be effected as of the date of the application to register.

(3) In this section the expressions "conveyance on sale" and "assignment on sale" mean an instrument made on sale by virtue whereof there is conferred or completed or completed a title under which an application for registration as first proprietor of land may be made under this Act, and include a conveyance or assignment by way of exchange where money is paid for equality of exchange, but do not include an enfranchisement or extinguishment of manorial incidents, whether under the Law of Property Act 1922, or otherwise, or an assignment or surrender of a lease to the owner of the immediate reversion containing a declaration that the term is to merge in such reversion.   **[616]**

NOTES
Sub-s (1): words in square brackets substituted by the Land Registration Act 1986, s 2(1).

124. Compulsory provisions bind the Crown

This Part of this Act, as respects transactions completed after the commencement of this Act, binds the Crown.   **[617]–[618]**

PART XII

ADMINISTRATIVE AND JUDICIAL PROVISIONS

His Majesty's Land Registry

126. His Majesty's Land Registry

(1) There shall continue to be an office in London to be called His Majesty's Land Registry, the business of which shall be conducted by a registrar to be appointed by the Lord Chancellor and known as the Chief Land Registrar, with such officers (namely, registrars, assistant registrars, clerks, messengers, and servants), as the Lord Chancellor, with the concurrence of the Treasury as to number, may appoint.

(2) . . .

(3) The Chief Land Registrar, registrars, assistant registrars, clerks, messengers, and servants shall receive such salaries or remuneration as the Treasury may from time to time direct.

(4) The salaries of the Chief Land Registrar, registrars, assistant registrars, clerks, messengers, and servants, and such incidental expenses of carrying this Act into effect as may be sanctioned by the Treasury, shall continue to be paid out of money provided by Parliament.

(5) The Lord Chancellor may make regulations for the land registry, and for assigning the duties to the respective officers, and determining the acts of the registrar which may be done by a registrar or assistant registrar, and for altering or adding to the official styles of the Chief Land Registrar and other officers of the land registry. Subject to such regulations, anything authorised or

required by this Act to be done to or by the registrar shall be done to or by the Chief Land Registrar . . .

(6) The Lord Chancellor may also make regulations as to the conduct of business at the land registry during any vacancy in the office of Chief Land Registrar, and for distributing the duties amongst the respective officers, and for assigning to a registrar or assistant registrar all or any of the functions and authorities by this Act or any other Act assigned to or conferred on the registrar, and all acts done by a registrar or assistant registrar under any such regulations shall have the same effect in all respects as if they had been done by the Chief Land Registrar.

[(6A) The fact that the Chief Land Registrar and other officers of the Land Registry are not required to be legally qualified is not to be taken as preventing the making of regulations under this section which provide for certain acts to be done by an officer who is legally qualified.]

(7) There shall continue to be a seal of the land registry and any document purporting to be sealed with that seal shall be admissible in evidence.   **[619]**

NOTES
Sub-s (2): repealed by the Administration of Justice Act 1956, s 57(2), Sch 2.
Sub-s (5): words omitted repealed by the Statute Law (Repeals) Act 1986.
Sub-s (6A): inserted by the Courts and Legal Services Act 1990, s 125(2), Sch 17, para 2.

127. Conduct of business by registrar

Subject to the provisions of this Act, the Chief Land Registrar shall conduct the whole business of registration under this Act, and shall frame and cause to be printed and circulated or otherwise promulgated such forms and directions as he may deem requisite or expedient for facilitating proceedings under this Act.
[620]

128. Power for registrar to summon witnesses

(1) The Chief Land Registrar, or any officer of the land registry authorised by him in writing, may administer an oath or take a statutory declaration in pursuance of this Act in that behalf for any of the purposes of this Act, and the Chief Land Registrar may, by summons under the seal of the land registry, require the attendance of all such persons as he may think fit in relation to the registration of any title; he may also, by a like summons, require any person having the custody of any map, survey, or book made or kept in pursuance of any Act of Parliament to produce such map, survey, or book for his inspection; he may examine upon oath any person appearing before him and administer an oath accordingly; and he may allow to every person summoned by him the reasonable charges of his attendance:

Provided that no person shall be required to attend in obedience to any summons or to produce such documents as aforesaid unless the reasonable charges of his attendance and of the production of such documents be paid or tendered to him.

(2) Any charges allowed by the registrar in pursuance of this section shall be deemed to be charges incurred in or about proceedings for registration and may be dealt with accordingly.

(3) If any person, after the delivery to him of such summons as aforesaid, or of a copy thereof, and payment or tender of his resonable charges for attendance, wilfully neglects or refuses to attend in pursuance of such summons, or to

produce such maps, surveys, books, or other documents as he may be required to produce under the provisions of this Act, or to answer upon oath or otherwise such questions as may be lawfully put to him by the registrar under the powers of this Act, he shall be liable on summary conviction to a fine not exceeding [level 2 on the standard scale].   **[621]**

NOTES

Sub-s (3): maximum fine increased by the Criminal Law Act 1977, s 31(6), and converted to a level on the standard scale by the Criminal Justice Act 1982, ss 37, 46.

129. Interchange of information between Land Registry and other Department

The Commissioners of Inland Revenue and other Government Departments, and local authorities, may furnish to the registrar on his request such particulars and information in regard to land and charges, and the registrar may in like manner furnish to the Commissioners of Inland Revenue, other Government Departments, and local authorities on their request such particulars and information as they are respectively by law entitled to require owners of property to furnish to them direct.   **[622]**

130. Statutory acknowledgements on return of documents

When any document is delivered or returned by the registrar to any person he may, at the cost of the registry, require such person to give a statutory acknowledgement of the right of the registrar and his successors in office to production of such document and to delivery of copies thereof, and may endorse notice of such right on the document, and the acknowledgement shall not be liable to stamp duty.   **[623]**

131. Indemnity to officers of registry

The Chief Land Registrar shall not, nor shall a registrar or assistant registrar nor any person acting under the authority of the Chief Land Registrar or a registrar or assistant registrar, or under any order or general rule made in pursuance of this Act, be liable to any action or proceeding for or in respect of any act or matter done or omitted to be done in good faith in the exercise or supposed exercise of the powers of this Act, or any order or general rule made in pursuance of this Act.   **[624]**

District Registries

132. Power to form district registries by general orders

(1) The Lord Chancellor, with the concurrence of the Treasury, shall have power by general orders from time to time to do all or any of the following things:—

    (*a*) To create district registries for the purposes of registration of titles to land within the defined districts respectively, and to alter any districts which may have been so created:

    (*b*) To fix, by notice to be published in the Gazette, the time for the commencement of registration at a district registry so created of titles to land within a district so defined:

    (*c*) To direct registration of land to be commenced in any one or more district or districts pursuant to any such notice:

    (*d*) To appoint district registrars, assistant district registrars, clerks, messengers, and servants to perform the business of registration in any district which may from time to time be created a district for registration under this Act:

(e) To provide for the mode in which district registrars are to be remunerated:

(f) To modify the provisions of this Act with respect to the formation and constitution of district registries, except the provision relating to the qualifications of district registrars, and assistant district registrars.

(2) A person shall not be qualified to be appointed district registrar under this Act unless he [has a 10 year general qualification, within the meaning of section 71 of the Courts and Legal Services Act 1990], and a person shall not be qualified to be appointed an assistant district registrar under this Act unless he [has a 5 year general qualification, within the meaning of that section].

(3) A district registrar or assistant district registrar may, with the assent of the Lord Chancellor, follow another calling.

(4) A seal shall be prepared for each district registry and any instrument purporting to be sealed with such seal shall be admissible in evidence.   **[625]**

NOTES
    Sub-s (2): words in square brackets substituted by the Courts and Legal Services Act 1990, s 71(2), Sch 10, para 3.

133. Powers of district registrar, and appeals from him

Subject to general rules each district registrar, and assistant district registrar shall, as regards the land within his jurisdiction, have the same powers and indemnity as are herein given to the registrars and assistant registrars in the land registry, and there shall be the same right to appeal as in the case of the registrar; an order of a district registrar may be enforced and any breach thereof punished in like manner as if the order had been made by the Chief Land Registrar:

Provided that the Lord Chancellor may, by general rules, make provision—

(a) for the duties of a district registrar as regards all or any of the proceedings preliminary to first registration, or as regards any matters which the district registrar has to determine, or any other matters being performed by the Chief Land Registrar or a registrar or assistant registrar in the land registry; and

(b) for any district registrar obtaining directions from or acting with the sanction of the Chief Land Registrar or a registrar or assistant registrar.   **[626]**

134. Application of general orders, etc, to districts

The general orders, rules, forms, directions, and fees for the time being applying to and payable in the land registry shall also apply to and be payable in all the district registries, subject to any alteration or addition for the time being made for any district by the Lord Chancellor with the advice and assistance of the Rule Committee, and, so far as they relate to fees, with the concurrence of the Treasury.   **[627]–[629]**

Provisions as to the Land Registry Act 1862

137. Provisions as to the Land Registry Act 1862

(1) No application for the registration of an estate under the Land Registry Act of 1862 shall be entertained.

(2) The Lord Chancellor may, by order, provide for the registration under this Act, without cost to the parties interested, of all titles registered under the Land Registry Act 1862, and care shall be taken in such order to protect any rights acquired in pursuance of registration under such last-mentioned Act, . . . and until such estate is registered under this Act, the Act of 1862 shall apply thereto in the same manner as if this Act had not been passed.

(3) The officers of the land registry shall for all the purposes of the Land Registry Act 1862, so far as it remains in operation, and for all the purposes of the Improvement of Land Act 1864 . . . be deemed to be officers acting under the Land Registry Act 1862, and having to discharge the duties belonging to officers acting under those Acts as occasion may require. **[630]**

NOTES

Sub-s (2): words omitted repealed by the Statute Law (Repeals) Act 1986.

Sub-s (3): words omitted repealed by the Administration of Justice Act 1965, s 34(1), Sch 2.

Description and Powers of the Court

[138. Jurisdiction of High Court and county courts

(1) Any jurisdiction conferred on the High Court by this Act or by the Land Registration and Land Charges Act 1971 may also be exercised, to such extent as may be prescribed, by county courts.

(2) Subject to the enactments relating to the Supreme Court of Judicature for the time being in force, all matters within the jurisdiction of the High Court under this Act or the said Act of 1971 shall be assigned to the Chancery Division of that court.

(3) Where the county court has jurisdiction under this Act or that Act it shall have all the powers of the High Court for the purposes of that jurisdiction.

(4) The Lord Chancellor may assign any duties of the High Court under this Act or that Act to any particular judge or judges of the High Court.] **[631]**

NOTES

Substituted by the Administration of Justice Act 1982, s 67, Sch 5.

139. Powers of court in action for specific performance

(1) Where an action is instituted for the specific performance of a contract relating to registered land, or a registered charge, the court having cognizance of the action may, by summons, or by such other mode as it deems expedient, cause all or any parties who have registered interests or rights in the registered land or charge, or have entered up notices, cautions, restrictions, or inhibitions against the same to appear in such action, and show cause why such contract should not be specifically performed, and the court may direct that any order made by the court in the action shall be binding on such parties or any of them.

(2) All costs incurred by any parties so appearing in an action to enforce against a vendor specific performance of his contract to sell any registered land or charge shall be taxed as between solicitor and client, and, unless the court otherwise orders, be paid by the vendor. **[632]**

140. Power of registrar to state case for the court

(1) Whenever, upon the examination of the title to any interest in land, the registrar entertains a doubt as to any matter of law or fact arising upon such title, he may (whether or not the matter has been referred to a conveyancing counsel in the prescribed manner), upon the application of any party interested in such land—

> (a) refer a case for the opinion of the High Court and the court may direct an issue to be tried before a jury for the purpose of determining any fact;
> (b) name the parties to such case;
> (c) give directions as to the manner in which proceedings in relation thereto are to be brought before the court.

(2) The opinion of any court to whom any case is referred by the registrar shall be conclusive on all the parties to the case, unless the court permits an appeal.   **[633]**

141. Intervention of court in case of persons under disability

Where a person under disability, or person outside the jurisdiction of the High Court, or person yet unborn, is interested in the land in respect of the title to which any question arises as aforesaid, any other person interested in such land may apply to the court for a direction that the opinion of the court shall be conclusively binding on the person under disability, person outside the jurisdiction, or unborn person.   **[634]**

142. Power for court to bind interests of persons under disability

(1) The Court shall hear the allegations of all parties appearing.

(2) The court may disapprove altogether or may approve, either with or without modification, of the directions of the registrar respecting any case referred to the court.

(3) The court may, if necessary, appoint a guardian, next friend or other person to appear on behalf of any person under disability, person outside the jurisdiction, or unborn person.

(4) If the court is satisfied that the interest of any person under disability, outside the jurisdiction, or unborn, will be sufficiently represented in any case, it shall make an order declaring that all persons, with the exceptions, if any, named in the order, are to be conclusively bound, and thereupon all persons with such exceptions, if any, as aforesaid, shall be conclusively bound by any decision of the court in which any such person is concerned.   **[635]**

143. Appeals

(1) Any person aggrieved by any order of a judge of a county court may, within the prescribed time and in the prescribed manner, appeal to the High Court.

(2) The court on hearing such appeal may give judgment affirming, reversing, or modifying the order appealed from, and may finally decide thereon, and make such order as to costs in the court below and of the appeal as may be agreeable to justice; and if the court alter or modify the order, the order so altered or modified shall be of like effect as if it were the order of the county court.

The High Court may also, in cases where the court thinks it expedient so to do, instead of making a final order, remit the case, with such directions as the court may think fit, to the court below.

(3) Any person aggrieved by an order made under this Act by the High Court otherwise than on appeal from a county court, . . . may appeal within the prescribed time in the same manner and with the same incidents in and with which orders made by the High Court . . . in cases within the ordinary jurisdiction of such court may be appealed from.   [636]

NOTES
Sub-s (3): words omitted repealed by the Courts Act 1971, s 56(4), Sch 11, Part II.

PART XIII
RULES, FEE ORDERS, REGULATIONS, SHORT TITLE, COMMENCEMENT
AND EXTENT

144. Power to make general rules

(1) Subject to the provisions of this Act, the Lord Chancellor may, with the advice and assistance of a judge of the Chancery Division of the High Court [nominated by the Lord Chancellor], the Chief Land Registrar, and three other persons, one to be chosen by the General Council of the Bar, one by [the Minister of Agriculture, Fisheries and Food], and one by the Council of the Law Society (which body of persons are in this Act referred to as the Rule Committee), make general rules for all or any of the following purposes:—

(i) For regulating the mode in which the register is to be made and kept;

(ii) For prescribing the forms to be observed, the precautions to be taken, the instruments to be used, the notices to be given, and the evidence to be adduced in all proceedings before the registrar or in connexion with registration, and in particular with respect to the reference to a conveyancing counsel of any title to land proposed to be registered with an absolute title;

(iii) For regulating the procedure on application for first registration, provided that the applicant or his solicitor shall not be bound to make any declaration where a documentary title is shown which would operate as a guarantee in regard to matters not disclosed by the abstract;

(iv) For enabling registration with a possessory title to be provisionally effected pending the investigation of the title;

(v) For regulating the custody of any documents from time to time coming into the hands of the registrar, with power to direct the destruction of any such documents where they have become altogether superseded by entries in the register, or have ceased to have any effect;

(vi) For the taxation of costs charged by solicitors . . . in or incidental to or consequential on the registration of an estate in land or any other matter required to be done for the purpose of carrying this Act into execution, and for determining the persons by whom such costs are to be paid;

(vii) For carrying out the provisions of this Act with respect to compulsory registration;

    (viii) For adapting to sub-mortgages and to incumbrances prior to registration the provisions of this Act with regard to charges;

    (ix) For the conduct of official searches . . .;

    (x) For enabling cautions to be entered against the registration of possessory and qualified titles as qualified, good leasehold, or absolute and against the registration of good leasehold title as absolute;

    (xi) For enabling a mortgagee by deposit to give notice to the registrar by registered letter or otherwise of the deposit or intended deposit with him of the land certificate, or charge certificate: Provided that the fee for the entry of any such notice shall not exceed [5p];

    (xii) For allowing the insertion in the register, and in land certificates, of the price paid or value declared on first registrations, transfers, and transmissions of land;

    (xiii) For making such adaptations as changes in the general law (including charges effected by the Law of Property Act 1922, or any Acts of the present session of Parliament amending or re-enacting any provisions of that Act) may render expedient, with a view to the practice under this Act being from time to time adapted, so far as expedient, the practice in force in regard to unregistered land;

    (xiv) For enabling the registrar, without further investigation, to accept a title as absolute or good leasehold, in proper cases, on the faith of certificates given by counsel or solicitors or both;

    (xv) For clearing the registered title on suitable occasions, and for enabling the registrar to permit any person interested to inspect entries on the register which have been cancelled, whether or not the title has been closed;

    (xvi) For giving notice on land certificates of the general effect of registration;

    (xvii) For the registration, by way of notice, on the first registration of the land, of any easement, right, or privilege, created by an instrument and operating at law which appears to affect adversely the land, and so far as practicable by reference to the instrument creating the same;

    (xviii) For enabling any person who acquires any such easement, right, or privilege, after the date of first registration of the land, to require (subject to notice being given to the owner of the servient land) entry to be made in the register of notice of the same, and so far as practicable by reference to the instrument creating the right;

    (xix) For enabling the first or any subsequent proprietor to require that notice of his title to any such right or interest, whether acquired under an instrument or by prescription or otherwise, being appurtenant or appendant to the registered land, be entered on the register, and, so far as practicable, by reference to the instrument (if any) creating the right or interest, and for prescribing the effect of any such entry;

    (xx) For providing for the registration of the title to an annuity or a rentcharge in possession (either perpetual or for a term of years absolute), or to mines and minerals when held separately from the surface, and as to notices to be entered on any exception of mines and minerals; and for preventing the registration of the benefit of any easement, right, privilege, or restrictive covenant, otherwise than as belonging to registered land;

(xxi) For regulating the issue and forms of certificates, and, if deemed desirable, for prescribing any special notification on the certificate to be given by way of warning when incumbrances, notices, and other adverse entries appear on the register;

(xxii) For providing for the cases in which the registrar may grant a certificate that an intended disposition is authorised and will be registered if presented;

(xxiii) For prescribing the effect of priority notices . . .;

(xxiv) For enabling a proprietor of any registered land or charge to register not more than three addresses (including, if he thinks fit, the address of his solicitor or firm of solicitors) to which notices are to be sent;

(xxv) For providing any special precautions to be taken against forgery when the land certificate is not in the possession of the proprietor of the registered land;

(xxvi) For prescribing any matter by this Act directed or authorised to be prescribed and for effecting anything with respect to which rules are by this Act authorised or required to be made;

(xxvii) For adapting the provisions of this Act relating to transfers of registered land to other dispositions authorised to be made by a proprietor;

(xxviii) For prescribing—

(a) the procedure to be adopted when land is or becomes subject to any charitable, ecclesiastical or public trusts,

(b) any consents to be given before a title to such land is registered,

(c) the duties, if any, to be performed by the managing trustees or committee, and

(d) the restrictions, if any, to be entered on the register in regard to such land;

(xxix) For enabling entries to be made in the register on the surrender, extinguishment or discharge of any subsisting interest without previously registering the title to the interest which is merged or extinguished;

(xxx) For enabling such alterations to be made in the register as may be consequential on the conversion of perpetually renewable leases into long terms by the Law of Property Act 1922, as amended;

(xxxi) For regulating any matter to be prescribed or in respect of which rules are to or may be made under this Act and any other matter or thing, whether similar or not to those above mentioned, in respect of which it may be expedient to make rules for the purpose of carrying this Act into execution.

(2) Any rules made in pursuance of this section shall be of the same force as if enacted in this Act.

(3) Any rules made in pursuance of this section shall be laid before both Houses of Parliament within three weeks after they are made, if Parliament be then sitting, and if Parliament be not then sitting, within three weeks after the beginning of the then next session of Parliament.   **[637]**

NOTES

Sub-s (1): first words in square brackets substituted by the Administration of Justice Act 1982, s 67, Sch 5; second words in square brackets substituted by virtue of the Transfer of Functions (Ministry of Food) Order 1955, SI 1955 No 554; words omitted from para (vi) repealed by the

Solicitors, Public Notaries, etc, Act 1949, s 1, Sch 2; in para (ix) words omitted repealed by the Land Registration Act 1988, ss 1(2), 2, Schedule; in para (xi) sum in square brackets substituted by virtue of the Decimal Currency Act 1969, s 10(1); in para (xxiii) words omitted repealed by the Land Registration Act 1986, s 5(5)(c).

145. Power to make Fee Orders and principles on which fees determined

(1) The Lord Chancellor may, with the advice and assistance of the Rule Committee and with the concurrence of the Treasury, make orders with respect to the amount of fees payable under this Act, regard being had to the following matters:—

    (a) In the case of the registration of an estate in land or of any transfer of an estate in land on the occasion of a sale, to the value of the estate as determined by the amount of purchase money; and

    (b) In the case of the registration of an estate in land, or of any transfer of an estate in land not upon a sale, to the value of the estate, to be ascertained in such manner as may be prescribed; and

    (c) In the case of registration of a charge or of any transfer of a charge, to the amount of such charge.

(2) Where the personal representatives of a deceased person are registered as proprietors of the registered land on his death, a fee shall not be chargeable for registering any disposition of the land by them unless the disposition is for valuable consideration.

(3) Specially reduced fees may be authorised to be charged on the registration of title to land wholly acquired for the purpose of being used as a street, or for street widening or improvements, or when acquired by a Government Department, a local authority, or other statutory body for permanent objects not involving a resale or other disposition.

(4) . . .

(5) The Lord Chancellor may, with the consent of the Treasury, by order, from time to time provide for the manner in which the money advanced for the acquisition of the site and the erection of new offices at the registry (so far as not already provided for by the existing sinking fund) shall be repaid, secured, or otherwise provided for; and also for the manner in which accounts of receipts and expenditure as between the several departments of the land registry are to be kept.   **[638]**

NOTES

    Sub-s (4): repealed by the Land Registration Act 1936, ss 7, 9 Schedule.

147. Repeals, savings and construction

(1) . . . without prejudice to the provisions of section thirty-eight of the Interpretation Act 1889:—

    (a) Nothing in this repeal shall, as otherwise expressly provided in this Act, affect any transfer of any interest in land or entry in the register made before the commencement of this Act, or any title or right acquired or appointment made before the commencement of this Act:

    (b) Nothing in this repeal shall affect any rules, regulations, orders, or other instruments made under any enactment so repealed, but all such rules, regulations, orders, and instruments shall, until superseded, continue in force as if made under the corresponding provision of this Act:

(c) Nothing in this repeal shall affect the tenure of office or salary or right to pension or superannuation allowance of any officer appointed before the commencement of this Act:

(d) References in any document to any enactment repealed by this Act shall be construed as references to the corresponding provisions of this Act.

(2) References to registration under the Land Charges Act 1925, apply to any registration made under any other statute which is by the Land Charges Act 1925, to have effect as if the registration had been made under that Act.

[639]

NOTES

Sub-s (1): words omitted repealed by the Statute Law Revision Act 1950.

148. Short title, commencement and extent

(1) This Act may be cited as the Land Registration Act 1925.

(2) This Act shall come into operation on the first day of January nineteen hundred and twenty-six, but shall be deemed to come into operation immediately after the Law of Property Act 1925, the Settled Land Act 1925, the Land Charges Act 1925, the Trustee Act 1925, and the Administration of Estates Act 1925, come into operation.

(3) This Act extends to England and Wales only.   **[640]**

ADMINISTRATION OF ESTATES ACT 1925
(c 23)

ARRANGEMENT OF SECTIONS

PART I
DEVOLUTION OF REAL ESTATE

PART II
EXECUTORS AND ADMINISTRATORS

General Provisions

An Act to consolidate Enactments relating to the Administration of the Estates of Deceased Persons   **[9 April 1925]**

PART I

DEVOLUTION OF REAL ESTATE

1. Devolution of real estate on personal representative

(1) Real estate to which a deceased person was entitled for an interest not ceasing on his death shall on his death, and notwithstanding any testamentary disposition thereof, devolve from time to time on the personal representative of the deceased, in like manner as before the commencement of this Act chattels real devolved on the personal representative from time to time of a deceased person.

(2) The personal representatives for the time being of a deceased person are deemed in law his heirs and assigns within the meaning of all trusts and powers.

(3) The personal representatives shall be the representative of the deceased in regard to his real estate to which he was entitled for an interest not ceasing on his death as well as in regard to his personal estate. **[641]**

2. Application to real estate of law affecting chattels real

(1) Subject to the provisions of this Act, all enactments and rules of law, and all jurisdiction of any court with respect to the appointment of administrators or to probate or letters of administration, or to dealings before probate in the case of chattels real, and with respect to costs and other matters in the administration of personal estate, in force before the commencement of this Act, and all powers, duties, rights, equities, obligations, and liabilities of a personal representative in force at the commencement of this Act with respect to chattels real, shall apply and attach to the personal representative and shall have effect with respect to real estate vested in him, and in particular all such powers of disposition and dealing as were before the commencement of this Act exercisable as respects chattels real by the survivor or survivors of two or more personal representatives, as well as by a single personal representative, or by all the personal representatives together, shall be exercisable by the personal representatives or representative of the deceased with respect to his real estate.

(2) Where as respects real estate there are two or more personal representatives, a conveyance of real estate devolving under this Part of this Act shall not, save as otherwise provided as respects trust estates including settled land, be made without the concurrence therein of all such representatives or an order of the court, but where probate is granted to one or some of two or more persons named as executors, whether or not power is reserved to the other or others to prove, any conveyance of the real estate may be made by the proving executor or executors for the time being, without an order of the court, and shall be as effectual as if all the persons named as executors had concurred therein.

(3) Without prejudice to the rights and powers of a personal representative, the appointment of a personal representative in regard to real estate shall not, save as hereinafter provided, affect—

    (*a*) any rule as to marshalling or as to administration of assets;
    (*b*) the beneficial interest in real estate under any testamentary disposition;
    (*c*) any mode of dealing with any beneficial interest in real estate, or the proceeds of sale thereof;

(*d*) the right of any person claiming to be interested in the real estate to take proceedings for the protection or recovery thereof against any person other than the personal representative.   **[642]**

3. Interpretation of Part I

(1) In this Part of this Act "real estate" includes—

(i) Chattels real, and land in possession, remainder, or reversion, and every interest in or over land to which a deceased person was entitled at the time of his death; and

(ii) Real estate held on trust (including settled land) or by way of mortgage or security, but not money to arise under a trust for sale of land, nor money secured or charged on land.

(2) A testator shall be deemed to have been entitled at his death to any interest in real estate passing under any gift contained in his will which operates as an appointment under a general power to appoint by will, or operates under the testamentary power conferred by statute to dispose of an entailed interest.

(3) An entailed interest of a deceased person shall (unless disposed of under the testamentary power conferred by statute) be deemed an interest ceasing on his death, but any further or other interest of the deceased in the same property in remainder or reversion which is capable of being disposed of by his will shall not be deemed to be an interest so ceasing.

(4) The interest of a deceased person under a joint tenancy where another tenant survives the deceased is an interest ceasing on his death.

(5) On the death of a corporator sole his interest in the corporation's real and personal estate shall be deemed to be an interest ceasing on his death and shall devolve to his successor.

This subsection applies on the demise of the Crown as respects all property, real and personal, vested in the Crown as a corporation sole.   **[643]**

PART II

EXECUTORS AND ADMINISTRATORS

General Provisions

5. Cesser of right of executor to prove

Where a person appointed executor by a will—

(i) survives the testator but dies without having taken out probate of the will; or

(ii) is cited to take out probate of the will and does not appear to the citation; or

(iii) renounces probate of the will;

his rights in respect of the executorship shall wholly cease, and the representation to the testator and the administration of his real and personal estate shall devolve and be committed in like manner as if that person had not been appointed executor.   **[644]**

6. Withdrawal of renunciation

(1) Where an executor who has renounced probate has been permitted, whether before or after the commencement of this Act, to withdraw the renunciation

and prove the will, the probate shall take effect and be deemed always to have taken effect without prejudice to the previous acts and dealings of and notices to any other personal representative who has previously proved the will or taken out letters of administration, and a memorandum of the subsequent probate shall be endorsed on the original probate or letters of administration.

(2) This section applies whether the testator died before or after the commencement of this Act.   **[645]**

7. Executor of executor represents original testator

(1) An executor of a sole or last surviving executor of a testator is the executor of that testator.

This provision shall not apply to an executor who does not prove the will of his testator, and, in the case of an executor who on his death leaves surviving him some other executor of his testator who afterwards proves the will of that testator, it shall cease to apply on such probate being granted.

(2) So long as the chain of such representation is unbroken, the last executor in the chain is the executor of every preceding testator.

(3) The chain of such representation is broken by—
    (*a*) an intestacy; or
    (*b*) the failure of a testator to appoint an executor; or
    (*c*) the failure to obtain probate of a will;
but is not broken by a temporary grant of administration if probate is subsequently granted.

(4) Every person in the chain of representation to a testator—
    (*a*) has the same rights in respect of the real and personal estate of that testator as the original executor would have had if living; and
    (*b*) is, to the extent to which the estate whether real or personal of that testator has come to his hands, answerable as if he were an original executor.   **[646]**

8. Right of proving executors to exercise powers

(1) Where probate is granted to one or some of two or more persons named as executors, whether or not power is reserved to the others or other to prove, all the powers which are by law conferred on the personal representative may be exercised by the proving executor or executors for the time being and shall be as effectual as if all the persons named as executors had concurred therein.

(2) This section applies whether the testator died before or after the commencement of this Act.   **[647]**

9. Vesting of estate of intestate between death and grant of administration

Where a person dies intestate, his real and personal estate, until administration is granted in respect thereof, shall vest in the Probate Judge in the same manner and to the same extent as formerly in the case of personal estate it vested in the ordinary.   **[648]**

15. Executor not to act while administration is in force

Where administration has been granted in respect of any real or personal estate of a deceased person, no person shall have power to bring any action or otherwise act as executor of the deceased person in respect of the estate comprised in or affected by the grant until the grant has been recalled or revoked.   **[649]**

17. Continuance of legal proceedings after revocation of temporary administration

[(1)] If, while any legal proceeding is pending in any court by or against an administrator to whom a temporary administration has been granted, that administration is revoked, that court may order that the proceeding be continued by or against the new personal representative in like manner as if the same had been originally commenced by or against him, but subject to such conditions and variations, if any, as that court directs.

[(2) The county court has jurisdiction under this section where the proceedings are pending in that court.]   **[650]**

NOTES
   Sub-s (1): numbered as such by the County Courts Act 1984, s 148(1), Sch 2, para 11.
   Sub-s (2): added by the County Courts Act 1984, s 148(1), Sch 2, para 11.

21. Rights and liabilities of administrator

Every person to whom administration of the real and personal estate of a deceased person is granted, shall, subject to the limitations contained in the grant, have the same rights and liabilities and be accountable in like manner as if he were the executor of the deceased.   **[651]**

[21A. A Debtor who becomes creditor's executor by representation or administrator to account for debt to estate

(1) Subject to subsection (2) of this section, where a debtor becomes his deceased creditor's executor by representation or administrator—

   (*a*) his debt shall thereupon be extinguished; but
   (*b*) he shall be accountable for the amount of the debt as part of the creditor's estate in any case where he would be so accountable if he had been appointed as an executor by the creditor's will.

(2) Subsection (1) of this section does not apply where the debtor's authority to act as executor or administrator is limited to part only of the creditor's estate which does not include the debt; and a debtor whose debt is extinguished by virtue of paragraph (*a*) shall not be accountable for its amount by virtue of paragraph (*b*) of that subsection in any case where the debt was barred by the Limitation Act 1939 before he became the creditor's executor or administrator.

(3) In this section "debt" includes any liability, and "debtor" and "creditor" shall be construed accordingly.]   **[652]**

NOTES
   Inserted by the Limitation Amendment Act 1980, s 10.

Special Provisions as to Settled Land

22. Special executors as respects settled land

(1) A testator may appoint, and in default of such express appointment shall be deemed to have appointed, as his special executors in regard to settled land, the

persons, if any, who are at his death the trustees of the settlement thereof, and probate may be granted to such trustees specially limited to the settled land.

In this subsection "settled land" means land vested in the testator which was settled previously to his death and not by his will.

(2) A testator may appoint other persons either with or without such trustees as aforesaid or any of them to be his general executors in regard to his other property and assets.   **[653]**

23. Provisions where, as respects settled land, representation is not granted to the trustees of the settlement

(1) Where settled land becomes vested in a personal representative, not being a trustee of the settlement, upon trust to convey the land to or assent to the vesting thereof in the tenant for life or statutory owner in order to give effect to a settlement created before the death of the deceased and not by his will, or would on the grant of representation to him, have become so vested, such representative may—

   (a) before representation has been granted, renounce his office in regard only to such settled land without renouncing it in regard to other property;
   (b) after representation has been granted, apply to the court for revocation of the grant in regard to the settled land without applying in regard to other property.

(2) Whether such renunciation or revocation is made or not, the trustees of the settlement, or any person beneficially interested thereunder, may apply to the High Court for an order appointing a special or additional personal representative in respect of the settled land, and a special or additional personal representative, if and when appointed under the order, shall be in the same position as if representation had originally been granted to him alone in place of the original personal representative, if any, or to him jointly with the original personal representative, as the case may be, limited to the settled land, but without prejudice to the previous acts and dealings, if any, of the personal representative originally constituted or the effect of notices given to such personal representative.

(3) The court may make such order as aforesaid subject to such security, if any, being given by or on behalf of the special or additional personal representative, as the court may direct, and shall, unless the court considers that special considerations apply, appoint such persons as may be necessary to secure that the persons to act as representatives in respect of the settled land shall, if willing to act, be the same persons as are the trustees of the settlement, and an office copy of the order when made shall be furnished to the [principal registry of the Family Division of the High Court] for entry, and a memorandum of the order shall be endorsed on the probate or administration.

(4) The person applying for the appointment of a special or additional personal representative shall give notice of the application to the [principal registry of the Family Division of the High Court] in the manner prescribed.

(5) Rules of court may be made for prescribing for all matters required for giving effect to the provisions of this section, and in particular—

   (a) for notice of any application being given to the proper officer;
   (b) for production of orders, probates, and administration to the registry;

(c) for the endorsement on a probate or administration of a memorandum of an order, subject or not to any exceptions;

(d) for the manner in which the costs are to be borne;

(e) for protecting purchasers and trustees and other persons in a fiduciary position, dealing in good faith with or giving notices to a personal representative before notice of any order has been endorsed on the probate or administration or a pending action has been registered in respect of the proceedings. **[654]**

NOTES

Sub-s (3): words in square brackets substituted by the Administration of Justice Act 1970, s 1(6), Sch 2, para 3.

Sub-s (4): words in square brackets substituted by the Administration of Justice Act 1970, s 1(6), Sch 2, para 3.

24. Power for special personal representatives to dispose of settled land

(1) The special personal representatives may dispose of the settled land without the concurrence of the general personal representatives, who may likewise dispose of the other property and assets of the deceased without the concurrence of the special personal representatives.

(2) In this section the expression "special personal representatives" means the representatives appointed to act for the purposes of settled land and includes any original personal representative who is to act with an additional personal representative for those purposes. **[655]**

Duties, Rights and Obligations

[25. Duty of personal representatives

The personal representative of a deceased person shall be under a duty to—

(a) collect and get in the real and personal estate of the deceased and administer it according to law;

(b) when required to do so by the court, exhibit on oath in the court a full inventory of the estate and when so required render an account of the administration of the estate to the court;

(c) when required to do so by the High Court, deliver up the grant of probate or administration to that court.] **[656]**

NOTES

Substituted by the Administration of Estates Act 1971, s 9

26. Rights of action by and against personal representative

(1), (2) . . .

(3) A personal representative may distrain for arrears of a rentcharge due or accruing to the deceased in his lifetime on the land affected or charged therewith, so long as the land remains in the possession of the person liable to pay the rentcharge or of the persons deriving title under him, and in like manner as the deceased might have done had he been living.

(4) A personal representative may distrain upon land for arrears of rent due or accruing to the deceased in like manner as the deceased might have done had he been living.

Such arrears may be distrained for after the termination of the lease or tenancy as if the term or interest had not determined, if the distress is made—

(a) within six months after the termination of the lease or tenancy;

(b) during the continuance of the possession of the lessee or tenant from whom the arrears were due.

The statutory enactments relating to distress for rent apply to any distress made pursuant to this subsection,

(5), (6) . . .   **[657]**

NOTES

Sub-ss (1), (2), (5), (6): repealed by the Law Reform (Miscellaneous Provisions) Act 1934, s 1(7).

27. Protection of persons on probate or administration

(1) Every person making or permitting to be made any payment or disposition in good faith under a representation shall be indemnified and protected in so doing, notwithstanding any defect or circumstance whatsoever affecting the validity of the representation.

(2) Where a representation is revoked, all payments and dispositions made in good faith to a personal representative under the representation before the revocation thereof are a valid discharge to the person making the same; and the personal representative who acted under the revoked representation may retain and reimburse himself in respect of any payments or dispositions made by him which the person to whom representation is afterwards granted might have properly made.   **[658]**

28. Liability of person fraudulently obtaining or retaining estate of deceased

If any person, to the defrauding of creditors or without full valuable consideration, obtains, receives or holds any real or personal estate of a deceased person or effects the release of any debt or liability due to the estate of the deceased, he shall be charged as executor in his own wrong to the extent of the real and personal estate received or coming to his hands, or the debt or liability released, after deducting—

(a) any debt for valuable consideration and without fraud due to him from the deceased person at the time of his death; and

(b) any payment made by him which might properly be made by a personal representative.   **[659]**

29. Liability of estate of personal representative

Where a person as personal representative of a deceased person (including an executor in his own wrong) wastes or converts to his own use any part of the real or personal estate of the deceased, and dies, his personal representative shall to the extent of the available assets of the defaulter be liable and chargeable in respect of such waste or conversion in the same manner as the defaulter would have been if living.   **[660]**

30. Provisions applicable where administration granted to nominee of the Crown

(1) Where the administration of the real and personal estate of any deceased person is granted to a nominee of the Crown (whether the Treasury Solicitor, or a person nominated by the Treasury Solicitor, or any other person), any legal proceeding by or against that nominee for the recovery of the real or personal estate, or any part or share thereof, shall be of the same character, and be instituted and carried on in the same manner, and be subject to the same rules of law and equity (including, except as otherwise provided by this Act, the rules

of limitation under the statutes of limitation or otherwise), in all respects as if the administration had been granted to such nominee as one of the persons interested under this Act in the estate of the deceased.

(2) An information or other proceeding on the part of His Majesty shall not be filed or instituted, and a petition of right shall not be presented, in respect of the real or personal estate of any deceased person or any part or share thereof, or any claim thereon, except ... subject to the same rules of law and equity within and subject to which a proceeding for the like purposes might be instituted by or against a subject.

(3) The Treasury Solicitor shall not be required, when applying for or obtaining administration of the estate of a deceased person for the use or benefit of His Majesty, to deliver, nor shall ... the High Court or the Commissioners of Inland Revenue be entitled to receive in connexion with any such application or grant of administration, any affidavit, statutory declaration, account, certificate, or other statement verified on oath; but the Treasury Solicitor shall deliver and the said Division and Commissioners respectively shall accept, in lieu thereof, an account or particulars of the estate of the deceased signed by or on behalf of the Treasury Solicitor.

(4) References in sections two, four ... and seven of the Treasury Solicitor Act, 1876, and in subsection (3) of section three of the Duchy of Lancaster Act, 1920, to "personal estate" shall include real estate.   **[661]**

NOTES
  Sub-s (2): words omitted repealed by the Limitation Act 1939, s 34(4), Schedule.
  Sub-s (3): words omitted repealed by the Administration of Justice Act 1970, s 54, Sch 11.
  Sub-s (4): words omitted repealed by the Statute Law (Repeals) Act 1981.

31. Power to make rules

Provision may be made by rules of court for giving effect to the provisions of this Part of this Act so far as relates to real estate and in particular for adapting the procedure and practice on the grant of letters of administration to the case of real estate.   **[662]**

PART III

ADMINISTRATION OF ASSETS

32. Real and personal estate of deceased are assets for payment of debts

(1) The real and personal estate, whether legal or equitable, of a deceased person, to the extent of his beneficial interest therein, and the real and personal estate of which a deceased person in pursuance of any general power (including the statutory power to dispose of entailed interests) disposes by his will, are assets for payment of his debts (whether by specialty or simple contract) and liabilities, and any disposition by will inconsistent with this enactment is void as against the creditors, and the court shall if necessary, administer the property for the purpose of the payment of the debts and liabilities.

This subsection takes effect without prejudice to the rights of incumbrancers.

(2) If any person to whom any such beneficial interest devolves, or is given, or in whom any such interest vests, disposes thereof in good faith before an

action is brought or process is sued out against him, he shall be personally liable for the value of the interest so disposed of by him, but that interest shall not be liable to be taken in execution in the action or under the process.   **[663]**

33. Trust for sale

(1) On the death of a person intestate as to any real or personal estate, such estate shall be held by his personal representatives—

    (*a*) as to the real estate upon trust to sell the same; and

    (*b*) as to the personal estate upon trust to call in sell and convert into money such part thereof as may not consist of money,

with power to postpone such sale and conversion for such a period as the personal representatives, without being liable to account, may think proper, and so that any reversionary interest be not sold until it falls into possession, unless the personal representatives see special reason for sale, and so also that, unless required for purposes of administration owing to want of other assets, personal chattels be not sold except for special reason.

(2) Out of the net money to arise from the sale and conversion of such real and personal estate (after payment of costs), and out of the ready money of the deceased (so far as not disposed of by his will, if any), the personal representative shall pay all such funeral, testamentary and administration expenses, debts and other liabilities as are properly payable thereout having regard to the rules of administration contained in this Part of this Act, and out of the residue of the said money the personal representative shall set aside a fund sufficient to provide for any pecuniary legacies bequeathed by the will (if any) of the deceased.

(3) During the minority of any beneficiary or the subsistence of any life interest and pending the distribution of the whole or any part of the estate of the deceased, the personal representatives may invest the residue of the said money, or so much thereof as may not have been distributed, in any investments for the time being authorised by statute for the investment of trust money, with power, at the discretion of the personal representatives, to change such investments for others of a like nature.

(4) The residue of the said money and any investments for the time being representing the same, including (but without prejudice to the trust for sale) any part of the estate of the deceased which may be retained unsold and is not required for the administration purposes aforesaid, is in this Act referred to as "the residuary estate of the intestate."

(5) The income (including net rents and profits of real estate and chattels real after payment of rates, taxes, rent, costs of insurance, repairs and other outgoings properly attributable to income) of so much of the real and personal estate of the deceased as may not be disposed of by his will, if any, or may not be required for the administration purposes aforesaid, may, however such estate is invested, as from the death of the deceased, be treated and applied as income, and for that purpose any necessary apportionment may be made between tenant for life and remainderman.

(6) Nothing in this section affects the rights of any creditor of the deceased or the rights of the Crown in respect of death duties.

(7) Where the deceased leaves a will, this section has effect subject to the provisions contained in the will.   **[664]**

34. Administration of assets

(1), (2) . . .

(3) Where the estate of a deceased person is solvent his real and personal estate shall, subject to rules of court and the provisions hereinafter contained as to charges on property of the deceased, and to the provisions, if any, contained in his will, be applicable towards the discharge of the funeral, testamentary and administration expenses, debts and liabilities payable thereout in the order mentioned in Part II of the First Schedule to this Act. **[665]**

NOTES

Sub-s (1): repealed by the Insolvency Act 1985, s 235, Sch 10, Part III.

Sub-s (2): repealed by the Administration of Estates Act 1971, s 12(2), (4), (6), Sch 2, Part II.

35. Charges on property of deceased to be paid primarily out of the property charged

(1) Where a person dies possessed of, or entitled to, or, under a general power of appointment (including the statutory power to dispose of entailed interests) by his will disposes of, an interest in property, which at the time of his death is charged with the payment of money, whether by way of legal mortgage, equitable charge or otherwise (including a lien for unpaid purchase money), and the deceased has not by will deed or other document signified a contrary or other intention, the interest so charged, shall as between the different persons claiming through the deceased, be primarily liable for the payment of the charge; and every part of the said interest, according to its value, shall bear a proportionate part of the charge on the whole thereof.

(2) Such contrary or other intention shall not be deemed to be signified—

> (a) by a general direction for the payment of debts or of all the debts of the testator out of his personal estate, or his residuary real and personal estate, or his residuary real estate; or
>
> (b) by a charge of debts upon any such estate;

unless such intention is further signified by words expressly or by necessary implication referring to all or some part of the charge.

(3) Nothing in this section affects the right of a person entitled to the charge to obtain payment or satisfaction thereof either out of the other assets of the deceased or otherwise. **[666]**

36. Effect of assent or conveyance by personal representative

(1) A personal representative may assent to the vesting, in any person who (whether by devise, bequest, devolution, appropriation or otherwise) may be entitled thereto, either beneficially or as a trustee or personal representative, of any estate or interest in real estate to which the testator or intestate was entitled or over which he exercised a general power of appointment by his will, including the statutory power to dispose of entailed interests, and which devolved upon the personal representative.

(2) The assent shall operate to vest in that person the estate or interest to which the assent relates, and, unless a contrary intention appears, the assent shall relate back to the death of the deceased.

(3) The statutory covenants implied by a person being expressed to convey as personal representative, may be implied in an assent in like manner as in a conveyance by deed.

(4) An assent to the vesting of a legal estate shall be in writing, signed by the personal representative, and shall name the person in whose favour it is given and shall operate to vest in that person the legal estate to which it relates; and an assent not in writing or not in favour of a named person shall not be effectual to pass a legal estate.

(5) Any person in whose favour an assent or conveyance of a legal estate is made by a personal representative may require that notice of the assent or conveyance be written or endorsed on or permanently annexed to the probate or letters of administration, at the cost of the estate of the deceased, and that the probate or letters of administration be produced, at the like cost, to prove that the notice has been placed thereon or annexed thereto.

(6) A statement in writing by a personal representative that he has not given or made an assent or conveyance in respect of a legal estate, shall, in favour of a purchaser, but without prejudice to any previous disposition made in favour of another purchaser deriving title mediately or immediately under the personal representative, be sufficient evidence that an assent or conveyance has not been given or made in respect of the legal estate to which the statement relates, unless notice of a previous assent or conveyance affecting that estate has been placed on or annexed to the probate or administration.

A conveyance by a personal representative of a legal estate to a purchaser accepted on the faith of such a statement shall (without prejudice as aforesaid and unless notice of a previous assent or conveyance affecting that estate has been placed on or annexed to the probate or administration) operate to transfer or create the legal estate expressed to be conveyed in like manner as if no previous assent or conveyance had been made by the personal representative.

A personal representative making a false statement, in regard to any such matter, shall be liable in like manner as if the statement had been contained in a statutory declaration.

(7) An assent or conveyance by a personal representative in respect of a legal estate shall, in favour of a purchaser, unless notice of a previous assent or conveyance affecting that legal estate has been placed on or annexed to the probate or administration, be taken as sufficient evidence that the person in whose favour the assent or conveyance is given or made is the person entitled to have the legal estate conveyed to him, and upon the proper trusts, if any, but shall not otherwise prejudicially affect the claim of any person rightfully entitled to the estate vested or conveyed or any charge thereon.

(8) A conveyance of a legal estate by a personal representative to a purchaser shall not be invalidated by reason only that the purchaser may have notice that all the debts, liabilities, funeral, and testamentary or administration expenses, duties, and legacies of the deceased have been discharged or provided for.

(9) An assent or conveyance given or made by a personal representative shall not, except in favour of a purchaser of a legal estate, prejudice the right of the personal representative or any other person to recover the estate or interest to which the assent or conveyance relates, or to be indemnified out of such estate or interest against any duties, debts, or liability to which such estate or interest would have been subject if there had not been any assent or conveyance.

(10) A personal representative may, as a condition of giving an assent or making a conveyance, require security for the discharge of any such duties, debt, or liability, but shall not be entitled to postpone the giving of an assent merely by reason of the subsistence of any such duties, debt or liability if

reasonable arrangements have been made for discharging the same; and an assent may be given subject to any legal estate or charge by way of legal mortgage.

(11) This section shall not operate to impose any stamp duty in respect of an assent, and in this section "purchaser" means a purchaser for money or money's worth.

(12) This section applies to assents and conveyances made after the commencement of this Act, whether the testator or intestate died before of after such commencement. **[667]**

37. Validity of conveyance not affected by revocation of representation

(1) All conveyances of any interest in real or personal estate made to a purchaser either before or after the commencement of this Act by a person to whom probate or letters of administration have been granted are valid, notwithstanding any subsequent revocation or variation, either before or after the commencement of this Act, of the probate or administration.

(2) This section takes effect without prejudice to any order of the court made before the commencement of this Act, and applies whether the testator or intestate died before or after such commencement. **[668]**

38. Right to follow property and powers of the court in relation thereto

(1) An assent or conveyance by a personal representative to a person other than a purchaser does not prejudice the rights of any person to follow the property to which the assent or conveyance relates, or any property representing the same, into the hands of the person in whom it is vested by the assent or conveyance, or of any other person (not being a purchaser) who may have received the same or in whom it may be vested.

(2) Notwithstanding any such assent or conveyance the court may, on the application of any creditor or other person interested,—

> (a) order a sale, exchange, mortgage, charge, lease, payment, transfer or other transaction to be carried out which the court considers requisite for the purpose of giving effect to the rights of the persons interested;
> (b) declare that the person, not being a purchaser, in whom the property is vested is a trustee for those purposes;
> (c) give directions respecting the preparation and execution of any conveyance or other instrument or as to any other matter required for giving effect to the order;
> (d) make any vesting order, or appoint a person to convey in accordance with the provisions of the Trustee Act 1925.

(3) This section does not prejudice the rights of a purchaser or a person deriving title under him, but applies whether the testator or intestate died before or after the commencement of this Act.

[(4) The county court has jurisdiction under this section where the estate in respect of which the application is made does not exceed in amount or value the county court limit.] **[669]**

NOTES
Sub-s (4): added by the County Courts Act 1984, s 148(1), Sch 2, para 12.

39. Powers of management

(1) In dealing with the real and personal estate of the deceased his personal representatives shall, for purposes of administration, or during a minority of any beneficiary or the subsistence of any life interest, or until the period of distribution arrives, have—

> (i) the same powers and discretions, including power to raise money by mortgage or charge (whether or not by deposit of documents), as a personal representative had before the commencement of this Act, with respect to personal estate vested in him, and such power of raising money by mortgage may in the case of land be exercised by way of legal mortgage; and
>
> (ii) all the powers, discretions and duties conferred or imposed by law on trustees holding land upon an effectual trust for sale (including power to overreach equitable interests and powers as if the same affected the proceeds of sale); and
>
> (iii) all the powers conferred by statute on trustees for sale, and so that every contract entered into by a personal representative shall be binding on and be enforceable against and by the personal representative for the time being of the deceased, and may be carried into effect, or be varied or rescinded by him, and, in the case of a contract entered into by a predecessor, as if it had been entered into by himself.

(2) Nothing in this section shall affect the right of any person to require an assent or conveyance to be made.

(3) This section applies whether the testator or intestate died before or after the commencement of this Act.   [670]

40. Powers of personal representative for raising money, etc

(1) For giving effect to beneficial interests the personal representative may limit or demise land for a term of years absolute, with or without impeachment for waste, to trustees on usual trusts for raising or securing any principal sum and the interest thereon for which the land, or any part thereof, is liable, and may limit or grant a rentcharge for giving effect to any annual or periodical sum for which the land or the income thereof or any part thereof is liable.

(2) This section applies whether the testator or intestate died before or after the commencement of this Act.   [671]

41. Powers of personal representative as to appropriation

(1) The personal representative may appropriate any part of the real or personal estate, including things in action, of the deceased in the actual condition or state of investment thereof at the time of appropriation in or towards satisfaction of any legacy bequeathed by the deceased, or of any other interest or share in his property, whether settled or not, as to the personal representative may seem just and reasonable, according to the respective rights of the persons interested in the property of the deceased:

> Provided that—
>
> (i) an appropriation shall not be made under this section so as to affect prejudicially any specific devise or bequest;
>
> (ii) an appropriation of property, whether or not being an investment authorised by law or by the will, if any, of the deceased for the

investment of money subject to the trust, shall not (save as hereinafter mentioned) be made under this section except with the following consents:—

(*a*) when made for the benefit of a person absolutely and beneficially entitled in possession, the consent of that person;

(*b*) when made in respect of any settled legacy share or interest, the consent of either the trustee thereof, if any (not being also the personal representative), or the person who may for the time being be entitled to the income:
If the person whose consent is so required as aforesaid is an infant or [is incapable by reason of mental disorder within the meaning of [the Mental Health Act 1983], of managing and administering his property and affairs] the consent shall be given on his behalf by his parents or parent, testamentary or other guardian . . . or receiver, or if, in the case of an infant, there is no such parent or guardian, by the court on the application of his next friend;

(iii) no consent (save of such trustee as aforesaid) shall be required on behalf of a person who may come into existence after the time of appropriation, or who cannot be found or ascertained at that time;

(iv) if no [receiver is acting for a person suffering from mental disorder] then, if the appropriation is of an investment authorised by law or by the will, if any, of the deceased for the investment of money subject to the trust, no consent shall be required on behalf of the [said person];

(v) if, independently of the personal representative, there is no trustee of a settled legacy share or interest, and no person of full age and capacity entitled to the income thereof, no consent shall be required to an appropriation in respect of such legacy share or interest, provided that the appropriation is of an investment authorised as aforesaid.

[(1A) The county court has jurisdiction under proviso (ii) to subsection (1) of this section where the estate in respect of which the application is made does not exceed in amount or value the county court limit.]

(2) Any property duly appropriated under the powers conferred by this section shall thereafter be treated as an authorised investment, and may be retained or dealt with accordingly.

(3) For the purposes of such appropriation, the personal representative may ascertain and fix the value of the respective parts of the real and personal estate and the liabilities of the deceased as he may think fit, and shall for that purpose employ a duly qualified valuer in any case where such employment may be necessary; and may make any conveyance (including an assent) which may be requisite for giving effect to the appropriation.

(4) An appropriation made pursuant to this section shall bind all persons interested in the property of the deceased whose consent is not hereby made requisite.

(5) The personal representative shall, in making the appropriation, have regard to the rights of any person who may thereafter come into existence, or

who cannot be found or ascertained at the time of appropriation, and of any other person whose consent is not required by this section.

(6) This section does not prejudice any other power of appropriation conferred by law or by the will (if any) of the deceased, and takes effect with any extended powers conferred by the will (if any) of the deceased, and where an appropriation is made under this section, in respect of a settled legacy, share or interest, the property appropriated shall remain subject to all trusts for sale and powers of leasing, disposition, and management or varying investments which would have been applicable thereto or to the legacy, share or interest in respect of which the appropriation is made, if no such appropriation had been made.

(7) If after any real estate has been appropriated in purported exercise of the powers conferred by this section, the person to whom it was conveyed disposes of it or any interest therein, then, in favour of a purchaser, the appropriation shall be deemed to have been made in accordance with the requirements of this section and after all requisite consents, if any, had been given.

(8) In this section, a settled legacy, share or interest includes any legacy, share or interest to which a person is not absolutely entitled in possession at the date of the appropriation, also an annuity, and "purchaser" means a purchaser for money or money's worth.

(9) This section applies whether the deceased died intestate or not, and whether before or after the commencement of this Act, and extends to property over which a testator exercises a general power of appointment, including the statutory power to dispose of entailed interests, and authorises the setting apart of a fund to answer an annuity by means of the income of that fund or otherwise.   [672]

NOTES

Sub-s (1): first, third and fourth words in square brackets substituted and words omitted repealed by the Mental Health Act 1959, s 149(1), Sch 7, Part I; second words in (inner) square brackets in para (ii) substituted by the Mental Health Act 1983, s 148, Sch 4, para 7.

Sub-s (1A): inserted by the County Courts Act 1984, s 148(1), Sch 2, para 13.

42. Power to appoint trustees of infants' property

(1) Where an infant is absolutely entitled under the will or on the intestacy of a person dying before or after the commencement of this Act (in this subsection called "the deceased") to a devise or legacy, or to the residue of the estate of the deceased, or any share therein, and such devise, legacy, residue or share is not under the will, if any, of the deceased, devised or bequeathed to trustees for the infant, the personal representatives of the deceased may appoint a trust corporation or two or more individuals not exceeding four (whether or not including the personal representatives or one or more of the personal representatives), to be the trustee or trustees of such devise, legacy, residue or share for the infant, and to be trustees of any land devised or any land being or forming part of such residue or share for the purposes of the Settled Land Act 1925, and of the statutory provisions relating to the management of land during a minority, and may execute or do any assurance or thing requisite for vesting such devise, legacy, residue or share in the trustee or trustees so appointed.

On such appointment the personal representatives, as such, shall be discharged from all further liability in respect of such devise, legacy, residue, or share, and the same may be retained in its existing condition or state of investment, or may be converted into money, and such money may be invested in any authorised investment.

(2) Where a personal representative has before the commencement of this Act retained or sold any such devise, legacy, residue or share, and invested the same or the proceeds thereof in any investments in which he was authorised to invest money subject to the trust, then, subject to any order of the court made before such commencement, he shall not be deemed to have incurred any liability on that account, or by reason of not having paid or transferred the money or property into court.   [673]

43. Obligations of personal representative as to giving possession of land and powers of the court

(1) A personal representative, before giving an assent or making a conveyance in favour of any person entitled, may permit that person to take possession of the land, and such possession shall not prejudicially affect the right of the personal representative to take or resume possession nor his power to convey the land as if he were in possession thereof, but subject to the interest of any lessee, tenant or occupier in possession or in actual occupation of the land.

(2) Any person who as against the personal representative claims possession of real estate, or the appointment of a receiver thereof, or a conveyance thereof, or an assent to the vesting thereof, or to be registered as proprietor thereof under the Land Registration Act 1925, may apply to the court for directions with reference thereto, and the court may make such vesting or other order as may be deemed proper, and the provisions of the Trustee Act 1925, relating to vesting orders and to the appointment of a person to convey, shall apply.

(3) This section applies whether the testator or intestate died before or after the commencement of this Act.

[(4) The county court has jurisdiction under this section where the estate in respect of which the application is made does not exceed in amount or value the county court limit.]   [674]

NOTES
   Sub-s (4): added by the County Courts Act 1984, s 148(1), Sch 2, para 14.

44. Power to postpone distribution

Subject to the foregoing provisions of this Act, a personal representative is not bound to distribute the estate of the deceased before the expiration of one year from the death.   [675]

PART IV

DISTRIBUTION OF RESIDUARY ESTATE

45. Abolition of descent to heir, curtesy, dower and escheat

(1) With regard to the real estate and personal inheritance of every person dying after the commencement of this Act, there shall be abolished—

   (a) All existing modes rules and canons of descent, and of devolution by special occupancy or otherwise, of real estate, or of a personal inheritance, whether operating by the general law or by the custom of gavelkind or borough english or by any other custom of any county, locality, or manor, or otherwise howsoever; and

(b) Tenancy by the curtesy and every other estate and interest of a husband in real estate as to which his wife dies intestate, whether arising under the general law or by custom or otherwise; and

(c) Dower and freebench and every other estate and interest of a wife in real estate as to which her husband dies intestate, whether arising under the general law or by custom or otherwise: Provided that where a right (if any) to freebench or other like right has attached before the commencement of this Act which cannot be barred by a testamentary or other disposition made by the husband, such right shall, unless released, remain in force as an equitable interest; and

(d) Escheat to the Crown or the Duchy of Lancaster or the Duke of Cornwall or to a mesne lord for want of heirs.

(2) Nothing in this section affects the descent or devolution of an entailed interest.　　　　　**[676]**

46. Succession to real and personal estate on intestacy

(1) The residuary estate of an intestate shall be distributed in the manner or be held on the trusts mentioned in this section, namely:—

[(i) If the intestate leaves a husband or wife, then in accordance with the following Table:

TABLE

If the intestate—

(1) leaves— 　(a) no issue, and 　(b) no parent, or brother or sister of the whole blood, or issue of a brother or sister of the whole blood	the residuary estate shall be held in trust for the surviving husband or wife absolutely.
(2) leaves issue (whether or not persons mentioned in subparagraph (b) above also survive)	the surviving husband or wife shall take the personal chattels absolutely and, in addition, the residuary estate of the intestate (other than the personal chattels) shall stand charged with the payment of a [fixed net sum], free of death duties and costs, to the surviving husband or wife with interest thereon from the date of the death . . . [at such rate as the Lord Chancellor may specify by order] until paid or appropriated, and, subject to providing for that sum and the interest thereon, the residuary estate (other than the personal chattels) shall be held— 　(a) as to one half upon trust for the surviving husband or wife during his or her life, and, subject to such life interest, on the statutory trusts for the issue of the intestate, and 　(b) as to the other half, on the statutory trusts for the issue of the intestate.

(3) leaves one or more of the following, that is to say, a parent, a brother or sister of the whole blood, or issue of a brother or sister of the whole blood, but leaves no issue

the surviving husband or wife shall take the personal chattels absolutely and, in addition, the residuary estate of the intestate (other than the personal chattels) shall stand charged with the payment of a [fixed net sum], free of death duties and costs, to the surviving husband or wife with interest thereon from the date of the death ... [at such rate as the Lord Chancellor may specify by order] until paid or appropriated, and, subject to providing for that sum and the interest thereon, the residuary estate (other than the personal chattels) shall be held—

(a) as to one half in trust for the surviving husband or wife absolutely, and

(b) as to the other half—

(i) where the intestate leaves one parent or both parents (whether or not brothers or sisters of the intestate or their issue also survive) in trust for the parent absolutely or, as the case may be, for the two parents in equal shares absolutely

(ii) where the intestate leaves no parent, on the statutory trusts for the brothers and sisters of the whole blood of the intestate.

[The fixed net sums referred to in paragraphs (2) and (3) of this Table shall be of the amounts provided by or under section 1 of the Family Provision Act 1966]]

(ii) If the intestate leaves issue but no husband or wife, the residuary estate of the intestate shall be held on the statutory trusts for the issue of the intestate;

(iii) If the intestate leaves [no husband or wife and] no issue but both parents, then ... the residuary estate of the intestate shall be held in trust for the father and mother in equal shares absolutely;

(iv) If the intestate leaves [no husband or wife and] no issue but one parent, then ... the residuary estate of the intestate shall be held in trust for the surviving father or mother absolutely;

(v) If the intestate leaves no [husband or wife and no issue and no] parent, then ... the residuary estate of the intestate shall be held in trust for the following persons living at the death of the intestate, and in the following order and manner, namely:—

First, on the statutory trusts for the brothers and sisters of the whole blood of the intestate; but if no person takes an absolutely vested interest under such trusts; then

Secondly, on the statutory trusts for the brothers and sisters of the half blood of the intestate; but if no person takes an absolutely vested interest under such trusts; then

Thirdly, for the grandparents of the intestate and, if more than one survive the intestate, in equal shares; but if there is no member of this class; then

Fourthly, on the statutory trusts for the uncles and aunts of the intestate (being brothers or sisters of the whole blood of a parent of the intestate); but if no person takes an absolutely vested interest under such trusts; then

Fifthly, on the statutory trusts for the uncles and aunts of the intestate (being brothers or sisters of the half blood of a parent of the intestate) . . .

(vi) In default of any person taking an absolute interest under the foregoing provisions, the residuary estate of the intestate shall belong to the Crown or to the Duchy of Lancaster or to the Duke of Cornwall for the time being, as the case may be, as bona vacantia, and in lieu of any right to escheat.

The Crown or the said Duchy or the said Duke may (without prejudice to the powers reserved by section nine of the Civil List Act 1910, or any other powers), out of the whole or any part of the property devolving on them respectively, provide, in accordance with the existing practice, for dependents, whether kindred or not, of the intestate, and other persons for whom the intestate might reasonably have been expected to make provision.

[(1A) The power to make orders under subsection (1) above shall be exercisable by statutory instrument subject to annulment in pursuance of a resolution of either House of Parliament; and any such order may be varied or revoked by a subsequent order made under the power.]

(2) A husband and wife shall for all purposes of distribution or division under the foregoing provisions of this section be treated as two persons.

[(3) Where the intestate and the intestate's husband or wife have died in circumstances rendering it uncertain which of them survived the other and the intestate's husband or wife is by virtue of section one hundred and eighty-four of the Law of Property Act 1925, deemed to have survived the intestate, this section shall, nevertheless, have effect as respects the intestate as if the husband or wife had not survived the intestate.

(4) The interest payable on [the fixed net sum] payable to a surviving husband or wife shall be primarily payable out of income.]   [677]

NOTES

Sub-s (1): para (i) substituted by the Intestates' Estates Act 1952, s 1, first and third words in square brackets substituted and words at the end of the table added by the Family Provision Act 1966, s 1, second and fourth words in square brackets substituted by the Administration of Justice Act 1977, s 28(1)(a) and words omitted repealed by the Statute Law (Repeals) Act 1981; in para (iii) words in square brackets inserted and words omitted repealed by the Intestates' Act 1952, s 1; in para (iv) words in square brackets inserted and words omitted repealed by the Intestates' Act 1952, s 1; in para (v) words in square brackets substituted and words omitted repealed by the Intestates' Act 1952, s 1.

Sub-s (1A): inserted by the Administration of Justice Act 1977, s 28(1).

Sub-s (3): added by the Intestates' Estates Act 1952, s 1(4).

Sub-s (4): added by the Intestates' Estates Act 1952, s 1(4); words in square brackets substituted by the Family Provision Act 1966, s 1.

47. Statutory trusts in favour of issue and other classes of relatives of intestate

(1) Where under this Part of this Act the residuary estate of an intestate, or any part thereof, is directed to be held on the statutory trusts for the issue of the intestate, the same shall be held upon the following trusts, namely:—

    (i) In trust, in equal shares if more than one, for all or any the children or child of the intestate, living at the death of the intestate, who attain the age of [eighteen] years or marry under that age, and for all or any of the issue living at the death of the intestate who attain the age of [eighteen] years or marry under that age of any child of the intestate who predeceases the intestate, such issue to take through all degrees, according to their stocks, in equal shares if more than one, the share which their parent would have taken if living at the death of the intestate, and so that no issue shall take whose parent is living at the death of the intestate and so capable of taking;

    (ii) The statutory power of advancement, and the statutory provisions which relate to maintenance and accumulation of surplus income, shall apply, but when an infant marries such infant shall be entitled to give valid receipts for the income of the infant's share or interest;

    (iii) Where the property held on the statutory trusts for issue is divisible into shares, then any money or property which, by way of advancement or on the marriage of a child of the intestate, has been paid to such child by the intestate or settled by the intestate for the benefit of such child (including any life or less interest and including property covenanted to be paid or settled) shall, subject to any contrary intention expressed or appearing from the circumstances of the case, be taken as being so paid or settled in or towards satisfaction of the share of such child or the share which such child would have taken if living at the death of the intestate, and shall be brought into account, at a valuation (the value to be reckoned as at the death of the intestate), in accordance with the requirements of the personal representatives;

    (iv) The personal representatives may permit any infant contingently interested to have the use and enjoyment of any personal chattels in such manner and subject to such conditions (if any) as the personal representatives may consider reasonable, and without being liable to account for any consequential loss.

(2) If the trusts in favour of the issue of the intestate fail by reason of no child or other issue attaining an absolutely vested interest—

    (a) the residuary estate of the intestate and the income thereof and all statutory accumulations, if any, of the income thereof, or so much thereof as may not have been paid or applied under any power affecting the same, shall go, devolve and be held under the provisions of this Part of this Act as if the intestate had died without leaving issue living at the death of the intestate;

    (b) references in this Part of this Act to the intestate "leaving no issue" shall be construed as "leaving no issue who attain an absolutely vested interest";

    (c) references in this Part of this Act to the intestate "leaving issue" or "leaving a child or other issue" shall be construed as "leaving issue who attain an absolutely vested interest."

(3) Where under this Part of this Act the residuary estate of an intestate or

any part thereof is directed to be held on the statutory trusts for any class of relatives of the intestate, other than issue of the intestate, the same shall be held on trusts corresponding to the statutory trusts for the issue of the intestate (other than the provision for bringing any money or property into account) as if such trusts (other than as aforesaid) were repeated with the substitution of references to the members or member of that class for references to the children or child of the intestate.

[(4) References in paragraph (i) of subsection (1) of the last foregoing section to the intestate leaving, or not leaving, a member of the class consisting of brothers or sisters of the whole blood of the intestate and issue of brothers or sisters of the whole blood of the intestate shall be construed as references to the intestate leaving, or not leaving, a member of that class who attains an absolutely vested interest.]

(5) . . .   **[678]**

NOTES
 Sub-s (1): words in square brackets substituted in relation to the estate of an intestate dying after 1 January 1970, by the Family Law Reform Act 1969, s 3(2).
 Sub-s (4): added by the Intestates' Estates Act 1952, s 1(3)(c).
 Sub-s (5): added by the Intestates' Act 1952, s 1(3)(c); repealed by the Family Provision Act 1966, ss 9, 10, Sch 2.

[47A. Right of surviving spouse to have his own life interest redeemed

(1) Where a surviving husband or wife is entitled to the interest in part of the residuary estate, and so elects, the personal representative shall purchase or redeem the life interest by paying the capital value thereof to the tenant for life, or the persons deriving title under the tenant for life, and the costs of the transaction; and thereupon the residuary estate of the intestate may be dealt with and distributed free from the life interest.

(2) . . .

(3) An election under this section shall only be exercisable if at the time of the election the whole of the said part of the residuary estate consists of property in possession, but, for the purposes of this section, a life interest in property partly in possession and partly not in possession shall be treated as consisting of two separate life interests in those respective parts of the property.

[(3A) The capital value shall be reckoned in such manner as the Lord Chancellor may by order direct, and an order under this subsection may include transitional provisions.

(3B) The power to make orders under subsection (3A) above shall be exercisable by statutory instrument subject to annulment in pursuance of a resolution of either House of Parliament; and any such order may be varied or revoked by a subsequent order made under the power.]

(4) . . .

(5) An election under this section shall be exercisable only within the period of twelve months from the date on which representation with respect to the estate of the intestate is first taken out:

Provided that if the surviving husband or wife satisfies the court that the limitation to the said period of twelve months will operate unfairly—

    (*a*) in consequence of the representation first taken out being probate of a will subsequently revoked on the ground that the will was invalid, or

    (*b*) in consequence of a question whether a person had an interest in the estate, or as to the nature of an interest in the estate, not having been determined at the time when representation was first taken out, or

    (*c*) in consequence of some other circumstances affecting the administration or distribution of the estate,

the court may extend the said period.

(6) An election under this section shall be exercisable, except where the tenant for life is the sole personal representative, by notifying the personal representative (or, where there are two or more personal representatives of whom one is the tenant for life, all of them except the tenant for life) in writing; and a notification in writing under this subsection shall not be revocable except with the consent of the personal representative.

(7) Where the tenant for life is the sole personal representative an election under this section shall not be effective unless written notice thereof is given to the [[Senior Registrar] of the Family Division of the High Court] within the period within which it must be made; and provision may be made by probate rules for keeping a record of such notices and making that record available to the public.

In this subsection the expression "probate rules" means rules [of court made under section 127 of the Supreme Court Act 1981].

(8) An election under this section by a tenant for life who is an infant shall be as valid and binding as it would be if the tenant for life were of age; but the personal representative shall, instead of paying the capital value of the life interest to the tenant for life, deal with it in the same manner as with any other part of the residuary estate to which the tenant for life is absolutely entitled.

(9) In considering for the purposes of the foregoing provisions of this section the question when representation was first taken out, a grant limited to settled land or to trust property shall be left out of account and a grant limited to real estate or to personal estate shall be left out of account unless a grant limited to the remainder of the estate has previously been made or is made at the same time.]   **[679]**

NOTES

    Inserted by the Intestates' Estates Act 1952, s 2.

    Sub-ss (2), (4): repealed by the Administration of Justice Act 1977, ss 28(2), 32(4), Sch 5, Part VI.

    Sub-s (3A): inserted by the Administration of Justice Act 1977, s 28(3).

    Sub-s (3B): inserted by the Administration of Justice Act 1977, s 28(3).

    Sub-s (7): first words in square brackets substituted by the Administration of Justice Act 1970, s 1(6), Sch 2, para 4, words in square brackets therein and third words in square brackets substituted by the Supreme Court Act 1981, s 152(1), Sch 5.

---

48. Powers of personal representative in respect of interests of surviving spouse

(1) . . .

    (2) The personal representatives may raise—

    (*a*) [the fixed net sum] or any part thereof and the interest thereon payable to the surviving husband or wife of the intestate on the security of the whole or any part of the residuary estate of the intestate (other than the personal chattels), so far as that estate may be sufficient for the purpose of the said sum and interest may not have been satisfied by an appropriation under the statutory power available in that behalf; and

(b) in like manner the capital sum, if any, required for the purchase or redemption of the life interest of the surviving husband or wife of the intestate, or any part thereof not satisfied by the application for that purpose of any part of the residuary estate of the intestate;

and in either case the amount, if any, properly required for the payment of the costs of the transaction. **[680]**

NOTES
Sub-s (1): repealed by the Intestates' Estates Act 1952, s 2.
Sub-s (2): words in square brackets substituted by the Family Provision Act 1966, s 1.

49. Application to cases of partial intestacy

[(1)] Where any person dies leaving a will effectively disposing of part of his property, this Part of this Act shall have effect as respects the part of his property not so disposed of subject to the provisions contained in the will and subject to the following modifications:—

[(aa) where the deceased leaves a husband or wife who acquires any beneficial interests under the will of the deceased (other than personal chattels specifically bequeathed) the references in this Part of this Act to [the fixed net sum] payable to a surviving husband or wife, and to interest on that sum, shall be taken as references to the said sum diminished by the value at the date of death of the said beneficial interests, and to interest on that sum as so diminished, and accordingly, where the said value exceeds the said sum, this Part of this Act shall have effect as if references to the said sum, and interest thereon, were omitted];

(a) The requirements [of section forty-seven of this Act] as to bringing property into account shall apply to any beneficial interests acquired by any issue of the deceased under the will of the deceased, but not to beneficial interests so acquired by any other persons;

(b) The personal representative shall, subject to his rights and powers for the purposes of administration, be a trustee for the persons entitled under this Part of this Act in respect of the part of the estate not expressly disposed of unless it appears by the will that the personal representative is intended to take such part beneficially.

[(2) References in the foregoing provisions of this section to beneficial interests acquired under a will shall be construed as including a reference to a beneficial interest acquired by virtue of the exercise by the will of a general power of appointment (including the statutory power to dispose of entailed interests), but not of a special power of appointment.

(3) For the purposes of paragraph (aa) in the foregoing provisions of this section the personal representative shall employ a duly qualified valuer in any case where such employment may be necessary.

(4) The references in subsection (3) of section forty-seven A of this Act to property are references to property comprised in the residuary estate and, accordingly, where a will of the deceased creates a life interest in property in possession, and the remaining interest in that property forms part of the residuary estate, the said references are references to that remaining interest (which, until the life interest determines, is property not in possession).] **[681]**

NOTES
    Sub-s (1): numbered as such and para (*aa*) inserted by the Intestates' Estates Act 1952, s 3, words
in square brackets substituted by the Family Provision Act 1966, s 1; in para (*a*) words in square
brackets inserted by the Intestates' Estates Act 1952, s 3.
    Sub-s (2): added by the Intestates' Estates Act 1952, s 3.
    Sub-s (3): added by the Intestates' Estates Act 1952, s 3.
    Sub-s (4): added by the Intestates' Estates Act 1952, s 3.

50. Construction of documents

(1) References to any Statutes of Distribution in an instrument inter vivos made or in a will coming into operation after the commencement of this Act, shall be construed as references to this Part of this Act; and references in such an instrument or will to statutory next of kin shall be construed, unless the context otherwise requires, as referring to the persons who would take beneficially on an intestacy under the foregoing provisions of this Part of this Act.

(2) Trusts declared in an instrument inter vivos made, or in a will coming into operation, before the commencement of this Act by reference to the Statutes of Distribution, shall, unless the contrary thereby appears, be construed as referring to the enactments (other than the Intestates' Estates Act 1890) relating to the distribution of effects of intestates which were in force immediately before the commencement of this Act.

[(3) In subsection (1) of this section the reference to this Part of this Act, or the foregoing provisions of this Part of this Act, shall in relation to an instrument inter vivos made, or a will or codicil coming into operation, after the coming into force of section 18 of the Family Law Reform Act 1987 (but not in relation to instruments inter vivos made or wills or codicils coming into operation earlier) be construed as including references to that section.] **[682]**

NOTES
    Sub-s (3): added by the Family Law Reform Act 1987, s 33(1), Sch 2, para 3.

51. Savings

(1) Nothing in this Part of this Act affects the right of any person to take beneficially, by purchase, as heir either general or special.

(2) The foregoing provisions of this Part of this Act do not apply to any beneficial interest in real estate (not including chattels real) to which a [person of unsound mind] or defective living and of full age at the commencement of this Act, and unable, by reason of his incapacity, to make a will, who thereafter dies intestate in respect of such interest without having recovered his testamentary capacity, was entitled at his death, and any such beneficial interest (not being an interest ceasing on his death) shall, without prejudice to any will of the deceased, devolve in accordance with the general law in force before the commencement of this Act applicable to freehold land, and that law shall, notwithstanding any repeal, apply to the case.

For the purposes of this subsection, a [person of unsound mind] or defective who dies intestate as respects any beneficial interest in real estate shall not be deemed to have recovered his testamentary capacity unless his . . . receiver has been discharged.

(3) Where an infant dies after the commencement of this Act without having been married, and independently of this subsection he would, at his death, have been equitably entitled under a settlement (including a will) to a

vested estate in fee simple or absolute interest in freehold land, or in any property settled to devolve therewith or as freehold land, such infant shall be deemed to have had an entailed interest, and the settlement shall be construed accordingly.

(4) This Part of this Act does not affect the devolution of an entailed interest as an equitable interest. [683]

NOTES
Sub-s (2): words in square brackets substituted by the Mental Treatment Act 1930, s 20(5); words omitted repealed by the Mental Health Act 1959, s 149(2), Sch 8.

52. Interpretation of Part IV

In this Part of this Act "real and personal estate" means every beneficial interest (including rights of entry and reverter) of the intestate in real and personal estate which (otherwise than in right of a power of appointment or of the testamentary power conferred by statute to dispose of entailed interests) he could, if of full age and capacity, have disposed of by his will [and references (however expressed) to any relationship between two persons shall be construed in accordance with section 1 of the Family Law Reform Act 1987]. [684]

NOTES
Words in square brackets added by the Family Law Reform Act 1987, s 33(1), Sch 2, para 4.

PART V

SUPPLEMENTAL

53. General savings

(1) Nothing in this Act shall derogate from the powers of the High Court which exist independently of this Act or alter the distribution of business between the several divisions of the High Court, or operate to transfer any jurisdiction from the High Court to any other court.

(2) Nothing in this Act shall affect any unrepealed enactment in a public general Act dispensing with probate or administration as respects personal estate not including chattels real.

(3) ... [685]

NOTES
Sub-s (3): repealed by the Finance Act 1975, ss 52(2), 59(5), Sch 13, Part I.

54. Application of Act

Save as otherwise expressly provided, this Act does not apply in any case where the death occurred before the commencement of this Act. [686]

55. Definitions

In this Act, unless the context otherwise requires, the following expressions have the meanings hereby assigned to them respectively, that is to say:—

(1) (i) "Administration" means, with reference to the real and personal estate of a deceased person, letters of administration whether general or limited, or with the will annexed or otherwise:

      (ii) "Administrator" means a person to whom administration is granted:

(iii) "Conveyance" includes a mortgage, charge by way of legal mortgage, lease, assent, vesting, declaration, vesting instrument, disclaimer, release and every other assurance of property or of an interest therein by any instrument, except a will, and "convey" has a corresponding meaning, and "disposition" includes a "conveyance" also a devise bequest and an appointment of property contained in a will, and "dispose of" has a corresponding meaning:

[(iiiA) "the County Court limit", in relation to any enactment contained in this Act, means the amount for the time being specified by an Order in Council under section 145 of the County Courts Act 1984 as the county court limit for the purposes of that enactment (or, where no such Order in Council has been made, the corresponding limit specified by Order in Council under section 192 of the County Courts Act 1959);]

(iv) "the Court" means the High Court and also the county court, where that court has jurisdiction ...

(v) "Income" includes rents and profits:

(vi) "Intestate" includes a person who leaves a will but dies intestate as to some beneficial interest in his real or personal estate:

(vii) "Legal estates" mean the estates charges and interests in or over land (subsisting or created at law) which are by statute authorised to subsist or to be created at law; and "equitable interests" mean all other interests and charges in or over land or in the proceeds of sale thereof:

(viii) "[Person of unsound mind]" includes a [person of unsound mind] whether so found or not, and in relation to a [person of unsound mind] not so found; ... and "defective" includes every person affected by the provisions of section one hundred and sixteen of the Lunacy Act 1890, as extended by section sixty-four of the Mental Deficiency Act 1913, and for whose benefit a receiver has been appointed:

(ix) "Pecuniary legacy" includes an annuity, a general legacy, a demonstrative legacy so far as it is not discharged out of the designated property, and any other general direction by a testator for the payment of money, including all death duties free from which any devise, bequest, or payment is made to take effect:

(x) "Personal chattels" mean carriages, horses, stable furniture and effects (not used for business purposes), motor cars and accessories (not used for business purposes), garden effects, domestic animals, plate, plated articles, linen, china, glass, books, pictures, prints, furniture, jewellery, articles of household or personal use or ornament, musical and scientific instruments and apparatus, wines, liquors and consumable stores, but do not include any chattels used at the death of the intestate for business purposes nor money or securities for money:

(xi) "Personal representative" means the executor, original or by representation, or administrator for the time being of a deceased person, and as regards any liability for the payment of death duties includes any person who takes possession of or intermeddles with the property of a deceased person without the authority of the personal representatives or the court, and "executor" includes a person deemed to be appointed executor as respects settled land:

(xii) "Possession" includes the receipt of rents and profits or the right to receive the same, if any:

 (xiii) "Prescribed" means prescribed by rules of court . . . :

 (xiv) "Probate" means the probate of a will:

 [(xv) "Probate judge" means the President of the Family Division of the High Court:]

 (xvi) . . .

 (xvii) "Property" includes a thing in action and any interest in real or personal property:

 (xviii) "Purchaser" means a lessee, mortgagee, or other person who in good faith acquires an interest in property for valuable consideration, also an intending purchaser and "valuable consideration" includes marriage, but does not include a nominal consideration in money:

 (xix) "Real estate" save as provided in Part IV of this Act means real estate, including chattels real, which by virtue of Part I of this Act devolves on the personal representative of a deceased person:

 (xx) "Representation" means the probate of a will and administration, and the expression "taking out representation" refers to the obtaining of the probate of a will or of the grant of administration:

 (xxi) "Rent" includes a rent service or a rentcharge, or other rent, toll, duty, or annual or periodical payment in money or money's worth, issuing out of or charged upon land, but does not include mortgage interest; and "rentcharge" includes a fee farm rent:

 (xxii) . . .

 (xxiii) "Securities" include stocks, funds, or shares:

 (xxiv) "Tenant for life," "statutory owner," "land," "settled land," "settlement," "trustees of the settlement," "term of years absolute," "death duties," and "legal mortgage," have the same meanings as in the Settled Land Act 1925, and "entailed interest" and "charge by way of legal mortgage" have the same meanings as in the Law of Property Act 1925:

 (xxv) "Treasury solicitor" means the solicitor for the affairs of His Majesty's Treasury, and includes the solicitor for the affairs of the Duchy of Lancaster:

 (xxvi) "Trust corporation" means the public trustee or a corporation either appointed by the court in any particular case to be a trustee or entitled by rules made under subsection (3) of section four of the Public Trustee Act 1906, to act as custodian trustee:

 (xxvii) "Trust for sale," in relation to land, means an immediate binding trust for sale, whether or not exercisable at the request or with the consent of any person, and with or without a power at discretion to postpone the sale; and "power to postpone a sale" means power to postpone in the exercise of a discretion:

 (xxviii) "Will" includes codicil.

(2) References to a child or issue living at the death of any person include child or issue en ventre sa mere at the death.

(3) References to the estate of a deceased person include property over which the deceased exercises a general power of appointment (including the statutory power to dispose of entailed interests) by his will. **[687]**

NOTES

 Sub-s (1): para (iiiA) inserted by the County Courts Act 1984, s 148(1), Sch 2, para 15; words omitted from para (iv) repealed by the Courts Act 1971, s 56(4), Sch 11, Part II; words omitted from para (viii) repealed by the Mental Health Act 1959, s 149(2), Sch 8, Part I, and words in square brackets substituted by the Mental Treatment Act 1930, s 20(5); words omitted from para (xiii) repealed by the Supreme Court Act 1981, s 152(4), Sch 7; para (xv) substituted by the Administration of Justice Act 1970, s 1(6), Sch 2, para 5; paras (xvi), (xxii) repealed by the Supreme Court Act 1981, s 152(4), Sch 7.

57. Application to Crown

(1) The provisions of this Act bind the Crown and the Duchy of Lancaster, and the Duke of Cornwall for the time being as respects the estates of persons dying after the commencement of this Act, but not so as to affect the time within which proceedings for the recovery of real or personal estate vesting in or devolving on His Majesty in right of His Crown, or His Duchy of Lancaster, or on the Duke of Cornwall, may be instituted.

(2) Nothing in this Act in any manner affects or alters the descent or devolution of any property for the time being vested in His Majesty either in right of the Crown or of the Duchy of Lancaster or of any property for the time being belonging to the Duchy of Cornwall. **[688]**

58. Short title, commencement and extent

(1) This Act may be cited as the Administration of Estates Act 1925.

(2) ...

(3) This Act extends to England and Wales only: **[689]**

NOTES
Sub-s (2): repealed by the Statute Law Revision Act 1950.

SCHEDULES
SCHEDULE 1
Section 34

PART II
Order of Application of Assets where the Estate is Solvent

1. Property of the deceased undisposed of by will, subject to the retention thereout of a fund sufficient to meet any pecuniary legacies.

2. Property of the deceased not specifically devised or bequeathed but included (either by a specific or general description) in a residuary gift, subject to the retention out of such property of a fund sufficient to meet any pecuniary legacies, so far as not provided for as aforesaid.

3. Property of the deceased specifically appropriated or devised or bequeathed (either by a specific or general description) for the payment of debts.

4. Property of the deceased charged with, or devised or bequeathed (either by a specific or general description) subject to a charge for the payment of debts.

5. The fund, if any, retained to meet pecuniary legacies.

6. Property specifically devised or bequeathed, rateably according to value,

7. Property appointed by will under a general power, including the statutory power to dispose of entailed interests, rateably according to value.

8. The following provisions shall also apply—

(a) The order of application may be varied by the will of the deceased.

(b) . . .   **[690]**

NOTES
Para 8: words omitted repealed by the Finance (No 2) Act 1983, s 16(4), Sch 2, Part II.

LAW OF PROPERTY (AMENDMENT) ACT 1926
(c 11)

An Act to amend certain enactments relating to the Law of Property and Trustees
[16 June 1926]

1. Conveyances of legal estates subject to certain interests

(1) Nothing in the Settled Land Act 1925, shall prevent a person on whom the powers of a tenant for life are conferred by paragraph (ix) of subsection (1) of section twenty of that Act from conveying or creating a legal estate subject to a prior interest as if the land had not been settled land.

(2) In any of the following cases, namely—

(a) where a legal estate has been conveyed or created under subsection one of this section, or under section sixteen of the Settled Land Act 1925, subject to any prior interest, or

(b) where before the first day of January, nineteen hundred and twenty-six, land has been conveyed to a purchaser for money or money's worth subject to any prior interest whether or not on the purchase the land was expressed to be exonerated from, or the grantor agreed to indemnify the purchaser against, such prior interest,

the estate owner for the time being of the land subject to such prior interest may, notwithstanding any provision contained in the Settled Land Act 1925, but without prejudice to any power whereby such prior interest is capable of being overreached, convey or create a legal estate subject to such prior interest as if the instrument creating the prior interest was not an instrument or one of the instruments constituting a settlement of the land.

(3) In this section "interest" means an estate, interest, charge or power of charging subsisting, or capable of arising or of being exercised, under a settlement, and, where a prior interest arises under the exercise of a power, "instrument" includes both the instrument conferring the power and the instrument exercising it.   **[691]**

3. Meaning of "trust corporation"

(1) For the purposes of the Law of Property Act 1925, the Settled Land Act 1925, the Trustee Act 1925, the Administration of Estates Act 1925, and the [Supreme Court Act 1981], the expression "Trust Corporation" includes the Treasury Solicitor, the Official Solicitor and any person holding any other official position prescribed by the Lord Chancellor, and, in relation to the property of a bankrupt and property subject to a deed of arrangement, includes the trustee in bankruptcy and the trustee under the deed respectively, and, in relation to charitable ecclesiastical and public trusts, also includes any local or public authority so prescribed, and any other corporation constituted under the laws of the United Kingdom or any part thereof which satisfies the Lord Chancellor that it undertakes the administration of any such trusts without remuneration, or that by its constitution it is required to apply the whole of its

net income after payment of outgoings for charitable ecclesiastical or public purposes, and is prohibited from distributing, directly or indirectly, any part thereof by way of profits amongst any of its members, and is authorised by him to act in relation to such trusts as a trust corporation.

(2) For the purposes of this provision, the expression "Treasury Solicitor" means the solicitor for the affairs of His Majesty's Treasury, and includes the solicitor for the affairs of the Duchy of Lancaster. **[692]**

NOTES
Sub-s (1): words in square brackets substituted by the Supreme Court Act 1981, s 152(1), Sch 5.

LANDLORD AND TENANT ACT 1927
(c 36)

An Act to provide for the payment of compensation for improvements and goodwill to tenants of premises used for business purposes, or the grant of a new lease in lieu thereof; and to amend the law of landlord and tenant

[22 December 1927]

PART I
COMPENSATION FOR IMPROVEMENTS AND GOODWILL ON THE TERMINATION OF TENANCIES OF BUSINESS PREMISES

3. Landlord's right to object

(1) Where a tenant of a holding to which this Part of this Act applies proposes to make an improvement on his holding, he shall serve on his landlord notice of his intention to make such improvement, together with a specification and plan showing the proposed improvement and the part of the existing premises affected thereby, and if the landlord, within three months after the service of the notice, serves on the tenant notice of objection, the tenant may, in the prescribed manner, apply to the tribunal, and the tribunal may, after ascertaining that notice of such intention has been served upon any superior landlords interested and after giving such persons an opportunity of being heard, if satisfied that the improvement—

(a) is of such a nature as to be calculated to add to the letting value of the holding at the termination of the tenancy; and
(b) is reasonable and suitable to the character thereof; and
(c) will not diminish the value of any other property belonging to the same landlord, or to any superior landlord from whom the immediate landlord of the tenant directly or indirectly holds;

and after making such modifications (if any) in the specification or plan as the tribunal thinks fit, or imposing such other conditions as the tribunal may think reasonable, certify in the prescribed manner that the improvement is a proper improvement:

Provided that, if the landlord proves that he has offered to execute the improvement himself in consideration of a reasonable increase of rent, or of such increase of rent as the tribunal may determine, the tribunal shall not give a certificate under this section unless it is subsequently shown to the satisfaction of the tribunal that the landlord has failed to carry out his undertaking.

(2) In considering whether the improvement is reasonable and suitable to the character of the holding, the tribunal shall have regard to any evidence brought before it by the landlord or any superior landlord (but not any other person) that the improvement is calculated to injure the amenity or convenience of the neighbourhood.

(3) The tenant shall, at the request of any superior landlord or at the request of the tribunal, supply such copies of the plans and specifications of the proposed improvement as may be required.

(4) Where no such notice of objection as aforesaid to a proposed improvement has been served within the time allowed by this section, or where the tribunal has certified an improvement to be a proper improvement, it shall be lawful for the tenant as against the immediate and any superior landlord to execute the improvement according to the plan and specification served on the landlord, or according to such plan and specification as modified by the tribunal or by agreement between the tenant and the landlord or landlords affected, anything in any lease of the premises to the contrary notwithstanding:

Provided that nothing in this subsection shall authorise a tenant to execute an improvement in contravention of any restriction created or imposed—

  (a) for naval, military or air force purposes;
  (b) for civil aviation purposes under the powers of the Air Navigation Act 1920;
  (c) for securing any rights of the public over the foreshore or bed of the sea.

(5) A tenant shall not be entitled to claim compensation under this Part of this Act in respect of any improvement unless he has, or his predecessors in title have, served notice of the proposal to make the improvement under this section, and (in case the landlord has served notice of objection thereto) the improvement has been certified by the tribunal to be a proper improvement and the tenant has complied with the conditions, if any, imposed by the tribunal, nor unless the improvement is completed within such time after the service on the landlord of the notice of the proposed improvement as may be agreed between the tenant and the landlord or may be fixed by the tribunal, and where proceedings have been taken before the tribunal, the tribunal may defer making any order as to costs until the expiration of the time so fixed for the completion of the improvement.

(6) Where a tenant has executed an improvement of which he has served notice in accordance with this section and with respect to which either no notice of objection has been served by the landlord or a certificate that it is a proper improvement has been obtained from the tribunal, the tenant may require the landlord to furnish to him a certificate that the improvement has been duly executed; and if the landlord refuses or fails within one month after the service of the requisition to do so, the tenant may apply to the tribunal who, if satisfied that the improvement has been duly executed, shall give a certificate to that effect.

Where the landlord furnishes such a certificate, the tenant shall be liable to pay any reasonable expenses incurred for the purpose by the landlord, and if any question arises as to the reasonableness of such expenses, it shall be determined by the tribunal.   **[692A]**

PART II

GENERAL AMENDMENTS OF THE LAW OF LANDLORD AND TENANT

18. Provisions as to covenants to repair

(1) Damages for a breach of a covenant or agreement to keep or put premises in repair during the currency of a lease, or to leave or put premises in repair at the termination of a lease, whether such covenant or agreement is expressed or implied, and whether general or specific, shall in no case exceed the amount (if any) by which the value of the reversion (whether immediate or not) in the premises is diminished owing to the breach of such covenant or agreement as aforesaid; and in particular no damage shall be recovered for a breach of any such covenant or agreement to leave or put premises in repair at the termination of a lease, if it is shown that the premises, in whatever state of repair they might be, would at or shortly after the termination of the tenancy have been or be pulled down, or such structural alterations made therein as would render valueless the repairs covered by the covenant or agreement.

(2) A right of re-entry or forfeiture for a breach of any such covenant or agreement as aforesaid shall not be enforceable, by action or otherwise, unless the lessor proves that the fact that such a notice as is required by section one hundred and forty-six of the Law of Property Act 1925, had been served on the lessee was known either—

    (*a*) to the lessee; or

    (*b*) to an under-lessee holding under an under-lease which reserved a nominal reversion only to the lessee; or

    (*c*) to the person who last paid the rent due under the lease either on his own behalf or as agent for the lessee or under-lessee;

and that a time reasonably sufficient to enable the repairs to be executed had elapsed since the time when the fact of the service of the notice came to the knowledge of any such person.

Where a notice has been sent by registered post addressed to a person at his last known place of abode in the United Kingdom, then, for the purposes of this subsection, that person shall be deemed, unless the contrary is proved, to have had knowledge of the fact that the notice had been served as from the time at which the letter would have been delivered in the ordinary course of post.

This subsection shall be construed as one with section one hundred and forty-six of the Law of Property Act 1925.

(3) This section applies whether the lease was created before or after the commencement of this Act.   **[693]**

19. Provisions as to covenants not to assign, etc, without licence or consent

(1) In all leases whether made before or after the commencement of this Act containing a covenant condition or agreement against assigning, under-letting, charging or parting with the possession of demised premises or any part thereof without licence or consent, such covenant condition or agreement shall, notwithstanding any express provision to the contrary, be deemed to be subject—

    (*a*) to a proviso to the effect that such licence or consent is not to be unreasonably withheld, but this proviso does not preclude the right of the landlord to require payment of a reasonable sum in respect of any legal or other expenses incurred in connection with such licence or consent; and

(b) (if the lease is for more than forty years, and is made in consideration wholly or partially of the erection, or the substantial improvement, addition or alteration of buildings, and the lessor is not a Government department or local or public authority, or a statutory or public utility company) to a proviso to the effect that in the case of any assignment, under-letting, charging or parting with the possession (whether by the holders of the lease or any under-tenant whether immediate or not) effected more than seven years before the end of the term no consent or licence shall be required, if notice in writing of the transaction is given to the lessor within six months after the transaction is effected.

(2) In all leases whether made before or after the commencement of this Act containing a covenant condition or agreement against the making of improvements without licence or consent, such covenant condition or agreement shall be deemed, notwithstanding any express provision to the contrary, to be subject to a proviso that such licence or consent is not to be unreasonably withheld; but this proviso does not preclude the right to require as a condition of such licence or consent the payment of a reasonable sum in respect of any damage to or diminution in the value of the premises or any neighbouring premises belonging to the landlord, and of any legal or other expenses properly incurred in connection with such licence or consent nor, in the case of an improvement which does not add to the letting value of the holding, does it preclude the right to require as a condition of such licence or consent, where such a requirement would be reasonable, an undertaking on the part of the tenant to reinstate the premises in the condition in which they were before the improvement was executed.

(3) In all leases whether made before or after the commencement of this Act containing a covenant condition or agreement against the alteration of the user of the demised premises, without licence or consent, such covenant condition or agreement shall, if the alteration does not involve any structural alteration of the premises, be deemed, notwithstanding any express provision to the contrary, to be subject to a proviso that no fine or sum of money in the nature of a fine, whether by way of increase of rent or otherwise, shall be payable for or in respect of such licence or consent; but this proviso does not preclude the right of the landlord to require payment of a reasonable sum in respect of any damage to or diminution in the value of the premises or any neighbouring premises belonging to him and of any legal or other expenses incurred in connection with such licence or consent.

Where a dispute as to the reasonableness of any such sum has been determined by a court of competent jurisdiction, the landlord shall be bound to grant the licence or consent on payment of the sum so determined to be reasonable.

(4) This section shall not apply to leases of agricultural holdings within the meaning of the [Agricultural Holdings Act 1986], and paragraph (b) of subsection (1), subsection (2) and subsection (3) of this section shall not apply to mining leases. **[694]**

NOTES
  Sub-s (4): words in square brackets substituted by the Agricultural Holdings Act 1986, s 100, Sch 14, para 15.

23. Service of notices

(1) Any notice, request, demand or other instrument under this Act shall be in writing and may be served on the person on whom it is to be served either personally, or by leaving it for him at his last known place of abode in England or Wales, or by sending it through the post in a registered letter addressed to him there, or, in the case of a local or public authority or a statutory or a public utility company, to the secretary or other proper officer at the principle office of such authority or company, and in the case of a notice to a landlord, the person on whom it is to be served shall include any agent of the landlord duly authorised in that behalf.

(2) Unless or until a tenant of a holding shall have received notice that the person theretofore entitled to the rents and profits of the holding (hereinafter referred to as "the original landlord") has ceased to be so entitled, and also notice of the name and address of the person who has become entitled to such rents and profits, any claim, notice, request, demand, or other instrument, which the tenant shall serve upon or deliver to the original landlord shall be deemed to have been served upon or delivered to the landlord of such holding.

[694A]

26. Short title, commencement and extent

(1) This Act may be cited as the Landlord and Tenant Act 1927.

(2) ...

(3) This Act shall extend to England and Wales only.

AGRICULTURAL CREDITS ACT 1928
(c 43)
ARRANGEMENT OF SECTIONS

PART II
AGRICULTURAL SHORT-TERM CREDITS

PART III
GENERAL

An Act to secure, by means of the formation of a company and the assistance thereof out of public funds, the making of loans for agricultural purposes on favourable terms, and to facilitate the borrowing of money on the security of farming stock and other agricultural assets, and for purposes connected therewith

[3 August 1928]

PART II
AGRICULTURAL SHORT-TERM CREDITS

5. Agricultural charges on farming stock and assets

(1) It shall be lawful for a farmer as defined by this Act by instrument in writing to create in favour of a bank as so defined a charge (hereinafter referred to as an agricultural charge) on all or any of the farming stock and other agricultural assets belonging to him as security for sums advanced or to be advanced to him or paid or to be paid on his behalf under any guarantee by the bank and interest, commission and charges thereon.

(2) An agricultural charge may be either a fixed charge, or a floating charge, or both a fixed and a floating charge.

(3) The property affected by a fixed charge shall be such property forming part of the farming stock and other agricultural assets belonging to the farmer at the date of the charge as may be specified in the charge, but may include—

   (*a*) in the case of live stock, any progeny thereof which may be born after the date of the charge; and
   (*b*) in the case of agricultural plant, any plant which may whilst the charge is in force be substituted for the plant specified in the charge.

(4) The property affected by a floating charge shall be the farming stock and other agricultural assets from time to time belonging to the farmer, or such part thereof as is mentioned in the charge.

(5) The principal sum secured by an agricultural charge may be either a specified amount, or a fluctuating amount advanced on current account not exceeding at any one time such amount (if any) as may be specified in the charge, and in the latter case the charge shall not be deemed to be redeemed by reason only of the current account having ceased to be in debit.

(6) An agricultural charge may be in such form and made upon such conditions as the parties thereto may agree, and sureties may be made parties thereto.

(7) For the purposes of this Part of this Act—

   "Farmer" means any person (not being an incorporated company or society) who, as tenant or owner of an agricultural holding, cultivates the holding for profit; and "agriculture" and "cultivation" shall be deemed to include horticulture, and the use of land for any purpose of husbandry, inclusive of the keeping or breeding of live stock, poultry, or bees, and the growth of fruit, vegetables, and the like;
   ["Bank" means the Bank of England, [an institution authorised under the Banking Act 1987], ... or the post office, in the exercise of its powers to provide banking services.]
   "Farming stock" means crops or horticultural produce, whether growing or severed from the land, and after severance whether subjected to any treatment or process of manufacture or not; live stock, including poultry and bees, and the produce and progeny thereof; any other agricultural or horticultural produce whether subjected to any treatment or process of manufacture or not; seeds and manures; agricultural vehicles, machinery, and other plant; agricultural tenant's fixtures and other agricultural fixtures which a tenant is by law authorised to remove;

"Other agricultural assets" means a tenant's right to compensation under the [Agricultural Holdings Act 1986, except under section 60(2)(*b*) or 62,], for improvements, damage by game, disturbance or otherwise, and any other tenant right.   **[694B]**

NOTES
   Sub-s (7): definition "Bank" substituted by the Banking Act 1979, s 51(1), Sch 6, paras 2, 14, words in square brackets substituted by the Banking Act 1987, s 108(1), Sch 6, para 2, words omitted repealed by the Trustee Savings Banks Act 1985, ss 4(3), 7(3), Sch 4; in definition "Other agricultural assets" words in square brackets substituted by the Agricultural Holdings Act 1986, s 100, Sch 14, para 16.
   Modifications: by virtue of the Banking Coordination (Second Council Directive) Regulations 1992, SI 1992 No 3218, reg 82(1), Sch 10, Part I, para 3, sub-s (7) of this section has effect as if the reference to an institution authorised under the Banking Act included a reference to a European deposit-taker.

6. Effect of fixed charge

(1) A fixed charge shall, so long as the charge continues in force, confer on the bank the following rights and impose upon the bank the following obligations, that is to say:—

  (*a*) a right, upon the happening of any event specified in the charge as being an event authorising the seizure of property subject to the charge, to take possession of any property so subject;

  (*b*) where possession of any property has been so taken, a right, after an interval of five clear days or such less time as may be allowed by the charge, to sell the property either by auction or, if the charge so provides, by private treaty, and either for a lump sum payment or payment by instalments;

  (*c*) an obligation, in the event of such power of sale being exercised, to apply the proceeds of sale in or towards the discharge of the moneys and liabilities secured by the charge, and the cost of seizure and sale, and to pay the surplus (if any) of the proceeds to the farmer.

(2) A fixed charge shall, so long as the charge continues in force, impose on the farmer the following obligations:—

  (*a*) an obligation whenever he sells any of the property, or receives any money in respect of other agricultural assets comprised in the charge, forthwith to pay to the bank the amount of the proceeds of the sale or the money so received, except to such extent as the charge otherwise provides or the bank otherwise allows; the sums so paid to be applied, except so far as otherwise agreed, by the bank in or towards the discharge of moneys and liabilities secured by the charge;

  (*b*) an obligation in the event of the farmer receiving any money under any policy of insurance on any of the property comprised in the charge, or any money paid by way of compensation under the Diseases of Animals Acts 1894 to 1927 in respect of the destruction of any live stock comprised in the charge, or by way of compensation under the Destructive Insects and Pests Acts 1877 to 1927 in respect of the destruction of any crops comprised in the charge, forthwith to pay the amount of the sums so received to the bank, except to such extent as the charge otherwise provides or the bank otherwise allows; the sums so paid to be applied, except so far as otherwise agreed by the bank, in or towards the discharge of the moneys and liabilities secured by the charge.

(3) Subject to compliance with the obligations so imposed, a fixed charge

shall not prevent the farmer selling any of the property subject to the charge, and neither the purchaser, nor, in the case of a sale by auction, the auctioneer, shall be concerned to see that such obligations are complied with notwithstanding that he may be aware of the existence of the charge.

(4) Where any proceeds of sale which in pursuance of such obligation as aforesaid ought to be paid to the bank are paid to some other person, nothing in this Act shall confer on the bank a right to recover such proceeds from that other person unless the bank proves that such other person knew that the proceeds were paid to him in breach of such obligation as aforesaid, but such other person shall not be deemed to have such knowledge by reason only that he has notice of the charge. **[694C]**

NOTES
    Diseases of Animals Acts 1894 to 1927: see now the Animal Health Act 1981.
    Destructive Insects and Pests Act 1877 to 1927: see now the Plant Health Act 1967.

7. Effect of floating charge

(1) An agricultural charge creating a floating charge shall have the like effect as if the charge had been created by a duly registered debenture issued by a company:

Provided that—

    (a) the charge shall become a fixed charge upon the property comprised in the charge as existing at the date of its becoming a fixed charge—

        (i) upon [bankruptcy order] being made against the farmer;
        (ii) upon the death of the farmer;
        (iii) upon the dissolution of partnership in the case where the property charged is partnership property;
        (iv) upon notice in writing to that effect being given by the bank on the happening of any event which by virtue of the charge confers on the bank the right to give such a notice;

    (b) the farmer, whilst the charge remains a floating charge, shall be subject to the like obligation as in the case of a fixed charge to pay over to the bank the amount received by him by way of proceeds of sale, in respect of other agricultural assets, under policies of insurance, or by way of compensation, and the last foregoing section shall apply accordingly: Provided that it shall not be necessary for a farmer to comply with such obligation if and so far as the amount so received is expended by him in the purchase of farming stock which on purchase becomes subject to the charge. **[694D]**

NOTES
    Words in square brackets substituted by the Insolvency Act 1985, s 235, Sch 8, para 6.

8. Supplemental provisions as to agricultural charges

(1) An agricultural charge shall have effect notwithstanding anything in the Bills of Sale Acts 1878 and 1882 and shall not be deemed to be a bill of sale within the meaning of those Acts.

(2) Agricultural charges shall in relation to one another have priority in accordance with the times at which they are respectively registered under this Part of this Act.

(3) Where an agricultural charge creating a floating charge has been made,

an agricultural charge purporting to create a fixed charge on, or a bill of sale comprising any of the property comprised in the floating charge shall, as respects the property subject to the floating charge, be void so long as the floating charge remains in force.

(4) ...

(5) Where a farmer who is adjudged bankrupt has created in favour of a bank an agricultural charge on any of the farming stock or other agricultural assets belonging to him, and the charge was created within three months of the date of the presentation of the bankruptcy petition and operated to secure any sum owing to the bank immediately prior to the giving of the charge, then, unless it is proved that the farmer immediately after the execution of the charge was solvent, the amount which but for this provision would have been secured by the charge shall be reduced by the amount of the sum so owing to the bank immediately prior to the giving of the charge, but without prejudice to the bank's right to enforce any other security for that sum or to claim payment thereof as an unsecured debt.

(6) Where after the passing of this Act the farmer has mortgaged his interest in the land comprised in the holding, then, if growing crops are included in an agricultural charge, the rights of the bank under the charge in respect of the crops shall have priority to those of the mortgagee, whether in possession or not, and irrespective of the dates of the mortgage and charge.

(7) An agricultural charge shall be no protection in respect of property included in the charge which but for the charge would have been liable to distress for rent, taxes, or rates.

(8) An instrument creating an agricultural charge shall be exempt from stamp duty.   **[694E]**

NOTES

    Sub-s (4): repealed by the Insolvency Act 1985, s 235, Sch 10, Part III.

9. Registration of agricultural charges

(1) Every agricultural charge shall be registered under this Act within seven clear days after the execution thereof, and, if not so registered, shall be void as against any person other than the farmer:

Provided that the High Court on proof that omission to register within such time as aforesaid was accidental or due to inadvertence may extend the time for registration on such terms as the Court thinks fit.

(2) The Land Registrar shall keep at the Land Registry a register of agricultural charges in such form and containing such particulars as may be prescribed.

(3) Registration of an agricultural charge shall be effected by sending by post to the Land Registrar at the Land Registry a memorandum of the instrument creating the charge and such particulars of the charge as may be prescribed, together with the prescribed fee; and the Land Registrar shall enter the particulars in the register and shall file the memorandum.

(4) The register kept and the memoranda filed under this section shall at all reasonable times be open to inspection by any person on payment (except where the inspection is made by or on behalf of a bank) of the prescribed fee, and any

person inspecting the register or any such filed memorandum on payment (except as aforesaid) of the prescribed fee may make copies or extracts therefrom.

(5) Any person may on payment of the prescribed fee require to be furnished with a copy of any entry in the register or of any filed memorandum or any part thereof certified to be a true copy by the Land Registrar.

(6) Registration of an agricultural charge may be proved by the production of a certified copy of the entry in the register relating to the charge, and a copy of any entry purporting to be certified as a true copy by the Land Registrar shall in all legal proceedings be evidence of the matters stated therein without proof of the signature or authority of the person signing it.

[(7) The Schedule to this Act shall have effect in relation to official searches in the register of agricultural charges.]

(8) Registration of an agricultural charge under this section shall be deemed to constitute actual notice of the charge, and of the fact of such registration, to all persons and for all purposes connected with the property comprised in the charge, as from the date of registration or other prescribed date, and so long as the registration continues in force:

Provided that, where an agricultural charge created in favour of a bank is expressly made for securing a current account or other further advances, the bank, in relation to the making of further advances under the charge, shall not be deemed to have notice of another agricultural charge by reason only that it is so registered if it was not so registered at the time when the first-mentioned charge was created or when the last search (if any) by or on behalf of the bank was made, whichever last happened.

(9) The Lord Chancellor may make regulations prescribing anything which under this section is to be prescribed, subject as respects fees to the approval of the Treasury, and generally as to the keeping of the register and the filing of memoranda, the removal of entries from the register on proof of discharge, and the rectification of the register.   [694F]

NOTES
   Sub-s (7): substituted by the Land Charges Act 1972, s 18(1), Sch 3, para 7.

10. Restriction on publication of agricultural charges

(1) It shall not be lawful to print for publication or publish any list of agricultural charges or of the names of farmers who have created agricultural charges.

(2) If any person acts in contravention of this section, he shall in respect of each offence be liable on summary conviction to a fine not exceeding [level 2 on the standard scale]:

Provided that no person other than a proprietor, editor, master printer, or publisher, shall be liable to be convicted under this section.

(3) No prosecution for an offence under this section shall be commenced without the consent of the Attorney-General.

(4) For the purpose of this section, "publication" means the issue of copies to the public, and "publish" has a corresponding meaning, and without prejudice to the generality of the foregoing definition the confidential notification by an association representative of a particular trade to its members trading or

carrying on business in the district in which property subject to an agricultural charge is situate of the creation of the charge shall not be deemed to be publication for the purposes of this section. **[694G]**

NOTES

Sub-s (2): maximum fine increased by the Criminal Law Act 1977, s 31(6), and converted to a level on the standard scale by the Criminal Justice Act 1982, ss 37, 46.

11. Frauds by farmers

(1) If, with intent to defraud, a farmer who has created an agricultural charge—

(*a*) fails to comply with the obligations imposed by this Act as to the payment over to the bank of any sums received by him by way of proceeds of sale, or in respect of other agricultural assets, or under a policy of insurance or by way of compensation; or

(*b*) removes or suffers to be removed from his holding any property subject to the charge;

he shall be guilty of a misdemeanour and liable on conviction on indictment to penal servitude for a term not exceeding three years.

(2) . . . **[694H]**

NOTES

Sub-s (2): repealed by the Magistrates' Courts Act 1952, s 132, Sch 6.

Misdemeanour: see now the Magistrates' Courts Act 1980, s 17, Sch 1, para 20.

Penal servitude: see now the Criminal Justice Act 1948, s 1(1), (2).

13. Rights of tenants

Any farmer being the tenant of an agricultural holding shall have the right to create an agricultural charge notwithstanding any provision in his contract of tenancy to the contrary. **[694I]**

14. Provisions as to agricultural societies

(1) A debenture issued by a society registered under the Industrial and Provident Societies Acts 1893 to 1928, creating in favour of a bank a floating charge on property which is farming stock within the meaning of this Part of this Act, may be registered in like manner as an agricultural charge, and section nine of this Act shall apply to such a charge in like manner as it applies to an agricultural charge, and the charge if so registered shall as respects such property be valid notwithstanding anything in the Bills of Sale Acts 1878 and 1882, and shall not be deemed to be a bill of sale within the meaning of those Acts:

Provided that, where any such charge is so registered, notice thereof signed by the secretary of the society shall be sent to the central office established under the Friendly Societies Act 1896 and registered there.

(2) Any such debenture may create a floating charge on any farming stock the property in which is vested in the society. **[694J]**

NOTES

Industrial and Provident Societies Acts 1893 to 1928: see now the Industrial and Provident Societies Act 1965.

Friendly Societies Act 1896: see now the Friendly Societies Act 1974.

PART III

GENERAL

15. Short title, commencement and extent

(1) This Act may be cited as the Agricultural Credits Act 1928.

(2) . . .

(3) This Act shall not (except as otherwise expressly provided) extend to Scotland or Northern Ireland.   **[694K]**

NOTES
Sub-s (2): repealed by the Statute Law Revision Act 1950.

LAW OF PROPERTY (AMENDMENT) ACT 1929
(c 9)

An Act to amend the provisions of the Law of Property Act, 1925, relating to relief against forfeiture of under-leases   [5 February 1929]

1. Relief of under-lessees against breach of covenant

Nothing in subsection (8), subsection (9) or subsection (10) of section one hundred and forty-six of the Law of Property Act 1925 (which relates to restrictions on and relief against forfeiture of leases and under-leases), shall affect the provisions of subsection (4) of the said section.   **[695]**

2. Short title

This Act may be cited as the Law of Property (Amendment) Act 1929, and the Law of Property Act 1925, the Law of Property (Amendment) Act 1926, so far as it amends that Act, and this Act may be cited together as the Law of Property Acts 1925 to 1929.   **[696]**

LAW OF PROPERTY (ENTAILED INTERESTS) ACT 1932
(c 27)

An Act to prevent the conversion of entailed interests into absolute interests and the destruction of interests expectant thereon by the statutory trusts for sale, and to define the expression "rent charge in possession"   [16 June 1932]

2. Definition of rent charge

For removing doubt it is hereby declared that a rent charge (not being a rent charge limited to take effect in remainder after or expectant on the failure or determination of some other interest) is a rent charge in possession within the meaning of paragraph (*b*) of subsection (2) of section one of the Law of Property Act 1925, notwithstanding that the payments in respect thereof are limited to commence or accrue at some time subsequent to its creation.   **[697]**

3. Short title and construction

(1) This Act may be cited as the Law of Property (Entailed Interests) Act 1932, and so far as it amends any Act shall be construed as one with that Act.

(2) The Law of Property Acts 1925 to 1929, and this Act, so far as it amends those Acts, may be cited together as the Law of Property Acts 1925 to 1932.

[698]

PUBLIC HEALTH ACT 1936
(c 49)

An Act to consolidate with amendments certain enactments relating to public health
[31 July 1936]

PART XII
GENERAL
Provisions as to recovery of expenses, etc

291. Certain expenses recoverable from owners to be a charge on the premises: power to order payment by instalments

(1) Where a local authority have incurred expenses for the repayment of which the owner of the premises in respect of which the expenses were incurred is liable, either under this Act or under any enactment repealed thereby, or by agreement with the authority, those expenses, together with interest from the date of service of a demand for the expenses, may be recovered by the authority from the person who is the owner of the premises at the date when the works are completed, or, if he has ceased to be the owner of the premises before the date when a demand for the expenses is served, either from him or from the person who is the owner at the date when the demand is served, and, as from the date of the completion of the works, the expenses and interest accrued due thereon shall, until recovered, be a charge on the premises and on all estates and interests therein.

(2) A local authority may by order declare any expenses recoverable by them under this section to be payable with interest by instalments within a period not exceeding thirty years, until the whole amount is paid; and any such instalments and interest, or any part thereof, may be recovered from the owner or occupier for the time being of the premises in respect of which the expenses were incurred, and, if recovered from the occupier, may be deducted by him from the rent of the premises:

Provided that an occupier shall not be required to pay at any one time any sum in excess of the amount which was due from him on account of rent at, or has become due from him on account of rent since, the date on which he received a demand from the local authority together with a notice requiring him not to pay rent to his landlord without deducting the sum so demanded.

An order may be made under this subsection at any time with respect to any unpaid balance of expenses and accrued interest so, however, that the period for repayment shall not in any case extend beyond thirty years from the service of the first demand for the expenses.

(3) The rate of interest chargeable under subsection (1) or subsection (2) of this section shall be such [reasonable] rate as the authority may determine:

. . .

(4) A local authority shall, for the purpose of enforcing a charge under this section, have all the same powers and remedies under the Law of Property Act 1925, and otherwise as if they were mortgagees by deed having powers of sale and lease, of accepting surrenders of leases and of appointing a receiver. **[699]**

NOTES

Sub-s (3): word in square brackets inserted and proviso repealed by the Local Government, Planning and Land Act 1980, s 1(6), Sch 6.

LEASEHOLD PROPERTY (REPAIRS) ACT 1938
(c 34)

ARRANGEMENT OF SECTIONS

An Act to amend the law as to the enforcement by landlords of obligations to repair and similar obligations arising under leases [23 June 1938]

1. Restriction on enforcement of repairing covenants in long leases of small houses

(1) Where a lessor serves on a lessee under sub-section (1) of section one hundred and forty-six of the Law of Property Act 1925, a notice that relates to a breach of a covenant or agreement to keep or put in repair during the currency of the lease [all or any of the property comprised in the lease], and at the date of the service of the notice [three] years or more of the term of the lease remain unexpired, the lessee may within twenty-eight days from that date serve on the lessor a counter-notice to the effect that he claims the benefit of this Act.

(2) A right to damages for a breach of such a covenant as aforesaid shall not be enforceable by action commenced at any time at which [three] years or more of the term of the lease remain unexpired unless the lessor has served on the lessee not less than one month before the commencement of the action such a

notice as is specified in subsection (1) of section one hundred and forty-six of the Law of Property Act 1925, and where a notice is served under this subsection, the lessee may, within twenty-eight days from the date of the service thereof, serve on the lessor a counter-notice to the effect that he claims the benefit of this Act.

(3) Where a counter-notice is served by a lessee under this section, then, notwithstanding anything in any enactment or rule of law, no proceedings, by action or otherwise, shall be taken by the lessor for the enforcement of any right of re-entry or forfeiture under any proviso or stipulation in the lease for breach of the covenant or agreement in question, or for damages for breach thereof, otherwise than with the leave of the court.

(4) A notice served under subsection (1) of section one hundred and forty-six of the Law of Property Act 1925, in the circumstances specified in subsection (1) of this section, and a notice served under subsection (2) of this section shall not be valid unless it contains a statement, in characters not less conspicuous than those used in any other part of the notice, to the effect that the lessee is entitled under this Act to serve on the lessor a counter-notice claiming the benefit of this Act, and a statement in the like characters specifying the time within which, and the manner in which, under this Act a counter-notice may be served and specifying the name and address for service of the lessor.

(5) Leave for the purposes of this section shall not be given unless the lessor proves—

(a) that the immediate remedying of the breach in question is requisite for preventing substantial diminution in the value of his reversion, or that the value thereof has been substantially diminished by the breach;

(b) that the immediate remedying of the breach is required for giving effect in relation to the [premises] to the purposes of any enactment, or of any byelaw or other provision having effect under an enactment, [or for giving effect to any order of a court or requirement of any authority under any enactment or any such byelaw or other provision as aforesaid];

(c) in a case in which the lessee is not in occupation of the whole of the [premises as respects which the covenant or agreement is proposed to be enforced], that the immediate remedying of the breach is required in the interests of the occupier of [those premises] or of part thereof;

(d) that the breach can be immediately remedied at an expense that is relatively small in comparison with the much greater expense that would probably be occasioned by postponement of the necessary work; or

(e) special circumstances which in the opinion of the court, render it just and equitable that leave should be given.

(6) The court may, in granting or in refusing leave for the purposes of this section impose such terms and conditions on the lessor or on the lessee as it may think fit. **[700]**

NOTES

Sub-s (1): words in square brackets substituted by the Landlord and Tenant Act 1954, s 51(2), (5).
Sub-s (2): words in square brackets substituted by the Landlord and Tenant Act 1954, s 51(2), (5).
Sub-s (5): words in square brackets substituted by the Landlord and Tenant Act 1954, s 51(2), (5).

2. Restriction on right to recover expenses of survey, etc

A lessor on whom a counter-notice is served under the preceding section shall not be entitled to the benefit of subsection (3) of section one hundred and forty-six of the Law of Property Act 1925, (which relates to costs and expenses incurred by a lessor in reference to breaches of covenant), so far as regards any costs or expenses incurred in reference to the breach in question, unless he makes an application for leave for the purposes of the preceding section, and on such an application the court shall have power to direct whether and to what extent the lessor is to be entitled to the benefit thereof.   **[701]**

3. Saving for obligation to repair on taking possession

This Act shall not apply to a breach of a covenant or agreement in so far as it imposes on the lessee an obligation to put [premises] in repair that is to be performed upon the lessee taking possession of the premises or within a reasonable time thereafter.   **[702]**

NOTES
  Word in square brackets substituted by the Landlord and Tenant Act 1954, s 51(2).

5. Application to past breaches

This Act applies to leases created, and to breaches occurring, before or after the commencement of this Act.   **[703]**

6. Court having jurisdiction under this Act

(1) In this Act the expression "the court" means the county court, except in a case which any proceedings by action for which leave may be given would have to be taken in a court other than the county court, and means in the said excepted case that other court.

(2) ...   **[704]**

NOTES
  Sub-s (2): repealed by the County Courts Act 1959, s 204, Sch 3.

7. Application of certain provisions of 15 and 16 Geo 5 c 20

(1) In this Act the expressions "lessor", "lessee" and "lease" have the meanings assigned to them respectively by sections one hundred and forty-six and one hundred and fifty-four of the Law of Property Act 1925, except that they do not include any reference to such a grant as is mentioned in the said section one hundred and forty-six, or to the person making, or to the grantee under such a grant, or to persons deriving title under such a person; and "lease" means a lease for a term of [seven years or more, not being a lease of an agricultural holding within the meaning of the [Agricultural Holdings Act 1986]].

(2) The provisions of section one hundred and ninety-six of the said Act (which relate to the service of notices) shall extend to notices and counter-notices required or authorised by this Act.   **[705]**

NOTES
  Sub-s (1): first words in square brackets substituted by the Landlord and Tenant Act 1954, s 51(2), words in square brackets therein substituted by the Agricultural Holdings Act 1986, s 100, Sch 14, para 7.

8. Short title and extent

(1) This Act may be cited as the Leasehold Property (Repairs) Act 1938.

(2) This Act shall not extend to Scotland or to Northern Ireland. **[706]**

INTESTATES' ESTATES ACT 1952
(c 64)

An Act to amend the law of England and Wales, about the property of persons dying intestate; to amend the Inheritance (Family Provision) Act, 1938; and for purposes connected therewith [30 October 1952]

PART I

AMENDMENTS OF LAW OF INTESTATE SUCCESSION

5. Rights of surviving spouse as respects the matrimonial home

The Second Schedule to this Act shall have effect for enabling the surviving husband or wife of a person dying intestate after the commencement of this Act to acquire the matrimonial home. **[707]**

PART III

GENERAL

9. Short title and commencement

(1) This Act may be cited as the Intestates' Estates Act 1952.

(2) This Act shall come into operation on the first day of January, nineteen hundred and fifty-three. **[708]**

SCHEDULES
SCHEDULE 2

Section 5

RIGHTS OF SURVIVING SPOUSE AS RESPECTS THE MATRIMONIAL HOME

1.—(1) Subject to the provisions of this Schedule, where the residuary estate of the intestate comprises of interest in a dwelling-house in which the surviving husband or wife was resident at the time of the intestate's death, the surviving husband or wife may require the personal representative in exercise of the power conferred by section forty-one of the principal Act (and with due regard to the requirements of that section as to valuation) to appropriate the said interest in the dwelling-house in or towards satisfaction of any absolute interest of the surviving husband or wife in the real and personal estate of the intestate.

(2) The right conferred by this paragraph shall not be exercisable where the interest is—

(a) a tenancy which at the date of the death of the intestate was a tenancy which would determine within the period of two years from that date; or

(b) a tenancy which the landlord by notice given for that date could determine within the remainder of that period.

(3) Nothing in subsection (5) of section forty-one of the principal Act (which requires the personal representative, in making an appropriation to any person under that section, to have regard to the rights of others) shall prevent the personal representative from giving effect to the right conferred by this paragraph.

(4) The reference in this paragraph to an absolute interest in the real and personal estate of the intestate includes a reference to the capital value of a life interest which the surviving husband or wife has under this Act elected to have redeemed.

(5) Where part of a building was, at the date of the death of the intestate, occupied as a separate dwelling, that dwelling shall for the purposes of this Schedule be treated as a dwelling-house.

2. Where—

(a) the dwelling-house forms part of a building and an interest in the whole of the building is comprised in the residuary estate; or

(b) the dwelling-house is held with agricultural land and an interest in the agricultural land is comprised in the residuary estate; or

(c) the whole or part of the dwelling-house was at the time of the intestate's death used as a hotel or lodging house; or

(d) a part of the dwelling-house was at the time of the intestate's death used for purposes other than domestic purposes,

the right conferred by paragraph 1 of this Schedule shall not be exercisable unless the court, on being satisfied that the exercise of that right is not likely to diminish the value of assets in the residuary estate (other than the said interest in the dwelling-house or make them more difficult to dispose of, so orders.

3.—(1) The right conferred by paragraph 1 of this Schedule.

(a) shall not be exercisable after the expiration of twelve months from the first taking out of representation with respect to the intestate's estate;

(b) shall not be exercisable after the death of the surviving husband or wife

(c) shall be exercisable, except where the surviving husband or wife is the sole personal representative, by notifying the personal representative (or, where there are two or more personal representatives of whom one is the surviving husband or wife, all of them except the surviving husband or wife) in writing.

(2) A notification in writing under paragraph (c) of the foregoing sub-paragraph shall not be revocable except with the consent of the personal representative; but the surviving husband or wife may require the personal representative to have the said interest in the dwelling-house valued in accordance with section forty-one of the principal Act and to inform him or her of the result of that valuation before he or she decides whether to exercise the right.

(3) Subsection (9) of the section forty-seven A added to the principal Act by section two of this Act shall apply for the purposes of the construction of the reference in this paragraph to the first taking out of representation, and the promise to subsection (5) of that section shall apply for the purpose of enabling the surviving husband or wife to apply for an extension of the period of twelve months mentioned in this paragraph.

4.—(1) During the period of twelve months mentioned in paragraph 3 of this Schedule the personal representative shall not without the written consent of the surviving husband or wife sell or otherwise dispose of the said interest in the dwelling-house except in the course of administration owing to want of other assets.

(2) An application to the court under paragraph 2 of this Schedule may be made by the personal representative as well as by the surviving husband or wife, and if, on an application under that paragraph, the court does not order that the right conferred by paragraph 1 of this Schedule shall be exercisable by the surviving husband or wife, the court may authorise the personal representative to dispose of the said interest in the dwelling-house within the said period of twelve months.

(3) Where the court under sub-paragraph (3) of paragraph 3 of this Schedule extends the said period of twelve months, the court may direct that this paragraph shall apply in relation to the extended period as it applied in relation to the original period of twelve months.

(4) This paragraph shall not apply where the surviving husband or wife is the sole personal representative or one of two or more personal representatives.

(5) Nothing in this paragraph shall confer any right on the surviving husband or wife as against a purchaser from the personal representative.

5.—(1) Where the surviving husband or wife is one of two or more personal representatives, the rule that a trustee may not be a purchaser of trust property shall not prevent the surviving husband or wife from purchasing out of the estate of the intestate an interest in a dwelling-house in which the surviving husband or wife was resident at the time of the intestate's death.

(2) The power of appropriation under section forty-one of the principal Act shall include power to appropriate an interest in a dwelling-house in which the surviving husband or wife was resident at the time of the intestate's death partly in satisfaction of an interest of the surviving husband or wife in the real and personal estate of the intestate and partly in return for a payment of money by the surviving husband or wife to the personal representative.

6.—(1) Where the surviving husband or wife is a person of unsound mind or a defective, a requirement or consent under this Schedule may be made or given on his or her behalf by the committee or receiver, if any, or, where there is no committee or receiver, by the court.

(2) A requirement or consent made or given under this Schedule by a surviving husband or wife who is an infant shall be as valid and binding as it would be if he or she were of age, and, as respects an appropriation in pursuance of paragraph 1 of this Schedule, the provisions of section forty-one of the principal Act as to obtaining the consent of the infant's parent or guardian, or of the court on behalf of the infant, shall not apply.

7.—(1) Except where the context otherwise requires, references in this Schedule to a dwelling-house include references to any garden or portion of ground attached to and usually occupied with the dwelling-house or otherwise required for the amenity or convenience of the dwelling-house.

(2) This Schedule shall be construed as one with Part IV of the principal Act.   [709]

NOTES

Principal Act: Administration of Estates Act 1925.

RECREATIONAL CHARITIES ACT 1958
(c 17)

An Act to declare charitable under the law of England and Wales the provision in the interests of social welfare of facilities for recreation or other leisure-time occupation, to make similar provision as to certain trusts heretofore established for carrying out social welfare activities within the meaning of the Miners' Welfare Act 1952, to enable laws for corresponding purposes to be passed by the Parliament of Northern Ireland, and for purposes connected therewith
[13 March 1958]

1. General provision as to recreational and similar trusts, etc

(1) Subject to the provisions of this Act, it shall be and be deemed always to have been charitable to provide, or assist in the provision of, facilities for

recreation or other leisure-time occupation, if the facilities are provided in the interests of social welfare:

Provided that nothing in this section shall be taken to derogate from the principle that a trust or institution to be charitable must be for the public benefit.

(2) The requirement of the foregoing subsection that the facilities are provided in the interests of social welfare shall not be treated as satisfied unless—

    (*a*) the facilities are provided with the object of improving the conditions of life for the persons for whom the facilities are primarily intended; and

    (*b*) either—

        (i) those persons have need of such facilities as aforesaid by reason of their youth, age, infirmity or disablement, poverty or social and economic circumstances; or

        (ii) the facilities are to be available to the members or female members of the public at large.

(3) Subject to the said requirement, subsection (1) of this section applies in particular to the provision of facilities at village halls, community centres and women's institutes, and to the provision and maintenance of grounds and buildings to be used for purposes of recreation or leisure-time occupation, and extends to the provision of facilities for those purposes by the organising of any activity.   **[710]**

6. Short title and extent

(1) This Act may be cited as the Recreational Charities Act 1958.

(2) Sections one and two of this Act shall affect the law of Scotland and Northern Ireland only in so far as they affect the operation of the Income Tax Acts or of other enactments in which references to charity are to be construed in accordance with the law of England and Wales [or, without prejudice to the foregoing generality, of the Local Government (Financial Provisions, etc) (Scotland) Act 1962.]   **[711]**

NOTES

    Sub-s (2): words in square brackets added by the Local Government (Financial Provisions, etc) (Scotland) Act 1962, s 12(1), Sch 2.

MATRIMONIAL CAUSES (PROPERTY AND MAINTENANCE) ACT 1958
(c 35)

An Act to enable the power of the court in matrimonial proceedings to order alimony, maintenance or the securing of a sum of money to be exercised at any time after a decree; to provide for the setting aside of dispositions of property made for the purpose of reducing the assets available for satisfying such an order; to enable the court after the death of a party to a marriage which has been dissolved or annulled to make provision out of his estate in favour of the other party; and to extend the powers of the court under section seventeen of the Married Women's Property Act 1882   *[7 July 1958]*

7. Extension of s 17 of Married Women's Property Act 1882

(1) Any right of a wife, under section seventeen of the Married Women's Property Act 1882 to apply to a judge of the High Court or of a county court, in any question between husband and wife as to the title to or possession of property, shall include the right to make such an application where it is claimed by the wife that her husband has had in his possession or under his control—

    (*a*) money to which, or to a share of which, she was beneficially entitled (whether by reason that it represented the proceeds of property to which, or to an interest in which, she was beneficially entitled, or for any other reason), or

    (*b*) property (other than money) to which, or to an interest in which, she was beneficially entitled,

and that either that money or other property has ceased to be in his possession or under his control or that she does not know whether it is still in his possession or under his control.

(2) Where, on an application made to a judge of the High Court or of a county court under the said section seventeen, as extended by the preceding subsection, the judge is satisfied—

    (*a*) that the husband has had in his possession or under his control money or other property as mentioned in paragraph (*a*) or paragraph (*b*) of the preceding subsection, and

    (*b*) that he has not made to the wife, in respect of that money or other property, such payment or disposition as would have been appropriate in the circumstances,

the power to make orders under that section shall be extended in accordance with the next following subsection.

(3) Where the last preceding subsection applies, the power to make orders under the said section seventeen shall include power for the judge to order the husband to pay to the wife—

    (*a*) in a case falling within paragraph (*a*) of subsection (1) of this section, such sum in respect of the money to which the application relates, or the wife's share thereof, as the case may be, or

    (*b*) in a case falling within paragraph (*b*) of the said subsection (1), such sum in respect of the value of the property to which the application relates, or the wife's interest therein, as the case may be,

as the judge may consider appropriate.

(4) Where on an application under the said section seventeen as extended by this section it appears to the judge that there is any property which—

    (*a*) represents the whole or part of the money or property in question, and

    (*b*) is property in respect of which an order could have been made under that section if an application had been made by the wife thereunder in a question as to the title to or possession of that property,

the judge (either in substitution for or in addition to the making of an order in accordance with the last preceding subsection) may make any order under that section in respect of that property which he could have made on such an application as is mentioned in paragraph (*b*) of this subsection.

(5) The preceding provisions of this section shall have effect in relation to a husband as they have effect in relation to a wife, as if any reference to the husband were a reference to the wife and any reference to the wife were a reference to the husband.

[(6) Any power of a judge which is exercisable on an application under the said section seventeen shall be exercisable in relation to an application made under that section as extended by this section.]

(7) For the avoidance of doubt it is hereby declared that any power conferred by the said section seventeen to make orders with respect to any property includes power to order a sale of the property.   [712]

NOTES

Sub-s (6): substituted by the Matrimonial and Family Proceedings Act 1984, s 46(1), Sch 1.

VARIATION OF TRUSTS ACT 1958
(c 53)

An Act to extend the jurisdiction of courts of law to vary trusts in the interests of beneficiaries and sanction dealings with trust property   [23 July 1958]

1. Jurisdiction of courts to vary trusts

(1) Where property, whether real or personal, is held on trusts arising, whether before or after the passing of this Act, under any will, settlement or other disposition, the court may if it thinks fit by order approve on behalf of—

(a) any person having, directly or indirectly, an interest, whether vested or contingent, under the trusts who by reason of infancy or other incapacity is incapable of assenting, or

(b) any person (whether ascertained or not) who may become entitled, directly or indirectly, to an interest under the trusts as being at a future date or on the happening of a future event a person of any specified description or a member of any specified class of persons, so however that this paragraph shall not include any person who would be of that description, or a member of that class, as the case may be, if the said date had fallen or the said event had happened at the date of the application to the court, or

(c) any person unborn, or

(d) any person in respect of any discretionary interest of his under protective trusts where the interest of the principal beneficiary has not failed or determined,

any arrangement (by whomsoever proposed, and whether or not there is any other person beneficially interested who is capable of assenting thereto) varying or revoking all or any of the trusts, or enlarging the powers of the trustees of managing or administering any of the property subject to the trusts:

Provided that except by virtue of paragraph (d) of this subsection the court shall not approve an arrangement on behalf of any person unless the carrying out thereof would be for the benefit of that person.

(2) In the foregoing subsection "protective trusts" means the trusts specified in paragraphs (i) and (ii) of subsection (1) of section thirty-three of the Trustee

Act 1925, or any like trusts, "the principal beneficiary" has the same meaning as in the said subsection (1) and "discretionary interest" means an interest arising under the trust specified in paragraph (ii) of the said subsection (1) or any like trust.

(3) . . . the jurisdiction conferred by subsection (1) of this section shall be exercisable by the High Court, except that the question whether the carrying out of any arrangement would be for the benefit of a person falling within paragraph (*a*) of the said subsection (1) shall be determined by order of [the authority having jurisdiction under [Part VII of the Mental Health Act 1983], if that person is a patient within the meaning of [the said Part VII]].

(4) . . .

(5) Nothing in the foregoing provisions of this section shall apply to trusts affecting property settled by Act of Parliament.

(6) Nothing in this section shall be taken to limit the powers conferred by section sixty-four of the Settled Land Act 1925, section fifty-seven of the Trustee Act 1925, or [the powers of the authority having jurisdiction under [Part VII of the Mental Health Act 1983]]. **[713]**

NOTES

Sub-s (3): words omitted repealed by the County Courts Act 1959, s 204, Sch 3; first words in square brackets substituted by the Mental Health Act 1959, s 149(1), Sch 7, Part I, second words in square brackets substituted by the Mental Health Act 1983, s 148, Sch 4, para 14.

Sub-s (4): repealed by the County Courts Act 1959, s 204, Sch 3.

Sub-s (6): first words in square brackets substituted by the Mental Health Act 1959, s 149(1), Sch 7, Part I, words in square brackets therein substituted by the Mental Health Act 1983, s 148, Sch 4, para 14.

2. Extent and provisions as to Northern Ireland

(1) This Act shall not extend to Scotland.

(2) The foregoing section shall not extend to Northern Ireland . . . **[714]**

NOTES

Sub-s (2): words omitted repealed by the Northern Ireland Constitution Act 1973, s 41(1), Sch 6, Part I.

3. Short title

This Act may be cited as the Variation of Trusts Act 1958. **[715]**

RIGHTS OF LIGHT ACT 1959
(c 56)

ARRANGEMENT OF SECTIONS

An Act to amend the law relating to rights of light, and for purposes connected therewith [16 July 1959]

2. Registration of notice in lieu of obstruction of access of light

(1) For the purpose of preventing the access and use of light from being taken to be enjoyed without interruption, any person who is an owner of land (in this and the next following section referred to as "servient land") over which light passes to a dwelling-house, workshop or other building (in this and the next following section referred to as "the dominant building") may apply to the local authority in whose area the dominant building is situated for the registration of a notice under this section.

(2) An application for the registration of a notice under this section shall be in the prescribed form and shall—

(a) indentify the servient land and the dominant building in the prescribed manner, and

(b) state that the registration of a notice in pursuance of the application is intended to be equivalent to the obstruction of the access of light to the dominant building across the servient land which would be caused by the erection, in such position on the servient land as may be specified in the application, of an opaque structure of such dimensions (including, if the application so states, unlimited height) as may be so specified.

(3) Any such application shall be accompanied by one or other of the following certificates issued by the Lands Tribunal, that is to say,—

(a) a certificate certifying that adequate notice of the proposed application has been given to all persons who, in the circumstances existing at the time when the certificate is issued, appear to the Lands Tribunal to be persons likely to be affected by the registration of a notice in pursuance of the application;

(b) a certificate certifying that, in the opinion of the Lands Tribunal, the case is one of exceptional urgency, and that accordingly a notice should be registered forthwith as a temporary notice for such period as may be specified in the certificate.

(4) Where application is duly made to a local authority for the registration of a notice under this section, it shall be the duty of [that authority to register the notice in the appropriate local land charges register, and—

(a) any notice so registered under this section shall be a local land charge; but

(b) section 5(1) and (2) and section 10 of the Local Charges Act 1975 shall not apply in relation thereto].

(5) Provision shall be made by rules under section three of the Lands Tribunal Act 1949 for regulating proceedings before the Lands Tribunal with respect to the issue of certificates for the purposes of this section, and, subject to the approval of the Treasury, the fees chargeable in respect of those proceedings; and, without prejudice to the generality of subsection (6) of that section, any such rules made for the purposes of this section shall include provision—

(a) for requiring applicants for certificates under paragraph (a) of sub-section (3) of this section to give such notices, whether by way of advertisement or otherwise, and to produce such documents and provide such information, as may be determined by or under the rules;

    (b) for determining the period to be specified in a certificate issued under paragraph (b) of subsection (3) of this section; and

    (c) in connection with any certificate issued under the said paragraph (b), for enabling a further certificate to be issued in accordance (subject to the necessary modifications) with paragraph (a) of subsection (3) of this section.   **[716]**

NOTES

    Sub-s (4): words in square brackets substituted by the Local Land Charges Act 1975, s 17(2), Sch 1.

3. Effect of registered notice and proceedings relating thereto

(1) Where, in pursuance of an application made in accordance with the last preceding section, a notice is registered thereunder, then, for the purpose of determining whether any person is entitled (by virtue of the Prescription Act 1832, or otherwise) to a right to the access of light to the dominant building across the servient land, the access of light to that building across that land shall be treated as obstructed to the same extent, and with the like consequences, as if an opaque structure, of the dimensions specified in the application,—

    (a) had, on the date of registration of the notice, been erected in the position on the servient land specified in the application, and had been so erected by the person who made the application, and

    (b) had remained in that position during the period for which the notice has effect and had been removed at the end of that period.

(2) For the purposes of this section a notice registered under the last preceding section shall be taken to have effect until either—

    (a) the registration is cancelled, or

    (b) the period of one year beginning with the date of registration of the notice expires, or

    (c) in the case of a notice registered in pursuance of an application accompanied by a certificate issued under paragraph (b) of subsection (3) of the last preceding section, the period specified in the certificate expires without such a further certificate as is mentioned in paragraph (c) of subsection (5) of that section having before the end of that period been lodged with the local authority,

and shall cease to have effect on the occurrence of any one of those events.

(3) Subject to the following provisions of this section, any person who, if such a structure as is mentioned in subsection (1) of this section had been erected as therein mentioned, would have had a right of action in any court in respect of that structure, on the grounds that he was entitled to a right to the access of light to the dominant building across the servient land, and that the said right was infringed by that structure, shall have the like right of action in that court in respect of the registration of a notice under the last preceding section:

    Provided that an action shall not be begun by virtue of this subsection after the notice in question has ceased to have effect.

(4) Where, at any time during the period for which a notice registered under the last preceding section has effect, the circumstances are such that, if the

access of light to the dominant building had been enjoyed continuously from a date one year earlier than the date on which the enjoyment thereof in fact began, a person would have had a right of action in any court by virtue of the last preceding subsection in respect of the registration of the notice, that person shall have the like right of action in that court by virtue of this subsection in respect of the registration of the notice.

(5) The remedies available to the plaintiff in an action brought by virtue of subsection (3) or subsection (4) of this section (apart from any order as to costs) shall be such declaration as the court may consider appropriate in the circumstances, and an order directing the registration of the notice to be cancelled or varied, as the court may determine.

(6) For the purposes of section four of the Prescription Act 1832 (under which a period of enjoyment of any of the rights to which that Act applies is not to be treated as interrupted except by a matter submitted to or acquiesced in for one year after notice thereof)—

    (a) as from the date of registration of a notice under the last preceding section, all persons interested in the dominant building or any part thereof shall be deemed to have notice of the registration thereof and of the person on whose application it was registered;

    (b) until such time as an action is brought by virtue of subsection (3) or subsection (4) of this section in respect of the registration of a notice under the last preceding section, all persons interested in the dominant building or any part thereof shall be deemed to acquiesce in the obstruction which, in accordance with subsection (1) of this section, is to be treated as resulting from the registration of the notice;

    (c) as from the date on which such an action is brought, no person shall be treated as submitting to or acquiescing in that obstruction:

Provided that, if in any such action, the court decides against the claim of the plaintiff, the court may direct that the preceding provisions of this subsection shall apply in relation to the notice as if that action had not been brought. **[717]**

4. Application to Crown Land

(1) Subject to the next following subsection, this Act shall apply in relation to land in which there is a Crown or Duchy interest as it applies in relation to land in which there is no such interest.

(2) Section three of the Prescription Act 1832, as modified by the preceding provisions of this Act, shall not by virtue of this section be construed as applying to any land to which (by reason that there is a Crown or Duchy interest therein) that section would not apply apart from this Act.

(3) In this section "Crown or Duchy interest" means an interest belonging to Her Majesty in right of the Crown or of the Duchy of Lancaster, or belonging to the Duchy of Cornwall, or belonging to a government department, or held in trust for Her Majesty for the purposes of a government department. **[718]**

5. Power to make rules

(1) . . .

(2) Any rules made [under section 14 of the Local Land Charges Act 1975 for the purposes of section 2 of this Act] shall (without prejudice to the inclusion

therein of other provisions as to cancelling or varying the registration of notices or agreements) include provision for giving effect to any order of the court under subsection (5) of section three of this Act. **[719]**

NOTES

Sub-s (1): repealed by the Local Land Charges Act 1975, s 19(1), Sch 2.

Sub-s (2): words in square brackets substituted by the Local Land Charges Act 1975, s 17(2), Sch 1.

7. Interpretation

(1) In this Act, except in so far as the context otherwise requires, the following expressions have the meanings hereby assigned to them respectively, that is to say:—

"action" includes a counterclaim, and any reference to the plaintiff in an action shall be construed accordingly;

["local authority", in relation to land in a district or a London borough, means the council of the district or borough, and, in relation to land in the City of London, means the Common Council of the City;]

"owner", in relation to any land, means a person who is the estate owner in respect of the fee simple thereof, or is entitled to a tenancy thereof (within the meaning of the Landlord and Tenant Act 1954) for a term of years certain of which, at the time in question, not less than seven years remain unexpired, or is a mortgagee in possession (within the meaning of the Law of Property Act 1925) where the interest mortgaged is either the fee simple of the land or such a tenancy thereof;

"prescribed" means prescribed by rules made by virtue of subsection (6) of section fifteen of the Land Charges Act 1925 as applied by section five of this Act:

(2) References in this Act to any enactment shall, except where the context otherwise requires, be construed as references to that enactment as amended by or under any other enactment. **[720]**

NOTES

Sub-s (1): definition "local authority" substituted by the Local Land Charges Act 1975, s 17(2), Sch 1.

8. Short title, commencement and extent

(1) This Act may be cited as the Rights of Light Act 1959.

(2) This Act, except sections one and six thereof, shall come into operation at the end of the period of three months beginning with the day on which it is passed.

(3) This Act shall not extend to Scotland.

(4) This Act . . . shall not extend to Northern Ireland. **[721]–[734]**

NOTES

Sub-s (4): words omitted repealed by the Northern Ireland Constitution Act 1973, s 41(1), Sch 6.

TRUSTEE INVESTMENTS ACT 1961
(c 62)

ARRANGEMENT OF SECTIONS

An Act to make fresh provision with respect to investment by trustees and persons having the investment powers of trustees, and by local authorities, and for purposes connected therewith   [3 August 1961]

1. New powers of investment of trustees

(1) A trustee may invest any property in his hands, whether at the time in a state of investment or not, in any manner specified in Part I or II of the First Schedule to this Act or, subject to the next following section, in any manner specified in Part III of that Schedule, and may also from time to time vary any such investments.

(2) The supplemental provisions contained in Part IV of that Schedule shall have effect for the interpretation and for restricting the operation of the said Parts I to III.

(3) No provision relating to the powers of the trustee contained in any instrument (not being an enactment or an instrument made under an enactment) made before the passing of this Act shall limit the powers conferred by this section, but those powers are exerciseable only in so far as a contrary intention is not expressed in any Act or instrument made under an enactment, whenever passed or made, and so relating or in any other instrument so relating which is made after the passing of this Act.

For the purposes of this subsection any rule of the law of Scotland whereby a testamentary writing may be deemed to be made on a date other than that on which it was actually executed shall be disregarded.

(4) In this Act "narrower-range investment" means an investment falling within Part I or II of the First Schedule to this Act and "wider-range investment" means an investment falling within Part III of that Schedule. **[735]**

2. Restrictions on wider-range investment

(1) A trustee shall not have power by virtue of the foregoing section to make or retain any wider-range investment unless the trust fund has been divided into two parts (hereinafter referred to as the narrower-range part and the wider-range part), the parts being, subject to the provisions of this Act, equal in value at the time of the division; and where such a division has been made no subsequent division of the same fund shall be made for the purposes of this section, and no property shall be transferred from one part of the fund to the other unless either—

(a) the transfer is authorised or required by the following provisions of this Act, or

(b) a compensating transfer is made at the same time.

In this section "compensating transfer", in relation to any transferred property, means a transfer in the opposite direction of property of equal value.

(2) Property belonging to the narrower-range part of a trust fund shall not by virtue of the foregoing section be invested except in narrower-range investments, and any property invested in any other manner which is or becomes comprised in that part of the trust fund shall either be transferred to the wider-range part of the fund, with a compensating transfer, or be reinvested in narrower-range investments as soon as may be.

(3) Where any property accrues to a trust fund after the fund has been divided in pursuance of subsection (1) of this section, then—

(a) if the property accrues to the trustee as owner or former owner of property comprised in either part of the fund, it shall be treated as belonging to that part of the fund;

(b) in any other case, the trustee shall secure, by apportionment of the accruing property or the transfer of property from one part of the fund to the other, or both, that the value of each part of the fund is increased by the same amount.

Where a trustee acquires property in consideration of a money payment the acquisition of the property shall be treated for the purposes of this section as investment and not as the accrual of property to the trust fund, notwithstanding that the amount of the consideration is less than the value of the property acquired; and paragraph (a) of this subsection shall not include the case of a dividend or interest becoming part of a trust fund.

(4) Where in the exercise of any power or duty of a trustee property falls to be taken out of the trust fund, nothing in this section shall restrict his discretion as to the choice of property to be taken out. **[736]**

3. Relationship between Act and other powers of investment

(1) The powers conferred by section one of this Act are in addition to and not in derogation from any power conferred otherwise than by this Act of investment or postponing conversion exerciseable by a trustee (hereinafter referred to as a "special power").

(2) Any special power (however expressed) to invest property in any investment for the time being authorised by law for the investment of trust property, being a power conferred on a trustee before the passing of this Act or conferred on him under any enactment passed before the passing of this Act, shall have effect as a power to invest property in like manner and subject to the like provisions as under the foregoing provisions of this Act.

(3) In relation to property, including wider-range but not including

narrower-range investments,—

(a) which a trustee is authorised to hold apart from—

    (i) the provisions of section one of this Act or any of the provisions of Part I of the Trustee Act 1925, or any of the provisions of the Trusts (Scotland) Act 1921, or

    (ii) any such power to invest in authorised investments as is mentioned in the foregoing subsection, or

(b) which became part of a trust fund in consequence of the exercise by the trustee, as owner of property falling within this subsection, of any power conferred by subsection (3) or (4) of section ten of the Trustee Act 1925, or paragraph (o) or (p) of subsection (1) of section four of the Trusts (Scotland) Act 1921,

the foregoing section shall have effect subject to the modifications set out in the Second Schedule to this Act.

(4) The foregoing subsection shall not apply where the powers of the trustee to invest or postpone conversion have been conferred or varied—

(a) by an order of any court made within the period of ten years ending with the passing of this Act, or

(b) by any enactment passed, or instrument having effect under an enactment made, within that period, being an enactment or instrument relating specifically to the trusts in question; or

(c) by an enactment contained in a local Act of the present Session;

but the provisions of the Third Schedule to this Act shall have effect in a case falling within this subsection. **[737]**

4. Interpretation of references to trust property and trust funds

(1) In this Act "property" includes real or personal property of any description, including money and things in action:

Provided that it does not include an interest in expectancy, but the falling into possession of such an interest, or the receipt of proceeds of the sale thereof, shall be treated for the purposes of this Act as an accrual of property to the trust fund.

(2) So much of the property in the hands of a trustee shall for the purposes of this Act constitute one trust fund as is held on trusts which (as respects the beneficiaries or their respective interests or the purposes of the trust or as

respects the powers of the trustee) are not identical with those on which any other property in his hands is held.

(3) Where property is taken out of a trust fund by way of appropriation so as to form a separate fund, and at the time of the appropriation the trust fund had (as to the whole or a part thereof) been divided in pursuance of subsection (1) of section two of this Act, or that subsection as modified by the Second Schedule to this Act, then if the separate fund is so divided the narrower-range and wider-range parts of the separate fund may be constituted so as either to be equal, or to bear to each other the same proportion as the two corresponding parts of the fund out of which it was so appropriated (the values of those parts of those funds being ascertained as at the time of appropriation), or some intermediate proportion.

(4) . . .   [738]

NOTES
Sub-s (4): applies to Scotland only.

5. Certain valuations to be conclusive for purposes of division of trust fund

(1) If for the purposes of section two or four of this Act or the Second Schedule thereto a trustee obtains, from a person reasonably believed by the trustee to be qualified to make it, a valuation in writing of any property, the valuation shall be conclusive in determining whether the division of the trust fund in pursuance of subsection (1) of the said section two, or any transfer or apportionment of property under that section or the said Second Schedule, has been duly made.

(2) The foregoing subsection applies to any such valuation notwithstanding that it is made by a person in the course of his employment as an officer or servant.   [739]

6. Duty of trustees in choosing investments

(1) In the exercise of his powers of investment a trustee shall have regard—

> (a) to the need for diversification of investments of the trust, in so far as is appropriate to the circumstances of the trust;
> (b) to the suitability to the trust of investments of the description of investment proposed and of the investment proposed as an investment of that description.

(2) Before exercising any power conferred by section one of this Act to invest a manner specified in Part II or III of the First Schedule to this Act, or before investing in any such manner in the exercise of a power falling within subsection (2) of section three of this Act, a trustee shall obtain and consider proper advice on the question whether the investment is satisfactory having regard to the matters mentioned in paragraphs (a) and (b) of the foregoing subsection.

(3) A trustee retaining any investment made in the exercise of such a power and in such a manner as aforesaid shall determine at what intervals the circumstances, and in particular the nature of the investment, make it desirable to obtain such advice as aforesaid, and shall obtain and consider such advice accordingly.

(4) For the purposes of the two foregoing subsections, proper advice is the advice of a person who is reasonably believed by the trustee to be qualified by his ability in and practical experience of financial matters; and such advice may

be given by a person notwithstanding that he gives it in the course of his employment as an officer or servant.

(5) A trustee shall not be treated as having complied with subsection (2) or (3) of this section unless the advice was given or has been subsequently confirmed in writing.

(6) Subsections (2) and (3) of this section shall not apply to one of two or more trustees where he is the person giving the advice required by this section to his co-trustee or co-trustees, and shall not apply where powers of a trustee are lawfully exercised by an officer or servant competent under subsection (4) of this section to give proper advice.

(7) Without prejudice to section eight of the Trustee Act 1925, or section thirty of the Trusts (Scotland) Act 1921 (which relate to valuation, and the proportion of the value to be lent, where a trustee lends on the security of property) the advice required by this section shall not include, in the case of a loan on the security of freehold or leasehold property in England and Wales or Northern Ireland or on heritable security in Scotland, advice on the suitability of the particular loan. **[740]**

7. Application of ss 1–6 to persons, other than trustees, having trustee investment powers

(1) Where any persons, not being trustees, have a statutory power of making investments which is or includes power—

    (a) to make the like investments as are authorised by section one of the Trustee Act 1925, or section ten of the Trusts (Scotland) Act 1921, or

    (b) to make the like investments as trustees are for the time being by law authorised to make,

however the power is expressed, the foregoing provisions of this Act shall with the necessary modifications apply in relation to them as if they were trustees:

Provided that property belonging to a Consolidated Loans Fund or any other fund applicable wholly or partly for the redemption of debt shall not by virtue of the foregoing provisions of this Act be invested or held invested in any manner specified in paragraph 6 of Part II of the First Schedule to this Act or in wider-range investments.

(2) Where, in the exercise of powers conferred by any enactment, an authority to which paragraph 9 of Part II of the First Schedule to this Act applies uses money belonging to any fund for a purpose for which the authority has power to borrow, the foregoing provisions of this Act, as applied by the foregoing subsection, shall apply as if there were comprised in the fund (in addition to the actual content thereof) property, being narrower-range investments, having a value equal to so much of the said money as for the time being has not been repaid to the fund, and accordingly any repayment of such money to the fund shall not be treated for the said purposes as the accrual of property to the fund:

Provided that nothing in this subsection shall be taken to require compliance with any of the provisions of section six of this Act in relation to the exercise of such powers as aforesaid.

(3) In this section "Consolidated Loans Fund" means a fund established under section fifty-five of the Local Government Act 1958, and includes a loans fund established under [Schedule 3 to the Local Government (Scotland) Act

1975] and "statutory power" means a power conferred by an enactment passed before the passing of this Act or by any instrument made under any such enactment. **[741]**

NOTES
Sub-s (3): words in square brackets substituted by the Local Government and Planning (Scotland) Act 1982, s 66(1), Sch 3, para 4.

8. Application of ss 1–6 in special cases

(1) In relation to persons to whom this section applies—

    (*a*) notwithstanding anything in subsection (3) of section one of this Act, no provision of any enactment passed, or instrument having effect under an enactment and made, before the passing of this Act shall limit the powers conferred by the said section one;

    (*b*) subsection (1) of the foregoing section shall apply where the power of making investments therein mentioned is or includes a power to make some only of the investments mentioned in paragraph (*a*) or (*b*) of that subsection.

(2) This section applies to—

    (*a*) the persons for the time being authorised to invest funds of the Duchy of Lancaster;

    (*b*) any persons specified in an order made by the Treasury by statutory instrument, being persons (whether trustees or not) whose power to make investments is conferred by or under any enactment contained in a local or private Act.

(3) An order of the Treasury made under the foregoing subsection may provide that the provisions of sections one to six of this Act (other than the provisions of subsection (3) of section one) shall, in their application to any persons specified therein, have effect subject to such exceptions and modifications as may be specified. **[742]**

9. Supplementary provisions as to investments

(1) ...

(2) It is hereby declared that the power to subscribe for securities conferred by subsection (4) of the said section ten includes power to retain them for any period for which the trustee has power to retain the holding in respect of which the right to subscribe for the securities was offered, but subject to any conditions subject to which the trustee has that power. **[743]**

NOTES
Sub-s (1): amends the Trustee Act 1925, s 10.

11. Local Authority investment schemes

(1) Without prejudice to powers conferred by or under any other enactment, any authority to which this section applies may invest property held by the authority in accordance with a scheme submitted to the Treasury by any association of local authorities ... and approved by the Treasury as enabling investments to be made collectively without in substance extending the scope of powers of investment.

(2) A scheme under this section may apply to a specified authority or to a specified class of authorities, may make different provisions as respects different

authorities or different classes of authorities or as respects different descriptions of property or property held for different purposes, and may impose restrictions on the extent to which the power controlled by the foregoing subsection shall be exerciseable.

(3) In approving a scheme under this section, the Treasury may direct that [the Financial Services Act 1986], shall not apply to dealings undertaken or documents issued for the purposes of the scheme, or to such dealings or documents of such descriptions as may be specified in the direction.

(4) The authorities to which this section applies are—
   (a) in England and Wales the council of a county, a ... borough ... a district or a [parish, the common] Council of the City of London [the Broads Authority] [, ... a joint authority established by Part IV of the Local Government Act 1985] ... and the Council of the Isles of Scilly;
   (b) in Scotland, a local authority within the meaning of the Local Government (Scotland) Act 1947;
   (c) in any part of Great Britain, a joint board or joint committee constituted to discharge or advise on the discharge of the functions of any two or more of the authorities mentioned in the foregoing paragraphs (including a joint committee established by [those authorities acting in combination in accordance with regulations made under section 7 of the Superannuation Act 1972];
   (d) in Northern Ireland, a district council established under the Local Government Act (Northern Ireland) 1972, and the Northern Ireland Local Government Officers' Superannuation Committee established under the Local Government (Superannuation) Act (Northern Ireland) 1950.   **[744]**

NOTES
   Sub-s (1): words omitted repealed by the London Government Act 1963, s 93(1), Sch 8, Part II and by the Local Government Act 1985, s 102, Sch 17.
   Sub-s (3): words in square brackets substituted by the Financial Services Act 1986, s 212(2), Sch 16, para 2.
   Sub-s (4): in para (a), first words in square brackets substituted by the Water Act 1989, s 190, Sch 25, para 29, second words in square brackets inserted by the Norfolk and Suffolk Broads Act 1988, s 21, Sch 6, third words in square brackets inserted by the Local Government Act 1985, s 84, Sch 14, para 38, first words omitted repealed by the London Government Act 1963, s 93(1), Sch 18, Part II, second words omitted repealed by the Local Government Act 1972, s 272(1), Sch 30, third words omitted repealed by the Education Reform Act 1988, s 237, Sch 13, Part I, fourth words omitted repealed by the Local Government Act 1985, s 102, Sch 17; in para (c) words in square brackets substituted by the Superannuation Act 1972, s 29(1), Sch 6, para 40; in para (d) words in square brackets substituted by the Transfer of Functions (Local Government, etc) (Northern Ireland) Order 1973, SR & O (NI) 1973 No 256, art 3, Sch 2.

12. Power to confer additional powers of investment

(1) Her Majesty may by Order in Council extend the powers of investment conferred by section one of this Act by adding to Part I, Part II or Part III of the First Schedule to this Act any manner of investment specified in the Order.

(2) Any Order under this section shall be subject to annulment in pursuance of a resolution of either House of Parliament.   **[745]**

13. Power to modify provisions as to division of trust fund

(1) The Treasury may by order made by statutory instrument direct that, subject to subsection (3) of section four of this Act, any division of a trust fund made in pursuance of subsection (1) of section two of this Act during the continuance in

force of the order shall be made so that the value of the wider-range part at the time of the division bears to the then value of the narrower-range part such proportion, greater than one but not greater than three to one, as may be prescribed by the order; and in this Act "the prescribed proportion" means the proportion for the time being prescribed under this subsection.

(2) A fund which has been divided in pursuance of subsection (1) of section two of this Act before the coming into operation of an order under the foregoing subsection may notwithstanding anything in that subsection be again divided (once only) in pursuance of the said subsection (1) during the continuance in force of the order.

(3) If an order is made under subsection (1) of this section, then as from the coming into operation of the order—

(*a*) paragraph (*b*) of subsection (3) of section two of this Act and subparagraph (*b*) of paragraph 3 of the Second Schedule thereto shall have effect with the substitution, for the words from "each" to the end, of the words "the wider-range part of the fund is increased by an amount which bears the prescribed proportion to the amount by which the value of the narrower-range part of the fund is increased";

(*b*) subsection (3) of section four of this Act shall have effect as if for the words "so as either" to "each other" there were substituted the words "so as to bear to each other either the prescribed proportion or".

(4) An order under this section may be revoked by a subsequent order thereunder prescribing a greater proportion.

(5) An order under this section shall not have effect unless approved by a resolution of each House of Parliament. **[746]**

15. Saving for powers of court

The enlargement of the investment powers of trustees by this Act shall not lessen any power of a court to confer wider powers of investment on trustees, or affect the extent to which any such power is to be exercised. **[747]**

16. Minor and consequential amendments and repeals

(1) The provisions of the Fourth Schedule to this Act (which contain minor amendments and amendments consequential on the foregoing provisions of this Act) shall have effect.

(2) . . . **[748]**

NOTES
Sub-s (2): repealed by the Statute Law (Repeals) Act 1974.

17. Short title, extent and construction

(1) This Act may be cited as the Trustee Investments Act 1961.

(2) Sections eleven and sixteen of this Act shall extend to Northern Ireland, but except as aforesaid and except so far as any other provisions of the Act apply by virtue of subsection (1) of section one of the Trustee Act (Northern Ireland) 1958, or any other enactment of the Parliament of Northern Ireland, to trusts the execution of which is governed by the law in force in Northern Ireland, this Act does not apply to such trusts.

(3) So much of section sixteen of this Act as relates to [the National Savings Bank] . . . shall extend to the Isle of Man and the Channel Islands.

(4) Except where the context otherwise requires, in this Act, in its application to trusts the execution of which is governed by the law in force in England and Wales, expressions have the same meaning as in the Trustee Act 1925.

(5) . . . [749]

NOTES
Sub-s (3): words in square brackets substituted by the Post Office Act 1969, ss 94, 114, Sch 6, Part III; words omitted repealed by the Trustee Savings Banks Act 1985, ss 4(3), 7(3), Sch 4.
Sub-s (5): applies to Scotland only.

SCHEDULES
SCHEDULE 1

Section 1

MANNER OF INVESTMENT

PART I
NARROWER-RANGE INVESTMENTS NOT REQUIRING ADVICE

1. In Defence Bonds, National Savings Certificates Ulster Savings Certificates, [Ulster Development Bonds] [National Development Bonds], [British Savings Bonds], [National Savings Income Bonds] [National Savings Deposit Bonds] [National Savings Indexed-Income Bonds], [National Savings Capital Bonds], [National Savings FIRST Option Bonds].

2. In deposits in [the National Savings Bank], . . . and deposits in a bank or department thereof certified under subsection (3) of section nine of the Finance Act 1956. [750]

NOTES
Para 1: first words in square brackets added by the Trustee Investments (Additional Powers) (No 2) Order 1962, SI 1962 No 2611, art 1; second words in square brackets added by the Trustee Investments (Additional Powers) Order 1964, SI 1964 No 703, art 1; third words in square brackets added by the Trustee Investments (Additional Powers) Order 1968, SI 1968 No 470, art 1; fourth words in square brackets added by the Trustee Investments (Additional Powers) Order 1982, SI 1982 No 1086, art 2; fifth words in square brackets added by the Trustee Investments (Additional Powers) (No 2) Order 1983, SI 1983 No 1525, art 2; sixth words in square brackets added by the Trustee Investments (Additional Powers) Order 1985, SI 1985 No 1780, art 2; seventh words in square brackets added by the Trustee Investments (Additional Powers) Order 1988, SI 1988 No 2254, art 2; eighth words in square brackets added by the Trustee Investments (Additional Powers) Order 1992, SI 1992 No 1738, art 2.
Para 2: words in square brackets substituted by the Post Office Act 1969, ss 94, 114, Sch 6, Part III; words omitted repealed by the Trustee Savings Bank Act 1986, s 36(2), Sch 6.

PART II
NARROWER-RANGE OF INVESTMENTS REQUIRING ADVICE

1. In securities issued by Her Majesty's Government in the United Kingdom, the Government of Northern Ireland or the Government of the Isle of Man, not being securities falling within Part I of this Schedule and being fixed-interest securities registered in the United Kingdom or the Isle of Man, Treasury Bills or Tax Reserve Certificates [or any variable interest securities issued by Her Majesty's Government in the United Kingdom and registered in the United Kingdom].

2. In any securities the payment of interest on which is guaranteed by Her Majesty's Government in the United Kingdom or the Government of Northern Ireland.

3. In fixed-interest securities issued in the United Kingdom by any public authority or nationalised industry or undertaking in the United Kingdom.

4. In fixed-interest securities issued in the United Kingdom by the government of any overseas territory within the Commonwealth or by any public or local authority within such a territory, being securities registered in the United Kingdom.

References in this paragraph to an overseas territory or to the government of such a territory shall be construed as if they occurred in the Overseas Service Act 1958.

[4A. In securities issued in the United Kingdom by the government of an overseas territory within the Commonwealth or by any public or local authority within such a territory, being securities registered in the United Kingdom and in respect of which the rate of interest is variable by reference to one or more of the following:—

　　(*a*) the Bank of England's minimum lending rate;
　　(*b*) the average rate of discount on allotment on 91-day Treasury bills;
　　(*c*) a yield on 91-day Treasury bills;
　　(*d*) a London sterling inter-bank offered rate;
　　(*e*) a London sterling certificate of deposit rate.

References in this paragraph to an overseas territory or to the government of such a territory shall be construed as if they occurred in the Overseas Service Act 1958.]

5. In fixed-interest securities issued in the United Kingdom by [the African Development Bank, the Asian Development Bank, the Caribbean Development Bank, [European Bank for Reconstruction and Development,] the International Finance Corporation, the International Monetary Fund or by] the International Bank for Reconstruction and Development, being securities registered in the United Kingdom.

[In fixed-interest securities issued in the United Kingdom by the Inter-American Development Bank.]

[In fixed interest securities issued in the United Kingdom by [the European Atomic Energy Community, the European Economic Community,] the European Investment Bank or by the European Coal and Steel Community, being securities registered in the United Kingdom.]

[5A. In securities issued in the United Kingdom by

　　　　(i) the International Bank for Reconstruction and Development or by the European Investment Bank or by the European Coal and Steel Community, being securities registered in the United Kingdom or
　　　　(ii) the Inter-American Development Bank

being securities in respect of which the rate of interest is variable by reference to one or more of the following:—

　　(*a*) the Bank of England's minimum lending rate;
　　(*b*) the average rate of discount on allotment on 91-day Treasury bills;
　　(*c*) a yield on 91-day Treasury bills;
　　(*d*) a London sterling inter-bank offered rate;
　　(*e*) a London sterling certificate of deposit rate.]

[5B. In securities issued in the United Kingdom by the African Development Bank, the Asian Development Bank, the Caribbean Development Bank, the European Atomic Energy Community, [European Bank for Reconstruction and Development,] the European Economic Community, the International Finance Corporation or by the International Monetary Fund, being securities registered in the United Kingdom and in respect of which the rate of interest is variable by reference to one or more of the following:—

　　(*a*) The average rate of discound on allotment on 91-day Treasury Bills;
　　(*b*) a yield on 91-day Treasury Bills;
　　(*c*) a London sterling inter-bank offered rate;
　　(*d*) a London sterling certificate of deposit rate.]

6. In debentures issued in the United Kingdom by a company incorporated in the United Kingdom, being debentures registered in the United Kingdom.

7. In stock of the Bank of Ireland. [In Bank of Ireland 7 per cent. Loan Stock 1968/ 91].

8. ....

9. In loans to any authority to which this paragraph applies charged on all or any of the revenues of the authority or on a fund into which all or any of those revenues are payable, in any fixed-interest securities issued in the United Kingdom by any such authority for the purpose of borrowing money so charged, and in deposits with any such authority by way of temporary loan made on the giving of a receipt for the loan by the treasurer or other similar officer of the authority and on the giving of an undertaking by the authority that, if requested to charge the loan as aforesaid, it will either comply with the request or repay the loan.

This paragraph applies to the following authorities, that is to say—

(a) any local authority in the United Kingdom;
(b) any authority all the members of which are appointed or elected by one or more local authorities in the United Kingdom;
(c) any authority the majority of the members of which are appointed or elected by one or more local authorities in the United Kingdom, being an authority which by virtue of any enactment has power to issue a precept to a local authority in England and Wales, or a requisition to a local authority in Scotland, or to the expenses of which, by virtue of any enactment, a local authority in the United Kingdom is or can be required to contribute;
(d) the Receiver for the Metropolitan Police District or a combined police authority (within the meaning of the Police Act 1946);
(e) the Belfast City and District Water Commissioners;
[(f) the Great Ouse Water Authority];
[(g) any district council in Northern Ireland];
[(h) . . .;
(i) any residuary body established by section 57 of the Local Government Act 1985.]

[9A. In any securities issued in the United Kingdom by any authority to which paragraph 9 applies for the purpose of borrowing money charged on all or any of the revenues of the authority or on a fund into which all or any of those revenues are payable and being securities in respect of which the rate of interest is variable by reference to one or more of the following:—

(a) the Bank of England's minimum lending rate;
(b) the average rate of discount on allotment on 91-day Treasury bills;
(c) a yield on 91-day Treasury bills;
(d) a London sterling inter-bank offered rate;
(e) a London sterling certificate of deposit rate.]

10. *In debentures or in the guaranteed or preference stock of any incorporated company, being statutory water undertakers within the meaning of the Water Act 1945, or any corresponding enactment in force in Northern Ireland, and having during each of the ten years immediately preceding the calendar year in which the investment was made paid a dividend of not less than five per cent. on its ordinary shares.*

[10A. In any units, or other shares of the investments subject to the trusts, of a unit trust scheme which, at the time of investment, is an authorised unit trust, within the meaning of *section 358 of the Income and Corporation Taxes Act 1970, in relation to which, by virtue of section 60 of the Finance Act 1980, section 354 of the said Act of 1970 does not apply* [subsection (1) of section 468 of the Income and Corporation Taxes Act 1988, in relation to which that subsection does not, by virtue of subsection (5) of that section, apply].]

11 .... .

[12. In deposits with a building society within the meaning of the Building Societies Act 1986.]

13. In mortgages of freehold property in England and Wales or Northern Ireland and of leasehold property in those countries of which the unexpired term at the time of investment is not less than sixty years, and in loans on heritable security in Scotland.

14. In perpetual rent-charges charged on land in England and Wales or Northern Ireland and fee-farm rents (not being rent-charges) issuing out of such land, and in feu-duties or ground annuals in Scotland.

[15. In Certificates of Tax Deposit.] **[751]**

NOTES

Para 1: words in square brackets added by the Trustee Investments (Additional Powers) Order 1977, SI 1977 No 831, art 3.

Para 4A: inserted by the Trustee Investments (Additional Powers) (No 2) Order 1977, SI 1977 No 1878, art 3.

Para 5: first words in square brackets inserted by the Trustee Investments (Additional Powers) Order 1983, SI 1983 No 772, art 2, words in square brackets therein inserted by the Trustee Investments (Additional Powers) Order 1991, SI 1991 No 999, art 2; third words in square brackets inserted by the Trustee Investments (Additional Powers) (No 2) Order 1964, SI 1964 No 1404, art 1; fourth words in square brackets inserted by the Trustee Investments (Additional Powers) Order 1972, SI 1972 No 1818, art 3, words in square brackets therein inserted by the Trustee Investments (Additional Powers) Order 1983, SI 1983 No 772, art 2.

Para 5A: inserted by the Trustee Investments (Additional Powers) (No 2) Order 1977, SI 1977 No 1878, art 3.

Para 5B: inserted by the Trustee Investments (Additional Powers) Order 1983, SI 1983 No 772, art 2; words in square brackets inserted by the Trustee Investments (Additional Powers) Order 1991, SI 1991 No 999, art 2.

Para 7: words in square brackets inserted by the Trustee Investments (Additional Powers) Order 1966, SI 1966 No 401, art 1.

Para 9: sub-para (*f*) added by the Trustee Investments (Additional Powers) Order 1962, SI 1962 No 658, art 1; sub-para (*g*) added by the Trustee Investments (Additional Powers) Order 1973, SI 1973 No 1332, art 3; sub-para (*h*) added by the Trustee Investments (Additional Powers) Order 1986, SI 1986 No 601, art 2, repealed by the Education Reform Act 1988, s 237, Sch 13, Part I; para (*i*) added by the Trustee Investments (Additional Powers) Order 1986, SI 1986 No 601, art 2.

Para 9A: inserted by the Trustee Investments (Additional Powers) (No 2) Order 1977, SI 1977 No 1878, art 3.

Para 10: repealed, except insofar as it relates to the debentures or guaranteed or preference stock of a company which is a statutory water undertaker within the meaning of an enactment in Northern Ireland by the Water Act 1989, s 190(1), Sch 25, para 29.

Para 10A: inserted by the Finance Act 1982, s 150; words in italics repealed with savings and subsequent words in square brackets substituted with savings in relation to the year of assessment 1988-89 and subsequent years of assessment, by the Income and Corporation Taxes Act 1988, s 844, Sch 29, para 32: for savings see Sch 30 thereof.

Para 11: repealed by the Trustee Savings Bank Act 1976, s 36(2), Sch 6.

Para 12: substituted by the Building Societies Act 1986, s 120, Sch 18, Part I, para 4(2).

Para 15: added by the Trustee Investments (Additional Powers) Order 1975, SI 1975 No 1710, art 3.

PART III

WIDER-RANGE INVESTMENTS

1. In any securities issued in the United Kingdom by a company incorporated in the United Kingdom, being securities registered in the United Kingdom and not being securities falling within Part II of this Schedule.

[2. In shares in a building society within the meaning of the Building Societies Act 1986.]

[3. In any units of an authorised unit trust scheme within the meaning of the Financial Services Act 1986] **[752]**

NOTES

Para 2: substituted by the Building Societies Act 1986, s 120, Sch 18, Part I, para 4(3).

Para 3: substituted by the Financial Services Act 1986, s 212(2), Sch 16, para 2.

PART IV

SUPPLEMENTAL

1. The securities mentioned in Parts I to III of this Schedule do not include any securities where the holder can be required to accept repayment of the principal, or the payment of any interest, otherwise than in sterling.

2. The securities mentioned in paragraphs 1 to 8 of Part II, other than Treasury Bills or Tax Reserve Certificates, securities issued before the passing of this Act by the Government of the Isle of Man, securities falling within paragraph 4 of the said Part II issued before the passing of this Act or securities falling within paragraph 9 of that Part, and the securities mentioned in paragraph 1 of Part III of this Schedule, do not include—

    (a) securities the price of which is not quoted on *a recognised stock exchange within the meaning of the Prevention of Fraud (Investments) Act 1958, or the Belfast stock exchange* [a recognised investment exchange within the meaning of the Financial Services Act 1986];

    (b) shares or debenture stock not fully paid up (except shares or debenture stock which by the terms of issue are required to be fully paid up within nine months of the date of issue).

3. The securities mentioned in paragraph 6 of Part II and paragraph 1 of Part III of this Schedule do not include—

    (a) shares or debentures of an incorporated company of which the total issued and paid up share capital is less than one million pounds;

    (b) shares or debentures of an incorporated company which has not in each of the five years immediately preceding the calendar year in which the investment is made paid a dividend on all the shares issued by the company, excluding any shares issued after the dividend was declared and any shares which by their terms of issue did not rank for the dividend for that year.

For the purposes of sub-paragraph (b) of this paragraph a company formed—

    (i) to take over the business of another company or other companies, or

    (ii) to acquire the securities of, or control of, another company or other companies,

or for either of those purposes and for other purposes shall be deemed to have paid a dividend as mentioned in that sub-paragraph in any year in which such a dividend has been paid by the other company or all the other companies, as the case may be.

[For the purposes of sub-paragraph (b) of this paragraph in relation to investment in shares or debentures of a successor company within the meaning of the Electricity (Northern Ireland) Order 1992 the company shall be deemed to have paid a dividend as mentioned in that sub-paragraph—

    (iii) in every year preceding the calendar year in which the transfer date within the meaning of Part III of that Order of 1992 falls ("the first investment year") which is included in the relevant five years; and

    (iv) in the first investment year, if that year is included in the relevant five years and that company does not in fact pay such a dividend in that year; and

"the relevant five years" means the five years immediately preceding the year in which the investment in question is made or proposed to be made.]

[3A. . . .]

4. In this Schedule, unless the context otherwise requires, the following expressions have the meanings hereby respectively assigned to them, that is to say—

    "debenture" includes debenture stock and bonds, whether constituting a charge on assets or not, and loan stock or notes;

    "enactment" includes an enactment of the Parliament of Northern Ireland;

    "fixed-interest securities" means securities which under their terms of issue bear a fixed rate of interest;

    "local authority" in relation to the United Kingdom, means any of the following authorities—

        (a) in England and Wales, the council of a county, a ... borough ... an urban or rural district or a parish, the Common Council of the City of London [the Greater London Council] and the Council of the Isles of Scilly;

        (b) in Scotland, a local authority within the meaning of the Local Government (Scotland) Act 1947;

(c) ...
...
"securities" includes shares, debentures [units within paragraph 3 of Part III of this Schedule], Treasury Bills and Tax Reserve Certificates;
"shares" includes stock;
"Treasury Bills" includes ... bills issued by Her Majesty's Government in the United Kingdom and Northern Ireland Treasury Bills.

5. It is hereby declared that in this Schedule "mortgage", in relation to freehold or leasehold property in Northern Ireland, includes a registered charge which, by virtue of subsection (4) of section forty of the Local Registration of Title (Ireland) Act 1891, or any other enactment, operates as a mortgage by deed.

6. References in this Schedule to an incorporated company are references to a company incorporated by or under any enactment and include references to a body of persons established for the purpose of trading for profit and incorporated by Royal Charter.

7. ...   [753]

NOTES
Para 2: words in square brackets substituted by the Financial Services Act 1986, s 212(2), Sch 16, para 2.
Para 3A: inserted by the Housing (Consequential Provisions) Act 1985, s 4, Sch 2, para 5; repealed by the Building Societies Act 1986, s 120, Sch 19, Part I.
Para 4: in definition "local authority", first words omitted repealed by the London Government Act 1963, s 93(1), Sch 18 Part II, second words omitted repealed by the Local Government Act 1972, s 272(1), Sch 30, sub para (c) repealed by the Statute Law (Repeals) Act 1981, words in square brackets inserted by the London Government Act 1963, s 83(1), Sch 17; definitions "ordinary deposits" and "special investment" repealed by the Trustee Savings Banks Act 1976, s 36(2), Sch 6; in definition "securities" words in square brackets inserted by the Financial Services Act 1986, s 212(2), Sch 16, para 2; in definition "Treasury Bills", words omitted repealed by the National Loans Act 1968, s 24(2), Sch 6, Part 1.
Para 7: repealed by the Building Societies Act 1986, s 120, Sch 19, Part I.

SCHEDULE 2
Section 3
MODIFICATION OF S 2 IN RELATION TO PROPERTY FALLING WITHIN S 3(3)

1. In this Schedule "special-range property" means property falling within subsection (3) of section three of this Act.

2. (1) Where a trust fund includes special-range property, subsection (1) of section two of this Act shall have effect as if references to the trust fund were references to so much thereof as does not consist of special-range property, and the special-range property shall be carried to a separate part of the fund.

(2) Any property which—

(a) being property belonging to the narrower-range or wider-range part of a trust fund, is converted into special-range property, or
(b) being special-range property, accrues to a trust fund after the division of the fund or part thereof in pursuance of subsection (1) of section two of this Act or of that subsection as modified by sub-paragraph (1) of this paragraph,

shall be carried to such a separate part of the fund as aforesaid; and subsections (2) and (3) of the said section two shall have effect subject to this sub-paragraph.

3. Where property carried to such a separate part as aforesaid is converted into property other than special-range property,—

(a) it shall be transferred to the narrower-range part of the fund or the wider-range part of the fund or apportioned between them, and
(b) any transfer of property from one of those parts to the other shall be made which is necessary to secure that the value of each of those parts of the fund is increased by the same amount.   [754]

SCHEDULE 3

Section 3

PROVISIONS SUPPLEMENTARY TO S 3(4)

1. Where in a case falling within subsection (4) of section three of this Act, property belonging to the narrower-range part of a trust fund—

(a) is invested otherwise than in a narrower-range investment, or

(b) being so invested, is retained and not transferred or as soon as may be reinvested as mentioned in subsection (2) of section two of this Act.

then, so long as the property continues so invested and comprised in the narrower-range part of the fund, section one of this Act shall not authorise the making or retention of any wider-range investment.

2. Section four of the Trustee Act 1925, or section thirty-three of the Trusts (Scotland) Act, 1921 (which relieve a trustee from liability for retaining an investment which has ceased to be authorised), shall not apply where an investment ceased to be authorised in consequence of the foregoing paragraph. **[755]**

SCHEDULE 4

Section 16

MINOR AND CONSEQUENTIAL AMENDMENTS

1. (1) References in the Trustee Act 1925, except in subsection (2) of section sixty-nine of that Act, to section one of that Act or to provisions which include that section shall be construed respectively as references to section one of this Act and as including references to section one of this Act.

(2) References in the Trusts (Scotland) Act 1921, to section ten or eleven of that Act, or to provisions which include either of those sections, shall be construed respectively as references to section one of this Act and as including references to that section.

2–6 . . . **[756]**

NOTES

Para 2: repealed by the Building Societies Act 1962, s 131, Sch 10, Part I.
Para 3: repealed by the Water Act 1989, s 190(3), Sch 27, Part II.
Paras 4, 5: repealed by the National Savings Bank Act 1971, s 28, Sch 2.
Para 6: repealed by the Housing (Consequential Provisions) Act 1985, s 3, Sch 1, Part I.

WILLS ACT 1963

(c 44)

ARRANGEMENT OF SECTIONS

An Act to repeal the Wills Act 1861 and make new provision in lieu thereof; and to provide that certain testamentary instruments shall be probative for the purpose of the conveyance of heritable property in Scotland [31 July 1963]

1. General rule as to formal validity

A will shall be treated as properly executed if its execution conformed to the internal law in force in the territory where it was executed, or in the territory where, at the time of its execution or of the testator's death, he was domiciled or had his habitual residence, or in a state of which, at either of those times, he was a national. **[757]**

2. Additional rules

(1) Without prejudice to the preceding section, the following shall be treated as properly executed—

    (*a*) a will executed on board a vessel or aircraft of any description, if the execution of the will conformed to the internal law in force in the territory with which, having regard to its registration (if any) and other relevant circumstances, the vessel or aircraft may be taken to have been most closely connected;

    (*b*) a will so far as it disposes of immovable property, if its execution conformed to the internal law in force in the territory where the property was situated;

    (*c*) a will so far as it revokes a will which under this Act would be treated as properly executed or revokes a provision which under this Act would be treated as comprised in a properly executed will, if the execution of the later will conformed to any law by reference to which the revoked will or provision would be so treated;

    (*d*) a will so far as it exercises a power of appointment, if the execution of the will conformed to the law governing the essential validity of the power.

(2) A will so far as it exercises a power of appointment shall not be treated as improperly executed by reason only that its execution was not in accordance with any formal requirements contained in the instrument creating the power. **[758]**

3. Certain requirements to be treated as formal

Where (whether in pursuance of this Act or not) a law in force outside the United Kingdom falls to be applied in relation to a will, any requirement of that law whereby special formalities are to be observed by testators answering a particular description, or witnesses to the execution of a will are to possess certain qualifications, shall be treated, notwithstanding any rule of that law to the contrary, as a formal requirement only. **[759]**

4. Construction of wills

The construction of a will shall not be altered by reason of any change in the testator's domicile after the execution of the will. **[760]**

6. Interpretation

(1) In this Act—

    "internal law" in relation to any territory or state means the law which would apply in a case where no question of the law in force in any other territory or state arose;

    "state" means a territory or group of territories having its own law of nationality;

    "will" includes any testamentary instrument or act, and "testator" shall be construed accordingly.

(2) Where under this Act the internal law in force in any territory or state is to be applied in the case of a will, but there are in force in that territory or state

two or more systems of internal law relating to the formal validity of wills, the system to be applied shall be ascertained as follows—

    (*a*) if there is in force throughout the territory or state a rule indicating which of those systems can properly be applied in the case in question, that rule shall be followed; or

    (*b*) if there is no such rule, the system shall be that with which the testator was most closely connected at the relevant time, and for this purpose the relevant time is the time of the testator's death where the matter is to be determined by reference to circumstances prevailing at his death, and the time of execution of the will in any other case.

(3) In determining for the purposes of this Act whether or not the execution of a will conformed to a particular law, regard shall be had to the formal requirements of that law at the time of execution, but this shall not prevent account being taken of an alteration of law affecting wills executed at that time if the alteration enables the will to be treated as properly executed. **[761]**

7. Short title commencement, repeal and extent

(1) This Act may be cited as the Wills Act 1963.

(2) This Act shall come into operation on 1st January 1964.

(3) ...

(4) This Act shall not apply to a will of a testator who died before the time of the commencement of this Act and shall apply to a will of a testator who dies after that time whether the will was executed before or after that time, but so that the repeal of the Wills Act 1861 shall not invalidate a will executed before that time.

(5) It is hereby declared that this Act extends to Northern Ireland, and for the purposes of section 6 of the Government of Ireland Act 1920 this Act shall be deemed to be an Act passed before the appointed day within the meaning of that section. **[762]**

NOTES
    Sub-s (3): repeals the Wills Act 1861.

PERPETUITIES AND ACCUMULATIONS ACT 1964
(c 55)

ARRANGEMENT OF SECTIONS

Perpetuities

An Act to modify the law of England and Wales relating to the avoidance of future interests in property on grounds of remoteness and governing accumulations of income from property [16 July 1964]

Perpetuities

1. Power to specify perpetuity period

(1) Subject to section 9(2) of this Act and subsection (2) below, where the instrument by which any disposition is made so provides, the perpetuity period applicable to the disposition under the rule against perpetuities, instead of being of any other duration, shall be of a duration equal to such number of years not exceeding eighty as is specified in that behalf in the instrument.

(2) Subsection (1) above shall not have effect where the disposition is made in exercise of a special power of appointment, but where a period is specified under that subsection in the instrument creating such a power the period shall apply in relation to any disposition under the power as it applies in relation to the power itself. **[763]**

2. Presumptions and evidence as to future parenthood

(1) Where in any proceedings there arises on the rule against perpetuities a question which turns on the ability of a person to have a child at some future time, then—

> (*a*) subject to paragraph (*b*) below, it shall be presumed that a male can have a child at the age of fourteen years or over, but not under that age, and that a female can have a child at the age of twelve years or over, but not under that age or over the age of fifty-five years; but
>
> (*b*) in the case of a living person evidence may be given to show that he or she will or will not be able to have a child at the time in question.

(2) Where any such question is decided by treating a person as unable to have a child at a particular time, and he or she does so, the High Court may make such order as it thinks fit for placing the persons interested in the property comprised in the disposition, so far as may be just, in the position they would have held if the question had not been so decided.

(3) Subject to subsection (2) above, where any such question is decided in relation to a disposition by treating a person as able or unable to have a child at a particular time, then he or she shall be so treated for the purpose of any question which may arise on the rule against perpetuities in relation to the same disposition in any subsequent proceedings.

(4) In the foregoing provisions of this section references to having a child are references to begetting or giving birth to a child, but those provisions (except subsection (1)(*b*)) shall apply in relation to the possibility that a person will at any time have a child by adoption, legitimation or other means as they apply to his or her ability at that time to beget or give birth to a child.   **[764]**

3. Uncertainty as to remoteness

(1) Where, apart from the provisions of this section and sections 4 and 5 of this Act, a disposition would be void on the ground that the interest disposed of might not become vested until too remote a time, the disposition shall be treated, until such time (if any) as it becomes established that the vesting must occur, if at all, after the end of the perpetuity period, as if the disposition were not subject to the rule against perpetuities; and its becoming so established shall not affect the validity of anything previously done in relation to the interest disposed of by way of advancement, application of intermediate income or otherwise.

(2) Where, apart from the said provisions, a disposition consisting of the conferring of a general power of appointment would be void on the ground that the power might not become exercisable until too remote a time, the disposition shall be treated, until such time (if any) as it becomes established that the power will not be exercisable within the perpetuity period, as if the disposition were not subject to the rule against perpetuities.

(3) Where, apart from the said provisions, a disposition consisting of the conferring of any power, option or other right would be void on the ground that the right might be exercised at too remote a time, the disposition shall be treated as regards any exercise of the right within the perpetuity period as if it were not subject to the rule against perpetuities and, subject to the said provisions, shall be treated as void for remoteness only if, and so far as, the right is not fully exercised within that period.

(4) Where this section applies to a disposition and the duration of the perpetuity period is not determined by virtue of section 1 or 9(2) of this Act, it shall be determined as follows:—

    (*a*) where any persons falling within subsection (5) below are individuals in being and ascertainable at the commencement of the perpetuity period the duration of the period shall be determined by reference to their lives and no others, but so that the lives of any description of persons falling within paragraph (*b*) or (*c*) of that subsection shall be disregarded if the number of persons of that description is such as to render it impracticable to ascertain the date of death of the survivor;

    (*b*) where there are no lives under paragraph (*a*) above the period shall be twenty-one years.

(5) The said persons are as follows:—

    (*a*) the person by whom the disposition was made;

    (*b*) a person to whom or in whose favour the disposition was made, that is to say—

        (i) in the case of a disposition to a class of persons, any member or potential member of the class;

        (ii) in the case of an individual disposition to a person taking only on certain conditions being satisfied, any person as to whom some of the conditions are satisfied and the remainder may in time be satisfied;

(iii) in the case of a special power of appointment exercisable in favour of members of a class, any member or potential member of the class;

(iv) in the case of a special power of appointment exercisable in favour of one person only, that person or, where the object of the power is ascertainable only on certain conditions being satisfied, any person as to whom some of the conditions are satisfied and the remainder may in time be satisfied;

(v) in the case of any power, option or other right, the person on whom the right is conferred;

(c) a person having a child or grandchild within sub-paragraphs (i) to (iv) of paragraph (b) above, or any of whose children or grandchildren, if subsequently born, would by virtue of his or her descent fall within those sub-paragraphs;

(d) any person on the failure or determination of whose prior interest the disposition is limited to take effect. **[765]**

4. Reduction of age and exclusion of class members to avoid remoteness

(1) Where a disposition is limited by reference to the attainment by any person or persons of a specified age exceeding twenty-one years, and it is apparent at the time the disposition is made or becomes apparent at a subsequent time—

(a) that the disposition would, apart from this section, be void for remoteness, but

(b) that it would not be so void if the specified age had been twenty-one years,

the disposition shall be treated for all purposes as if, instead of being limited by reference to the age in fact specified, it had been limited by reference to the age nearest to that age which would, if specified instead, have prevented the disposition from being so void.

(2) Where in the case of any disposition different ages exceeding twenty-one years are specified in relation to different persons—

(a) the reference in paragraph (b) of subsection (1) above to the specified age shall be construed as a reference to all the specified ages, and

(b) that subsection shall operate to reduce each such age so far as is necessary to save the disposition from being void for remoteness.

(3) Where the inclusion of any persons, being potential members of a class or unborn persons who at birth would become members or potential members of the class, prevents the foregoing provisions of this section from operating to save a disposition from being void for remoteness, those persons shall thenceforth be deemed for all the purposes of the disposition to be excluded from the class, and the said provisions shall thereupon have effect accordingly.

(4) Where, in the case of a disposition to which subsection (3) above does not apply, it is apparent at the time the disposition is made or becomes apparent at a subsequent time that, apart from this subsection, the inclusion of any persons, being potential members of a class or unborn persons who at birth would become members or potential members of the class, would cause the disposition to be treated as void for remoteness, those persons shall, unless their exclusion would exhaust the class, thenceforth be deemed for all the purposes of the disposition to be excluded from the class.

(5) Where this section has effect in relation to a disposition to which section 3 above applies, the operation of this section shall not affect the validity of

anything previously done in relation to the interest disposed of by way of advancement, application of intermediate income or otherwise.

(6) . . .

[(7) For the avoidance of doubt it is hereby declared that a question arising under section 3 of this Act or subsection (1)(*a*) above of whether a disposition would be void apart from this section is to be determined as if subsection (6) above had been a separate section of this Act.]   **[766]**

NOTES
Sub-s (6): repeals the Law of Property Act 1925, s 163.
Sub-s (7): added by the Children Act 1975, s 108(1)(*a*), Sch 3.

5. Condition relating to death of surviving spouse

Where a disposition is limited by reference to the time of death of the survivor of a person in being at the commencement of the perpetuity period and any spouse of that person, and that time has not arrived at the end of the perpetuity period, the disposition shall be treated for all purposes, where to do so would save it from being void for remoteness, as if it had instead been limited by reference to the time immediately before the end of that period.   **[767]**

6. Saving and acceleration of expectant interests

A disposition shall not be treated as void for remoteness by reason only that the interest disposed of is ulterior to and dependent upon an interest under a disposition which is so void, and the vesting of an interest shall not be prevented from being accelerated on the failure of a prior interest by reason only that the failure arises because of remoteness.   **[768]**

7. Powers of appointment

For the purposes of the rule against perpetuities, a power of appointment shall be treated as a special power unless—

    (*a*) in the instrument creating the power it is expressed to be exercisable by one person only, and

    (*b*) it could, at all times during its currency when that person is of full age and capacity, be exercised by him so as immediately to transfer to himself the whole of the interest governed by the power without the consent of any other person or compliance with any other condition, not being a formal condition relating only to the mode of exercise of the power:

Provided that for the purpose of determining whether a disposition made under a power of appointment exercisable by will only is void for remoteness, the power shall be treated as a general power where it would have fallen to be so treated if exercisable by deed.   **[769]**

8. Administrative powers of trustees

(1) The rule against perpetuities shall not operate to invalidate a power conferred on trustees or other persons to sell, lease, exchange or otherwise dispose of any property for full consideration, or to do any other act in the administration (as opposed to the distribution) of any property, and shall not prevent the payment to trustees or other persons of reasonable remuneration for their services.

(2) Subsection (1) above shall apply for the purpose of enabling a power to

be exercised at any time after the commencement of this Act notwithstanding that the power is conferred by an instrument which took effect before that commencement.   [770]

9. Options relating to Land

(1) The rule against perpetuities shall not apply to a disposition consisting of the conferring of an option to acquire for valuable consideration an interest reversionary (whether directly or indirectly) on the term of a lease if—

   (a) the option is exercisable only by the lessee or his successors in title, and

   (b) it ceases to be exercisable at or before the expiration of one year following the determination of the lease.

This subsection shall apply in relation to an agreement for a lease as it applies in relation to a lease, and "lessee" shall be construed accordingly.

(2) In the case of a disposition consisting of the conferring of an option to acquire for valuable consideration any interest in land, the perpetuity period under the rule against perpetuities shall be twenty-one years, and section 1 of this Act shall not apply:

Provided that this subsection shall not apply to a right of pre-emption conferred on a public or local authority in respect of land used or to be used for religious purposes where the right becomes exercisable only if the land ceases to be used for such purposes.   [771]

10. Avoidance of contractual and other rights in cases of remoteness

Where a disposition inter vivos would fail to be treated as void for remoteness if the rights and duties thereunder were capable of transmission to persons other than the original parties and had been so transmitted, it shall be treated as void as between the person by whom it was made and the person to whom or in whose favour it was made or any successor of his, and no remedy shall lie in contract or otherwise for giving effect to it or making restitution for its lack of effect.   [772]

11. Rights for enforcement of rentcharges

(1) The rule against perpetuities shall not apply to any powers or remedies for recovering or compelling the payment of an annual sum to which section 121 or 122 of the Law of Property Act 1925 applies, or otherwise becoming exercisable or enforceable on the breach of any condition or other requirement relating to that sum.

(2) . . .   [773]

NOTES

Sub-s (2): amends the Law of Property Act 1925, s 121(6).

---

12. Possibilities of reverter, conditions subsequent, exceptions and reservations

(1) In the case of—

   (a) a possibility of reverter on the determination of a determinable fee simple, or

   (b) a possibility of a resulting trust on the determination of any other determinable interest in property,

the rule against perpetuities shall apply in relation to the provision causing the interest to be determinable as it would apply if that provision were expressed in the form of a condition subsequent giving rise, on breach thereof, to a right of re-entry or an equivalent right in the case of property other than land, and where the provision falls to be treated as void for remoteness the determinable interest shall become an absolute interest.

(2) Where a disposition is subject to any such provision, or to any such condition subsequent, or to any exception or reservation, the disposition shall be treated for the purposes of this Act as including a separate disposition of any rights arising by virtue of the provision, condition subsequent, exception or reservation.   [774]

Accumulations

13. Amendment of s 164 of Law of Property Act 1925

(1) The periods for which accumulations of income under a settlement or other disposition are permitted by section 164 of the Law of Property Act 1925 shall include—

  (*a*) a term of twenty-one years from the date of the making of the disposition, and

  (*b*) the duration of the minority or respective minorities of any person or persons in being at that date.

(2) It is hereby declared that the restrictions imposed by the said section 164 apply in relation to a power to accumulate income whether or not there is a duty to exercise that power, and that they apply whether or not the power to accumulate extends to income produced by the investment of income previously accumulated.   [775]

14. Right to stop accumulations

Section 2 above shall apply to any question as to the right of beneficiaries to put an end to accumulations of income under any disposition as it applies to questions arising on the rule against perpetuities.   [776]

Supplemental

15. Short title, interpretation and extent

(1) This Act may be cited as the Perpetuities and Accumulations Act 1964.

  (2) In this Act—

  "disposition" includes the conferring of a power of appointment and any other disposition of an interest in or right over property, and references to the interest disposed of shall be construed accordingly;
  "in being" means living or en ventre sa mere;
  "power of appointment" includes any discretionary power to transfer a beneficial interest in property without the furnishing of valuable consideration;
  "will" includes a codicil;

and for the purposes of this Act a disposition contained in a will shall be deemed to be made at the death of the testator.

(3) For the purposes of this Act a person shall be treated as a member of a class if in his case all the conditions identifying a member of the class are

satisfied, and shall be treated as a potential member if in his case some only of those conditions are satisfied but there is a possibility that the remainder will in time be satisfied.

(4) Nothing in this Act shall affect the operation of the rule of law rendering void for remoteness certain dispositions under which property is limited to be applied for purposes other than the benefit of any person or class of persons in cases where the property may be so applied after the end of the perpetuity period.

(5) The foregoing sections of this Act shall apply (except as provided in section 8(2) above) only in relation to instruments taking effect after the commencement of this Act, and in the case of an instrument made in the exercise of a special power of appointment shall apply only where the instrument creating the power takes effect after that commencement;

Provided that section 7 above shall apply in all cases for construing the foregoing reference to a special power of appointment.

(6) This Act shall apply in relation to a disposition made otherwise than by an instrument as if the disposition had been contained in an instrument taking effect when the disposition was made. [777]

LAW OF PROPERTY (JOINT TENANTS) ACT 1964
(c 63)

ARRANGEMENT OF SECTIONS

An Act to amend the law with respect to land vested in joint tenants [31 July 1964]

1. Assumptions on sale of land by survivor of joint tenants

(1) For the purposes of section 36(2) of the Law of Property Act 1925, as amended by section 7 of and the Schedule to the Law of Property (Amendment) Act 1926, the survivor of two or more joint tenants shall in favour of a purchaser of the legal estate, be deemed to be solely and beneficially interested if he conveys as beneficial owner or the conveyance includes a statement that he is so interested.

Provided that the foregoing provisions of this subsection shall not apply if, at any time before the date of the conveyance by the survivor—

(a) a memorandum of severance (that is to say a note or memorandum signed by the joint tenants or one of them and recording that the joint tenancy was severed in equity on a date therein specified) had been endorsed on or annexed to the conveyance by virtue of which the legal estate was vested in the joint tenants; or

(b) [a bankruptcy order] made against any of the joint tenants, or a petition for such an order, had been registered under the Land Charges Act 1925, being an order or petition of which the purchaser has notice, by virtue of the registration, on the date of the conveyance by the survivor.

(2) The foregoing provisions of this section shall apply with the necessary modifications in relation to a conveyance by the personal representatives of the survivor of joint tenants as they apply in relation to a conveyance by such a survivor.   **[778]**

NOTES

Sub-s (1): words in square brackets substituted by the Insolvency Act 1985, s 235, Sch 8, para 13.

2. Retrospective and transitional provisions

Section 1 of this Act shall be deemed to have come into force on 1st January 1926, and for the purposes of that section in its application to a conveyance executed before the passing of this Act a statement signed by the vendor or by his personal representatives that he was solely and beneficially interested shall be treated as if it had been included in the conveyance.   **[779]**

3. Exclusion of registered land

This Act shall not apply to any land the title of which has been registered under the provisions of the Land Registration Acts 1925 and 1936.   **[780]**

4. Short title, construction, citation and extent

(1) This Act may be cited as the Law of Property (Joint Tenants) Act 1964, and shall be construed as one with the Law of Property Act 1925.

(2) The Law of Property Acts 1925 to 1932, and this Act, may be cited together as the Law of Property Acts 1925 to 1964.

(3) This Act extends to England and Wales only.   **[781]**

COMMONS REGISTRATION ACT 1965
(c 64)

ARRANGEMENT OF SECTIONS

An Act to provide for the registration of common land and of town or village greens;
   to amend the law as to prescriptive claims to rights of common; and for purposes
   connected therewith   [5 August 1965]

1. Registration of commons and towns or village greens and ownership of and rights over them

(1) There shall be registered, in accordance with the provisions of this Act and
subject to the exceptions mentioned therein,—

   (a) land in England or Wales which is common land or a town or village
       green;
   (b) rights of common over such land; and
   (c) persons claiming to be or found to be owners of such land or becoming
       the owners thereof by virtue of this Act;

and no rights of common over land which is capable of being registered under
this Act shall be registered under the Land Registration Acts 1925 and 1936.

(2) After the end of such period, not being less than three years from the
commencement of this Act, as the Minister may by order determine—

   (a) no land capable of being registered under this Act shall be deemed to
       be common land or a town or village green unless it is so registered;
       and
   (b) no rights of common shall be exercisable over any such land unless
       they are registered either under this Act or under the Land Registration
       Acts 1925 and 1936.

(3) Where any land is registered under this Act but no person is registered
as the owner thereof under this Act or under the Land Registration Acts 1925
and 1936, it shall—

   (a) if it is a town or village green, be vested in accordance with the
       following provisions of this Act; and
   (b) if it is common land, be vested as Parliament may hereafter
       determine.   [782]

2. Registration authorities

(1) The registration authority for the purposes of this Act shall be—

   (a) in relation to any land situated in any county . . . , the council of that
       county [or, if the county is a metropolitan county, the council of the
       metropolitan district in which the land is situated] . . . ; and
   (b) in relation to any land situated in Greater London, the [council of the
       London borough in which the land is situated];

except where an agreement under this section otherwise provides.

(2) Where part of any land is in the area of one registration authority and
part in that of another the authorities may by agreement provide for one of
them to be the registration authority in relation to the whole of the land.   [783]

NOTES
  Sub-s (1): in para (*a*) words omitted repealed by the Local Government Act 1972, s 272(1), Sch 30, words in square brackets inserted by the Local Government Act 1985, s 16, Sch 8, para 10; in para (*b*) words in square brackets inserted by the Local Government Act 1985, s 16, Sch 8, para 10.

3. The registers

(1) For the purposes of registering such land as is mentioned in section 1(1) of this Act and rights of common over and ownership of such land every registration authority shall maintain—

    (*a*) a register of common land; and
    (*b*) a register of town or village greens;

and regulations under this Act may require or authorise a registration authority to note on those registers such other information as may be prescribed.

(2) Any register maintained under this Act shall be open to inspection by the public at all reasonable times. **[784]**

4. Provisional registration

(1) Subject to the provisions of this section, a registration authority shall register any land as common land or a town or village green or, as the case may be, any rights of common over or ownership of such land, on application duly made to it and accompanied by such declaration and such other documents (if any) as may be prescribed for the purpose of verification or of proving compliance with any prescribed conditions.

(2) An application for the registration of any land as common land or as a town or village green may be made by any person, and a registration authority—

    (*a*) may so register any land notwithstanding that no application for that registration has been made, and
    (*b*) shall so register any land in any case where it registers any rights over it under this section.

(3) No person shall be registered under this section as the owner of any land which is registered under the Land Registration Acts 1925 and 1936 and no person shall be registered under this section as the owner of any other land unless the land itself is registered under this section.

(4) Where, in pursuance of an application under this section, any land would fall to be registered as common land or as a town or village green, but the land is already so registered, the registration authority shall not register it again but shall note the application in the register.

(5) A registration under this section shall be provisional only until it has become final under the following provisions of this Act.

(6) An application for registration under this section shall not be entertained if made after such date, not less than three years from the commencement of this Act, as the Minister may by order specify; and different dates may be so specified for different classes of applications.

(7) Every local authority shall take such steps as may be prescribed for informing the public of the period within which and the manner in which applications for registration under this section may be made. **[785]**

5. Notification of, and objections to, registration

(1) A registration authority shall give such notices and take such other steps as may be prescribed for informing the public of any registration made by it under section 4 of this Act, of the times and places where copies of the relevant entries in the register may be inspected and of the period during which and the manner in which objections to the registration may be made to the authority.

(2) The period during which objections to any registration under section 4 of this Act may be made shall be such period, ending not less than two years after the date of the registration, as may be prescribed.

(3) Where any land or rights over land are registered under section 4 of this Act but no person is so registered as the owner of the land the registration authority may, if it thinks fit, make an objection to the registration notwithstanding that it has no interest in the land.

(4) Where an objection to a registration under section 4 of this Act is made, the registration authority shall note the objection on the register and shall give such notice as may be prescribed to the person (if any) on whose application the registration was made and to any person whose application is noted under section 4(4) of this Act.

(5) Where a person to whom notice has been given under subsection (4) of this section so requests or where the registration was made otherwise than on the application of any person, the registration authority may, if it thinks fit, cancel or modify a registration to which objection is made under this section.

(6) Where such an objection is made, then, unless the objection is withdrawn or the registration cancelled before the end of such period as may be prescribed, the registration authority shall refer the matter to a Commons Commissioner.

(7) An objection to the registration of any land as common land or as a town or village green shall be treated for the purposes of this Act as being also an objection to any registration (whenever made) under section 4 of this Act of any rights over the land.

(8) A registration authority shall take such steps as may be prescribed for informing the public of any objection which they have noted on the register under this section and of the times and places where copies of the relevant entries in the register may be inspected.

(9) Where regulations under this Act require copies of any entries in a register to be sent by the registration authority to another local authority they may require that other authority to make the copies available for inspection in such manner as may be prescribed.   **[786]**

6. Disposal of disputed claims

(1) The Commons Commissioner to whom any matter has been referred under section 5 of this Act shall inquire into it and shall either confirm the registration, with or without modifications, or refuse to confirm it; and the registration shall, if it is confirmed, become final, and, if the confirmation is refused, become void,—

    (a) if no appeal is brought against the confirmation or refusal, at the end of the period during which such an appeal could have been brought;

    (b) if such an appeal is brought, when it is finally disposed of.

(2) On being informed in the prescribed manner that a registration has

become final (with or without modifications) or has become void a registration authority shall indicate that fact in the prescribed manner in the register and, if it has become void, cancel the registration.

(3) Where the registration of any land as common land or as a town or village green is cancelled (whether under this section or under section 5(5) of this Act) the registration authority shall also cancel the registration of any person as the owner thereof.   **[787]**

7. Finality of undisputed registrations

(1) If no objection is made to a registration under section 4 of this Act or if all objections made to such a registration are withdrawn the registration shall become final at the end of the period during which such objections could have been made under section 5 of this Act or, if an objection made during that period is withdrawn after the end thereof, at the date of the withdrawal.

(2) Where by virtue of this section a registration has become final the registration authority shall indicate that fact in the prescribed manner in the register.   **[788]**

8. Vesting of unclaimed land

(1) Where the registration under section 4 of this Act of any land as common land or as a town or village green has become final but no person is registered under that section as the owner of the land, then unless the land is registered under the Land Registration Acts 1925 and 1936, the registration authority shall refer the question of the ownership of the land to a Commons Commissioner.

(2) After the registration authority has given such notices as may be prescribed, the Commons Commissioner shall inquire into the matter and shall, if satisfied that any person is the owner of the land, direct the registration authority to register that person accordingly; and the registration authority shall comply with the direction.

(3) If the Commons Commissioner is not so satisfied and the land is a town or village green he shall direct the registration authority to register as the owner of the land the local authority specified in subsection (5) of this section; and the registration authority shall comply with the direction.

(4) On the registration under this section of a local authority as the owner of any land the land shall vest in that local authority and, if the land is not regulated by a scheme under the Commons Act 1899, sections 10 and 15 of the Open Spaces Act 1906 (power to manage and make byelaws) shall apply in relation to it as if that local authority had acquired the ownership under the said Act of 1906.

[(5) Subject to subsection (6) of this section, the local authority in which any land is to be vested under this section is—

    (a) if the land is in a parish or community where there is a parish or community council, that council, but, if the land is regulated by a scheme under the Commons Act 1899, only if the powers of management under Part I of that Act are, in accordance with arrangements under Part VI of the Local Government Act 1972, being exercised by the parish or community council;

    (b) if the land is in a London borough, the council of that borough; and

    (c) in any other case, the council of the district in which the land is situated.

(6) Where—

    (*a*) any land has been vested in a district council in accordance with subsection (5)(*c*) of this section, and

    (*b*) after the land has been so vested a parish or community council comes into being for the parish or community in which the land is situated (whether by the establishment of a new council or by adding that parish or community to a group of parishes or communities for which a council has already been established),

then, if the circumstances are such that, had the direction under subsection (3) of this section been given at a time after the parish or community council had come into being, the land would in accordance with subsection (5)(*a*) of this section have been vested in the parish or community council, the district council shall, if requested to do so by the parish or community council, direct the registration authority to register the parish or community council, in place of the district council, as the owner of the land; and the registration authority shall comply with any such direction.

(7) The council of any district, parish or community affected by any registration made in pursuance of subsection (6) above shall pay to the other of those councils so affected such sum, if any, as may be agreed between them to be appropriate to take account of any sums received or to be received, or any expenditure incurred or to be incurred, in respect of the land concerned, and, in default of agreement, the question of what sum, if any, is appropriate for that purpose shall be determined by arbitration.]   **[789]**

NOTES

    Sub-ss (5)–(7): substituted, for sub-s (5), as originally enacted, by the Local Government Act 1972, s 189(2).

9. Protection of unclaimed common land

Where the registration under section 4 of this Act of any land as common land has become final but no person is registered under this Act or the Land Registration Acts 1925 and 1936 as the owner of the land, then, until the land is vested under any provision hereafter made by Parliament, any local authority in whose area the land or part of the land is situated may take such steps for the protection of the land against unlawful interference as could be taken by an owner in possession of the land, and may (without prejudice to any power exercisable apart from this section) institute proceedings for any offence committed in respect of that land.   **[790]**

10. Effect of registration

The registration under this Act of any land as common land or as a town or village green, or of any rights of common over any such land, shall be conclusive evidence of the matters registered, as at the date of registration, except where the registration is provisional only.   **[791]**

11. Exemption from registration

(1) The foregoing provisions of this Act shall not apply to the New Forest or Epping Forest nor to any land exempted from those provisions by an order of the Minister, and shall not be taken to apply to the Forest of Dean.   **[792]**

12. Subsequent registration under Land Registration Acts 1925 and 1936

The following provisions shall have effect with respect to the registration under the Land Registration Act 1925 and 1936 of any land after the ownership of the land has been registered under this Act, that is to say—

    (*a*) section 123 of the Land Registration Act 1925 (compulsory registration of title on sale) shall have effect in relation to the land whether or not the land is situated in an area in which an Order in Council under section 120 of that Act is for the time being in force, unless the registration under this Act is provisional only; and

    (*b*) if the registration authority is notified by the Chief Land Registrar that the land has been registered under the Land Registration Acts 1925 and 1936 the authority shall delete the registration of the ownership under this Act and indicate in the register in the prescribed manner that it has been registered under those Acts.   **[793]**

13. Amendment of registers

Regulations under this Act shall provide for the amendment of the registers maintained under this Act where—

    (*a*) any land registered under this Act ceases to be common land or a town or village green; or

    (*b*) any land becomes common land or a town or village green; or

    (*c*) any rights registered under this Act are apportioned, extinguished or released, or are varied or transferred in such circumstances as may be prescribed;

. . .   **[794]**

NOTES

    Words omitted repealed by the Law of Property Act 1969, s 16(2), Sch 2, Part I.

14. Rectification of registers

The High Court may order a register maintained under this Act to be amended if—

    (*a*) the registration under this Act of any land or rights of common has become final and the court is satisfied that any person was induced by fraud to withdraw an objection to the registration or to refrain from making such an objection; or

    (*b*) the register has been amended in pursuance of section 13 of this Act and it appears to the court that no amendment or a different amendment ought to have been made and that the error cannot be corrected in pursuance of regulations made under this Act;

and, in either case, the court deems it just to rectify the register.   **[795]**

15. Quantification of certain grazing rights

(1) Where a right of common consists of or includes a right, not limited by number, to graze animals or animals of any class, it shall for the purposes of registration under this Act be treated as exercisable in relation to no more animals, or animals of that class, than a definite number.

(2) Any application for the registration of such a right shall state the number of animals to be entered in the register or, as the case may be, the numbers of animals of different classes to be so entered.

(3) When the registration of such a right has become final the right shall accordingly be exercisable in relation to animals not exceeding the number or numbers registered or such other number or numbers as Parliament may hereafter determine.   **[796]**

16. Disregard of certain interruptions in prescriptive claims to rights of common

(1) Where during any period a right of common claimed over any land was not exercised, but during the whole or part of that period either—

(*a*) the land was requisitioned; or

(*b*) where the right claimed is a right to graze animals, the right could not be or was not exercised for reasons of animal health;

that period or part shall be left out of account, both—

(i) in determining for the purposes of the Prescription Act 1832 whether there was an interruption within the meaning of that Act of the actual enjoyment of the right; and

(ii) in computing the period of thirty or sixty years mentioned in section 1 of that Act.

(2) For the purposes of the said Act any objection under this Act to the registration of a right of common shall be deemed to be such a suit or action as is referred to in section 4 of that Act.

(3) In this section "requisitioned" means in the possession of a Government department in the exercise or purported exercise of powers conferred by regulations made under the Emergency Powers (Defence) Act 1939 or by Part VI of the Requisitioned Land and War Works Act 1945; and in determining in any proceedings and question arising under this section whether any land was requisitioned during any period a document purporting to be a certificate to that effect issued by a Government department shall be admissible in evidence.

(4) Where it is necessary for the purposes of this section to establish that a right to graze animals on any land could not be or was not exercised for reasons of animal health it shall be sufficient to prove either—

(*a*) that the movement of the animals to that land was prohibited or restricted by or under the Diseases of Animals Act 1950 or any enactment repealed by that Act; or

(*b*) that the land was not, but some other land was, approved for grazing under any scheme in force under that Act or any such enactment and the animals were registered, or were undergoing tests with a view to registration, under the scheme.   **[797]**

17. Commons Commissioners and assessors

(1) The Lord Chancellor shall—

(*a*) appoint to be Commons Commissioners such number of [persons who have a 7 year general qualification, within the meaning of section 71 of the Courts and Legal Services Act 1990,] as he may determine; and

(*b*) draw up from time to time revise a panel of assessors to assist the Commons Commissioners in dealing with cases calling for special knowledge;

and shall appoint one of the Commons Commissioners to be Chief Commons Commissioner.

[*(1A) A Commons Commissioner shall vacate his office on the day on which he attains the age of seventy years; but this subsection is subject to section 26(4) to (6) of the Judicial Pensions and Retirement Act 1993 (power of Lord Chancellor to authorise continuance in office up to the age of seventy-five years).*]

(2) Any matter referred under this Act to a Commons Commissioner shall be dealt with by such one of the Commissioners as the Chief Commons Commissioner may determine, and that Commissioner may sit with an assessor selected by the Chief Commons Commissioner from the panel appointed under this section.

(3) If at any time the Chief Commons Commissioner is for any reason unable to act, the Lord Chancellor may appoint another Commons Commissioner to act in his stead.

(4) A Commons Commissioner may order any party to any proceedings before him to pay to any other party to the proceedings any costs incurred by that party in respect of the proceedings; and any costs so awarded shall be taxed in the county court according to such of the scales prescribed by county court rules for proceedings in the county court as may be directed by the order, but subject to any modifications specified in the direction, or, if the order gives no direction, by the county court, and shall be recoverable in like manner as costs awarded in the county court.

(5) The Minister shall pay to the Commons Commissioners and assessors appointed under this section such fees and such travelling and other allowances as the Minister may, with the approval of the Treasury, determine, and shall provide the Commons Commissioners with such services and facilities as appear to him required for the discharge of their functions.   **[798]**

NOTES
    Sub-s (1): words in square brackets substituted by the Courts and Legal Services Act 1990, s 71(2), Sch 10, para 26.
    Sub-s (1A): prospectively added with savings by the Judicial Pensions and Retirement Act 1993, ss 26, 27, Sch 6, para 26, Sch 7.

18. Appeals from Commons Commissioners

(1) Any person aggrieved by the decision of a Commons Commissioner as being erroneous in point of law may, within such time as may be limited by rule of court, require the Commissioner to state a case for the decision of the High Court.

(2) So much of section 63(1) of the Supreme Court of Judicature (Consolidation) Act 1925 as requires appeals to the High Court to be heard and determined by a Divisional Court shall not apply to an appeal by way of case stated under this section, but no appeal to the Court of Appeal shall be brought against the decision of the High Court in such a case except with the leave of that Court or the Court of Appeal.   **[799]**

19. Regulations

(1) The Minister may make regulations—
    (a) for prescribing the form of the registers to be maintained under this Act and of any applications and objections to be made and notices and certificates to be given thereunder;
    (b) for regulating the procedure of registration authorities in dealing with applications for registration and with objections;

 (c) for prescribing the steps to be taken by registration authorities for the information of other local authorities and of the public in cases where registrations are cancelled or modified;

 (d) for requiring registration authorities to supply by post, on payment of such fee as may be prescribed, such information relating to the entries in the registers kept by them as may be prescribed;

 (e) for regulating the procedure of the Commons Commissioners and, in particular, for providing for the summoning of persons to attend and give evidence and produce documents and for authorising the administration of oaths, and for enabling any inquiry or proceedings begun by or before one Commons Commissioner to be continued by or before another;

 (f) for enabling an application for the registration of rights of common attached to any land to be made either by the landlord or by the tenant and for regulating the procedure where such an application is made by both;

 (g) for enabling the Church Commissioners to act with respect to any land or rights belonging to an ecclesiastical benefice of the Church of England which is vacant;

 (h) for treating any registration conflicting with another registration as an objection to the other registration;

 (i) for requiring, before applications for registration are entertained, the taking of such steps as may be specified in the regulations for the information of persons having interests in any land affected by the registration;

 (j) for the correction of errors and omissions in the registers;

 (k) for prescribing anything required or authorised to be prescribed by this Act.

(2) The regulations may make provision for the preparation of maps to accompany applications for registration and the preparation, as part of the registers, of maps showing any land registered therein and any land to which rights of common registered therein are attached, and for requiring registration authorities to deposit copies of such maps with such Government departments and other authorities as may be prescribed.

(3) The regulations may prescribe the payment of a fee not exceeding five pounds on an application made after the end of such period as may be specified in the regulations.

(4) The regulations may make different provision with respect to different circumstances.

(5) Regulations under this Act shall be made by statutory instrument which shall be subject to annulment in pursuance of a resolution of either House of Parliament.   **[800]**

20. Orders

(1) Any order made by the Minister under any provision of this Act may be varied or revoked by subsequent order made thereunder.

(2) Any such order, other than an order made under section 11 of this Act, shall be made by statutory instrument.

(3) Any statutory instrument made under this section shall be subject to annulment in pursuance of a resolution of either House of Parliament.   **[801]**

21. Savings

(1) Section 1(2) of this Act shall not affect the application to any land registered under this Act of section 193 or section 194 of the Law of Property Act 1925 (rights of access to, and restriction on inclosure of, land over which rights of common are exercisable).

(2) Section 10 of this Act shall not apply for the purpose of deciding whether any land forms part of a highway.   **[802]**

22. Interpretation

(1) In this Act, unless the context otherwise requires,—

"common land" means—

    (*a*) land subject to rights of common (as defined in this Act) whether those rights are exercisable at all times or only during limited periods;

    (*b*) waste land of a manor not subject to rights of common;

but does not include a town or village green or any land which forms part of a highway;

"land" includes land covered with water;

"local authority" means . . . the council of a county, . . . London borough or county district, the council of a parish . . . ;

"the Minister" means [the Secretary of State];

"prescribed" means prescribed by regulations under this Act;

"registration" includes an entry in the register made in pursuance of section 13 of this Act;

"rights of common" includes cattlegates or beastgates (by whatever name known) and rights of sole or several vesture or herbage or of sole or several pasture, but does not include rights held for a term of years or from year to year;

"town or village green" means land which has been allotted by or under any Act for the exercise or recreation of the inhabitants of any locality or on which the inhabitants of any locality have a customary right to indulge in lawful sports and pastimes or on which the inhabitants of any locality have indulged in such sports and pastimes as of right for not less than twenty years.

(2) References in this Act to the ownership and the owner of any land are references to the ownership of a legal estate in fee simple in any land and to the person holding that estate, and references to land registered under the Land Registration Acts 1925 and 1936 are references to land the fee simple of which is so registered.   **[803]**

NOTES

    Sub-s (1): in definition "local authority" first words omitted repealed by the Local Government Act 1985, s 102, Sch 17; other words omitted repealed by the Local Government Act 1972, s 272(1), Sch 30; in definition "the Minister" words in square brackets substituted by virtue of the Ministry of Land and Natural Resources (Dissolution) Order 1967, SI 1967 No 156, art 2 and the Secretary of State for the Environment Order 1970, SI 1970 No 1681, art 2.

23. Application to Crown

(1) This Act shall apply in relation to land in which there is a Crown or Duchy interest as it applies in relation to land in which there is no such interest.

(2) In this section "Crown or Duchy interest" means an interest belonging

to Her Majesty in right of the Crown or of the Duchy of Lancaster, or belonging to the Duchy of Cornwall, or belonging to a Government department, or held in trust for Her Majesty for the purposes of a Government department.　　**[804]**

24. Expenses

There shall be defrayed out of moneys provided by Parliament any expenses of the Minister under this Act and any increase attributable to this Act in the sums payable under any other Act out of moneys so provided.　　**[805]**

25. Short title, commencement and extent

(1)　This Act may be cited as the Commons Registration Act 1965.

(2)　This Act shall come into force on such day as the Minister may by order appoint, and different days may be so appointed for different purposes; and any reference in any provision to the commencement of this Act is a reference to the date on which that provision comes into force.

(3)　This Act does not extend to Scotland or to Northern Ireland.　　**[806]**

LAND REGISTRATION ACT 1966
(c 39)

An Act to alter the provisions of Part XI of the Land Registration Act 1925 relating to the making of orders creating areas of compulsory registration, to restrict the rights under that Act to register unregistered land in other areas, to amend its provisions relating to losses indemnifiable under that Act and to releal section 11 of the Small Holdings and Allotments Act 1926　　[13 December 1966]

1. Amendments of Land Registration Act 1925

(2)　Applications under sections 4 and 8 of the said Act (first registration of title) as respects land outside an area of compulsory registration shall not be entertained except in such classes of cases as the registrar may, by notice published in such way as appears to him appropriate, from time to time specify and in those cases the registrar may require the applicant under either of those sections to show that there are special considerations which make it expedient to grant the application.

In this subsection "area of compulsory registration" means an area as respects which an Order in Council made or having effect under the said section 120 is in force.　　**[807]**

MISREPRESENTATION ACT 1967
(c 7)

ARRANGEMENT OF SECTIONS

*An Act to amend the law relating to innocent misrepresentations and to amend
sections 11 and 35 of the Sale of Goods Act 1893*   [22 March 1967]

1. Removal of certain bars to rescission for innocent misrepresentation

Where a person has entered into a contract after a misrepresentation has been
made to him, and—

(*a*) the misrepresentation has become a term of the contract; or
(*b*) the contract has been performed;

or both, then, if otherwise he would be entitled to rescind the contract without
alleging fraud, he shall be so entitled, subject to the provisions of this Act,
notwithstanding the matters mentioned in paragraphs (*a*) and (*b*) of this
section.   **[808]**

2. Damages for misrepresentation

(1) Where a person has entered into a contract after a misrepresentation has
been made to him by another party thereto and as a result thereof he has suffered
loss, then, if the person making the misrepresentation would be liable to
damages in respect thereof had the misrepresentation been made fraudulently,
that person shall be so liable notwithstanding that the misrepresentation was
not made fraudulently, unless he proves that he had reasonable ground to
believe and did believe up to the time the contract was made that the facts
represented were true.

(2) Where a person has entered into a contract after a misrepresentation
has been made to him otherwise than fraudulently, and he would be entitled, by
reason of the misrepresentation, to rescind the contract, then, if it is claimed, in
any proceedings arising out of the contract, that the contract ought to be or has
been rescinded the court or arbitrator may declare the contract subsisting and
award damages in lieu of rescission, if of opinion that it would be equitable to
do so, having regard to the nature of the misrepresentation and the loss that
would be caused by it if the contract were upheld, as well as to the loss that
rescission would cause to the other party.

(3) Damages may be awarded against a person under subsection (2) of this
section whether or not he is liable to damages under subsection (1) thereof, but
where he is so liable any award under the said subsection (2) shall be taken into
account in assessing his liability under the said subsection (1).   **[809]**

[3. Avoidance of certain provisions excluding liability for misrepresentation

If a contract contains a term which would exclude or restrict—

(*a*) any liability to which a party to a contract may be subject by reason
of any misrepresentation made by him before the contract was made;
or
(*b*) any remedy available to another party to the contract by reason of
such a misrepresentation,

that term shall be of no effect except in so far as it satisfies the requirement of reasonableness as stated in section 11(1) of the Unfair Contract Terms Act 1977; and it is for those claiming that the term satisfies that requirement to show that it does.] **[810]**

NOTES
Substituted by the Unfair Contract Terms Act 1977, s 8(1).

5. Saving for past transactions

Nothing in this Act shall apply in relation to any misrepresentation or contract of sale which is made before the commencement of this Act. **[811]**

6. Short title, commencement and extent

(1) This Act may be cited as the Misrepresentation Act 1967.

(2) This Act shall come into operation at the expiration of the period of one month beginning with the date on which it is passed.

(3) ...

(4) This Act does not extend to Northern Ireland. **[812]**

NOTES
Sub-s (3): applies to Scotland only.

WILLS ACT 1968
(c 28)

An Act to restrict the operation of section 15 of the Wills Act 1837 [30 May 1968]

1. Restriction of operation of Wills Act 1837, s 15

(1) For the purposes of section 15 of the Wills Act 1837 (avoidance of gifts to attesting witnesses and their spouses) the attestation of a will by a person to whom or to whose spouse there is given or made any such disposition as is described in that section shall be disregarded if the will is duly executed without his attestation and without that of any other such person.

(2) This section applies to the will of any person dying after the passing of this Act, whether executed before or after the passing of this Act. **[813]**

2. Short title and extent

(1) This Act may be cited as the Wills Act 1968.

(2) This Act does not extend to Scotland or Northern Ireland. **[814]**

FAMILY LAW REFORM ACT 1969
(c 46)

ARRANGEMENT OF SECTIONS

PART I
REDUCTION OF AGE OF MAJORITY AND RELATED PROVISIONS

An Act to amend the law relating to the age of majority, to persons who have not attained that age and to the time when a particular age is attained; to amend the law relating to the property rights of illegitimate children and of other persons whose relationship is traced through an illegitimate link; to make provision for the use of blood tests for the purpose of determining the paternity of any person in civil proceedings; to make provision with respect to the evidence required to rebut a presumption of legitimacy and illegitimacy; to make further provision, in connection with the registration of the birth of an illegitimate child, for entering the name of the father; and for connected purposes [25 July 1969]

PART I
REDUCTION OF AGE OF MAJORITY AND RELATED PROVISIONS

1. Reduction of age of majority from 21 to 18

(1) As from the date on which this section comes into force a person shall attain full age on attaining the age of eighteen instead of on attaining the age of twenty-one; and a person shall attain full age on that date if he has then already attained the age of eighteen but not the age of twenty-one.

(2) The foregoing subsection applies for the purposes of any rule of law, and, in the absence of a definition or of any indication of a contrary intention, for the construction of "full age", "infant", "infancy", "minor", "minority" and similar expressions in—

(a) any statutory provision, whether passed or made before, on or after the date on which this section comes into force; and

(b) any deed, will or other instrument of whatever nature (not being a statutory provision) made on or after that date.

(3) In the statutory provisions specified in Schedule 1 to this Act for any reference to the age of twenty-one years there shall be substituted a reference to the age of eighteen years; but the amendment by this subsection of the provisions specified in Part II of that Schedule shall be without prejudice to any power of amending or revoking those provisions.

(4) This section does not affect the construction of any such expression as is referred to in subsection (2) of this section in any of the statutory provisions described in Schedule 2 to this Act, and the transitional provisions and savings contained in Schedule 3 to this Act shall have effect in relation to this section.

(5) The Lord Chancellor may by order made by statutory instrument amend

any provision in any local enactment passed on or before the date on which this section comes into force (not being a provision described in paragraph 2 of Schedule 2 to this Act) by substituting a reference to the age of eighteen years for any reference therein to the age of twenty-one years; and any statutory instrument containing an order under this subsection shall be subject to annulment in pursuance of a resolution of either House of Parliament.

(6) In this section "statutory provision" means any enactment (including, except where the context otherwise requires, this Act) and any order, rule, regulation, byelaw or other instrument made in the exercise of a power conferred by any enactment.

(7) Notwithstanding any rule of law, a will or codicil executed before the date on which this section come into force shall not be treated for the purposes of this section as made on or after that date by reason only that the will or codicil is confirmed by a codicil executed on or after that date.   **[815]**

3. Provisions relating to wills and intestacy

(3) Any will which—

(a) has been made, whether before or after the coming into force of this section, by a person under the age of eighteen; and

(b) is valid by virtue of the provisions of section 11 of the said Act of 1837 and the said Act of 1918,

may be revoked by that person notwithstanding that he is still under that age whether or not the circumstances are then such that he would be entitled to make a valid will under those provisions.   **[816]**

9. Time at which a person attains a particular age

(1) The time at which a person attains a particular age expressed in years shall be the commencement of the relevant anniversary of the date of his birth.

(2) This section applies only where the relevant anniversary falls on a date after that on which this section comes into force, and, in relation to any enactment, deed, will or other instrument, has effect subject to any provision therein.   **[817]**

LAW OF PROPERTY ACT 1969
(c 59)

ARRANGEMENT OF SECTIONS

PART III

AMENDMENT OF LAW RELATING TO DISPOSITIONS OF ESTATES AND INTERESTS IN LAND AND TO LAND CHARGES

An Act to amend Part II of the Landlord and Tenant Act 1954; to provide for the closing of the Yorkshire deeds registries; to amend the law relating to dispositions of estates and interests in land and to land charges; to make further provision as to the powers of the Lands Tribunal and court in relation to restrictive covenants affecting land; and for purposes connected with those matters   [22 October 1969]

PART III

AMENDMENT OF LAW RELATING TO DISPOSITIONS OF ESTATES AND INTERESTS IN LAND AND TO LAND CHARGES

23. Reduction of statutory period of title

Section 44 (1) of the Law of Property Act 1925 (under which the period of commencement of title which may be required under a contract expressing no contrary intention is thirty years except in certain cases) shall have effect, in its application to contracts made after the commencement of this Act, as if it specified fifteen years instead of thirty years as the period of commencement of title which may be so required.   **[818]**

24. Contracts for purchase of land affected by land charge, etc

(1) Where under a contract for the sale or other disposition of any estate or interest in land the title to which is not registered under the Land Registration Act 1925 or any enactment replaced by it any question arises whether the purchaser had knowledge, at the time of entering into the contract, of a registered land charge, that question shall be determined by reference to his actual knowledge and without regard to the provisions of section 198 of the Law of Property Act 1925 (under which registration under the Land Charges Act 1925 or any enactment replaced by it is deemed to constitute actual notice).

(2) Where any estate or interest with which such a contract is concerned is affected by a registered land charge and the purchaser, at the time of entering into the contract, had not received notice and did not otherwise actually know that the estate or interest was affected by the charge, any provision of the contract shall be void so far as it purports to exclude the operation of subsection (1) above or to exclude or restrict any right or remedy that might otherwise be exercisable by the purchaser on the ground that the estate or interest is affected by the charge.

(3) In this section—

"purchaser" includes a lessee, mortgagee or other person acquiring or intending to acquire an estate or interest in land; and

"registered land charge" means any instrument or matter registered, otherwise than in a register of local land charges, under the Land Charges Act 1925 or any Act replaced by it.

(4) For the purposes of this section any knowledge acquired in the course of

a transaction by a person who is acting therein as counsel, or as solicitor or other agent, for another shall be treated as the knowledge of that other.

(5) This section does not apply to contracts made before the commencement of this Act. **[819]**

25. Compensation in certain cases for loss due to undisclosed land charges

(1) Where a purchaser of any estate or interest in land under a disposition to which this section applies has suffered loss by reason that the estate or interest is affected by a registered land charge, then if—

    (*a*) the date of completion was after the commencement of this Act; and

    (*b*) on that date the purchaser had no actual knowledge of the charge; and

    (*c*) the charge was registered against the name of an owner of an estate in the land who was not as owner of any such estate a party to any transaction, or concerned in any event, comprised in the relevant title;

the purchaser shall be entitled to compensation for the loss.

(2) For the purposes of subsection (1)(*b*) above, the question whether any person had actual knowledge of a charge shall be determined without regard to the provisions of section 198 of the Law of Property Act 1925 (under which registration under the Land Charges Act 1925 or any enactment replaced by it is deemed to constitute actual notice).

(3) Where a transaction comprised in the relevant title was effected or evidenced by a document which expressly provided that it should take effect subject to an interest or obligation capable of registration in any of the relevant registers, the transaction which created that interest or obligation shall be treated for the purposes of subsection (1)(*c*) above as comprised in the relevant title.

(4) Any compensation for loss under this section shall be paid by the Chief Land Registrar, and where the purchaser of the estate or interest in question has incurred expenditure for the purpose—

    (*a*) of securing that the estate or interest is no longer affected by the registered land charge or is so affected to a less extent; or

    (*b*) of obtaining rompensation under this section;

the amount of the compensation shall include the amount of the expenditure (so far as it would not otherwise fall to be treated as compensation for loss) reasonably incurred by the purchaser for that purpose.

(5) In the case of an action to recover compensation under this section, the cause of action shall be deemed for the purposes of [the Limitation Act 1980] to accrue at the time when the registered land charge affecting the estate or interest in question comes to the notice of the purchaser.

(6) Any proceedings for the recovery of compensation under this section shall be commenced in the High Court; and if in such proceedings the High Court dismisses a claim to compensation it shall not order the purchaser to pay the Chief Land Registrar's costs unless it considers that it was unreasonable for the purchaser to commence the proceedings.

(7) ...

(8) Where compensation under this section has been paid in a case where

the purchaser would have had knowledge of the registered land charge but for the fraud of any person, the Chief Land Registrar, on behalf of the Crown, may recover the amount paid from that person.

(9) This section applies to the following dispositions, that is to say—

(a) any sale or exchange and, subject to the following provisions of this subsection, any mortgage of an estate or interest in land;

(b) any grant of a lease for a term of years derived out of a leasehold interest;

(c) any compulsory purchase, by whatever procedure, of land; and

(d) any conveyance of a fee simple in land under Part I of the Leasehold Reform Act 1967;

but does not apply to the grant of a term of years derived out of the freehold or the mortgage of such a term by the lessee; and references in this section to a purchaser shall be construed accordingly.

(10) In this section—

"date of completion", in relation to land which vests in the Land Commission or another acquiring authority by virtue of a general vesting declaration under the Land Commission Act 1967 or the Town and Country Planning Act 1968, means the date on which it so vests;

"mortgage" includes any charge;

"registered land charge" means any instrument or matter registered, otherwise than in a register of local land charges, under the Land Charges Act 1925 or any Act replaced by it, except that—

(a) in relation to an assignment of a lease or underlease or a mortgage by an assignee under such an assignment, it does not include any instrument or matter affecting the title to the freehold or to any relevant leasehold reversion; and

(b) in relation to the grant of an underlease or the mortgage by the underlessee of the term of years created by an underlease, it does not include any instrument or matter affecting the title to the freehold or to any leasehold reversion superior to the leasehold interest out of which the term of years is derived;

"relevant registers" means the registers kept under section 1 of the Land Charges Act 1925;

"relevant title" means—

(a) in relation to a disposition made under a contract, the title which the purchaser was, apart from any acceptance by him (by agreement or otherwise) of a shorter or an imperfect title, entitled to require; or

(b) in relation to any other disposition, the title which he would have been entitled to require if the disposition had been made under a contract to which section 44(1) of the Law of Property Act 1925 applied and that contract had been made on the date of completion.

(11) For the purposes of this section any knowledge acquired in the course of a transaction by a person who is acting therein as counsel, or as solicitor or other agent, for another shall be treated as the knowledge of that other.   **[820]**

NOTES

Sub-s (5): words in square brackets substituted by the Limitation Act 1980, s 40(2), Sch 3, para 9.

Sub-s (7): repealed by the Land Charges Act 1972, s 18(3), Sch 5.

Part V

Supplementary Provisions

31. Short title, commencement and extent

(1) This Act may be cited as the Law of Property Act 1969.

(2) This Act, except section 28(6), shall come into force on 1st January 1970.

(3) This Act does not extend to Scotland or Northern Ireland.   **[821]**

ADMINISTRATION OF JUSTICE ACT 1970
(c 31)

An Act to make further provision about the courts (including assizes), their business, jurisdiction and procedure; to enable a High Court judge to accept appointment as arbitrator or umpire under an arbitration agreement; to amend the law respecting the enforcement of debt and other liabilities; to amend section 106 of the Rent Act 1968; and for miscellaneous purposes connected with the administration of justice   [29 May 1970]

Part IV

Actions by Mortgagees for Possession

36. Additional powers of court in action by mortgagee for possession of dwelling-house

(1) Where the mortgagee under a mortgage of land which consists of or includes a dwelling-house brings an action in which he claims possession of the mortgaged property, not being an action for foreclosure in which a claim for possession of the mortgaged property is also made, the court may exercise any of the powers conferred on it by subsection (2) below if it appears to the court that in the event of its exercising the power the mortgagor is likely to be able within a reasonable period to pay any sums due under the mortgage or to remedy a default consisting of a breach of any other obligation arising under or by virtue of the mortgage.

(2) The court—

    (*a*) may adjourn the proceedings, or

    (*b*) on giving judgment, or making an order, for delivery of possession of the mortgaged property, or at any time before the execution of such judgment or order, may—

        (i) stay or suspend execution of the judgment or order, or

        (ii) postpone the date for delivery of possession,

for such period or periods as the court thinks reasonable.

(3) Any such adjournment, stay, suspension or postponement as is referred to in subsection (2) above may be made subject to such conditions with regard to payment by the mortgagor of any sum secured by the mortgage or the remedying of any default as the court thinks fit.

(4) The court may from time to time vary or revoke any condition imposed by virtue of this section.

(5) This section shall have effect in relation to such an action as is referred to in subsection (1) above begun before the date on which this section comes into force unless in that action judgment has been given, or an order made, for delivery of possession of the mortgaged property and that judgment or order was executed before that date.

(6) In the application of this section to Northern Ireland, "the court" means a judge of the High Court in Northern Ireland, and in subsection (1) the words from "not being" to "made" shall be omitted.   **[822]**

39. Interpretation of Part IV

(1) In this Part of this Act—

"dwelling-house" includes any building or part thereof which is used as a dwelling;

"mortgage" includes a charge and "mortgagor" and "mortgagee" shall be construed accordingly;

"mortgagor" and "mortgagee" includes any person deriving title under the original mortgagor or mortgagee.

(2) The fact that part of the premises comprised in a dwelling-house is used as a shop or office or for business, trade or professional purposes shall not prevent the dwelling-house from being a dwelling-house for the purposes of this Part of this Act.   **[823]**

LAW REFORM (MISCELLANEOUS PROVISIONS) ACT 1970
(c 33)

An Act to abolish actions for breach of promise of marriage and make provision with respect to the property of, and gifts between, persons who have been engaged to marry; to abolish the right of a husband to claim damages for adultery with his wife; to abolish actions for the enticement of harbouring of a spouse, or for the enticement, seduction or harbouring of a child; to make provision with respect to the maintenance of survivors of void marriages; and for purposes connected with the matters aforesaid   [29 May 1970]

Legal consequences of termination of contract to marry

2. Property of engaged couples

(1) Where an agreement to marry is terminated, any rule of law relating to the rights of husbands and wives in relation to property in which either or both has or have a beneficial interest, including any such rule as explained by section 37 of the Matrimonial Proceedings and Property Act 1970, shall apply, in relation to any property in which either or both of the parties to the agreement had a beneficial interest while the agreement was in force, as it applies in relation to property in which a husband or wife has a beneficial interest.

(2) Where an agreement to marry is terminated, section 17 of the Married Women's Property Act 1882 and section 7 of the Matrimonial Causes (Property and Maintenance) Act 1958 (which sections confer power on a judge of the High Court or a county court to settle disputes between husband and wife about property) shall apply, as if the parties were married, to any dispute between, or

claim by, one of them in relation to property in which either or both had a beneficial interest while the agreement was in force; but an application made by virtue of this section to the judge under the said section 17, as originally enacted or as extended by the said section 7, shall be made within three years of the termination of the agreement.   **[824]**

MATRIMONIAL PROCEEDINGS AND PROPERTY ACT 1970
(c 45)

An Act to make fresh provision for empowering the court in matrimonial proceedings to make orders ordering either spouse to make financial provision for, or transfer property to, the other spouse or a child of the family, orders for the variation of ante-nuptial and post-nuptial settlements, orders for the custody and education of children and orders varying, discharging or suspending orders made in such proceedings; to make other amendments of the law relating to matrimonial proceedings; to abolish the right to claim restitution of conjugal rights; to declare what interest in property is acquired by a spouse who contributes to its improvement; to make provision as to a spouse's rights of occupation under section 1 of the Matrimonial Homes Act 1967 in certain cases; to extend section 17 of the Married Women's Property Act 1882 and section 7 of the Matrimonial Causes (Property and Maintenance) Act 1958; to amend the law about the property of a person whose marriage is the subject of a decree of judicial separation dying intestate; to abolish the agency of necessity of a wife; and for purposes connected with the matters aforesaid   [29 May 1970]

PART II
MISCELLANEOUS PROVISIONS
Provisions relating to property of married persons

37. Contributions by spouse in money or money's worth to the improvement of property

It is hereby declared that where a husband or wife contributes in money or money's worth to the improvement of real or personal property in which or in the proceeds of sale of which either or both of them has or have a beneficial interest, the husband or wife so contributing shall, if the contribution is of a substantial nature and subject to any agreement between them to the contrary express or implied, be treated as having then acquired by virtue of his or her contribution a share or an enlarged share, as the case may be, in that beneficial interest of such an extent as may have been then agreed or, in default of such agreement, as may seem in all the circumstances just to any court before which the question of the existence or extent of the beneficial interest of the husband or wife arises (whether in proceedings between them or in any other proceedings).   **[825]**

39. Extension of s 17 of Married Women's Property Act 1882

An application may be made to the High Court or a county court under section 17 of the Married Women's Property Act 1882 (powers of the court in disputes between husband and wife about property) (including that section as extended by section 7 of the Matrimonial Causes (Property and Maintenance) Act 1958) by either of the parties to a marriage notwithstanding that their marriage has been dissolved or annulled so long as the application is made within the period of three years beginning with the date on which the marriage was dissolved or annulled; and references in the said section 17 and the said section 7 to a husband or a wife shall be construed accordingly. **[826]**

POWERS OF ATTORNEY ACT 1971
(c 27)

ARRANGEMENT OF SECTIONS

An Act to make new provision in relation to powers of attorney and the delegation by trustees of their trusts, powers and discretions [12 May 1971]

1. Execution of powers of attorney

(1) An instrument creating a power of attorney shall be [executed as a deed by] the donor of the power.

(2) ...

(3) This section is without prejudice to any requirement in, or having effect under, any other Act as to the witnessing of instruments creating powers of attorney and does not affect the rules relating to the execution of instruments by bodies corporate. **[827]**

NOTES
Sub-s (1): words in square brackets substituted by the Law of Property (Miscellaneous Provisions) Act 1989, s 1, Sch 1, para 6.
Sub-s (2): repealed by the Law of Property (Miscellaneous Provisions) Act 1989, ss 1, 4, Sch 1, para 6, Sch 2.

3. Proof of instruments creating powers of attorney

(1) The contents of an instrument creating a power of attorney may be proved by means of a copy which—

(a) is a reproduction of the original made with a photographic or other device for reproducing documents in facsimile; and

(b) contains the following certificate or certificates signed by the donor of the power or by a solicitor [duly certificated notary public] or stockbroker, that is to say—

(i) a certificate at the end to the effect that the copy is a true and complete copy of the original; and

(ii) if the original consists of two or more pages, a certificate at the end of each page of the copy to the effect that it is a true and complete copy of the corresponding page of the original.

(2) Where a copy of an instrument creating a power of attorney has been made which complies with subsection (1) of this section, the contents of the instrument may also be proved by means of a copy of that copy if the further copy itself complies with that subsection, taking references in it to the original as references to the copy from which the further copy is made.

(3) In this section ["duly certificated notary public" has the same meaning as it has in the Solicitors Act 1974 by virtue of section 87(1) of that Act and] "stockbroker" means a member of any stock exchange within the meaning of the Stock Transfer Act 1963 or the Stock Transfer Act (Northern Ireland) 1963.

(4) This section is without prejudice to section 4 of the Evidence and Powers of Attorney Act 1940 (proof of deposited instruments by office copy) and to any other method of proof authorised by law.

(5) For the avoidance of doubt, in relation to an instrument made in Scotland the references to a power of attorney in this section and in section 4 of the Evidence and Powers of Attorney Act 1940 include references to a factory and commission. **[828]**

NOTES

Sub-s (1): words in square brackets inserted by the Courts and Legal Services Act 1990, s 125(2), Sch 17, para 4.

Sub-s (3): words in square brackets inserted by the Courts and Legal Services Act 1990, s 125(2), Sch 17, para 4.

4. Powers of attorney given as security

(1) Where a power of attorney is expressed to be irrevocable and is given to secure—

(a) a proprietary interest of the donee of the power; or

(b) the performance of an obligation owed to the donee,

then, so long as the donee has that interest or the obligation remains undischarged, the power shall not be revoked—

(i) by the donor without the consent of the donee; or

(ii) by the death, incapacity or bankruptcy of the donor or, if the donor is a body corporate, by its winding up or dissolution.

(2) A power of attorney given to secure a proprietary interest may be given to the person entitled to the interest and persons deriving title under him to that interest, and those persons shall be duly constituted donees of the power for all purposes of the power but without prejudice to any right to appoint substitutes given by the power.

(3) This section applies to powers of attorney whenever created. **[829]**

5. Protection of donee and third persons where power of attorney is revoked

(1) A donee of a power of attorney who acts in pursuance of the power at a time when it has been revoked shall not, by reason of the revocation, incur any liability (either to the donor or to any other person) if at that time he did not know that the power had been revoked.

(2) Where a power of attorney has been revoked and a person, without knowledge of the revocation, deals with the donee of the power, the transaction between them shall, in favour of that person, be as valid as if the power had then been in existence.

(3) Where the power is expressed in the instrument creating it to be irrevocable and to be given by way of security then, unless the person dealing with the donee knows that it was not in fact given by way of security, he shall be entitled to assume that the power is incapable of revocation except by the donor acting with the consent of the donee and shall accordingly be treated for the purposes of subsection (2) of this section as having knowledge of the revocation only if he knows that it has been revoked in that manner.

(4) Where the interest of a purchaser depends on whether a transaction between the donee of a power of attorney and another person was valid by virtue of subsection (2) of this section, it shall be conclusively presumed in favour of the purchaser that that person did not at the material time know of the revocation of the power if—

    (a) the transaction between that person and the donee was completed within twelve months of the date on which the power came into operation; or

    (b) that person makes a statutory declaration, before or within three months after the completion of the purchase, that he did not at the material time know of the revocation of the power.

(5) Without prejudice to subsection (3) of this section, for the purposes of this section knowledge of the revocation of power of attorney includes knowledge of the occurrence of any event (such as the death of the donor) which has the effect of revoking the power.

(6) In this section "purchaser" and "purchase" have the meaning specified in section 205(1) of the Law of Property Act 1925.

(7) This section applies whenever the power of attorney was created but only to acts and transactions after the commencement of this Act.   **[830]**

6. Additional protection for transferees under stock exchange transactions

(1) Without prejudice to section 5 of this Act, where—

    (a) the donee of a power of attorney executes, as transferor, an instrument transferring registered securities; and

    (b) the instrument is executed for the purposes of a stock exchange transaction,

it shall be conclusively presumed in favour of the transferee that the power had not been revoked at the date of the instrument if a statutory declaration to that effect is made by the donee of the power on or within three months after that date.

(2) In this section "registered securities" and "stock exchange transaction" have the same meanings as in the Stock Transfer Act 1963.   **[831]**

7. Execution of instruments etc by donee of power of attorney

[(1) If the donee of a power of attorney is an individual, he may, if he thinks fit—

    (a) execute any instrument with his own signature, and]

(*b*) do any other thing in his own name,

by the authority of the donor of the power; and any document executed or thing done in that manner shall be as effective as if executed or done by the donee with the signature . . ., or, as the case may be, in the name, of the donor of the power.

(2) For the avoidance of doubt it is hereby declared that an instrument to which subsection (3) . . . of section 74 of the Law of Property Act 1925 applies may be executed either as provided in [that subsection] or as provided in this section.

(3) This section is without prejudice to any statutory direction requiring an instrument to be executed in the name of an estate owner within the meaning of the said Act of 1925.

(4) This section applies whenever the power of attorney was created.

[832]–[833]

NOTES
Sub-s (1): words in square brackets substituted and words omitted repealed by the Law of Property (Miscellaneous Provisions) Act 1989, ss 1, 4, Sch 1, para 7, Sch 2.
Sub-s (2): words in square brackets substituted and words omitted repealed by the Law of Property (Miscellaneous Provisions) Act 1989, ss 1, 4, Sch 1, para 7, Sch 2.

8. . . .

NOTES
This section repeals the Law of Property Act 1925, s 129.

9. Power to delegate trusts etc by power of attorney

(1) Section 25 of the Trustee Act 1925 (power to delegate trusts etc, during absence abroad) shall be amended as follows:

(2), (3) . . .

(4) This section applies whenever the trusts, powers or discretions in question arose but does not invalidate anything done by virtue of the said section 25 as in force at the commencement of this Act. **[834]**

NOTES
Sub-ss (2), (3): amend the Trustee Act 1925, s 25.

10. Effect of general power of attorney in specified form

(1) Subject to subsection (2) of this section, a general power of attorney in the form set out in Schedule 1 to this Act, or in a form to the like effect but expressed to be made under this Act, shall operate to confer—

(*a*) on the donee of the power; or
(*b*) if there is more than one donee, on the donees acting jointly or acting jointly or severally, as the case may be,

authority to do on behalf of the donor anything which he can lawfully do by an attorney.

(2) This section does not apply to functions which the donor has as a trustee or personal representative or as a tenant for life or statutory owner within the meaning of the Settled Land Act 1925. **[835]**

11. Short title, repeals, consequential amendments, commencement and extent

(1) This Act may be cited as the Powers of Attorney Act 1971.

(2) The enactments specified in Schedule 2 to this Act are hereby repealed to the extent specified in the third column of that Schedule.

(3) . . .

(4) This Act shall come into force on 1st October 1971.

(5) Section 3 of this Act extends to Scotland and Northern Ireland but, save as aforesaid, this Act extends to England and Wales only.   **[836]**

NOTES
    Sub-s (3): in part amends the Law of Property Act 1925, s 125(2); remainder repealed by the Supreme Court Act 1981, s 152(4), Sch 7.

SCHEDULES
SCHEDULE 1

Section 10

FORM OF GENERAL POWER OF ATTORNEY FOR PURPOSES OF SECTION 10

THIS GENERAL POWER OF ATTORNEY is made this   day of   19   by AB of

I appoint CD of [or CD of   and EF of   jointly or jointly and severally] to be my attorney[s] in accordance with section 10 of the Powers of Attorney Act 1971.

IN WITNESS etc.,   **[837]**

SCHEDULE 2

Section 11(2)

REPEALS

Chapter	Short Title	Extent of Repeal
15 & 16 Geo 5 c 19	The Trustee Act 1925	Section 29.
15 & 16 Geo 5 c 20	The Law of Property Act 1925	Sections 123 and 124. Section 125(1). Sections 126 to 129.
15 & 16 Geo 5 c 49	The Supreme Court of Judicature (Consolidation) Act 1925	Section 219(1).
4 & 5 Eliz 2 c 46	The Administration of Justice Act 1956	Section 18.

[838]

LAND REGISTRATION AND LAND CHARGES ACT 1971
(c 54)

ARRANGEMENT OF SECTIONS

PART I

AMENDMENT OF LAND REGISTRATION ACTS 1925 TO 1966

*An Act to amend the Land Registration Acts 1925 to 1966; to amend the Land
Charges Act 1925 and related enactments; and for connected purposes*
[27 July 1971]

Part I

Amendment of Land Registration Acts 1925 to 1966

1. Payment of indemnity

(1) Any indemnity payable after the commencement of this section under any provision of the Land Registration Act 1925, including so much of any indemnity which has become so payable at any time before then as has not then been paid, shall, instead of being paid out of the insurance fund, be paid by the registrar out of moneys provided by Parliament; and no other person shall thereafter be under any liability to pay any such indemnity.

(2) Any money which at the commencement of this section stands to the credit of the insurance fund shall be paid into the Consolidated Fund, and any other assets then comprised in the insurance fund shall be realised forthwith, and the proceeds thereof shall be paid into the Consolidated Fund; and as soon as its assets have been so dealt with, the insurance fund shall cease to exist.

(3) In this section "the insurance fund" means the insurance fund established under the Land Transfer Act 1897.   **[839]**

2. Determination of questions as to right to or amount of indemnity

(1) If any question arises as to whether a person is entitled to an indemnity under any provision of the Land Registration Act 1925 or as to the amount of any such indemnity, he may apply to the court to have that question determined.

(2) Section 83(5)(*c*) of the Land Registration Act 1925 (by virtue of which no indemnity is payable under that Act on account of costs incurred in taking or defending any legal proceedings without the consent of the registrar) shall not apply to the costs of an application to the court under subsection (1) above or of any legal proceedings arising out of such an application; and as regards any such application or proceedings section 131 of that Act (which provides that the registrar, among others, shall not be liable to any action or proceeding for or in respect of anything done or omitted as there mentioned) shall not apply to the registrar.

(3) On an application under subsection (1) above the court shall not order the applicant, even if unsuccessful, to pay any costs except his own unless it considers that the application was unreasonable.

(4) . . .

(5) Nothing in this section shall be taken to preclude the registrar from settling by agreement claims for indemnity under the Land Registration Act 1925.

(6) Where any such question as is mentioned in subsection (1) above has

arisen (whether before or after the passing of this Act) before the time of the commencement of this section and has not before that time been referred to the court in pursuance of rules under the Land Registration Act 1925, that subsection shall apply to it notwithstanding that it arose before that time; but where any such question has been so referred before that time, it shall be determined as if this section and, so far as it relates to the repeal of section 83(7) of the Land Registration Act 1925 and section 1(3) of the Land Registration Act 1966, section 14(2)(*b*) of this Act had not come into force.   **[840]**

NOTES
   Sub-s (4): repeals the Land Registration Act 1925, s 83(7) and substitutes s 83(8).

3. Right to indemnity not to be excluded by reason of act etc not amounting to fraud or lack of proper care

(1) ...

(2) Subsection (1) above shall have effect in relation to any claim for indemnity made before the time of the commencement of this section and not settled by agreement or finally determined before that time, as well as to all such claims made after that time.   **[841]**

NOTES
   Sub-s (1): amends the Land Registration Act 1925, s 83(5)(*a*), and repeals the Land Registration Act 1966, s 1(4).

4. Souvenir land

(1) The Lord Chancellor may by rules made with the advice and assistance of the Rule Committee make provision—

   (*a*) for enabling the registrar, in such circumstances and subject to such conditions as may be specified in the rules, to declare any area of land to be subject to a souvenir land scheme if the registrar is satisfied that the land comprised in that area consists wholly or mainly of land which has been or is proposed to be disposed of (by way of sale or otherwise) in souvenir plots or of which part has been, and the remainder is proposed to be, so disposed of;

   (*b*) with respect to the cancellation of declarations and the extension or reduction of the area to which any declaration relates;

   (*c*) for authorising or requiring the registrar not to accept applications under the Land Registration Act 1925 relating to souvenir land or cautions or other documents relating to such land;

   (*d*) for excepting souvenir land from the operation of section 123 of that Act (effect of that Act in areas where registration is compulsory);

   (*e*) for securing that transactions relating to souvenir land which is registered land take effect as if the souvenir land in question were not registered land; and

   (*f*) generally for modifying or excluding in relation to souvenir land the operation of any provision contained in the Land Registration Acts 1925 to 1966 or any general rules thereunder.

(2) Rules under this section may include such supplemental, consequential or incidental provision as may appear to the Lord Chancellor to be necessary or expedient for the purposes of the rules, and may make different provision for souvenir land in general and souvenir land so far as it consists or does not consist of souvenir plots, and for other different circumstances.

(3) The power to make rules under this section shall be exercisable by statutory instrument, and a statutory instrument containing any such rules shall be laid before Parliament after being made.

(4) Section 131 of the Land Registration Act 1925 (indemnity to officers of registry) shall apply in relation to rules made under section as it applies in relation to general rules made in pursuance of that Act.

(5) For the purposes of this section—

"declaration" means a declaration by the registrar, made in pursuance of rules under this section made by virtue of subsection (1) (*a*) above, that an area of land is subject to a souvenir land scheme;

"souvenir land" means land situated within an area in respect of which a declaration is for the time being in force;

"souvenir plot" means any piece of land which, being of inconsiderable size and little or no practical utility, is unlikely to be wanted in isolation except for the sake of pure ownership or for sentimental reasons or commemorative purposes.   **[842]–[848]**

DEFECTIVE PREMISES ACT 1972
(c 35)

ARRANGEMENT OF SECTIONS

An Act to impose duties in connection with the provision of dwellings and otherwise to amend the law of England and Wales as to liability for injury or damage caused to persons through defects in the state of premises   **[29 June 1972]**

1. Duty to build dwellings properly

(1) A person taking on work for or in connection with the provision of a dwelling (whether the dwelling is provided by the erection or by the conversion or enlargement of a building) owes a duty—

(*a*) if the dwelling is provided to the order of any person, to that person; and

(*b*) without prejudice to paragraph (*a*) above, to every person who acquires an interest (whether legal or equitable) in the dwelling;

to see that the work which he takes on is done in a workmanlike or, as the case may be, professional manner, with proper materials and so that as regards that work the dwelling will be fit for habitation when completed.

(2) A person who takes on any such work for another on terms that he is to do it in accordance with instructions given by or on behalf of that other shall, to the extent to which he does it properly in accordance with those instructions, be treated for the purposes of this section as discharging the duty imposed on him

by subsection (1) above except where he owes a duty to that other to warn him
of any defects in the instructions and fails to discharge that duty.

(3) A person shall not be treated for the purposes of subsection (2) above as
having given instructions for the doing of work merely because he has agreed to
the work being done in a specified manner, with specified materials or to a
specified design.

(4) A person who—

   (a) in the course of a business which consists of or includes providing or
       arranging for the provision of dwellings or installations in dwellings;
       or
   (b) in the exercise of a power of making such provision or arrangements
       conferred by or by virtue of any enactment;

arranges for another to take on work for or in connection with the provision of
a dwelling shall be treated for the purposes of this section as included among
the persons who have taken on the work.

(5) Any cause of action in respect of a breach of the duty imposed by this
section shall be deemed, for the purposes of the Limitation Act 1939, the Law
Reform (Limitation of Actions, &c.) Act 1954 and the Limitation Act 1963, to
have accrued at the time when the dwelling was completed, but if after that
time a person who has done work for or in connection with the provision of the
dwelling does further work to rectify the work he has already done, any such
cause of action in respect of that further work shall be deemed for those purposes
to have accrued at the time when the further work was finished.   **[849]**

2. Cases excluded from the remedy under section 1

(1) Where—

   (a) in connection with the provision of a dwelling or its first sale or letting
       for habitation any rights in respect of defects in the state of the
       dwelling are conferred by an approved scheme to which this section
       applies on a person having or acquiring an interest in the dwelling;
       and
   (b) it is stated in a document of a type approved for the purposes of this
       section that the requirements as to design or construction imposed by
       or under the scheme have, or appear to have, been substantially
       complied with in relation to the dwelling;

no action shall be brought by any person having or acquiring an interest in the
dwelling for breach of the duty imposed by section 1 above in relation to the
dwelling.

(2) A scheme to which this section applies—

   (a) may consist of any number of documents and any number of
       agreements or other transactions between any number of persons; but
   (b) must confer, by virtue of agreements entered into with persons having
       or acquiring an interest in the dwellings to which the scheme applies,
       rights on such persons in respect of defects in the state of the dwellings.

(3) In this section "approved" means approved by the Secretary of State,
and the power of the Secretary of State to approve a scheme or document for
the purposes of this section shall be exercisable by order, except that any
requirements as to construction or design imposed under a scheme to which this
section applies may be approved by him without making any order or, if he
thinks fit, by order.

(4) The Secretary of State—

    (*a*) may approve a scheme or document for the purposes of this section with or without limiting the duration of his approval; and

    (*b*) may by order revoke or vary a previous order under this section or, without such an order, revoke or vary a previous approval under this section given otherwise than by order.

(5) The production of a document purporting to be a copy of an approval given by the Secretary of State otherwise than by order and certified by an officer of the Secretary of State to be a true copy of the approval shall be conclusive evidence of the approval, and without proof of the handwriting or official position of the person purporting to sign the certificate.

(6) The power to make an order under this section shall be exercisable by statutory instrument which shall be subject to annulment in pursuance of a resolution by either House of Parliament.

(7) Where an interest in a dwelling is compulsorily acquired—

    (*a*) no action shall be brought by the acquiring authority for breach of the duty imposed by section 1 above in respect of the dwelling; and

    (*b*) if any work for or in connection with the provision of the dwelling was done otherwise than in the course of a business by the person in occupation of the dwelling at the time of the compulsory acquisition, the acquiring authority and not that person shall be treated as the person who took on the work and accordingly as owing that duty.

[850]

3. Duty of care with respect to work done on premises not abated by disposal of premises

(1) Where work of construction, repair, maintenance or demolition or any other work is done on or in relation to premises, any duty of care owed, because of the doing of the work, to persons who might reasonably be expected to be affected by defects in the state of the premises created by the doing of the work shall not be abated by the subsequent disposal of the premises by the person who owed the duty.

(2) This section does not apply—

    (*a*) in the case of premises which are let, where the relevant tenancy of the premises commenced, or the relevant tenancy agreement of the premises was entered into, before the commencement of this Act;

    (*b*) in the case of premises disposed of in any other way, when the disposal of the premises was completed, or a contract for their disposal was entered into, before the commencement of this Act; or

    (*c*) in either case, where the relevant transaction disposing of the premises is entered into in pursuance of an enforceable option by which the consideration for the disposal was fixed before the commencement of this Act.

[851]

4. Landlord's duty of care in virtue of obligation or right to repair premises demised

(1) Where premises are let under a tenancy which puts on the landlord an obligation to the tenant for the maintenance or repair of the premises, the landlord owes to all persons who might reasonably be expected to be affected by defects in the state of the premises a duty to take such care as is reasonable in

all the circumstances to see that they are reasonably safe from personal injury or from damage to their property caused by a relevant defect.

(2) The said duty is owed if the landlord knows (whether as the result of being notified by the tenant or otherwise) or if he ought in all the circumstances to have known of the relevant defect.

(3) In this section "relevant defect" means a defect in the state of the premises existing at or after the material time and arising from, or continuing because of, an act or omission by the landlord which constitutes or would if he had had notice of the defect, have constituted a failure by him to carry out his obligation to the tenant for the maintenance or repair of the premises; and for the purposes of the foregoing provision "the material time" means—

(*a*) where the tenancy commenced before this Act, the commencement of this Act; and

(*b*) in all other cases, the earliest of the following times, that is to say—

(i) the time when the tenancy commences;

(ii) the time when the tenancy agreement is entered into;

(iii) the time when possession is taken of the premises in contemplation of the letting.

(4) Where premises are let under a tenancy which expressly or impliedly gives the landlord the right to enter the premises to carry out any description of maintenance or repair of the premises, then, as from the time when he first is, or by notice or otherwise can put himself, in a position to exercise the right and so long as he is or can put himself in that position, he shall be treated for the purposes of subsections (1) to (3) above (but for no other purpose) as if he were under an obligation to the tenant for that description of maintenance or repair of the premises; but the landlord shall not owe the tenant any duty by virtue of this subsection in respect of any defect in the state of the premises arising from, or continuing because of, a failure to carry out an obligation expressly imposed on the tenant by the tenancy.

(5) For the purposes of this section obligations imposed or rights given by any enactment in virtue of a tenancy shall be treated as imposed or given by the tenancy.

(6) This section applies to a right of occupation given by contract or any enactment and not amounting to a tenancy as if the right were a tenancy, and "tenancy" and cognate expressions shall be construed accordingly.   **[852]**

5. Application to Crown

This Act shall bind the Crown, but as regards the Crown's liability in tort shall not bind the Crown further than the Crown is made liable in tort by the Crown Proceedings Act 1947.   **[853]**

6. Supplemental

(1) In this Act—

"disposal", in relation to premises, includes a letting, and an assignment or surrender of a tenancy, of the premises and the creation by contract of any other right to occupy the premises, and "dispose" shall be construed accordingly;

"personal injury" includes any disease and any impairment of a person's physical or mental condition;

"tenancy" means—

(a) a tenancy created either immediately or derivatively out of the freehold, whether by a lease or underlease, by an agreement for a lease or underlease or by a tenancy agreement, but not including a mortgage term or any interest arising in favour of a mortgagor by his attorning tenant to his mortgagee; or

(b) a tenancy at will or a tenancy on sufferance; or

(c) a tenancy, whether or not constituting a tenancy at common law, created by or in pursuance of any enactment;

and cognate expressions shall be construed accordingly.

(2) Any duty imposed by or enforceable by virtue of any provision of this Act is in addition to any duty a person may owe apart from that provision.

(3) Any term of an agreement which purports to exclude or restrict, or has the effect of excluding or restricting, the operation of any of the provisions of this Act, or any liability arising by virtue of any such provision, shall be void.

(4) ...   [854]

NOTES

Sub-s (4): repeals the Occupiers' Liability Act 1957, s 4.

7. Short title, commencement and extent

(1) This Act may be cited as the Defective Premises Act 1972.

(2) This Act shall come into force on 1st January 1974.

(3) This Act does not extend to Scotland or Northern Ireland.   [855]

LAND CHARGES ACT 1972
(c 61)

ARRANGEMENT OF SECTIONS

An Act to consolidate certain enactments relating to the registration of land charges and other instruments and matters affecting land   [9 August 1972]

Preliminary

1. The registers and the index

(1) The registrar shall continue to keep at the registry in the prescribed manner the following registers, namely—

(a) a register of land charges;
(b) a register of pending actions;
(c) a register of writs and orders affecting land;
(d) a register of deeds of arrangement affecting land;
(e) a register of annuities,

and shall also continue to keep there an index whereby all entries made in any of those registers can readily be traced.

(2) Every application to register shall be in the prescribed form and shall contain the prescribed particulars.

[(3) Where any charge or other matter is registrable in more than one of the registers kept under this Act, it shall be sufficient if it is registered in one such register, and if it is so registered the person entitled to the benefit of it shall not be prejudicially affected by any provision of this Act as to the effect of non-registration in any other such register.

(3A) Where any charge or other matter is registrable in a register kept under this Act and was also, before the commencement of the Local Land Charges Act 1975, registrable in a local land charges register, then, if before the commencement of the said Act it was registered in the appropriate local land charges register, it shall be treated for the purposes of the provisions of this Act as to the effect of non-registration as if it had been registered in the appropriate register under this Act; and any certificate setting out the result of an official search of the appropriate local land charges register shall, in relation to it, have effect as if it were a certificate setting out the result of an official search under this Act.]

(4) Schedule 1 to this Act shall have effect in relation to the register of annuities.

(5) An office copy of an entry in any register kept under this section shall be admissible in evidence in all proceedings and between all parties to the same extent as the original would be admissible.

(6) Subject to the provisions of this Act, registration may be vacated pursuant to an order of the court.

[[(6A) The county courts have jurisdiction under subsection (6) above—

(a) in the case of a land charge of Class C(i), C(ii) or D(i), if the amount does not exceed £30,000;

(b) in the case of a land charge of Class C(iii), if it is for a specified capital sum of money not exceeding £30,000 or, where it is not for a specified capital sum, if the capital value of the land affected does not exceed £30,000;

(c) in the case of a land charge of Class A, Class B, Class C(iv), Class D(ii), Class D(iii) or Class E if the capital value of the land affected does not exceed £30,000;

(d) in the case of a land charge of Class F, if the land affected by it is the subject of an order made by the court under section 1 of the Matrimonial Homes Act 1983 or an application for an order under that section relating to that land has been made to the court;

(e) in a case where an application under section 23 of the Deeds of Arrangement Act 1914 could be entertained by the court.]

(6B) . . .]]

(7) In this section "index" includes any device or combination of devices serving the purpose of an index.   **[856]**

NOTES

Commencement: 1 July 1991 (sub-s (6A)); 1 August 1977 (sub-ss (3), (3A)); 29 January 1973 (remainder) (SI 1972 No 2058, SI 1977 No 984).

Sub-ss (3), (3A): substituted for sub-s (3), as originally enacted, by the Local Land Charges Act 1975, s 17(1)(a).

Sub-s (6A): inserted by the County Courts Act 1984, s 148(1), Sch 2, para 16; substituted by the High Court and County Courts Jurisdiction Order 1991, SI 1991 No 724, art 2(8), Schedule.

Sub-s (6B): inserted by the County Courts Act 1984, s 148(1), Sch 2, para 16; repealed by the High Court and County Courts Jursidiction Order 1991, SI 1991 No 724, art 2(8), Schedule.

Registration in register of land charges

2. The register of land charges

(1) If a charge on or obligation affecting land falls into one of the classes described in this section, it may be registered in the register of land charges as a land charge of that class.

(2) A Class A land charge is—

(a) a rent or annuity or principal money payable by instalments or otherwise, with or without interest, which is not a charge created by deed but is a charge upon land (other than a rate) created pursuant to the application of some person under the provisions of any Act of Parliament, for securing to any person either the money spent by him or the costs, charges and expenses incurred by him under such Act, or the money advanced by him for repaying the money spent or the costs, charges and expenses incurred by another person under the authority of an Act of Parliament; or

(b) a rent or annuity or principal money payable as mentioned in paragraph (a) above which is not a charge created by deed but is a charge upon land (other than a rate) created pursuant to the application of some person under any of the enactments mentioned in Schedule 2 to this Act.

(3) A Class B land charge is a charge on land (not being a local land charge ...) of any of the kinds described in paragraph (*a*) of subsection (2) above, created otherwise than pursuant to the application of any person.

(4) A Class C land charge is any of the following [(not being a local land charge)], namely—

    (i) a puisne mortgage;
    (ii) a limited owner's charge;
    (iii) a general equitable charge;
    (iv) an estate contract;

and for this purpose—

    (i) a puisne mortgage is a legal mortgage which is not protected by a deposit of documents relating to the legal estate affected;
    (ii) a limited owner's charge is an equitable charge acquired by a tenant for life or statutory owner under [[the Inheritance Tax Act 1984] or under] any other statute by reason of the discharge by him of any [capital transfer tax] or other liabilities and to which special priority is given by the statute;
    (iii) a general equitable charge is any equitable charge which—

        (*a*) is not secured by a deposit of documents relating to the legal estate affected; and
        (*b*) does not arise or affect an interest arising under a trust for sale or a settlement; and
        (*c*) is not a charge given by way of indemnity against rents equitably apportioned or charged exclusively on land in exoneration of other land and against the breach or non-observance of covenants or conditions; and
        (*d*) is not included in any other class of land charge;

    (iv) an estate contract is a contract by an estate owner or by a person entitled at the date of the contract to have a legal estate conveyed to him to convey or create a legal estate, including a contract conferring either expressly or by statutory implication a valid option to purchase, a right of pre-emption or any other like right.

(5) A Class D land charge is any of the following [(not being a local land charge)], namely—

    (i) an Inland Revenue Charge;
    (ii) a restrictive covenant;
    (iii) an equitable easement;

and for this purpose—

    (i) an Inland Revenue charge is a charge on land, being a charge acquired by the Board under [the Inheritance Tax Act 1984];
    (ii) a restrictive covenant is a covenant or agreement (other than a covenant or agreement between a lessor and a lessee) restrictive of the user of land and entered into on or after 1st January 1926;
    (iii) an equitable easement is an easement, right or privilege over or affecting land created or arising on or after 1st January 1926, and being merely an equitable interest.

(6) A Class E land charge is an annuity created before 1st January 1926 and not registered in the register of annuities.

(7) A Class F land charge is a charge affecting any land by virtue of the [Matrimonial Homes Act 1983].

(8) A charge or obligation created before 1st January 1926 can only be registered as a Class B land charge or a Class C land charge if it is acquired under a conveyance made on or after that date.

(9) ... **[857]**

NOTES
Sub-s (3): words omitted repealed by the Local Land Charges Act 1975, s 19, Sch 2.
Sub-s (4): first words in square brackets inserted by the Local Land Charges Act 1975, s 17(1)(*b*); second and final words in square brackets substituted by the Finance Act 1975, s 52(1), Sch 12, paras 2, 18, words "the Inheritance Tax Act 1984" substituted by the Inheritance Tax Act 1984, s 276, Sch 8, para 3.
Sub-s (5): first words in square brackets inserted by the Local Land Charges Act 1975, s 17(1)(*b*); second words in square brackets substituted by the Inheritance Tax Act 1984, s 276, Sch 8, para 3.
Sub-s (7): words in square brackets substituted by the Matrimonial Homes Act 1983, s 12, Sch 2.
Sub-s (9): repealed by the Finance Act 1977, s 59, Sch 9.
Capital transfer tax: except in relation to a liability to tax arising before 25 July 1986 capital transfer tax shall be known as inheritance tax and the Capital Transfer Tax Act 1984 may be cited as the Inheritance Tax Act 1984, by virtue of the Finance Act 1986, s 100.

3. Registration of land charges

(1) A land charge shall be registered in the name of the estate owner whose estate is intended to be affected.

(2) A land charge registered before 1st January 1926 under any enactment replaced by the Land Charges Act 1925 in the name of a person other than the estate owner may remain so registered until it is registered in the name of the estate owner in the prescribed manner.

(3) A puisne mortgage created before 1st January 1926 may be registered as a land charge before any transfer of the mortgage is made.

(4) The expenses incurred by the person entitled to the charge in registering a land charge of Class A, Class B or Class C (other than an estate contract) or by the Board in registering an Inland Revenue charge shall be deemed to form part of the land charge, and shall be recoverable accordingly on the day for payment of any part of the land charge next after such expenses are incurred.

(5) Where a land charge is not created by an instrument, short particulars of the effect of the charge shall be furnished with the application to register the charge.

(6) An application to register an Inland Revenue charge shall state the [tax] in respect of which the charge is claimed and, so far as possible, shall define the land affected, and such particulars shall be entered or referred to in the register.

(7) In the case of a land charge for securing money created by a company before 1st January 1970 or so created at any time as a floating charge, registration under *any of the enactments mentioned in subsection (8) below* [Part XII, or Chapter III of Part XXIII, of the Companies Act 1985 (or corresponding earlier enactments)] shall be sufficient in place of registration under this Act, and shall have effect as if the land charge had been registered under this Act.

(8) *The enactments* [The corresponding earlier enactments] referred to in

subsection (7) above are section 93 of the Companies (Consolidation) Act 1908, section 79 of the Companies Act 1929 . . . section 95 of the Companies Act 1948 [and sections 395 to 398 of the Companies Act 1985] [as originally enacted].

[858]

NOTES
 Sub-s (6): word in square brackets substituted by the Finance Act 1975, s 52, Sch 12, paras 2, 18(1), (4).
 Sub-s (7): words in italics prospectively repealed and words in square brackets immediately following prospectively substituted by the Companies Act 1989, s 107, Sch 16, para 1(2).
 Sub-s (8): words in italics prospectively repealed and words in square brackets immediately following prospectively substituted and third words in square brackets prospectively added by the Companies Act 1989, s 107, Sch 16, para 1(3); second words in square brackets substituted and words omitted repealed by the Companies Consolidation (Consequential Provisions) Act 1985, s 30, Sch 2.

4. Effect of land charges and protection of purchasers

(1) A land charge of Class A (other than a land improvement charge registered after 31st December 1969) or of Class B shall, when registered, take effect as if it had been created by a deed of charge by way of legal mortgage, but without prejudice to the priority of the charge.

(2) A land charge of Class A created after 31st December 1888 shall be void as against a purchaser of the land charged with it or of any interest in such land, unless the land charge is registered in the register of land charges before the completion of the purchase.

(3) After the expiration of one year from the first conveyance occurring on or after 1st January 1889 of a land charge of Class A created before that date the person entitled to the land charge shall not be able to recover the land charge or any part of it as against a purchaser of the land charged with it or of any interest in the land, unless the land charge is registered in the register of land charges before the completion of the purchase.

(4) If a land improvement charge was registered as a land charge of Class A before 1st January 1970, any body corporate which, but for the charge, would have power to advance money on the security of the estate or interest affected by it shall have that power notwithstanding the charge.

(5) A land charge of Class B and a land charge of Class C (other than an estate contract) created or arising on or after 1st January 1926 shall be void as against a purchaser of the land charged with it, or of any interest in such land, unless the land charge is registered in the appropriate register before the completion of the purchase.

(6) An estate contract and a land charge of Class D created or entered into on or after 1st January 1926 shall be void as against a purchaser for money or money's worth [(or, in the case of an Inland Revenue charge, a purchaser within the meaning of [the Inheritance Tax Act 1984)]] of a legal estate in the land charged with it, unless the land charge is registered in the appropriate register before the completion of the purchase.

(7) After the expiration of one year from the first conveyance occurring on or after 1st January 1926 of a land charge of Class B or Class C created before that date the person entitled to the land charge shall not be able to enforce or recover the land charge or any part of it as against a purchaser of the land charged with it, or of any interest in the land, unless the land charge is registered in the appropriate register before the completion of the purchase.

(8) A land charge of Class F shall be void as against a purchaser of the land charged with it, or of any interest in such land, unless the land charge is registered in the appropriate register before the completion of the purchase.

[859]

NOTES

Sub-s (6): first words in square brackets inserted by the Finance Act 1975, s 52, Sch 12, paras 2, 18(1), (5), words in square brackets therein substituted by the Inheritance Tax Act 1984, ss 274, 276, Sch 8, para 13.

Capital transfer tax: except in relation to a liability to tax arising before 25 July 1986 capital transfer tax shall be known as inheritance tax and the Capital Transfer Tax Act 1984 may be cited as the Inheritance Tax Act 1984, by virtue of the Finance Act 1986, s 100.

Registration in registers of pending actions, writs and orders and deeds of arrangement

5. The register of pending actions

(1) There may be registered in the register of pending actions—

    (*a*) a pending land action;
    (*b*) a petition in bankruptcy filed on or after 1st January 1926.

(2) Subject to general rules under section 16 of this Act, every application for registration under this section shall contain particulars of the title of the proceedings and the name, address and description of the estate owner or other person whose estate or interest is intended to be affected.

(3) An application for registration shall also state—

    (*a*) if it relates to a pending land action, the court in which and the day on which the action was commenced; and
    (*b*) if it relates to a petition in bankruptcy, the court in which and the day on which the petition was filed.

(4) The registrar shall forthwith enter the particulars in the register, in the name of the estate owner or other person whose estate or interest is intended to be affected.

(5) An application to register a petition in bankruptcy against a firm shall state the names and addresses of the partners, and the registration shall be effected against each partner as well as against the firm.

(6) No fee shall be charged for the registration of a petition in bankruptcy if the application for registration is made by the registrar of the court in which the petition is filed.

(7) A pending land action shall not bind a purchaser without express notice of it unless it is for the time being registered under this section.

(8) A petition in bankruptcy shall not bind a purchaser of a legal estate in good faith, for money or money's worth, . . ., unless it is for the time being registered under this section.

(9) . . .

(10) The court, if it thinks fit, may upon the determination of the proceedings, or during the pendency of the proceedings if satisfied that they are not prosecuted in good faith, make an order vacating a registration under this section, and direct the party on whose behalf it was made to pay all or any of the costs and expenses occasioned by the registration and by its vacation.

[(11) The county court has jurisdiction under subsection (10) of this section where the action was brought or the petition in bankruptcy was filed in that court.]   **[860]**

NOTES

Sub-s (8): words omitted repealed by the Insolvency Act 1985, s 235, Sch 8, para 21, Sch 10, Part III.

Sub-s (9): repealed by the Insolvency Act 1985, s 235, Sch 10, Part III.

Sub-s (11): added by the County Courts Act 1984, s 148(1), Sch 2, para 17.

6. The register of writs and orders affecting land

(1) There may be registered in the register of writs and orders affecting land—

     (a) any writ or order affecting land issued or made by any court for the purpose of enforcing a judgment or recognisance;

     (b) any order appointing a receiver or sequestrator of land;

     [(c) any bankruptcy order, whether or not the bankrupt's estate is known to include land;]

     [(d) any access order under the access to Neighbouring Land Act 1992.]

(2) Every entry made pursuant to this section shall be made in the name of the estate owner or other person whose land, if any, is affected by the writ or order registered.

(3) No fee shall be charged for the registration of a [bankruptcy order] if the application for registration is made by an official receiver.

(4) Except as provided by subsection (5) below and by [section 37(5) of the Supreme Court Act 1981] and [section 107(3) of the County Courts Act 1984] (which make special provision as to receiving orders in respect of land of judgment debtors) every such writ and order as is mentioned in subsection (1) above, and every delivery in execution or other proceeding taken pursuant to any such writ or order, or in obedience to any such writ or order, shall be void as against a purchaser of the land unless the writ or order is for the time being registered under this section.

[(5) Subject to subsection (6) below, the title of a trustee in bankruptcy shall be void as against a purchaser of a legal estate in good faith for money or money's worth unless the bankruptcy order is for the time being registered under this section.]

(6) Where a petition in bankruptcy has been registered under section 5 above, the title of the trustee in bankruptcy shall be void as against a purchaser of a legal estate in good faith for money or money's worth . . . claiming under a conveyance made after the date of registration, unless at the date of the conveyance either the registration of the petition is in force or a receiving order on the petition is registered under this section.   **[861]**

NOTES

Sub-s (1): para (c) added by the Insolvency Act 1985, s 235, Sch 8, para 21; para (d) added by the Access to Neighbouring Land Act 1992, s 5(1).

Sub-s (3): words in square brackets substituted by the Insolvency Act 1985, s 235, Sch 8, para 21.

Sub-s (4): first words in square brackets substituted by the Supreme Court Act 1981, s 152(1), Sch 5; second words in square brackets substituted by the County Courts Act 1984, s 148(1), Sch 2, para 18.

Sub-s (5): substituted by the Insolvency Act 1985, s 235, Sch 8, para 21.

Sub-s (6): words omitted repealed by the Insolvency Act 1985, s 235, Sch 8, para 21, Sch 10, Part III.

7. The register of deeds of arrangement affecting land

(1) The deed of arrangement affecting land may be registered in the register of deeds of arrangement affecting land, in the name of the debtor, on the application of a trustee of the deed or a creditor assenting to or taking the benefit of the deed.

(2) Every deed of arrangement shall be void as against a purchaser of any land comprised in it or affected by it unless it is for the time being registered under this section. **[862]**

8. Expiry and renewal of registrations

A registration under section 5, section 6 or section 7 of this Act shall cease to have effect at the end of the period of five years from the date on which it is made, but may be renewed from time to time and, if so renewed, shall have effect for five years from the date of renewal. **[863]**

Searches and official searches

9. Searches

(1) Any person may search in any register kept under this Act on paying the prescribed fee.

(2) Without prejudice to subsection (1) above, the registrar may provide facilities for enabling persons entitled to search in any such register to see photographic or other images or copies of any portion of the register which they may wish to examine. **[864]**

10. Official searches

(1) Where any person requires search to be made at the registry for entries of any matters or documents, entries of which are required or allowed to be made in the registry by this Act, he may make a requisition in that behalf to the registrar, which may be either—

    (a) a written requisition delivered at or sent by post to the registry; or

    (b) a requisition communicated by teleprinter, telephone or other means in such manner as may be prescribed in relation to the means in question, in which case it shall be treated as made to the registrar if, but only if, he accepts it;

and the registrar shall not accept a requisition made in accordance with paragraph (b) above unless it is made by a person maintaining a credit account at the registry, and may at his discretion refuse to accept it notwithstanding that it is made by such a person.

(2) The prescribed fee shall be payable in respect of every requisition made under this section; and that fee—

    (a) in the case of a requisition made in accordance with subsection (1)(a) above, shall be paid in such manner as may be prescribed for the purposes of this paragraph unless the requisition is made by a person maintaining a credit account at the registry and the fee is debited to that account;

    (b) in the case of a requisition made in accordance with subsection (1)(b) above, shall be debited to the credit account of the person by whom the requisition is made.

(3) Where a requisition is made under subsection (1) above and the fee

payable in respect of it is paid or debited in accordance with subsection (2) above, the retistrar shall thereupon make the search required and—

    (a) shall issue a certificate setting out the result of the search; and

    (b) without prejudice to paragraph (a) above, may take such other steps as he considers appropriate to communicate that result to the person by whom the requisition was made.

(4) In favour of a purchaser or an intending purchaser, as against persons interested under or in respect of matters or documents entries of which are required or allowed as aforesaid, the certificate, according to its tenor, shall be conclusive, affirmatively or negatively, as the case may be.

(5) If any officer, clerk or person employed in the registry commits, or is party or privy to, any act of fraud or collusion, or is wilfully negligent, in the making of or otherwise in relation to any certificate under this section, he shall be guilty of an offence and shall be liable on conviction on indictment to imprisonment for a term not exceeding two years, or on summary conviction to imprisonment for a term not exceeding three months or to a fine not exceeding [the prescribed sum], or to both such imprisonment and fine.

(6) Without prejudice to subsection (5) above, no officer, clerk or person employed in the registry shall, in the absence of fraud on his part, be liable for any loss which may be suffered—

    (a) by reason of any discrepancy between—

        (i) the particulars which are shown in a certificate under this section as being the particulars in respect of which the search for entries was made, and

        (ii) the particulars in respect of which a search for entries was required by the person who made the requisition; or

    (b) by reason of any communication of the result of a search under this section made otherwise than by issuing a certificate under this section. **[865]**

NOTES

    Sub-s (5): words in square brackets substituted by the Magistrates' Courts Act 1980, s 32(2).

Miscellaneous and supplementary

11. Date of effective registration and priority notices

(1) Any person intending to make an application for the registration of any contemplated charge, instrument or other matter in pursuance of this Act or any rule made under this Act may give a priority notice in the prescribed form at least the relevant number of days before the registration is to take effect.

(2) Where a notice is given under subsection (1) above, it shall be entered in the register to which the intended application when made will relate.

(3) If the application is presented within the relevant number of days thereafter and refers in the prescribed manner to the notice, the registration shall take effect as if the registration has been made at the time when the charge, instrument or matter was created, entered into, made or arose, and the date at which the registration so takes effect shall be deemed to be the date of registration.

(4) Where—

    (a) any two charges, instruments or matters are contemporaneous; and (*b*) one of them (whether or not protected by a priority notice) is subject to or dependent on the other; and

    (*c*) the latter is protected by a priority notice,

the subsequent or dependent charge, instrument or matter shall be deemed to have been created, entered into or made, or to have arisen, after the registration of the other.

(5) Where a purchaser has obtained a certificate under section 10 above, any entry which is made in the register after the date of the certificate and before the completion of the purchase, and is not made pursuant to a priority notice entered on the register on or before the date of the certificate, shall not affect the purchaser if the purchase is completed before the expiration of the relevant number of days after the date of the certificate.

(6) The relevant number of days is—

    (*a*) for the purposes of subsections (1) and (5) above, fifteen;

    (*b*) for the purposes of subsection (3) above, thirty;

or such other number as may be prescribed; but in reckoning the relevant number of days for any of the purposes of this section any days when the registry is not open to the public shall be excluded. **[866]**

12. Protection of solicitors, trustees, etc

A solicitor, or a trustee, personal representative, agent or other person in a fiduciary losition, shall not be answerable—

    (*a*) in respect of any loss occasioned by reliance on an office copy of an entry in any register kept under this Act;

    (*b*) for any loss that may arise from error in a certificate under section 10 above obtained by him. **[867]**

13. Saving for overreaching powers

(1) The registration of any charge, annuity or other interest under this Act shall not prevent the charge, annuity or interest being overreached under any other Act, except where otherwise provided by that other Act.

(2) The registration as a land charge of a puisne mortgage, or charge shall not operate to prevent that mortgage or charge being overreached in favour of a prior mortgagee or a person deriving title under him where, by reason of a sale or foreclosure, or otherwise, the right of the puisne mortgagee or subsequent chargee to redeem is barred. **[868]**

14. Exclusion of matters affecting registered land or created by instruments necessitating registration of land

(1) This Act shall not apply to instruments or matters required to be registered or re-registered on or after 1st January 1926, if and so far as they affect registered land, and can be protected under the Land Registration Act 1925 by lodging or registering a creditor's notice, restriction, caution, inhibition or other notice.

(2) Nothing in this Act imposes on the registrar any obligation to ascertain whether or not an instrument or matter affects registered land.

(3) Where an instrument executed on or after 27th July 1971 conveys, grants or assigns an estate in land and creates a land charge affecting that estate, this Act shall not apply to the land charge, so far as it affects that estate, if under section 123 of the Land Registration Act 1925 (effect of that Act in areas where

registration is compulsory) the instrument will, unless the necessary application for registration under that Act is made within the time allowed by or under that section, become void so far as respects the conveyance, grant or assignment of that estate. **[869]**

15. Application to the Crown

(1) This Act binds the Crown, but nothing in this Act shall be construed as rendering land owned by or occupied for the purposes of the Crown subject to any charge to which, independently of this Act, it would not be subject.

(2) References in this Act to restrictive covenants include references to any conditions, stipulations or restrictions imposed on or after 1st January 1926, by virtue of section 137 of the Law of Property Act 1922, for the protection of the amenities of royal parks, gardens and palaces. **[870]**

16. General rules

(1) The Lord Chancellor may, with the concurrence of the Treasury as to fees, make such general rules as may be required for carrying this Act into effect, and in particular—

    (a) as to forms and contents of applications for registration, modes of identifying where practicable the land affected, requisitions for and certificates of official searches, and regulating the practice of the registry in connection therewith;

    (b) for providing for the mode of registration of a land charge (and in the case of a puisne mortgage, general equitable charge, estate contract, restrictive covenant or equitable easement by reference to the instrument imposing or creating the charge, interest or restriction, or an extract from that instrument) and for the cancellation without an order of court of the registration of a land charge, on its cesser, or with the consent of the person entitled to it, or on sufficient evidence being furnished that the land charge has been overreached under the provisions of any Act or otherwise;

    (c) for determining the date on which applications and notices shall be treated for the purposes of section 11 of this Act as having been made or given;

    (d) for determining the times and order at and in which applications and priority notices are to be registered;

    (e) for varying the relevant number of days for any of the purposes of section 11 of this Act;

    (f) for enabling the registrar to provide credit accounting facilities in respect of fees payable by virtue of this Act;

    (g) for treating the debiting of such a fee to a credit account maintained at the registry as being, for such purposes of this Act or of the rules as may be specified in the rules, payment of that fee;

    (h) for the termination or general suspension of any credit accounting facilities provided under the rules or for their withdrawal or suspension in particular cases at the discretion of the registrar;

    (j) for requiring the registrar to take steps in relation to any instrument or matter in respect of which compensation has been claimed under section 25 of the Law of Property Act 1969 which would be likely to bring that instrument or matter to the notice of any person who subsequently makes a search of the registers kept under section 1 of this Act or requires such a search to be made in relation to the estate or interest affected by the instrument or matter; and (*k*) for authorising the use of the index kept under this Act in any manner which will serve that purpose, notwithstanding that its use in that manner is not otherwise authorised by or by virtue of this Act.

(2) The power of the Lord Chancellor, with the concurrence of the Secretary of State, to make [rules under section [412 of the Insolvency Act 1986]] shall include power to make rules as respects the registration and re-registration of a petition in bankruptcy under section 5 of this Act and [a bankruptcy order] under section 6 of this Act, as if the registration and re-registration were required [by [Parts VIII to XI] of that Act.   **[871]**

NOTES

Sub-s (2): first, third and fourth words in square brackets substituted by the Insolvency Act 1985, s 235, Sch 8, para 21, words "412 of the Insolvency Act 1986" and "Parts VIII to XI" substituted by the Insolvency Act 1986, s 439(2), Sch 14.

17. Interpretation

(1) In this Act, unless the context otherwise requires,—

"annuity" means a rentcharge or an annuity for a life or lives or for any term of years or greater estate determinable on a life or on lives and created after 25th April 1855 and before 1st January 1926, but does not include an annuity created by a marriage settlement or will;

"the Board" means the Commissioners of Inland Revenue;

"conveyance" includes a mortgage, charge, lease, assent, vesting declaration, vesting instrument, release and every other aseurance of property, or of an interest in property, by any instrument except a will, and "convey" has a corresponding meaning;

"court" means the High Court, or the county court in a case where that court has jurisdiction;

"deed of arrangement" has the same meaning as in the Deeds of Arrangement Act 1914;

"estate owner", "legal estate", "equitable interest", "trust for sale", "charge by way of legal mortgage", [and "will"] have the same meanings as in the Law of Property Act 1925;

"judgment" includes any order or decree having the effect of a judgment;

"land" includes land of any tenure and mines and minerals, whether or not severed from the surface, buildings or parts of buildings (whether the division is horizontal, vertical or made in any other way) and other corporeal hereditaments, also a manor, an advowson and a rent and other incorporeal hereditaments, and an easement, right, privilege or benefit in, over or derived from land, but not an undivided share in land, and "hereditament" means real property which, on an intestacy occurring before 1st January 1926, might have devolved on an heir;

"land improvement charge" means any charge under the Improvement of Land Act 1864 or under any special improvement Act within the meaning of the Improvement of Land Act 1899;

"pending land action" means any action or proceeding pending in court relating to land or any interest in or charge on land;

"prescribed" means prescribed by rules made pursuant to this Act;

"purchaser" means any person (including a mortgagee or lessee) who, for valuable consideration, takes any interest in land or in a charge on land, and "purchase" has a corresponding meaning;

"registrar" means the Chief Land Registrar, "registry" means Her Majesty's Land Registry, and "registered land" has the same meaning as in the Land Registration Act 1925;

"tenant for life", "statutory owner", "vesting instrument" and "settlement" have the same meanings as in the Settled Land Act 1925.

(2) For the purposes of any provision in this Act requiring or authorising anything to be done at or delivered or sent to the registry, any reference to the registry shall, if the registrar so directs, be read as a reference to such office of the registry (whether in London or elsewhere) as may be specified in the direction.

(3) Any reference in this Act to any enactment is a reference to it as amended by or under any other enactment, including this Act. **[872]**

NOTES

Sub-s (1): words in square brackets substituted by the Finance Act 1975, s 52(1), Sch 12, paras 2, 18(1), (6).

18. Consequential amendments, repeals, savings, etc

(1) Schedule 3 to this Act, which contains consequential amendments of other Acts, shall have effect.

(2) . . .

(3) The enactments specified in Schedule 5 to this Act are hereby repealed to the extent specified in the third column of that Schedule.

(4) . . .

(5) In so far as any entry in a register or instrument made or other thing whatsoever done under any enactment repealed by this Act could have been made or done under a corresponding provision in this Act, it shall have effect as if made or done under that corresponding provision; and for the purposes of this provision any entry in a register which under section 24 of the Land Charges Act 1925 had effect as if made under that Act shall, so far as may be necessary for the continuity of the law, be treated as made under this Act.

(6) Any enactment or other document referring to an enactment repealed by this Act or to an enactment repealed by the Land Charges Act 1925 shall, as far as may be necessary for preserving its effect, be construed as referring, or as including a reference, to the corresponding enactment in this Act.

(7) Nothing in the foregoing provisions of this section shall be taken as prejudicing the operation of section 38 of the Interpretation Act 1889 (which relates to the effect of repeals). **[873]**

NOTES

Sub-s (2): repealed by the Local Land Charges Act 1975, s 19(1), Sch 2.
Sub-s (4): revokes the Land Charges Rules 1972, SI 1972 No 50.

19. Short title, commencement and extent

(1) This Act may be cited as the Land Charges Act 1972.

(2) This Act shall come into force on such day as the Lord Chancellor may by order made by statutory instrument appoint; and different days may be so appointed for different purposes.

(3) This Act extends to England and Wales only. **[874]**

SCHEDULES
SCHEDULE 1

Section 1

ANNUITIES

1. No further entries shall be made in the register of annuities.

2. An entry of an annuity made in the register of annuities before 1st January 1926 may be vacated in the prescribed manner on the prescribed evidence as to satisfaction, cesser or discharge being furnished.

3. The register shall be closed when all the entries in it have been vacated or the prescribed evidence of the satisfaction, cesser or discharge of all the annuities has been furnished.

4. An annuity which before 1st January 1926 was capable of being registered in the register of annuities shall be void as against a creditor or a purchaser of any interest in the land charged with the annuity unless the annuity is for the time being registered in the register of annuities or in the register of land charges. **[875]**

SCHEDULE 2

Section 2

CLASS A LAND CHARGES

1. Charges created pursuant to applications under the enactments mentioned in this Schedule may be registered as land charges of Class A by virtue of paragraph (*b*) of section 2(2) of this Act:—

(*a*)The Tithe Act 1918 (8 & 9 Geo 5 c 54)	Sections 4(2) and 6(1) (charge of consideration money for redemption of tithe rentcharge).
(*b*) The Tithe Annuities Apportionment Act 1921 (11 & 12 Geo 5 c 20)	Section 1 (charge of apportioned part of tithe redemption annuity).
(*c*) The Landlord and Tenant Act 1927 (17 & 18 Geo 5 c 36)	Paragraph (7) of Schedule 1 (charge in respect of improvements to business premises).
(*d*) [The Land Drainage Act 1991 (c 59)]	[Section 34(2)] (charge in respect of sum paid in communication of certain obligations to repair banks, watercourses etc.).
(*e*) The Tithe Act 1936 (26 Geo 5 & 1 Edw 8 c 43)	Section 30(1) (charge for redemption of corn rents etc.).
(*f*) The Civil Defence Act 1939 (2 & 3 Geo 6 c 31)	Sections 18(4) and 19(1) (charges in respect of civil defence works).
(*g*) The Agricultural Holdings Act 1948 (11 & 12 Geo 6 c 63)	[Section 74 (charge in respect of sums due to] occupier of agricultural holding). . . .
	Section 82 (charge in favour of landlord of agricultural holding in respect of compensation for or cost of certain improvements).
(*h*) The Corn Rents Act 1963 (1963 c 14)	Section 1 (5) (charge under a scheme for the apportionment or redemption of corn rents or other payments in lieu of tithes).
[(*i*) The Agricultural Holdings Act 1986	Section 85 (charges in respect of sums due to tenant of agricultural holding).
	Section 86 (charges in favour of landlord of agricultural holdings in respect of compensation for or cost of certain improvements).]

2. The following provisions of paragraph 1 above shall cease to have effect upon the coming into operation of the first scheme under the Corn Rents Act 1963, that is to say:—

(a) in sub-paragraph (a), the words "and 6(1)"; and
(b) sub-paragraph (e).

3. [The reference in paragraph 1(g) above to section 74 of the Agricultural Holdings Act 1948 and the references in paragraph (i) above to section 85 and 86 of the Agricultural Holdings Act 1986] include references to any previous similar enactment. **[876]**

NOTES
Para 1: first and second words in square brackets substituted by the Water Consolidation (Consequential Provisions) Act 1991, s 2, Sch 1, para 21; third words in square brackets substituted, final words in square brackets added and words omitted repealed by the Agricultural Holdings Act 1986, ss 100, 101, Sch 14, para 51, Sch 15, Part I.
Para 3: words in square brackets substituted by the Agricultural Holdings Act 1986, s 100, Sch 14, para 51.

LOCAL GOVERNMENT ACT 1972
(c 70)

An Act to make provision with respect to local government and the functions of local authorities in England and Wales; to amend Part II of the Transport Act 1968; to confer rights of appeal in respect of decisions relating to licences under the Home Counties (Music and Dancing) Licensing Act 1926; to make further provision with respect to magistrates' courts committees; to abolish certain inferior courts of record; and for connected purposes [26 October 1972]

PART VII

MISCELLANEOUS POWERS OF LOCAL AUTHORITIES

Land transactions—principal councils

123. Disposal of land by principal councils

(1) Subject to the following provisions of this section, a principal council may dispose of land held by them in any manner they wish.

(2) Except with the consent of the Secretary of State, a council shall not dispose of land under this section, otherwise than by way of a short tenancy, for a consideration less than the best that can reasonably be obtained.

[(2A) A principal council may not dispose under subsection (1) above of any land consisting or forming part of an open space unless before disposing of the land they cause notice of their intention to do so, specifying the land in question, to be advertised in two consecutive weeks in a newspaper circulating in the area in which the land is situated, and consider any objections to the proposed disposal which may be made to them.

(2B) Where by virtue of subsection (2A) above a council dispose of land which is held—

(a) for the purposes of section 164 of the Public Health Act 1875 (pleasure grounds); or
(b) in accordance with section 10 of the Open Spaces Act 1906 (duty of local authority to maintain open spaces and burial grounds),

the land shall by virtue of the disposal be freed from any trust arising solely by virtue of its being land held in trust for enjoyment by the public in accordance with the said section 164 or, as the case may be, the said section 10.]

(3)–(5) . . .

(6) Capital money received in respect of a disposal under this section of land held for charitable purposes shall be applied in accordance with any directions given under [the Charities Act 1993].

(7) For the purposes of this section a disposal of land is a disposal by way of a short tenancy if it consists—

   (*a*) of the grant of a term not exceeding seven years, or
   (*b*) of the assignment of a term which at the date of the assignment has not more than seven years to run,

and in this section "public trust land" has the meaning assigned to it by section 122(6) above.   **[876A]**

NOTES
   Sub-s (2A): inserted by the Local Government, Planning and Land Act 1980, s 113, Sch 23, para 14.
   Sub-s (2B): inserted by the Local Government, Planning and Land Act 1980, s 113, Sch 23, para 14.
   Sub-ss (3)–(5): repealed by the Local Government, Planning and Land Act 1980, s 194, Sch 34, Part XIII.
   Sub-s (6): repealed for certain purposes by the Local Government and Housing Act 1989, s 194, Sch 12, Part I; words in square brackets substituted by the Charities Act 1993, s 98(1), Sch 6, para 12.

ADMINISTRATION OF JUSTICE ACT 1973
(c 15)

An Act to amend the law relating to justices of the peace and to make further provision with respect to the administration of justice and matters connected therewith   [18 April 1973]

PART II

MISCELLANEOUS

8. Extension of powers of court in action by mortgagee of dwelling-house

(1) Where by a mortgage of land which consists of or includes a dwelling-house, or by any agreement between the mortgagee under such a mortgage and the mortgagor, the mortgagor is entitled or is to be permitted to pay the principal sum secured by instalments or otherwise to defer payment of it in whole or in part, but provision is also made for earlier payment in the event of any default by the mortgagor or of a demand by the mortgagee or otherwise, then for purposes of section 36 of the Administration of Justice Act 1970 (under which a court has power to delay giving a mortgagee possession of the mortgaged property so as to allow the mortgagor a reasonable time to pay any sums due under the mortgage) a court may treat as due under the mortgage on account of the principal sum secured and of interest on it only such amounts as the mortgagor would have expected to be required to pay if there had been no such provision for earlier payment.

(2) A court shall not exercise by virtue of subsection (1) above the powers conferred by section 36 of the Administration of Justice Act 1970 unless it

appears to the court not only that the mortgagor is likely to be able within a reasonable period to pay any amounts regarded (in accordance with subsection (1) above) as due on account of the principal sum secured, together with the interest on those amounts, but also that he is likely to be able by the end of that period to pay any further amounts that he would have expected to be required to pay by then on account of that sum and of interest on it if there had been no such provision as is referred to in subsection (1) above for earlier payment.

(3) Where subsection (1) above would apply to an action in which a mortgagee only claimed possession of the mortgaged property, and the mortgagee brings an action for foreclosure (with or without also claiming possession of the property), then section 36 of the Administration of Justice Act 1970 together with subsections (1) and (2) above shall apply as they would apply if it were an action in which the mortgagee only claimed possession of the mortgaged property, except that—

(a) section 36(2)(b) shall apply only in relation to any claim for possession; and

(b) section 36(5) shall not apply.

(4) For purposes of this section the expressions "dwelling-house", "mortgage", "mortgagee" and "mortgagor" shall be construed in the same way as for the purposes of Part IV of the Administration of Justice Act 1970.

(5) This section shall have effect in relation to an action begun before the date on which this section comes into force if before that date judgment has not been given, nor an order made, in that action for delivery of possession of the mortgaged property and, where it is a question of subsection (3) above, an order *nisi* for foreclosure has not been made in that action.

(6) In the application of this section to Northern Ireland, subsection (3) shall be omitted. **[877]**

MATRIMONIAL CAUSES ACT 1973
(c 18)

An Act to consolidate certain enactments relating to matrimonial proceedings, maintenance agreements, and declarations of legitimacy, validity of marriage and British nationality, with amendments to give effect to recommendations of the Law Commission [23 May 1973]

PART I
DIVORCE, NULLITY AND OTHER MATRIMONIAL SUITS
Other matrimonial suits

18. Effects of judicial separation

(1) Where the court grants a decree of judicial separation it shall no longer be obligatory for the petitioner to cohabit with the respondent.

(2) If while a decree of judicial separation is in force and the separation is continuing either of the parties to the marriage dies intestate as respects all or any of his or her real or personal property, the property as respects which he or she died intestate shall devolve as if the other party to the marriage had then been dead.

(3) Notwithstanding anything in section 2(1)(*a*) of the Matrimonial Proceedings (Magistrates' Courts) Act 1960, a provision in force under an order made, or having effect as if made, under that section exempting one party to a marriage from the obligation to cohabit with the other shall not have effect as a decree of judicial separation for the purposes of subsection (2) above. **[878]**

PART II

FINANCIAL RELIEF FOR PARTIES TO MARRIAGE AND CHILDREN OF FAMILY

Ancillary relief in connection with divorce proceedings, etc

23. Financial provision orders in connection with divorce proceedings, etc.

(1) On granting a decree of divorce, a decree of nullity of marriage or a decree of judicial separation or at any time thereafter (whether, in the case of a decree of divorce or of nullity of marriage, before or after the decree is made absolute), the court may make any one or more of the following orders, that is to say—

   (*a*) an order that either party to the marriage shall make to the other such periodical payments, for such term, as may be specified in the order;

   (*b*) an order that either party to the marriage shall secure to the other to the satisfaction of the court such periodical payments, for such term, as may be so specified;

   (*c*) an order that either party to the marriage shall pay to the other such lump sum or sums as may be so specified;

   (*d*) an order that a party to the marriage shall make to such person as may be specified in the order for the benefit of a child of the family, or to such a child, such periodical payments, for such term, as may be so specified;

   (*e*) an order that a party to the marriage shall secure to such person as may be so specified for the benefit of such a child, or to such a child, to the satisfaction of the court, such periodical payments, for such term, as may be so specified;

   (*f*) an order that a party to the marriage shall pay to such person as may be so specified for the benefit of such a child, or to such a child, such lump sum as may be so specified;

subject, however, in the case of an order under paragraph (*d*), (*e*) or (*f*) above, to the restrictions imposed by section 29(1) and (3) below on the making of financial provision orders in favour of children who have attained the age of eighteen.

(2) The court may also, subject to those restrictions, make any one or more of the orders mentioned in subsection (1)(*d*), (*e*) and (*f*) above—

   (*a*) in any proceedings for divorce, nullity or marriage or judicial separation, before granting a decree; and

   (*b*) where any such proceedings are dismissed after the beginning of the trial, either forthwith or within a reasonable period after the dismissal.

(3) Without prejudice to the generality of subsection (1)(*c*) or (*f*) above—

   (*a*) an order under this section that a party to a marriage shall pay a lump sum to the other party may be made for the purpose of enabling that other party to meet any liabilities or expenses reasonably incurred by him or her in maintaining himself or herself or any child of the family before making an application for an order under this section in his or her favour;

(b) an order under this section for the payment of a lump sum to or for the benefit of a child of the family may be made for the purpose of enabling any liabilities or expenses reasonably incurred by or for the benefit of that child before the making of an application for an order under this section in his favour to be met; and

(c) an order under this section for the payment of a lump sum may provide for the payment of that sum by instalments of such amount as may be specified in the order and may require the payment of the instalments to be secured to the satisfaction of the court.

(4) The power of the court under subsection (1) or (2)(a) above to make an order in favour of a child of the family shall be exercisable from time to time; and where the court makes an order in favour of a child under subsection (2)(b) above, it may from time to time, subject to the restrictions mentioned in subsection (1) above, make a further order in his favour of any of the kinds mentioned in subsection (1)(d), (e) or (f) above.

(5) Without prejudice to the power to give a direction under section 30 below for the settlement of an instrument by conveyancing counsel, where an order is made under subsection (1)(a), (b) or (c) above on or after granting a decree of divorce or nullity or marriage, neither the order nor any settlement made in pursuance of the order shall take effect unless the decree has been made absolute.

[(6) Where the court—

(a) makes an order under this section for the payment of a lump sum; and
(b) directs—

(i) that payment of that sum or any part of it shall be deferred; or
(ii) that that sum or any part of it shall be paid by instalments,

the court may order that the amount deferred or the instalments shall carry interest at such rate as may be specified by the order from such date, not earlier than the date of the order, as may be so specified, until the date when payment of it is due.] **[879]**

24. Property adjustment orders in connection with divorce proceedings, etc

(1) On granting a decree of divorce, a decree of nullity of marriage or a decree of judicial separation or at any time thereafter (whether, in the case of a decree of divorce or of nullity of marriage, before or after the decree is made absolute), the court may make any one or more of the following orders, that is to say—

(a) an order that a party to the marriage shall transfer to the other party, to any child of the family or to such person as may be specified in the order for the benefit of such a child such property as may be so specified, being property to which the first-mentioned party is entitled, either in possession or reversion;

(b) an order that a settlement of such property as may be so specified, being property to which a party to the marriage is so entitled, be made to the satisfaction of the court for the benefit of the other party to the marriage and of the children of the family or either or any of them;

(c) an order varying for the benefit of the parties to the marriage and of the children of the family or either or any of them any ante-nuptial or post-nuptial settlement (including such a settlement made by will or codicil) made on the parties to the marriage;

(d) an order extinguishing or reducing the interest of either of the parties to the marriage under any such settlement;

subject, however, in the case of an order under paragraph (*a*) above, to the restrictions imposed by section 29(1) and (3) below on the making of orders for a transfer of property in favour of children who have attained the age of eighteen.

(2) The court may make an order under subsection (1)(*c*) above notwithstanding that there are no children of the family.

(3) Without prejudice to the power to give a direction under section 30 below for the settlement of an instrument by conveyancing counsel, where an order is made under this section on or after granting a decree of divorce or nullity of marriage, neither the order nor any settlement made in pursuance of the order shall take effect unless the decree has been made absolute.   **[880]**

[24A. Orders for sale of property

(1) Where the court makes under section 23 or 24 of this Act a secured periodical payments order, an order for the payment of a lump sum or a property adjustment order, then, on making that order or at any time thereafter, the court may make a further order for the sale of such property as may be specified in the order, being property in which or in the proceeds of sale of which either or both of the parties to the marriage has or have a beneficial interest, either in possession or reversion.

(2) Any order made under subsection (1) above may contain such consequential or supplementary provisions as the court thinks fit and, without prejudice to the generality of the foregoing provision, may include—

   (*a*) provision requiring the making of a payment out of the proceeds of sale of the property to which the order relates, and
   (*b*) provision requiring any such property to be offered for sale to a person, or class of persons, specifed in the order.

(3) Where an order is made under subsection (1) above on or after the grant of a decree of divorce or nullity of marriage, the order shall not take effect unless the decree has been made absolute.

(4) Where an order is made under subsection (1) above, the court may direct that the order, or such provision thereof as the court may specify, shall not take effect until the occurrence of an event specified by the court or the expiration of a period so specified.

(5) Where an order under subsection (1) above contains a provision requiring the proceeds of sale of the property to which the order relates to be used to secure periodical payments to a party to the marriage, the order shall cease to have effect on the death or re-marriage of that person.

[(6) Where a party to a marriage has a beneficial interest in any property, or in the proceeds of sale thereof, and some other person who is not a party to the marriage also has a beneficial interest in that property or in the proceeds of sale thereof, then, before deciding whether to make an order under this section in relation to that property, it shall be the duty of the court to give that other person an opportunity to make representations with respect to the order; and any representations made by that other person shall be included among the circumstances to which the court is required to have regard under section 25(1) below.]]   **[881]**

NOTES
Inserted by the Matrimonial Homes and Property Act 1981, s 7.

Sub-s (6): added by the Matrimonial and Family Proceedings Act 1984, s 46(1), Sch 1.

[25. Matters to which court is to have regard in deciding how to exercise its powers under ss 23, 24 and 24A

(1) It shall be the duty of the court in deciding whether to exercise its powers under section 23, 24 or 24A above and, if so, in what manner, to have regard to all the circumstances of the case, first consideration being given to the welfare while a minor of any child of the family who has not attained the age of eighteen.

(2) As regards the exercise of the powers of the court under section 23(1)(*a*), (*b*) or (*c*), 24 or 24A above in relation to a party to the marriage, the court shall in particular have regard to the following matters—

(*a*) the income, earning capacity, property and other financial resources which each of the parties to the marriage has or is likely to have in the foreseeable future, including in the case of earning capacity any increase in that capacity which it would in the opinion of the court be reasonable to expect a party to the marriage to take steps to acquire;

(*b*) the financial needs, obligations and responsibilities which each of the parties to the marriage has or is likely to have in the foreseeable future;

(*c*) the standard of living enjoyed by the family before the breakdown of the marriage;

(*d*) the age of each party to the marriage and the duration of the marriage;

(*e*) any physical or mental disability of either of the parties to the marriage;

(*f*) the contributions which each of the parties has made or is likely in the foreseeable future to make to the welfare of the family, including any contribution by looking after the home or caring for the family;

(*g*) the conduct of each of the parties, if that conduct is such that it would in the opinion of the court be inequitable to disregard it;

(*h*) in the case of proceedings for divorce or nullity of marriage, the value to each of the parties to the marriage of any benefit (for example, a pension) which, by reason of the dissolution or annulment of the marriage, that party will lose the chance of acquiring.

(3) As regards the exercise of the powers of the court under section 23(1)(*d*), (*e*) or (*f*), (2) or (4), 24 or 24A above in relation to a child of the family, the court shall in particular have regard to the following matters—

(*a*) the financial needs of the child;

(*b*) the income, earning capacity (if any), property and other financial resources of the child;

(*c*) any physical or mental disability of the child;

(*d*) the manner in which he was being and in which the parties to the marriage expected him to be educated or trained;

(*e*) the considerations mentioned in relation to the parties to the marriage in paragraphs (*a*), (*b*), (*c*) and (*e*) of subsection (2) above.

(4) As regards the exercise of the powers of the court under section 23(1)(*d*), (*e*) or (*f*), (2) or (4), 24 or 24A above against a party to a marriage in favour of a child of the family who is not the child of that party, the court shall also have regard—

(*a*) to whether that party assumed any responsibility for the child's maintenance, and, if so, to the extent to which, and the basis upon which, that party assumed such responsibility and to the length of time for which that party discharged such responsibility;

(*b*) to whether in assuming and discharging such responsibility that party did so knowing that the child was not his or her own;

(*c*) to the liability of any other person to maintain the child.] **[882]**

NOTES

Substituted together with s 25A for s 25, as originally enacted, by the Matrimonial and Family Proceedings Act 1984, s 3.

[25A. Exercise of court's powers in favour of party to marriage on decree of divorce or nullity of marriage

(1) Where on or after the grant of a decree of divorce or nullity of marriage the court decides to exercise its powers under section 23(1)(*a*), (*b*) or (*c*), 24 or 24A above in favour of a party to the marriage, it shall be the duty of the court to consider whether it would be appropriate so to exercise those powers that the financial obligations of each party towards the other will be terminated as soon after the grant of the decree as the court considers just and reasonable.] **[882A]**

...

NOTES

Substituted together with s 25 for s 25, as orginally enacted, by the Matrimonial and Family Proceedings Act 1984, s 3.

29. Duration of continuing financial provision orders in favour of children, and age limit on making certain orders in their favour

(1) Subject to subsection (3) below, no financial provision order and no order for a transfer of property under section 24(1)(*a*) above shall be made in favour of a child who has attained the age of eighteen.

(2) The term to be specified in a periodical payments or secured periodical payments order in favour of a child may begin with the date of the making of an application for the order in question or any later date [or a date ascertained in accordance with subsection (5) or (6) below] but—

(*a*) shall not in the first instance extend beyond the date of the birthday of the child next following his attaining the upper limit of the compulsory school age (*that is to say, the age that is for the time being that limit by virtue of section 35 of the Education Act 1944 together with any Order in Council made under that section*) (construed in accordance with section 277 of the Education Act 1993) [unless the court considers that in the circumstances of the case the welfare of the child requires that it should extend to a later date]; and

(*b*) shall not in any event, subject to subsection (3) below, extend beyond the date of the child's eighteenth birthday.

(3) Subsection (1) above, and paragraph (*b*) of subsection (2), shall not apply in the case of a child, if it appears to the court that—

(*a*) the child is, or will be, or if an order were made without complying with either or both of those provisions would be, receiving instruction at an educational establishment or undergoing training for a trade, profession or vocation, whether or not he is also, or will also be, in gainful employment; or

(*b*) there are special circumstances which justify the making of an order without complying with either or both of those provisions.

(4) Any periodical payments order in favour of a child shall, notwithstanding anything in the order, cease to have effect on the death of the person liable to

make payments under the order, except in relation to any arrears due under the order on the date of the death.

[(5) Where—

(a) a maintenance assessment ("the current assessment") is in force with respect to a child; and

(b) an application is made under Part II of this Act for a periodical payments or secured periodical payments order in favour of that child—

(i) in accordance with section 8 of the Child Support Act 1991, and

(ii) before the end of the period of 6 months beginning with the making of the current assessment

the term to be specified in any such order made on that application may be expressed to begin on, or at any time after, the earliest permitted date.

(6) For the purposes of subsection (5) above, "the earliest permitted date" is whichever is the later of—

(a) the date 6 months before the application is made; or

(b) the date on which the current assessment took effect or, where successive maintenance assessments have been continuously in force with respect to a child, on which the first of those assessments took effect.

(7) Where—

(a) a maintenance assessment ceases to have effect or is cancelled by or under any provision of the Child Support Act 1991; and

(b) an application is made, before the end of the period of 6 months beginning with the relevant date, for a periodical payments or secured periodical payments order in favour of a child with respect to whom that maintenance assessment was in force immediately before it ceased to have effect or was cancelled,

the term to be specified in any such order made on that application may begin with the date on which that maintenance assessment ceased to have effect or, as the case may be, the date with effect from which it was cancelled, or any later date.

(8) In subsection (7)(b) above—

(a) where the maintenance assessment ceased to have effect, the relevant date is the date on which it so ceased; and

(b) where the maintenance assessment was cancelled, the relevant date is the later of—

(i) the date on which the person who cancelled it did so, and

(ii) the date from which the cancellation first had effect.] **[883]**

NOTES

Commencement: 5 April 1993 (sub-ss (5)–(8)); 1 January 1974 (remainder) (SI 1973 No 1972).

Sub-s (2): first words in square brackets inserted by the Maintenance Orders (Backdating) Order 1993, SI 1993 No 623, art 2, Sch 1, para 1; words in italics prospectively repealed and second words in square brackets prospectively substituted by the Education Act 1993, s 307(1), Sch 19, para 53; third words in square brackets substituted by the Matrimonial and Family Proceedings Act 1984, s 5(4).

Sub-s (5): added by the Maintenance Orders (Backdating) Order 1993, SI 1993 No 623, art 2, Sch 1, para 2.

Sub-s (6): added by the Maintenance Orders (Backdating) Order 1993, SI 1993 No 623, art 2, Sch 1, para 2.

Sub-s (7): added by the Maintenance Orders (Backdating) Order 1993, SI 1993 No 623, art 2, Sch 1, para 2.
Sub-s (8): added by the Maintenance Orders (Backdating) Order 1993, SI 1993 No 623, art 2, Sch 1, para 2.

CONSUMER CREDIT ACT 1974
(c 39)

ARRANGEMENT OF SECTIONS

An Act to establish for the protection of consumers a new system, administered by the Director General of Fair Trading, of licensing and other control of traders concerned with the provision of credit, or the supply of goods on hire or hire-purchase, and their transactions, in place of the present enactments regulating moneylenders, pawnbrokers and hire-purchase traders and their transactions, and for related matters   [31 July 1974]

PART II

CREDIT AGREEMENTS, HIRE AGREEMENTS AND LINKED TRANSACTIONS

8. Consumer credit agreements

(1) A personal credit agreement is an agreement between an individual ("the debtor") and any other person ("the creditor") by which the creditor provides the debtor with credit of any amount.

(2) A consumer credit agreement is a personal credit agreement by which the creditor provides the debtor with credit not exceeding [£15,000].

(3) A consumer credit agreement is a regulated agreement within the meaning of this Act if it is not an agreement (an "exempt agreement") specified in or under section 16.   **[884]**

NOTES

Sub-s (2): sum in square brackets substituted by the Consumer Credit (Increase of Monetary Limits) Order 1983, SI 1983 No 1878, art 4, Schedule, Part II.

15. Consumer hire agreements

(1) A consumer hire agreement is an agreement made by a person with an individual (the "hirer") for the bailment or (in Scotland) the hiring of goods to the hirer, being an agreement which—

    (a) is not a hire-purchase agreement, and
    (b) is capable of subsisting for more than three months, and
    (c) does not require the hirer to make payments exceeding [£15,000].

(2) A consumer hire agreement is a regulated agreement if it is not an exempt agreement.   **[885]**

NOTES

Sub-s (1): sum in square brackets substituted by the Consumer Credit (Increase of Monetary Limits) Order 1983, SI 1983 No 1878, art 4, Schedule, Part II.

16. Exempt agreements

(1) This Act does not regulate a consumer credit agreement where the creditor is a local authority . . ., or a body specified, or of a description specified, in an order made by the Secretary of State, being—

    (a) an insurance company,
    (b) a friendly society,
    (c) an organisation of employers or organisation of workers,
    (d) a charity,
    (e) a land improvement company, . . .
    (f) a body corporate named or specifically referred to in any public general Act [, or
    [(ff) a body corporate named or specifically referred to in an order made under—

section 156(4), 444(1) or 447(2)(*a*) of the Housing Act 1985,
section 2 of the Home Purchase Assistance and Housing
Corporation Guarantee Act 1978 or section 31 of the Tenants'
Rights, &c. (Scotland) Act 1980, or
Article 154(1)(*a*) or 156AA of the Housing (Northern Ireland)
Order 1981 or Article 10(6A) of the Housing (Northern Ireland)
Order 1983; or]

(*g*) a building society] [, or
(*h*) an authorised institution or wholly-owned subsidiary (within the
meaning of the Companies Act 1985) of such an institution.]

(2) Subsection (1) applies only where the agreement is—

(*a*) a debtor-creditor-supplier agreement financing—

(i) the purchase of land, or
(ii) the provision of dwellings on any land,
and secured by a land mortgage on that land, or

(*b*) a debtor-creditor agreement secured by any land mortgage; or
(*c*) a debtor-creditor-supplier agreement financing a transaction which is
a linked transaction in relation to—

(i) an agreement falling within paragraph (*a*), or
(ii) an agreement falling within paragraph (*b*) financing—

(*aa*) the purchase of any land, or
(*bb*) the provision of dwellings on any land,

and secured by a land mortgage on the land referred to in
paragraph (*a*) or, as the case may be, the land referred to in
subparagraph (ii).

(3) The Secretary of State shall not make, vary or revoke an order—

(*a*) under subsection (1)(*a*) without consulting the Minister of the Crown
responsible for insurance companies,
(*b*) under subsection (1)(*b*) . . . without consulting the Chief Registrar of
Friendly Societies,
(*c*) under subsection (1)(*d*) without consulting the Charity Commissioners, . . .
(*d*) under subsection (1)(*e*) [, (*f*) or (*ff*)] without consulting any Minister
of the Crown with responsibilities concerning the body in question
[or
(*e*) under subsection (1)(*g*) without consulting the Building Societies
Commission and the Treasury] [or
(*f*) under subsection (1)(*h*) without consulting the Treasury and the Bank
of England.]

(4) An order under subsection (1) relating to a body may be limited so as to
apply only to agreements by that body of a description specified in the order.

(5) The Secretary of State may by order provide that this Act shall not
regulate other consumer credit agreements where—

(*a*) the number of payments to be made by the debtor does not exceed the
number specified for that purpose in the order, or
(*b*) the rate of the total charge for credit does not exceed the rate so
specified, or
(*c*) an agreement has a connection with a country outside the United
Kingdom.

(6) The Secretary of State may by order provide that this Act shall not regulate consumer hire agreements of a description specified in the order where—

    (*a*) the owner is a body corporate authorised by or under any enactment to supply electricity, gas or water, and
    (*b*) the subject of the agreement is a meter or metering equipment,

[or where the owner is a public telecommunications operator specified in the order].

[(6A) This Act does not regulate a consumer credit agreement where the creditor is a housing authority and the agreement is secured by a land mortgage of a dwelling.

(6B) In subsection (6A) "housing authority" means—

    (*a*) as regards England and Wales, [the Housing Corporation, Housing for Wales and] an authority or body within section 80(1) of the Housing Act 1985 (the landlord condition for secure tenancies), other than a housing association or a housing trust which is a charity;
    (*b*) as regards Scotland, a development corporation established under an order made, or having effect as if made under the New Towns (Scotland) Act 1968, the Scottish Special Housing Association or the Housing Corporation;
    (*c*) as regards Northern Ireland, the Northern Ireland Housing Executive.]

(7) Nothing in this section affects the application of sections 137 to 140 (extortionate credit bargains).

(8) . . .

(9) In the application of this section to Northern Ireland subsection (3) shall have effect as if any reference to a Minister of the Crown were a reference to a Northern Ireland department, any reference to the Chief Registrar of Friendly Societies were a reference to the Registrar of Friendly Societies for Northern Ireland, and any reference to the Charity Commissioners were a reference to the Department of Finance for Northern Ireland.   **[886]**

NOTES

    Sub-s (1): words omitted repealed and para (*g*) added by the Building Societies Act 1986, s 120, Sch 18, Part I, para 10(2), Sch 19, Part I; para (*ff*) inserted by the Housing and Planning Act 1986, s 22(2), (4), with respect to agreements made after 7 January 1987; para (*h*) added by the Banking Act 1987, s 88.

    Sub-s (3): words omitted from para (*b*) repealed by the Employment Protection Act 1975, s 125(3), Sch 18; word omitted from para (*c*) repealed and para (*e*) added by the Building Societies Act 1986, s 120, Sch 18, Part I, para 10(3), Sch 19, Part I; in para (*d*) words in square brackets substituted with respect to agreements made after 7 January 1987 by the Housing and Planning Act 1986, s 22(2), (4); para (*f*) added by the Banking Act 1987, s 88.

    Sub-s (6): words in square brackets substituted by the Telecommunications Act 1984, s 109, Sch 4, para 60.

    Sub-s (6A): inserted with respect to agreements made after 7 January 1987 by the Housing and Planning Act 1986, s 22.

    Sub-s (6B): inserted with respect to agreements made after 7 January 1987 by the Housing and Planning Act 1986, s 22; amended by the Housing Act 1988, s 140, Sch 17, Part I.

    Sub-s (8): applies to Scotland only.

PART V

ENTRY INTO CREDIT OR HIRE AGREEMENTS

Preliminary matters

58. Opportunity for withdrawal from prospective land mortgage

(1) Before sending to the debtor or hirer, for his signature, an unexecuted agreement in a case where the prospective regulated agreement is to be secured on land (the "mortgaged land"), the creditor or owner shall give the debtor or hirer a copy of the unexecuted agreement which contains a notice in the prescribed form indicating the right of the debtor or hirer to withdraw from the prospective agreement, and how and when the right is exercisable, together with a copy of any other document referred to in the unexecuted agreement.

(2) Subsection (1) does not apply to—

     (*a*) a restricted-use credit agreement to finance the purchase of the mortgaged land, or

     (*b*) an agreement for a bridging loan in connection with the purchase of the mortgaged land or other land.   **[887]**

PART VII

DEFAULT AND TERMINATION

Default notices

87. Need for default notice

(1) Service of a notice on the debtor or hirer in accordance with section 88 (a "default notice") is necessary before the creditor or owner can become entitled, by reason of any breach by the debtor or hirer of a regulated agreement,—

     (*a*) to terminate the agreement, or

     (*b*) to demand earlier payment of any sum, or

     (*c*) to recover possession of any goods or land, or

     (*d*) to treat any right conferred on the debtor or hirer by the agreement as terminated, restricted or deferred, or

     (*e*) to enforce any security.

         [887A]

. . .

Further restriction of remedies for default

92. Recovery of possession of goods or land

(1) Except under an order of the court, the creditor or owner shall not be entitled to enter any premises to take possession of goods subject to a regulated hire-purchase agreement, regulated conditional sale agreement or regulated consumer hire agreement.

(2) At any time when the debtor is in breach of a regulated conditional sale agreement relating to land, the creditor is entitled to recover possession of the

land from the debtor, or any person claiming under him, on an order of the court only.

(3) An entry in contravention of subsection (1) or (2) is actionable as a breach of statutory duty.   [888]

PART VIII

SECURITY

Land mortgages

126. Enforcement of land mortgages

A land mortgage securing a regulated agreement is enforceable (so far as provided in relation to the agreement) on an order of the court only.   [889]

PART IX

JUDICIAL CONTROL

Extortionate credit bargains

137. Extortionate credit bargains

(1) If the court finds a credit bargain extortionate it may reopen the credit agreement so as to do justice between the parties.

(2) In this section and sections 138 to 140—

(*a*) "credit agreement" means any agreement between an individual (the "debtor") and any other person (the "creditor") by which the creditor provides the debtor with credit of any amount, and

(*b*) "credit bargain"—

(i) where no transaction other than the credit agreement is to be taken into account in computing the total charge for credit, means the credit agreement, or

(ii) where one or more other transactions are to be so taken into account, means the credit agreement and those other transactions, taken together.   [890]

138. When bargains are extortionate

(1) A credit bargain is extortionate if it—

(*a*) requires the debtor or a relative of his to make payments (whether unconditionally, or on certain contingencies) which are grossly exorbitant, or

(*b*) otherwise grossly contravenes ordinary principles of fair dealing.

(2) In determining whether a credit bargain is extortionate, regard shall be had to such evidence as is adduced concerning—

(*a*) interest rates prevailing at the time it was made,

(*b*) the factors mentioned in subsections (3) to (5), and

(*c*) any other relevant considerations.

(3) Factors applicable under subsection (2) in relation to the debtor include—

(*a*) his age, experience, business capacity and state of health; and (*b*) the degree to which, at the time of making the credit bargain, he was under financial pressure, and the nature of that pressure.

(4) Factors applicable under subsection (2) in relation to the creditor include—

(*a*) the degree of risk accepted by him, having regard to the value of any security provided;

(*b*) his relationship to the debtor; and

(*c*) whether or not a colourable cash price was quoted for any goods or services included in the credit bargain.

(5) Factors applicable under subsection (2) in relation to a linked transaction include the question how far the transaction was reasonably required for the protection of debtor or creditor, or was in the interest of the debtor. **[891]**

139. Reopening of extortionate agreements

(1) A credit agreement may, if the court thinks just, be reopened on the ground that the credit bargain is extortionate—

(*a*) on an application for the purpose made by the debtor or any surety to the High Court, county court or sheriff court; or

(*b*) at the instance of the debtor or a surety in any proceedings to which the debtor and creditor are parties, being proceedings to enforce the agreement, any security relating to it, or any linked transaction; or

(*c*) at the instance of the debtor or a surety in other proceedings in any court where the amount paid or payable under the credit agreement is relevant.

(2) In reopening the agreement, the court may, for the purpose of relieving the debtor or a surety from payment of any sum in excess of that fairly due and reasonable, by order—

(*a*) direct accounts to be taken, or (in Scotland) an accounting to be made, between any persons,

(*b*) set aside the whole or part of any obligation imposed on the debtor or surety by the credit bargain or any related agreement,

(*c*) require the creditor to repay the whole or part of any sum paid under the credit bargain or any related agreement by the debtor or a surety, whether paid to the creditor or any other person,

(*d*) direct the return to the surety of any property provided for the purposes of the security, or

(*e*) alter the terms of the credit agreement or any security instrument.

(3) An order may be made under subsection (2) notwithstanding that its effect is to place a burden on the creditor in respect of an advantage unfairly enjoyed by another person who is a party to a linked transaction.

(4) An order under subsection (2) shall not alter the effect of any judgment.

(5) In England and Wales, an application under subsection (1)(*a*) shall be brought only in the county court in the case of—

(*a*) a regulated agreement, or

(*b*) an agreement (not being a regulated agreement) under which the creditor provides the debtor with fixed-sum credit . . . or running-account credit . . .

[(5A) . . .]

(6) . . .

(7) In Northern Ireland an application under subsection (1)(*a*) may be brought in the county court in the case of—

   (*a*) a regulated agreement, or
   (*b*) an agreement (not being a regulated agreement) under which the creditor provides the debtor with fixed-sum credit not exceeding [£15,000] or running-account credit on which the credit limit does not exceed [£15,000].   **[892]**

NOTES

Sub-s (5): words omitted repealed by the High Court and County Courts Jurisdiction Order 1991, SI 1991 No 724, art 2(8), Schedule.

Sub-s (5A): inserted by the Administration of Justice Act 1982, s 37, Sch 3, Part I, para 4; repealed by the High Court and County Courts Jurisdiction Order 1991, SI 1991 No 724, art 2(8), Schedule.

Sub-s (6): applies to Scotland only.

Sub-s (7): sums in square brackets substituted by virtue of the County Courts (Financial Limits) Order (Northern Ireland) 1992, SR 1993 No 282.

140. Interpretation of sections 137 to 139

Where the credit agreement is not a regulated agreement, expressions used in sections 137 to 139 which, apart from this section, apply only to regulated agreements, shall be construed as nearly as may be as if the credit agreement were a regulated agreement.   **[893]**

PART XII

SUPPLEMENTAL

Interpretation

189. Definitions

(1) In this Act, unless the context otherwise requires—

   "advertisement" includes every form of advertising, whether in a publication, by television or radio, by display of notices, signs, labels, showcards or goods, by distribution of samples, circulars, catalogues, price lists or other material, by exhibition of pictures, models or films, or in any other way, and references to the publishing of advertisements shall be construed accordingly;

   "advertiser" in relation to an advertisement, means any person indicated by the advertisement as willing to enter into transactions to which the advertisement relates;

   "ancillary credit business" has the meaning given by section 145(1);

   "antecedent negotiations" has the meaning given by section 56;

   "appeal period" means the period beginning on the first day on which an appeal to the Secretary of State may be brought and ending on the last day on which it may be brought or, if it is brought, ending on its final determination, or abandonment;

   . . .

   "associate" shall be construed in accordance with section 184;

   ["authorised institution" means an institution authorised under the Banking Act 1987;]

   "bill of sale" has the meaning given by section 4 of the Bills of Sale Act 1878 or, for Northern Ireland, by section 4 of the Bills of Sale (Ireland) Act 1879;

["building society" means a building society within the meaning of the Building Societies Act 1986;]

"business" includes profession or trade, and references to a business apply subject to subsection (2);

"cancellable agreement" means a regulated agreement which, by virtue of section 67, may be cancelled by the debtor or hirer;

"canvass" shall be construed in accordance with sections 48 and 153;

"cash" includes money in any form;

"charity" means as respects England and Wales a charity registered under [the Charities Act 1993] or an exempt charity (within the meaning of that Act), and as respects Scotland and Northern Ireland an institution or other organisation established for charitable purposes only ("organisation" including any persons administering a trust and "charitable" being construed in the same way as if it were contained in the Income Tax Acts);

"conditional sale agreement" means an agreement for the sale of goods or land under which the purchase price or part of it is payable by instalments, and the property in the goods or land is to remain in the seller (notwithstanding that the buyer is to be in possession of the goods or land) until such conditions as to the payment of instalments or otherwise as may be specified in the agreement are fulfilled;

"consumer credit agreement" has the meaning given by section 8, and includes a consumer credit agreement which is cancelled under section 69(1), or becomes subject to section 69(2), so far as the agreement remains in force;

"consumer credit business" means any business so far as it comprises or relates to the provision of credit under regulated consumer credit agreements;

"consumer hire agreement" has the meaning given by section 15;

"consumer hire business" means any business so far as it comprises or relates to the bailment or (in Scotland) the hiring of goods under regulated consumer hire agreements;

"controller", in relation to a body corporate, means a person—

(a) in accordance with whose directions or instructions the directors of the body corporate or of another body corporate which is its controller (or any of them) are accustomed to act, or

(b) who, either alone or with any associate or associates, is entitled to exercise or control the exercise of, one third or more of the voting power at any general meeting of the body corporate or of another body corporate which is its controller;

"copy" shall be construed in accordance with section 180;

. . .

"court" means in relation to England and Wales the county court, in relation to Scotland the sheriff court and in relation to Northern Ireland the High Court or the county court;

"credit" shall be construed in accordance with section 9;

"credit-broker" means a person carrying on a business of credit brokerage;

"credit brokerage" has the meaning given by section 145(2);

"credit limit" has the meaning given by section 10(2);

"creditor" means the person providing credit under a consumer credit agreement or the person to whom his rights and duties under the agreement have passed by assignment or operation of law, and in relation to a prospective consumer credit agreement, includes the prospective creditor;

"credit reference agency" has the meaning given by section 145(8);

"credit-sale agreement" means an agreement for the sale of goods, under which the purchase price or part of it is payable by instalments, but which is not a conditional sale agreement;

"credit-token" has the meaning given by section 14(1);

"credit-token agreement" means a regulated agreement for the provision of credit in connection with the use of a credit-token;

"debt-adjusting" has the meaning given by section 145(5);

"debt-collecting" has the meaning given by section 145(7);

"debt-counselling" has the meaning given by section 145(6);

"debtor" means the individual receiving credit under a consumer credit agreement or the person to whom his rights and duties under the agreement have passed by assignment or operation of law, and in relation to a prospective consumer credit agreement includes the prospective debtor;

"debtor-creditor agreement" has the meaning given by section 13;

"debtor-creditor-supplier agreement" has the meaning given by section 12;

"default notice" has the meaning given by section 87(1);

"deposit" means any sum payable by a debtor or hirer by way of deposit or down-payment, or credited or to be credited to him on account of any deposit or down-payment, whether the sum is to be or has been paid to the creditor or owner or any other person, or is to be or has been discharged by a payment of money or a transfer or delivery of goods or by any other means;

"Director" means the Director General of Fair Trading;

"electric line" has the meaning given by [the Electricity Act 1989] or, for Northern Ireland, [the Electricity (Northern Ireland) Order 1992];

"embodies" and related words shall be construed with subsection (4);

"enforcement authority" has the meaning given by section 161(1);

"enforcement order" means an order under section 65(1), 105(7)(*a*) or (*b*), 111(2) or 124(1) or (2);

"executed agreement" means a document, signed by or on behalf of the parties, embodying the terms of a regulated agreement, or such of them as have been reduced to writing;

"exempt agreement" means an agreement specified in or under section 16;

"finance" means to finance wholly or partly and "financed" and "refinanced" shall be construed accordingly;

"file" and "copy of the file" have the meanings given by section 158(5);

"fixed-sum credit" has the meaning given by section 10(1)(*b*);

"friendly society" means a society registered under the Friendly Societies Acts 1896 to 1971 *or a society within the meaning of the Friendly Societies Act (Northern Ireland) 1970*;

"future arrangements" shall be construed in accordance with section 187;

"general notice" means a notice published by the Director at a time and in a mannner appearing to him suitable for securing that the notice is seen within a reasonable time by persons likely to be affected by it;

"give", means, deliver or send by post to;

"goods", has the meaning given by section [section 61(1) of the Sale of Goods Act 1979];

"group licence" has the meaning given by section 22(1)(*b*);

"High Court" means Her Majesty's High Court of Justice, or the Court of Session in Scotland or the High Court of Justice in Northern Ireland;

"hire-purchase agreement" means an agreement, other than a conditional sale agreement, under which—

    (*a*) goods are bailed or (in Scotland) hired in return for periodical payments by the person to whom they are bailed or hired, and

    (*b*) the property in the goods will pass to that person if the terms of the agreement are complied with and one or more of the following occurs—

        (i) the exercise of an option to purchase by that person,

        (ii) the doing of any other specified act by any party to the agreement,

        (iii) the happening of any other specified event;

"hirer" means the individual to whom goods are bailed or (in Scotland) hired under a consumer hire agreement, or the person to whom his rights and duties under the agreement have passed by assignment or operation of law, and in relation to a prospective consumer hire agreement includes the prospective hirer;

"individual" includes a partnership or other unincorporated body of persons not consisting entirely of bodies corporate;

"installation" means—

    (*a*) the installing of any electric line or any gas or water pipe,

    (*b*) the fixing of goods to the premises where they are to be used, and the alteration of premises to enable goods to be used on them,

    (*c*) where it is reasonably necessary that goods should be constructed or erected on the premises where they are to be used, any work carried out for the purpose of constructing or erecting them on those premises;

"insurance company" has the meaning given by section [section 96(1) of the Insurance Companies Act 1982], but does not include a friendly society or an organisation of workers or organisation of employers;

"judgment" includes an order or decree made by any court;

"land", includes an interest in land, and in relation to Scotland includes heritable subjects of whatever description;

"land improvement company" means an improvement company as defined by section 7 of the Improvement of Land Act 1899;

"land mortgage" includes any security charged on land;

"licence" means a licence under Part III (including that Part as applied to ancillary credit businesses by section 147);

"licensed", in relation to any act, means authorised by a licence to do the act or cause or permit another person to do it;

"licensee", in the case of a group licence, includes any person covered by the licence;

"linked transaction" has the meaning given by section 19(1);

"local authority", in relation to England and Wales, means . . ., a county council, a London borough council, a district council, the Common Council of the City of London, or the Council of Isles of Scilly, and in relation to Scotland, means a regional, islands or district council, and, in relation to Northern Ireland, means a district council;

. . .

"modifying agreement" has the meaning given by section 82(2);

. . .

"multiple agreement" has the meaning given by section 18(1);

"negotiator" has the meaning given by section 56(1);

"non-commercial agreement" means a consumer credit agreement or a consumer hire agreement not made by the creditor or owner in the course of a business carried on by him;

"notice" means notice in writing;

"notice of cancellation" has the meaning given by section 69(1);

"owner" means a person who bails or (in Scotland) hires out goods under a consumer hire agreement or the person to whom his rights and duties under the agreement have passed by assignment or operation of law, and in relation to a prospective consumer hire agreement, includes the prospective bailor or persons from whom the goods are to be hired;

"pawn" means any article subject to a pledge;

"pawn-receipt" has the meaning given by section 114;

"pawnee" and "pawnor" include any person to whom the rights and duties of the original pawnee or the original pawnor, as the case may be, have passed by assignment or operation of law;

"payment" includes tender;

"personal credit agreement" has the meaning given by section 8(1);

"pledge" means the pawnee's rights over an article taken in pawn;

"prescribed" means prescribed by regulations made by the Secretary of State;

"pre-existing arrangements" shall be construed in accordance with section 187;

"principal agreement" has the meaning given by section 19(1);

"protected goods" has the meaning given by section 90(7);

"quotation" has the meaning given by section 52(1)(*a*);

"redemption period" has the meaning given by section 116(3);

"register" means the register kept by the Director under section 35;

"regulated agreement" means a consumer credit agreement, or consumer hire agreement, other than an exempt agreement, and "regulated" and "unregulated" shall be construed accordingly;

"regulations" means regulations made by the Secretary of State;

"relative", except in section 184, means a person who is an associate by virtue of section 184(1);

"representation" includes any condition or warranty, and any other statement or undertaking, whether oral or in writing;

"restricted-use credit agreement" and "restricted-use credit" have the meanings given by section 11(1);

"rules of court", in relation to Northern Ireland means, in relation to the High Court, rules made under section 7 of the Northern Ireland Act 1962, and, in relation to any other court, rules made by the authority having for the time being power to make rules regulating the practice and procedure in that court;

"running-account credit" shall be construed in accordance with section 10;

"security", in relation to an actual or prospective consumer credit agreement or consumer hire agreement, or any linked transaction, means a mortgage, charge, pledge, bond, debenture, indemnity, guarantee, bill, note or other right provided by the debtor or hirer, or at his request (express or implied), to secure the carrying out of the obligations of the debtor or hirer under the agreement;

"security instrument" has the meaning given by section 105(2);

"serve on" means deliver or send by post to;

"signed" shall be construed in accordance with subsection (3);

"small agreement" has the meaning given by section 17(1), and "small" in relation to an agreement within any category shall be construed accordingly;

"specified fee" shall be construed in accordance with section 2(4) and (5);

"standard licence" has the meaning given by section 22(1)(*a*);

"supplier" has the meaning given by section 11(1)(*b*) or 12(*c*) or 13(*c*) or, in relation to an agreement falling within section 11(1)(*a*), means the creditor, and includes a person to whom the rights and duties of a supplier (as so defined) have passed by assignment or operation of law, or (in relation to a prospective agreement) the prospective supplier;

"surety" means the person by whom any security is provided, or the person to whom his rights and duties in relation to the security have passed by assignment or operation of law;

"technical grounds" shall be construed in accordance with subsection (5);

"time order" has the meaning given by section 129(1);

"total charge for credit" means a sum calculated in accordance with regulations under section 20(1);

"total price" means the total sum payable by the debtor under a hire-purchase agreement or a conditional sale agreement, including any sum payable on the exercise of an option to purchase, but excluding any sum payable as a penalty or as compensation or damages for a breach of the agreement;

"unexecuted agreement" means a document embodying the terms of a prospective regulated agreement, or such of them as it is intended to reduce to writing;

"unlicensed" means without a licence but applies only in relation to acts for which a licence is required;

"unrestricted-use credit agreement" and "unrestricted-use credit" have the meanings given by section 11(2);

"working day" means any day other than—

    (*a*) Saturday or Sunday,

    (*b*) Christmas Day or Good Friday,

    (*c*) a bank holiday within the meaning given by section 1 of the Banking and Financial Dealings Act 1971. **[893A]**

NOTES

Sub-s (1): definition "authorised institution" inserted by the Banking Act 1987, s 88; definition "building society" substituted by the Building Societies Act 1986, s 120, Sch 18, para 10; in definition "charity" words in square brackets substituted by the Charities Act 1993, s 98(1), Sch 6, para 30; in definition "electric line" first words in square brackets substituted by the Electricity Act 1989, s 112(1), Sch 16, para 17, second words in square brackets substituted by the Electricity (Northern Ireland) Order 1992, SI 1992 No 231, art 95(1), Sch 12, para 15; in definition "friendly society" words in italics prospectively repealed by the Friendly Societies Act 1992, s 120, Sch 22, Part I; in definition "goods" words in square brackets substituted by the Sale of Goods Act 1979, s 63, Sch 2, para 18; in definition "insurance company" words in square brackets substituted by the Insurance Companies Act 1982, s 99(2), Sch 5, para 14; in definition "local authority" words omitted repealed by the Local Government Act 1985, s 102, Sch 17; other words omitted apply to Scotland only.

INHERITANCE (PROVISION FOR FAMILY AND DEPENDANTS) ACT 1975

(c 63)

ARRANGEMENT OF SECTIONS

Powers of court to order financial provision from deceased's estate

*An Act to make fresh provisions for empowering the court to make orders for the
making out of the estate of a deceased person of provision for the spouse, former
spouse, child, child of the family or dependant of that person; and for matters
connected therewith*   [12 November 1975]

Powers of court to order financial provision from deceased's estate

1. Application for financial provision from deceased's estate

(1) Where after the commencement of this Act a person dies domiciled in
England and Wales and is survived by any of the following persons—

   (a) the wife or husband of the deceased;
   (b) a former wife or former husband of the deceased who has not
       remarried;
   (c) a child of the deceased;

(*d*) any person (not being a child of the deceased) who, in the case of any marriage to which the deceased was at any time a party, was treated by the deceased as a child of the family in relation to that marriage;

(*e*) any person (not being a person included in the foregoing paragraphs of this subsection) who immediately before the death of the deceased was being maintained, either wholly or partly, by the deceased;

that person may apply to the court for an order under section 2 of this Act on the ground that the disposition of the deceased's estate effected by his will or the law relating to intestacy, or the combination of his will and that law, is not such as to make reasonable financial provision for the applicant.

(2) In this Act "reasonable financial provision"—

(*a*) in the case of an application made by virtue of subsection (1)(*a*) above by the husband or wife of the deceased (except where the marriage with the deceased was the subject of a decree of judicial separation and at the date of death the decree was in force and the separation was continuing), means such financial provision as it would be reasonable in all the circumstances of the case for a husband or wife to receive, whether or not that provision is required for his or her maintenance;

(*b*) in the case of any other application made by virtue of subsection (1) above, means such financial provision as it would be reasonable in all the circumstances of the case for the applicant to receive for his maintenance.

(3) For the purposes of subsection (1)(*e*) above, a person shall be treated as being maintained by the deceased, either wholly or partly, as the case may be, if the deceased, otherwise than for full valuable consideration, was making a substantial contribution in money or money's worth towards the reasonable needs of that person. **[894]**

2. Powers of court to make orders

(1) Subject to the provisions of this Act, where an application is made for an order under this section, the court may, if it is satisfied that the disposition of the deceased's estate effected by his will or the law relating to intestacy, or the combination of his will and that law, is not such as to make reasonable financial provision for the applicant, make any one or more of the following orders—

(*a*) an order for the making to the applicant out of the net estate of the deceased of such periodical payments and for such term as may be specified in the order;

(*b*) an order for the payment to the applicant out of that estate of a lump sum of such amount as may be so specified;

(*c*) an order for the transfer to the applicant of such property comprised in that estate as may be so specified;

(*d*) an order for the settlement for the benefit of the applicant of such property comprised in that estate as may be so specified;

(*e*) an order for the acquisition out of property comprised in that estate of such property as may be so specified and for the transfer of the property so acquired to the applicant or for the settlement thereof for his benefit;

(*f*) an order varying any ante-nuptial or post-nuptial settlement (including such a settlement made by will) made on the parties to a marriage to which the deceased was one of the parties, the variation being for the benefit of the surviving party to that marriage, or any child of that marriage, or any person who was treated by the deceased as a child of the family in relation to that marriage.

(2) An order under subsection (1)(*a*) above providing for the making out of the net estate of the deceased of periodical payments may provide for—

    (*a*) payments of such amount as may be specified in the order,

    (*b*) payments equal to the whole of the income of the net estate or of such portion thereof as may be so specified,

    (*c*) payments equal to the whole of the income of such part of the net estate as the court may direct to be set aside or appropriated for the making out of the income thereof of payments under this section,

or may provide for the amount of the payments or any of them to be determined in any other way the court thinks fit.

(3) Where an order under subsection (1)(*a*) above provides for the making of payments of an amount specified in the order, the order may direct that such part of the net estate as may be so specified shall be set aside or appropriated for the making out of the income thereof of those payments; but no larger part of the net estate shall be so set aside or appropriated than is sufficient, at the date of the order, to produce by the income thereof the amount required for the making of those payments.

(4) An order under this section may contain such consequential and supplemental provisions as the court thinks necessary or expedient for the purpose of giving effect to the order or for the purpose of securing that the order operates fairly as between one beneficiary of the estate of the deceased and another and may, in particular, but without prejudice to the generality of this subsection—

    (*a*) order any person who holds any property which forms part of the net estate of the deceased to make such payment or transfer such property as may be specified in the order;

    (*b*) varying the disposition of the deceased's estate effected by the will or the law relating to intestacy, or by both the will and the law relating to intestacy, in such manner as the court thinks fair and reasonable having regard to the provisions of the order and all the circumstances of the case;

    (*c*) confer on the trustees of any property which is the subject of an order under this section such powers as appear to the court to be necessary or expedient.   **[895]**

3. Matters to which court is to have regard in exercising powers under s 2

(1) Where an application is made for an order under section 2 of this Act, the court shall, in determining whether the disposition of the deceased's estate effected by his will or the law relating to intestacy, or the combination of his will and that law, is such as to make reasonable financial provision for the applicant and, if the court considers that reasonable financial provision has not been made, in determining whether and in what manner it shall exercise its powers under that section, have regard to the following matters, that is to say—

    (*a*) the financial resources and financial needs which the applicant has or is likely to have in the forseeable future;

    (*b*) the financial resources and financial needs which any other applicant for an order under section 2 of this Act has or is likely to have in the foreseeable future;

(c) the financial resources and financial needs which any beneficiary of the estate of the deceased has or is likely to have in the foreseeable future;

(d) any obligations and responsibilities which the deceased had towards any applicant for an order under the said section 2 or towards any beneficiary of the estate of the deceased;

(e) the size and nature of the net estate of the deceased;

(f) any physical or mental disability of any applicant for an order under the said section 2 or any beneficiary of the estate of the deceased;

(g) any other matter, including the conduct of the applicant or any other person, which in the circumstances of the case the court may consider relevant.

(2) Without prejudice to the generality of paragraph (g) of subsection (1) above, where an application for an order under section 2 of this Act is made by virtue of section 1(1)(a) or 1(1)(b) of this Act, the court shall, in addition to the matters specifically mentioned in paragraphs (a) to (f) of that subsection, have regard to—

(a) the age of the applicant and the duration of the marriage;

(b) the contribution made by the applicant to the welfare of the family of the deceased, including any contribution made by looking after the home or caring for the family;

and, in the case of an application by the wife or husband of the deceased, the court shall also, unless at the date of death a decree of judicial separation was in force and the separation was continuing, have regard to the provision which the applicant might reasonably have expected to receive if on the day on which the deceased died the marriage, instead of being terminated by death, had been terminated by a decree of divorce.

(3) Without prejudice to the generality of paragraph (g) of subsection (1) above, where an application for an order under section 2 of this Act is made by virtue of section 1(1)(c) or 1(1)(d) of this Act, the court shall, in addition to the matters specifically mentioned in paragraphs (a) to (f) of that subsection, have regard to the manner in which the applicant was being or in which he might expect to be educated or trained, and where the application is made by virtue of section 1(1)(d) the court shall also have regard—

(a) to whether the deceased had assumed any responsibility for the applicant's maintenance and, if so, to the extent to which and the basis upon which the deceased assumed that responsibility and to the length of time for which the deceased discharged that responsibility;

(b) to whether in assuming and discharging that responsibility the deceased did so knowing that the applicant was not his own child;

(c) to the liability of any other person to maintain the applicant.

(4) Without prejudice to the generality of paragraph (g) of subsection (1) above, where an application for an order under section 2 of this Act is made by virtue of section 1(1)(e) of this Act, the court shall, in addition to the matters specifically mentioned in paragraphs (a) to (f) of that subsection, have regard to the extent to which and the basis upon which the deceased assumed responsibility for the maintenance of the applicant, and to the length of time for which the deceased discharged that responsibility.

(5) In considering the matters to which the court is required to have regard under this section, the court shall take into account the facts as known to the court at the date of the hearing.

(6) In considering the financial resources of any person for the purposes of this section the court shall take into account his earning capacity and in considering the financial needs of any person for the purposes of this section the court shall take into account his financial obligations and responsibilities. **[896]**

4. Time-limit for applications

An application for an order under section 2 of this Act shall not, except with the permission of the court, be made after the end of the period of six months from the date on which representation with respect to the estate of the deceased is first taken out. **[897]**

5. Interim orders

(1) Where an application for an order under section 3 of this Act it appears to the court-

    (a) that the applicant is in immediate need of financial assistance, but it is not yet possible to determine what order (if any) should be made under that section; and

    (b) that property forming part of the net estate of the deceased is or can be made available to meet the need of the applicant;

the court may order that, subject to such conditions or restrictions, if any, as the court may impose and to any further order of the court, there shall be paid to the applicant out of the net estate of the deceased such sum or sums and (if more than one) at such intervals as the court thinks reasonable; and the court may order that, subject to the provisions of this Act, such payments are to be made until such date as the court may specify, not being later than the date on which the court either makes an order under the said section 2 or decides not to exercise its powers under that section.

(2) Subsections (2), (3) and (4) of section 2 of this Act shall apply in relation to an order under this section as they apply in relation to an order under that section.

(3) In determining what order, if any, should be made under this section the court shall, so far as the urgency of the case admits, have regard to the same matters as those to which the court is required to have regard under section 3 of this Act.

(4) An order made under section 2 of this Act may provide that any sum paid to the applicant by virtue of this section shall be treated to such an extent and in such manner as may be provided by that order as having been paid on account of any payment provided for by that order. **[898]**

6. Variation, discharge, etc of orders for periodical payments

(1) Subject to the provisions of this Act, where the court has made an order under section 2(1)(a) of this Act (in this section referred to as "the original order") for the making of periodical payments to any person (in this section referred to as "the original recipient"), the court, on an application under this section, shall have power by order to vary or discharge the original order or to suspend any provision of it temporarily and to revive the operation of any provision so suspended.

(2) Without prejudice to the generality of subsection (1) above, an order made on an application for the variation of the original order may—

  (*a*) provide for the making out of any relevant property of such periodical payments and for such term as may be specified in the order to any person who has applied, or would but for section 4 of this Act be entitled to apply, for an order under section 2 of this Act (whether or not, in the case of any application, an order was made in favour of the applicant);

  (*b*) provide for the payment out of any relevant property of a lump sum of such amount as may be so specified to the original recipient or to any such person as is mentioned in paragraph (*a*) above;

  (*c*) provide for the transfer of the relevant property, or such part thereof as may be so specified, to the original recipient or to any such person as is so mentioned.

(3) Where the original order provides that any periodical payments payable thereunder to the original recipient are to cease on the occurrence of an event specified in the order (other than the remarriage of a former wife or former husband) or on the expiration of a period so specified, then, if, before the end of the period of six months from the date of the occurrence of that event or of the expiration of that period, an application is made for an order under this section, the court shall have power to make any order which it would have had power to make if the application had been made before the date (whether in favour of the original recipient or any such person as is mentioned in subsection (2)(*a*) above and whether having effect from that date or from such later date as the court may specify).

(4) Any reference in this section to the original order shall include a reference to an order made under this section and any reference in this section to the original recipient shall include a reference to any person to whom periodical payments are required to be made by virtue of an order under this section.

(5) An application under this section may be made by any of the following persons, that is to say—

  (*a*) any person who by virtue of section 1(1) of this Act has applied, or would but for section 4 of this Act be entitled to apply, for an order under section 2 of this Act,

  (*b*) the personal representatives of the deceased,

  (*c*) the trustees of any relevant property, and

  (*d*) any beneficiary of the estate of the deceased.

(6) An order under this section may only affect—

  (*a*) property the income of which is at the date of the order applicable wholly or in part for the making of periodical payments to any person who has applied for an order under this Act, or

  (*b*) in the case of an application under subsection (3) above in respect of payments which have ceased to be payable on the occurrence of an event or the expiration of a period, property the income of which was so applicable immediately before the occurrence of that event or the expiration of that period, as the case may be,

and any such property as is mentioned in paragraph (*a*) or (*b*) above is in subsections (2) and (5) above referred to as "relevant property".

(7) In exercising the powers conferred by this section the court shall have regard to all circumstances of the case, including any change in any of the matters to which the court was required to have regard when making the order to which the application relates.

(8) Where the court makes an order under this section, it may give such consequential directions as it thinks necessary or expedient having regard to the provisions of the order.

(9) No such order as is mentioned in section 2(1)(*d*), (*e*) or (*f*), 9, 10 or 11 of this Act shall be made on an application under this section.

(10) For the avoidance of doubt it is hereby declared that, in relation to an order which provides for the making of periodical payments which are to cease on the occurrence of an event specified in the order (other than the remarriage of a former wife or former husband) or on the expiration of a period so specified, the power to vary an order includes power to provide for the making of periodical payments after the expiration of that period or the occurrence of that event.   **[899]**

7. Payment of lump sums by instalments

(1) An order under section 2(1)(*b*) or 6(2)(*b*) of this Act for the payment of a lump sum may provide for the payment of that sum by instalments of such amount as may be specified in the order.

(2) Where an order is made by virtue of subsection (1) above, the court shall have power, on an application made by the person to whom the lump sum is payable, by the personal representatives of the deceased or by the trustees of the property out of which the lump sum is payable, to vary that order by varying the number of instalments payable, the amount of any instalment and the date on which any instalment becomes payable.   **[900]**

Property available for financial provision

8. Property treated as part of "net estate"

(1) Where a deceased person has in accordance with the provisions of any enactment nominated any person to receive any sum of money or other property on his death and that nomination is in force at the time of his death, that sum of money, after deducting therefrom any [inheritance tax] payable in respect thereof, or that other property, to the extent of the value thereof at the date of the death of the deceased after deducting therefrom any [inheritance tax] so payable, shall be treated for the purposes of this Act as part of the net estate of the deceased; but this subsection shall not render any person liable for having paid that sum or transferred that other property to the person named in the nomination in accordance with the directions given in the nomination.

(2) Where any sum of money or other property is received by any person as a donatio mortis causa made by a deceased person, that sum of money, after deducting therefrom any [inheritance tax] payable thereon, or that other property, to the extent of the value thereof at the date of the death of the deceased after deducting therefrom any [inheritance tax] so payable, shall be treated for the purposes of this Act as part of the net estate of the deceased; but this subsection shall not render any person liable for having paid that sum or transferred that other property in order to give effect to that donatio mortis causa.

(3) The amount of [inheritance tax] to be deducted for the purposes of this

section shall not exceed the amount of that tax which has been borne by the person nominated by the deceased or, as the case may be, the person who has received a sum of money or other property as a donatio mortis causa.   **[901]**

NOTES
   Capital transfer tax: except in relation to a liability to tax arising before 25 July 1986 capital transfer tax shall be known as inheritance tax and the Capital Transfer Tax Act 1984 may be cited as the Inheritance Tax Act 1984, by virtue of the Finance Act 1986, s 100.

9. Property held on a joint tenancy

(1) Where a deceased person was immediately before his death beneficially entitled to a joint tenancy of any property, then, if, before the end of the period of six months from the date on which representation with respect to the estate of the deceased was first taken out, an application is made for an order under section 2 of this Act, the court for the purpose of facilitating the making of financial provision for the applicant under this Act may order that the deceased's severable share of that property, at the value thereof immediately before his death, shall, to such extent as appears to the court to be just in all the circumstances of the case, be treated for the purposes of this Act as part of the net estate of the deceased.

(2) In determining the extent to which any severable share is to be treated as part of the net estate of the deceased by virtue of an order under subsection (1) above, the court shall have regard to any [inheritance tax] payable in respect of that severable share.

(3) Where an order is made under subsection (1) above, the provisions of this section shall not render any person liable for anything done by him before the order was made.

(4) For the avoidance of doubt it is hereby declared that for the purposes of this section there may be a joint tenancy of a chose in action.   **[902]**

NOTES
   Capital transfer tax: except in relation to a liability to tax arising before 25 July 1986 capital transfer tax shall be known as inheritance tax and the Capital Transfer Tax Act 1984 may be cited as the Inheritance Tax Act 1984, by virtue of the Finance Act 1986, s 100.

Powers of court in relation to transactions intended to defeat applications for financial provision

10. Dispositions intended to defeat applications for financial provision

(1) Where an application is made to the court for an order under section 2 of this Act, the applicant may, in the proceedings on that application, apply to the court for an order under subsection (2) below.

(2) Where on an application under subsection (1) above the court is satisfied—

   (a) that, less than six years before the date of the death of the deceased, the deceased with the intention of defeating an application for financial provision under this Act made a disposition, and
   (b) that full valuable consideration for that disposition was not given by the person to whom or for the benefit of whom the disposition was made (in this section referred to as "the donee") or by any other person, and

(c) that the exercise of the powers conferred by this section would facilitate the making of financial provision for the applicant under this Act,

then, subject to the provisions of this section and of sections 12 and 13 of this Act, the court may order the donee (whether or not at the date of the order he holds any interest in the property disposed of to him or for his benefit by the deceased) to provide, for the purpose of the making of that financial provision, such sum of money or other property as may be specified in the order.

(3) Where an order is made under subsection (2) above as respects any disposition made by the deceased which consisted of the payment of money to or for the benefit of the donee, the amount of any sum of money or the value of any property ordered to be provided under that subsection shall not exceed the amount of the payment made by the deceased after deducting therefrom any [inheritance tax] borne by the donee in respect of that payment.

(4) Where an order is made under subsection (2) above as respects any disposition made by the deceased which consisted of the transfer of property (other than a sum of money) to or for the benefit of the donee, the amount of any sum of money or the value of any property ordered to be provided under that subsection shall not exceed the value at the date of the death of the deceased of the property disposed of by him to or for the benefit of the donee (or if that property has been disposed of by the person to whom it was transferred by the deceased, the value at the date of that disposal thereof) after deducting therefrom any capital transfer tax borne by the donee in respect of the transfer of that property by the deceased.

(5) Where an application (in this subsection referred to as "the original application") is made for an order under subsection (2) above in relation to any disposition, then, if on an application under this subsection by the donee or by any applicant for an order under section 2 of this Act the court is satisfied—

(a) that, less than six years before the date of the death of the deceased, the deceased with the intention of defeating an application for financial provision under this Act made a disposition other than the disposition which is the subject of the original application, and

(b) that full valuable consideration for that other disposition was not given by the person to whom or for the benefit of whom that other disposition was made or by any other person,

the court may exercise in relation to the person to whom or for the benefit of whom that other disposition was made the powers which the court would have had under subsection (2) above if the original application had been made in respect of that other disposition and the court had been satisifed as to the matters set out in paragraphs (a), (b) and (c) of that subsection; and where any application is made under this subsection, any reference in this section (except in subsection (2)(b)) to the donee shall include a reference to the person to whom or for the benefit of whom that other disposition was made.

(6) In determining whether and in what manner to exercise its powers under this section, the court shall have regard to the circumstances in which any disposition was made and any valuable consideration which was given therefor, the relationship, if any, of the donee to the deceased, the conduct and financial resources of the donee and all the other circumstances of the case.

(7) In this section "disposition" does not include—

(a) any provision in a will, any such nomination as is mentioned in section 8(1) of this Act or any donatio mortis causa, or

(b) any appointment of property made, otherwise than by will, in the exercise of a special power of appointment,

but, subject to these exceptions, includes any payment of money (including the payment of a premium under a policy of assurance) and any conveyance, assurance, appointment or gift of property of any description, whether made by an instrument or otherwise.

(8) The privisions of this section do not apply to any disposition made before the commencement of this Act. **[903]**

NOTES

Capital transfer tax: except in relation to a liability to tax arising before 25 July 1986 capital transfer tax shall be known as inheritance tax and the Capital Transfer Tax Act 1984 may be cited as the Inheritance Tax Act 1984, by virtue of the Finance Act 1986, s 100.

11. Contracts to leave property by will

(1) Where an application is made to a court for an order under section 2 of this Act, the applicant may, in the proceedings on that application, apply to the court for an order under this section.

(2) Where on an application under subsection (1) above the court is satisfied—

    (a) that the deceased made a contract by which he agreed to leave by his will a sum of money or other property to any person or by which he agreed that a sum of money or other property would be paid or transferred to any person out of his estate, and

    (b) that the deceased made that contract with the intention of defeating an application for financial provision under this Act, and

    (c) that when the contract was made full valuable consideration for that contract was not given or promised by the person with whom or for the benefit of whom the contract was made (in this section referred to as "the donee") or by any other person, and

    (d) that the exercise of the powers conferred by this section would facilitate the making of financial provision for the applicant under this Act,

then, subject to the provisions of this section and of sections 12 and 13 of this Act, the court may make any one or more of the following orders, that is to say—

    (i) if any money has been paid or any other property has been transferred to or for the benefit of the donee in accordance with the contract, an order directing the donee to provide, for the purpose of the making of that financial provision, such sum of money or other property as may be specified in the order;

    (ii) if the money or all the money has not been paid or the property or all the property has not been transferred in accordance with the contract, an order directing the personal representatives not to make any payment or transfer any property, or not to make any further payment or transfer any further property, as the case may be, in accordance therewith or directing the personal representatives only to make such payment or transfer such property as may be specified in the order.

(3) Notwithstanding anything in subsection (2) above, the court may exercise its powers thereunder in relation to any contract made by the deceased only to the extent that the court considers that the amount of any sum of money

paid or to be paid or the value of any property transferred or to be transferred in accordance with the contract exceeds the value of any valuable consideration given or to be given for that contract, and for this purpose the court shall have regard to the value of property at the date of the hearing.

(4) In determining whether and in what manner to exercise its powers under this section, the court shall have regard to the circumstances in which the contract was made, the relationship, if any, of the donee to the deceased, the conduct and financial resources of the donee and all the other circumstances of the case.

(5) Where an order has been made under subsection (2) above in relation to any contract the rights of any person to enforce that contract or to recover damages or to obtain other relief for the breach thereof shall be subject to any adjustment made by the court under section 12(3) of this Act and shall survive to such extent only as is consistent with giving effect to the terms of that order.

(6) The provisions of this section do not apply to a contract made before the commencement of this Act.   **[904]**

12. Provisions supplementary to ss 10 and 11

(1) Where the exercise of any of the powers conferred by section 10 or 11 of this Act is conditional on the court being satisfied that a disposition or contract was made by a deceased person with the intention of defeating an application for financial provision under this Act, that condition shall be fulfilled if the court is of the opinion that, on a balance of probabilities, the intention of the deceased (though not necessarily his sole intention) in making the disposition or contract was to prevent an order for financial provision being made under this Act or to reduce the amount of the provision which might otherwise be granted by an order thereunder.

(2) Where an application is made under section 11 of this Act with respect to any contract made by the deceased and no valuable consideration was given or promised by any person for that contract then, notwithstanding anything in subsection (1) above, it shall be presumed, unless the contrary is shown, that the deceased made that contract with the intention of defeating an application for financial provision under this Act.

(3) Where the court makes an order under section 10 or 11 of this Act it may give such consequential directions as it thinks fit (including directions requiring the making of any payment or the transfer of any property) for giving effect to the order or for securing a fair adjustment of the rights of the persons affected thereby.

(4) Any power conferred on the court by the said section 10 or 11 to order the donee, in relation to any disposition or contract, to provide any sum of money or other property shall be exercisable in like manner in relation to the personal representative of the donee, and—

(a) any reference in section 10(4) to the disposal of property by the donee shall include a reference to disposal by the personal representative of the donee, and

(b) any reference in section 10(5) to an application by the donee under that subsection shall include a reference to an application by the personal representative of the donee;

but the court shall not have power under the said section 10 or 11 to make an order in respect of any property forming part of the estate of the donee which has been distributed by the personal representative; and the personal representative shall not be liable for having distributed any such property before he has notice of the making of an application under the said section 10 or 11 on the ground that he ought to have taken into account the possibility that such an application would be made.   **[905]**

13. Provisions as to trustees in relation to ss 10 and 11

(1) Where an application is made for—

    (*a*) an order under section 10 of this Act in respect of a disposition made by the deceased to any person as a trustee, or

    (*b*) an order under section 11 of this Act in respect of any payment made or property transferred, in accordance with a contract made by the deceased, to any person as a trustee,

the powers of the court under the said section 10 or 11 to order that trustee to provide a sum of money or other property shall be subject to the following limitation (in addition, in a case of an application under section 10, to any provision regarding the deduction of [inheritance tax]) namely, that the amount of any sum of money or the value of any property ordered to be provided—

    (i) in the case of an application in respect of a disposition which consisted of the payment of money or an application in respect of the payment of money in accordance with a contract, shall not exceed the aggregate of so much of that money as is at the date of the order in the hands of the trustee and the value at that date of any property which represents that money or is derived therefrom and is at that date in the hands of the trustee;

    (ii) in the case of an application in respect of a disposition which consisted of the transfer of property (other than a sum of money) or an application in respect of the transfer of property (other than a sum of money) in accordance with a contract, shall not exceed the aggregate of the value at the date of the order of so much of that property as is at that date in the hands of the trustee and the value at that date of any property which represents the first mentioned property or is derived therefrom and is at that date in the hands of the trustee.

(2) Where any such application is made in respect of a disposition made to any person as a trustee or in respect of any payment made or property transferred in pursuance of a contract to any person as a trustee, the trustee shall not be liable for having distributed any money or other property on the ground that he ought to have taken into account the possibility that such an application would be made.

(3) Where any such application is made in respect of a disposition made to any person as a trustee or in respect of any payment made or property transferred in accordance with a contract to any person as a trustee, any reference in the said section 10 or 11 to the donee shall be construed as including a reference to the trustee or trustees for the time being of the trust in question and any reference in subsection (1) or (2) above to a trustee shall be construed in the same way.   **[906]**

NOTES

    Capital transfer tax: except in relation to a liability to tax arising before 25 July 1986 capital transfer tax shall be known as inheritance tax and the Capital Transfer Tax Act 1984 may be cited as the Inheritance Tax Act 1984, by virtue of the Finance Act 1986, s 100.

Special provisions relating to cases of divorce, separation, etc

14. Provision as to cases where no financial relief was granted in divorce proceedings, etc

(1) Where, within twelve months from the date on which a decree of divorce or nullity of marriage has been made absolute or a decree of judicial separation has been granted, a party to the marriage dies and—

(a) an application for a financial provision order under section 23 of the Matrimonial Causes Act 1973 or a property adjustment order under section 24 of that Act has not been made by the other party to that marriage, or

(b) such an application has been made but the proceedings thereon have not been determined at the time of the death of the deceased,

then, if an application for an order under section 2 of this Act is made by that other party, the court shall, notwithstanding anything in section 1 or section 3 of this Act, have power, if it thinks it just to do so, to treat that party for the purposes of that application as if the decree of divorce or nullity of marriage had not been made absolute or the decree of judicial separation had not been granted, as the case may be.

(2) This section shall not apply in relation to a decree of judicial separation unless at the date of the death of the deceased the decree was in force and the separation was continuing.   **[907]**

15. Restriction imposed in divorce proceedings, etc on application under this Act

[(1) On the grant of a decree of divorce, a decree of nullity of marriage or a decree of judicial separation or at any time thereafter the court, if it considers it just to do so, may, on the application of either party to the marriage, order that the other party to the marriage shall not on the death of the applicant be entitled to apply for an order under section 2 of this Act.

In this subsection "the court" means the High Court or, where a county court has jurisdiction by virtue of Part V of the Matrimonial and Family Proceedings Act 1984, a county court.]

(2) In the case of a decree of divorce or nullity of marriage an order may be made under subsection (1) above before or after the decree is made absolute, but if it is made before the decree is made absolute it shall not take effect unless the decree is made absolute.

(3) Where an order made under subsection (1) above on the grant of a decree of divorce or nullity of marriage has come into force with respect to a party to a marriage, then, on the death of the other party to that marriage, the court shall not entertain any application for an order under section 2 of this Act made by the first-mentioned party.

(4) Where an order made under subsection (1) above on the grant of a decree of judicial separation has come into force with respect to any party to a marriage, then, if the other party to that marriage dies while the decree is in force and the separation is continuing, the court shall not entertain any application for an order under section 2 of this Act made by the first-mentioned party.   **[908]**

NOTES

Sub-s (1): substituted by the Matrimonial and Family Proceedings Act 1964, s 8.

[15A. Restriction imposed in proceedings under Matrimonial and Family Proceedings Act 1984 on application under this Act

(1) On making an order under section 17 of the Matrimonial and Family Proceedings Act 1984 (orders for financial provision and property adjustment following overseas divorces, etc.) the court, if it considers it just to do so, may, on the application of either party to the marriage, order that the other party to the marriage shall not on the death of the applicant be entitled to apply for an order under section 2 of this Act.

In this subsection "the court" means the High Court or, where a county court has jurisdiction by virtue of Part V of the Matrimonial and Family Proceedings Act 1984, a county court.

(2) Where an order under subsection (1) above has been made with respect to a party to a marriage which has been dissolved or annulled, then, on the death of the other party to that marriage, the court shall not entertain an application under section 2 of this Act made by the first-mentioned party.

(3) Where an order under subsection (1) above has been made with respect to a party to a marriage the parties to which have been legally separated, then, if the other party to the marriage dies while the legal separation is in force, the court shall not entertain an application under section 2 of this Act made by the first-mentioned party.] **[909]**

NOTES
  Inserted by the Matrimonial and Family Proceedings Act 1984, s 25.

16. Variation and discharge of secured periodical payments orders made under Matrimonial Causes Act 1973

(1) Where an application for an order under section 2 of this Act is made to the court by any person who was at the time of the death of the deceased entitled to payments from the deceased under a secured periodical payments order made under the Matrimonial Causes Act 1973, then, in the proceedings on that application, the court shall have power, if an application is made under this section by that person or by the personal representative of the deceased, to vary or discharge that periodical payments order or to revive the operation of any provision thereof which has been suspended under section 31 of that Act.

(2) In exercising the powers conferred by this section the court shall have regard to all the circumstances of the case, including any order which the court proposes to make under section 2 or section 5 of this Act and any change (whether resulting from the death of the deceased or otherwise) in any of the matters to which the court was required to have regard when making the secured periodical payments order.

(3) The powers exercisable by the court under this section in relation to an order shall be exercisable also in relation to any instrument executed in pursuance of the order. **[910]**

17. Variation and revocation of maintenance agreements

(1) Where an application for an order under section 2 of this Act is made to the court by any person who was at the time of the death of the deceased entitled to payments from the deceased under a maintenance agreement which provided for the continuation of payments under the agreement after the death of the deceased, then, in the proceedings on that application, the court shall have

power, if an application is made under this section by that person or by the personal representative of the deceased, to vary or revoke that agreement.

(2) In exercising the powers conferred by this section the court shall have regard to all the circumstances of the case, including any order which the court proposes to make under section 2 or section 5 of this Act and any change (whether resulting from the death of the deceased or otherwise) in any of the circumstances in the light of which the agreement was made.

(3) If a maintenance agreement is varied by the court under this section the like consequences shall ensue as if the variation had been made immediately before the death of the deceased by agreement between the parties and for valuable consideration.

(4) In this section "maintenance agreement", in relation to a deceased person, means any agreement made, whether in writing or not and whether before or after the commencement of this Act, by the deceased with any person with whom he entered into a marriage, being an agreement which contained provisions governing the rights and liabilities towards one another when living separately of the parties to that marriage (whether or not the marriage has been dissolved or annulled) in respect of the making or securing of payments or the disposition or use of any property, including such rights and liabilities with respect to the maintenance or education of any child, whether or not a child of the deceased or a person who was treated by the deceased as a child of the family in relation to that marriage.   **[911]**

18. Availability of court's powers under this Act in applications under ss 31 and 36 of the Matrimonial Causes Act 1973

(1) Where—

    (*a*) a person against whom a secured periodical payments order was made under the Matrimonial Causes Act 1973 has died and an application is made under section 31(6) of that Act for the variation or discharge of that order or for the revival of the operation of any provision thereof which has been suspended, or

    (*b*) a party to a maintenance agreement within the meaning of section 34 of that Act has died, the agreement being one which provides for the continuation of payments thereunder after the death of one of the parties, and an application is made under section 36(1) of that Act for the alteration of the agreement under section 35 thereof.

the court shall have power to direct that the application made under the said section 31(6) or 36(1) shall be deemed to have been accompanied by an application for an order under section 2 of this Act.

(2) Where the court gives a direction under subsection (1) above it shall have power, in the proceedings on the application under the said section 31(6) or 36(1), to make any order which the court would have had power to make under the provisions of this Act if the application under the said section 31(6) or 36(1), as the case may be, had been made jointly with an application for an order under the said section 2; and the court shall have power to give such consequential directions as may be necessary for enabling the court to exercise any of the powers available to the court under this Act in the case of an application for an order under section 2.

(3) Where an order made under section 15(1) of this Act is in force with

respect to a party to a marriage, the court shall not give a direction under subsection (1) above with respect to any application made under the said section 31(6) or 36(1) by that party on the death of the other party.   **[912]**

Miscellaneous and supplementary provisions

19. Effect, duration and form of orders

(1) Where an order is made under section 2 of this Act then for all purposes, including the purposes of the enactments relating to [inheritance tax], the will or the law relating to intestacy, or both the will and the law relating to intestacy, as the case may be, shall have effect and be deemed to have had effect as from the deceased's death subject to the provisions of the order.

(2) Any order made under section 2 or 5 of this Act in favour of—

    (*a*) an applicant who was the former husband or former wife of the deceased, or

    (*b*) an applicant who was the husband or wife of the deceased in a case where the marriage with the deceased was the subject of a decree of judicial separation and at the date of death the decree was in force and the separation was continuing,

shall, in so far as it provides for the making of periodical payments, cease to have effect on the remarriage of the applicant, except in relation to any arrears due under the order on the date of the remarriage.

(3) A copy of every order made under this Act [other than an order made under section 15(1) of this Act] shall be sent to the principal registry of the Family Division for entry and filing, and a memorandum of the order shall be endorsed on, or permanently annexed to, the probate or letters of administration under which the estate is being administered.   **[913]**

NOTES
    Sub-s (3): words in square brackets inserted by the Administration of Justice Act 1982, s 52.
    Capital transfer tax: except in relation to a liability to tax arising before 25 July 1986 capital transfer tax shall be known as inheritance tax and the Capital Transfer Tax Act 1984 may be cited as the Inheritance Tax Act 1984, by virtue of the Finance Act 1986, s 100.

20. Provisions as to personal representatives

(1) The provisions of this Act shall not render the personal representative of a deceased person liable for having distributed any part of the estate of the deceased, after the end of the period of six months from the date on which representation with respect to the estate of the deceased is first taken out, on the ground that he ought to have taken into account the possibility—

    (*a*) that the court might permit the making of an application for an order under section 2 of this Act after the end of that period, or

    (*b*) that, where an order has been made under the said section 2, the court might exercise in relation thereto the powers conferred on it by section 6 of this Act,

but this subsection shall not prejudice any power to recover, by reason of the making of an order under this Act, any part of the estate so distributed.

(2) Where the personal representative of a deceased person pays any sum directed by an order under section 5 of this Act to be paid out of the deceased's net estate, he shall not be under any liability by reason of that estate not being

sufficient to make the payment, unless at the time of making the payment he has reasonable cause to believe that the estate is not sufficient.

(3) Where a deceased person entered into a contract by which he agreed to leave by his will any sum of money or other property to any person or by which he agreed that a sum of money or other property would be paid or transferred to any person out of his estate, then, if the personal representative of the deceased has reason to believe that the deceased entered into the contract with the intention of defeating an application for financial provision under this Act, he may, notwithstanding anything in that contract, postpone the payment of that sum of money or the transfer of that property until the expiration of the period of six months from the date on which representation with respect to the estate of the deceased is first taken out or, if during that period an application is made for an order under section 2 of this Act, until the determination of the proceedings on that application.   **[914]**

21. Admissibility as evidence of statements made by deceased

In any proceedings under this Act a statement made by the deceased, whether orally or in a document or otherwise, shall be admissible under section 2 of the Civil Evidence Act 1968 as evidence of any fact stated therein in like manner as if the statement were a statement falling within section 2(1) of that Act; and any reference in that Act to a statement admissible, or given or proposed to be given, in evidence under section 2 thereof or to the admissibility or the giving in evidence of a statement by virtue of that section or to any statement falling within section 2(1) of that Act shall be construed accordingly.   **[915]–[916]**

23. Determination of date on which representation was first taken out

In considering for the purposes of this Act when representation with respect to the estate of a deceased person was first taken out, a grant limited to settled land or to trust property shall be left out of account, and a grant limited to real estate or to personal estate shall be left out of account unless a grant limited to the remainder of the estate has previously been made or is made at the same time.
                                                                        [917]

24. Effect of this Act on s 46(1)(vi) of Administration of Estates Act 1925

Section 46(1)(vi) of the Administration of Estates Act 1925, in so far as it provides for the devolution of property on the Crown, the Duchy of Lancaster or the Duke of Cornwall as bona vacantia, shall have effect subject to the provisions of this Act.   **[918]**

25. Interpretation

(1) In this Act—

    "beneficiary", in relation to the estate of a deceased person, means—

        (a) a person who under the will of the deceased or under the law relating to intestacy is beneficially interested in the estate or would be so interested if an order had not been made under this Act, and

        (b) a person who has received any sum of money or other property which by virtue of section 8(1) or 8(2) of this Act is treated as part of the net estate of the deceased or would have received that sum or other property if an order had not been made under this Act;

    "child" includes an illegitimate child and a child en ventre sa mere at the death of the deceased;

    "the court" [unless the context otherwise requires] means the High Court, or where a county court has jurisdiction by virtue of section 22 of this Act, a county court;

["former wife" or "former husband" means a person whose marriage with the deceased was during the lifetime of the deceased either—

(a) dissolved or annulled by a decree of divorce or a decree of nullity of marriage granted under the law of any part of the British Islands, or

(b) dissolved or annulled in any country or territory outside the British Islands by a divorce or annulment which is entitled to be recognised as valid by the law of England and Wales;]

"net estate", in relation to a deceased person, means—

(a) all property of which the deceased had power to dispose by his will (otherwise than by virtue of a special power of appointment) less the amount of his funeral, testamentary and administration expenses, debts and liabilities, including any [inheritance tax] payable out of his estate on his death;

(b) any property in respect of which the deceased held a general power of appointment (not being a power exercisable by will) which has not been exercised;

(c) any sum of money or other property which is treated for the purposes of this Act as part of the net estate of the deceased by virtue of section 8(1) or (2) of this Act;

(d) any property which is treated for the purposes of this Act as part of the net estate of the deceased by virtue of an order made under section 9 of the Act;

(e) any sum of money or other property which is, by reason of a disposition or contract made by the deceased, ordered under section 10 or 11 of this Act to be provided for the purpose of the making of financial provision under this Act;

"property" includes any chose in action;

"reasonable financial provision" has the meaning assigned to it by section 1 of this Act;

"valuable consideration" does not include marriage or a promise of marriage;

"will" includes codicil.

(2) For the purposes of paragraph (a) of the definition of "net estate" in subsection (1) above a person who is not of full age and capacity shall be treated as having power to dispose by will of all property of which he would have had power to dispose by will if he had been of full age and capacity.

(3) Any reference in this Act to provision out of the net estate of a deceased person includes a reference to provision extending to the whole of that estate.

(4) For the purposes of this Act any reference to a wife or husband shall be treated as including a reference to a person who in good faith entered into a void marriage with the deceased unless either—

(a) the marriage of the deceased and that person was dissolved or annulled during the lifetime of the deceased and the dissolution or annulment is recognised by the law of England and Wales, or

(b) that person has during the lifetime of the deceased entered into a later marriage.

(5) Any reference in this Act to remarriage or to a person who has remarried includes a reference to a marriage which is by law void or voidable or to a person who has entered into such a marriage, as the case may be, and a marriage shall be treated for the purposes of this Act as a remarriage, in relation to any

party thereto, notwithstanding that the previous marriage of that party was void or voidable.

(6) Any reference in this Act to an order or decree made under the Matrimonial Causes Act 1973 or under any section of that Act shall be construed as including a reference to an order or decree which is deemed to have been made under that Act or under that section thereof, as the case may be.

(7) Any reference in this Act to any enactment is a reference to that enactment as amended by or under any subsequent enactment.   **[919]**

NOTES
Sub-s (1): in definition "court" words in square brackets inserted by the Matrimonial and Family Proceedings Act 1984, s 8; definitions "former wife" and "former husband" substituted by the Matrimonial and Family Proceedings Act 1984, s 25.
Capital transfer tax: except in relation to a liability to tax arising before 25 July 1986 capital transfer tax shall be known as inheritance tax and the Capital Transfer Tax Act 1984 may be cited as the Inheritance Tax Act 1984, by virtue of the Finance Act 1986, s 100.

26. Consequential amendments, repeals and transitional provisions

(1) . . .

(2) Subject to the provisions of this section, the enactments specified in the Schedule to this Act are hereby repealed to the extent specified in the third column of the Schedule; . . .

(3) The repeal of the said enactments shall not affect their operation in relation to any application made thereunder (whether before or after the commencement of this Act) with reference to the death of any person who died before the commencement of this Act.

(4) Without prejudice to the provisions of section 38 of the Interpretation Act 1889 (which relates to the effect of repeals) nothing in any repeal made by this Act shall affect any order made or direction given under any enactment repealed by this Act, and, subject to the provisions of this Act, every such order or direction (other than an order made under section 4A of the Inheritance (Family Provision) Act 1938 or section 28A of the Matrimonial Causes Act 1965) shall, if it is in force at the commencement of this Act or is made by virtue of subsection (2) above, continue in force as if it had been made under section 2(1)(a) of this Act, and for the purposes of section 6(7) of this Act the court in exercising its powers under that section in relation to an order continued in force by this subsection shall be required to have regard to any change in any of the circumstances to which the court would have been required to have regard when making that order if the order had been made with reference to the death of any person who died after the commencement of this Act.   **[920]**

NOTES
Sub-s (1): amends the Matrimonial Causes Act 1973, s 36.
Sub-s (2): words omitted amend the Matrimonial Causes Act 1973, Sch 2, para 5(2).
Interpretation Act 1889, s 38: see now the Interpretation Act 1978, ss 16(1), 17(2)(a) of, and Sch 2, para 3 to, that Act.

27. Short title, commencement and extent

(1) This Act may be cited as the Inheritance (Provision for Family and Dependants) Act 1975.

(2) This Act does not extend to Scotland or Northern Ireland.

(3) This Act shall come into force on 1st April 1976.   **[921]**

LOCAL LAND CHARGES ACT 1975
(c 76)

ARRANGEMENT OF SECTIONS

Definition of local land charges

An Act to make fresh provision for and in connection with the keeping of local land
   charges registers and the registration of matters therein [12 November 1975]

Definition of local land charges

1. Local land charges

(1) A charge or other matter affecting land is a local land charge if it falls within
any of the following descriptions and is not one of the matters set out in section
2 below:—

  (*a*) any charge acquired either before or after the commencement of this
      Act by a local authority, water authority [sewerage undertaker] or new
      town development corporation under the Public Health Acts 1936
      and 1937, . . . the Public Health Act 1961 or [the Highways Act 1980
      (or any Act repealed by that Act)] [or the Building Act 1984], or any
      similar charge acquired by a local authority under any other Act,
      whether passed before or after this Act, being a charge that is binding
      on successive owners of the land affected;

  (*b*) any prohibition of or restriction on the use of land—

  (i) imposed by a local authority on or after 1st January 1926 (including any prohibition or restriction embodied in any condition attached to a consent, approval or licence granted by a local authority on or after that date), or
  (ii) enforceable by a local authority under any covenant or agreement made with them on or after that date,

being a prohibition or restriction binding on successive owners of the land affected;

  (c) any prohibition of or restriction on the use of land—

  (i) imposed by a Minister of the Crown or government department on or after the date of the commencement of this Act (including any prohibition or restriction embodied in any condition attached to a consent, approval or licence granted by such a Minister or department on or after that date), or
  (ii) enforceable by such a Minister or department under any covenant or agreement made with him or them on or after that date, being a prohibition or restriction binding on successive owners of the land affected;

  (d) any positive obligation affecting land enforceable by a Minister of the Crown, government department or local authority under any covenant or agreement made with him or them on or after the date of the commencement of this Act and binding on successive owners of the land affected;

  (e) any charge or other matter which is expressly made a local land charge by any statutory provision not contained in this section.

(2) For the purposes of subsection (1)(a) above, any sum which is recoverable from successive owners or occupiers of the land in respect of which the sum is recoverable shall be treated as a charge, whether the sum is expressed to be a charge on the land or not.

[(3) For the purposes of this section and section 2 of this Act, the Broads Authority shall be treated as a local authority.]   **[922]**

NOTES
  Sub-s (1): first words in square brackets inserted by the Water Act 1989, s 190(1), Sch 25, para 52; words omitted repealed and second words in square brackets substituted by the Highways Act 1980, s 343(2), Sch 24, para 26; third words in square brackets inserted by the Building Act 1984, s 133(1), Sch 6, para 16.
  Sub-s (3): added by the Norfolk and Suffolk Broads Act 1988, s 21, Sch 6, para 14.

2. Matters which are not local charges

The following matters are not local charges:—

  (a) a prohibition or restriction enforceable under a covenant or agreement made between a lessor and lessee;
  (b) a positive obligation enforceable under a covenant or agreement made between a lessor and lessee;
  (c) a prohibition or restriction enforceable by a Minister of the Crown, government department or local authority under any covenant or agreement, being a prohibition or restriction binding on successive owners of the land affected by reason of the fact that the covenant or agreement is made for the benefit of land of the Minister, government department or local authority;
  (d) a prohibition or restriction embodied in any bye-laws;

(*e*) a condition or limitation subject to which planning permission was granted at any time before the commencement of this Act or was or is (at any time) deemed to be granted under any statutory provision relating to town and country planning, whether by a Minister of the Crown, government department or local authority;

(*f*) a prohibition or restriction embodied in a scheme under the Town and Country Planning Act 1932 or any enactment repealed by that Act;

(*g*) a prohibition or restriction enforceable under a forestry dedication covenant entered into pursuant to section 5 of the Forestry Act 1967;

(*h*) a prohibition or restriction affecting the whole of any of the following areas:—

    (i) England, Wales or England and Wales;

    (ii) England, or England and Wales, with the exception of, or of any part of, Greater London;

    (iii) Greater London. **[923]**

Local Land charges registers, registration and related matters

3. Registering authorities, local land charges registers, and indexes

(1) Each of the following local authorities—

(*a*) the council of any district;

(*b*) the council of any London borough; and

(*c*) the Common Council of the City of London,

shall be a registering authority for the purposes of this Act.

(2) There shall continue to be kept for the area of each registering authority—

(*a*) a local land charges register, and

(*b*) an index whereby all entries made in that register can readily be traced,

and as from the commencement of this Act the register and index kept for the area of a registering authority shall be kept by that authority.

[(3) Neither a local land charges register nor an index such as is mentioned in subsection (2)(*b*) above need be kept in documentary form.]

(4) For the purposes of this Act the area of the Common Council of the City of London includes the Inner Temple and the Middle Temple. **[924]**

NOTES

Sub-s (3): substituted by the Local Government (Miscellaneous Provisions) Act 1982, s 34(*a*).

4. The appropriate local land charges register

In this Act ... , unless the context otherwise requires, "the appropriate local land charges register", in relation to any land or to a local land charge, means the local land charges register for the area in which the land or, as the case may be, the land affected by the charge is situated or, if the land in question is situated in two or more areas for which local land charges registers are kept, each of the local land charges registers kept for those areas respectively. **[925]**

NOTES

Words omitted repealed by the Interpretation Act 1978, s 25(1), Sch 3.

5. Registration

(1) Subject to subsection (6) below, where the originating authority as respects a local land charge are the registering authority, it shall be their duty to register it in the appropriate local land charges register.

(2) Subject to subsection (6) below, where the originating authority as respects a local land charge are not the registering authority, it shall be the duty of the originating authority to apply to the registering authority for its registration in the appropriate local land charges register and upon any such application being made it shall be the duty of the registering authority to register the charge accordingly.

(3) The registration in a local land charges register of a local charge, or of any matter which when registered becomes a local land charge, shall be carried out by reference to the land affected or such part of it as is situated in the area for which the register is kept.

(4) In this Act, "the originating authority", as respects a local land charge, means the Minister of the Crown, government department, local authority or other person by whom the charge is brought into existence or by whom, on its coming into existence, the charge is enforceable; and for this purpose—

    (*a*) where a matter that is a local land charge consists of or is embodied in, or is otherwise given effect by, an order, scheme or other instrument made or confirmed by a Minister of the Corwn or government department on the application of another authority the charge shall be treated as brought into existence by that other authority; and

    (*b*) a local land charge brought into existence by a Minister of the Crown or government department on an appeal from a decision or determination of another authority or in the exercise of powers ordinarily exercisable by another authority shall be treated as brought into existence by that other authority.

(5) The registration of a local land charge may be cancelled pursuant to an order of the court.

(6) Where a charge or other matter is registrable in a local land charges register and before the commencement of this Act was also registrable in a register kept under the Land Charges Act 1972, then, if before the commencement of this Act it was registered in a register kept under that Act, there shall be no duty to register it, or to apply for its registration, under this Act and section 10 below shall not apply in relation to it.   [926]

6. Local authority's right to register a general charge against land in certain circumstances

(1) Where a local authority have incurred any expenditure in respect of which, when any relevant work is completed and any requisite resolution is passed or order is made, there will arise in their favour a local land charge (in this section referred to as "the specific charge"), the following provisions of this section shall apply.

(2) At any time before the specific charge comes into existence, a general charge against the land, without any amount being specified, may be registered in the appropriate local land charges register by the registering authority if they are the originating authority and, if they are not, shall be registered therein by them if the originating authority make an application for that purpose.

(3) A general charge registered under this section shall be a local land charge, but section 5(1) and (2) above shall not apply in relation to such a charge.

(4) If a general charge is registered under this section pursuant to an application by the originating authority, they shall, when the specific charge comes into existence, notify the registering authority of that fact, and any such notification shall be treated as an application (subject to subsection (5) below) for the cancellation of the general charge and the registration of the specific charge.

(5) Where a general charge is registered under this section its registration shall be cancelled within such period starting with the day on which the specific charge comes into existence, and not being less than 1 year, as may be prescribed, and the specific charge shall not be registered before the general charge is cancelled.

(6) If the registration of the general charge is duly cancelled within the period specified in subsection (5) above and the specific charge is registered forthwith upon the cancellation or was discharged before the cancellation, then, for the purposes of section 10 below, the specific charge shall be treated as having come into existence at the time when the general charge was cancelled.
[927]

7. Effect of registering certain financial charges

A local land charge falling within section 1(1)(*a*) above shall, when registered, take effect as if it had been created by a deed of charge by way of legal mortgage within the meaning of the Law of Property Act 1925, but without prejudice to the priority of the charge.   **[928]**

Searches

8. Personal searches

(1) Any person may search in any local land charges register on paying the prescribed fee.

[(1A) If a local land charges register is kept otherwise than in documentary form, the entitlement of a person to search in it is satisfied if the registering authority makes the portion of it which he wishes to examine available for inspection in visible and legible form.]

(2) Without prejudice to [subsection (1) and (1A)] above, a registering authority may provide facilities for enabling persons entitled to search in the authority's local land charges register to see photographic or other images or copies of any portion of the register which they may wish to examine.   **[929]**

NOTES
  Sub-s (1A): inserted by the Local Government (Miscellaneous Provisions) Act 1982, s 34(*b*).
  Sub-s (2): words in square brackets substituted by the Local Government (Miscellaneous Provisions) Act 1982, s 34(*c*).

9. Official searches

(1) Where any person requires an official search of the appropriate local land charges register to be made in respect of any land, he may make a requisition in that behalf of the registering authority.

(2) *A requisition under this section must be in writing, and* for the purposes of serving any such requisition on the Common Council of the City of London section 231 (1) of the Local Government Act 1972 shall apply in relation to that Council as it applies in relation to a local authority within the meaning of that Act.

(3) The prescribed fee shall be payable in the prescribed manner in respect of every requisition made under this section.

(4) Where a requisition is made to a registering authority under this section and the fee payable in respect of it is paid in accordance with subsection (3) above, the registering authority shall thereupon make the search required and shall issue an official certificate setting out the result of the search.   **[930]**

NOTES
Sub-s (2): words in italics prospectively repealed by the Local Government and Housing Act 1989, ss 158, 194, Sch 12, Part II.

Compensation for non-registration or defective official search certificate

10. Compensation for non-registration or defective official search certificate

(1) Failure to register a local land charge in the appropriate local land charges register shall not affect the enforceability of the charge but where a person has purchased any land affected by a local land charge, then—

(*a*) in a case where a material personal search of the appropriate local land charges register was made in respect of the land in question before the relevant time, if at the time of the search the charge was in existence but not registered in that register; or

[(*aa*) in a case where the appropriate local land charges register kept otherwise than in documentary form and a material personal search of that register was made in respect of the land in question before the relevant time, if the entitlement to search in that register conferred by section 8 above was not satisfied as mentioned in subsection (1A) of that section; or]

(*b*) in a case where a material official search of the appropriate local land charges register was made in respect of the land in question before the relevant time, if the charge was in existence at the time of the search but (whether registered or not) was not shown by the official search certificate as registered in that register,

the purchaser shall (subject to section 11(1) below) be entitled to compensation for any loss suffered by him [in consequence].

(2) At any time when rules made under this Act make provision for local land charges registers to be divided into parts then, for the purposes of subsection (1) above—

(*a*) a search (whether personal or official) of a part or parts only of any such register shall not constitute a search of that register in relation to any local land charge registrable in a part of the register not searched; and

(*b*) a charge shall not be taken to be registered in the appropriate local land charges register unless registered in the appropriate part of the register.

(3) For the purposes of this section—

(*a*) a person purchases land where, for valuable consideration, he acquires any interest in land or the proceeds of sale of land, and this includes cases where he acquires as lessee or mortgagee and shall be treated as including cases where an interest is conveyed or assigned at his direction to another person;

(*b*) the relevant time—

(i) where the acquisition of the interest in question was preceded by a contract for its acquisition, other than a qualified liability contract, is the time when that contract was made;

(ii) in any other case, is the time when the purchaser acquired the interest in question or, if he acquired it under a disposition which took effect only when registered under the Land Registration Act 1925, the time when that disposition was made; and for the purposes of sub-paragraph (i) above, a qualified liability contract is a contract containing a term the effect of which is to make the liability of the purchaser dependent upon, or avoidable by reference to, the outcome of a search for local land charges affecting the land to be purchased;

(*c*) a personal search is material if, but only if—

(i) it is made after the commencement of this Act, and

(ii) it is made by or on behalf of the purchaser or, before the relevant time, the purchaser or his agent has knowledge of the result of it;

(*d*) an official search is material if, but only if—

(i) it is made after the commencement of this Act, and

(ii) it is requisitioned by or on behalf of the purchaser or, before the relevant time, the purchaser or his agent has knowledge of the contents of the official search certificate.

(4) Any compensation for loss under this section shall be paid by the registering authority in whose area the land affected is situated; and where the purchaser has incurred expenditure for the purpose of obtaining compensation under this section, the amount of the compensation shall include the amount of the expenditure reasonably incurred by him for that purpose (so far as that expenditure would not otherwise fall to be treated as loss for which he is entitled to compensation under this section).

(5) Where any compensation for loss under this section is paid by a registering authority in respect of a local land charge as respects which they are not the originating authority, then, unless an application for registration of the charge was made to the registering authority by the originating authority in time for it to be practicable for the registering authority to avoid incurring liability to pay that compensation, an amount equal thereto shall be recoverable from the originating authority by the registering authority.

(6) Where any compensation for loss under this section is paid by a registering authority, no part of the amount paid, or of any corresponding amount paid to that authority by the originating authority under subsection (5) above, shall be recoverable by the registering authority or the originating authority from any other person except as provided by subsection (5) above or under a policy of insurance or on grounds of fraud.

(7) In the case of an action to recover compensation under this section the cause of action shall be deemed for the purposes of the Limitation Act 1939 to accrue at the time when the local land charge comes to the notice of the purchaser; and for the purposes of this subsection the question when the charge

came to his notice shall be determined without regard to the provisions of section 198 of the Law of Property Act 1925 (under which registration under certain enactments is deemed to constitute actual notice).

[(8) Where the amount claimed by way of compensation under this section does not exceed £5,000, proceedings for the recovery of such compensation may be begun in a county court.]

(9) If in any proceedings for the recovery of compensation under this section he court dismisses a claim to compensation, it shall not order the purchaser to pay the registering authority's costs unless it considers that it was unreasonable for the purchaser to commence the proceedings.   **[931]**

NOTES

Commencement: 1 July 1991 (sub-s (8)); 1 August 1977 (remainder) (SI 1971 No 984).

Sub-s (1): para (*aa*) inserted and other words in square brackets substitutued by the Local Government (Miscellaneous Provisions) Act 1982, s 34(*d*).

Sub-s (8): substituted for sub-ss (8), (8A) by the High Court and County Courts Jurisdiction Order 1991, SI 1991 No 724, art 2(8), Schedule; sub-s (8A) originally inserted by the County Courts Act 1984, s 148(1), Sch 2, para 57.

11. Mortgages, trusts for sale and settled land

(1) Where there appear to be grounds for a claim under section 10 above in respect of an interest that is subject to a mortgage—

    (*a*) the claim may be made by any mortgagee of the interest as if he were the person entitled to that interest but without prejudice to the making of a claim by that person;

    (*b*) no compensation shall be payable under that section in respect of the interest of the mortgagee (as distinct from the interest which is subject to the mortgage);

    (*c*) any compensation payable under that section in respect of the interest that is subject to the mortgage shall be paid to the mortgagee or, if there is more than one mortgagee, to the first mortgagee and shall in either case be applied by him as if it were proceeds of sale.

(2) Where an interest is held on trust for sale any compensation payable in respect of it under section 10 above shall be dealt with as if it were proceeds of sale arising under the trust.

(3) Where an interest is settled land for the purposes of the Settled Land Act 1925 any compensation payable in respect of it under section 10 above shall be treated as capital money arising under that Act.   **[932]**

Miscellaneous and supplementary

12. Office copies as evidence

An office copy of an entry in any local land charges register shall be admissible in evidence in all proceedings and between all parties to the same extent as the original would be admissible.   **[933]**

13. Protection of solicitors, trustees etc

A solicitor or a trustee, personal representative, agent or other person in a fiduciary position, shall not be answerable in respect of any loss occasioned by reliance on an erroneous official search certificate or an erroneous office copy of an entry in a local land charges register.   **[934]**

16. Interpretation

(1) In this Act, except where the context otherwise requires—

"the appropriate local land charges register" has the meaning provided by section 4 above;

"the court" means the High Court, or the county court in a case where the county court has jurisdiction;

"land" includes mines and minerals, whether or not severed from the surface, buildings or parts of buildings (whether the division is horizontal, vertical or made in any other way) and other corporeal hereditaments;

"official search certificate" means a certificate issued pursuant to section 9(4) above;

"the originating authority", as respects a local land charge, has the meaning provided by section 5(4) above;

"personal search" means a search pursuant to section 8 above;

"prescribed" means prescribed by rules made under section 14 above;

"the registering authority", in relation to any land or to a local land charge, means the registering authority in whose area the land or, as the case may be, the land affected by the charge is situated, or, if the land in question is situated in the areas of two or more registering authorities each of those authorities respectively;

"statutory provision" means a provision of this Act or of any other Act or Measure, whenever passed, or a provision of any rules, regulations, order or similar instrument made (whether before or after the passing of this Act) under an Act, whenever passed.

(2) Except in so far as the context otherwise requires, any reference in this Act to an enactment is a reference to that enactment as amended, extended or applied by or under any other enactment, including this Act. **[935]**

20. Short title etc

(1) This Act may be cited as the Local Land Charges Act 1975.

(2) This Act binds the Crown, but nothing in this Act shall be taken to render land owned by or occupied for the purposes of the Crown subject to any charge to which, independently of this Act, it would not be subject.

(3) This Act shall come into force on such day as the Lord Chancellor may by order made by statutory instrument appoint.

(4) This Act extends to England and Wales only. **[936]**

RENTCHARGES ACT 1977
(c 30)

ARRANGEMENT OF SECTIONS

Prohibition and extinguishment

An Act to prohibit the creation, and provide for the extinguishment, apportionment and redemption, of certain rentcharges   [22 July 1977]

Prohibition and extinguishment

1. Meaning of "rentcharge"

For the purposes of this Act "rentcharge" means any annual or other periodic sum charged on or issuing out of land, except—

     (*a*)   rent reserved by a lease or tenancy, or
     (*b*)   any sum payable by way of interest.   **[937]**

2. Creation of rentcharges prohibited

(1) Subject to this section, no rentcharge may be created whether at law or in equity after the coming into force of this section.

(2) Any instrument made after the coming into force of this section shall, to the extent that it purports to create a rentcharge the creation of which is prohibited by this section, be void.

(3) This section does not prohibit the creation of a rentcharge—

     (*a*)   which has the effect of making the land on which the rent is charged settled land by virtue of section 1(1)(*v*) of the Settled Land Act 1925;
     (*b*)   which would have that effect but for the fact that the land on which the rent is charged is already settled land or is held on trust for sale;
     (*c*)   which is an estate rentcharge;
     (*d*)   under any Act of Parliament providing for the creation of rentcharges in connection with the execution of works on land (whether by way of improvements, repairs or otherwise) or the commutation of any obligation to do any such work; or

(e) by, or in accordance with the requirements of, any order of a court.

(4) For the purposes of this section "estate rentcharge" means (subject to subsection (5) below) a rentcharge created for the purpose—

(a) of making covenants to be performed by the owner of the land affected by the rentcharge enforceable by the rent owner against the owner for the time being of the land; or

(b) of meeting, or contributing towards, the cost of the performance by the rent owner of covenants for the provision of services, the carrying out of maintenance or repairs, the effecting of insurance or the making of any payment by him for the benefit of the land affected by the rentcharge or for the benefit of that and other land.

(5) A rentcharge of more than a nominal amount shall not be treated as an estate rentcharge for the purposes of this section unless it represents a payment for the performance by the rent owner of any such covenant as is mentioned in subsection (4)(b) above which is reasonable in relation to that covenant.   **[938]**

3. Extinguishment of rentcharges

(1) Subject to this section, every rentcharge shall (if it has not then ceased to have effect) be extinguished at the expiry of the period of 60 years beginning—

(a) with the passing of this Act, or

(b) with the date on which the rentcharge first became payable, whichever is the later; and accordingly the land on which it was charged or out of which it issued shall, at the expiration of that period, be discharged and freed from the rentcharge.

(2) The extinguishment of a rentcharge under this section shall not affect the exercise by any person of any right or remedy for the recovery of any rent which accrues before the rentcharge is so extinguished.

(3) This section shall not have the effect of extinguishing any rentcharge—

(a) which is, by virtue of any enactment or agreement or by custom, charged on or otherwise payable in relation to land wholly or partly in lieu of tithes; or

(b) which is of a kind referred to in subsection (3) of section 2 above (disregarding subsection (5) of that section).

(4) Subsection (1) above shall not apply to a variable rentcharge; but where such a rentcharge ceases to be variable, subsection (1) above shall apply as if the date on which the rentcharge first became payable were the date on which it ceased to be variable.

(5) For the purposes of subsection (4) above, a rentcharge shall (at any time) be treated as variable if at any time thereafter the amount of the rentcharge will, or may, vary in accordance with the provisions of the instrument under which it is payable.   **[939]**

Apportionment

4. Application for apportionment

(1) The owner of any land which is affected by a rentcharge which also affects land which is not in his ownership may, subject to this section, apply to the Secretary of State for an order apportioning the rentcharge between that land and the remaining land affected by the rentcharge.

(2) The owner of any land which is affected by a rentcharge which does not affect land not in his ownership may apply to the Secretary of State for an order apportioning the rentcharge between such parts of his land as may be specified in the application.

(3) No application for apportionment may be made under this section in respect of—

(a) a rentcharge of a kind mentioned in section 2(3)(d) or 3(3)(a) above, or

(b) land affected by a rentcharge which also affects other land, if the whole of that other land is exonerated or indemnified from the whole of the rentcharge by means of a charge on the first mentioned land.

(4) Every application—

(a) under subsection (1) above, shall specify the amount (if any) equitably apportioned to the applicant's land, and

(b) under subsection (2) above, shall specify the applicant's proposal for apportioning the rentcharge between the parts of his land specified in the application.

(5) Subject to subsection (4) above, every application under this section shall be in such form and shall contain such information and be accompanied by such documents as may be prescribed by regulations.

(6) In any case where the Secretary of State considers that any additional document or information ought to be furnished by the applicant he may require the applicant—

(a) to deliver to him such documents (including documents of title and, in the case of registered land, an authority to inspect the register), and

(b) to furnish him with such information, as the Secretary of State may specify.

(7) Where an applicant's documents of title are in the custody of a mortgagee the the mortgagee shall, if requested to do so by the Secretary of State for the purpose of an application made under this section, deliver those documents to the Secretary of State on such terms as to their custody and return as the mortgagee may reasonably require.   **[940]**

5. Apportionment

(1) Where an application for apportionment is made under section 4 above and the Secretary of State is satisfied that he is in a position to do so, he shall prepare a draft order for apportionment of the rentcharge.

(2) If the application is made under section 4(1) above, the amount specified in the draft order as being that part of the rentcharge apportioned to the applicant's land shall be—

(a) the amount specified in the application as the amount equitably apportioned to that land; or

(b) where no amount has been equitably apportioned to that land, such amount as the Secretary of State considers appropriate.

(3) If the application is made under section 4(2) above, the amounts specified in the draft order as apportioned between the parts of the applicant's land specified in the application shall be those proposed in the application.

(4) A copy of the draft order shall be served by the Secretary of State on the

person appearing to him to be the rent owner or his agent, and, in a case falling within subsection (2)(*b*) above, on such persons as appear to him to be the owners of the land affected by the rentcharge.

(5) After service of a draft order on the rent owner or his agent under subsection (4) above, the rent owner may, before the expiry of the period of 21 days beginning with the date on which the draft order is served (or such longer period, not exceeding the period of 42 days beginning with that date, as the Secretary of State may in a particular case allow)—

    (*a*) object to it on the ground that such an apportionment would provide insufficient security for any part of the rentcharge;

    (*b*) make an application to the effect that in the event of the apportionment not exceeding the sum mentioned in section 7(2) below, a condition should be imposed under that section.

(6) Where a draft order is served under subsection (4) above on a person who is the owner of any land affected by the rentcharge, that person may, before the expiry of the period of 21 days beginning with the date on which the draft order is served (or such longer period, not exceeding the period of 42 days beginning with that date, as the Secretary of State may in a particular case allow), make representations to the Secretary of State concerning the apportionment specified in the draft order.

(7) Any objection, application or representations under subsection (5) or (6) above shall be made in writing.

(8) An objection under subsection (5) above shall state what apportionment (if any) would in the opinion of the rent owner provide sufficient security for the rentcharge or, as the case may be, part of the rentcharge.

(9) The Secretary of State shall consider any objection duly made under subsection (5) above and any representations duly made under subsection (6) above and, if he is satisfied that the draft order should be modified—

    (*a*) in the case of an objection, in order to preserve for the rent owner sufficient security for each apportioned part of the rentcharge, or

    (*b*) to take account of any such representations,

he shall make such modifications in the draft order as appear to him to be appropriate.

(10) Where—

    (*a*) the relevant period has expired without any objection or representation having been duly made, or

    (*b*) an objection has, or any representations have, been duly made and the objection has, or, as the case may be, all the representations have, been considered by the Secretary of State,

the Secretary of State shall, if the applicant has not then withdrawn his application and the Secretary of State is satisfied that it is appropriate to do so, make an order (an "apportionment order") in the form of the draft but incorporating—

    (i) any modifications made by the Secretary of State in accordance with subsection (9) above, and

    (ii) where appropriate, a condition imposed by virtue of section 7(2) below.

(11) Immediately after making an apportionment order the Secretary of State shall serve copies of the order on the applicant and on the person appearing

to him to be the rent owner or his agent, and, in a case falling within subsection (2)(*b*) above, on those persons on whom copies of the draft order were served under subsection (4) above.

(12) In a case where modifications have been made in a draft order under subsection (9) above, the Secretary of State shall not make an apportionment order without giving the applicant an opportunity to withdraw his application.

[941]

6. Appeal

(1) Where the applicant or the rent owner or, in a case falling within section 5 (2)(*b*) above, any other person who is the owner of any land affected by the rentcharge, is aggrieved by the terms of an apportionment order, he may appeal to the Lands Tribunal.

(2) Where an appeal has been duly made to the Lands Tribunal under this section, the Tribunal shall—

    (*a*) confirm the order, or

    (*b*) set it aside, and, subject to section 7(2) below, make such other order apportioning the rentcharge as it thinks fit.   **[942]**

7. Effect of apportionment order

(1) An apportionment order shall, subject to subsection (2) below, have effect—

    (*a*) on the expiry of the period of 28 days beginning with the day on which it is made, or

    (*b*) where an appeal against the order has been duly made under section 6 above, on such day as the Lands Tribunal shall specify.

(2) If—

    (*a*) in the case of an application made under section 4(1) above, the part of the rentcharge apportioned to the applicant's land, or

    (*b*) in the case of an application under section 4(2) above, any apportioned part of the rentcharge,

does not exceed the annual sum of £5, then, subject to subsection (3) below, it shall, where an application has been duly made under section 5(5)(*b*) above, be made a condition of the apportionment order that it shall have effect only for the purpose of the redemption of tht part of the rentcharge in accordance with the following provisions of this Act.

(3) The Secretary of State shall not impose a condition under subsection (2) above in any case where he considers that, having regard to all the circumstances, to do so would cause the applicant to suffer financial hardship.

(4) In the case of an application under section 4(1) above, the effect of an apportionment order shall (subject to subsection (2) above) be to release the applicant's land from any part of the rentcharge not apportioned to it and to release the remaining land affected by the rentcharge from such part (if any) of the rentcharge as is apportioed to the applicant's land.

(5) In the case of an application under section 4(2) above, the effect of an apportionment order shall (subject to subsection (2) above) be to release each part of the applicant's land from any part of the rentcharge not apportioned to it.

(6) The Secretary of State may by regulations specify, in substitution for the sum mentioned in subsection (2) above, such other annual sum as he considers appropriate.   **[943]**

Redemption

8. Application for redemption certificate

(1) The owner of any land affected by a rentcharge may apply to the Secretary of State, in accordance with this section, for a certificate (in this Act referred to as a "redemption certificate") certifying that the rentcharge has been redeemed.

(2) Every application under this section shall be in such form and shall contain such information and be accompanied by such documents as may be prescribed by regulations.

(3) In any case where the Secretary of State considers that any additional document or information ought to be furnished by the applicant he may require the applicant—

(*a*) to deliver to him such documents (including documents of title and, in the case of registered land, an authority to inspect the register), and
(*b*) to furnish him with such information.

as the Secretary of State may specify.

(4) No application may be made under this section in respect of a rentcharge of a kind mentioned in section 2(3) or 3(3)(*a*) above.

(5) An application under this section may only be made—

(*a*) if the period for which the rentcharge concerned would remain payable if it were not redeemed is ascertainable, and
(*b*) in the case of a rentcharge which has at any time been a variable rentcharge, if it has ceased to be variable at the time of making the application.

For the purposes of this section a rentcharge shall (at any time) be treated as variable if at any time thereafter the amount of the rentcharge will, or may, vary in accordance with the provisions of the instrument under which it is payable.

(6) Where an applicant's documents of title are in the custody of a mortgagee the mortgagee shall, if requested to do so by the Secretary of State for the purpose of an application made under this section, deliver those documents to the Secretary of State on such terms as to their custody and return as the mortgagee may reasonably require.   **[944]**

9. Issue of redemption certificate

(1) Whre an application for a redemption certificate has been duly made under section 8 above, the Secretary of State shall serve notice of the application ("notice of application") on the person appearing to him to be the rent owner in relation to the rentcharge to which the application relates or his agent.

(2) A notice of application shall require the person on whom it is served to notify the Secretary of State, before the expiry of the period of 21 days beginning with the date on which the notice of application is served, whether or not he is the rent owner in relation to that rentcharge.

(3) Notification under subsection (2) above shall be given in the form

prescribed by regulations and shall contain such information, and be accompanied by such documents, as may be so prescribed.

(4) Where the Secretary of State hs been duly notified under subsection (2) above, or the period mentioned in that subsection has expired without his being so notified, he shall serve a notice ("instructions for redemption") on the applicant for the redemption certificate—

> (*a*) specifying the sum required to redeem the rentcharge 'the "redemption price") calculated in accordance with section 10(1) below, and
> (*b*) naming the person (determined in accordance with section 10(2) below), if any, appearing to the Secretary of State to be the person to whom the redemption price should be paid by the applicant.

(5) After service of instructions for redemption, the Secretary of State shall issue the applicant with a redemption certificate on proof—

> (*a*) that the applicant has, before the expiry of the period of 28 days beginning with the date on which the instructions are served—
>> (i) paid the amount specified as the redemption price to the person named in the instructions as the person to whom payment should be made, or
>> (ii) where no person is so named, paid that amount into court in accordance with section 10(4) below, or
> (*b*) in a case where the applicant has been authorised to do so under subsection (6) below, that he has paid that amount into court in accordance with section 10(4) below before the expiry of that period (or such longer period as the Secretary of State may allow).

(6) For the purposes of subsection (5)(*b*) above, the Secretary of State may authorise payment into court in any case where he is satisfied that the applicant is unable to effect payment in accordance with the instructions for redemption or that it would be unreasonable to require him to do so.   **[945]**

10. Provisions supplemental to section 9

(1) For the purposes of section 9 above, the redemption price shall be calculated by applying the formula:—

$$P = £\frac{R}{Y} - \frac{R}{Y(1+Y)^n}$$

.

where:—

P = the redemption price;

R = the annual amount of the rentcharge to be redeemed;

Y = the yield, expressed as a decimal fraction, from $2\frac{1}{2}$ per cent. Consolidated Stock; and

n = the period, expressed in years (taking any part of a year as a whole year), for which the rentcharge would remain payable if it were not redeemed.

In calculating the yield from $2\frac{1}{2}$ per cent. Consolidated Stock, the price of that stock shall be taken to be the middle market price at the close of business on the last trading day in the week before that in which instructions for redemption are served under section 9(4) above.

(2) For the purposes of section 9(4)(*b*) above, the person to whom the redemption price should be paid is—

(*a*) in a case where the rentcharge was subject to a mortgage, the mortgagee or, if there is more than one mortgagee, the first mortgagee;

(*b*) in a case where the rentcharge was not subject to a mortgage but was settled land or was subject to a trust for sale, the trustees;

(*c*) in any other case, the rent owner.

(3) Where a redemption certicate has been issued under section 9 above—

(*a*) it shall have the effect of releasing the applicant's land from the rentcharge concerned, but

(*b*) it shall not affect the exercise by the rent owner of any right or remedy for the recovery of any rent which accrues before the date on which it was issued.

(4) Where a payment is made into court for the purposes of section 9 above, the sum concerned shall—

(*a*) if it does not exceed [£5,000], be paid into the county court, and

(*b*) in any other case, be paid into the High Court.

[(4A) . . .]

(5) Any person who, in notifying the Secretary of State under section 9(2) above, makes a statement which he knows to be false in a material particular, or recklessly makes any statement which is so false, shall be guilty of an offence punishable on summary conviction by a fine not exceeding [level 5 on the standard scale]. **[946]**

NOTES
Sub-s (4): sum in square brackets substituted by the High Court and County Courts Jurisdiction Order 1991, SI 1991 No 724, art 2(8), Schedule.
Sub-s (4A): inserted by the County Courts Act 1984, s 148(1), Sch 2, para 63; repealed by the High Court and County Courts Jurisdiction Order 1991, SI 1991 No 724, art 2(8), Schedule.
Sub-s (5): maximum fine converted to a level on the standard scale by the Criminal Justice Act 1982, ss 37, 46.

Miscellaneous and general

11. Implied covenants

(1) Where any land affected by a rentcharge created after the passing of this Act by virtue of section 2(3)(*a*) or (*b*) above—

(*a*) is conveyed for consideration in money or money's worth, and

(*b*) remains affected by the rentcharge or by any part of it,

the following provisions of this section shall have effect in place of those of section 77 of the Law of Property Act 1925, in respect of the covenants deemed to be included and implied in the conveyance.

(2) In addition to the covenants implied under section 76 of the Law of Property Act 1925, there shall be deemed to be included and implied in the conveyance covenants by the conveying party or joint and several convenants by the conveying parties (if more than one) with the grantee (or with each of the grantees) in the following terms:—

(*a*) that the conveying party will at all times from the date of the conveyance duly pay the rentcharge (or part of the rentcharge) and keep the grantee and those deriving title under him and their respective estates and effects indemnified against all claims and demands whatsoever in respect of the rentcharge; and (*b*) that the conveying party will (at his expense), in the event of the rentcharge (or part of the rentcharge) ceasing to affect the land conveyed, furnish evidence of that fact to the grantee and those deriving title under him.

(3) The benefit of the covenants deemed to be included and implied in a conveyance, by virtue of subsection (2) above, shall be annexed and incident to and shall go with the estate or interest of the implied covenantee and shall be capable of being enforced by every person in whom the estate or interest is from time to time vested.

(4) Any stipulation which is contained in an agreement and which is inconsistent with, or designed to prevent the operation of, the said covenants (or any part of them) shall be void.   **[947]**

12. Regulations

(1) Regulations under any provision of this Act shall be made by the Secretary of State and shall be contained in a statutory instrument, which shall be subject to annulment in pursuance of a resolution of either House of Parliament.

(2) Regulations under any provision of this Act may contain such incidental and supplemental provisions as the Secretary of State considers appropriate and may make different provisions in relation to different cases or classes of case and in relation to different circumstances.   **[948]**

13. Interpretation

(1) In this Act—

"apportionment, in relation to a rentcharge, includes an apportionment which provides for the amount apportioned to any part of the land affected by the rentcharge to be nil;

"apportionment order" means an order made under section 5(10) above or, where appropriate, an order made by the Lands Tribunal under section 6(2)(*b*) above;

"conveyance" has the same meaning as in section 205(1) of the Law of Property Act 1925;

"land" has the same meaning as in section 205(1) of the Law of Property Act 1925;

"legal apportionment" and "equitable apportionment" in relation to a rentcharge mean, respectively—

(*a*) any apportionment of the rentcharge which is binding on the rent owner, and
(*b*) any apportionment or exoneration of the rentcharge which is not binding on the rent owner;

"owner", in relation to any land, means a person, other than a mortgagee not in possession, who is for the time being entitled to dispose of the fee simple of the land, whether in possession or in reversion, and includes a person holding or entitled to the rents and profits of the land under a lease or agreement;

"redemption certificate" has the meaning given in section 8(1) above;

"rent owner", in relation to a rentcharge, means the person entitled to the rentcharge or empowered to dispose of it absolutely or to give an absolute discharge for the capital value thereof.

(2) The provisions of this Act relating to the redemption and apportionment of rentcharges shall apply equally to the redemption and further apportionment if legally apportioned parts of rentcharges.

(3) Subject to section 3(4) above, a rentcharge shall be treated for the purposes of this Act as becoming payable on the first day of the first period in respect of which it is to be paid. **[949]**

14. Application to Crown

(1) This Act shall apply in relatin to any land in which there subsists a Crown interest as it applies in relation to land in which no such interest subsists.

(2) In this section "Crown interest" means an interest which belongs to Her Majesty in right of the Crown or of the Duchy of Lancaster or to the Duchy of Cornwall or to a government department, or which is held in trust for Her Majesty for the purposes of a government department. **[950]**

15. Expenses

(1) Any expenses incurred by the Secretary of State in consequence of this Act shall be paid out of money provided by Parliament.

(2) Subject to any provision made by regulations, any expenses incurred by any person in connection with an application for an apportionment order or for a redemption certificate under this Act shall be borne by that person.

(3) Regulations under subsection (2) above shall, in particular, provide for the reasonable expenses of a mortgagee, incurred in complying with a request under section 4(7) or 8(6) above, to be borne by the applicant. **[951]**

16. Service of notices, etc.

(1) Any document required to be served under this Act may be served on the person to be served either by delivering it to him, or by leaving it at his proper address, or by sending it by post.

(2) Any such document required to be served on a body corporate or a firm shall be duly served if it is served on the secretary or clerk of that body or a partner of that firm.

(3) For the purposes of this section, and of section 26 of the Interpretation Act 1889, in its application to this section, the proper address of a person shall be—

>   (a) in the case of a secretary or clerk of a body corporate, that of the registered or principal office of that body;
>   (b) in the case of a partner of a firm, that of the principal office of the firm;
>   (c) in any other case, the last known address of the person to be served.
>   **[952]**

18. Short title etc

(1) This Act may be cited as the Rentcharges Act 1977.

(2) The following provisions shall come into force on the expiry of the period of one month beginning with the date on which this Act is passed:—

(*a*) sections 1 to 3;

(*b*) sections 12 to 15, in section 17, subsection (1) (so far as it relates to paragraph 2 of Schedule 1), subsection (2) (except as it applies to the entries in Schedule 2 relating to section 10 of the Inclosure Act 1854 and section 191 of the Law of Property Act 1925) and subsections (3) and (6), and this section;

and the remaining provisions of this Act shall come into force on such day as the Secretary of State may by order appoint.

(3) This Act does not extend to Scotland or Northern Ireland.   **[953]**

PROTECTION FROM EVICTION ACT 1977
(c 43)

ARRANGEMENT OF SECTIONS

PART I
UNLAWFUL EVICTION AND HARASSMENT

An Act to consolidate section 16 of the Rent Act 1957 and Part III of the Rent Act 1965, and related enactments   [29 July 1977]

PART I
UNLAWFUL EVICTION AND HARASSMENT

1. Unlawful eviction and harassment of occupier

(1) In this section "residential occupier", in relation to any premises, means a person occupying the premises as a residence, whether under a contract or by virtue of any enactment or rule of law giving him the right to remain in occupation or restricting the right of any other person to recover possession of the premises.

(2) If any person unlawfully deprives the residential occupier of any premises of his occupation of the premises or any part thereof, or attempts to do so, he shall be guilty of an offence unless he proves that he believed, and had reasonable cause to believe, that the residential occupier had ceased to reside in the premises.

(3) If any person with intent to cause the residential occupier of any premises—

> (a) to give up the occupation of the premises or any part thereof; or
> (b) to refrain from exercising any right or pursuing any remedy in respect of the premises or part thereof;

does acts [likely] to interfere with the peace or comfort of the residential occupier or members of his household, or persistently withdraws or withholds services reasonably required for the occupation of the premises as a residence, he shall be guilty of an offence.

[(3A) Subject to subsection (3B) below, the landlord of a residential occupier or an agent of the landlord shall be guilty of an offence if—

> (a) he does acts likely to interfere with the peace or comfort of the residential occupier or members of his household, or
> (b) he persistently withdraws or withholds services reasonably required for the occupation of the premises in question as a residence,

and (in either case) he knows, or has reasonable cause to believe, that that conduct is likely to cause the residential occupier to give up the occupation of the whole or part of the premises or to refrain from exercising any right or pursuing any remedy in respect of the whole or part of the premises.

(3B) A person shall not be guilty of an offence under subsection (3A) above if he proves that he had reasonable grounds for doing the acts or withdrawing or withholding the services in question.

(3C) In subsection (3A) above "landlord", in relation to a residential occupier of any premises, means the person who, but for—

> (a) the residential occupier's right to remain in occupation of the premises, or
> (b) a restriction on the person's right to recover possession of the premises,

would be entitled to occupation of the premises and any superior landlord under whom that person derives title.]

(4) A person guilty of an offence under this section shall be liable—

> (a) on summary conviction, to a fine not exceeding [the prescribed sum] or to imprisonment for a term not exceeding 6 months or to both;
> (b) on conviction on indictment, to a fine or to imprisonment for a term not exceeding 2 years or to both.

(5) Nothing in this section shall be taken to prejudice any liability or remedy to which a person guilty of an offence thereunder may be subject in civil proceedings.

(6) Where an offence under this section committed by a body corporate is proved to have been committed with the consent or connivance of, or to be attributable to any neglect on the part of, any director, manager or secretary or other similar officer of the body corporate or any person who was purporting to act in any such capacity, he as well as the body corporate shall be guilty of that

offence and shall be liable to be proceeded against and punished accordingly.

[954]

NOTES
 Sub-s (3): word in square brackets substituted with respect to acts done after 15 January 1989 by the Housing Act 1988, s 29.
 Sub-s (3A): inserted with respect to acts done after 15 January 1989 by the Housing Act 1988, s 29.
 Sub-s (3B): inserted with respect to acts done after 15 January 1989 by the Housing Act 1988, s 29.
 Sub-s (3C): inserted with respect to acts done after 15 January 1989 by the Housing Act 1988, s 29.
 Sub-s (4): words in square brackets substituted by the Magistrates' Court Act 1980, s 32(2).

2. Restriction on re-entry without due process of law

Where any premises are let as a dwelling on a lease which is subject to a right of re-entry or forfeiture it shall not be lawful to enforce that right otherwise than by proceedings in the court while any person is lawfully residing in the premises or part of them. **[955]**

3. Prohibition of eviction without due process of law

(1) Where any premises have been let as a dwelling under a tenancy which is [neither a statutorily protected tenancy nor an excluded tenancy] and—

    (*a*) the tenancy (in this section referred to as the former tenancy) has come to an end, but

    (*b*) the occupier continues to reside in the premises or part of them,

it shall not be lawful for the owner to enforce against the occupier, otherwise than by proceedings in the court, his right to recover possession of the premises.

(2) In this section "the occupier", in relation to any premises, means any person lawfully residing in the premises or part of them at the termination of the former tenancy.

[(2A) Subsections (1) and (2) above apply in relation to any restricted contract (within the meaning of the Rent Act 1977) which—

    (*a*) creates a licence; and

    (*b*) is entered into after the commencement of section 69 of the Housing Act 1980;

as they apply in relation to a restricted contract which creates a tenancy.]

[(2B) Subsections (1) and (2) above apply in relation to any premises occupied as a dwelling under a licence, other than an excluded licence, as they apply in relation to premises let as a dwelling under a tenancy, and in those subsections the expressions "let" and "tenancy" shall be construed accordingly.

(2C) References in the preceding provisions of this section and section 4(2A) below to an excluded tenancy do not apply to—

    (*a*) a tenancy entered into before the date on which the Housing Act 1988 came into force, or

    (*b*) a tenancy entered into on or after that date but pursuant to a contract made before that date,

but, subject to that, "excluded tenancy" and "excluded licence" shall be construed in accordance with section 3A below.]

(3) This section shall, with the necessary modifications, apply where the

owner's right to recover possession arises on the death of the tenant under a statutory tenancy within the meaning of the Rent Act 1977 or the Rent (Agriculture) Act 1976.   **[956]**

NOTES
  Sub-s (1): words in square brackets substituted by the Housing Act 1988, s 30(1).
  Sub-s (2A): inserted by the Housing Act 1980, s 69(1).
  Sub-s (2B): inserted by the Housing Act 1988, s 30(2).
  Sub-s (2C): inserted by the Housing Act 1988, s 30(2).

[3A. Excluded tenancies and licences

(1) Any reference in this Act to an excluded tenancy or an excluded licence is a reference to a tenancy or licence which is excluded by virtue of any of the following provisions of this section.

(2) A tenancy or licence is excluded if—

    (*a*) under its terms the occupier shares any accommodation with the landlord or licensor; and

    (*b*) immediately before the tenancy or licence was granted and also at the time it comes to an end, the landlord or licensor occupied as his only or principal home premises of which the whole or part of the shared accommodation formed part.

(3) A tenancy or licence is also excluded if—

    (*a*) under its terms the occupier shares any accommodation with a member of the family of the landlord or licensor;

    (*b*) immediately before the tenancy or licence was granted and also at the time it comes to an end, the member of the family of the landlord or licensor occupied as his only or principal home premises of which the whole or part of the shared accommodation formed part; and

    (*c*) immediately before the tenancy or licence was granted and also at the time it comes to an end, the landlord or licensor occupied as his only or principal home premises in the same building as the shared accommodation and that building is not a purpose-built block of flats.

(4) For the purposes of subsections (2) and (3) above, an occupier shares accommodation with another person if he has the use of it in common with that person (whether or not also in common with others) and any reference in those subsections to shared accommodation shall be construed accordingly, and if, in relation to any tenancy or licence, there is at any time more than one person who is the landlord or licensor, any reference in those subsections to the landlord or licensor shall be construed as a reference to any one of those persons.

(5) In subsections (2) to (4) above—

    (*a*) "accommodation" includes neither an area used for storage nor a staircase, passage, corridor or other means of access;

    (*b*) "occupier" means, in relation to a tenancy, the tenant and, in relation to a licence, the licensee; and

    (*c*) "purpose-built block of flats" has the same meaning as in Part III of Schedule 1 to the Housing Act 1988;

and section 113 of the Housing Act 1985 shall apply to determine whether a person is for the purposes of subsection (3) above a member of another's family as it applies for the purposes of Part IV of that Act.

(6) A tenancy or licence is excluded if it was granted as a temporary expedient to a person who entered the premises in question or any other

premises as a trespasser (whether or not, before the beginning of that tenancy or licence, another tenancy or licence to occupy the premises or any other premises had been granted to him).

(7) A tenancy or licence is excluded if—

    (a) it confers on the tenant or licensee the right to occupy the premises for a holiday only, or

    (b) it is granted otherwise than for money or money's worth.

(8) A licence is excluded if it confers rights of occupation in a hostel, within the meaning of the Housing Act 1985, which is provided by—

    (a) the council of a county, district or London Borough, the Common Council of the City of London, the Council of the Isles of Scilly, the Inner London Education Authority, a joint authority within the meaning of the Local Government Act 1985 or a residuary body within the meaning of that Act;

    (b) a development corporation within the meaning of the New Towns Act 1981;

    (c) the Commission for the New Towns;

    (d) an urban development corporation established by an order under section 135 of the Local Government, Planning and Land Act 1980;

    (e) a housing action trust established under Part III of the Housing Act 1988;

    (f) the Development Board for Rural Wales;

    (g) the Housing Corporation or Housing for Wales;

    (h) a housing trust which is a charity or a registered housing association, within the meaning of the Housing Associations Act 1985; or

    (i) any other person who is, or who belongs to a class of person which is, specified in an order made by the Secretary of State.

(9) The power to make an order under subsection (8)(i) above shall be exercisable by statutory instrument which shall be subject to annulment in pursuance of a resolution of either House of Parliament.]   **[957]**

NOTES
    Inserted by the Housing Act 1988, s 31.

---

4. Special provisions for agricultural employees

(1) This section shall apply where the tenant under the former tenancy (within the meaning of section 3 of this Act) occupied the premises under the terms of his employment as a person employed in agriculture, as defined in section 1 of the Rent (Agriculture) Act 1976, but is not a statutory tenant as defined in that Act.

(2) In this section "the occupier", in relation to any premises means—

    (a) the tenant under the former tenancy; or

    (b) the widow or widower of the tenant under the former tenancy residing with him at his death or, if the former tenant leaves no such widow or widower, any member of his family residing with him at his death.

[(2A) In accordance with section 3(2B) above, any reference in subsections (1) and (2) above to the tenant under the former tenancy includes a reference to the licensee under a licence (other than an excluded licence) which has come to an end (being a licence to occupy premises as a dwelling); and in the following provisions of this section the expressions "tenancy" and "rent" and any other expressions referable to a tenancy shall be construed accordingly.]

(3) Without prejudice to any power of the court apart from this section to postpone the operation or suspend the execution of an order for possession, if in proceedings by the owner against the occupier the court makes an order for the possession of the premises the court may suspend the execution of the order on such terms and conditions, including conditions as to the payment by the occupier of arrears of rent, mesne profits and otherwise as the court thinks reasonable.

(4) Where the order for possession is made within the period of 6 months beginning with the date when the former tenancy came to an end, then, without prejudice to any powers of the court under the preceding provisions of this section or apart from this section to postpone the operation or suspend the execution of the order for a longer period, the court shall suspend the execution of the order for the remainder of the said period of 6 months unless the court—

    (*a*) is satisfied either—

        (i) that other suitable accommodation is, or will within that period be made, available to the occupier; or

       (ii) that the efficient management of any agricultural land or the efficient carrying on of any agricultural operations would be seriously prejudiced unless the premises are available for occupation by a person employed or to be employed by the owner; or

      (iii) that greater hardship (being hardship in respect of matters other than the carrying on of such a business as aforesaid) would be caused by the suspension of the order until the end of that period than by its execution within that period; or

      (iv) that the occupier, or any person residing or lodging with the occupier, has been causing damage to the premises or has been guilty of conduct which is a nuisance or annoyance to persons occupying other premises; and

    (*b*) considers that it would be reasonable not to suspend the execution of the order for the remainder of that period.

(5) Where the court suspends the execution of an order for possession under subsection (4) above it shall do so on such terms and conditions, including conditions as to the payment by the occupier of arrears of rent, mesne profits and otherwise as the court thinks reasonable.

(6) A decision of the court not to suspend the execution of the order under subsection (4) above shall not prejudice any other power of the court to postpone the operation or suspend the execution of the order for the whole or part of the period of 6 months mentioned in that subsection.

(7) Where the court has, under the preceding provisions of this section, suspended the execution of an order for possession, it may from time to time vary the period of suspension or terminate it and may vary any terms and conditions imposed by virtue of this section.

(8) In considering whether or how to exercise its powers under subsection (3) above, the court shall have regard to all the circumstances and, in particular, to—

    (*a*) whether other suitable accommodation is or can be made available to the occupier;

    (*b*) whether the efficient management of any agricultural land or the efficient carrying on of any agricultural operations would be seriously prejudiced unless the premises were available for occupation by a person employed or to be employed by the owner; and

(c) whether greater hardship would be caused by the suspension of the execution of the order than by its execution without suspension or further suspension.

(9) Where in proceedings for the recovery of possession of the premises the court makes an order for possession but suspends the execution of the order under this section, it shall make no order for costs, unless it appears to the court, having regard to the conduct of the owner or of the occupier, that there are special reasons for making such an order.

(10) Where, in the case of an order for possession of the premises to which subsection (4) above applies, the execution of the order is not suspended under that subsection or, the execution of the order having been so suspended, the suspension is terminated, then, if it is subsequently made to appear to the court that the failure to suspend the execution of the order or, as the case may be, the termination of the suspension was—

(a) attributable to the provisions of paragraph (a)(ii) of subsection (4), and

(b) due to misrepresentation or concealment of material facts by the owner of the premises,

the court may order the owner to pay to the occupier such sum as appears sufficient as compensation for damage or loss sustained by the occupier as a result of that failure or termination.　　　　　　　　　　　　　　**[958]**

NOTES

Sub-s (2A): inserted by the Housing Act 1988, s 30(3).

PART II

NOTICE TO QUIT

5. Validity of notices to quit

(1) [Subject to subsection (1B) below] no notice by a landlord or a tenant to quit any premises let (whether before or after the commencement of this Act) as a dwelling shall be valid unless—

(a) it is in writing and contains such information as may be prescribed, and

(b) it is given not less than 4 weeks before the date on which it is to take effect.

(1A) Subject to subsection (1B) below, no notice by a licensor or a licensee to determine a periodic licence to occupy premises as a dwelling (whether the licence was granted before or after the passing of this Act) shall be valid unless—

(a) it is in writing and contains such information as may be prescribed, and

(b) it is given not less than 4 weeks before the date on which it is to take effect.

(1B) Nothing in subsection (1) or subsection (1A) above applies to—

(a) premises let on an excluded tenancy which is entered into on or after the date on which the Housing Act 1988 came into force unless it is entered into pursuant to a contract made before that date; or (*b*) premises occupied under an excluded licence.]

(2) In this section "prescribed" means prescribed by regulations made by the Secretary of State by statutory instrument, and a statutory instrument containing any such regulations shall be subject to annulment in pursuance of a resolution of either House of Parliament.

(3) Regulations under this section may make different provision in relation to different descriptions of lettings and different circumstances. **[959]**

NOTES
Sub-s (1): words in square brackets inserted by the Housing Act 1988, s 32(1).
Sub-s (1A): inserted by the Housing Act 1988, s 32(2).
Sub-s (1B): inserted by the Housing Act 1988, s 32(2).

PART III

SUPPLEMENTAL PROVISIONS

8. Interpretation

(1) In this Act "statutorily protected tenancy" means—

   (*a*) a protected tenancy within the meaning of the Rent Act 1977 or a tenancy to which Part I of the Landlord and Tenant Act 1954 applies;
   (*b*) a protected occupancy or statutory tenancy as defined in the Rent (Agriculture) Act 1976;
   (*c*) a tenancy to which Part II of the Landlord and Tenant Act 1954 applies;
   (*d*) a tenancy of an agricultural holding within the meaning of the [Agricultural Holdings Act 1986];
   [(*e*) an assured tenancy or assured agricultural occupancy under Part I of the Housing Act 1988];
   [(*f*) a tenancy to which Schedule 10 to the Local Government and Housing Act 1989 applies].

(2) For the purposes of Part I of this Act a person who, under the terms of his employment, had exclusive possession of any premises other than as a tenant shall be deemed to have been a tenant and the expressions "let" and "tenancy" shall be construed accordingly.

(3) In Part I of this Act "the owner", in relation to any premises, means the person who, as against the occupier, is entitled to possession thereof.

[(4) In this Act "excluded tenancy" and "excluded licence" have the meaning assigned by section 3A of this Act.

(5) If, on or after the date on which the Housing Act 1988 came into force, the terms of an excluded tenancy or excluded licence entered into before that date are varied, then—

   (*a*) if the variation affects the amount of the rent which is payable under the tenancy or licence, the tenancy or licence shall be treated for the purposes of sections 3(2C) and 5(1B) above as a new tenancy or licence entered into at the time of the variation; and
   (*b*) if the variation does not affect the amount of the rent which is so payable, nothing in this Act shall affect the determination of the question whether the variation is such as to give rise to a new tenancy or licence.

(6) Any reference in subsection (5) above to a variation affecting the amount

of the rent which is payable under a tenancy or licence does not include a reference to—

> (a) a reduction or increase effected under Part III or Part VI of the Rent Act 1977 (rents under regulated tenancies and housing association tenancies), section 78 of that Act (power of rent tribunal in relation to restricted contracts) or sections 11 to 14 of the Rent (Agriculture) Act 1976; or
>
> (b) a variation which is made by the parties and has the effect of making the rent expressed to be payable under the tenancy or licence the same as a rent for the dwelling which is entered in the register under Part IV or section 79 of the Rent Act 1977.] **[960]**

NOTES

Sub-s (1): in para (d) words in square brackets substituted by the Agricultural Holdings Act 1986, s 100, Sch 14, para 61; para (e) added by the Housing Act 1988, s 33(2); para (f) added by the Local Government and Housing Act 1989, s 194(1), Sch 11, para 54.

Sub-s (4): added by the Housing Act 1988, s 33(3).

Sub-s (5): added by the Housing Act 1988, s 33(3).

Sub-s (6): added by the Housing Act 1988, s 33(3).

9. The court for purposes of Part I

(1) The court for the purposes of Part I of this Act shall, subject to this section, be—

> (a) the county court, in relation to premises with respect to which the county court has for the time being jurisdiction in actions for the recovery of land; and
>
> (b) the High Court, in relation to other premises.

(2) Any powers of a county court in proceedings for the recovery of possession of any premises in the circumstances mentioned in section 3(1) of this Act may be exercised with the leave of the judge by any registrar of the court, except in so far as rules of court otherwise provide.

(3) Nothing in this Act shall affect the jurisdiction of the High Court in proceedings to enforce a lessor's right of re-entry or forfeiture or to enforce a mortgagee's right of possession in a case where the former tenancy was not binding on the mortgagee.

(4) Nothing in this Act shall affect the operation of—

> (a) section 59 of the Pluralities Act 1838;
>
> (b) section 19 of the Defence Act 1842;
>
> (c) section 6 of the Lecturers and Parish Clerks Act 1844;
>
> (d) paragraph 3 of Schedule 1 to the Sexual Offences Act 1956; or
>
> (e) section 13 of the Compulsory Purchase Act 1965. **[961]**

13. Short title, etc

(1) This Act may be cited as the Protection from Eviction Act 1977.

(2) This Act shall come into force on the expiry of the period of one month beginning with the date on which it is passed.

(3) This Act does not extend to Scotland or Northern Ireland.

(4) References in this Act to any enactment are references to that enactment as amended, and include references thereto as applied by any other enactment including, except where the context otherwise requires, this Act. **[962]**

INTERPRETATION ACT 1978
(c 30)

An Act to consolidate the Interpretation Act 1889 and certain other enactments relating to the construction and operation of Acts of Parliament and other instruments, with amendments to give effect to recommendations of the Law Commission and the Scottish Law Commission [20 July 1978]

Interpretation and construction

7. References to service by post

Where an Act authorises or requires any document to be served by post (whether the expression "serve" or the expression "give" or "send" or any other expression is used) then, unless the contrary intention appears, the service is deemed to be effected by properly addressing, pre-paying and posting a letter containing the document and, unless the contrary is proved, to have been effected at the time at which the letter would be delivered in the ordinary course of post. **[963]**

9. References to time of day

Subject to section 3 of the Summer Time Act 1972 (construction of references to points of time during the period of summer time), whenever an expression of time occurs in an Act, the time referred to shall, unless it is otherwise specifically stated, be held to be Greenwich mean time. **[963A]**

Miscellaneous

19. Citation of other Acts

(1) Where an Act cites another Act by year, statute, session or chapter, or a section or other portion of another Act by number or letter, the reference shall, unless the contrary intention appears, be read as referring—

    (a) in the case of Acts included in any revised edition of the statutes printed by authority, to that edition;

    (b) in the case of Acts not so included but included in the edition prepared under the direction of the Record Commission, to that edition;

    (c) in any other case, to the Acts printed by the Queen's Printer, or under the superintendence or authority of Her Majesty's Stationery Office.

    . . . **[963B]**

Supplementary

23. Application to other instruments

. . .

(3) Sections 9 and 19(1) also apply to deeds and other instruments and documents as they apply to Acts and subordinate legislation; and in the application of section 17(2)(a) to Acts passed or subordinate legislation made after the commencement of this Act, the reference to any other enactment includes any deed or other instrument or document.

    . . . **[963C]**

ESTATE AGENTS ACT 1979
(c 38)

An Act to make provision with respect to the carrying on of and to persons who carry on, certain activities in connection with the disposal and acquisition of interests in land; and for purposes connected therewith   [4 April 1979]

CLIENTS' MONEY AND ACCOUNTS

12. Meaning of "clients' money" etc

(1) In this Act "clients' money", in relation to a person engaged in estate agency work, means any money received by him in the course of that work which is a contract or pre-contract deposit—

    (a) in respect of the acquisition of an interest in land in the United kingdom, or

    (b) in respect of a connected contract,

whether that money is held or received by him as agent, bailee, stakeholder or in any other capacity.

(2) In this Act "contract deposit" means any sum paid by a purchaser—

    (a) which in whole or in part is, or is intended to form part of, the consideration for acquiring such an interest as is referred to in subsection (1)(a) above or for a connected contract; and

    (b) which is paid by him at or after the time at which he acquires the interest or enters into an enforceable contract to acquire it.

(3) In this Act "pre-contract deposit" means any sum paid by any person—

    (a) in whole or in part as an earnest of his intention to acquire such an interest as is referred to in subsection (1)(a) above, or

    (b) in whole or in part towards meeting any liability of his in respect of the consideration for the acquisition of such an interest which will arise if he acquires or enters into an enforceable contract to acquire the interest, or

    (c) in respect of a connected contract.

and which is paid by him at a time before he either acquires the interest or enters into an enforceable contract to acquire it.

(4) In this Act "connected contract", in relation to the acquisition of an interest in land, means a contract which is conditional upon such an acquisition or upon entering into an enforceable contract for such an acquisition (whether or not it is also conditional on other matters).   **[964]**

13. Clients' money held on trust or as agent

(1) It is hereby declared that clients' money received by any person in the course of estate agency work in England, Wales or Northern Ireland—

    (a) is held by him on trust for the person who is entitled to call for it to be paid over to him or to be paid on his direction or to have it otherwise credited to him, or

    (b) if it is received by him as stakeholder, is held by him on trust for the person who may become so entitled on the occurrence of the event against which the money is held.

(2) . . .

(3) The provisions of sections 14 and 15 below as to the investment of clients' money, the keeping of accounts and records and accounting for interest shall have effect in place of the corresponding duties which would be owed by a person holding clients' money as trustee, or in Scotland as agent, under the general law.

(4) Where an order of the Director under section 3 above has the effect of prohibiting a person from holding clients' money the order may contain provision—

  (a) appointing another person as trustee, or in Scotland as agent, in place of the person to whom the order relates to hold and deal with clients' money held by that person when the order comes into effect; and

  (b) requiring the expenses and such reasonable remuneration of the new trustee or agent as may be specified in the order to be paid by the person to whom the order relates or, if the order so provides, out of the clients' money;

but nothing in this subsection shall affect the power conferred by section 41 of the Trustee Act 1925 or section 40 of the Trustee Act (Northern Ireland) 1958 to appoint a new trustee to hold clients' money.

(5) For the avoidance of doubt it is hereby declared that the fact that any person has or may have a lien on clients' money held by him does not affect the operation of this section and also that nothing in this section shall prevent such a lien from being given effect. **[965]**

NOTES
  Sub-s (2): applies to Scotland only.

SUPPLEMENTARY

36. Short title, commencement and extent

(1) This Act may be cited as the Estate Agents Act 1979.

(2) This Act shall come into force on such day as the Secretary of State may by order made by statutory instrument appoint and different days may be so appointed for different provisions and for different purposes.

(3) This Act extends to Northern Ireland. **[966]**

CHARGING ORDERS ACT 1979
(c 53)

An Act to make provision for imposing charges to secure payment of money due, or to become due, under judgments or orders of court; to provide for restraining and prohibiting dealings with, and the making of payments in respect of, certain securities; and for connected purposes [6 December 1979]

Charging orders

1. Charging orders

(1) Where, under a judgment or order of the High Court or a county court, a person (the "debtor") is required to pay a sum of money to another person (the "creditor") then, for the purpose of enforcing that judgment or order, the appropriate court may make an order in accordance with the provisions of this Act imposing on any such property of the debtor as may be specified in the

order a charge for securing the payment of any money due or to become due under the judgment or order.

(2) The appropriate court is—

 (*a*) in a case where the property to be charged is a fund in court, the court in which that fund is lodged;

 (*b*) in a case where paragraph (*a*) above does not apply and the order to be enforced is a maintenance order of the High Court, the High Court or a county court;

 (*c*) in a case where neither paragraph (*a*) nor paragraph (*b*) above applies and the judgment or order to be enforced is a judgment or order of the High Court for a sum exceeding [the county court limit], the High Court [or a county court]; and

 (*d*) in any other case, a county court.

In this section ["county court limit" means the county court limit for the time being specified in an Order in Council under [section 145 of the County Courts Act 1984], as the county court limit for the purposes of this section and] "maintenance order" has the same meaning as in section 2(*a*) of the Attachment of Earnings Act 1971.

(3) An order under subsection (1) above is referred to in this Act as a "charging order".

(4) Where a person applies to the High Court for a charging order to enforce more than one judgment or order, that court shall be the appropriate court in relation to the application if it would be the appropriate court, apart from this subsection, on an application relating to one or more of the judgments or orders concerned.

(5) In deciding whether to make a charging order the court shall consider all the circumstances of the case and, in particular, any evidence before it as to—

 (*a*) the personal circumstances of the debtor, and

 (*b*) whether any other creditor of the debtor would be likely to be unduly prejudiced by the making of the order.   **[967]**

NOTES

 Sub-s (2): first words in square brackets substituted by the Administration of Justice Act 1982, ss 34, 37, Sch 3, Part II, paras 3, 6, words in square brackets therein substituted by the County Courts Act 1984, s 148(1), Sch 2, para 71.

2. Property which may be charged

(1) Subject to subsection (3) below, a charge may be imposed by a charging order only on—

 (*a*) any interest held by the debtor beneficially—

  (i) in any asset of a kind mentioned in subsection (2) below, or

  (ii) under any trust; or

 (*b*) any interest held by a person as trustee of a trust ("the trust"), if the interest is in such an asset or is an interest under another trust and—

  (i) the judgment or order in respect of which a charge is to be imposed was made against that person as trustee of the trust, or

  (ii) the whole beneficial interest under the trust is held by the debtor unencumbered and for his own benefit, or

      (iii) in a case where there are two or more debtors all of whom are liable to the creditor for the same debt, they together hold the whole beneficial interest under the trust unencumbered and for their own benefit.

(2) The assets referred to in subsection (1) above are—

  (*a*) land,

  (*b*) securities of any of the following kinds—

     (i) government stock,

    (ii) stock of any body (other than a building society) incorporated within England and Wales,

   (iii) stock of any body incorporated outside England and Wales or of any state or territory outside the United Kingdom, being stock registered in a register kept at any place within England and Wales,

   (iv) units of any unit trust in respect of which a register of the unit holders is kept at any place within England and Wales, or

  (*c*) funds in court.

(3) In any case where a charge is imposed by a charging order on any interest in an asset of a kind mentioned in paragraph (*b*) or (*c*) of subsection (2) above, the court making the order may provide for the charge to extend to any interest or dividend payable in respect of the asset. **[968]**

3. Provisions supplementing sections 1 and 2

(1) A charging order may be made either absolutely or subject to conditions as to notifying the debtor or as to the time when the charge is to become enforceable, or as to other matters.

(2) The Land Charges Act 1972 and the Land Registration Act 1925 shall apply in relation to charging orders as they apply in relation to other orders or writs issued or made for the purpose of enforcing judgments.

(3) . . .

(4) Subject to the provisions of this Act, a charge imposed by a charging order shall have the like effect and shall be enforceable in the same courts and in the same manner as an equitable charge created by the debtor by writing under his hand.

(5) The court by which a charging order was made may at any time, on the application of the debtor or of any person interested in any property to which the order relates, make an order discharging or varying the charging order.

(6) Where a charging order has been protected by an entry registered under the Land Charges Act 1972 or the Land Registration Act 1925, an order under subsection (5) above discharging the charging order may direct that the entry be cancelled.

(7) The Lord Chancellor may by order made by statutory instrument amend section 2(2) of this Act by adding to, or removing from, the kinds of asset for the time being referred to there, any asset of a kind which in his opinion ought to be so added or removed.

(8) Any order under subsection (7) above shall be subject to annulment in pursuance of a resolution of either House of Parliament. **[969]**

NOTES
Sub-s (3): amends the Land Registration Act 1925, s 49.

LIMITATION ACT 1980
(c 58)

ARRANGEMENT OF SECTIONS

An Act to consolidate the Limitation Acts 1939 to 1980   [13 November 1980]

PART I

ORDINARY TIME LIMITS FOR DIFFERENT CLASSES OF ACTION

Actions founded on simple contract

5. Time limit for actions founded on simple contract

An action founded on simple contract shall not be brought after the expiration
of six years from the date on which the cause of action accrued.   **[970]**

Actions to recover land and rent

15. Time limit for actions to recover land

(1) No action shall be brought by any person to recover any land after the
expiration of twelve years from the date on which the right of action accrued to
him or, if it first accrued to some person through whom he claims, to that
person.

(2) Subject to the following provisions of this section, where—

    (*a*) the estate or interest claimed was an estate or interest in reversion or
remainder or any other future estate or interest and the right of action
to recover the land accrued on the date on which the estate or interest
fell into possession by the determination of the preceding estate or
interest; and

    (*b*) the person entitled to the preceding estate or interest (not being a term
of years absolute) was not in possession of the land on that date;

no action shall be brought by the person entitled to the succeeding estate or
interest after the expiration of twelve years from the date on which the right of
action accrued to the person entitled to the preceding estate or interest or six
years from the date on which the right of action accrued to the person entitled
to the succeeding estate or interest, whichever period last expires.

(3) Subsection (2) above shall not apply to any estate or interest which falls
into possession on the determination of an entailed interest and which might
have been barred by the person entitled to the entailed interest.

(4) No person shall bring an action to recover any estate or interest in land
under an assurance taking effect after the right of action to recover the land had

accrued to the person by whom the assurance was made or some person through whom he claimed or some person entitled to a preceding estate or interest, unless the action is brought within the period during which the person by whom the assurance was made could have brought such an action.

(5) Where any person is entitled to any estate or interest in land in possession and, while so entitled, is also entitled to any future estate or interest in that land, and his right to recover the estate or interest in possession is barred under this Act, no action shall be brought by that person, or by any person claiming through him, in respect of the future estate or interest, unless in the meantime possession of the land has been recovered by a person entitled to an intermediate estate or interest.

(6) Part I of Schedule 1 to this Act contains provisions for determining the date of accrual of rights of action to recover land in the cases there mentioned.

(7) Part II of that Schedule contains provisions modifying the provisions of this section in their application to actions brought by, or by a person claiming through, the Crown or any spiritual or eleemosynary corporation sole. **[971]**

16. Time limit for redemption actions

When a mortgagee of land has been in possession of any of the mortgaged land for a period of twelve years, no action to redeem the land of which the mortgagee has been so in possession shall be brought after the end of that period by the mortgagor or any person claiming through him. **[972]**

17. Extinction of title to land after expiration of time limit

Subject to—

(*a*) section 18 of this Act; and
(*b*) section 75 of the Land Registration Act 1925;

at the expiration of the period prescribed by this Act for any person to bring an action to recover land (including a redemption action) the title of that person to the land shall be extinguished. **[973]**

18. Settled land and land held on trust

(1) Subject to section 21(1) and (2) of this Act, the provisions of this Act shall apply to equitable interests in land, including interests in the proceeds of the sale of land held upon trust for sale, as they apply to legal estates.

Accordingly a right of action to recover the land shall, for the purposes of this Act but not otherwise, be treated as accruing to a person entitled in possession to such an equitable interest in the like manner and circumstances, and on the same date, as it would accrue if his interest were a legal estate in the land (and any relevant provision of Part I of Schedule 1 to this Act shall apply in any such case accordingly).

(2) Where the period prescribed by this Act has expired for the bringing of an action to recover land by a tenant for life or a statutory owner of settled land—

(*a*) his legal estate shall not be extinguished if and so long as the right of action to recover the land of any person entitled to a beneficial interest in the land either has not accrued or has not been barred by this Act; and

(b) the legal estate shall accordingly remain vested in the tenant for life or statutory owner and shall devolve in accordance with the Settled Land Act 1925;

but if and when every such right of action has been barred by this Act, his legal estate shall be extinguished.

(3) Where any land is held upon trust (including a trust for sale) and the period prescribed by this Act has expired for the bringing of an action to recover the land by the trustees, the estate of the trustees shall not be extinguished if and so long as the right of action to recover the land of any person entitled to a beneficial interest in the land or in the proceeds of sale either has not accrued or has not been barred by this Act; but if and when every such right of action has been so barred the estate of the trustees shall be extinguished.

(4) Where—

(a) any settled land is vested in a statutory owner; or
(b) any land is held upon trust (including a trust for sale);

an action to recover the land may be brought by the statutory owner or trustees on behalf of any person entitled to a beneficial interest in possession in the land or in the proceeds of sale whose right of action has not been barred by this Act, notwithstanding that the right of action of the statutory owner or trustees would apart from this provision have been barred by this Act. **[974]**

19. Time limit for actions to recover rent

No action shall be brought, or distress made, to recover arrears of rent, or damages in respect of arrears of rent, after the expiration of six years from the date on which the arrears became due. **[975]**

Actions to recover money secured by a mortgage or charge or to recover proceeds of the sale of land

20. Time limit for action to recover money secured by a mortgage or charge or to recover proceeds of the sale of land

(1) No action shall be brought to recover—

(a) any principal sum of money secured by a mortgage or other charge on property (whether real or personal); or
(b) proceeds of the sale of land;

after the expiration of twelve years from the date on which the right to receive the money accrued.

(2) No foreclosure action in respect of mortgaged personal property shall be brought after the expiration of twelve years from the date on which the right to foreclose accrued.

But if the mortgagee was in possession of the mortgaged property after that date, the right to foreclose on the property which was in his possession shall not be treated as having accrued for the purposes of this subsection until the date on which his possession discontinued.

(3) The right to receive any principal sum of money secured by a mortgage or other charge and the right to foreclose on the property subject to the mortgage or charge shall not be treated as accruing so long as that property comprises any future interest or any life insurance policy which has not matured or been determined.

(4) Nothing in this section shall apply to a foreclosure action in respect of mortgaged land, but the provisions of this Act relating to actions to recover land shall apply to such an action.

(5) Subject to subsections (6) and (7) below, no action to recover arrears of interest payable in respect of any sum of money secured by a mortgage or other charge or payable in respect of proceeds of the sale of land, or to recover damages in respect of such arrears shall be brought after the expiration of six years from the date on which the interest became due.

(6) Where—

    (*a*) a prior mortgagee or other incumbrancer has been in possession of the property charged; and

    (*b*) an action is brought within one year of the discontinuance of that possession by the subsequent incumbrancer;

the subsequent incumbrancer may recover by that action all the arrears of interest which fell due during the period of possession by the prior incumbrancer or damages in respect of those arrears, notwithstanding that the period exceeded six years.

(7) Where—

    (*a*) the property subject to the mortgage or charge comprises any future interest or life insurance policy; and

    (*b*) it is a term of the mortgage or charge that arrears of interest shall be treated as part of the principal sum of money secured by the mortgage or charge;

interest shall not be treated as becoming due before the right to recover the principal sum of money has accrued or is treated as having accrued.　　　　**[976]**

Actions in respect of trust property or the personal estate of deceased persons

21. Time limit for actions in respect of trust property

(1) No period of limitation prescribed by this Act shall apply to an action by a beneficiary under a trust, being an action—

    (*a*) in respect of any fraud or fraudulent breach of trust to which the trustee was a party or privy; or

    (*b*) to recover from the trustee trust property or the proceeds of trust property in the possession of the trustee, or previously received by the trustee and converted to his use.

(2) Where a trustee who is also a beneficiary under the trust receives or retains trust property or its proceeds as his share on a distribution of trust property under the trust, his liability in any action brought by virtue of subsection (1)(*b*) above to recover that property or its proceeds after the expiration of the period of limitation prescribed by this Act for bringing an action to recover trust property shall be limited to the excess over his proper share.

This subsection only applies if the trustee acted honestly and reasonably in making the distribution.

(3) Subject to the preceding provisions of this section, an action by a beneficiary to recover trust property or in respect of any breach of trust, not being an action for which a period of limitation is prescribed by any other

provision of this Act, shall not be brought after the expiration of six years from the date on which the right of action accrued.

For the purposes of this subsection, the right of action shall not be treated as having accrued to any beneficiary entitled to a future interest in the trust property until the interest fell into possession.

(4) No beneficiary as against whom there would be a good defence under this Act shall derive any greater or other benefit from a judgment or order obtained by any other beneficiary than he could have obtained if he had brought the action and this Act had been pleaded in defence. **[977]**

22. Time limit for actions claiming personal estate of a deceased person

Subject to section 21(1) and (2) of this Act—

(*a*) no action in respect of any claim to the personal estate of a deceased person or to any share or interest in any such estate (whether under a will or on intestacy) shall be brought after the expiration of twelve years from the date on which the right to receive the share or interest accrued; and

(*b*) no action to recover arrears of interest in respect of any legacy, or damages in respect of such arrears, shall be brought after the expiration of six years from the date on which the interest became due. **[978]**

Actions for an account

23. Time limit in respect of actions for an account

An action for an account shall not be brought after the expiration of any time limit under this Act which is applicable to the claim which is the basis of the duty to account. **[979]**

Miscellaneous and supplemental

26. Administration to date back to death

For the purposes of the provisions of this Act relating to actions for the recovery of land and advowsons an administrator of the estate of a deceased person shall be treated as claiming as if there had been no interval of time between the death of the deceased person and the grant of the letters of administration. **[980]**

27. Cure of defective disentailing assurance

(1) This section applies where—

(*a*) a person entitled in remainder to an entailed interest in any land makes an assurance of his interest which fails to bar the issue in tail or the estates and interests taking effect on the determination of the entailed interest, or fails to bar those estates and interests only; and

(*b*) any person takes possession of the land by virtue of the assurance.

(2) If the person taking possession of the land by virtue of the assurance, or any other person whatsoever (other than a person entitled to possession by virtue of the settlement) is in possession of the land for a period of twelve years from the commencement of the time when the assurance could have operated as an effective bar, the assurance shall thereupon operate, and be treated as

having always operated, to bar the issue in tail and the estates and interests taking effect on the determination of the entailed interest.

(3) The reference in subsection (2) above to the time when the assurance could have operated as an effective bar is a reference to the time at which the assurance, if it had then been executed by the person entitled to the entailed interest, would have operated, without the consent of any other person, to bar the issue in tail and the estates and interests taking effect on the determination of the entailed interest.   **[981]**

PART II

EXTENSION OR EXCLUSION OF ORDINARY TIME LIMITS

Disability

28. Extension of limitation period in case of disability

(1) Subject to the following provisions of this section, if on the date when any right of action accrued for which a period of limitation is prescribed by this Act, the person to whom it accrued was under a disability, the action may be brought at any time before the expiration of six years from the date when he ceased to be under a disability or died (whichever first occurred) notwithstanding that the period of limitation has expired.

(2) This section shall not affect any case where the right of action first accrued to some person (not under a disability) through whom the person under a disability claims.

(3) When a right of action which has accrued to a person under a disability accrues, on the death of that person while still under a disability, to another person under a disability, no further extension of time shall be allowed by reason of the disability of the second person.

(4) No action to recover land or money charged on land shall be brought by virtue of this section by any person after the expiration of thirty years from the date on which the right of action accrued to that person or some person through whom he claims.

[(4A) If the action is one to which section 4A of this Act applies, subsection (1) above shall have effect as if for the words from "at any time" to "occurred)" there were substituted the words "by him at any time before the expiration of three years from the date when he ceased to be under a disability".]

(5) If the action is one to which section 10 of this Act applies, subsection (1) above shall have effect as if for the words "six years" there were substituted the words "two years".

(6) If the action is one to which section 11 or 12(2) of this Act applies, subsection (1) above shall have effect as if for the words "six years" there were substituted the words "three years".

[(7) If the action is one to which section 11A of this Act applies or one by virtue of section 6(1)(*a*) of the Consumer Protection Act 1987 (death caused by defective product), subsection (1) above—

(*a*) shall not apply to the time limit prescribed by subsection (3) of the said section 11A or to that time limit as applied by virtue of section 12(1) of this Act; and

(*b*) in relation to any other time limit prescribed by this Act shall have
effect as if for the words "six years" there were substituted the words
"three years".]   **[982]**

NOTES
Sub-s (4A): inserted by the Administration of Justice Act 1985, s 57(3).
Sub-s (7): added by the Consumer Protection Act 1987, s 6, Sch 1, para 4.

**[28A. Extension for cases where the limitation period is the period under section
14A(4)(*b*)**

(1) Subject to subsection (2) below, if in the case of any action for which a period
of limitation is prescribed by section 14A of this Act—

    (*a*) the period applicable in accordance with subsection (4) of that section
is the period mentioned in paragraph (*b*) of that subsection;

    (*b*) on the date which is for the purposes of that section the starting date
for reckoning that period the person by reference to whose knowledge
that date fell to be determined under subsection (5) of that section was
under a disability; and

    (*c*) section 28 of this Act does not apply to the action;

the action may be brought at any time before the expiration of three years from
the date when he ceased to be under a disability or died (whichever first
occurred) notwithstanding that the period mentioned above has expired.

(2) An action may not be brought by virtue of subsection (1) above after the
end of the period of limitation prescribed by section 14B of this Act.]   **[983]**

NOTES
Inserted by the Latent Damage Act 1986, s 2(1).

Acknowledgment and part payment

29. Fresh accrual of action on acknowledgment or part payment

(1) Subsections (2) and (3) below apply where any right of action (including a
foreclosure action) to recover land or an advowson or any right of a mortgagee
of personal property to bring a foreclosure action in respect of the property has
accrued.

(2) If the person in possession of the land, benefice or personal property in
question acknowledges the title of the person to whom the right of action has
accrued—

    (*a*) the right shall be treated as having accrued on and not before the date
of the acknowledgment; and

    (*b*) in the case of a right of action to recover land which has accrued to a
person entitled to an estate or interest taking effect on the
determination of an entailed interest against whom time is running
under section 27 of this Act, section 27 shall thereupon cease to apply
to the land.

(3) In the case of a foreclosure or other action by a mortgagee, if the person
in possession of the land, benefice or personal property in question or the person
liable for the mortgage debt makes any payment in respect of the debt (whether
of principal or interest) the right shall be treated as having accrued on and not
before the date of the payment.

(4) Where a mortgagee is by virtue of the mortgage in possession of any
mortgaged land and either—

    (*a*) receives any sum in respect of the principal or interest of the mortgage
debt; or

(*b*) acknowledges the title of the mortgagor, or his equity of redemption;

an action to redeem the land in his possession may be brought at any time before the expiration of twelve years from the date of the payment or acknowledgment.

(5) Subject to subsection (6) below, where any right of action has accrued to recover—

(*a*) any debt or other liquidated pecuniary claim; or
(*b*) any claim to the personal estate of a deceased person or to any share or interest in any such estate;

and the person liable or accountable for the claim acknowledges the claim or makes any payment in respect of it the right shall be treated as having accrued on and not before the date of the acknowledgment or payment.

(6) A payment of a part of the rent or interest due at any time shall not extend the period for claiming the ramainder then due, but any payment of interest shall be treated as a payment in respect of the principal debt.

(7) Subject to subsection (6) above, a current period of limitation may be repeatedly extended under this section by further acknowledgments or payments, but a right of action, once barred by this Act, shall not be revived by any subsequent acknowledgment or payment. **[984]**

30. Formal provisions as to acknowledgments and part payments

(1) To be effective for the purposes of section 29 of this Act, an acknowledgment must be in writing and signed by the person making it.

(2) For the purposes of section 29, any acknowledgment or payment—

(*a*) may be made by the agent of the person by whom it is required to be made under that section; and
(*b*) shall be made to the person, or to an agent of the person, whose title or claim is being acknowledged or, as the case may be, in respect of whose claim the payment is being made. **[985]**

31. Effect of acknowledgment or part payment on persons other than the maker or recipient

(1) An acknowledgment of the title to any land, benefice, or mortgaged personalty by any person in possession of it shall bind all other persons in possession during the ensuing period of limitation.

(2) A payment in respect of a mortgage debt by the mortgagor or any other person liable for the debt, or by any person in possession of the mortgaged property, shall, so far as any right of the mortgagee to foreclose or otherwise to recover the property is concerned, bind all other persons in possession of the mortgaged property during the ensuing period of limitation.

(3) Where two or more mortgagees are by virtue of the mortgage in possession of the mortgaged land, an acknowledgment of the mortgagor's title or of his equity of redemption by one of the mortgagees shall only bind him and his successors and shall not bind any other mortgagee or his successors.

(4) Where in a case within subsection (3) above the mortgagee by whom the acknowledgment is given is entitled to a part of the mortgaged land and not to any ascertained part of the mortgage debt the mortgagor shall be entitled to redeem that part of the land on payment, with interest, of the part of the

mortgage debt which bears the same proportion to the whole of the debt as the value of the part of the land bears to the whole of the mortgaged land.

(5) Where there are two or more mortgagors, and the title or equity of redemption of one of the mortgagors is acknowledged as mentioned above in this section, the acknowledgment shall be treated as having been made to all the mortgagors.

(6) An acknowledgment of any debt or other liquidated pecuniary claim shall bind the acknowledgor and his successors but not any other person.

(7) A payment made in respect of any debt or other liquidated pecuniary claim shall bind all persons liable in respect of the debt or claim.

(8) An acknowledgment by one of several personal representatives of any claim to the personal estate of a deceased person or to any share or interest in any such estate, or a payment by one of several personal representatives in respect of any such claim, shall bind the estate of the deceased person.

(9) In this section "successor", in relation to any mortgagee or person liable in respect of any debt or claim, means his personal representatives and any other person on whom the rights under the mortgage or, as the case may be, the liability in respect of the debt or claim devolve (whether on death or bankruptcy or the disposition of property or the determination of a limited estate or interest in settled property or otherwise). **[986]**

Fraud, concealment and mistake

32. Postponement of limitation period in case of fraud, concealment or mistake

(1) Subject to [subsections (3) and (4A)] below, where in the case of any action for which a period of limitation is prescribed by this Act, either—

    (*a*) the action is based upon the fraud of the defendant; or

    (*b*) any fact relevant to the plaintiff's right of action has been deliberately concealed from him by the defendant; or

    (*c*) the action is for relief from the consequences of a mistake;

the period of limitation shall not begin to run until the plaintiff has discovered the fraud, concealment or mistake (as the case may be) or could with reasonable diligence have discovered it.

References in this subsection to the defendant include references to the defendant's agent and to any person through whom the defendant claims and his agent.

(2) For the purposes of subsection (1) above, deliberate commission of a breach of duty in circumstances in which it is unlikely to be discovered for some time amounts to deliberate concealment of the facts involved in that breach of duty.

(3) Nothing in this section shall enable any action—

    (*a*) to recover, or recover the value of, any property; or

    (*b*) to enforce any charge against, or set aside any transaction affecting, any property;

to be brought against the purchaser of the property or any person claiming through him in any case where the property has been purchased for valuable consideration by an innocent third party since the fraud or concealment or (as the case may be) the transaction in which the mistake was made took place.

(4) A purchaser is an innocent third party for the purposes of this section—

    (*a*) in the case of fraud or concealment of any fact relevant to the plaintiff's right of action, if he was not a party to the fraud or (as the case may be) to the concealment of that fact and did not at the time of the purchase know or have reason to believe that the fraud or concealment had taken place; and

    (*b*) in the case of mistake, if he did not at the time of the purchase know or have reason to believe that the mistake had been made.

[(4A) Subsection (1) above shall not apply in relation to the time limit prescribed by section 11A(3) of this Act or in relation to that time limit as applied by virtue of section 12(1) of this Act.]

[(5) Sections 14A and 14B of this Act shall not apply to any action to which subsection (1)(*b*) above applies (and accordingly the period of limitation referred to in that subsection, in any case to which either of those sections would otherwise apply, is the period applicable under section 2 of this Act).]   **[987]**

NOTES
    Sub-s (1): words in square brackets substituted by the Consumer Protection Act 1987, s 6, Sch 1, para 5.
    Sub-s (4A): inserted by the Consumer Protection Act 1987, s 6, Sch 1, para 5.
    Sub-s (5): added by the Latent Damage Act 1986, s 2(2).

Discretionary exclusion of time limit for actions in respect of personal injuries or death

33. Discretionary exclusion of time limit for actions in respect of personal injuries or death

(1) If it appears to the court that it would be equitable to allow an action to proceed having regard to the degree to which—

    (*a*) the provisions of section 11 [or 11A] of this Act prejudice the plaintiff or any person whom he represents; and

    (*b*) any decision of the court under this subsection would prejudice the defendant or any person whom he represents;

the court may direct that those provisions shall not apply to the action, or shall not apply to any specified cause of action to which the action relates.

[(1A) The court shall not under this section disapply—

    (*a*) subsection (3) of section 11A; or

    (*b*) where the damages claimed by the plaintiff are confined to damages for loss of or damage to any property, any other provision in its application to an action by virtue of Part I of the Consumer Protection Act 1987.]

(2) The court shall not under this section disapply section 12(1) except where the reason why the person injured could no longer maintain an action was because of the time limit in section 11 [or subsection (4) of section 11A].

If, for example, the person injured could at his death no longer maintain an action under the Fatal Accidents Act 1976 because of the time limit in Article 29 in Schedule 1 to the Carriage by Air Act 1961, the court has no power to direct that section 12(1) shall not apply.

(3) In acting under this section the court shall have regard to all the circumstances of the case and in particular to—

(*a*) the length of, and the reasons for, the delay on the part of the plaintiff;
(*b*) the extent to which, having regard to the delay, the evidence adduced or likely to be adduced by the plaintiff or the defendant is or is likely to be less cogent than if the action had been brought within the time allowed by section 11[, by section 11A] or (as the case may be) by section 12;
(*c*) the conduct of the defendant after the cause of action arose, including the extent (if any) to which he responded to requests reasonably made by the plaintiff for information or inspection for the purpose of ascertaining facts which were or might be relevant to the plaintiff's cause of action against the defendant;
(*d*) the duration of any disability of the plaintiff arising after the date of the accrual of the cause of action;
(*e*) the extent to which the plaintiff acted promptly and reasonably once he knew whether or not the act or omission of the defendant, to which the injury was attributable, might be capable at that time of giving rise to an action for damages;
(*f*) the steps, if any, taken by the plaintiff to obtain medical, legal or other expert advice and the nature of any such advice he may have received.

(4) In a case where the person injured died when, because of section 11 [or subsection (4) of section 11A], he could no longer maintain an action and recover damages in respect of the injury, the court shall have regard in particular to the length of, and the reasons for, the delay on the part of the deceased.

(5) In a case under subsection (4) above, or any other case where the time limit, or one of the time limits, depends on the date of knowledge of a person other than the plaintiff, subsection (3) above shall have effect with appropriate modifications, and shall have effect in particular as if references to the plaintiff included references to any person whose date of knowledge is or was relevant in determining a time limit.

(6) A direction by the court disapplying the provisions of section 12(1) shall operate to disapply the provisions to the same effect in section 1(1) of the Fatal Accidents Act 1976.

(7) In this section "the court" means the court in which the action has been brought.

(8) References in this section to section 11 [or 11A] include references to that section as extended by any of the preceding provisions of this Part of this Act or by any provision of Part III of this Act.   [988]

NOTES
    Sub-s (1): words in square brackets inserted by the Consumer Protection Act 1987, s 6, Sch 1, para 6.
    Sub-s (1A) inserted by the Consumer Protection Act 1987, s 6, Sch 1, para 6.
    Sub-s (2): words in square brackets inserted by the Consumer Protection Act 1987, s 6, Sch 1, para 6.
    Sub-s (3): words in square brackets inserted by the Consumer Protection Act 1987, s 6, Sch 1, para 6.
    Sub-s (4): words in square brackets inserted by the Consumer Protection Act 1987, s 6, Sch 1, para 6.
    Sub-s (8): words in square brackets inserted by the Consumer Protection Act 1987, s 6, Sch 1, para 6.

PART III

MISCELLANEOUS AND GENERAL

35. New claims in pending actions: rules of court

(1) For the purposes of this Act, any new claim made in the course of any action shall be deemed to be a separate action and to have been commenced—

    (a) in the case of a new claim made in or by way of third party proceedings, on the date on which those proceedings were commenced; and

    (b) in the case of any other new claim, on the same date as the original action.

(2) In this section a new claim means any claim by way of set-off or counterclaim, and any claim involving either—

    (a) the addition or substitution of a new cause of action; or

    (b) the addition or substitution of a new party;

and "third party proceedings" means any proceedings brought in the course of any action by any party to the action against a person not previously a party to the action, other than proceedings brought by joining any such person as defendant to any claim already made in the original action by the party bringing the proceedings.

(3) Except as provided by section 33 of this Act or by rules of court, neither the High Court nor any county court shall allow a new claim within subsection (1)(b) above, other than an original set-off or counterclaim, to be made in the course of any action after the expiry of any time limit under this Act which would affect a new action to enforce that claim.

For the purposes of this subsection, a claim is an original set-off or an original counterclaim if it is a claim made by way of set-off or (as the case may be) by way of counterclaim by a party who has not previously made any claim in the action.

(4) Rules of court may provide for allowing a new claim to which subsection (3) above applies to be made as there mentioned, but only if the conditions specified in subsection (5) below are satisfied, and subject to any further restrictions the rules may impose.

(5) The conditions referred to in subsection (4) above are the following—

    (a) in the case of a claim involving a new cause of action, if the new cause of action arises out of the same facts or substantially the same facts as are already in issue on any claim previously made in the original action; and

    (b) in the case of a claim involving a new party, if the addition or substitution of the new party is necessary for the determination of the original action.

(6) The addition or substitution of a new party shall not be regarded for the purposes of subsection (5)(b) above as necessary for the determination of the original action unless either—

    (a) the new party is substituted for a party whose name was given in any claim made in the original action in mistake for the new party's name; or (*b*) any claim already made in the original action cannot be maintained by or against an existing party unless the new party is joined or substituted as plaintiff or defendant in that action.

(7) Subject to subsection (4) above, rules of court may provide for allowing a party to any action to claim relief in a new capacity in respect of a new cause of action notwithstanding that he had no title to make that claim at the date of the commencement of the action.

This subsection shall not be taken as prejudicing the power of rules of court to provide for allowing a party to claim relief in a new capacity without adding or substituting a new cause of action.

(8) Subsections (3) to (7) above shall apply in relation to a new claim made in the course of third party proceedings as if those proceedings were the original action, and subject to such other modifications as may be prescribed by rules of court in any case or class of case.

(9) . . . **[989]**

NOTES
Sub-s (9): repealed by the Supreme Court Act 1981, s 152(4), Sch 7.

36. Equitable jurisdiction and remedies

(1) The following time limits under this Act, that is to say—

    (*a*) the time limit under section 2 for actions founded on tort;
  [(*aa*)the time limit under section 4A for actions for libel or slander;]
    (*b*) the time limit under section 5 for actions founded on simple contract;
    (*c*) the time limit under section 7 for actions to enforce awards where the submission is not by an instrument under seal;
    (*d*) the time limit under section 8 for actions on a specialty;
    (*e*) the time limit under section 9 for actions to recover a sum recoverable by virtue of any enactment; and
    (*f*) the time limit under section 24 for actions to enforce a judgment;

shall not apply to any claim for specific performance of a contract or for an injunction or for other equitable relief, except in so far as any such time limit may be applied by the court by analogy in like manner as the corresponding time limit under any enactment repealed by the Limitation Act 1939 was applied before 1st July 1940.

(2) Nothing in this Act shall affect any equitable jurisdiction to refuse relief on the ground of acquiescence or otherwise. **[990]**

NOTES
Sub-s (1): para (*aa*) inserted by the Administration of Justice Act 1985, s 57(5).

38. Interpretation

(1) In this Act, unless the context otherwise requires—

    "action" includes any proceeding in a court of law, including an ecclesiastical court;
    "land" includes corporeal hereditaments, tithes and rentcharges and any legal or equitable estate or interest therein, including an interest in the proceeds of the sale of land held upon trust for sale, but except as provided above in this definition does not include any incorporeal hereditament;

"personal estate" and "personal property" do not include chattels real;

"personal injuries" includes any disease and any impairment of a person's physical or mental condition, and "injury" and cognate expressions shall be construed accordingly;

"rent" includes a rentcharge and a rentservice; "rentcharge" means any annuity or periodical sum of money charged upon or payable out of land, except a rent service or interest on a mortgage on land;

"settled land", "statutory owner" and "tenant for life" have the same meanings respectively as in the Settled Land Act 1925;

"trust" and "trustee" have the same meanings respectively as in the Trustee Act 1925; and

"trust for sale" has the same meaning as in the Law of Property Act 1925.

(2) For the purposes of this Act a person shall be treated as under a disability while he is an infant, or of unsound mind.

(3) For the purposes of subsection (2) above a person is of unsound mind if he is a person who, by reason of mental disorder within the meaning of the [Mental Health Act 1983], is incapable of managing and administering his property and affairs.

(4) Without prejudice to the generality of subsection (3) above, a person shall be conclusively presumed for the purposes of subsection (2) above to be of unsound mind—

> (*a*) while he is liable to be detained or subject to guardianship under [the Mental Health Act 1983 (otherwise than by virtue of section 35 or 89)]; and
>
> [(*b*) while he is receiving treatment as an in-patient in any hospital within the meaning of the Mental Health Act 1983 or mental nursing home within the meaning of the Nursing Homes Act 1975 without being liable to be detained under the said Act of 1983 (otherwise than by virtue of section 35 or 89), being treatment which follows without any interval a period during which he was liable to be detained or subject to guardianship under the Mental Health Act 1959, or the said Act of 1983 (otherwise than by virtue of section 35 or 89) or by virtue of any enactment repealed or excluded by the Mental Health Act 1959].

(5) Subject to subsection (6) below, a person shall be treated as claiming through another person if he became entitled by, through, under, or by the act of that other person to the right claimed, and any person whose estate or interest might have been barred by a person entitled to an entailed interest in possession shall be treated as claiming through the person so entitled.

(6) A person becoming entitled to any estate or interest by virtue of a special power of appointment shall not be treated as claiming through the appointor.

(7) References in this Act to a right of action to recover land shall include references to a right to enter into possession of the land or, in the case of rentcharges and tithes, to distrain for arrears of rent or tithe, and references to the bringing of such an action shall include references to the making of such an entry or distress.

(8) References in this Act to the possession of land shall, in the case of tithes and rentcharges, be construed as references to the receipt of the tithe or rent, and references to the date of dispossession or discontinuance of possession of land shall, in the case of rent charges, be construed as references to the date of the last receipt of rent.

(9) References in Part II of this Act to a right of action shall include references to—

    (*a*) a cause of action;

    (*b*) a right to receive money secured by a mortgage or charge on any property;

    (*c*) a right to recover proceeds of the sale of land; and

    (*d*) a right to receive a share or interest in the personal estate of a deceased person.

(10) References in Part II to the date of the accrual of a right of action shall be construed—

    (*a*) in the case of an action upon a judgment, as references to the date on which the judgment became enforceable; and

    (*b*) in the case of an action to recover arrears of rent or interest, or damages in respect of arrears of rent or interest, as references to the date on which the rent or interest became due.   **[991]**

NOTES

Sub-s (3): words in square brackets substituted by the Mental Health Act 1983, s 148, Sch 4, para 55.

Sub-s (4): words in square brackets substituted by the Mental Health Act 1983, s 148, Sch 4, para 55.

41. Short title, commencement and extent

(1) This Act may be cited as the Limitation Act 1980.

(2) This Act, except section 35, shall come into force on 1st May 1981.

. . .   **[992]**

SCHEDULES

SCHEDULE 1

Section 15(6), (7)

PROVISIONS WITH RESPECT TO ACTIONS TO RECOVER LAND

PART I

ACCRUAL OF RIGHTS OF ACTION TO RECOVER LAND

Accrual of right of action in case of present interests in land

1. Where the person bringing an action to recover land, or some person through whom he claims, has been in possession of the land, and has while entitled to the land been dispossessed or discontinued his possession, the right of action shall be treated as having accrued on the date of the dispossession or discontinuance.

2. Where any person brings an action to recover any land of a deceased person (whether under a will or on intestacy) and the deceased person—

    (*a*) was on the date of his death in possession of the land or, in the case of a rentcharge created by will or taking effect upon his death, in possession of the land charged; and

    (*b*) was the last person entitled to the land to be in possession of it;

the right of action shall be treated as having accrued on the date of his death.

3. Where any person brings an action to recover land, being an estate or interest in possession assured otherwise than by will to him, or to some person through whom he claims, and—

    (*a*) the person making the assurance was on the date when the assurance took effect in possession of the land or, in the case of a rentcharge created by the assurance, in possession of the land charged; and (*b*) no person has been in possession of the land by virtue of the assurance;

the right of action shall be treated as having accrued on the date when the assurance took effect.

Accrual of right of action in case of future interests

4. The right of action to recover any land shall, in a case where—

(*a*) the estate or interest claimed was an estate or interest in reversion or remainder or any other future estate or interest; and

(*b*) no person has taken possession of the land by virtue of the estate or interest claimed;

be treated as having accrued on the date on which the estate or interest fell into possession by the determination of the preceding estate or interest.

5.—(1) Subject to sub-paragraph (2) below, a tenancy from year to year or other period, without a lease in writing, shall for the purposes of this Act be treated as being determined at the expiration of the first year or other period; and accordingly the right of action of the person entitled to the land subject to the tenancy shall be treated as having accrued at the date on which in accordance with this sub-paragraph the tenancy is determined.

(2) Where any rent has subsequently been received in respect of the tenancy, the right of action shall be treated as having accrued on the date of the last receipt of rent.

6.—(1) Where—

(*a*) any person is in possession of land by virtue of a lease in writing by which a rent of not less than ten pounds a year is reserved; and

(*b*) the rent is received by some person wrongfully claiming to be entitled to the land in reversion immediately expectant on the determination of the lease; and

(*c*) no rent is subsequently received by the person rightfully so entitled;

the right of action to recover the land of the person rightfully so entitled shall be treated as having accrued on the date when the rent was first received by the person wrongfully claiming to be so entitled and not on the date of the determination of the lease.

(2) Sub-paragraph (1) above shall not apply to any lease granted by the Crown.

Accrual of right of action in case of forfeiture or breach of condition

7.—(1) Subject to sub-paragraph (2) below, a right of action to recover land by virtue of a forfeiture or breach of condition shall be treated as having accrued on the date on which the forfeiture was incurred or the condition broken.

(2) If any such right has accrued to a person entitled to an estate or interest in reversion or remainder and the land was not recovered by virtue of that right, the right of action to recover the land shall not be treated as having accrued to that person until his estate or interest fell into possession, as if no such forfeiture or breach of condition had occurred.

Right of action not to accrue or continue unless there is adverse possession

8.—(1) No right of action to recover land shall be treated as accruing unless the land is in the possession of some person in whose favour the period of limitation can run (referred to below in this paragraph as "adverse possession"); and where under the preceding provisions of this Schedule any such right of action is treated as accruing on a certain date and no person is in adverse possession on that date, the right of action shall not be treated as accruing unless and until adverse possession is taken of the land.

(2) Where a right of action to recover land has accrued and after its accrual, before the right is barred, the land ceases to be in adverse possession, the right of action shall no longer be treated as having accrued and no fresh right of action shall be treated as accruing unless and until the land is again taken into adverse possession.

(3) For the purposes of this paragraph—

(*a*) possession of any land subject to a rentcharge by a person (other than the person entitled to the rentcharge) who does not pay the rent shall be treated as adverse possession of the rentcharge; and

(*b*) receipt of rent under a lease by a person wrongfully claiming to be entitled to the land in reversion immediately expectant on the determination of the lease shall be treated as adverse possession of the land.

(4) For the purpose of determining whether a person occupying any land is in adverse possession of the land it shall not be assumed by implication of law that his occupation is by permission of the person entitled to the land merely by virtue of the fact that his occupation is not inconsistent with the latter's present or future enjoyment of the land.

This provision shall not be taken as prejudicing a finding to the effect that a person's occupation of any land is by implied permission of the person entitled to the land in any case where such a finding is justified on the actual facts of the case.

Possession of beneficiary not adverse to others interested in settled land or land held on trust for sale

9. Where any settled land or any land held on trust for sale is in the possession of a person entitled to a beneficial interest in the land or in the proceeds of sale (not being a person solely or absolutely entitled to the land or the proceeds), no right of action to recover the land shall be treated for the purposes of this Act as accruing during that possession to any person in whom the land is vested as tenant for life, statutory owner or trustee, or to any other person entitled to a beneficial interest in the land or the proceeds of sale. **[993]**

PART II

Modifications of Section 15 where Crown or certain Corporations Sole are involved

10. Subject to paragraph 11 below, section 15(1) of this Act shall apply to the bringing of an action to recover any land by the Crown or by any spiritual or eleemosynary corporation sole with the substitution for the reference to twelve years of a reference to thirty years.

11.—(1) An action to recover foreshore may be brought by the Crown at any time before the expiration of sixty years from the date mentioned in section 15(1) of this Act.

(2) Where any right of action to recover land which has ceased to be foreshore but remains in the ownership of the Crown accrued when the land was foreshore, the action may be brought at any time before the expiration of—

(*a*) sixty years from the date of accrual of the right of action; or

(*b*) thirty years from the date when the land ceased to be foreshore:

whichever period first expires.

(3) In this paragraph "foreshore" means the shore and bed of the sea and of any tidal water, below the line of the medium high tide between the spring tides and the neap tides.

12. Notwithstanding section 15(1) of this Act, where in the case of any action brought by a person other than the Crown or a spiritual or eleemosynary corporation sole the right of action first accrued to the Crown or any such corporation sole through whom the person in question claims, the action may be brought at any time before the expiration of—

(*a*) the period during which the action could have been brought by the Crown or the corporation sole; or

(*b*) twelve years from the date on which the right of action accrued to some person other than the Crown or the corporation sole;

whichever period first expires.

13. Section 15(2) of this Act shall apply in any case where the Crown or a spiritual or eleemosynary corporation sole is entitled to the succeeding estate or interest with the substitution—

(*a*) for the reference to twelve years of a reference to thirty years; and
(*b*) for the reference to six years of a reference to twelve years. [994]

HIGHWAYS ACT 1980
(c 66)

ARRANGEMENT OF SECTIONS

PART III
CREATION OF HIGHWAYS

PART IV
MAINTENANCE OF HIGHWAYS

Highways maintainable at public expense

Methods whereby highways may become maintainable at public expense

PART VIII
STOPPING UP AND DIVERSION OF HIGHWAYS AND STOPPING UP OF MEANS OF ACCESS TO HIGHWAYS

Stopping up and diversion of highways

PART IX
LAWFUL AND UNLAWFUL INTERFERENCE WITH HIGHWAYS AND STREETS

Damage to highways, streets etc

PART XI
MAKING UP OF PRIVATE STREETS

The private street works code

PART XIV

MISCELLANEOUS AND SUPPLEMENTARY PROVISIONS

Savings etc

An Act to consolidate the Highways Acts 1959 to 1971 and related enactments, with amendments to give effect to recommendations of the Law Commission
[13 November 1980]

PART III

CREATION OF HIGHWAYS

25. Creation of footpath or bridleway by agreement

(1) A local authority may enter into an agreement with any person having the necessary power in that behalf for the dedication by that person of a footpath or bridleway over land in their area.

An agreement under this section is referred to in this Act as a "public path creation agreement".

(2) For the purposes of this section "local authority"—

(*a*) in relation to land outside Greater London means a county council, a district council or a joint planning board within the meaning of [the Town and Country Planning Act 1990], being a board for an area which comprises any part of a National Park; and

(*b*) in relation to land in Greater London means . . . a London borough council or the Common Council.

(3) Before entering into an agreement under this section a local authority shall consult any other local authority or authorities in whose area the land concerned is situated.

(4) An agreement under this section shall be on such terms as to payment or otherwise as may be specified in the agreement and may, if it is so agreed, provide for the dedication of the footpath or bridleway subject to limitations or conditions affecting the public right of way over it.

(5) Where a public path creation agreement has been made it shall be the duty of the local authority who are a party to it to take all necessary steps for securing that the footpath or bridleway is dedicated in accordance with it.

[(6) As soon as may be after the dedication of a footpath or bridleway in accordance with a public path creation agreement, the local authority who are party to the agreement shall give notice of the dedication by publication in at least one local newspaper circulating in the area in which the land to which the agreement relates is situated.]   **[995]**

NOTES
    Sub-s (2): words in square brackets substituted by the Planning (Consequential Provisions) Act 1990, s 4, Sch 2, para 45; words omitted repealed by the Local Government Act 1985, s 102, Sch 17.
    Sub-s (6): added by the Wildlife and Countryside Act 1981, s 64.

26. Compulsory powers for creation of footpaths and bridleways

(1) Where it appears to a local authority that there is need for a footpath or bridleway over land in their area and they are satisfied that, having regard to—

  (a) the extent to which the path or way would add to the convenience or enjoyment of a substantial section of the public, or to the convenience of persons resident in the area, and

  (b) the effect which the creation of the path or way would have on the rights of persons interested in the land, account being taken of the provisions as to compensation contained in section 28 below,

it is expedient that the path or way should be created, the authority may by order made by them and submitted to and confirmed by the Secretary of State, or confirmed by them as an unopposed order, create a footpath or bridleway over the land.

An order under this section is referred to in this Act as a "public path creation order"; and for the purposes of this section "local authority" has the same meaning as in section 25 above.

(2) Where it appears to the Secretary of State in a particular case that there is need for a footpath or bridleway as mentioned in subsection (1) above, and he is satisfied as mentioned in that subsection, he may, after consultation with each body which is a local authority for the purposes of this section in relation to the land concerned, make a public path creation order creating the footpath or bridleway.

(3) A local authority shall, before exercising any power under this section, consult any other local authority or authorities in whose area the land concerned is situated.

(4) A right of way created by a public path creation order may be either unconditional or subject to such limitations or conditions as may be specified in the order.

(5) A public path creation order shall be in such form as may be prescribed by regulations made by the Secretary of State, and shall contain a map, on such scale as may be so prescribed, defining the land over which a footpath or bridleway is thereby created.

(6) Schedule 6 to this Act shall have effect as to the making, confirmation, validity and date of operation of public path creation orders.   **[996]**

27. Making up of new footpaths and bridleways

(1) On the dedication of a footpath or bridleway in pursuance of a public path creation agreement, or on the coming into operation of a public path creation order, being—

> (a) an agreement or order made by a local authority who are not the highway authority for the path in question,or
>
> (b) an order made by the Secretary of State under section 26(2) above in relation to which he directs that this subsection shall apply,

the highway authority shall survey the path or way and shall certify what work (if any) appears to them to be necessary to bring it into a fit condition for use by the public as a footpath or bridleway, as the case may be, and shall serve a copy of the certificate on the local authority mentioned in paragraph (a) above or, where paragraph (b) applies, on such local authority as the Secretary of State may direct.

(2) It shall be the duty of the highway authority to carry out any works specified in a certificate under subsection (1) above, and where the authority have carried out the work they may recover from the authority on whom a copy of the certificate was served any expenses reasonably incurred by them in carrying out that work, including any expenses so incurred in the discharge of any liability for compensation in respect of the carrying out thereof.

(3) Notwithstanding anything in the preceding provisions of this section, where an agreement or order is made as mentioned in subsection (1)(a) above, the local authority making the agreement or order may—

> (a) with the consent of the highway authority carry out (in place of the highway authority) the duties imposed by that subsection on the highway authority; and
>
> (b) carry out any works which, apart from this subsection, it would be the duty of the highway authority to carry out under subsection (2) above.

(4) Where the Secretary of State makes a public path creation order under section 26(2) above, he may direct that subsection (5) below shall apply.

(5) Where the Secretary of State gives such a direction—

> (a) the local authority who, on the coming into force of the order, became the highway authority for the path or way in question shall survey the path or way and shall certify what work (if any) appears to them to be necessary to bring it into a fit condition for use by the public as a footpath or bridleway, as the case may be, and shall furnish the Secretary of State with a copy of the certificate;
>
> (b) if the Secretary of State is not satisfied with a certificate made under the foregoing paragraph, he shall either cause a local inquiry to be held or shall give to the local authority an opportunity of being heard by a person appointed by him for the purpose and, after considering the report of the person appointed to hold the inquiry or the person so appointed as aforesaid, shall make such order either confirming or varying the certificate as he may think fit; and
>
> (c) subject to the provisions of the last foregoing paragraphs, it shall be the duty of the highway authority to carry out the work specified in a certificate made by them under paragraph (a) above.

(6) In this section "local authority" means any council or any such joint planning board as is mentioned in section 25(2)(a) above. **[997]**

28. Compensation for loss caused by public path creation order

(1) Subject to the following provisions of this section, if, on a claim made in accordance with this section, it is shown that the value of an interest of a person in land is depreciated, or that a person has suffered damage by being disturbed in his enjoyment of land, in consequence of the coming into operation of a public path creation order, the authority by whom the order was made shall pay to that person compensation equal to the amount of the depreciation or damage.

(2) A claim for compensation under this section shall be made within such time and in such manner as may be prescribed by regulations made by the Secretary of State, and shall be made to the authority by whom the order was made.

(3) For the purposes of the application of this section to an order made by the Secretary of State under section 26(2) above, references in this section to the authority by whom the order was made are to be construed as references to such one of the authorities referred to in that subsection as may be nominated by the Secretary of State for the purposes of this subsection.

(4) Nothing in this section confers on any person, in respect of a footpath or bridleway created by a public path creation order, a right to compensation for depreciation of the value of an interest in the land, or for disturbance in his enjoyment of land, not being in either case land over which the path or way was created or land held therewith, unless the creation of the path or way would have been actionable at his suit if it had been effected otherwise than in the exercise of statutory powers.

(5) In this section "interest", in relation to land, includes any estate in land and any right over land, whether the right is exercisable by virtue of the ownership of an interest in land or by virtue of a licence or agreement, and in particular includes sporting rights. **[998]**

29. Protection for agriculture and forestry

In the exercise of their functions under this Part of this Act relating to the making of public path creation agreements and public path creation orders it shall be the duty of councils and joint planning boards to have due regard to the needs of agriculture and forestry. **[999]**

30. Dedication of highway by agreement with parish or community council

(1) The council of a parish or community may enter into an agreement with any person having the necessary power in that behalf for the dedication by that person of a highway over land in the parish or community or an adjoining parish or community in any case where such a dedication would in the opinion of the council be beneficial to the inhabitants of the parish or community or any part thereof.

(2) Where the council of a parish or community have entered into an agreement under subsection (1) above for the dedication of a highway they may carry out any works (including works of maintenance or improvement) incidental to or consequential on the making of the agreement or contribute towards the expense of carrying out such works, and may agree or combine with the council of any other parish or community to carry out such works or to make such a contribution. **[1000]**

31. Dedication of way as highway presumed after public use for 20 years

(1) Where a way over any land, other than a way of such a character that use of it by the public could not give rise at common law to any presumption of dedication, has been actually enjoyed by the public as of right and without interruption for a full period of 20 years, the way is to be deemed to have been dedicated as a highway unless there is sufficient evidence that there was no intention during that period to dedicate it.

(2) The period of 20 years referred to in subsection (1) above is to be calculated retrospectively from the date when the right of the public to use the way is brought into question, whether by a notice such as is mentioned in subsection (3) below or otherwise.

(3) Where the owner of the land over which any such way as aforesaid passes—

    (a) has erected in such manner as to be visible to persons using the way a notice inconsistent with the dedication of the way as a highway, and

    (b) has maintained the notice after the 1st January 1934, or any later date on which it was erected,

the notice, in the absence of proof of a contrary intention, is sufficient evidence to negative the intention to dedicate the way as a highway.

(4) In the case of land in the possession of a tenant for a term of years, or from year to year, any person for the time being entitled in reversion to the land shall, notwithstanding the existence of the tenancy, have the right to place and maintain such a notice as is mentioned in subsection (3) above, so, however, that no injury is done thereby to the business or occupation of the tenant.

(5) Where a notice erected as mentioned in subsection (3) above is subsequently torn down or defaced, a notice given by the owner of the land to the appropriate council that the way is not dedicated as a highway is, in the absence of proof of a contrary intention, sufficient evidence to negative the intention of the owner of the land to dedicate the way as a highway.

(6) An owner of land may at any time deposit with the appropriate council—

    (a) a map of the land on a scale of not less than 6 inches to 1 mile, and

    (b) a statement indicating what ways (if any) over the land he admits to have been dedicated as highways;

and, in any case in which such a deposit has been made, statutory declarations made by that owner or by his successors in title and lodged by him or them with the appropriate council at any time—

    (i) within six years from the date of the deposit, or

    (ii) within six years from the date on which any previous declaration was last lodged under this section,

to the effect that no additional way (other than any specifically indicated in the declaration) over the land delineated on the said map has been dedicated as a highway since the date of the deposit, or since the date of the lodgment of such previous declaration, as the case may be, are, in the absence of proof of a contrary intention, sufficient evidence to negative the intention of the owner or his successors in title to dedicate any such additional way as a highway.

(7) For the purposes of the foregoing provisions of this section "owner", in relation to any land, means a person who is for the time being entitled to dispose of the fee simple in the land; and for the purposes of subsections (5) and (6) above "the appropriate council" means the council of the county [, metropolitan

district] or London borough in which the way (in the case of subsection (5)) or the land (in the case of subsection (6)) is situated or, where the way or land is situated in the City, the Common Council.

(8) Nothing in this section affects any incapacity of a corporation or other body or person in possession of land for public or statutory purposes to dedicate a way over that land as a highway if the existence of a highway would be incompatible with those purposes.

(9) Nothing in this section operates to prevent the dedication of a way as a highway being presumed on proof of user for any less period than 20 years, or being presumed or proved in any circumstances in which it might have been presumed or proved immediately before the commencement of this Act.

(10) Nothing in this section or section 32 below affects [section 56(1) of the Wildlife and Countryside Act 1981 (which provides that a definitive map and statment] are conclusive evidence as to the existence of the highways shown on the map and as to certain particulars contained in the statement) . . .

(11) For the purposes of this section "land" includes land covered with water. **[1001]**

NOTES
Sub-s (7): words in square brackets inserted by the Local Government Act 1985, s 8, Sch 4, para 7.
Sub-s (10): words in square brackets substituted and words omitted repealed by the Wildlife and Countryside Act 1981, s 72(11).

33. Protection of rights of reversioners

The person entitled to the remainder or reversion immediately expectant upon the determination of a tenancy for life, or pour autre vie, in land shall have the like remedies by action for trespass or an injunction to prevent the acquisition by the public of a right of way over that land as if he were in possession thereof. **[1002]**

35. Creation of walkways by agreement

(1) An agreement under this section may be entered into—

    (*a*) by a local highway authority, after consultation with the council of any [non-metropolitan] district in which the land concerned is situated;

    (*b*) by a [non-metropolitan] district council, either alone or jointly with the local highway authority, after consultation with the local highway authority.

(2) An agreement under this section is an agreement with any person having an interest in any land on which a building is, or is proposed to be, situated, being a person who by virtue of that interest has the necessary power in that behalf,—

    (*a*) for the provision of ways over, through or under parts of the building, or the building when constructed, as the case may be, or parts of any structure attached, or to be attached, to the building; and

    (*b*) for the dedication by that person of those ways as footpaths subject to such limitations and conditions, if any, affecting the public right of way thereover as may be specified in the agreement and to any rights reserved by the agreement to that person and any person deriving title to the land under him.

A footpath created in pursuance of an agreement under this section is referred to below as a "walkway".

(3) An agreement under this section may make provision for—

    (*a*) the maintenance, cleansing and drainage of any walkway to which the agreement relates;

    (*b*) the lighting of such walkway and of that part of the building or structure which will be over or above it;

    (*c*) the provision and maintenance of support for such walkway;

    (*d*) entitling the authority entering into the agreement or, where the agreement is entered into jointly by a [non-metropolitan] district council and a local highway authority, either of those authorities to enter on any building or structure in which such walkway will be situated and to execute any works necessary to secure the performance of any obligation which any person is for the time being liable to perform by virtue of the agreement or of subsection (4) below;

    (*e*) the making of payments by the authority entering into the agreement or, where the agreement is entered into jointly by a [non-metropolitan] district council and a local highway authority, either of those authorities to any person having an interest in the land or building affected by the agreement;

    (*f*) the termination, in such manner and subject to such conditions as may be specified in the agreement, of the right of the public to use such walkway;

    (*g*) any incidental and consequential matters.

(4) Any covenant (whether positive or restrictive) contained in an agreement under this section and entered into by a person having an interest in any land affected by the agreement shall be binding upon persons deriving title to the land under the covenantor to the same extent as it is binding upon the covenantor notwithstanding that it would not have been binding upon those persons apart from the provisions of this subsection, and shall be enforceable against those persons by the local highway authority.

(5) A covenant contained in an agreement under this section and entered into by a person having an interest in any land affected by the agreement is a local land charge.

(6) Where an agreement has been entered into under this section the appropriate authority may make byelaws regulating—

    (*a*) the conduct of persons using any walkway to which the agreement relates;

    (*b*) the times at which any such walkway may be closed to the public;

    (*c*) the placing or retention of anything (including any structure or projection) in, on or over any such walkway.

(7) For the purposes of subsection (6) above, "the appropriate authority" means—

    (*a*) where the agreement was entered into by a local highway authority, that authority;

    (*b*) where the agreement was entered into by a [non-metropolitan] district council alone, that council;

    (*c*) where the agreement was entered into by a district council jointly with the local highway authority, the local highway authority; but in cases falling within paragraph (*c*) above the local highway authority shall before making any byelaw consult the district council, and in exercising his power of confirmation the Minister shall have regard to any dispute between the local highway authority and the district council.

(8) Not less than 2 months before an authority propose to make byelaws under subsection (6) above they shall display in a conspicuous position on or adjacent to the walkway in question notice of their intention to make such byelaws.

(9) A notice under subsection (8) above shall specify the place where a copy of the proposed byelaws may be inspected and the period, which shall not be less than 6 weeks from the date on which the notice was first displayed as aforesaid, within which representations may be made to the authority, and the authority shall consider any representations made to them within that period.

(10) The Minister of the Crown having power by virtue of section 236 of the Local Government Act 1972 to confirm byelaws made under subsection (6) above may confirm them with or without modifications; and if he proposes to confirm them with modifications he may, before confirming them, direct the authority by whom they were made to give notice of the proposed modifications to such persons and in such manner as may be specified in the direction.

(11) Subject to subsection (12) below, the Minister, after consulting such representative organisations as he thinks fit, may make regulations—

(a) for preventing any enactment or instrument relating to highways or to things done on or in connection with highways from applying to walkways which have been, or are to be, created in pursuance of agreements under this section or to things done on or in connection with such walkways;

(b) for amending, modifying or adapting any such enactment or instrument in its application to such walkways;

(c) without prejudice to the generality of paragraphs (a) and (b) above, for excluding, restricting or regulating the rights of statutory undertakers, . . . [. . . and the operators of telecommunications code systems to place] and maintain apparatus in, under, over, along or across such walkways;

(d) without prejudice as aforesaid, for defining the circumstances and manner in which such walkways may be closed periodically or temporarily or stopped up and for prescribing the procedure to be followed before such a walkway is stopped up.

(12) Regulations under this section shall not exclude the rights of statutory undertakers, . . . [. . . and the operators of telecommunications code systems to place] and maintain apparatus in, under, along or across any part of a walkway, being a part which is not supported by any structure.

(13) Without prejudice to subsection (11) above, regulations under this section may make different provisions for different classes of walkways and may include such incidental, supplemental and consequential provisions (and, in particular, provisions relating to walkways provided in pursuance of agreements made before the coming into operation of the regulations) as appear to the Minister to be expedient for the purposes of the regulations.

(14) Nothing in this section is to be taken as affecting any other provision of this Act, or any other enactment, by virtue of which highways may be created.   **[1003]**

NOTES

Sub-s (1): words in square brackets inserted by the Local Government Act 1985, s 8, Sch 4, para 9.

Sub-s (3): words in square brackets inserted by the Local Government Act 1985, s 8, Sch 4, para 9.

Sub-s (7): words in square brackets inserted by the Local Government Act 1985, s 8, Sch 4, para 9.

Sub-s (11): words in square brackets substituted by the Telecommunications Act 1984, s 109, Sch 4, para 76; words omitted repealed by the Water Act 1989, s 190(3), Sch 27, Part I.

Sub-s (12): words in square brackets substituted by the Telecommunications Act 1984, s 8, Sch 4, para 9; words omitted repealed by the Water Act 1989, s 190(3), Sch 27, Part I.

PART IV

MAINTENANCE OF HIGHWAYS

Highways maintainable at public expense

36. Highways maintainable at public expense

(1) All such highways as immediately before the commencement of this Act were highways maintainable at the public expense for the purposes of the Highways Act 1959 continue to be so maintainable (subject to this section and to any order of a magistrates' court under section 47 below) for the purposes of this Act.

(2) Without prejudice to any other enactment (whether contained in this Act or not) whereby a highway may become for the purposes of this Act a highway maintainable at the public expense, and subject to this section and section 232(7) below, and to any order of a magistrates' court under section 47 below, the following highways (not falling within subsection (1) above) shall for the purposes of this Act be highways maintainable at the public expense:—

(a) a highway constructed by a highway authority, otherwise than on behalf of some other person who is not a highway authority;

(b) a highway constructed by a council within their own area under [Part II of the Housing Act 1985], other than one in respect of which the local highway authority are satisfied that it has not been properly constructed, and a highway constructed by a council outside their own area under [the said Part II], being, in the latter case, a highway the liability to maintain which is, by virtue of [the said Part II], vested in the council who are the local highway authority for the area in which the highway is situated;

(c) a highway that is a trunk road or a special road; . . .

(d) a highway, being a footpath or bridleway, created in consequence of a public path creation order or a public path diversion order or in consequence of an order made by the Minister of Transport or the Secretary of State under [section 247 of the Town and Country Planning Act 1990 or by a competent authority under section 257 of that Act], or dedicated in pursuance of a public path creation agreement;

[(e) a highway, being a footpath or bridleway, created in consequence of a rail crossing diversion order, or of an order made under section 14 or 16 of the Harbours Act 1964, or of an order made under section 1 or 3 of the Transport and Works Act 1992.]

(3) Paragraph (c) of subsection (2) above is not to be construed as referring to a part of a trunk road or special road consisting of a bridge or other part which a person is liable to maintain under a charter or special enactment, or by reason of tenure, enclosure or prescription.

[(3A) Paragraph (*e*) of subsection (2) above shall not apply to a footpath or bridleway, or to any part of a footpath or bridleway, which by virtue of an order of a kind referred to in that subsection is maintainable otherwise than at the public expense.]

(4) Subject to subsection (5) below, where there occurs any event on the occurrence of which, under any rule of law relating to the duty of maintaining a highway by reason of tenure, enclosure or prescription, a highway would, but for the enactment which abrogated the former rule of law under which a duty of maintaining highways fell on the inhabitants at large (section 38(1) of the Highways Act 1959) or any other enactment, become, or cease to be, maintainable by the inhabitants at large of any area, the highway shall become, or cease to be, a highway which for the purposes of this Act is a highway maintainable at the public expense.

(5) A highway shall not by virtue of subsection (4) above become a highway which for the purposes of this Act is a highway maintainable at the public expense unless either—

(*a*) it was a highway before 31st August 1835; or
(*b*) it became a highway after that date and has at some time been maintainable by the inhabitants at large of any area or a highway maintainable at the public expense;

and a highway shall not by virtue of that subsection cease to be a highway maintainable at the public expense if it is a highway which under any rule of law would become a highway maintainable by reason of enclosure but is prevented from becoming such a highway by section 51 below.

(6) The council of every county [, metropolitan district] and London borough and the Common Council shall cause to be made, and shall keep corrected up to date, a list of the streets within their area which are highways maintainable at the public expense.

(7) Every list made under subsection (6) above shall be kept deposited at the offices of the council by whom it was made and may be inspected by any person free of charge at all reasonable hours and in the case of a list made by the council of a county, the county council shall supply to the council of each district in the county an up to date list of the streets within the area of the district that are highways maintainable at the public expense, and the list so supplied shall be kept deposited at the office of the district council and may be inspected by any person free of charge at all reasonable hours. **[1004]**

NOTES
    Commencement: 31 January 1993 (sub-s (3A)); 1 January 1981 (remainder) (SI 1992 No 3144).
    Sub-s (2): in para (*b*) words in square brackets substituted by the Housing (Consequential Provisions) Act 1985, s 4, Sch 2, para 47; word omitted from para (*c*) repealed and para (*e*) added by the Transport and Works Act 1992, ss 64(2), (3), 68, Sch 4, Part I; in para (*d*) words in square brackets substituted by the Planning (Consequential Provisions) Act 1990, s 4, Sch 2, para 45(3).
    Sub-s (3A): inserted by the Transport and Works Act 1992, s 64(4).
    Sub-s (6): words in square brackets inserted by the Local Government Act 1985, s 8, Sch 4, para 7.

Methods whereby highways may become maintainable at public expense

38. Power of highway authorities to adopt by agreement

(1) Subject to subsection (2) below, where any person is liable under a special enactment or by reason of tenure, enclosure or prescription to maintain a highway, the Minister, in the case of a trunk road, or a local highway authority,

in any other case, may agree with that person to undertake the maintenance of that highway; and where an agreement is made under this subsection the highway to which the agreement relates shall, on such date as may be specified in the agreement, become for the purposes of this Act a highway maintainable at the public expense and the liability of that person to maintain the highway shall be extinguished.

(2) A local highway authority shall not have power to make an agreement under subsection (1) above with respect to a highway with respect to which they or any other highway authority have power to make an agreement under Part V or Part XII of this Act.

[(3) A local highway authority may agree with any person to undertake the maintenance of a way—

(a) which that person is willing and has the necessary power to dedicate as a highway, or

(b) which is to be constructed by that person, or by a highway authority on his behalf, and which he proposes to dedicate as a highway;

and where an agreement is made under this subsection the way to which the agreement relates shall, on such date as may be specified in the agreement, become for the purposes of this Act a highway maintainable at the public expense.

(3A) The Minister may agree with any person to undertake the maintenance of a road—

(a) which that person is willing and has the necessary power to dedicate as a highway, or

(b) which is to be constructed by that person, or by a highway authority on his behalf, and which he proposes to dedicate as a highway,

and which the Minister proposes should become a trunk road; and where an agreement is made under this subsection the road shall become for the purposes of this Act a highway maintainable at the public expense on the date on which an order comes into force under section 10 directing that the road become a trunk road or, if later, the date on which the road is opened for the purposes of through traffic.]

(4) Without prejudice to the provisions of subsection (3) above and subject to the following provisions of this section, a local highway authority may, by agreement with railway, canal or tramway undertakers, undertake to maintain as part of a highway maintainable at the public expense a bridge or viaduct which carries the railway, canal or tramway of the undertakers over such a highway or which is intended to carry such a railway, canal or tramway over such a highway and is to be constructed by those undertakers or by the highway authority on their behalf.

(5) ...

(6) An agreement under this section may contain such provisions as to the dedication as a highway of any road or way to which the agreement relates, the bearing of the expenses of the construction, maintenance or improvement of any highway, road, bridge or viaduct to which the agreement relates and other relevant matters as the authority making the agreement think fit.   **[1005]**

NOTES
Commencement: 1 November 1991 (sub-ss (3), (3A)); 1 January 1981 (remainder) (SI 1991 No 2288).
Sub-ss (3), (3A): substituted for sub-s (3), as originally enacted, by the New Roads and Street Works Act 1991, s 22(1).

Sub-s (5): repealed by the Local Government Act 1985, s 102, Sch 17.

PART VIII
STOPPING UP AND DIVERSION OF HIGHWAYS AND STOPPING UP OF MEANS OF
ACCESS TO HIGHWAYS

Stopping up and diversion of highways

118. Stopping up of footpaths and bridleways

(1) Where it appears to a council as respects a footpath or bridleway in their
area (other than one which is a trunk road or a special road) that it is expedient
that the path or way should be stopped up on the ground that it is not needed
for public use, the council may by order made by them and submitted to and
confirmed by the Secretary of State, or confirmed as an unopposed order,
extinguish the public right of way over the path or way.

An order under this section is referred to in this Act as a "public path
extinguishment order".

(2) The Secretary of State shall not confirm a public path extinguishment
order, and a council shall not confirm such an order as an unopposed order,
unless he or, as the case may be, they are satisfied that it is expedient so to do
having regard to the extent (if any) to which it appears to him or, as the case
may be, them that the path or way would, apart from the order, be likely to be
used by the public, and having regard to the effect which the extinguishment of
the right of way would have as respects land served by the path or way, account
being taken of the provisions as to compensation contained in section 28 above
as applied by section 121(2) below.

(3) A public path extinguishment order shall be in such form as may be
prescribed by regulations made by the Secretary of State and shall contain a
map, on such scale as may be so prescribed, defining the land over which the
public right of way is thereby extinguished.

(4) Schedule 6 to this Act has effect as to the making, confirmation, validity
and date of operation of public path extinguishment orders.

(5) Where, in accordance with regulations made under paragraph 3 of the
said Schedule 6, proceedings preliminary to the confirmation of the public path
extinguishment order are taken concurrently with proceedings preliminary to
the confirmation of a public path creation [, public path diversion order or rail
crossing diversion order] then, in considering—

    (*a*) under subsection (1) above whether the path or way to which the
        public path extinguishment order relates is needed for public use, or
    (*b*) under subsection (2) above to what extent (if any) that path or way
        would apart from the order be likely to be used by the public,

the council or the Secretary of State, as the case may be, may have regard to the
extent to which the public path creation [, public path diversion order or rail
crossing diversion order] would provide an alternative path or way.

(6) For the purposes of subsections (1) and (2) above, any temporary
circumstances preventing or diminishing the use of a path or way by the public
shall be disregarded.

(7) In this section and in sections [118A] to 121 below "council" includes a joint planning board, within the meaning of [the Town and Country Planning Act 1990], for an area which comprises any part of a National Park.   **[1006]**

NOTES
Sub-s (5): words in square brackets substituted by the Transport and Works Act 1992, s 47, Sch 2, para 2.
Sub-s (7): figure in square brackets substituted by the Transport and Works Act 1992, s 47, Sch 2, para 2; words in square brackets substituted by the Planning (Consequential Provisions) Act 1990, s 4, Sch 2, para 45.

119. Diversion of footpaths and bridleways

(1) [Where it appears to a council as respects a footpath or bridleway in their area (other than one that is a trunk road or special road) that, in the interests of the owner, lessee or occupier of land crossed by the path or way or of the public, it is expedient that the line of the path or way, or part of that line, should be divered (whether on to land of the same or]

  (*a*) create, as from such date as may be specified in the order, any such new footpath or bridleway as appears to the council requisite for effecting the diversion, and
  (*b*) extinguish, as from such date as may be so specified in accordance with the provisions of subsection (3) below, the public right of way over so much of the path or way as appears to the council requisite as aforesaid.

An order under this section is referred to in this Act as a "public path diversion order".

(2) A public path diversion order shall not alter a point of termination of the path or way—

  (*a*) if that point is not on a highway, or
  (*b*) (where it is on a highway) otherwise than to another point which is on the same highway, or a highway connected with it, and which is substantially as convenient to the public.

(3) Where it appears to the council that work requires to be done to provide necessary facilities for the convenient exercise of any such new public right of way as is mentioned in subsection (1)(*a*) above, the date specified under subsection (1)(*b*) above shall be later than the date specified under subsection (1)(*a*) by such time as appears to the council requisite for enabling the work to be carried out.

(4) A right of way created by a public path diversion order may be either unconditional or (whether or not the right of way extinguished by the order was subject to limitations or conditions of any description) subject to such limitations or conditions as may be specified in the order.

(5) Before determining to make a public path diversion order [on the representations of an owner, lessee or occupier of land crossed by the path or way, the council may require him] to enter into an agreement with them to defray, or to make such contribution as may be specified in the agreement towards,—

  (*a*) any compensation which may become payable under section 28 above as applied by section 121(2) below, or (*b*) where the council are the highway authority for the path or way in question, any expenses which they may incur in bringing the new site of the path or way into fit condition for use for the public, or

(*c*) where the council are not the highway authority, any expenses which may become recoverable from them by the highway authority under the provisions of section 27(2) above as applied by subsection (9) below.

(6) The Secretary of State shall not confirm a public path diversion order, and a council shall not confirm such an order as an unopposed order, unless he or, as the case may be, they are satisfied that the diversion to be effected by it is expedient as mentioned in subsection (1) above, and further that the path or way will not be substantially less convenient to the public in consequence of the diversion and that it is expedient to confirm the order having regard to the effect which—

(*a*) the diversion would have on public enjoyment of the path or way as a whole,

(*b*) the coming into operation of the order would have as respects other land served by the existing public right of way, and

(*c*) any new public right of way created by the order would have as respects the land over which the right is so created and any land held with it,

so, however, that for the purposes of paragraphs (*b*) and (*c*) above the Secretary of State or, as the case may be, the council shall take into account the provisions as to compensation referred to in subsection (5)(*a*) above.

(7) A public path diversion order shall be in such form as may be prescribed by regulations made by the Secretary of State and shall contain a map, on such scale as may be so prescribed,—

(*a*) showing the existing site of so much of the line of the path or way as is to be diverted by the order and the new site to which it is to be diverted,

(*b*) indicating whether a new right of way is created by the order over the whole of the new site or whether some part of it is already comprised in a footpath or bridleway, and

(*c*) where some part of the new site is already so comprised, defining that part.

(8) Schedule 6 to this Act has effect as to the making, confirmation, validity and date of operation of public path diversion orders.

(9) Section 27 above (making up of new footpaths and bridleways) applies to a footpath or bridleway created by a public path diversion order with the substitution, for references to a public path creation order, of references to a public path diversion order and, for references to section 26(2) above, of references to section 120(3) below.   **[1007]**

NOTES
    Sub-s (1): words in square brackets substituted by the Wildlife and Countryside Act 1981, s 63, Sch 16.
    Sub-s (5): words in square brackets substituted by the Wildlife and Countryside Act 1981, s 63, Sch 16.

PART IX

LAWFUL AND UNLAWFUL INTERFERENCE WITH HIGHWAYS AND STREETS

Damage to highways, streets etc

[134. Ploughing etc of footpath or bridleway

(1) Where in the case of any footpath or bridleway (other than a field-edge path) which passes over a field or enclosure consisting of agricultural land, or land which is being brought into use for agriculture—

    (*a*) the occupier of the field or enclosure desires in accordance with the rules of good husbandry to plough, or otherwise disturb the surface of, all or part of the land comprised in the field or enclosure, and

    (*b*) it is not reasonably convenient in ploughing, or otherwise disturbing the surface of, the land to avoid disturbing the surface of the path or way so as to render it inconvenient for the exercise of the public right of way,

the public right of way shall be subject to the condition that the occupier has the right so to plough or otherwise disturb the surface of the path or way.

(2) Subsection (1) above does not apply in relation to any excavation or any engineering operation.

(3) Where the occupier has disturbed the surface of a footpath or bridleway under the right conferred by subsection (1) above he shall within the relevant period, or within an extension of that period granted under subsection (8) below,—

    (*a*) so make good the surface of the path or way to not less than its minimum width as to make it reasonably convenient for the exercise of the right of way; and

    (*b*) so indicate the line of the path or way on the ground to not less than its minimum width that it is apparent to members of the public wishing to use it.

(4) If the occupier fails to comply with the duty imposed by subsection (3) above he is guilty of an offence and liable to a fine not exceeding level 3 on the standard scale.

(5) Proceedings for an offence under this section in relation to a footpath or bridleway shall be brought only by the highway authority or the council of the non-metropolitan district, parish or community in which the offence is committed.

(6) Without prejudice to section 130 (protection of public rights) above, it is the duty of the highway authority to enforce the provisions of this section.

(7) For the purposes of this section "the relevant period",—

    (*a*) where the disturbance of the surface of the path or way is the first disturbance for the purposes of the sowing of a particular agricultural crop, means fourteen days beginning with the day on which the surface of the path or way was first disturbed for those purposes; or

    (*b*) in any other case, means twenty-four hours beginning with the time when it was disturbed.

(8) On an application made to the highway authority before the disturbance

or during the relevant period, the authority may grant an extension of that period for an additional period not exceeding twenty-eight days.

(9) In this section "minimum width", in relation to a highway, has the same meaning as in Schedule 12A to this Act.] **[1008]**

NOTES
Commencement: 13 August 1990.
Substituted by the Rights of Way Act 1990, s 1(3).

[135. Authorisation of other works disturbing footpath or bridleway

(1) Where the occupier of any agricultural land, or land which is being brought into use for agriculture, desires to carry out in relation to that land an excavation or engineering operation, and the excavation or operation—

   (*a*) is reasonably necessary for the purposes of agriculture, but
   (*b*) will so disturb the surface of a footpath or bridleway which passes over that land as to render it inconvenient for the exercise of the public right of way,

he may apply to the highway authority for an order that the public right of way shall be subject to the condition that he has the right to disturb the surface by that excavation or operation during such period, not exceeding three months, as is specified in the order ("the authorisation period").

(2) The highway authority shall make an order under subsection (1) above if they are satisfied either—

   (*a*) that it is practicable temporarily to divert the path or way in a manner reasonably convenient to users; or
   (*b*) that it is practicable to take adequate steps to ensure that the path or way remains sufficiently convenient, having regard to the need for the excavation or operation, for temporary use while it is being carried out.

(3) An order made by a highway authority under subsection (1) above—

   (*a*) may provide for the temporary diversion of the path or way during the authorisation period, but shall not divert it on to land not occupied by the applicant unless written consent to the making of the order has been given by the occupier of that land, and by any other person whose consent is needed to obtain access to it;
   (*b*) may include such conditions as the authority reasonably think fit for the provision, either by the applicant or by the authority at the expense of the applicant, of facilities for the convenient use of any such diversion, including signposts and other notices, stiles, bridges, and gates;
   (*c*) shall not affect the line of a footpath or bridleway on land not occupied by the applicant;

and the authority shall cause notices of any such diversion, together with a plan showing the effect of the diversion and the line of the alternative route provided, to be prominently displayed throughout the authorisation period at each end of the diversion.

(4) An order made by a highway authority under subsection (1) above may include such conditions as the authority reasonably think fit—

   (*a*) for the protection and convenience during the authorisation period of users of the path or way;

(*b*) for making good the surface of the path or way to not more than its
minimum width before the expiration of the authorisation period;
(*c*) for the recovery from the applicant of expenses incurred by the
authority in connection with the order.

(5) An order under this section shall not authorise any interference with the
apparatus or works of any statutory undertakers.

(6) If the applicant fails to comply with a condition imposed under
subsection (3)(*b*) or (4)(*a*) or (*b*) above he is guilty of an offence and liable to a
fine not exceeding level 3 on the standard scale.

(7) Proceedings for an offence under this section in relation to a footpath or
bridleway shall be brought only by the highway authority or (with the consent
of the highway authority) the council of the non-metropolitan district, parish or
community in which the offence is committed.

(8) Without prejudice to section 130 (protection of public rights) above, it is
the duty of the highway authority to enforce the provisions of this section.

(9) In this section "minimum width", in relation to a highway, has the same
meaning as in Schedule 12A to this Act.]   **[1009]**

NOTES
   Commencement: 13 August 1990.
   Substituted by the Rights of Way Act 1990, s 1(4).

PART XI

MAKING UP OF PRIVATE STREETS

The private street works code

205. Street works in private streets

(1) Where a private street is not, to the satisfaction of the street works authority,
sewered, levelled, paved, metalled, flagged, channelled, made good and lighted,
the authority may from time to time resolve with respect to the street to execute
street works and, subject to the private street works code, the expenses incurred
by the authority in executing those works shall be apportioned between the
premises fronting the street.

(2) Where the authority resolve to execute street works with respect to a
part only of the street (other than a part extending for the whole of the length of
the street), the expenses incurred by them in executing the works shall be
apportioned only between the premises fronting the length of the street which
constitutes or comprises that part.

(3) Where an authority have passed a resolution under subsection (1) above,
the proper officer of the council shall prepare—
(*a*) a specification of the street works referred to in the resolution, with
any necessary plans and sections,
(*b*) an estimate of the probable expenses of the works, and
(*c*) a provisional apportionment apportioning the estimated expenses
between the premises liable to be charged with them under the private
street works code;
and the specification, plans, sections, estimate and provisional apportionment
shall comprise the particulars specified in paragraphs 1 to 4 of Schedule 16 to
this Act and shall be submitted to the authority, who may by a further resolution

(hereafter in the private street works code referred to as "the resolution of approval") approve them with or without modification or addition as they think fit.

(4) If, in the case of a street outside Greater London, the street works referred to in the resolution under subsection (1) above include the sewering of the street, the proper officer of the county council shall, when preparing the specification required by subsection (3) above, consult the council of the district in which the street works are to be carried out.

(5) After the resolution of approval has been passed, a notice containing the particulars specified in paragraph 5 of Schedule 16 to this Act shall—

(a) be published once in each of 2 successive weeks in a local newspaper circulating in the area of the street works authority, and

(b) be posted in a prominent position in or near to the street to which the resolution relates once at least in each of 3 successive weeks, and

(c) within 7 days from the date of the first publication under paragraph (a) above, be served on the owners of the premises shown in the provisional apportionment as liable to be charged;

and during one month from the said date a copy of the resolution of approval, and the approved documents or copies of them certified by the proper officer of the council, shall be kept deposited and open to inspection free of charge at all reasonable hours at the offices of the street works authority and also, [in the case of a street situated in a non-metropolitan district, at the offices of the council of that district].

(6) Where a notice is served on an owner of premises under subsection (5)(c) above it shall be accompanied by a statement of the sum apportioned on those premises by the provisional apportionment. **[1010]**

NOTES

Sub-s (5): words in square brackets substituted by the Local Government Act 1985, s 8, Sch 4, para 34.

206. Incidental works

A street works authority may include in street works to be executed under the private street works code with respect to a street any works which they think necessary for bringing the street, as regards sewerage, drainage, level, or other matters, into conformity with any other streets, whether maintainable at the public expense or not, including the provision of separate sewers for the reception of sewage and of surface water respectively. **[1011]**

207. Provisional apportionment of expenses

(1) In a provisional apportionment of expenses of street works under the private street works code, the apportionment of expenses between the premises liable to be charged with them shall, subject to the provisions of this section, be made according to the frontage of the respective premises.

(2) The street works authority may, if they think just, resolve that in settling the apportionment regard shall be had to the following considerations:—

(a) the greater or less degree of benefit to be derived by any premises from the street works;

(b) the amount and value of any work already done by the owners or occupiers of any premises.

(3) The authority may—

(a) if they think just, include in the apportionment any premises which do not front the street, but have access to it through a court, passage, or otherwise, and which will, in the opinion of the authority, be benefited by the works, and

(b) fix, by reference to the degree of benefit to be derived by those premises, the amount to be apportioned on them.   **[1012]**

208. Objections to proposed works

(1) Within one month from the date of the first publication of a notice under section 205(5)(a) above, an owner of premises shown in a provisional apportionment of expenses as liable to be charged with any part of the expenses of executing street works with respect to a private street or a part of a private street may, by notice to the street works authority, object to their proposals on any of the following grounds:—

(a) that the alleged private street is not a private street or, as the case may be, that the alleged part of a private street is not a part of a private street;

(b) that there has been some material informality, defect or error in, or in respect of, the resolution, notice, plans, sections or estimate;

(c) that the proposed works are insufficient or unreasonable;

(d) that the estimated expenses of the proposed works are excessive;

(e) that any premises ought to be excluded from or inserted in the provisional apportionment;

(f) that the provisional apportionment is incorrect in respect of some matter of fact to be specified in the objection or, where the provisional apportionment is made with regard to other considerations than frontage, in respect of the degree of benefit to be derived by any premises, or of the amount or value of any work already done by the owner or occupier of premises.

(2) Where premises are owned jointly by 2 or more persons, a notice under subsection (1) above may be given on behalf of those persons by one of their number, if he is authorised in writing by a majority of them to do so.   **[1013]**

209. Hearing and determination of objections

(1) If an objection is made under section 208 above within the period there specified, and is not withdrawn, the street works authority may, after the expiration of that period, apply to a magistrates' court to appoint a time for hearing and determining all objections so made within that period, and shall serve on the objectors notice of the time and place so appointed.

(2) At the hearing the court shall hear and determine the objections in the same manner as nearly as may be as if the authority were proceeding summarily against the objectors to enforce payment of a sum of money summarily recoverable.

The court may quash in whole or in part or may amend the resolution of approval, specification, plans, sections, estimate and provisional apportionment, or any of them, on the application either of an objector or of the authority, and may also, if it thinks fit, adjourn the hearing and direct further notices to be given.

(3) The costs of any proceedings before a magistrates' court in relation to objections under the private street works code are in the discretion of the court,

and the court may, if it thinks fit, direct that the whole or a part of any costs ordered to be paid by an objector or objectors are to be paid in the first instance by the authority, and charged as part of the expenses of the works on the premises of the objector, or, as the case may be, on the premises of the objectors in such proportions as may appear just. [1014]

210. Power to amend specification, apportionment, etc

(1) Subject to the provisions of this section, the street works authority may from time to time amend the specification, plans, sections, estimate and provisional apportionment for any street works proposed under section 205 above.

(2) If the street works authority propose to amend the estimate so as to increase the amount of it, then, before the amendment is made, a notice containing the particulars specified in paragraph 6 of Schedule 16 to this Act shall—

(a) be published once in each of 2 successive weeks in a local newspaper circulating in the area of the street works authority, and

(b) be posted in a prominent position in or near to the street to which the resolution of approval relates once at least in each of 3 successive weeks, and

(c) within 7 days from the date of the first publication under paragraph (a) above, be served on the owners of the premises shown in the provisional apportionment as liable to be charged;

and, during one month from the said date, a document certified by the proper officer of the council giving details of the the estimate and of the consequential amendment of the provisional apportionment shall be kept deposited and open to inspection free of charge at all reasonable hours at the offices of the street works authority and also, [in the case of a street situated in a non-metropolitan district], at the offices of the council of that district].

(3) Where a notice is served on an owner of premises under subsection (2)(c) above it shall be accompanied by a statement of the sum apportioned on those premises by the provisional apportionment as proposed to be amended.

(4) Within one month from the date of the first publication of a notice under subsection (2)(a) above, objections may be made and, if made, shall be heard and determined in like manner, and subject to the like provisions with respect to the persons entitled to be heard and otherwise, as objections under section 208 above. [1015]

NOTES
Sub-s (2): words in square brackets substituted by the Local Government Act 1985, s 8, Sch 4, para 34.

211. Final apportionment and objections to it

(1) When any street works to be executed under the private street works code have been completed, and the expenses of them ascertained, the proper officer of the council shall make a final apportionment by dividing the expenses in the same proportions as those in which the estimated expenses were divided in the original or amended provisional apportionment, as the case may be, and notice of the final apportionment shall be served on the owners of the premises affected by it.

(2) Within one month from the date on which notice of the final apportionment is served on him, the owner of any premises shown in the

apportionment as liable to be charged may, by notice to the authority, object to the apportionment on the following grounds, or any of them:—

    (*a*) that there has been an unreasonable departure from the specification, plans and sections;

    (*b*) that the actual expenses have without sufficient reason exceeded the estimated expenses by more than 15 per cent.;

    (*c*) that the apportionment has not been made in accordance with this section

Objections under this section shall be determined in the like manner, and subject to the like provisions with respect to the persons entitled to be heard and otherwise, as objections to the provisional apportionment.

(3) The final apportionment, subject to any amendment made to it by a court on the hearing of objections to it under this section, is conclusive for all purposes. **[1016]**

212. Recovery of expenses and charges thereof on premises

(1) A street works authority may from time to time recover from the owner for the time being of any premises in respect of which any sum is due for expenses of street works the whole or any portion of that sum together with interest at such reasonable rates as the authority may determine from the date of the final apportionment.

(2) The sum apportioned on any premises by the final apportionment or, as the case may be, by that apportionment as amended by a court, together with interest from the date of the final apportionment is, until recovered, a charge on the premises and on all estates and interests therein.

(3) A street works authority, for the purpose of enforcing a charge under subsection (2) above before it is registered under the Local Land Charges Act 1975, have the same powers and remedies under the Law of Property Act 1925 and otherwise as if they were mortgagees by deed having powers of sale and lease and of appointing a receiver.

(4) A street works authority may by order declare the expenses apportioned on any premises by a final apportionment made by the proper officer of the council or, as the case may be, by that apportionment as amended by a court, to be payable by annual instalments within a period not exceeding 30 years, together with interest from the date of the final apportionment; and any such instalment and interest, or any part thereof, may be recovered from the owner or occupier for the time being of the premises.

Schedule 13 to this Act applies in relation to any sum paid by an occupier of premises under this subsection. **[1017]**

213. Power for limited owners to borrow for expenses

The owners of any premises, if they are persons who under the Compulsory Purchase Act 1965 are empowered to sell and convey or release lands, may charge those premises with—

    (*a*) such sum as may be necessary to defray the whole or a part of any expenses which the owners of, or any other person in respect of, those premises for the time being are liable to defray under the private street works code, and (*b*) the expenses of making such a charge;

and, for securing the repayment of that sum with interest, may mortgage the premises to any person advancing that sum so, however, that the principal due on any such mortgage shall be repaid by equal yearly or half-yearly payments within 20 years. **[1018]**

The advance payments code

219. Payments to be made by owners of new buildings in respect of street works

(1) Subject to the provisions of this section, where—

(*a*) it is proposed to erect a building for which plans are required to be deposited with the local authority in accordance with building regulations, and

(*b*) the building will have a frontage on a private street in which the street works authority have power under the private street works code to require works to be executed or to execute works,

no work shall be done in or for the purpose of erecting the building unless the owner of the land on which it is to be erected or a previous owner thereof has paid to the street works authority, or secured to the satisfaction of that authority the payment to them of, such sum as may be required under section 220 below in respect of the cost of street works in that street.

(2) If work is done in contravention of subsection (1) above, the owner of the land on which the building is to be erected and, if he is a different person, the person undertaking the erection of the building is guilty of an offence and liable to a fine not exceeding [level 3 on the standard scale], and any further contravention in respect of the same building constitutes a new offence and may be punished accordingly.

Proceedings under this subsection shall not be taken by any person other than the street works authority.

(3) Where the person undertaking the erection of the building is not the owner of the land on which it is to be erected and is charged with an offence under subsection (2) above, it shall be a defence for him to prove that he had reasonable grounds for believing that the sum required under section 220 below had been paid or secured by the owner of the land in accordance with subsection (1) above.

(4) This section does not apply—

(*a*) where the owner of the land on which the building is to be erected will be exempt, by virtue of a provision in the private street works code, from liability to expenses incurred in respect of street works in the private street in question;

(*b*) where the building proposed to be erected will be situated in the curtilage of, and be appurtenant to, an existing building;

(*c*) where the building is proposed to be erected in a parish or community and plans for the building were deposited with the district council or, according to the date of deposit, the rural district council before the date on which the New Streets Act 1951, or the advance payments code (either in this Act or in the Highways Act 1959) was applied in the parish or community or, as the case may require, in the part of the parish or community in which the building is to be erected;

(*d*) where an agreement has been made by any person with the street works authority under section 38 above providing for the carrying out at the expense of that person of street works in the whole of the street or a part of the street comprising the whole of the part on which the frontage of the building will be, and for securing that the street or the part thereof, on completion of the works, will become a highway maintainable at the public expense;

(e) where the street works authority, being satisfied that the whole of the street or such a part thereof as aforesaid is not, and is not likely within a reasonable time to be, substantially built-up or in so unsatisfactory a condition as to justify the use of powers under the private street works code for securing the carrying out of street works in the street or part thereof, by notice exempt the building from this section;

(f) where the street works authority, being satisfied that the street is not, and is not likely within a reasonable time to become, joined to a highway maintainable at the public expense, by notice exempt the building from this section;

(g) where the whole street, being less than 100 yards in length, or a part of the street not less than 100 yards in length and comprising the whole of the part on which the frontage of the building will be, was on the material date built-up to such an extent that the aggregate length of the frontages of the buildings on both sides of the street or part constituted at least one half of the aggregate length of all the frontages on both sides of the street or part;

(h) where (in a case not falling within paragraph (g) above) the street works authority, being satisfied that the whole of the street was on the material date substantially built-up, by notice exempt the building from this section;

(i) where the building is proposed to be erected on land belonging to, or in the possession of—

  (i) the British Railways Board, ... the British Waterways Board, [London Regional Transport], ... any wholly-owned subsidiary (within the meaning of the Transport Act 1968) or joint subsidiary (within the meaning of section 51(5) of that Act) of any of those bodies [other than London Regional Transport, or any subsidiary (whether wholly-owned or not) of London Regional Transport (within the meaning of the London Regional Transport Act 1984)];

  (ii) the council of a county, district or London borough ... or the Common Council;

  (iii) the Commission for the New Towns or a new town development corporation;

(j) where the building is to be erected by a company the objects of which include the provision of industrial premises for use by persons other than the company, being a company the constitution of which prohibits the distribution of the profits of the company to its members, and the cost of the building is to be defrayed wholly or mainly by a government department;

(k) where the street works authority, being satisfied—

  (i) that more than three-quarters of the aggregate length of all the frontages on both sides of the street, or of a part of the street not less than 100 yards in length and comprising the whole of the part on which the frontage of the building will be, consists, or is at some future time likely to consist, of the frontages of industrial premises, and

(ii) that their powers under the private street works code are not likely to be exercised in relation to the street, or to that part of it, as the case may be, within a reasonable time,

by resolution exempt the street, or that part of it, from this section.

(5) Where a sum has been paid or secured under this section by the owner of the land in relation to a building proposed to be erected on it, and thereafter a notice is served under subsection (4) above exempting the building from this section, or a resolution is passed under paragraph (*k*) of that subsection exempting the street or part of a street on which the building will have a frontage from this section, the street works authority shall refund that sum to the person who is for the time being owner of the land or shall release the security, as the case may be.

Where the said sum was paid, and after the payment but before the service of the said notice or the passing of the said resolution, as the case may be, the land in respect of which it was paid was divided into 2 or more parts each having a frontage on the private street in question, the sum is to be treated for the purposes of this subsection as apportioned between the owners of the land according to their respective frontages.

(6) For the purposes of this section "the material date" is—

(*a*) in relation to a building proposed to be erected in an area which before 1st April 1974 was a rural district or a contributory place within a rural district, the date on which the New Streets Act 1951 or the advance payments code (either in this Act or in the Highways Act 1959) was applied in that area;

(*b*) in relation to a building proposed to be erected anywhere else, 1st October 1951. **[1019]**

NOTES
Sub-s (2): maximum fine increased and converted to a level on the standard scale by the Criminal Justice Act 1982, ss 37, 38, 46.
Sub-s (4): first words omitted repealed by the Transport Act 1981, s 14, Sch 4, para 6; second words omitted repealed by the Statute Law (Repeals) Act 1989; third words omitted repealed, first words in square brackets substituted and second words in square brackets inserted by the London Regional Transport Act 1984, s 71(3), Sch 6, para 20, Sch 7; fourth words omitted repealed by the Local Government Act 1985, s 102, Sch 17.

220. Determination of liability for, and amount of, payments

(1) In a case to which section 219 above applies the street works authority shall, within 6 weeks from the passing of any required plans relating to the erection of a building deposited with them or, in a case to which subsection (2) below applies, with the district council, serve a notice on the person by or on whose behalf the plans were deposited requiring the payment or the securing under section 219 above of a sum specified in the notice.

In this subsection and subsection (2) below "required plans" means plans required to be deposited with the local authority in accordance with building regulations.

(2) Where (outside Greater London) the advance payments code is in force in the whole or any part of a [non-metropolitan] district, the district council, in any case to which section 219 above may be applicable, shall within one week from the date of the passing of any required plans deposited with them relating to the erection of a building in an area in which that code is in force inform the street works authority that the plans have been passed.

(3) Subject to the provisions of this section, the sum to be specified in a notice under subsection (1) above is such sum as, in the opinion of the street works authority, would be recoverable under the private street works code in respect of the frontage of the proposed building on the private street if the authority were then to carry out such street works in the street as they would require under that code before declaring the street to be a highway which for the purposes of this Act is a highway maintainable at the public expense.

In this subsection a reference to a street does not include a reference to a part of a street, except to a part which the street works authority think fit to treat as constituting a separate street for the purposes of this subsection and which comprises the whole of the part on which the frontage of the building will be.

(4) If, at any time after the service of a notice under subsection (1) above, the street works authority—

(*a*) are of opinion that the sum specified in the notice exceeds such sum as in their opinion would be recoverable as mentioned in subsection (3) above if they were then to carry out such street works as are so mentioned, or

(*b*) are of opinion that no sum would be so recoverable,

they may, by a further notice, served on the person who is for the time being owner of the land on which the building is to be, or has been, erected, substitute a smaller sum for the sum specified in the notice served under subsection (1) above or, as the case may be, intimate that no sum falls to be paid or secured.

This subsection does not apply where a sum has been paid or secured in compliance with a notice served under subsection (1) above and the case is one in which the authority have power to make a refund or release under section 221(1) below.

(5) Where, under a local Act, the erection of buildings on land having a frontage on a new street is prohibited until works for the construction or sewering of the street have been carried out in accordance with byelaws, the amount of the sum to be specified in a notice served under this section shall be calculated as if those works had been carried out.

(6) Where a notice is served on any person under this section (other than a notice intimating that no sum falls to be paid or secured) that person or, if he is a different person, the owner of the land on which the building is to be, or has been erected, may, not later than one month from the date of the service of the notice, appeal to the Minister and the Minister may substitute a smaller sum for the sum specified by the street works authority.

On an appeal under this subsection, the Minister shall give the appellant an opportunity of being heard before a person appointed by the Minister.

(7) Where a sum has been paid or secured in compliance with a notice served under subsection (1) above and a notice is subsequently served under subsection (4) above substituting a smaller sum for the sum specified in the first-mentioned notice or intimating that no sum falls to be paid or secured, the street works authority—

(*a*) if the sum was paid, shall refund the amount of the excess or, as the case may be, the whole sum to the person who is for the time being owner of the land on which the building is to be, or has been, erected;

(*b*) if the sum was secured and the person whose property is security for the payment of it is for the time being owner of that land, shall release the security to the extent of the excess or, as the case may be, the whole security;

(c) if the sum was secured and the person whose property is security for the payment of it is not for the time being owner of that land, shall pay to that owner an amount equal to the excess or, as the case may be, the whole sum, and are entitled to realise the security for the purpose of recovering the amount so paid.

(8) Where land in respect of which a sum has been paid or secured in compliance with a notice under subsection (1) above is subsequently divided into 2 or more parts so that 2 or more owners would, if street works were carried out, incur liability in respect of it, the sum is to be treated as apportioned between those owners according to their respective frontages and, if the sum was secured and the security is the property of one only of those owners, the street works authority—

(a) are required under subsection (7)(b) above to release the security only to the extent of the amount apportioned to the owner, and

(b) are entitled to realise the security for the purpose of recovering the amount or amounts paid to the other owner or owners under subsection (7)(c) above.

(9) Where a security is realised for the purpose of recovering an amount paid by a street works authority under subsection (7)(c) above, and the sum produced by realising the security exceeds the amount so paid, the amount of the excess shall be held by the authority and dealt with under the advance payments code as if it had been an amount paid under section 219 above on the date on which the security was realised. **[1020]**

NOTES
Sub-s (2): words in square brackets inserted by the Local Government Act 1985, s 8, Sch 4, para 35.

221. Refunds etc where work done otherwise than at expense of street works authority

(1) Where—

(a) a sum has been paid or secured under section 219 above by the owner of land in respect of the cost of street works to be carried out in the private street on which that land has a frontage, and

(b) any street works are subsequently carried out in the private street in respect of that frontage to the satisfaction of but otherwise than at the expense of the street works authority,

the authority may refund to the person at whose expense the works are carried out the whole or such proportion of that sum or, as the case may be, release the whole or such part of the security, as in their opinion represents the amount by which the liability of the owner of that land in respect of street works has been reduced as a result of the carrying out of the street works in question.

Where the person at whose expense the works are carried out is not the person who is for the time being owner of that land no refund or release shall be made under this subsection unless the owner has been notified of the proposal to make the refund or release and has been afforded an opportunity of making representations to the street works authority in relation to it.

(2) Where any land which has a frontage on a private street, and in respect of which a sum has been paid or secured under section 219 above, is subsequently

divided into 2 or more parts each having a frontage on that private street, the sum is to be treated as apportioned between the owners thereof according to their respective frontages, and subsection (1) above has effect accordingly.

(3) Where—

    (a) a sum has been paid or secured under section 219 above by the owner of land in respect of the cost of street works to be carried out in the private street on which that land has a frontage, and

    (b) thereafter the street works authority enter into an agreement with any person under section 38 above providing for the carrying out at the expense of that person of street works in respect of that frontage,

that agreement may also provide for the refund of the said sum or a part of it either without interest or with interest at such rate as may be specified in the agreement, or for the release of the whole or a part of the security, as the case may be. **[1021]**

222. Sums paid or secured to be in discharge of further liability for street works

(1) Where a sum has been paid or secured under section 219 above by the owner of land in respect of the cost of street works to be carried out in the private street on which that land has a frontage, the liability of that owner or any subsequent owner of that land in respect of the carrying out of street works in that street under the private street works code ("the street works liability") is, as respects that frontage, to be deemed to be discharged to the extent of the sum so paid or secured.

(2) If, when the street is declared to be a highway which for the purposes of this Act is a highway maintainable at the public expense, the said sum is found to exceed the total street works liability in respect of that frontage or there is no such liability because the street was not made up at the expense of the street works authority, the street works authority—

    (a) if the sum was paid, shall refund the amount of the excess or, as the case may be, the whole sum to the person who is for the time being owner of the land;

    (b) if the sum was secured and the person whose property is security for the payment of it is for the time being owner of the land, shall release the security to the extent of the excess or, as the case may be, the whole security;

    (c) if the sum was secured and the person whose property is security for the payment of it is not for the time being owner of the land, shall pay to that owner an amount equal to the excess or, as the case may be, the whole sum, and are entitled to realise the security for the purpose of recovering the amount so paid.

(3) Where land in respect of which a sum has been paid or secured under section 219 above is subsequently divided into 2 or more parts so that 2 or more owners incur or would incur the street works liability, the sum is to be treated as apportioned between those owners according to their respective frontages, and if the sum was secured and the security is the property of one only of those owners the street works authority—

    (a) are required under subsection (2)(b) above to release the security only to the extent to which the amount apportioned to that owner exceeds his street works liability or, as the case may be, to the extent of the whole of that amount, and (*b*) are entitled to realise the security for the purpose of recovering the amount or amounts paid to the other owner or owners under subsection (2)(*c*) above.

(4) Where any refund, release or payment has been made under section 220(7) above, or under section 221 above, the foregoing provisions of this section have effect as if for references therein to a sum paid or secured there were substituted references to any sum remaining paid or secured.   **[1022]**

223. Determination to cease to have effect when plans not proceeded with

(1) Where, on the occasion of the deposit of plans for the erection of a building, the amount to be paid or secured under section 219 above has been determined under section 220 above, and subsequently—

(*a*) the local authority, under [section 32 of the Building Act 1984], declare the deposit of the plans to be of no effect, or
(*b*) before any work has been done in or for the purpose of erecting the building the owner gives notice to the local authority of his intention not to proceed with the building,

the said determination and any payment made or security given in accordance with it are, unless there have already been carried out or commenced in the street under the private street works code street works in respect of which the owner of the land on which the building was to be erected is liable, of no effect for the purposes of this Part of this Act.

(2) Where by virtue of subsection (1) above a determination is of no effect and a sum has been paid or security given in accordance with it, the street works authority—

(*a*) if the sum was paid, shall refund it to the person who is for the time being owner of the land;
(*b*) if the sum was secured and the person whose property is security for the payment of it is for the time being owner of the land, shall release the security;
(*c*) if the sum was secured and the person whose property is security for the payment of it is not for the time being owner of the land, shall pay to that owner an amount equal to the said sum, and are entitled to realise the security for the purpose of recovering the amount so paid.

(3) Where land in respect of which a sum has been paid or secured as mentioned in subsection (2) above is subsequently divided into 2 or more parts so that 2 or more owners would, if street works were carried out, incur liability in respect thereof, the sum is to be treated as apportioned between those owners according to their respective frontages and, if the sum was secured and the security is the property of one only of those owners, the street works authority—

(*a*) are required under subsection (2)(*b*) above to release the security only to the extent of the amount apportioned to that owner, and
(*b*) are entitled to realise the security for the purpose of recovering the amount or amounts paid to the other owner or owners under subsection (2)(*c*) above.

(4) Where any refund, release or payment has been made under section 220(7) above, or under section 221 above, subsections (2) and (3) above have effect as if for references in those subsections to a sum paid and security given there were substituted references to, respectively, any sum remaining paid and any remaining security.

(5) Where—

    (a) a person notifies the local authority in accordance with subsection (1)(b) above of his intention not to proceed with the building and by reason thereof a determination is of no effect, and

    (b) subsequently notice is given to the local authority by the owner of the land that he intends to proceed with the building in accordance with the plans as originally deposited,

the notice to be served under subsection (1) of section 220 above by the street works authority shall, in lieu of being served as required by that subsection, be served on him within one month from the date of the service of the notice of his intention to proceed with the building, and section 220 has effect accordingly.

(6) Where the advance payments code is in force in the whole or any part of a [non-metropolitan] district, the district council, in any case to which this section may be applicable, shall within one week inform the county council of the happening of any of the following events:—

    (a) the making of any declaration that the deposit of plans relating to the erection of a building is of no effect,

    (b) the giving of any notice by an owner of his intention not to proceed with a building, and

    (c) the giving of any notice by an owner of his intention to proceed with the building in accordance with the plans as originally deposited.

[1023]

NOTES

    Sub-s (1): words in square brackets substituted by the Building Act 1984, s 133(1), Sch 6, para 21.
    Sub-s (6): words in square brackets inserted by the Local Government Act 1985, s 8, Sch 4, para 35.

224. Certain matters to be local land charges

(1) The matters specified in subsection (2) below are local land charges.

(2) The matters referred to in subsection (1) above are:—

    (a) notices served by a street works authority under section 220(1) or (4) above;

    (b) determinations by the Minister under section 220(6) above;

    (c) payments made and securities given under section 219 above;

    (d) notices served under subsection (4)(e), (f) or (h) of section 219 above exempting a building from that section;

    (e) resolutions passed under subsection (4)(k) of section 219 above exempting a street or a part of a street from that section; and

    (f) refunds made and releases of securities granted under section 221, 222 or 223 above.

(3) As respects any matter that is a local land charge by virtue of this section, the street works authority for the street concerned are, notwithstanding anything in section 5(4) of the Local Land Charges Act 1975, to be treated as the originating authority for the purposes of that Act. **[1024]**

225. Interest on sums paid under advance payments code

(1) Any sum paid by the owner of land to a street works authority under section 219 above, in so far as it continues to be held by the authority, carries simple interest at the appropriate rate from the date of payment until such time as the sum or a part of it remaining so held—

(*a*) falls to be set off under section 222 above against the liability of the owner of the land in respect of the carrying out of street works; or

(*b*) falls to be refunded in full under the provisions of the advance payments code;

and the interest shall be held by the authority until that time and dealt with under those provisions as if it formed part of the said sum.

This subsection does not apply to any sum in so far as it is repaid under any such agreement as is referred to in section 221(3) above.

(2) For the purposes of the advance payments code interest on any sum held by a street works authority shall be calculated in respect of each financial year during which it accrues at the appropriate rate prevailing at the commencement of that financial year.

(3) In this section "the appropriate rate" means the rate at the material time determined by the Treasury in respect of local loans for periods of 10 years on the security of local rates (being a determination under section 6(2) of the National Loans Act 1968, and subject to any relevant direction under the said section 6(2)). **[1025]**

General

228. Adoption of private street after execution of street works

(1) When any street works have been executed in a private street, the street works authority may, by notice displayed in a prominent position in the street, declare the street to be a highway which for the purposes of this Act is a highway maintainable at the public expense, and on the expiration of one month from the day on which the notice was first so displayed the street shall, subject to subsections (2) to (4) below, become such a highway.

(2) A street shall not become a highway maintainable at the public expense by virtue of subsection (1) above if, within the period there mentioned, the owner of the street or, if more than one, the majority in number of the owners of the street, by notice to the authority object; but within 2 months from the expiration of that period the street works authority may apply to a magistrates' court for an order overruling the objection.

(3) If an order overruling an objection under subsection (2) above is made pursuant to an application under that subsection and no appeal against the order is brought within the time limited for such an appeal, the street or part in question shall become a highway maintainable at the public expense on the expiration of that time.

(4) Where such an order is made or refused and an appeal, or an appeal arising out of that appeal, is brought against or arises out of the order or refusal, then—

(*a*) if the final determination of the matter is in favour of the authority, or

(*b*) the appeal is abandoned by the objectors,

the street shall become a highway maintainable at the public expense on that final determination or, as the case may be, on the abandonment of the appeal.

(5) Notwithstanding anything in any other enactment or provision, for the purposes of this section the time for bringing or seeking leave for any appeal (including an application for certiorari) is 2 months from the date of the decision

or of the conclusion of the proceedings appealed against, unless apart from this subsection the time is less than that period; and no power, however worded, to enlarge any such time is exercisable for the purposes of this section.

(6) Where street works have been executed in a part only of a street (other than a part extending for the whole of the length of the street), subsections (1) to (4) above have effect as if for references in those subsections to the street there were substituted references to the length of the street which constitutes or comprises that part.

(7) If all street works (whether or not including lighting) have been executed in a private street to the satisfaction of the street works authority, then, on the application of the majority in rateable value of the owners of premises in the street, the street works authority shall, within the period of 3 months from the date of the application, by notice displayed in a prominent position in the street, declare the street to be a highway which for the purposes of this Act is a highway maintainable at the public expense and thereupon the street shall become such a highway.

In this subsection a reference to a street does not include a reference to a part of a street. **[1026]**

229. Power of majority of frontagers to require adoption where advance payments made

(1) Where a majority in number of the owners of land having a frontage on a built-up private street, or as many of those owners as have between them more than half the aggregate length of all the frontages on both sides of the street, by notice request the street works authority to exercise their powers under the private street works code so as—

　(a) to secure the carrying out of such street works in that street as the street works authority require under that code before declaring the street to be a highway which for the purposes of this Act is a highway maintainable at the public expense, and

　(b) to declare the street to be such a highway,

the street works authority shall proceed to exercise their powers accordingly.

(2) Subsection (1) above does not apply unless, in at least one case, a payment has been made or security has been given under section 219 above by the owner of land having a frontage on the street and the payment has not been refunded, or the security released or realised, under subsection (5) of that section, or under section 223 above.

(3) For the purposes of this section a street is to be deemed to be built-up if the aggregate length of the frontages of the buildings on both sides of the street constitutes at least one half of the aggregate length of all the frontages on both sides of the street.

(4) This section does not apply in relation to a part of a street unless it is a part not less than 100 yards in length which the owners of land having a frontage on that part of the street elect to treat as constituting a street for the purposes of this section. **[1027]**

235. Evasion of private street works expenses by owners

(1) Where a street works authority are empowered by section 212 above to recover any sum from the owner of any premises, and the authority are unable

by the exercise of their powers (other than powers conferred by this section) to recover that sum, then if—

    (*a*) the said premises were previously transferred by a person ("the transferor") who at the time of the transfer was the owner of other premises adjoining those premises, and

    (*b*) a magistrates' court is satisfied that the transfer was intended for the purpose of evading the payment of expenses of street works,

the court may make an order under this section.

(2) An order under this section shall provide that, to such extent as the court making the order may determine, the street works authority may recover the said sum, and, where that sum is payable under an order made under section 212(4) above or section 305(2) below, any further sums which may fall due under that order, from the transferor.

(3) In this section "transfer" includes any disposal of land whether by way of sale, lease, exchange, gift or otherwise. **[1028]**

PART XIV

MISCELLANEOUS AND SUPPLEMENTARY PROVISIONS

Savings etc

345. Short title, commencement and extent

(1) This Act may be cited as the Highways Act 1980.

(2) This Act shall come into force on 1st January 1981.

(3) This Act (except paragraph 18(*c*) of Schedule 24) extends to England and Wales only. **[1029]**

SUPREME COURT ACT 1981
(c 54)

ARRANGEMENT OF SECTIONS

PART II

JURISDICTION

THE HIGH COURT

Powers

An Act to consolidate with amendments the Supreme Court of Judicature (Consolidation) Act 1925 and other enactments relating to the Supreme Court in England and Wales and the administration of justice therein; to repeal certain obsolete or unnecessary enactments so relating; to amend Part VIII of the Mental Health Act 1959, the Courts-Martial (Appeals) Act 1968, the Arbitration Act 1979 and the law relating to county courts; and for connected purposes [28 July 1981]

PART II

JURISDICTION

THE HIGH COURT

Powers

[35A. Power of High Court to award interest on debts and damages

(1) Subject to rules of court, in proceedings (whenever instituted) before the High Court for the recovery of a debt or damages there may be included in any sum for which judgment is given simple interest, at such rate as the court thinks fit or as rules of court may provide, on all or any part of the debt or damages in respect of which judgment is given, or payment is made before judgment, for all or any part of the period between the date when the cause of action arose and—

(*a*) in the case of any sum paid before judgment, the date of the payment; and

(*b*) in the case of the sum for which judgment is given, the date of the judgment.

(2) In relation to a judgment given for damages for personal injuries or death which exceed £200 subsection (1) shall have effect—

(*a*) with the substitution of "shall be included" for "may be included"; and

(*b*) with the addition of "unless the court is satisfied that there are special reasons to the contrary" after "given", where first occurring.

(3) Subject to rules of court, where—

(*a*) there are proceedings (whenever instituted) before the High Court for the recovery of a debt; and

(*b*) the defendant pays the whole debt to the plaintiff (otherwise than in pursuance of a judgment in the proceedings),

the defendant shall be liable to pay the plaintiff simple interest at such rate as the court thinks fit or as rules of court may provide on all or any part of the debt for all or any part of the period between the date when the cause of action arose and the date of the payment.

(4) Interest in respect of a debt shall not be awarded under this section for a period during which, for whatever reason, interest on the debt already runs.

(5) Without prejudice to the generality of section 84, rules of court may provide for a rate of interest by reference to the rate specified in section 17 of the Judgments Act 1838 as that section has effect from time to time or by reference to a rate for which any other enactment provides.

(6) Interest under this section may be calculated at different rates in respect of different periods.

(7) In this section "plaintiff" means the person seeking the debt or damages and "defendant" means the person from whom the plaintiff seeks the debt or damages and "personal injuries" includes any disease and any impairment of a person's physical or mental condition.

(8) Nothing in this section affects the damages recoverable for the dishonour of a bill of exchange.] **[1030]**

NOTES

Inserted by the Administration of Justice Act 1982, s 15(1), Sch 1, Part I.

37. Powers of High Court with respect to injunctions and receivers

(1) The High Court may by order (whether interlocutory or final) grant an injunction or appoint a receiver in all cases in which it appears to the court to be just and convenient to do so.

(2) Any such order may be made either unconditionally or on such terms and conditions as the court thinks just.

(3) The power of the High Court under subsection (1) to grant an interlocutory injunction restraining a party to any proceedings from removing from the jurisdiction of the High Court, or otherwise dealing with, assets located within that jurisdiction shall be exercisable in cases where that party is, as well as in cases where he is not, domiciled, resident or present within that jurisdiction.

(4) The power of the High Court to appoint a receiver by way of equitable execution shall operate in relation to all legal estates and interests in land; and that power—

(*a*) may be exercised in relation to an estate or interest in land whether or not a charge has been imposed on that land under section 1 of the Charging Orders Act 1979 for the purpose of enforcing the judgment, order or award in question; and

(*b*) shall be in addition to, and not in derogation of, any power of any court to appoint a receiver in proceedings for enforcing such a charge.

(5) Where an order under the said section 1 imposing a charge for the purpose of enforcing a judgment, order or award has been, or has effect as if, registered under section 6 of the Land Charges Act 1972, subsection (4) of the said section 6 (effect of non-registration of writs and orders registrable under that section) shall not apply to an order appointing a receiver made either—

(*a*) in proceedings for enforcing the charge; or

(*b*) by way of equitable execution of the judgment, order or award or, as the case may be, of so much of it as requires payment of moneys secured by the charge. **[1031]**

38. Relief against forfeiture for non-payment of rent

(1) In any action in the High Court for the forfeiture of a lease for non-payment of rent, the court shall have power to grant relief against forfeiture in a summary manner, and may do so subject to the same terms and conditions as to the payment of rent, costs or otherwise as could have been imposed by it in such an action immediately before the commencement of this Act.

(2) Where the lessee or a person deriving title under him is granted relief under this section, he shall hold the demised premises in accordance with the terms of the lease without the necessity for a new lease. **[1032]**

GENERAL PROVISIONS
Law and equity

49. Concurrent administration of law and equity

(1) Subject to the provisions of this or any other Act, every court exercising jurisdiction in England or Wales in any civil cause or matter shall continue to administer law and equity on the basis that, wherever there is any conflict or variance between the rules of equity and the rules of the common law with reference to the same matter, the rules of equity shall prevail.

(2) Every such court shall give the same effect as hitherto—

(*a*) to all equitable estates, titles, rights, reliefs, defences and counter-claims, and to all equitable duties and liabilities; and

(*b*) subject thereto, to all legal claims and demands and all estates, titles, rights, duties, obligations and liabilities existing by the common law or by any custom or created by any statute,

and, subject to the provisions of this or any other Act, shall so exercise its jurisdiction in every cause or matter before it as to secure that, as far as possible, all matters in dispute between the parties are completely and finally determined, and all multiplicity of legal proceedings with respect to any of those matters is avoided.

(3) Nothing in this Act shall affect the power of the Court of Appeal or the High Court to stay any proceedings before it, where it thinks fit to do so, either of its own motion or on the application of any person, whether or not a party to the proceedings. **[1033]**

50. Power to award damages as well as, or in substitution for, injunction or specific performance

Where the Court of Appeal or the High Court has jurisdiction to entertain an application for an injunction or specific performance, it may award damages in addition to, or in substitution for, an injunction or specific performance. **[1034]**

PART V

PROBATE CAUSES AND MATTERS

Powers of Court in relation to personal representatives

113. Power of court to sever grant

(1) Subject to subsection (2), the High Court may grant probate or administration in respect of any part of the estate of a deceased person, limited in any way the court thinks fit.

(2) Where the estate of a deceased person is known to be insolvent, the grant of representation to it shall not be severed under subsection (1) except as regards a trust estate in which he had no beneficial interest.   **[1035]**

114. Number of personal representatives

(1) Probate or administration shall not be granted by the High Court to more than four persons in respect of the same part of the estate of a deceased person.

(2) Where under a will or intestacy any beneficiary is a minor or a life interest arises, any grant of administration by the High Court shall be made either to a trust corporation (with or without an individual) or to not less than two individuals, unless it appears to the court to be expedient in all the circumstances to appoint an individual as sole administrator.

(3) For the purpose of determining whether a minority or life interest arises in any particular case, the court may act on such evidence as may be prescribed.

(4) If at any time during the minority of a beneficiary or the subsistence of a life interest under a will or intestacy there is only one personal representative (not being a trust corporation), the High Court may, on the application of any person interested or the guardian or receiver of any such person, and in accordance with probate rules, appoint one or more additional personal representatives to act while the minority or life interest subsists and until the estate is fully administered.

(5) An appointment of an additional personal representative under subsection (4) to act with an executor shall not have the effect of including him in any chain of representation.   **[1036]**

115. Grants to trust corporations

(1) The High Court may—

    (*a*) where a trust corporation is named in a will as executor, grant probate to the corporation either solely or jointly with any other person named in the will as executor, as the case may require; or

    (*b*) grant administration to a trust corporation, either solely or jointly with another person;

and the corporation may act accordingly as executor or administrator, as the case may be.

(2) Probate or administration shall not be granted to any person as nominee of a trust corporation.

(3) Any officer authorised for the purpose by a trust corporation or its directors or governing body may, on behalf of the corporation, swear affidavits, give security and do any other act which the court may require with a view to

the grant to the corporation of probate or administration; and the acts of an officer so authorised shall be binding on the corporation.

[*(4) Subsections (1) to (3) shall also apply in relation to any body which is exempt from the provisions of section 23(1) of the Solicitors Act 1974 (unqualified persons not to prepare papers for probate etc.) by virtue of any of paragraphs (e) to (h) of subsection (2) of that section.*] **[1037]**

NOTES

Sub-s (4): prospectively added by the Courts and Legal Services Act 1990, s 54(2).

116. Power of court to pass over prior claims to grant

(1) If by reason of any special circumstances it appears to the High Court to be necessary or expedient to appoint as administrator some person other than the person who, but for this section, would in accordance with probate rules have been entitled to the grant, the court may in its discretion appoint as administrator such person as it thinks expedient.

(2) Any grant of administration under this section may be limited in any way the court thinks fit. **[1038]**

117. Administration pending suit

(1) Where any legal proceedings concerning the validity of the will of a deceased person, or for obtaining, recalling or revoking any grant, are pending, the High Court may grant administration of the estate of the deceased person in question to an administrator pending suit, who shall, subject to subsection (2), have all the rights, duties and powers of a general administrator.

(2) An administrator pending suit shall be subject to the immediate control of the court and act under its direction; and, except in such circumstances as may be prescribed, no distribution of the estate, or any part of the estate, of the deceased person in question shall be made by such an administrator without the leave of the court.

(3) The court may, out of the estate of the deceased, assign an administrator pending suit such reasonable remuneration as it thinks fit. **[1039]**

118. Effect of appointment of minor as executor

Where a testator by his will appoints a minor to be an executor, the appointment shall not operate to vest in the minor the estate, or any part of the estate, of the testator, or to constitute him a personal representative for any purpose, unless and until probate is granted to him in accordance with probate rules. **[1040]**

119. Administration with will annexed

(1) Administration with the will annexed shall be granted, subject to and in accordance with probate rules, in every class of case in which the High Court had power to make such a grant immediately before the commencement of this Act.

(2) Where administration with the will annexed is granted, the will of the deceased shall be performed and observed in the same manner as if probate of it had been granted to an executor. **[1041]**

120. Power to require administrators to produce sureties

(1) As a condition of granting administration to any person the High Court may, subject to the following provisions of this section and subject to and in accordance with probate rules, require one or more sureties to guarantee that they will make good, within any limit imposed by the court on the total liability of the surety or sureties, any loss which any person interested in the administration of the estate of the deceased may suffer in consequence of a breach by the administrator of his duties as such.

(2) A guarantee given in pursuance of any such requirement shall enure for the benefit of every person interested in the administration of the estate of the deceased as if contained in a contract under seal made by the surety or sureties with every such person and, where there are two or more sureties, as if they had bound themselves jointly and severally.

(3) No action shall be brought on any such guarantee without the leave of the High Court.

(4) Stamp duty shall not be chargeable on any such guarantee.

(5) This section does not apply where administration is granted to the Treasury Solicitor, the Official Solicitor, the Public Trustee, the Solicitor for the affairs of the Duchy of Lancaster or the Duchy of Cornwall or the Crown Solicitor for Northern Ireland, or to the consular officer of a foreign state to which section 1 of the Consular Conventions Act 1949 applies, or in such other cases as may be prescribed.   **[1042]**

Revocation of grants and cancellation of resealing at instance of court

121. Revocation of grants and cancellation of resealing at instance of court

(1) Where it appears to the High Court that a grant either ought not to have been made or contains an error, the court may call in the grant and, if satisfied that it would be revoked at the instance of a party interested, may revoke it.

(2) A grant may be revoked under subsection (1) without being called in, if it cannot be called in.

(3) Where it appears to the High Court that a grant resealed under the Colonial Probates Acts 1892 and 1927 ought not to have been resealed, the court may call in the relevant document and, if satisfied that the resealing would be cancelled at the instance of a party interested, may cancel the resealing.

In this and the following subsection "the relevant document" means the original grant or, where some other document was sealed by the court under those Acts, that document.

(4) A resealing may be cancelled under subsection (3) without the relevant document being called in, if it cannot be called in.   **[1043]**

Interpretation of Part V and other probate provisions

128. Interpretation of Part V and other probate provisions

In this Part, and in the other provisions of this Act relating to probate causes and matters, unless the context otherwise requires—

"administration" includes all letters of administration of the effects of deceased persons, whether with or without a will annexed, and whether granted for general, special or limited purposes;

"estate" means real and personal estate, and "real estate" includes—

(a) chattels real and land in possession, remainder or reversion and every interest in or over land to which the deceased person was entitled at the time of his death, and

(b) real estate held on trust or by way of mortgage or security, but not money to arise under a trust for sale of land, nor money secured or charged on land;

"grant" means a grant of probate or administration;

"non-contentious or common form probate business" means the business of obtaining probate and administration where there is no contention as to the right thereto, including—

(a) the passing of probates and administrations through the High Court in contentious cases where the contest has been terminated,

(b) all business of a non-contentious nature in matters of testacy and intestacy not being proceedings in any action, and

(c) the business of lodging caveats against the grant of probate or administration;

"Principal Registry" means the Principal Registry of the Family Division;

"probate rules" means rules of court made under section 127;

"trust corporation" means the Public Trustee or a corporation either appointed by the court in any particular case to be a trustee or authorised by rules made under section 4(3) of the Public Trustee Act 1906 to act as a custodian trustee;

"will" includes a nuncupative will and any testamentary document of which probate may be granted. **[1044]**

WILDLIFE AND COUNTRYSIDE ACT 1981
(1981 c 69)

ARRANGEMENT OF SECTIONS

PART II
NATURE CONSERVATION, COUNTRYSIDE AND NATIONAL PARKS

Countryside

An Act to repeal and re-enact with amendments the Protection of Birds Acts 1954 to 1967 and the Conservation of Wild Creatures and Wild Plants Act 1975; to prohibit certain methods of killing or taking wild animals; to amend the law relating to protection of certain mammals; to restrict the introduction of certain animals and plants; to amend the Endangered Species (Import and Export) Act 1976; to amend the law relating to nature conservation, the countryside and National Parks and to make provision with respect to the Countryside Commission; to amend the law relating to public rights of way; and for connected purposes   [30 October 1981]

PART II

NATURE CONSERVATION, COUNTRYSIDE
AND NATIONAL PARKS

Countryside

39. Management agreements with owners and occupiers of land

(1) A relevant authority may, for the purpose of conserving or enhancing the natural beauty or amenity of any land which is both in the countryside and within their area or promoting its enjoyment by the public, make an agreement (in this section referred to as a "management agreement") with any person having an interest in the land with respect to the management of the land during a specified term or without limitation of the duration of the agreement.

(2) Without prejudice to the generality of subsection (1), a management agreement—

(*a*) may impose on the person having an interest in the land restrictions as respects the method of cultivating the land, its use for agricultural purposes or the exercise of rights over the land and may impose obligations on that person to carry out works or agricultural or forestry operations or do other things on the land;

(*b*) may confer on the relevant authority power to carry out works for the purpose of performing their functions under the 1949 Act and the 1968 Act; and

(*c*) may contain such incidental and consequential provisions (including provisions for the making of payments by either party to the other) as appear to the relevant authority to be necessary or expedient for the purposes of the agreement.

(3) The provisions of a management agreement with any person interested in the land shall, unless the agreement otherwise provides, be binding on persons deriving title under or from that person and be enforceable by the relevant authority against those persons accordingly.

(4) Schedule 2 to the Forestry Act 1967 (power for tenant for life and others to enter into forestry dedication covenants) shall apply to management agreements as it applies to forestry dedication covenants.

(5) In this section "the relevant authority" mean—

(*a*) as respects land in a National Park [and outside a metropolitan county], the county planning authority;

[(*aa*) as respects land within the Broads, the Broads Authority;]

(*b*) . . .

(*c*) as respects any other land, the local planning authority.

(6) The powers conferred by this section on a relevant authority shall be in addition to and not in derogation of any powers conferred on such an authority by or under any enactment. **[1044A]**

NOTES

Sub-s (5): words in square brackets in para (*a*) inserted and para (*b*) repealed by the Local Government Act 1985, ss 7, 102, Sch 3, para 7, Sch 17; para (*aa*) inserted by the Norfolk and Suffolk Broads Act 1988, s 2, Sch 3, Part I.

1949 Act: National Parks and Access to Countryside Act 1949.

1968 Act: Countryside Act 1968.

PART III

PUBLIC RIGHTS OF WAY

Ascertainment of public rights of way

53. Duty to keep definitive map and statement under continuous review

(1) In the Part "definitive map and statement", in relation to any area, means, subject to section 57(3)—

(*a*) the latest revised map and statement prepared in definitive form for that area under section 33 of the 1949 Act; or

(*b*) where no such map and statement have been so prepared, the original definitive map and statement prepared for that area under section 32 of that Act; or

(*c*) where no such map and statement have been so prepared, the map and statement prepared for that area under section 55(3).

(2) As regards every definitive map and statement, the surveying authority shall—

(*a*) as soon as reasonably practicable after the commencement date, by order make such modifications to the map and statement as appear to them to be requisite in consequence of the occurrence, before that date, of any of the events specified in subsection (3); and

(*b*) as from that date, keep the map and statement under continuous review and as soon as reasonably practicable after the occurrence, on or after that date, of any of those events, by order make such modifications to the map and statement as appear to them to be requisite in consequence of the occurrence of that event.

(3) The events referred to in subsection (2) are as follows—

(*a*) the coming into operation of any enactment or instrument, or any other event, whereby—

(i) a highway shown or required to be shown in the map and statement has been authorised to be stopped up, diverted, widened or extended;

(ii) a highway shown or required to be shown in the map and statement as a highway of a particular description has ceased to be a highway of that description; or

(iii) a new right of way has been created over land in the area to which the map relates, being a right of way such that the land over which the right subsists is a public path;

(*b*) the expiration, in relation to any way in the area to which the map relates, of any period such that the enjoyment by the public of the way during that period raises a presumption that the way has been dedicated as a public path;

(c) the discovery by the authority of evidence which (when considered with all other relevant evidence available to them) shows—

   (i) that a right of way which is not shown in the map and statement subsists or is reasonably alleged to subsist over land in the area to which the map relates, being a right of way to which this Part applies;

   (ii) that a highway shown in the map and statement as a highway of a particular description ought to be there shown as a highway of a different description; or

   (iii) that there is no public right of way over land shown in the map and statement as a highway of any description, or any other particulars contained in the map and statement require modification.

(4) The modifications which may be made by an order under subsection (2) shall include the addition to the statement of particulars as to—

(a) the position and width of any public path or byway open to all traffic which is or is to be shown on the map; and

(b) any limitations or conditions affecting the public right of way thereover.

(5) Any person may apply to the authority for an order under subsection (2) which makes such modifications as appear to the authority to be requisite in consequence of the occurrence of one or more events falling within paragraph (b) or (c) of subsection (3); and the provisions of Schedule 14 shall have effect as to the making and determination of applications under this subsection.

(6) Orders under subsection (2) which make only such modifications as appear to the authority to be requisite in consequence of the occurrence of one or more events falling within paragraph (a) of subsection (3) shall take effect on their being made; and the provisions of Schedule 15 shall have effect as to the making, validity and date of coming into operation of other orders under subsection (2). **[1045]**

NOTES
1949 Act: National Parks and Acces to the Countryside Act 1949.

54. Duty to reclassify roads used as public paths

(1) As regards every definitive map and statement, the surveying authority shall, as soon as reasonably practicable after the commencement date—

(a) carry out a review of such of the particulars contained in the map and statement as relate to roads used as public paths; and

(b) by order make such modifications to the map and statement as appear to the authority to be requisite to give effect to subsections (2) and (3);

and the provisions of Schedule 15 shall have effect as to the making, validity and date of coming into operation of orders under this subsection.

(2) A definitive map and statement shall show every road used as a public path by one of the three following descriptions, namely—

(a) a byway open to all traffic;

(b) a bridleway;

(*c*) a footpath,

and shall not employ the expression "road used as a public path" to describe any way.

(3) A road used as a public path shall be shown in the definitive map and statement as follows—

  (*a*) if a public right of way for vehicular traffic has been shown to exist, as a byway open to all traffic;

  (*b*) if paragraph (*a*) does not apply and public bridleway rights have not been shown not to exist, as a bridlewy; and

  (*c*) if neither paragraph (*a*) nor paragraph (*b*) applies, as a footpath.

(4) Each way which, in pursuance of an order under subsection (1), is shown in the map and statement by any of the three descriptions shall, as from the coming into operation of the order, be a highway maintainable at the public expense; and each way which, in pursuance of paragraph 9 of Part III of Schedule 3 to the 1968 Act, is so shown shall continue to be so maintainable.

(5) In this section "road used a a public path" means a way which is shown in the definitive map and statement as a road used as a public path.

(6) In subsections (2)(*a*) and (5) of section 51 of the 1949 Act (long distance routes) references to roads used as public paths shall include references to any way shown in a definitive map and statement as a byway open to all traffic.

(7) Nothing in this section or section 53 shall limit the operation of traffic orders under the Road Traffic Regulation Act [1984] or oblige a highway authority to provide, on a way shown in a definitive map and statement as a byway open to all traffic, a metalled carriage-way or a carriage-way which is by any other means provided with a surface suitable for the passage of vehicles.

[1046]

NOTES
  Sub-s (7): date in square brackets substituted by the Road Traffic Regulations Act 1984, s 146, Sch 13.
  1949 Act: National Parks and Access to the Countryside Act 1949.
  1968 Act: Countryside Act 1968.

56. Effect of definitive map and statement

(1) A definitive map and statement shall be conclusive evidence as to the particulars contained therein to the following extent, namely—

  (*a*) where the map shows a footpath, the map shall be conclusive evidence that there was at the relevant date a highway as shown on the map, and that the public had thereover a right of way on foot, so however that this paragraph shall be without prejudice to any question whether the public had at that date any right of way other than that right;

  (*b*) where the map shows a bridleway, the map shall be conclusive evidence that there was at the relevant date a highway as shown on the map, and that the public had thereover at that date a right of way on foot and a right of way on horseback or leading a horse, so however that this paragraph shall be without prejudice to any question whether the public had at that date any right of way other than those rights;

  (*c*) where the map shows a byway open to all traffic, the map shall be conclusive evidence that there was at the relevant date a highway as shown on the map, and that the public had thereover at that date a right of way for vehicular and all other kinds of traffic;

(*d*) where the map shows a road used as a public path, the map shall be conclusive evidence that there was at the relevant date a highway as shown on the map, and that the public had thereover at that date a right of way on foot and a right of way on horseback or leading a horse, so however that this paragraph shall be without prejudice to any question whether the public had at that date any right of way other than those rights; and

(*e*) where by virtue of the foregoing paragraphs the map is conclusive evidence, as at any date, as to a highway shown thereon, any particulars contained in the statement as to the position or width thereof shall be conclusive evidence as to the position or width thereof at that date, and any particulars so contained as to limitations or conditions affecting the public right of way shall be conclusive evidence that at the said date the said right was subject to those limitations or conditions, but without prejudice to any question whether the right was subject to any other limitations or conditions at that date.

(2) For the purposes of this section "the relevant date"—

(*a*) in relation to any way which is shown on the map otherwise than in pursuance of an order under the foregoing provisions of this Part, means the date specified in the statement as the relevant date for the purposes of the map;

(*b*) in relation to any way which is shown on the map in pursuance of such an order, means the date which, in accordance with subsection (3), is specified in the order as the relevant date for the purposes of the order.

(3) Every order under the foregoing provisions of this Part shall specify, as the relevant date for the purposes of the order, such date, not being earlier than six months before the making of the order, as the authority may determine.

(4) A document purporting to be certified on behalf of the surveying authority to be a copy of or of any part of a definitive map or statement as modified in accordance with the provisions of this Part shall be receivable in evidence and shall be deemed, unless the contrary is shown, to be such a copy.

(5) Where it appears to the Secretary of State that paragraph (*d*) of subsection (1) can have no further application, he may by order made by statutory instrument repeal that paragraph. **[1047]**

58. Application of ss 53 to 57 to inner London

(1) Subject to subsection (2), the foregoing provisions of this Part shall not apply to any area to which this subsection applies; and this subsection applies to any area which, immediaely before 1st April 1965, formed part of the administrative county of London.

(2) A London borough council may by resolution adopt the said foregoing provisions as respects any part of their area specified in the resolution, being a part to which subsection (1) applies, and those provisions shall thereupon apply accordingly.

(3) Where by virtue of a resolution under subsection (2), the said foregoing provisions apply to any area, those provisions shall have effect in relation thereto as if for references to the commencement date there were substituted references to the date on which the resolution comes into operation. **[1048]**

59. Prohibition on keeping bulls on land crossed by public rights of way

(1) If, in a case not falling within subsection (2), the occupier of a field or enclosure crossed by a right of way to which this Part applies permits a bull to be at large in the field or enclosure, he shall be liable on summary conviction to a fine not exceeding [level 3 on the standard scale].

(2) Subsection (1) shall not apply to any bull which—

(*a*) does not exceed the age of ten months; or
(*b*) is not of a recognised dairy breed and is at large in any field or enclosure in which cows or heifers are also at large

(3) Nothing in any byelaws, whenever made, shall make unlawful any act which is, or but for subsection (2) would be, made unlawful by subsection (1).

(4) In this section "recognised dairy breed" means one of the following breeds, namely, Ayrshire, British Friesian, British Holstein, Dairy Shorthorn, Guernsey, Jersey and Kerry.

(5) The Secretary of State may by order add any breed to, or remove any breed from, subsection (4); and an order under this subsection shall be made by statutory instrument which shall be subject to annulment in pursuance of a resolution of either House of Parliament.   **[1049]**

NOTES
    Sub-s (1): maximum fine converted to level on the standard scale by the Criminal Justice Act 1982, ss 37, 46.

66. Interpretation of Part III

(1) In this Part—

"bridleway" means a highway over which the public have the following, but no other, rights of way, that is to say, a right of way on foot and a right of way on horseback or leading a horse, with or without a right to drive animals of any description along the highway;
"byway open to all traffic" means a highway over which the public have a right of way for vehicular and all other kinds of traffic, but which is used by the public mainly for the purpose for which footpaths and bridleways are so used;
"definitive map and statement" has the meaning given by section 53(1);
"footpath" means a highway over which the public have a right of way on foot only, other than such a highway at the side of a public road;
"horse" includes a pony, ass and mule, and "horseback" shall be construed accordingly;
"public path" means a highway being either a footpath or a bridleway;
"right of way to which this Part applies" means a right of way such that the land over which the right subsists is a public path or a byway open to all traffic;
["surveying authority", in relation to any area, means the county council, metropolitan district council or London borough council whose area includes that area.]

(2) A highway at the side of a river, canal or other inland navigation shall not be excluded from any definition contained in subsection (1) by reason only

that the public have a right to use the highway for purposes of navigation, if the highway would fall within that definition if the public had no such right thereover.   **[1050]**

NOTES
    Sub-s (1): definition "surveying authority" substituted by the Local Government Act 1985, s 7, Sch 3, para 7.

LOCAL GOVERNMENT (MISCELLANEOUS PROVISIONS) ACT 1982
(c 30)

An Act to make amendments for England and Wales of provisions of that part of the law relating to local authorities or highways which is commonly amended by local Acts; to make provision for the control of sex establishments; to make further provision for the control of refreshment premises and for consultation between local authorities in England and Wales and fire authorities with regard to fire precautions for buildings and caravan sites; to repeal the Theatrical Employers Registration Acts 1925 and 1928; to make further provision as to the enforcement of section 8 of the Public Utilities Street Works Act 1950 and sections 171 and 174 of the Highways Act 1980; to make provision in connection with the computerisation of local land charges registers', to make further provision in connection with the acquisition of land and rights over land by boards constituted in pursuance of section 1 of the Town and Country Planning Act 1971 or reconstituted in pursuance of Schedule 17 to the Local Government Act 1972; to exclude from the definition of "construction or maintenance work" in section 20 of the Local Government, Planning and Land Act 1980 work undertaken by local authorities and development bodies pursuant to certain agreements with the [Training Commission] which specify the work to be undertaken and under which the Commission agrees to pay the whole or part of the cost of the work so specified; to define "year" for the purposes of Part III of the said Act of 1980; to amend section 140 of the Local Government Act 1972 and to provide for the insurance by local authorities of persons voluntarily assisting probation committees; to make provision for controlling nuisance and disturbance on educational premises; to amend section 137 of the Local Government Act 1972; to make further provision as to arrangements made by local authorities under the Employment and Training Act 1973; to extend the duration of certain powers to assist industry or employment conferred by local Acts; to make corrections and minor improvements in certain enactments relating to the local administration of health and planning functions; and for connected purposes   [13 July 1982]

NOTES
    Words in square brackets substituted by virtue of the Employment Act 1988, s 24.

PART XII
MISCELLANEOUS

33. Enforceability by local authorities of certain covenants relating to land

(2) If, in a case where this section applies,—

(*a*) the instrument contains a covenant on the part of any person having an interest in land, being a covenant to carry out any works or do any other thing on or in relation to that land, and

(*b*) the instrument defines the land to which the covenant relates, being land in which that person has an interest at the time the instrument is executed, and

(*c*) the covenant is expressed to be one to which this section or section 126 of the Housing Act 1974 (which is superseded by this section) applies,

the covenant shall be enforceable (without any limit of time) against any person deriving title from the original covenantor in respect of his interest in any of the land defined as mentioned in paragraph (*b*) above and any person deriving title under him in respect of any lesser interest in that land as if that person had also been an original covenanting party in respect of the interest for the time being held by him.   **[1050A]**

ADMINISTRATION OF JUSTICE ACT 1982
(c 53)

ARRANGEMENT OF SECTIONS

PART IV
WILLS

Rectification and interpretation of wills

Registration of wills

An Act to make further provision with respect to the administration of justice and matters connected therewith; to amend the law relating to actions for damages for personal injuries, including injuries resulting in death, and to abolish certain actions for loss of services; to amend the law relating to wills; to make further provision with respect to funds in court, statutory deposits and schemes for the common investment of such funds and deposits and certain other funds; to amend the law relating to deductions by employers under attachment of earnings orders; to make further provision with regard to penalties that may be awarded by the Solicitors' Disciplinary Tribunal under section 47 of the Solicitors Act 1974; to make further provision for the appointment of justices of the peace in England and Wales and in relation to temporary vacancies in the membership of the Law Commission; to enable the title register kept by the Chief Land Registrar to be kept otherwise than in documentary form; and to authorise the payment of travelling, subsistence and financial loss allowances for justices of the peace in Northern Ireland   [28 October 1982]

PART IV

WILLS

Rectification and interpretation of wills

20. Rectification

(1) If a court is satisfied that a will is so expressed that it fails to carry out the testator's intentions, in consequence—

(a) of a clerical error; or

(b) of a failure to understand his instructions,

it may order that the will shall be rectified so as to carry out his intentions.

(2) An application for an order under this section shall not, except with the permission of the court, be made after the end of the period of six months from the date on which representation with respect to the estate of the deceased is first taken out.

(3) The provisions of this section shall not render the personal representatives of a deceased person liable for having distributed any part of the estate of the deceased, after the end of the period of six months from the date on which representation with respect to the estate of the deceased is first taken out, on the ground that they ought to have taken into account the possibility that the court might permit the making of an application for an order under this section after the end of that period; but this subsection shall not prejudice any power to recover, by reason of the making of an order under this section, any part of the estate so distributed.

(4) In considering for the purposes of this section when representation with respect to the estate of a deceased person was first taken out, a grant limited to settled land or to trust property shall be left out of account, and a grant limited to real estate or to personal estate shall be left out of account unless a grant limited to the remainder of the estate has previously been made or is made at the same time.   **[1051]**

21. Interpretation of wills — general rules as to evidence

(1) This section applies to a will—

(a) in so far as any part of it is meaningless;

(b) in so far as the language used in any part of it is ambiguous on the face of it;

(c) in so far as evidence, other than evidence of the testator's intention, shows that the language used in any part of it is ambiguous in the light of surrounding circumstances.

(2) In so far as this section applies to a will extrinsic evidence, including evidence of the testator's intention, may be admitted to assist in its interpretation.   **[1052]**

22. Presumption as to effect of gifts to spouses

Except where a contrary intention is shown it shall be presumed that if a testator devises or bequeaths property to his spouse in terms which in themselves would give an absolute interest to the spouse, but by the same instrument purports to give his issue an interest in the same property, the gift to the spouse is absolute notwithstanding the purported gift to the issue.   **[1053]**

Registration of wills

23. Deposit and registration of wills of living persons

(1) The following, namely—

    (*a*) the Principal Registry of the Family Division of the High Court of Justice;

    (*b*) the Keeper of the Registers of Scotland; and

    (*c*) the Probate and Matrimonial Office of the Supreme Court of Northern Ireland,

shall be registering authorities for the purposes of this section.

(2) Each registering authority shall provide and maintain safe and convenient depositories for the custody of the wills of living persons.

(3) Any person may deposit his will in such a depository in accordance with regulations under section 25 below and on payment of the prescribed fee.

(4) It shall be the duty of a registering authority to register in accordance with regulations under section 25 below—

    (*a*) any will deposited in a depository maintained by the authority; and

    (*b*) any other will whose registration is requested under Article 6 of the Registration Convention.

(5) A will deposited in a depository provided—

    (*a*) under section 172 of the Supreme Court of Judicature (Consolidation) Act 1925 or section 126 of the Supreme Court Act 1981; or

    (*b*) under Article 27 of the Administration of Estates (Northern Ireland) Order 1979,

shall be treated for the purposes of this section as if it had been deposited under this section.

(6) In this section "prescribed" means—

    (*a*) in the application of this section to England and Wales, prescribed by an order under section 130 of the Supreme Court Act 1981;

    (*b*) in its application to Scotland, prescribed by an order under section 26 below; and

    (*c*) in its application to Northern Ireland, prescribed by an order under section 116 of the Judicature (Northern Ireland) Act 1978.   **[1054]**

NOTES

Commencement: To be appointed.

24. Designation of Principal Registry as national body under Registration Convention

(1) The Principal Registry of the Family Division of the High Court of Justice shall be the national body for the purposes of the Registration Convention, and shall accordingly have the functions assigned to the national body by the Registration Convention including, without prejudice to the general application of the Convention to the Principal Registry by virtue of this section, the functions—

    (*a*) of arranging for the registration of wills in other Contracting States as provided for in Article 6 of the Convention;

(b) of receiving and answering requests for information arising from the national bodies of other Contracting States.

(2) In this Part of this Act "the Registration Convention" means the Convention on the Establishment of a Scheme of Registration of Wills concluded at Basle on 16th May 1972. **[1055]**

NOTES

Commencement: To be appointed.

25. Regulations as to deposit and registration of wills

(1) Regulations may make provision—

    (a) as to the conditions for the deposit of a will;

    (b) as to the manner of and procedure for—

        (i) the deposit and registration of a will; and

        (ii) the withdrawal of a will which has been deposited; and

        (iii) the cancellation of the registration of a will; and

    (c) as to the manner in which the Principal Registry of the Family Division is to perform its functions as the national body under the Registration Convention.

(2) Regulations under this section may contain such incidental or supplementary provisions as the authority making the regulations considers appropriate.

(3) Any such regulations are to be made—

    (a) for England and Wales, by the President of the Family Division of the High Court of Justice, with the concurrence of the Lord Chancellor;

    (b) for Scotland, by the Secretary of State after consultation with the Lord President of the Court of Session; and

    (c) for Northern Ireland, by the Northern Ireland Supreme Court Rules Committee, with the concurrence of the Lord Chancellor.

(4) Regulations made by virtue of subsection (1)(c) above shall be made by the Lord Chancellor.

(5) Subject to subsection (6) below, regulations under this section shall be made by statutory instrument and shall be laid before Parliament after being made.

(6) Regulations for Northern Ireland shall be statutory rules for the purposes of the Statutory Rules (Northern Ireland) Order 1979; and any such statutory rule shall be laid before Parliament after being made in like manner as a statutory instrument and section 4 of the Statutory Instruments Act 1946 shall apply accordingly.

(7) The Statutory Instruments Act 1946 shall apply to a statutory instrument containing regulations made in accordance with subsection (3)(a) or (c) above as if the regulations had been made by a Minister of the Crown.

(8) Any regulations made under section 172 of the Supreme Court of Judicature (Consolidation) Act 1925 or section 126 of the Supreme Court Act 1981 shall have effect for the purposes of this Part of this Act as they have effect for the purposes of the enactment under which they were made. **[1056]**

NOTES
Commencement: To be appointed.

MATRIMONIAL HOMES ACT 1983
(c 19)

ARRANGEMENT OF SECTIONS

An Act to consolidate certain enactments relating to the rights of a husband or wife to occupy a dwelling house that has been a matrimonial home   [9 May 1983]

1. Rights concerning matrimonial home where one spouse has no estate, etc

(1) Where one spouse is entitled to occupy a dwelling house by virtue of a beneficial estate or interest or contract or by virtue of any enactment giving him or her the right to remain in occupation, and the other spouse is not so entitled, then, subject to the provisions of this Act, the spouse not so entitled shall have the following rights (in this Act referred to as "rights of occupation")—

     (a) if in occupation, a right not to be evicted or excluded from the dwelling house or any part thereof by the other spouse except with the leave of the court given by an order under this section;

     (b) if not in occupation, a right with the leave of the court so given to enter into and occupy the dwelling house.

(2) So long as one spouse has rights of occupation, either of the spouses may apply to the court for an order—

     (a) declaring, enforcing, restricting or terminating those rights, or

     (b) prohibiting, suspending or restricting the exercise by either spouse of the right to occupy the dwelling house, or

     (c) requiring either spouse to permit the exercise by the other of that right.

(3) On an application for an order under this section, the court may make such order as it thinks just and reasonable having regard to the conduct of the

spouses in relation to each other and otherwise, to their respective needs and financial resources, to the needs of any children and to all the circumstances of the case, and, without prejudice to the generality of the foregoing provision—

(a) may except part of the dwelling house from a spouse's rights of occupation (and in particular a part used wholly or mainly for or in connection with the trade, business or profession of the other spouse),

(b) may order a spouse occupying the dwelling house or any part thereof by virtue of this section to make periodical payments to the other in respect of the occupation,

(c) may impose on either spouse obligations as to the repair and maintenance of the dwelling house or the discharge of any liabilities in respect of the dwelling house.

(4) Orders under this section may, in so far as they have a continuing effect, be limited so as to have effect for a period specified in the order or until further order.

(5) Where a spouse is entitled under this section to occupy a dwelling house or any part thereof, any payment or tender made or other thing done by that spouse in or towards satisfaction of any liability of the other spouse in respect of rent, rates, mortgage payments or other outgoings affecting the dwelling house shall, whether or not it is made or done in pursuance of an order under this section, be as good as if made or done by the other spouse.

(6) A spouse's occupation by virtue of this section shall, for the purposes of the Rent (Agriculture) Act 1976, and of the Rent Act 1977 (other than Part V and sections 103 to 106), be treated as possession by the other spouse and [for purposes of Part IV of the Housing Act 1985 [and Part I of the Housing Act 1988] (secured tenancies)] be treated as occupation by the other spouse.

(7) Where a spouse is entitled under this section to occupy a dwelling house or any part thereof and makes any payment in or towards satisfaction of any liability of the other spouse in respect of mortgage payments affecting the dwelling house, the person to whom the payment is made may treat it as having been made by that other spouse, but the fact that that person has treated any such payment as having been so made shall not affect any claim of the first-mentioned spouse against the other to an interest in the dwelling house by virtue of the payment.

(8) Where a spouse is entitled under this section to occupy a dwelling house or part thereof by reason of an interest of the other spouse under a trust, all the provisions of subsections (5) to (7) above shall apply in relation to the trustees as they apply in relation to the other spouse.

(9) The jurisdiction conferred on the court by this section shall be exercisable by the High Court or by a county court, and shall be exercisable by a county court notwithstanding that by reason of the amount of the net annual value for rating of the dwelling house or otherwise the jurisdiction would not but for this subsection be exercisable by a county court.

(10) This Act shall not apply to a dwelling house which has at no time been a matrimonial home of the spouses in question; and a spouse's rights of occupation shall continue only so long as the marriage subsists and the other spouse is entitled as mentioned in subsection (1) above to occupy the dwelling house, except where provision is made by section 2 of this Act for those rights to be a charge on an estate or interest in the dwelling house.

(11) It is hereby declared that a spouse who has an equitable interest in a

dwelling house or in the proceeds of sale thereof, not being a spouse in whom is vested (whether solely or as a joint tenant) a legal estate in fee simple or a legal term of years absolute in the dwelling house, is to be treated for the purpose only of determining whether he or she has rights of occupation under this section as not being entiled to occupy the dwelling house by virtue of that interest.   **[1057]**

NOTES
    Sub-s (6): first words in square brackets substituted by the Housing (Consequential Provisions) Act 1985, s 4, Sch 2, para 56, words in square brackets therein inserted by the Housing Act 1988, s 140, Sch 17, Part I.

2. Effect of rights of occupation as charge on dwelling house

(1) Where, at any time during the subsistence of a marriage, one spouse is entitled to occupy a dwelling house by virtue of a beneficial estate or interest, then the other spouse's rights of occupation shall be a charge on that estate or interest, having the like priority as if it were an equitable interest created at whichever is the latest of the following dates, that is to say—

  (a) the date when the spouse so entitled acquires the estate or interest,
  (b) the date of the marriage, and
  (c) the 1st January 1968 (which is the date of commencement of the Act of 1967).

(2) If, at any time when a spouse's rights of occupation are a charge on an interest of the other spouse under a trust, there are, apart from either of the spouses, no persons, living or unborn, who are or could become beneficiaries under the trust, then those rights shall be a charge also on the estate or interest of the trustees for the other spouse, having the like priority as if it were an equitable interest created (under powers overriding the trusts) on the date when it arises.

(3) In determining for purposes of subsection (2) above whether there are any persons who are not, but could become, beneficiaries under the trust, there shall be disregarded any potential exercise of a general power of appointment exercisable by either or both of the spouses alone (whether or not the exercise of it requires the consent of another person).

(4) Notwithstanding that a spouse's rights of occupation are a charge on an estate or interest in the dwelling house, those rights shall be brought to an end by—

  (a) the death of the other spouse, or
  (b) the termination (otherwise than by death) of the marriage,

unless in the event of a matrimonial dispute or estrangement the court sees fit to direct otherwise by an order made under section 1 above during the subsistence of the marriage.

(5) Where a spouse's rights of occupation are a charge on the estate or interest of the other spouse or of trustees for the other spouse—

  (a) any order under section 1 above against the other spouse shall, except in so far as the contrary intention appears, have the like effect against persons deriving title under the other spouse or under the trustees and affected by the charge, and
  (b) subsections (2) to (8) of section 1 above shall apply in relation to any person deriving title under the other spouse or under the trustees and affected by the charge as they apply in relation to the other spouse.

(6) Where—

    (a) a spouse's rights of occupation are a charge on an estate or interest in the dwelling house, and

    (b) that estate or interest is surrendered so as to merge in some other estate or interest expectant thereon in such circumstances that, but for the merger, the person taking the estate or interest surrendered would be bound by the charge,

the surrender shall have effect subject to the charge and the persons thereafter entitled to the other estate or interest shall, for so long as the estate or interest surrendered would have endured if not so surrendered, be treated for all purposes of this Act as deriving title to the other estate or interest under the other spouse or, as the case may be, under the trustees for the other spouse, by virtue of the surrender.

(7) . . .

(8) Where the title to the legal estate by virtue of which a spouse is entitled to occupy a dwelling house (including any legal estate held by trustees for that spouse) is registered under the Land Registration Act 1925 or any enactment replaced by that Act—

    (a) registration of a land charge affecting the dwelling house by virtue of this Act shall be effected by registering a notice under that Act, and

    (b) a spouse's rights of occupation shall not be an overriding interest within the meaning of that Act affecting the dwelling house notwithstanding that the spouse is in actual occupation of the dwelling house.

(9) A spouse's rights of occupation (whether or not constituting a charge) shall not entitle that spouse to lodge a caution under section 54 of the Land Registration Act 1925.

(10) Where—

    (a) a spouse's rights of occupation are a charge on the estate of the other spouse or of trustees for the other spouse, and

    (b) that estate is the subject of a mortgage within the meaning of the Law of Property Act 1925,

then, if, after the date of creation of the mortgate, the charge is registered under section 2 of the Land Charges Act 1972, the charge shall, for the purposes of section 94 of that Act of 1925 (which regulates the rights of mortgagees to make further advances ranking in priority to subsequent mortgages), be deemed to be mortgage subsequent in date to the first-mentioned mortgage.

(11) It is hereby declared that a charge under subsection (1) or (2) above is not registrable under section 2 of the Land Charges Act 1972 or subsection (8) above unless it is a charge on a legal estate.   **[1058]**

NOTES

    Sub-s (7): repealed by the Insolvency Act 1985, s 235, Sch 10, Part III.

    The Act of 1967: Matrimonial Homes Act 1967.

3. Restriction on registration where spouse entitled to more than one charge

Where one spouse is entitled by virtue of section 2 above to a registrable charge in respect of each of two or more dwelling houses, only one of the charges to which that spouse is so entitled shall be registered under section 2 of the Land Charges Act 1972 or section 2(8) above at any one time, and if any of those charges is registered under either of those provisions the Chief Land Registrar, on being satisfied that any other of them is so registered, shall cancel the registration of the charge first registered. **[1059]**

4. Contract for sale of house affected by registered charge to include term requiring cancellation of registration before completion

(1) Where one spouse is entitled by virtue of section 2 above to a charge on an estate in a dwelling house and the charge is registered under section 2 of the Land Charges Act 1972 or section 2(8) above, it shall be a term of any contract for the sale of that estate whereby the vendor agrees to give vacant possession of the dwelling house on completion of the contract that the vendor will before such completion procure the cancellation of the registration of the charge at his expense.

(2) Subsection (1) above shall not apply to any such contract made by a vendor who is entitled to sell the estate in the dwelling house freed from any such charge.

(3) If, on the completion of such a contract as is referred to in subsection (1) above, there is delivered to the purchaser or his solicitor an application by the spouse entitled to the charge for the cancellation of the registration of that charge, the term of the contract for which subsection (1) above provides shall be deemed to have been performed.

(4) This section applies only if and so far as a contrary intention is not expressed in the contract.

(5) This section shall apply to a contract for exchange as it applies to a contract for sale.

(6) This section shall, with the necessary modifications, apply to a contract for the grant of a lease or underlease of a dwelling house as it applies to a contract for the sale of an estate in a dwelling house. **[1060]**

5. Cancellation of registration after termination of marriage, etc

(1) Where a spouse's rights of occupation are a charge on an estate in a dwelling house and the charge is registered under section 2 of the Land Charges Act 1972 or section 2(8) above, the Chief Land Registrar shall, subject to subsection (2) below, cancel the registration of the charge if he is satisfied—

    (a) by the production of a certificate or other sufficient evidence, that either spouse is dead, or

    (b) by the production of an official copy of a decree of a court, that the marriage in question has been terminated otherwise than by death, or

    (c) by the production of an order of the court, that the spouse's rights of occupation constitution the charge have been terminated by the order.

    (2) Where—

    (a) the marriage in question has been terminated by the death of the spouse entitled to an estate in the dwelling house or otherwise than by death, and

    (b) an order affecting the charge of the spouse not so entitled had been made by virtue of section 2(4) above,

then if, after the making of the order, registration of the charge was renewed or the charge registered in pursuance of subsection (3) below, the Chief Land Registrar shall not cancel the registration of the charge in accordance with subsection (1) above unless he is also satisified that the order has ceased to have effect.

(3) Where such an order has been made, then, for the purposes of subsection (2) above, the spouse entitled to the charge affected by the order may—

(a) if before the date of the order the charge was registered under section 2 of the Land Charges Act 1972 or section 2(8) above, renew the registration of the charge, and

(b) if before the said date the charge was not so registered, register the charge under section 2 of the Land Charges Act 1972 or section 2(8) above.

(4) Renewal of the registration of a charge in pursuance of subsection (3) above shall be effected in such manner as may be prescribed, and an application for such renewal or for registration of a chrage in pursuance of that subsection shall contain such particulars of any order affecting the charge made by virtue of section 2(4) above as may be prescribed.

(5) The renewal in pursuance of subsection (3) above of the registration of a charge shall not affect the priority of the charge.

(6) In this section "prescribed" means prescribed by rules made under section 16 of the Land Charges Act 1972 or section 144 of the Land Registration Act 1925, as the circumstances of the case require. **[1061]**

6. Release of rights of occupation and postponement of priority of charges

(1) A spouse entitled to rights of occupation may by a release in writing release those rights or release them as respects part only of the dwelling house affected by them.

(2) Where a contract is made for the sale of an estate or interest in a dwelling house, or for the grant of a lease or underlease of a dwelling house, being (in either case) a dwelling house affected by a charge registered under section 2 of the Land Charges Act 1972 or section 2(8) above, then, without prejudice to subsection (1) above, the rights of occupation constituting the charge shall be deemed to have been released on the happening of whichever of the following events first occurs—

(a) the delivery to the purchaser or lessee, as the case may be, or his solicitor on completion of the contract of an application by the spouse entitled to the charge for the cancellation of the registration of the charge, or

(b) the lodging of such an application at Her Majesty's Land Registry.

(3) A spouse entitled by virtue of section 2 above to a charge on an estate or interest may agree in writing that any other charge on, or interest in, that estate or interest shall rank in priority to the charge to which that spouse is so entitled. **[1062]**

7. Transfer of certain tenancies on divorce, etc

Schedule 1 to this Act shall have effect. **[1063]**

8. Dwelling house subject to mortgage

(1) In determining for the purposes of the foregoing provisions of this Act (including Schedule 1) whether a spouse or former spouse is entitled to occupy a dwelling house by virtue of an estate or interest, there shall be disregarded any

right to possession of the dwelling house conferred on a mortgagee of the dwelling house under or by virtue of his mortgage, whether the mortgagee is in possession or not; but the other spouse shall not by virtue of the rights of occupation conferred by this Act have any larger right against the morgagee to occupy the dwelling house than the one first mentioned has by virtue of his or her estate or interest and of any contract with the mortgagee, unless under section 2 above those rights of occupation are a charge, affecting the mortgagee, on the estate or interest mortgaged.

(2) Where a mortgagee of land which consists of or includes a dwelling house brings an action in any court for the enforcement of his security, a spouse who is not a party to the action and who is enabled by section 1(5) or (8) above to meet the mortgagor's liabilities under the mortgage, on applying to the court at any time before the action is finally disposed of in that court, shall be entiled to be made a party to the action if the court—

    (*a*) does not see special reason against it, and

    (*b*) is satisfied that the applicant may be expected to make such payments or do such things in or towards satisfaction of the mortgagor's liabilities or obligations as might affect the outcome of the proceedings or that the expectation of it should be considered under section 36 of the Administration of Justice Act 1970.

(3) Where a mortgagee of land which consists or substantially consists of a dwelling house brings an action for the enforcement of his security, and at the relevant time there is—

    (*a*) in the case of unregistered land, a land charge of Class F registered against the person who is the estate owner at the relevant time or any person who, where the estate owner is a trustee, preceded him as trustee during the subsistence of the mortgage, or

    (*b*) in the case of registered land, a subsisting registration of a notice under section 2(8) above or a notice or caution under section 2(7) of the Act of 1967,

notice of the action shall be served by the mortgagee on the person on whose behalf the land charge is registered or the notice or caution entered, if that person is not a party to the action.

(4) For the purposes of subsection (3) above, if there has been issued a certificate of the result of an official search made on behalf of the mortgagee which would disclose any land charge of Class F, notice or caution within subsection (3)(*a*) or (*b*) above, and the action is commenced within the priority period, the relevant time is the date of that certificate; and in any other case the relevant time is the time when the action is commenced.

(5) In subsection (4) above, "priority period" means, for both registered and unregistered land, the period for which, in accordance with section 11(5) and (6) of the Land Charges Act 1972, a certificate on an official search operates in favour of a purchaser. **[1064]**

NOTES

    Act of 1967: Matrimonial Homes Act 1967.

9. Rights concerning matrimonial home where both spouses have estate, etc

(1) Where each of two spouses is entitled, by virtue of a legal estate vested in them jointly, to occupy a dwelling house in which they have or at any time have had a matrimonial home, either of them may apply to the court, with respect to

the exercise during the subsistence of the marriage of the right to occupy the dwelling house, for an order prohibiting, suspending or restricting its exercise by the other or requiring the other to permit its exercise by the applicant.

(2) In relation to orders under this section, section 1(3), (4) and (9) above shall apply as they apply in relation to orders under that section.

(3) Where each of two spouses is entitled to occupy a dwelling house by virtue of a contract, or by virtue of any enactment giving them the right to remain in occupation, this section shall apply as it applies where they are entitled by virtue of a legal estate vested in them jointly.

(4) In determining for the purposes of this section whether two spouses are entitled to occupy a dwelling house, there shall be disregarded any right to possession of the dwelling house conferred on a mortgagee of the dwelling house under or by virtue of his mortgage, whether the mortgagee is in possession or not.   **[1065]**

10. Interpretation

(1) In this Act—

"Act of 1967" means the Matrimonial Homes Act 1967;
"Act of 1981" means the Matrimonial Homes and Property Act 1981;
"dwelling house" includes any building or part thereof which is occupied as a dwelling, and any yard, garden, garage or outhouse belonging to the dwelling house and occupied therewith;
"mortgage" includes a charge and "mortgagor" and "mortgagee" shall be construed accordingly;
"morgagor" and "mortgagee" includes any person deriving title under the original mortgagor or mortgagee;
"rights of occupation" has the meaning assigned to it in section 1(1) above.

(2) It is hereby declared that this Act applies as between a husband and a wife notwithstanding that the marriage in question was entered into under a law which permits polygamy (whether or not either party to the marriage in question has for the time being any spouse additional to the other party).

(3) References in this Act to registration under section 2(8) above include (as well as references to registration by notice under section 2(7) of the Act of 1967) references to registration by caution duly lodged under the said section 2(7) before the 14th February 1983 (the date of commencement of section 4(2) of the Act of 1981).   **[1066]**

11. Transitional provision

Neither section 2(9) above, nor the repeal by section 4(2) of the Act of 1981 of the words "or caution" in section 2(7) of the Act of 1967, affects a caution duly lodged as respects any estate of interest before the said 14th February 1983.
            [1067]

NOTES
  Act of 1981: Matrimonial Homes and Property Act 1981.
  Act of 1967: Matrimonial Homes Act 1967.

12. Consequential amendments and repeals

(1) The Acts specified in Schedule 2 to this Act shall have effect subject to the amendments specified in that Schedule.

(2) The Acts specified in Schedule 3 to this Act are repealed to the extent specified in the third column of that Schedule. **[1068]**

13. Short title, commencement and extent

(1) This Act may be cited as the Matrimonial Homes Act 1983.

(2) This Act shall come into force at the end of the period of three months beginning with the day on which it is passed.

(3) This Act does not extend to Scotland or Northern Ireland. **[1069]**

SCHEDULES

SCHEDULE 1

Section 7

TRANSFER OF CERTAIN TENANCIES ON DIVORCE, ETC

PART I

General

1.—(1) Where one spouse is entitled, either in his or her own right or jointly with the other spouse, to occupy a dwelling house by virtue of—

    (*a*) a protected tenancy or statutory tenancy within the meaning of the Rent Act 1977, or

    (*b*) a statutory tenancy within the meaning of the Rent (Agriculture) Act 1976, or

    (*c*) a secure tenancy [within the meaning of section 79 of the Housing Act 1985], [or

    (*d*) an assured tenancy or assured agricultural occupancy, within the meaning of Part I of the Housing Act 1988,]

then, on granting a decree of divorce, a decree of nullity of marriage or a decree of judicial separation, or at any time thereafter (whether, in the case of a decree of divorce or nullity of marriage, before or after the decree is made absolute), the court by which the decree is granted may make an order under Part II below.

(2) References in this Schedule to a spouse being entitled to occupy a dwelling house by virtue of a protected, statutory or secure tenancy [or an assured tenancy or assured agricultural occupancy] apply whether that entitlement is in his or her own right, or jointly with the other spouse. **[1070]**

NOTES
Para 1: first words in square brackets substituted by the Housing (Consequential Provisions) Act 1985, s 4, Sch 2, para 56; second and third words in square brackets inserted by the Housing Act 1988, s 40, Sch 17, Part I.

PART II

Protected or secure tenancy

2.—(1) Where a spouse is entitled to occupy the dwelling house by virtue of a protected tenancy within the meaning of the Rent Act 1977, or a secure tenancy [within the meaning of the Housing Act 1985] or [an assured tenancy or assured agricultural occupancy within the meaning of the Housing Act 1988], the court may by order direct that, as from such date as may be specified in the order, there shall, by virtue of the order and without further assurance, be transferred to, and vested in, the other spouse—

(*a*) the estate or interest which the spouse so entitled had in the dwelling house immediately before that date by virtue of the lease or agreement creating the tenancy and any assignment of that lease or agreemet, with all rights, privileges and appurtenances attaching to that estate or interest but subject to all covenants, obligations, liabilities and incumbrances to which it is subject; and
(*b*) where the spouse so entitled is an assignee of such lease or agreement, the liability of that spouse under any covenant of indemnity by the assignee expressed or implied in the assignment of the lease or agreement to that spouse.

(2) Where an order is made under this paragraph, any liability or obligation to which the spouse so entitled is subject under any covenant having reference to the dwelling house in the lease or agreement, being a liability or obligation falling due to be discharged or performed on or after the date so specified, shall not be enforceable against that spouse.

(3) Where the spouse so entitled is a successor [within the meaning of Part IV of the Housing Act 1985], his or her former spouse (or, in the case of judicial separation, his or her spouse) shall be deemed also to be a successor within the meaning of that Chapter.

[(4) Where the spouse so entitled is for the purposes of section 17 of the Housing Act 1988 a successor in relation to the tenancy or occupancy, his or her former spouse (or, in the case of judicial separation, his or her spouse) shall be deemed to be a successor in relation to the tenancy or occupancy for the purposes of that section.

(5) If the transfer under sub-paragraph (1) above is of an assured agricultural occupancy, then, for the purposes of Chapter III of Part I of the Housing Act 1988,—

(*a*) the agricultural worker condition shall be fulfilled with respect to the dwelling-house while the spouse to whom the assured agricultural occupancy is transferred continues to be the occupier under that occupancy; and
(*b*) that condition shall be treated as so fulfilled by virtue of the same paragraph of Schedule 3 to the Housing Act 1988 as was applicable before the transfer.]

Statutory tenancy within the meaning of the Rent Act 1977

3.—(1) Where the spouse is entitled to occupy the dwelling house by virtue of a statutory tenancy within the meaning of the Rent Act 1977, the court may by order direct that, as from such date as may be specified in the order, that spouse shall cease to be entitled to occupy the dwelling house and that the other spouse shall be deemed to be the tenant or, as the case may be, the sole tenant under that statutory tenancy.

(2) The question whether the provisions of paragraphs 1 to 3 or, as the case may be, paragraphs 5 to 7 of Schedule 1 to the Rent Act 1977 as to the succession by the surviving spouse of a deceased tenant, or by a member of the deceased tenant's family, to the right to retain possession are capable of having effect in the event of the death of the person deemed by an order under this paragraph to be the tenant or sole tenant under the statutory tenancy shall be determined according as those provisions have or have not already had effect in relation to the statutory tenancy.

Statutory tenancy within the meaning of the Rent (Agriculture) Act 1976

4. Where the spouse is entitled to occupy the dwelling house by virtue of a statutory tenancy within the meaning of the Rent (Agriculture) Act 1976, the court may by order direct that, as from such date as may be specified in the order, that spouse shall cease to be entitled to occupy the dwelling house and that the other spouse shall be deemed to be the tenant or, as the case may be, the sole tenant under that statutory tenancy; and a spouse who is deemed as aforesaid to be the tenant under a statutory tenancy shall be (within the meaning of that Act) a statutory tenant in this own right, or a statutory tenant by succession, according as the other spouse was a statutory tenant in his own or a statutory tenant by succession.   **[1071]**

NOTES

Para 2: first words in square brackets in sub-para (1) and words in square brackets in sub-para (3) substituted by the Housing (Consequential Provisions) Act 1985, s 4, Sch 2, para 56; second words in square brackets in sub-para (1) inserted and sub-paras (4), (5) added by the Housing Act 1988, s 140, Sch 17, Part I.

PART III

Ancillary jurisdiction

5. Where the court makes an order under Part II of this Schedule, it may by the order direct that both spouses shall be jointly and severally liable to discharge or perform any or all of the liabilities and obligations in respect of the dwelling house (whether arising under the tenancy or otherwise) which have at the date of the order fallen due to be discharged or performed by one only of the spouses or which, but for the direction, would before the date specified as the date on which the order is to take effect fall due to be discharged or performed by one only of them; and where the court gives such a direction it may further direct that either spouse shall be liable to indemnify the other in whole or in part against any payment made or expenses incurred by the other in discharging or performing any such liability or obligation.

Date when order is to take effect

6. In the case of a decree of divorce or nullity of marriage, the date specified in an order under Part II of this Schedule as the date on which the order is to take effect shall not be earlier than the date on which the decree is made absolute.

Remarriage of either spouse

7. If after the grant of a decree dissolving or annulling a marriage either spouse remarries, that spouse shall not be entitled to apply, by reference to the grant of that decree, for an order under Part II of this Schedule.

Rules of court

8.—(1) Rules of court shall be made requiring the court before it makes an order under this Schedule to give the landlord of the dwelling house to which the order will relate an opportunity of being heard.

(2) Rules of court may provide that an application for an order under this Schedule shall not, without the leave of the court by which the decree of divorce, nullity of marriage or judicial separation was granted, be made after the expiration of such period from the grant of the decree as may be prescribed by the rules.

(3), (4) . . .

Savings for sections 1 and 2 of this Act

9. Where a spouse is entitled to occupy a dwelling house by virtue of a tenancy, this Schedule shall not effect the operation of sections 1 and 2 of this Act in relation to the other spouse's rights of occupation, and the court's power to make orders under this Schedule shall be in addition to the powers conferred by those sections.

Interpretation

10.—(1) In this Schedule—

. . .

. . .

"landlord" includes any person from time to time deriving title under the original landlord and also includes, in relation to any dwelling house, any person other than the tenant who is, or but for Part VII of the Rent Act 1977 or Part II of the Rent (Agriculture) Act 1976 would be, entitled to possession of the dwelling house;

"tenancy" includes sub-tenancy.

(2) For the avoidance of doubt it is hereby declared that the reference in paragraph 7 above to remarriage includes a reference to a marriage which is by law void or voidable. **[1072]**

NOTES

Para 8: sub-paras (3), (4) repealed by the Matrimonial and Family Proceedings Act 1984, s 36(3), Sch 3.

Para 10: definitions omitted repealed by the Matrimonial and Family Proceedings Act 1984, s 46(3), Sch 3.

COUNTY COURTS ACT 1984
(c 28)

ARRANGEMENT OF SECTIONS

An Act to consolidate certain enactments relating to county courts   [26 June 1984]

PART II

JURISDICTION AND TRANSFER OF PROCEEDINGS

Actions of contract and tort

16 Money recoverable by statute

A county court shall have jurisdiction to hear and determine an action for the recovery of a sum recoverable by virtue of any enactment for the time being in force, if—

(*a*) it is not provided by that or any other enactment that such sums shall only be recoverable in the High Court or shall only be recoverable summarily; . . .

(*b*) . . .   **[1073]**

NOTES

Words omitted repealed by the High Court and County Courts Jurisdiction Order 1991, SI 1991 No 724, art 2(8), Schedule.

Recovery of land and cases where title in question

21. Actions for recovery of land and actions where title is in question

(1) A county court shall have jurisdiction to hear and determine any action for the recovery of land . . .

(2) A county court shall have jurisdiction to hear and determine any action in which the title to any hereditament comes in question . . .

(3) Where a mortgage of land consists of or includes a dwelling-house and no part of the land is situated in Greater London then, subject to subsection (4), if a county court has jurisdiction by virtue of this section to hear and determine an action in which the mortgagee under that mortgage claims possession of the mortgaged property, no court other than a county court shall have jurisdiction to hear and determine that action.

(4) Subsection (3) shall not apply to an action for foreclosure or sale in which a claim for possession of the mortgaged property is also made.

(5), (6) . . .

(7) In this section—

"dwelling-house" includes any building or part of a building which is used as a dwelling;

"mortgage" includes a charge and "mortgagor" and "mortgagee" shall be construed accordingly;

"mortgagor" and "mortgagee" includes any person deriving title under the original mortgagor or mortgagee.

(8) The fact that part of the premises comprised in a dwelling-house is used as a shop or office or for business, trade or professional purposes shall not prevent the dwelling-house from being a dwelling-house for the purposes of this section.

(9) This section does not apply to a mortgage securing an agreement which is a regulated agreement within the meaning of the Consumer Credit Act 1974.

[1074]–[1075]

NOTES
Sub-s (1): words omitted repealed by the High Court and County Courts Jurisdiction Order 1991, SI 1991 No 724, art 2(8), Schedule.
Sub-s (2): words omitted repealed by the High Court and County Courts Jurisdiction Order 1991, SI 1991 No 724, art 2(8), Schedule.
Sub-ss (5), (6): repealed by the High Court and County Courts Jurisdiction Order 1991, No 724, art 2(8), Schedule.

Equity proceedings

23. Equity jurisdiction

A county court shall have all the jurisdiction of the High Court to hear and determine—

(*a*) proceedings for the administration of the estate of a deceased person, where the estate does not exceed in amount or value the county court limit;

(*b*) proceedings—

(i) for the execution of any trust, or

(ii) for a declaration that a trust subsists, or

(iii) under section 1 of the Variation of Trusts Act 1958,

where the estate or fund subject, or alleged to be subject, to the trust does not exceed in amount or value the county court limit;

(*c*) proceedings for foreclosure or redemption of any mortgage or for enforcing any charge or lien, where the amount owing in respect of the mortgage, charge or lien does not exceed the county court limit;

(*d*) proceedings for the specific performance, or for the rectification, delivery up or cancellation, of any agreement for the sale, purchase or lease of any property, where, in the case of a sale or purchase, the purchase money, or in the case of a lease, the value of the property, does not exceed the county court limit;

(*e*) proceedings relating to the maintenance or advancement of a minor, where the property of the minor does not exceed in amount or value the county court limit;

(*f*) proceedings for the dissolution or winding-up of any partnership (whether or not the existence of the partnerships is in dispute), where the whole assets of the partnership do not exceed in amount or value the county court limit;

(*g*) proceedings for relief against fraud or mistake, where the damage sustained or the estate or fund in respect of which relief is sought does not exceed in amount or value the county court limit. **[1076]**

24. Jurisdiction by agreement in certain equity proceedings

(1) If, as respects any proceedings to which this section applies, the parties agree, by a memorandum signed by them or by their respective [legal representatives] or agents, that a county court specified in the memorandum shall have jurisdiction in the proceedings, that court shall, notwithstanding anything in any enactment, have jurisdiction to hear and determine the proceedings accordingly.

(2) Subject to subsection (3), this section applies to any proceedings in which a county court would have jurisdiction by virtue of—

(*a*) section 113(3) of the Settled Land Act 1925,

(*b*) section 63A of the Trustee Act 1925,

    (c) sections 3(7), . . . 49(4), 66(4), 89(7), 90(3), 91(8), 92(2), 136(3), . . .
        181(2), 188(2) of, and paragraph 3A of Part III and paragraph 1(3A)
        and (4A) of Part IV of Schedule 1 to, the Law of Property Act 1925,
    (d) sections 17(2), 38(4), 41(1A), and 43(4) of the Administration of
        Estates Act 1925,
    (e) section 6(1) of the Leasehold Property (Repairs) Act 1938,
    (f) sections 1(6A) and 5(11) of the Land Charges Act 1972, and
    (g) sections 23 and 25 of this Act,
but for the limits of the jurisdiction of the court provided in those enactments.

    (3) This section does not apply to proceedings under section 1 of the
Variation of Trusts Act 1958.   **[1077]**

NOTES
    Sub-s (1): words in square brackets substituted by the Courts and Legal Services Act 1990,
s 125(3), Sch 18, para 49(3).
    Sub-s (2): words omitted repealed by the High Court and County Courts Jurisdiction Order
1991, SI 1991 No 724, art 2(8), Schedule.

Family provision proceedings

25. Jurisdiction under Inheritance (Provision for Family and Dependants) Act 1975

A county court shall have jurisdiction to hear and determine any application for
an order under section 2 of the Inheritance (Provision for Family and
Dependants) Act 1975 (including any application for permission to apply for
such an order and any application made, in the proceedings on an application
for such an order, for an order under any other provision of that Act) . . . **[1078]**

NOTES
    Words omitted repealed by the High Court and County Courts Jurisdiction Order 1991, SI 1991
No 724, art 2(8), Schedule.

PART IX

MISCELLANEOUS AND GENERAL

Forfeiture for non-payment of rent

138. Provisions as to forfeiture for non-payment of rent

(1) This section has effect where a lessor is proceeding by action in a county
court (being an action in which the county court has jurisdiction) to enforce
against a lessee a right of re-entry or forfeiture in respect of any land for non-
payment of rent.

    (2) If the lessee pays into court [or to the lessor] not less than 5 clear days
before the return day all the rent in arrear and the costs of the action, the action
shall cease, and the lessee shall hold the land according to the lease without any
new lease.

    (3) If—
    (a) the action does not cease under subsection (2); and
    (b) the court at the trial is satisfied that the lessor is entitled to enforce the
        right of re-entry or forfeiture,
the court shall order possession of the land to be given to the lessor at the
expiration of such period, not being less than 4 weeks from the date of the order,

as the court thinks fit, unless within that period the lessee pays into court [or to the lessor] all the rent in arrear and the costs of the action.

(4) The court may extend the period specified under subsection (3) at any time before possession of the land is recovered in pursuance of the order under that subsection.

(5) ... if—

(a) within the period specified in the order; or
(b) within that period as extended under subsection (4),

the lessee pays into court [or to the lessor]—

(i) all the rent in arrear; and
(ii) the costs of the action,

he shall hold the land according to the lease without any new lease.

(6) Subsection (2) shall not apply where the lessor is proceeding in the same action to enforce a right of re-entry or forfeiture on any other ground as well as for non-payment of rent, or to enforce any other claim as well as the right of re-entry or forfeiture and the claim for arrears of rent.

(7) If the lessee does not—

(a) within the period specified in the order; or
(b) within that period as extended under subsection (4), pay into court [or to the lessor]—

(i) all the rent in arrear; and
(ii) the costs of the action,

the order shall be [enforceable] in the prescribed manner and so long as the order remains unreversed the lessee shall [, subject to subsections (8) and (9A),] be barred from all relief.

(8) The extension under subsection (4) of a period fixed by a court shall not be treated as relief from which the lessee is barred by subsection (7) if he fails to pay into court [or to the lessor] all the rent in arrear and the costs of the action within that period.

(9) Where the court extends a period under subsection (4) at a time when—

(a) that period has expired; and
(b) a warrant has been issued for the possession of the land, the court shall suspend the warrant for the extended period; and, if, before the expiration period, the lessee pays into court [or to the lessor] all the rent in arrear and all the costs of the action, the court shall cancel the warrant.

[(9A) Where the lessor recovers possession of the land at any time after the making of the order under subsection (3) (whether as a result of the enforcement of the order or otherwise) the lessee may, at any time within six months from the date on which the lessor recovers possession, apply to the court for relief; and on any such application the court may, if it thinks fit, grant to the lessee such relief, subject to such terms and conditions, as it thinks fit.

(9B) Where the lessee is granted relief on an application under subsection (9A) he shall hold the land according to the lease without any new lease.

(9C) An application under subsection (9A) may be made by a person with an interest under a lease of the land derived (whether immediately or otherwise) from the lessee's interest therein in like manner as if he were the lessee; and on any such application the court may make an order which (subject to such terms and conditions as the court thinks fit) vests the land in such a person, as lessee of the lessor, for the remainder of the term of the lease under which he has any such interest as aforesaid, or for any lesser term.

In this subsection any reference to the land includes a reference to a part of the land.]

(10) Nothing in this section or section 139 shall be taken to affect—

    (*a*) the power of the court to make any order which it would otherwise have power to make as respects a right of re-entry or forfeiture on any ground other than non-payment of rent; or

    (*b*) section 146(4) of the Law of Property Act 1925 (relief against forfeiture). **[1079]**

NOTES
    Commencement: 1 July 1991 (sub-s (3A)); 1 October 1986 (sub-ss (9A)–(9C)); 1 August 1984 (remainder).
    Sub-s (2): words in square brackets inserted by the Courts and Legal Services Act 1990, s 125(2), Sch 17, para 17.
    Sub-s (3): words in square brackets inserted by the Courts and Legal Services Act 1990, s 125(2), Sch 17, para 17.
    Sub-s (5): words omitted repealed by the Administration of Justice Act 1985, ss 55(2), 67(2), Sch 8, Part III; words in square brackets inserted by the Courts and Legal Services Act 1990, s 125(2), Sch 17, para 17.
    Sub-s (7): first words in square brackets inserted by the Courts and Legal Services Act 1990, s 125(2), Sch 17, para 17; second words in square brackets substituted and third words in square brackets inserted by the Administration of Justice Act 1985, s 55(3).
    Sub-s (9): words in square brackets inserted by the Courts and Legal Services Act 1990, s 125(2), Sch 17, para 17.
    Sub-s (9A): inserted by the Administration of Justice Act 1985, s 55(4).
    Sub-s (9B): inserted by the Administration of Justice Act 1985, s 55(4).
    Sub-s (9C): inserted by the Administration of Justice Act 1985, s 55(4).

139. Service of summons and re-entry

(1) In a case where section 138 has effect, if—

    (*a*) one-half-year's rent is in arrear at the time of the commencement of the action; and

    (*b*) the lessor has a right to re-enter for non-payment of that rent; and

    (*c*) no sufficient distress is to be found on the premises countervailing the arrears then due,

the service of the summons in the action in the prescribed manner shall stand in lieu of a demand and re-entry.

(2) Where a lessor has enforced against a lessee, by re-entry without action, a right of re-entry or forfeiture as respects any land for non-payment of rent, the lessee may . . . at any time within six months from the date on which the lessor re-entered apply to the county court for relief, and on any such application the court may, if it thinks fit, grant to the lessee such relief as the High Court could have granted.

[(3) Subsections (9B) and (9C) of section 138 shall have effect in relation to an application under subsection (2) of this section as they have effect in relation to an application under subsection (9A) of that section.] **[1080]**

NOTES

Sub-s (2): words omitted repealed by the High Court and County Courts Jurisdiction Order 1991, SI 1991 No 724, art 2(8), Schedule.

Sub-s (3): added by the Administration of Justice Act 1985, s 55(5).

140. Interpretation of sections 138 and 139

For the purposes of sections 138 and 139—

"lease" includes—

    (*a*) an original or derivative under-lease;

    (*b*) an agreement for a lease where the lessee has become entitled to have his lease granted; and

    (*c*) a grant at a fee farm rent, or under a grant securing a rent by condition;

"lessee" includes—

    (*a*) an original or derivative under-lessee;

    (*b*) the persons deriving title under a lessee;

    (*c*) a grantee under a grant at a fee farm rent, or under a grant securing a rent by condition; and

    (*d*) the persons deriving title under such a grantee;

"lessor" includes—

    (*a*) an original or derivative under-lessor;

    (*b*) the persons deriving title under a lessor;

    (*c*) a person making a grant at a fee farm rent, or a grant securing a rent by condition; and

    (*d*) the persons deriving title under such a grantor;

"under-lease" includes an agreement for an under-lease where the under-lessee has become entitled to have his underlease granted; and

"under-lessee" includes any person deriving title under an under-lessee.

[1081]

Power to raise monetary limits

145. Power to raise monetary limits

(1) If it appears to Her Majesty in Council—

    (*a*) that the county court limit for the purposes of any enactment referring to that limit, or

    (*b*) that the higher limit or the lower limit referred to in section 20 of this Act,

should be increased, Her Majesty may by Order in Council direct that the limit in question shall be such amount as may be specified in the Order.   **[1082]**

General

147. Interpretation

(1) In this Act, unless the context otherwise requires—

    . . .

"the county court limit" means—

(a) in relation to any enactment contained in this Act for which a limit is for the time being specified by an Order under section 145, that limit,

(b) . . .

(c) in relation to any enactment contained in this Act and not within paragraph (a) . . ., the county court limit for the time being specified by any other Order in Council or order defining the limit of county court jurisdiction for the purposes of that enactment;

. . .

(2), (3) . . . **[1083]**

NOTES

Sub-s (1): in definition "the county court limit" words omitted repealed by the High Court and County Courts Jurisdiction Order 1991, SI 1991 No 724, art 2(8), Schedule; other definitions omitted are outside the scope of this work.

Sub-ss (2), (3): repealed by the Local Government Finance (Repeals, Savings and Consequential Amendments) Order 1990, SI 1990 No 776, art 3(1), Sch 1.

MATRIMONIAL AND FAMILY PROCEEDINGS ACT 1984
(c 42)

An Act to amend the Matrimonial Causes Act 1973 so far as it restricts the time within which proceedings for divorce or nullity of marriage can be instituted; to amend that Act, the Domestic Proceedings and Magistrates' Courts Act 1978 and the Magistrates' Courts Act 1980 so far as they relate to the exercise of the jurisdiction of courts in England and Wales to make provision for financial relief or to exercise related powers in matrimonial and certain other family proceedings; to make provision for financial relief to be available where a marriage has been dissolved or annulled, or the parties to a marriage have been legally separated, in a country overseas; to make related amendments in the Maintenance Orders (Reciprocal Enforcement) Act 1972 and the Inheritance (Provision for Family and Dependants) Act 1975; to make provision for the distribution and transfer between the High Court and county courts of, and the exercise in those courts of jurisdiction in, family business and family proceedings and to repeal and re-enact with amendments certain provisions conferring on designated county courts jurisdiction in matrimonial proceedings; to impose a duty to notify changes of address on persons liable to make payments under maintenance orders enforceable under Part II of the Maintenance Orders Act 1950 or Part I of the Maintenance Orders Act 1958; and for connected purposes [12 July 1984]

PART III

FINANCIAL RELIEF IN ENGLAND AND WALES AFTER OVERSEAS DIVORCE ETC

Orders for financial provision and property adjustment

17. Orders for financial provision and property adjustment

(1) Subject to section 20 below, the court on an application by a party to a marriage for an order for financial relief under this section, may make any one

or more of the orders which it could make under Part II of the 1973 Act if a decree of divorce, a decree of nullity of marriage or a decree of judicial separation in respect of the marriage had been granted in England and Wales, that is to say—

(a) any order mentioned in section 23(1) of the 1973 Act (financial provision orders);

(b any order mentioned in section 24(1) of that Act (property adjustment orders).

(2) Subject to section 20 below, where the court makes a secured periodical payments order, an order for the payment of a lump sum or a property adjustment order under subsection (1) above, then, on making that order or at any time thereafter, the court may make any order mentioned in section 24A(1) of the 1973 Act (orders for sale of property) which the court would have power to make if the order under subsection (1) above had been made under Part II of the 1973 Act. **[1084]**

NOTES

1973 Act: Matrimonial Causes Act 1973.

18. Matters to which the court is to have regard in exercising its powers under s 17

(1) In deciding whether to exercise its powers under section 17 above and, if so, in what manner the court shall act in accordance with this section.

(2) The court shall have regard to all the circumstances of the case, first consideration being given to the welfare while a minor of any child of the family who has not attained the age of eighteen.

(3) As regards the exercise of those powers in relation to a party to the marriage, the court shall in particular have regard to the matters mentioned in section 25(2)(a) to (h) of the 1973 Act and shall be under duties corresponding with those imposed by section 25A(1) and (2) of the 1973 Act where it decides to exercise under section 17 above powers corresponding with the powers referred to in those subsections.

(4) As regards the exercise of those powers in relation to a child of the family, the court shall in particular have regard to the matters mentioned in section 25(3)(a) to (e) of the 1973 Act.

(5) As regards the exercise of those powers against a party to the marriage in favour of a child of the family who is not the child of that party, the court shall also have regard to the matters mentioned in section 25(4)(a) to (c) of the 1973 Act.

(6) Where an order has been made by a court outside England and Wales for the making of payments or the transfer of property by a party to the marriage, the court in considering in accordance with this section the financial resources of the other party to the marriage or a child of the family shall have regard to the extent to which that order has been complied with or is likely to be complied with. **[1085]**

NOTES

1973 Act: Matrimonial Causes Act 1973.

20. Restriction of powers of court where jurisdiction depends on matrimonial home in England or Wales

(1) Where the court has jurisdiction to entertain an application for an order for financial relief by reason only of the situation in England or Wales of a dwelling-house which was a matrimonial home of the parties, the court may make under section 17 above any one or more of the following orders (but no other)—

> (*a*) an order that either party to the marriage shall pay to the other such lump sum as may be specified in the order;
>
> (*b*) an order that a party to the marriage shall pay to such person as may be so specified for the benefit of a child of the family, or to such a child, such lump sum as may be so specified;
>
> (*c*) an order that a party to the marriage shall transfer to the other party, to any child of the family or to such person as may be so specified for the benefit of such a child, the interest of the first-mentioned party in the dwelling-house, or such part of that interest as may be so specified;
>
> (*d*) an order that a settlement of the interest of a party to the marriage in the dwelling-house, or such part of that interest as may be so specified, be made to the satisfaction of the court for the benefit of the other party to the marriage and of the children of the family or either or any of them;
>
> (*e*) an order varying for the benefit of the parties to the marriage and of the children of the family or either or any of them any ante-nuptial or post-nuptial settlement (including such a settlement made by will or codicil) made on the parties to the marriage so far as that settlement relates to an interest in the dwelling-house;
>
> (*f*) an order extinguishing or reducing the interest of either of the parties to the marriage under any such settlement so far as that interest is an interest in the dwelling-house;
>
> (*g*) an order for the sale of the interest of a party to the marriage in the dwelling-house.

(2) Where, in the circumstances mentioned in subsection (1) above, the court makes an order for the payment of a lump sum by a party to the marriage, the amount of the lump sum shall not exceed, or where more than one such order is made the total amount of the lump sum shall not exceed in aggregate, the following amount, that is to say—

> (*a*) if the interest of that party in the dwelling-house is sold in pursuance of an order made under subsection (1)(*g*) above, the amount of the proceeds of the sale of that interest after deducting therefrom any costs incurred in the sale thereof;
>
> (*b*) if the interest of that party is not so sold, the amount which in the opinion of the court represents the value of that interest.

(3) Where the interest of a party to the marriage in the dwelling-house is held jointly or in common with any other person or persons—

> (*a*) the reference in subsection (1)(*g*) above to the interest of a party to the marriage shall be construed as including a reference to the interest of that other person, or the interest of those other persons, in the dwelling-house, and

(*b*) the reference in subsection (2)(*a*) above to the amount of the proceeds of a sale ordered under subsection (1)(*g*) above shall be construed as a reference to that part of those proceeds which is attributable to the interest of that party to the marriage in the dwelling-house.   **[1086]**

COMPANIES ACT 1985
(c 6)

ARRANGEMENT OF SECTIONS

An Act to consolidate the greater part of the Companies Acts   [11 March 1985]

PART I

FORMATION AND REGISTRATION OF COMPANIES; JURIDICIAL STATUS AND
MEMBERSHIP

CHAPTER III

A COMPANY'S CAPACITY; FORMALITIES OF CARRYING ON BUSINESS

[35. A company's capacity not limited by its memorandum

(1) The validity of an act done by a company shall not be called into question
on the ground of lack of capacity by reason of anything in the company's
memorandum.

(2) A member of a company may bring proceedings to restrain the doing of
an act which but for subsection (1) would be beyond the company's capacity;
but no such proceedings shall lie in respect of an act to be done in fulfilment of
a legal obligation arising from a previous act of the company.

(3) It remains the duty of the directors to observe any limitations on their
powers flowing from the company's memorandum; and action by the directors
which but for subsection (1) would be beyond the company's capacity may only
be ratified by the company by special resolution.

A resolution ratifying such action shall not affect any liability incurred by the directors or any other person; relief from any such liability must be agreed to separately by special resolution.

(4) The operation of this section is restricted by [section 65(1) of the Charities Act 1993] and section 112(3) of the Companies Act 1989 in relation to companies which are charities; and section 322A below (invalidity of certain transactions to which directors or their associates are parties) has effect notwithstanding this section.]   **[1086A]**

NOTES
Commencement: 4 February 1991.
Substituted with savings, together with ss 35A, 35B, by the Companies Act 1989, s 108(1).
Sub-s (4): words in square brackets substituted by the Charities Act 1993, s 98(1), Sch 6, para 20(1), (2).
Section 35B not reproduced.

[35A. Power of directors to bind the company

(1) In favour of a person dealing with a company in good faith, the power of the board of directors to bind the company, or authorise others to do so, shall be deemed to be free of any limitation under the company's constitution.

(2) For this purpose—

    (*a*) a person "deals with" a company if he is a party to any transaction or other act to which the company is a party;

    (*b*) a person shall not be regarded as acting in bad faith by reason only of his knowing that an act is beyond the powers of the directors under the company's constitution; and

    (*c*) a person shall be presumed to have acted in good faith unless the contrary is proved.

(3) The references above to limitations on the directors' power under the company's constitution include limitations deriving—

    (*a*) from a resolution of the company in general meeting or a meeting of any class of shareholders, or

    (*b*) from any agreement between the members of the company or of any class of shareholders.

(4) Subsection (1) does not affect any right of a member of the company to bring proceedings to restrain the doing of an act which is beyond the powers of the directors; but no such proceedings shall lie in respect of an act to be done in fulfilment of a legal obligation arising from a previous act of the company.

(5) Nor does that subsection affect any liability incurred by the directors, or any other person, by reason of the directors' exceeding their powers.

(6) The operation of this section is restricted by [section 65(1) of the Charities Act 1993] and section 112(3) of the Companies Act 1989 in relation to companies which are charities; and section 322A below (invalidity of certain transactions to which directors or their associates are parties) has effect notwithstanding this section.]   **[1086B]**

NOTES
Commencement: 4 February 1991.
Substituted with savings, together with ss 35, 35B, by the Companies Act 1989, s 108(1).
Sub-s (6): words in square brackets substituted by the Charities Act 1993, s 98(1), Sch 6, para 20(1), (2).

[36. Company contracts: England and Wales

Under the law of England and Wales a contract may be made—

    (*a*) by a company, by writing under its common seal, or

    (*b*) on behalf of a company, by any person acting under its authority, express or implied;

and any formalities required by law in the case of a contract made by an individual also apply, unless a contrary intention appears, to a contract made by or on behalf of a company.] **[1086C]**

NOTES
    Commencement: 31 July 1990.
    Substituted by the Companies Act 1989, s 130(1).

[36A. Execution of documents: England and Wales

(1) Under the law of England and Wales the following provisions have effect with respect to the execution of documents by a company.

(2) A document is executed by a company by the affixing of its common seal.

(3) A company need not have a common seal, however, and the following subsections apply whether it does or not.

(4) A document signed by a director and the secretary of a company, or by two directors of a company, and expressed (in whatever form of words) to be executed by the company has the same effect as if executed under the common seal of the company.

(5) A document executed by a company which makes it clear on its face that it is intended by the person or persons making it to be a deed has effect, upon delivery, as a deed; and it shall be presumed, unless a contrary intention is proved, to be delivered upon its being so executed.

(6) In favour of a purchaser a document shall be deemed to have been duly executed by a company if it purports to be signed by a director and the secretary of the company, or by two directors of the company, and, where it makes it clear on its face that it is intended by the person or persons making it to be a deed, to have been delivered upon its being executed.

A "purchaser" means a purchaser in good faith for valuable consideration and includes a lessee, mortgagee or other person who for valuable consideration acquires an interest in property.] **[1086D]**

NOTES
    Commencement: 31 July 1990.
    Inserted by the Companies Act 1989, s 130(2).

Part XII

Registration of Charges

NOTES
    Sections 395–408 and 410–423 are prospectively substituted by new ss 395–420 by the Companies Act 1989, ss 92–104. Sections 409, 424 are prospectively replaced by new ss 703A–703N by the Companies Act 1989, ss 92(*b*), 105, Sch 15.

CHAPTER I

REGISTRATION OF CHARGES (ENGLAND AND WALES)

395. Certain charges void if not registered

(1) Subject to the provisions of this Chapter, a charge created by a company registered in England and Wales and being a charge to which this section applies is, so far as any security on the company's property or undertaking is conferred by the charge, void against the liquidator [or administrator] and any creditor of the company, unless the prescribed particulars of the charge together with the instrument (if any) by which the charge is created or evidenced, are delivered to or received by the registrar of companies for registration in the manner required by this Chapter within 21 days after the date of the charge's creation.

(2) Subsection (1) is without prejudice to any contract or obligation for repayment of the money secured by the charge; and when a charge becomes void under this section, the money secured by it immediately becomes payable.   **[1087]**

NOTES

See note preceding this section.

Sub-s (1): words in square brackets substituted by the Insolvency Act 1985, s 109, Sch 6, para 10.

396. Charges which have to be registered

(1) Section 395 applies to the following charges—

    (a) a charge for the purpose of securing any issue of debentures,

    (b) a charge on uncalled share capital of the company,

    (c) a charge created or evidenced by an instrument which, if executed by an individual, would require registration as a bill of sale,

    (d) a charge on land (wherever situated) or any interest in it, but not including a charge for any rent or other periodical sum issuing out of the land,

    (e) a charge on book debts of the company,

    (f) a floating charge on the company's undertaking or property,

    (g) a charge on calls made but not paid,

    (h) a charge on a ship or aircraft, or any share in a ship,

    (j) a charge on goodwill, on a patent or a licence under a patent, on a trademark or on a copyright or a licence under a copyright [or on any intellectual property].

(2) Where a negotiable instrument has been given to secure the payment of any book debts of a company, the deposit of the instrument for the purpose of securing an advance to the company is not, for purposes of section 395, to be treated as a charge on those book debts.

(3) The holding of debentures entitling the holder to a charge on land is not for purposes of this section deemed to be an interest in land.

[(3A) The following are "intellectual property" for the purposes of this section—

    (a) any patent, trade mark, service mark, registered design, copyright or design right;

    (b) any licence under or in respect of any such right.]

(4) In this Chapter, "charge" includes mortgage.   **[1088]**

NOTES

See note preceding s 395 at para **[1087]**.

Sub-s (1): in sub-para (*j*), words in italics prospectively repealed and subsequent words in square brackets prospectively substituted by the Copyright, Designs and Patents Act 1988, s 303(1), Sch 7, para 31(2); in original sub-para (*j*) reference to trade mark includes reference to service mark, by virtue of the Patents, Designs and Marks Act 1986, s 2(3), Sch 2, Part I.

Sub-s (3A): prospectively inserted by the Copyright, Designs and Patents Act 1988, s 303(1), Sch 7, para 31(2).

397. Formalities of registration (debentures)

(1) Where a series of debentures containing, or giving by reference to another instrument, any charge to the benefit of which the debenture holders of that series are entitled pari passu is created by a company, it is for purposes of section 395 sufficient if there are delivered to or received by the registrar, within 21 days after the execution of the deed containing the charge (or, if there is no such deed, after the execution of any debentures of the series), the following particulars in the prescribed form—

> *(a) the total amount secured by the whole series, and*
> *(b) the dates of the resolutions authorising the issue of the series and the date of the covering deed (if any) by which the security is created or defined, and*
> *(c) a general description of the property charged, and*
> *(d) the names of the trustees (if any) for the debenture holders,*

together with the deed containing the charge or, if there is no such deed, one of the debentures of the series:

Provided that there shall be sent to the registrar of companies, for entry in the register, particulars in the prescribed form of the date and amount of each issue of debentures of the series, but any omission to do this does not affect the validity of any of those debentures.

(2) Where any commission, allowance or discount has been paid or made either directly or indirectly by a company to a person in consideration of his—

> *(a) subscribing or agreeing to subscribe, whether absolutely or conditionally, for debentures of the company, or*
> *(b) procuring or agreeing to procure subscriptions, whether absolute or conditional, for such debentures,*

the particulars required to be sent for registration under section 395 shall include particulars as to the amount or rate per cent of the commission, discount or allowance so paid or made, but omission to do this does not affect the validity of the debentures issued.

(3) The deposit of debentures as security for a debt of the company is not, for the purposes of subsection (2), treated as the issue of the debentures at a discount.

[1088A]

NOTES

See note preceding s 395 at para **[1087]**.

398. Verification of charge on property outside United Kingdom

(1) In the case of a charge created out of the United Kingdom comprising property situated outside the United Kingdom, the delivery to and the receipt by the registrar of companies of a copy (verified in the prescribed manner) of the instrument by which the charge is created or evidenced has the same effect for purposes of sections 395 to 398 as the delivery and receipt of the instrument itself.

(2) In that case, 21 days after the date on which the instrument or copy could, in due course of post (and if despatched with due diligence), have been received in the United Kingdom are substituted for the 21 days mentioned in section 395(1) (or

as the case may be, section 397(1)) as the time within which the particulars and instrument or copy are to be delivered to the registrar.

(3) Where a charge is created in the United Kingdom but comprises property outside the United Kingdom, the instrument creating or purporting to create the charge may be sent for registration under section 395 notwithstanding that further proceedings may be necessary to make the charge valid or effectual according to the law of the country in which the property is situated.

(4) Where a charge comprises property situated in Scotland or Northern Ireland and registration in the country where the property is situated is necessary to make the charge valid or effectual according to the law of that country, the delivery to and receipt by the registrar of a copy (verified in the prescribed manner) of the instrument by which the charge is created or evidenced, together with a certificate in the prescribed form stating that the charge was presented for registration in Scotland or Northern Ireland (as the case may be) on the date on which it was so presented has, for purposes of sections 395 to 398, the same effect as the delivery and receipt of the instrument itself.   **[1088B]**

NOTES
    See note preceding s 395 at para **[1087]**.

399. Company's duty to register charges it creates

(1) It is a company's duty to send to the registrar of companies for registration the particulars of every charge created by the company and of the issues of debentures of a series requiring registration under sections 395 to 398; but registration of any such charge may be effected on the application of any person interested in it.

(2) Where registration is effected on the application of some person other than the company, that person is entitled to recover from the company the amount of any fees properly paid by him to the registrar on the registration.

(3) If a company fails to comply with subsection (1), then, unless the registration has been effected on the application of some other person, the company and every officer of it who is in default is liable to a fine and, for continued contravention, to a daily default fine.   **[1088C]**

NOTES
    See note preceding s 395 at para **[1087]**.

400. Charges existing on property acquired

(1) This section applies where a company registered in England and Wales acquires property which is subject to a charge of any such kind as would, if it had been created by the company after the acquisition of the property, have been required to be registered under this Chapter.

(2) The company shall cause the prescribed particulars of the charge, together with a copy (certified in the prescribed manner to be a correct copy) of the instrument (if any) by which the charge was created or is evidenced, to be delivered to the registrar of companies for registration in manner required by this Chapter within 21 days after the date on which the acquisition is completed.

(3) However, if the property is situated and the charge was created outside Great Britain, 21 days after the date on which the copy of the instrument could in due course of post, and if despatched with due diligence, have been received in the United Kingdom is substituted for the 21 days above-mentioned as the time within which the particulars and copy of the instrument are to be delivered to the registrar.

(4) If default is made in complying with this section, the company and every officer of it who is in default is liable to a fine and, for continued contravention, to a daily default fine. **[1088D]**

401. Register of charges to be kept by registrar of companies

(1) The registrar of companies shall keep, with respect to each company, a register in the prescribed form of all the charges requiring registration under this Chapter; and he shall enter in the register with respect to such charges the following particulars—

(a) in the case of a charge to the benefit of which the holders of a series of debentures are entitled, the particulars specified in section 397(1),

(b) in the case of any other charge—

(i) if it is a charge created by the company, the date of its creation, and if it is a charge which was existing on property acquired by the company, the date of the acquisition of the property, and

(ii) the amount secured by the charge, and

(iii) short particulars of the property charged, and

(iv) the persons entitled to the charge.

(2) The registrar shall give a certificate of the registration of any charge registered in pursuance of this Chapter, stating the amount secured by the charge.

The certificate—

(a) shall be either signed by the registrar, or authenticated by his official seal, and

(b) is conclusive evidence that the requirements of this Chapter as to registration have been satisfied.

(3) The register kept in pursuance of this section shall be open to inspection by any person. **[1088E]**

NOTES
See note preceding s 395 at para **[1087]**.

402. Endorsement of certificate on debentures

(1) The company shall cause a copy of every certificate of registration given under section 401 to be endorsed on every debenture or certificate of debenture stock which is issued by the company, and the payment of which is secured by the charge so registered.

(2) But this does not require a company to cause a certificate of registration of any charge so given to be endorsed on any debenture or certificate of debenture stock issued by the company before the charge was created.

(3) If a person knowingly and wilfully authorises or permits the delivery of a debenture or certificate of debenture stock which under this section is required to have endorsed on it a copy of a certificate of registration, without the copy being so endorsed upon it, he is liable (without prejudice to any other liability) to a fine. **[1088F]**

NOTES
See note preceding s 395 at para **[1087]**.

403. Entries of satisfaction and release

(1) The registrar of companies, on receipt of a statutory declaration in the prescribed form verifying, with respect to a registered charge,—

    (a) that the debt for which the charge was given has been paid or satisfied in whole or in part, or

    (b) that part of the property or undertaking charged has been released from the charge or has ceased to form part of the company's property or undertaking,

may enter on the register a memorandum of satisfaction in whole or in part, or of the fact that part of the property or undertaking has been released from the charge or has ceased to form part of the company's property or undertaking (as the case may be).

(2) Where the registrar enters a memorandum of satisfaction in whole, he shall if required furnish the company with a copy of it. **[1088G]**

NOTES
See note preceding s 395 at para **[1087]**.

404. Rectification of register of charges

(1) The following applies if the court is satisfied that the omission to register a charge within the time required by this Chapter or that the omission or mis-statement of any particular with respect to any such charge or in a memorandum of satisfaction was accidental, or due to inadvertence or to some other sufficient cause, or is not of a nature to prejudice the position of creditors or shareholders of the company, or that on other grounds it is just and equitable to grant relief.

(2) The court may, on the application of the company or a person interested, and on such terms and conditions as seem to the court just and expedient, order that the time for registration shall be extended or, as the case may be, that the omission or mis-statement shall be rectified. **[1088H]**

NOTES
See note preceding s 395 at para **[1087]**.

405. Registration of enforcement of security

(1) If a person obtains an order for the appointment of a receiver or manager of a company's property, or appoints such a receiver or manager under powers contained in an instrument, he shall within 7 days of the order or of the appointment under those powers, give notice of the fact to the registrar of companies; and the registrar shall enter the fact in the register of charges.

(2) Where a person appointed receiver or manager of a company's property under powers contained in an instrument ceases to act as such receiver or manager, he shall, on so ceasing, give the registrar notice to that effect, and the registrar shall enter the fact in the register of charges.

(3) A notice under this section shall be in the prescribed form.

(4) If a person makes default in complying with the requirements of this section, he is liable to a fine and, for continued contravention, to a daily default fine. **[1088I]**

NOTES
See note preceding s 395 at para **[1087]**.

406. Companies to keep copies of instruments creating charges

(1) Every company shall cause a copy of every instrument creating a charge requiring registration under this Chapter to be kept at its registered office.

(2) In the case of a series of uniform debentures, a copy of one debenture of the series is sufficient. **[1088J]**

NOTES
See note preceding s 395 at para **[1087]**.

407. Company's register of charges

(1) Every limited company shall keep at its registered office a register of charges and enter in it all charges specifically affecting property of the company and all floating charges on the company's undertaking or any of its property.

(2) The entry shall in each case give a short description of the property charged, the amount of the charge and, except in the case of securities to bearer, the names of the persons entitled to it.

(3) If an officer of the company knowingly and wilfully authorises or permits the omission of an entry required to be made in pursuance of this section, he is liable to a fine. **[1088K]**

NOTES
See note preceding s 395 at para **[1087]**.

408. Right to inspect instruments which create charges, etc

(1) The copies of instruments creating any charge requiring registration under this Chapter with the registrar of companies, and the register of charges kept in pursuance of section 407, shall be open during business hours (but subject to such reasonable restrictions as the company in general meeting may impose, so that not less than 2 hours in each day be allowed for inspection) to the inspection of any creditor or member of the company without fee.

(2) The register of charges shall also be open to the inspection of any other person on payment of such fee, not exceeding 5 pence, for each inspection, as the company may prescribe.

(3) If inspection of the copies referred to, or of the register, is refused, every officer of the company who is in default is liable to a fine and, for continued contravention, to a daily default fine.

(4) If such a refusal occurs in relation to a company registered in England and Wales, the court may by order compel an immediate inspection of the copies or register. **[1088L]**

NOTES
See note preceding s 395 at para **[1087]**.

409. Charges on property in England and Wales created by overseas company

(1) This Chapter extends to charges on property in England and Wales which are created, and to charges on property in England and Wales which is acquired, by a company (whether a company within the meaning of this Act or not) incorporated outside Great Britain which has an established place of business in England and Wales.

(2) In relation to such a company, sections 406 and 407 apply with the substitution, for the reference to the company's registered office, of a reference to its principal place of business in England and Wales. **[1088M]**

NOTES
See note preceding s 395 at para **[1087]**.

CHAPTER II
REGISTRATION OF CHARGES (SCOTLAND)

410. Charges void unless registered

(1) The following provisions of this Chapter have effect for the purpose of securing the registration in Scotland of charges created by companies.

(2) Every charge created by a company, being a charge to which this section applies, is, so far as any security on the company's property or any part of it is conferred by the charge, void against the liquidator [or administrator] and any creditor of the company unless the prescribed particulars of the charge, together with a copy (certified in the prescribed manner to be a correct copy) of the instrument (if any) by which the charge is created or evidenced, are delivered to or received by the registrar of companies for registration in the manner required by this Chapter within 21 days after the date of the creation of the charge.

(3) Subsection (2) is without prejudice to any contract or obligation for repayment of the money secured by the charge; and when a charge becomes void under this section the money secured by it immediately becomes payable.

(4) This section applies to the following charges—

   (a) a charge on land wherever situated, or any interest in such land (not including a charge for any rent, ground annual or other periodical sum payable in respect of the land, but including a charge created by a heritable security within the meaning of section 9(8) of the Conveyancing and Feudal Reform (Scotland) Act 1970),
   (b) a security over the uncalled share capital of the company,
   (c) a security over incorporeal moveable property of any of the following categories—

      (i) the book debts of the company,
      (ii) calls made but not paid,
      (iii) goodwill,
      (iv) a patent or a licence under a patent,
      (v) a trademark,
      (vi) a copyright or a licence under a copyright,
   [(vii) a registered design or a licence in respect of such a design,
      (viii) a design right or a licence under a design right,]

   (d) a security over a ship or aircraft or any share in a ship, and
   (e) a floating charge.

(5) In this Chapter "company" (except in section 424) means an incorporated company registered in Scotland; "registrar of companies" means the registrar or other officer performing under this Act the duty of registration of companies in Scotland; and references to the date of creation of a charge are—

   (a) in the case of a floating charge, the date on which the instrument creating the floating charge was executed by the company creating the charge, and

(b) in any other case, the date on which the right of the person entitled to the benefit of the charge was constituted as a real right. **[1088N]**

NOTES
See note preceding s 395 at para **[1087]**.
Sub-s (2): words in square brackets inserted by the Insolvency Act 1985, s 109(1), Sch 6, para 10.
Sub-s (3): paras (c)(vii), (viii) added by the Copyright, Designs and Patents Act 1988, s 303(1), Sch 7, para 31(3).

411. Charges on property outside United Kingdom

(1) In the case of a charge created out of the United Kingdom comprising property situated outside the United Kingdom, the period of 21 days after the date on which the copy of the instrument creating it could (in due course of post, and if despatched with due diligence) have been received in the United Kingdom is substituted for the period of 21 days after the date of the creation of the charge as the time within which, under section 410(2), the particulars and copy are to be delivered to the registrar.

(2) Where a charge is created in the United Kingdom but comprises property outside the United Kingdom, the copy of the instrument creating or purporting to create the charge may be sent for registration under section 410 notwithstanding that further proceedings may be necessary to make the charge valid or effectual according to the law of the country in which the property is situated. **[1088O]**

NOTES
See note preceding s 395 at para **[1087]**.

412. Negotiable instrument to secure book debts

Where a negotiable instrument has been given to secure the payment of any book debts of a company, the deposit of the instrument for the purpose of securing an advance to the company is not, for purposes of section 410, to be treated as a charge on those book debts. **[1088P]**

NOTES
See note preceding s 395 at para **[1087]**.

413. Charges associated with debentures

(1) The holding of debentures entitling the holder to a charge on land is not, for the purposes of section 410, deemed to be an interest in land.

(2) Where a series of debentures containing, or giving by reference to any other instrument, any charge to the benefit of which the debenture-holders of that series are entitled pari passu, is created by a company, it is sufficient for purposes of section 410 if there are delivered to or received by the registrar of companies within 21 days after the execution of the deed containing the charge or if there is no such deed, after the execution of any debentures of the series, the following particulars in the prescribed form—

(a) the total amount secured by the whole series,
(b) the dates of the resolutions authorising the issue of the series and the date of the covering deed (if any) by which the security is created or defined,
(c) a general description of the property charged,
(d) the names of the trustees (if any) for the debenture holders, and
(e) in the case of a floating charge, a statement of any provisions of the charge and of any instrument relating to it which prohibit or restrict or regulate the power of the company to grant further securities ranking in priority to, or pari passu with, the floating charge, or which vary or otherwise regulate

the order of ranking of the floating charge in relation to subsisting securities,

together with a copy of the deed containing the charge or, if there is no such deed, of one of the debentures of the series :

Provided that where more than one issue is made of debentures in the series, there shall be sent to the registrar of companies for entry in the register particulars (in the prescribed form) of the date and amount of each issue of debentures of the series, but any omission to do this does not affect the validity of any of those debentures.

(3) Where any commission, allowance or discount has been paid or made, either directly or indirectly, by a company to any person in consideration of his subscribing or agreeing to subscribe, whether absolutely or conditionally, for any debentures of the company, or procuring or agreeing to procure subscriptions (whether absolute or conditional) for any such debentures, the particulars required to be sent for registration under section 410 include particulars as to the amount or rate per cent of the commission, discount or allowance so paid or made; but any omission to do this does not affect the validity of the debentures issued.

The deposit of any debentures as security for any debt of the company is not, for purposes of this subsection, treated as the issue of the debentures at a discount.

[1088Q]

NOTES

See note preceding s 395 at para **[1087]**.

414. Charge by way of ex facie absolute disposition, etc

(1) For the avoidance of doubt, it is hereby declared that, in the case of a charge created by way of an ex facie absolute disposition or assignation qualified by a back letter or other agreement, or by a standard security qualified by an agreement, compliance with section 410(2) does not of itself render the charge unavailable as security for indebtedness incurred after the date of compliance.

(2) Where the amount secured by a charge so created is purported to be increased by a further back letter or agreement, a further charge is held to have been created by the ex facie absolute disposition or assignation or (as the case may be) by the standard security, as qualified by the further back letter or agreement; and the provisions of this Chapter apply to the further charge as if—

  (a) references in this Chapter (other than in this section) to the charge were references to the further charge, and
  (b) references to the date of the creation of the charge were references to the date on which the further back letter or agreement was executed. **[1088R]**

NOTES

See note preceding s 395 at para **[1087]**.

415. Company's duty to register charges created by it

(1) It is a company's duty to send to the registrar of companies for registration the particulars of every charge created by the company and of the issues of debentures of a series requiring registration under sections 410 to 414; but registration of any such charge may be effected on the application of any person interested in it.

(2) Where registration is effected on the application of some person other than the company, that person is entitled to recover from the company the amount of any fees properly paid by him to the registrar on the registration.

(3) If a company makes default in sending to the registrar for registration the particulars of any charge created by the company or of the issues of debentures of a series requiring registration as above mentioned, then, unless the registration has been effected on the application of some other person, the company and every officer of it who is in default is liable to a fine and, for continued contravention, to a daily default fine. **[1088S]**

NOTES
See note preceding s 395 at para **[1087]**.

416. Duty to register charges existing on property acquired

(1) Where a company acquires any property which is subject to a charge of any kind as would, if it had been created by the company after the acquisition of the property, have been required to be registered under this Chapter, the company shall cause the prescribed particulars of the charge, together with a copy (certified in the prescribed manner to be a correct copy) of the instrument (if any) by which the charge was created or is evidenced, to be delivered to the registrar of companies for registration in the manner required by this Chapter within 21 days after the date on which the transaction was settled.

(2) If, however, the property is situated and the charge was created outside Great Britain, 21 days after the date on which the copy of the instrument could (in due course of post, and if despatched with due diligence) have been received in the United Kingdom are substituted for 21 days after the settlement of the transaction as the time within which the particulars and the copy of the instrument are to be delivered to the registrar.

(3) If default is made in complying with this section, the company and every officer of it who is in default is liable to a fine and, for continued contravention, to a daily default fine. **[1088T]**

NOTES
See note preceding s 395 at para **[1087]**.

417. Register of charges to be kept by registrar of companies

(1) The registrar of companies shall keep, with respect to each company, a register in the prescribed form of all the charges requiring registration under this Chapter, and shall enter in the register with respect to such charges the particulars specified below.

(2) In the case of a charge to the benefit of which the holders of a series of debentures are entitled, there shall be entered in the register the particulars specified in section 413(2).

(3) In the case of any other charge there shall be entered—

    (a) if it is a charge created by the company, the date of its creation, and if it was a charge existing on property acquired by the company, the date of the acquisition of the property,

    (b) the amount secured by the charge,

    (c) short particulars of the property charged,

    (d) the persons entitled to the charge, and

    (e) in the case of a floating charge, a statement of any of the provisions of the charge and of any instrument relating to it which prohibit or restrict or regulate the company's power to grant further securities ranking in priority to, or pari passu with, the floating charge, or which vary or otherwise

regulate the order of ranking of the floating charge in relation to subsisting securities.

(4) The register kept in pursuance of this section shall be open to inspection by any person. **[1088U]**

NOTES

See note preceding s 395 at para **[1087]**.

418. Certificate of registration to be issued

(1) The registrar of companies shall give a certificate of the registration of any charge registered in pursuance of this Chapter.

(2) The certificate—

    (a) shall be either signed by the registrar, or authenticated by his official seal,

    (b) shall state the name of the company and the person first-named in the charge among those entitled to the benefit of the charge (or, in the case of a series of debentures, the name of the holder of the first such debenture to be issued) and the amount secured by the charge, and

    (c) is conclusive evidence that the requirements of this Chapter as to registration have been complied with. **[1088V]**

NOTES

See note preceding s 395 at para **[1087]**.

419. Entries of satisfaction and relief

(1) The registrar of companies, on application being made to him in the prescribed form, and on receipt of a statutory declaration in the prescribed form verifying, with respect to any registered charge,—

    (a) that the debt for which the charge was given has been paid or satisfied in whole or in part, or

    (b) that part of the property charged has been released from the charge or has ceased to form part of the company's property,

may enter on the register a memorandum of satisfaction (in whole or in part) regarding that fact.

(2) Where the registrar enters a memorandum of satisfaction in whole, he shall, if required, furnish the company with a copy of the memorandum.

(3) Without prejudice to the registrar's duty under this section to require to be satisfied as above mentioned, he shall not be so satisfied unless—

    (a) the creditor entitled to the benefit of the floating charge, or a person authorised to do so on his behalf, certifies as correct the particulars submitted to the registrar with respect to the entry on the register of a memorandum under this section, or

    (b) the court, on being satisfied that such certification cannot readily be obtained, directs him accordingly.

(4) Nothing in this section requires the company to submit particulars with respect to the entry in the register of a memorandum of satisfaction where the company, having created a floating charge over all or any part of its property, disposes of part of the property subject to the floating charge.

(5) A memorandum or certification required for the purposes of this section shall be in such form as may be prescribed. **[1088W]**

NOTES
See note preceding s 395 at para **[1087]**.

420. Rectification of register

The court, on being satisfied that the omission to register a charge within the time required by this Act or that the omission or mis-statement of any particular with respect to any such charge or in a memorandum of satisfaction was accidental, or due to inadvertence or to some other sufficient cause, or is not of a nature to prejudice the position of creditors or shareholders of the company, or that it is on other grounds just and equitable to grant relief, may, on the application of the company or any person interested, and on such terms and conditions as seem to the court just and expedient, order that the time for registration shall be extended or (as the case may be) that the omission or mis-statement shall be rectified. **[1088X]**

NOTES
See note preceding s 395 at para **[1087]**.

421. Copies of instruments creating charges to be kept by company

(1) Every company shall cause a copy of every instrument creating a charge requiring registration under this Chapter to be kept at the company's registered office.

(2) In the case of a series of uniform debentures, a copy of one debenture of the series is sufficient. **[1088Y]**

NOTES
See note preceding s 395 at para **[1087]**.

422. Company's register of charges

(1) Every company shall keep at its registered office a register of charges and enter in it all charges specifically affecting property of the company, and all floating charges on any property of the company.

(2) There shall be given in each case a short description of the property charged, the amount of the charge and, except in the case of securities to bearer, the names of the persons entitled to it.

(3) If an officer of the company knowingly and wilfully authorises or permits the omission of an entry required to be made in pursuance of this section, he is liable to a fine. **[1088Z]**

NOTES
See note preceding s 395 at para **[1087]**.

423. Right to inspect copies of instruments, and company's register

(1) The copies of instruments creating charges requiring registration under this Chapter with the registrar of companies, and the register of charges kept in pursuance of section 422, shall be open during business hours (but subject to such reasonable restrictions as the company in general meeting may impose, so that not less than 2 hours in each day be allowed for inspection) to the inspection of any creditor or member of the company without fee.

(2) The register of charges shall be open to the inspection of any other person on payment of such fee, not exceeding 5 pence for each inspection, as the company may prescribe.

(3) If inspection of the copies or register is refused, every officer of the company who is in default is liable to a fine and, for continued contravention, to a daily default fine.

(4) If such a refusal occurs in relation to a company, the court may by order compel an immediate inspection of the copies or register.   **[1088AA]**

NOTES
    See note preceding s 395 at para **[1087]**.

424. Extension of Chapter II

(1) This Chapter extends to charges on property in Scotland which are created, and to charges on property in Scotland which is acquired, by a company incorporated outside Great Britain which has a place of business in Scotland.

(2) In relation to such a company, sections 421 and 422 apply with the substitution, for the reference to the company's registered office, of a reference to its principal place of business in Scotland.   **[1088AB]**

NOTES
    See note preceding s 395 at para **[1087]**.

NOTES
    Ss 395–420 (new provisions relating to the registration of charges with respect to companies registered in Great Britain) are prospectively substituted in place of ss 395–408 (at paras **[1087]**–**[1088L]**), 410–423 (at paras **[1088N]**–**[1088AA]**), by the Companies Act 1989, ss 92–104 as follows.

[Registration in the company charges register

395. Introductory provisions

(1) The purpose of this Part is to secure the registration of charges on a company's property.

    (2) In this Part—
       "charge" means any form of security interest (fixed or floating) over property, other than an interest arising by operation of law; and
       "property", in the context of what is the subject of a charge, includes future property.

    (3) It is immaterial for the purposes of this Part where the property subject to a charge is situated.

    (4) References in this Part to "the registrar" are—
       (a) in relation to a company registered in England and Wales, to the registrar of companies for England and Wales, and
       (b) in relation to a company registered in Scotland, to the registrar of companies for Scotland;
and references to registration, in relation to a charge, are to registration in the register kept by him under this Part.]   **[1088AC]**

NOTES
    See note preceding this section.

[396. Charges requiring registration

(1) The charges requiring registration under this Part are—

(*a*) a charge on land or any interest in land, other than—

    (i) in England and Wales, a charge for rent or any other periodical sum issuing out of the land,

    (ii) in Scotland, a charge for any rent, ground annual or other periodical sum payable in respect of the land;

(*b*) a charge on goods or any interest in goods, other than a charge under which the chargee is entitled to possession either of the goods or of a document of title to them;

(*c*) a charge on intangible movable property (in Scotland, incorporeal moveable property) of any of the following descriptions—

    (i) goodwill,

    (ii) intellectual property,

    (iii) book debts (whether book debts of the company or assigned to the company),

    (iv) uncalled share capital of the company or calls made but not paid;

(*d*) a charge for securing an issue of debentures; or

(*e*) a floating charge on the whole or part of the company's property.

(2) The descriptions of charge mentioned in subsection (1) shall be construed as follows—

(*a*) a charge on a debenture forming part of an issue or series shall not be treated as falling within paragraph (*a*) or (*b*) by reason of the fact that the debenture is secured by a charge on land or goods (or on an interest in land or goods);

(*b*) in paragraph (*b*) "goods" means any tangible movable property (in Scotland, corporeal moveable property) other than money;

(*c*) a charge is not excluded from paragraph (*b*) because the chargee is entitled to take possession in case of default or on the occurrence of some other event;

(*d*) in paragraph (*c*)(ii) "intellectual property" means—

    (i) any patent, trade mark, service mark, registered design, copyright or design right, or

    (ii) any licence under or in respect of any such right;

(*e*) a debenture which is part of an issue or series shall not be treated as a book debt for the purposes of paragraph (*c*)(iii);

(*f*) the deposit by way of security of a negotiable instrument given to secure the payment of book debts shall not be treated for the purposes of paragraph (*c*)(iii) as a charge on book debts;

(*g*) a shipowner's lien on subfreights shall not be treated as a charge on book debts for the purposes of paragraph (*c*)(iii) or as a floating charge for the purposes of paragraph (*e*).

(3) Whether a charge is one requiring registration under this Part shall be determined—

(*a*) in the case of a charge created by a company, as at the date the charge is created, and

(*b*) in the case of a charge over property acquired by a company, as at the date of the acquisition.

(4) The Secretary of State may by regulations amend subsections (1) and (2) so as to add any description of charge to, or remove any description of charge from, the charges requiring registration under this Part.

(5) Regulations under this section shall be made by statutory instrument

which shall be subject to annulment in pursuance of a resolution of either House of Parliament.

(6) In the following provisions of this Part references to a charge are, unless the context otherwise requires, to a charge requiring registration under this Part.

Where a charge not otherwise requiring registration relates to property, by virtue of which it requires to be registered and to other property, the references are to the charge so far as it relates to property of the former description.]

[1088AD]

NOTES
See note preceding s 395 at para **[1088AC]**.

[397. The companies charges register

(1) The registrar shall keep for each company a register, in such form as he thinks fit, of charges on property of the company.

(2) The register shall consist of a file containing with respect to each charge the particulars and other information delivered to the registrar under the provisions of this Part.

(3) Any person may require the registrar to provide a certificate stating the date on which any specified particulars of, or other information relating to, a charge were delivered to him.
　(4)　The certificate shall be signed by the registrar or authenticated by his official seal.
　(5)　The certificate shall be conclusive evidence that the specified particulars or other information were delivered to the registrar no later than the date stated in the certificate; and it shall be presumed unless the contrary is proved that they were not delivered earlier than that date.]　　　　　　　　　　　　　　　　　　　　　**[1088AE]**

NOTES
See note preceding s 395 at para **[1088AC]**.

[398. Company's duty to deliver particulars of charge for registration

(1) It is the duty of a company which creates a charge, or acquires property subject to a charge—
　(*a*)　to deliver the prescribed particulars of the charge, in the prescribed form, to the registrar for registration, and
　(*b*)　to do so within 21 days after the date of the charge's creation or, as the case may be, the date of the acquisition;
but particulars of a charge may be delivered for registration by any person interested in the charge.

(2) Where the particulars are delivered for registration by a person other than the company concerned, that person is entitled to recover from the company the amount of any fees paid by him to the registrar in connection with the registration.

(3) If a company fails to comply with subsection (1), then, unless particulars of the charge have been delivered for registration by another person, the company and every officer of it who is in default is liable to a fine.

(4) Where prescribed particulars in the prescribed form are delivered to the

registrar for registration, he shall file the particulars in the register and shall note, in such form as he thinks fit, the date on which they were delivered to him.

(5) The registrar shall send to the company and any person appearing from the particulars to be the chargee, and if the particulars were delivered by another person interested in the charge to that person, a copy of the particulars filed by him and of the note made by him as to the date on which they were delivered.] **[1088AF]**

NOTES
See note preceding s 395 at para **[1088AC]**.

[399. Effect of failure to deliver particulars for registration

(1) Where a charge is created by a company and no prescribed particulars in the prescribed form are delivered for registration within the period of 21 days after the date of the charge's creation, the charge is void against—

(*a*) an administrator or liquidator of the company, and
(*b*) any person who for value acquires an interest in or right over property subject to the charge,

where the relevant event occurs after the creation of the charge, whether before or after the end of the 21 day period.

This is subject to section 400 (late delivery of particulars).

(2) In this Part "the relevant event" means—

(*a*) in relation to the voidness of a charge as against an administrator or liquidator, the beginning of the insolvency proceedings, and
(*b*) in relation to the voidness of a charge as against a person acquiring an interest in or right over property subject to a charge, the acquisition of that interest or right;

and references to "a relevant event" shall be construed accordingly.

(3) Where a relevant event occurs on the same day as the charge is created, it shall be presumed to have occurred after the charge is created unless the contrary is proved.] **[1088AG]**

NOTES
See note preceding s 395 at para **[1088AC]**.

[400. Late delivery of particulars

(1) Where prescribed particulars of a charge created by a company, in the prescribed form, are delivered for registration more than 21 days after the date of the charge's creation, section 399(1) does not apply in relation to relevant events occurring after the particulars are delivered.

(2) However, where in such a case—

(*a*) the company is at the date of delivery of the particulars unable to pay its debts, or subsequently becomes unable to pay its debts in consequence of the transaction under which the charge is created, and
(b) insolvency proceedings begin before the end of the relevant period beginning with the date of delivery of the particulars,

the charge is void as against the administrator or liquidator.

(3) For this purpose—

(*a*) the company is "unable to pay its debts" in the circumstances specified in section 123 of the Insolvency Act 1986; and

(*b*) the "relevant period" is—

    (i) two years in the case of a floating charge created in favour of a person connected with the company (within the meaning of section 249 of that Act),

    (ii) one year in the case of a floating charge created in favour of a person not so connected, and

    (iii) six months in any other case.

(4) Where a relevant event occurs on the same day as the particulars are delivered, it shall be presumed to have occurred before the particulars are delivered unless the contrary is proved.] **[1088AH]**

NOTES
See note preceding s 395 at para **[1088AC]**.

[401. Delivery of further particulars

(1) Further particulars of a charge, supplementing or varying the registered particulars, may be delivered to the registrar for registration at any time.

(2) Further particulars must be in the prescribed form signed by or on behalf of both the company and the chargee.

(3) Where further particulars are delivered to the registrar for registration and appear to him to be duly signed, he shall file the particulars in the register and shall note, in such form as he thinks fit, the date on which they were delivered to him.

(4) The registrar shall send to the company and any person appearing from the particulars to be the chargee, and if the particulars were delivered by another person interested in the charge to that other person, a copy of the further particulars filed by him and of the note made by him as to the date on which they were delivered.] **[1088AI]**

NOTES
See note preceding s 395 at para **[1088AC]**.

[402. Effect of omissions and errors in registered particulars

(1) Where the registered particulars of a charge created by a company are not complete and accurate, the charge is void, as mentioned below, to the extent that rights are not disclosed by the registered particulars which would be disclosed if they were complete and accurate.

(2) The charge is void to that extent, unless the court on the application of the chargee orders otherwise, as against—

(*a*) an administrator or liquidator of the company, and

(*b*) any person who for value acquires an interest in or right over property subject to the charge,

where the relevant event occurs at a time when the particulars are incomplete or inaccurate in a relevant respect.

(3) Where a relevant event occurs on the same day as particulars or further particulars are delivered, it shall be presumed to have occurred before those particulars are delivered unless the contrary is proved.

(4) The court may order that the charge is effective as against an administrator or liquidator of the company if it is satisfied—

    (*a*) that the omission or error is not likely to have misled materially to his prejudice any unsecured creditor of the company, or

    (*b*) that no person became an unsecured creditor of the company at a time when the registered particulars of the charge were incomplete or inaccurate in a relevant respect.

(5) The court may order that the charge is effective as against a person acquiring an interest in or right over property subject to the charge if it is satisfied that he did not rely, in connection with the acquisition, on registered particulars which were incomplete or inaccurate in a relevant respect.

(6) For the purposes of this section an omission or inaccuracy with respect to the name of the chargee shall not be regarded as a failure to disclose the rights of the chargee.] **[1088AJ]**

NOTES

    See note preceding s 395 at para **[1088AC]**.

[403. Memorandum of charge ceasing to affect company's property

(1) Where a charge of which particulars have been delivered ceases to affect the company's property, a memorandum to that effect may be delivered to the registrar for registration.

(2) The memorandum must be in the prescribed form signed by or on behalf of both the company and the chargee.

(3) Where a memorandum is delivered to the registrar for registration and appears to him to be duly signed, he shall file it in the register, and shall note, in such form as he thinks fit, the date on which it was delivered to him.

(4) The registrar shall send to the company and any person appearing from the memorandum to be the chargee, and if the memorandum was delivered by another person interested in the charge to that person, a copy of the memorandum filed by him and of the note made by him as to the date on which it was delivered.

(5) If a duly signed memorandum is delivered in a case where the charge in fact continues to affect the company's property, the charge is void as against—

    (*a*) an administrator or liquidator of the company, and

    (*b*) any person who for value acquires an interest in or right over property subject to the charge,

where the relevant event occurs after the delivery of the memorandum.

(6) Where a relevant event occurs on the same day as the memorandum is delivered, it shall be presumed to have occurred before the memorandum is delivered unless the contrary is proved.] **[1088AK]**

NOTES

    See note preceding s 395 at para **[1088AC]**.

[Further provisions with respect to voidness of charges

404. Exclusion of voidness as against unregistered charges

(1) A charge is not void by virtue of this Part as against a subsequent charge unless some or all of the relevant particulars of that charge are duly delivered for registration—

(a) within 21 days after the date of its creation, or

(b) before complete and accurate relevant particulars of the earlier charge are duly delivered for registration.

(2) Where relevant particulars of the subsequent charge so delivered are incomplete or inaccurate, the earlier charge is void as against that charge only to the extent that rights are disclosed by registered particulars of the subsequent charge duly delivered for registration before the corresponding relevant particulars of the earlier charge.

(3) The relevant particulars of a charge for the purposes of this section are those prescribed particulars relating to rights inconsistent with those conferred by or in relation to the other charge.]   **[1088AL]**

NOTES

See note preceding s 395 at para **[1088AC]**.

[405. Restrictions on voidness by virtue of this Part

(1) A charge is not void by virtue of this Part as against a person acquiring an interest in or right over property where the acquisition is expressly subject to the charge.

(2) Nor is a charge void by virtue of this Part in relation to any property by reason of a relevant event occurring after the company which created the charge has disposed of the whole of its interest in that property.]   **[1088AM]**

NOTES

See note preceding s 395 at para **[1088AC]**.

[406. Effect of exercise of power of sale

(1) A chargee exercising a power of sale may dispose of property to a purchaser freed from any interest or right arising from the charge having become void to any extent by virtue of this Part—

(a) against an administrator or liquidator of the company, or

(b) against a person acquiring a security interest over property subject to the charge;

and a purchaser is not concerned to see or inquire whether the charge has become so void.

(2) The proceeds of the sale shall be held by the chargee in trust to be applied—

First, in discharge of any sum effectively secured by prior incumbrances to which the sale is not made subject;

Second, in payment of all costs, charges and expenses properly incurred by him in connection with the sale, or any previous attempted sale, of the property;

Third, in discharge of any sum effectively secured by the charge and incumbrances ranking *pari passu* with the charge;

Fourth, in discharge of any sum effectively secured by incumbrances ranking after the charge;

and any residue is payable to the company or to a person authorised to give a receipt for the proceeds of the sale of the property.

(3) For the purposes of subsection (2)—

(*a*) prior incumbrances include any incumbrance to the extent that the charge is void as against it by virtue of this Part; and

(*b*) no sum is effectively secured by a charge to the extent that it is void as against an administrator or liquidator of the company.

(4) In this section—

(*a*) references to things done by a chargee include things done by a receiver appointed by him, whether or not the receiver acts as his agent;

(*b*) "power of sale" includes any power to dispose of, or grant an interest out of, property for the purpose of enforcing a charge (but in relation to Scotland does not include the power to grant a lease), and references to "sale" shall be construed accordingly; and

(*c*) "purchaser" means a person who in good faith and for valuable consideration acquires an interest in property.

(5) The provisions of this section as to the order of application of the proceeds of sale have effect subject to any other statutory provision (in Scotland, any other statutory provision or rule of law) applicable in any case.

(6) Where a chargee exercising a power of sale purports to dispose of property freed from any such interest or right as is mentioned in subsection (1) to a person other than a purchaser, the above provisions apply, with any necessary modifications, in relation to a disposition to a purchaser by that person or any successor in title of his.

(7) In Scotland, subsections (2) and (7) of section 27 of the Conveyancing and Feudal Reform (Scotland) Act 1970 apply to a chargee unable to obtain a discharge for any payment which he is required to make under subsection (2) above as they apply to a creditor in the circumstances mentioned in those subsections.] **[1088AN]**

NOTES
See note preceding s 395 at para **[1088AC]**.

[407. Effect of voidness on obligation secured

(1) Where a charge becomes void to any extent by virtue of this Part, the whole of the sum secured by the charge is payable forthwith on demand; and this applies notwithstanding that the sum secured by the charge is also the subject of other security.

(2) Where the charge is to secure the repayment of money, the references in subsection (1) to the sum secured include any interest payable.] **[1088AO]**

NOTES
See note preceding s 395 at para **[1088AC]**.

[Additional information to be registered

408. Particulars of taking up of issue of debentures

(1) Where particulars of a charge for securing an issue of debentures have been delivered for registration, it is the duty of the company—

(*a*) to deliver to the registrar for registration particulars in the prescribed form of the date on which any debentures of the issue are taken up, and of the amount taken up, and (*b*) to do so before the end of the period of 21 days after the date on which they are taken up.

(2) Where particulars in the prescribed form are delivered to the registrar for registration under this section, he shall file them in the register.

(3) If a company fails to comply with subsection (1), the company and every officer of it who is in default is liable to a fine.]   **[1088AP]**

NOTES
See note preceding s 395 at para **[1088AC]**.

[409. Notice of appointment of receiver or manager, &c

(1) If a person obtains an order for the appointment of a receiver or manager of a company's property, or appoints such a receiver or manager under powers contained in an instrument, he shall within seven days of the order or of the appointment under those powers, give notice of that fact in the prescribed form to the registrar for registration.

(2) Where a person appointed receiver or manager of a company's property under powers contained in an instrument ceases to act as such receiver or manager, he shall, on so ceasing, give notice of that fact in the prescribed form to the registrar for registration.

(3) Where a notice under this section in the prescribed form is delivered to the registrar for registration, he shall file it in the register.

(4) If a person makes default in complying with the requirements of subsection (1) or (2), he is liable to a fine.

(5) This section does not apply in relation to companies registered in Scotland (for which corresponding provision is made by sections 53, 54 and 62 of the Insolvency Act 1986).]   **[1088AQ]**

NOTES
See note preceding s 395 at para **[1088AC]**.

[410. Notice of crystallisation of floating charge, &c

(1) The Secretary of State may by regulations require notice in the prescribed form to be given to the registrar of—

  (*a*) the occurrence of such events as may be prescribed affecting the nature of the security under a floating charge of which particulars have been delivered for registration, and
  (*b*) the taking of such action in exercise of powers conferred by a fixed or floating charge of which particulars have been delivered for registration, or conferred in relation to such a charge by an order of the court, as may be prescribed.

(2) The regulations may make provision as to—

  (*a*) the persons by whom notice is required to be, or may be, given, and the period within which notice is required to be given;
  (*b*) the filing in the register of the particulars contained in the notice and the noting of the date on which the notice was given; and
  (*c*) the consequences of failure to give notice.
  (3) As regards the consequences of failure to give notice of an event causing a floating charge to crystallise, the regulations may include provision to the effect that the crystallisation—

    (*a*) shall be treated as ineffective until the prescribed particulars are delivered, and

    (*b*) if the prescribed particulars are delivered after the expiry of the prescribed period, shall continue to be ineffective against such persons as may be prescribed,

subject to the exercise of such powers as may be conferred by the regulations on the court.

(4) The regulations may provide that if there is a failure to comply with such of the requirements of the regulations as may be prescribed, such persons as may be prescribed are liable to a fine.

(5) Regulations under this section shall be made by statutory instrument which shall be subject to annulment in pursuance of a resolution of either House of Parliament.

(6) Regulations under this section shall not apply in relation to a floating charge created under the law of Scotland by a company registered in Scotland.]

[1088AR]

NOTES

   See note preceding s 395 at para **[1088AC]**.

[*Copies of instruments and register to be kept by company*

411. Duty to keep copies of instruments and register

(1) Every company shall keep at its registered office a copy of every instrument creating or evidencing a charge over the company's property.

    In the case of a series of uniform debentures, a copy of one debenture of the series is sufficient.

(2) Every company shall also keep at its registered office a register of all such charges, containing entries for each charge giving a short description of the property charged, the amount of the charge and (except in the case of securities to bearer) the names of the persons entitled to it.

(3) This section applies to any charge, whether or not particulars are required to be delivered to the registrar for registration.

(4) If a company fails to comply with any requirement of this section, the company and every officer of it who is in default is liable to a fine.]   **[1088AS]**

NOTES

   See note preceding s 395 at para **[1088AC]**.

[412. Inspection of copies and register

(1) The copies and the register referred to in section 411 shall be open to the inspection of any creditor or member of the company without fee; and to the inspection of any other person on payment of such fee as may be prescribed.

(2) Any person may request the company to provide him with a copy of—

    (*a*) any instrument creating or evidencing a charge over the company's property, or

    (*b*) any entry in the register of charges kept by the company, on payment of such fee as may be prescribed.

This subsection applies to any charge, whether or not particulars are required to be delivered to the registrar for registration.

(3) The company shall send the copy to him not later than ten days after the day on which the request is received or, if later, on which payment is received.

(4) If inspection of the copies or register is refused, or a copy requested is not sent within the time specified above—

    (a) the company and every officer of it who is in default is liable to a fine, and

    (b) the court may by order compel an immediate inspection of the copies or register or, as the case may be, direct that the copy be sent immediately.] **[1088AT]**

NOTES
See note preceding s 395 at para **[1088AC]**.

[Supplementary provisions

413. Power to make further provision by regulations

(1) The Secretary of State may by regulations make further provision as to the application of the provisions of this Part in relation to charges of any description specified in the regulations.

Nothing in the following provisions shall be construed as restricting the generality of that power.

(2) The regulations may require that where the charge is contained in or evidenced or varied by a written instrument, there shall be delivered to the registrar for registration, instead of particulars or further particulars of the charge, the instrument itself or a certified copy of it together with such particulars as may be prescribed.

(3) The regulations may provide that a memorandum of a charge ceasing to affect property of the company shall not be accepted by the registrar unless supported by such evidence as may be prescribed, and that a memorandum not so supported shall be treated as not having been delivered.

(4) The regulations may also provide that where the instrument creating the charge is delivered to the registrar in support of such a memorandum, the registrar may mark the instrument as cancelled before returning it and shall send copies of the instrument cancelled to such persons as may be prescribed.

(5) The regulations may exclude or modify, in such circumstances and to such extent as may be prescribed, the operation of the provisions of this Part relating to the voidness of a charge.

(6) The regulations may require, in connection with the delivery of particulars, further particulars or a memorandum of the charge's ceasing to affect property of the company, the delivery of such supplementary information as may be prescribed, and may—

    (a) apply in relation to such supplementary information any provisions of this Part relating to particulars, further particulars or such a memorandum, and

    (b) provide that the particulars, further particulars or memorandum shall be treated as not having been delivered until the required supplementary information is delivered.

(7) Regulations under this section shall be made by statutory instrument which shall be subject to annulment in pursuance of a resolution of either House of Parliament.] **[1088AU]**

NOTES
See note preceding s 395 at para **[1088AC]**.

[414. Date of creation of charge

(1) References in this Part to the date of creation of a charge by a company shall be construed as follows.

(2) A charge created under the law of England and Wales shall be taken to be created—

(*a*) in the case of a charge created by an instrument in writing, when the instrument is executed by the company or, if its execution by the company is conditional, upon the conditions being fulfilled, and

(*b*) in any other case, when an enforceable agreement is entered into by the company conferring a security interest intended to take effect forthwith or upon the company acquiring an interest in property subject to the charge.

(3) A charge created under the law of Scotland shall be taken to be created—

(*a*) in the case of a floating charge, when the instrument creating the floating charge is executed by the company, and

(*b*) in any other case, when the right of the person entitled to the benefit of the charge is constituted as a real right.

(4) Where a charge is created in the United Kingdom but comprises property outside the United Kingdom, any further proceedings necessary to make the charge valid or effectual under the law of the country where the property is situated shall be disregarded in ascertaining the date on which the charge is to be taken to be created.] **[1088AV]**

NOTES
See note preceding s 395 at para **[1088AC]**.

[415. Prescribed particulars and related expressions

(1) References in this Part to the prescribed particulars of a charge are to such particulars of, or relating to, the charge as may be prescribed.

(2) The prescribed particulars may, without prejudice to the generality of subsection (1), include—

(*a*) whether the company has undertaken not to create other charges ranking in priority to or *pari passu* with the charge, and

(*b*) whether the charge is a market charge within the meaning of Part VII of the Companies Act 1989 or a charge to which the provisions of that Part apply as they apply to a market charge.

(3) References in this Part to the registered particulars of a charge at any time are to such particulars and further particulars of the charge as have at that time been duly delivered for registration.

(4) References in this Part to the registered particulars of a charge being

complete and accurate at any time are to their including all the prescribed particulars which would be required to be delivered if the charge were then newly created.]   **[1088AW]**

NOTES

See note preceding s 395 at para **[1088AC]**.

[416. Notice of matters disclosed on register

(1) A person taking a charge over a company's property shall be taken to have notice of any matter requiring registration and disclosed on the register at the time the charge is created.

(2) Otherwise, a person shall not be taken to have notice of any matter by reason of its being disclosed on the register or by reason of his having failed to search the register in the course of making such inquiries as ought reasonably to be made.

(3) The above provisions have effect subject to any other statutory provision as to whether a person is to be taken to have notice of any matter disclosed on the register.]   **[1088AX]**

NOTES

See note preceding s 395 at para **[1088AC]**.

[417. Power of court to dispense with signature

(1) Where it is proposed to deliver further particulars of a charge, or to deliver a memorandum of a charge ceasing to affect the company's property, and—

    (a) the chargee refuses to sign or authorise a person to sign on his behalf, or cannot be found, or

    (b) the company refuses to authorise a person to sign on its behalf,

the court may on the application of the company or the chargee, or of any other person having a sufficient interest in the matter, authorise the delivery of the particulars or memorandum without that signature.

(2) The order may be made on such terms as appear to the court to be appropriate.

(3) Where particulars or a memorandum are delivered to the registrar for registration in reliance on an order under this section, they must be accompanied by an office copy of the order.

In such a case the references in sections 401 and 403 to the particulars or memorandum being duly signed are to their being otherwise duly signed.

(4) The registrar shall file the office copy of the court order along with the particulars or memorandum.]   **[1088AY]**

NOTES

See note preceding s 395 at para **[1088AC]**.

[418. Regulations

Regulations under any provision of this Part, or prescribing anything for the purposes of any such provision—

    (a) may make different provision for different cases, and

(*b*) may contain such supplementary, incidental and transitional provisions as appear to the Secretary of State to be appropriate.] **[1088AZ]**

NOTES
See note preceding s 395 at para **[1088AC]**.

[419. Minor definitions

(1) In this Part—

"chargee" means the person for the time being entitled to exercise the security rights conferred by the charge;

"issue of debentures" means a group of debentures, or an amount of debenture stock, secured by the same charge; and

"series of debentures" means a group of debentures each containing or giving by reference to another instrument a charge to the benefit of which the holders of debentures of the series are entitled *pari passu*.

(2) References in this Part to the creation of a charge include the variation of a charge which is not registrable so as to include property by virtue of which it becomes registrable.

The provisions of section 414 (construction of references to date of creation of charge) apply in such a case with any necessary modifications.

(3) References in this Part to the date of acquisition of property by a company are—

(*a*) in England and Wales, to the date on which the acquisition is completed, and

(*b*) in Scotland, to the date on which the transaction is settled.

(4) In the application of this Part to a floating charge created under the law of Scotland, references to crystallisation shall be construed as references to the attachment of the charge.

(5) References in this Part to the beginning of insolvency proceedings are to—

(*a*) the presentation of a petition on which an administration order or winding-up order is made, or

(*b*) the passing of a resolution for voluntary winding up.]   **[1088BA]**

NOTES
See note preceding s 395 at para **[1088AC]**.

[420. Index of defined expressions

The following Table shows the provisions of this Part defining or otherwise explaining expressions used in this Part (other than expressions used only in the same section)—

charge	sections 395(2) and 396(6)
charge requiring registration	section 396
chargee	section 419(1)
complete and accurate (in relation to registered particulars)	section 415(4)
creation of charge	section 419(2)
crystallisation (in relation to Scottish floating charge)	section 419(4)
date of acquisition (of property by a company)	section 419(3)

date of creation of charge	section 414
further particulars	section 401
insolvency proceedings, beginning of	section 419(5)
issue of debentures	section 419(1)
memorandum of charge ceasing to affect company's property	section 403
prescribed particulars	section 415(1) and (2)
property	section 395(2)
registered particulars	section 415(3)
registrar and registration in relation to a charge	section 395(4)
relevant event	section 399(2)
series of debentures	section 419(1).]

[1088BB]

NOTES
See note preceding s 395 at para **[1088AC]**.

PART XX

WINDING UP OF COMPANIES REGISTERED UNDER THIS ACT OR THE FORMER
COMPANIES ACTS

CHAPTER VI

MATTERS ARISING SUBSEQUENT TO WINDING UP

654. Property of dissolved company to be bona vacantia

(1) When a company is dissolved, all property and rights whatsoever vested in or held on trust for the company immediately before its dissolution (including leasehold property, but not including property held by the company on trust for any other person) are deemed to be bona vacantia and—

    (*a*) accordingly belong to the Crown, or to the Duchy of Lancaster or to the Duke of Cornwall for the time being (as the case may be), and

    (*b*) vest and may be dealt with in the same manner as other bona vacantia accruing to the Crown, to the Duchy of Lancaster or to the Duke of Cornwall.

(2) Except as provided by the section next following, the above has effect subject to and without prejudice to any order made by the court under section 651 or 653. **[1089]**

NOTES
Chapter III of Part XXIII (ss 703A–703N) prospectively inserted by the Companies Act 1989, s 105, Sch 15, as follows.

[CHAPTER III

REGISTRATION OF CHARGES

703A. Introductory provisions

(1) The provisions of this Chapter have effect for securing the registration in Great Britain of charges on the property of a registered oversea company.

(2) Section 395(2) and (3) (meaning of "charge" and "property") have effect for the purposes of this Chapter.

(3) A "registered oversea company", in relation to England and Wales or Scotland, means an oversea company which—

[(a) has duly delivered documents under paragraph 1 of Schedule 21A to the registrar for that part of Great Britain and has not subsequently given notice to him under section 695A(3) that it has closed the branch in respect of which the documents were registered, or

(b)] has duly delivered documents to the registrar for that part of Great Britain under section 691 and has not subsequently given notice to him under section 696(4) that it has ceased to have an established place of business in that part.

(4) References in this Chapter to the registrar shall be construed in accordance with section 703E below and references to registration, in relation to a charge, are to registration in the register kept by him under this Chapter.]

[1089A]

NOTES
See note preceding this section.
Sub-s (3): words in square brackets inserted by the Oversea Companies and Credit and Financial Institutions (Branch Disclosure) Regulations 1992, SI 1992 No 3179, reg 4, Sch 3, para 12.

[703B. Charges requiring registration]

(1) The charges requiring registration under this Chapter are those which if created by a company registered in Great Britain would require registration under Part XII of this Act.

(2) Whether a charge is one requiring registration under this Chapter shall be determined—

[(a) in the case of a charge over property of a company at the date when it becomes a registered oversea company, as at that date,]
(b) in the case of a charge created by a registered oversea company, as at the date the charge is created, and
(c) in the case of a charge over property acquired by a registered oversea company, as at the date of the acquisition.

(3) In the following provisions of this Chapter references to a charge are, unless the context otherwise requires, to a charge requiring registration under this Chapter.

Where a charge not otherwise requiring registration relates to property by virtue of which it requires to be registered and to other property, the references are to the charge so far as it relates to property of the former description.]

[1089B]

NOTES
See note preceding s 703A at para **[1089A]**.
Sub-s (2): para (a) substituted by the Oversea Companies and Credit and Financial Institutions (Branch Disclosure) Regulations 1992, SI 1992 No 3179, reg 4, Sch 3, para 13.

[703C. The register]

(1) The registrar shall keep for each registered oversea company a register, in such form as he thinks fit, of charges on property of the company.

(2) The register shall consist of a file containing with respect to each such

charge the particulars and other information delivered to the registrar under or by virtue of the following provisions of this Chapter.

(3) Section 397(3) to (5) (registrar's certificate as to the date of delivery of particulars) applies in relation to the delivery of any particulars or other information under this Chapter.] **[1089C]**

NOTES

See note preceding s 703A at para **[1089A]**.

[703D. Company's duty to deliver particulars of charges for registration

(1) If when an oversea company

　[(a) delivers documents for registration under paragraph 1 of Schedule 21A—

　　　(i) in respect of a branch in England and Wales, or
　　　(ii) in respect of a branch in Scotland,

　　　for the first time since becoming a company to which section 690A applies, or

　(b) delivers documents for registration under section 691,]

any of its property is situated in Great Britain and subject to a charge, it is the company's duty at the same time to deliver the prescribed particulars of the charge, in the prescribed form, to the registrar for registration.

　[(1A) Subsection (1) above does not apply in relation to a charge if—

　(a) the particulars of it required to be delivered under that subsection have already been so delivered to the registrar to whom the documents mentioned in subsection (1) above are delivered, and
　(b) the company has at all times since they were so delivered to him been a registered oversea company in relation to the part of Great Britain for which he is registrar.]

(2) Where a registered oversea company—

　(a) creates a charge on property situated in Great Britain, or
　(b) acquires property which is situated in Great Britain and subject to a charge,

it is the company's duty to deliver the prescribed particulars of the charge in the prescribed form, to the registrar for registration within 21 days after the date of the charge's creation or, as the case may be, the date of the acquisition.

This subsection does not apply if the property subject to the charge is at the end of that period no longer situated in Great Britain.

(3) Where the preceding subsections do not apply and property of a registered oversea company is for a continuous period of four months situated in Great Britain and subject to a charge, it is the company's duty before the end of that period to deliver the prescribed particulars of the charge, in the prescribed form, to the registrar for registration.

(4) Particulars of a charge required to be delivered under subsection (1), (2) or (3) may be delivered for registration by any person interested in the charge.

(5) If a company fails to comply with subsection (1), (2) or (3), then, unless particulars of the charge have been delivered for registration by another person, the company and every officer of it who is in default is liable to a fine.

(6) Section 398(2), (4) and (5) (recovery of fees paid in connection with

registration, filing of particulars in register and sending of copy of particulars filed and note as to date) apply in relation to particulars delivered under this Chapter. **[1089D]**

NOTES
See note preceding s 703A at para **[1089A]**.
Sub-s (1): words in square brackets substituted by the Oversea Companies and Credit and Financial Institutions (Branch Disclosure) Regulations 1992, SI 1992 No 3179, reg 4, Sch 3, para 14.
Sub-s (1A): inserted by the Oversea Companies and Credit and Financial Institutions (Branch Disclosure) Regulations 1992, SI 1992 No 3179, reg 4, Sch 3, para 14.

[703E. Registrar to whom particulars, &c to be delivered

(1) The particulars required to be delivered by section 703D(1) (charges over property of oversea company becoming registered in a part of Great Britain) shall be delivered to the registrar to whom the documents are delivered under [paragraph 1 of Schedule 21A or, as the case may be,] section 691.

(2) The particulars required to be delivered by section 703D(2) or (3) (charges over property of registered oversea company) shall be delivered—

[(*a*) where the company is a company to which section 690A applies—

(i) if it has registered a branch in one part of Great Britain but has not registered a branch in the other, to the registrar for the part in which it has registered a branch,

(ii) if it has registered a branch in both parts of Great Britain but the property subject to the charge is situated in one part of Great Britain only, to the registrar for that part, and

(iii) in any other case, to the registrars for both parts of Great Britain; and

(*b*) where the company is a company to which section 691 applies—

(i) if it is registered in one part of Great Britain and not in the other, to the registrar for the part in which it is registered,

(ii) if it is registered in both parts of Great Britain but the property subject to the charge is situated in one part of Great Britain only, to the registrar for that part, and

(iii) in any other case, to the registrar for both parts of Great Britain.]

(3) Other documents required or authorised by virtue of this Chapter to be delivered to the registrar shall be delivered to the registrar or registrars to whom particulars of the charge to which they relate have been, or ought to have been, delivered.

(4) [If a company ceases to be a registered oversea company in relation to either part of Great Britain, charges over property of the company shall cease to be subject to the provisions of this Chapter, as regards registration in that part of Great Britain, as from the date on which the notice under section 695A(3) or, as the case may be, 696(3) is given.]

This is without prejudice to rights arising by reason of events occurring before that date.] **[1089E]**

NOTES
See note preceding s 703A at para **[1089A]**.
Sub-s (1): words in square brackets inserted by the Oversea Companies and Credit and Financial Institutions (Branch Disclosure) Regulations 1992, SI 1992 No 3179, reg 4, Sch 3, para 15.

Sub-s (2): words in square brackets substituted by the Oversea Companies and Credit and Financial Institutions (Branch Disclosure) Regulations 1992, SI 1992 No 3179, reg 4, Sch 3, para 15.

Sub-s (4): words in square brackets substituted by the Oversea Companies and Credit and Financial Institutions (Branch Disclosure) Regulations 1992, SI 1992 No 3179, reg 4, Sch 3, para 15.

[703F. Effect of failure to deliver particulars, late delivery and effect of errors and omissions

(1) The following provisions of Part XII—

    (*a*) section 399 (effect of failure to deliver particulars),

    (*b*) section 400 (late delivery of particulars), and

    (*c*) section 402 (effect of errors and omissions in particulars delivered),

apply, with the following modifications, in relation to a charge created by a registered oversea company of which particulars are required to be delivered under this Chapter.

(2) Those provisions do not apply to a charge of which particulars are required to be delivered under section 703D(1) (charges existing when company delivers documents under section 691).

(3) In relation to a charge of which particulars are required to be delivered under section 703D(3) (charges registrable by virtue of property being within Great Britain for requisite period), the references to the period of 21 days after the charge's creation shall be construed as references to the period of four months referred to in that subsection.] **[1089F]**

NOTES

    See note preceding s 703A at para **[1089A]**.

[703G. Delivery of further particulars or memorandum

Sections 401 and 403 (delivery of further particulars and memorandum of charge ceasing to affect company's property) apply in relation to a charge of which particulars have been delivered under this Chapter.] **[1089G]**

NOTES

    See note preceding s 703A at para **[1089A]**.

[703H. Further provisions with respect to voidness of charges

(1) The following provisions of Part XII apply in relation to the voidness of a charge by virtue of this Chapter—

    (*a*) section 404 (exclusion of voidness as against unregistered charges),

    (*b*) section 405 (restrictions on cases in which charge is void),

    (*c*) section 406 (effect of exercise of power of sale), and

    (*d*) section 407 (effect of voidness on obligation secured).

(2) In relation to a charge of which particulars are required to be delivered under section 703D(3) (charges registrable by virtue of property being within Great Britain for requisite period), the reference in section 404 to the period of 21 days after the charge's creation shall be construed as a reference to the period of four months referred to in that subsection.] **[1089H]**

NOTES

    See note preceding s 703A at para **[1089A]**.

[703I. Additional information to be registered

(1) Section 408 (particulars of taking up of issue of debentures) applies in relation to a charge of which particulars have been delivered under this Chapter.

(2) Section 409 (notice of appointment of receiver or manager) applies in relation to the appointment of a receiver or manager of property of a registered oversea company.

(3) Regulations under section 410 (notice of crystallisation of floating charge, &c) may apply in relation to a charge of which particulars have been delivered under this Chapter; but subject to such exceptions, adaptations and modifications as may be specified in the regulations.] **[1089I]**

NOTES
See note preceding s 703A at para **[1089A]**.

[703J. Copies of instruments and register to be kept by company

(1) Sections 411 and 412 (copies of instruments and register to be kept by company) apply in relation to a registered oversea company and any charge over property of the company situated in Great Britain.

(2) They apply to any charge, whether or not particulars are required to be delivered to the registrar.

(3) In relation to such a company the references to the company's registered office shall be construed as references to its principal place of business in Great Britain.] **[1089J]**

NOTES
See note preceding s 703A at para **[1089A]**.

[703K. Power to make further provision by regulations

(1) The Secretary of State may by regulations make further provision as to the application of the provisions of this Chapter, or the provisions of Part XII applied by this Chapter, in relation to charges of any description specified in the regulations.

(2) The regulations may apply any provisions of regulations made under section 413 (power to make further provision with respect to application of Part XII) or make any provision which may be made under that section with respect to the application of provisions of Part XII.] **[1089K]**

NOTES
See note preceding s 703A at para **[1089A]**.

[703L. Provisions as to situation of property

(1) The following provisions apply for determining for the purposes of this Chapter whether a vehicle which is the property of an oversea company is situated in Great Britain—

    (*a*) a ship, aircraft or hovercraft shall be regarded as situated in Great Britain if, and only if, it is registered in Great Britain;

    (*b*) any further description of vehicle shall be regarded as situated in Great Britain on a day if, and only if, at any time on that day the management of the vehicle is directed from a place of business of the company in Great Britain;

and for the purposes of this Chapter a vehicle shall not be regarded as situated in one part of Great Britain only.

(2) For the purposes of this Chapter as it applies to a charge on future property, the subject-matter of the charge shall be treated as situated in Great Britain unless it relates exclusively to property of a kind which cannot, after being acquired or coming into existence, be situated in Great Britain; and references to property situated in a part of Great Britain shall be similarly construed.]   **[1089L]**

NOTES
    See note preceding s 703A at para **[1089A]**.

[703M. Other supplementary provisions

The following provisions of Part XII apply for the purposes of this Chapter—

    (*a*) section 414 (construction of references to date of creation of charge),
    (*b*) section 415 (prescribed particulars and related expressions),
    (*c*) section 416 (notice of matters disclosed in the register),
    (*d*) section 417 (power of court to dispense with signature),
    (*e*) section 418 (regulations) and
    (*f*) section 419 (minor definitions).]   **[1089M]**

NOTES
    See note preceding s 703A at para **[1089A]**.

[703N. Index of defined expressions

The following Table shows the provisions of this Chapter and Part XII defining or otherwise explaining expressions used in this Chapter (other than expressions used only in the same section)—

charge	sections 703A(2), 703B(3) and 395(2)
charge requiring registration	sections 703B(1) and 396
creation of charge	sections 703M(f) and 419(2)
date of acquisition (of property by a company)	sections 703M(*f*) and 419(3)
date of creation of charge	sections 703M(a) and 414
property	sections 703A(2) and 395(2)
registered oversea company	section 703A(3)
registrar and registration in relation to a charge	sections 703A(4) and 703E
situated in Great Britain	
in relation to vehicles	section 703L(1)
in relation to future property	section 703L(2).".

                                                  [1089N]

NOTES
    See note preceding s 703A at para **[1089A]**.

[711A. Exclusion of deemed notice

(1) A person shall not be taken to have notice of any matter merely because of its being disclosed in any document kept by the registrar of companies (and thus available for inspection) or made available by the company for inspection.

(2) This does not affect the question whether a person is affected by notice

of any matter by reason of a failure to make such inquiries as ought reasonably to be made.

(3) In this section "document" includes any material which contains information.

(4) Nothing in this section affects the operation of—

    (*a*) section 416 of this Act (under which a person taking a charge over a company's property is deemed to have notice of matters disclosed on the companies charges register), or

    (*b*) section 198 of the Law of Property Act 1925 as it applies by virtue of section 3(7) of the Land Charges Act 1972 (under which the registration of certain land charges under Part XII, or Chapter III of Part XXIII, of this Act is deemed to constitute actual notice for all purposes connected with the land affected).]   **[1090]**

NOTES

Prospectively inserted by the Companies Act 1989, s 142(1).

CHARITIES ACT 1985

(c 20)

ARRANGEMENT OF SECTIONS

An Act to make further provision with respect to charities in England and Wales
[23 May 1985]

2. Resolution by trustees of old charity to alter objects

(1) This section applies, subject to subsection (11) below, to a local charity for the relief of poverty, where—

    (a) at least 50 years have elapsed since the date of the charity's foundation, or

    (b) it is subject to a scheme (whether established by the court or by the Commissioners) for the joint administration of two or more charities, and in the case of each of the charities comprised in the scheme at least 50 years have elapsed since the date of its foundation.

(2) If the charity trustees are of the opinion—

    (a) that the objects of the charity may fairly be considered obsolete or lacking in usefulness, or impossible of achievement, having regard to the period that has elapsed since the charity was founded, the social and economic

changes that have taken place in that period and other circumstances (if any) relevant to the functioning and administration of the charity, and

(b) that an alteration of the charity's objects is required in order that the charity's resources may be applied to better effect, consistently with the spirit of the original gift,

they may (subject to the following provisions) pass a resolution that the trusts of the charity be modified by replacing the objects of the charity by other objects, being in law charitable, specified in the resolution.

(3) The objects so specified must be, in the trustees' opinion, not so far dissimilar in character to those of the original charitable gift that this modification of the charity's trusts would constitute an unjustifiable departure from the intentions of the founder of the charity, or violate the spirit of the gift.

(4) The trustees must take such steps as are reasonably open to them to secure the approval to the proposed alteration of objects of any person identifiable as having been the founder of the charity.

(5) The resolution of the trustees must be unanimous and be in the form set out in Schedule 1 to this Act, or as near to that form as circumstances may admit.

(6) Having passed the resolution, the trustees shall—

(a) give such public notice that they have done so as they think reasonable and justified, having regard to the resources of the charity and the extent of its area of benefit, and

(b) send copies of the resolution to the Commissioners and to the appropriate local authority, accompanied in each case by a statement of their reasons for being of the opinions specified in subsections (2) and (3) above.

The trustees need not comply with paragraph (a) of this subsection if they consider that, in all the circumstances, no useful purpose would be served by giving public notice of the resolution.

(7) The Commissioners may, when considering the resolution, require the trustees to provide additional information or explanation as to the circumstances in and by reference to which they have determined to act under this section or as to their compliance with this section; and the Commissioners shall take into consideration any representations made to them by the appropriate local authority and others appearing to them to be interested.

(8) The Commissioners shall, not less than six weeks or more than 3 months from the time when they receive a copy of the resolution from the trustees—

(a) if it appears to them that the requirements of this section are satisfied in respect of the resolution, and that the proposed alteration of objects is justified in all the circumstances (treating the trustees' opinion under subsections (2) and (3) as prima facie well-founded and not to be set aside in the absence of contrary considerations), give to the trustees notice of their concurrence with the resolution, or

(b) give them notice that they require further time in which to consider the case (but so that not more than an additional 6 months shall be taken for that purpose), or

(c) give them notice that they do not concur with the resolution.

Any notice given by the Commissioners under this subsection (including any notice of concurrence, or non-concurrence, given after they have taken further time for consideration) shall be in writing, and they shall send a copy of it to the appropriate local authority.

(9) If the Commissioners give notice of their concurrence with the resolution then, with effect from the date specified in the notice the trusts of the charity shall, by virtue of this section, be deemed modified in accordance with the terms of the resolution, and the trust instrument shall have effect accordingly.

(10) References in this section to a charity's trust instrument include any document which for the time being lays down or regulates the manner in which the charity's property may or must be applied.

(11) This section does not apply to an exempt charity or a charity which is a company or other body corporate.

(12) Section 4(6)(b) of the Act of 1960 (duty to give notice etc. to the Commissioners) does not apply where the trusts of a charity are modified by virtue of this section. **[1091]**

NOTES
Repealed with savings by the Charities Act 1992, s 78(2), Sch 7 and the Charities Act 1992 (Commencement No 1 and Transitional Provisions) Order 1992, SI 1992 No 1900, art 2(5).
Act of 1960: Charities Act 1960.

3. Power for certain charity trustees to transfer whole property to another charity

(1) Subject to and in accordance with this section, the trustees of a registered charity, or a charity which is not required to be registered, may pass a resolution that the whole property of the charity be transferred to another charity, being a registered charity or a charity that is not required to be registered, to be held and applied by, and as property of, that other charity.

(2) Such a resolution shall not have effect unless in the case of the charity first-mentioned ("the transferor charity") its gross income in the preceding accounting period was £200 or less; and the trustees must, before passing such a resolution—

(a) obtain from the trustees of the other charity ("the transferee charity") written confirmation that they are willing to accept a transfer of property under this section, and

(b) have formed the opinion that the objects of the transferee charity are not so far dissimilar in character to those of the original charitable gift that the proposed transfer would constitute an unjustifiable departure from the intentions of the founder of the transferor charity or violate the spirit of the gift.

(3) The trustees must also take such steps as are reasonably open to them to secure the approval to the proposed transfer of any person identifiable as having been the founder of the charity.

(4) The resolution of the trustees must be unanimous, and must be in the form set out in Schedule 2 to this Act, or as near to that form as circumstances may admit.

(5) Having passed the resolution, the trustees shall—

(a) give such public notice that they have done so as they think reasonable and justified, having regard to the resources of the charity and the extent of its area of benefit, and

(b) send copies of the resolution to the Commissioners and, if it is a local charity for the relief of poverty, to the appropriate local authority, accompanied in each case by a statement of their reasons for wishing to effect a transfer of property under this section.

The trustees need not comply with paragraph (a) of this subsection if they consider that, in all the circumstances, no useful purpose would be served by giving public notice of the resolution.

(6) The Commissioners may, when considering the resolution, require the trustees to provide additional information or explanation as to the circumstances in and by reference to which they have determined to act under this section or as to their compliance with this section; and the Commissioners shall take into consideration any representations made to them by the appropriate local authority and others appearing to them to be interested.

(7) The Commissioners shall, not less than six weeks or more than 3 months from the time when they receive a copy of the resolution from the trustees—

(a) if it appears to them that the requirements of this section are satisfied in respect of the resolution and that it is a proper case (treating the trustees' opinion under subsection (2)(b) as prima facie well-founded and not to be set aside in the absence of contrary considerations), give to the trustees notice of their concurrence with the resolution, or

(b) give them notice that they require further time in which to consider the case (but so that not more than an additional 6 months shall be taken for that purpose), or

(c) give them notice that they do not concur with the resolution.

Any notice given by the Commissioners under this subsection (including any notice of concurrence, or non-concurrence, given after they have taken further time for consideration) shall be in writing, and if a copy of the resolution has been sent to the appropriate local authority under subsection (5)(b), they shall send a copy of any such notice to that authority.

(8) If the Commissioners give notice of their concurrence with the resolution, the trustees of the transferor charity shall on receipt of the notice make arrangements for the transfer of the whole property of the charity to the trustees of the transferee charity, to be acquired by that charity on the terms of this section.

(9) Those terms are as follows—

(a) all property acquired from the transferor charity which was expendable as income in the hands of that charity is to be treated as expendable in the hands of the transferee charity;

(b) any property of the transferor charity which was not expendable as income, having formed part of that charity's permanent endowment, is to remain subject to the same restrictions on expenditure as applied before the transfer;

(c) the whole property acquired by the transferee charity is to be held and applied for the objects of that charity.

(10) For the purpose of enabling any property to be transferred under this section, the Commissioners shall have power, at the request of the trustees of the transferor charity to make orders vesting any property of that charity in the trustees of the transferee charity.

(11) This section does not apply to a charity falling within paragraph (g) of Schedule 2 to the Act of 1960 or a charity which is a company or other body corporate. **[1092]**

NOTES

Repealed with savings by the Charities Act 1992, s 78(2), Sch 7 and the Charities Act 1992 (Commencement No 1 and Transitional Provisions) Order 1992, SI 1992 No 1900, art 2(5).

Act of 1960: Charities Act 1960.

4. Power for very small charities to spend capital

(1) Where, in the case of a charity having a permanent endowment—

> *(a) the value of the endowment is £25 or less and the endowment does not consist of or comprise any land or interest in land, and*
>
> *(b) the charity's gross income in the preceding accounting period was £5 or less, and*
>
> *(c) the charity trustees are of the opinion that the property of the charity is too small, in relation to its objects, for any useful purpose to be achieved by the expenditure of income alone,*

the trustees may pass a resolution that the charity ought to be freed from any restrictions imposed by law with respect to expenditure of capital.

(2) Before passing such a resolution, the trustees must consider whether any reasonable possibility exists of effecting a transfer of the charity's property to another charity under section 3 of this Act (disregarding any such transfer as would, in the trustees' opinion, impose on their charity an unacceptable burden of costs).

(3) The resolution of the trustees must be unanimous, and be in the form set out in Schedule 3 to this Act, or as near to that form as circumstances may admit.

(4) Having passed the resolution, the trustees shall send a copy of it to the Commissioners and shall then have power by virtue of this section to expend any property of the charity without regard to any restriction imposed by law and applying to the expenditure of capital but not to the expenditure of income.

(5) This section does not apply to a charity falling within paragraph (g) of Schedule 2 to the Act of 1960. **[1093]**

NOTES

Repealed with savings by the Charities Act 1992, s 78(2), Sch 7 and the Charities Act 1992 (Commencement No 1 and Transitional Provisions) Order 1992, SI 1992 No 1900, art 2(5).
Act of 1960: Charities Act 1960.

5. Financial limits

(1) The Secretary of State may, if he thinks it expedient with a view to increasing the number of charities which may take advantage of the provisions of the Charities Acts specially applicable to small charities, by order in a statutory instrument, alter the money sums specified in—

> *(a) section 18(5) of the Act of 1960 (persons who may, in the case of small charities, apply to the Commissioners for exercise of their jurisdiction under that section), and*
>
> *(b) section 3(2) of this Act,*

or either of those sums.

(2) The Secretary of State may, if he thinks it expedient in consequence of changes in the value of money, by order in a statutory instrument, alter the money sums specified in paragraphs (a) and (b) of section 4(1) of this Act.

(3) A statutory instrument under this section shall be subject to annulment in pursuance of a resolution of either House of Parliament. **[1094]**

NOTES

Repealed with savings by the Charities Act 1992, s 78(2), Sch 7 and the Charities Act 1992 (Commencement No 1 and Transitional Provisions) Order 1992, SI 1992 No 1900, art 2(5).
Act of 1960: Charities Act 1960.

6. Interpretation

(1) References in this Act to a local charity for the relief of poverty are to a registered charity, not being an ecclesiastical charity, having the following characteristics—

    (a) the sole or primary object of the charity is the relief of poverty (within any meaning given to that expression under the law of charitable trusts as applied for the time being), and

    (b) it is established for purposes which are by their nature or by the trusts of the charity directed wholly or mainly to the benefit of a particular area in England and Wales (in this section referred to as "the area of benefit"), and—

        (i) the area of benefit is, or falls wholly within, the area of not more than five adjoining parishes or of one county or of Greater London, or

        (ii) the area that would have been the area of benefit when the charity was originally established was, or fell wholly within, the area of one or more parishes specified in the trusts.

(2) In this Act "appropriate local authority", in relation to a local charity for the relief of poverty, means any local authority for an area which is the area of benefit or within which the whole or any part of the area of benefit falls, being the council of a non-metropolitan county, metropolitan district or London borough or the Common Council of the City of London.

(3) In this Act—

    (a) "accounting period" means a period of not more than 15 months or less than 12 months;

    (b) "the Act of 1960" means the Charities Act 1960;

    (c) "parish" includes ecclesiastical and local government parish and, in Wales, a community under the Local Government Act 1972;

    (d) "registered" means registered in the register of charities maintained by the Commissioners under Part II of the Act of 1960;

    (e) any reference to the trustees of a charity is to the persons having the general control and management of its administration;

and (subject as above) sections 45 and 46 of the Act of 1960 (interpretation) have effect for the purposes of this Act as they have effect for the purposes of that Act.

                                          [1095]

NOTES

    Repealed with savings by the Charities Act 1992, s 78(2), Sch 7 and the Charities Act 1992 (Commencement No 1 and Transitional Provisions) Order 1992, SI 1992 No 1900, art 2(5).

7. Citation, etc

(1) This Act may be cited as the Charities Act 1985; and the Act of 1960 and this Act may be cited together as the Charities Act 1960 and 1985.

(2) This Act shall come into force on a day appointed by the Secretary of State by order in a statutory instrument and different days may be appointed for different provisions and for different purposes.

(3) This Act shall not extend to Scotland or Northern Ireland.   **[1096]**

NOTES

    Repealed with savings by the Charities Act 1992, s 78(2), Sch 7 and the Charities Act 1992 (Commencement No 1 and Transitional Provisions) Order 1992, SI 1992 No 1900, art 2(5).

    Act of 1960: Charities Act 1960.

SCHEDULES
SCHEDULE 1

Section 2

FORM OF RESOLUTION BY CHARITY TRUSTEES UNDER SECTION 2

WHEREAS we are the trustees of the .. .. Charity, being a charity to which section 2 of the Charities Act 1985 applies:

AND WHEREAS we are of the opinion—
 *(a) that the objects of the charity may fairly be considered obsolete or lacking in usefulness, or impossible of achievement, having regard to the period that has elapsed since the charity was founded, the social and economic changes that have taken place in that period and other circumstances relative to the functioning and administration of the charity, as follows
 .. ..

 (relevant circumstances, if any to be specified)
 and
 (b) that an alteration of the charity's objects, as set out in .. ..

 (here specify the applicable trust instrument) is required in order that the charity's resources may be applied to better effect, consistently with the spirit of the original gift:

AND WHEREAS alternative objects, being in law charitable, are specified in the schedule to this resolution and are in our opinion not so far dissimilar in character to those of the original charitable gift that this modification of the charity's trust would constitute an unjustifiable departure from the intentions of the founder of the charity, or violate the spirit of the gift:

AND WHEREAS as we have complied with section 2(4) of the said Act of 1985:

NOW THEREFORE we, the trustees of the said charity, under and in pursuance of section 2 of the Charities Act 1985, hereby resolve that the trusts of the charity be modified by replacing the objects set out in the trust instrument by the alternative objects specified in the schedule.

Signed: .. ..
.. ..
.. ..

TRUSTEES
OF THE .. .. ..
.. CHARITY

*Delete any words or phrases not applicable.

Schedule to this Resolution

ALTERNATIVE OBJECTS PROPOSED TO REPLACE THOSE SET OUT IN THE TRUST INSTRUMENT

.. .. **[1097]**

NOTES
 Repealed with savings by the Charities Act 1992, s 78(2), Sch 7 and the Charities Act 1992 (Commencement No 1 and Transitional Provisions) Order 1992, SI 1992 No 1900, art 2(5).

SCHEDULE 2

Section 3

FORM OF RESOLUTION BY CHARITY TRUSTEES UNDER SECTION 3

WHEREAS we are the trustees of the .. .. Charity, of which the gross income in the preceding accounting period was £ .. .. :

AND WHEREAS we think it expedient that the whole property of the charity be transferred to another charity, to be held and applied for, and as property of, that other charity:

AND WHEREAS we have obtained from the trustees of the .. .. (here name proposed transferee charity), written confirmation that they are willing to accept a transfer of property under section 3 of the Charities Act 1985:

AND WHEREAS we have formed the opinion that the objects of the .. .. Charity are not so far dissimilar in character to those of the original charitable gift that the proposed transfer would constitute an unjustifiable departure from the intentions of the founder of the .. .. Charity, or violate the spirit of the gift:

AND WHEREAS we have complied with section 3(3) of the said Act of 1985:

NOW THEREFORE we, the trustees of the .. .. Charity, under and in pursuance of section 3 of the Charities Act 1985, hereby resolve that the whole property of the charity, including its permanent endowment, be transferred to the .. .. Charity.

Signed: .. ..
.. ..
TRUSTEES
OF THE .. .. ..
.. CHARITY **[1098]**

NOTES
Repealed with savings by the Charities Act 1992, s 78(2), Sch 7 and the Charities Act 1992 (Commencement No 1 and Transitional Provisions) Order 1992, SI 1992 No 1900, art 2(5).

SCHEDULE 3
Section 4
FORM OF RESOLUTION BY CHARITY TRUSTEES UNDER SECTION 4

WHEREAS we are the trustees of the .. .. Charity:

AND WHEREAS the value of the charity's permanent endowment is £ .. .. .. (or thereabouts), and the endowment does not consist of or comprise land or any interest in land, and its gross income in the last preceding accounting period was £ .. .. :

AND WHEREAS we are of the opinion that the property of the charity is too small, in relation to its objects, for any useful purpose to be achieved by the expenditure of income alone:

AND WHEREAS we have complied with section 4(2) of the Charities Act 1985:

NOW THEREFORE we, the trustees of the said charity, under and in pursuance of section 4 of the Charities Act 1985, hereby resolve that the charity ought to be freed from any restrictions imposed by law with respect to expenditure of capital.

Signed: .. ..
.. ..
.. ..
TRUSTEES
OF THE .. .. ..
.. CHARITY **[1099]**

NOTES
Repealed with savings by the Charities Act 1992, s 78(2), Sch 7 and the Charities Act 1992 (Commencement No 1 and Transitional Provisions) Order 1992, SI 1992 No 1900, art 2(5).

ENDURING POWERS OF ATTORNEY ACT 1985
(c 29)

ARRANGEMENT OF SECTIONS

Enduring powers of attorney

An Act to enable powers of attorney to be created which will survive any subsequent mental incapacity of the donor and to make provision in connection with such powers   **[26 June 1985]**

Enduring powers of attorney

1. Enduring power of attorney to survive mental incapacity of donor

(1) Where an individual creates a power of attorney which is an enduring power within the meaning of this Act then—

(a) the power shall not be revoked by any subsequent mental incapacity of his; but

(b) upon such incapacity supervening the donee of the power may not do anything under the authority of the power except as provided by subsection (2) below or as directed or authorised by the court under section 5 unless or, as the case may be, until the instrument creating the power is registered by the court under section 6; and

(c) section 5 of the Powers of Attorney Act 1971 (protection of donee and third persons) so far as applicable shall apply if and so long as paragraph (b) above operates to suspend the donee's authority to act under the power as if the power had been revoked by the donor's mental incapacity.

(2) Notwithstanding subsection (1)(*b*) above, where the attorney has made an application for registration of the instrument then, until the application has been initially determined, the attorney may take action under the power—

    (*a*) to maintain the donor or prevent loss to his estate; or

    (*b*) to maintain himself or other persons in so far as section 3(4) permits him to do so.

(3) Where the attorney purports to act as provided by subsection (2) above then, in favour of a person who deals with him without knowledge that the attorney is acting otherwise than in accordance with paragraph (*a*) or (*b*) of that subsection, the transaction between them shall be as valid as if the attorney were acting in accordance with paragraph (*a*) or (*b*).   **[1100]**

2. Characteristics of an enduring power

(1) Subject to subsections (7) to (9) below and section 11, a power of attorney is an enduring power within the meaning of this Act if the instrument which creates the power—

    (*a*) is in the prescribed form; and

    (*b*) was executed in the prescribed manner by the donor and the attorney; and

    (*c*) incorporated at the time of execution by the donor the prescribed explanatory information.

(2) The Lord Chancellor shall make regulations as to the form and execution of instruments creating enduring powers and the regulations shall contain such provisions as appear to him to be appropriate for securing—

    (*a*) that no document is used to create an enduring power which does not incorporate such information explaining the general effect of creating or accepting the power as may be prescribed; and

    (*b*) that such instruments include statements to the following effect—

        (i) by the donor, that he intends the power to continue in spite of any intervening mental incapacity of his;

       (ii) by the donor, that he read or had read to him the information explaining the effect of creating the power;

      (iii) by the attorney, that he understands the duty of registration imposed by this Act.

(3) Regulations under subsection (2) above—

    (*a*) may include different provision for cases where more than one attorney is to be appointed by the instrument than for cases where only one attorney is to be appointed; and

    (*b*) may, if they amend or revoke any regulations previously made under that subsection, include saving and transitional provisions.

(4) Regulations under subsection (2) above shall be made by statutory instrument which shall be subject to annulment in pursuance of a resolution of either House of Parliament.

(5) An instrument in the prescribed form purporting to have been executed in the prescribed manner shall be taken, in the absence of evidence to the contrary, to be a document which incorporated at the time of execution by the donor the prescribed explanatory information.

(6) Where an instrument differs in an immaterial respect in form or mode of expression from the prescribed form the instrument shall be treated as sufficient in point of form and expression.

(7) A power of attorney cannot be an enduring power unless, when he executes the instrument creating it, the attorney is—

(*a*) an individual who has attained eighteen years and is not bankrupt; or
(*b*) a trust corporation.

(8) A power of attorney under section 25 of the Trustee Act 1925 (power to delegate trusts etc. by power of attorney) cannot be an enduring power.

(9) A power of attorney which gives the attorney a right to appoint a substitute or successor cannot be an enduring power.

(10) An enduring power shall be revoked by the bankruptcy of the attorney whatever the circumstances of the bankruptcy.

(11) An enduring power shall be revoked on the exercise by the court of any of its powers under Part VII of the Mental Health Act 1983 if, but only if, the court so directs.

(12) No disclaimer of an enduring power, whether by deed or otherwise, shall be valid unless and until the attorney gives notice of it to the donor or, where section 4(6) or 7(1) applies, to the court.

(13) In this section "prescribed" means prescribed under subsection (2) above.   **[1101]**

3. Scope of authority etc of attorney under enduring power

(1) An enduring power may confer general authority (as defined in subsection (2) below) on the attorney to act on the donor's behalf in relation to all or a specified part of the property and affairs of the donor or may confer on him authority to do specified things on the donor's behalf and the authority may, in either case, be conferred subject to conditions and restrictions.

(2) Where an instrument is expressed to confer general authority on the attorney it operates to confer, subject to the restriction imposed by subsection (5) below and to any conditions or restrictions contained in the instrument, authority to do on behalf of the donor anything which the donor can lawfully do by an attorney.

(3) Subject to any conditions or restrictions contained in the instrument, an attorney under an enduring power, whether general or limited, may (without obtaining any consent) execute or exercise all or any of the trusts, powers or discretions vested in the donor as trustee and may (without the concurrence of any other person) give a valid receipt for capital or other money paid.

(4) Subject to any conditions or restrictions contained in the instrument, an attorney under an enduring power, whether general or limited, may (without obtaining any consent) act under the power so as to benefit himself or other persons than the donor to the following extent but no further, that is to say—

(*a*) he may so act in relation to himself or in relation to any other person if the donor might be expected to provide for his or that person's needs respectively; and
(*b*) he may do whatever the donor might be expected to do to meet those needs.

(5) Without prejudice to subsection (4) above but subject to any conditions or restrictions contained in the instrument, an attorney under an enduring power, whether general or limited, may (without obtaining any consent) dispose of the property of the donor by way of gift to the following extent but no further, that is to say—

    (a) he may make gifts of a seasonal nature or at a time, or on an anniversary, of a birth or marriage, to persons (including himself) who are related to or connected with the donor, and

    (b) he may make gifts to any charity to whom the donor made or might be expected to make gifts,

provided that the value of each such gift is not unreasonable having regard to all the circumstances and in particular the size of the donor's estate.   **[1102]**

Action on actual or impending incapacity of donor

4. Duties of attorney in event of actual or impending incapacity of donor

(1) If the attorney under an enduring power has reason to believe that the donor is or is becoming mentally incapable subsections (2) to (6) below shall apply.

(2) The attorney shall, as soon as practicable, make an application to the court for the registration of the instrument creating the power.

(3) Before making an application for registration the attorney shall comply with the provisions as to notice set out in Schedule 1.

(4) An application for registration shall be made in the prescribed form and shall contain such statements as may be prescribed.

(5) The attorney may, before making an application for the registration of the instrument, refer to the court for its determination any question as to the validity of the power and he shall comply with any direction given to him by the court on that determination.

(6) No disclaimer of the power shall be valid unless and until the attorney gives notice of it to the court.

(7) Any person who, in an application for registration, makes a statement which he knows to be false in a material particular shall be liable—

    (a) on conviction on indictment, to imprisonment for a term not exceeding two years or to a fine, or both; and

    (b) on summary conviction, to imprisonment for a term not exceeding six months or to a fine not exceeding the statutory maximum, or both.

(8) In this section and Schedule 1 "prescribed" means prescribed by rules of the court.   **[1103]**

5. Functions of court prior to registration

Where the court has reason to believe that the donor of an enduring power may be, or may be becoming, mentally incapable and the court is of the opinion that it is necessary, before the instrument creating the power is registered, to exercise any power with respect to the power of attorney or the attorney appointed to act under it which would become exercisable under section 8(2) on its registration, the court may exercise that power under this section and may do so whether the attorney has or has not made an application to the court for the registration of the instrument. **[1104]**

6. Functions of court on application for registration

(1) In any case where—

    (*a*) an application for registration is made in accordance with section 4(3) and (4), and

    (*b*) neither subsection (2) nor subsection (4) below applies,

the court shall register the instrument to which the application relates.

(2) Where it appears to the court that there is in force under Part VII of the Mental Health Act 1983 an order appointing a receiver for the donor but the power has not also been revoked then, unless it directs otherwise, the court shall not exercise or further exercise its functions under this section but shall refuse the application for registration.

(3) Where it appears from an application for registration that notice of it has not been given under Schedule 1 to some person entitled to receive it (other than a person in respect of whom the attorney has been dispensed or is otherwise exempt from the requirement to give notice) the court shall direct that the application be treated for the purposes of this Act as having been made in accordance with section 4(3), if the court is satisfied that, as regards each such person—

    (*a*) it was undesirable or impracticable for the attorney to give him notice; or

    (*b*) no useful purpose is likely to be served by giving him notice.

(4) If, in the case of an application for registration—

    (*a*) a valid notice of objection to the registration is received by the court before the expiry of the period of five weeks beginning with the date or, as the case may be, the latest date on which the attorney gave notice to any person under Schedule 1, or

    (*b*) it appears from the application that there is no one to whom notice has been given under paragraph 1 of that Schedule, or

    (*c*) the court has reason to believe that appropriate inquiries might bring to light evidence on which the court could be satisfied that one of the grounds of objection set out in subsection (5) below was established,

the court shall neither register the instrument nor refuse the application until it has made or caused to be made such inquiries (if any) as it thinks appropriate in the circumstances of the case.

(5) For the purposes of this Act a notice of objection to the registration of an instrument is valid if the objection is made on one or more of the following grounds, namely—

    (*a*) that the power purported to have been created by the instrument was not valid as an enduring power of attorney;

    (*b*) that the power created by the instrument no longer subsists;

    (*c*) that the application is premature because the donor is not yet becoming mentally incapable;

    (*d*) that fraud or undue pressure was used to induce the donor to create the power;

(e) that, having regard to all the circumstances and in particular the attorney's relationship to or connection with the donor, the attorney is unsuitabe to be the donor's attorney.

(6) If, in a case where subsection (4) above applies, any of the grounds of objection in subsection (5) above is established to the satisfaction of the court, the court shall refuse the application but if, in such a case, it is not so satisfied, the court shall register the instrument to which the application relates.

(7) Where the court refuses an application for registration on ground (d) or (e) in subsection (5) above it shall by order revoke the power created by the instrument.

(8) Where the court refuses an application for registration on any ground other than that specified in subsection (5)(c) above the instrument shall be delivered up to be cancelled, unless the court otherwise directs.   **[1105]**

Legal position after registration

7. Effect and proof of registration etc

(1) The effect of the registration of an instrument under section 6 is that—

    (a) no revocation of the power by the donor shall be valid unless and until the court confirms the revocation under section 8(3);

    (b) no disclaimer of the power shall be valid unless and until the attorney gives notice of it to the court;

    (c) the donor may not extend or restrict the scope of the authority conferred by the instrument and no instruction or consent given by him after registration shall, in the case of a consent, confer any right and, in the case of an instruction, impose or confer any obligation or right on or create any liability of the attorney or other persons having notice of the instruction or consent.

(2) Subsection (1) above applies for so long as the instrument is registered under section 6 whether or not the donor is for the time being mentally incapable.

(3) A document purporting to be an office copy of an instrument registered under this Act [or under the Enduring Powers of Attorney (Northern Ireland) Order 1987] shall, in any part of the United Kingdom, be evidence of the contents of the instrument and of the fact that it has been so registered.

(4) Subsection (3) above is without prejudice to section 3 of the Powers of Attorney Act 1971 (proof by certified copies) and to any other method of proof authorised by law.   **[1106]**

NOTES

    Sub-s (3): words in square brackets inserted by the Enduring Powers of Attorney (Northern Ireland Consequential Amendment) Order 1987, SI 1987 No 1628, art 2.

8. Functions of court with respect to registered power

(1) Where an instrument has been registered under section 6, the court shall have the following functions with respect to the power and the donor of and the attorney appointed to act under the power.

    (2) The court may—

(*a*) determine any question as to the meaning or effect of the instrument;
(*b*) give directions with respect to—

    (i) the management or disposal by the attorney of the property and affairs of the donor;
    (ii) the rendering of accounts by the attorney and the production of the records kept by him for the purpose;
    (iii) the remuneration or expenses of the attorney, whether or not in default of or in accordance with any provision made by the instrument, including directions for the repayment of excessive or the payment of additional remuneration;

(*c*) require the attorney to furnish information or produce documents or things in his possession as attorney;
(*d*) give any consent or authorisation to act which the attorney would have to obtain from a mentally capable donor;
(*e*) authorise the attorney to act so as to benefit himself or other persons than the donor otherwise than in accordance with section 3(4) and (5) (but subject to any conditions or restrictions contained in the instrument);
(*f*) relieve the attorney wholly or partly from any liability which he has or may have incurred on account of a breach of his duties as attorney.

(3) On application made for the purpose by or on behalf of the donor, the court shall confirm the revocation of the power if satisfied that the donor has done whatever is necessary in law to effect an express revocation of the power and was mentally capable of revoking a power of attorney when he did so (whether or not he is so when the court considers the application).

(4) The court shall cancel the registration of an instrument registered under section 6 in any of the following circumstances, that is to say—

(*a*) on confirming the revocation of the power under subsection (3) above or receiving notice of disclaimer under section 7(1)(*b*);
(*b*) on giving a direction revoking the power on exercising any of its powers under Part VII of the Mental Health Act 1983;
(*c*) on being satisfied that the donor is and is likely to remain mentally capable;
(*d*) on being satisfied that the power has expired or has been revoked by the death or bankruptcy of the donor or the death, mental incapacity or bankruptcy of the attorney or, if the attorney is a body corporate, its winding up or dissolution;
(*e*) on being satisfied that the power was not a valid and subsisting enduring power when registration was effected;
(*f*) on being satisfied that fraud or undue pressure was used to induce the donor to create the power; or
(*g*) on being satisfied that, having regard to all the circumstances and in particular the attorney's relationship to or connection with the donor, the attorney is unsuitable to be the donor's attorney.

(5) Where the court cancels the registration of an instrument on being satisfied of the matters specified in paragraph (*f*) or (*g*) of subsection (4) above it shall by order revoke the power created by the instrument.

(6) On the cancellation of the registration of an instrument under subsection (4) above except paragraph (*c*) the instrument shall be delivered up to be cancelled, unless the court otherwise directs. **[1107]**

Protection of attorney and third parties

9. Protection of attorney and third persons where power invalid or revoked

(1) Subsections (2) and (3) below apply where an instrument which did not create a valid power of attorney has been registered under section 6 (whether or not the registration has been cancelled at the time of the act or transaction in question).

(2) An attorney who acts in pursuance of the power shall not incur any liability (either to the donor or to any other person) by reason of the non-existence of the power unless at the time of acting he knows—

(a) that the instrument did not create a valid enduring power; or

(b) that an event has occurred which, if the instrument had created a valid enduring power, would have had the effect of revoking the power; or

(c) that, if the instrument had created a valid enduring power, the power would have expired before that time.

(3) Any transaction between the attorney and another person shall, in favour of that person, be as valid as if the power had then been in existence, unless at the time of the transaction that person has knowledge of any of the matters mentioned in subsection (2) above.

(4) Where the interest of a purchaser depends on whether a transaction between the attorney and another person was valid by virtue of subsection (3) above, it shall be conclusively presumed in favour of the purchaser that the transaction was valid if—

(a) the transaction between that person and the attorney was completed within twelve months of the date on which the instrument was registered; or

(b) that person makes a statutory declaration, before or within three months after the completion of the purchase, that he had no reason at the time of the transaction to doubt that the attorney had authority to dispose of the property which was the subject of the transaction.

(5) For the purposes of section 5 of the Powers of Attorney Act 1971 (protection of attorney and third persons where action is taken under the power of attorney in ignorance of its having been revoked) in its application to an enduring power the revocation of which by the donor is by virtue of section 7(1)(a) above invalid unless and until confirmed by the court under section 8(3) above, knowledge of the confirmation of the revocation is, but knowledge of the unconfirmed revocation is not, knowledge of the revocation of the power.

(6) Schedule 2 shall have effect to confer protection in cases where the instrument failed to create a valid enduring power and the power has been revoked by the donor's mental incapacity.

(7) In this section "purchaser" and "purchase" have the meanings specified in section 205(1) of the Law of Property Act 1925.   **[1108]**

Supplementary

10. Application of Mental Health Act provisions relating to the court

(1) The provisions of Part VII of the Mental Health Act 1983 (relating to the Court of Protection) specified below shall apply to persons within and

proceedings under this Act in accordance with the following paragraphs of this subsection and subsection (2) below, that is to say—

   (*a*) section 103 (functions of Visitors) shall apply to persons within this Act as it applies to the persons mentioned in that section;

   (*b*) section 104 (powers of judge) shall apply to proceedings under this Act with respect to persons within this Act as it applies to the proceedings mentioned in subsection (1) of that section;

   (*c*) section 105(1) (appeals to nominated judge) shall apply to any decision of the Master of the Court of Protection or any nominated officer in proceedings under this Act as it applies to any decision to which that subsection applies and an appeal shall lie to the Court of Appeal from any decision of a nominated judge whether given in the exercise of his original jurisdiction or on the hearing of an appeal under section 105(1) as extended by this paragraph;

   (*d*) section 106 except subsection (4) (rules of procedure) shall apply to proceedings under this Act and persons within this Act as it applies to the proceedings and persons mentioned in that section.

(2) Any functions conferred or imposed by the provisions of the said Part VII applied by subsection (1) above shall be exercisable also for the purposes of this Act and the persons who are "within this Act" are the donors of and attorneys under enduring powers of attorney whether or not they would be patients for the purposes of the said Part VII.

(3) In this section "nominated judge" and "nominated officer" have the same meanings as in Part VII of the Mental Health Act 1983.   **[1109]**

11. Application to joint and joint and several attorneys

(1) An instrument which appoints more than one person to be an attorney cannot create an enduring power unless the attorneys are appointed to act jointly or jointly and severally.

(2) This Act, in its application to joint attorneys, applies to them collectively as it applies to a single attorney but subject to the modifications specified in Part I of Schedule 3.

(3) This Act, in its application to joint and several attorneys, applies with the modifications specified in subsections (4) to (7) below and in Part II of Schedule 3.

(4) A failure, as respects any one attorney, to comply with the requirements for the creation of enduring powers, shall prevent the instrument from creating such a power in his case without however affecting its efficacy for that purpose as respects the other or others or its efficacy in his case for the purpose of creating a power of attorney which is not an enduring power.

(5) Where one or more but not both or all the attorneys makes or joins in making an application for registration of the instrument then—

   (*a*) an attorney who is not an applicant as well as one who is may act pending the initial determination of the application as provided in section 1(2) (or under section 5);

   (*b*) notice of the application shall also be given under Schedule 1 to the other attorney or attorneys; and

   (*c*) objection may validly be taken to the registration on a ground relating to an attorney or to the power of an attorney who is not an applicant as well as to one or the power of one who is an applicant.

(6) The court shall not refuse under section 6(6) to register an instrument because a ground of objection to an attorney or power is established if an enduring power subsists as respects some attorney who is not affected thereby but shall give effect to it by the prescribed qualification of the registration.

(7) The court shall not cancel the registration of an instrument under section 8(4) for any of the causes vitiating registration specified in that subsection if an enduring power subsists as respects some attorney who is not affected thereby but shall give effect to it by the prescribed qualification of the registration.

(8) In this section—

"prescribed" means prescribed by rules of the court; and

"the requirements for the creation of enduring powers" means the provisions of section 2 other than subsections (10) to (12) and of regulations under subsection (2) of that section.   **[1110]**

12. Power of Lord Chancellor to modify pre-registration requirements in certain cases

(1) The Lord Chancellor may by order exempt attorneys of such descriptions as he thinks fit from the requirements of this Act to give notice to relatives prior to registration.

(2) Subject to subsection (3) below, where an order is made under this section with respect to attorneys of a specified description then, during the currency of the order, this Act shall have effect in relation to any attorney of that description with the omission of so much of section 4(3) and Schedule 1 as requires notice of an application for registration to be given to relatives.

(3) Notwithstanding that an attorney under a joint or joint and several power is of a description specified in a current order under this section, subsection (2) above shall not apply in relation to him if any of the other attorneys under the power is not of a description specified in that or another current order under this section.

(4) The power to make an order under this section shall be exercisable by statutory instrument which shall be subject to annulment in pursuance of a resolution of either House of Parliament.   **[1111]**

13. Interpretation

(1) In this Act—

"the court", in relation to any functions under this Act, means the authority having jurisdiction under Part VII of the Mental Health Act 1983;

"enduring power" is to be construed in accordance with section 2;

"mentally incapable" or "mental incapacity", except where it refers to revocation at common law, means, in relation to any person, that he is incapable by reason of mental disorder of managing and administering his property and affairs and "mentally capable" and "mental capacity" shall be construed accordingly;

"mental disorder" has the same meaning as it has in the Mental Health Act 1983;

"notice" means notice in writing;

"rules of the court" means rules under Part VII of the Mental Health Act 1983 as applied by section 10;

. . .

"trust corporation" means the Public Trustee or a corporation either appointed by the High Court or a county court (according to their respective jurisdictions) in any particular case to be a trustee or entitled by rules under section 4(3) of the Public Trustee Act 1906 to act as custodian trustee.

(2) Any question arising under or for the purposes of this Act as to what the donor of the power might at any time be expected to do shall be determined by assuming that he had full mental capacity at the time but otherwise by reference to the circumstances existing at that time.   **[1112]**

NOTES
   Sub-s (1): definition "statutory maximum" repealed by the SL(R)A 1993, s 1(1), Sch 1, Pt XIV.

14. Short title, commencement and extent

(1) This Act may be cited as the Enduring Powers of Attorney Act 1985.

(2) This Act shall come into force on such day as the Lord Chancellor appoints by order made by statutory instrument.

(3) This Act extends to England and Wales only except that section 7(3) and section 10(1)(*b*) so far as it applies section 104(4) of the Mental Health Act 1983 extend also to Scotland and Northern Ireland.   **[1113]**

SCHEDULES

SCHEDULE 1

Section 4(3)

NOTIFICATION PRIOR TO REGISTRATION

PART I

Duty to Give Notice to Relatives and Donor

Duty to give notice to relatives

1. Subject to paragraph 3 below, before making an application for registration the attorney shall give notice of his intention to do so to all those persons (if any) who are entitled to receive notice by virtue of paragraph 2 below.

2.—(1) Subject to the limitations contained in sub-paragraphs (2) to (4) below, persons of the following classes (referred to in this Act as "relatives") are entitled to receive notice under paragraph 1 above—

   (*a*) the donor's husband or wife;
   (*b*) the donor's children;
   (*c*) the donor's parents;
   (*d*) the donor's brothers and sisters, whether of the whole or half blood;
   (*e*) the widow or widower of a child of the donor;
   (*f*) the donor's grandchildren;
   (*g*) the children of the donor's brothers and sisters of the whole blood;
   (*h*) the children of the donor's brothers and sisters of the half blood;
   (*i*) the donor's uncles and aunts of the whole blood; and
   (*j*) the children of the donor's uncles and aunts of the whole blood.

(2) A person is not entitled to receive notice under paragraph 1 above if—

   (*a*) his name or address is not known to the attorney and cannot be reasonably ascertained by him; or
   (*b*) the attorney has reason to believe that he has not attained eighteen years or is mentally incapable.

(3) Except where sub-paragraph (4) below applies, no more than three persons are entitled to receive notice under paragraph 1 above and, in determining the persons who are so entitled, persons falling within class (*a*) of sub-paragraph (1) above are to be preferred to persons falling with class (*b*) of that sub-paragraph, persons falling within class (*b*) are to be preferred to persons falling within class (*c*) of that sub-paragraph; and so on.

(4) Notwithstanding the limit of three specified in sub-paragraph (3) above, where—

   (*a*) there is more than one person falling within any of classes (*a*) to (*j*) of sub-paragraph (1) above, and
   (*b*) at least one of those persons would be entitled to receive notice under paragraph 1 above,

then, subject to sub-paragraph (2) above, all the persons falling within that class are entitled to receive notice under paragraph 1 above.

3.—(1) An attorney shall not be required to give notice under paragraph 1 above to himself or to any other attorney under the power who is joining in making the application, notwithstanding that he or, as the case may be, the other attorney is entitled to receive notice by virtue of paragraph 2 above.

(2) In the case of any person who is entitled to receive notice under paragraph 1 above, the attorney, before applying for registration, may make an application to the court to be dispensed from the requirement to give him notice; and the court shall grant the application if it is satisfied—

   (*a*) that it would be undesirable or impracticable for the attorney to give him notice; or
   (*b*) that no useful purpose is likely to be served by giving him notice.

Duty to give notice to donor

4.—(1) Subject to sub-paragraph (2) below, before making an application for registration the attorney shall give notice of his intention to do so to the donor.

(2) Paragraph 3(2) above shall apply in relation to the donor as it applies in relation to a person who is entitled to receive notice under paragraph 1 above.   **[1114]**

PART II

Contents of Notices

5. A notice to relatives under this Schedule—

   (*a*) shall be in the prescribed form;
   (*b*) shall state that the attorney proposes to make an application to the Court of Protection for the registration of the instrument creating the enduring power in question;
   (*c*) shall inform the person to whom it is given that he may object to the proposed registration by notice in writing to the Court of Protection before the expiry of the period of four weeks beginning with the day on which the notice under this Schedule was given to him;
   (*d*) shall specify, as the grounds on which an objection to registration may be made, the grounds set out in section 6(5).

6. A notice to the donor under this Schedule—

   (*a*) shall be in the prescribed form;
   (*b*) shall contain the statement mentioned in paragraph 5(*b*) above; and
   (*c*) shall inform the donor that, whilst the instrument remains registered, any revocation of the power by him will be ineffective unless and until the revocation is confirmed by the Court of Protection.   **[1115]**

PART III
Duty to Give Notice to Other Attorneys

7.—(1) Subject to sub-paragraph (2) below, before making an application for registration an attorney under a joint and several power shall give notice of his intention to do so to any other attorney under the power who is not joining in making the application; and paragraphs 3(2) and 5 above shall apply in relation to attorneys entitled to receive notice by virtue of this paragraph as they apply in relation to persons entitled to receive notice by virtue of paragraph 2 above.

(2) An attorney is not entitled to receive notice by virtue of this paragraph if—

    (*a*) his address is not known to the applying attorney and cannot reasonably be ascertained by him; or

    (*b*) the applying attorney has reason to believe that he has not attained eighteen years or is mentally incapable.   **[1116]**

PART IV
Supplementary

8.—(1) For the purposes of this Schedule an illegitimate child shall be treated as if he were the legitimate child of his mother and father.

(2) Notwithstanding anything in section 7 of the Interpretation Act 1978 (construction of references to service by post), for the purposes of this Schedule a notice given by post shall be regarded as given on the date on which it was posted.   **[1117]**

SCHEDULE 2
Section 9(6)
FURTHER PROTECTION OF ATTORNEY AND THIRD PERSONS

1. Where—

    (*a*) an instrument framed in a form prescribed under section 2(2) creates a power which is not a valid enduring power; and

    (*b*) the power is revoked by the mental incapacity of the donor, paragraphs 2 and 3 below shall apply, whether or not the instrument has been registered.

2. An attorney who acts in pursuance of the power shall not, by reason of the revocation, incur any liability (either to the donor or to any other person) unless at the time of acting he knows—

    (*a*) that the instrument did not create a valid enduring power; and

    (*b*) that the donor has become mentally incapable.

3. Any transaction between the attorney and another person shall, in favour of that person, be as valid as if the power had then been in existence, unless at the time of the transaction that person knows—

    (*a*) that the instrument did not create a valid enduring power; and

    (*b*) that the donor has become mentally incapable.

4. Section 9(4) shall apply for the purpose of determining whether a transaction was valid by virtue of paragraph 3 above as it applies for the purpose of determining whether a transaction was valid by virtue of section 9(3).   **[1118]**

SCHEDULE 3

JOINT AND JOINT AND SEVERAL ATTORNEYS

PART I

Joint Attorneys

1. In section 2(7), the reference to the time when the attorney executes the instrument shall be read as a reference to the time when the second or last attorney executes the instrument.

2. In section 2(9) and (10), the reference to the attorney shall be read as a reference to any attorney under the power.

3. In section 5, references to the attorney shall be read as including references to any attorney under the power.

4. Section 6 shall have effect as if the ground of objection to the registration of the instrument specified in subsection (5)(*e*) applied to any attorney under the power.

5. In section 8(2), references to the attorney shall be read as including references to any attorney under the power.

6. In section 8(4), references to the attorney shall be read as including references to any attorney under the power.   **[1119]**

PART II

Joint and Several Attorneys

7. In section 2(10), the reference to the bankruptcy of the attorney shall be construed as a reference to the bankruptcy of the last remaining attorney under the power; and the bankruptcy of any other attorney under the power shall cause that person to cease to be attorney, whatever the circumstances of the bankruptcy.

8. The restriction upon disclaimer imposed by section 4(6) applies only to those attorneys who have reason to believe that the donor is or is becoming mentally incapable.   **[1120]**

ADMINISTRATION OF JUSTICE ACT 1985

(c 61)

An Act to make further provision with respect to the administration of justice and matters connected therewith; to amend the Solicitors Act 1974; to regulate the provision of solicitors' services in the case of incorporated practices; to regulate the provision of conveyancing services by persons practising as licensed conveyancers; to make further provision with respect to complaints relating to the provision of legal aid services; to amend the law relating to time limits for actions for libel and slander; and to make further provision with respect to arbitrations and proceedings in connection with European patents

[30 October 1985]

PART IV

THE SUPREME COURT AND COUNTY COURTS

Proceedings relating to estates of deceased persons and trusts

47. Power of High Court to make judgments binding on persons who are not parties

(1) This section applies to actions in the High Court relating to the estates of deceased persons or to trusts and falling within any description specified in rules of court.

(2) Rules of court may make provision for enabling any judgment given in an action to which this section applies to be made binding on persons who—

(a) are or may be affected by the judgment and would not otherwise be bound by it; but

(b) have in accordance with the rules been given notice of the action and of such matters connected with it as the rules may require.

(3) Different provision may be made under this section in relation to actions of different descriptions. **[1121]**

50. Power of High Court to appoint substitute for, or to remove, personal representative

(1) Where an application relating to the estate of a deceased person is made to the High Court under this subsection by or on behalf of a personal representative of the deceased or a beneficiary of the estate, the court may in its discretion—

(a) appoint a person (in this section called a substituted personal representative) to act as personal representative of the deceased in place of the existing personal representative or representatives of the deceased or any of them; or

(b) if there are two or more existing personal representatives of the deceased, terminate the appointment of one or more, but not all, of those persons.

(2) Where the court appoints a person to act as a substituted personal representative of a deceased person, then—

(a) if that person is appointed to act with an executor or executors the appointment shall (except for the purpose of including him in any chain of representation) constitute him executor of the deceased as from the date of the appointment; and

(b) in any other case the appointment shall constitute that person administrator of the deceased's estate as from the date of the appointment.

(3) The court may authorise a person appointed as a substituted personal representative to charge remuneration for his services as such, on such terms (whether or not involving the submission of bills of charges for taxation by the court) as the court may think fit.

(4) Where an application relating to the estate of a deceased person is made to the court under subsection (1), the court may if it thinks fit, proceed as if the application were, or included, an application for the appointment under the Judicial Trustees Act 1896 of a judicial trustee in relation to that estate.

(5) In this section "beneficiary", in relation to the estate of a deceased person, means a person who under the will of the deceased or under the law relating to intestacy is beneficially interested in the estate.

(6) ... **[1122]**

NOTES
Sub-s (6): amends the Judicial Trustees Act 1896, s 1.

HOUSING ACT 1985
(c 68)

ARRANGEMENT OF SECTIONS

An Act to consolidate the Housing Acts (except those provisions consolidated in the Housing Associations Act 1985 and the Landlord and Tenant Act 1985), and certain related provisions, with amendments to give effect to recommendations of the Law Commission   [30 October 1985]

PART IV

SECURE TENANCIES AND RIGHTS OF SECURE TENANTS

Security of tenure

79. Secure tenancies

(1) A tenancy under which a dwelling-house is let as a separate dwelling is a secure tenancy at any time when the conditions described in sections 80 and 81 as the landlord condition and the tenant condition are satisfied.

(2) Subsection (1) has effect subject to—

    (*a*)   the exceptions in Schedule 1 (tenancies which are not secure tenancies),
    (*b*)   sections 89(3) and (4) and 90(3) and (4) (tenancies ceasing to be secure after death of tenant), and
    (*c*)   sections 91(2) and 93(2) (tenancies ceasing to be secure in consequence of assignment or subletting).

(3) The provisions of this Part apply in relation to a licence to occupy a dwelling-house (whether or not granted for a consideration) as they apply in relation to a tenancy.

(4) Subsection (3) does not apply to a licence granted as a temporary expedient to a person who entered the dwelling-house or any other land as a trespasser (whether or not, before the grant of that licence, another licence to occupy that or another dwelling-house had been granted to him).   **[1123]**

80. The landlord condition

(1) The landlord condition is that the interest of the landlord belongs to one of the following authorities or bodies—

     a local authority,
     a new town corporation,
     [a housing action trust]
     an urban development corporation,
     the Development Board for Rural Wales,
     the Housing Corporation,
     a housing trust which is a charity, or
     a housing association or housing co-operative to which this section applies.

    (2) This section applies to—

(a) a registered housing association other than a co-operative housing association, and

(b) an unregistered housing association which is a co-operative housing association.

(3) If a co-operative housing association ceases to be registered, it shall, within the period of 21 days beginning with the date on which it ceases to be registered, notify each of its tenants who thereby becomes a secure tenant, in writing, that he has become a secure tenant.

[(4) This section applies to a housing co-operative within the meaning of section 27B (agreements under certain superseded provisions) where the dwelling-house is comprised in a housing co-operative agreement within the meaning of that section.]   **[1124]**

NOTES

Sub-s (1): words in square brackets inserted by the Housing Act 1988, s 83(2); words in italics repealed with savings by the Housing Act 1988, s 140, Sch 18.

Sub-s (2): repealed with savings by the Housing Act 1988, s 140, Sch 18.

Sub-s (4): substituted by the Housing and Planning Act 1986, s 24(2), Sch 5, Part II, para 26.

81. The tenant condition

The tenant condition is that the tenant is an individual and occupies the dwelling-house as his only or principal home; or, where the tenancy is a joint tenancy, that each of the joint tenants is an individual and at least one of them occupies the dwelling-house as his only or principal home.   **[1125]**

Succession on death of tenant

89. Succession to periodic tenancy

. . .

(3) Where there is no person qualified to succeed the tenant and the tenancy is vested or otherwise disposed of in the course of the administration of the tenant's estate, the tenancy ceases to be a secure tenancy unless the vesting or other disposal is in pursuance of an order made under section 24 of the Matrimonial Causes Act 1973 (property adjustment orders in connection with matrimonial proceedings).

(4) A tenancy which ceases to be a secure tenancy by virtue of this section cannot subsequently become a secure tenancy.   **[1126]**

90. Devolution of term certain

. . .

(3) The tenancy ceases to be a secure tenancy on being vested or otherwise disposed of in the course of administration of the tenant's estate, unless—

(a) the vesting or other disposal is in pursuance of an order made under section 24 of the Matrimonial Causes Act 1973 (property adjustment orders in connection with matrimonial proceedings), or

(b) the vesting or other disposal is to a person qualified to succeed the tenant.

. . .   **[1127]**

Assignment, lodgers and subletting

91. Assignment in general prohibited

(1) A secure tenancy which is—

    (*a*) a periodic tenancy, or
    (*b*) a tenancy for a term certain granted on or after 5th November 1982,

is not capable of being assigned except in the cases mentioned in subsection (3).

(2) If a secure tenancy for a term certain granted before 5th November 1982 is assigned, then, except in the cases mentioned in subsection (3), it ceases to be a secure tenancy and cannot subsequently become a secure tenancy.

(3) The exceptions are—

    (*a*) an assignment in accordance with section 92 (assignment by way of exchange);
    (*b*) an assignment in pursuance of an order made under section 24 of the Matrimonial Causes Act 1973 (property adjustment orders in connection with matrimonial proceedings);
    (*c*) an assignment to a person who would be qualified to succeed the tenant if the tenant died immediately before the assignment. **[1128]**

92. Assignments by way of exchange

(1) It is a term of every secure tenancy that the tenant may, with the written consent of the landlord, assign the tenancy to another secure tenant who satisfies the condition in subsection (2) [or an assured tenant who satisfies the conditions in subsection (2A)].

(2) The condition is that the other secure tenant has the written consent of his landlord to an assignment of his tenancy either to the first-mentioned tenant or to another secure tenant who satisfies the condition in this subsection.

[(2A) The conditions to be satisfied with respect to an assured tenant are—

    (*a*) that the landlord under his assured tenancy is either the Housing Corporation, Housing for Wales, a registered housing association or a housing trust which is a charity; and
    (*b*) that he intends to assign his assured tenancy to the secure tenant referred to in subsection (1) or to another secure tenant who satisfies the condition in subsection (2).]

(3) The consent required by virtue of this section shall not be withheld except on one or more of the grounds set out in Schedule 3, and if withheld otherwise than on one of those grounds shall be treated as given.

(4) The landlord may not rely on any of the grounds set out in Schedule 3 unless he has, within 42 days of the tenant's application for the consent, served on the tenant a notice specifying the ground and giving particulars of it.

(5) Where rent lawfully due from the tenant has not been paid or an obligation of the tenancy has been broken or not performed, the consent required by virtue of this section may be given subject to a condition requiring the tenant to pay the outstanding rent, remedy the breach or perform the obligation.

(6) Except as provided by subsection (5), a consent required by virtue of this section cannot be given subject to a condition, and a condition imposed otherwise than as so provided shall be disregarded.   **[1129]**

NOTES
   Commencement: 16 November 1989 (sub-s (2A)); 1 April 1986 (remainder).
   Sub-s (1): words in square brackets added by the Local Government and Housing Act 1989, s 163(2).
   Sub-s (2A): inserted by the Local Government and Housing Act 1989, s 163(3).

93. Lodgers and subletting

(1) It is a term of every secure tenancy that the tenant—
   (a) may allow any persons to reside as lodgers in the dwelling-house, but
   (b) will not, without the written consent of the landlord, sublet or part with possession of part of the dwelling-house.

(2) If the tenant under a secure tenancy parts with the possession of the dwelling-house or sublets the whole of it (or sublets first part of it and then the remainder), the tenancy ceases to be a secure tenancy and cannot subsequently become a secure tenancy.   **[1130]**

94. Consent to subletting

(1) This section applies to the consent required by virtue of section 93(1)(b) (landlord's consent to subletting of part of dwelling-house).

(2) Consent shall not be unreasonably withheld (and if unreasonably withheld shall be treated as given), and if a question arises whether the withholding of consent was unreasonable it is for the landlord to show that it was not.

(3) In determining that question the following matters, if shown by the landlord, are among those to be taken into account—
   (a) that the consent would lead to overcrowding of the dwelling-house within the meaning of Part X (over-crowding);
   (b) that the landlord proposes to carry out works on the dwelling-house, or on the building of which it forms part, and that the proposed works will affect the accommodation likely to be used by the sub-tenant who would reside in the dwelling-house as a result of the consent.

(4) Consent may be validly given notwithstanding that it follows, instead of preceding, the action requiring it.

(5) Consent cannot be given subject to a condition (and if purporting to be given subject to a condition shall be treated as given unconditionally).

(6) Where the tenant has applied in writing for consent, then—
   (a) if the landlord refuses to give consent, it shall give the tenant a written statement of the reasons why consent was refused, and
   (b) if the landlord neither gives nor refuses to give consent within a reasonable time, consent shall be taken to have been withheld. **[1131]**

95. Assignment or subletting where tenant condition not satisfied

(1) This section applies to a tenancy which is not a secure tenancy but would be if the tenant condition referred to in section 81 (occupation by the tenant) were satisfied.

(2) Sections 91 and 93(2) (restrictions on assignment or subletting of whole dwelling-house) apply to such a tenancy as they apply to a secure tenancy, except that—

    (*a*) section 91(3)(*b*) and (*c*) (assignments excepted from restrictions) do not apply to such a tenancy for a term certain granted before 5th November 1982, and

    (*b*) references to the tenancy ceasing to be secure shall be disregarded, without prejudice to the application of the remainder of the provisions in which those references occur. **[1132]**

PART V

THE RIGHT TO BUY

The right to buy

118. The right to buy

(1) A secure tenant has the right to buy, that is to say, the right, in the circumstances and subject to the conditions and exceptions stated in the following provisions of this Part—

    (*a*) if the dwelling-house is a house and the landlord owns the freehold, to acquire the freehold of the dwelling-house;

    (*b*) if the landlord does not own the freehold or if the dwelling-house is a flat (whether or not the landlord owns the freehold), to be granted a lease of the dwelling-house.

(2) Where a secure tenancy is a joint tenancy then, whether or not each of the joint tenants occupies the dwelling-house as his only or principal home, the right to buy belongs jointly to all of them or to such one or more of them as may be agreed between them; but such an agreement is not valid unless the person or at least one of the persons to whom the right to buy is to belong occupies the dwelling-house as his only or principal home. **[1133]**

NOTES

Modifications: see the Housing (Extension of Right to Buy) Order 1993, SI 1993 No 2240, art 3, Schedule, para 1, the Housing (Preservation of Right to Buy) Regulations 1993, SI 1993 No 2241, reg 2(1), Sch 1, paras 1–3 and the Local Government Reorganisation (Preservation of Right to Buy) Order 1986, SI 1986 No 2092, art 6, Sch 1, paras 1, 2.

See further: the Housing (Consequential Provisions) Act 1985, s 5(1), Sch 3, para 2.

Purchase price

126. Purchase price

(1) The price payable for a dwelling-house on a conveyance or grant in pursuance of this Part is—

    (*a*) the amount which under section 127 is to be taken as its value at the relevant time, less

    (*b*) the discount to which the purchaser is entitled under this Part.

(2) References in this Part to the purchase price include references to the consideration for the grant of a lease. **[1134]**

NOTES

Modifications: see the Housing (Extension of Right to Buy) Order 1993, SI 1993 No 2240, art 3, Schedule, para 13, the Housing (Preservation of Right to Buy) Regulations 1993, SI 1993 No 2241, reg 2(1), Sch 1, para 2.

See further: the Housing (Consequential Provisions) Act 1985, s 5(1), Sch 3, para 2.

127. Value of dwelling-house

(1) The value of a dwelling-house at the relevant time shall be taken to be the price which at that time it would realise if sold on the open market by a willing vendor—

    (*a*) on the assumptions stated for a conveyance in subsection (2) and for a grant in subsection (3), . . .

    (*b*) disregarding any improvements made by any of the persons specified in subsection (4) and any failure by any of those persons to keep the dwelling-house in good internal repair [, and

    (*c*) on the assumption that any service charges or improvement contributions payable will not be less than the amounts to be expected in accordance with the estimates contained in the landlord's notice under section 125].

(2) For a conveyance the assumptions are—

    (*a*) that the vendor was selling for an estate in fee simple with vacant possession,

    (*b*) that neither the tenant nor a member of his family residing with him wanted to buy, and

    (*c*) that the dwelling-house was to be conveyed with the same rights and subject to the same burdens as it would be in pursuance of this Part.

(3) For the grant of a lease the assumptions are—

    (*a*) that the vendor was granting a lease with vacant possession for the appropriate term defined in paragraph 12 of Schedule 6 (but subject to sub-paragraph (3) of that paragraph),

    (*b*) that neither the tenant nor a member of his family residing with him wanted to take the lease,

    (*c*) that the ground rent would not exceed £10 per annum, and

    (*d*) that the grant was to be made with the same rights and subject to the same burdens as it would be in pursuance of this Part.

(4) The persons referred to in subsection (1)(*b*) are—

    (*a*) the secure tenant,

    (*b*) any person who under the same tenancy was a secure tenant before him, and

    (*c*) any member of his family who, immediately before the secure tenancy was granted, was a secure tenant of the same dwelling-house under another tenancy,

but do not include, in a case where the secure tenant's tenancy has at any time been assigned by virtue of section 92 (assignments by way of exchange), a person who under that tenancy was a secure tenant before the assignment.

[1135]

NOTES

    Modifications: see the Housing (Extension of Right to Buy) Order 1993, SI 1993 No 2240, art 3, Schedule, para 14, the Housing (Preservation of Right to Buy) Regulations 1993, SI 1993 No 2241, reg 2(1), Sch 1, paras 1, 2, 10 and the Local Government Reorganisation (Preservation of Right to Buy) Order 1986, SI 1986 No 2092, art 6, Sch 1, paras 1, 7.

    See further: the Housing (Consequential Provisions) Act 1985, s 5(1), Sch 3, para 2.

129. Discount

    [(1) Subject to the following provisions of this Part, a person exercising the right to buy is entitled to a discount of a percentage calculated by reference to the period which is to be taken into account in accordance with Schedule 4 (qualifying period for right to buy and discount).

(2) The discount is, subject to any order under subsection (2A)—

(*a*) in the case of a house, 32 per cent. plus one per cent. for each complete year by which the qualifying period exceeds two years, up to a maximum of 60 per cent.;

(*b*) in the case of a flat, 44 per cent. plus two per cent. for each complete year by which the qualifying period exceeds two years, up to a maximum of 70 per cent.

(2A) The Secretary of State may by order made with the consent of the Treasury provide that, in such cases as may be specified in the order—

(*a*) the minimum percentage discount,

(*b*) the percentage increase for each complete year of the qualifying period after the first two, or

(*c*) the maximum percentage discount,

shall be such percentage, higher than that specified in subsection (2), as may be specified in the order.

(2B) An order—

(*a*) may make different provision with respect to different cases or descriptions of case,

(*b*) may contain such incidental, supplementary or transitional provisions as appear to the Secretary of State to be necessary or expedient, and

(*c*) shall be made by statutory instrument and shall not be made unless a draft of it has been laid before and approved by resolution of each House of Parliament.]

(3) Where joint tenants exercise the right to buy, Schedule 4 shall be construed as if for the secure tenant there were substituted that one of the joint tenants whose substitution will produce the largest discount. **[1136]**

NOTES
   Sub-s (1)–(2B): substituted for sub-ss (1), (2) as originally enacted by the Housing and Planning Act 1986, s 2(1), (2).
   Modifications: see the Housing (Extension of Right to Buy) Order 1993, SI 1993 No 2240, art 3, Schedule, para 16, the Housing (Preservation of Right to Buy) Regulations 1993, SI 1993 No 2241, reg 2(1), Sch 1, para 1 and the Local Government Reorganisation (Preservation of Right to Buy) Order 1986, SI 1986 No 2092, art 6, Sch 1, para 1.
   See further: the Housing (Consequential Provisions) Act 1985, s 5(1), Sch 3, para 2.

The right to a mortgage

132. The right to a mortgage

(1) A secure tenant who has the right to buy has the right, subject to the following provisions of this Part—

(a) to leave the whole or part of the aggregate amount mentioned in section 133(1) outstanding on the security of a first mortgage of the dwelling-house, or

(b) if the landlord is a housing association, to have the whole or part of that amount advanced to him on that security by the [Corporation];

and in this Act that right is referred to as "the right to a mortgage".

(2) Where the right to buy belongs jointly to two or more persons, the right to a mortgage also belongs to them jointly.   **[1137]**

NOTES

Repealed with savings by the Leasehold Reform, Housing and Urban Development Act 1993, s 187(2), Sch 22 and the Leasehold Reform, Housing and Urban Development Act 1993 (Commencement and Transitional Provisions No 1) Order 1993, SI 1993 No 2134, art 4, Sch 1, para 4.

Sub-s (1): word in square brackets substituted by the Housing Act 1988, s 140, Sch 17, Part II.

Modifications: see the Housing (Preservation of Right to Buy) Regulations 1993, SI 1993 No 2241, reg 2(1), Sch 1, paras 1, 2 and the Local Government Reorganisation (Preservation of Right to Buy) Order 1986, SI 1986 No 2092, art 6, Sch 1, paras 1, 10.

See further: the Housing (Consequential Provisions) Act 1985, s 5(1), Sch 3, para 2.

133. The amount to be secured

(1) The amount which a secure tenant exercising the right to a mortgage is entitled to leave outstanding, or have advanced to him, on the security of the dwelling-house is, subject to the limit imposed by this section, the aggregate of—

(a) *the purchase price,*
(b) *so much of the costs incurred by the landlord or the [Corporation] as is chargeable to the tenant under section 178(2) (costs), and*
(c) *any costs incurred by the tenant and defrayed on his behalf by the landlord or the [Corporation].*

(2) The limit is that the amount which the tenant is entitled to leave outstanding or have advanced to him on the security of the dwelling-house may not exceed—

(a) *where the right to a mortgage belongs to one person, the amount to be taken into account, in accordance with regulations under this section, as his available annual income multiplied by such factor as, under the regulations, is appropriate to it;*
(b) *where the right to a mortgage belongs to more than one person, the aggregate of the amounts to be taken into account in accordance with the regulations as the available annual income of each of them, after multiplying each of those amounts by the factor appropriate to it under the regulations.*

(3) The Secretary of State may by regulations make provision for calculating the amount which is to be taken into account under this section as a person's available annual income and for specifying a factor appropriate to it; and the regulations—

(a) *may provide for arriving at a person's available annual income by deducting from the sums taken into account as his annual income sums related to his needs and commitments, and may exclude sums from those to be taken into account as a person's annual income, and*
(b) *may specify different amounts and different factors for different circumstances.*

(4) Where the amount which a secure tenant is entitled to leave outstanding on the security of the dwelling-house is reduced by the limit imposed by this section, the landlord may, if it thinks fit and the tenant agrees, treat him as entitled to leave outstanding on that security such amount exceeding the limit, but not exceeding the aggregate mentioned in subsection (1), as the landlord may determine.

(5) References in this Part to a secure tenant being entitled, or treated as entitled, to a "full mortgage" are to his being entitled, or treated as entitled, to leave

*outstanding or have advanced to him on the security of the dwelling-house an amount
equal to the aggregate mentioned in subsection (1).*

(6) *Regulations under this section—*

(a) *may make different provision with respect to different cases or descriptions
of case, including different provision for different areas, and*

(b) *shall be made by statutory instrument which shall be subject to annulment
in pursuance of a resolution of either House of Parliament.* **[1138]**

NOTES

Repealed with savings by the Leasehold Reform, Housing and Urban Development Act 1993,
s 187(2), Sch 22 and the Leasehold Reform, Housing and Urban Development Act 1993
(Commencement and Transitional Provisions No 1) Order 1993, SI 1993 No 2134, art 4, Sch 1, para
4.

Sub-s (1): words in square brackets substituted by the Housing Act 1988, s 140, Sch 17, Part II.

Modifications: see the Housing (Preservation of Right to Buy) Regulations 1993, SI 1993
No 2241, reg 2(1), Sch 1, paras 1, 2 and the Local Government Reorganisation (Preservation of
Right to Buy) Order 1986, SI 1986 No 2092, art 6, Sch 1, paras 1, 11.

See further: the Housing (Consequential Provisions) Act 1985, s 5(1), Sch 3, para 2.

Completion of purchase in pursuance of right to buy

138. Duty of landlord to convey freehold or grant lease

(1) Where a secure tenant has claimed to exercise the right to buy and that right
has been established, then, as soon as all matters relating to the grant *and to the
amount to be left outstanding or advanced on the security of the dwelling-house* have
been agreed or determined, the landlord shall make to the tenant—

(a) if the dwelling-house is a house and the landlord owns the freehold, a
grant of the dwelling-house for an estate in fee simple absolute, or

(b) if the landlord does not own the freehold or if the dwelling-house is a
flat (whether or not the landlord owns the freehold), a grant of a lease
of the dwelling-house,

in accordance with the following provisions of this Part.

(2) If the tenant has failed to pay the rent or any other payment due from
him as a tenant for a period of four weeks after it had been lawfully demanded
from him, the landlord is not bound to comply with subsection (1) while the
whole or part of that payment remains outstanding.

(3) The duty imposed on the landlord by subsection (1) is enforceable by
injunction. **[1138A]**

NOTES

Sub-s (1): words in italics repealed with savings by the Leasehold Reform, Housing and Urban
Development Act 1993, s 187(2), Sch 2 and the Leasehold Reform, Housing and Urban Development
Act 1993 (Commencement and Transitional Provisions No 1) Order 1993, SI 1993 No 2134, art 4,
Sch 1, para 4.

Modifications: see the Housing (Extension of Right to Buy) Order 1993, SI 1993 No 2240, art 3,
Schedule, para 20, the Housing (Preservation of Right to Buy) Regulations 1993, SI 1993 No 2241,
reg 2(1), Sch 1, paras 1, 2 and the Local Government Reorganisation (Preservation of Right to Buy)
Order 1986, SI 1986 No 2092, art 6, Sch 1, paras 1, 16.

See further: the Housing (Consequential Provisions) Act 1985, s 5(1), Sch 3, para 2.

Provisions affecting future disposals

155. Repayment of discount on early disposal

(1) A conveyance of the freehold or grant of a lease in pursuance of this Part
shall contain (unless, in the case of a conveyance or grant in pursuance of the

right to buy, there is no discount) a covenant binding on the secure tenant and his successors in title to the following effect.

(2) In the case of a conveyance or grant in pursuance of the right to buy, the covenant shall be to pay to the landlord on demand, if within a period of [three years] there is a relevant disposal which is not an exempted disposal (but if there is more than one such disposal, then only on the first of them), the discount to which the secure tenant was entitled, reduced by [one third] for each complete year which has elapsed after the conveyance or grant and before the disposal.

(3) In the case of a grant in pursuance of the right to be granted a shared ownership lease, the covenant shall be to pay to the landlord on demand, if within a period of [three years] commencing with the acquisition by the tenant of his initial share or the acquisition by him of an additional share there is a relevant disposal which is not an exempted disposal (but if there is more than one such disposal, then only on the first of them), the aggregate of—

(a) the effective discount (if any) to which the tenant was entitled on the acquisition of his initial share, and

(b) for each additional share, the effective discount (if any) to which the tenant was entitled on the acquisition of that share,

reduced, in each case, by [one third] for each complete year which has elapsed after the acquisition and before the disposal.

[(3) In the case of a conveyance or grant in pursuance of the right to acquire on rent to mortgage terms, the covenant shall be to pay to the landlord on demand, if within the period of three years commencing with the making of the initial payment there is a relevant disposal which is not an exempted disposal (but if there is more than one such disposal, then only on the first of them), the discount (if any) to which the tenant was entitled on the making of—

(*a*) the initial payment,

(*b*) any interim payment made before the disposal, or

(*c*) the final payment if so made,

reduced, in each case, by one-third for each complete year which has elapsed after the making of the initial payment and before the disposal.]

[(3A) Where a secure tenant has served on his landlord an operative notice of delay, as defined in section 153A,—

(*a*) the three years referred to in subsection (2) shall begin from a date which precedes the date of the conveyance of the freehold or grant of the lease by a period equal to the time (or, if there is more than one such notice, the aggregate of the times) during which, by virtue of section 153B, any payment of rent falls to be taken into account in accordance with subsection (3) of that section; and

(b) any reference in subsection (3) (other than paragraph (a) thereof) to the acquisition of the tenant's initial share shall be construed as a reference to a date which precedes that acquisition by the period referred to in paragraph (a) of this subsection.

[(*b*) any reference in subsection (3) (other than paragraph (*a*) thereof) to the making of the initial payment shall be construed as a reference to the date which precedes that payment by the period referred to in paragraph (*a*) of this subsection.]] **[1139]**

NOTES

Commencement: 11 October 1993 (sub-s (3)); 10 March 1989 (sub-s (3A)); 1 April 1986 (remainder).

Sub-s (2): words in square brackets substituted by the Housing and Planning Act 1986, s 2(3).

Sub-s (3): substituted with savings by the Leasehold Reform, Housing and Urban Development Act 1993, s 120(1) and the Leasehold Reform, Housing and Urban Development Act 1993 (Commencement and Transitional Provisions No 1) Order 1993, SI 1993 No 2134, art 4, Sch 1, para 4; in original sub-s (3) words in square brackets substituted by the Housing and Planning Act 1986, s 2(3).

Sub-s (3A): inserted by the Housing Act 1988, s 140, Sch 17, Part I; para (*b*) substituted with savings by the Leasehold Reform, Housing and Urban Development Act 1993, s 120(2) and the Leasehold Reform, Housing and Urban Development Act 1993 (Commencement and Transitional Provisions No 1) Order 1993, SI 1993 No 2134, art 4, Sch 1, para 4.

Modifications: see the Housing (Extension of Right to Buy) Order 1993, SI 1993 No 2240, art 3, Schedule, para 41, the Housing (Preservation of Right to Buy) Regulations 1993, SI 1993 No 2241, reg 2(1), Sch 1, paras 1, 20 and the Local Government Reorganisation (Preservation of Right to Buy) Order 1986, SI 1986 No 2092, art 6, Sch 1, paras 1, 21.

See further: the Housing (Consequential Provisions) Act 1985, s 5(1), Sch 3, para 2.

156. Liability to repay is a charge on the premises

(1) The liability that may arise under the covenant required by section 155 is a charge on the dwelling-house, taking effect as if it had been created by deed expressed to be by way of legal mortgage.

(2) The charge has priority immediately after any legal charge securing an amount—

(a) left outstanding by the tenant in exercising the right to buy or the right to be granted a shared ownership lease, or

(b) advanced to him by an approved lending institution for the purpose of enabling him to exercise that right, or

(c) further advanced to him by that institution;

but the landlord may at any time by written notice served on an approved lending institution postpone the charge taking effect by virtue of this section to a legal charge securing an amount advanced or further advanced to the tenant by that institution.

[(2) Subject to subsections (2A) and (2B), the charge has priority as follows—

(*a*) if it secures the liability that may arise under the covenant required by section 155(2), immediately after any legal charge securing an amount advanced to the secure tenant by an approved lending institution for the purpose of enabling him to exercise the right to buy;

(*b*) if it secures the liability that may arise under the covenant required by section 155(3), immediately after the mortgage—

(i) which is required by section 151B (mortgage for securing redemption of landlord's share), and

(ii) which, by virtue of subsection (2) of that section, has priority immediately after any legal charge securing an amount advanced to the secure tenant by an approved lending institution for the purpose of enabling him to exercise the right to acquire on rent to mortgage terms.

(2A) The following, namely—

(*a*) any advance which is made otherwise than for the purpose mentioned in paragraph (*a*) or (*b*) of subsection (2) and is secured by a legal charge having priority to the charge taking effect by virtue of this section, and

(*b*) any further advance which is so secured,

shall rank in priority to that charge if, and only if, the landlord by written notice served on the institution concerned gives its consent; and the landlord shall so give its consent if the purpose of the advance or further advance is an approved purpose.

(2B) The landlord may at any time by written notice served on an approved lending institution postpone the charge taking effect by virtue of this section to any advance or further advance which—

    (*a*) is made to the tenant by that institution, and

    (*b*) is secured by a legal charge not having priority to that charge;

and the landlord shall serve such a notice if the purpose of the advance or further advance is an approved purpose.]

(3) A charge taking effect by virtue of this section is a land charge for the purposes of section 59 of the Land Registration Act 1925 notwithstanding subsection (5) of that section (exclusion of mortgages), and subsection (2) of that section applies accordingly with respect to its protection and realisation.

[(3A) The covenant required by section 155 (covenant for repayment of discount) does not, by virtue of its binding successors in title of the tenant, bind a person exercising rights under a charge having priority over the charge taking effect by virtue of this section, or a person deriving title under him; and a provision of the conveyance or grant, or of a collateral agreement, is void in so far as it purports to authorise a forfeiture, or to impose a penalty or disability, in the event of any such person failing to comply with that covenant.]

(4) The approved lending institutions for the purposes of this section are—

    the [Corporation],

    a building society,

    a bank,

    a trustee savings bank,

    an insurance company,

    a friendly society,

and any body specified, or of a class or description specified, in an order made by the Secretary of State with the consent of the Treasury.

[(4A) The approved purposes for the purposes of this section are—

    (*a*) to enable the tenant to make an interim or final payment,

    (*b*) to enable the tenant to defray, or to defray on his behalf, any of the following—

        (i) the cost of any works to the dwelling-house,

        (ii) any service charge payable in respect of the dwelling-house for works, whether or not to the dwelling-house, and

        (iii) any service charge or other amount payable in respect of the dwelling-house for insurance, whether or not of the dwelling-house, and

    (*c*) to enable the tenant to discharge, or to discharge on his behalf, any of the following—

        (i) so much as is still outstanding of any advance or further advance which ranks in priority to the charge taking effect by virtue of this section,

        (ii) any arrears of interest on such an advance or further advance, and

        (iii) any costs and expenses incurred in enforcing payment of any such interest, or repayment (in whole or in part) of any such advance or further advance.

(4B) Where different parts of an advance or further advance are made for different purposes, each of those parts shall be regarded as a separate advance or further advance for the purposes of this section.]

(5) An order under subsection (4)—

    (*a*) shall be made by statutory instrument, and

    (*b*) may make different provision with respect to different cases or descriptions of case, including different provision for different areas.

(6) Before making an order varying or revoking a previous order, the Secretary of State shall give an opportunity for representations to be made on behalf of any body which, if the order were made, would cease to be an approved lending institution for the purposes of this section.   **[1140]**

NOTES

    Commencement: 11 October 1993 (sub-ss (2)–(2B), (4A), (4B)); 7 January 1987 (sub-s (3A)); 1 April 1986 (remainder).

    Sub-ss (2)–(2B): substituted with savings for sub-s (2), as originally enacted, by the Leasehold Reform, Housing and Urban Development Act 1993, s 120(3) and the Leasehold Reform, Housing and Urban Development Act 1993 (Commencement and Transitional Provisions No 1) Order 1993, SI 1993 No 2134, art 4, Sch 1, para 4.

    Sub-s (3A): inserted by the Housing and Planning Act 1987, s 24(1), Sch 5, para 1.

    Sub-s (4): word in square brackets substituted by the Housing Act 1988, s 140, Sch 17, Part II.

    Sub-ss (4A), (4B): inserted with savings by the Leasehold Reform, Housing and Urban Development Act 1993, s 120(4) and the Leasehold Reform, Housing and Urban Development Act 1993 (Commencement and Transitional Provisions No 1) Order 1993, SI 1993 No 2134, art 4, Sch 1, para 4.

    Modifications: see the Housing (Extension of Right to Buy) Order 1993, SI 1993 No 2240, art 3, Schedule, para 42, the Housing (Preservation of Right to Buy) Regulations 1993, SI 1993 No 2241, reg 2(1), Sch 1, paras 1, 2, 21 and the Local Government Reorganisation (Preservation of Right to Buy) Order 1986, SI 1986 No 2092, art 6, Sch 1, paras 1, 22.

    See further: the Housing (Consequential Provisions) Act 1985, s 5(1), Sch 3, para 2.

157. Restriction on disposal of dwelling-houses in National Parks, etc

(1) Where in pursuance of this Part a conveyance or grant is executed by a local authority, the Development Board for Rural Wales or a housing association ("the landlord") of a dwelling-house situated in—

    (*a*) a National Park,

    (*b*) an area designated under section 87 of the National Parks and Access to the Countryside Act 1949 as an area of outstanding natural beauty, or

    (*c*) an area designated by order of the Secretary of State as a rural area,

the conveyance or grant may contain a covenant limiting the freedom of the tenant (including any successor in title of his and any person deriving title under him or such a successor) to dispose of the dwelling-house in the manner specified below.

(2) The limitation is, subject to subsection (4), that until such time (if any) as may be notified in writing by the landlord to the tenant or a successor in title of his

    [(*a*)] there will be no relevant disposal which is not an exempted disposal without the written consent of the landlord; but that consent shall not be withheld if the disposal is to a person satisfying the condition stated in subsection (3) [and—

    (*b*) there will be no disposal by way of tenancy or licence without the written consent of the landlord unless the disposal is to a person satisfying that condition or by a person whose only or principal home is and, throughout the duration of the tenancy or licence, remains the dwelling-house].

(3) The condition is that the person to whom the disposal is made (or, if it is made to more than one person, at least one of them) has, throughout the period of three years immediately preceding the application for consent [or, in the case of a disposal by way of tenancy or licence, preceding the disposal]—

    (*a*) had his place of work in a region designated by order of the Secretary of State which, or part of which, is comprised in the National Park or area, or

    (*b*) had his only or principal home in such a region;

or has had the one in part or parts of that period and the other in the remainder; but the region need not have been the same throughout the period.

(4) If the Secretary of State or, where the landlord is a housing association, the [Corporation], consents, the limitation specified in subsection (2) may be replaced by the following limitation, that is to say, that until the end of the period of ten years beginning with the conveyance or grant there will be no relevant disposal which is not an exempted disposal, unless in relation to that or a previous such disposal—

    (*a*) the tenant (or his successor in title or the person deriving title under him or his successor) has offered to reconvey the dwelling-house, or as the case may be surrender the lease, to the landlord for such consideration as is mentioned in section 158, and

    (*b*) the landlord has refused the offer or has failed to accept it within one month after it was made.

(5) The consent of the Secretary of State or the [Corporation] under subsection (4) may be given subject to such conditions as he or, as the case may be, the Corporation, thinks fit.

(6) A disposal in breach of such a covenant as is mentioned in subsection (1) is void [and, so far as it relates to disposals by way of tenancy or licence, such a covenant may be enforced by the landlord as if—

    (*a*) the landlord were possessed of land adjacent to the house concerned; and

    (*b*) the covenant were expressed to be made for the benefit of such adjacent land].

[(6A) Any reference in the preceding provisions of this section to a disposal by way of tenancy or licence does not include a reference to a relevant disposal or an exempted disposal.]

(7) Where such a covenant imposes the limitation specified in subsection (2), the limitation is a local land charge and the Chief Land Registrar shall enter the appropriate restriction on the register of title as if application therefor had been made under section 58 of the Land Registration Act 1925.

(8) An order under this section—

    (*a*) may make different provision with respect to different cases or descriptions of case, including different provision for different areas, and

    (*b*) shall be made by statutory instrument which shall be subject to annulment in pursuance of a resolution of either House of Parliament. **[1141]**

NOTES

    Sub-s (2): para (*a*) numbered as such and para (*b*) added by the Housing Act 1988, s 126.
    Sub-s (3): words in square brackets inserted by the Housing Act 1988, s 126.
    Sub-s (4): word in square brackets substituted by the Housing Act 1988, s 140, Sch 17, Part II.

Sub-s (5): word in square brackets substituted by the Housing Act 1988, s 140, Sch 17, Part II.
Sub-s (6): words in square brackets added by the Housing Act 1988, s 126.
Sub-s (6A): inserted by the Housing Act 1988, s 126.
Modifications: see the Housing (Extension of Right to Buy) Order 1993, SI 1993 No 2240, art 3, Schedule, para 44, the Housing (Preservation of Right to Buy) Regulations 1993, SI 1993 No 2241, reg 2(1), Sch 1, paras 1, 2, 22 and the Local Government Reorganisation (Preservation of Right to Buy) Order 1986, SI 1986 No 2092, art 6, Sch 1, paras 1, 23.
See further: the Housing (Consequential Provisions) Act 1985, s 5(1), Sch 3, para 2.

159. Relevant disposals

(1) A disposal, whether of the whole or part of the dwelling-house, is a relevant disposal for the purposes of this Part if it is—

> (a) a further conveyance of the freehold or an assignment of the lease, or
>
> (b) the grant of a lease (other than a mortgage term) for a term of more than 21 years otherwise than at a rack rent

(2) For the purposes of subsection (1)(b) it shall be assumed—

> (a) that any option to renew or extend a lease or sub-lease, whether or not forming part of a series of options, is exercised, and
>
> (b) that any option to terminate a lease or sub-lease is not exercised.

[1142]

NOTES
Modifications: see the Housing (Extension of Right to Buy) Order 1993, SI 1993 No 2240, art 3, Schedule, para 46 and the Housing (Preservation of Right to Buy) Regulations 1993, SI 1993 No 2241, reg 2(1), Sch 1, para 2.
See further: the Housing (Consequential Provisions) Act 1985, s 5(1), Sch 3, para 2.

163. Treatment of options

(1) For the purposes of this Part the grant of an option enabling a person to call for a relevant disposal which is not an exempted disposal shall be treated as such a disposal made to him.

(2) For the purposes of section 157(2) (requirement of consent to disposal of dwelling-house in National Park, etc.) a consent to such a grant shall be treated as a consent to a disposal in pursuance of the option.   **[1143]**

NOTES
Modifications: see the Housing (Preservation of Right to Buy) Regulations 1993, SI 1993 No 2241, reg 2(1), Sch 1, para 2 and the Local Government Reorganisation (Preservation of Right to Buy) Order 1986, SI 1986, No 2092, art 6, Sch 1, para 25.
See further: the Housing (Consequential Provisions) Act 1985, s 5(1), Sch 3, para 2.

PART XVIII

MISCELLANEOUS AND GENERAL PROVISIONS

Enforceability of covenants, &c

609. Enforcement of covenants against owner for the time being

Where—

> (a) a local housing authority have disposed of land held by them for any of the purposes of this Act and the person to whom the disposal was made has entered into a covenant with the authority concerning the land, or

(b) an owner of any land has entered into a covenant with the local
housing authority concerning the land for the purposes of any of the
provisions of this Act,

the authority may enforce the covenant against the persons deriving title under
the covenantor, notwithstanding that the authority are not in possession of or
interested in any land for the benefit of which the covenant was entered into, in
like manner and to the like extent as if they had been possessed of or interested
in such land.   **[1143A]**

Final provisions

625. Short title, commencement and extent

. . .

(3) This Act extends to England and Wales only.   **[1143B]**

SCHEDULES
SCHEDULE 1
Section 79

TENANCIES WHICH ARE NOT SECURE TENANCIES

Long leases

1. A tenancy is not a secure tenancy if it is a long tenancy.

Premises occupied in connection with employment

2.—(1) A tenancy is not a secure tenancy if the tenant is an employee of the landlord
or of—

a local authority,
a new town corporation,
[a housing action trust],
an urban development corporation,
the Development Board for Rural Wales, or
the governors of an aided school,

and his contract of employment requires him to occupy the dwelling-house for the better
performance of his duties.

(2) A tenancy is not a secure tenancy if the tenant is a member of a police force and
the dwelling-house is provided for him free of rent and rates in pursuance of regulations
made under section 33 of the Police Act 1964 (general regulations as to government,
administration and conditions of service of police forces).

(3) A tenancy is not a secure tenancy if the tenant is an employee of a fire authority
(within the meaning of the Fire Services Acts 1947 to 1959) and—

(a) his contract of employment requires him to live in close proximity to a
particular fire station, and
(b) the dwelling-house was let to him by the authority in consequence of that
requirement.

(4) A tenancy is not a secure tenancy if—

(a) within the period of three years immediately preceding the grant the conditions
mentioned in sub-paragraph (1), (2) or (3) have been satisfied with respect to a
tenancy of the dwelling-house, and
(b) before the grant the landlord notified the tenant in writing of the circumstances
in which this exception applies and that in its opinion the proposed tenancy
would fall within this exception,

until the periods during which those conditions are not satisfied with respect to the
tenancy amount in aggregate to more than three years.

(5) In this paragraph "contract of employment" means a contract of service or apprenticeship, whether express or implied and (if express) whether oral or in writing.

Land acquired for development

3.—(1) A tenancy is not a secure tenancy if the dwelling-house is on land which has been acquired for development and the dwelling-house is used by the landlord, pending development of the land, as temporary housing accommodation.

(2) In this paragraph "development" has the meaning given by [section 55 of the Town and Country Planning Act 1990] (general definition of development for purposes of that Act).

Accommodation for homeless persons

4.—(1) A tenancy granted in pursuance of—

  (*a*) section 63 (duty to house pending inquiries in case of apparent priority need),
  (*b*) section 65(3) (duty to house temporarily person found to have priority need but to have become homeless intentionally), or
  (*c*) section 68(1) (duty to house pending determination whether conditions for referral of application are satisfied),

is not a secure tenancy before the expiry of the period of twelve months beginning with the date specified in sub-paragraph (2), unless before the expiry of that period the tenant is notified by the landlord that the tenancy is to be regarded as a secure tenancy.

(2) The date referred to in sub-paragraph (1) is the date on which the tenant received the notification required by section 64(1) (notification of decision on question of homelessness or threatened homelessness) or, if he received a notification under section 68(3) (notification of which authority has duty to house), the date on which he received that notification.

Temporary accommodation for persons taking up employment

5.—(1) A tenancy is not a secure tenancy before the expiry of one year from the grant if—

  (*a*) the person to whom the tenancy was granted was not, immediately before the grant, resident in the district in which the dwelling-house is situated,
  (*b*) before the grant of the tenancy, he obtained employment, or an offer of employment, in the district or its surrounding area,
  (*c*) the tenancy was granted to him for the purpose of meeting his need for temporary accommodation in the district or its surrounding area in order to work there, and of enabling him to find permanent accommodation there, and
  (*d*) the landlord notified him in writing of the circumstances in which this exception applies and that in its opinion the proposed tenancy would fall within this exception;

unless before the expiry of that year the tenant has been notified by the landlord that the tenancy is to be regarded as a secure tenancy.

(2) In this paragraph—

"district" means district of a local housing authority; and
"surrounding area", in relation to a district, means the area consisting of each district that adjoins it.

Short-term arrangements

6. A tenancy is not a secure tenancy if—

  (*a*) the dwelling-house has been leased to the landlord with vacant possession for use as temporary housing accommodation,
  (*b*) the terms on which it has been leased include provision for the lessor to obtain vacant possession from the landlord on the expiry of a specified period or when required by the lessor,
  (*c*) the lessor is not a body which is capable of granting secure tenancies, and

(*d*) the landlord has no interest in the dwelling-house other than under the lease in question or as a mortgagee.

Temporary accommodation during works

7. A tenancy is not a secure tenancy if—

(*a*) the dwelling-house has been made available for occupation by the tenant (or a predecessor in title of his) while works are carried out on the dwelling-house which he previously occupied as his home, and

(*b*) the tenant or predecessor was not a secure tenant of that other dwelling-house at the time when he ceased to occupy it as his home.

Agricultural holdings

8. A tenancy is not a secure tenancy if the dwelling-house is comprised in an agricultural holding (within the meaning of the [Agricultural Holdings Act 1986]) and is occupied by the person responsible for the control (whether as tenant or as servant or agent of the tenant) of the farming of the holding.

Licensed premises

9. A tenancy is not a secure tenancy if the dwelling-house consists of or includes premises licensed for the sale of intoxicating liquor for consumption on the premises.

Student lettings

10.—(1) A tenancy of a dwelling-house is not a secure tenancy before the expiry of the period specified in sub-paragraph (3) if—

(*a*) it is granted for the purpose of enabling the tenant to attend a designated course at an educational establishment, and

(*b*) before the grant of the tenancy the landlord notified him in writing of the circumstances in which this exception applies and that in its opinion the proposed tenancy would fall within this exception;

unless the tenant has before the expiry of that period been notified by the landlord that the tenancy is to be regarded as a secure tenancy.

(2) A landlord's notice under sub-paragraph (1)(*b*) shall specify the educational establishment which the person concerned proposes to attend.

(3) The period referred to in sub-paragraph (1) is—

(*a*) in a case where the tenant attends a designated course at the educational establishment specified in the landlord's notice, the period ending six months after the tenant ceases to attend that (or any other) designated course at that establishment;

(*b*) in any other case, the period ending six months after the grant of the tenancy.

(4) In this paragraph—

"designated course" means a course of any kind designated by regulations made by the Secretary of State for the purposes of this paragraph

"educational establishment" means a university or [institution which provides higher education or further education (or both); and for the purposes of this definition "higher education" and "further education" have the same meaning as in the Education Act 1944].

(5) Regulations under sub-paragraph (4) shall be made by statutory instrument and may make different provision with respect to different cases or descriptions of case, including different provision for different areas.

1954 Act tenancies

11. A tenancy is not a secure tenancy if it is one to which Part II of the Landlord and Tenant Act 1954 applies (tenancies of premises occupied for business purposes).

Almshouses

[12. A licence to occupy a dwelling-house is not a secure tenancy if—

(a) the dwelling-house is an almshouse, and
(b) the licence was granted by or on behalf of a charity which—

(i) is authorised under its trusts to maintain the dwelling-house as an almshouse, and
(ii) has no power under its trusts to grant a tenancy of the dwelling-house;

and in this paragraph "almshouse" means any premises maintained as an almshouse, whether they are called an almshouse or not; and "trusts", in relation to a charity, means the provisions establishing it as a charity and regulating its purposes and administration, whether those provisions take effect by way of trust or not.]   **[1144]**

NOTES

Commencement: 1 September 1992 (para 12); 1 April 1986 (remainder).
Para 2: words in square brackets inserted by the Housing Act 1988, s 83(1), (6).
Para 3: words in square brackets substituted by the Planning (Consequential Provisions) Act 1990, s 4, Sch 2, para 71(6).
Para (8): words in square brackets substituted by the Agricultural Holdings Act 1986, s 100, Sch 14, para 63.
Para 10: words in square brackets substituted by the Education Reform Act 1988, s 237(1), Sch 12, para 95.
Para 12: substituted by the Charities Act 1992, s 78(1), Sch 6, para 12.

SCHEDULE 3

Section 92
GROUNDS FOR WITHHOLDING CONSENT TO ASSIGNMENT BY WAY OF EXCHANGE

Ground 1

The tenant or the proposed assignee is obliged to give up possession of the dwelling-house of which he is the secure tenant in pursuance of an order of the court, or will be so obliged at a date specified in such an order.

Ground 2

Proceedings have been begun for possession of the dwelling-house of which the tenant or the proposed assignee is the secure tenant on one or more of grounds 1 to 6 in Part I of Schedule 2 (grounds on which possession may be ordered despite absence of suitable alternative accommodation), or there has been served on the tenant or the proposed assignee a notice under section 83 (notice of proceedings for possession) which specifies one or more of those grounds and is still in force.

Ground 3

The accommodation afforded by the dwelling-house is substantially more extensive than is reasonably required by the proposed assignee.

Ground 4

The extent of the accommodation afforded by the dwelling-house is not reasonably suitable to the needs of the proposed assignee and his family.

Ground 5

The dwelling-house—

(*a*) forms part of or is within the curtilage of a building which, or so much of it as is held by the landlord, is held mainly for purposes other than housing purposes and consists mainly of accommodation other than housing accommodation, or is situated in a cemetery, and

(*b*) was let to the tenant or a predecessor in title of his in consequence of the tenant or predecessor being in the employment of—

the landlord,
a local authority,
a new town corporation,
[a housing action trust]
the Development Board for Rural Wales,
an urban development corporation, or
the governors of an aided school.

Ground 6

The landlord is a charity and the proposed assignee's occupation of the dwelling-house would conflict with the objects of the charity.

Ground 7

The dwelling-house has features which are substantially different from those of ordinary dwelling-houses and which are designed to make it suitable for occupation by a physically disabled person who requires accommodation of the kind provided by the dwelling-house and if the assignment were made there would no longer be such a person residing in the dwelling-house.

Ground 8

The landlord is a housing association or housing trust which lets dwelling-houses only for occupation (alone or with others) by persons whose circumstances (other than merely financial circumstances) make it especially difficult for them to satisfy their need for housing and if the assignment were made there would no longer be such a person residing in the dwelling-house.

Ground 9

The dwelling-house is one of a group of dwelling-houses which it is the practice of the landlord to let for occupation by persons with special needs and a social service or special facility is provided in close proximity to the group of dwelling-houses in order to assist persons with those special needs and if the assignment were made there would no longer be a person with those special needs residing in the dwelling-house.

[*Ground 10*

The dwelling-house is the subject of a management agreement under which the manager is a housing association of which at least half the members are tenants of dwelling-houses subject to the agreement, at least half the tenants of the dwelling-houses are members of the association and the proposed assignee is not, and is not willing to become, a member of the association.]   **[1145]**

NOTES
    Ground 5: words in square brackets inserted by the Housing Act 1988, s 83(6).
    Ground 10: added by the Housing and Planning Act 1986, s 24(1), Sch 5, para 7.

LANDLORD AND TENANT ACT 1985
(c 70)

ARRANGEMENT OF SECTIONS

Implied terms as to fitness for human habitation

An Act to consolidate certain provisions of the law of landlord and tenant formerly found in the Housing Acts, together with the Landlord and Tenant Act 1962, with amendments to give effect to recommendations of the Law Commission

[30 October 1985]

Implied terms as to fitness for human habitation

8. Implied terms as to fitness for human habitation

(1) In a contract to which this section applies for the letting of a house for human habitation there is implied, notwithstanding any stipulation to the contrary—

    (*a*) a condition that the house is fit for human habitation at the commencement of the tenancy, and

    (*b*) an undertaking that the house will be kept by the landlord fit for human habitation during the tenancy.

(2) The landlord, or a person authorised by him in writing, may at reasonable times of the day, on giving 24 hours' notice in writing, to the tenant or occupier, enter premises to which this section applies for the purpose of viewing their state and condition.

(3) This section applies to a contract if—

    (*a*) the rent does not exceed the figure applicable in accordance with subsection (4), and

    (*b*) the letting is not on such terms as to the tenant's responsibility as are mentioned in subsection (5).

(4) The rent limit for the application of this section is shown by the following Table, by reference to the date of making of the contract and the situation of the premises;

TABLE

Date of making contract	Rent limit
Before 31st July 1923.	In London: £40.
	Elsewhere: £26 or £16 (see Note 1)
On or after 31st July 1923 and before 6th July 1957.	In London: £40.
	Elsewhere: £26.
On or after 6th July 1957.	In London: £80.
	Elsewhere: £52.

NOTES

1. The applicable figure for contracts made before 31st July 1923 is £26 in the case of premises situated in a borough or urban district which at the date of the contract had according to the last published census a population of 50,000 or more. In the case of a house situated elsewhere, the figure is £16.

2. The references to "London" are, in relation to contracts made before 1st April 1965, to the administrative county of London and, in relation to contracts made on or after that date, to Greater London exclusive of the outer London boroughs.

(5) This section does not apply where a house is let for a term of three years or more (the lease not being determinable at the option of either party before the expiration of three years) upon terms that the tenant puts the premises into a condition reasonably fit for human habitation.

(6) In this section "house" includes—

(a) a part of a house, and
(b) any yard, garden, outhouses and appurtenances belonging to the house or usually enjoyed with it.   **[1146]**

10. Fitness for human habitation

In determining for the purposes of this Act whether a house is unfit for human habitation, regard shall be had to its condition in respect of the following matters—

repair,
stability,
freedom from damp,
internal arrangement,
natural lighting,
ventilation,
water supply,
drainage and sanitary conveniences,
facilities for preparation and cooking of food and for the disposal of waste water;

and the house shall be regarded as unfit for human habitation if, and only if, it is so far defective in one or more of those matters that it is not reasonably suitable for occupation in that condition.   **[1147]**

Repairing obligations

11. Repairing obligations in short leases

(1) In a lease to which this section applies (as to which, see sections 13 and 14) there is implied a covenant by the lessor—

    (*a*) to keep in repair the structure and exterior of the dwelling-house (including drains, gutters and external pipes),

    (*b*) to keep in repair and proper working order the installations in the dwelling-house for the supply of water, gas and electricity and for sanitation (including basins, sinks, baths and sanitary conveniences, but not other fixtures, fittings and appliances for making use of the supply of water, gas or electricity), and

    (*c*) to keep in repair and proper working order the installations in the dwelling-house for space heating and heating water.

[(1A) If a lease to which this section applies is a lease of a dwelling-house which forms part only of a building, then, subject to subsection (1B), the covenant implied by subsection (1) shall have effect as if—

    (*a*) the reference in paragraph (*a*) of that subsection to the dwelling-house included a reference to any part of the building in which the lessor has an estate or interest; and

    (*b*) any reference in paragraphs (*b*) and (*c*) of that subsection to an installation in the dwelling-house included a reference to an installation which, directly or indirectly, serves the dwelling-house and which either—

        (i) forms part of any part of a building in which the lessor has an estate or interest; or

        (ii) is owned by the lessor or under his control.

(1B) Nothing in subsection (1A) shall be construed as requiring the lessor to carry out any works or repairs unless the disrepair (or failure to maintain in working order) is such as to affect the lessee's enjoyment of the dwelling-house or of any common parts, as defined in section 60(1) of the Landlord and Tenant Act 1987, which the lessee, as such, is entitled to use.]

(2) The covenant implied by subsection (1) ("the lessor's repairing covenant") shall not be construed as requiring the lessor—

    (*a*) to carry out works or repairs for which the lessee is liable by virtue of his duty to use the premises in a tenant-like manner, or would be so liable but for an express covenant on his part,

    (*b*) to rebuild or reinstate the premises in the case of destruction or damage by fire, or by tempest, flood or other inevitable accident, or

    (*c*) to keep in repair or maintain anything which the lessee is entitled to remove from the dwelling-house.

(3) In determining the standard of repair required by the lessor's repairing covenant, regard shall be had to the age, character and the dwelling-house and the locality in which it is situated.

[(3A) In any case where—

    (*a*) the lessor's repairing covenant has effect as mentioned in subsection (1A), and

    (*b*) in order to comply with the covenant the lessor needs to carry out works or repairs otherwise than in, or to an installation in, the dwelling-house, and

(c) the lessor does not have a sufficient right in the part of the building or the installation concerned to enable him to carry out the required works or repairs,

then, in any proceedings relating to a failure to comply with the lessor's repairing covenant, so far as it requires the lessor to carry out the works or repairs in question, it shall be a defence for the lessor to prove that he used all reasonable endeavours to obtain, but was unable to obtain, such rights as would be adequate to enable him to carry out the works or repairs.]

(4) A covenant by the lessee for the repair of the premises is of no effect so far as it relates to the matters mentioned in subsection (1)(a) to (c), except so far as it imposes on the lessee any of the requirements mentioned in subsection (2)(a) or (c).

(5) The reference in subsection (4) to a covenant by the lessee for the repair of the premises includes a covenant—

(a) to put in repair or deliver up in repair,
(b) to paint, point or render,
(c) to pay money in lieu of repairs by the lessee, or
(d) to pay money on account of repairs by the lessor.

(6) In a case in which the lessor's repairing covenant is implied there is also implied a covenant by the lessee that the lessor, or any person authorised by him in writing, may at reasonable times of the day and on giving 24 hours' notice in writing to the occupier, enter the premises comprised in the lease for the purpose of viewing their condition and state of repair.   **[1148]**

NOTES
Commencement: 15 January 1989 (sub-ss (1A), (1B), (3A)); 1 April 1986 (remainder).
Sub-s (1A): inserted with savings by the Housing Act 1988, s 116.
Sub-s (1B): inserted with savings by the Housing Act 1988, s 116.
Sub-s (3A): inserted with savings by the Housing Act 1988, s 116.

12. Restriction on contracting out of s 11

(1) A covenant or agreement, whether contained in a lease to which section 11 applies or in an agreement collateral to such a lease, is void in so far as it purports—

(a) to exclude or limit the obligations of the lessor or the immunities of the lessee under that section, or
(b) to authorise any forfeiture or impose on the lessee any penalty, disability or obligation in the event of his enforcing or relying upon those obligations or immunities,

unless the inclusion of the provision was authorised by the county court.

(2) The county court may, by order made with the consent of the parties, authorise the inclusion in a lease, or in an agreement collateral to a lease, of provisions excluding or modifying in relation to the lease, the provisions of section 11 with respect to the repairing obligations of the parties if it appears to the court that it is reasonable to do so, having regard to all the circumstances of the case, including the other terms and conditions of the lease.   **[1149]**

13. Leases to which s 11 applies: general rule

(1) Section 11 (repairing obligations) applies to a lease of a dwelling-house granted on or after 24th October 1961 for a term of less than seven years.

(2) In determining whether a lease is one to which section 11 applies—

    (*a*) any part of the term which falls before the grant shall be left out of account and the lease shall be treated as a lease for a term commencing with the grant,

    (*b*) a lease which is determinable at the option of the lessor before the expiration of seven years from the commencement of the term shall be treated as a lease for a term of less than seven years, and

    (*c*) a lease (other than a lease to which paragraph (*b*) applies) shall not be treated as a lease for a term of less than seven years if it confers on the lessee an option for renewal for a term which, together with the original term, amounts to seven years or more.

(3) This section has effect subject to—

section 14 (leases to which section 11 applies: exceptions), and

section 32(2) (provisions not applying to tenancies within Part II of the Landlord and Tenant Act 1954).   **[1150]**

14. Leases to which s 11 applies: exceptions

(1) Section 11 (repairing obligations) does not apply to a new lease granted to an existing tenant, or to a former tenant still in possession, if the previous lease was not a lease to which section 11 applied (and, in the case of a lease granted before 24th October 1961, would not have been if it had been granted on or after that date).

(2) In subsection (1)—

"existing tenant" means a person who is when, or immediately before, the new lease is granted, the lessee under another lease of the dwelling-house;

"former tenant still in possession" means a person who—

    (*a*) was the lessee under another lease of the dwelling-house which terminated at some time before the new lease was granted, and

    (*b*) between the termination of that other lease and the grant of the new lease was continuously in possession of the dwelling-house or of the rents and profits of the dwelling-house; and

"the previous lease" means the other lease referred to in the above definitions.

(3) Section 11 does not apply to a lease of a dwelling-house which is a tenancy of an agricultural holding within the meaning of the [Agricultural Holdings Act 1986].

(4) Section 11 does not apply to a lease granted on or after 3rd October 1980 to—

a local authority,

a new town corporation,

an urban development corporation,

the Development Board for Rural Wales,

a registered housing association,

a co-operative housing association, or

an educational institution or other body specified, or of a class specified, by regulations under section 8 of the Rent Act 1977 [or paragraph 8 of Schedule 1 to the Housing Act 1988] (bodies making student lettings)

[a housing action trust established under Part III of the Housing Act 1988].

(5) Section 11 does not apply to a lease granted on or after 3rd October 1980 to—

  (a) Her Majesty in right of the Crown (unless the lease is under the management of the Crown Estate Commissioners), or

  (b) a government department or a person holding in trust for Her Majesty for the purposes of a government department.   **[1151]**

NOTES

  Sub-s (3): words in square brackets substituted by the Agricultural Holdings Act 1986, s 100, Sch 14, para 64.

  Sub-s (4): first words in square brackets inserted by the Local Government and Housing Act 1989, s 194, Sch 11, para 89; second words in square brackets added with savings by the Housing Act 1988, s 116.

15. Jurisdiction of county court

The county court has jurisdiction to make a declaration that section 11 (repairing obligations) applies, or does not apply, to a lease—

  (a) whatever the net annual value of the property in question, and

  (b) notwithstanding that no other relief is sought than a declaration.   **[1152]**

16. Meaning of "lease" and related expressions

In sections 11 to 15 (repairing obligations in short leases)—

  (a) "lease" does not include a mortgage term;

  (b) "lease of a dwelling-house" means a lease by which a building or part of a building is let wholly or mainly as a private residence, and "dwelling-house" means that building or part of a building;

  (c) "lessee" and "lessor" mean, respectively, the person for the time being entitled to the term of a lease and to the reversion expectant on it.   **[1153]**

17. Specific performance of landlord's repairing obligations

(1) In proceedings in which a tenant of a dwelling alleges a breach on the part of his landlord of a repairing covenant relating to any part of the premises in which the dwelling is comprised, the court may order specific performance of the covenant whether or not the breach relates to a part of the premises let to the tenant and notwithstanding any equitable rule restricting the scope of the remedy, whether on the basis of a lack of mutuality or otherwise.

(2) In this section—

  (a) "tenant" includes a statutory tenant,

  (b) in relation to a statutory tenant the reference to the premises let to him is to the premises of which he is a statutory tenant,

  (c) "landlord", in relation to a tenant, includes any person against whom the tenant has a right to enforce a repairing covenant, and

  (d) "repairing covenant" means a covenant to repair, maintain, renew, construct or replace any property.   **[1154]**

Final provisions

40. Short title, commencement and extent

. . .

(3) This Act extends to England and Wales.   **[1154A]**

AGRICULTURAL HOLDINGS ACT 1986
(c 5)

ARRANGEMENT OF SECTIONS

PART I

INTRODUCTORY

PART III

NOTICES TO QUIT

Notices to quit whole or part of agricultural holding

Notices to quit part of agricultural holding

PART VII

MISCELLANEOUS AND SUPPLEMENTAL

SCHEDULES

*An Act to consolidate certain enactments relating to agricultural holdings, with
amendments to give effect to recommendations of the Law Commission*
　　　　　　　　　　　　　　　　　　　　　　　　[18 March 1986]

PART I

INTRODUCTORY

1. Principal definitions

(1) In this Act "agricultural holding" means the aggregate of the land (whether
agricultural land or not) comprised in a contract of tenancy which is a contract
for an agricultural tenancy, not being a contract under which the land is let to
the tenant during his continuance in any office, appointment or employment
held under the landlord.

(2) For the purposes of this section, a contract of tenancy relating to any
land is a contract for an agricultural tenancy if, having regard to—

　(*a*) the terms of the tenancy,

(b) the actual or contemplated use of the land at the time of the conclusion of the contract and subsequently, and

(c) any other relevant circumstances,

the whole of the land comprised in the contract, subject to such exceptions only as do not substantially affect the character of the tenancy, is let for use as agricultural land.

(3) A change in user of the land concerned subsequent to the conclusion of a contract of tenancy which involves any breach of the terms of the tenancy shall be disregarded for the purpose of determining whether a contract which was not originally a contract for an agricultural tenancy has subsequently become one unless it is effected with the landlord's permission, consent or acquiescence.

(4) In this Act "agricultural land" means—

(a) land used for agriculture which is so used for the purposes of a trade or business, and

(b) any other land which, by virtue of a designation under section 109(1) of the Agriculture Act 1947, is agricultural land within the meaning of that Act.

(5) In this Act "contract of tenancy" means a letting of land, or agreement for letting land, for a term of years or from year to year; and for the purposes of this definition a letting of land, or an agreement for letting land, which, by virtue of subsection (6) of section 149 of the Law of Property Act 1925, takes effect as such a letting of land or agreement for letting land as is mentioned in that subsection shall be deemed to be a letting of land or, as the case may be, an agreement for letting land, for a term of years.   **[1155]**

2. Restriction on letting agricultural land for less than from year to year

(1) An agreement to which this section applies shall take effect, with the necessary modifications, as if it were an agreement for the letting of land for a tenancy from year to year unless the agreement was approved by the Minister before it was entered into.

(2) Subject to subsection (3) below, this section applies to an agreement under which—

(a) any land is let to a person for use as agricultural land for an interest less than a tenancy from year to year, or

(b) a person is granted a licence to occupy land for use as agricultural land,

if the circumstances are such that if his interest were a tenancy from year to year he would in respect of that land be the tenant of an agricultural holding.

(3) This section does not apply to an agreement for the letting of land, or the granting of a licence to occupy land—

(a) made (whether or not it expressly so provides) in contemplation of the use of the land only for grazing or mowing (or both) during some specified period of the year, or

(b) by a person whose interest in the land is less than a tenancy from year to year and has not taken effect as such a tenancy by virtue of this section.

(4) Any dispute arising as to the operation of this section in relation to any agreement shall be determined by arbitration under this Act.   **[1156]**

PART III

NOTICES TO QUIT

Notices to quit whole or part of agricultural holding

25. Length of notice to quit

(1) A notice to quit an agricultural holding or part of an agricultural holding shall (notwithstanding any provision to the contrary in the contract of tenancy of the holding) be invalid if it purports to terminate the tenancy before the expiry of twelve months from the end of the then current year of tenancy.

(2) Subsection (1) above shall not apply—

(a) where the tenant is insolvent,
(b) to a notice given in pursuance of a provision in the contract of tenancy authorising the resumption of possession of the holding or some part of it for some specified purpose other than the use of the land for agriculture,
(c) to a notice given by a tenant to a sub-tenant,
(d) where the tenancy is one which, by virtue of subsection (6) of section 149 of the Law of Property Act 1925, has taken effect as such a term of years as is mentioned in that subsection.

(3) Where on a reference under section 12 above with respect to an agricultural holding the arbitrator determines that the rent payable in respect of the holding shall be increased, a notice to quit the holding given by the tenant at least six months before it purports to take effect shall not be invalid by virtue of subsection (1) above if it purports to terminate the tenancy at the end of the year of the tenancy beginning with the date as from which the increase of rent is effective.

(4) On an application made to the Tribunal with respect to an agricultural holding under paragraph 9 of Part II of Schedule 3 to this Act, the Tribunal may, if they grant a certificate in accordance with the application—

(a) specify in the certificate a minimum period of notice for termination of the tenancy (not being a period of less than two months), and
(b) direct that that period shall apply instead of the period of notice required in accordance with subsection (1) above;

and in any such case a notice to quit the holding which states that the Tribunal have given a direction under this subsection shall not be invalid by virtue of subsection (1) above if the notice given is not less than the minimum notice specified in the certificate.

(5) A notice to quit within subsection (3) or (4) above shall not be invalid by virtue of any term of the contract of tenancy requiring a longer period of notice to terminate the tenancy, and a notice to quit within subsection (4) above shall not be invalid by reason of its terminating at a date other than the end of a year of the tenancy. **[1157]**

Notices to quit part of agricultural holding

31. Notice to quit part of holding valid in certain cases

(1) A notice to quit part of an agricultural holding held on a tenancy from year to year given by the landlord of the holding shall not be invalid on the ground that it relates to part only of the holding if it is given—

(a) for the purpose of adjusting the boundaries between agricultural units or amalgamating agricultural units or parts of such units, or

(b) with a view to the use of the land to which the notice relates for any of the objects mentioned in subsection (2) below,

and the notice states that it is given for that purpose or with a view to any such use, as the case may be.

(2) The objects referred to in subsection (1) above are—

(a) the erection of cottages or other houses for farm labourers, whether with or without gardens;

(b) the provision of gardens for cottages or other houses for farm labourers;

(c) the provision of allotments;

(d) the letting of land (with or without other land) as a smallholding under Part III of the Agriculture Act 1970;

(e) the planting of trees;

(f) the opening or working of a deposit of coal, ironstone, limestone, brick-earth or other mineral, or a stone quarry or a clay, sand or gravel pit, or the construction of any works or buildings to be used in connection therewith;

(g) the making of a watercourse or reservoir;

(h) the making of a road, railway, tramroad, siding, canal or basin, or a wharf, pier, or other work connected therewith. **[1158]**

PART VII

MISCELLANEOUS AND SUPPLEMENTAL

89. Power of limited owners to apply capital for improvements

(1) Where under powers conferred by the Settled Land Act 1925 or the Law of Property Act 1925 capital money is applied in or about the execution of any improvement specified in Schedule 7 to this Act no provision shall be made for requiring the money or any part of it to be replaced out of income, and accordingly any such improvement shall be deemed to be an improvement authorised by Part I of Schedule 3 to the Settled Land Act 1925.

(2) Where under powers conferred by the Universities and College Estates Act 1925 capital money is applied in payment for any improvement specified in Schedule 7 to this Act no provision shall be made for replacing the money out of income unless the Minister requires such provision to be made under section 26(5) of that Act or, in the case of a university or college to which section 2 of the Universities and College Estates Act 1964 applies, it appears to the university or college to be necessary to make such provision under the said section 26(5) as modified by Schedule 1 to the said Act of 1964. **[1159]**

102. Citation, commencement and extent

. . .

(3) . . . , this Act extends to England and Wales only. **[1159A]**

SCHEDULES

SCHEDULE 7

Sections 64, 66 etc

LONG-TERM IMPROVEMENTS BEGUN ON OR AFTER 1ST MARCH 1948 FOR WHICH COMPENSATION IS PAYABLE

PART I

Improvements to which Consent of Landlord Required

1. Making or planting of osier beds.
2. Making of water meadows.
3. Making of watercress beds.
4. Planting of hops.
5. Planting of orchards of fruit bushes.
6. Warping or weiring of land.
7. Making of gardens.
8. Provision of underground tanks.   **[1160]**

PART II

Improvements to which Consent of Landlord or Approval of Tribunal Required

9. Erection, alteration or enlargement of buildings, and making or improvement of permanent yards.

10. Carrying out works in compliance with an improvement notice served, or an undertaking accepted, under Part VII of the Housing Act 1985 or Part VIII of the Housing Act 1974.

11. Erection or construction of loading platforms, ramps, hard standings for vehicles or other similar facilities.

12. Construction of silos.

13. Claying of land.

14. Marling of land.

15. Making or improvement of roads or bridges.

16. Making or improvement of water courses, culverts, ponds, wells or reservoirs, or of works for the application of water power for agricultural or domestic purposes or of works for the supply, distribution or use of water for such purposes (including the erection or installation of any structures or equipment which form part of or are to be used for or in connection with operating any such works).

17. Making or removal of permanent fences.

18. Reclaiming of waste land.

19. Making or improvement of embankments or sluices.

20. Erection of wirework for hop gardens.

21. Provision of permanent sheep-dipping accommodation.

22. Removal of bracken, gorse, tree roots, boulders or other like obstructions to cultivation.

23. Land drainage (other than improvements falling within paragraph 1 of Schedule 8 to this Act).

24. Provision or laying-on of electric light or power.

25. Provision of facilities for the storage or disposal of sewage or farm waste.

26. Repairs to fixed equipment, being equipment reasonably required for the proper farming of the holding, other than repairs which the tenant is under an obligation to carry out.

27. The grubbing up of orchards or fruit bushes.

28. Planting trees otherwise than as an orchard and bushes other than fruit bushes.

                                                                              [1161]

LAND REGISTRATION ACT 1986
(c 26)

An Act to make amendments of the Land Registration Act 1925 relating to the conversion of title and to leases, to abolish the Minor Interests Index, and for connected purposes [26 June 1986]

5. Abolition of Minor Interests Index

(1) In section 102 of the 1925 Act, subsection (2) (under which priorities between certain dealings with equitable interests are regulated by the order of lodging of priority cautions and inhibitions) is repealed, and accordingly—

(a) the index maintained for the purposes of that subsection and known as the Minor Interests Index shall cease to be kept, and

(b) any question of priority which would have fallen to be determined in accordance with that subsection shall be determined in accordance with the rule of law referred to in section 137(1) of the Law of Property Act 1925 (which applies to dealings with equitable interests in land the rule commonly known as the rule in *Dearle v. Hall*).

(2) The following provisions have effect for the purposes of the application of the rule in *Dearle v. Hall*, and of sections 137 and 138 of the Law of Property Act 1925, to dealings in respect of which a priority caution or inhibition was entered in the Minor Interests Index—

(a) the notice of the making of the entry which was given under the Land Registration Rules 1925 before the commencement of this Act to the proprietor or, in the case of settled land, to the trustees of the settlement, shall be treated for those purposes as a notice of the dealing to which the entry relates given (at the time it was issued by the registrar) by the person on whose behalf the entry was made to the trustees or other persons appropriate to receive it for the purposes of establishing priority under the rule in *Dearle v. Hall*;

(b) where a trust corporation has been nominated to receive notices of dealings in accordance with section 138, subsection (4) of that section (under which the notice does not affect priority until received by the corporation) does not apply but the trustees shall, if the notice has not already been transmitted to the corporation, deliver it or send it by post to the corporation as soon as practicable after the commencement of this Act.

(3) A person who suffers loss as a result of the operation of this section is entitled to be indemnified in the same way as a person suffering loss by reason of an error or omission in the register, except that in relation to a claim under this subsection the reference in section 83(6)(a) of the 1925 Act (restriction on amount of indemnity in certain cases) to the value of the relevant estate, interest or charge at the time when the error or omission was made shall be construed as a reference to its value immediately before the commencement of this Act.

(4) For the purposes of subsection (3) above, a loss resulting from trustees failing to comply with their duty under subsection (2)(b) above shall be treated as a loss resulting from the operation of this section; but this is without prejudice to the liability of the trustees for breach of that duty or to the registrar's right of recourse against them under section 83(10) of the 1925 Act (under which the registrar may enforce a right which a person indemnified would have been

entitled to enforce in relation to a matter in respect of which an indemnity has been paid).

(5) ... **[1162]**

NOTES
Sub-s (5): amends the Land Registration Act 1925, ss 54, 102, 144.
1925 Act: Land Registration Act 1925.

6. Citation etc

(1) This Act may be cited as the Land Registration Act 1986.

(2) The Land Registration Acts 1925 to 1971 and this Act may be cited together as the Land Registration Acts 1925 to 1986.

(3) This Act shall be construed as one with the 1925 Act.

(4) This Act shall come into force on such day as the Lord Chancellor may appoint by order made by statutory instrument.

(5) This Act extends to England and Wales only. **[1163]**

INSOLVENCY ACT 1986
(c 45)

ARRANGEMENT OF SECTIONS

An Act to consolidate the enactments relating to company insolvency and winding up (including the winding up of companies that are not insolvent, and of unregistered companies); enactments relating to the insolvency and bankruptcy of individuals; and other enactments bearing on those two subject matters, including the functions and qualification of insolvency practitioners, the public administration of insolvency, the penalisation and redress of malpractice and wrongdoing, and the avoidance of certain transactions at an undervalue

[25 July 1986]

THE SECOND GROUP OF PARTS: INSOLVENCY OF INDIVIDUALS; BANKRUPTCY:
PART IX BANKRUPTCY

CHAPTER I BANKRUPTCY PETITIONS; BANKRUPTCY ORDERS

Commencement and duration of bankruptcy; discharge

278. Commencement and continuance

The bankruptcy of an individual against whom a bankruptcy order has been made—

     (a) commences on the day on which the order is made, and
     (b) continues until the individual is discharged under the following provisions of this Chapter.   **[1163A]**

CHAPTER II PROTECTION OF BANKRUPT'S ESTATE AND INVESTIGATION OF HIS
AFFAIRS

283. Definition of bankrupt's estate

(1) Subject as follows, a bankrupt's estate for the purposes of any of this Group of Parts comprises—

     (a) all property belonging to or vested in the bankrupt at the commencement of the bankruptcy, and
     (b) any property which by virtue of any of the following provisions of this Part is comprised in that estate or is treated as falling within the preceding paragraph.

(2) Subsection (1) does not apply to—

(a) such tools, books, vehicles and other items of equipment as are necessary to the bankrupt for use personally by him in his employment, business or vocation;

(b) such clothing, bedding, furniture, household equipment and provisions as are necessary for satisfying the basic domestic needs of the bankrupt and his family.

This subsection is subject to section 308 in Chapter IV (certain excluded property reclaimable by trustee).

(3) Subsection (1) does not apply to—

(a) property held by the bankrupt on trust for any other person, or

(b) the right of nomination to a vacant ecclesiastical benefice.

[(3A) Subject to section 308A in Chapter IV, subsection (1) does not apply to—

(a) a tenancy which is an assured tenancy or an assured agricultural occupancy, within the meaning of Part I of the Housing Act 1988, and the terms of which inhibit an assignment as mentioned in section 127(5) of the Rent Act 1977, or

(b) a protected tenancy, within the meaning of the Rent Act 1977, in respect of which, by virtue of any provision of Part IX of that Act, no premium can lawfully be required as a condition of assignment, or

(c) a tenancy of a dwelling-house by virtue of which the bankrupt is, within the meaning of the Rent (Agriculture) Act 1976, a protected occupier of the dwelling-house, and terms of which inhibit an assignment as mentioned in section 127(5) of the Rent Act 1977, or

(d) a secure tenancy, within the meaning of Part IV of the Housing Act 1985, which is not capable of being assigned, except in the cases mentioned in section 91(3) of that Act.]

(4) References in any of this Group of Parts to property, in relation to a bankrupt, include references to any power exercisable by him over or in respect of property except in so far as the power is exercisable over or in respect of property not for the time being comprised in the bankrupt's estate and—

(a) is so exercisable at a time after either the official receiver has had his release in respect of that estate under section 299(2) in Chapter III or a meeting summoned by the trustee of that estate under section 331 in Chapter IV has been held, or

(b) cannot be so exercised for the benefit of the bankrupt;

and a power exercisable over or in respect of property is deemed for the purposes of any of this Group of Parts to vest in the person entitled to exercise it at the time of the transaction or event by virtue of which it is exercisable by that person (whether or not it becomes so exercisable at that time).

(5) For the purposes of any such provision in this Group of Parts, property comprised in a bankrupt's estate is so comprised subject to the rights of any person other than the bankrupt (whether as a secured creditor of the bankrupt or otherwise) in relation thereto, but disregarding—

(a) any rights in relation to which a statement such as is required by section 269(1)(a) was made in the petition on which the bankrupt was adjudged bankrupt, and

(b) any rights which have been otherwise given up in accordance with the rules.

(6) This section has effect subject to the provisions of any enactment not contained in this Act under which any property is to be excluded from a bankrupt's estate. **[1164]**

NOTES
   Sub-s (3A): inserted by the Housing Act 1988, s 117(1).

284. Restrictions on dispositions of property

(1) Where a person is adjudged bankrupt, any disposition of property made by that person in the period to which this section applies is void except to the extent that it is or was made with the consent of the court, or is or was subsequently ratified by the court.

(2) Subsection (1) applies to a payment (whether in cash or otherwise) as it applies to a disposition of property and, accordingly, where any payment is void by virtue of that subsection, the person paid shall hold the sum paid for the bankrupt as part of his estate.

(3) This section applies to the period beginning with the day of the presentation of the petition for the bankruptcy order and ending with the vesting, under Chapter IV of this Part, of the bankrupt's estate in a trustee.

(4) The preceding provisions of this section do not give a remedy against any person—

    (a) in respect of any property or payment which he received before the commencement of the bankruptcy in good faith, for value and without notice that the petition had been presented, or

    (b) in respect of any interest in property which derives from an interest in respect of which there is, by virtue of this subsection, no remedy.

(5) Where after the commencement of his bankruptcy the bankrupt has incurred a debt to a banker or other person by reason of the making of a payment which is void under this section, that debt is deemed for the purposes of any of this Group of Parts to have been incurred before the commencement of the bankruptcy unless—

    (a) that banker or person had notice of the bankruptcy before the debt was incurred, or

    (b) it is not reasonably practicable for the amount of the payment to be recovered from the person to whom it was made.

(6) A disposition of property is void under this section notwithstanding that the property is not or, as the case may be, would not be comprised in the bankrupt's estate; but nothing in this section affects any disposition made by a person of property held by him on trust for any other person. **[1165]**

CHAPTER IV ADMINISTRATION BY TRUSTEE

Acquisition, control and realisation of bankrupt's estate

306. Vesting of bankrupt's estate in trustee

(1) The bankrupt's estate shall vest in the trustee immediately on his appointment taking effect or, in the case of the official receiver, on his becoming trustee.

(2) Where any property which is, or is to be, comprised in the bankrupt's

estate vests in the trustee (whether under this section or under any other provision of this Part), it shall so vest without any conveyance, assignment or transfer. **[1166]**

307. After-acquired property

(1) Subject to this section and section 309, the trustee may by notice in writing claim for the bankrupt's estate any property which has been acquired by, or has devolved upon, the bankrupt since the commencement of the bankruptcy.

(2) A notice under this section shall not be served in respect of—

    (a) any property falling within subsection (2) or (3) of section 283 in Chapter II,

    (b) any property which by virtue of any other enactment is excluded from the bankrupt's estate, or

    (c) without prejudice to section 280(2)(c) (order of court on application for discharge), any property which is acquired by or, devolves upon, the bankrupt after his discharge.

(3) Subject to the next subsection, upon the service on the bankrupt of a notice under this section the property to which the notice relates shall vest in the trustee as part of the bankrupt's estate; and the trustee's title to that property has relation back to the time at which the property was acquired by, or devolved upon, the bankrupt.

(4) Where, whether before or after service of a notice under this section—

    (a) a person acquires property in good faith, for value and without notice of the bankruptcy, or

    (b) a banker enters into a transaction in good faith and without such notice,

the trustee is not in respect of that property or transaction entitled by virtue of this section to any remedy against that person or banker, or any person whose title to any property derives from that person or banker.

(5) References in this section to property do not include any property which, as part of the bankrupt's income, may be the subject of an income payments order under section 310. **[1167]**

313. Charge on bankrupt's home

(1) Where any property consisting of an interest in a dwelling house which is occupied by the bankrupt or by his spouse or former spouse is comprised in the bankrupt's estate and the trustee is, for any reason, unable for the time being to realise that property, the trustee may apply to the court for an order imposing a charge on the property for the benefit of the bankrupt's estate.

(2) If on an application under this section the court imposes a charge on any property, the benefit of that charge shall be comprised in the bankrupt's estate and is enforceable, up to the value from time to time of the property secured, for the payment of any amount which is payable otherwise than to the bankrupt out of the estate and of interest on that amount at the prescribed rate.

(3) An order under this section made in respect of property vested in the trustee shall provide, in accordance with the rules, for the property to cease to be comprised in the bankrupt's estate and, subject to the charge (and any prior charge), to vest in the bankrupt.

(4) Subsections (1) and (2) and (4) to (6) of section 3 of the Charging Orders

Act 1979 (supplemental provisions with respect to charging orders) have effect in relation to orders under this section as in relation to charging orders under that Act. **[1168]**

314. Powers of trustee

(1) The trustee may—

    (a) with the permission of the creditors' committee or the court, exercise any of the powers specified in Part I of Schedule 5 to this Act, and

    (b) without that permission, exercise any of the general powers specified in Part II of that Schedule.

(2) With the permission of the creditors' committee or the court, the trustee may appoint the bankrupt—

    (a) to superintend the management of his estate or any part of it,

    (b) to carry on his business (if any) for the benefit of his creditors, or

    (c) in any other respect to assist in administering the estate in such manner and on such terms as the trustee may direct.

(3) A permission given for the purposes of subsection (1)(a) or (2) shall not be a general permission but shall relate to a particular proposed exercise of the power in question; and a person dealing with the trustee in good faith and for value is not to be concerned to enquire whether any permission required in either case has been given.

(4) Where the trustee has done anything without the permission required by subsection (1)(a) or (2), the court or the creditors' committee may, for the purpose of enabling him to meet his expenses out of the bankrupt's estate, ratify what the trustee has done.

But the committee shall not do so unless it is satisfied that the trustee has acted in a case of urgency and has sought its ratification without undue delay.

(5) Part III of Schedule 5 to this Act has effect with respect to the things which the trustee is able to do for the purposes of, or in connection with, the exercise of any of his powers under any of this Group of Parts.

(6) Where the trustee (not being the official receiver) in exercise of the powers conferred on him by any provision in this Group of Parts—

    (a) disposes of any property comprised in the bankrupt's estate to an associate of the bankrupt, or

    (b) employs a solicitor,

he shall, if there is for the time being a creditors' committee, give notice to the committee of that exercise of his powers.

(7) Without prejudice to the generality of subsection (5) and Part III of Schedule 5, the trustee may, if he thinks fit, at any time summon a general meeting of the bankrupt's creditors.

Subject to the preceding provisions in this Group of Parts, he shall summon such a meeting if he is requested to do so by a creditor of the bankrupt and the request is made with the concurrence of not less than one-tenth, in value, of the bankrupt's creditors (including the creditor making the request).

(8) Nothing in this Act is to be construed as restricting the capacity of the trustee to exercise any of his powers outside England and Wales. **[1169]**

Disclaimer of onerous property

315. Disclaimer (general power)

(1) Subject as follows, the trustee may, by the giving of the prescribed notice, disclaim any onerous property and may do so notwithstanding that he has taken possession of it, endeavoured to sell it or otherwise exercised rights of ownership in relation to it.

(2) The following is onerous property for the purposes of this section, that is to say—

> (a) any unprofitable contract, and
> (b) any other property comprised in the bankrupt's estate which is unsaleable or not readily saleable, or is such that it may give rise to a liability to pay money or perform any other onerous act.

(3) A disclaimer under this section—

> (a) operates so as to determine, as from the date of the disclaimer, the rights, interests and liabilities of the bankrupt and his estate in or in respect of the property disclaimed, and
> (b) discharges the trustee from all personal liability in respect of that property as from the commencement of his trusteeship,

but does not, except so far as is necessary for the purpose of releasing the bankrupt, the bankrupt's estate and the trustee from any liability, affect the rights or liabilities of any other person.

(4) A notice of disclaimer shall not be given under this section in respect of any property that has been claimed for the estate under section 307 (after-acquired property) or 308 (personal property of bankrupt exceeding reasonable replacement value) [or 308A], except with the leave of the court.

(5) Any person sustaining loss or damage in consequence of the operation of a disclaimer under this section is deemed to be a creditor of the bankrupt to the extent of the loss damage and accordingly may prove for the loss or damage as a bankruptcy debt. **[1170]**

NOTES

Sub-s (4): words in square brackets inserted by the Housing Act 1988, s 117(4).

CHAPTER V EFFECT OF BANKRUPTCY ON CERTAIN RIGHTS, TRANSACTIONS, ETC

Rights of occupation

337. Rights of occupation of bankrupt

(1) This section applies where—

> (a) a person who is entitled to occupy a dwelling house by virtue of a beneficial estate or interest is adjudged bankrupt, and
> (b) any persons under the age of 18 with whom that person had at some time occupied that dwelling house had their home with that person at the time when the bankruptcy petition was presented and at the commencement of the bankruptcy.

(2) Whether or not the bankrupt's spouse (if any) has rights of occupation under the Matrimonial Homes Act 1983—

> (a) the bankrupt has the following rights as against the trustee of his estate—

(i) if in occupation, a right not to be evicted or excluded from the dwelling house or any part of it, except with the leave of the court,

(ii) if not in occupation, a right with the leave of the court to enter into and occupy the dwelling house, and

(b) the bankrupt's rights are a charge, having the like priority as an equitable interest created immediately before the commencement of the bankruptcy, on so much of his estate or interest in the dwelling house as vests in the trustee.

(3) The Act of 1983 has effect, with the necessary modifications, as if—

(a) the rights conferred by paragraph (a) of subsection (2) were rights of occupation under that Act,

(b) any application for leave such as is mentioned in that paragraph were an application for an order under section 1 of that Act, and

(c) any charge under paragraph (b) of that subsection on the estate or interest of the trustee were a charge under that Act on the estate or interest of a spouse.

(4) Any application for leave such as is mentioned in subsection (2)(a) or otherwise by virtue of this section for an order under section 1 of the Act of 1983 shall be made to the court having jurisdiction in relation to the bankruptcy.

(5) On such an application the court shall make such order under section 1 of the Act of 1983 as it thinks just and reasonable having regard to the interests of the creditors, to the bankrupt's financial resources, to the needs of the children and to all the circumstances of the case other than the needs of the bankrupt.

(6) Where such an application is made after the end of the period of one year beginning with the vesting (under Chapter IV of this Part) of the bankrupt's estate in a trustee, the court shall assume, unless the circumstances of the case are exceptional, that the interests of the bankrupt's creditors outweigh all other considerations. **[1171]**

338. Payments in respect of premises occupied by bankrupt

Where any premises comprised in a bankrupt's estate are occupied by him (whether by virtue of the preceding section or otherwise) on condition that he makes payments towards satisfying any liability arising under a mortgage of the premises or otherwise towards the outgoings of the premises, the bankrupt does not, by virtue of those payments, acquire any interest in the premises. **[1172]**

Adjustment of prior transactions, etc

339. Transactions at an undervalue

(1) Subject as follows in this section and sections 341 and 342, where an individual is adjudged bankrupt and he has at a relevant time (defined in section 341) entered into a transaction with any person at an undervalue, the trustee of the bankrupt's estate may apply to the court for an order under this section.

(2) The court shall, on such an application, make such order as it thinks fit for restoring the position to what it would have been if that individual had not entered into that transaction.

(3) For the purposes of this section and sections 341 and 342, an individual enters into a transaction with a person at an undervalue if—

(a) he makes a gift to that person or he otherwise enters into a transaction with that person on terms that provide for him to receive no consideration,

(b) he enters into a transaction with that person in consideration of marriage, or

(c) he enters into a transaction with that person for a consideration the value of which, in money or money's worth, is significantly less than the value, in money or money's worth, of the consideration provided by the individual. **[1173]**

340. Preferences

(1) Subject as follows in this and the next two sections, where an individual is adjudged bankrupt and he has at a relevant time (defined in section 341) given a preference to any person, the trustee of the bankrupt's estate may apply to the court for an order under this section.

(2) The court shall, on such an application, make such order as it thinks fit for restoring the position to what it would have been if that individual had not given that preference.

(3) For the purposes of this and the next two sections, an individual gives a preference to a person if—

(a) that person is one of the individual's creditors or a surety or guarantor for any of his debts or other liabilities, and

(b) the individual does anything or suffers anything to be done which (in either case) has the effect of putting that person into a position which, in the event of the individual's bankruptcy, will be better than the position he would have been in if that thing had not been done.

(4) The court shall not make an order under this section in respect of a preference given to any person unless the individual who gave the preference was influenced in deciding to give it by a desire to produce in relation to that person the effect mentioned in subsection (3)(b) above.

(5) An individual who has given a preference to a person who, at the time the preference was given, was an associate of his (otherwise than by reason only of being his employee) is presumed, unless the contrary is shown, to have been influenced in deciding to give it by such a desire as is mentioned in subsection (4).

(6) The fact that something has been done in pursuance of the order of a court does not, without more, prevent the doing or suffering of that thing from constituting the giving of a preference. **[1174]**

341. "Relevant time" under ss 339, 340

(1) Subject as follows, the time at which an individual enters into a transaction at an undervalue or gives a preference is a relevant time if the transaction is entered into or the preference given—

(a) in the case of a transaction at an undervalue, at a time in the period of 5 years ending with the day of the presentation of the bankruptcy petition on which the individual is adjudged bankrupt,

(b) in the case of a preference which is not a transaction at an undervalue and is given to a person who is an associate of the individual (otherwise than by reason only of being his employee), at a time in the period of 2 years ending with that day, and

(c) in any other case of a preference which is not a transaction at an undervalue, at a time in the period of 6 months ending with that day.

(2) Where an individual enters into a transaction at an undervalue or gives a preference at a time mentioned in paragraph (a), (b) or (c) of subsection (1) (not being, in the case of a transaction at an undervalue, a time less than 2 years before the end of the period mentioned in paragraph (a)), that time is not a relevant time for the purposes of sections 339 and 340 unless the individual—

(a) is insolvent at that time, or
(b) becomes insolvent in consequence of the transaction or preference;

but the requirements of this subsection are presumed to be satisfied, unless the contrary is shown, in relation to any transaction at an undervalue which is entered into by an individual with a person who is an associate of his (otherwise than by reason only of being his employee).

(3) For the purposes of subsection (2), an individual is insolvent if—

(a) he is unable to pay his debts as they fall due, or
(b) the value of his assets is less than the amount of his liabilities, taking into account his contingent and prospective liabilities.

(4) A transaction entered into or preference given by a person who is subsequently adjudged bankrupt on a petition under section 264(1)(d) (criminal bankruptcy) is to be treated as having been entered into or given at a relevant time for the purposes of sections 339 and 340 if it was entered into or given at any time on or after the date specified for the purposes of this subsection in the criminal bankruptcy order on which the petition was based.

(5) No order shall be made under section 339 or 340 by virtue of subsection (4) of this section where an appeal is pending (within the meaning of section 277) against the individual's conviction of any offence by virtue of which the criminal bankruptcy order was made. **[1175]**

NOTES
Sub-ss (4), (5): prospectively repealed by the Criminal Justice Act 1988, s 170(2), Sch 16.

342. Orders under ss 339, 340

(1) Without prejudice to the generality of section 339(2) or 340(2), an order under either of those sections with respect to a transaction or preference entered into or given by an individual who is subsequently adjudged bankrupt may (subject as follows)—

(a) require any property transferred as part of the transaction, or in connection with the giving of the preference, to be vested in the trustee of the bankrupt's estate as part of that estate;
(b) require any property to be so vested if it represents in any person's hands the application either of the proceeds of sale of property so transferred or of money so transferred;
(c) release or discharge (in whole or in part) any security given by the invididual;
(d) require any person to pay, in respect of benefits received by him from the individual, such sums to the trustee of his estate as the court may direct;
(e) provide for any surety or guarantor whose obligations to any person were released or discharged (in whole or in part) under the transaction or by the giving of the preference to be under such new or revived obligations to that person as the court thinks appropriate;

(*f*) provide for security to be provided for the discharge of any obligation imposed by or arising under the order, and for such an obligation to be charged on any property and for the security or charge to have the same priority as a security or charge released or discharged (in whole or in part) under the transaction or by the giving of the preference; and

(*g*) provide for the extent to which any person whose property is vested by the order in the trustee of the bankrupt's estate, or on whom obligations are imposed by the order, is to be able to prove in the bankruptcy for debts or other liabilities which arose from, or were released or discharged (in whole or in part) under or by, the transaction or the giving of the preference.

(2) An order under section 339 or 340 may affect the property of, or impose any obligation on, any person whether or not he is the person with whom the individual in question entered into the transaction or, as the case may be, the person to whom the preference was given; but such an order—

(*a*) shall not prejudice any interest in property which was acquired from a person other than that individual and was acquired in good faith, for value and without notice of the relevant circumstances, or prejudice any interest deriving from such an interest, and

(*b*) shall not require a person who received a benefit from the transaction or preference in good faith, for value and without notice of the relevant circumstances to pay a sum to the trustee of the bankrupt's estate, except where he was a party to the transaction or the payment is to be in respect of a preference given to that person at a time when he was a creditor of that individual.

(3) Any sums required to be paid to the trustee in accordance with an order under section 339 or 340 shall be comprised in the bankrupt's estate.

(4) For the purposes of this section the relevant circumstances, in relation to a transaction or preference, are—

(*a*) the circumstances by virtue of which an order under section 339 or 340 could be made in respect of the transaction or preference if the individual in question were adjudged bankrupt within a particular period after the transaction is entered into or the preference given, and

(*b*) if that period has expired, the fact that that individual has been adjudged bankrupt within that period. **[1176]**

343. Extortionate credit transactions

(1) This section applies where a person is adjudged bankrupt who is or has been a party to a transaction for, or involving, the provision to him of credit.

(2) The court may, on the application of the trustee of the bankrupt's estate, make an order with respect to the transaction if the transaction is or was extortionate and was not entered into more than 3 years before the commencement of the bankruptcy.

(3) For the purposes of this section a transaction is extortionate if, having regard to the risk accepted by the person providing the credit—

(*a*) the terms of it are or were such as to require grossly exorbitant payments to be made (whether unconditionally or in certain contingencies) in respect of the provision of the credit, or

(b) it otherwise grossly contravened ordinary principles of fair dealing;

and it shall be presumed, unless the contrary is proved, that a transaction with respect to which an application is made under this section is or, as the case may be, was extortionate.

(4) An order under this section with respect to any transaction may contain such one or more of the following as the court thinks fit, that is to say—

  (a) provision setting aside the whole or part of any obligation created by the transaction;
  (b) provision otherwise varying the terms of the transaction or varying the terms on which any security for the purposes of the transaction is held;
  (c) provision requiring any person who is or was party to the transaction to pay to the trustee any sums paid to that person, by virtue of the transaction, by the bankrupt;
  (d) provision requiring any person to surrender to the trustee any property held by him as security for the purposes of the transaction;
  (e) provision directing accounts to be taken between any persons.

(5) Any sums or property required to be paid or surrendered to the trustee in accordance with an order under this section shall be comprised in the bankrupt's estate.

(6) Neither the trustee of a bankrupt's estate nor an undischarged bankrupt is entitled to make an application under section 139(1)(a) of the Consumer Credit Act 1974 (re-opening of extortionate credit agreements) for any agreement by which credit is or has been provided to the bankrupt to be re-opened.

But the powers conferred by this section are exercisable in relation to any transaction concurrently with any powers exercisable under this Act in relation to that transaction as a transaction at an undervalue.   **[1177]**

THE THIRD GROUP OF PARTS: MISCELLANEOUS MATTERS BEARING ON BOTH COMPANY AND INDIVIDUAL INSOLVENCY; GENERAL INTERPRETATION; FINAL PROVISIONS

PART XVI PROVISIONS AGAINST DEBT AVOIDANCE (ENGLAND AND WALES ONLY)

423. Transactions defrauding creditors

(1) This section relates to transactions entered into at an undervalue; and a person enters into such a transaction with another person if—

  (a) he makes a gift to the other person or he otherwise enters into a transaction with the other on terms that provide for him to receive no consideration;
  (b) he enters into a transaction with the other in consideration of marriage; or
  (c) he enters into a transaction with the other for a consideration the value of which, in money or money's worth, is significantly less than the value, in money or money's worth, of the consideration provided by himself.

(2) Where a person has entered into such a transaction, the court may, if satisfied under the next subsection, make such order as it thinks fit for—

  (a) restoring the position to what it would have been if the transaction had not been entered into, and

(b) protecting the interests of persons who are victims of the transaction.

(3) In the case of a person entering into such a transaction, an order shall only be made if the court is satisfied that it was entered into by him for the purpose—

    (a) of putting assets beyond the reach of a person who is making, or may at some time make, a claim against him, or

    (b) of otherwise prejudicing the interests of such a person in relation to the claim which he is making or may make.

(4) In this section "the court" means the High Court or—

    (a) if the person entering into the transaction is an individual, any other court which would have jurisdiction in relation to a bankruptcy petition relating to him;

    (b) if that person is a body capable of being wound up under Part IV or V of this Act, any other court having jurisdiction to wind it up.

(5) In relation to a transaction at an undervalue, references here and below to a victim of the transaction are to a person who is, or is capable of being, prejudiced by it; and in the following two sections the person entering into the transaction is referred to as "the debtor". **[1178]**

424. Those who may apply for an order under s 423

(1) An application for an order under section 423 shall not be made in relation to a transaction except—

    (a) in a case where the debtor has been adjudged bankrupt or is a body corporate which is being wound up or in relation to which an administration order is in force, by the official receiver, by the trustee of the bankrupt's estate or the liquidator or administrator of the body corporate or (with the leave of the court) by a victim of the transaction;

    (b) in a case where a victim of the transaction is bound by a voluntary arrangement approved under Part I or Part VIII of this Act, by the supervisor of the voluntary arrangement or by any person who (whether or not so bound) is such a victim; or

    (c) in any other case, by a victim of the transaction.

(2) An application made under any of the paragraphs of subsection (1) is to be treated as made on behalf of every victim of the transaction. **[1179]**

PART XVII MISCELLANEOUS AND GENERAL

426. Co-operation between courts exercising jurisdiction in relation to insolvency

(1) An order made by a court in any part of the United Kingdom in the exercise of jurisdiction in relation to insolvency law shall be enforced in any other part of the United Kingdom as if it were made by a court exercising the corresponding jurisdiction in that other part.

(2) However, without prejudice to the following provisions of this section, nothing in subsection (1) requires a court in any part of the United Kingdom to enforce, in relation to property situated in that part, any order made by a court in any other part of the United Kingdom.

(3) The Secretary of State, with the concurrence in relation to property situated in England and Wales of the Lord Chancellor, may by order make provision for securing that a trustee or assignee under the insolvency law of any

part of the United Kingdom has, with such modifications as may be specified in the order, the same rights in relation to any property situated in another part of the United Kingdom as he would have in the corresponding circumstances if he were a trustee or assignee under the insolvency law of that other part.

(4) The courts having jurisdiction in relation to insolvency law in any part of the United Kingdom shall assist the courts having the corresponding jurisdiction in any other part of the United Kingdom or any relevant country or territory.

(5) For the purposes of subsection (4) a request made to a court in any part of the United Kingdom by a court in any other part of the United Kingdom or in a relevant country or territory is authority for the court to which the request is made to apply, in relation to any matters specified in the request, the insolvency law which is applicable by either court in relation to comparable matters falling within its jurisdiction.

In exercising its discretion under this subsection, a court shall have regard in particular to the rules of private international law.

(6) Where a person who is a trustee or assignee under the insolvency law of any part of the United Kingdom claims property situated in any other part of the United Kingdom (whether by virtue of an order under subsection (3) or otherwise), the submission of that claim to the court exercising jurisdiction in relation to insolvency law in that other part shall be treated in the same manner as a request made by a court for the purpose of subsection (4).

(7) Section 38 of the Criminal Law Act 1977 (execution of warrant of arrest throughout the United Kingdom) applies to a warrant which, in exercise of any jurisdiction in relation to insolvency law, is issued in any part of the United Kingdom for the arrest of a person as it applies to a warrant issued in that part of the United Kingdom for the arrest of a person charged with an offence.

(8) Without prejudice to any power to make rules of court, any power to make provision by subordinate legislation for the purpose of giving effect in relation to companies or individuals to the insolvency law of any part of the United Kingdom includes power to make provision for the purpose of giving effect in that part to any provision made by or under the preceding provisions of this section.

(9) An order under subsection (3) shall be made by statutory instrument subject to annulment in pursuance of a resolution of either House of Parliament.

(10) In this section "insolvency law" means—

(*a*) in relation to England and Wales, provision made by or under this Act or sections 6 to 10, 12, 15, 19(*c*) and 20 (with Schedule 1) of the Company Directors Disqualification Act 1986 and extending to England and Wales;

(*b*) in relation to Scotland, provision extending to Scotland and made by or under this Act, sections 6 to 10, 12, 15, 19(*c*) and 20 (with Schedule 1) of the Company Directors Disqualification Act 1986, Part XVIII of the Companies Act or the Bankruptcy (Scotland) Act 1985;

(*c*) in relation to Northern Ireland, provision made by or under [the Insolvency (Northern Ireland) Order 1989];

(*d*) in relation to any relevant country or territory, so much of the law of that country or territory as corresponds to provisions falling within any of the foregoing paragraphs;

and references in this subsection to any enactment include, in relation to any time before the coming into force of that enactment the corresponding enactment in force at that time.

(11) In this section "relevant country or territory" means—

    (*a*) any of the Channel Islands or the Isle of Man, or

    (*b*) any country or territory designated for the purposes of this section by the Secretary of State by order made by statutory instrument.

[(12) In the application of this section to Northern Ireland—

    (*a*) for any reference to the Secretary of State there is substituted a reference to the Department of Economic Development in Northern Ireland;

    (*b*) in subsection (3) for the words "another part of the United Kingdom" and the words "that other part" there are substituted the words "Northern Ireland";

    (*c*) for subsection (9) there is substituted the following susection—

        "(9) An order made under subsection (3) by the Department of Economic Development in Northern Ireland shall be a statutory rule for the purposes of the Statutory Rules (Northern Ireland) Order 1979 and shall be subject to negative resolution within the meaning of section 41(6) of the Interpretation Act (Northern Ireland) 1954.".] **[1180]**

NOTES

    Commencement: 1 October 1991 (sub-s (12)); 29 December 1986 (remainder).

    Sub-s (10): words in square brackets substituted by the Insolvency (Northern Ireland) Order 1989, SI 1989 No 2405, art 381(2), Sch 9, para 41.

    Sub-s (12): added by the Insolvency (Northern Ireland) Order 1989, SI 1989 No 2405, art 381(2), Sch 9, para 41.

440. Extent (Scotland)

. . .

    (2) The following provisions of this Act do not extend to Scotland—

    . . .

    (*b*) the second Group of Parts; **[1180A]**

441. Extent (Northern Ireland)

(1) The following provisions of this Act extend to Northern Ireland—

    (*a*) sections . . . 426, . . . **[1180B]**

RECOGNITION OF TRUSTS ACT 1987
(c 14)

An Act to enable the United Kingdom to ratify the Convention on the law applicable to trusts and on their recognition which was signed on behalf of the United Kingdom on 10th January 1986 [9 April 1987]

1. Applicable law and recognition of trusts

(1) The provisions of the Convention set out in the Schedule to this Act shall have the force of law in the United Kingdom.

(2) Those provisions shall, so far as applicable, have effect not only in relation to the trusts described in Articles 2 and 3 of the Convention but also in relation to any other trusts of property arising under the law of any part of the United Kingdom or by virtue of a judicial decision whether in the United Kingdom or elsewhere.

(3) In accordance with Articles 15 and 16 such provisions of the law as are there mentioned shall, to the extent there specified, apply to the exclusion of the other provisions of the Convention.

(4) In Article 17 the reference to a State includes a reference to any country or territory (whether or not a party to the Convention and whether or not forming part of the United Kingdom) which has its own system of law.

(5) Article 22 shall not be construed as affecting the law to be applied in relation to anything done or omitted before the coming into force of this Act.

[1181]

2. Extent

(1) This Act extends to Northern Ireland.

(2) Her Majesty may by Order in Council direct that this Act shall also form part of the law of the Isle of Man, any of the Channel Islands or any colony.

(3) An Order in Council under subsection (2) above may modify this Act in its application to any of the territories there mentioned and may contain such supplementary provisions as Her Majesty considers appropriate.

(4) An Order in Council under subsection (2) above shall be subject to annulment in pursuance of a resolution of either House of Parliament.   **[1182]**

3. Short title, commencement and application to the Crown

(1) This Act may be cited as the Recognition of Trusts Act 1987.

(2) This Act shall come into force on such date as the Lord Chancellor and the Lord Advocate may appoint by an order made by statutory instrument.

(3) This Act binds the Crown.   **[1183]**

SCHEDULE

Section 1

CONVENTION ON THE LAW APPLICABLE TO TRUSTS AND ON THEIR RECOGNITION

CHAPTER I SCOPE

Article 1

This Convention specifies the law applicable to trusts and governs their recognition.

Article 2

For the purposes of this Convention, the term "trust" refers to the legal relationship created— inter vivos or on death— by a person, the settlor, when assets have been placed under the control of a trustee for the benefit of a beneficiary or for a specified purpose.

A trust has the following characteristics—

(*a*) the assets constitute a separate fund and are not a part of the trustee's own estate;

(*b*) title to the trust assets stands in the name of the trustee or in the name of another person on behalf of the trustee;

(*c*) the trustee has the power and the duty, in respect of which he is accountable, to manage, employ or dispose of the assets in accordance with the terms of the trust and the special duties imposed upon him by law.

The reservation by the settlor of certain rights and powers, and the fact that the trustee may himself have rights as a beneficiary, are not necessarily inconsistent with the existence of a trust.

Article 3

The Convention applies only to trusts created voluntarily and evidenced in writing.

Article 4

The Convention does not apply to preliminary issues relating to the validity of wills or of other acts by virtue of which assets are transferred to the trustee.

Article 5

The Convention does not apply to the extent that the law specified by Chapter II does not provide for trusts or the category of trusts involved.   **[1184]**

CHAPTER II APPLICABLE LAW

Article 6

A trust shall be governed by the law chosen by the settlor. The choice must be express or be implied in the terms of the instrument creating or the writing evidencing the trust, interpreted, if necessary, in the light of the circumstances of the case.

Where the law chosen under the previous paragraph does not provide for trusts or the category of trust involved, the choice shall not be effective and the law specified in Article 7 shall apply.

Article 7

Where no applicable law has been chosen, a trust shall be governed by the law with which it is most closely connected.

In ascertaining the law with which a trust is most closely connected reference shall be made in particular to—

(*a*) the place of administration of the trust designated by the settlor;

(*b*) the situs of the assets of the trust;

(*c*) the place of residence or business of the trustee;

(*d*) the objects of the trust and the places where they are to be fulfilled.

Article 8

The law specified by Article 6 or 7 shall govern the validity of the trust, its construction, its effects and the administration of the trust. In particular that law shall govern—

(*a*) the appointment, resignation and removal of trustees, the capacity to act as a trustee, and the devolution of the office of trustee;

(*b*) the rights and duties of trustees among themselves;

(*c*) the right of trustees to delegate in whole or in part the discharge of their duties or the exercise of their powers;

(*d*) the power of trustees to administer or to dispose of trust assets, to create security interests in the trust assets, or to acquire new assets;

(*e*) the powers of investment of trustees;

(*f*) restrictions upon the duration of the trust, and upon the power to accumulate the income of the trust;

(*g*) the relationships between the trustees and the beneficiaries including the personal liability of the trustees to the beneficiaries;

(*h*) the variation or termination of the trust;

(*i*) the distribution of the trust assets;

(*j*) the duty of trustees to account for their administration.

Article 9

In applying this Chapter a severable aspect of the trust, particularly matters of administration, may be governed by a different law.

Article 10

The law applicable to the validity of the trust shall determine whether that law or the law governing a severable aspect of the trust may be replaced by another law.　　**[1185]**

CHAPTER III RECOGNITION

Article 11

A trust created in accordance with the law specified by the preceding Chapter shall be recognised as a trust.

Such recognition shall imploy, as a minimum, that the trust property constitutes a separate fund, that the trustee may sue and be sued in his capacity as trustee, and that he may appear or act in this capacity before a notary or any person acting in an official capacity.

In so far as the law applicable to the trust requires or provides, such recognition shall imply in particular—

(*a*) that personal creditors of the trustee shall have no recourse against the trust assets;

(*b*) that the trust assets shall not form part of the trustee's estate upon his insolvency or bankruptcy;

(*c*) that the trust assets shall not form part of the matrimonial property of the trustee or his spouse nor part of the trustee's estate upon his death;

(*d*) that the trust assets may be recovered when the trustee, in breach of trust, has mingled trust assets with his own property or has alienated trust assets. However, the rights and obligations of any third party holder of the assets shall remain subject to the law determined by the choice of law rules of the forum.

Article 12

Where the trustee desires to register assets, movable or immovable, or documents of title to them, he shall be entitled, in so far as this is not prohibited by or inconsistent with the law of the State where registration is sought, to do so in his capacity as trustee or in such other way that the existence of the trust is disclosed.

Article 14

The Convention shall not prevent the application of rules of law more favourable to the recognition of trusts. **[1186]**

CHAPTER IV GENERAL CLAUSES

Article 15

The Convention does not prevent the application of provisions of the law designated by the conflicts rules of the forum, in so far as those provisions cannot be derogated from by voluntary act, relating in particular to the following matters—

(*a*) the protection of minors and incapable parties;
(*b*) the personal and proprietary effects of marriage;
(*c*) succession rights, testate and intestate, especially the indefeasible shares of spouses and relatives;
(*d*) the transfer of title property and security interests in property;
(*e*) the protection of creditors in matters of insolvency;
(*f*) the protection, in other respects, of third parties acting in good faith.

If recognition of a trust is prevented by application of the preceding paragraph, the court shall try to give effect to the objects of the trust by other means.

Article 16

The Convention does not prevent the application of those provisions of the law of the forum which must be applied even to international situations, irrespective of rules of conflict of laws.

Article 17

In the Convention the word "law" means the rules of law in force in a State other than its rules of conflict of laws.

Article 18

The provisions of the Convention may be disregarded when their application would be manifestly incompatible with public policy.

Article 22

The Convention applies to trusts regardless of the date on which they were created. **[1187]**

REVERTER OF SITES ACT 1987

(c 15)

ARRANGEMENT OF SECTIONS

An Act to amend the law with respect to the reverter of sites that have ceased to be used for particular purposes; and for connected purposes   [9 April 1987]

1. Right of reverter replaced by trust for sale

(1) Where any relevant enactment provides for land to revert to the ownership of any person at any time, being a time when the land ceases, or has ceased for a specified period, to be used for particular purposes, that enactment shall have effect, and (subject to subsection (4) below) shall be deemed always to have had effect, as if it provided (instead of for the reverter) for the land to be vested after that time, on the trust arising under this section, in the persons in whom it was vested immediately before that time.

(2) Subject to the following provisions of this Act, the trust arising under this section in relation to any land is a trust to sell the land and to stand possessed of the net proceeds of sale (after payment of costs and expenses) and of the net rents and profits until sale (after payment of rates, taxes, costs of insurance, repairs and other outgoings) upon trust for the persons who but for this Act would from time to time be entitled to the ownership of the land by virtue of its reverter.

(3) Where—

(*a*) a trust in relation to any land has arisen or is treated as having arisen under this section at such a time as is mentioned in subsection (1) above; and

(*b*) immediately before that time the land was vested in any persons in their capacity as the minister and churchwardens of any parish,

those persons shall be treated as having become trustees for sale under this section in that capacity and, accordingly, their interest in the land shall pass and, if the case so requires, be treated as having passed to their successors from time to time.

(4) This section shall not confer any right on any person as a beneficiary—

(*a*) in relation to any property in respect of which that person's claim was statute-barred before the commencement of this Act, or in relation to any property derived from any such property; or

(*b*) in relation to any rents or profits received, or breach of trust committed, before the commencement of this Act;

and anything validly done before the commencement of this Act in relation to any land which by virtue of this section is deemed to have been held at the time on trust for sale shall, if done by the beneficiaries, be deemed, so far as necessary for preserving its validity, to have been done by the trustees.

(5) Where any property is held by any persons as trustees of a trust which has arisen under this section and, in consequence of subsection (4) above, there are no beneficiaries of that trust, the trustees shall have no power to act in relation to that property except—

(*a*) for the purposes for which they could have acted in relation to that property if this Act had not been passed; or (*b*) for the purpose of securing the establishment of a scheme under section 2 below or the making of an order under section 2 of the Education Act 1973 (special powers as to trusts for religious education).

(6) In this section—

"churchwardens" includes chapel wardens;

"minister" includes a rector, vicar or perpetual curate; and

"parish" includes a parish of the Church in Wales;

and the reference to a person's claim being statute-barred is a reference to the Limitation Act 1980 providing that no proceedings shall be brought by that person to recover the property in respect of which the claim subsists.   **[1188]**

2. Charity Commissioners' schemes

(1) Subject to the following provisions of this section and to sections 3 and 4 below, where any persons hold any property as trustees of a trust which has arisen under section 1 above, the Charity Commissioners may, on the application of the trustees, by order establish a scheme which—

(*a*) extinguishes the rights of beneficiaries under the trust; and

(*b*) requires the trustees to hold the property on trust for such charitable purposes as may be specified in the order.

(2) Subject to subsections (3) and (4) below, an order made under this section—

(*a*) may contain any such provision as may be contained in an order made by the High Court for establishing a scheme for the administration of a charity; and

(*b*) shall have the same effect as an order so made.

(3) The charitable purposes specified in an order made under this section on an application with respect to any trust shall be as similar in character as the Charity Commissioners think is practicable in all the circumstances to the purposes (whether charitable or not) for which the trustees held the relevant land before the cesser of use in consequence of which the trust arose; but in determining the character of the last-mentioned purposes the Commissioners, if they think it appropriate to do so, may give greater weight to the persons or locality benefited by the purposes than to the nature of the benefit.

(4) An order made under this section on an application with respect to any trust shall be so framed as to secure that if a person who—

(*a*) but for the making of the order would have been a beneficiary under the trust; and

(*b*) has not consented to the establishment of a scheme under this section,

notifies a claim to the trustees within the period of five years after the date of the making of the order, that person shall be paid an amount equal to the value of his rights at the time of their extinguishment.

(5) The Charity Commissioners shall not make any order under this section establishing a scheme unless—

(*a*) the requirements of section 3 below with respect to the making of the application for the order are satisfied or, by virtue of subsection (4) of that section, do not apply;

(*b*) one of the conditions specified in subsection (6) below is fulfilled;

(*c*) public notice of the Commissioners' proposals has been given inviting representations to be made to them within a period specified in the notice, being a period ending not less than one month after the date of the giving of the notice; and

(*d*) that period has ended and the Commissioners have taken into consideration any representations which have been made within that period and not withdrawn.

(6) The conditions mentioned in subsection (5)(*b*) above are—

(*a*) that there is no claim by any person to be a beneficiary in respect of rights proposed to be extinguished—

   (i) which is outstanding; or

   (ii) which has at any time been accepted as valid by the trustees or by persons whose acceptance binds the trustees; or

   (iii) which has been upheld in proceedings that have been concluded;

(*b*) that consent to the establishment of a scheme under this section has been given by every person whose claim to be a beneficiary in respect of those rights is outstanding or has been so accepted or upheld.

(7) The Charity Commissioners shall refuse to consider an application under this section unless it is accompanied by a statutory declaration by the applicants—

(*a*) that the requirements of section 3 below are satisfied with respect to the making of the application or, if the declaration so declares, do not apply; and

(*b*) that a condition specified in subsection (6) above and identified in the declaration is fulfilled;

and the declaration shall be conclusive for the purposes of this section of the matters declared therein.

(8) A notice given for the purposes of subsection (5)(*c*) above shall contain such particulars of the Commissioners' proposals, or such directions for obtaining information about them, and shall be given in such manner, as they think sufficient and appropriate; and a further such notice shall not be required where the Commissioners decide, before proceeding with any proposals of which notice has been so given, to modify them. **[1189]**

3. Applications for schemes

(1) Where an application is made under section 2 above by the trustees of any trust that has arisen under section 1 above, the requirements of this section are satisfied with respect to the making of that application if, before the application is made—

(*a*) notices under subsection (2) below have been published in two national newspapers and in a local newspaper circulating in the locality where the relevant land is situated;

(*b*) each of those notices specified a period for the notification to the trustees of claims by beneficiaries, being a period ending not less than three months after the date of publication of the last of those notices to be published;

(*c*) that period has ended;

(*d*) for a period of not less than twenty-one days during the first month of that period, a copy of one of those notices was affixed to some object on the relevant land in such a position and manner as, so far as practicable, to make the notice easy for members of the public to see and read without going on to the land; and (*e*) the trustees have considered what other steps could be taken to trace the persons who are or may be beneficiaries and to inform those persons of the application to be made under section 2 above and have taken such of the steps considered by them as it was reasonably practicable for them to take.

(2) A notice under this subsection shall—

(*a*) set out the circumstances that have resulted in a trust having arisen under section 1 above;

(*b*) state that an application is to be made for the establishment of a scheme with respect to the property subject to the trust; and

(*c*) contain a warning to every beneficiary that, if he wishes to oppose the extinguishment of his rights, he should notify his claim to the trustees in the manner, and within the period, specified in the notice.

(3) Where at the time when the trustees publish a notice for the purposes of subsection (2) above—

(*a*) the relevant land is not under their control; and

(*b*) it is not reasonably practicable for them to arrange for a copy of the notice to be affixed as required by paragraph (*d*) of subsection (1) above to some object on the land,

that paragraph shall be disregarded for the purposes of this section.

(4) The requirements of this section shall not apply in the case of an application made in respect of any trust if—

(*a*) the time when that trust is treated as having arisen was before the commencement of this Act; and

(*b*) more than twelve years have elapsed since that time. **[1190]**

4. Provisions supplemental to ss 2 and 3

(1) Where an order is made under section 2 above—

(*a*) public notice of the order shall be given in such manner as the Charity Commissioners think sufficient and appropriate; and

(*b*) a copy of the order shall, for not less than one month after the date of the giving of the notice, be available for public inspection at all reasonable times at the Commissioners' office and at some convenient place in the locality where the relevant land is situated;

and a notice given for the purposes of paragraph (*a*) above shall contain such particulars of the order, or such directions for obtaining information about it, as the Commissioners think sufficient and appropriate.

(2) Subject to subsection (3) below, an appeal against an order made under section 2 above may be brought in the High Court by any of the following, that is to say—

(*a*) the Attorney General;

(*b*) the trustees of the trust established under the order;

(*c*) a beneficiary of, or the trustees of, the trust in respect of which the application for the order had been made;

(*d*) any person interested in the purposes for which the last-mentioned trustees or any of their predecessors held the relevant land before the cesser of use in consequence of which the trust arose under section 1 above;

(*e*) any two or more inhabitants of the locality where that land is situated.

(3) An appeal shall not be brought under subsection (2) above against any order—

(*a*) after the end of the period of three months beginning with the day following the date on which public notice of the order is given; or

(*b*) without either a certificate by the Charity Commissioners that it is a proper case for an appeal or the leave of the High Court,

unless it is brought by the Attorney General.

(4) Sections 40 [, 40A] and 42 of the Charities Act 1960 (supplemental provisions with respect to orders and appeals) shall apply in relation to, and to appeals against, orders under section 2 above as they apply in relation to, and to appeals against, orders under that Act.

(5) Trustees of a trust which has arisen under section 1 above may pay or apply capital money for any of the purposes of section 2 or 3 above or of this section. **[1191]**

NOTES

Sub-s (4): figure in square brackets inserted by the Charities Act 1992, s 78(1), Sch 6, para 16.

5. Orders under the Education Act 1973

(1) An order made under section 2 of the Education Act 1973 (special powers as to certain trusts for religious education) with respect to so much of any endowment as consists of—

(*a*) land in relation to which a trust under section 1 above has arisen or will arise after the land ceased or ceases to be used for particular purposes; or

(*b*) any other property subject to a trust under that section,

may extinguish any rights to which a person is or may become entitled as a beneficiary under the trust.

(2) The Secretary of State shall not by an order under section 2 of the said Act of 1973 extinguish any such rights unless he is satisfied that all reasonably practicable steps to trace the persons who are or may become entitled to any of those rights have been taken and either—

(*a*) that there is no claim by any person to be a person who is or may become so entitled—

(i) which is outstanding; or

(ii) which has at any time been accepted as valid by the trustees or by persons whose acceptance binds or will bind the trustees; or

(iii) which has been upheld in proceedings that have been concluded; or

(*b*) that consent to the making of an order under section 2 of the said Act of 1973 has been given by every person whose claim to be such a person is outstanding or has been so accepted or upheld.

(3) Where applications for the extinguishment of the rights of any beneficiaries are made with respect to the same trust property both to the Secretary of State under section 2 of the said Act of 1973 and to the Charity Commissioners under section 2 above, the Commissioners shall not consider, or further consider, the application made to them, unless the Secretary of State either—

    (*a*) consents to the application made to the Charity Commissioners being considered before the application made to him; or

    (*b*) disposes of the application made to him without extinguishing the rights of one or more of the beneficiaries.

(4) Trustees of a trust which has arisen under section 1 above may pay or apply capital money for the purposes of any provision of this section or section 2 of the said Act of 1973. **[1192]**

6. Classification of status etc of land before reverter

(1) Nothing in this Act shall require any land which is or has been the subject of any grant, conveyance or other assurance under any relevant enactment to be treated as or as having been settled land.

(2) It is hereby declared—

    (*a*) that the power conferred by section 14 of the School Sites Act 1841 (power of sale etc.) is exercisable at any time in relation to land in relation to which (but for the exercise of the power) a trust might subsequently arise under section 1 above; and

    (*b*) that the exercise of that power in respect of any land prevents any trust from arising under section 1 above in relation to that land or any land representing the proceeds of sale of that land. **[1193]**

7. Construction

(1) In this Act—

"relevant enactment" means any enactment contained in—

    (*a*) the School Sites Acts;

    (*b*) the Literary and Scientific Institutions Act 1854; or

    (*c*) the Places of Worship Sites Act 1873;

"relevant land", in relation to a trust which has arisen under section 1 above, means the land which but for this Act would have reverted to the persons who are the first beneficiaries under the trust.

(2) In this Act references to land include references to—

    (*a*) any part of any land which has been the subject of a grant, conveyance or other assurance under any relevant enactment; and

    (*b*) any land an interest in which (including any future or contingent interest arising under any such enactment) belongs to the Crown, the Duchy of Lancaster or the Duchy of Cornwall.

(3) For the purposes of this Act a claim by any person to be a beneficiary under a trust is outstanding if—

    (*a*) it has been notified to the trustees;

    (*b*) it has not been withdrawn; and

    (*c*) proceedings for determining whether it should be upheld have not been commenced or (if commenced) have not been concluded.

(4) For the purposes of this Act proceedings shall not, in relation to any person's claim, be treated as concluded where the time for appealing is unexpired or an appeal is pending unless that person has indicated his intention not to appeal or, as the case may be, not to continue with the appeal. **[1194]**

8. Consequential amendments, repeals and saving

(1) The Secretary of State shall not make a determination under paragraph 7 of Schedule 1 to the Education Act 1946 (payment to local education authority of proceeds of sale of voluntary school) in respect of any property subject to a trust which has arisen under section 1 above unless he is satisfied that adequate steps have been taken to protect the interests of the beneficiaries under the trust.

(2) . . .

(3) The enactments mentioned in the Schedule to this Act are hereby repealed to the extent specified in the third column of that Schedule.

(4) The repeals contained in the Schedule to this Act shall not affect the operation at any time after the commencement of this Act of so much of any order made before the commencement of this Act under section 2 of the Education Act 1973 as has excluded the operation of the third proviso to section 2 of the School Sites Act 1841.   **[1195]**

NOTES

    Sub-s (2): amends the Law of Property Act 1925, s 3(3).

9. Short title, commencement and extent

(1) This Act may be cited as the Reverter of Sites Act 1987.

(2) This Act shall come into force on such day as the Lord Chancellor may by order made by statutory instrument appoint.

(3) This Act shall extend to England and Wales only.   **[1196]**

SCHEDULE

Section 8

REPEALS

Chapter	Short title	Extent of repeal
15 & 16 Geo 5 c 20	The Law of Property Act 1925	In section 3(3), the words "of a statutory or other right of reverter, or". In section 7(1), the words "the School Sites Acts".
1973 c 16	The Education Act 973	In section 2(3) the words from "and in the case of" onwards.

[1197]

FAMILY LAW REFORM ACT 1987
(c 42)

ARRANGEMENT OF SECTIONS

PART I

GENERAL PRINCIPLE

*An Act to reform the law relating to the consequences of birth outside marriage ; to
make further provision with respect to the rights and duties of parents and the
determination of parentage ; and for connected purposes*   [15 May 1987]

Part I

General Principle

1. General principle

(1) In this Act and enactments passed and instruments made after the coming
into force of this section, references (however expressed) to any relationship
between two persons shall, unless the contrary intention appears, be construed
without regard to whether or not the father and mother of either of them, or the
father and mother of any peson through whom the relationship is deduced, have
or had been married to each other at any time.

(2) In this Act and enactments passed after the coming into force of this
section, unless the contrary intention appears—

    (*a*) references to a person whose father and mother were married to each
        other at the time of his birth include; and

    (*b*) references to a person whose father and mother were not married to
        each other at the time of his birth do not include,

references to any person whom subsection (3) below applies, and cognate
references shall be construed accordingly.

(3) This subsection applies to any person who—

    (*a*) is treated as legitimate by virtue of section 1 of the Legitimacy Act
        1976;

    (*b*) is a legitimated person within the meaning of section 10 of that Act;

    (*c*) is an adopted child within the meaning of Part IV of that Act 1976;
        or

    (*d*) is otherwise treated in law as legitimate.

(4) For the purpose of construing references falling within subsection (2)
above, the time of a person's birth shall be taken to include any time during the
period beginning with—

    (*a*) the insemination resulting in his birth; or

    (*b*) where there was no such insemination, his conception,

and (in either case) ending with his birth.   **[1198]**

Part III

Property Rights

18. Succession on intestacy

(1) In Part IV of the Administration of Estates Act 1925 (which deals with the
distribution of the estate of an intestate), references (however expressed) to any

relationship between two persons shall be construed in accordance with section 1 above.

(2) For the purposes of subsection (1) above and that Part of that Act, a person whose father and mother were not married to each other at the time of his birth shall be presumed not to have been survived by his father, or by any person related to him only through his father, unless the contrary is shown.

(3) In section 50(1) of that Act (which relates to the construction of documents), the reference to Part IV of that Act, or to the foregoing provisions of that Part, shall in relation to an instrument inter vivos made, or a will or codicil coming into operation, after the coming into force of this section (but not in relation to instruments inter vivos made or wills or codicils coming into operation earlier) be construed as including references to this section.

(4) This section does not affect any rights under the intestacy of a person dying before the coming into force of this section.   **[1199]**

19. Dispositions of property

(1) In the following dispositions, namely—

    (*a*) dispositions inter vivos made on or after the date on which this section comes into force; and

    (*b*) dispositions by will or codicil where the will or codicil is made on or after that date,

references (whether express or implied) to any relationship between two persons shall be construed in accordance with section 1 above.

(2) It is hereby declared that the use, without more, of the word "heir" or "heirs" or any expression which is used to create an entailed interest in real or personal property does not show a contrary intention for the purposes of section 1 as applied by subsection (1) above.

(3) In relation to the dispositions mentioned in subsection (1) above, section 33 of the Trustee Act 1925 (which specifies the trust implied by a direction that income is to be held on protective trusts for the benefit of any person) shall have effect as if any reference (however expressed) to any relationship between two persons were constructed in accordance with section 1 above.

(4) Where under any disposition of real or personal property, any interest in such property is limited (whether subject to any preceding limitation or charge or not) in such a way that it would, apart from this section, devolve (as nearly as the law permits) along with a dignity or title of honour, then—

    (*a*) whether or not the disposition contains an express reference to the dignity or title of honour; and

    (*b*) whether or not the property or some interest in the property may in some event become severed from it,

nothing in this section shall operate to sever the property or any interest in it from the dignity or title, but the property or interest shall devolve in all respects as if this section had not been enacted.

(5) This section is without prejudice to section 42 of the Adoption Act 1976 (construction of dispositions in cases of adoption).

(6) In this section "disposition" means a disposition, including an oral disposition, of real or personal property whether inter vivos or by will or codicil.

(7) Notwithstanding any rule of law, a disposition made by will or codicil

executed before the date on which this section comes into force shall not be treated for the purposes of this section as made on or after that date by reason only that the will or codicil is confirmed by a codicil executed on or after that date.   **[1200]**

21. Entitlement to grant of probate etc

(1) For the purpose of determining the person or persons who would in accordance with probate rules be entitled to a grant of probate or administration in respect of the estate of a deceased person, the deceased shall be presumed, unless the contrary is shown, not to have been survived—

> (*a*) by any person related to him whose father and mother were not married to each other at the time of his birth; or
>
> (*b*) by any person whose relationship with him is deduced through such a person as is mentioned in paragraph (*a*) above.

(2) In this section "probate rules" means rules of court made under section 127 of the Supreme Court Act 1981.

(3) This section does not apply in relation to the estate of a person dying before the coming into force of this section.   **[1201]**

LANDLORD AND TENANT ACT 1988
(c 26)

ARRANGEMENT OF SECTIONS

An Act to make new provision for imposing statutory duties in connection with covenants in tenancies against assigning, underletting, charging or parting with the possession of premises without consent   [29 July 1988]

1. Qualified duty to consent to assigning, underletting etc of premises

(1) This section applies in any case where—

> (*a*) a tenancy includes a covenant on the part of the tenant not to enter into one or more of the following transactions, that is—
>
> > (i) assigning,
> > (ii) underletting,
> > (iii) charging, or
> > (iv) parting with the possession of,
> >
> > the premises comprised in the tenancy or any part of the premises without the consent of the landlord or some other person, but
>
> (*b*) the covenant is subject to the qualification that the consent is not to be unreasonably withheld (whether or not it is also subject to any other qualification).

(2) In this section and section 2 of this Act—

(*a*) references to a proposed transaction are to any assignment, underletting, charging or parting with possession to which the covenant relates, and

(*b*) references to the person who may consent to such a transaction are to the person who under the covenant may consent to the tenant entering into the proposed transaction.

(3) Where there is served on the person who may consent to a proposed transaction a written application by the tenant for consent to the transaction, he owes a duty to the tenant within a reasonable time—

(*a*) to give consent, except in a case where it is reasonable not to give consent,

(*b*) to serve on the tenant written notice of his decision whether or not to give consent specifying in addition—

(i) if the consent is given subject to conditions, the conditions,
(ii) if the consent is withheld, the reasons for withholding it.

(4) Giving consent subject to any condition that is not a reasonable condition does not satisfy the duty under subsection (3)(*a*) above.

(5) For the purposes of this Act it is reasonable for a person not to give consent to a proposed transaction only in a case where, if he withheld consent and the tenant completed the transaction, the tenant would be in breach of a covenant.

(6) It is for the person who owed any duty under subsection (3) above—

(*a*) if he gave consent and the question arises whether he gave it within a reasonable time, to show that he did,

(*b*) if he gave consent subject to any condition and the question arises whether the condition was a reasonable condition, to show that it was,

(*c*) if he did not give consent and the question arises whether it was reasonable for him not to do so, to show that it was reasonable,

and, if the question arises whether he served notice under that subsection within a reasonable time, to show that he did.   **[1202]**

2. Duty to pass on applications

(1) If, in a case where section 1 of this Act applies, any person receives a written application by the tenant for consent to a proposed transaction and that person—

(*a*) is a person who may consent to the transaction or (though not such a person) is the landlord, and

(*b*) believes that another person, other than a person who he believes has received the application or a copy of it, is a person who may consent to the transaction,

he owes a duty to the tenant (whether or not he owes him any duty under section 1 of this Act) to take such steps as are reasonable to secure the receipt within a reasonable time by the other person of a copy of the application.

(2) The reference in section 1(3) of this Act to the service of an application on a person who may consent to a proposed transaction includes a reference to the receipt by him of an application or a copy of an application (whether it is for his consent or that of another).   **[1203]**

3. Qualified duty to approve consent by another

(1) This section applies in any case where—

>   (*a*) a tenancy includes a covenant on the part of the tenant not without the approval of the landlord to consent to the sub-tenant—

>>   (i) assigning,
>>   (ii) underletting,
>>   (iii) charging, or
>>   (iv) parting with the possession of,

the premises comprised in the sub-tenancy or any part of the premises, but

>   (*b*) the covenant is subject to the qualification that the approval is not to be unreasonably withheld (whether or not it is also subject to any other qualification).

(2) Where there is served on the landlord a written application by the tenant for approval or a copy of a written application to the tenant by the sub-tenant for consent to a transaction to which the covenant relates the landlord owes a duty to the sub-tenant within a reasonable time—

>   (*a*) to give approval, except in a case where it is reasonable not to give approval,
>   (*b*) to serve on the tenant and the sub-tenant written notice of his decision whether or not to give approval specifying in addition—

>>   (i) if approval is given subject to conditions, the conditions,
>>   (ii) if approval is withheld, the reasons for withholding it.

(3) Giving approval subject to any condition that is not a reasonable condition does not satisfy the duty under subsection (2)(*a*) above.

(4) For the purposes of this section it is reasonable for the landlord not to give approval only in a case where, if he withheld approval and the tenant gave his consent, the tenant would be in breach of covenant.

(5) It is for a landlord who owed any duty under subsection (2) above—

>   (*a*) if he gave approval and the question arises whether he gave it within a reasonable time, to show that he did,
>   (*b*) if he gave approval subject to any condition and the question arises whether the condition was a reasonable condition, to show that it was,
>   (*c*) if he did not give approval and the question arises whether it was reasonable for him not to do so, to show that it was reasonable,

and, if the question arises whether he served notice under that subsection within a reasonable time, to show that he did.   **[1204]**

4. Breach of duty

A claim that a person has broken any duty under this Act may be made the subject of civil proceedings in like manner as any other claim in tort for breach of statutory duty.   **[1205]**

5. Interpretation

(1) In this Act—

>   "covenant" includes condition and agreement,
>   "consent" includes licence,
>   "landlord" includes any superior landlord from whom the tenant's immediate landlord directly or indirectly holds,

"tenancy", subject to subsection (3) below, means any lease or other tenancy (whether made before or after the coming into force of this Act) and includes—

(*a*) a sub-tenancy, and
(*b*) an agreement for a tenancy

and references in this Act to the landlord and to the tenant are to be interpreted accordingly, and

"tenant", where the tenancy is affected by a mortgage (within the meaning of the Law of Property Act 1925) and the mortgagee proposes to exercise his statutory or express power of sale, includes the mortgagee.

(2) An application or notice is to be treated as served for the purposes of this Act if—

(*a*) served in any manner provided in the tenancy, and
(*b*) in respect of any matter for which the tenancy makes no provision, served in any manner provided by section 23 of the Landlord and Tenant Act 1927.

(3) This Act does not apply to a secure tenancy (defined in section 79 of the Housing Act 1985).

(4) This Act applies only to applications for consent or approval served after its coming into force. **[1206]**

6. Application to Crown

This Act binds the Crown; but as regards the Crown's liability in tort shall not bind the Crown further than the Crown is made liable in tort by the Crown Proceedings Act 1947. **[1207]**

7. Short title, commencement and extent

(1) This Act may be cited as the Landlord and Tenant Act 1988.

(2) This Act shall come into force at the end of the period of two months beginning with the day on which it is passed.

(3) This Act extends to England and Wales only. **[1208]**

HOUSING ACT 1988
(c 50)

ARRANGEMENT OF SECTIONS

PART I
RENTED ACCOMMODATION:

CHAPTER I ASSURED TENANCIES

Meaning of assured tenancy etc

An Act to make further provision with respect to dwelling-houses let on tenancies or occupied under licences; to amend the Rent Act 1977 and the Rent (Agriculture) Act 1976; to establish a body, Housing for Wales, having functions relating to housing associations; to amend the Housing Associations Act 1985 and to repeal and re-enact with amendments certain provisions of Part II of that Act;

to make provision for the establishment of housing action trusts for areas designated by the Secretary of State; to confer on persons approved for the purpose the right to acquire from public sector landlords certain dwelling-houses occupied by secure tenants; to make further provision about rent officers, the administration of housing benefit and rent allowance subsidy, the right to buy, repair notices and certain disposals of land and the application of capital money arising thereon; to make provision consequential upon the Housing (Scotland) Act 1988; and for connected purposes [15 November 1988]

PART I

RENTED ACCOMMODATION

CHAPTER I ASSURED TENANCIES

Meaning of assured tenancy etc

1. Assured tenancies

(1) A tenancy under which a dwelling-house is let as a separate dwelling is for the purposes of this Act an assured tenancy if and so long as—

    (a) the tenant or, as the case may be, each of the joint tenants is an individual; and

    (b) the tenant or, as the case may be, at least one of the joint tenants occupies the dwelling-house as his only or principal home; and

    (c) the tenancy is not one which, by virtue of subsection (2) or subsection (6) below, cannot be an assured tenancy.

(2) Subject to subsection (3) below, if and so long as a tenancy falls within any paragraph in Part I of Schedule 1 to this Act, it cannot be an assured tenancy; and in that Schedule—

    (a) "tenancy" means a tenancy under which a dwelling-house is let as a separate dwelling;

    (b) Part II has effect for determining the rateable value of a dwelling-house for the purposes of Part I; and

    (c) Part III has effect for supplementing paragraph 10 in Part I.

[(2A) The Secretary of State may by order replace any amount referred to in paragraphs 2 and 3A of Schedule 1 to this Act by such amount as is specified in the order; and such an order shall be made by statutory instrument which shall be subject to annulment in pursuance of a resolution of either House of Parliament.]

(3) Except as provided in Chapter V below, at the commencement of this Act, a tenancy—

    (a) under which a dwelling-house was then let as a separate dwelling, and

    (b) which immediately before that commencement was an assured tenancy for the purposes of sections 56 to 58 of the Housing Act 1980 (tenancies granted by approved bodies),

shall become an assured tenancy for the purposes of this Act.

(4) In relation to an assured tenancy falling within subsection (3) above—

    (a) Part I of Schedule 1 to this Act shall have effect, subject to subsection (5) below, as if it consisted only of paragraphs 11 and 12; and

    (b) sections 56 to 58 of the Housing Act 1980 (and Schedule 5 to that Act) shall not apply after the commencement of this Act.

(5) In any case where—

    (*a*) immediately before the commencement of this Act the landlord under a tenancy is a fully mutual housing association, and

    (*b*) at the commencement of this Act the tenancy becomes an assured tenancy by virtue of subsection (3) above,

then, so long as that association remains the landlord under that tenancy (and under any statutory periodic tenancy which arises on the coming to an end of that tenancy), paragraph 12 of Schedule 1 to this Act shall have effect in relation to that tenancy with the omission of sub-paragraph (1)(*h*).

(6) If, in pursuance of its duty under—

    (*a*) section 63 of the Housing Act 1985 (duty to house pending inquiries in case of apparent priority need),

    (*b*) section 65(3) of that Act (duty to house temporarily person found to have priority need but to have become homeless intentionally), or

    (*c*) section 68(1) of that Act (duty to house pending determination whether conditions for referral of application are satisfied),

a local housing authority have made arrangements with another person to provide accommodation, a tenancy granted by that other person in pursuance of the arrangements to a person specified by the authority cannot be an assured tenancy before the expiry of the period of twelve months beginning with the date specified in subsection (7) below unless, before the expiry of that period, the tenant is notified by the landlord (or, in the case of joint landlords, at least one of them) that the tenancy is to be regarded as an assured tenancy.

(7) The date referred to in subsection (6) above is the date on which the tenant received the notification required by section 64(1) of the Housing Act 1985 (notification of decision on question of homelessness or threatened homelessness) or, if he received a notification under section 68(3) of that Act (notification of which authority has duty to house), the date on which he received that notification. **[1209]**

NOTES
    Commencement: 1 April 1990 (sub-s (2A)); 15 January 1989 (remainder).
    Sub-s (2A): inserted by the References to Rating (Housing) Regulations 1990, SI 1990 No 434, reg 2, Schedule, para 27.

2. Letting of a dwelling-house together with other land

(1) If, under a tenancy, a dwelling-house is let together with other land, then, for the purposes of this Part of this Act,—

    (*a*) if and so long as the main purpose of the letting is the provision of a home for the tenant or, where there are joint tenants, at least one of them, the other land shall be treated as part of the dwelling-house; and

    (*b*) if and so long as the main purpose of the letting is not as mentioned in paragraph (*a*) above, the tenancy shall be treated as not being one under which a dwelling-house is let as a separate dwelling.

(2) Nothing in subsection (1) above affects any question whether a tenancy is precluded from being an assured tenancy by virtue of any provision of Schedule 1 to this Act. **[1210]**

3. Tenant sharing accommodation with persons other than landlord

(1) Where a tenant has the exclusive occupation of any accommodation (in this section referred to as "the separate accommodation") and—

    (a) the terms as between the tenant and his landlord on which he holds the separate accomodation include the use of other accommodation (in this section referred to as "the shared accommodation") in common with another person or other persons, not being or including the landlord, and

    (b) by reason only of the circumstances mentioned in paragraph (a) above, the separate accommodation would not, apart from this section, be a dwelling-house let on an assured tenancy,

the separate accommodation shall be deemed to be a dwelling-house let on an assured tenancy and the following provisions of this section shall have effect.

(2) For the avoidance of doubt it is hereby declared that where, for the purpose of determining the rateable value of the separate accommodation, it is necessary to make an apportionment under Part II of Schedule 1 to this Act, regard is to be had to the circumstances mentioned in subsection (1)(a) above.

(3) While the tenant is in possession of the separate accommodation, any term of the tenancy terminating or modifying, or providing for the termination or modification of, his right to the use of any of the shared accommodation which is living accommodation shall be of no effect.

(4) Where the terms of the tenancy are such that, at any time during the tenancy, the persons in common with whom the tenant is entitled to the use of the shared accommodation could be varied or their number could be increased, nothing in subsection (3) above shall prevent those terms from having effect so far as they relate to any such variation or increase.

(5) In this section "living accommodation" means accommodation of such a nature that the fact that it constitutes or is included in the shared accommodation is sufficient, apart from this section, to prevent the tenancy from constituting an assured tenancy of a dwelling-house. **[1211]**

4. Certain sublettings not to exclude any part of sublessor's premises from assured tenancy

(1) Where the tenant of a dwelling-house has sub-let a part but not the whole of the dwelling-house, then, as against his landlord or any superior landlord, no part of the dwelling-house shall be treated as excluded from being a dwelling-house let on an assured tenancy by reason only that the terms on which any person claiming under the tenant holds any part of the dwelling-house include the use of accommodation in common with other persons.

(2) Nothing in this section affects the rights against, and liabilities to, each other of the tenant and any person claiming under him, or of any two such persons. **[1212]**

Security of tenure

5. Security of tenure

(1) An assured tenancy cannot be brought to an end by the landlord except by obtaining an order of the court in accordance with the following provisions of this Chapter or Chapter II below or, in the case of a fixed term tenancy which contains power for the landlord to determine the tenancy in certain

circumstances, by the exercise of that power and, accordingly, the service by the landlord of a notice to quit shall be of no effect in relation to a periodic assured tenancy.

(2) If an assured tenancy which is a fixed term tenancy comes to an end otherwise than by virtue of—

(a) an order of the court, or

(b) a surrender or other action on the part of the tenant,

then, subject to section 7 and Chapter II below, the tenant shall be entitled to remain in possession of the dwelling-house let under that tenancy and, subject to subsection (4) below, his right to possession shall depend upon a periodic tenancy arising by virtue of this section.

(3) The periodic tenancy referred to in subsection (2) above is one—

(a) taking effect in possession immediately on the coming to an end of the fixed term tenancy;

(b) deemed to have been granted by the person who was the landlord under the fixed term tenancy immediately before it came to an end to the person who was then the tenant under that tenancy;

(c) under which the premises which are let are the same dwelling-house as was let under the fixed term tenancy;

(d) under which the periods of the tenancy are the same as those for which rent was last payable under the fixed term tenancy; and

(e) under which, subject to the following provisions of this Part of this Act, the other terms are the same as those of the fixed term tenancy immediately before it came to an end, except that any term which makes provision for determination by the landlord or the tenant shall not have effect while the tenancy remains an assured tenancy.

(4) The periodic tenancy referred to in subsection (2) above shall not arise if, on the coming to an end of the fixed term tenancy, the tenant is entitled, by virtue of the grant of another tenancy, to possession of the same or substantially the same dwelling-house as was let to him under the fixed term tenancy.

(5) If, on or before the date on which a tenancy is entered into or is deemed to have been granted as mentioned in subsection (3)(b) above, the person who is to be the tenant under that tenancy—

(a) enters into an obligation to do any act which (apart from this subsection) will cause the tenancy to come to an end at a time when it is an assured tenacy, or

(b) executes, signs or gives any surrender, notice to quit or other document which (apart from this subsection) has the effect of bringing the tenancy to an end at a time when it is an assured tenancy,

the obligation referred to in paragraph (a) above shall not be enforceable or, as the case may be, the surrender, notice to quit or other document referred to in paragraph (b) above shall be of no effect.

(6) If, by virtue of any provision of this Part of this Act, Part I of Schedule 1 to this Act has effect in relation to a fixed term tenancy as if it consisted only of paragraphs 11 and 12, that Part shall have the like effect in relation to any periodic tenancy which arises by virtue of this section on the coming to an end of the fixed term tenancy.

(7) Any reference in this Part of this Act to a statutory periodic tenancy is a reference to a periodic tenancy arising by virtue of this section. **[1213]**

6. Fixing of terms of statutory periodic tenancy

(1) In this section, in relation to a statutory periodic tenancy,—

    (a) "the former tenancy" means the fixed term tenancy on the coming to an end of which the statutory periodic tenancy arises; and

    (b) "the implied terms" means the terms of the tenancy which have effect by virtue of section 5(3)(e) above, other than terms as to the amount of the rent;

but nothing in the following provisions of this section applies to a statutory periodic tenancy at a time when, by virtue of paragraph 11 or paragraph 12 in Part 1 of Schedule 1 to this Act, it cannot be an assured tenancy.

(2) Not later than the first anniversary of the day on which the former tenancy came to an end, the landlord may serve on the tenant, or the tenant may serve on the landlord, a notice in the prescribed form proposing terms of the statutory periodic tenancy different from the implied terms and, if the landlord or the tenant considers it appropriate, proposing an adjustment of the amount of the rent to take account of the proposed terms.

(3) Where a notice has been served under subsection (2) above,—

    (a) within the period of three months beginning on the date on which the notice was served on him, the landlord or the tenant, as the case may be, may, by an application in the prescribed form, refer the notice to a rent assessment committee under subsection (4) below; and

    (b) if the notice is not so referred, then, with effect from such date, not falling within the period referred to in paragraph (a) above, as may be specified in the notice, the terms proposed in the notice shall become terms of the tenancy in substitution for any of the implied terms dealing with the same subject matter and the amount of the rent shall be varied in accordance with any adjustment so proposed.

(4) Where a notice under subsection (2) above is referred to a rent assessment committee, the committee shall consider the terms proposed in the notice and shall determine whether those terms, or some other terms (dealing with the same subject matter as the proposed terms), are such as, in the committee's opinion, might reasonably be expected to be found in an assured periodic tenancy of the dwelling-house concerned, being a tenancy—

    (a) which begins on the coming to an end of the former tenancy; and

    (b) which is granted by a willing landlord on terms which, except in so far as they relate to the subject matter of the proposed terms, are those of the statutory periodic tenancy at the time of the committee's consideration.

(5) Whether or not a notice under subsection (2) above proposes an adjustment of the amount of the rent under the statutory periodic tenancy, where a rent assessment committee determine any terms under subsection (4) above, they shall, if they consider it appropriate, specify such an adjustment to take account of the terms so determined.

(6) In making a determination under subsection (4) above, or specifying an adjustment of an amount of rent under subsection (5) above, there shall be disregarded any effect on the terms or the amount of the rent attributable to the granting of a tenancy to a sitting tenant.

(7) Where a notice under subsection (2) above is referred to a rent assessment

committee, then, unless the landlord and the tenant otherwise agree, with effect from such date as the committee may direct—

(a) the terms determined by the committee shall become terms of the statutory periodic tenancy in substitution for any of the implied terms dealing with the same subject matter; and

(b) the amount of the rent under the statutory periodic tenancy shall be altered to accord with any adjustment specified by the committee;

but for the purposes of paragraph (b) above the committee shall not direct a date earlier than the date specified, in accordance with subsection (3)(b) above, in the notice referred to them.

(8) Nothing in this section requires a rent assessment committee to continue with a determination under subsection (4) above if the landlord and tenant give notice in writing that they no longer require such a determination or if the tenancy has come to an end. **[1214]**

7. Orders for possession

(1) The court shall not make an order for possession of a dwelling-house let on an assured tenancy except on one or more of the grounds set out in Schedule 2 to this Act; but nothing in this Part of this Act relates to proceedings for possession of such a dwelling-house which are brought by a mortgagee, within the meaning of the Law of Property Act 1925, who has lent money on the security of the assured tenancy.

(2) The following provisions of this section have effect, subject to section 8 below, in relation to proceedings for the recovery of possession of a dwelling-house let on an assured tenancy.

(3) If the court is satisfied that any of the grounds in Part I of Schedule 2 to this Act is established then, subject to [subsections (5A) and (6)] below, the court shall make an order for possession.

(4) If the court is satisfied that any of the grounds in Part II of Schedule 2 to this Act is established, then, subject to [subsections (5A) and (6)] below, the court may make an order for possession if it considers it reasonable to do so.

(5) Part III of Schedule 2 to this Act shall have effect for supplementing Ground 9 in that Schedule and Part IV of that Schedule shall have effect in relation to notices given as mentioned in Grounds 1 to 5 of that Schedule.

[(5A) The court shall not make an order for possession of a dwelling-house let on an assured periodic tenancy arising under Schedule 10 to the Local Government and Housing Act 1989 on any of the following grounds, that is to say,—

(a) Grounds 1, 2 and 5 in Part I of Schedule 2 to this Act;

(b) Ground 16 in Part II of that Schedule; and

(c) if the assured periodic tenancy arose on the termination of a former 1954 Act tenancy, within the meaning of the said Schedule 10, Ground 6 in Part I of Schedule 2 to this Act.]

(6) The court shall not make an order for possession of a dwelling-house to take effect at a time when it is let on an assured fixed term tenancy unless—

(a) the ground for possession is Ground 2 or Ground 8 in Part I of Schedule 2 to this Act or any of the grounds in Part II of that Schedule, other than Ground 9 or Ground 16; and (*b*) the terms of the tenancy make provision for it to be brought to an end on the ground in question (whether that provision takes the form of a provision for re-entry, for forfeiture, for determination by notice or otherwise).

(7) Subject to the preceding provisions of this section, the court may make an order for possession of a dwelling-house on grounds relating to a fixed term tenancy which has come to an end; and where an order is made in such circumstances, any statutory periodic tenancy which has arisen on the ending of the fixed term tenancy shall end (without any notice and regardless of the period) on the day on which the order takes effect. **[1215]**

NOTES
Commencement: 1 April 1990 (sub-s (5A)); 15 January 1989 (remainder).
Sub-s (3): words in square brackets substituted by the Local Government and Housing Act 1989, s 194, Sch 11, para 101.
Sub-s (4): words in square brackets substituted by the Local Government and Housing Act 1989, s 194, Sch 11, para 101.
Sub-s (5A): inserted by the Local Government and Housing Act 1989, s 194, Sch 11, para 101.

8. Notice of proceedings for possession

(1) The court shall not entertain proceedings for possession of a dwelling-house let on an assured tenancy unless—

(*a*) the landlord or, in the case of joint landlords, at least one of them has served on the tenant a notice in accordance with this section and the proceedings are begun within the time limits stated in the notice in accordance with subsections (3) and (4) below; or

(*b*) the court considers it just and equitable to dispense with the requirement of such a notice.

(2) The court shall not make an order for possession on any of the grounds in Schedule 2 to this Act unless that ground and particulars of it are specified in the notice under this section; but the grounds specified in such a notice may be altered or added to with the leave of the court.

(3) A notice under this section is one in the prescribed form informing the tenant that—

(*a*) the landlord intends to begin proceedings for possession of the dwelling-house on one or more of the grounds specified in the notice; and

(*b*) those proceedings will not begin earlier than a date specified in the notice which, without prejudice to any additional limitation under subsection (4) below, shall not be earlier than the expiry of the period of two weeks from the date of service of the notice; and

(*c*) those proceedings will not begin later than twelve months from the date of service of the notice.

(4) If a notice under this section specifies, in accordance with subsection (3)(*a*) above, any of Grounds 1, 2, 5 to 7, 9 and 16 in Schedule 2 to this Act (whether with or without other grounds), the date specified in the notice as mentioned in subsection (3)(*b*) above shall not be earlier than—

(*a*) two months from the date of service of the notice; and

(*b*) if the tenancy is a periodic tenancy, the earliest date on which, apart from section 5(1) above, the tenancy could be brought to an end by a notice to quit given by the landlord on the same date as the date of service of the notice under this section.

(5) The court may not exercise the power conferred by subsection (1)(*b*) above if the landlord seeks to recover possession on Ground 8 in Schedule 2 to this Act.

(6) Where a notice under this section—

    (*a*) is served at a time when the dewlling-house is let on a fixed term tenancy, or

    (*b*) is served after a fixed term tenancy has come to an end but relates (in whole or in part) to events occurring during that tenancy,

the notice shall have effect notwithstanding that the tenant becomes or has become tenant under a statutory periodic tenancy arising on the coming to an end of the fixed term tenancy. **[1216]**

9. Extended discretion of court in possession claims

(1) Subject to subsection (6) below, the court may adjourn for such period or periods as it thinks fit proceedings for possession of a dwelling-house let on an assured tenancy.

(2) On the making of an order for possession of a dwelling-house let on an assured tenancy or at any time before the execution of such an order, the court, subject to subsection (6) below, may—

    (*a*) stay or suspend excecution of the order, or

    (*b*) postpone the date of possession,

for such period or periods as the court thinks just.

(3) On any such adjournment as is referred to in subsection (1) above or on any such stay, suspension or postponement as is referred to in subsection (2) above, the court, unless it considers that to do so would cause exceptional hardship to the tenant or would otherwise be unreasonable, shall impose conditions with regard to payment by the tenant of arrears of rent (if any) and rent or payments in respect of occupation after the termination of the tenancy (mesne profits) and may impose such other conditions as it thinks fit.

(4) If such conditions as are referred to in subsection (3) above are complied with, the court may, if it thinks fit, discharge or rescind any such order as is referred to in subsection (2) above.

(5) In any case where—

    (*a*) at a time when proceedings are brought for possession of a dwelling-house let on an assured tenancy, the tenant's spouse or former spouse, having rights of occupation under the Matrimonial Homes Act 1983, is in occupation of the dwelling-house, and

    (*b*) the assured tenancy is terminated as a result of those proceedings,

the spouse or former spouse, so long as he or she remains in occupation, shall have the same rights in relation to, or in connection with, any such adjournment as is referred to in subsection (1) above or any such stay, suspension or postponement as is referred to in subsection (2) above, as he or she would have if those rights of occupation were not affected by the termination of the tenancy.

(6) This section does not apply if the court is satisfied that the landlord is entitled to possession of the dwelling-house—

    (*a*) on any of the grounds in Part I of Schedule 2 to this Act; or

    (*b*) by virtue of subsection (1) or subsection (4) of section 21 below. **[1217]**

10. Special provisions applicable to shared accommodation

(1) This section applies in a case falling within subsection (1) of section 3 above and expressions used in this section have the same meaning as in that section.

(2) Without prejudice to the enforcement of any order made under subsection (3) below, while the tenant is in possession of the separate accommodation, no order shall be made for possession of any of the shared accommodation, whether on the application of the immediate landlord of the tenant or on the application of any person under whom that landlord derives title, unless a like order has been made, or is made at the same time, in respect of the separate accommodation; and the provisions of section 6 above shall have effect accordingly.

(3) On the application of the landlord, the court may make such order as it thinks just either—

    (a) terminating the right of the tenant to use the whole or any part of the shared accommodation other than living accommodation; or

    (b) modifying his right to use the whole or any part of the shared accommodation, whether by varying the persons or increasing the number of persons entitled to the use of that accommodation or otherwise.

(4) No order shall be made under subsection (3) above so as to effect any termination or modification of the rights of the tenant which, apart from section 3(3) above, could not be effected by or under the terms of the tenancy. **[1218]**

11. Payment of removal expenses in certain cases

(1) Where a court makes an order for possession of a dwelling-house let on an assured tenancy on Ground 6 or Ground 9 in Schedule 2 to this Act (but not on any other ground), the landlord shall pay to the tenant a sum equal to the reasonable expenses likely to be incurred by the tenant in removing from the dwelling-house.

(2) Any question as to the amount of the sum referred to in subsection (1) above shall be determined by agreement between the landlord and the tenant or, in default of agreement, by the court.

(3) Any sum payable to a tenant by virtue of this section shall be recoverable as a civil debt due from the landlord. **[1219]**

12. Compensation for misrepresentation or concealment

Where a landlord obtains an order for possession of a dwelling-house let on an assured tenancy on one or more of the grounds in Schedule 2 to this Act and it is subsequently made to appear to the court that the order was obtained by misrepresentation or concealment of material facts, the court may order the landlord to pay to the former tenant such sum as appears sufficient as compensation for damage or loss sustained by that tenant as a result of the order. **[1220]**

Rent and other terms

13. Increases of rent under assured periodic tenancies

(1) This section applies to—

    (*a*) a statutory periodic tenancy other than one which, by virtue of paragraph 11 or paragraph 12 in Part I of Schedule 1 to this Act, cannot for the time being be an assured tenancy; and

    (*b*) any other periodic tenancy which is an assured tenancy, other than one in relation to which there is a provision, for the time being binding on the tenant, under which the rent for a particular period of the tenancy will or may be greater than the rent for an earlier period.

(2) For the purpose of securing an increase in the rent under a tenancy to which this section applies, the landlord may serve on the tenant a notice in the prescribed form proposing a new rent to take effect at the beginning of a new period of the tenancy specified in the notice, being a period beginning not earlier than—

    (*a*) the minimum period after the date of the service of the notice; and

    (*b*) except in the case of a statutory periodic tenancy, the first anniversary of the date on which the first period of the tenancy began; and

    (*c*) if the rent under the tenancy has previously been increased by virtue of a notice under this subsection or a determination under section 14 below, the first anniversary of the date on which the increased rent took effect.

(3) The minimum period referred to in subsection (2) above is—

    (*a*) in the case of a yearly tenancy, six months;

    (*b*) in the case of a tenancy where the period is less than a month, one month; and

    (*c*) in any other case, a period equal to the period of the tenancy.

(4) Where a notice is served under subsection (2) above, a new rent specified in the notice shall take effect as mentioned in the notice unless, before the beginning of the new period specified in the notice,—

    (*a*) the tenant by an application in the prescribed form refers the notice to a rent assessment committee; or

    (*b*) the landlord and the tenant agree on a variation of the rent which is different from that proposed in the notice or agree that the rent should not be varied.

(5) Nothing in this section (or in section 14 below) affects the right of the landlord and the tenant under an assured tenancy to vary by agreement any term of the tenancy (including a term relating to rent). **[1221]**

14. Determination of rent by rent assessment committee

(1) Where, under subsection (4)(*a*) of section 13 above, a tenant refers to a rent assessment committee a notice under subsection (2) of that section, the committee shall determine the rent at which, subject to subsections (2) and (4) below, the committee consider that the dwelling-house concerned might reasonably be expected to be let in the open market by a willing landlord under an assured tenancy—

    (*a*) which is a periodic tenancy having the same periods as those of the tenancy to which the notice relates;

    (*b*) which begins at the beginning of the new period specified in the notice;

    (*c*) the terms of which (other than relating to the amount of the rent) are the same as those of the tenancy to which the notice relates; and

    (*d*) in respect of which the same notices, if any, have been given under any of Grounds 1 to 5 of Schedule 2 to this Act, as have been given (or have effect as if given) in relation to the tenancy to which the notice relates.

(2) In making a determination under this section, there shall be disregarded—

(a) any effect on the rent attributable to the granting of a tenancy to a sitting tenant;

(b) any increase in the value of the dwelling-house attributable to a relevant improvement carried out by a person who at the time it was carried out was the tenant, if the improvement—

    (i) was carried out otherwise than in pursuance of an obligation to his immediate landlord, or

    (ii) was carried out pursuant to an obligation to his immediate landlord being an obligation which did not relate to the specific improvement concerned but arose by reference to consent given to the carrying out of that improvement; and

(c) any reduction in the value of the dwelling-house attributable to a failure by the tenant to comply with any terms of the tenancy.

(3) For the purposes of subsection (2)(b) above, in relation to a notice which is referred by a tenant as mentioned in subsection (1) above, an improvement is a relevant improvement if either it was carried out during the tenancy to which the notice relates or the following conditions are satisfied, namely—

(a) that it was carried out not more than twenty-one years before the date of service of the notice; and

(b) that, at all times during the period beginning when the improvement was carried out and ending on the date of service of the notice, the dwelling-house has been let under an assured tenancy; and

(c) that, on the coming to an end of an assured tenancy at any time during that period, the tenant (or, in the case of joint tenants, at least one of them) did not quit.

[(3A) In making a determination under this section in any case where under Part I of the Local Government Finance Act 1992 the landlord or a superior landlord is liable to pay council tax in respect of a hereditament ("the relevant hereditament") of which the dwelling-house forms part, the rent assessment committee shall have regard to the amount of council tax which, as at the date on which the notice under section 13(2) above was served, was set by the billing authority—

(a) for the financial year in which that notice was served, and

(b) for the category of dwellings within which the relevant hereditament fell on that date,

but any discount or other reduction affecting the amount of council tax payable shall be disregarded.

(3B) In subsection (3A) above—

(a) "hereditament" means a dwelling within the meaning of Part I of the Local Government Finance Act 1992,

(b) "billing authority" has the meaning as in that Part of that Act, and

(c) "category of dwellings" has the same meaning as in section 30(1) and (2) of that Act.]

(4) In this section "rent" does not include any service charge, within the meaning of section 18 of the Landlord and Tenant Act 1985, but, subject to that, includes any sums payable by the tenant to the landlord on account of the

use of furniture [, in respect of council tax] or for any of the matters referred to in subsection (1)(*a*) of that section, whether or not those sums are separate from the sums payable for the occupation of the dwelling-house concerned or are payable under separate agreements.

(5) Where any rates in respect of the dwelling-house concerned are borne by the landlord or a superior landlord, the rent assessment committee shall make their determination under this section as if the rates were not so borne.

(6) In any case where—

(*a*) a rent assessment committee have before them at the same time the reference of a notice under section 6(2) above relating to a tenancy (in this subsection referred to as "the section 6 reference") and the reference of a notice under section 13(2) above relating to the same tenancy (in this subsection referred to as "the section 13 reference"), and

(*b*) the date specified in the notice under section 6(2) above is not later than the first day of the new period specified in the notice under section 13(2) above, and

(*c*) the committee propose to hear the two references together,

the committee shall make a determination in relation to the section 6 reference before making their determination in relation to the section 13 reference and, accordingly, in such a case the reference in subsection (1)(*c*) above to the terms of the tenancy to which the notice relates shall be construed as a reference to those terms as varied by virtue of the determination made in relation to the section 6 reference.

(7) Where a notice under section 13(2) above has been referred to a rent assessment committee, then, unless the landlord and the tenant otherwise agree, the rent determined by the committee (subject, in a case where subsection (5) above applies, to the addition of the appropriate amount in respect of rates) shall be the rent under the tenancy with effect from the beginning of the new period specified in the notice or, if it appears to the rent assessment committee that that would cause undue hardship to the tenant, with effect from such later date (not being later than the date the rent is determied) as the committee may direct.

(8) Nothing in this section requires a rent assessment committee to continue with their determination of a rent for a dwelling-house if the landlord and tenant give notice in writing that they no longer require such a determination or if the tenancy has come to an end.   **[1222]**

NOTES
    Commencement: 1 April 1993 (sub-ss (3A), (3B)); 15 January 1989 (remainder).
    Sub-s (3A): inserted with savings by the Local Government Finance (Housing) (Consequential Amendments) Order 1993, SI 1993 No 651, arts 1(2), 2(1), Sch 1, para 17(2).
    Sub-s (3B): inserted with savings by the Local Government Finance (Housing) (Consequential Amendments) Order 1993, SI 1993 No 651, arts 1(2), 2(1), Sch 1, para 17(2).
    Sub-s (4): words in square brackets inserted with savings by the Local Government Finance (Housing) (Consequential Amendments) Order 1993, SI 1993 No 651, arts 1(2), 2(1), Sch 1, para 17(3).

[14A. Interim increase before 1st April 1994 of rent under assured periodic tenancies in certain cases where landlord liable for council tax

(1) In any case where—

(*a*) under Part I of the Local Government Finance Act 1992 the landlord of a dwelling-house let under an assured tenancy to which section 13 above applies or a superior landlord is liable to pay council tax in respect of a dwelling (within the meaning of that Part of that Act) which includes that dwelling-house,

(b) under the terms of the tenancy (or an agreement collateral to the tenancy) the tenant is liable to make payments to the landlord in respect of council tax,

(c) the case falls within subsection (2) or subsection (3) below, and

(d) no previous notice under this subsection has been served in relation to the dwelling-house,

the landlord may serve on the tenant a notice in the prescribed form proposing an increased rent to take account of the tenant's liability to make payments to the landlord in respect of council tax, such increased rent to take effect at the beginning of a new period of the tenency specified in the notice being a period beginning not earlier than one month after the date on which the notice was served.

(2) The case falls within this subsection if—

(a) the rent under the tenancy has previously been increased by virtue of a notice under section 13(2) above or a determination under section 14 above, and

(b) the first anniversary of the date on which the increased rent took effect has not yet occurred.

(3) The case falls within this subsection if a notice has been served under section 13(2) above before 1st April 1993 but no increased rent has taken effect before that date.

(4) No notice may be served under subsection (1) above after 31st march 1994.

(5) Where a notice is served under subsection (1) above, the new rent specified in the notice shall take effect as mentioned in the notice unless, before the beginning of the new period specified in the notice—

(a) the tenant by an application in the prescribed form refers the notice to a rent assessment committee, or

(b) the landlord and the tenant agree on a variation of the rent which is different from that proposed in the notice or agree that the rent should not be varied.

(6) Nothing in this section (or in section 14B below) affects the right of the landlord and the tenant under an assured tenancy to vary by agreement any term of the tenancy (including a term relating to rent).]   **[1222A]**

NOTES
Commencement: 1 April 1993.
Inserted by the Local Government Finance (Housing) (Consequential Amendments) Order 1993, SI 1993 No 651, art 2(2), Sch 2, para 8.

[14B. Interim determination of rent by rent assessment committee

(1) Where, under subsection (5)(a) of section 14A above, a tenant refers to a rent assessment committee a notice under subsection (1) of that section, the committee shall determine the amount by which, having regard to the provisions of section 14(3A) above, the existing rent might reasonably be increased to take account of the tenant's liability to make payments to the landlord in respect of council tax.

(2) Where a notice under section 14A(1) above has been referred to a rent assessment committee, then, unless the landlord and the tenant otherwise agree, the existing rent shall be increased by the amount determined by the committee with effect from the beginning of the new period specified in the notice or, if it appears to the committee that that would cause undue hardship to the tenant, with effect from such later date (not being later than the date the increase is determined) as the committee may direct.

(3) In any case where—

(a) a rent assessment committee have before them at the same time the reference of a notice under section 13(2) above relating to a tenancy (in this subsection referred to as "the section 13 reference") and the reference of a notice under section 14A(1) above relating to the same tenancy (in this subsection referred to as "the section 14A reference"); and

(b) the committee propose to hear the two references together,

the committee shall make a determination in relation to the section 13 reference before making their determination in relation to the section 14A reference, and if in such a case the date specified in the notice under section 13(2) above is later than the date specified in the notice under section 14A(1) above, the rent determined under the section 14A reference shall not take effect until the date specified in the notice under section 13(2).

(4) In this section "rent" has the same meaning as in section 14 above; and section 14(4) above applies to a determination under this section as it applies to a determination under that section.]   **[1222B]**

NOTES
Commencement: 1 April 1993.
Inserted by the Local Government Finance (Housing) (Consequential Amendments) Order 1993, SI 1993 No 651, art 2(2), Sch 2, para 8.

15. Limited prohibition on assignment etc without consent

(1) Subject to subsection (3) below, it shall be an implied term of every assured tenancy which is a periodic tenancy that, except with the consent of the landlord, the tenant shall not—

(a) assign the tenancy (in whole or in part); or

(b) sub-let or part with possession of the whole or any part of the dwelling-house let on the tenancy.

(2) Section 19 of the Landlord and Tenant Act 1927 (consents to assign not to be unreasonably withheld etc.) shall not apply to a term which is implied into an assured tenancy by subsection (1) above.

(3) In the case of a periodic tenancy which is not a statutory periodic tenancy [or an assured periodic tenancy arising under Schedule 10 to the Local Government and Housing Act 1989] subsection (1) above does not apply if—

(a) there is a provision (whether contained in the tenancy or not) under which the tenant is prohibited (whether absolutely or conditionally) from assigning or sub-letting or parting with possession or is permitted (whether absolutely or conditionally) to assign, sub-let or part with possession; or

(b) a premium is required to be paid on the grant or renewal of the tenancy.

(4) In subsection (3)(b) above "premium" includes—

(a) any fine or other like sum;
(b) any other pecuniary consideration in addition to rent; and
(c) any sum paid by way of deposit, other than one which does not exceed one-sixth of the annual rent payable under the tenancy immediately after the grant or renewal in question.   **[1223]**

NOTES
Sub-s (3): words in square brackets inserted by the Local Government and Housing Act 1989, s 194, Sch 11, para 102.

16. Access for repairs

It shall be an implied term of every assured tenancy that the tenant shall afford to the landlord access to the dwelling-house let on the tenancy and all reasonable facilities for executing therein any repairs which the landlord is entitled to execute.   **[1224]**

Miscellaneous

17. Succession to assured periodic tenancy by spouse

(1) In any case where—

(a) the sole tenant under an assured periodic tenancy dies, and
(b) immediately before the death, the tenant's spouse was occupying the dwelling-house as his or her only or principal home, and
(c) the tenant was not himself a successor, as defined in subsection (2) or subsection (3) below,

then, on the death, the tenancy vests by virtue of this section in the spouse (and, accordingly, does not devolve under the tenant's will or intestacy).

(2) For the purposes of this section, a tenant is a successor in relation to a tenancy if—

(a) the tenancy became vested in him either by virtue of this section or under the will or intestacy of a previous tenant; or
(b) at some time before the tenant's death the tenancy was a joint tenancy held by himself and one or more other persons and, prior to his death, he became the sole tenant by survivorship; or
(c) he became entitled to the tenancy as mentioned in section 39(5) below.

(3) For the purposes of this section, a tenant is also a successor in relation to a tenancy (in this subsection referred to as "the new tenancy") which was granted to him (alone or jointly with others) if—

(a) at some time before the grant of the new tenancy, he was, by virtue of subsection (2) above, a successor in relation to an earlier tenancy of the same or substantially the same dwelling-house as is let under the new tenancy; and
(b) at all times since he became such a successor he has been a tenant (alone or jointly with others) of the dwelling-house which is let under the new tenancy or of a dwelling-house which is substantially the same as that dwelling-house.

(4) For the purposes of this section, a person who was living with the tenant as his or her wife or husband shall be treated as the tenant's spouse.

(5) If, on the death of the tenant, there is, by virtue of subsection (4) above, more than one person who fulfils the condition in subsection (1)(b) above, such

one of them as may be decided by agreement or, in default of agreement, by the county court shall be treated as the tenant's spouse for the purposes of this section.   **[1225]**

18. Provisions as to reversions on assured tenancies

(1) If at any time—

(a) a dwelling-house is for the time being lawfully let on an assured tenancy, and

(b) the landlord under the assured tenancy is himself a tenant under a superior tenancy; and

(c) the superior tenancy comes to an end,

then, subject to subsection (2) below, the assured tenancy shall continue in existence as a tenancy held of the person whose interest would, apart from the continuance of the assured tenancy, entitle him to actual possession of the dwelling-house at that time.

(2) Subsection (1) above does not apply to an assured tenancy if the interest which, by virtue of that subsection, would become that of the landlord, is such that, by virtue of Schedule 1 to this Act, the tenancy could not be an assured tenancy.

(3) Where, by virtue of any provision of this Part of this Act, an assured tenancy which is a periodic tenancy (including a statutory periodic tenancy) continues beyond the beginning of a reversionary tenancy which was granted (whether before, on or after the commmencement of this Act) so as to begin on or after—

(a) the date on which the previous contractual assured tenancy came to an end, or

(b) a date on which, apart from any provision of this Part, the periodic tenancy could have been brought to an end by the landlord by notice to quit,

the reversionary tenancy shall have effect as if it had been granted subject to the periodic tenancy.

(4) The reference in subsection (3) above to the previous contractual assured tenancy applies only where the periodic tenancy referred to in that subsection is a statutory periodic tenancy and is a reference to the fixed-term tenancy which immediately preceded the statutory periodic tenancy.   **[1226]**

19. Restriction on levy of distress for rent

(1) Subject to subsection (2) below, no distress for the rent of any dwelling-house let on an assured tenancy shall be levied except with the leave of the county court; and, with respect to any application for such leave, the court shall have the same powers with respect to adjournment, stay, suspension, postponement and otherwise as are conferred by section 9 above in relation to proceedings for possession of such a dwelling-house.

(2) Nothing in subsection (1) above applies to distress levied under section 102 of the County Courts Act 1984.   **[1227]**

CHAPTER II ASSURED SHORTHOLD TENANCIES

20. Assured shorthold tenancies

(1) Subject to subsection (3) below, an assured shorthold tenancy is an assured tenancy—

    (a) which is a fixed term tenancy granted for a term certain of not less than six months; and

    (b) in respect of which there is no power for the landlord to determine the tenancy at any time earlier than six months from the beginning of the tenancy; and

    (c) in respect of which a notice is served as mentioned in subsection (2) below.

(2) The notice referred to in subsection (1)(c) above is one which—

    (a) is in such form as may be prescribed;

    (b) is served before the assured tenancy is entered into;

    (c) is served by the person who is to be the landlord under the assured tenancy on the person who is to be the tenant under that tenancy; and

    (d) states that the assured tenancy to which it relates is to be a shorthold tenancy.

(3) Notwithstanding anything in subsection (1) above, where—

    (a) immediately before a tenancy (in this subsection referred to as "the new tenancy") is granted, the person to whom it is granted or, as the case may be, at least one of the persons to whom it is granted was a tenant under an assured tenancy which was not a shorthold tenancy, and

    (b) the new tenancy is granted by the person who, immediately before the beginning of the tenancy, was the landlord under the assured tenancy referred to in paragraph (a) above,

the new tenancy cannot be an assured shorthold tenancy.

    (4) Subject to subsection (5) below, if, on the coming to an end of an assured shorthold tenancy (including a tenancy which was an assured shorthold but ceased to be assured before it came to an end), a new tenancy of the same or substantially the same premises comes into being under which the landlord and the tenant are the same as at the coming to an end of the earlier tenancy, then, if and so long as the new tenancy is an assured tenancy, it shall be an assured shorthold tenancy, whether or not it fulfils the conditions in paragraphs (a) to (c) of subsection (1) above.

    (5) Subsection (4) above does not apply if, before the new tenancy is entered into (or, in the case of a statutory periodic tenancy, takes effect in possession), the landlord serves notice on the tenant that the new tenancy is not to be a shorthold tenancy.

    (6) In the case of joint landlords—

    (a) the reference in subsection (2)(c) above to the person who is to be the landlord is a reference to at least one of the persons who are to be joint landlords; and

    (b) the reference in subsection (5) above to the landlord is a reference to at least one of the joint landlords.

(7) Section 14 above shall apply in relation to an assured shorthold tenancy as if in subsection (1) of that section the reference to an assured tenancy were a reference to an assured shorthold tenancy. **[1228]**

21. Recovery of possession on expiry or termination of assured shorthold tenancy

(1) Without prejudice to any right of the landlord under an assured shorthold tenancy to recover possession of the dwelling-house let on the tenancy in accordance with Chapter I above, on or after the coming to an end of an assured shorthold tenancy which was a fixed term tenancy, a court shall make an order for possession of the dwelling-house if it is satisfied—

    (*a*) that the assured shorthold tenancy has come to an end and no further assured tenancy (whether shorthold or not) is for the time being in existence, other than [an assured shorthold periodic tenancy (whether statutory or not)]; and

    (*b*) the landlord or, in the case of joint landlords, at least one of them has given to the tenant not less than two months' notice stating that he requires possession of the dwelling-house.

(2) A notice under paragraph (*b*) of subsection (1) above may be given before or on the day on which the tenancy comes to an end; and that subsection shall have effect notwithstanding that on the coming to an end of the fixed term tenancy a statutory periodic tenancy arises.

(3) Where a court makes an order for possession of a dwelling-house by virtue of subsection (1) above, any statutory periodic tenancy which has arisen on the coming to an end of the assured shorthold tenancy shall end (without further notice and regardless of the period) on the day on which the order takes effect.

(4) Without prejudice to any such right as is referred to in subsection (1) above, a court shall make an order for possession of a dwelling-house let on an assured shorthold tenancy which is a periodic tenancy if the court is satisfied—

    (*a*) that the landlord or, in the case of joint landlords, at least one of them has given to the tenant a notice stating that, after a date specified in the notice, being the last day of a period of the tenancy and not earlier than two months after the date the notice was given, possession of the dwelling-house is required by virtue of this section; and

    (*b*) that the date specified in the notice under paragraph (*a*) above is not earlier than the earliest day on which, apart from section 5(1) above, the tenancy could be brought to an end by a notice to quit given by the landlord on the same date as the notice under paragraph (*a*) above. **[1229]**

NOTES
    Sub-s (1): words in square brackets substituted by the Local Government and Housing Act 1989, s 194, Sch 11, para 103.

22. Reference of excessive rents to rent assessment committee

(1) Subject to section 23 and subsection (2) below, the tenant under an assured shorthold tenancy in respect of which a notice was served as mentioned in section 20(2) above may make an application in the prescribed form to a rent assessment committee for a determination of the rent which, in the committee's opinion, the landlord might reasonably be expected to obtain under the assured shorthold tenancy.

(2) No application may be made under this section if—

(a) the rent payable under the tenancy is a rent previously determined under this section; or

(b) the tenancy is an assured shorthold tenancy falling within subsection (4) of section 20 above (and, accordingly, is one in respect of which notice need not have been served as mentioned in subsection (2) of that section).

(3) Where an application is made to a rent assessment committee under subsection (1) above with respect to the rent under an assured shorthold tenancy, the committee shall not make such a determination as is referred to in that subsection unless they consider—

(a) that there is a sufficient number of similar dwelling-houses in the locality let on assured tenancies (whether shorthold or not); and

(b) that the rent payable under the assured shorthold tenancy in question is significantly higher than the rent which the landlord might reasonably be expected to be able to obtain under the tenancy, having regard to the level of rents payable under the tenancies referred to in paragraph (a) above.

(4) Where, on an application under this section, a rent assessment committee make a determination of a rent for an assured shorthold tenancy—

(a) the determination shall have effect from such date as the committee may direct, not being earlier than the date of the application;

(b) if, at any time on or after the determination takes effect, the rent which, apart from this paragraph, would be payable under the tenancy exceeds the rent so determined, the excess shall be irrecoverable from the tenant; and

(c) no notice may be served under section 13(2) above with respect to a tenancy of the dwelling-house in question until after the first anniversary of the date on which the determination takes effect.

(5) Subsections (4), (5) and (8) of section 14 above apply in relation to a determination of rent under this section as they apply in relation to a determination under that section and, accordingly, where subsection (5) of that section applies, any reference in subsection (4)(b) above to rent is a reference to rent exclusive of the amount attributable to rates. **[1230]**

23. Termination of rent assessment committee's functions

(1) If the Secretary of State by order made by statutory instrument so provides, section 22 above shall not apply in such cases or to tenancies of dwelling-houses in such areas or in such other circumstances as may be specified in the order.

(2) An order under this section may contain such transitional, incidental and supplementary provisions as appear to the Secretary of State to be desirable.

(3) No order shall be made under this section unless a draft of the order has been laid before, and approved by a resolution of, each House of Parliament. **[1231]**

CHAPTER IV
PROTECTION FROM EVICTION

27. Damages for unlawful eviction

(1) This section applies if, at any time after 9th June 1988, a landlord (in this section referred to as "the landlord in default") or any person acting on behalf

of the landlord in default unlawfully deprives the residential occupier of any premises of his occupation of the whole or part of the premises.

(2) This section also applies if, at any time after 9th June 1988, a landlord (in this section referred to as "the landlord in default") or any person acting on behalf of the landlord in default—

    (*a*) attempts unlawfully to deprive the residential occupier of any premises of his occupation of the whole or part of the premises, or

    (*b*) knowing or having reasonable cause to believe that the conduct is likely to cause the residential occupier of any premises—

        (i) to give up his occupation of the premises or any part thereof, or

        (ii) to refrain from exercising any right or pursuing any remedy in respect of the premises or any part thereof,

    does acts likely to interfere with the peace or comfort of the residential occupier or members of his household, or persistently withdraws or withholds services reasonably required for the occupation of the premises as a residence,

and, as a result, the residential occupier gives up his occupation of the premises as a residence.

(3) Subject to the following provisions of this section, where this section applies, the landlord in default shall, by virtue of this section, be liable to pay to the former residential occupier, in respect of his loss of the right to occupy the premises in question as his residence, damages assessed on the basis set out in section 28 below.

(4) Any liability arising by virtue of subsection (3) above—

    (*a*) shall be in the nature of a liability in tort; and

    (*b*) subject to subsection (5) below, shall be in addition to any liability arising apart from this section (whether in tort, contract or otherwise).

(5) Nothing in this section affects the right of a residential occupier to enforce any liability which arises apart from this section in respect of his loss of the right to occupy premises as his residence; but damages shall not be awarded both in respect of such a liability and in respect of a liability arising by virtue of this section on account of the same loss.

(6) No liability shall arise by virtue of subsection (3) above if—

    (*a*) before the date on which proceedings to enforce the liability are finally disposed of, the former residential occupier is reinstated in the premises in question in such circumstances that he becomes again the residential occupier of them; or

    (*b*) at the request of the former residential occupier, a court makes an order (whether in the nature of an injunction or otherwise) as a result of which he is reinstated as mentioned in paragraph (*a*) above;

and, for the purposes of paragraph (*a*) above, proceedings to enforce a liability are finally disposed of on the earliest date by which the proceedings (including any proceedings on or in consequence of an appeal) have been determined and any time for appealing or further appealing has expired, except that if any appeal is abandoned, the proceedings shall be taken to be disposed of on the date of the abandonment.

(7) If, in proceedings to enforce a liability arising by virtue of subsection (3) above, it appears to the court—

(*a*) that, prior to the event which gave rise to the liability, the conduct of the former residential occupier or any person living with him in the premises concerned was such that it is reasonable to mitigate the damages for which the landlord in default would otherwise be liable, or

(*b*) that, before the proceedings were begun, the landlord in default offered to reinstate the former residential occupier in the premises in question and either it was unreasonable of the former residential occupier to refuse that offer or, if he had obtained alternative accommodation before the offer was made, it would have been unreasonable of him to refuse that offer if he had not obtained that accommodation,

the court may reduce the amount of damages which would otherwise be payable to such amount as it thinks appropriate.

(8) In proceedings to enforce a liability arising by virtue of subsection (3) above, it shall be a defence for the defendant to prove that he believed, and had reasonable cause to believe—

(*a*) that the residential occupier has ceased to reside in the premises in question at the time when he was deprived of occupation as mentioned in subsection (1) above or, as the case may be, when the attempt was made or the acts were done as a result of which he gave up his occupation of those premises; or

(*b*) that, where the liability would otherwise arise by virtue only of the doing of acts or the withdrawal or withholding of services, he had reasonable grounds for doing the acts or withdrawing or withholding the services in question.

(9) In this section—

(*a*) "residential occupier", in relation to any premises, has the same meaning as in section 1 of the 1977 Act;

(*b*) "the right to occupy", in relation to a residential occupier, includes any restriction on the right of another person to recover possession of the premises in question;

(*c*) "landlord", in relation to a residential occupier, means the person who, but for the occupier's right to occupy, would be entitled to occupation of the premises and any superior landlord under whom that person derives title;

(*d*) "former residential occupier", in relation to any premises, means the person who was the residential occupier until he was deprived of or gave up his occupation as mentioned in subsection (1) or subsection (2) above (and, in relation to a former residential occupier, "the right to occupy" and "landlord" shall be construed accordingly).   **[1231A]**

NOTES
1977 Act: Protection from Eviction Act 1977.

28. The measure of damages

(1) The basis for the assessment of damages referred to in section 27(3) above is the difference in value, determined as at the time immediately before the residential occupier ceased to occupy the premises in question as his residence, between—

(*a*) the value of the interest of the landlord in default determined on the assumption that the residential occupier continues to have the same right to occupy the premises as before that time; and

(*b*) the value of that interest determined on the assumption that the residential occupier has ceased to have that right.

(2) In relation to any premises, any reference in this section to the interest of the landlord in default is a reference to his interest in the building in which the premises in question are comprised (whether or not that building contains any other premises) together with its curtilage.

(3) For the purposes of the valuations referred to in subsection (1) above, it shall be assumed—

(*a*) that the landlord in default is selling his interest on the open market to a willing buyer;

(*b*) that neither the residential occupier nor any member of his family wishes to buy; and

(*c*) that it is unlawful to carry out any substantial development of any of the land in which the landlord's interest subsists or to demolish the whole or part of any building on that land.

(4) In this section "the landlord in default" has the same meaning as in section 27 above and subsection (9) of that section applies in relation to this section as it applies in relation to that.

(5) Section 113 of the Housing Act 1985 (meaning of "members of a person's family") applies for the purposes of subsection (3)(*b*) above.

(6) The reference in subsection (3)(*c*) above to substantial development of any of the land in which the landlord's interest subsists is a reference to any development other than—

(*a*) development for which planning permission is granted by a general development order for the time being in force and which is carried out so as to comply with any condition or limitation subject to which planning permission is so granted; or

(*b*) a change of use resulting in the building referred to in subsection (2) above or any part of it being used as, or as part of, one or more dwelling-houses;

and in this subsection "general development order" [has the same meaning given in section 56(6) of the Town and Country Planning Act 1990] and other expressions have the same meaning as in that Act. **[1231B]**

NOTES
Sub-s (6): words in square brackets substituted by the Planning (Consequential Provisions) Act 1990, s 4, Sch 2, para 79(1).

33. Interpretation of Chapter IV and the 1977 Act

(1) In this Chapter "the 1977 Act" means the Protection from Eviction Act 1977.

(2), (3) . . . **[1231C]**

PART V

MISCELLANEOUS AND GENERAL

Supplementary

141. Short title, commencement and extent

. . .

(5) Parts I . . . of this Act . . . extend to England and Wales only.

(6) This Act does not extend to Northern Ireland.   **[1231D]**

SCHEDULES

SCHEDULE 1

Section 1

TENANCIES WHICH CANNOT BE ASSURED TENANCIES

PART I

THE TENANCIES

Tenancies entered into before commencement

1. A tenancy which is entered into before, or pursuant to a contract made before, the commencement of this Act.

Tenancies of dwelling-houses with high rateable values

[2. (1) A tenancy—

(*a*) which is entered into on or after 1st April 1990 (otherwise than, where the dwelling-house had a rateable value on 31st March 1990, in pursuance of a contract made before 1st April 1990), and

(*b*) under which the rent payable for the time being is payable at a rate exceeding £25,000 a year.

(2) In sub-paragraph (1) "rent" does not include any sum payable by the tenant as is expressed (in whatever terms) to be payable in respect of rates [council tax], services, management, repairs, maintenance or insurance, unless it could not have been regarded by the parties to the tenancy as a sum so payable.

2A. A tenancy—

(*a*) which was entered into before the 1st April 1990, or on or after that date in pursuance of a contract made before that date, and

(*b*) under which the dwelling-house had a rateable value on the 31st March 1990 which, if it is in Greater London, exceeded £1,500 and, if it is elsewhere, exceeded £750.]

Tenancies at a low rent

[3. A tenancy under which for the time being no rent is payable.

3A. A tenancy—

(*a*) which is entered into on or after 1st April 1990 (otherwise than, where the dwelling-house had a rateable value on 31st March 1990, in pursuance of a contract made before 1st April 1990), and

(*b*) under which the rent payable for the time being is payable at a rate of, if the dwelling-house is in Greater London, £1,000 or less a year and, if it is elsewhere, £250 or less a year.

3B. A tenancy—

(a) which was entered into before 1st April 1990 or, where the dwelling-house had a rateable value on the 31st March 1990, on or after 1st April 1990 in pursuance of a contract made before that date, and

(b) under which the rent for the time being payable is less than two-thirds of the rateable value of the dwelling-house on 31st March 1990.

3C. Paragraph 2(2) above applies for the purposes of paragraphs 3, 3A and 3B as it applies for the purposes of paragraph 2(1).]

Business tenancies

4. A tenancy to which Part II of the Landlord and Tenant Act 1954 applies (business tenancies).

Licensed premises

5. A tenancy under which the dwelling-house consists of or comprises premises licensed for the sale of intoxicating liquors for consumption on the premises.

Tenancies of agricultural land

6.—(1) A tenancy under which agricultural land, exceeding two acres, is let together with the dwelling-house.

(2) In this paragraph "agricultural land" has the meaning set out in section 26(3)(a) of the General Rate Act 1967 (exclusion of agricultural land and premises from liability for rating).

Tenancies of agricultural holdings

7. A tenancy under which the dwelling-house—

(a) is comprised in an agricultural holding (within the meaning of the Agricultural Holdings Act 1986); and

(b) is occupied by the person responsible for the control (whether as tenant or as servant or agent of the tenant) of the farming of the holding.

Lettings to students

8.—(1) A tenancy which is granted to a person who is pursuing, or intends to pursue, a course of study provided by a specified educational institution and is so granted either by that institution or by another specified institution or body of persons.

(2) In sub-paragraph (1) above "specified" means specified, or of a class specified, for the purposes of this paragraph by regulations made by the Secretary of State by statutory instrument.

(3) A statutory instrument made in the exercise of the power conferred by sub-paragraph (2) above shall be subject to annulment in pursuance of a resolution of either House of Parliament.

Holiday lettings

9. A tenancy the purpose of which is to confer on the tenant the right to occupy the dwelling-house for a holiday.

Resident landlords

10.—(1) A tenancy in respect of which the following conditions are fulfilled—

(a) that the dwelling-house forms part only of a building and, except in a case where the dwelling-house also forms part of a flat, the building is not a purpose-built block of flats; and

(b) that, subject to Part III of this Schedule, the tenancy was granted by an individual who, at the time when the tenancy was granted, occupied as his only or principal home another dwelling-house which,—

   (i) in the case mentioned in paragraph (*a*) above, also forms part of the flat; or

   (ii) in any other case, also forms part of the building; and

(*c*) that, subject to Part III of this Schedule, at all times since the tenancy was granted the interest of the landlord under the tenancy has belonged to an individual who, at the time he owned that interest, occupied as his only or principal home another dwelling-house which,—

   (i) in the case mentioned in paragraph (*a*) above, also formed part of the flat; or

   (ii) in any other case, also formed part of the building; and

(*d*) that the tenancy is not one which is excluded from this sub-paragraph by sub-paragraph (3) below.

(2) If a tenancy was granted by two or more persons jointly, the reference in sub-paragraph (1)(*b*) above to an individual is a reference to any one of those persons and if the interest of the landlord is for the time being held by two or more persons jointly, the reference in sub-paragraph (1)(*c*) above to an individual is a reference to any one of those persons.

(3) A tenancy (in this sub-paragraph referred to as "the new tenancy") is excluded from sub-paragraph (1) above if—

(*a*) it is granted to a person (alone, or jointly with others) who, immediately before it was granted, was a tenant under an assured tenancy (in this sub-paragraph referred to as "the former tenancy") of the same dwelling-house or of another dwelling-house which forms part of the building in question; and

(*b*) the landlord under the new tenancy and under the former tenancy is the same person or, if either of those tenancies is or was granted by two or more persons jointly, the same person is the landlord or one of the landlords under each tenancy.

Crown tenancies

11.—(1) A tenancy under which the interest of the landlord belongs to Her Majesty in right of the Crown or to a government department or is held in trust for Her Majesty for the purposes of a government department.

(2) The reference in sub-paragraph (1) above to the case where the interest of the landlord belongs to Her Majesty in right of the Crown does not include the case where that interest is under the management of the Crown Estate Commissioners.

Local authority tenancies etc.

12.—(1) A tenancy under which the interest of the landlord belongs to—

(*a*) a local authority, as defined in sub-paragraph (2) below;

(*b*) the Commission for the New Towns;

(*c*) the Development Board for Rural Wales;

(*d*) an urban development corporation established by an order under section 135 of the Local Government, Planning and Land Act 1980;

(*e*) a development corporation, within the meaning of the New Towns Act 1981;

(*f*) an authority established under section 10 of the Local Government Act 1985 (waste disposal authorities);

(*g*) a residuary body, within the meaning of the Local Government Act 1985;

(*h*) a fully mutual housing association; or

(*i*) a housing action trust established under Part III of this Act.

(2) The following are local authorities for the purposes of sub-paragraph (1)(*a*) above—

(*a*) the council of a county, district or London borough;

(*b*) the Common Council of the City of London;

(*c*) the Council of the Isles of Scilly;

(*d*) the Broads Authority;

(*e*) the Inner London Education Authority; and

(*f*) a joint authority, within the meaning of the Local Government Act 1985.

Transitional cases

13.—(1) A protected tenancy, within the meaning of the Rent Act 1977.

(2) A housing association tenancy, within the meaning of Part VI of that Act.

(3) A secure tenancy.

(4) Where a person is a protected occupier of a dwelling-house, within the meaning of the Rent (Agriculture) Act 1976, the relevant tenancy, within the meaning of that Act, by virtue of which he occupies the dwelling-house. **[1232]**

NOTES
 Commencement: 1 April 1990 (paras 2, 2A, 3–3C); 15 January 1989 (remainder).
 Para 2: substituted together with para 2A, for para 2 as originally enacted, by the References to Rating (Housing) Regulations 1990, SI 1990 No 434, reg 2, Schedule, para 29; words in square brackets inserted by the Local Government Finance (Housing) (Consequential Amendments) Order 1993, SI 1993 No 651, art 2(1), Sch 1, para 19.
 Para 2A: substituted together with para 2, for para 2 as originally enacted, by the References to Rating (Housing) Regulations 1990, SI 1990 No 434, reg 2, Schedule, para 29.
 Para 3: substituted together with paras 3A–3C, for para 3 as originally enacted, by the References to Rating (Housing) Regulations 1990, SI 1990 No 434, reg 2, Schedule, para 30.
 Para 3A: substituted together with paras 3, 3B, 3C, for para 3 as originally enacted, by the References to Rating (Housing) Regulations 1990, SI 1990 No 434, reg 2, Schedule, para 30.
 Para 3B: substituted together with paras 3, 3A, 3C, for para 3 as originally enacted, by the References to Rating (Housing) Regulations 1990, SI 1990 No 434, reg 2, Schedule, para 30.
 Para 3C: substituted together with paras 3–3B, for para 3 as originally enacted, by the References to Rating (Housing) Regulations 1990, SI 1990 No 434, reg 2, Schedule, para 30.

PART II

RATEABLE VALUES

14.—(1) The rateable value of a dwelling-house at any time shall be ascertained for the purposes of Part I of this Schedule as follows—

 (a) if the dwelling-house is a hereditament for which a rateable value is then shown in the valuation list, it shall be that rateable value;

 (b) if the dwelling-house forms part only of such a hereditament or consists of or forms part of more than one such hereditament, its rateable value shall be taken to be such value as is found by a proper apportionment or aggregation of the rateable value or values so shown.

(2) Any question arising under this Part of this Schedule as to the proper apportionment or aggregation of any value or values shall be determined by the county court and the decision of that court shall be final.

15. Where, after the time at which the rateable value of a dwelling-house is material for the purposes of any provision of Part I of this Schedule, the valuation list is altered so as to vary the rateable value of the hereditament of which the dwelling-house consists (in whole or in part) or forms part and the alteration has effect from that time or from an earlier time, the rateable value of the dwelling-house at the material time shall be ascertained as if the value shown in the valuation list at the material time had been the value shown in the list as altered.

16. Paragraphs 14 and 15 above apply in relation to any other land which, under section 2 of this Act, is treated as part of a dwelling-house as they apply in relation to the dwelling-house itself. **[1233]**

PART III

PROVISIONS FOR DETERMINING APPLICATION OF PARAGRAPH 10 (RESIDENT LANDLORDS)

17.—(1) In determining whether the condition in paragraph 10(1)(*c*) above is at any time fulfilled with respect to a tenancy, there shall be disregarded—

(*a*) any period of not more than twenty-eight days, beginning with the date on which the interest of the landlord under the tenancy becomes vested at law and in equity in an individual who, during that period, does not occupy as his only or principal home another dwelling-house which forms part of the building or, as the case may be, flat concerned;

(*b*) if, within a period falling within paragraph (*a*) above, the individual concerned notifies the tenant in writing of his intention to occupy as his only or principal home another dwelling-house in the building or, as the case may be, flat concerned, the period beginning with the date on which the interest of the landlord under the tenancy becomes vested in that individual as mentioned in that paragraph and ending—

    (i) at the expiry of the period of six months beginning on that date, or

    (ii) on the date on which that interest ceases to be so vested, or

    (iii) on the date on which that interest becomes again vested in such an individual as is mentioned in paragraph 10(1)(*c*) or the condition in that paragraph becomes deemed to be fulfilled by virtue of paragraph 18(1) or paragraph 20 below,

whichever is the earlier; and

(*c*) any period of not more than two years beginning with the date on which the interest of the landlord under the tenancy becomes, and during which it remains, vested—

    (i) in trustees as such; or

    (ii) by virtue of section 9 of the Administration of Estates Act 1925, in the Probate Judge, within the meaning of that Act.

(2) Where the interest of the landlord under a tenancy becomes vested at law and in equity in two or more persons jointly, of whom at least one was an individual, sub-paragraph (1) above shall have effect subject to the following modifications—

(*a*) in paragraph (*a*) for the words from "an individual" to "occupy" there shall be substituted "the joint landlords if, during that period none of them occupies"; and

(*b*) in paragraph (*b*) for the words "the individual concerned" there shall be substituted "any of the joint landlords who is an individual" and for the words "that individual" there shall be substituted "the joint landlords".

18.—(1) During any period when—

(*a*) the interest of the landlord under the tenancy referred to in paragraph 10 above is vested in trustees as such, and

(*b*) that interest is or, if it is held on trust for sale, the proceeds of its sale are held on trust for any person who or for two or more persons of whom at least one occupies as his only or principal home a dwelling-house which forms part of the building or, as the case may be, flat referred to in paragraph 10(1)(*a*),

the condition in paragraph 10(1)(*c*) shall be deemed to be fulfilled and accordingly, no part of that period shall be disregarded by virtue of paragraph 17 above.

(2) If a period during which the condition in paragraph 10(1)(*c*) is deemed to be fulfilled by virtue of sub-paragraph (1) above comes to an end on the death of a person who was in occupation of a dwelling-house as mentioned in paragraph (*b*) of that sub-paragraph, then, in determining whether that condition is at any time thereafter fulfilled, there shall be disregarded any period—

(*a*) which begins on the date of the death;

(*b*) during which the interest of the landlord remains vested as mentioned in sub-paragraph (1)(*a*) above; and

(*c*) which ends at the expiry of the period of two years beginning on the date of the death or on any earlier date on which the condition in paragraph 10(1)(*c*) becomes again deemed to be fulfilled by virtue of sub-paragraph (1) above.

19. In any case where—

(*a*) immediately before a tenancy comes to an end the condition in paragraph 10(1)(*c*) is deemed to be fulfilled by virtue of paragraph 18(1) above, and

(b) on the coming to an end of that tenancy the trustees in whom the interest of the landlord is vested grant a new tenancy of the same or substantially the same dwelling-house to a person (alone or jointly with others) who was the tenant or one of the tenants under the previous tenancy,

the condition in paragraph 10(1)(b) above shall be deemed to be fulfilled with respect to the new tenancy.

20.—(1) The tenancy referred to in paragraph 10 above falls within this paragraph if the interest of the landlord under the tenancy becomes vested in the personal representatives of a deceased person acting in that capacity.

(2) If the tenancy falls within this paragraph, the condition in paragraph 10(1)(c) shall be deemed to be fulfilled for any period, beginning with the date on which the interest becomes vested in the personal representatives and not exceeding two years, during which the interest of the landlord remains so vested.

21. Throughout any period which, by virtue of paragraph 17 or paragraph 18(2) above, falls to be disregarded for the purpose of determining whether the condition in paragraph 10(1)(c) is fulfilled with respect to a tenancy, no order shall be made for possession of the dwelling-house subject to that tenancy, other than an order which might be made if that tenancy were or, as the case may be, had been an assured tenancy.

22. For the purposes of paragraph 10 above, a building is a purpose-built block of flats if as constructed it contained, and it contains, two or more flats; and for this purpose "flat" means a dwelling-house which—

(a) forms part only of a building; and
(b) is separated horizontally from another dwelling-house which forms part of the same building. **[1234]**

SCHEDULE 2

Section 7

GROUNDS FOR POSSESSION OF DWELLING-HOUSES LET ON ASSURED TENANCIES

PART I

GROUNDS ON WHICH COURT MUST ORDER POSSESSION

Ground 1

Not later than the beginning of the tenancy the landlord gave notice in writing to the tenant that possession might be recovered on this ground or the court is of the opinion that it is just and equitable to dispense with the requirement of notice and (in either case)—

(a) at some time before the beginning of the tenancy, the landlord who is seeking possession or, in the case of joint landlords seeking possession, at least one of them occupied the dwelling-house as his only or principal home; or
(b) the landlord who is seeking possession or, in the case of joint landlords seeking possession, at least one of them requires the dwelling-house as his or his spouse's only or principal home and neither the landlord (or, in the case of joint landlords, any one of them) nor any other person who, as landlord, derived title under the landlord who gave the notice mentioned above acquired the reversion on the tenancy for money or money's worth.

Ground 2

The dwelling-house is subject to a mortgage granted before the beginning of the tenancy and—

(a) the mortgagee is entitled to exercise a power of sale conferred on him by the mortgage or by section 101 of the Law of Property Act 1925; and
(b) the mortgagee requires possession of the dwelling-house for the purpose of disposing of it with vacant possession in exercise of that power; and

(*c*) either notice was given as mentioned in Ground 1 above or the court is satisfied that it is just and equitable to dispense with the requirement of notice;

and for the purposes of this ground "mortgage" includes a charge and "mortgagee" shall be construed accordingly.

Ground 3

The tenancy is a fixed term tenancy for a term not exceeding eight months and—

(*a*) not later than the beginning of the tenancy the landlord gave notice in writing to the tenant that possession might be recovered on this ground; and

(*b*) at some time within the period of twelve months ending with the beginning of the tenancy, the dwelling-house was occupied under a right to occupy it for a holiday.

Ground 4

The tenancy is a fixed term tenancy for a term not exceeding twelve months and—

(*a*) not later than the beginning of the tenancy the landlord gave notice in writing to the tenant that possession might be recovered on this ground; and

(*b*) at some time within the period of twelve months ending with the beginning of the tenancy, the dwelling-house was let on a tenancy falling within paragrpah 8 of Schedule 1 to this Act.

Ground 5

The dwelling-house is held for the purpose of being available for occupation by a minister of religion as a residence from which to perform the duties of his office and—

(*a*) not later than the beginning of the tenancy the landlord gave notice in writing to the tenant that possession might be recovered on this ground; and

(*b*) the court is satisfied that the dwelling-house is required for occupation by a minister of religion as such a residence.

Ground 6

The landlord who is seeking possession or, if that landlord is a registered housing association or charitable housing trust, a superior landlord intends to demolish or reconstruct the whole or a substantial part of the dwelling-house or to carry out substantial works on the dwelling-house or any part thereof or any building of which it forms part and the following conditions are fulfilled—

(*a*) the intended work cannot reasonably be carried out without the tenant giving up possession of the dwelling-house because—

(i) the tenant is not willing to agree to such a variation of the terms of the tenancy as would give such access and other facilities as would permit the intended work to be carried out, or

(ii) the nature of the intended work is such that no such variation is practicable, or

(iii) the tenant is not willing to accept an assured tenancy of such part only of the dwelling-house (in this sub-paragraph referred to as "the reduced part") as would leave in the possession of his landlord so much of the dwelling-house as would be reasonable to enable the intended work to be carried out and, where appropriate, as would give such access and other facilities over the reduced part as would permit the intended work to be carried out, or

(iv) the nature of the intended work is such that such a tenancy is not practicable; and

(*b*) either the landlord seeking possession acquired his interest in the dwelling-house before the grant of the tenancy or that interest was in existence at the time of that grant and neither that landlord (or, in the case of joint landlords, any of them) nor any other person who, alone or jointly with others, has acquired that interest since that time acquired it for money or money's worth; and

    (c) the assured tenancy on which the dwelling-house is let did not come into being by virtue of any provision of Schedule 1 to the Rent Act 1977, as amended by Part I of Schedule 4 to this Act or, as the case may be, section 4 of the Rent (Agriculture) Act 1976, as amended by Part II of that Schedule.

For the purposes of this ground, if, immediately before the grant of the tenancy, the tenant to whom it was granted or, if it was granted to joint tenants, any of them was the tenant or one of the joint tenants [of the dwelling-house concerned] under an earlier assured tenancy [or as the case may be, under a tenancy to which Schedule 10 to the Local Government and Housing Act 1989 applied], any reference in paragraph (b) above to the grant of the tenancy is a reference to the grant of that earlier assured tenancy [or, as the case may be, to the grant of the tenancy to which the said Schedule 10 applied].

For the purposes of this ground "registered housing association" has the same meaning as in the Housing Associations Act 1985 and "charitable housing trust" means a housing trust, within the meaning of that Act, which is a charity, within the meaning of [the Charities Act 1993].

[For the purposes of this ground, every acquisition under Part IV of this Act shall be taken to be an acquisition for money or money's worth; and in any case where—

    (i) the tenancy (in this paragraph referred to as "the current tenancy") was granted to a person (alone or jointly with others) who, immediately before it was granted, was a tenant under a tenancy of a different dwelling-house (in this paragraph referred to as "the earlier tenancy"), and

    (ii) the landlord under the current tenancy is the person who, immediately before that tenancy was granted, was the landlord under the earlier tenancy, and

    (iii) the condition in paragraph (b) above could not have been fulfilled with respect to the earlier tenancy by virtue of an acquisition under Part IV of this Act (including one taken to be such an acquisition by virtue of the previous operation of this paragraph),

the acquisition of the landlord's interest under the current tenancy shall be taken to have been under that Part and the landlord shall be taken to have acquired that interest after the grant of the current tenancy.]

Ground 7

The tenancy is a periodic tenancy (including a statutory periodic tenancy) which has devolved under the will or intestacy of the former tenant and the proceedings for the recovery of possession are begun not later than twelve months after the death of the former tenant or, if the court so directs, after the date on which, in the opinion of the court, the landlord or, in the case of joint landlords, any one of them became aware of the former tenant's death.

For the purposes of this ground, the acceptance by the landlord of rent from a new tenant after the death of the former tenant shall not be regarded as creating a new periodic tenancy, unless the landlord agrees in writing to a change (as compared with the tenancy before the death) in the amount of the rent, the period of the tenancy, the premises which are let or any other term of the tenancy.

Ground 8

Both at the date of the service of the notice under section 8 of this Act relating to the proceedings for possession and at the date of the hearing—

    (a) if rent is payable weekly or fortnightly, at least thirteen weeks' rent is unpaid;

    (b) if rent is payable monthly, at least three months' rent is unpaid;

    (c) if rent is payable quarterly, at least one quarter's rent is more than three months in arrears; and

    (d) if rent is payable yearly, at least three months' rent is more than three months in arrears;

and for the purpose of this ground "rent" means rent lawfully due from the tenant.

[1235]

NOTES

Ground 6: first, third and fifth words in square brackets inserted and second words in square brackets substituted by the Local Government and Housing Act 1989, s 194, Sch 11, paras 108, 109; fourth words in square brackets substituted by the Charities Act 1993, s 98(1), Sch 6, para 30.

PART II
GROUNDS ON WHICH COURT MAY ORDER POSSESSION

Ground 9

Suitable alternative accommodation is available for the tenant or will be available for him when the order for possession takes effect.

Ground 10

Some rent lawfully due from the tenant—

(a) is unpaid on the date on which the proceedings for possession are begun; and
(b) except where subsection (1)(b) of section 8 of this Act applies, was in arrears at the date of the service of the notice under that section relating to those proceedings.

Ground 11

Whether or not any rent is in arrears on the date on which proceedings for possession are begun, the tenant has persistently delayed paying rent which has become lawfully due.

Ground 12

Any obligation of the tenancy (other than one related to the payment of rent) has been broken or not performed.

Ground 13

The condition of the dwelling-house or any of the common parts has deteriorated owing to acts of waste by, or the neglect or default of, the tenant or any other person residing in the dwelling-house and, in the case of an act of waste by, or the neglect or default of, a person lodging with the tenant or a sub-tenant of his, the tenant has not taken such steps as he ought reasonably to have taken for the removal of the lodger or sub-tenant.

For the purposes of this ground, "common parts" means any part of a building comprising the dwelling-house and any other premises which the tenant is entitled under the terms of the tenancy to use in common with the occupiers of other dwelling-houses in which the landlord has an estate or interest.

Ground 14

The tenant or any other person residing in the dwelling-house has been guilty of conduct which is a nuisance or annoyance to adjoining occupiers, or has been convicted of using the dwelling-house or allowing the dwelling-house to be used for immoral or illegal purposes.

Ground 15

The condition of any furniture provided for use under the tenancy has, in the opinion of the court, deteriorated owing to ill-treatment by the tenant or any other person residing in the dwelling-house and, in the case of ill-treatment by a person lodging with the tenant or by a sub-tenant of his, the tenant has not taken such steps as he ought reasonably to have taken for the removal of the lodger or sub-tenant.

Ground 16

The dwelling-house was let to the tenant in consequence of his employment by the landlord seeking possession or a previous landlord under the tenancy and the tenant has ceased to be in that employment.

[For the purposes of this ground, at a time when the landlord is or was the Secretary of State, employment by a health service body, as defined in section 60(7) of the National Health Service and Community Care Act 1990, shall be regarded as employment by the Secretary of State.] **[1236]**

NOTES

Ground 16: words in square brackets added by the National Health Service and Community Care Act 1990, s 60, Sch 8, para 10.

PART III

SUITABLE ALTERNATIVE ACCOMMODATION

1. For the purposes of Ground 9 above, a certificate of the local housing authority for the district in which the dwelling-house in question is situated, certifying that the authority will provide suitable alternative accommodation for the tenant by a date specified in the certificate, shall be conclusive evidence that suitable alternative accommodation will be available for him by that date.

2. Where no such certificate as is mentioned in paragraph 1 above is produced to the court, accommodation shall be deemed to be suitable for the purposes of Ground 9 above if it consists of either—

(a) premises which are to be let as a separate dwelling such that they will then be let on an assured tenancy, other than—
  (i) a tenancy in respect of which notice is given not later than the beginning of the tenancy that possession might be recovered on any of Grounds 1 to 5 above, or
  (ii) an assured shorthold tenancy, within the meaning of Chapter II of Part I of this Act, or

(b) premises to be let as a separate dwelling on terms which will, in the opinion of the court, afford to the tenant security of tenure reasonably equivalent to the security afforded by Chapter I of Part I of this Act in the case of an assured tenancy of a kind mentioned in sub-paragraph (a) above,

and, in the opinion of the court, the accommodation fulfils the relevant conditions as defined in paragraph 3 below.

3.—(1) For the purposes of paragraph 2 above, the relevant conditions are that the accommodation is reasonably suitable to the needs of the tenant and his family as regards proximity to place of work, and either—

(a) similar as regards rental and extent to the accommodation afforded by dwelling-houses provided in the neighbourhood by any local housing authority for persons whose needs as regards extent are, in the opinion of the court, similar to those of the tenant and of his family; or

(b) reasonably suitable to the means of the tenant and to the needs of the tenant and his family as regards extent and character; and

that if any furniture was provided for use under the assured tenancy in question, furniture is provided for use in the accommodation which is either similar to that so provided or is reasonably suitable to the needs of the tenant and his family.

(2) For the purposes of sub-paragraph (1)(a) above, a certificate of a local housing authority stating—

(a) the extent of the accommodation afforded by dwelling-houses provided by the authority to meet the needs of tenants with families of such number as may be specified in the certificate, and

(b) the amount of the rent charged by the authority for dwelling-houses affording accommodation of that extent, shall be conclusive evidence of the facts so stated.

4. Accommodation shall not be deemed to be suitable to the needs of the tenant and his family if the result of their occupation of the accommodation would be that it would be an overcrowded dwelling-house for the purposes of Part X of the Housing Act 1985.

5. Any document purporting to be a certificate of a local housing authority named therein issued for the purposes of this Part of this Schedule and to be signed by the proper officer of that authority shall be received in evidence and, unless the contrary is shown, shall be deemed to be such a certificate without further proof.

6. In this Part of this Schedule "local housing authority" and "district", in relation to such an authority, have the same meaning as in the Housing Act 1985.　　**[1237]**

Part IV
Notices Relating to Recovery of Possession

7. Any reference in Grounds 1 to 5 in Part I of this Schedule or in the following provisions of this Part to the landlord giving a notice in writing to the tenant is, in the case of joint landlords, a reference to at least one of the joint landlords giving such a notice.

8.—(1) If, not later than the beginning of a tenancy (in this paragraph referred to as "the earlier tenancy"), the landlord gives such a notice in writing to the tenant as is mentioned in any of Grounds 1 to 5 in Part I of this Schedule, then, for the purposes of the ground in question and any further application of this paragraph, that notice shall also have effect as if it had been given immediately before the beginning of any later tenancy falling within sub-paragraph (2) below.

(2) Subject to sub-paragraph (3) below, sub-paragraph (1) above applies to a later tenancy—

    (*a*) which takes effect immediately on the coming to an end of the earlier tenancy; and

    (*b*) which is granted (or deemed to be granted) to the person who was the tenant under the earlier tenancy immediately before it came to an end; and

    (*c*) which is of substantially the same dwelling-house as the earlier tenancy.

(3) Sub-paragraph (1) above does not apply in relation to a later tenancy if, not later than the beginning of the tenancy, the landlord gave notice in writing to the tenant that the tenancy is not one in respect of which possession can be recovered on the ground in question.

9. Where paragraph 8(1) above has effect in relation to a notice given as mentioned in Ground 1 in Part I of this Schedule, the reference in paragraph (*b*) of that ground to the reversion on the tenancy is a reference to the reversion on the earlier tenancy and on any later tenancy falling within paragraph 8(2) above.

10. Where paragraph 8(1) above has effect in relation to a notice given as mentioned in Ground 3 or Ground 4 in Part I of this Schedule, any second or subsequent tenancy in relation to which the notice has effect shall be treated for the purpose of that ground as beginning at the beginning of the tenancy in respect of which the notice was actually given.

11. Any reference in Grounds 1 to 5 in Part I of this Schedule to a notice being given not later than the beginning of the tenancy is a reference to its being given not later than the day on which the tenancy is entered into and, accordingly, section 45(2) of this Act shall not apply to any such reference.　　**[1238]**

LAW OF PROPERTY (MISCELLANEOUS PROVISIONS) ACT 1989
(c 34)

ARRANGEMENT OF SECTIONS

An Act to make new provision with respect to deeds and their execution and contracts for the sale or other disposition of interests in land; and to abolish the rule of law known as the rule in Bain v Fothergill   [27 July 1989]

1. Deeds and their execution

(1) Any rule of law which—

    (*a*) restricts the substances on which a deed may be written;

    (*b*) requires a seal for the valid execution of an instrument as a deed by an individual; or

    (*c*) requires authority by one person to another to deliver an instrument as a deed on his behalf to be given by deed,

is abolished.

(2) An instrument shall not be a deed unless—

    (*a*) it makes it clear on its face that it is intended to be a deed by the person making it or, as the case may be, by the parties to it (whether by describing itself as a deed or expressing itself to be executed or signed as a deed or otherwise); and

    (*b*) it is validly executed as a deed by that person or, as the case may be, one or more of those parties.

(3) An instrument is validly executed as a deed by an individual if, and only if—

    (*a*) it is signed—

        (i) by him in the presence of a witness who attests the signature; or

        (ii) at his direction and in his presence and the presence of two witnesses who each attest the signature; and

    (*b*) it is delivered as a deed by him or a person authorised to do so on his behalf.

(4) In subsections (2) and (3) above "sign", in relation to an instrument, includes making one's mark on the instrument and "signature" is to be construed accordingly.

(5) Where a solicitor [, duly certificated notary public] or licensed conveyancer, or an agent or employee of a solicitor [, duly certificated notary public] or licensed conveyancer, in the course of or in connection with a

transaction involving the disposition or creation of an interest in land, purports to deliver an instrument as a deed on behalf of a party to the instrument, it shall be conclusively presumed in favour of a purchaser that he is authorised so to deliver the instrument.

(6) In subsection (5) above—

"disposition" and "purchaser" have the same meanings as in the Law of Property Act 1925;

["duly certificated notary public" has the same meaning as it has in the Solicitors Act 1974 by virtue of section 87 of that Act;] and

"interest in land" means any estate, interest or charge in or over land or in or over the proceeds of sale of land.

(7) Where an instrument under seal that constitutes a deed is required for the purposes of an Act passed before this section comes into force, this section shall have effect as to signing, sealing or delivery of an instrument by an individual in place of any provision of that Act as to signing, sealing or delivery.

(8) The enactments mentioned in Schedule 1 to this Act (which in consequence of this section require amendments other than those provided by subsection (7) above) shall have effect with the amendments specified in that Schedule.

(9) Nothing in subsection (1)(*b*), (2), (3), (7) or (8) above applies in relation to deeds required or authorised to be made under—

(*a*) the seal of the county palatine of Lancaster;

(*b*) the seal of the Duchy of Lancaster; or

(*c*) the seal of the Duchy of Cornwall.

(10) The references in this section to the execution of a deed by an individual do not include execution by a corporation sole and the reference in subsection (7) above to signing, sealing or delivery by an individual does not include signing, sealing or delivery by such a corporation.

(11) Nothing in this section applies in relation to instruments delivered as deeds before this section comes into force.   **[1239]**

NOTES

Commencement: 31 July 1990 (SI 1990 No 1175).

Sub-s (5): words in square brackets inserted by the Courts and Legal Services Act 1990, s 125(2), Sch 17, para 20.

Sub-s (6): words in square brackets inserted by the Courts and Legal Services Act 1990, s 125(2), Sch 17, para 20.

2. Contracts for sale etc of land to be made by signed writing

(1) A contract for the sale or other disposition of an interest in land can only be made in writing and only by incorporating all the terms which the parties have expressly agreed in one document or, where contracts are exchanged, in each.

(2) The terms may be incorporated in a document either by being set out in it or by reference to some other document.

(3) The document incorporating the terms or, where contracts are exchanged, one of the documents incorporating them (but not necessarily the same one) must be signed by or on behalf of each party to the contract.

(4) Where a contract for the sale or other disposition of an interest in land

satisfies the conditions of this section by reason only of the rectification of one or more documents in pursuance of an order of a court, the contract shall come into being, or be deemed to have come into being, at such time as may be specified in the order.

(5) This section does not apply in relation to—

(*a*) a contract to grant such a lease as is mentioned in section 54(2) of the Law of Property Act 1925 (short leases);

(*b*) a contract made in the course of a public auction; or

(*c*) a contract regulated under the Financial Services Act 1986;

and nothing in this section affects the creation or operation of resulting, implied or constructive trusts.

(6) In this section—

"disposition" has the same meaning as in the Law of Property Act 1925;

"interest in land" means any estate, interest or charge in or over land or in or over the proceeds of sale of land.

(7) Nothing in this section shall apply in relation to contracts made before this section comes into force.

(8) Section 40 of the Law of Property Act 1925 (which is superseded by this section) shall cease to have effect.   **[1240]**

NOTES
    Commencement: 27 September 1989.

3. Abolition of rule in Bain v Fothergill

The rule of law known as the rule in *Bain v Fothergill* is abolished in relation to contracts made after this section comes into force.   **[1241]**

NOTES
    Commencement: 27 September 1989.

4. Repeals

The enactments mentioned in Schedule 2 to this Act are repealed to the extent specified in the third column of that Schedule.   **[1242]**

NOTES
    Commencement: 31 July 1990 (certain purposes); 27 September 1989 (remaining purposes) (SI 1990 No 1175).

5. Commencement

(1) The provisions of this Act to which this subsection applies shall come into force on such day as the Lord Chancellor may by order made by statutory instrument appoint.

(2) The provisions to which subsection (1) above applies are—

(*a*) section 1 above; and

(*b*) section 4 above, except so far as it relates to section 40 of the Law of Property Act 1925.

(3) The provisions of this Act to which this subsection applies shall come into force at the end of the period of two months beginning with the day on which this Act is passed.

(4) The provisions of this Act to which subsection (3) above applies are—

(*a*) sections 2 and 3 above; and

(*b*) section 4 above, so far as it relates to section 40 of the Law of Property Act 1925.   **[1243]**

NOTES

Commencement: 27 July 1989.

6. Citation

(1) This Act may be cited as the Law of Property (Miscellaneous Provisions) Act 1989.

(2) This Act extends to England and Wales only.   **[1244]**

NOTES

Commencement: 27 July 1989.

SCHEDULES
SCHEDULE 1

Section 1

CONSEQUENTIAL AMENDMENTS RELATING TO DEEDS

. . .   **[1245]**

NOTES

Commencement: 31 July 1990 (SI 1990 No 1175).

This Schedule amends the Law of Property Act 1925 and the Powers of Attorney Act 1971.

SCHEDULE 2

Section 4

REPEALS

. . .   **[1246]**

NOTES

Commencement: 31 July 1990 (in part); 27 September 1989 (remainder) (SI 1990 No 1175).

This Schedule contains repeals only.

TOWN AND COUNTRY PLANNING ACT 1990
(c 8)

ARRANGEMENT OF SECTIONS

PART III
CONTROL OVER DEVELOPMENT

Meaning of development

*An Act to consolidate certain enactments relating to town and country planning
(excluding special controls in respect of buildings and areas of special
architectural or historic interest and in respect of hazardous substances) with
amendments to give effect to recommendations of the Law Commission*
[24 May 1990]

PART III

CONTROL OVER DEVELOPMENT

Meaning of development

55. Meaning of "development" and "new development"

(1) Subject to the following provisions of this section, in this Act, except where
the context otherwise requires, "development," means the carrying out of
building, engineering, mining or other operations in, on, over or under land, or
the making of any material change in the use of any buildings or other land.

[(1A) For the purposes of this Act "building operations" includes—

(*a*) demolition of buildings;
(*b*) rebuilding;
(*c*) structural alterations of or additions to buildings; and
(*d*) other operations normally undertaken by a person carrying on business
as a builder.]

(2) The following operations or uses of land shall not be taken for the
purposes of this Act to involve development of the land—

(*a*) the carrying out for the maintenance, improvement or other alteration
of any building of works which—

(i) affect only the interior of the building, or
(ii) do not materially affect the external appearance of the building,

and are not works for making good war damage or works begun after
5th December 1968 for the alteration of a building by providing
additional space in it underground;
(*b*) the carrying out on land within the boundaries of a road by a local
highway authority of any works required for the maintenance or
improvement of the road;
(*c*) the carrying out by a local authority or statutory undertakers of any
works for the purpose of inspecting, repairing or renewing any sewers,

mains, pipes, cables or other apparatus, including the breaking open
of any street or other land for that purpose;

(*d*) the use of any buildings or other land within the curtilage of a
dwellinghouse for any purpose incidental to the enjoyment of the
dwellinghouse as such;

(*e*) the use of any land for the purposes of agriculture or forestry (including
afforestation) and the use for any of those purposes of any building
occupied together with land so used;

(*f*) in the case of buildings or other land which are used for a purpose of
any class specified in an order made by the Secretary of State under
this section, the use of the buildings or other land or, subject to the
provisions of the order, of any part of the buildings or the other land,
for any other purpose of the same class;

[(*g*) the demolition of any description of building specified in a direction
given by the Secretary of State to local planning authorities generally
or to a particular local planning authority.]

(3) For the avoidance of doubt it is hereby declared that for the purposes of
this section—

(*a*) the use as two or more separate dwellinghouses of any building
previously used as a single dwellinghouse involves a material change
in the use of the building and of each part of it which is so used;

(*b*) the deposit of refuse or waste materials on land involves a material
change in its use, notwithstanding that the land is comprised in a site
already used for that purpose, if—

(i) the superficial area of the deposit is extended, or

(ii) the height of the deposit is extended and exceeds the level of the
land adjoining the site.

(4) For the purposes of this Act mining operations include—

(*a*) the removal of material of any description—

(i) from a mineral-working deposit;

(ii) from a deposit of pulverised fuel ash or other furnace ash or
clinker; or

(iii) from a deposit of iron, steel or other metallic slags; and

(*b*) the extraction of minerals from a disused railway embankment.

[(4A) Where the placing or assembly of any tank in any part of any inland
waters for the purpose of fish farming there would not, apart from this
subsection, involve development of the land below, this Act shall have effect as
if the tank resulted from carrying out engineering operations over that land;
and in this subsection—

"fish farming" means the breeding, rearing or keeping of fish or shellfish
(which includes any kind of crustacean and mollusc);

"inland waters" means waters which do not form part of the sea or of any
creek, bay or estuary or of any river as far as the tide flows; and

"tank" includes any cage and any other structure for use in fish farming.]

(5) Without prejudice to any regulations made under the provisions of this
Act relating to the control of advertisements, the use for the display of
advertisements of any external part of a building which is not normally used for
that purpose shall be treated for the purposes of this section as involving a
material change in the use of that part of the building.

(6) . . .   [1247]

NOTES
    Commencement: 27 July 1992 (sub-s (1A)); 2 January 1992 (sub-s (4A)); 24 August 1990
(remainder) (SI 1991 No 2728, SI 1991 No 2905, SI 1992 No 1279).
    Sub-s (1A): inserted by the Planning and Compensation Act 1991, s 13(1).
    Sub-s (2): para (*g*) added by the Planning and Compensation Act 1991, s 13(2).
    Sub-s (4A): inserted by the Planning and Compensation Act 1991, s 14.
    Sub-s (6): repealed by the Planning and Compensation Act 1991, ss 31, 84, Sch 6, para 9, Sch 19,
Parts I, II.

Other controls over development

[106. Planning obligations

(1) Any person interested in land in the area of a local planning authority may,
by agreement or otherwise, enter into an obligation (referred to in this section
and sections 106A and 106B as "a planning obligation"), enforceable to the
extent mentioned in subsection (3)—

    (*a*) restricting the development or use of the land in any specified way;

    (*b*) requiring specified operations or activities to be carried out in, on,
under or over the land;

    (*c*) requiring the land to be used in any specified way; or

    (*d*) requiring a sum or sums to be paid to the authority on a specified date
or dates or periodically.

(2) A planning obligation may—

    (*a*) be unconditional or subject to conditions;

    (*b*) impose any restriction or requirement mentioned in subsection (1)(*a*)
to (*c*) either indefinitely or for such period or periods as may be
specified; and

    (*c*) if it requires a sum or sums to be paid, require the payment of a
specified amount or an amount determined in accordance with the
instrument by which the obligation is entered into and, if it requires
the payment of periodical sums, require them to be paid indefinitely
or for a specified period.

(3) Subject to subsection (4) a planning obligation is enforceable by the
authority identified in accordance with subsection (9)(*d*)—

    (*a*) against the person entering into the obligation; and

    (*b*) against any person deriving title from that person.

(4) The instrument by which a planning obligation is entered into may
provide that a person shall not be bound by the obligation in respect of any
period during which he no longer has an interest in the land.

(5) A restriction or requirement imposed under a planning obligation is
enforceable by injunction.

(6) Without prejudice to subsection (5), if there is a breach of a requirement
in a planning obligation to carry out any operations in, on, under or over the
land to which the obligation relates, the authority by whom the obligation is
enforceable may—

    (*a*) enter the land and carry out the operations; and

    (*b*) recover from the person or persons against whom the obligation is
enforceable any expenses reasonably incurred by them in doing so.

(7) Before an authority exercise their power under subsection (6)(*a*) they

shall give not less than twenty-one days' notice of their intention to do so to any person against whom the planning obligation is enforceable.

(8) Any person who wilfully obstructs a person acting in the exercise of a power under subsection (6)(*a*) shall be guilty of an offence and liable on summary conviction to a fine not exceeding level 3 on the standard scale.

(9) A planning obligation may not be entered into except by an instrument executed as a deed which—

(*a*) states that the obligation is a planning obligation for the purposes of this section;

(*b*) identifies the land in which the person entering into the obligation is interested;

(*c*) identifies the person entering into the obligation and states what his interest in the land is; and

(*d*) identifies the local planning authority by whom the obligation is enforceable.

(10) A copy of any such instrument shall be given to the authority so identified.

(11) A planning obligation shall be a local land charge and for the purposes of the Local Land Charges Act 1975 the authority by whom the obligation is enforceable shall be treated as the originating authority as respects such a charge.

(12) Regulations may provide for the charging on the land of—

(*a*) any sum or sums required to be paid under a planning obligation; and

(*b*) any expenses recoverable by a local planning authority under subsection (6)(*b*),

and this section and sections 106A and 106B shall have effect subject to any such regulations.

(13) In this section "specified" means specified in the instrument by which the planning obligation is entered into and in this section and section 106A "land" has the same meaning as in the Local Land Charges Act 1975.] **[1248]**

NOTES

Commencement: 25 October 1991 (SI 1991 No 2272).

Substituted, together with ss 106A, 106B, for s 106 as originally enacted, by the Planning and Compensation Act 1991, s 12(1).

[106A. Modification and discharge of planning obligations

(1) A planning obligation may not be modified or discharged except—

(*a*) by agreement between the authority by whom the obligation is enforceable and the person or persons against whom the obligation is enforceable; or

(*b*) in accordance with this section and section 106B.

(2) An agreement falling within subsection (1)(*a*) shall not be entered into except by an instrument executed as a deed.

(3) A person against whom a planning obligation is enforceable may, at any time after the expiry of the relevant period, apply to the local planning authority by whom the obligation is enforceable for the obligation—

(*a*) to have effect subject to such modifications as may be specified in the application; or (*b*) to be discharged.

(4) In subsection (3) "the relevant period" means—

    (*a*) such period as may be prescribed; or
    (*b*) if no period is prescribed, the period of five years beginning with the date on which the obligation is entered into.

(5) An application under subsection (3) for the modification of a planning obligation may not specify a modification imposing an obligation on any other person against whom the obligation is enforceable.

(6) Where an application is made to an authority under subsection (3), the authority may determined—

    (*a*) that the planning obligation shall continue to have effect without modification;
    (*b*) if the obligation no longer serves a useful purpose, that it shall be discharged; or
    (*c*) if the obligation continues to serve a useful purpose, but would serve that purpose equally well if it had effect subject to the modifications specified in the application, that it shall have effect subject to those modifications.

(7) The authority shall give notice of their determination to the applicant within such period as may be prescribed.

(8) Where an authority determine that a planning obligation shall have effect subject to modifications specified in the application, the obligation as modified shall be enforceable as if it had been entered into on the date on which notice of the determination was given to the applicant.

(9) Regulations may make provision with respect to—

    (*a*) the form and content of applications under subsection (3);
    (*b*) the publication of notices of such applications;
    (*c*) the procedures for considering any representations made with respect to such applications; and
    (*d*) the notices to be given to applicants of determinations under subsection (6).

(10) Section 84 of the Law of Property Act 1925 (power to discharge or modify restrictive covenants affecting land) does not apply to a planning obligation.]   **[1249]**

NOTES

    Commencement: 9 November 1992 (certain purposes); 25 November 1991 (remaining purposes) (SI 1991 No 2728, SI 1992 No 2831).
    Substituted, together with ss 106, 106B, for s 106 as originally enacted, by the Planning and Compensation Act 1991, s 12(1).

[106B. Appeals

(1) Where a local planning authority—

    (*a*) fail to give notice as mentioned in section 106A(7); or
    (*b*) determine that a planning obligation shall continue to have effect without modification,

the applicant may appeal to the Secretary of State.

(2) For the purposes of an appeal under subsection (1)(*a*), it shall be assumed

that the authority have determined that the planning obligation shall continue to have effect without modification.

(3) An appeal under this section shall be made by notice served within such period and in such manner as may be prescribed.

(4) Subsections (6) to (9) of section 106A apply in relation to appeals to the Secretary of State under this section as they apply in relation to applications to authorities under that section.

(5) Before determining the appeal the Secretary of State shall, if either the applicant or the authority so wish, give each of them an opportunity of appearing before and being heard by a person appointed by the Secretary of State for the purpose.

(6) The determination of an appeal by the Secretary of State under this section shall be final.

(7) Schedule 6 applies to appeals under this section.] **[1250]**

NOTES
    Commencement: 9 November 1992 (certain purposes); 25 November 1991 (remaining purposes) (SI 1991 No 2728, SI 1992 No 2831).
    Substituted, together with ss 106, 106A, for s 106 as originally enacted, by the Planning and Compensation Act 1991, s 12(1).

PART VII

ENFORCEMENT

Established use certificates

[191. Certificate of lawfulness of existing use or development

(1) If any person wishes to ascertain whether—

    (*a*) any existing use of buildings or other land is lawful;
    (*b*) any operations which have been carried out in, on, over or under land are lawful; or
    (*c*) any other matter constituting a failure to comply with any condition or limitation subject to which planning permission has been granted is lawful,

he may make an application for the purpose to the local planning authority specifying the land and describing the use, operations or other matter.

(2) For the purposes of this Act uses and operations are lawful at any time if—

    (*a*) no enforcement action may then be taken in respect of them (whether because they did not involve development or require planning permission or because the time for enforcement action has expired or for any other reason); and
    (*b*) they do not constitute a contravention of any of the requirements of any enforcement notice then in force.

(3) For the purposes of this Act any matter constituting a failure to comply with any condition or limitation subject to which planning permission has been granted is lawful at any time if—

    (*a*) the time for taking enforcement action in respect of the failure has then expired; and

(b) it does not constitute a contravention of any of the requirements of any enforcement notice or breach of condition notice then in force.

(4) If, on an application under this section, the local planning authority are provided with information satisfying them of the lawfulness at the time of the application of the use, operations or other matter described in the application, or that description as modified by the local planning authority or a description substituted by them, they shall issue a certificate to that effect; and in any other case they shall refuse the application.

(5) A certificate under this section shall—

    (a) specify the land to which it relates;

    (b) describe the use, operations or other matter in question (in the case of any use falling within one of the classes specified in an order under section 55(2)(f), identifying it by reference to that class);

    (c) give the reasons for determining the use, operations or other matter to be lawful; and

    (d) specify the date of the application for the certificate.

(6) The lawfulness of any use, operations or other matter for which a certificate is in force under this section shall be conclusively presumed.

(7) A certificate under this section in respect of any use shall also have effect, for the purposes of the following enactments, as if it were a grant of planning permission—

    (a) section 3(3) of the Caravan Sites and Control of Development Act 1960;

    (b) section 5(2) of the Control of Pollution Act 1974; and

    (c) section 36(2)(a) of the Environmental Protection Act 1990.]   **[1251]**

NOTES
    Commencement: 27 July 1992 (certain purposes); 25 November 1991 (remaining purposes) (SI 1991 No 2728, SI 1992 No 1630).
    Substituted by the Planning and Compensation Act 1991, s 10(1).

[192. Certificate of lawfulness of proposed use or development

(1) If any person wishes to ascertain whether—

    (a) any proposed use of buildings or other land; or

    (b) any operations proposed to be carried out in, on, over or under land,

would be lawful, he may make an application for the purpose to the local planning authority specifying the land and describing the use or operations in question.

(2) If, on an application under this section, the local planning authority are provided with information satisfying them that the use or operations described in the application would be lawful if instituted or begun at the time of the application, they shall issue a certificate to that effect; and in any other case they shall refuse the application.

(3) A certificate under this section shall—

    (a) specify the land to which it relates;

    (b) describe the use or operations in question (in the case of any use falling within one of the classes specified in an order under section 55(2)(f), identifying it by reference to that class);

    (c) give the reasons for determining the use or operations to be lawful; and (*d*) specify the date of the application for the certificate.

(4) The lawfulness of any use or operations for which a certificate is in force under this section shall be conclusively presumed unless there is a material change, before the use is instituted or the operations are begun, in any of the matters relevant to determining such lawfulness.] **[1252]**

NOTES
Commencement: 27 July 1992 (SI 1992 No 1630).
Substituted by the Planning and Compensation Act 1991, s 10(1).

PART IX

ACQUISITION AND APPROPRIATION OF LAND FOR PLANNING PURPOSES, ETC

Extinguishment of certain rights affecting acquired or appropriated land

237. Power to override easements and other rights

(1) Subject to subsection (3), the erection, construction or carrying out or maintenance of any building or work on land which has been acquired or appropriated by a local authority for planning purposes (whether done by the local authority or by a person deriving title under them) is authorised by virtue of this section if it is done in accordance with planning permission, notwithstanding that it involves—

(*a*) interference with an interest or right to which this section applies, or
(*b*) a breach of a restriction as to the user of land arising by virtue of a contract.

(2) Subject to subsection (3), the interests and rights to which this section applies are any easement, liberty, privilege, right or advantage annexed to land and adversely affecting other land, including any natural right to support.

(3) Nothing in this section shall authorise interference with any right of way or right of laying down, erecting, continuing or maintaining apparatus on, under or over land which is—

(*a*) a right vested in or belonging to statutory undertakers for the purpose of the carrying on of their undertaking, or
(*b*) a right conferred by or in accordance with the telecommunications code on the operator of a telecommunications code system.

(4) In respect of any interference or breach in pursuance of subsection (1), compensation—

(*a*) shall be payable under section 63 or 68 of the Lands Clauses Consolidation Act 1845 or under section 7 or 10 of the Compulsory Purchase Act 1965, and
(*b*) shall be assessed in the same manner and subject to the same rules as in the case of other compensation under those sections in respect of injurious affection where—

    (i) the compensation is to be estimated in connection with a purchase under those Acts, or
    (ii) the injury arises from the execution of works on land acquired under those Acts.

(5) Where a person deriving title under the local authority by whom the land in question was acquired or appropriated—

(*a*) is liable to pay compensation by virtue of subsection (4), and (*b*) fails to discharge that liability,

the liability shall be enforceable against the local authority.

(6) Nothing in subsection (5) shall be construed as affecting any agreement between the local authority and any other person for indemnifying the local authority against any liability under that subsection.

(7) Nothing in this section shall be construed as authorising any act or omission on the part of any person which is actionable at the suit of any person on any grounds other than such an interference or breach as is mentioned in subsection (1). **[1253]**

NOTES
Commencement: 24 August 1990.

ACCESS TO NEIGHBOURING LAND ACT 1992
(c 23)

ARRANGEMENT OF SECTIONS

An Act to enable persons who desire to carry out works to any land which are reasonably necessary for the preservation of that land to obtain access to neighbouring land in order to do so; and for purposes connected therewith
[16 March 1992]

1. Access orders

(1) A person—

    (*a*) who, for the purpose of carrying out works to any land (the "dominant land"), desires to enter upon any adjoining or adjacent land (the "servient land"), and

    (*b*) who needs, but does not have, the consent of some other person to that entry,

may make an application to the court for an order under this section ("an access order") against that other person.

(2) On an application under this section, the court shall make an access order if, and only if, it is satisfied—

    (*a*) that the works are reasonably necessary for the preservation of the whole or any part of the dominant land; and

    (*b*) that they cannot be carried out, or would be substantially more difficult to carry out, without entry upon the servient land;

but this subsection is subject to subsection (3) below.

(3) The court shall not make an access order in any case where it is satisfied that, were it to make such an order—

(*a*) the respondent or any other person would suffer interference with, or disturbance of, his use or enjoyment of the servient land, or

(*b*) the respondent, or any other person (whether of full age or capacity or not) in occupation of the whole or any part of the servient land, would suffer hardship,

to such a degree by reason of the entry (notwithstanding any requirement of this Act or any term or condition that may be imposed under it) that it would be unreasonable to make the order.

(4) Where the court is satisfied on an application under this section that it is reasonably necessary to carry out any basic preservation works to the dominant land, those works shall be taken for the purposes of this Act to be reasonably necessary for the preservation of the land; and in this subsection "basic preservation works" means any of the following, that is to say—

(*a*) the maintenance, repair or renewal of any part of a building or other structure comprised in, or situate on, the dominant land;

(*b*) the clearance, repair or renewal of any drain, sewer, pipe or cable so comprised or situate;

(*c*) the treatment, cutting back, felling, removal or replacement of any hedge, tree, shrub or other growing thing which is so comprised and which is, or is in danger of becoming, damaged, diseased, dangerous, insecurely rooted or dead;

(*d*) the filling in, or clearance, of any ditch so comprised;

but this subsection is without prejudice to the generality of the works which may, apart from it, be regarded by the court as reasonably necessary for the preservation of any land.

(5) If the court considers it fair and reasonable in all the circumstances of the case, works may be regarded for the purposes of this Act as being reasonably necessary for the preservation of any land (or, for the purposes of subsection (4) above, as being basic preservation works which it is reasonably necessary to carry out to any land) notwithstanding that the works incidentally involve—

(*a*) the making of some alteration, adjustment or improvement to the land, or

(*b*) the demolition of the whole or any part of a building or structure comprised in or situate upon the land.

(6) Where any works are reasonably necessary for the preservation of the whole or any part of the dominant land, the doing to the dominant land of anything which is requisite for, incidental to, or consequential on, the carrying out of those works shall be treated for the purposes of this Act as the carrying out of works which are reasonably necessary for the preservation of that land; and references in this Act to works, or to the carrying out of works, shall be construed accordingly.

(7) Without prejudice to the generality of subsection (6) above, if it is reasonably necessary for a person to inspect the dominant land—

(*a*) for the purpose of ascertaining whether any works may be reasonably necessary for the preservation of the whole or any part of that land,

(*b*) for the purpose of making any map or plan, or ascertaining the course of any drain, sewer, pipe or cable, in preparation for, or otherwise in connection with, the carrying out of works which are so reasonably necessary, or

(*c*) otherwise in connection with the carrying out of any such works,

the making of such an inspection shall be taken for the purposes of this Act to be the carrying out to the dominant land of works which are reasonably necessary for the preservation of that land; and references in this Act to works, or to the carrying out of works, shall be construed accordingly. **[1254]**

NOTES
Commencement: 31 January 1993 (SI 1992 No 3349).

2. Terms and conditions of access orders

(1) An access order shall specify—

> (a) the works to the dominant land that may be carried out by entering upon the servient land in pursuance of the order;
> (b) the particular area of servient land that may be entered upon by virtue of the order for the purpose of carrying out those works to the dominant land; and
> (c) the date on which, or the period during which, the land may be so entered upon;

and in the following provisions of this Act any reference to the servient land is a reference to the area specified in the order in pursuance of paragraph (b) above.

(2) An access order may impose upon the applicant or the respondent such terms and conditions as appear to the court to be reasonably necessary for the purpose of avoiding or restricting—

> (a) any loss, damage, or injury which might otherwise be caused to the respondent or any other person by reason of the entry authorised by the order; or
> (b) any inconvenience or loss of privacy that might otherwise be so caused to the respondent or any other person.

(3) Without prejudice to the generality of subsection (2) above, the terms and conditions which may be imposed under that subsection include provisions with respect to—

> (a) the manner in which the specified works are to be carried out;
> (b) the days on which, and the hours between which, the work involved may be executed;
> (c) the persons who may undertake the carrying out of the specified works or enter upon the servient land under or by virtue of the order;
> (d) the taking of any such precautions by the applicant as may be specified in the order.

(4) An access order may also impose terms and conditions—

> (a) requiring the applicant to pay, or to secure that such person connected with him as may be specified in the order pays, compensation for—
>> (i) any loss, damage or injury, or
>> (ii) any substantial loss of privacy or other substantial inconvenience,
>
> which will, or might, be caused to the respondent or any other person by reason of the entry authorised by the order;
> (b) requiring the applicant to secure that he, or such person connected with him as may be specified in the order, is insured against any such risks as may be so specified; or
> (c) requiring such a record to be made of the condition of the servient land, or of such part of it as may be so specified, as the court may

consider expedient with a view to facilitating the determination of any question that may arise concerning damage to that land.

(5) An access order may include provision requiring the applicant to pay the respondent such sum by way of consideration for the privilege of entering the servient land in pursuance of the order as appears to the court to be fair and reasonable having regard to all the circumstances of the case, including, in particular—

(a) the likely financial advantage of the order to the applicant and any persons connected with him; and

(b) the degree of inconvenience likely to be caused to the respondent or any other person by the entry;

but no payment shall be ordered under this subsection if and to the extent that the works which the applicant desires to carry out by means of the entry are works to residential land.

(6) For the purposes of subsection (5)(a) above, the likely financial advantage of an access order to the applicant and any persons connected with him shall in all cases be taken to be a sum of money equal to the greater of the following amounts, that is to say—

(a) the amount (if any) by which so much of any likely increase in the value of any land—

(i) which consists of or includes the dominant land, and

(ii) which is owned or occupied by the same person as the dominant land,

as may reasonably be regarded as attributable to the carrying out of the specified works exceeds the likely cost of carrying out those works with the benefit of the access order; and

(b) the difference (if it would have been possible to carry out the specified works without entering upon the servient land) between—

(i) the likely cost of carrying out those works without entering upon the servient land; and

(ii) the likely cost of carrying them out with the benefit of the access order.

(7) For the purposes of subsection (5) above, "residential land" means so much of any land as consists of—

(a) a dwelling or part of a dwelling;

(b) a garden, yard, private garage or outbuilding which is used and enjoyed wholly or mainly with a dwelling; or

(c) in the case of a building which includes one or more dwellings, any part of the building which is used and enjoyed wholly or mainly with those dwellings or any of them.

(8) The persons who are to be regarded for the purposes of this section as "connected with" the applicant are—

(a) the owner of any estate or interest in, or right over, the whole or any part of the dominant land;

(b) the occupier of the whole or any part of the dominant land; and

(c) any person whom the applicant may authorise under section 3(7) below to exercise the power of entry conferred by the access order.

(9) The court may make provision—

(a) for the reimbursement by the applicant of any expenses reasonably incurred by the respondent in connection with the application which are not otherwise recoverable as costs;

(b) for the giving of security by the applicant for any sum that might become payable to the respondent or any other person by virtue of this section or section 3 below. **[1255]**

NOTES
Commencement: 31 January 1993 (SI 1992 No 3349).

3. Effect of access order

(1) An access order requires the respondent, so far as he has power to do so, to permit the applicant or any of his associates to do anything which the applicant or associate is authorised or required to do under or by virtue of the order or this section.

(2) Except as otherwise provided by or under this Act, an access order authorises the applicant or any of his associates, without the consent of the respondent,—

(a) to enter upon the servient land for the purpose of carrying out the specified works;

(b) to bring on to that land, leave there during the period permitted by the order and, before the end of that period, remove, such materials, plant and equipment as are reasonably necessary for the carrying out of those works; and

(c) to bring on to that land any waste arising from the carrying out of those works, if it is reasonably necessary to do so in the course of removing it from the dominant land;

but nothing in this Act or in any access order shall authorise the applicant or any of his associates to leave anything in, on or over the servient land (otherwise than in discharge of their duty to make good that land) after their entry for the purpose of carrying out works to the dominant land ceases to be authorised under or by virtue of the order.

(3) An access order requires the applicant—

(a) to secure that any waste arising from the carrying out of the specified works is removed from the servient land forthwith;

(b) to secure that, before the entry ceases to be authorised under or by virtue of the order, the servient land is, so far as reasonably practicable, made good; and

(c) to indemnify the respondent against any damage which may be caused to the servient land or any goods by the applicant or any of his associates which would not have been so caused had the order not been made;

but this subsection is subject to subsections (4) and (5) below.

(4) In making an access order, the court may vary or exclude, in whole or in part,—

(a) any authorisation that would otherwise be conferred by subsection (2)(b) or (c) above; or

(b) any requirement that would otherwise be imposed by subsection (3) above.

(5) Without prejudice to the generality of subsection (4) above, if the court is satisfied that it is reasonably necessary for any such waste as may arise from

the carrying out of the specified works to be left on the servient land for some period before removal, the access order may, in place of subsection (3)(*a*) above, include provision—

(*a*) authorising the waste to be left on that land for such period as may be permitted by the order; and

(*b*) requiring the applicant to secure that the waste is removed before the end of that period.

(6) Where the applicant or any of his associates is authorised or required under or by virtue of an access order or this section to enter, or do any other thing, upon the servient land, he shall not (as respects that access order) be taken to be a trespasser from the beginning on account of his, or any other person's, subsequent conduct.

(7) For the purposes of this section, the applicant's "associates" are such number of persons (whether or not servants or agents of his) whom he may reasonably authorise under this subsection to exercise the power of entry conferred by the access order as may be reasonably necessary for carrying out the specified works.   **[1256]**

NOTES
Commencement: 31 January 1993 (SI 1992 No 3349).

4. Persons bound by access order, unidentified persons and bar on contracting out

(1) In addition to the respondent, an access order shall, subject to the provisions of the Land Charges Act 1972 and the Land Registration Act 1925, be binding on—

(*a*) any of his successors in title to the servient land; and

(*b*) any person who has an estate or interest in, or right over, the whole or any part of the servient land which was created after the making of the order and who derives his title to that estate, interest or right under the respondent;

and references to the respondent shall be construed accordingly.

(2) If and to the extent that the court considers it just and equitable to allow him to do so, a person on whom an access order becomes binding by virtue of subsection (1)(*a*) or (*b*) above shall be entitled, as respects anything falling to be done after the order becomes binding on him, to enforce the order or any of its terms or conditions as if he were the respondent, and references to the respondent shall be construed accordingly.

(3) Rules of court may—

(*a*) provide a procedure which may be followed where the applicant does not know, and cannot reasonably ascertain, the name of any person whom he desires to make respondent to the application; and

(*b*) make provision enabling such an applicant to make such a person respondent by description instead of by name;

and in this subsection "applicant" includes a person who proposes to make an application for an access order.

(4) Any agreement, whenever made, shall be void if and to the extent that it would, apart from this subsection, prevent a person from applying for an access order or restrict his right to do so.   **[1257]**

NOTES
Commencement: 31 January 1993 (SI 1992 No 3349).

5. Registration of access orders and of applications for such orders

(1)–(3) ...

    (4) In any case where—

        (*a*) an access order is discharged under section 6(1)(*a*) below, and

        (*b*) the order has been protected by an entry registered under the Land Charges Act 1972 or by a notice or caution under the Land Registration Act 1925,

the court may by order direct that the entry, notice or caution shall be cancelled.

    (5) The rights conferred on a person by or under an access order are not capable of constituting an overriding interest within the meaning of the Land Registration Act 1925, notwithstanding that he or any other person is in actual occupation of the whole or any part of the servient land in question.

    (6) An application for an access order shall be regarded as a pending land action for the purposes of the Land Charges Act 1972 and the Land Registration Act 1925. **[1258]**

NOTES
Commencement: 31 January 1993 (SI 1992 No 3349).
Sub-s (1): amends the Land Charges Act 1972, s 6(1).
Sub-ss (2), (3): amend the Land Registration Act 1925, s 49(1) and add s 64(7).

6. Variation of orders and damages for breach

(1) Where an access order or an order under this subsection has been made, the court may, on the application of any party to the proceedings in which the order was made or of any other person on whom the order is binding—

    (*a*) discharge or vary the order or any of its terms or conditions;

    (*b*) suspend any of its terms or conditions; or

    (*c*) revive any term or condition suspended under paragraph (*b*) above;

and in the application of subsections (1) and (2) of section 4 above in relation to an access order, any order under this subsection which relates to the access order shall be treated for the purposes of those subsections as included in the access order.

    (2) If any person contravenes or fails to comply with any requirement, term or condition imposed upon him by or under this Act, the court may, without prejudice to any other remedy available, make an order for the payment of damages by him to any other person affected by the contravention or failure who makes an application for relief under this subsection. **[1259]**

NOTES
Commencement: 31 January 1993 (SI 1992 No 3349).

7. Jurisdiction over, and allocation of, proceedings

(1) The High Court and the county courts shall both have jurisdiction under this Act.

    (2) ...

    (3) The amendment by subsection (2) above of provisions contained in an

order shall not be taken to have prejudiced any power to make further orders revoking or amending those provisions. **[1260]**

NOTES
Commencement: 31 January 1993 (SI 1992 No 3349).
Sub-s (2): amends the High Court and County Courts Jurisdiction Order 1991, SI 1991 No 724, art 4 and inserts art 6A.

8. Interpretation and application

(1) Any reference in this Act to an "entry" upon any servient land includes a reference to the doing on that land of anything necessary for carrying out the works to the dominant land which are reasonably necessary for its preservation; and "enter" shall be construed accordingly.

(2) This Act applies in relation to any obstruction of, or other interference with, a right over, or interest in, any land as it applies in relation to an entry upon that land; and "enter" and "entry" shall be construed accordingly.

(3) In this Act—

"access order" has the meaning given by section 1(1) above;
"applicant" means a person making an application for an access order and, subject to section 4 above, "the respondent" means the respondent, or any of the respondents, to such an application;
"the court" means the High Court or a county court;
"the dominant land" and "the servient land" respectively have the meanings given by section 1(1) above, but subject, in the case of servient land, to section 2(1) above;
"land" does not include a highway;
"the specified works" means the works specified in the access order in pursuance of section 2(1)(*a*) above. **[1261]**

NOTES
Commencement: 31 January 1993 (SI 1992 No 3349).

9. Short title, commencement and extent

(1) This Act may be cited as the Access to Neighbouring Land Act 1992.

(2) This Act shall come into force on such day as the Lord Chancellor may by order made by statutory instrument appoint.

(3) This Act extends to England and Wales only. **[1262]**

NOTES
Commencement: 31 January 1993 (SI 1992 No 3349).

TIMESHARE ACT 1992
(c 35)

An Act to provide for rights to cancel certain agreements about timeshare accommodation [16 March 1992]

1. Application of Act

(1) In this Act—

> (*a*) "timeshare accommodation" means any living accommodation, in the United Kingdom or elsewhere, used or intended to be used, wholly or partly, for leisure purposes by a class of persons (referred to below in this section as "timeshare users") all of whom have rights to use, or participate in arrangements under which they may use, that accommodation, or accommodation within a pool of accommodation to which that accommodation belongs, for intermittent periods of short duration, and
> (*b*) "timeshare rights" means rights by virtue of which a person becomes or will become a timeshare user, being rights exercisable during a period of not less than three years.

(2) For the purposes of subsection (1)(*a*) above—

> (*a*) "accommodation" means accommodation in a building or in a caravan (as defined in section 29(1) of the Caravan Sites and Control of Development Act 1960), and
> (*b*) a period of not more than one month, or such other period as may be prescribed, is a period of short duration.

(3) Subsection (1)(*b*) above does not apply to a person's rights—

> (*a*) as the owner of any shares or securities,
> (*b*) under a contract of employment (as defined in section 153 of the Employment Protection (Consolidation) Act 1978) or a policy of insurance, or
> (*c*) by virtue of his taking part in a collective investment scheme (as defined in section 75 of the Financial Services Act 1986),

or to such rights as may be prescribed.

(4) In this Act "timeshare agreement" means, subject to subsection (6) below, an agreement under which timeshare rights are conferred or purport to be conferred on any person and in this Act, in relation to a timeshare agreement—

> (*a*) references to the offeree are to the person on whom timeshare rights are conferred, or purport to be conferred, and
> (*b*) references to the offeror are to the other party to the agreement,

and, in relation to any time before the agreement is entered into, references in this Act to the offeree or the offeror are to the persons who become the offeree and offeror when it is entered into.

(5) In this Act "timeshare credit agreement" means, subject to subsection (6) below, an agreement, not being a timeshare agreement—

    (*a*) under which a person (referred to in this Act as the "creditor") provides or agrees to provide credit for or in respect of a person who is the offeree under a timeshare agreement, and

    (*b*) when the credit agreement is entered into, the creditor knows or has reasonable cause to believe that the whole or part of the credit is to be used for the purpose of financing the offeree's entering into a timeshare agreement.

(6) An agreement is not a timeshare agreement or a timeshare credit agreement if, when entered into, it may be cancelled by virtue of section 67 of the Consumer Credit Act 1974.

(7) This Act applies to any timeshare agreement or timeshare credit agreement if—

    (*a*) the agreement is to any extent governed by the law of the United Kingdom or of a part of the United Kingdom, or

    (*b*) when the agreement is entered into, one or both of the parties are in the United Kingdom.

(8) In the application of this section to Northern Ireland—

    (*a*) for the reference in subsection (2)(*a*) above to section 29(1) of the Caravan Sites and Control of Development Act 1960 there is substituted a reference to section 25(1) of the Caravans Act (Northern Ireland) 1963, and

    (*b*) for the reference in subsection (3)(*b*) above to section 153 of the Employment Protection (Consolidation) Act 1978 there is substituted a reference to article 2(2) of the Industrial Relations (Northern Ireland) Order 1976.   **[1263]**

NOTES

Commencement: 12 October 1992 (SI 1992 No 1941).

2. Obligation to give notice of right to cancel timeshare agreement

(1) A person must not in the course of a business enter into a timeshare agreement to which this Act applies as offeror unless the offeree has received, together with a document setting out the terms of the agreement or the substance of those terms, notice of his right to cancel the agreement.

(2) A notice under this section must state—

    (*a*) that the offeree is entitled to give notice of cancellation of the agreement to the offeror at any time on or before the date specified in the notice, being a day falling not less than fourteen days after the day on which the agreement is entered into, and

    (*b*) that if the offeree gives such a notice to the offeror on or before that date he will have no further rights or obligations under the agreement, but will have the right to recover any sums paid under or in contemplation of the agreement.

(3) A person who contravenes this section is guilty of an offence and liable—

    (*a*) on summary conviction, to a fine not exceeding the statutory maximum, and (*b*) on conviction on indictment, to a fine. **[1264]**

NOTES
Commencement: 12 October 1992 (SI 1992 No 1941).

3. Obligation to give notice of right to cancel timeshare credit agreement

(1) A person must not in the course of a business enter into a timeshare credit agreement to which this Act applies as creditor unless the offeree has received, together with a document setting out the terms of the agreement or the substance of those terms, notice of his right to cancel the agreement.

(2) A notice under this section must state—

    (*a*) that the offeree is entitled to give notice of cancellation of the agreement to the creditor at any time on or before the date specified in the notice, being a day falling not less than fourteen days after the day on which the agreement is entered into, and

    (*b*) that, if the offeree gives such a notice to the creditor on or before that date, then—

        (i) so far as the agreement relates to repayment of credit and payment of interest, it shall have effect subject to section 7 of this Act, and

        (ii) subject to sub-paragraph (i) above, the offeree will have no further rights or obligations under the agreement. **[1265]**

NOTES
Commencement: 12 October 1992 (SI 1992 No 1941).

4. Provisions supplementary to sections 2 and 3

(1) Sections 2 and 3 of this Act do not apply where, in entering into the agreement, the offeree is acting in the course of a business.

(2) A notice under section 2 or 3 must be accompanied by a blank notice of cancellation and any notice under section 2 or 3 of this Act or blank notice of cancellation must—

    (*a*) be in such form as may be prescribed, and

    (*b*) comply with such requirements (whether as to type, size, colour or disposition of lettering, quality or colour of paper, or otherwise) as may be prescribed for securing that the notice is prominent and easily legible.

(3) An agreement is not invalidated by reason of a contravention of section 2 or 3. **[1266]**

NOTES
Commencement: 12 October 1992 (SI 1992 No 1941).

5. Right to cancel timeshare agreement

(1) Where a person—

    (*a*) has entered, or proposes to enter, into a timeshare agreement to which this Act applies as offeree, and

    (*b*) has received the notice required under section 2 of this Act before entering into the agreement,

the agreement may not be enforced against him on or before the date specified in the notice in pursuance of subsection (2)(*a*) of that section and he may give notice of cancellation of the agreement to the offeror at any time on or before that date.

(2) Subject to subsection (3) below, where a person who enters into a timeshare agreement to which this Act applies as offeree has not received the notice required under section 2 of this Act before entering into the agreement, the agreement may not be enforced against him and he may give notice of cancellation of the agreement to the offeror at any time.

(3) If in a case falling within subsection (2) above the offeree affirms the agreement at any time after the expiry of the period of fourteen days beginning with the day on which the agreement is entered into—

(a) subsection (2) above does not prevent the agreement being enforced against him, and
(b) he may not at any subsequent time give notice of cancellation of the agreement to the offeror.

(4) The offeree's giving, within the time allowed under this section, notice of cancellation of the agreement to the offeror at a time when the agreement has been entered into shall have the effect of cancelling the agreement.

(5) The offeree's giving notice of cancellation of the agreement to the offeror before the agreement has been entered into shall have the effect of withdrawing any offer to enter into the agreement.

(6) Where a timeshare agreement is cancelled under this section, then, subject to subsection (9) below—

(a) the agreement shall cease to be enforceable, and
(b) subsection (8) below shall apply.

(7) Subsection (8) below shall also apply where giving a notice of cancellation has the effect of withdrawing an offer to enter into a timeshare agreement.

(8) Where this subsection applies—

(a) any sum which the offeree has paid under or in contemplation of the agreement to the offeror, or to any person who is the offeror's agent for the purpose of receiving that sum, shall be recoverable from the offeror by the offeree and shall be due and payable at the time the notice of cancellation is given, but
(b) no sum may be recovered by or on behalf of the offeror from the offeree in respect of the agreement.

(9) Where a timeshare agreement includes provision for providing credit for or in respect of the offeree, then, notwithstanding the giving of notice of cancellation under this section, so far as the agreement relates to repayment of the credit and payment of interest—

(a) it shall continue to be enforceable, subject to section 7 of this Act, and
(b) the notice required under section 2 of this Act must also state that fact. **[1267]**

NOTES

Commencement: 12 October 1992 (SI 1992 No 1941).

6. Right to cancel timeshare credit agreement

(1) Where a person—

(a) has entered into a timeshare credit agreement to which this Act applies as offeree, and

(b) has received the notice required under section 3 of this Act before entering into the agreement,

he may give notice of cancellation of the agreement to the creditor at any time on or before the date specified in the notice in pursuance of subsection (2)(a) of that section.

(2) Subject to subsection (3) below, where a person who enters into a timeshare credit agreement to which this Act applies as offeree has not received the notice required under section 3 of this Act before entering into the agreement, he may give notice of cancellation of the agreement to the creditor at any time.

(3) If in a case falling within subsection (2) above the offeree affirms the agreement at any time after the expiry of the period of fourteen days beginning with the day on which the agreement is entered into, he may not at any subsequent time give notice of cancellation of the agreement to the creditor.

(4) The offeree's giving, within the time allowed under this section, notice of cancellation of the agreement to the creditor at a time when the agreement has been entered into shall have the effect of cancelling the agreement.

(5) Where a timeshare credit agreement is cancelled under this section—

(a) the agreement shall continue in force, subject to section 7 of this Act, so far as it relates to repayment of the credit and payment of interest, and

(b) subject to paragraph (a) above, the agreement shall cease to be enforceable. **[1268]**

NOTES
Commencement: 12 October 1992 (SI 1992 No 1941).

7. Repayment of credit and interest

(1) This section applies following—

(a) the giving of notice of cancellation of a timeshare agreement in accordance with section 5 of this Act in a case where subsection (9) of that section applies, or

(b) the giving of notice of cancellation of a timeshare credit agreement in accordance with section 6 of this Act.

(2) If the offeree repays the whole or a portion of the credit—

(a) before the expiry of one month following the giving of the notice, or

(b) in the case of a credit repayable by instalments, before the date on which the first instalment is due,

no interest shall be payable on the amount repaid.

(3) If the whole of a credit repayable by instalments is not repaid on or before the date specified in subsection (2)(b) above, the offeree shall not be liable to repay any of the credit except on receipt of a request in writing in such form as may be prescribed, signed by or on behalf of the offeror or (as the case may be) creditor, stating the amounts of the remaining instalments (recalculated by the offeror or creditor as nearly as may be in accordance with the agreement and without extending the repayment period), but excluding any sum other than principal and interest. **[1269]**

NOTES
Commencement: 12 October 1992 (SI 1992 No 1941).

8. Defence of due diligence

(1) In proceedings against a person for an offence under section 2(3) of this Act it shall be a defence for that person to show that he took all reasonable steps and exercised all due diligence to avoid committing the offence.

(2) Where in proceedings against a person for such an offence the defence provided by subsection (1) above involves an allegation that the commission of the offence was due—

(a) to the act or default of another, or
(b) to reliance on information given by another,

that person shall not, without the leave of the court, be entitled to rely on the defence unless he has served a notice under subsection (3) below on the person bringing the proceedings not less than seven clear days before the hearing of the proceedings or, in Scotland, the diet of trial.

(3) A notice under this subsection shall give such information identifying or assisting in the identification of the person who committed the act or default or gave the information as is in the possession of the person serving the notice at the time when he serves it.   **[1270]**

NOTES
Commencement: 12 October 1992 (SI 1992 No 1941).

9. Liability of person other than principal offender

(1) Where the commission by a person of an offence under section 2(3) of this Act is due to the act or default of some other person, that other person is guilty of the offence and may be proceeded against and punished by virtue of this section whether or not proceedings are taken against the first-mentioned person.

(2) Where a body corporate is guilty of an offence under section 2(3) of this Act (including where it is so guilty by virtue of subsection (1) above) in respect of an act or default which is shown to have been committed with the consent or connivance of, or to be attributable to neglect on the part of, a director, manager, secretary or other similar officer of the body corporate or a person who was purporting to act in such a capacity, he (as well as the body corporate) is guilty of the offence and liable to be proceeded against and punished accordingly.

(3) Where the affairs of a body corporate are managed by its members, subsection (2) above applies in relation to the acts and defaults of a member in connection with his functions of management as if he were a director of the body corporate.

(4) Where an offence under section 2(3) of this Act committed in Scotland by a Scottish partnership is proved to have been committed with the consent or connivance of, or to be attributable to neglect on the part of, a partner, he (as well as the partnership) is guilty of the offence and liable to be proceeded against and punished accordingly.   **[1271]**

NOTES
Commencement: 12 October 1992 (SI 1992 No 1941).

10. Enforcement

The Schedule to this Act (which makes provision about enforcement) shall have effect. **[1272]**

NOTES
Commencement: 12 October 1992 (SI 1992 No 1941).

11. Prosecution time limit

(1) No proceedings for an offence under section 2(3) of this Act or paragraph 4(3) or 5(1) of the Schedule to this Act shall be commenced after—

> (*a*) the end of the period of three years beginning with the date of the commission of the offence, or
>
> (*b*) the end of the period of one year beginning with the date of the discovery of the offence by the prosecutor,

whichever is the earlier.

(2) For the purposes of this section a certificate signed by or on behalf of the prosecutor and stating the date on which the offence was discovered by him shall be conclusive evidence of that fact; and a certificate stating that matter and purporting to be so signed shall be treated as so signed unless the contrary is proved.

(3) In relation to proceedings in Scotland, subsection (3) of section 331 of the Criminal Procedure (Scotland) Act 1975 (date of commencement of proceedings) shall apply for the purposes of this section as it applies for the purposes of that. **[1273]**

NOTES
Commencement: 12 October 1992 (SI 1992 No 1941).

12. General provisions

(1) For the purposes of this Act, a notice of cancellation of an agreement is a notice (however expressed) showing that the offeree wishes unconditionally to cancel the agreement, whether or not it is in a prescribed form.

(2) The rights conferred and duties imposed by sections 2 to 7 of this Act are in addition to any rights conferred or duties imposed by or under any other Act.

(3) For the purposes of this Act, if the offeree sends a notice by post in a properly addressed and pre-paid letter the notice is to be treated as given at the time of posting.

(4) This Act shall have effect in relation to any timeshare agreement or timeshare credit agreement notwithstanding any agreement or notice.

(5) For the purposes of the Consumer Credit Act 1974, a transaction done under or for the purposes of a timeshare agreement is not, in relation to any regulated agreement (within the meaning of that Act), a linked transaction.

(6) In this Act—

> "credit" includes a cash loan and any other form of financial accommodation,
>
> "notice" means notice in writing,
>
> "order" means an order made by the Secretary of State, and

"prescribed" means prescribed by an order.

(7) An order under this Act may make different provision for different cases or circumstances.

(8) Any power under this Act to make an order shall be exercisable by statutory instrument and a statutory instrument containing an order under this Act (other than an order made for the purposes of section 13(2) of this Act) shall be subject to annulment in pursuance of a resolution of either House of Parliament.   **[1274]**

NOTES
Commencement: 12 October 1992 (SI 1992 No 1941).

13. Short title, etc

(1) This Act may be cited as the Timeshare Act 1992.

(2) This Act shall come into force on such day as may be prescribed.

(3) This Act extends to Northern Ireland.   **[1275]**

NOTES
Commencement: 12 October 1992 (SI 1992 No 1941).

SCHEDULE
Section 10

ENFORCEMENT

Enforcement authority

1.—(1) Every local weights and measures authority in Great Britain shall be an enforcement authority for the purposes of this Schedule, and it shall be the duty of each such authority to enforce the provisions of this Act within their area.

(2) The Department of Economic Development in Northern Ireland shall be an enforcement authority for the purposes of this Schedule, and it shall be the duty of the Department to enforce the provisions of this Act within Northern Ireland.

Prosecutions

2.—(1) ...

(2) Nothing in paragraph 1 above shall authorise a local weights and measures authority to bring proceedings in Scotland for an offence.

Powers of officers of enforcement authority

3.—(1) If a duly authorised officer of an enforcement authority has reasonable grounds for suspecting that an offence under section 2 of this Act has been committed, he may—

(a) require a person carrying on or employed in a business to produce any book or document relating to the business, and take copies of it or any entry in it, or

(b) require such a person to produce in a visible and legible documentary form any information so relating which is contained in a computer, and take copies of it,

for the purposes of ascertaining whether such an offence has been committed.

(2) If such an officer has reasonable grounds for believing that any documents may be required as evidence in proceedings for such an offence, he may seize and detain them and shall, if he does so, inform the person from whom they are seized.

(3) The powers of an officer under this paragraph may be exercised by him only at a reasonable hour and on production (if required) of his credentials.

(4) Nothing in this paragraph requires a person to produce, or authorises the taking from a person of, a document which he could not be compelled to produce in civil proceedings before the High Court or (in Scotland) the Court of Session.

4.—(1) A person who—

(*a*) intentionally obstructs an officer of an enforcement authority acting in pursuance of this Schedule,

(*b*) without reasonable excuse fails to comply with a requirement made of him by such an officer under paragraph 3(1) above, or

(*c*) without reasonable excuse fails to give an officer of an enforcement authority acting in pursuance of this Schedule any other assistance or information which the officer has reasonably required of him for the purpose of the performance of the officer's functions under this Schedule,

is guilty of an offence.

(2) A person guilty of an offence under sub-paragraph (1) above is liable on summary conviction to a fine not exceeding level 5 on the standard scale.

(3) If a person, in giving information to an officer of an enforcement authority who is acting in pursuance of this Schedule—

(*a*) makes a statement which he knows is false in a material particular, or

(*b*) recklessly makes a statement which is false in a material particular,

he is guilty of an offence.

(4) A person guilty of an offence under sub-paragraph (3) above is liable—

(*a*) on summary conviction, to a fine not exceeding the statutory maximum, and

(*b*) on conviction on indictment, to a fine.

Disclosure of information

5.—(1) If a person discloses to another any information obtained in the exercise of functions under this Schedule he is guilty of an offence unless the disclosure was made—

(*a*) in or for the purpose of the performance by him or any other person of any such function, or

(*b*) for a purpose specified in section 38(2)(*a*), (*b*) or (*c*) of the Consumer Protection Act 1987 (enforcement of various enactments; compliance with Community obligations; and civil or criminal proceedings).

(2) A person guilty of an offence under sub-paragraph (1) above is liable—

(*a*) on summary conviction, to a fine not exceeding the statutory maximum, and

(*b*) on conviction on indictment, to a fine.

Privilege against self-incrimination

6. Nothing in this Schedule requires a person to answer any question or give any information if to do so might incriminate him. **[1276]**

NOTES

Commencement: 12 October 1992 (SI 1992 No 1941).
Para 2: sub-para (1) amends the Fair Trading Act 1973, s 130(1).

CHARITIES ACT 1992

(c 41)

An Act to amend the Charities Act 1960 and make other provision with respect to charities; to regulate fund-raising activities carried on in connection with charities and other institutions; to make fresh provision with respect to public charitable collections; and for connected purposes [16 March 1992]

PART I

CHARITIES

Charity property

36. Removal of requirements under statutory provisions for consent to dealings with charity land

(1) Any provision—

(*a*) establishing or regulating a particular charity and contained in, or having effect under, any Act of Parliament, or

(*b*) contained in the trusts of a charity,

shall cease to have effect if and to the extent that it provides for dispositions of, or other dealings with, land held by or in trust for the charity to require the consent of the Commissioners (whether signified by order or otherwise).

(2) Any provision of an order or scheme under the Education Act 1944 or the Education Act 1973 relating to a charity shall cease to have effect if and to the extent that it requires, in relation to any sale, lease or other disposition of land held by or in trust for the charity, approval by the Commissioners or the Secretary of State of the amount for which the land is to be sold, leased or otherwise disposed of.

(3) In this section "land" means land in England or Wales. **[1277]**

NOTES

Commencement: 1 January 1993 (SI 1992 No 1900).

CHARITIES ACT 1993
(c 10)

ARRANGEMENT OF SECTIONS

PART I

THE CHARITY COMMISSIONERS AND THE OFFICIAL CUSTODIAN FOR CHARITIES

PART II

REGISTRATION AND NAMES OF CHARITIES

Registration of charities

PART IV

APPLICATION OF PROPERTY CY-PRÈS AND ASSISTANCE AND SUPERVISION OF CHARITIES BY COURT AND COMMISSIONERS

Extended powers of court and variation of charters

An Act to consolidate the Charitable Trustees Incorporation Act 1872 and, except for certain spent or transitional provisions, the Charities Act 1960 and Part I of the Charities Act 1992 [27 May 1993]

PART I

THE CHARITY COMMISSIONERS AND THE OFFICIAL CUSTODIAN FOR CHARITIES

1. The Charity Commissioners

(1) There shall continue to be a body of Charity Commissioners for England and Wales, and they shall have such functions as are conferred on them by this Act in addition to any functions under any other enactment for the time being in force.

(2) The provisions of Schedule 1 to this Act shall have effect with respect to the constitution and proceedings of the Commissioners and other matters relating to the Commissioners and their officers and employees.

(3) The Commissioners shall (without prejudice to their specific powers and duties under other enactments) have the general function of promoting the effective use of charitable resources by encouraging the development of better methods of administration, by giving charity trustees information or advice on any matter affecting the charity and by investigating and checking abuses.

(4) It shall be the general object of the Commissioners so to act in the case

of any charity (unless it is a matter of altering its purposes) as best to promote and make effective the work of the charity in meeting the needs designated by its trusts; but the Commissioners shall not themselves have power to act in the administration of a charity.

(5) The Commissioners shall, as soon as possible after the end of every year, make to the Secretary of State a report on their operations during that year, and he shall lay a copy of the report before each House of Parliament.

[1278]

NOTES
Commencement: 1 August 1993.

2. The official custodian for charities

(1) There shall continue to be an officer known as the official custodian for charities (in this Act referred to as "the official custodian") whose function it shall be to act as trustee for charities in the cases provided for by this Act; and the official custodian shall be by that name a corporation sole having perpetual succession and using an official seal which shall be officially and judicially noticed.

(2) Such officer of the Commissioners as they may from time to time designate shall be the official custodian.

(3) The official custodian shall perform his duties in accordance with such general or special directions as may be given him by the Commissioners, and his expenses (except those re-imbursed to him or recovered by him as trustee for any charity) shall be defrayed by the Commissioners.

(4) Anything which is required to or may be done by, to or before the official custodian may be done by, to or before any officer of the Commissioners generally or specially authorised by them to act for him during a vacancy in his office or otherwise.

(5) The official custodian shall not be liable as trustee for any charity in respect of any loss or of the mis-application of any property unless it is occasioned by or through the wilful neglect or default of the custodian or of any person acting for him; but the Consolidated Fund shall be liable to make good to a charity any sums for which the custodian may be liable by reason of any such neglect or default.

(6) The official custodian shall keep such books of account and such records in relation thereto as may be directed by the Treasury and shall prepare accounts in such form, in such manner and at such times as may be so directed.

(7) The accounts so prepared shall be examined and certified by the Comptroller and Auditor General, and the report to be made by the Commissioners to the Secretary of State for any year shall include a copy of the accounts so prepared for any period ending in or with the year and of the certificate and report of the Comptroller and Auditor General with respect to those accounts.

[1279]

NOTES
Commencement: 1 August 1993.

PART II

REGISTRATION AND NAMES OF CHARITIES

Registration of charities

3. The register of charities

(1) The Commissioners shall continue to keep a register of charities, which shall be kept by them in such manner as they think fit.

(2) There shall be entered in the register every charity not excepted by subsection (5) below; and a charity so excepted (other than one excepted by paragraph (*a*) of that subsection) may be entered in the register at the request of the charity, but (whether or not it was excepted at the time of registration) may at any time, and shall at the request of the charity, be removed from the register.

(3) The register shall contain—
  (*a*) the name of every registered charity; and
  (*b*) such other particulars of, and such other information relating to, every such charity as the Commissioners think fit.

(4) Any institution which no longer appears to the Commissioners to be a charity shall be removed from the register, with effect, where the removal is due to any change in its purposes or trusts, from the date of that change; and there shall also be removed from the register any charity which ceases to exist or does not operate.

(5) The following charities are not required to be registered—
  (*a*) any charity comprised in Schedule 2 to this Act (in this Act referred to as an "exempt charity");
  (*b*) any charity which is excepted by order or regulations;
  (*c*) any charity which has neither—
    (i) any permanent endowment, nor
    (ii) the use or occupation of any land,

  and whose income from all sources does not in aggregate amount to more than £1,000 a year;

and no charity is required to be registered in respect of any registered place of worship.

. . .

(7) It shall be the duty—
  (*a*) of the charity trustees of any charity which is not registered nor excepted from registration to apply for it to be registered, and to supply the documents and information required by subsection (6) above; and
  (*b*) of the charity trustees (or last charity trustees) of any institution which is for the time being registered to notify the Commissioners if it ceases to exist, or if there is any change in its trusts or in the particulars of it entered in the register, and to supply to the Commissioners particulars of any such change and copies of any new trusts or alterations of the trusts.

. . .

(12) If the Secretary of State thinks it expedient to do so—

(*a*) in consequence of changes in the value of money, or

(*b*) with a view to extending the scope of the exception provided for by subsection (5)(*c*) above,

he may by order amend subsection (5)(*c*) by substituting a different sum for the sum for the time being specified there.

(13) The reference in subsection (5)(*b*) above to a charity which is excepted by order or regulations is to a charity which—

(*a*) is for the time being permanently or temporarily excepted by order of the Commissioners; or

(*b*) is of a description permanently or temporarily excepted by regulations made by the Secretary of State,

and which complies with any conditions of the exception.

(14) In this section "registered place of worship" means any land or building falling within section 9 of the Places of Worship Registration Act 1855 (that is to say, the land and buildings which if the Charities Act 1960 had not been passed, would by virtue of that section as amended by subsequent enactments be partially exempted from the operation of the Charitable Trusts Act 1853), and for the purposes of this subsection "building" includes part of a building.

[1280]

NOTES

Commencement: 1 August 1993.

PART IV

APPLICATION OF PROPERTY CY-PRÈS AND ASSISTANCE AND SUPERVISION OF CHARITIES BY COURT AND COMMISSIONERS

Extended powers of court and variation of charters

13. Occasions for applying property cy-près.

(1) Subject to subsection (2) below, the circumstances in which the original purposes of a charitable gift can be altered to allow the property given or part of it to be applied cy-près shall be as follows—

(*a*) where the original purposes, in whole or in part—

(i) have been as far as may be fulfilled; or

(ii) cannot be carried out, or not according to the directions given and to the spirit of the gift; or

(*b*) where the original purposes provide a use for part only of the property available by virtue of the gift; or

(*c*) where the property available by virtue of the gift and other property applicable for similar purposes can be more effectively used in conjunction, and to that end can suitably, regard being had to the spirit of the gift, be made applicable to common purposes; or

(*d*) where the original purposes were laid down by reference to an area which then was but has since ceased to be a unit for some other purpose, or by reference to a class of persons or to an area which has for any reason since ceased to be suitable, regard being had to the spirit of the gift, or to be practical in administering the gift; or

(*e*) where the original purposes, in whole or in part, have, since they were laid down,—

(i) been adequately provided for by other means; or

(ii) ceased, as being useless or harmful to the community or for other reasons, to be in law charitable; or

(iii) ceased in any other way to provide a suitable and effective method of using the property available by virtue of the gift, regard being had to the spirit of the gift.

(2) Subsection (1) above shall not affect the conditions which must be satisfied in order that property given for charitable purposes may be applied cy-près except in so far as those conditions require a failure of the original purposes.

(3) References in the foregoing subsections to the original purposes of a gift shall be construed, where the application of the property given has been altered or regulated by a scheme or otherwise, as referring to the purposes for which the property is for the time being applicable.

(4) Without prejudice to the power to make schemes in circumstances falling within subsection (1) above, the court may by scheme made under the court's jurisdiction with respect to charities, in any case where the purposes for which the property is held are laid down by reference to any such area as is mentioned in the first column in Schedule 3 to this Act, provide for enlarging the area to any such area as is mentioned in the second column in the same entry in that Schedule.

(5) It is hereby declared that a trust for charitable purposes places a trustee under a duty, where the case permits and requires the property or some part of it to be applied cy-près, to secure its effective use for charity by taking steps to enable it to be so applied. **[1281]**

NOTES

Commencement: 1 August 1993.

14. Application cy-près of gifts of donors unknown or disclaiming

(1) Property given for specific charitable purposes which fail shall be applicable cy-près as if given for charitable purposes generally, where it belongs—

(a) to a donor who after—

(i) the prescribed advertisements and inquiries have been published and made, and

(ii) the prescribed period beginning with the publication of those advertisements has expired,

cannot be identified or cannot be found; or

(b) to a donor who has executed a disclaimer in the prescribed form of his right to have the property returned.

(2) Where the prescribed advertisements and inquiries have been published and made by or on behalf of trustees with respect to any such property, the trustees shall not be liable to any person in respect of the property if no claim by him to be interested in it is received by them before the expiry of the period mentioned in subsection (1)(a)(ii) above.

(3) For the purposes of this section property shall be conclusively presumed (without any advertisement or inquiry) to belong to donors who cannot be identified, in so far as it consists—

(a) of the proceeds of cash collections made by means of collecting boxes or by other means not adapted for distinguishing one gift from another; or (*b*) of the proceeds of any lottery, competition, entertainment, sale or similar money-raising activity, after allowing for property given to provide prizes or articles for sale or otherwise to enable the activity to be undertaken.

(4) The court may by order direct that property not falling within subsection (3) above shall for the purposes of this section be treated (without any advertisement or inquiry) as belonging to donors who cannot be identified where it appears to the court either—

    (*a*) that it would be unreasonable, having regard to the amounts likely to be returned to the donors, to incur expense with a view to returning the property; or

    (*b*) that it would be unreasonable, having regard to the nature, circumstances and amounts of the gifts, and to the lapse of time since the gifts were made, for the donors to expect the property to be returned.

(5) Where property is applied cy-près by virtue of this section, the donor shall be deemed to have parted with all his interest at the time when the gift was made; but where property is so applied as belonging to donors who cannot be identified or cannot be found, and is not so applied by virtue of subsection (3) or (4) above—

    (*a*) the scheme shall specify the total amount of that property; and

    (*b*) the donor of any part of that amount shall be entitled, if he makes a claim not later than six months after the date on which the scheme is made, to recover from the charity for which the property is applied a sum equal to that part, less any expenses properly incurred by the charity trustees after that date in connection with claims relating to his gift; and

    (*c*) the scheme may include directions as to the provision to be made for meeting any such claim.

(6) Where—

    (*a*) any sum is, in accordance with any such directions, set aside for meeting any such claims, but

    (*b*) the aggregate amount of any such claims actually made exceeds the relevant amount,

then, if the Commissioners so direct, each of the donors in question shall be entitled only to such proportion of the relevant amount as the amount of his claim bears to the aggregate amount referred to in paragraph (*b*) above; and for this purpose "the relevant amount" means the amount of the sum so set aside after deduction of any expenses properly incurred by the charity trustees in connection with claims relating to the donors' gifts.

(7) For the purposes of this section, charitable purposes shall be deemed to "fail" where any difficulty in applying property to those purposes makes that property or the part not applicable cy-près available to be returned to the donors.

(8) In this section "prescribed" means prescribed by regulations made by the Commissioners; and such regulations may, as respects the advertisements which are to be published for the purposes of subsection (1)(*a*) above, make provision as to the form and content of such advertisements as well as the manner in which they are to be published.

(9) Any regulations made by the Commissioners under this section shall be published by the Commissioners in such manner as they think fit.

(10) In this section, except in so far as the context otherwise requires, references to a donor include persons claiming through or under the original donor, and references to property given include the property for the time being representing the property originally given or property derived from it.

(11) This section shall apply to property given for charitable purposes, notwithstanding that it was so given before the commencement of this Act.

[1282]

NOTES

Commencement: 1 August 1993.

15. Charities governed by charter, or by or under statute

(1) Where a Royal charter establishing or regulating a body corporate is amendable by the grant and acceptance of a further charter, a scheme relating to the body corporate or to the administration of property held by the body (including a scheme for the cy-près application of any such property) may be made by the court under the court's jurisdiction with respect to charities notwithstanding that the scheme cannot take effect without the alteration of the charter, but shall be so framed that the scheme, or such part of it as cannot take effect without the alteration of the charter, does not purport to come into operation unless or until Her Majesty thinks fit to amend the charter in such manner as will permit the scheme or that part of it to have effect.

(2) Where under the court's jurisdiction with respect to charities or the corresponding jurisdiction of a court in Northern Ireland, or under powers conferred by this Act or by any Northern Ireland legislation relating to charities, a scheme is made with respect to a body corporate, and it appears to Her Majesty expedient, having regard to the scheme, to amend any Royal charter relating to that body, Her Majesty may, on the application of that body, amend the charter accordingly by Order in Council in any way in which the charter could be amended by the grant and acceptance of a further charter; and any such Order in Council may be revoked or varied in like manner as the charter it amends.

(3) The jurisdiction of the court with respect to charities shall not be excluded or restricted in the case of a charity of any description mentioned in Schedule 4 to this Act by the operation of the enactments or instruments there mentioned in relation to that description, and a scheme established for any such charity may modify or supersede in relation to it the provision made by any such enactment or instrument as if made by a scheme of the court, and may also make any such provision as is authorised by that Schedule. **[1283]**

NOTES

Commencement: 1 August 1993.

Property vested in official custodian

21. Entrusting charity property to official custodian, and termination of trust

(1) The court may by order—

    (*a*) vest in the official custodian any land held by or in trust for a charity;

    (*b*) authorise or require the persons in whom any such land is vested to transfer it to him; or (*c*) appoint any person to transfer any such land to him;

but this subsection does not apply to any interest in land by way of mortgage or other security.

(2) Where property is vested in the official custodian in trust for a charity, the court may make an order discharging him from the trusteeship as respects all or any of that property.

(3) Where the official custodian is discharged from his trusteeship of any property, or the trusts on which he holds any property come to an end, the court may make such vesting orders and give such directions as may seem to the court to be necessary or expedient in consequence.

(4) No person shall be liable for any loss occasioned by his acting in conformity with an order under this section or by his giving effect to anything done in pursuance of such an order, or be excused from so doing by reason of the order having been in any respect improperly obtained.   **[1284]**

NOTES
Commencement: 1 August 1993.

22. Supplementary provisions as to property vested in official custodian

(1) Subject to the provisions of this Act, where property is vested in the official custodian in trust for a charity, he shall not exercise any powers of management, but he shall as trustee of any property have all the same powers, duties and liabilities, and be entitled to the same rights and immunities, and be subject to the control and orders of the court, as a corporation appointed custodian trustee under section 4 of the Public Trustee Act 1906 except that he shall have no power to charge fees.

(2) Subject to subsection (3) below, where any land is vested in the official custodian in trust for a charity, the charity trustees shall have power in his name and on his behalf to execute and do all assurances and things which they could properly execute or do in their own name and on their own behalf if the land were vested in them.

(3) If any land is so vested in the official custodian by virtue of an order under section 18 above, the power conferred on the charity trustees by subsection (2) above shall not be exercisable by them in relation to any transaction affecting the land, unless the transaction is authorised by order of the court or of the Commissioners.

(4) Where any land is vested in the official custodian in trust for a charity, the charity trustees shall have the like power to make obligations entered into by them binding on the land as if it were vested in them; and any covenant, agreement or condition which is enforceable by or against the custodian by reason of the land being vested in him shall be enforceable by or against the charity trustees as if the land were vested in them.

(5) In relation to a corporate charity, subsections (2), (3) and (4) above shall apply with the substitution of references to the charity for references to the charity trustees.

(6) Subsections (2), (3) and (4) above shall not authorise any charity trustees or charity to impose any personal liability on the official custodian.

(7) Where the official custodian is entitled as trustee for a charity to the custody of securities or documents of title relating to the trust property, he may

permit them to be in the possession or under the control of the charity trustees
without thereby incurring any liability.   **[1285]**

NOTES
Commencement: 1 August 1993.

Establishment of common investment or deposit funds

24. Schemes to establish common investment funds

(1) The court or the Commissioners may by order make and bring into effect
schemes (in this section referred to as "common investment schemes") for the
establishment of common investment funds under trusts which provide—

    (*a*) for property transferred to the fund by or on behalf of a charity
        participating in the scheme to be invested under the control of trustees
        appointed to manage the fund; and

    (*b*) for the participating charities to be entitled (subject to the provisions
        of the scheme) to the capital and income of the fund in shares
        determined by reference to the amount or value of the property
        transferred to it by or on behalf of each of them and to the value of
        the fund at the time of the transfers.

(2) The court or the Commissioners may make a common investment
scheme on the application of any two or more charities.

(3) A common investment scheme may be made in terms admitting any
charity to participate, or the scheme may restrict the right to participate in any
manner.

(4) A common investment scheme may make provision for, and for all
matters connected with, the establishment, investment, management and
winding up of the common investment fund, and may in particular include
provision—

    (*a*) for remunerating persons appointed trustees to hold or manage the
        fund or any part of it, with or without provision authorising a person
        to receive the remuneration notwithstanding that he is also a charity
        trustee of or trustee for a participating charity;

    (*b*) for restricting the size of the fund, and for regulating as to time,
        amount or otherwise the right to transfer property to or withdraw it
        from the fund, and for enabling sums to be advanced out of the fund
        by way of loan to a participating charity pending the withdrawal of
        property from the fund by the charity;

    (*c*) for enabling income to be withheld from distribution with a view to
        avoiding fluctuations in the amounts distributed, and generally for
        regulating distributions of income;

    (*d*) for enabling money to be borrowed temporarily for the purpose of
        meeting payments to be made out of the funds;

    (*e*) for enabling questions arising under the scheme as to the right of a
        charity to participate, or as to the rights of participating charities, or
        as to any other matter, to be conclusively determined by the decision
        of the trustees managing the fund or in any other manner;

    (*f*) for regulating the accounts and information to be supplied to
        participating charities.

(5) A common investment scheme, in addition to the provision for property
to be transferred to the fund on the basis that the charity shall be entitled to a
share in the capital and income of the fund, may include provision for enabling

sums to be deposited by or on behalf of a charity on the basis that (subject to the provisions of the scheme) the charity shall be entitled to repayment of the sums deposited and to interest thereon at a rate determined by or under the scheme; and where a scheme makes any such provision it shall also provide for excluding from the amount of capital and income to be shared between charities participating otherwise than by way of deposit such amounts (not exceeding the amounts properly attributable to the making of deposits) as are from time to time reasonably required in respect of the liabilities of the fund for the repayment of deposits and for the interest on deposits, including amounts required by way of reserve.

(6) Except in so far as a common investment scheme provides to the contrary, the rights under it of a participating charity shall not be capable of being assigned or charged, nor shall any trustee or other person concerned in the management of the common investment fund be required or entitled to take account of any trust or other equity affecting a participating charity or its property or rights.

(7) The powers of investment of every charity shall include power to participate in common investment schemes unless the power is excluded by a provision specifically referring to common investment schemes in the trusts of the charity.

(8) A common investment fund shall be deemed for all purposes to be a charity; and if the scheme admits only exempt charities, the fund shall be an exempt charity for the purposes of this Act.

(9) Subsection (8) above shall apply not only to common investment funds established under the powers of this section, but also to any similar fund established for the exclusive benefit of charities by or under any enactment relating to any particular charities or class of charity. **[1286]**

NOTES
  Commencement: 1 August 1993.

PART V
CHARITY LAND

36. Restrictions on dispositions

(1) Subject to the following provisions of this section and section 40 below, no land held by or in trust for a charity shall be sold, leased or otherwise disposed of without an order of the court or of the Commissioners.

(2) Subsection (1) above shall not apply to a disposition of such land if—

  (a) the disposition is made to a person who is not—

  (i) a connected person (as defined in Schedule 5 to this Act), or
  (ii) a trustee for, or nominee of, a connected person; and

  (b) the requirements of subsection (3) or (5) below have been complied with in relation to it.

(3) Except where the proposed disposition is the granting of such a lease as is mentioned in subsection (5) below, the charity trustees must, before entering into an agreement for the sale, or (as the case may be) for a lease or other disposition, of the land—

(*a*) obtain and consider a written report on the proposed disposition from a qualified surveyor instructed by the trustees and acting exclusively for the charity;

(*b*) advertise the proposed disposition for such period and in such manner as the surveyor has advised in his report (unless he has there advised that it would not be in the best interests of the charity to advertise the proposed disposition); and

(*c*) decide that they are satisfied, having considered the surveyor's report, that the terms on which the disposition is proposed to be made are the best that can reasonably be obtained for the charity.

(4) For the purposes of subsection (3) above a person is a qualified surveyor if—

(*a*) he is a fellow or professional associate of the Royal Institution of Chartered Surveyors or of the Incorporated Society of Valuers and Auctioneers or satisfies such other requirement or requirements as may be prescribed by regulations made by the Secretary of State; and

(*b*) he is reasonably believed by the charity trustees to have ability in, and experience of, the valuation of land of the particular kind, and in the particular area, in question;

and any report prepared for the purposes of that subsection shall contain such information, and deal with such matters, as may be prescribed by regulations so made.

(5) Where the proposed disposition is the granting of a lease for a term ending not more than seven years after it is granted (other than one granted wholly or partly in consideration of a fine), the charity trustees must, before entering into an agreement for the lease—

(*a*) obtain and consider the advice on the proposed disposition of a person who is reasonably believed by the trustees to have the requisite ability and practical experience to provide them with competent advice on the proposed disposition; and

(*b*) decide that they are satisfied, having considered that person's advice, that the terms on which the disposition is proposed to be made are the best that can reasonably be obtained for the charity.

(6) Where—

(*a*) any land is held by or in trust for a charity, and

(*b*) the trusts on which it is so held stipulate that it is to be used for the purposes, or any particular purposes, of the charity,

then (subject to subsections (7) and (8) below and without prejudice to the operation of the preceding provisions of this section) the land shall not be sold, leased or otherwise disposed of unless the charity trustees have previously—

(i) given public notice of the proposed disposition, inviting representations to be made to them within a time specified in the notice, being not less than one month from the date of the notice; and

(ii) taken into consideration any representations made to them within that time about the proposed disposition.

(7) Subsection (6) above shall not apply to any such disposition of land as is there mentioned if—

(*a*) the disposition is to be effected with a view to acquiring by way of replacement other property which is to be held on the trusts referred to in paragraph (*b*) of that subsection; or

(b) the disposition is the granting of a lease for a term ending not more than two years after it is granted (other than one granted wholly or partly in consideration of a fine).

(8) The Commissioners may direct—

(a) that subsection (6) above shall not apply to dispositions of land held by or in trust for a charity or class of charities (whether generally or only in the case of a specified class of dispositions or land, or otherwise as may be provided in the direction), or

(b) that that subsection shall not apply to a particular disposition of land held by or in trust for a charity,

if, on an application made to them in writing by or on behalf of the charity or charities in question, the Commissioners are satisfied that it would be in the interests of the charity or charities for them to give the direction.

(9) The restrictions on disposition imposed by this section apply notwithstanding anything in the trusts of a charity; but nothing in this section applies—

(a) to any disposition for which general or special authority is expressly given (without the authority being made subject to the sanction of an order of the court) by any statutory provision contained in or having effect under an Act of Parliament or by any scheme legally established; or

(b) to any disposition of land held by or in trust for a charity which—

(i) is made to another charity otherwise than for the best price that can reasonably be obtained, and

(ii) is authorised to be so made by the trusts of the first-mentioned charity; or

(c) to the granting, by or on behalf of a charity and in accordance with its trusts, of a lease to any beneficiary under those trusts where the lease—

(i) is granted otherwise than for the best rent that can reasonably be obtained; and

(ii) is intended to enable the demised premises to be occupied for the purposes, or any particular purposes, of the charity.

(10) Nothing in this section applies—

(a) to any disposition of land held by or in trust for an exempt charity;

(b) to any disposition of land by way of mortgage or other security; or

(c) to any disposition of an advowson.

(11) In this section "land" means land in England or Wales.   **[1287]**

NOTES
Commencement: 1 August 1993.

37. Supplementary provisions relating to dispositions

(1) Any of the following instruments, namely—

(a) any contract for the sale, or for a lease or other disposition, of land which is held by or in trust for a charity, and

(b) any conveyance, transfer, lease or other instrument effecting a disposition of such land,

shall state—

(i) that the land is held by or in trust for a charity,

(ii) whether the charity is an exempt charity and whether the disposition is one falling within paragraph (*a*), (*b*) or (*c*) of subsection (9) of section 36 above, and

(iii) if it is not an exempt charity and the disposition is not one falling within any of those paragraphs, that the land is land to which the restrictions on disposition imposed by that section apply.

(2) Where any land held by or in trust for a charity is sold, leased or otherwise disposed of by a disposition to which subsection (1) or (2) of section 36 above applies, the charity trustees shall certify in the instrument by which the disposition is effected—

(*a*) (where subsection (1) of that section applies) that the disposition has been sanctioned by an order of the court or of the Commissioners (as the case may be), or

(*b*) (where subsection (2) of that section applies) that the charity trustees have power under the trusts of the charity to effect the disposition, and that they have complied with the provisions of that section so far as applicable to it.

(3) Where subsection (2) above has been complied with in relation to any disposition of land, then in favour of a person who (whether under the disposition or afterwards) acquires an interest in the land for money or money's worth, it shall be conclusively presumed that the facts were as stated in the certificate.

(4) Where—

(*a*) any land held by or in trust for a charity is sold, leased or otherwise disposed of by a disposition to which subsection (1) or (2) of section 36 above applies, but

(*b*) subsection (2) above has not been complied with in relation to the disposition,

then in favour of a person who (whether under the disposition or afterwards) in good faith acquires an interest in the land for money or money's worth, the disposition shall be valid whether or not—

(i) the disposition has been sanctioned by an order of the court or of the Commissioners, or

(ii) the charity trustees have power under the trusts of the charity to effect the disposition and have complied with the provisions of that section so far as applicable to it.

(5) Any of the following instruments, namely—

(*a*) any contract for the sale, or for a lease or other disposition, of land which will, as a result of the disposition, be held by or in trust for a charity, and

(*b*) any conveyance, transfer, lease or other instrument effecting a disposition of such land,

shall state—

(i) that the land will, as a result of the disposition, be held by or in trust for a charity,

(ii) whether the charity is an exempt charity, and

(iii) if it is not an exempt charity, that the restrictions on disposition imposed by section 36 above will apply to the land (subject to subsection (9) of that section).

(6) In section 29(1) of the Settled Land Act 1925 (charitable and public trusts)—

   (a) the requirement for a conveyance of land held on charitable, ecclesiastical or public trusts to state that it is held on such trusts shall not apply to any instrument to which subsection (1) above applies; and

   (b) the requirement imposed on a purchaser, in the circumstances mentioned in section 29(1) of that Act, to see that any consents or orders requisite for authorising a transaction have been obtained shall not apply in relation to any disposition in relation to which subsection (2) above has been complied with;

and expressions used in this subsection which are also used in that Act have the same meaning as in that Act.

(7) Where—

   (a) the disposition to be effected by any such instrument as is mentioned in subsection (1)(b) or (5)(b) above will be a registered disposition, or

   (b) any such instrument will on taking effect be an instrument to which section 123(1) of the Land Registration Act 1925 (compulsory registration of title) applies,

the statement which, by virtue of subsection (1) or (5) above, is to be contained in the instrument shall be in such form as may be prescribed.

(8) Where—

   (a) an application is duly made—

      (i) for registration of a disposition of registered land, or

      (ii) for registration of a person's title under a disposition of unregistered land, and

   (b) the instrument by which the disposition is effected contains a statement complying with subsections (5) and (7) above, and

   (c) the charity by or in trust for which the land is held as a result of the disposition is not an exempt charity,

the registrar shall enter in the register, in respect of the land, a restriction in such form as may be prescribed.

(9) Where—

   (a) any such restriction is entered in the register in respect of any land, and

   (b) the charity by or in trust for which the land is held becomes an exempt charity,

the charity trustees shall apply to the registrar for the restriction to be withdrawn; and on receiving any application duly made under this subsection the registrar shall withdraw the restriction.

(10) Where—

   (a) any registered land is held by or in trust for an exempt charity and the charity ceases to be an exempt charity, or

   (b) any registered land becomes, as a result of a declaration of trust by the registered proprietor, land held in trust for a charity (other than an exempt charity),

the charity trustees shall apply to the registrar for such a restriction as is mentioned in subsection (8) above to be entered in the register in respect of the land; and on receiving any application duly made under this subsection the registrar shall enter such a restriction in the register in respect of the land.

(11) In this section—

    (a) references to a disposition of land do not include references to—

        (i) a disposition of land by way of mortgage or other security,

        (ii) any disposition of an advowson, or

        (iii) any release of a rentcharge failing within section 40(1) below; and

    (b) "land" means land in England or Wales;

and subsections (7) to (10) above shall be construed as one with the Land Registration Act 1925. **[1288]**

NOTES
Commencement: 1 August 1993.

38. Restrictions on mortgaging

(1) Subject to subsection (2) below, no mortgage of land held by or in trust for a charity shall be granted without an order of the court or of the Commissioners.

(2) Subsection (1) above shall not apply to a mortgage of any such land by way of security for the repayment of a loan where the charity trustees have, before executing the mortgage, obtained and considered proper advice, given to them in writing, on the matters mentioned in subsection (3) below.

(3) Those matters are—

    (a) whether the proposed loan is necessary in order for the charity trustees to be able to pursue the particular course of action in connection with which the loan is sought by them;

    (b) whether the terms of the proposed loan are reasonable having regard to the status of the charity as a prospective borrower; and

    (c) the ability of the charity to repay on those terms the sum proposed to be borrowed.

(4) For the purposes of subsection (2) above proper advice is the advice of a person—

    (a) who is reasonably believed by the charity trustees to be qualified by his ability in and practical experience of financial matters; and

    (b) who has no financial interest in the making of the loan in question;

and such advice may constitute proper advice for those purposes notwithstanding that the person giving it does so in the course of his employment as an officer or employee of the charity or of the charity trustees.

(5) This section applies notwithstanding anything in the trusts of a charity; but nothing in this section applies to any mortgage for which general or special authority is given as mentioned in section 36(9)(a) above.

(6) In this section—

"land" means land in England or Wales;

"mortgage" includes a charge.

(7) Nothing in this section applies to an exempt charity. **[1289]**

NOTES
Commencement: 1 August 1993.

39. Supplementary provisions relating to mortgaging

(1) Any mortgage of land held by or in trust for a charity shall state—

   (*a*) that the land is held by or in trust for a charity,
   (*b*) whether the charity is an exempt charity and whether the mortgage is one falling within subsection (5) of section 38 above, and
   (*c*) if it is not an exempt charity and the mortgage is not one falling within that subsection, that the mortgage is one to which the restrictions imposed by that section apply;

and where the mortgage will be a registered disposition any such statement shall be in such form as may be prescribed.

(2) Where subsection (1) or (2) of section 38 above applies to any mortgage of land held by or in trust for a charity, the charity trustees shall certify in the mortgage—

   (*a*) (where subsection (1) of that section applies) that the mortgage has been sanctioned by an order of the court or of the Commissioners (as the case may be), or
   (*b*) (where subsection (2) of that section applies) that the charity trustees have power under the trusts of the charity to grant the mortgage, and that they have obtained and considered such advice as is mentioned in that subsection.

(3) Where subsection (2) above has been complied with in relation to any mortgage, then in favour of a person who (whether under the mortgage or afterwards) acquires an interest in the land in question for money or money's worth, it shall be conclusively presumed that the facts were as stated in the certificate.

(4) Where—

   (*a*) subsection (1) or (2) of section 38 above applies to any mortgage of land held by or in trust for a charity, but
   (*b*) subsection (2) above has not been complied with in relation to the mortgage,

then in favour of a person who (whether under the mortgage or afterwards) in good faith acquires an interest in the land for money or money's worth, the mortgage shall be valid whether or not—

   (i) the mortgage has been sanctioned by an order of the court or of the Commissioners, or
   (ii) the charity trustees have power under the trusts of the charity to grant the mortgage and have obtained and considered such advice as is mentioned in subsection (2) of that section.

(5) In section 29(1) of the Settled Land Act 1925 (charitable and public trusts)—

   (*a*) the requirement for a mortgage of land held on charitable, ecclesiastical or public trusts (as a "conveyance" of such land for the purposes of that Act) to state that it is held on such trusts shall not apply to any mortgage to which subsection (1) above applies; and
   (*b*) the requirement imposed on a mortgagee (as a "purchaser" for those purposes), in the circumstances mentioned in section 29(1) of that Act, to see that any consents or orders requisite for authorising a transaction have been obtained shall not apply in relation to any mortgage in relation to which subsection (2) above has been complied with;

and expressions used in this subsection which are also used in that Act have the same meaning as in that Act.

(6) In this section—

"mortgage" includes a charge, and "mortgagee" shall be construed accordingly;

"land" means land in England or Wales;

"prescribed" and "registered disposition" have the same meaning as in the Land Registration Act 1925.   **[1290]**

NOTES
Commencement: 1 August 1993.

PART IX

MISCELLANEOUS

Powers of investment

70. Relaxation of restrictions on wider-range investments

(1) The Secretary of State may by order made with the consent of the Treasury—

(a) direct that, in the case of a trust fund consisting of property held by or in trust for a charity, any division of the fund in pursuance of section 2(1) of the Trustee Investments Act 1961 (trust funds to be divided so that wider-range and narrower-range investments are equal in value) shall be made so that the value of the wider-range part at the time of the division bears to the then value of the narrower-range part such proportion as is specified in the order;

(b) provide that, in its application in relation to such a trust fund, that Act shall have effect subject to such modifications so specified as the Secretary of State considers appropriate in consequence of, or in connection with, any such direction.

(2) Where, before the coming into force of an order under this section, a trust fund consisting of property held by or in trust for a charity has already been divided in pursuance of section 2(1) of that Act, the fund may, notwithstanding anything in that provision, be again divided (once only) in pursuance of that provision during the continuance in force of the order.

(3) No order shall be made under this section unless a draft of the order has been laid before and approved by a resolution of each House of Parliament.

(4) Expressions used in this section which are also used in the Trustee Investments Act 1961 have the same meaning as in that Act.

(5) In the application of this section to Scotland, "charity" means a recognised body within the meaning of section 1(7) of the Law Reform (Miscellaneous Provisions) (Scotland) Act 1990.   **[1291]**

NOTES
Commencement: 1 August 1993.

71. Extension of powers of investment

(1) The Secretary of State may by regulations made with the consent of the Treasury make, with respect to property held by or in trust for a charity, provision authorising a trustee to invest such property in any manner specified

in the regulations, being a manner of investment not for the time being included in any Part of Schedule 1 to the Trustee Investments Act 1961.

(2) Regulations under this section may make such provision—

(*a*) regulating the investment of property in any manner authorised by virtue of subsection (1) above, and

(*b*) with respect to the variation and retention of investments so made,

as the Secretary of State considers appropriate.

(3) Such regulations may, in particular, make provision—

(*a*) imposing restrictions with respect to the proportion of the property held by or in trust for a charity which may be invested in any manner authorised by virtue of subsection (1) above, being either restrictions applying to investment in any such manner generally or restrictions applying to investment in any particular such manner;

(*b*) imposing the like requirements with respect to the obtaining and consideration of advice as are imposed by any of the provisions of section 6 of the Trustee Investments Act 1961 (duty of trustees in choosing investments).

(4) Any power of investment conferred by any regulations under this section—

(*a*) shall be in addition to, and not in derogation from, any power conferred otherwise than by such regulations; and

(*b*) shall not be limited by the trusts of a charity (in so far as they are not contained in any Act or instrument made under an enactment) unless it is excluded by those trusts in express terms;

but any such power shall only be exercisable by a trustee in so far as a contrary intention is not expressed in any Act or in any instrument made under an enactment and relating to the powers of the trustee.

(5) No regulations shall be made under this section unless a draft of the regulations has been laid before and approved by a resolution of each House of Parliament.

(6) In this section "property"—

(*a*) in England and Wales, means real or personal property of any description, including money and things in action, but does not include an interest in expectancy; and

(*b*) in Scotland, means property of any description (whether heritable or moveable, corporeal or incorporeal) which is presently enjoyable, but does not include a future interest, whether vested or contingent;

and any reference to property held by or in trust for a charity is a reference to property so held, whether it is for the time being in a state of investment or not.

(7) In the application of this section to Scotland, "charity" means a recognised body within the meaning of section 1(7) of the Law Reform (Miscellaneous Provisions) (Scotland) Act 1990. **[1292]**

NOTES

Commencement: 1 August 1993.

96. Construction of references to a "charity" or to particular classes of charity

. . .

(3) A charity shall be deemed for the purposes of this Act to have a permanent endowment unless all property held for the purposes of the charity may be expended for those purposes without distinction between capital and income, and in this Act "permanent endowment" means, in relation to any charity, property held subject to a restriction on its being expended for the purposes of the charity.

. . . **[1293]**

NOTES
Commencement: 1 August 1993.

97. General interpretation

(1) In this Act, except in so far as the context otherwise requires—

"charitable purposes" means purposes which are exclusively charitable according to the law of England and Wales;

"charity trustees" means the persons having the general control and management of the administration of a charity;

"the Commissioners" means the Charity Commissioners for England and Wales;

"company" means a company formed and registered under the Companies Act 1985 or to which the provisions of that Act apply as they apply to such a company;

"the court" means the High Court and, within the limits of its jurisdiction, any other court in England and Wales having a jurisdiction in respect of charities concurrent (within any limit of area or amount) with that of the High Court, and includes any judge or officer of the court exercising the jurisdiction of the court;

"financial year"—

(a) in relation to a charity which is a company, shall be construed in accordance with section 223 of the Companies Act 1985; and

(b) in relation to any other charity, shall be construed in accordance with regulations made by virtue of section 42(2) above;

but this definition is subject to the transitional provisions in section 99(4) below and Part II of Schedule 8 to this Act;

"gross income", in relation to charity, means its gross recorded income from all sources including special trusts;

"independent examiner", in relation to a charity, means such a person as is mentioned in section 43(3)(a) above;

"institution" includes any trust or undertaking;

"the official custodian" means the official custodian for charities;

"permanent endowment" shall be construed in accordance with section 96(3) above;

"the register" means the register of charities kept under section 3 above and "registered" shall be construed accordingly;

"special trust" means property which is held and administered by or on behalf of a charity for any special purposes of the charity, and is so held and administered on separate trusts relating only to that property but a special trust shall not, by itself, constitute a charity for the purposes of Part VI of this Act;

"trusts" in relation to a charity, means the provisions establishing it as a charity and regulating its purposes and administration, whether those provisions take effect by way of trust or not, and in relation to other institutions has a corresponding meaning.

...   **[1294]**

NOTES
Commencement: 1 August 1993.

100. Short title and extent

(1) This Act may be cited as the Charities Act 1993.

(2) Subject to subsection (3) to (6) below, this Act extends only to England and Wales.

(3) Section 10 above and this section extend to the whole of the United Kingdom.

(4) Section 15(2) extends also to Northern Ireland.

(5) Sections 70 and 71 and so much of section 86 as relates to those sections extend also to Scotland.

...   **[1295]**

NOTES
Commencement: 1 August 1993.

SCHEDULES

SCHEDULE 2

Sections 3, 96

Exempt Charities

The following institutions, so far as they are charities, are exempt charities within the meaning of this Act, that is to say—

(a) any institution which, if the Charities Act 1960 had not been passed, would be exempted from the powers and jurisdiction, under the Charitable Trusts Acts 1853 to 1939, of the Commissioners or Minister of Education (apart from any power of the Commissioners or Minister to apply those Acts in whole or in part to charities otherwise exempt) by the terms of any enactment not contained in those Acts other than section 9 of the Places of Worship Registration Act 1855;

(b) the universities of Oxford, Cambridge, London, Durham and Newcastle, the colleges and halls in the universities of Oxford, Cambridge, Durham and Newcastle, Queen Mary and Westfield College in the University of London and the colleges of Winchester and Eton;

(c) any university, university college, or institution connected with a university or university college, which Her Majesty declares by Order in Council to be an exempt charity for the purposes of this Act;

(d) a grant-maintained school;

[(da) the School Curriculum and Assessment Authority;]

(e) *the National Curriculum Council;*

(f) *the Curriculum Council for Wales;*

[(f)the Curriculum and Assessment Authority for Wales;]

(g) *the School Examinations and Assessment Council;*

(h) a higher education corporation;

(i) a successor company to a higher education corporation (within the meaning of section 129(5) of the Education Reform Act 1988) at a time when an institution conducted by the company is for the time being designated under that section;

(*j*) a further education corporation;

(*k*) the Board of Trustees of the Victoria and Albert Museum;

(*l*) the Board of Trustees of the Science Museum;

(*m*) the Board of Trustees of the Armouries;

(*n*) the Board of Trustees of the Royal Botanic Gardens, Kew;

(*o*) the Board of Trustees of the National Museums and Galleries on Merseyside;

(*p*) the trustees of the British Museum and the trustees of the Natural History Museum;

(*q*) the Board of Trustees of the National Gallery;

(*r*) the Board of Trustees of the Tate Gallery;

(*s*) the Board of Trustees of the National Portrait Gallery;

(*t*) the Board of Trustees of the Wallace Collection;

(*u*) the Trustees of the Imperial War Museum;

(*v*) the Trustees of the National Maritime Museum;

(*w*) any institution which is administered by or on behalf of an institution included above and is established for the general purposes of, or for any special purpose of or in connection with, the last-mentioned institution;

(*x*) the Church Commissioners and any institution which is administered by them;

(*y*) any registered society within the meaning of the Industrial and Provident Societies Act 1965 and any registered society or branch within the meaning of the Friendly Societies Act 1974;

(*z*) the Board of Governors of the Museum of London;

(*za*) the British Library Board;

[(*zb*)the National Lottery Charities Board.] **[1296]**

NOTES

Commencement: 1 August 1993.

Para (*da*) inserted, paras (*e*), (*g*) prospectively repealed and para (*f*) prospectively substituted by the Education Act 1993, ss 253(2), 307(1), (3), Sch 15, para 5, Sch 19, para 175, Sch 21, Part II; para (*zb*) added by the National Lottery etc Act 1993, s 37, Sch 4, para 12.

SCHEDULE 5

Section 36(2)

MEANING OF "CONNECTED PERSON" FOR PURPOSES OF SECTION 36(2)

1.   In section 36(2) of this Act "connected person", in relation to a charity, means—

(*a*) a charity trustee or trustee for the charity;

(*b*) a person who is the donor of any land to the charity (whether the gift was made on or after the establishment of the charity);

(*c*) a child, parent, grandchild, grandparent, brother or sister of any such trustee or donor;

(*d*) an officer, agent or employee of the charity;

(*e*) the spouse of any person falling within any of sub-paragraphs (*a*) to (*d*) above;

(*f*) an institution which is controlled—

(i) by any person failing within any of sub-paragraphs (*a*) to (*e*) above, or

(ii) by two or more such persons taken together; or

(*g*) a body corporate in which—

(i) any connected person falling within any of sub-paragraphs (*a*) to (f) above has a substantial interest, or

(ii) two or more such persons, taken together, have a substantial interest.

2.—(1) In paragraph 1(*c*) above "child" includes a stepchild and an illegitimate child.

(2) For the purposes of paragraph 1(*e*) above a person living with another as that person's husband or wife shall be treated as that person's spouse.

3. For the purposes of paragraph 1(f) above a person controls an institution if he is able to secure that the affairs of the institution are conducted in accordance with his wishes.

4.—(1) For the purposes of paragraph 1(*g*) above any such connected person as is there mentioned has a substantial interest in a body corporate if the person or institution in question—

    (*a*) is interested in shares comprised in the equity share capital of that body of a nominal value of more than one-fifth of that share capital, or

    (*b*) is entitled to exercise, or control the exercise of, more than one-fifth of the voting power at any general meeting of that body.

(2) The rules set out in Part I of Schedule 13 to the Companies Act 1985 (rules for interpretation of certain provisions of that Act) shall apply for the purposes of sub-paragraph (1) above as they apply for the purposes of section 346(4) of that Act ("connected persons" etc).

(3) In this paragraph "equity share capital" and "share" have the same meaning as in that Act.   **[1297]–[1299]**

NOTES

Commencement: 1 August 1993.

PART 2
STATUTORY INSTRUMENTS

LAND REGISTRATION RULES 1925
(SR & O 1925 NO 1093)

NOTES
Made: 3 November 1925.
Authority: Land Registration Act 1925, s 144.

ARRANGEMENT OF RULES

PRELIMINARY

PART I
THE REGISTER

PART II
FIRST REGISTRATION AND CONVERSION

General Provisions

Part III

Registered Dealings with Registered Land:
As to Registered Dispositions Generally

(i) Form

PRELIMINARY

1. Interpretation

(1) In these rules "the Act" means the Land Registration Act 1925, and words or expressions defined in the Act have the same meanings in these rules.

(2) The Interpretation Act 1889 is to apply for the purpose of the interpretation of these rules as it applies for the purpose of the interpretation of an Act of Parliament, except so far as it may be inconsistent with the Act or these rules.

(3) "Statutory declaration" includes affidavit.

(4) "Forms" in these rules, means the Forms in the Schedule hereto.

[(5) The "Companies Acts" mean the Companies Act 1985, any Acts amending or replacing that Act and any former enactment relating to companies.]

[(5A) "Proper office" means the district land registry designated as the proper office by Article 2(2) of the Land Registration (District Registries) Order 1991.]

[(5B) In rules 24, 83 and 85 "day" means a day on which the Land Registry is open to the public and in rules 83, 84 and 85 "application" means an application for making, rectifying or cancelling any entry in the register of a registered title.]

[(5C) Except for the purpose of rule 300 any reference in these rules to a solicitor shall be construed as including a reference to a licensed conveyancer within the meaning of section 11(2) of the Administration of Justice Act 1985 and any reference to a person's solicitor shall be construed as including a reference to a licensed conveyancer acting for that person.]

[(5D) "Charity" and "charity trustees" have the same meaning as in sections 96 and 97(1) of the Charities Act 1993 respectively.]

[(5E) "the official custodian" means the official custodian for charities.]

[(5F) "Exempt charity" has the same meaning as in section 96 of the Charities Act 1993.]

[(5G) "Trusts" in relation to a charity has the same meaning as in section 97(1) of the Charities Act 1993.]

[(5H) In rules 42, 90, 267, 306(2) and 310(1) "Registry" shall include any premises where documents are stored on behalf of the Registrar.]

(6) The marginal notes to these rules shall not affect the construction thereof. **[1300]**

NOTES
Commencement: 28 March 1994 (paras (5A), (5H)); 1 August 1993 (paras (5D), (5F), (5G)); 1 January 1993 (para (5E)); 1 June 1989 (para (5C)); 1 January 1979 (para (5B)); before 1 January 1970 (remainder).
Para (5): substituted by the Land Registration (Companies and Insolvency) Rules 1986, SI 1986 No 2116, r 2.
Para (5A): inserted by the Land Registration Rules 1978, SI 1978 No 1601, r 2; substituted by the Land Registration Rules 1993, SI 1993 No 3275, r 3(1).
Para (5B): inserted by the Land Registration Rules 1978, SI 1978 No 1601, r 2.
Para (5C): inserted by the Land Registration Rules 1989, SI 1989 No 801, r 2.
Para (5D): inserted by the Land Registration (Charities) Rules 1992, SI 1992 No 3005, r 2; substituted by the Land Registration (Charities) Rules 1993, SI 1993 No 1704, r 2.
Para (5E): inserted by the Land Registration (Charities) Rules 1992, SI 1992 No 3005, r 2.
Para (5F): inserted by the Land Registration (Charities) Rules 1992, SI 1992 No 3005, r 2; substituted by the Land Registration (Charities) Rules 1993, SI 1993 No 1704, r 2.
Para (5G): inserted by the Land Registration (Charities) Rules 1993, SI 1993 No 1704, r 2.
Para (5H): inserted by the Land Registration Rules 1993, SI 1993 No 3275, r 3(2).
Interpretation Act 1889: see now the Interpretation Act 1978.

PART I

THE REGISTER

2. Parts of Register and title number

The register shall consist of three parts, called the Property Register, the Proprietorship Register, and the Charges Register. The title to each registered property shall bear a distinguishing number. **[1301]**

3. Property Register

The Property Register shall contain—

(1) The description of the land and estate comprised in the title, with a reference to the General Map or to the filed plan of the land referred to in Part V of these rules.

(2) Such notes as have to be entered relating—

    (*a*) to the ownership of the mines and minerals;

    (*b*) to exemption from any of the overriding interests mentioned in Section 70 of the Act;

    (*c*) to easements, rights, privileges, conditions and covenants for the benefit of the land, and other like matters. **[1302]**

NOTES

  The Act: Land Registration Act 1925.

4. Additions to and removals from register

Where land is removed from, or, with the consent of the Registrar, added to a title, the register shall be cleared and a new edition thereof made showing the land comprised in the title after the addition or removal and the subsisting entries relating thereto, or, where for reasons of expense or otherwise this is not practicable, the register shall be amended to show the land which has been added or removed. **[1303]**

5. Leasehold land rentcharges and land subject thereto

(1) In the case of leasehold land there shall be entered in the Property Register a reference to the registered lease, and such particulars of the lease, and of the exceptions or reservations therefrom (if any) as the applicant may desire, and the Registrar approve; and a reference to the lessor's title, if registered.

(2) In the case of rentcharges created by an instrument, that instrument shall be referred to in the Property Register.

(3) Where land is acquired in consideration of the reservation of a rentcharge and the grant of the land contains any exceptions or reservations, that grant shall be referred to in the Property Register. **[1304]**

6. Proprietorship Register

The Proprietorship Register shall state the nature of the title, and shall contain the name, address, and description of the proprietor of the land, and cautions, inhibitions, and restrictions affecting his right of disposing thereof. **[1305]**

7. Charges Register

The Charges Register shall contain—

    (*a*) incumbrances subsisting at the date of first registration;

    (*b*) subsequent charges, and other incumbrances (including notices of leases and other notices of adverse interests or claims permitted by the Act);

    (*c*) such notes as have to be entered relating to covenants, conditions, and other rights adversely affecting the land;

    (*d*) all such dealings with registered charges and incumbrances as are capable of registration. **[1306]**

[7A. Entry in the day list

(1) There shall be kept, in relation to the relevant title numbers, a record (known as the "day list") of the date of delivery of every pending application for first registration and every pending application for making, rectifying or cancelling any entry in the register of a registered title.

(2) The day list may be kept by means of a computer.] **[1307]**

NOTES
Inserted by the Land Registration Rules 1978, SI 1978 No 1601, r 3.

8. Index Map and Parcels Index

(1) Index Maps shall be kept in the Registry which shall show the position and extent of every registered estate, provided that, where practicable, the General Map shall be used for this purpose.

(2) Where the General Map is used as the Index Map the current number under which each estate is registered shall be shown in the Parcels Index.

(3) Where there is a separate Index Map, the number under which each estate was first registered shall be shown thereon, or, where practicable, the current title number. **[1308]**

[9. Index of proprietors' names

(1) There shall also be kept an index of proprietors' names showing in respect of the register of each title the name of the proprietor of the land and of the proprietor of any registered charge, together in each case with the title number:

Provided that it shall not be necessary for there to be entered in the index either:

   (a) the name of any building society, local authority or government department as proprietor of a charge, or

   (b) until such time as the Lord Chancellor shall direct, the name of any corporate or joint proprietor of land or of a charge registered as proprietor prior to 1 May 1972.

(2) Any person may apply in Form 104 for a search to be made in the index in respect of either his own name, or the name of some other person in whose property he is able to satisfy the Registrar that he is interested generally (for instance, as his trustee in bankruptcy or his personal representative).

(3) On receiving any such application the Registrar shall make the search and shall supply the applicant with details of every entry in the index relating to the particulars stated in the application . . .

(4) In this rule "index" includes any device or combination of devices serving the purpose of an index.] **[1309]**

NOTES
Substituted by the Land Registration Rules 1976, SI 1976 No 1332, r 2(1).
Para (3): words omitted revoked by the Land Registration Rules 1993, SI 1993 No 3275, r 4.

[10. List of pending applications for first registration

Until the estate in land comprised in a pending application for first registration is shown on the Index Map, the title number and a short description of the land shall be entered in a list of pending applications for first registration.]

NOTES

Substituted by the Land Registration Rules 1978, SI 1978 No 1601, r 4.

13. Correction of register

Where any clerical error or error of a like nature is discovered in the register, or in any plan or document referred to therein, which can be corrected without detriment to any registered interest, the registrar may (if he thinks fit, and after giving any notices, and calling for any evidence or obtaining any assent he may deem proper) cause the necessary correction to be made. **[1313]**

14. Registrations in error

Where it is proved to the satisfaction of the Registrar that the whole of the land comprised in a title, or too large a part to be properly dealt with under the last preceding rule, has been registered in error, the Registrar may enter notice of the fact in the register, and he may either—

    (*a*) with the consent of the proprietor and of all other persons appearing by the register to be interested in the land, or

    (*b*) after notice to the persons aforesaid and such inquiry, if any, as he may consider proper, and upon the production of such evidence as he may deem necessary;

cancel the registration wholly or to the extent required. **[1314]**

15. Production of certificates

For the purpose of these rules the Registrar may make such order as to the production of the land and charge certificates (if any) as may be deemed necessary. **[1315]**

16. Cancellation of determined entries

The Registrar may, at any time, after such inquiry and notices, if any, as he may consider proper, and upon the production of such evidence as is required by these rules or as he may deem necessary, withdraw from the register by cancellation or otherwise any lease, incumbrance, charge, note, notice, or other entry, which he is satisfied has determined, or ceased, or been discharged, or for any other reason no longer affects or relates to registered land. **[1316]**

[17. New editions of the register

(1) The Registrar may at any time when he considers it desirable, make a new edition of the register containing only the subsisting entries, and he may, in doing so, make any rearrangement that may appear to him conducive to clarity, including the altering of the number of the title and, subject to paragraph (2), the division of the title into two or more titles.

(2) A rearrangement of the register which includes the division of the title into two or more titles shall only be made under paragraph (1) on the application of the registered proprietor of the land, or after notice to the registered proprietor of the land and the registered proprietor of any charge.

(3) Such arrangements shall be made as to the recalling of the land and charge certificates and for the issue of new certificates as may be necessary.]

[1317]

NOTES

Commencement: 28 March 1994.

Substituted by the Land Registration Rules 1993, SI 1993 No 3275, r 5.

18. Registration under one or more numbers

Where several plots of land are vested in the same proprietor they may be registered under one number or several numbers as the Registrar may consider most convenient for the purpose of saving expense and facilitating future transactions.   **[1318]**

PART II

FIRST REGISTRATION AND CONVERSION

General Provisions

19. Form of application

Application for first registration shall be made by delivering . . . a written application to the effect of Forms 1, 2, 3 or 5, as the case may require.   **[1319]**

NOTES
   Words omitted revoked by the Land Registration Rules 1978, SI 1978 No 1601, r 6.

20. Documents to be delivered with application for first registration

The application shall (unless the Registrar shall otherwise direct) be accompanied by—

> (i) all such original deeds and documents relating to the title as the applicant has in his possession or under his control, including opinions of counsel, abstracts of title, contracts for or conditions of sale, requisitions, replies and other like documents, in regard to the title,
>
> (ii) a copy or sufficient abstract of the latest document of title, not being a document of record,
>
> (iii) sufficient particulars, by plan or otherwise, to enable the land to be fully identified on the Ordnance Map or Land Registry General Map,
>
> (iv) a list in triplicate of all documents delivered.   **[1320]**

21. Lease and certified copy to accompany application

(1) In the case of leasehold land, a certified copy of the lease, or if approved by the Registrar, an abstract or other sufficient evidence of its contents, shall be deposited with the application if the original lessee is the applicant, and in other cases likewise if required by the Registrar.

(2) In all cases the lease itself shall accompany the application if in the possession or control of the applicant.   **[1321]**

22. Registration of a nominee

When the application is for registration in the name of a nominee, the consent in writing of the nominee shall be delivered with the application, together with a statement that the applicant is not in a fiduciary position in regard to the land.   **[1322]**

23. Foreshore

Where any land included in an application for registration comprises foreshore, the fact shall be stated in the application, and such notices (if any) as may be required by Section 97 of the Act shall be served through the Registry.   **[1323]**

NOTES
The Act: Land Registration Act 1925.

[24. Delivery of applications for first registration

(1) Every application for first registration shall be delivered at the proper office and, when so delivered, shall be allotted a title number and shall be dated as of the day on which it is deemed by this rule to have been delivered.

(2) Every application for first registration delivered at the proper office after 9.30 hours on one day and before or at 9.30 hours on the next day shall be deemed to have been delivered at the same time, namely, immediately after 9.30 hours on the second day.

(3) For the purpose of this rule an application for first registration includes the lodging of a priority notice under rule 71 of these rules and a caution against first registration under section 53 of the Act.

[(4) If under this rule an application (other than the lodging of a priority notice under rule 71 of these rules and a caution against first registration under section 53 of the Act) would otherwise be required to be delivered to two or more proper offices it may be delivered to any one of those proper offices and if so delivered shall be treated as duly delivered to all of those proper offices.]]

[1324]

NOTES
Commencement: 2 April 1990 (para (4)); 1 October 1986 (remainder).
Substituted by the Land Registration (Delivery of Applications) Rules 1986, SI 1986 No 1534, r 4.
Para (4): added by the Land Registration Rules 1990, SI 1990 No 314, r 7.
The Act: Land Registration Act 1925.

25. Examination of title by Registrar

Where land is proposed to be registered with absolute or good leasehold title, the title shown by the documents accompanying the application shall be examined by or under the superintendence of the Registrar; and he may make such searches and enquiries and give such notices to tenants and occupiers and other persons as he may deem expedient. **[1325]**

26. Reference to special conveyancing or other counsel

The whole or any portion of the examination of the title may be referred by the Registrar, if he thinks fit, for the opinion of one of the special conveyancing counsel for the purposes of these rules, and the Registrar may act on such opinion:

Provided that where the title has already been examined on a sale by counsel of not less than 7 years' standing the Registrar may act on his opinion, or he may refer the application to him for further consideration and act on his further opinion. **[1326]**

27. Searches and enquiries by the Registrar

All searches, official certificates of search and enquiries which the Registrar may consider necessary in the examination of, or in relation to, the title shall be made or obtained by such person and in such manner as the Registrar shall direct. **[1327]**

28. Modifications of examinations of title by Registrar

Where either—

    (*a*) the land has been sold or purchased under an order of the Court, or

    (*b*) it shall appear to the Registrar that the title has been sufficiently investigated on a transaction for value,

the examination of the title may be modified in such manner as the Registrar may think fit.　　　　　　　　　　　　　　　　　　　　**[1328]**

[29. Certificate by a solicitor as to title on first registration

On an application for first registration following a sale of freehold or leasehold land or the grant of a lease where the land comprises only a single house or flat, including any yard, garden or outhouse belonging thereto the Registrar may, if he thinks fit, register a title as absolute or good leasehold on production of a certificate by a solicitor at the expense of the applicant, to the effect that—

    (*a*) he acted for the applicant on the purchase or the grant of the lease which induced the registration;

    (*b*) he investigated, or caused to be investigated, the title in the usual way on the applicant's behalf and made, or caused to be made, all necessary searches;

    (*c*) he believes that the applicant is, and has been since the date of the acquisition, in undisputed possession of the land or in receipt of the rents and profits thereof;

    (*d*) he is not aware of any question or doubt affecting the applicant's title or of any claim to the land adverse to the interest of the applicant;

    (*e*) the applicant has not entered into any arrangement or created any incumbrance requiring entry on the register except as may be stated in the certificate; and

    (*f*) he is not aware of any other matters affecting the applicant's title except as may be referred to in the assurance to the applicant or stated in the certificate.]　　　　　　　　　　　　　　**[1329]–[1330]**

NOTES

    Commencement: 1 June 1989.

    Substituted by the Land Registration Rules 1989, SI 1989 No 801, r 3.

31. Advertisements

Save as hereinafter expressly provided, before any registration is completed with absolute or good leasehold title, an advertisement shall be inserted in the Gazette and in such local or other newspaper or newspapers, if any, and in such manner as shall be decided by the Registrar in each case.　　　　**[1331]**

32. Contents of advertisements

The advertisement shall give the name and address of the person to be registered, a short description of the land, and the situation thereof, and shall require objections (if any) to be made before the expiration of a stated period, not less than fourteen days from the appearance of the advertisement in the Gazette.

　　　　　　　　　　　　　　　　　　　　　　　　　　[1332]

33. Advertisements when dispensed with

Where the original lessee is registered as first proprietor, or if the land be situated in a district in which registration of title is compulsory on sale, and the applicant is a purchaser on a sale completed within the year preceding the application, an advertisement shall not, unless the Registrar thinks it necessary or advisable, be issued. **[1333]**

34. Objections to registration

(1) Any person may, by notice in writing, signed by himself or his solicitor and delivered at the Registry before the completion of the registration, object to the registration.

(2) Such notice shall state concisely the grounds of the objection and give an address in the United Kingdom of the person objecting, to which all notices and other communications for him may be sent through the post. **[1334]**

35. Hearing of objections

(1) The Registrar shall thereupon give notice to the applicant of the objection, and the title shall not be registered until the objection has been withdrawn or otherwise disposed of.

(2) The applicant may obtain an appointment before the Registrar for the hearing of any objection, as prescribed by these rules, and the objector shall be given at least seven clear days' notice of such appointment. **[1335]**

36. Provisional possessory registration

No registration with absolute title shall be made unless and until the Registrar approves of the title, but if the applicant desires it, registration with a possessory title may be provisionally effected pending the investigation of title. **[1336]**

37. Prima facie evidence on first registration

Where the applicant has no documents of title in his possession or under his control a statutory declaration by the applicant in Form 4 may, if the Registrar is satisfied on enquiry or otherwise that the applicant is in possession or receipt of the rents and profits of the land, be taken as prima facie evidence of his right to apply for registration as first proprietor. **[1337]**

38. Marking of Deeds in Possessory Titles

In the case of registration with a possessory title the Registrar may

(1) act upon a Statutory declaration by the solicitor of the applicant that the documents produced affect the land included in the application for registration and are all the deeds necessary to be marked for the purposes of Section 16 of the Act, or

(2) dispense with the production of such deeds, on being furnished with a like Statutory declaration showing cause why they cannot be produced. **[1338]**

39. Restraint on alienation

Where the estate of the first registered proprietor is or may be subject to a restraint on alienation, the Registrar shall enter a restriction protecting any such restraint in such manner and form as he shall think fit.

Provided that—

(a) where a married woman is entitled to land without power of anticipation, or;

(*b*) notwithstanding the restraint, the land can be disposed of under the Settled Land Act 1925;

the restriction applicable to settled land shall be employed.   **[1339]**

40. Entry of incumbrances in the Register

Incumbrances, conditions, and other burdens (including fee farm grants, or other grants reserving rents or services) to which the land may be subject, shall be entered in the register and may be entered either directly, or by reference to the instruments by which they are created, or by setting out extracts therefrom.
          [1340]

41. Adverse easements

(1) Notice of an easement, right, or privilege created by an instrument and operating at law which appears to the Registrar to affect adversely tte land shall, if the Registrar thinks fit, be entered in the register.

(2) Such entry shall, so far as practicable and convenient, be by reference to the instrument by which the easement, right or privilege is created or by setting out an extract therefrom.   **[1341]**

42. Completion of registration

When—

    (*a*) all objections (if any) have been disposed of,

    (*b*) the time fixed by the advertisements and notices (if any) has expired,

    (*c*) it has been determined with what title the registration is to be made, and the requirements of Sections 14 and 16 of the Act have been complied with,

the registration shall be completed as of the day on which, and of the priority in which, the application was delivered, and the document of title, other than such as have under the Act or rules to be retained in the Registry, shall be delivered to the applicant.   **[1342]**

NOTES
    The Act: Land Registration Act 1925.

Leasehold Land

44. Registration of and dealing with underleases

Where any intermediate leasehold interest subsists between the freehold reversion and the leasehold estate which is the subject of registration, the words "lessor" and "lease," in these rules and in Sections 10 and 23 of the Act, shall be read as applying to a sub-lessor and a sub-lease.   **[1343]**

NOTES
    The Act: Land Registration Act 1925.

[45. Leases prohibiting or restricting dealings inter vivos

On the registration of any leasehold land held under a lease containing a prohibition or restriction on dealings therewith inter vivos, notice shall be entered in the register that all estates, rights, interests, powers, and remedies arising upon, or by reason of, any dealing made in breach of the prohibition or restriction are excepted from the effect of registration.]   **[1344]**

NOTES
Substituted by the Land Registration Rules 1986, SI 1986 No 2118, r 3.

46. Notice of lease

(1) Where a lease, affecting land already registered, is registered in pursuance of these rules, notice of the registration thereof shall be given to the proprietor of the freehold land or of the superior lease out of which the lease is derived, as the case may be.

(2) If no valid objection be made within seven days after service of the notice, or if the proprietor of the freehold or of the superior lease consents in writing (by himself or his solicitor) to the application, the lease shall be noted against the title to the freehold or to the superior lease in the same manner as notices of leases have to be entered under Section 48 of the Act and these rules.
[1345]

47. Lease and reversionary lease

Where a lease in possession and a reversionary lease to take effect in possession upon, or at any time within one month after, the expiration of the first-mentioned lease, are so held that the interest under both instruments belongs to the same person in the same right, such leases, so far as they relate to lands comprised in both instruments, shall be deemed for the purposes of Section 8 of the Act, and of these rules, to create one continuous term. **[1346]**

NOTES
The Act: Land Registration Act 1925.

Conversion of Possessory into Absolute or Good Leasehold Title

[48. Application for conversion under section 77 of the Act and section 1(2) of the Land Registration Act 1986

(1) An application for conversion by the proprietor of the land shall be made in Form 6 and, except where made under section 77(2)(*b*) or by virtue of section 1(2)(*b*) of the Land Registration Act 1986, shall be accompanied by all the documents of or relating to the title and, in the case of an application for converson for absolute leasehold title, to the freehold and to any intermediate leasehold.

(2) Before complying with the application, the Registrar—

    (*a*) shall serve notice on such persons as he considers necessary, including notice to owners of neighbouring property, who may be entitled to enforce restrictive conditions affecting the land;

    (*b*) may at the applicant's expense insert notice of the application in such newspaper or newspapers as he may direct;

    (*c*) may make such enquiries on the land or elsewhere as he may consider necessary.] **[1347]**

NOTES
Substituted by the Land Registration Rules 1986, SI 1986 No 2118, r 4.
The Act: Land Registration Act 1925.

*Manors, Advowsons, Rents, Tithe Rentcharges and other
Incorporeal Hereditaments, Mines and Minerals severed from the Land, Cellars,
Flats and similar Hereditaments*

50. Registration of incorporeal hereditaments

Application for registration of manors, advowsons, rents, tithe rentcharges, or
other incorporeal hereditaments, mines and minerals severed from the land,
cellars, flats, and other similar hereditaments, not including an undivided share,
shall be made according to the rules above prescribed, and shall be proceeded
with in the same manner, subject only to such modifications as the nature of the
case may require and the Registrar may approve:

Provided that where a rentcharge is created by an instrument, that
instrument shall be referred to in the register.   **[1348]**

51. Registration of a manor

On the registration of a manor the applicant shall leave in the Registry a plan
of the lands (if any) alleged to be the demesne lands of the manor, provided that
if the applicant leaves in the Registry a reference to the General Map showing
with sufficient accuracy the land affected by his application, it shall not be
necessary for him to leave, deposit, or furnish any plan.   **[1349]**

52. Registration of a rent, etc

On the registration of a rent or tithes or rentcharge in lieu of tithe the applicant
shall leave in the Registry, with the application, a plan of the lands out of which
they are issuing, so far as they can be conveniently identified and described, or
such other information as may be necessary for identifying such lands, so far as
practicable, on the Ordnance Map:

Provided that if the applicant leaves in the Registry a reference to the
General Map showing with sufficient accuracy the land affected by his
application, it shall not be necessary for him to leave, deposit, or furnish any
plan.   **[1350]**

53. Registration of mines and minerals

On the registration of mines and minerals severed from the land, a plan showing
as accurately as is practicable the surface under which the mines and minerals
lie, shall be deposited in the Registry, together with such other plans, sections,
and further descriptions (if any) as the Registrar may deem necessary for the
purpose of identifying such mines and minerals, together with full particulars
of any appurtenant rights of access, or rights incidental to the working of the
mines and minerals that may be subsisting and intended to be entered in the
register:

Provided that if the applicant leaves in the Registry a reference to the
General Map showing with sufficient accuracy the land affected by his
application, it shall not be necessary for him to leave, deposit, or furnish any
plan.   **[1351]**

Settled Land

54. Registration of a flat, tunnel, etc

On the registration of a proprietor of a flat or floor, or part of a flat or floor, of a
house or of a cellar or tunnel or other underground space apart from the surface,

a plan shall be furnished of the surface under or over which the tenement to be registered lies, and such further verbal or other description as the Registrar may deem necessary, together with notes of any appurtenant rights of access, whether held in common with others or not, or obligations affecting other tenements for the benefit of the tenement the title to which is being registered:

Provided that if the applicant leaves in the Registry a reference to the General Map showing with sufficient accuracy the land affected by his application, it shall not be necessary for him to leave, deposit, or furnish any plan.   **[1352]–[1353]**

56. Settled land; restriction required

Where application is made for registration of settled land, a statement in writing of the proper restriction shall be left with the application, or the Registrar shall be furnished with the information necessary to enable him to frame the proper restriction.   **[1354]**

57. Principle governing restrictions

In framing restrictions for the protection of persons interested in settled land, it shall not be the duty of the trustees of the settlement or of the Registrar to protect the interests of any person who would not have been a necessary party to a disposition thereof under the powers of the Settled Land Act 1925, as extended by the settlement, if the land had been unregistered; but it shall be the duty of the trustees, or, if there are no trustees, of the Registrar, to give notice of the restrictions to such of the beneficiaries (if any) as the Registrar shall direct, and any such person can, if he desires (but at his own risk), lodge a caution or apply for an inhibition.   **[1355]**

58. Forms of restrictions applicable to settled land

(1) The restrictions given in Forms 9 to 11 shall apply respectively to the various cases set forth in those forms, and may be modified according to circumstances as the parties may require and the Registrar may deem fit.

(2) For the purposes of those restrictions, references to the powers conferred by the Settled Land Act 1925 shall include any powers conferred by the settlement in extension of those statutory powers.   **[1356]**

59. Settlement may be filed

(1) The settlement, whether consisting of one or two or more documents, or a copy or abstract thereof, may be filed in the Registry for safe custody and future reference.

(2) It shall not be referred to in the register, but shall be filed separately under the number of the title to which it relates.   **[1357]**

Land held for Charitable Uses

[60. Applications for first registration of land held for Charitable Uses

(1) Any application under sections 4 and 8 of the Act for first registration of land held by or in trust for a charity shall be made by the charity trustees or, where the charity is a company or other body corporate, by that company or other body corporate.

(2) Paragraph (1) above applies to an application for the registration as proprietor of—

    (*a*) the charity trustees;
    (*b*) the charity;
    (*c*) the official custodian;
    (*d*) any other trustee for the charity.

(3) Where the person to be registered as proprietor is the official custodian, there shall be produced to the registrar—

    (*a*) a certified copy of the order of the court made under section 21(1) of the Charities Act 1993; or
    (*b*) a certified copy of an order of the Charity Commissioners made under sections 16 or 18 of the Charities Act 1993; or
    (*c*) a statement by the solicitor to the charity as to the statute which vested the land in the official custodian;

and in every case the address of the charity trustees shall be given to the registrar and, if so desired, the address of the official custodian, for the purposes of rule 315 (addresses for service of notices).

(4) Where the charity trustees have been incorporated under Part VII of the Charities Act 1993 the trustees shall produce to the registrar with the application a certified copy of the certificate granted by the Charity Commissioners under section 50 of that Act.

(5) Where the charity is subject to the provisions of the Universities and College Estates Acts 1925 and 1964 the application shall be accompanied by a certificate to that effect.

(6) Where the charity trustees, the charity, the official custodian or other trustees for the charity are registered as proprietor the registrar shall enter the appropriate restriction in the register.

(7) In this rule the appropriate restriction means—

    (*a*) in the case of a charity which is not an exempt charity, a restriction in form 12;
    (*b*) in the case of an exempt charity which is not subject to the Universities and College Estates Acts 1925 and 1964, a restriction in form 12A;
    (*c*) in the case of an exempt charity which is subject to the Universities and College Estates Acts 1925 and 1964, a restriction in form 12B;
    (*d*) where the title concerned is a rentcharge, a restriction in form 12C;
    (*e*) in the case of land vested in the official custodian under section 18 of the Charities Act 1993, a restriction in form 12D.]   **[1358]**

NOTES
    Commencement: 1 August 1993.
    Substituted by the Land Registration (Charities) Rules 1993, SI 1993 No 1704, r 3.
    The Act: Land Registration Act 1925.

[61. Statements to be contained in instruments effecting a disposition in favour of a charity

The statement required by section 37(5) of the Charities Act 1993 to be inserted into any conveyance, lease or other instrument to which section 123(1) of the Act applies and which will result in land being held by or in trust for a charity shall be in the following form:

    "The land conveyed (or as the case may be) will, as a result of this conveyance (or as the case may be), be held by or in trust for the (named) charity and either the charity is an exempt charity or the charity is not an exempt charity and the restrictions on disposition imposed by section 36 of the Charities Act 1993 will apply to the land (subject to subsection (9) of that section)".]   **[1359]**

NOTES
Commencement: 1 August 1993.
Substituted by the Land Registration (Charities) Rules 1993, SI 1993 No 1704, r 4.
The Act: Land Registration Act 1925.

[62. Statements to be contained in instruments effecting a disposition by a charity

The statement required by section 37(1) of the Charities Act 1993 to be inserted into any conveyance, lease or other instrument to which section 123(1) of the Act applies effecting a disposition of unregistered land held by or in trust for a charity shall be in the following form:

"The land conveyed (or as the case may be) is held by or in trust for a charity by the vendor (or as the case may be) and

the charity is an exempt charity

or

the charity is not an exempt charity and the conveyance (or as the case may be) is one falling within paragraph (*a*), (*b*) or (*c*) as the case may be) of subsection (9) of section 36 of the Charities Act 1993

or

the charity is not an exempt charity and the restrictions on disposition imposed by section 36 of the Charities Act 1993 apply to the land (subject to subsection (9) of that section)."]   **[1360]**

NOTES
Commencement: 1 August 1993.
Substituted by the Land Registration (Charities) Rules 1993, SI 1993 No 1704, r 5.
The Act: Land Registration Act 1925.

Small Holdings

63. Registration under Small Holdings Act 1908 to 1919

Application by a County Council for registration as proprietor of land acquired pursuant to the Small Holdings and Allotments Acts 1908 to 1919 shall be made in Form 5 and shall be accompanied by the conveyance to the Council, and a certified copy thereof, and a note shall be made in the Proprietorship Register that the land was acquired for the purpose of small holdings under the Small Holdings and Allotments Acts 1908 to 1919.   **[1361]**

NOTES
Small Holdings and Allotments Acts 1908 to 1919: see now the Agriculture Act 1947, s 67, Sch 8.

Cautions against Entry of Land on the Register

64. Form of cautions against first registration

A caution against entry of land on the register, lodged under Section 53 of the Act, shall be in Form 13, and shall be signed by the cautioner or his solicitor, and shall contain an address for service in the United Kingdom, and shall refer to, and be accompanied by, sufficient particulars, by plan or otherwise, to identify on the Ordnance Map or the Land Registry General Map, the land to which the caution relates.   **[1362]**

NOTES
The Act: Land Rgistration Act 1925.

65. Cautions against registration of manors, etc

In the case of a manor or an advowson or other incorporeal hereditament, the names of the county and parish or place, and such other particulars (if any) as the Registrar may deem necessary, shall be furnished.   **[1363]**

66. Form of statutory declaration

The statutory declaration in support of the caution shall be in Form 14, and shall be delivered with the caution.   **[1364]**

67. Period for objections

The period to be limited by the notice to be served of the cautigner under Subsection (3) of Section 53 of the Act shall be fourteen days, or such other period (not being less than seven days) as the Registrar may under special circumstances direct. The notice shall be in Form 15.   **[1365]**

NOTES
The Act: Land Registration Act 1925.

68. Withdrawal of caution

(1) The caution may at any time be withdrawn in respect of the whole or any part of the land to which it relates upon an application for that purpose in Form 16, signed by the cautioner or his solicitor, or the person entitled to the benefit of the caution or his solicitor.

(2) Where the withdrawal is in respect of a part only of the land the application shall refer to, and be accompanied by, sufficient particulars, by plan or otherwise, to identify on the Ordnance Map or on the General Map the part to which the withdrawal relates.   **[1366]**

69. Consent by cautioner

At any time after the notice required by Subsection (3) of Section 53 of the Act has been served, the cautioner may, by writing signed by himself or his solicitor, consent to the registration, and the consent may be either absolute, or conditional on some special entry being made on the register.   **[1367]–[1368]**

NOTES
The Act: Land Registration Act 1925.

Priority Notices against First Registration

71. Form and effect of Priority Notices against first registration

(1) A person entitled to apply for registration as first proprietor of land (whether his application requires the consent of any other person or not) or his solicitor, or, with his consent in writing, any other person or his solicitor, may lodge at the Registry a notice (to be called a Priority Notice) in Form 17, reserving

priority for a specified application intended to be subsequently made, and a written acknowledgment of the receipt of the notice shall be given him.

(2) If within fourteen days from the lodgment of the notice or within such further time as the Registrar shall think fit, application is made in accordance with the notice and is accompanied by the acknowledgment, it shall be dealt with in priority to any other application affecting the same land which may have been made in the meantime.

(3) On the expiration of the period fixed as aforesaid for the operation of the notice it may be cancelled.   **[1369]**

Dealings prior to Registration

72. Dealings by persons having right to apply for first registration

(1) Where a person having the right to apply for registration as first proprietor desires to deal with the land in any way permitted by the Act before he is himself registered as proprietor he may do so in the manner, and subject to the conditions, which would be applicable if he were in fact the registered proprietor. In the case of a transfer, the transferee shall be deemed to be the applicant for first registration and shall be entered on the register accordingly.

(2) Subject to any prior rights obtained by registration under the Act and rules, a dealing so made shall, when completed by registration, have the same effect as if the person making it were registered as proprietor.

(3) Provided that a dealing, other than a lease, shall not be accepted for registration until an application has been made for the registration of the estate to which it relates, and if the application for registration of the estate is subsequently refused, or withdrawn, or abandoned, the registration of such dealing shall be annulled.   **[1370]**

NOTES
   The Act: Land Registration Act 1925.

73. Effect of dealings prior to first registration

(1) Pursuant to Subsection (2) of Section 123 of the Act, it is hereby provided that any dealing with land which takes place between the date of a conveyance, grant, or assignment necessitating compulsory registration of land and the date of application to register, shall (subject to the provisions of Subsection (1) of the said Section) take effect as if it had taken place after the date of first registration, which shall be effected as of the date of the application to register.

(2) Where a dealing is a charge or other incumbrance, capable of registration in the Charges Register of the title affected, the person for the time being entitled to it shall have power to lodge an application on behalf of the proper applicant for the first registration of the estate on which such charge or incumbrance has been created.   **[1371]**

NOTES
   The Act: Land Registration Act 1925.

PART III

REGISTERED DEALINGS WITH REGISTERED LAND:
As to Registered Dispositions Generally

(i) Form

74. Forms to be used

The forms in the Schedule hereto shall be used in all matters to which they refer, or are capable of being applied or adapted, with such alterations and additions, if any, as are necessary or desired and the Registrar allows.   [1372]

75. Instruments where no form is prescribed

Instruments for which no form is provided or to which the scheduled forms cannot conveniently be adapted, shall be in such form as the Registrar shall direct or allow, the scheduled forms being followed as nearly as circumstances will permit.   [1373]

76. Implied covenants

For the purpose of introducing the covenants implied under Sections 76 and 77 of the Law of Property Act 1925, a person may, in a registered disposition, be expressed to execute, transfer, or charge as beneficial owner, as settlor, as trustee, as mortgagee, as personal representative of a deceased person, as committee of a lunatic, or as receiver of a defective, or under an order of the court: and an instrument of transfer or charge, and any instrument affecting registered land, or a registered charge, may be expressed accordingly, but no reference to covenants implied under Section 76 aforesaid shall be entered in the register.   [1374]

77. Special provisions as to implied covenants

Pursuant to Subsection (2) of Section 38 of the Act, it is hereby provided that—

(1) Any covenant implied by virtue of Section 76 of the Law of Property Act 1925 in a disposition of registered land shall take effect as though the disposition was expressly made subject to—

   (a) all charges and other interests appearing or protected on the register at the time of the execution of the disposition and affecting the title of the covenantor;

   (b) any overriding interests of which the purchaser has notice and subject to which it would have taken effect, had the land been unregistered; and

(2) The benefit of any covenant implied under Sections 76 and 77 aforesaid, or either of them shall, on and after the registration of the disposition in which it is implied, be annexed and incident to and shall go with the registered proprietorship of the interest for the benefit of which it is given and shall be capable of being enforced by the proprietor for the time being thereof.

(3) The provisions of this rule are in addition to and not in substitution for the other provisions relating to covenants contained in the said Act.

(4) Provided that where covenants are to be implied under Section 77 aforesaid, with or without modification, express reference shall be made in the disposition to that section or to the Parts of the 2nd Schedule to that Act in which the covenants are set out.   [1375]

NOTES
The Act: Land Registration Act 1925.

78. Power for Registrar to decline to enter improper forms

If it appears to the Registrar that any instrument or entry proposed to be entered or made in the register is improper in form or in substance, or is not clearly expressed, or does not indicate with sufficient precision the particular interest or land which it is intended to affect, or refers only to matters which are not the subject of registration under the Act, or, being a condition, does not run with the land, or is not capable of being legally annexed thereto, or of affecting assigns by registration of a notice or other entry, or being a restriction, is unreasonable or calculated to cause inconvenience, or is otherwise expressed in a manner inconsistent with the principles upon which the register is to be kept, he may decline to enter the same in the register, either absolutely or subject only to such modifications therein as he shall approve; or he may himself, with the applicant's consent, settle the form of the entry to be made. **[1376]**

NOTES
The Act: Land Registration Act 1925.

79. Identification of specific parts dealt with

An instrument dealing with part of the land comprised in a title shall be accompanied by a plan signed by the grantor and by or on behalf of the grantee, showing the land dealt with unless such part is clearly defined on the filed plan of the land or the General Map, in which case it may be defined by reference to the filed plan or General Map, as the case may be. **[1377]**

80. Particular forms prescribed by statute for corporations, etc

Where, under or by virtue of any statute, or other sufficient authority, a public body, corporation, company or society is empowered or required to take conveyances or mortgages or to execute deeds and instruments in any particular form or style, all transfers and other instruments requiring registration may be adapted to such form and style, and for that purpose the scheduled forms may be modified in such manner as the Registrar may from time to time direct or approve.

Where the form prescribed by the statute or authority names no definite transferee, the entry in the register may be adapted to the form. **[1378]**

81. Instruments by persons entitled to be registered as proprietor

An instrument executed under Section 37 of the Act, or under the rules relating to dealings prior to first registration, by a person entitled to be registered as proprietor of any interest in land, or of a charge, before he has been registered as such, shall be in the same form as is required for a disposition by the proprietor with such modification, if any, as may be necessary to define clearly the land affected. But no registration of such instrument shall be made until the person executing the same has been registered as proprietor, or his right to be so registered has been shown to the satisfaction of the Registrar. **[1379]**

NOTES
The Act: Land Registration Act 1925.

(ii) Execution and Attestation

[82. Instruments executed by attorney

(1) If any instrument executed by an attorney is delivered at the Registry, there shall be furnished to the registrar either the instrument creating the power of attorney, or a copy by means of which its contents may be proved under either section 3 of the Powers of Attorney Act 1971 or section 7(3) of the Enduring Powers of Attorney Act 1985 or a document which complies with section 4 of the Evidence and Powers of Attorney Act 1940.

(2) If an Order pursuant to section 8 of the Enduring Powers of Attorney Act 1985 has been made with respect to a power or the donor thereof or the attorney appointed thereunder the order or an office copy or copy certified pursuant to rule 309 shall be furnished to the registrar.

(3) The registrar may retain any instrument creating a power of attorney or any order or any copy or document produced pursuant to this rule.

(4) If any transaction between the donee of a power of attorney and the person dealing with him is not completed within twelve months of the date on which the power came into operation, evidence shall be produced to the registrar to satisfy him that the power had not been revoked at the time of the transaction.

(5) When the power was in a form prescribed under section 2(2) of the Enduring Powers of Attorney Act 1985 the evidence that the power had not been revoked shall, unless the registrar otherwise directs, consist of a statutory declaration by the person dealing with the donee of the power that he did not, at the time of the completion of the transaction:

(a) know of any revocation of the power whether by the donor or by an Order of the Court of Protection;

(b) know of the occurrence of any event (such as the death of the donor or the bankruptcy of the donor or of any donee or a direction by the Court of Protection on exercising its powers under Part VII of the Mental Health Act 1983 which had the effect of revoking the power;

(c) know that the power was not a valid enduring power of attorney and had been revoked by the donor's mental incapacity.

(6) In any case to which paragraph (5) above does not apply the evidence that the power has not been revoked shall, unless the registrar otherwise directs, consist of a statutory declaration by the person dealing with the donee that he did not, at the time of the completion of the transaction:

(a) know of any revocation of the power

(b) know of the occurrence of any event (such as the death, bankruptcy or other incapacity of the donor) which had the effect of revoking the power.

Provided that where the power was expressed in the instrument creating it to be irrevocable and to be given by way of security the statutory declaration shall be to the effect that the declarant did not know that the power was not in fact given by way of security and did not know that the power had been revoked by the donor acting with the consent of the donee.]   **[1380]**

NOTES

Substituted by the Land Registration (Powers of Attorney) Rules 1986, SI 1986 No 1537, r 2.

(iii) Registration

[83. Delivery of applications

(1) Every application shall be delivered at the proper office and, when so delivered, shall be allocated an official reference number and shall be dated as of the day on which it is deemed under rule 85 of these rules to have been delivered.

[(2) If under this rule an application would otherwise be required to be delivered to two or more proper offices it may be delivered to any one of those proper offices and if so delivered shall be treated as duly delivered to all of those proper offices.]

[(3) The application shall be completed by registration as of the day on which and, subject to the effect of any provisions of the Act or of any rules made thereunder, of the priority in which it is deemed to have been delivered.] **[1381]**

NOTES
Commencement: 2 April 1990 (para (2)); 1 January 1979 (remainder).
Substituted by the Land Registration Rules 1978, SI 1978 No 1601, r 8.
Para (2): inserted by the Land Registration Rules 1990, SI 1990 No 314, r 9.
Para (3): renumbered as such by the Land Registration Rules 1990, SI 1990 No 314, r 9.

[84. Priority of applications

(1) Where two or more applications relating to a particular title are deemed to have been delivered at the same time, the order in which, as between each other, they shall rank in priority shall, subject to the effect of any provision of the Act or of any rules made thereunder, be determined in the manner prescribed by this rule.

(2) Where the applications are made by the same applicant, they shall rank in such order as he shall specify.

(3) Where the applications are not made by the same applicant, they shall rank in such order as may be agreed between the applicants or, failing agreement, as may be determined under rule 298 of these rules.

(4) Where one transaction is dependent upon another the registrar may assume (unless or until the contrary appears) that the applicant or applicants have specified or agreed that the applications shall have priority so as to give effect to the sequence of the instruments effecting the transactions.] **[1382]**

NOTES
Substituted by the Land Registration Rules 1978, SI 1978 No 1601, r 9.
The Act: Land Registration Act 1925.

[85. Date of delivery of applications

Every application delivered at a proper office after 9.30 hours on one day and before or at 9.30 hours on the next day shall be deemed to have been delivered at the same time, namely, immediately after 9.30 hours on the second day.]
[1383]

NOTES
Commencement: 2 April 1990.
Substituted by the Land Registration Rules 1990, SI 1990 No 314, r 10.

86. Alterations in instruments after delivery

(1) If any alteration is required to be made in an instrument after it has been delivered for registration, it may, before any entry in respect thereof has been made in the register, and, if the Registrar shall think fit, be withdrawn from registration and returned for the purpose of alteration and re-execution.

(2) The re-execution must be by all persons whose interests appear to be affected by the instrument, whether it was originally so executed by them or not.

(3) On re-delivery at the Registry, the dealing shall be registered as of the date and priority of such re-delivery.   **[1384]**

87. Instruments affecting two or more titles

(1) Where an instrument or application affects two or more titles or two or more charges it may, on the written application of the person delivering it for registration, be registered as to some or one only of the titles or charges affected thereby.

(2) An instrument so registered may be afterwards registered as to any of the other titles or charges affected thereby, but shall not affect any title or charge as to which it has not been registered.   **[1385]**

90. Retention of documents in Registry

Except where otherwise provided by the Act or these rules, all deeds, applications, and other documents on which any entry in the register is founded shall be retained, and shall not be taken away from the Registry, except under a written order of the registrar or an order from the court.   **[1386]**

NOTES
The Act: Land Registration Act 1925.

91. Endorsement of registration with lesser

(1) Where registered leasehold land is held under a lease which requires a disposition to be produced to the lessor or his agent, or to be produced to and endorsed by him, such a stipulation shall, as regards any transfer or charge, be sufficiently complied with by production of the instrument or a copy thereof to him and by endorsement, if required, of the instrument of transfer or charge or of a copy thereof, or, after the registration thereof, by production, if required, of the land certificate or charge certificate, as the case may be, and by endorsement on the lease.

(2) Such endorsement shall not be made on the land or charge certificate, and if so made, after the commencement of the Act, shall be void. **[1387]–[1389]**

(iv) Stamp Duty

94. Stamping of deeds off the register

Where an application or instrument capable of registration is made or executed for the sole purpose of carrying out on the register a transaction already effected by a deed or other instrument not capable of registration, the Inland Revenue stamp on the transaction shall be affixed to or impressed on the last-mentioned deed or instrument, and the registered instrument shall bear no stamp duty:

Provided that the stamped instrument shall, before the completion of the registration, be produced to an officer of the Registry, to show that all duty payable in respect of the transaction has been paid.   **[1390]**

95. Questions as to sufficiency of stamp

(1) When, upon the delivery of any instrument for registration, a question arises whether such instrument, or any other instrument produced under the last preceding rule, is sufficiently stamped, and the applicant for registration, or his solicitor, gives a written undertaking that he will within a time fixed by the Registrar procure and furnish the necessary evidence that the instrument so delivered or produced either then was or has subsequently been sufficiently stamped, the instrument may be returned, for the purpose of procuring of such evidence, to the person who delivered or produced it.

(2) If such instrument is subsequently, within the time fixed, delivered or produced at the Registry, with the proper evidence that it is, when so delivered or produced, sufficiently stamped, the registration shall be completed as of the date of the original application.

(3) If, at the expiration of the time fixed, the written undertaking has not been complied with, the application shall be cancelled.   **[1391]**

(v) Deeds and Instruments off the Register

96. Certificate as to the necessity of deeds off the register

Pursuant to Section 39 of the Act it is hereby provided that, where a transaction (though relating exclusively to registered land or to a registered charge) is of such a character (by reason, for instance, of its being accompanied by lengthy recitals or personal covenants not affecting the substance of the transaction in relation to the registered land or charge or if its being closely involved with other transactions or of its being necessary that duplicates should be held by different persons) as to render it necessary or useful that the registered disposition should be accompanied by an additional deed or instrument, the Registrar may issue a certificate to that effect in such form as he shall think fit, and in that case the additional deed or instrument shall, if in accordance with such certificate, be an exception within the meaning of the said Section and shall not be rendered void by that Section.   **[1392]**

NOTES
    The Act: Land Registration Act 1925.

97. Minor interests in mortgage debts

Section 101 of the Act shall, so far as applicable, apply to a minor interest in a debt secured by a registered charge, as if that debt had been referred to in place of registered land.   **[1393]**

98. Form of transfer

A transfer of the land comprised in a freehold title shall be made by an instrument in Forms 19 or 20.   **[1394]**

99. Transfer of land into settlement

A transfer of land into settlement shall be made by a vesting transfer in one of the Forms 21 or 22, with the addition of the proper restrictions to be entered in the register, according to the principles prescribed by these rules, and the Registrar shall, on receipt thereof, register the transferee (being the tenant for life of full age, statutory owner or personal representative, as the case may require) named therein as the proprietor of the land, and shall enter in the register the restrictions contained in the transfer. **[1395]**

100. Registered land brought into settlement

Where registered land has been settled and the existing registered proprietor is the tenant for life under the settlement, the proprietor shall make a declaration in Form 23 and shall apply for the registration of a restriction in Form 9, or such other restriction as may be required, having regard to the terms of the settlement and the Settled Land Act 1925. **[1396]**

101. Land bought with capital money

Where registered land is acquired with capital money the transfer shall be in Form 24. **[1397]**

102. Transfer to statutory owners

A transfer to the statutory owners under Subsection (2) of Section 91 of the Act shall not refer to the settlement and shall be in the ordinary form, with the addition of a restriction against any disposition not authorised by the Settled Land Act 1925 or the settlement. **[1398]**

NOTES
The Act: Land Registration Act 1925.

103. Creation of interests affecting settled land in priority to the settlement

Pursuant to Subsection (2) of Section 87 of the Act it is hereby provided as follows:—

    (i) Where a proprietor or the personal representative of a deceased proprietor has power under a settlement to create a legal estate in priority to the settlement, he may do so by any document sufficient at law to create it.

    (ii) The document shall be completed by registration and shall be a registered disposition and shall vest a legal estate in the grantee.

    (iii) On production of such a document purporting to be in exercise of such a power executed by such proprietor or personal representative the Registrar shall, without enquiry as to the existence or terms of the power, register notice of the estate created as an incumbrance on the land, and shall inform all persons, appearing by the register to be interested, that he has done so.

    (iv) The registration of such a notice shall not confer on the grantee any greater estate or interest, as against the other persons interested under the settlement, than it would have conferred if the land had not been on the register. **[1399]**

NOTES
The Act: Land Registration Act 1925.

104. Duty to apply for restrictions when land is settled

(1) On the creation of a settlement it shall be the duty of the proprietor, or (if there is no proprietor) the personal representatives of a deceased proprietor, to

apply to the Registrar for the entry of such restrictions or inhibitions or notices as may be appropriate to the case.

The application shall state that they are required for the protection of the minor interests under the settlement.

(2) The Registrar shall enter such restrictions, inhibitions or notices without enquiry as to the terms of the settlement provided they are not in his opinion unreasonable or calculated to cause inconvenience, and shall inform all persons, appearing by the register to be affected thereby, that he has done so.

(3) Nothing in this rule shall affect the rights and powers of a personal representative for purposes of administration. **[1400]**

105. Discharge from liability in respect of minor interests under a settlement

Where a proprietor or personal representative of a deceased proprietor has, in good faith, complied with the requirements of the Act in executing a vesting deed, assent or transfer of land or discharge of trustees and in applying for the necessary and proper restrictions or other entries (if any) that may be required for the protection of minor interests under a settlement, he shall be absolutely discharged from all liability in respect of the equitable interests and powers taking effect under the settlement, and shall be entitled to be kept indemnified at the cost of the trust estate from all liabilities affecting the settled land, but the proprietor for the time being (not being a purchaser for value or his successor in title) shall hold the land upon the trusts (if any) affecting the same. **[1401]**

NOTES
   The Act: Land Registration Act 1925.

106. Release of land from minor interests under a settlement

Where the trustees of a settlement desire to release registered land from the minor interests under such settlement they may do so by any document sufficient at law to release it, and, on an application made for that purpose, effect shall be given to the transaction by making the consequential alterations in the register. **[1402]**

107. Transfer of land in consideration of a rent

(1) A transfer of land in consideration or partly in consideration of a rent may be made by the proprietor of the land by an instrument in any form legally sufficient for the purpose of which the Registrar may approve.

(2) The transferee shall be registered as the proprietor of the land, and the rent shall be entered in the Charges Register as an incumbrance. **[1403]**

108. Separate title for proprietor of a rent

The transferor shall be registered as the proprietor of the rent under a separate title, and a reference to that title shall be made in the title of the transferee.
[1404]

109. Implied covenants on a transfer of freehold land subject to a rent

On a transfer of freehold land subject to an existing rent, covenants (similar to those implied by Section 24 of the Act on a transfer of leasehold land) shall be implied under Section 77 of the Law of Property Act 1925, but such implication may be negatived by adding suitable words to the instrument of transfer as in Form 33, and in that case a note thereof shall be entered in the register.

If it is desired to substitute modified covenants for the covenants implied by this rule, the necessary variations may be made in the transfer.   **[1405]**

NOTES
The Act: Land Registration Act 1925.

110. Covenants for indemnity

On a transfer of land subject to a charge or other incumbrance appearing on the register, or, in the case of a possessory or qualified title, an incumbrance not affected by the registration, covenants by either party to pay the money owing and to indemnify the other party may be added to the instrument of transfer and may be noted on the register.   **[1406]**

111. Transfers excepting minerals

(1) A transfer of land—

    (*a*) without the mines and minerals shall be made by an instrument in Form 25,

    (*b*) with certain specified mines and minerals shall be made by an instrument in Form 26,

    (*c*) with the mines and minerals, except certain specified mines and minerals, shall be made by an instrument in Form 27.

(2) The transferee shall be registered as proprietor of the land, with a note to the effect that the mines and minerals (or that the mines and minerals other than certain specified mines and minerals; or that certain specified mines and minerals, as the case may be) are excepted.

(3) The transferor shall, if entitled to the excepted mines and minerals, be registered as the proprietor thereof, with an absolute, qualified, good leasehold, or possessory title, according to the circumstances of the case.

(4) In any such transfer rights to work the mines and minerals, or in relation to the surface or any strata of minerals, may be reserved or granted.   **[1407]**

112. Transfers of minerals

(1) A transfer

    (*a*) of mines and minerals without the land shall be made by an instrument in Form 28,

    (*b*) of certain specified mines and minerals without the land shall be made by an instrument in Form 29,

    (*c*) without the land, of the mines and minerals, except certain specified mines and minerals, shall be made by an instrument in Form 30.

(3) The transferee shall be registered as the proprietor of the mines and minerals transferred, with an absolute, qualified, good leasehold, or possessory title, according to the circumstances of the case; and a note shall be entered against the transferor's title to the effect that the mines and minerals (or that certain specified mines and minerals; or that the mines and minerals other than certain specified mines and minerals, as the case may be) have been transferred.

(3) In any such transfer rights to work the mines and minerals, or in relation to the surface or any strata of minerals, may be reserved or granted.   **[1408]**

113. Instruments transferring mines and minerals apart from the surface and vice versa, granting rent-charges or leases, etc

(1) An instrument under Sections 18 or 21 of the Act transferring mines and minerals apart from the surface or the surface without all or any of the mines and minerals, or granting a rentcharge issuing out of freehold or leasehold land, or a lease or sub-lease of land, shall refer to the land by means of its title number and, if part only of the land in the title is to be affected, to a plan (signed by the grantor and by or on behalf of the grantee) enabling it to be identified on the filed plan of the land or, where the part dealt with is clearly defined on the General Map, by reference to that Map.

(2) Such an instrument transferring, granting, leasing or sub-leasing an easement, right or privilege in, over or derived from registered land, shall, as regards the servient tenement, refer to it by means of its title number and, if part only of the land in the title is to be affected, to a plan (signed by the grantor and by or on behalf of the grantee) or other description enabling it to be identified on the filed plan or the Land Registry General Map.

(3) As regards the dominant tenement the land shall, if and so far as it is registered, be referred to in like manner, and if and so far as it is not registered shall be referred to by a plan (similarly signed) or other description enabling it to be identified on the Ordnance Map.   **[1409]**

NOTES
    The Act: Land Registration Act 1925.

114. Sale by chargee

A transfer of land in exercise of a power of sale contained in a registered charge shall be made by an instrument in Form 31.   **[1410]**

115. Transfer of leasehold land

(1) A transfer of leasehold land shall be made by an instrument in Form 32, and all or any of the covenants implied by Section 24 of the Act on a transfer of leasehold land may, if it is desired, be negatived by adding suitable words to the instrument of transfer, and in that case an entry negativing the implied covenants shall be entered in the register.

(2) If it is desired to substitute modified covenants, by reference to Section 77 of the Law of Property Act 1925 or otherwise, for the covenants implied by Section 24, the necessary variations may be made in the transfer.   **[1411]**

NOTES
    The Act: Land Registration Act 1925.

116. Disposition of leasehold land subject to a rent

A disposition of leasehold land subject to a rent (whether legally apportioned or not) and to a rent legally apportioned shall be made by an instrument in Forms 33 or 34 or as near thereto as circumstances will permit.   **[1412]**

117. Variation of implied covenants

On a transfer of part of the land held under a lease, the covenants implied by Section 24 of the Act, or Section 77 of the Law of Property Act 1925, may, if it is desired, be modified or negatived by adding suitable words to the instrument of transfer, and a note shall be made in the register.   **[1413]**

NOTES
The Act: Land Registration Act 1925.

118. Transfer for a small holding

On a sale by a county council of land subject to all or some of the conditions of Section 12 of the Small Holdings and Allotments Act 1908 the transfer shall be in Form 37 and a restriction and note in Form 39 shall be entered in the register.   **[1414]**

NOTES
Small Holdings and Allotments Act 1908, s 12: see now the Small Holdings and Allotments Act 1926, s 6 and the Agriculture Act 1947, s 67, Sch 8.

119. Transfer not for a small holding

On a sale by a county council of land free from all the conditions of Section 12 of the Small Holdings and Allotments Act 1908 the transfer shall be in Form 38, and all reference to the Small Holdings Act shall be cancelled on the register.

[1415]

NOTES
Small Holdings and Allotments Act 1908, s 12: see now the Small Holdings and Allotments Act 1926, s 6 and the Agriculture Act 1947, s 67, Sch 8.

120. Sales under Sec 12 of the Small Holdings Act 1908

On a sale made by a county council under Section 12 of the Small Holdings and Allotments Act 1908 no evidence shall be required by the Registrar as to the happening of any of the events mentioned in the said section as giving rise to the powers of the county council or the fulfilment of any of the provisions in that Section contained.   **[1416]**

NOTES
Small Holdings and Allotments Act 1908, s 12: see now the Small Holdings and Allotments Act 1926, s 6 and the Agriculture Act 1947, s 67, Sch 8.

121. Transfer to a company or other corporation

(1) A transfer of land to an incorporated company or other corporation, sole or aggregate, shall be made by an instrument in Form 35, and, save as mentioned in this rule, shall refer to the licence in mortmain or statute enabling the corporation to acquire or hold the land.

(2) If the licence or statute contains any limit to the extent of land which may be acquired or held or any provisions as to the purposes for which it may be used, a statement showing that the land transferred, together with any land already acquired or held under such licence or statute, does not exceed such limit, and, showing also the purposes for which the land is to be used, shall be added.

(3) Such statements shall be proved by statutory declaration or otherwise as the Registrar may direct.

(4) Provided that—

    (*a*) a transfer of land from the Ecclesiastical Commissioners to an incumbent or other ecclesiastical corporation shall be exempt from the provisions of this rule;

(*b*) where a company is incorporated for profit under the Companies Acts, it shall not be necessary to refer to those Acts, but the memorandum and articles of association shall be produced to show that the statutory powers of acquisition and disposition are not affected.   **[1417]**

[122. Dispositions in favour of a charity

(1) A disposition or dealing in favour of a charity shall comply with this rule.

(2) The statement required by section 37(5) of the Charities Act 1993 to be inserted into any instrument effecting a disposition which will result in the land being held by or in trust for a charity shall be in the following form:

"The land transferred (or as the case may be) will, as a result of this transfer (or as the case may be), be held by or in trust for the (named) charity and either the charity is an exempt charity or the charity is not an exempt charity and the restrictions on disposition imposed by section 36 of the Charities Act 1993 will apply to the land (subject to subsection (9) of that section)."

(3) Where the charity trustees have been incorporated under Part VII of the Charities Act 1993 they shall be described in the instrument effecting the disposition as:

"a body corporate under Part VII of the Charities Act 1993"

(4) Where the charity is subject to the provisions of the Universities and College Estates Acts 1925 and 1964 the instrument effecting the disposition shall contain the following statement:

"The provisions of the Universities and College Estates Acts 1925 and 1964 apply to the charity".]   **[1418]**

NOTES
Commencement: 1 August 1993.
Substituted by the Land Registration (Charities) Rules 1993, SI 1993 No 1704, r 7.

[123. Applications for the registration of dispositions or dealings with titles to be held by or in trust for a charity

(1) Any application to register a disposition of land under sections 19, 22 or 26 of the Act which, when registered, will be held by or in trust for a charity shall be made by the charity trustees or, where the charity is a company or other body corporate, by that company or other body corporate.

(2) Paragraph (1) above applies to an application for the registration of—
   (*a*) the charity trustees;
   (*b*) the charity;
   (*c*) the official custodian;
   (*d*) any other trustee for the charity.

(3) Where the person to be registered as proprietor is the official custodian, there shall be produced to the registrar—
   (*a*) a certified copy of an order of the court made under section 21(1) of the Charities Act 1993; or
   (*b*) a certified copy of an order of the Charity Commissioners made under sections 16 or 18 of the Charities Act 1993,

and the address of the charity trustees shall be stated in the application and, if so desired, that of the official custodian, for the purposes of rule 315 (addresses for service of notices).

(4) Where the charity trustees have been incorporated under Part VII of the Charities Act 1993 the trustees shall produce to the registrar with the application a certified copy of the certificate granted by the Charity Commissioners under section 50 of that Act.

(5) Where the charity trustees, the charity, the official custodian or any other trustee for the charity, are registered as proprietor the registrar shall enter the appropriate restriction in the register.

(6) In this rule the appropriate restriction means—

> (*a*) in the case of a charity which is not an exempt charity, a restriction in form 12;
>
> (*b*) in the case of an exempt charity which is not subject to the Universities and College Estates Acts 1925 and 1964, a restriction in form 12A;
>
> (*c*) in the case of an exempt charity which is subject to the Universities and College Estates Acts 1925 and 1964, a restriction in form 12B;
>
> (*d*) where the title concerned is a rentcharge, a restriction in form 12C;
>
> (*e*) in the case of land vested in the official custodian under section 18 of the Charities Act 1993, a restriction in form 12D.

(7) The registrar may, before completing the registration, require the production of a certified copy of the charitable trust deed, will, statute, memorandum or articles of association, order of the court or of the Charity Commissioners or other instrument or direction defining the trusts under which the title will be held.] **[1419]**

NOTES
Commencement: 1 August 1993.
Substituted by the Land Registration (Charities) Rules 1993, SI 1993 No 1704, r 7.
The Act: Land Registration Act 1925.

[124. Duties of charity trustees and others to make applications where a registered title is held by or in trust for a charity

(1) In this rule the expression "the appropriate restriction" has the same meaning as in rule 123(6).

(2) Where registered land not previously held by or in trust for a charity becomes so held, the charity trustees or the charity shall apply for the appropriate restriction to be entered.

(3) Where a registered proprietor is a company or other body corporate which becomes a charity it shall apply for the appropriate restriction to be entered.

(4) Where registered land is held by or in trust for a charity which becomes an exempt charity, the charity trustees or the charity shall apply for the appropriate restriction to be entered.

(5) Where, under rule 131, the registrar enters as proprietor a person who is or holds on trust for a charity the registrar shall also enter the appropriate restriction.

(6) Where in relation to a charity or charity trustees the Charity

Commissioners have taken any action under the provisions of section 18(1), (2), or (4) of the Charities Act 1993 they may apply for the entry of a restriction in Form 12D on the register of any title held by or in trust for that chairty.] **[1420]**

NOTES
Commencement: 1 August 1993.
Substituted by the Land Registration (Charities) Rules 1993, SI 1993 No 1704, r 8.

125. Entry of incumbent on a transfer to the Ecclesiastical Commissioners

Where by virtue of any Act of Parliament a conveyance to the Ecclesiastical Commissioners would have the effect of vesting any land, either immediately or at a subsequent time, in an incumbent or any other ecclesiastical corporation sole and his successors, the Registrar may, on production of a transfer to the Ecclesiastical Commissioners, together with a certificate by them in Form 40, or to the like effect, enter such incumbent, or other ecclesiastical corporation, and his successors as proprietor. **[1421]**

126. Entry of incumbent upon creation of a new parish

(1) When by virtue of the New Parishes Acts 1843 to 1884 any land would upon the creation of a new parish become vested in an incumbent and his successors, and the last preceding rule shall be inapplicable, the Registrar may on production of—

  (a) the land certificate,
  (b) the consent of the Proprietor of the land,
  (c) a certificate by the Ecclesiastical Commissioners, in Form 41, or to the like effect,

enter such incumbent as proprietor.

(2) If the proprietor refuses to give his consent, or his consent can only be obtained after undue delay or expense, the Registrar may, after due notice under these rules to the proprietor, and such further evidence (if any) as he may deem sufficient, make the entry without production of the consent or the land certificate. **[1422]**

NOTES
New Parishes Acts 1843 to 1884: see now New Parishes Measure 1943.

127. Entry of Ecclesiastical Commissioners etc, as proprietor

(1) Where by—

  (a) a scheme of the Ecclesiastical Commissioners and an Order in Council ratifying the same, or
  (b) other instrument taking effect on publication in the Gazette made pursuant to the provisions of any Act of Parliament relating to or administered by the Ecclesiastical Commissioners, or
  (c) any conveyance authorised by any such Act.

any land shall be expressed or declared to be transferred or vested to or in the Ecclesiastical Commissioners, or to or in any ecclesiastical corporation, aggregate or sole, or any person, and it shall be necessary or deemed desirable by the Ecclesiastical Commissioners to enter the transferee on the register, the Registrar may (on production of the land certificate, and the consent of the proprietor of the land and of a certificate by the Ecclesiastical Commissioners in Form 42, or to, the like effect, and of the King's printer's copy of the Gazette containing such publication), enter such ecclesiastical corporation or the Ecclesiastical Commissioners, or such person, as proprietor.

(2) The consent of the proprietor to the scheme, testified by his signing or sealing the same, shall be a sufficient consent for the purposes of this rule, and the King's printer's copy of the Gazette containing it shall be sufficient evidence of such consent. **[1423]**

[128. Dispositions and other dealings by a charity

(1) A disposition or dealing by a charity shall comply with the requirements of this rule.

(2) The statement required by section 37(1) of the Charities Act 1993 to be inserted into any instrument effecting a disposition of registered land held by or in trust for a charity (other than a charge of registered land) shall be in the following form:

"The land transferred (or as the case may be) is held by or in trust for a charity by the proprietor and

the charity is an exempt charity

or

the charity is not an exempt charity and the transfer (or as the case may be) is one falling within paragraph (*(a), (b) or (c) as the case may be*) of subsection (9) of section 36 of the Charities Act 1993

or

the charity is not an exempt charity and the restrictions on disposition imposed by section 36 of the Charities Act 1993 apply to the land (subject to subsection (9) of that section)."

(3) The statement required by section 39(1) of the Charities Act 1993 to be inserted into any charge of registered land held by or in trust for a charity shall be in the following form:

"The land charged is held by or in trust for a charity by the proprietor and

the charity is an exempt charity

or

the charity is not an exempt charity and the charge is one falling within subsection (5) of section 38 of the Charities Act 1993

or

the charity is not an exempt charity and the charge is one to which the restrictions imposed by section 38 of the Charities Act 1993 apply."] **[1424]–[1426]**

NOTES
Commencement: 1 August 1993.
Substituted by the Land Registration (Charities) Rules 1993, SI 1993 No 1704, r 9.

131. Where power of disposing of registered land has become vested in some person other than the proprietor

Where the power of disposing of registered land has, by the operation of any statute or statutory power or by Order of Court or by paramount title, become vested in some person other than the proprietor (as, for instance, in the case of a deed poll executed under Section 77 of the Lands Clauses Consolidation Act 1845, or of a vesting in a co-tenant for life of full age, or the trustees of a settlement in the case of an infant under the First Schedule to the Law of Property Act 1925, or the Second Schedule to the Settled Land Act 1925, or of a declaration express or implied vesting an estate made under any statute, or of a sale by a mortgagee with a title paramount to the title registered) and the proprietor refuses to execute a transfer, or his execution of a transfer cannot be obtained, or can only be obtained after undue delay or expense, the Registrar may—

    (a) after due notice under these rules to such proprietor,
    (b) on production of the land certificate, unless an order to the contrary is made by the Registrar,
    (c) on such other evidence as he may deem sufficient,

make such entry in or correction of the register as under the circumstances he shall deem fit, for the purpose of vesting the registered land in the same person in whom the legal estate would have been vested if the land had not been registered. **[1427]–[1428]**

133. Registration of a personal representative, etc, under Sec 92 of the Act

An application, under the last paragraph of Section 92 of the Act, by a personal representative or tenant for life or statutory owner to be registered as proprietor of land, shall be in writing signed by the applicant or his solicitor and shall be accompanied by the land certificate and by evidence to the satisfaction of the Registrar that he would, by virtue of the Settled Land Act 1925 or the Law of Property Act 1925 be entitled to have the land vested in him. **[1429]**

NOTES
    The Act: Land Registration Act 1925.

134. Registration of trustees for sale under Sec 94 of the Act

An application under Subsection (3) of Section 94 of the Act by trustees for sale to be registered as proprietors of land shall be in writing signed by the applicants or their solicitor, and shall be accompanied by the land certificate and by evidence to the satisfaction of the Registrar that the land is by virtue of a specified statute made subject to a trust for sale and that the applicants are the trustees thereof. **[1430]**

NOTES
    The Act: Land Registration Act 1925.

135. Transfer imposing restrictive covenants

A transfer of land imposing restrictive covenants under Section 40 of the Act shall be made by an instrument in Form 43, and a certified copy thereof shall be lodged therewith. **[1431]**

NOTES
    The Act: Land Registration Act 1925.

136. Transfer by way of exchange

Where any registered land is exchanged for other registered land, the exchange shall be made by an instrument in Form 44. **[1432]**

137. Exchanges under an award

(1) Where an exchange is made under an order or award of the Board of Agriculture, the production of such an order or award, or a sealed copy thereof, together with the land certificate, shall be a sufficient authority to the Registrar to make such entries and alterations on the register as are required to complete the exchange.

(2) If the lands to be exchanged are not in the same condition with regard to registration—as, for instance, if one estate is registered with absolute title and the other with possessory title, or if one estate is subject to incumbrances and the other is not, or is subject to different incumbrances, or if one estate is already on the register and the other is not—the Registrar shall carry out the order or award in such manner as may be best calculated to give effect in the register to the provisions of the Inclosure Acts and Tithe Acts in regard to exchanges or any similar provision for the time being in force.   **[1433]**

Charges

[139. Charges and incorporated documents

(1) In this rule "incorporated document" means any separate document containing provisions intended by the parties to a charge on registered land to form part of the terms and conditions of the charge, which separate document is referred to in the charge, or in another incorporated document within the meaning thereof.

(2) A charge on registered land may be made by an instrument in Form 45 and a copy of the instrument of charge shall be delivered with it.

(3) Where a charge on registered land is not in Form 45 the requirement to deliver a copy of the instrument of charge extends to any incorporated document.

(4) The requirement in paragraph (3) to deliver an incorporated document shall be deemed to have been fulfilled if—

(a) in the case where the incorporated document is in a standard form which the Registrar has approved for the purpose of this paragraph, the charge refers to the incorporated document by means of a description approved by the Registrar;

(b) in the case of an incorporated document of a type approved by the Registrar, an undertaking has previously been given to the Registrar by the proprietor or intending proprietor of a charge (which undertaking has not been withdrawn) to deliver a copy of the terms of any particular incorporated document of that type when the Registrar so directs;

(c) in the case of a particular incorporated document, the Registrar accepts or has accepted an undertaking by the proprietor or intending proprietor of a charge to deliver a copy of the terms of that incorporated document when the Registrar so directs.

(5) Application for the approval of the Registrar for the purposes of paragraph (4) may be made to the Registrar at any time and any approval given by the Registrar under that paragraph may be—

(a) given subject to such conditions as he sees fit;

(b) modified or withdrawn by the Registrar at any time, but, in the case of approval given under paragraph (4)(a), not so as to impose on any person obligation to lodge the incorporated document in any case where the charge has already been registered.

(6) An undertaking given to the Registrar pursuant to paragraph (4)(*b*) may be withdrawn by the person who has given it upon his delivering to the Registrar notice in writing identifying the relevant undertaking and specifying a date upon which the withdrawal is to be treated as coming into effect (being a date at least 14 days after the date upon which the notice is delivered to the Registrar) and thereupon the person who has given the undertaking shall be treated as having been discharged from it but only in respect of incorporated documents of the type to which the undertaking relates which are incorporated into charges lodged for registration after the date specified in the notice.

(7) In relation to any particular incorporated document a person who has given an undertaking pursuant to paragraph (4)(*b*) or paragraph (4)(*c*) or has already given an undertaking pursuant to sub-paragraph (*b*) of this paragraph shall be discharged from that undertaking—

(*a*) upon his delivering to the Registrar a copy of the terms of the incorporated document; or

(*b*) where some other person who the Registrar is satisfied is competent to do so gives an undertaking in the same terms in substitution for it; or

(*c*) where the charge which incorporates the incorporated document has been wholly discharged.

(8) In relation to any particular incorporated document any person who has, pursuant to paragraph (4)(*b*), paragraph (4)(*c*) or paragraph (7)(*b*), given an undertaking which has not been withdrawn under paragraph (6) or in respect of which the person has not been discharged under paragraph (7), shall comply with it by delivering to the Registrar a copy of the terms of the incorporated document when directed by the Registrar.]   **[1434]**

NOTES
Commencement: 1 May 1991.
Substituted by the Land Registration (Charges) Rules 1990, SI 1990 No 2613, r 2.

[139A. Obligation to make further advances

(1) In this rule "incorporated document" has the same meaning as in Rule 139.

(2) The proprietor or intending proprietor of a charge who, under the terms of that charge, is under an obligation to make further advances may apply to the Registrar for a note of such obligation to be entered on the register for the purposes of section 30(4) of the Act.

(3) Except as provided in paragraph (4) below a separate application shall be made in Form 113.

(4) If a proprietor or intending proprietor of a charge so desires the application in Form 113 may be included in the instrument of charge or a deed of alteration of a registered charge but not in any incorporated document.

(5) The Registrar, on receipt of an application made under paragraph (3) or (4) above, shall give effect to it by adding a note to the entry of the charge in such terms as he considers appropriate, but he shall not be required to make any such note unless application is duly made in accordance with this rule.]

                                                                    [1434A]

NOTES
Commencement: 1 May 1991.
Inserted by the Land Registration (Charges) Rules 1990, SI 1990 No 2613, r 3.
The Act: Land Registration Act 1925.

140. Charge negativing or modifying implied covenants

The registration of an instrument of charge negativing or modifying the provisions of Sections 28, 29 and 34 of the Act, or any of them, shall for the purposes of those Sections be deemed a sufficient negative or contrary entry on the register.   **[1435]**

NOTES
The Act: Land Registration Act 1925.

141. Effect on powers, of the registration of a charge

(1) The proprietor of the land, while in possession, shall have all the powers of leasing and of accepting surrenders of leases conferred by Sections 99 and 100 of the Law of Property Act 1925, as extended by the instrument of charge or any instrument varying the terms thereof, but subject to any contrary intention expressed in any such instrument, a note of which intention shall, under an application to be made for that purpose, be entered in the register.

(2) The proprietor of a charge, while in possession, or after a receiver has been appointed, or such receiver on his behalf, shall have all the powers conferred by the said two Sections (as extended as aforesaid), but subject to any contrary intention expressed as aforesaid, a note of which intention shall, under an application to be made for that purpose, be entered in the register.

(3) The proprietor of an annual sum, within the meaning of Section 121 of the Law of Property Act 1925, charged on registered land or the income thereof, shall have power to create a term in accordance with that Section; and if that term would have been legal, or clothed with a legal estate (had the land not been registered), it may, on an application made for that purpose, be registered.

(4) Subject as aforesaid all dispositions, by the proprietor of the land, authorised by Sections 18 and 21 of the Act, shall, unless the proprietor of the charge concurs in the disposition, take effect subject to any charge registered at the time of the disposition.

(5) This rule has effect without prejudice to Section 104 of the Act.   **[1436]**

NOTES
The Act: Land Registration Act 1925.

142. Charges to secure an annuity or further advances

A charge to secure an annuity or to secure future advances may be made by an instrument in Forms 46 or 47, and Forms 46 or 47 may be combined with Form 45.   **[1437]**

143. Charges by purchaser of small holding

A charge to secure part of the purchase money on a sale by a county council under the Small Holdings and Allotments Act 1908 to 1919 and the Allotments Act 1922 shall be in Forms 48, 49 or 50, with such additions and modifications as the circumstances may require.   **[1438]**

NOTES
> Small Holdings and Allotments Acts 1908 to 1919: see now the Agriculture Act 1947, s 67, Sch 8.

144. Charge under Section 90 of the Act (settled land)

(1) A charge under Section 90 of the Act shall be in Form 45.

(2) It shall not refer to the settlement, but shall be accompanied by the land certificate and by such evidence or other particulars as may be necessary to satisfy the Registrar that it is created for securing money actually raised and that it is now capable of being overriden under the Settled Land Act 1925, or the Law of Property Act 1925.

(3) When registered it shall take effect and be dealt with in the same manner, by the same instruments, and with the same results in all respects as in the Act and these rules provided with regard to charges generally.

(4) Provided that, in cases in which under these rules, a charge does not take priority, according to date of registration, the requisite note shall be added and shall have effect accordingly. **[1439]**

NOTES
> The Act: Land Registration Act 1925.

[145. Certificate of registration under Companies Acts

(1) On the registration of a charge created by a company registered under the Companies Acts, there shall be produced to the Registrar a certificate under Section 395 of the Companies Act 1985 that such charge has been registered under that section.

(2) If no such certificate is produced a note shall be made in the register that the charge is subject to the provisions of section 395 of the said Act.] **[1440]**

NOTES
> Substituted by the Land Registration (Companies and Insolvency) Rules 1986, SI 1986 No 2116, r 3.

146. Mortgage debt held in shares

Where it appears from a charge that the money secured is advanced by two or more persons, but not on joint account, they shall be entered as joint proprietors of the charge as a whole, but the register may show the shares in which the money is held. **[1441]**

147. Entry to be made in register on foreclosure

Where the proprietor of a charge obtains an order for foreclosure absolute, the order, or an office copy thereof, shall be delivered to the Registrar, who shall thereupon enter the proprietor of the charge as proprietor (subject to prior charges) of the land the equity of redemption in which is foreclosed. The charge certificate shall accompany the application. **[1442]**

148. Effect of dispositions by proprietor of a charge

Subject to any entry to the contrary on the register, any disposition by the proprietor of a charge (other than a lease within Section 104 of the Act) shall have the same effect as dispositions under Sections 20, 23 and 40 of the Act, as the case may be, save that such dispositions shall be subject only to the

overriding interests (if any) and to the incumbrances and other entries (if any)
appearing on the register which have priority over the charge under which the
disposition is made.   **[1443]**

NOTES
   The Act: Land Registration Act 1925.

149. Declaration by the proprietor of a charge who has acquired a title by possession

(1) The declaration to be made pursuant to Subsection (2) of Section 34 of the
Act by the proprietor of a charge who has acquired a title by possession shall be
by a deed poll in Form 52, with such modifications (if any) as the circumstances
may require.

(2) The evidence in support shall consist of a statutory declaration by an
independent and trustworthy person as to the fact of the entry upon the land or
into receipt of the rents and profits and as to the possession having been
continuous and undisputed.

(3) The beneficial title to the equity of redemption must also, if required, be
proved to the satisfaction of the Registrar so as to show that there is no person
entitled to redeem.   **[1444]**

NOTES
   The Act: Land Registration Act 1925.

150. Alteration of terms of a registered charge

An application to alter the terms of a registered charge under Section 31 of the
Act shall be in Form 51, and shall be executed by the proprietors of the charge
and of the land and of every charge of equal or inferior priority prejudicially
affected by the alteration.   **[1445]**

NOTES
   The Act: Land Registration Act 1925.

[151. Discharge of a registered charge

A discharge wholly or in part of a registered charge shall be made by an
instrument in Form 53 and shall—

   (*a*) where the proprietor of the charge is an individual, be signed by him;
   (*b*) where the proprietor of the charge is a company registered under the
           Companies Acts, be executed—

        (i)   under seal in accordance with section 74(1) of the Law of Property
               Act 1925; or
        (ii) in accordance with section 36A of the Companies Act 1985; or
        (iii) otherwise in such manner as the Registrar is satisfied may be
               authorised under its articles of association;

   (*c*) where the proprietor of the charge is any other corporate body,
           either—

        (i)   be executed under seal in accordance with section 74(1) of the
               Law of Property Act 1925; or
        (ii) be signed or executed by such person as the Registrar is satisfied
               has authority, under the instrument or statute constituting or

regulating the affairs of the proprietor or otherwise, to bind the proprietor in the discharge of the charge;

but the Registrar shall be at liberty to accept and act upon any other proof of satisfaction of a charge which he may deem sufficient.] **[1446]–[1447]**

NOTES
Commencement: 1 May 1991.
Substituted by the Land Registration (Charges) Rules 1990, SI 1990 No 2613, r 4.

153. Transfer of a charge

A transfer of a charge shall be made by an instrument in Form 54. **[1448]**

154. Consolidation of charges

(1) Where a charge, whether affecting the whole or a part of the land comprised in a title, reserves the right to consolidate, it shall not on that account only be registered against any other land than that expressly described in it.

(2) But where the right reserved is to consolidate with a specified charge, or an application in writing is made to register the right in respect of a specified charge, the Registrar shall require the production of the land certificates of all the titles affected, and, on the production thereof, shall enter in the register a notice that the specified charges are consolidated. **[1449]**

155. Land charges when registered as charges

(1) Land charges for securing money, within the proviso to Subsection (2) of Section 59 of the Act, required to be registered before realisation (being Classes A and B and local land charges as defined in the Land Charges Act 1925), shall be deemed to be created by the person registered as proprietor of the land at the date of the charge, and shall be capable of registration accordingly.

(2) Where such a charge is registered, the term and covenants specified in Sections 27 and 28 of the Act shall not be implied, and the proprietor of the charge shall not by virtue of such registration be entitled to any rights under Section 34 of the Act to which he would not have been entitled if the charge had not been so registered. **[1450]**

NOTES
The Act: Land Registration Act 1925.

156. Notice of priority for any subsequent charge made for giving effect to a minor interest

(1) Where the proprietor would, if the land were not registered, be bound under Subsection (1) of Section 16 of the Settled Land Act 1925, to state in a mortgage of settled land that it shall take effect subject to any equitable charges or powers of charging which have priority, as in that section mentioned, he shall be bound to—

    (a) refer to the minor interest having such priority in the instrument of charge,
    (b) furnish such evidence respecting the minor interest for filing or otherwise as the Registrar may reasonably require.

(2) The entry of the charge in the register, containing such a reference, shall

be deemed a sufficient entry of notice on the register to secure the priority of any charge subsequently made for giving effect to the minor interest on the register.   **[1451]**

157. Claim that a charge has statutory priority

(1) Where a person registers a charge which, by virtue of some statute, he alleges to have priority over other charges upon the same land of earlier date, he shall (unless the charge contains such a statement) state in writing under what statute such priority is claimed.

(2) An entry shall be made in the register that a claim is made by the proprietor of the charge—

    (*a*) that it has priority under the statute referred to,
    (*b*) that it does not (as between itself and other registered charges of earlier date) rank according to the date of its creation, or to the order of entry in the register.   **[1452]**

158. Determination by Registrar of a claim to statutory priority of a charge

(1) If and when it becomes important to determine whether such claim to priority is well founded, any person interested may apply to the Registrar to determine the question in accordance with these rules.

(2) The Registrar may either himself determine all questions as to the priorities and relative rights of the parties, or may require the matter to be brought before the Court for decision.

(3) The result of the decision shall be entered in the register, and any necessary alterations shall be made therein.   **[1453]**

159. Paramount interests and provisional registration

The provisions of the rules relating to the giving effect of paramount interests and to provisional registration, with respect to registered land, shall apply, with the necessary modifications, to a registered charge.   **[1454]**

Adaptation to Incumbrances prior to Registration and to Sub-mortgages of the provisions of the Act with regard to Charges

160. Registration of proprietor of incumbrances prior to first registration of land

(1) Where it appears that any person is entitled to an incumbrance created prior to the first registration of land, the Registrar shall, on the application or with the consent of the person so entitled and on due proof of his title and after notice to the proprietor of the land, register such person as the proprietor of such incumbrance.

(2) Where there are two or more such incumbrances, their relative priorities shall not be affected by the registration of some or one of them only, or by the order in which such of them as are registered are entered in the register. **[1455]**

161. Dispositions of incumbrances

From and after the registration of the proprietor of an incumbrance, all transfers and other dispositions thereof or thereunder shall be entered in the register and shall (subject to any entry to the contrary in the register) rank, as between themselves, for purposes of priority in the order in which they are registered; and the incumbrance shall cease to be subject to the jurisdiction of any local Deed Registry. **[1456]**

162. Form of dispositions

The same forms shall be used and proceedings adopted as to transfers and other dispositions of or under incumbrances so registered as are required in the case of registered charges. **[1457]**

163. Sub-charge

(1) The proprietor of a charge or incumbrance may at any time charge the mortgage debt with the payment of money in the same manner as the proprietor of land can charge the land; and such charges are in these rules referred to as sub-charges.

(2) The proprietor of a sub-charge shall, subject to any entry to the contrary in the register, have the same powers of disposition, in relation to the land, as if he had been registered as proprietor of the principal charge. **[1458]**

164. Dispositions of sub-charges

(1) A sub-charge shall be completed, transferred, and discharged in the same form and manner as a charge.

(2) Subject to any entry in the register to the contrary—

    (*a*) a sub-charge shall, as against the person creating it, imply the same covenants and, as against that person and all persons over whose interests the charge confers power, confer the same powers and have the same effect as a charge,

    (*b*) registered sub-charges on the same charge or incumbrance shall, as between themselves, rank according to the order in which they are entered on the register and not according to the order in which they are created. **[1459]**

165. Production of certificate on registration

On the registration of a sub-charge, the charge certificate or incumbrance shall be produced and a note of the sub-charge shall be entered therein. **[1460]**

166. Form of certificates of incumbrance and sub-charge

(1) Certificates of incumbrance and of sub-charge shall be prepared in like forms and be issued and dealt with and may be used to create a lien by deposit in the same manner as charge certificates.

(2) They shall be produced on the same occasions and their production may be dispensed with on the same terms as charge certificates. **[1461]**

Transfer and Discharge

167. Form of transfer and discharge

A transfer of land combined with a discharge of a charge or incumbrance shall be made by an instrument in Form 55. **[1462]**

Transmissions of Land Charges
(i) On death

168. Registration of a personal representative

(1) On production of the probate or letters of administration of a sole (or sole surviving) proprietor of land or of a charge, dying after 1897, the personal representative named in such probate or letters shall be registered as proprietor in the place of the deceased proprietor with the addition of the words "executor *or* executrix (*or* administrator *or* administratrix) of [*name*] deceased."

(2) Provided that in the case of land settled previously to the death of the proprietor, the special personal representatives in whom the land vests under the Administration of Estates Act 1925 shall be registered as proprietors. **[1463]**

169. Registration of an additional executor

When, after an executor has been registered as proprietor under the preceding rule, another executor applies to be registered as proprietor jointly with him, the Registrar shall, after notice to the other executor, make the necessary alteration in the register upon production by the applicant, of the probate obtained by him; or, if he has not proved the will, of a statement in writing, signed by him, that he has applied for probate and desires to be registered accordingly. **[1464]**

170. Transfer, etc, by personal representative

Pursuant to Subsection (3) of Section 41 of the Act it is hereby provided that—

(1) The personal representative of a deceased proprietor may, without being himself registered, transfer any registered land or charge of which the deceased was registered as proprietor, or may dispose of it by way of assent or appropriation or vesting assent.

(2) If he transfers the transfer shall be in the usual form.

(3) If he assents or appropriates or executes a vesting assent the instrument shall be in Forms 56 or 57, as the case may be.

(4) On delivery of the transfer, assent, appropriation or vesting assent at the Registry, accompanied, if the personal representative is not already registered as proprietor, by the probate or letters of administration, the Registrar shall register the person named in the instrument for that purpose as proprietor, together with the restrictions (if any) contained therein.

(5) It shall not be the duty of the Registrar nor shall he be entitled to consider or to call for any information concerning the reason why any transfer is made, or as to terms of the will, and, whether he has notice or not of its contents, he shall be entitled to assume that the personal representative is acting (whether by transfer, assent or appropriation or vesting assent) correctly and within his powers. **[1465]**

NOTES
  The Act: Land Registration Act 1925.

171. Minorities

(1) Where a settlement is created or arises under a will or intestacy and an infant becomes beneficially entitled to an estate in fee simple or a term of years

absolute in the registered land, or would if he were of full age be or have the powers of a tenant for life, the statutory owners shall, after administration is completed as respects the registered land, direct the personal representatives to apply for the proper restrictions (if any) according to the principles prescribed by these rules.

(2) The application shall be in Form 76, and on receipt of an application from the personal representatives in that form, accompanied by the land certificate, it shall not be the duty of the Registrar, nor shall he be entitled to consider or call for any information concerning the reason why the application is made or as to the terms of the will or the devolution under the intestacy, or as to whether the direction by the statutory owners was actually given or not, or as to its terms, and whether he has notice of those matters or not, he shall be entitled to assume that the personal representatives are acting according to the directions given and that the directions were given by the statutory owners and were correct.

(3) Where under Subsection (3) of Section 19 of the Settled Land Act 1925 there is a tenant for life of full age, he shall be entitled to be registered as proprietor during any minority therein referred to, but subject to the prescribed restrictions.

(4) Nothing in this rule shall affect the right of statutory owners to be registered as proprietors. **[1466]**

172. Death of a joint proprietor

If one of two or more joint proprietors of land or of a charge dies, his name shall be withdrawn from the register on proof of death, or on production of probate or letters of administration, together with such other evidence (if any) as the Registrar may require. **[1467]**

173. Death of Official Receiver or trustee in bankruptcy

On the death of a proprietor registered as Official Receiver or trustee in bankruptcy, his personal representatives shall not be registered, but proceedings shall be taken in accordance with these rules to register his successor in office. **[1468]**

(ii) On Bankruptcy or Liquidation

[174. Registration of Official Receiver

(1) The Official Receiver may be registered as proprietor in place of the bankrupt on production to the Registrar of

   (*a*) an office copy of a bankruptcy order relating to the bankrupt and
   (*b*) a certificate signed by the Official Receiver that the land or charge is comprised in the bankrupt's estate.

(2) The Official Receiver may be registered as proprietor in place of a deceased proprietor on production of such evidence as the Registrar may require.

(3) Nothing in these rules shall affect the provisions of Section 103 of the Settled Land Act 1925.] **[1469]**

NOTES
    Substituted by the Land Registration (Companies and Insolvency) Rules 1986, SI 1986 No 2116,
r 4.

[175. Registration of trustee in bankruptcy in place of Official Receiver

Where the Official Receiver has been registered as proprietor and some other
person is subsequently appointed trustee, such person may be registered as
proprietor in the place of the Official Receiver on production of the evidence
required by rule 176(1)(*b*).]   **[1470]**

NOTES
    Substituted by the Land Registration (Companies and Insolvency) Rules 1986, SI 1986 No 2116,
r 4.

[176. Original registration of trustee in bankruptcy

(1) If the Official Receiver has not been registered as proprietor and some other
person has been appointed trustee of the bankrupt's estate, such person may be
registered as proprietor in place of the bankrupt on production to the Registrar
of—

(*a*) an office copy of a bankruptcy order relating to the bankrupt made by
a court having jurisdiction in insolvency,

(*b*) either a copy of his certificate of appointment as trustee by the meeting
of the bankrupt's creditors duly certified by the trustee or his solicitor
as being a true copy of the original or a copy of his certificate of
appointment as trustee by the Secretary of State or an office copy of
the order of the Court of his appointment as trustee and

(*c*) a certificate signed by the trustee that the land or charge is comprised
in the bankrupt's estate.

(2) A trustee in bankruptcy may be registered as proprietor in place of a
deceased proprietor on production of such evidence as the Registrar may
require.]   **[1471]**

NOTES
    Substituted by the Land Registration (Companies and Insolvency) Rules 1986, SI 1986 No 2116,
r 4.

[177. Words added in register

Where the Official Receiver or trustee in bankruptcy is registered as proprietor,
the words "Official Receiver" or "Trustee in bankruptcy of [*name*]" shall be
added to the register.]   **[1472]**

NOTES
    Substituted by the Land Registration (Companies and Insolvency) Rules 1986, SI 1986 No 2116,
r 4.

[179. Creditor's notice

(1) A creditor's notice shall be entered in the Proprietorship Register in the
following form:—

"Creditor's Notice in respect of a petition in bankruptcy presented in the
[*name*] Court (Court reference No .. ../ .. ..) protecting the rights of
all creditors (Land Charges Ref No .. ../ .. ..)."

(2) A creditors' notice shall be entered in the Charges Register in the following form:—

"Creditors' Notice in respect of a petition in bankruptcy against [*name of chargee*] presented in the [*name*] Court (Court reference No .. ../ .. ..) protecting the rights of all creditors (Land Charges Ref No .. ../ .. ..)."

(3) Notice of any such entry shall be given to the proprietor of the land or charge as appropriate.] **[1473]**

NOTES
Substituted by the Land Registration (Companies and Insolvency) Rules 1986, SI 1986 No 2116, r 6.

[180. Bankruptcy inhibition

(1) A bankruptcy inhibition shall be entered in the Proprietorship Register in the following form:—

"Bankruptcy Inhibition in pursuance of a bankruptcy order made by the [*name*] Court (Court reference No .. ../ .. ..). No disposition by the proprietor of the land or transmission is to be registered until a trustee in bankruptcy is registered (Land Charges Ref No .. ../ .. ..)."

(2) A bankruptcy inhibition shall be entered in the Charges Register in the following form:—

"Bankruptcy Inhibition in pursuance of a bankruptcy order made by the [*name*] Court (Court reference No .. ../ .. ..). No disposition or transmission of the charge dated .. .. is to be registered until a trustee in bankruptcy of the property of [*name of chargee*] is registered (Land Charges Ref No .. ../ .. ..)."

(3) Notice of any such entry shall be given to the proprietor of the land or charge as appropriate.] **[1474]**

NOTES
Substituted by the Land Registration (Companies and Insolvency) Rules 1986, SI 1986 No 2116, r 6.

[181. Action of the Registrar under Section 62 of the Act (bankruptcy)

Where:—

    (*a*) any doubt arises as to the identity of the debtor or bankrupt, or
    (*b*) the registration of a pending action in respect of a bankruptcy petition is vacated, or
    (*c*) the bankruptcy order is annulled, or
    (*d*) the bankruptcy proceedings do not affect or have ceased to affect the statutory powers of the bankrupt under the Act,

the Registrar shall as soon as practicable after receiving notice thereof and after making such enquiry and giving such notice (if any) as he shall deem necessary, take such action in the matter as he shall think advisable.] **[1475]**

NOTES
Substituted by the Land Registration (Companies and Insolvency) Rules 1986, SI 1986 No 2116, r 6.
The Act: Land Registration Act 1925.

[182. Mistake in bankruptcy order

Where a mistake has occurred in a bankruptcy order or where any amendment in the register appears to be required, it shall be the duty of the Official Receiver or the trustee in bankruptcy (if appointed), as soon as it comes to his knowledge, to notify such mistake or to suggest such amendment to the Registrar, who shall thereupon, after making such enquiries and giving such notices (if any) as he shall deem necessary, make such amendment in the register as may be necessary.] **[1476]**

NOTES
Substituted by the Land Registration (Companies and Insolvency) Rules 1986, SI 1986 No 2116, r 6.

[183. Trustee in bankruptcy vacating office

When a trustee in bankruptcy who has been registered as proprietor vacates his office as trustee because he ceases to be a person who is qualified to act as an insolvency practitioner under the Insolvency Act 1986 or any Act amending or replacing that Act or by release, resignation, death, removal from office or any other cause, the Official Receiver may be registered as proprietor; or, if some other person be appointed trustee, such person may be registered as proprietor on production of the evidence required by rule 176(1).] **[1477]**

NOTES
Substituted by the Land Registration (Companies and Insolvency) Rules 1986, SI 1986 No 2116, r 6.

184. Where property becomes divested

(1) Where the Official Receiver or a trustee has been registered as proprietor, and, by reason of any act or omission or order, his estate and interest in the property has become divested, he may give notice to the Registrar in Form 58.

(2) The notice shall be entered on the register, together with a general restriction against dealings until further order.

(3) On such entry being made the Official Receiver or trustee shall be exonerated from all such liability (if any) as may affect him in respect of the property by reason of his name being entered on the register as proprietor thereof.

(4) Where such notice has been entered on the register an entry may be made under these rules without notice to the proprietor, or inquiry as to his execution of a transfer. **[1478]**

[185. Administration orders and liquidation of a company

(1) When an administration order has been made by the Court in respect of a company under the provisions of the Insolvency Act 1986 the order and the appointment of the administrator named therein shall on his application and on production of an office copy thereof be noted in the register.

(2) When a company is in liquidation, any order, appointment or resolution appointing a liquidator shall be noted in the register on his application and on production of either an office copy of the order or a copy of the appointment or resolution certified by the liquidator or his solicitor as being a true copy of the original together with such other evidence as the Registrar may require.] **[1479]**

NOTES
Substituted by the Land Registration (Companies and Insolvency) Rules 1986, SI 1986 No 2116, r 7.

PART IV

MINOR ENTRIES IN THE REGISTER

186. Notices of leases or agreements

(1) An application to register notice of a lease or agreement for a lease, under Section 48 of the Act, may be made either by the lessee or by any person entitled to or interested in the lease or agreement or by the proprietor of the land against which the notice is to be entered.

(2) The application shall be accompanied by the lease or counterpart, or by the agreement or duplicate, as the case may be, also by a copy or full abstract thereof, and a copy or tracing of the plan (if any) thereon.

(3) Except where the application is made by the proprietor, it shall be accompanied also by either the consent of the proprietor in writing signed by himself or his solicitor, or by an order of the Court authorising the registration of the notice.

(4) Consent to the registration of a notice of a lease or agreement may be given either before or after its execution. **[1480]**

NOTES
The Act: Land Registration Act 1925.

187. When notice of a lease affects incumbrances

Where, after the creation of an incumbrance, a lease is executed which would, apart from the Act, be binding on the incumbrancer, and notice of such lease is registered under Section 48 of the Act, that notice shall be effectual against the incumbrancer, notwithstanding that his incumbrance was registered before the registration of the notice. **[1481]**

NOTES
The Act: Land Registration Act 1925.

188. Form of entry of notice of lease

The notice in the register shall give the term, and may include such other short particulars as can be conveniently entered. The lease or agreement shall be marked with a note of the entry and shall be returned to the applicant. **[1482]**

189. Statutory declaration where lease is not produced

If the lease or counterpart or the agreement or duplicate is not produced, a statutory declaration by the applicant or his solicitor, stating the reason of the non-production and verifying the copy or abstract, shall be furnished. **[1483]**

190. Notices under Section 49 of the Act (rights and claims)

(1) Application for the registration of notices of or claims in respect of any of the matters set out in Section 49 of the Act shall be in Form 59, and shall state concisely the facts or documents on which the claim depends.

(2) The evidence in support of the application shall be delivered therewith and the matter shall be proceeded with, and such entry made on the register as the Registrar shall direct.   **[1484]**

NOTES

The Act: Land Registration Act 1925.

[191. Where it appears to the Registrar upon first registration or conversion of a title that the land is subject to an Inland Revenue charge arising under Part III of the Finance Act 1975, or where the Commissioners of Inland Revenue apply under rule 190 of these Rules for the registration of notice of such a charge, the Registrar shall enter notice thereof in the charges register in Form 60.]   **[1485]**

NOTES

Substituted by the Land Registration (Capital Transfer Tax) Rules 1975, SI 1975 No 367, r 2.

[192. Notice of an Inland Revenue charge in Form 60 shall be cancelled by the Registrar as to the whole or, where appropriate, as to a part, of the land affected thereby on the production to him of a certificate given by the Commissioners of Inland Revenue in Form 61 or to the like effect but subject to any condition specified in the certificate as to the registration of a disposition to a purchaser.]   **[1486]**

NOTES

Substituted by the Land Registration (Capital Transfer Tax) Rules 1975, SI 1975 No 367, r 2.

[193. Notice of any liability for death duty (other than inheritance tax) shall be cancelled by the Registrar as to the whole or, where appropriate, as to a part, of the land affected thereby on the production to him of a certificate given by the Commissioners of Inland Revenue in Form 61 or to the like effect, or on the registration of a disposition which will override any charge for such duty.]   **[1487]**

NOTES

Substituted by the Land Registration (Capital Transfer Tax) Rules 1975, SI 1975 No 367, r 2.
Capital transfer tax: except in relation to a liability to tax arising before 25 July 1986 capital transfer tax shall be known as inheritance tax and the Capital Transfer Tax Act 1984 may be cited as the Inheritance Tax Act 1984, by virtue of the Finance Act 1986, s 100.

194. Exemption from land tax, tithe rent-charge

(1) Application to notify exemption from land tax, tithe rentcharge, and an annuity or charge for the redemption of tithe rentcharge, shall be made by delivering at the Registry the certificate of redemption or other necessary evidence, with a request to notify the exemption in the register.

(2) If the Registrar is satisfied by sufficient evidence that the claim to such exemption is well founded, he shall notify the fact in the Property Register.
                                                                                        [1488]

Mines and Minerals

195. Express registration of mines and minerals with the land

Where—

    (*a*) any mines and minerals have been opened and worked by the proprietor of the land or by his predecessors in title, or by any person claiming under him or them, and it does not appear on the examination of title or from any other source that the ownership of such mines and minerals is vested in any other person, or

(b) in any other case where it is proved to the satisfaction of the Registrar that the right to any mines and minerals, whether opened and worked or not, is vested in the proprietor,

the Registrar may cause him to be expressly registered as proprietor of such mines and minerals, by adding to the Property Register a note to the effect that they are included in the registration.   **[1489]**

196. Severance of mines and minerals from the land

Where it appears from the documents or abstract of title furnished, or from the admission of the proprietor of the land, or from any other source, that all or any of the mines and minerals are severed from the land, the Registrar shall enter a note in the Property Register that such mines and minerals are excepted from the registration.   **[1490]**

Miscellaneous entries

197. Notice of freedom from or the existence of overriding interests

(1) Where any person desires to have an entry made in the register of the freedom from or the existence of an overriding interest mentioned in Section 70 of the Act, the application shall be made in writing and shall state the particulars of the entry required to be made.

(2) If the applicant is the proprietor of the land or the liability, right, or interest has been created by the proprietor of the land, and if, in either case, there is no caution, restriction, or inhibition on the register, an entry of the existence of the liability, right, or interest may be made accordingly.

(3) In other cases evidence satisfactory to the Registrar shall be produced of the existence or discharge of the liability, right, or interest, as the case may require.

(4) The proprietor of the land, if not the applicant, shall have notice of the application, and the matter shall be proceeded with as the Registrar shall direct.

(5) Any entry of the existence of the liability, right, or interest, if made, shall be against the title in the Charges Register, and such entry shall be made so far as practicable and convenient by reference to the instrument creating the right or by setting out an extract therefrom.

(6) Any entry, showing that the registered land is free from any one or more of the liabilities, rights, or interest, mentioned in Section 70 of the Act shall be made in the Property Register.   **[1491]**

NOTES
  The Act: Land Registration Act 1925.

198. Notice to proprietor of servient tenement as to easement, etc

The notice required to be served on the proprietor of the servient tenement, before an entry can be made against it, of the existence of an easement, right, or privilege, not created by an instrument, shall be fourteen days or such longer period as the Registrar may deem advisable.   **[1492]**

199. Entry as to trivial rights not required

The Registrar shall not be required to enter notice of any liability, right, or interest which shall appear to him to be of a trivial or obvious character, or the entry of which on the register is likely to cause confusion or inconvenience.

[1493]

Miscellaneous Entries

200. Determination of registered estates

Where the title to a lease, rentcharge or other estate or interest has been registered under the Act, the determination thereof may be notified on the register, upon the production of a surrender or other sufficient release or discharge, executed by the proprietor thereof and every person appearing by the register to be interested therein.   **[1494]**

NOTES

   The Act: Land Registration Act 1925.

201. Determination of leases, etc, noted, where there has been no dealing

Where the title is not so registered, but a lease, incumbrance, rentcharge, easement, right or other interest is noted on the register as an incumbrance, and there has been no dealing therewith or transmission thereof, the determination may be notified on the register on production of the document (if any) creating it, with a sufficient release or discharge thereof executed by the incumbrancer named therein.   **[1495]**

202. Determination of leases, etc, noted where there has been a dealing

If, in the like case, there has been a dealing with or transmission of the incumbrance the application shall also be accompanied by sufficient evidence of the applicant's title (with an abstract if required by the Registrar), as in cases of examination of title on first registration.   **[1496]**

203. Method of entry of determination of leases, etc

(1) The determination may be notified on the register either by cancelling the original entry, or by noting the fact, as the Registrar may think fit.

(2) Where the title to the lease or other incumbrance has been registered such title shall be closed.   **[1497]**

204. Note of variation of lease, etc, on register

The variation of a lease or other estate, right, or interest registered or noted on the register shall be notified in such manner and on such evidence as the Registrar shall deem appropriate and sufficient.   **[1498]**

205. Restrictive covenants under a building scheme

On the determination, otherwise than by effluxion of time, of a lease, containing restrictive covenants which the Registrar has reason to believe may be enforceable by persons other than the lessor, the Registrar may, if he thinks fit, make an entry on the register to the effect that the land is subject to such liability (if any) as may be subsisting by reason of those covenants.   **[1499]**

206. Where lease may be treated as merged

Where—

 (*a*) the proprietor of any land, comprised in a leasehold title, becomes, by any means, the proprietor of the land comprised in the title against which the lease is noted as an incumbrance, or

 (*b*) a lease or agreement for a lease, noted as an incumbrance only, is vested in such proprietor,

the Registrar may, unless the contrary appears, treat the lease as merged, in which case the title shall be closed, or the note shall be cancelled, as the case may require. **[1500]**

207. Entries as to merged interests

Where any interest in land, situated in a compulsory area, would, on registration under a separate title, be immediately merged in a superior registered estate, or otherwise determined, it shall not be necessary to register such interest, but the Registrar shall have power to make such entries (if any) in the register of any superior registered estate as may be necessary, as if a separate title had been opened and closed on merger, or otherwise. **[1501]**

208. Production of determined leases

Where, under these rules, an entry is to be made of the determination of a lease, or agreement for a lease, or a note is to be cancelled, the lease or agreement shall be produced and marked with notice of the entry, and the land certificate of the title closed and the charge certificates (if any) thereon shall be delivered up and cancelled. **[1502]**

209. Lease determined as to part

When a lease or agreement for a lease has determined as to a part only of the land demised thereby or comprised therein, these rules shall apply so far as circumstances will admit. **[1503]**

210. Perpetually renewable leases and sub-leases

Where land comprised in a perpetually renewable lease or sub-lease has been registered before the commencement of the Act, then on any dealing therewith or transmission thereof, the Registrar shall make such alterations in the register as may be necessary to make it comply with the provisions relating to perpetually renewable leases and sub-leases contained in the Law of Property Act 1922 as amended. **[1504]**

NOTES
The Act: Land Registration Act 1925.

211. Dealing with an interest which is not a legal estate

On the occasion of the first dealing for value after the commencement of the Act with any interest (not being an undivided share in land) which is not a legal estate—as, for instance, a lease for life or lives or a term of years determinable with life or lives—the Registrar shall alter the entries in the register to such form as would have been adopted if the land had been registered after the commencement of the Act, and shall inform every person appearing by the register to be interested in the lease or other disposition that he has done so. **[1505]**

NOTES
The Act: Land Registration Act 1925.

212. Entry and discharge of restrictive covenants

Restrictive covenants created under Section 40, or noted against a title under Section 50 of the Act, shall be entered in the Charges Register, in the method directed by Section 50, and any release, waiver, discharge, or modification shall be noted on the register in such manner as the Registrar may direct. **[1506]**

NOTES
The Act: Land Registration Act 1925.

213. Entry restraining a disposition by a sole surviving proprietor

(1) An entry under Subsection (3) of Section 58 of the Act shall be in Form 62, and need only be made where, by law, the survivor of the joint proprietors will not have power to give a valid receipt for capital on a disposition of the land or charge, or where the Registrar, for any special reason, considers that such an entry would be desirable.

(2) Such an entry may at any time be made with the consent of joint proprietors entitled in their own right.

(3) No entry shall be made under this rule where the prescribed restrictions, applicable to settled land, are entered on the register. **[1507]**

NOTES
The Act: Land Registration Act 1925.

214. Production of the equitable title required before entry of a disposition

When such an entry has been made and the joint proprietors have been reduced to the number specified therein, the Registrar shall, before entering on the register any disposition by the proprietor, require the production of the equitable title; and may give such notices to the persons, or some or one of the persons, equitably entitled, as he may deem expedient. **[1508]**

Cautions (except Cautions against entry of Land on the Register)

215. Caution against dealings

(1) A caution against dealings with registered land or a registered charge, lodged under Section 54 of the Act, shall be in Form 63.

(2) A caution against the registration of a possessory or good leasehold or qualified title as good leasehold or qualified or absolute shall be in Form 69.

(3) The caution shall be signed by the cautioner or his solicitor and shall contain an address for service in the United Kingdom.

(4) The declaration in support of the caution shall be in Form 14, or to the like effect, and shall contain a reference to the land or charge to which it relates; and to the registered number of the title, and shall also state the nature of the interest of the cautioner in such land or charge. **[1509]**

NOTES
The Act: Land Registration Act 1925.

216. Particulars to be given to identify land affected by a caution

It shall not be necessary that the land to which a caution relates shall be described therein in any particular manner, if sufficient particulars are given by plan or otherwise to identify, on the proper Ordnance Map or the General Map, the land to which the caution is intended to apply. **[1510]**

217. Consent under a caution

Any consent given under Sections 55 and 56 of the Act by the cautioner or his personal representative shall be signed by him or his solicitor. **[1511]**

NOTES
The Act: Land Registration Act 1925.

218. Service of notice on cautioner

(1) On the application at any time in writing of the proprietor of the land or of a charge to which a caution relates, or when a dealing affecting such land or charge is brought in for registration without the consent of the cautioner, the notice under Section 55 of the Act shall be served on the cautioner.

(2) The period to be limited by such notice shall be fourteen days or such other period (not being less than seven days) as the Registrar may, under special circumstances, direct.

(3) The notice shall be in Form 70. **[1512]**

NOTES
The Act: Land Registration Act 1925.

219. Objection by cautioner to registration of a dealing

At any time before the expiration of the period limited by the notice, or such extension thereof as may be granted by the Registrar, the cautioner or his personal representative may show cause why the caution should continue to have effect, or why the dealing should not be registered—as, for instance, that it has been obtained by fraud or mistake, or that it is inconsistent with a prior dealing or with some adverse right or minor interest which would not be overridden if the land were not registered. **[1513]**

220. Hearing of cautioner by Registrar

(1) Cause may be shown either by the cautioner appearing before the Registrar or by his delivering a statement in writing, signed by him or his solicitor, setting forth the grounds on which cause is shown.

(2) The Registrar may thereupon either order that the caution shall thenceforth cease to have effect and that the entry thereof on the register be cancelled, or he may appoint a time for the proprietor or the applicant for registration, as the case may be, and the cautioner or his personal representative and such other persons (if any) as he may deem expedient, to appear before him.

(3) After hearing all such persons, and serving such notices (if any) as he shall think necessary, the Registrar shall make such order in the matter as he shall think just, as, for instance, that the caution shall continue to have effect, or that it shall cease to have effect and that the entry thereof on the register be cancelled, or that the registration be refused either with or without an inhibition

against registration at any future time, or that it be completed forthwith, or after an interval, or that it be completed conditionally or with some modification, or subject to the prior registration of a dealing in favour of the cautioner, or subject to some notice, condition, restriction, or inhibition under the Act.

(4) The Registrar may refer the matter, at any stage, or any question arising thereon, for the decision of the Court.   **[1514]**

221. Cancellation of a caution on expiry of notice

When the notice required by a caution has been given in respect of the whole of the land or charge affected thereby and the period named in the notice has expired, the caution shall, unless the Registrar shall otherwise direct, be deemed to be exhausted and shall be cancelled on the register.   **[1515]**

222. Cancellation of a caution on an application therefor

A caution may at any time be cancelled upon an application for that purpose in Form 71, signed by the cautioner or his personal representative, or his solicitor, and thereupon the entry thereof on the register shall be cancelled; but any liability previously incurred under the Act of a cautioner to indemnify or make compensation shall not be affected by such withdrawal.   **[1516]**

NOTES
  The Act: Land Registration Act 1925.

224. Withdrawal of mortgage caution

(1) A mortgage caution may be withdrawn at any time in the same manner and on the same conditions as an ordinary caution.

(2) A mortgage caution may be vacated, subject to the requisite evidence being furnished to the Registrar of the discharge of the mortgage.   **[1517]**

225. Dealing with land affected by a mortgage caution

On the lodgment for registration of any dealing with the land to which it relates, a mortgage caution shall be dealt with in the same manner as a caution under Section 54 of the Act, save that it cannot be warned off the register by service of notice on the cautioner; and the dealing, if registered, shall take effect subject to the rights, if any, protected by the mortgage caution.   **[1518]**

NOTES
  The Act: Land Registration Act 1925.

226. Registration of mortgage as a charge

(1) If and when application is made to register the mortgage as a charge, the registration of the charge and of all dealings and devolutions affecting the mortgage shall have the same priority as the mortgage cautions by which they were respectively protected on the register, or such of them as are then subsisting and capable of taking effect.

(2) If the applicant is the person appearing by the register to be entitled to the benefit of the mortgage caution, the registration shall be made forthwith, and the applicant or his nominee shall be entered as proprietor of the charge.

(3) In other cases the application must be accompanied by proof of the applicant's title and shall be proceeded with as the Registrar shall direct. **[1519]**

227. Effect of registration

On the registration of the mortgage as a charge, all mortgage cautions relating to it shall be cancelled.   **[1520]**

[228. Inspection otherwise than under authority of proprietor

(1) In this rule "a person interested" in relation to any land includes a tenant or a person interested in a charge or incumbrance to which the land is subject or a person interested [within the meaning hereof] defined in any adjoining land.

(2) A person interested in any registered land may inspect and obtain office copies of the Property Register and the filed plan of the title to that land.

(3) A tenant entitled to inspect the Proprietorship Register of a title under section 112C of the Act (right of residential tenant to search for landlord's name and address) may apply on Form 108 for the name and address of the proprietor of the land registered under that title to be disclosed to him.

(4) A person interested in any registered land may upon written application inspect and obtain office copies of the Proprietorship Register, the Charges Register and any document referred to in any entry of the title to that land, and the statutory declaration in support of a caution affecting that land, provided the person interested is a tenant entitled to inspect the same under section 112C of the Act or the Registrar is satisfied that such inspection is reasonable and proper and that either:

    (*a*) the person interested, by reason of the death of a sole proprietor, or for any other sufficient reason, cannot obtain the requisite authority for or consent to such inspection; or

    (*b*) no objection by the proprietor to such inspection has been received following notice given to the proprietor by the Registrar in such form and of such period (being not less than 3 days) as the Registrar may direct.]   **[1521]**

NOTES

    Substituted by the Land Registration Rules 1987, SI 1987 No 2214, r 2.

    Para (1): words in square brackets substituted by the Land Registration Rules 1989, SI 1989 No 801, r 4.

    The Act: Land Registration Act 1925.

[228A. Sub-mortgages of registered charges

The provisions of section 106 of the Land Registration Act 1925 (as substituted by section 26 (1) of the Administration of Justice Act 1977) shall, subject to any necessary modification, apply to a sub-mortgage created by the proprietor of a registered charge.]   **[1522]–[1523]**

NOTES

    Inserted by the Land Registration Rules 1977, SI 1977 No 2089, r 4.

Inhibitions

230. Application for an inhibition

(1) An application for an inhibition under Section 57 of the Act shall either be accompanied by the consent in writing of the proprietor of the land, or shall be supported by the statutory declaration of the applicant and such other evidence (if any) as the Registrar may deem necessary.

(2) Pending the result of any hearing before the Registrar as prescribed by these rules, the Registrar may, if for any reason he thinks it desirable, enter an inhibition preventing any dealing with the land or any charge thereon.   **[1524]**

NOTES
The Act: Land Registration Act 1925.

231. Cancellation of inhibition entered under order of Court

(1) Except as to inhibitions originally entered pursuant to an order of the Court, any application to discharge or cancel the same shall be made to the Registrar.

(2) The applications may be made by any person aggrieved by the inhibition.   **[1525]**

Benefices

232. Inhibition on the registration of incumbent

Where land is transferred to the incumbent of a benefice in his corporate capacity, an inhibition shall be entered in the register and on the land certificate in Form 73, or to the like effect.   **[1526]**

233. Sale by an incumbent

In the case of a sale by an incumbent under the Glebe Lands Act 1888, or any Act amending or extending the same, the receipt of the Minister of Agriculture for the purchase money shall be deemed to be a certificate for the purposes of Section 99 of the Act, and shall be a sufficient authority to the Registrar to register the transfer.   **[1527]**

NOTES
The Act: Land Registration Act 1925.

234. Certificate on sale by an incumbent

In all other cases of dispositions by incumbents the certificate to be given in accordance with Section 99 of the Act shall be in Form 74, or to the like effect.
                                                                              [1528]

NOTES
The Act: Land Registration Act 1925.

Restrictions

235. Application for a restriction

(1) An application for a restriction under Section 58 of the Act shall—
   (a) be in Form 75,
   (b) state the particulars of the restriction required to be entered on the register,
   (c) be signed by the applicant or his solicitor,
   (d) be proceeded with as the Registrar shall direct.

(2) An application to withdraw or modify any restriction shall be in Form 77, and shall be signed by all persons for the time being appearing by the register to be interested in the restriction, or their solicitors.   **[1529]**

NOTES
The Act: Land Registration Act 1925.

236. Application for a restriction by persons other than the proprietor

(1) An application for a restriction by persons other than the proprietor shall be in Form 75 modified as required to meet the circumstances of the case.

(2) It shall set out the grounds on which the application is made, and shall be accompanied by such evidence as the Registrar may direct. **[1530]**

Orders under inhibitions and restrictions

237. Order of Registrar in anticipation of a dealing

(1) Application may be made to the Registrar for an order under an inhibition or restriction, or a certificate under Section 89 of the Act, in anticipation of an intended dealing, and the Registrar may, on any such application, make an order or grant a certificate that the dealing be registered either unconditionally or subject to such limitations or conditions as he may think fit.

(2) The order need not be entered on the register, but shall be filed, and, so long as it is in force, shall be shown to any person searching the register. **[1531]**

NOTES
The Act: Land Registration Act 1925.

Ecclesiastical Commissioners

238. Powers of Ecclesiastical Commissioners

In order to give due effect to any arrangement with respect to land made under any of the Acts relating to or administered by the Ecclesiastical Commissioners, whether by scheme and Order in Council, grant, conveyance, transfer, or other instrument, the Ecclesiastical Commissioners shall be deemed to be persons interested within the meaning of Sections 54 and 57 of the Act. **[1532]**

NOTES
The Act: Land Registration Act 1925.

Notice of Deposit of Certificate

239. Notice of deposit of certificate

(1) Any person with whom a land certificate or charge certificate is deposited as security for money may, by registered letter or otherwise, in writing give notice to the Registrar of such deposit, and of his name and address.

(2) The notice shall describe (by reference to the district and parish or place and number of the title) the land to which the certificate relates.

(3) On receipt of such notice the Registrar shall enter notice of the deposit in the Charges Register, and shall give a written acknowledgment of its receipt.

(4) Such notice shall operate as a caution under Section 54 of the Act.

(5) The provisions of Section 66 of the Act, and of these rules, as respects the deposit of a charge certificate, shall apply to the deposit of a certificate of sub-charge or of an incumbrance in like manner. **[1533]**

NOTES
    The Act: Land Registration Act 1925.

240. Notice of intended deposit of certificate

A person applying for registration as proprietor of land or of a charge may, whether the land or charge is already registered or not, create a lien on the land or charge equivalent to that created by a deposit of a certificate by giving notice in writing, signed by himself, to the Registrar, that he intends to deposit the land certificate or charge certificate, when issued, with another person as security for money.   **[1534]**

241. Particulars to be given on notice of intended deposit

(1) The notice of such intended deposit shall state the name and address of the person with whom the certificate is to be deposited, and shall describe the land or charge to which the certificate relates by reference to the district or parish or place and number of the title or (in the case of unregistered land) by reference to the deed or document by which the land was last dealt with, or otherwise to the satisfaction of the Registrar.

(2) The Registrar shall enter notice of the intended deposit in the register and give a written acknowledgment of its receipt.   **[1535]**

242. Effect of notice of intended deposit

(1) A notice of intended deposit shall operate as a caution under Section 54 of the Act.

(2) The certificate shall, when issued or re-issued, be delivered by the Registrar to the person named in that behalf in the notice.   **[1536]**

NOTES
    The Act: Land Registration Act 1925.

243. When notice of deposit may not be entered

Notice of deposit or intended deposit of a certificate shall not be entered while another such notice is on the register, nor as to part only of the land or charge to which the certificate relates.   **[1537]**

244. Certificate left while notice of deposit on register

If, while a notice of deposit or intended deposit is on the register, the certificate is left in the Registry for any purpose, it shall be dealt with, notwithstanding the notice, and shall be returned to the person leaving it or as he may in writing direct.   **[1538]**

245. When new certificate may not be issued

So long as a notice of such deposit is on the register no new certificate shall be issued—

    (a) under Section 67 of the Act,
    (b) under Section 64 on a sale under a charge subsequent in priority to the notice of deposit, without notice similar to that given under a caution,
    (c) in the other cases mentioned in paragraphs (a) to (c) of Subsection (4) of Section 64, without a notice similar to that given under a caution.

[1539]

NOTES
The Act: Land Registration Act 1925.

246. Withdrawal of notice of deposit

The notice of deposit or notice of intended deposit may be withdrawn from the register on a written request or consent signed by the person entitled to the lien created by the deposit, or notice of intended deposit, or his successor in title; accompanied in either case by the land certificate, or charge certificate. **[1540]**

Entry of Value of Land on the Register

247. Value entered on register

(1) On the first registration of land, and on subsequent changes of proprietorship, the Registrar shall, [if the proprietor so requests], enter in the register and on the land certificate the price paid or value declared.

(2) ... **[1541]**

NOTES
Para (1): words in square brackets substituted by the Land Registration Rules 1976, SI 1976 No 1332, r 2(2).
Para (2): revoked by the Land Registration Rules 1976, r 3, Schedule.

Undivided shares

248. Registration of the entirety of the land

(1) The evidence to be furnished and the procedure to be adopted on the registration, under Section 78 of the Act, of the entirety of land shall be the same as that prescribed for an application for the first registration of land, with the necessary modifications.

(2) On the completion of the application the previous registration of the undivided share shall be annulled.

(3) Where two or more shares composing the entirety are registered in different modes of registration (for instance, if one is registered with absolute title and another with possessory title, or if two or more are registered with possessory title in the names of different persons at first proprietors or at different dates of first registration) the entirety shall nevertheless be registered in one mode only, and, if it be with possessory title, the name of the first proprietor and the date of first registration shall be those of the first proprietor of and the date of the registration of the entirety. **[1542]**

NOTES
The Act: Land Registration Act 1925.

Formal Alterations

249. Change of name, address, or description

The Registrar may, from time to time, make any formal alterations in the register as to any change in the name, address, or description of any proprietor or otherwise as he may deem proper. **[1543]**

PART V

MISCELLANEOUS

Acquisition of Rights by Prescription

250. Acquisition of adverse easements by prescription

(1) Pursuant to Subsection (5) of Section 75 of the Act, it is hereby provided that easements, rights and privileges adversely affecting registered land may be acquired in equity by prescription in the same manner and to the same extent as if the land were not registered.

(2) If any easement, right, or privilege so acquired is of such estate and nature as is capable of taking effect at law it shall take effect at law also, and in that case—

   (a) if it is an overriding interest, notice of it may be entered on the register if the Registrar thinks fit under Subsection (3) of Section 70 of the Act.
   (b) if it has been acquired for the benefit of registered land, it may, if the Registrar thinks fit, be registered as part of the description of the land. **[1544]**

NOTES
   The Act: Land Registration Act 1925.

Appurtenances and Easements

251. Registration vests appurtenances

The registration of a person as proprietor of land shall vest in him, together with the land, all rights, privileges, and appurtenances appertaining or reputed to appertain to the land or any part thereof, or, at the time of registration, demised, occupied, or enjoyed therewith, or reputed or known as part or parcel of or appurtenant to the land or any part thereof, including the appropriate rights and interests which, had there been a conveyance of the land or manor, would under Section 62 of the Law of Property Act 1925, have passed therewith. **[1545]**

252. Application for entry of appurtenant right on register

(1) Where the proprietor wishes (whether on first registration or at any other time) to have a specific entry on the register of any appurtenant right, capable of subsisting as a legal estate, to which he may be entitled, he may apply to the Registrar in writing, signed by himself or his solicitor, for such an entry to be made.

(2) The application shall state the nature of the right and shall furnish evidence of its existence. **[1546]**

253. Notice to be served regarding adverse rights

(1) The Registrar shall thereupon give such notice (if any) to the person in possession of the land affected as he may deem advisable.

(2) If the land affected is registered he shall give notice to the proprietor and to every person appearing by the register to be interested, and shall, if he thinks fit, enter notice of it against such land. **[1547]**

254. Entry of appurtenant right and its effect

(1) If the Registrar is satisfied that the right is capable of subsisting as a legal estate and appurtenant to the land, he may enter it as part of the description of the land in the Property Register, and the effect of such entry shall be to confer an absolute, good leasehold, qualified or possessory title to the right, according to the nature of the title to the land.

(2) If the Registrar is not satisfied that the right is appurtenant, he shall enter it with such qualification as he may deem advisable, or he may merely enter notice of the fact that the proprietor claims it.   **[1548]**

255. Entries by reference

The entry shall be made as far as practicable by reference to the instrument (if any) creating the right, or by setting out an extract therefrom.   **[1549]**

256. Transfer of benefit

On any registered disposition of the land or of a charge thereon, the benefit of the entry shall, on registration, but without prejudice to any express exception or reservation, accrue to the grantee as part of the registered estate.   **[1550]**

257. Positive registration

The benefit of an easement, right, or privilege shall not be entered on the register except as appurtenant to a registered estate, and then only if capable of subsisting as a legal estate.   **[1551]**

258. Adverse easements treated as overriding interests

Rights, privileges, and appurtenances appertaining or reputed to appertain to land or demised, occupied, or enjoyed therewith or reputed or known as part or parcel of or appurtenant thereto, which adversely affect registered land, are overriding interests within Section 70 of the Act, and shall not be deemed incumbrances for the purposes of the Act.   **[1552]**

NOTES
  The Act: Land Registration Act 1925.

Corporations, etc

259. Evidence required on registration of a corporation, etc

Where an application for registration as proprietors of land or of a charge is made by a corporation, or a body of trustees, in whom, as such, property from time to time vests, there shall be produced such evidence, if any, as the Registrar directs of incorporation, or of the provisions under which the property so vested as aforesaid, as the case may be, and in either case of the power to deal with the land or charge:

Provided that where a company is registered for profit under the Companies Acts, a copy of the memorandum and articles of association shall be furnished, but no further evidence shall be offered that it has power to acquire any interest in or charge on land, or to dispose of any such interest or charge unless the Registrar, in any specific case, requires evidence to be furnished. **[1553]–[1554]**

Certificates

261. Form of land certificate

A land certificate shall be in Form 78 and the Land Registry seal shall be affixed to it.   **[1555]**

262. Form of charge certificate

(1) A charge certificate shall certify the registration of the charge and shall contain—

(*a*) [either the original or] an office copy of the charge,
(*b*) a description (if no description is contained in the charge) of the land affected,
(*c*) the name and address of the proprietor of the charge,
(*d*) a list of the prior incumbrances (if any) appearing on the register.

(2) There shall also be added such further particulars if any, as the Registrar shall think fit, and the Land Registry seal shall be affixed to it.

(3) Notes of subsequent dealings affecting the charge shall from time to time be entered on the certificate, or a new certificate shall be issued in place thereof, as may be more convenient.   **[1556]**

NOTES
    Para (1): Words in square brackets inserted by the Land Registration Rules 1993, SI 1993 No 3275, r 7.

263. Authorised statements

A land certificate or charge certificate may contain a short statement of the general effect of registration and directions as to the general procedure on dealings and as to fees.   **[1557]**

264. Annexation of office copies

Where an office copy of an entry in the register or of the filed plan of the land or of any document filed in the Registry is annexed to any certificate, it shall for the purposes of Section 68 of the Act be deemed to be contained in the certificate itself.   **[1558]–[1559]**

NOTES
    The Act: Land Registration Act 1925.

266. When production of land certificate may be required, or new one issued

On any application for registration made by or with the consent of the proprietor of the land or of a charge or incumbrance, the Registrar may require the production of the land certificate or charge certificate or incumbrance, and may refuse to proceed with the application until the certificate is produced:

Provided that a new certificate may be issued, without the production of the original certificate, in any of the cases mentioned in Subsection (4) of Section 64 of the Act, but subject to such notices or enquiries (if any) being given or made as the Registrar may, in any case, deem necessary.   **[1560]**

NOTES
    The Act: Land Registration Act 1925.

267. Cancellation of certificate

When a certificate is produced on the closing of a title, the clearing of the register, or the discharge of a charge or incumbrance, the land or charge certificate (as the case may be) shall be retained in the Registry and cancelled.

[1561]

268. Purposes for which certificates may be retained

(1) The Registrar shall have power to retain a certificate produced under Section 64 of the Act for the purpose of making an entry thereon.

(2) On the registration of any transaction for which the production of a land certificate or charge certificate is required, the certificate shall, before it is re-issued, be made to correspond with the register. **[1562]**

NOTES
The Act: Land Registration Act 1925.

269. Certificate deposited for specified purpose only

(1) A certificate may be deposited in the Registry with written directions that it is to be held for a specified purpose only.

(2) Save for the purposes of the last preceding rule, a certificate so deposited shall not be used, or be deemed to be in the Registry for any other purpose, without the written consent of the person by whom such directions were given, or his successor in title or his solicitor. **[1563]**

270. Receipt for land certificate produced instead of land certificate

(1), (2) . . .

(3) When deposited pursuant to Section 65 of the Act, the land certificate need not be made to correspond with the register from time to time and a new certificate may be issued in place thereof on the cancellation of the charge or mortgage. **[1564]**

NOTES
Paras (1), (2): revoked by the Land Registration Rules 1930, SR & O 1930 No 211, r 5.
The Act: Land Registration Act 1925.

271. Lost certificates

(1) Where it is proved to the satisfaction of the Registrar that a certificate has been lost or destroyed, or that it is in the possession of a person out of the jurisdiction of the Court or its production cannot be obtained without undue delay or expense, he may issue a new one, after taking such indemnities as he may consider necessary, and after giving such public notice in the Gazette and in such local or other newspapers (if any) and in such manner as shall appear to him sufficient in each case.

(2) The notice shall give the name and address of the proprietor and the registered description of the land, and shall state that it is proposed to issue a new certificate and shall request any person in whose possession the certificate may be, or who has any objection to each issue, to inform the Registrar of the fact. **[1565]**

Maps and Verbal Descriptions of Land

272. Ordnance Map

The Ordnance Map shall be the basis of all registered descriptions of land.

[1566]

273. Land Registry General Map

(1) For the purpose of describing land, there shall be prepared and kept in the Registry a series of maps, which together shall be called the Land Registry General Map (in these rules referred to as the "General Map").

(2) Each of the series shall be either—

(a) an extract from the Ordnance Map revised and corrected to such extent as may be necessary; or

(b) a map based on and uniform with the Ordnance Map, and so constructed that every parcel shown on it can be accurately located on the Ordnance Map.

(3) Each of the series shall be marked in such a manner as to be easily identified as part of the General Map.

(4) Every parcel on the General Map shall be numbered for reference in such manner as and when the Registrar shall deem convenient.   **[1567]**

274. Parcels Index

(1) A Parcels Index shall be kept in the Registry containing any reference numbers on the parcels of registered land shown on the General Map, and showing, with regard to each of such parcels, the numbers of the titles, and, as respects land which has not been registered, of the cautions and priority notices against first registration (if any) relating to it.   **[1568]**

275. Extract from General Map

Where an office copy of or extract from the General Map is annexed to any certificate, it shall, for the purposes of Section 68 of the Act, be deemed to be contained in the certificate itself.   **[1569]**

NOTES
The Act: Land Registration Act 1925.

276. Fixed boundaries

If it is desired to indicate on the filed plan or General Map, or otherwise to define in the register, the precise position of the boundaries of the land or any parts thereof, notice shall be given to the owners and occupiers of the adjoining lands, in each instance, of the intention to ascertain and fix the boundary, with such plan, or tracing, or extract from the proposed verbal description of the land as may be necessary, to show clearly the fixed boundary proposed to be registered; and any question of doubt or dispute arising therefrom shall be dealt with as provided by these rules.   **[1570]**

277. Note as to fixed boundaries in register

When the position and description of the boundaries of the land have been thus ascertained and determined, the necessary particulars shall be added to the filed plan or General Map, and a note shall be made in the Property Register to the effect that the boundaries have been fixed. The plan or General Map shall then be deemed to define accurately the fixed boundaries. **[1571]**

278. General boundaries

(1) Except in cases in which it is noted in the Property Register that the boundaries have been fixed, the filed plan or General Map shall be deemed to indicate the general boundaries only.

(2) In such cases the exact line of the boundary will be left undetermined — as, for instance, whether it includes a hedge or wall and ditch, or runs along the centre of a wall or fence, or its inner or outer face, or how far it runs within or beyond it; or whether or not the land registered includes the whole or any portion of an adjoining road or stream.

(3) When a general boundary only is desired to be entered in the register, notice to the owners of the adjoining lands need not be given.

(4) This rule shall apply notwithstanding that a part or the whole of a ditch, wall, fence, road, stream, or other boundary is expressly included in or excluded from the title or that it forms the whole of the land comprised in the title. **[1572]**

279. Where physical boundaries do not exist

Where, and so far as, physical boundaries or boundary marks do not exist, the fullest available particulars of the boundaries shall be added to the filed plan or General Map. **[1573]**

280. Revision of Ordnance Map

(1) When the necessary plan or reference to the General Map cannot be prepared without a revision of the Ordnance Map or General Map, the Registrar shall, if required by the applicant, make the necessary revision.

(2) In districts where registration of title is compulsory, the revision shall be made without charge. **[1574]**

281. Verbal description of land

(1) When an applicant desires to enter any verbal particulars or description of land on the register, they shall be submitted to the Registrar for his approval.

(2) Such particulars shall contain a reference to the filed plan of the land or reference to the General Map, and shall be compared therewith by the Registrar. **[1575]**

282. Separate portions distinguished on map

When such particulars consist of or refer to a detailed list, by schedule or otherwise, of separate portions of the land, each portion so detailed shall be distinguished, if possible, by a number or other reference in the list and on the filed plan or General Map. **[1576]**

283. Particulars of changes in street names, etc

In districts where registration of title is compulsory, the Registrar shall be furnished by the local authorities with particulars of alterations of names and numbers of streets and houses from time to time made, for future reference; and any correction of the register rendered necessary by such alterations may be made.　　　　**[1577]**

284. Revision and correction of plans

(1) Renewal, revision, or correction of plans and verbal descriptions of land may be made at any time on the application in writing of the proprietor, upon the production of such evidence and the giving of such notices as the Registrar may deem necessary.

(2) Revision or correction of any part of the General Map may also be made at any time on the application of the proprietor of the land to which such part relates.　　　　**[1578]**

285. Conflict between verbal particulars and Map

The Registrar shall decide any question arising on a conflict between the verbal particulars and the filed plan or General Map. On such decision being given the particulars and the filed plan or General Map shall be altered accordingly.

[1579]–[1585]

Inspection, Searches and Copies of the Register

291. Conditions as to inspections

Every inspection shall be made in the presence of an officer of the Registry, and every copy or note of, or extract from any register or document in the custody of the Registrar shall be made by the person inspecting in pencil only. No ink shall be used.　　　　**[1585]**

295. Official search exonerates from responsibility for error

(1) When a solicitor or other person obtains an official certificate of the result of a search he shall not be answerable in respect of loss that may arise from any error therein.

(2) When the certificate is obtained by a solicitor acting for trustees, personal representatives, or other persons in a fiduciary position, those persons also shall not be so answerable.　　　　**[1586]–[1587]**

297. Inspection of register where land has been removed

(1) When any land has been removed from the register, the last proprietor of the land or of any charge thereon may, for a period of two years from the date of such removal, inspect the register and have office copies of the entries supplied to him.

(2) After two years from the removal no inspection shall be allowed, or office copy be issued, except by order of the Registrar, given after satisfying himself that the applicant is interested, and that the application is reasonable.

[1588]

Hearings before the Registrar

298. Hearing before the Registrar

(1) If any question, doubt, dispute, difficulty or complaint arises before the Registrar upon any application or during any investigation of title—

(*a*) as to the registration of a title, incumbrance, or charge,

(*b*) as to any dealing with any registered title, incumbrance, or charge, or any matter entered or noted in or omitted from the register, or

(*c*) as to the amendment or withdrawal from the register or production to the Registrar of any certificate or other document, or

(*d*) in any registration or other proceeding in the Registry, or

(*e*) as to any claim for indemnity,

(whether such questions relate to the construction, validity, or effect of any instrument, or the persons interested, or the nature or extent of their respective interests or powers, or as to order of priority, or the mode in which any entry should be made or dealt with in the register or otherwise), the Registrar shall hear and determine the matter and, subject to appeal to the Court, make such order in the matter as he shall think just.

(2) But the Registrar may, if he thinks fit, instead of deciding the question himself, refer the matter at any stage, or any question thereon, for the decision of the Court. **[1589]**

299. Appeal to the Court

Any person aggrieved by an order or decision of the Registrar may appeal to the Court. **[1590]**

300. Notice as to hearing to be served

Notice that the Registrar will hear and determine the matter at the Registry shall be served by him on all persons appearing to be interested, stating the time of such hearing and that such persons may attend before him at that time in person, or by his solicitor or counsel. **[1591]**

301. Notice of appeal to be entered in the register

No appeal from a decision or order of the Registrar, or (unless otherwise ordered) of the Court, shall affect any dealing for valuable consideration which has been duly registered before a notice in writing of the intention to appeal has been delivered at the Registry on the part of the alpellant. Such notice shall be entered in the register. **[1592]**

302. Service of an order of the Court on the Registrar

(1) Service on the Registrar of any order or office copy of any order of any Court shall be made by delivering the same at the Registry.

(2) When the order directs rectification of the register to be made, or any other act to be done, an application therefor shall be delivered at the same time, and the matter shall be proceeded with as the Registrar shall direct:

Provided that no such rectification, or act, shall be completed until the expiration of four clear days from the day on which the order is made. **[1593]**

References to Counsel

303. Special Conveyancing Counsel

(1) The Special Conveyancing Counsel for the purposes of these rules shall be the Conveyancing Counsel to the High Court, and such other barristers experienced in conveyancing as the Lord Chancellor shall from time to time appoint, and the business referred to them shall be distributed in rotation.

(2) Matters affecting a title which have already been dealt with by one of the Conveyancing Counsel, shall, so far as practicable, be referred to the same Counsel. But the Registrar may, if he thinks fit, under special circumstances, direct or transfer a reference to any one in particular of the Conveyancing Counsel. **[1594]**

304. Questions involving exceptional knowledge

When, in the course of any proceeding in the Registry, a question arises which, in the opinion of the Registrar, involves for its determination any special exceptional knowledge of some branch of law which rarely arises for consideration, the Registrar may obtain the advice or assistance therein of any competent person whom he may select, and may act upon his opinion. **[1595]**

Abatement

305. Continuation of application on death, etc

In case of death or transmission or change of interest pending an application for registration the proceedings shall not abate, but may be continued by any person, entitled to apply for registration who desires to adopt them. **[1596]**

Abstracts and Documents

306. Documents at Registry where retained, etc

(1) All abstracts and copies of documents and all documents for registration delivered at the Registry shall be retained there, pending completion of the registration to which they relate.

(2) Afterwards such of them as have not under these rules to be retained in the Registry shall be dealt with as the Registrar shall direct.

(3) Abstracts and documents left for reference or otherwise shall be examined and verified by such persons and in such manner as the Registrar shall direct. **[1597]**

307. Abstract may be required by Registrar

The Registrar may require an abstract or concise statement of any deeds and documents, delivered at the Registry for perusal in the course of any registration proceeding, to be furnished and duly verified. **[1598]**

308. Form of documents to be filed

All documents (other than maps or plans) to be filed in the Registry, shall be printed, type-written, lithographed, or written on stout paper, foolscap size, and shall allow a sufficient stitching margin, in order that they may be conveniently bound. **[1599]**

309. Documents to be certified

Every copy of a document delivered by a solicitor at the Registry shall be endorsed with his name and address, and shall be certified by him to be a true copy of the original. Such copy need not be stamped. **[1600]**

310. Return of certain documents and destruction permitted in certain cases

(1) All documents not required by the Act or rules to be retained in the Registry may, when no longer required, be returned to the persons who produced the same, or their successors in title, and the Registrar may direct the destruction of any documents which such persons decline to accept.

(2) The Registrar may also direct the destruction of any documents in his possession or custody where they have become altogether superseded by entries in the register, or have ceased to have any effect. **[1601]**

NOTES
   The Act: Land Registration Act 1925.

Preparation and Service of Notices and Summonses

311. Service of notices and summonses

(1) All notices and summonses (not being applications to the Court) required to be given or served for any purpose shall be prepared on the official forms and under the stamp of the Registry.

(2) If the service of the notices or summonses is personal, it shall be proved by statutory declaration.

(3) If the service is through the post, it shall be made by registered letter, in conformity with Section 79 of the Act; except in the case of notices of the receipt of instruments or applications for registration, which need not be registered. **[1602]**

NOTES
   The Act: Land Registration Act 1925.

312. Contents of notices

(1) Every notice issued or sent by or through the Registry (other than notices of the receipt of instruments or allocations for registration) shall fix a time within which any act or step required by such notice to be done or taken thereunder is to be done or taken; and shall state what will be the consequence of any omission to comply therewith.

(2) It shall also state in what manner and within what time any answer or objection or other communication arising out of such notice is to be made, and the address at or to which it is to be delivered or sent.

(3) All subsequent proceedings thereunder shall be conducted in accordance with these rules; and, so far as they do not apply, in such manner as the Registrar shall direct. **[1603]**

[313. Notice to be deemed to be received within seven days

(1) Every notice sent through the post shall, unless returned by the Post Office, be deemed to have been received by the person addressed seven days after its issue exclusive of the day of posting, and the time fixed by the notice for taking any step thereunder is to be calculated accordingly.

(2) Each such notice shall contain either a copy of paragraph (1) of this rule or an explanation of its effect.] **[1604]**

NOTES
Commencement: 1 June 1989.
Substituted by the Land Registration Rules 1989, SI 1989 No 801, r 5.

314. Return of notices by Post Office

On the return by the Post Office of any letter containing any notice, the Registrar
may either require any further notice to be given, or may authorise substituted
service of the notice; or may proceed without notice, if, under the circumstances,
and having regard to these rules, he shall think fit to do so.   **[1605]**

Addresses for Service

315. Notices to be sent to addresses for service

(1) The address of any person, as entered in the register, shall, unless he shall
otherwise direct, be his address for service.

(2) Any person may, if he desires, have three addresses entered in the
register, including (if he thinks fit) the address of his solicitor or firm of solicitors,
to each of which all notices and other communications to him are to be sent.
          [1606]

Statutory Declarations and Evidence on Oath

316. Statutory declarations and evidence on oath

(1) Statutory declarations made for the immediate purpose of being filed, read,
or used in the Registry are not chargeable with any Inland Revenue Stamp
Duty.

(2) Statutory declarations to be used in the course of registration may be
made before the Registrar, or any officer of the Registry authorised by him in
writing, or before any person authorised by law to take statutory declarations.

(3) All declarations shall be filed in the office, and office copies thereof shall
(if required) be taken for use.

(4) The Registrar may, if he thinks fit, require evidence to be given *viva voce*
before him on oath.   **[1607]**

Neglected Applications to be treated as withdrawn

[317. Applications not in order

(1) If an application is not in order the Registrar may raise such requisitions as
he may consider necessary and may specify a period (being not less than one
month) within which the applicant shall comply therewith and, if the applicant
fails to comply with the requisitions within that period, the Registrar may
cancel the application or may extend the period when this appears to him to be
reasonable in the circumstances.

(2) If an application appears to the Registrar to be substantially defective,
he may reject it on delivery or he may cancel it at any time thereafter.

[(3) Where a fee for an application (including any service for which a fee is
payable) is paid by means of a cheque and it comes to the notice of the Registrar
before the application has been completed that the cheque has not been
honoured, the application may be cancelled.]]   **[1608]**

NOTES
Commencement: 2 April 1990 (para (3)); 1 January 1979 (remainder).
Substituted by the Land Registration Rules 1978, SI 1978 No 1601, r 11.
Para (3): added by the Land Registration Rules 1990, SI 1990 No 314, r 12.

Summonses of Witnesses, and for Production of Documents, etc

319. Summonses by the Registrar

When any summons has been issued by the Registrar under Section 128 of the Act, to be served upon any person not bound to attend or produce documents at his own expense, the declaration, verifying the service thereof, shall also prove that the reasonable charges of the attendance of the person summoned, and of his production of the documents (if any) required to be produced, have been paid or tendered to him. **[1609]**

NOTES
The Act: Land Registration Act 1925.

320. Production of documents, etc

The Registrar shall have all the powers conferred by Sections 15 and 128 of the Act in all proceedings in the Registry, whether arising in relation to the registration of any land or title or otherwise. **[1610]**

NOTES
The Act: Land Registration Act 1925.

Costs

321. Orders and taxation

(1) All costs incurred in any proceeding in the Registry shall be in the discretion of the Registrar, having regard to the provisions as to costs contained in the Act and these rules.

(2) The costs shall, unless the parties otherwise agree, be taxed as the Registrar shall direct by the taxing officers of the Supreme Court.

(3) Any order made by the Registrar as to costs may be enforced in the mode provided by Section 17 of the Act with respect to costs, charges, and expenses incurred in or about proceedings for registration of land. **[1611]**

NOTES
The Act: Land Registration Act 1925.

Discretionary Power of Registrar

322. Power to relax regulations, etc

(1) The Registrar, if he so thinks fit, may, in any particular case, extend the time limited, or relax the regulations made by general rules, for any purpose; and may at any time adjourn any proceeding, and make any new appointment.

(2) If at any time he is of opinion that the production of any further documents, or evidence, or the giving of any further notices is necessary or desirable, he may refuse to complete or proceed with a registration, or to do any act, or make any entry until such further documents, or evidence, or notices have been supplied or given. **[1612]**

Holidays

323. Holidays

The Registry shall be open to the public daily, except on [Saturdays], Sundays, Good Friday, Easter Eve, Monday and Tuesday in Easter week, Monday in Whitsun week, Christmas Day, and the next following working day, and all days duly appointed by proclamation to be observed as days of general fast, humiliation, or thanksgiving, and any other days appointed by the Lord Chancellor in that behalf.   **[1613]**

NOTES
Word in square brackets inserted by the Land Registration Rules 1956, SI 1956 No 1024, r 2.

Short title and Commencement

325. Short title and commencement

These rules may be cited as the Land Registration Rules 1925, and shall come into operation on the first day of January, 1926.   **[1614]**

SCHEDULE

FORM 9.—*Restriction where Tenant for Life is registered as proprietor (r 58)*

No disposition under which capital money arises is to be registered unless the money is paid to A.B., of &c., and C.D., of &c. (the trustees of the settlement, of which there must be two and not more than four individuals, or a trust corporation), or into Court.

Except under an order of the Registrar, no disposition is to be registered unless authorised by the Settled Land Act 1925.

Note.—In cases where the Settlement so provides a further provision may be added to the Restriction that no transfer of the mansion house (shown on an attached plan or otherwise adequately described to enable it to be fully identified on the General Map, Ordnance Map, or Filed Plan) is to be registered without the consent of the said A.B. and C.D., or an Order of the Court.   **[1615]**

FORM 10.—*Restriction where Statutory owners or trustees holding on trust for sale are entered as proprietors (r 58)*

Except under an Order of the Registrar, no disposition is to be registered unless authorised by the Settled Land Act 1925 and except where the sole proprietor is a trust corporation, no disposition under which capital money arises is to be registered unless the money is paid to at least two proprietors.

Note.—This restriction does not apply where the statutory owners are not the trustees of the settlement.   **[1616]**

[FORM 12.—*Restriction applicable to a charity which is not an exempt charity (Rules 60(7) and 123(6))*

Except under an order of the registrar no disposition or dealing by the proprietor of the land is to be registered unless the instrument giving effect to it contains a certificate complying with section 37(2) or, in the case of a charge, with section 39(2) of the Charities Act 1993.]   **[1616A]**

NOTES
Commencement: 1 August 1993.
Substituted by the Land Registration (Charities) Rules 1993, SI 1993 No 1704, r 3(2), Schedule.

FORM 13.—*Caution (under Section 53 of the Act) against entry of Land on the Register (r 64)*

(Heading as in Form 1)

(*Date*). A.B. [*the cautioner*], of &c., is entitled to notice of any application that may be made for the registration of the freehold land (*or* leasehold land held under a lease dated, &c., and made between A.B., of &c., of the one part, and C.D., of the other part, for the term of .. .. years from (*date*) *or otherwise as the case may be*) shown and edged with red on the plan attached thereto.

(To be signed by the cautioner or his solicitor.)

Note.—The statutory declaration in support (in the next form) must set forth the interest in respect of which the cautioner claims to be entitled to object to any disposition of the land being made without his consent.

The form can be adapted to the case of a manor or an advowson or other incorporeal hereditament.

If the cautioner's address is not within the United Kingdom, an address for service within that area must also be given.

[*Note.*—Where sufficient particulars (by parcel number or otherwise), to enable the land to be fully identified on the General Map, Ordnance Map, or Filed Plan, can be furnished without a special plan, such particulars may be introduced into the form instead of the reference to a plan.]   **[1617]**

FORM 14.—*Statutory Declaration in support of a Caution (r 66, 215)*

(Heading as in Form 1)

I, A.B., of &c., solemnly and sincerely declare that I am interested in the land (*or*) charge, referred to in the caution now produced and shown to me marked, "A" [*here state the nature of the declarant's interest* "as beneficial owner in fee simple" "beneficially entitled to the lease referred to therein," "tenant for life within the meaning of the Settled Land Act 1925," "purchaser under a contract for sale, dated, &c.," "plaintiff in an action in the Chancery Division of the High Court of Justice, B. *v.* C., 1897, B. 145," "equitable mortgagee under a memorandum of charge dated .. .. under the hand of .. .. ," *or as the case may be*].

And I make, &c.

(To be declared by the cautioner, or, with the necessary alterations, by his solicitor.)
                                                                                   [1618]

FORM 17.—*Priority Notice (under Rule 71) for entry of Land on the Register*

(Heading as in Form 19)

To the Registrar.

Take notice that I, A.B., of &c., desire to reserve priority for an application for registration of myself as first proprietor of the freehold [leasehold] land shown and edged with red on the plan attached hereto, which I have contracted to purchase [for the residue of a term of .. .. years from the (*date*) created by a lease, dated the (*date*) and made between .. .. of .. .. and .. .. of .. ..].

(To be signed by the applicant or his solicitor)

Note.—Where sufficient particulars (by parcel number or otherwise), to enable the land to be fully identified on the General Map, Ordnance Map, or Filed Plan, can be furnished without a special plan, such particulars may be introduced into the form instead of the reference to a plan.   **[1619]**

[FORM 19.—*Transfer of Freehold Land (Whole) (r 98)*

H.M. LAND REGISTRY

Land Registration Acts 1925 to 1986

(County and District *or* London Borough) .. ..

Title No. .. ..

Property .. ..

Date .. ..

In consideration of   pounds (£) receipt of which is acknowledged (I) AB of &c., transfer(s) to CD of &c., the land comprised in the title above referred to.

where the transfer is to be executed personally by an individual add

(Signed as a deed *or* Signed and delivered)   (*Signature of AB*)

by AB in the presence of:

(Signature, name and address of witness)

where the transfer is to be executed by an individual directing another to sign on his behalf add

(Signed as a deed *or* Signed and delivered) by XY) at the direction and on behalf of AB in (his *or* her) presence and in the presence of: (*Signature of AB by XY*)

(Signatures, names and addresses of two witnesses)

where the transfer is to be executed by a company registered under the Companies Acts, using its common seal, add

The common seal of AB was affixed in the presence   (*Common seal of AB*)

of:

    Director .. ..

    Secretary .. ..

where the transfer is to be executed by a company registered under the Companies Acts, without using a common seal, add

(Signed as a deed *or* Signed and delivered) by AB acting by (a director and its secretary *or* two directors) .. .. .. Director

    .. .. .. (Secretary *or* Director)

Note.—Where the transfer is made under section 37 of the Act following a dealing with part only of the land comprised in a title, or is made under rule 72, the number of the title must be left blank, and instead of the words "the title above referred to" a reference to the last preceding document of title containing a description of the land must be inserted.

When the consideration is advanced by different persons in separate sums, or does not consist or wholly consist of money, its nature or the separate payments made may be concisely stated.

Where the transfer is to two or more jointly, there may be added to the form a declaration as to whether the survivor of the transferees can or cannot give a valid receipt for capital money arising on a disposition of the land, and provision may be made for the transferees to execute the transfer.

The amount of the consideration should be stated in words and repeated in figures— as, for instance, "thirty seven thousand pounds (£37,000)".

Where more convenient the parties may be defined by expressions such as "the Vendor", "the Purchaser", &c, and the instrument can be framed in the third person.

Where alternative wording is provided in the form only one of the alternatives should be used.

A person signing a transfer, whether as an individual party, as a witness or as director or secretary of a company, must sign manually and not in facsimile save where signature in facsimile is authorised by any statutue or statutory instrument.]   **[1620]**

NOTES
Commencement: 31 July 1990.
Substituted by the Land Registration (Execution of Deeds) Rules 1990, SI 1990 No 1010, r 2, Schedule.
The Act: Land Registration Act 1925.

FORM 20.—*Transfer of Freehold Land (Part) (r 98)*

As Form 19, adding after "the land" these words, "shown and edged with red on the accompaning plan and known as [and—*if it is desired that a particular verbal description be entered on the Register*—described in the Schedule hereto] being part of the land comprised in the title above referred to."

Add Schedule if desired.

(To be executed as Form 19 by the transferor. The plan must be signed by the .. .. transferor and by or on behalf of the transferee.)

Note.—Where sufficient particulars (by parcel number or otherwise), to enable, the land to be fully identified on the General Map, Ordnance Map, or Filed Plan, can be furnished without the special plan, such particulars may be introduced into the form instead of the reference to a plan.   **[1621]**

FORM 45.—*Charge (r 139)*

(Heading as in Form 19)

(*Date.*) In consideration of .. .. pounds (£ .. ..), I, A.B. of &c., hereby charge the land comprised in the title above referred to with the payment to C.D., of &c., on the .. .. of .. .. 19 , of the principal sum of £ .. .. , with interest at .. per cent. per annum, payable [half yearly, quarterly on the .. .. of .. .. &c., in every year.

(To be executed as Form 19)

Note.—Where the charge is made under Section 37 of the Act, and deals with part only of the land comprised in a title, or is made under Rule 73, the number of the title must be left blank, and instead of the words "the title above referred to" a reference to the last preceding document of title containing a description of the land must be inserted.

Where the consideration is advanced by different persons in separate sums or does not consist, or wholly consist, of money, its nature, or the separate payment made, may be concisely stated.

The amount of the consideration should be stated in words, and repeated in figures— as, for instance, "three hundred and seventy pounds (£370)."

Where the charge is to two or more jointly no addition need be made to the form.

Where the money is to be held in separate shares *after* "C.D., of part &c.," *insert in place of the text* "and E.F., of &c., jointly on the .. .. day of .. .. , 19 .. of the aggregate principal sum of &c [*as in text adding after* "every year"] which sum as to £ .. .. part thereof and the interest thereon belongs to the said C.D. and as to £ .. .. residue thereof and the interest thereon belongs to the said E.F.

Any of the following stipulations with any requisite variations may also be added at the end of the charge.

A.—*Stipulations negativing the Covenants implied in charges by Section 28 of the Act*

(1) No covenant is hereby implied to pay the principal or interest secured by the charge.

(2) No covenant is hereby implied as to payment of rent or performance or observance of the covenants or conditions of the registered lease, or as to indemnity in respect thereof.

B.—*Stipulations in charges excluding the provisions of Section 28 of the Act, and altering the priority of charges under Section 29 of the Act*

(1) The creditor shall have no power to enter on the land.

(2) The creditor shall have no power to enforce foreclosure or sale of the land.

(3) The creditor shall have no power of sale.

(4) The creditor may exercise the power of sale without notice.

(5) This charge shall rank *pari passu* with a charge of even date to .. .. of .. .. to secure .. .. *or* shall be the [first, second, third, &c., *as the case may be*] in order of priority of three charges of even date, one of which is to .. .. of .. .. to secure .. .. , another is to .. .. of .. .. to secure .. .. , and the other is this charge *or* shall have priority to a charge dated, &c., registered, &c., in favour of A.B., of &c., for .. .. (*or otherwise as the case may be*).

C.—*Miscellaneous Stipulations*

(1) The interest to be secured by the charge shall be reduced to .. .. per cent. in every (half year, quarter, &c.) in which it is paid within .. .. days after it becomes due.

(2) None of the principal secured by the charge shall be called in till the .. .. of .. .. 19 , unless the interest shall fail to be paid within .. .. days after it becomes due.

(3) None of the principal secured by the charge shall be paid off till the .. .. of .. ..each, 19 , unless the proprietor of the charge shall be willing to accept it.

(4) If the interest secured by the charge shall be paid within .. .. days after it becomes due the principal shall be payable by instalments of .. .. each, to be paid on the .. .. of .. .. and the .. .. of .. .. in every year, the first of such instalments to be paid on the .. .. of .. .. 19 :

Provided that on failure of payment of any instalment within .. .. days after it becomes due, the whole of the principal remaining owing on the said security shall become payable at once:

Provided nevertheless that the whole or any part (not less than .. .. at any one time) of the above mentioned principal may be paid off on giving one month's notice in writing of the intention to do so, and on paying up all arrears of interest that may be due at the time of such payment of principal.   **[1622]**

NOTES
The Act: Land Registration Act 1925.

FORM 53.—*Discharge of Registered Charge (r 151)*

(Heading as in Form 19)

(*Date.*) I, A.B., of &c., hereby admit that the charge dated (*date*), and registered (*date*), of which I am the proprietor, has been discharged.

(To be signed by the proprietor of the charge and attested.)

Note.—The discharge may be made as to part of the land only, by adding at the end "as to the land shown and edged with red on the accompanying plan, signed by me, being part of," or as to part of the money only by adding "to the extent of .. .."

Where the charge was for future advances or for an indefinite amount there must be added to the final discharge, for the purpose of stamp duty, a statement of the total amount or value of the money at any time secured.

Note.—Where sufficient particulars (by parcel number or otherwise), to enable the land to be fully identified on the General Map, Ordnance Map, or Filed Plan, can be furnished without a special plan, such particulars may be introduced into the form instead of the reference to a plan.   **[1623]**

FORM 63.—*Caution (under Section 54 of the Act) against Dealings with Registered Land or a Charge (r 215)*

(Heading as in Form 58)

(*Date.*) A.B. [*the cautioner*], of &c., requires that no dealing with the land (*or* charge) above referred to (*or* with the land shown and edged with red on the plan hereto) shall be registered until notice has been served upon him or his personal representative.

(To be signed by the cautioner or his solicitor)

Note.—If the cautioner's address is not within the United Kingdom, an address for service within that area must also be given.   **[1624]**

NOTES
The Act: Land Registration Act 1925.

FORM 70.—*Notice to a person who has lodged a Caution (r 218)*

(Heading as in Form 19 or 58)

Notice.—The caution lodged by you in this office on the (*date*), requiring that no dealing with the land (*or* charge) above referred to should be registered until notice had been served upon you, will cease to have any effect after the expiration of fourteen days next ensuing the date at which this notice is served, unless an order to the contrary is made by the Registrar.

Dated the .... day of .... 19 .   **[1624A]**

FORM 75.—*Application to register a Restriction under Section 58 of the Act (r 235)*

(Heading as in Form 19)

(*Date.*) A.B. (*the proprietor*), of &c., hereby applies to the Registrar to enter the following restriction against the title (*or* charge) above referred to.

Restriction.—Except under an Order of the Registrar, no disposition shall be registered without the consent of C.D., of &c. (or otherwise—*see* examples in Forms 9 to 11 or 12).   **[1624B]**

NOTES
The Act: Land Registration Act 1925.

FORM 80.—*Authority to inspect register (r 289)*

(Heading as in Form 19 or 58)

(*Date.*) I, A.B., of &c. (*the proprietor*), hereby authorise the bearer to apply at any time to the Registrar for information as to the entries in the register of the title [*or* charge above referred to at the above date].

(To be signed by A.B. or his solicitor)   **[1625]**

LAND REGISTRATION (MATRIMONIAL HOMES) RULES 1990
(SI 1990 No 1360)

NOTES
Made: 4 July 1990.
Authority: Land Registration Act 1925, s 144; Matrimonial Homes Act 1983, 5(4), (6).

1. Citation, Commencement and Interpretation

These rules may be cited as the Land Registration (Matrimonial Homes) Rules 1990 and shall come into force on 3rd December 1990.   **[1626]**

NOTES
Commencement: 3 December 1990.

2. (1) In these rules, unless the context otherwise requires:—

"The 1967 Act" means the Matrimonial Homes Act 1967;
"The 1983 Act" means the Matrimonial Homes Act 1983;
"proper office" means the district land registry designated as the proper office by Article 2(2) of the Land Registration (District Registries) Order 1989;

(2) A form referred to by number means the form so numbered in the Schedule to these rules.   **[1627]**

NOTES
Commencement: 3 December 1990.

3. Application to register notice

An application in pursuance of section 2(8) of the 1983 Act to register a notice shall be made in Form 99 to the proper office and, if at the date of the application an order has been made by virtue of section 2(4) of that Act, the application shall be accompanied by an official copy of the order for filing in the Registry.

[1628]

NOTES
Commencement: 3 December 1990.
1983 Act: Matrimonial Homes Act 1983.

4. Application to renew registration of notice or caution

(1) Where a notice has been registered in pursuance of section 2(7) of the 1967 Act or section 2(8) of the 1983 Act or, before 14th February 1983, a caution has been registered in pursuance of section 2(7) of the 1967 Act, an application to renew the registration under paragraph (*a*) of section 5(3) of the 1983 Act shall be made in Form 100 to the proper office and shall be accompanied by an official copy of the order referred to in the said paragraph (*a*) for filing in the Registry.

(2) If the registrar is satisfied that the application is in order he shall renew the registration by entering on the register a further notice or caution, as the case may require.   **[1629]**

NOTES
Commencement: 3 December 1990.
1967 Act: Matrimonial Homes Act 1967.

1983 Act: Matrimonial Homes Act 1983.

5. Warning off of cautions registered under section 2(7) of the 1967 Act

Where, before 14th February 1983, a caution has been registered in pursuance of section 2(7) of the 1967 Act, the registrar shall not be required, on the application of the proprietor of the land to which the caution relates, to serve the notice referred to in rule 218 of the Land Registration Rules 1925 except upon production of:

    (*a*) a release in writing of the rights of occupation protected by the caution; or

    (*b*) a statutory declaration that, as to the whole or any part of the land to which the caution relates, no charge under section 2 of the 1983 Act or section 2 of the 1967 act has ever arisen or, if such a charge has arisen, it is no longer subsisting. **[1630]**

NOTES
    Commencement: 3 December 1990.
    1967 Act: Matrimonial Homes Act 1967.
    1983 Act: Matrimonial Homes Act 1983.

6. Official search by mortgagee

(1) Where registered land which consists of or includes a dwelling house is subject to a registered charge, or to a mortgage which is protected by a notice or caution in accordance with section 106(3) of the Land Registration Act 1925, the proprietor of the registered charge, or as the case may be the mortgagee, may apply for an official certificate of the result of a search of the register for the purpose of section 8(4) of the 1983 Act.

(2) An application under paragraph (1) shall be in Form 106 and shall be delivered in duplicate at the proper office.

(3) An official certificate giving the result of the search shall be issued in the form set out under the heading "Official Certificate of Result of Search" in Form 106. **[1631]**

NOTES
    Commencement: 3 December 1990.
    The 1983 Act: Matrimonial Homes Act 1983.

7. Revocation

. . . **[1632]**

NOTES
    Commencement: 3 December 1990.
    This rule revokes SI 1983 No 40.

Rules 3, 4 and 6

SCHEDULE

Application for
**Registration of a Notice
of Rights of Occupation**

HM Land Registry

Form **99**

(Rule 3 Land Registration
(Matrimonial Homes) Rules 1990)

_____District Land Registry

1. Please insert details of the dwelling house against which you wish to register a notice of rights of occupation.	1. County and District or London Borough Title number Property
2. Please state your full name and address.	2.
3. Please state your husband's or wife's full name.	3.
4. Is there a subsisting Class F Land Charge in your favour affecting any other dwelling house? If "yes": (a) insert address of that dwelling house	4. YES/NO (a)
(b) if registered under the Land Charges Act 1972, please state registration number (c) if registered under the Land Registration Act 1925, please state title number	(b) L.C. number (c) Title number
5. Has an order been made under section 2(4) of the Matrimonial Homes Act 1983? If so, please enclose an official copy.	5. YES/NO

DECLARATION
I declare that the information given above is true and that I am entitled by virtue of section 2(1) or (2) of the Matrimonial Homes Act 1983 to a charge on the legal estate registered under the title mentioned in 1 above.

APPLICATION
I apply under section 2(8) of the Matrimonial Homes Act 1983 for registration, under section 49(1)(c) of the Land Registration Act 1925, of notice of a Class F Land Charge against the title mentioned in 1 above [and I apply for cancellation of the registration of the subsisting Class F Land Charge referred to in 4 above in accordance with section 3 of the Matrimonial Homes Act 1983.]

My signature
or signature of
applicant's solicitor

Date

Key number	If applicable, name and address, in Block Letters, of applicant's solicitor.
Reference	

[1633]

NOTES
Commencement: 3 December 1990.

Application for **Renewal of Registration of a Notice or a Caution in respect of Rights of Occupation**

HM Land Registry

Form

100

(Rule 4 Land Registration
(Matrimonial Homes) Rules 1990)

_____District Land Registry

County and District or London Borough _____
Title number _____
Property _____
_____
_____

Following an Order dated_____and made under section 2(4) of the
Matrimonial Homes Act 1983, [I,] [We, _____
of_____
solicitors acting for] _____
of_____
apply under section 5(3)(a) of the said Act for the renewal of the registration of the [notice]
[caution against dealings] registered against the above mentioned title on _____

_____.

An official copy of the said Order accompanies this application.

Signature of Applicant or Applicant's solicitor _____

Date _____   Telephone number_____

Reference _____   Key number (if any) _____

[1634]

NOTES
Commencement: 3 December 1990.

Application by **Mortgagee**   HM Land Registry   Form
for **Official Search** in
respect of **Rights of Occupation**

106

_____ District Land Registry

(Rule 6 Land Registration
(Matrimonial Homes) Rules 1990)

Please complete the numbered panels using BLOCK LETTERS.

1 County and District or London Borough:-	For official use only
2 Title number (one only per form) of the registered property:-	
3 Property:-	**6** I/We [as solicitors acting for] the before-mentioned mortgagee(s) apply pursuant to rule 6 of the Land Registration (Matrimonial Homes) Rules 1990 for an official certificate of the result of a search of the register of the above title for the purpose of section 8(4) of the Matrimonial Homes Act 1983 to ascertain whether any notice or caution is entered in that register to protect rights of occupation under that Act.
4 Full name of Mortgagee(s):-	Signed Date Telephone No.

5 Particulars of Mortgage:-   (Please enter X in the appropriate box.)

☐ Registered charge dated _____
numbered _____ in the Charges Register
OR

☐ Mortgage dated_____ protected
by notice entered on _____
in the Charges Register
OR

☐ Mortgage dated _____ protected
by caution entered on _____
in the Proprietorship Register

7 Key number	Complete this panel using BLOCK LETTERS and insert the name and address (including postcode) of the person to whom the official certificate of result of search is to be sent.
Reference	

Official Certificate of Result of Search

It is certified that the official search applied for has been made with the following result:

☐ [Notice of] [Caution to protect] rights of occupation under the Matrimonial Homes Act 1983 in favour of_____
_____

was registered on _____

☐ There is no entry in the register of a notice or caution to protect rights of occupation under the Matrimonial Homes Act 1983.

Date

[1635]

NOTES

Commencement: 3 December 1990.

ENDURING POWERS OF ATTORNEY (PRESCRIBED FORM) REGULATIONS 1990
(SI 1990 No 1376)

NOTES
  Made: 5 July 1990.
  Authority: Enduring Powers of Attorney Act 1985, s 2(2).

1. Citation and commencement

These Regulations may be cited as the Enduring Powers of Attorney (Prescribed Form) Regulations 1990 and shall come into force on 31st July 1990.   **[1636]**

NOTES
  Commencement: 31 July 1990.

2. Prescribed form

(1) Subject to paragraphs (2) and (3) of this regulation and to regulation 4, an enduring power of attorney must be in the form set out in the Schedule to these Regulations and must include all the explanatory information headed "About using this form" in Part A of the Schedule and all the relevant marginal notes to Parts B and C. It may also include such additions (including paragraph numbers) or restrictions as the donor may decide.

(2) In completing the form of enduring power of attorney—
  (a) there shall be excluded (either by omission or deletion)—
    (i) where the donor appoints only one attorney, everything between the square brackets on the first page of Part B; and
    (ii) one and only one of any pair of alternatives;
  (b) there may also be so excluded—
    (i) the words on the second page of Part B "subject to the following restrictions and conditions", if those words do not apply;
    (ii) the attestation details for a second witness in Parts B and C if a second witness is not required; and
    (iii) any marginal notes which correspond with any words excluded under the provisions of this paragraph and the two notes numbered 1 and 2 which appear immediately under the heading to Part C.

(3) The form of execution by the donor or by an attorney may be adapted to provide—
  (a) for a case where the donor or an attorney signs by means of a mark; and
  (b) for the case (dealt with in regulation 3) where the enduring power of attorney is executed at the direction of the donor or of an attorney;
and the form of execution by an attorney may be adapted to provide for execution by a trust corporation.

(4) Subject to paragraphs (1), (2) and (3) of this regulation and to regulation 4, an enduring power of attorney which seeks to exclude any provision contained in these Regulations is not a valid enduring power of attorney.   **[1637]**

NOTES
  Commencement: 31 July 1990.

Execution

3. (1) An enduring power of attorney in the form set out in the Schedule to these Regulations shall be executed by both the donor and the attorney, although not necessarily at the same time, in the presence of a witness, but not necessarily the same witness, who shall sign the form and give his full name and address.

(2) The donor and an attorney shall not witness the signature of each other nor one attorney the signature of another.

(3) Where an enduring power of attorney is executed at the direction of the donor—

    (*a*) it must be signed in the presence of two witnesses who shall each sign the form and give their full names and addresses; and

    (*b*) a statement that the enduring power of attorney has been executed at the direction of the donor must be inserted in Part B;

    (*c*) it must not be signed by either an attorney or any of the witnesses to the signature of either the donor or an attorney.

(4) Where an enduring power of attorney is executed at the direction of an attorney—

    (*a*) paragraph (3)(*a*) above applies; and

    (*b*) a statement that the enduring power of attorney has been executed at the direction of the attorney must be inserted in Part C;

    (*c*) it must not be signed by either the donor, an attorney or any of the witnesses to the signature of either the donor or an attorney.   **[1638]**

NOTES
   Commencement: 31 July 1990.

4. Where more than one attorney is appointed and they are to act jointly and severally, then at least one of the attorneys so appointed must execute the instrument for it to take effect as an enduring power of attorney, and only those attorneys who have executed the instrument shall have the functions of an attorney under an enduring power of attorney in the event of the donor's mental incapacity or of the registration of the power, whichever first occurs.   **[1639]**

NOTES
   Commencement: 31 July 1990.

5. Revocation

. . . except that—

    (*a*) a power executed in the form prescribed by those Regulations and executed by the donor before 31st July 1991 shall be capable (whether or not seals are affixed to it) of being a valid enduring power of attorney;

    (*b*) regulation 3(3) shall apply to a power executed by the donor before 31st July 1991 under the provisions of those Regulations and the form of enduring power of attorney prescribed by those Regulations may be modified accordingly.   **[1640]**

NOTES
   Commencement: 31 July 1990.
   Words omitted revoke the Enduring Powers of Attorney (Prescribed Form) Regulations 1987, SI 1987 No 1612.

Regulations 2 and 3   SCHEDULE

ENDURING POWER OF ATTORNEY

Part A: About using this form

1. **You may choose one attorney or more than one.** If you choose one attorney then you must delete everything between the square brackets on the first page of the form. If you choose more than one, you must decide whether they are able to act:
   - Jointly (that is, they must all act together and cannot act separately) or
   - Jointly and severally (that is, they can all act together but they can also act separately if they wish).
   On the first page of the form, show what you have decided by crossing out one of the alternatives.

2. **If you give your attorney(s) general power** in relation to all your property and affairs, it means that they will be able to deal with your money or property and may be able to sell your house.

3. **If you don't want your attorney(s) to have such wide powers,** you can include any restrictions you like. For example, you can include a restriction that your attorney(s) must not act on your behalf until they have reason to believe that you are becoming mentally incapable; or a restriction as to what your attorney(s) may do. Any restrictions you choose must be written or typed where indicated on the second page of the form.

4. **If you are a trustee** (and please remember that co-ownership of a home involves trusteeship), you should seek legal advice if you want your attorney(s) to act as a trustee on your behalf.

5. **Unless you put in a restriction preventing it** your attorney(s) will be able to use any of your money or property to make any provision which you yourself might be expected to make for their own needs or the needs of other people. Your attorney(s) will also be able to use your money to make gifts, but only for reasonable amounts in relation to the value of your money and property.

6. **Your attorney(s) can recover the out-of-pocket expenses** of acting as your attorney(s). If your attorney(s) are professional people, for example solicitors or accountants, they may be able to charge for their professional services as well. You may wish to provide expressly for remuneration of your attorney(s) (although if they are trustees they may not be allowed to accept it).

7. **If your attorney(s) have reason to believe** that you have become or are becoming mentally incapable of managing your affairs, your attorney(s) will have to apply to the Court of Protection for registration of this power.

8. **Before applying to the Court of Protection for registration** of this power, your attorney(s) must give written notice that that is what they are going to do, to you and your nearest relatives as defined in the Enduring Powers of Attorney Act 1985. You or your relatives will be able to object if you or they disagree with registration.

9. **This is a simplified explanation** of what the Enduring Powers of Attorney Act 1985 and the Rules and Regulations say. If you need more guidance, you or your advisers will need to look at the Act itself and the Rules and Regulations. The Rules are the Court of Protection (Enduring Powers of Attorney) Rules 1986 (Statutory Instrument 1986 No. 127). The Regulations are the Enduring Powers of Attorney (Prescribed Form) Regulations 1990 (Statutory Instrument 1990 No. 1376).

10. **Note to Attorney(s)**
    After the power has been registered you should notify the Court of Protection if the donor dies or recovers.

11. **Note to Donor**
    Some of these explanatory notes may not apply to the form you are using if it has already been adapted to suit your particular requirements.

YOU CAN CANCEL THIS POWER AT ANY TIME BEFORE IT HAS TO BE REGISTERED

[1641]

NOTES
    Commencement: 31 July 1990.

Part B: To be completed by the 'donor' (the person appointing the attorney(s))

Don't sign this form unless you understand what it means

Please read the notes in the margin
which follow and which are part of
the form itself.

Donor's name and address.

I _____

of _____

Donor's date of birth.

born on _____

appoint _____

See note 1 on the front of this form. If
you are appointing only one attorney
you should cross out everything
between the square brackets. If
appointing more than two attorneys
please give the additional name(s) on
an attached sheet.

of _____

• [and _____

   of _____

Cross out the one which does not
apply (see note 1 on the front of this
form).

   • jointly
   • jointly and severally]
to be my attorney(s) for the purpose of the Enduring Powers of Attorney Act
1985

Cross out the one which does not
apply (see note 2 on the front of this
form). Add any additional powers.

   • with general authority to act on my behalf
   • with authority to do the following on my behalf:

If you don't want the attorney(s) to
have general power, you must give
details here of what authority you are
giving the attorney(s).

in relation to

Cross out the one which does not
apply.

   • all my property and affairs:
   • the following property and affairs:

Part B: continued

Please read the notes in the margin which follow and which are part of the form itself.
If there are restrictions or conditions, insert them here; if not, cross out these words if you wish (see note 3 on the front of this form).

• subject to the following restrictions and conditions:

If this form is being signed at your direction:–
• the person signing must not be an attorney or any witness (to Parts B or C).
• you must add a statement that this form has been signed at your direction.
• a second witness is necessary (please see below).

Your signature (or mark).

I intend that this power shall continue even if I become mentally incapable

I have read or have had read to me the notes in Part A which are part of, and explain, this form.

Signed by me as a deed _____
and delivered

Date.
Someone must witness your signature.

on_____

Signature of witness.

in the presence of _____

Your attorney(s) cannot be your witness. It is not advisable for your husband or wife to be your witness.

Full name of witness_____

Address of witness _____

_____

_____

A second witness is only necessary if this form is not being signed by you personally but at your direction (for example, if a physical disability prevents you from signing).
Signature of second witness.

in the presence of _____

Full name of witness_____

Address of witness _____

_____

_____

[1642]

NOTES
Commencement: 31 July 1990.

Part C: To be completed by the attorney(s)

Note: 1.   This form may be adapted to provide for execution by a corporation

     2.   If there is more than one attorney additional sheets in the form as shown below must be added to this Part C

Please read the notes in the margin which follow and which are part of the form itself.

Don't sign this form before the donor has signed Part B or if, in your opinion, the donor was already mentally incapable at the time of signing Part B.

If this form is being signed at your direction:–

• the person signing must not be an attorney or any witness (to Parts B or C).

• you must add a statement that this form has been signed at your direction.

• a second witness is necessary (please see below).

Signature (or mark) of attorney.

Date.

Signature of witness.

The attorney must sign the form and his signature must be witnessed. The donor may not be the witness and one attorney may not witness the signature of the other.

A second witness is only necessary if this form is not being signed by you personally but at your direction (for example, if a physical disability prevents you from signing). Signature of second witness.

I understand that I have a duty to apply to the Court for the registration of this form under the Enduring Powers of Attorney Act 1985 when the donor is becoming or has become mentally incapable.

I also understand my limited power to use the donor's property to benefit persons other than the donor.

I am not a minor

Signed by me as a deed _____
and delivered

on_____

in the presence of _____

Full name of witness_____

Address of witness _____

_____

_____

in the presence of _____

Full name of witness_____

Address of witness _____

_____

_____

[1643]

NOTES
     Commencement: 31 July 1990.

LAND REGISTRATION (OPEN REGISTER) RULES 1991
(SI 1992 No 122)

NOTES
Made: 18 December 1991.
Authority: Land Registration Act 1925, s 144.

PART I

1. Citation, commencement and interpretation

(1) These Rules may be cited as the Land Registration (Open Register) Rules 1991 and shall come into force on 30th March 1992.

(2) In these Rules, unless the context otherwise requires:

"the Act" means the Land Registration Act 1925;

"caution title" means:

    (*a*) the document prepared by the registrar which records, under a distinguishing number, details of any caution against first registration lodged under section 53 of the Act and of the statutory declaration in support of that caution; and

    (*b*) the plan, referred to in that document, prepared by the registrar, showing the extent of the land affected by the caution;

"credit account" means an account authorised by the registrar under article 15(1) of the Land Registration Fees Order 1991;

"designated plan" means a plan which is a copy or extract from the Ordnance Map at the largest scale published for the area in which the land to which it relates is situated, such plan to have a length no greater than 297 mm and a width no greater than 210 mm (A4 paper size);

"Index Map section" means the document or documents comprising a single section of the Index Maps maintained by the registrar under rule 8 of the principal rules, and the associated Parcels Index (if any) maintained by the registrar under rule 274 of the principal rules;

"the 1990 Rules" means the Land Registration Rules 1990;

"the principal rules" means the Land Registration Rules 1925);

"proper office" means the district land registry designated as the proper office by article 2(2) of the Land Registration (District Registries) Order 1991;

"title plan" means the filed plan or portion of the General Map referred to in the register of a registered title.

(3) Except in rule 15, a form referred to by a number means the form so numbered in Schedule 1.

(4) Expressions used in these rules have, unless the contrary intention appears, the meaning which they bear in the principal rules. **[1644]**

NOTES
Commencement: 30 March 1992.

Part II

Applications Relating to Registered Titles

2. Application for office copies of the register or the title plan or for a certificate of inspection of the title plan

(1) Any person may apply for:

    (*a*) an office copy of the entries on the register of a registered title;

    (*b*) an office copy of the title plan of a registered title;

    (*c*) a certificate of inspection of the title plan of a registered title.

(2) Save as provided by rule 6(2), an application under paragraph (1) shall be made:

    (*a*) by delivering in documentary form an application in Form 109; or

    (*b*) by delivering the application, during the currency of any relevant notice given pursuant to rule 13, and subject to and in accordance with the limitations contained in that notice, by any means of communication, other than that referred to in sub-paragraph (*a*), and:

        (i) where the application is made by facsimile transmission the applicant shall provide Form 109 together with, when the application is for a certificate of the title plan and no estate plan has been approved, a designated plan of the land in respect of which the certificate is to be issued; and

        (ii) in any other case the applicant shall provide, in such order as may be required by that notice and, in the case of delivery by telephone, in such order as may be requested by the registrar, such particulars as are appropriate and are required for an application in Form 109. **[1645]**

NOTES
Commencement: 30 March 1992.

3. Application for office copies of documents referred to in the register

(1) Any person may apply for an office copy of a document referred to in the register of a registered title which is in the custody of the registrar (not being a lease or charge or a copy of a lease or charge).

(2) Save as provided by rule 6(2), an application under paragraph (1) shall be made:

    (*a*) by delivering in documentary form an application in Form 110; or

    (*b*) by delivering the application, during the currency of any relevant notice given pursuant to rule 13, and subject to and in accordance with the limitations contained in that notice, by any means of communication other than that referred to in sub-paragraph (*a*), and:

        (i) where the application is made by facsimile transmission the applicant shall provide Form 110; and

        (ii) in any other case the applicant shall provide, in such order as may be required by that notice and, in the case of delivery by telephone, in such order as may be requested by the registrar, such particulars as are appropriate and are required for an application in Form 110. **[1646]**

NOTES
Commencement: 30 March 1992.

4. Inspection of the register, title plan and documents referred to in the register

Save as provided by rule 6(2), an application for a personal inspection of:

    (a) the entries on the register of a registered title;

    (b) the title plan of a registered title;

    (c) a document referred to in the register of a registered title which is in the custody of the registrar (not being a lease or charge or a copy of a lease or charge);

shall be in Form 111. **[1647]**

NOTES
Commencement: 30 March 1992.

[4A. Inspection and copying of register entries—access by remote terminal

Access to the registrar's computer system, by means of a person's remote terminal, for the purpose of inspection and the making of copies of and extracts from entries on the register of a registered title held on that system is subject to the following conditions:

    (a) Such access may only be undertaken during the currency of a relevant notice given pursuant to rule 13, and subject to and in accordance with the limitations contained in that notice.

    (b) A person who wishes to apply for such access must provide such of the following particulars as may be required by the registrar:

        (i) The credit account number, name and telephone number of the person making the application.

        (ii) The title number of the registered title in respect of which the application is made.

        (iii) The property description of the land in respect of which the application is made.

        (iv) The relevant postcode.] **[1648]**

NOTES
Commencement: 28 March 1994.
Inserted by the Land Registration Rules 1993, SI 1993 No 3275, r 8.

5. Official certificate of inspection of title plan

(1) Where a person has applied under these rules for a certificate of inspection of the title plan, upon completion of the inspection an official certificate of inspection shall be issued.

(2) The official certificate of inspection shall be in Form 102 or to like effect.

(3) An official certificate of inspection of the title plan made pursuant to an application under these rules shall be regarded as an official search for the purposes of section 83(3) of the Act and rule 295 of the principal rules. **[1649]**

NOTES
Commencement: 30 March 1992.
The Act: Land Registration Act 1925.
Principal rules: Land Registration Rules 1925, SR & O 1925 No 1093.

6. Inspection in connection with criminal proceedings, receivership under certain Acts and insolvency

(1) If a person referred to in column 1 of Part 1 or Part 2 [or Part 3] of Schedule 2:

(*a*) applies in Form 112A or 112B [or 112C] whichever is appropriate to make an inspection under this rule in relation to a person specified in the application or to a property so specified; and

(*b*) gives the registrar the appropriate certificate (completed to contain all particulars required) referred to in column 2 of the said Schedule;

the registrar shall permit him to inspect and to obtain copies of and extracts from any document falling within section 112(2) of the Act and shall, if so requested (and notwithstanding rule 9 of the principal rules), provide him with the result of a search of the index of proprietors' names pursuant to the application.

(2) Where a person applies under paragraph (1) he may apply in Form 112A or 112B [or 112C] whichever is appropriate for inspection of or office copies of: the entries on the register of a registered title, the title plan of a registered title, a document referred to in the register of a registered title which is in the custody of the registrar or a caution title.

(3) An application under this rule shall be delivered to such office of the Registry as the registrar may direct.

(4) During the currency of any relevant notice given pursuant to rule 13, and subject to and in accordance with the limitations contained in that notice, any application under this rule may be made by facsimile transmission.

(5) In Schedule 2:

(*a*) references to senior executive officers include references to equivalent departmental grades;

(*b*) references to an official receiver are references to an official receiver for the purpose of the Insolvency Act 1986 or the Companies Act 1985 or a person acting as a deputy to such an official receiver:

(*c*) references to a trustee in bankruptcy are references to a trustee in bankruptcy of a person adjudged bankrupt in England and Wales or Northern Ireland or to a permanent or interim trustee in the sequestration of a debtor's estate in Scotland;

(*d*) references to the official assignee are references to the Official Assignee for bankruptcy for Northern Ireland or the Official Assignee for company liquidations for Northern Ireland; and

(*e*) references to a liquidator or administrator are respectively references to a liquidator or administrator appointed for the purposes of the Insolvency Act 1986.

[(6) In Form 112C and Schedule 2 references to tax are references to any of the taxes mentioned in the definition of tax in section 118(1) of the Taxes Management Act 1970.] **[1650]**

NOTES

Commencement: 28 March 1994 (para (6)); 30 March 1992 (remainder).

Para (1): words in square brackets inserted by the Land Registration Rules 1993, SI 1993 No 3275, r 9(1).

Para (2): words in square brackets inserted by the Land Registration Rules 1993, SI 1993 No 3275, r 9(2).

Para (6): added by the Land Registration Rules 1993, SI 1993 No 3275, r 9(3).

The Act: Land Registration Act 1925.

7. Inspection under a court order

In any case where a court (having power to do so) has ordered that a person may inspect and make copies of any document falling within section 112(2) of the Act, that person shall give to the registrar a document certified by the proper officer of the court to be a true copy of such order. **[1651]**

NOTES
Commencement: 30 March 1992.
The Act: Land Registration Act 1925.

PART III

8. Application for office copies of a caution title

(1) Any person may apply for an office copy of a caution title.

(2) Save as provided by rule 6(2), an application under paragraph (1) shall be made:

    (*a*) by delivering in documentary form an application in Form 110A; or

    (*b*) by delivering the application, during the currency of any relevant notice given pursuant to rule 13, and subject to and in accordance with the limitations contained in that notice, by any means of communication, other than that referred to in sub-paragraph (*a*), and:

        (i) where the application is made by facsimile transmission the applicant shall provide Form 110A; and

        (ii) in any other case the applicant shall provide, in such order as may be required by that notice and, in the case of delivery by telephone, in such order as may be requested by the registrar, such particulars as are appropriate and are required for an application in Form 110A.

(3) An office copy shall be issued without reference to any application or matter which may affect the subsistence of the caution against first registration recorded in the relevant caution title.   **[1652]**

NOTES
Commencement: 30 March 1992.

PART IV

OFFICIAL SEARCHES OF AND COPIES OF THE INDEX MAP

9. Application for and issue of Official Certificate of Search of Index Map

(1) Any person may apply for an official search of the Index Map or General Map and the Parcel Index and the list of pending applications for first registration kept under rule 10 of the principal rules.

(2) An application under paragraph (1) shall be made:

    (*a*) by delivering in documentary form an application in Form 96; or

    (*b*) by delivering the application, during the currency of any relevant notice given pursuant to rule 13, and subject to and in accordance with the limitations contained in that notice, by any means of communication, other than that referred to in sub-paragraph (*a*), and:

        (i) where the application is made by facsimile transmission the applicant shall provide Form 96; and

        (ii) in any other case the applicant shall provide, in such order as may be required by that notice and, in the case of delivery by telephone, in such order as may be requested by the registrar, such particulars as are appropriate and are required for an application in Form 96.

(3) If the registrar shall so require, an applicant shall provide to the registrar a copy or extract from the Ordnance Map on the largest scale published of the land to which the application relates.

(4) If the application is in order an official certificate of search shall be issued.

(5) An official certificate of search shall be issued in the form set out under the heading "Certificate of result of Official Search of the Index Map" in Form 96 or to like effect. **[1653]**

NOTES
Commencement: 30 March 1992.
Principal rules: Land Registration Rules 1925, SR & O 1925 No 1093.

10. Application for copies of Index Map sections

(1) Any person may apply for a copy of an Index Map section.

(2) An application under paragraph (1) shall be made by delivering in documentary form an application in Form 96B.

(3) A copy of an Index Map section provided by the registrar under this rule shall not constitute an office copy or extract for the purpose of section 113 of the Act or an official search for the purpose of section 83(3) of the Act or an official certificate of the result of a search for the purpose of rule 295 of the principal rules. **[1654]**

NOTES
Commencement: 30 March 1992.
The Act: Land Registration Act 1925.
Principal rules: Land Registration Rules 1925, SR & O 1925 No 1093.

PART V

[11. Delivery of applications

(1) Subject to rule 6(3) and to paragraph (2), an application made under these rules shall be delivered to the proper office.

(2) Any application of the type referred to in rule 13(4) shall be delivered to the registrar.] **[1665]**

NOTES
Commencement: 28 March 1994.
Substituted by the Land Registration Rules 1993, SI 1993 No 3275, r 10.

12. Separate applications for each title required in certain cases

(1) A separate application shall be delivered in respect of each registered title if the application is for:
  (a) office copies of the register or the title plan or for a certificate of inspection of the title plan made under rule 2;
  (b) office copies of documents referred to in the register made under rule 3;
  (c) inspection of the register, the title plan and documents referred to in the register made under rule 4.

(2) Where an application is made under rule 2 and the property described in accordance with panel 2 of Form 109 is registered under more than one title number, but the applicant fails to provide a title number or the title number provided does not relate to any part of the property described in accordance with panel 2 of that form, the registrar may:

    (*a*) deal with the application as though it referred only to such one of the title numbers under which the property or any part is registered as he shall choose, in which case in respect of the remaining title number or numbers there shall be deemed to have been no application; or

    (*b*) accept such application and if he does so it shall he deemed to be a separate application in respect of each title revealed; or

    (*c*) cancel the application.

(3) Where an application is made under rule 8, a separate application shall be delivered in respect of each caution title. **[1666]**

NOTES
Commencement: 30 March 1992.

13. Notice for the provision of additional arrangements for applications

(1) If the registrar is satisfied that adequate arrangements have been or will he made for dealing with the applications specified in paragraph (4) in accordance with this rule, he may, in such manner as he considers appropriate for informing persons who may wish to make applications under these rules, give notice to that effect specifying the class or classes of case covered by those arrangements; and such a notice may in particular, but without prejudice to the generality of the foregoing provision, specify the class or classes of case so covered by limiting them:

    (*a*) to one or more of the types of application mentioned in paragraph (4);

    (*b*) to applications made by a person maintaining a credit account;

    (*c*) to applications which relate to land within specified counties, districts, London Boroughs or other administrative areas;

    (*d*) to applications made between specified hours and on specified days (which need not be those between or on which the Registry is open to the public and may be different for applications of different types);

    (*e*) to delivery of applications by one or more means of communication;

    (*f*) when an application is made by facsimile transmission in Form 96 and refers to land shown on an accompanying plan, to any such application which is accompanied by a designated plan;

    (*g*) when an application is made under rule 2(2)(*b*) or 3(2)(*b*) [or 4A] to an application which states the relevant title number;

    (*h*) when an application is made under rule 8(2)(*b*), to an application which states the relevant distinguishing number of the caution title;

    (*i*) when an application is made for a certificate of inspection of the title plan of a registered title under rule 2(2)(*b*)(ii) to an application which provides the relevant plot number on the estate plan;

    (*j*) when an application is made under rule 9(2)(*b*)(ii) to an application which does not require a plan to identify the land to which the application relates.

(2) [Subject to paragraphs (3) and (3A)], a notice given pursuant to paragraph (1) shall be current from the time specified in that behalf in the notice; and either:

    (*a*) until the time, if any, specified in that behalf in the notice; or

(b) if no time of ceasing to be current is specified in the notice, indefinitely.

(3) A notice given pursuant to paragraph (1) may from time to time be varied, suspended, withdrawn, renewed or replaced by a further notice.

[(3A) If and so long as owing to the breakdown or other unavailability of facilities or data involved in giving effect to the arrangements made for dealing with applications covered by a notice given under paragraph (1) such arrangements cease, in whole or in part, to be effective, the notice shall cease, to the necessary extent, to be treated as current notwithstanding the absence of a variation, suspension or withdrawal thereof under paragraph (3).]

(4) The applications referred to in paragraph (1) are:

(a) an application for office copies of the register or the title plan or for a certificate of inspection of the title plan made under rule 2(2)(b);

(b) an application for office copies of documents referred to in the register made under rule 3(2)(b);

(c) an application for information or office copies made under rule 6(4);

(d) an application for an office copy of a caution title made under rule 8(2)(b);

(e) an application for an official certificate of search of the Index Map made under rule 9(2)(b).

[(f) an application for inspection and copying of register entries where access is by remote terminal under rule 4A.]

(5) Notwithstanding the provisions of rules 2(2)(b), 3(2)(b), 6(4), 8(2)(b) and 9(2)(b), the registrar may in his discretion refuse to accept an application made under any of those provisions in any individual case.   **[1667]**

NOTES
Commencement: 28 March 1994 (para (3A)); 30 March 1992 (remainder).
Para (1): words in square brackets inserted by the Land Registration Rules 1993, SI 1993 No 3275, r 11(1).
Para (2): words in square brackets inserted by the Land Registration Rules 1993, SI 1993 No 3275, r 11(2).
Para (3A): inserted by the Land Registration Rules 1993, SI 1993 No 3275, r 11(3).
Para (4): sub-para (f) added by the Land Registration Rules 1993, SI 1993 No 3275, r 11(4).

14. Certain applications not to be made by facsimile transmission

No application may be made by facsimile transmission under the principal rules; and no application may be so made under the Land Registration (Matrimonial Homes) Rules 1990.   **[1668]**

NOTES
Commencement: 30 March 1992.
Principal rules: Land Registration Rules 1925, SR & O 1925 No 1093.

15. Revocation

. . .   **[1669]**

NOTES
This rule revokes the Land Registration Rules 1925, SR & O 1925 No 1093, r 70, the Land Registration Rules 1990, SI 1990 No 314, rr 3, 4, 5 and the Land Registration (Open Register Rules) 1990, SI 1990 No 1362.

SCHEDULES

NOTES

The Schedules are not reproduced in this work.

FAMILY PROVISION (INTESTATE SUCCESSION) ORDER 1993
(SI 1993 No 2906)

NOTES

Made: 29 November 1993.
Authority: Family Provision Act 1966, s 1(1)(*a*), (*b*).

1. This Order may be cited as the Family Provision (Intestate Succession) Order 1993 and shall come into force on 1st December 1993. **[1670]**

2. In the case of a person dying after the coming into force of this Order, section 46(1) of the Administration of Estates Act 1925 shall apply as if the net sums charged by paragraph (i) on the residuary estate were:—

    (*a*) under paragraph (2) of the Table, the sum of £125,000; and
    (*b*) under paragraph (3) of the Table, the sum of £200,000. **[1671]**

THE LAND REGISTRATION (OFFICIAL SEARCHES) RULES 1993
(SI 1993 No 3276)

NOTES

Made: 14 December 1993.
Authority: Land Registration Act 1925, ss 112(2), 144.

PART I

1. Citation and commencement
These rules may be cited as the Land Registration (Official Searches) Rules 1993 and shall come into force on 28th March 1994. **[1672]**

NOTES

Commencement: 28 March 1994.

2. Interpretation
(1) In these rules, unless the context otherwise requires:

    "the Act" means the Land Registration Act 1925;
    "credit account" means an account authorised by the registrar under article 15(1) of the Land Registration Fees Order 1993;
    "day" except in rule 14(1)(*e*), means a day when the Land Registry is open to the public;

"day list" means the record kept pursuant to rule 7A of the principal rules;

"designated plan" means a plan which is a copy or extract from the Ordnance Map at the largest scale published for the area in which the land to which it relates is situated, such plan to have a length no greater than 297 mm and a width no greater than 210 mm (A4 paper size);

"official certificate of search" means a result of official search issued in accordance with rule 4 or 10;

"pending first registration application" means an application made under section 4 or 8 of the Act and entered on the day list but where the registration has not yet been completed;

"the principal rules" means the Land Registration Rules 1925;

"priority period" means the period beginning at the time when an application for an official search is deemed by virtue of paragraph (3) below to have been delivered and ending immediately after 0930 hours on the thirtieth day thereafter;

"proper office" means the district land registry designated as the proper office by article 2(2) of the Land Registration (District Registries) Order 1991;

"purchaser" means any person (including a lessee or chargee) who in good faith and for valuable consideration acquires or intends to acquire a legal estate in land and "purchase" has a corresponding meaning;

"search from date" means:

   (*a*) (i) the date stated on an office copy (either issued in response to an application made under rule 2 of the Land Registration (Open Register) Rules 1991 or issued under rule 4(3) or rule 10(3) of these rules) of the register of the relevant registered title as the date on which the entries shown on the said office copy were subsisting, provided that the said office copy was issued by the registrar not more than twelve months before the day upon which the relevant application under these rules was delivered or, in the case of an application for an official search with priority, was deemed by virtue of paragraph (3) below to have been delivered;

   (ii) the date stated at the time of an access by remote terminal, under rule 4A of the Land Registration (Open Register) Rules 1991, to the register of the relevant registered title as the date on which the entries accessed were subsisting, providing that the transmission by the registrar's computer system of the entries so accessed occurred not more than twelve months before the day upon which the relevant application under these rules was delivered or, in the case of an application for an official search with priority, was deemed by virtue of paragraph (3) below to have been delivered;

   (*b*) where the term is used in Form 94C and at D of Part I of Schedule 3, either a date within (*a*) or the date (or most recent date, if more than one) stated in the land or a charge certificate of the relevant registered title as the date on which that certificate was officially examined with the register.

(2) In these rules a form referred to by number means the form so numbered in Schedule 1.

(3) (*a*) An application for an official search with priority made by a

purchaser which is delivered under the provisions of rule 3(3)(*a*) or rule 3(3)(*b*)(ii) after 0930 hours on one day and before or at 0930 hours on the next day shall be deemed to have been delivered immediately before 0930 hours on the second day.

(*b*) An application for an official search with priority made by a purchaser which is delivered under the provisions of rule 3(3)(*b*)(i) or rule 3(3)(*b*)(iii) shall be deemed to have been delivered at the time notice of it is entered on the day list.

(4) Expressions used in these rules have, unless the contrary intention appears, the meaning which they bear in the principal rules. **[1673]**

NOTES
Commencement: 28 March 1994.

PART II
OFFICIAL SEARCHES WITH PRIORITY

3. Application for official search with priority by purchaser

(1) A purchaser may apply for an official search with priority of the register of the title to the land to which the purchase relates.

(2) Where land is subject to a pending first registration application a purchaser of such land may apply for an official search with priority in relation to that pending first registration application.

(3) An application for an official search with priority shall be made:

(*a*) by delivering in documentary form at the proper office an application on Form 94A or Form 94B, as appropriate; or

(*b*) during the currency of any relevant notice given pursuant to rule 14, and subject to and in accordance with the limitations contained in that notice, by delivering the application to the registrar, by any means of communication, other than that referred to in sub-paragraph (*a*) and;

    (i) where the application is made by telephone or orally the purchaser shall provide, in such order as may be requested, such of the particulars as are appropriate and are required for an application for an official search with priority in Form 94A or Form 94B;

    (ii) where the application is made by facsimile transmission the purchaser shall provide Form 94A or Form 94B, as appropriate, together with, where the application is in Form 94B (and the plot number or numbers of any relevant approved estate plan are not quoted), as designated plan of the land in respect of which the official search is to be made; and

    (iii) in any other case the purchaser shall provide, in such order as may be required by that notice, such of the particulars as are appropriate and are required for an application for an official search with priority in Form 94A or Form 94B.

(4) Where the application is made on Form 94B under paragraph (3)(*a*), unless the registrar otherwise allows:

(*a*) Form 94B and any plan accompanying the application, shall be delivered in duplicate;

(b) the application shall be accompanied by Form 94B (Result) in duplicate.

(5) Where the application is made under paragraph (3)(b)(ii) in Form 94B, the purchaser shll provide, unless the registrar otherwise allows, Form 94B (Result).   [1674]

NOTES
Commencement: 28 March 1994.

4. Entry of application on day list and issue of official certificate of search with priority

(1) If an application for an official search with priority is in order, notice of it shall be entered on the day list and upon completion of the official search with priority an official certificate of search shall be issued giving the result of the search as at the time and day it is deemed to have been delivered.

(2) An official certificate of search with priority of a register or in relation to a pending first registration application may, at the registrar's discretion, be issued in one, or more than one, of the following ways:

    (a) in the form set out under the heading "Official Certificate of Result of Search" in Form 94B (Result);

    (b) in documentary form;

    (c) during the currency of any relevant notice given pursuant to rule 14, and subject to and in accordance with the limitations contained in that notice, by any means of communication, other than the means referred to in sub-paragraphs (a) and (b).

(3) Subject to paragraphs (4) and (5), an official certificate of search issued under paragraph (2) shall include such information specified in Part I or Part II of Schedule 2 as the case may require and may be issued by reference to an office copy of the register.

(4) Where the official certificate of search is issued in Form 94B (Result) or in documentary form, under paragraph (2), together with the relevant application form, or a copy of that aplication form, it need not include any of the information referred to in paragraph (3) which appears on that application form.

(5) Where an official certificate of search is issued under paragraph (2)(c) and another official certificate of search is to be, or has been, issued under paragraph (2)(b) in respect of the same application, it need only include the information specified at A, F, G, and H, of Part I or A, H, and I of Part II of Schedule 2 as the case may require.   [1675]

NOTES
Commencement: 28 March 1994.

5. Inspection of applications for official searches with priority and official certificates of search with priority

During the priority period details in a visible and legible form:

    (a) of the application for official search with priority; and

    (b) of the official certificate of search with priority;

shall be made available for inspection by any person.   [1676]

NOTES
Commencement: 28 March 1994.

6. Priority of applications protected by an official search with priority of a register

Where a purchaser has applied for an official search with priority of a register, any entry which is made in that register during the priority period relating to that search shall be postponed to a subsequent application to register the instrument effecting the purchase and, if the purchase is dependent on a prior dealing, to a subsequent application to register the instrument effecting that dealing, provided each such subsequent application:

    (*a*) is deemed to have been delivered at the proper office within the priority period;

    (*b*) affects the same land or charge as the postponed entry; and

    (*c*) is in due course completed by registration.   **[1677]**

NOTES

Commencement: 28 March 1994.

7. Priority of applications protected by an official search with priority relating to a pending first registration application

(1) Paragraph (2) has effect where, with respect to a purchase of land which is subject to a pending first registration application:

    (*a*) the purchaser has applied for an official search with priority in relation to the pending first registration application; and

    (*b*) the pending first registration application is subsequently completed by registration of all or any part of the land comprised in that purchase.

(2) Any entry made in the register of title to the land pursuant to an application delivered or otherwise made during the priority period of the official search shall be postponed to any entry made pursuant to a subsequent application to register the instrument effecting the purchase and, if the purchase is dependent upon a prior dealing, a subsequent application to register the instrument effecting that dealing, provided each such subsequent application:

    (*a*) is deemed to have been delivered at the proper office within the priority period;

    (*b*) affects the same land or charge as the postponed entry; and

    (*c*) is in due course completed by registration.   **[1678]**

NOTES

Commencement: 28 March 1994.

8. Priority of concurrent applications for official searches with priority and concurrent official certificates of searches with priority

(1) Where two or more official certificates of search with priority relating to the same land or the same charge have been issued and are in operation pursuant to these rules, such certificates shall, as far as relates to the priority thereby conferred, take effect, unless the applicants otherwise agree, in the order in which the applications for official search with priority were deemed to have been delivered.

(2) Where two or more applications for official search with priority relating to the same land or the same charge are deemed to have been delivered at the same time the official certificates of search with priority shall, as far as relates to the priority thereby conferred, take effect in such order as may be agreed by

the applicants or, failing agreement, as may be determined under rule 298 of the principal rules.

(3) Where one transaction is dependent upon another the register may for the purposes of this rule assume (unless or until the contrary appears) that applicants for search with priority have agreed that their applications shall have priority as between each other so as to give effect to the sequence of the instruments effecting their transactions.

(4) Where an official search with priority has been made in respect of a particular registered title and an application relating to that title is deemed, by virtue of rule 85 of the principal rules, to have been delivered at the same time as the expiry of the priority period relating to that search, the time of the delivery of the application shall be deemed to be within that priority period.

(5) Where an official search with priority has been made in respect of a particular pending first registration application and a subsequent application relating to any land which is subject to the pending first registration application, or was so subject before completion of the registration of that land, is deemed, by virtue of rule 85 of the principal rules, to have been delivered at the same time as the expiry of the priority period relating to that search, the time of delivery of that subsequent application shall be deemed to be within that priority period.   **[1679]**

NOTES
  Commencement: 28 March 1994.

PART III

Official Search without Priority

9. Application for official search without priority

(1) A person (not being a purchaser requiring an official search with priority under Part II of these rules) may apply for an official search without priority of a register.

(2) An application for an official search without priority may be made:

   (*a*) by delivering in documentary form at the proper office an application on Form 94C; or
   (*b*) during the currency of any relevant notice given pursuant to rule 14, and subject to and in accordance with the limitations contained in that notice, by delivering the application to the registrar, by any means of communication, other than that referred to in sub-paragraph (*a*) and:

      (i) where the application is made by telephone or orally the applicant shall provide, in such order as may be requested, such of the particulars as are appropriate and are required by Form 94C;
      (ii) where the application is made by facsimile transmission the applicant shall provide Form 94C and if the application is in respect of part of the land in a registered title and the plot number or numbers of any relevant approved estate plan are not quoted, the applicant shall also provide a designated plan of the land in respect of which the official search is to be made; and
      (iii) in any other case the applicant shall provide, in such order as shall be required by that notice, such of the particulars as are appropriate and are required by Form 94C.

(3) Where the application is made under paragraph (2)(*a*), unless the registrar otherwise allows—

    (*a*) Form 94C and any plan accompanying the application, shall be delivered in duplicate;

    (*b*) the application shall be accompanied by Form 94C (Result) in duplicate.

(4) Where the application is made under paragraph (2)(*b*)(ii), the applicant shall provide, unless the registrar otherwise allows, Form 94C (Result). **[1680]**

NOTES

Commencement: 28 March 1994.

10. Issue of official certificate of search without priority

(1) On completion of the official search without priority an official certificate of search without priority shall be issued and such certificate shall not confer on the applicant priority for the registration of any dealing.

(2) An official certificate of search without priority may, at the registrar's discretion, be issued in one, or more than one, of the following ways:

    (*a*) in the form set out under the heading "Official Certificate of Result of Search" in Form 94C (Result);

    (*b*) in documentary form;

    (*c*) during the currency of any relevant notice given pursuant to rule 14, and subject to and in accordance with the limitations contained in that notice, by any means of communication, other than the means referred to in sub-paragraphs (*a*) and (*b*).

(3) Subject to paragraphs (4) and (5), an official certificate of search without priority issued under paragraph (2) shall include the information specified in Part I of Schedule 2 and may be issued by reference to an office copy of the register.

(4) Where the official certificate of search is issued in Form 94C (Result) or in documentary form, under paragraph (2), together with the relevant application form, or a copy of that application form, it need not include any of the information referred to in paragraph (3) which appears on that application form.

(5) Where an official certificate of search is issued under paragraph (2)(*c*) and another official certificate of search is to be, or has been, issued under paragraph (2)(*b*) in respect of the same application, it need only include the information specified at A, F, G, and H, of Part I of Schedule 2. **[1681]**

NOTES

Commencement: 28 March 1994.

PART IV

REQUEST FOR INFORMATION AND SEARCHES WITHOUT PRIORITY

11. Information requested by applicant making a telephone or oral application under rule 3(3)(*b*)(i) or rule 9(2)(*b*)(i) or an application by remote terminal under rule 3(3)(*b*)(iii) or rule 9(2)(*b*)(iii)

(1) If so requested by an applicant who is making a telephone or oral application under rule 3(3)(*b*)(i) or rule 9(2)(*b*)(i), the registrar may at his discretion, before

the official search has been completed in respect of such application, give to the applicant, by telephone or orally, details of:

    (*a*) in the case of an application for a search of the whole of, or part of, the land in a registered title:

        (i) any relevant adverse entry that has been made in the register since the search from date given in the application; and

        (ii) any relevant entry subsisting on the day list made pursuant to rule 7A of the principal rules, rule 4 of the Land Registration (Official Searches) Rules 1990 or rule 4 of these rules; and

    (*b*) in the case of an application for a search of the whole of, or part of, the land subject to a pending first registration application, any relevant entry subsisting on the day list made pursuant to rule 7A of the principal rules (and entered on the day list subsequent to the date upon which the pending first registration was deemed to be delivered), rule 4 of the Land Registration (Official Searches) Rules 1990 or rule 4 of these rules affecting the pending first registration application.

    (2) If so requested by an applicant who is making an application to the registrar's computer system from a remote terminal under rule 3(3)(*b*)(iii) or rule 9(2)(*b*)(iii), the registrar may at his discretion, before the official search has been completed in respect of such application, inform the applicant, by a transmission to the remote terminal, whether or not there have been any relevant entries of the kind referred to in paragraph (1)(*a*) or (*b*), but the registrar need not provide the applicant with details of any relevant entries.   **[1682]**

NOTES
    Commencement: 28 March 1994.

12. Search without priority by telephone

(1) During the currency of any relevant notice given pursuant to rule 14, and subject to and in accordance with the limitations contained in that notice, a person may apply to the registrar by telephone for a search without priority of the whole of, or (where the search is in respect of one or more plots on an approved estate plan) part of, the land in a registered title to ascertain whether:

    (*a*) any relevant adverse entry has been made in the register of the title since the search from date given in the application; and

    (*b*) there is any relevant entry subsisting on the day list made pursuant to rule 7A of the principal rules, rule 4 of the Land Registration (Official Searches) Rules 1990 or rule 4 of these rules affecting the title.

    (2) Where an application is made under paragraph (1) the particulars set out in Part I of Schedule 3 shall be supplied in such order as may be required by the notice referred to in paragraph (1).   **[1683]**

NOTES
    Commencement: 28 March 1994.

13. Result of search without priority by telephone

(1) The result of a search given by telephone pursuant to an application under rule 12 shall include the information set out in Part II of Schedule 3.

    (2) A search made pursuant to an application under rule 12 shall not confer upon the applicant priority for the registration of any dealing.   **[1684]**

NOTES
Commencement: 28 March 1994.

PART V

14. Notice for the provision of additional arrangements for searches

(1) If the registrar is satisfied that adequate arrangements have been or will be made for dealing with the applications for or results of search specified in paragraph (5) in accordance with this rule, he may, in such manner as he considers appropriate for informing persons who may wish to make applications under these rules, give notice to that effect specifying the class or classes of case covered by those arrangements; and such a notice may in particular, but without prejudice to the generality of the foregoing provision, specify the class or classes of case so covered by limiting them:

(a) to one or more of the types of application or result of search mentioned in paragraph (5);

(b) to applications for, or results in respect of, searches of the whole of the land in a registered title or the whole of the land subject to a pending first registration application;

(c) in the case of applications made as mentioned in paragraph (5), to applications made by a person maintaining a credit account;

(d) to applications which relate to land within specified counties, districts, London boroughs or other administrative areas;

(e) to applications made between specified hours and on specified days (which need not be those between or on which the Land Registry is open to the public and may be different for applications of different types);

(f) where an application is made under rule 3(3)(b) or 9(2)(b) or a result is issued under rule 4(2)(c) or 10(2)(c), to delivery of such application or to the issue of such result by one or more means of communication;

(g) where a result is issued under rule 4(2)(c) or rule 10(2)(c), to results of search which state, in the case of an official search of a register, that there are no adverse entries, no pending applications and no official searches which fall within paragraphs F, G or H of Part I of Schedule 2, or, in the case of an official search with priority in relation to a pending first registration application, that there are no pending applications and no official searches which fall within paragraphs H or I of Part II of Schedule 2;

(h) where an application is in respect of part of the land in a registered title, to an application which provides the relevant plot number on the approved estate plan.

(2) Subject to paragraphs (3) and (4), a notice given pursuant to paragraph (1) shall be current from the time specified in that behalf in the notice either:

(a) until the time, if any, specified in that behalf in the notice; or

(b) if no time of ceasing to be current is specified in the notice, indefinitely.

(3) A notice given pursuant to paragraph (1) may from time to time be varied, suspended, withdrawn, renewed or replaced by a further notice.

(4) If and so long as owing to the breakdown or other unavailability of facilities or data involved in giving effect to the arrangements made for dealing with applications for or results of search covered by a notice given under paragraph (1) such arrangements cease, in whole or in part, to be effective, the notice shall cease, to the necessary extent, to be treated as current notwithstand-

ing the absence of a variation, suspension or withdrawal thereof under paragraph (3).

(5) The applications for or results of search referred to in paragraph (1) are:

(a) an application for an official search with priority made under rule 3(3)(b);

(b) an official certificate of search with priority issued under rule 4(2)(c);

(c) an application for an official search without priority made under rule 9(2)(b);

(d) an official certificate of search without priority issued under rule 10(2)(c);

(e) an application for a search without priority by telephone under rule 12.

(6) Notwithstanding the provisions of rule 3(3)(b), 4(2)(c), 9(2)(b), 10(2)(c) and 12 the registrar may in his discretion refuse to accept an application made, or to issue a result, under any of those provisions in any individual case. **[1685]**

NOTES
Commencement: 28 March 1994.

15. Revocation

. . .   **[1686]**

NOTES
Commencement: 28 March 1994.
This rule revokes the Land Registration (Official Searches) Rules 1990, SI 1990 No 1361.

SCHEDULES

NOTES
The Schedules, consisting of various forms, are not reproduced in this work.

INDEX

References are to paragraph numbers